VICE & VIRTUE IN EVERYDAY LIFE
Introductory Readings in Ethics

VICE & VIRTUE IN EVERYDAY LIFE

Introductory Readings in Ethics

CHRISTINA SOMMERS
Clark University

FRED SOMMERS
Brandeis University

HARCOURT BRACE COLLEGE PUBLISHERS
Fort Worth   Philadelphia   San Diego
New York   Orlando   Austin   San Antonio
Toronto   Montreal   London   Sydney   Tokyo

Editor in Chief	Ted Buchholz
Acquisitions Editor	David Tatom
Project Editor	Laura Hanna
Production Manager	Kathleen Ferguson
Book Designer	Peggy Young

Address for Editorial Correspondence
Harcourt Brace College Publishers, 301 Commerce Street, Suite 3700, Fort Worth, TX 76102

Address for Orders
Harcourt Brace College Publishers, 6277 Sea Harbor Drive, Orlando, FL 32887
1-800-782-4479, or 1-800-433-0001 (in Florida)

Printed in the United States of America

Library of Congress Catalogue Number 92-71052

ISBN 0-15-500375-5

4 5 6 7 8 9 0 1 2   0 1 6   9 8 7 6 5 4

In the nineteenth century, moral philosophy was the most important course in a student's college career. The course was taken during the senior year and typically was taught by the college president. Now, after many years, normative ethics is flourishing again. Philosophy departments are attracting unprecedented numbers of students to courses in contemporary ethical problems, business ethics, medical ethics, and ethics for engineers, nurses, and social workers. We find dozens of journals, hundreds of texts and anthologies, and, according to a survey by the Hastings Center, 11,000 courses in applied ethics. It is too early to venture more than a suggestion as to what has occasioned the renaissance of normative ethics. Undoubtedly, the unsettling effects of rapid social and technological change are somehow implicated. But if we cannot confidently identify the cause of the renaissance, we can describe it and comment on its significance for moral education in America and Great Britain. And, without looking a gift horse in the mouth, we are permitted to criticize its direction. For not all is cause for self-congratulation.

In reading the articles selected for a course in applied ethics, students encounter arguments by philosophers who take strong stands on such important social questions as abortion, euthanasia, capital punishment, and censorship. By contrast, students may find little to read on private individual virtue and responsibility. Many college ethics courses are concerned primarily with the conduct and policies of schools, hospitals, courts, corporations, and governments. Again, the moral responsibilities of the students may be discussed only occasionally. Because most students are not likely to be personally involved in administering the death penalty or selecting candidates for kidney dialysis, and because most will never conduct recombinant DNA research or even undergo abortions, the effective purpose of such courses in applied ethics is to teach students how to form responsible opinions on social policies—a purpose that is more civic than personal. "Applying" ethics to modern life involves more than learning how to be for or against social and institutional policies. These are important goals, but they are not enough.

This anthology brings together classical and contemporary writings on such matters as courage, pride, wisdom, compassion, generosity, honor, and self-respect. The anthology also includes essays on such moral foibles as hypocrisy, self-deception, jealousy, revenge, and narcissism. More standard materials are included, among them chapters on theories of moral conduct, moral education, and contemporary social issues.

This third edition has been augmented by a chapter entitled "The Meaning of Life" which includes a range of authors from Job and T'ao Chi'en to Camus and Bertrand Russell.

The collection seeks to combine the virtues of current texts on applied ethics with the virtues of more traditional survey texts. In addition, the selections address lively and important issues in personal morality. Social ethics is only half of normative ethics. Private ethics, including the theory of virtue, is the other half. We believe we need more balanced and traditional fare. Hence, this anthology.

ACKNOWLEDGMENTS

For their review of the third edition manuscript, we express our appreciation to David Cheney, Bridgewater State College; Lawrence M. Hinman, University of San Diego; Alexander E. Hooke, Villa Julie College; and Robert K. Pring, Herkimer County Community College.

CHRISTINA SOMMERS
FRED SOMMERS

TABLE OF CONTENTS

Contents

Contents

INTRODUCTION

Why, in novels, films, and television programs, are villains so easily distinguishable from heroes? What is it about, say, Huckleberry Finn or the runaway slave Jim that is unmistakably good, and about Huck's father Pap and the Duke and King that is unmistakably bad? For generations children have loved Cinderella and despised her evil stepsisters. Our moral sympathies are in constant play. We root for the moral heroes of the prime-time shows and eagerly await the downfall of the villains they pursue.

The moral dimension of our everyday experience is a pervasive and inescapable fact. In an important sense we are all "moralizers," instinctively applying moral judgment to the fictional and real people of our acquaintance and, in reflective moments, to ourselves as well. Moral philosophy seeks to make sense of this moral dimension in our lives. One objective is moral self-knowledge and self-evaluation. This is notoriously difficult. It is one thing to recognize good and evil when we encounter it in literature or in our friends; it is quite another to recognize good and evil in ourselves. The philosophical study of morality, by its reasoned approach to the concepts that figure centrally in our moral judgments, can help us be more objective. In particular, it can help by alerting us to some of the characteristic

1

deceptions that prevent us from seeing our own moral virtues and defects.

The philosopher's approach to such concepts as good and evil or vice and virtue differs in important ways from that of the social scientist or theologian. A sociologist or an anthropologist, for example, describes and interprets a society's mores and, in contrast to the moral philosopher, usually is careful to keep the account morally neutral. A theologian will call on us to act in a particular way and to avoid certain sinful practices. By contrast, the moral philosopher, though not neutral, usually does not exhort to action. Instead, the moral philosopher will explain what makes an act right or a person virtuous. In discussing criteria of right action and virtuous character, the philosopher will try to show why certain traits, such as honesty, generosity, and courage, are worthy, and others, such as hypocrisy, selfishness, and cowardice, are not. More generally, the moral philosopher seeks a clear and well-reasoned answer to the question: "What is it to be moral?"

Moral philosophers have viewed this central question in two distinct ways. Some construe the question as asking what we, as responsible agents confronting decisions of right and wrong, ought to do. These moral philosophers, then, see it as their task to formulate general principles of behavior that define our duties by distinguishing right actions from wrong ones. A theory that emphasizes moral duties and actions is *action based*. A second approach—called *virtue based*—takes the central question of morality to be: "What sort of person should I be?" Here the emphasis is not so much on what to *do* as on what to *be*. For virtue-based theorists, the object of moral education is to produce a virtuous individual. They therefore have much to say about moral education and character development. By concentrating attention on character rather than action, the philosopher of virtue tacitly assumes that a virtuous person's actions generally fall within the range of what is right and fair.

In the modern period—beginning with David Hume and Immanuel Kant—moral philosophy has tended to be action based. The reader will learn some of the reasons underlying the recent neglect of virtue and character from selected essays by Bernard Mayo, Anthony Quinton, Bernard Williams, and Alasdair MacIntyre, who are among the growing number of philosophers who view an exclusively action-based approach as inadequate. We have attempted to give equal space to virtue-based theories.

The ten chapters of this third edition are distinguished thematically. The opening essays highlight the crucial importance of character and of the capacity for sympathy and compassion. These essays,
together with several other selections, suggest that being moral is
never simply a matter of knowing how one should act. Sociopaths
may be well aware of the right thing to do but, because they lack
human sympathy, simply not care enough to be moral except where
a display of moral behavior serves their individual purpose. All the
same, knowing how to act is essential to being moral. The essays in
Chapter Two are devoted to the exposition and criticism of several action-based theories such as act and rule utilitarianism and
Kantianism.

The selections on virtue and vice in Chapters Three and Four range
from classical to contemporary. Aristotle's (and Plato's) thesis that
happiness is tied to the moral virtues is a central theme. The religious
and philosophical discussions of vice and virtue differ in characteristic ways. For a theologian such as Augustine or Abelard, vice is sin
construed as rebellion against the decrees of God. For a philosopher
such as Aristotle or Plutarch, vice is more akin to physical illness or
deformity. The selections contain representative analyses of such virtues as generosity and wisdom, and such vices as envy and self-
deception.

Human beings are variously moral; the amoral personality and the
supermoral personality are extreme types. Not very long ago the
former type would have been called "nihilistic," but today the more
usual label is "sociopathic" or "psychopathic." The moral philosopher who is disposed to argue that amoralism is untenable naturally
prefers to condemn the amoralist as a pathological character type.
But the philosophers in Chapter Five are keenly aware that more
than name-calling is required if one is properly to answer the serious
question "Why be moral?" The other extreme type—the supermoralist—sometimes is characterized as saintly; the latter half of Chapter
Five examines the personality of "The Moral Saint." Oddly enough,
some moral philosophers are averse to moral saintliness as an ideal to
be pursued. Chapter Six, "Moral Education," continues the discussion of moral character, focusing on training and development. We
present several views on how best to educate children to become
morally sensitive and mature. Aristotle's classic position that moral
education uses reward and other reinforcements to habituate the child
to virtuous activity is followed by a contemporary theory (Lawrence

Kohlberg's) inspired by Plato's idea that morality is innate and that moral education proceeds by eliciting it in stages. In this chapter, we also consider the question of how to distinguish an effective but legitimate approach to education from an approach that wrongfully interferes with the child's autonomy through "indoctrination" and "thought control."

Part of being moral is respecting ourselves as well as respecting others. Respect for others is bound up with self-respect since we cannot respect ourselves as moral beings unless we value our respectful treatment of others. Chapter Seven includes discussions of the place of self-respect and dignity in the development of moral character.

The essays in Chapters Eight and Nine pertain primarily to that part of moral philosophy called applied ethics. The student will encounter philosophers arguing different sides of topical moral issues such as divorce, rearing of children, and duties to one's parents, as well as more general social issues such as the morality or immorality of our current practices in dealing with the problem of hunger in underdeveloped countries.

Human beings are conscious of themselves as finite creatures in the wider environment of a vast universe. Chapter Ten on the Meaning of Life focuses on the profound question of how we may see ourselves in this perspective. As significant? As doomed to futility and extinction? As "absurd"? Where does morality fit in? This last chapter presents a wide range of responses from Job and T'ao Chi'en in ancient times, to Leo Tolstoy and Bertrand Russell in our own times.

What, finally, may the open-minded and careful reader of a comprehensive text on moral philosophy expect to gain? First, if not foremost, the reader will acquire a great deal of knowledge of the classical approaches to moral philosophy and, with this, some sense of the moral tradition of Western civilization as Greek and Judeo-Christian thought have influenced it. Second, the reader will become aware of some of the central problem areas in ethics and will be in a better position to approach them with the confidence that comes with historical perspective and a sharpened moral insight. Social change and novel technologies bring about new problems, each with its moral dimension. Yet morality itself is not really changed in any radical way. There will always be a right and decent way to cope with the new situations that confront us.

4

Chapter One

GOOD AND EVIL

Much of moral philosophy is a disciplined effort to systematize and explain our most common convictions about good and evil and right and wrong. Proper ethical philosophy takes the simplest moral truths as its starting point. Almost no one doubts that cruelty is wrong. But philosophers differ on how to explain what is wrong about acting cruelly and even about the meaning of right and wrong. So we have various systems of moral theory. Inevitably we have the possibility that a philosopher may devise a pseudo-ethical doctrine that loses sight of basic intuitions about human dignity and elementary decency. When such a doctrine achieves currency and popular respectability, it becomes a powerful force for evil. For then, what passes as conventional wisdom allows the average person to behave in reprehensible but conventionally acceptable ways.

In Chapter One we find examples of the ways the moral intuitions of the individual may conflict with publicly accepted principles that are not grounded in respect for human dignity. In the first two selections, "From Cruelty to Goodness" by Philip Hallie and "The Conscience of Huckleberry Finn" by Jonathan Bennett, the moral failure of princple is easy to diagnose. A dominant group adopts a philosophy that permits it to confine its moral concern to those inside the

5

group, treating outsiders as beyond the moral pale; their pain, their dignity, even their very lives merit no moral consideration. Huckleberry Finn, being white, is within the moral domain. His mentors have taught him that he does not owe moral behavior to slaves. Yet Huck treats Jim, the runaway slave, as if he too deserves the respect due a white person. And therein lies Huck's conflict. Everything he conventionally believes tells him he is doing wrong in helping Jim elude his pursuers.

Mark Twain's account of the conflict between official "book" morality and the ground-level morality of an innately decent and sympathetic person is one of the best in literature. Usually the conflict is embodied in two protagonists (Victor Hugo's novel *Les Misérables* is an example), but Huck Finn's conflict is within himself. And we are glad that his decency is stronger than his book morality. Both Jonathan Bennett and Philip Hallie quote the Nazi officer Heinrich Himmler, one of the fathers of the "final solution," as a spokesman for those who advocate suspending all moral feeling toward a particular group. Interestingly, Himmler considered himself all the more moral for being above pitying the children and other innocent victims outside the domain of moral consideration. Indeed, we hear stories of Germans who were conscience-stricken because—against their principles—they allowed some Jews to escape.

Our dismay at man's inhumanity to man is qualified by the inspiring example of the residents of the French village Le Chambon-sur-Lignon who acted together to care for and save 6,000 Jews, mostly children, from the Nazis. Le Chambon is said to have been the safest place in Europe for a Jew during the Second World War. From his studies of the village, Hallie concludes that Le Chambon residents successfully combatted evil because they never allowed themselves to be blind to the victim's point of view. "When we are blind to that point of view we can countenance and perpetrate cruelty with impunity." The true morality of Le Chambon drives out false and hypocritical Nazi "decencies" that ignore the most elementary moral intuitions and that permit and encourage the horrors of Himmler's and Hitler's Germany.

The example of Le Chambon is the proper antidote to the moral apathy that is the condition of many people today, and which Martin Gansberg dramatically describes in "38 Who Saw Murder Didn't Call Police." In sharp contrast to the residents of Le Chambon, the spectators who witnessed the murder of Kitty Genovese were literally demoralized. Not only did they fail to intervene; they did not even call for help.

In his selection, Josiah Royce defends a morality that respects human dignity. Beginning from the axiom that we owe respect and decency to our neighbor, Royce confronts the question that the Nazi and all those who ignore the humanity of special groups pervert: Who, then, are our neighbors? Royce answers that our neighbors include anyone with feelings: "Pain is pain, joy is joy, everywhere even as in thee." Royce calls this the Moral Insight. He points out that treating strangers with care and solicitude is hardly unnatural; for each of us, our future self is like a stranger to us, yet we are naturally concerned with the welfare of that stranger.

The moral blindness that is the opposite of Royce's moral insight has tragic consequences for the victims whose humanity is ignored. The point is taken up by Hallie who complains that some moral philosophers who concentrate on the motives and character of evildoers often fail to attend to the suffering of the victims. Hallie argues that it is not the character of evildoers that is the crucial element of evil; but rather that evil mainly consists in the suffering caused by the perpetrators of evil. For Hallie, evil is what evil does. He therefore takes sharp issue with Bennett for saying that the Nazi who professes to be affected by the suffering he causes is in some respects morally superior to theologians like Jonathan Edwards who never actually harmed anyone but who claim to have no pity for the sinner who would suffer the torments of the damned.

Do we punish people for the evil they do or for what they are? Melville's *Billy Budd* is a classic on this question. Billy Budd is an exceptionally pure and good person who has committed a crime. We are tempted to say that Budd's fine character exculpates his crime. But this could be a dangerous doctrine if applied generally, since it challenges the principle that moral agents—including those of especially superior moral character—must be responsible to society for the consequences of their acts.

Nietzsche challenges the tradition of Western morality with its moral insights and its golden rule to refrain from doing to others what you would not want them to do to you. He characterizes this tradition that enjoins us to protect the weak and whose origins lie in the teachings of Judaism and Christianity as "sentimental weakness" and a "denial of life." According to Nietzsche, the tradition emasculates those who are strong, vital, and superior by forcing them to

7

attend to the weak and mediocre. Nietzsche was especially effective in suggesting that morality often is used in hypocritical ways to stifle initiative. Yet, on the whole, philosophers have rejected Nietzsche's heroic morality as tending to encourage a morally irresponsible exercise of power. This is perhaps unfair, since Nietzsche himself almost certainly would have looked with contempt upon such self-styled "heroes" as the leaders of Nazi Germany. Another reason seems more valid: Nietzsche's own ideal does in fact denigrate sympathy with the weak and helpless, and so fails to convince those of us who see moral heroism in the likes of Huckleberry Finn and the people of Le Chambon.

From Cruelty to Goodness

———————————————————— *☙☙—*

PHILIP HALLIE

Philip Hallie (b. 1922) is a professor of philosophy at
Wesleyan University. His published works include *The
Paradox of Cruelty* (1969) and *Lest Innocent Blood Be Shed*
(1979).

Hallie considers institutionalized cruelty and finds that,
besides physically assaulting its victims, it almost always
assaults their dignity and self-respect. As an example of
the antithesis of institutionalized cruelty, Hallie cites the
residents of the French village of Le Chambon who, at
grave risk to their lives, saved 6,000 Jews from the Nazis.
For him the opposite of being cruel is not merely ceasing
to be cruel; nor is it fighting cruelty with violence and
hatred (though this may be necessary). Rather, it is epit-
omized in the unambiguous and unpretentious goodness
of the citizens of Le Chambon who followed the positive
Biblical injunctions "Defend the fatherless" and "Be your
brother's keeper," as well as the negative injunctions
"Thou shalt not murder or betray."

I am a student of ethics, of good and evil; but my approach to these
two rather melodramatic terms is skeptical. I am in the tradition
of the ancient Greek *skeptikoi*, whose name means "inquirers" or

FROM CRUELTY TO GOODNESS © Institute of Society, Ethics and the Life Sciences, 360 Broadway,
Hastings-on-Hudson, NY 10706. Reprinted by permission of the copyright holder.

"investigators." And what we investigate is relationships among particular facts. What we put into doubt are the intricate webs of high-level abstractions that passed for philosophizing in the ancient world, and that still pass for philosophizing. My approach to good and evil emphasizes not abstract common nouns like "justice," but proper names and verbs. Names and verbs keep us close to the facts better than do our highfalutin common nouns. Names refer to particular people, and verbs connect subjects with predicates *in time,* while common nouns are above all this.

One of the words that is important to me is my own name. For me, philosophy is personal; it is closer to literature and history than it is to the exact sciences, closer to the passions, actions, and common sense of individual persons than to a dispassionate technical science. It has to do with the personal matter of wisdom. And so ethics for me is personal—my story, and not necessarily (though possibly) yours. It concerns particular people at particular times.

But ethics is more than such particulars. It involves abstractions, that is, rules, laws, ideals. When you look at the ethical magnates of history you see in their words and deeds two sorts of ethical rules: negative and positive. The negative rules are scattered throughout the Bible, but Moses brought down from Mount Sinai the main negative ethical rules of the West: Thou shalt not murder; thou shalt not betray. . . . The positive injunctions are similarly spread throughout the Bible. In the first chapter of the book of Isaiah we are told to ". . . defend the fatherless, plead for the widow . . ." The negative ethic forbids certain actions; the positive ethic demands certain actions. To follow the negative ethic is to be decent, to have clean hands. But to follow the positive ethic, to be one's brother's keeper, is to be more than decent—it is to be active, even aggressive. If the negative ethic is one of decency, the positive one is the ethic of riskful, strenuous nobility.

In my early studies of particularized ethical terms, I found myself dwelling upon negative ethics, upon prohibitions. And among the most conspicuous prohibitions I found embodied in history was the prohibition against deliberate harmdoing, against cruelty. "Thou shalt not be cruel" had as much to do with the nightmare of history as did the prohibitions against murder and betrayal. In fact, many of the Ten Commandments—especially those against murder, adultery, stealing, and betrayal—were ways of prohibiting cruelty.

Early in my research it became clear that there are various approaches to cruelty, as the different commandments suggest. For instance, there is the way reflected in the origins of the word "cruel." The Latin *crudus* is related to still older words standing for bloodshed, or raw flesh. According to the etymology of the word, cruelty involves the spilling of blood.

But modern dictionaries give the word a different meaning. They define it as "disposed to giving pain." They emphasize awareness, not simply bloodshed. After all, they seem to say, you cannot be cruel to a dead body. There is no cruelty without consciousness.

And so I found myself studying the kinds of awareness associated with the hurting of human beings. It is certainly true that for millennia in history and literature people have been torturing each other not only with hard weapons but also with hard words.

Still, the word "pain" seemed to be a simplistic and superficial way of describing the many different sorts of cruelty. In Reska Weiss's *Journey Through Hell* (London, 1961) there is a brief passage of one of the deepest cruelties that Nazis perpetrated upon extermination camp inmates. On a march

> Urine and excreta poured down the prisoners' legs, and by nightfall the excrement, which had frozen to our limbs, gave off its stench. . . .

And Weiss goes on to talk not in terms of "pain" or bloodshed, but in other terms:

> . . . We were really no longer human beings in the accepted sense. Not even animals, but putrefying corpses moving on two legs. . . .

There is one factor that the idea of "pain" and the simpler idea of bloodshed do not touch: cruelty, not playful, quotidian teasing or ragging, but cruelty (what the anti-cruelty societies usually call "substantial cruelty") involves the maiming of a person's dignity, the crushing of a person's self-respect. Bloodshed, the idea of pain (which is usually something involving a localizable occurrence, localizable in a tooth, in a head, in short, in the body), these are superficial ideas of cruelty. A whip, bleeding flesh, these are what the journalists of cruelty emphasize, following the etymology and dictionary meaning of the word. But the depths of an understanding of cruelty lie in the depths of an understanding of human dignity and of how you can maim it without bloodshed, and often without localizable bodily pain.

In excremental assault, in the process of keeping camp inmates from wiping themselves or from going to the latrine, and in making them drink water from a toilet bowl full of excreta (and the excreta of the guards at that) localizable pain is nothing. Deep humiliation is everything. We human beings believe in hierarchies, whether we are skeptics or not about human value. There is a hierarchical gap between shit and me. We are even above using the word. We are "above" walking around besmirched with feces. Our dignity, whatever the origins of that dignity may be, does not permit it. In order to be able to want to live, in order to be able to walk erect, we must respect ourselves as beings "higher" than our feces. When we feel that we are not "higher" than dirt or filth, then our lives are maimed at the very center, in the very depths, not merely in some localizable portion of our bodies. And when our lives are so maimed we become things, slaves, instruments. From ancient times until this moment, and as long as there will be human beings on this planet, there are those who know this and will use it, just as the Roman slave owners and the Southern American slave owners knew it when—one time a year—they encouraged the slaves to drink all the alcohol they could drink so that they could get bestially drunk and then even more bestially sick afterwards, under the eyes of their generous owners. The self-hatred, the loss of self-respect that the Saturnalia created in ancient Rome, say, made it possible to continue using the slaves as things, since they themselves came to think of themselves as things, as subhuman tools of the owners and the overseers.

Institutionalized cruelty, I learned, is the subtlest kind of cruelty. In episodic cruelty the victim knows he is being hurt, and his victimizer knows it too. But in a persistent pattern of humiliation that endures for years in a community, both the victim and the victimizer find ways of obscuring the harm that is being done. Blacks come to think of themselves as inferior, even esthetically inferior (black is "dirty"); and Jews come to think of themselves as inferior, even esthetically (dark hair and aquiline noses are "ugly"), so that the way they are being treated is justified by their "actual" inferiority, by the inferiority they themselves feel.

A similar process happens in the minds of the victimizers in institutionalized cruelty. They feel that since they are superior, even esthetically ("to be blonde is to be beautiful"), they deserve to do what they wish, deserve to have these lower creatures under their control. The words of Heinrich Himmler, head of the Nazi SS, in Posen in the year 1943 in a speech to his SS subordinates in a closed session, show how institutionalized cruelty can obscure harmdoing:

> . . . the words come so easily. "The Jewish people will be extermi-
> nated," says every party member, "of course. It's in our program . . .
> extermination. We'll take care of it." And then they come, these nice
> 80 million Germans, and every one of them has his decent Jew. Sure
> the others are swine, but his one is a fine Jew . . . Most of you will
> know what it means to have seen 100 corpses together, or 500 to 1000.
> To have made one's way through that, and . . . to have remained a
> decent person throughout, that is what has made us hard. That is a
> page of glory in our history. . . .

In this speech he was making a sharp distinction between the program of crushing the Jews and the personal sentiments of individual
Germans. The program stretched over years; personal sentiments
were momentary. He was pleading for the program, for institutionalized destruction.

But one of the most interesting parts of the speech occurs toward
the end of it:

> . . . in sum, we can say that we fulfilled the heaviest of tasks [de-
> stroying the Jews] in love to our people. And we suffered no harm in
> our essence, in our soul, in our character. . . .

Commitment that overrides all sentimentality transforms cruelty
and destruction into moral nobility, and commitment is the lifeblood
of an institution.

Cruelty and the Power Relationships

But when I studied all these ways that we have used the word "cruelty," I was nagged by the feeling that I had not penetrated into its
inner structure. I was classifying, sorting out symptoms; but symptoms are signals, and what were the symptoms signals *of?* I felt like
a person who had been studying cancer by sorting out brief pains
from persistent pains, pains in the belly from pains in the head. I was
being superficial, and I was not asking the question, "What are the
forces behind these kinds of cruelty?" I felt that there were such
forces, but as yet I had not touched them.

Then one day I was reading in one of the great autobiographies of
western civilization, Frederick Douglass's *Life and Times*. The

13

passage I was reading was about Douglass's thoughts on the origins of slavery. He was asking himself: "How could these whites keep us enslaved?" And he suddenly realized:

> My faculties and powers of body and soul are not my own, but are the property of a fellow-mortal in no sense superior to me, except that he has the physical power to compel me to be owned and controlled by him. By the combined physical force of the community I am his slave—a slave for life.

And then I saw that a disparity in power lay at the center of the dynamism of cruelty. If it was institutional cruelty it was in all likelihood a difference involving both verbal and physical power that kept the cruelty going. The power of the majority and the weakness of a minority were at the center of the institutional cruelty of slavery and of Nazi anti-Semitism. The whites not only outnumbered the blacks in America, but had economic and political ascendancy over them. But just as important as these "physical" powers was the power that words like "nigger" and "slave" gave the white majority. Their language sanctified if it did not create their power ascendancy over the blacks, and one of the most important projects of the slave-holders and their allies was that of seeing to it that the blacks them-selves thought of themselves in just these powerless terms. They utilized the language to convince not only the whites but the blacks themselves that blacks were weak in mind, in will power, and in worth. These words were like the excremental assault in the killing camps of the Nazis: they diminished both the respect the victimizers might have for their victims and the respect the victims might have for themselves.

It occurred to me that if a power differential is crucial to the idea of cruelty, then when that power differential is maintained, cruelty will tend to be maintained, and when that power differential is elim-inated, cruelty will tend to be eliminated. And this seemed to work. In all kinds of cruelty, violent and polite, episodic and institutional, when the victim arms himself with the appropriate strength, the cruelty diminishes or disappears. When Jews joined the Bush War-riors of France, the Maquis, and became powerful enough to strike at Vichy or the Nazis, they stopped being victims of French and Nazi cruelty. When Frederick Douglass learned to use the language with great skill and expressiveness, and when he learned to use his physical strength against his masters, the power differential between him and

his masters diminished, and so did their cruelty to him. In his autobiography he wrote:

> A man without force is without the essential dignity of humanity.
> Human nature is so constituted that it cannot honor a helpless man,
> though it can pity him, and even this it cannot do long if signs of
> power do not arise.

When I looked back at my own childhood in Chicago, I remembered that the physical and mental cruelties that I suffered in the
slums of the southwest side when I was about ten years old sharply
diminished and finally disappeared when I learned how to defend
myself physically and verbally. It is exactly this lesson that Douglass
learned while growing up in the cruel institution of slavery.

Cruelty then, whatever else it is, is a kind of power relationship,
an imbalance of power wherein the stronger party becomes the victimizer and the weaker becomes the victim. And since many general
terms are most swiftly understood in relationship with their opposites (just as "heavy" can be understood most handily in relationship
with what we mean by "light") the opposite of cruelty lay in a
situation where there is no imbalance of power. The opposite of
cruelty, I learned, was freedom from that unbalanced power relationship. Either the victim should get stronger and stand up to the victimizer, and thereby bring about a balance of their powers, or the
victim should free himself from the whole relationship by flight.

In pursuing this line of thought, I came to believe that, again,
dictionaries are misleading: many of them give "kindness" as the
antonym for "cruelty." In studying slavery in America and the concentration camps of central Europe I found that kindness could be
the ultimate cruelty, especially when it was given within that unbalanced power relationship. A kind overseer or a kind camp guard can
exacerbate cruelty, can remind his victim that there are other relationships than the relationship of cruelty, and can make the victim
deeply bitter, especially when he sees the self-satisfied smile of his
victimizer. He is being cruelly treated when he is given a penny or a
bun after having endured the crushing and grinding of his mental
and bodily well-being. As Frederick Douglass put it:

> The kindness of the slave-master only gilded the chain. It detracted
> nothing from its weight or strength. The thought that men are for
> other and better uses than slavery throve best under the gentle treat-
> ment of a kind master.

No, I learned, the opposite of cruelty is not kindness. The opposite of the cruelty of the overseer in American slavery was not the kindness of that overseer for a moment or for a day. An episodic kindness is not the opposite of an institutionalized cruelty. The opposite of institutionalized cruelty is freedom from the cruel relationship.

It is important to see how perspectival the whole meaning of cruelty is. From the perspective of the SS guard or the southern overseer, a bit of bread, a smile is indeed a diminution of cruelty. But in the relationship of cruelty, the point of view of the victimizer is of only minor importance; it is the point of view of the victim that is authoritative. The victim feels the suffering in his own mind and body, whereas the victimizer, like Himmler's "hard" and "decent" Nazi, can be quite unaware of that suffering. The sword does not feel the pain that it inflicts. Do not ask it about suffering.

Goodness Personified in Le Chambon

All these considerations drove me to write my book *The Paradox of Cruelty*. But with the book behind me, I felt a deep discontent. I saw cruelty as an embodiment, a particular case of evil. But if cruelty is one of the main evils of human history, why is the opposite of cruelty not one of the key goods of human history? Freedom from the cruel relationship, either by escaping it or by redressing the imbalance of power, was not essential to what western philosophers and theologians have thought of as goodness. Escape is a negative affair. Goodness has something positive in it, something triumphantly affirmative.

Hoping for a hint of goodness in the very center of evil, I started looking closely at the so-called "medical experiments" of the Nazis upon children, usually Jewish and Gypsy children, in the death camps. Here were the weakest of the weak. Not only were they despised minorities, but they were, as individuals, still in their nonage. They were dependents. Here the power imbalance between the cruel experimenters and their victims was at its greatest. But instead of seeing light or finding insight by going down into this hell, into the deepest depth of cruelty, I found myself unwillingly becoming part of the world I was studying. I found myself either yearning to be viciously cruel to the victimizers of the children, or I found myself feeling compassion for the children, feeling their despair and pain as they looked up at the men and women in white coats cutting off their fingertips one at a time, or breaking their slender bones, or wounding their internal organs. Either I became a would-be victimizer or one more Jewish victim, and in either case I was not achieving insight, only misery, like so many other students of the Holocaust. And when I was trying to be "objective" about my studies, when I was succeeding at being indifferent to both the victimizers and the victims of these cruel relationships, I became cold; I became another monster who could look upon the maiming of a child with an indifferent eye.

To relieve this unending suffering, from time to time I would turn to the literature of the French resistance to the Nazis. I had been trained by the U.S. Army to understand it. The resistance was a way of trying to redress the power imbalance between Hitler's Fortress Europe and Hitler's victims, and so I saw it as an enemy of cruelty. Still, its methods were often cruel like the methods of most power struggles, and I had little hope of finding goodness here. We soldiers violated the negative ethic forbidding killing in order, we thought, to follow the positive ethic of being our brothers' keepers.

And then one gray April afternoon I found a brief article on the French village of Le Chambon-sur-Lignon. I shall not analyze here the tears of amazement and gladness and release from despair—in short, of joy—that I shed when I first read that story. Tears themselves interest me greatly—but not the tears of melancholy hindsight and existential despair; rather the tears of awe you experience when the realization of an ideal suddenly appears before your very eyes or thunders inside your mind; these tears interest me.

And one of the reasons I wept at first reading about Le Chambon in those brief, inaccurate pages was that at last I had discovered an embodiment of goodness in opposition to cruelty. I had discovered in the flesh and blood of history, in people with definite names in a definite place at a definite time in the nightmare of history, what no classical or religious ethicist could deny was goodness.

The French Protestant village of Le Chambon, located in the Cévennes Mountains of southeastern France, and with a population of about 3,500, saved the lives of about 6,000 people, most of them Jewish children whose parents had been murdered in the killing camps of central Europe. Under a national government which was not only collaborating with the Nazi conquerors of France but frequently trying to outdo the Germans in anti-Semitism in order to

17

please their conquerors, and later under the day-to-day threat of destruction by the German Armed SS, they started to save children in the winter of 1940, the winter after the fall of France, and they continued to do so until the war in France was over. They sheltered the refugees in their own homes and in various houses they established especially for them; and they took many of them across the terrible mountains to neutral Geneva, Switzerland, in the teeth of French and German police and military power. The people of Le Chambon are poor, and the Huguenot faith to which they belong is a diminishing faith in Catholic and atheist France; but their spiritual power, their capacity to act in unison against the victimizers who surrounded them, was immense, and more than a match for the military power of those victimizers.

But for me as an ethicist the heart of the matter was not only their special power. What interested me was that they obeyed *both* the negative and the positive injunctions of ethics; they were good not only in the sense of trying to be their brothers' keepers, protecting the victim, "defending the fatherless," to use the language of Isaiah; they were also good in the sense that they obeyed the negative injunctions against killing and betraying. While those around them—including myself—were murdering in order presumably, to help mankind in some way or other, they murdered nobody, and betrayed not a single child in those long and dangerous four years. For me as an ethicist they were the embodiment of unambiguous goodness.

But for me as a student of cruelty they were something more: they were an embodiment of the opposite of cruelty. And so, somehow, at last, I had found goodness in opposition to cruelty. In studying their story, and in telling it in *Lest Innocent Blood Be Shed,* I learned that the opposite of cruelty is not simply freedom from the cruel relationship; it is *hospitality*. It lies not only in something negative, an absence of cruelty or of imbalance; it lies in unsentimental, efficacious love. The opposite of the cruelties of the camps was not the liberation of the camps, the cleaning out of the barracks and the cessation of the horrors. All of this was the *end* of the cruelty relationship, not the opposite of that relationship. And it was not even the end of it, because the victims would never forget and would remain in agony as long as they remembered their humiliation and suffering. No, the opposite of cruelty was not the liberation of the camps, not freedom; it was the hospitality of the people of Le Chambon, and of very few others during the Holocaust. The opposite of cruelty was the kind of goodness that happened in Le Chambon.

Let me explain the difference between liberation and hospitality by telling you about a letter I received a year ago from a woman who had been saved by the people of Le Chambon when she was a young girl. She wrote:

> Never was there a question that the Chambonnais would not share all they had with us, meager as it was. One Chambonnais once told me that even if there was less, they still would want more for us.

And she goes on:

> It was indeed a very different attitude from the one in Switzerland, which while saving us also resented us so much.
>
> If today we are not bitter people like most survivors it can only be due to the fact that we met people like the people of Le Chambon, who showed to us simply that life can be different, that there are people who care, that people can live together and even risk their own lives for their fellow man.

The Swiss liberated refugees and removed them from the cruel relationship; the people of Le Chambon did more. They taught them that goodness could conquer cruelty, that loving hospitality could remove them from the cruel relationship. And they taught me this, too.

It is important to emphasize that cruelty is not simply an episodic, momentary matter, especially institutional cruelty like that of Nazism or slavery. As we have seen throughout this essay, not only does it persist while it is being exerted upon the weak; *it can persist in the survivors* after they have escaped the power relationship. The survivors torture themselves, continue to suffer, continue to maim their own lives long after the actual torture is finished. The self-hatred and rage of the blacks and the despair of the native Americans and the Jews who have suffered under institutional crushing and maiming are continuations of original cruelties. And these continuations exist because only a superficial liberation from torture has occurred. The sword has stopped falling on their flesh in the old obvious ways, but the wounds still bleed. I am not saying that the village of Le Chambon healed these wounds—they go too deep. What I am saying is that the people I have talked to who were once children in Le Chambon have more hope for their species and more respect for themselves as human beings than most other survivors I have met. The enduring hospitality they met in Le Chambon helped them find realistic hope in a world of persisting cruelty.

What was the nature of this hospitality that saved and deeply changed so many lives? It is hard to summarize briefly what the Chambonnais did, and above all how they did it. The morning after a new refugee family came to town they would find on their front door a wreath with "*Bienvenue!*" "Welcome!" painted on a piece of cardboard attached to the wreath. Nobody knew who had brought the wreath; in effect, the whole town had brought it.

It was mainly the women of Le Chambon who gave so much more than shelter to these, the most hated enemies of the Nazis. There was Madame Barraud, a tiny Alsatian, who cared for the refugee boys in her house with all the love such a tiny body could hold, and who cared for the way they felt day and night. And there were others.

But there was one person without whom Le Chambon could not have become the safest place in Europe for Jews: the Huguenot minister of the village, André Trocmé. Trocmé was a passionately religious man. He was massive, more than six feet tall, blonde, with a quick temper. Once long after the war, while he was lecturing on the main project of his life, the promotion of the idea of nonviolence in international relations, one of the members of his audience started to whisper a few words to his neighbor. Trocmé let this go on for a few moments, then interrupted his speech, walked up to the astonished whisperer, raised his massive arm, pointed toward the door, and yelled, "Out! Out! Get out!" And the lecture was on nonviolence.

The center of his thought was the belief that God showed how important man was by becoming Himself a human being, and by becoming a particular sort of human being who was the embodiment of sacrificially generous love. For Trocmé, every human being was like Jesus, had God in him or her, and was just as precious as God Himself. And when Trocmé with the help of the Quakers and others organized his village into the most efficient rescue machine in Europe, he did so not only to save the Jews, but also to save the Nazis and their collaborators. He wanted to keep them from blackening their souls with more evil—he wanted to save them, the victimizers, from evil.

One of the reasons he was successful was that the Huguenots had been themselves persecuted for hundreds of years by the kings of France, and they knew what persecution was. In fact, when the people of Le Chambon took Jewish children and whole families across the mountains of southeastern France into neutral Switzerland, they often followed pathways that had been taken by Huguenots in their flight from the Dragoons of the French kings.

A particular incident from the story of Le Chambon during the Nazi occupation of France will explain succinctly why he was successful in making the village a village of refuge. But before I relate the story, I must point out that the people of the village did not think of themselves as "successful," let alone as "good." From their point of view, they did not do anything that required elaborate explanation. When I asked them why they helped these dangerous guests, they invariably answered, "What do you mean, 'Why'? Where else could they go? How could you turn them away? What is so special about being ready to help (*prête à servir*)? There was nothing else to do." And some of them laughed in amazement when I told them that I thought they were "good people." They saw no alternative to their actions and to the way they acted, and therefore they saw what they did as necessary, not something to be picked out for praise. Helping these guests was for them as natural as breathing or eating—one does not think of alternatives to these functions; they did not think of alternatives to sheltering people who were endangering not only the lives of their hosts but the lives of all the people of the village.

And now the story. One afternoon a refugee woman knocked on the door of a farmhouse outside the village. The farmers around the village proper were Protestants like most of the others in Le Chambon, but with one difference: they were mostly "Darbystes," followers of a strange Scot named Darby, who taught their ancestors in the nineteenth century to believe every word of the Bible, and indeed, who had them memorize the Bible. They were literal fundamentalists. The farm-woman opened the door to the refugee and invited her into the kitchen where it was warm. Standing in the middle of the floor the refugee, in heavily accented French, asked for eggs for her children. In those days of very short supplies, people with children often went to the farmers in the "gray market" (neither black nor exactly legal) to get necessary food. This was early in 1941, and the farmers were not yet accustomed to the refugees. The farm-woman looked into the eyes of the shawled refugee and asked, "Are you Jewish?" The woman started to tremble, but she could not lie, even though that question was usually the beginning of the end of life for Jews in Hitler's Fortress Europe. She answered, "Yes."

The woman ran from the kitchen to the staircase nearby, and while the refugee trembled with terror in the kitchen, she called up the stairs, "Husband, children, come down, come down! We have in our house at this very moment a representative of the Chosen People!"

Not all the Protestants in Le Chambon were Darbyste fundamentalists; but almost all were convinced that people are the children of God, and are as precious as God Himself. Their leaders were Huguenot preachers and their following of the negative and positive commandments of the Bible came in part from their personal generosity and courage, but also in part from the depths of their religious conviction that we are all children of God, and we must take care of each other lovingly. This combined with the ancient and deep historical ties between the Huguenots and the Jews of France and their own centuries of persecution by the Dragoons and Kings of France helped make them what they were, "always ready to help," as the Chambonnais saying goes.

A Choice of Perspectives

We have come a long way from cruelty to the people of Le Chambon, just as I have come a long way in my research from concrete evil to concrete goodness. Let me conclude with a point that has been alternately hinted at and stressed in the course of this essay.

A few months after *Lest Innocent Blood Be Shed* was published I received a letter from Massachusetts that opened as follows:

> I have read your book, and I believe that you mushy-minded moralists should be awakened to the facts. Nothing happened in Le Chambon, nothing of any importance whatsoever.
>
> The Holocaust, dear Professor, was like a geological event, like an earthquake. No person could start it; no person could change it; and no person could end it. And no small group of persons could do so either. It was the armies and the nations that performed actions that counted. Individuals did nothing. You sentimentalists have got to learn that the great masses and big political ideas make the difference. Your people and the people they saved simply do not exist . . .

Now between this position and mine there is an abyss that no amount of shouted arguments or facts can cross. And so I shall not answer this letter with a tightly organized reply. I shall answer it only by telling you that one of the reasons institutional cruelty exists and persists is that people believe that individuals can do nothing, that only vast ideologies and armies can act meaningfully. Every act of institutional cruelty—Nazism, slavery, and all the others—lives not with people in the concrete, but with abstractions that blind people to individuals. Himmler's speech to the SS leadership in 1943 is full of phrases like "exterminating a bacillus," and "The Jewish people will be exterminated." And in that speech he attacks any German who believes in "his decent Jew." Institutional cruelty, like other misleading approaches to ethics, blinds us to the victim's point of view; and when we are blind to that point of view we can countenance and perpetrate cruelty with impunity.

I have told you that I cannot and will not try to refute the letter from Massachusetts. I shall only summarize the point of view of this essay with another story.

I was lecturing a few months ago in Minneapolis, and when I finished talking about the Holocaust and the village of Le Chambon, a woman stood up and asked me if the village of Le Chambon was in the Department of Haute-Loire, the high sources of the Loire River. Obviously she was French, with her accent; and all French people know that there are many villages called "Le Chambon" in France, just as any American knows that there are many "Main Streets" in the United States. I said that Le Chambon was indeed in the Haute-Loire.

She said, "Then you have been speaking about the village that saved all three of my children. I want to thank you for writing this book, not only because the story will now be permanent, but also because I shall be able to talk about those terrible days with Americans now, for they will understand those days better than they have. You see, you Americans, though you sometimes cross the oceans, live on an island here as far as war is concerned . . ."

Then she asked to come up and say one sentence. There was not a sound, not even breathing, to be heard in the room. She came to the front of the room and said, "The Holocaust was storm, lightning, thunder, wind, rain, yes. And Le Chambon was the rainbow."

Only from her perspective can you understand the cruelty and the goodness I have been talking about, not from the point of view of the gentleman from Massachusetts. You must choose which perspective is best, and your choice will have much to do with your feelings

23

about the preciousness of life, and not only the preciousness of other people's lives. If the lives of others are precious to you, your life will become more precious to you.

STUDY QUESTIONS

1. Distinguish between positive and negative moral injunctions. Do you agree with Hallie that we need both for moral decency?
2. Do you agree with Hallie that cruelty is prevalent when a serious imbalance of power exists among people? Can we be cruel to our equals?
3. Why does Hallie deny that kindness is the opposite of cruelty? What does he consider to be cruelty's opposite?
4. What does the writer Terence des Pres mean when he says of Le Chambon, "Those events took place and therefore demand a place in our view of the world"?
5. Hallie cites Himmler as having compared the Jewish people to a bacillus that should be exterminated. Can you think of other examples of official dehumanization of one group by another dominant group? What role does such dehumanization play in making it possible for people, who think of themselves as decent and moral, to inflict terrible cruelties on the dehumanized population?

The Conscience of Huckleberry Finn

JONATHAN BENNETT

Jonathan Bennett (b. 1930) is a professor of philosophy at Syracuse University. He is the author of several books, including *Rationality* (1964), *Linguistic Behavior* (1976), *Events and their Names* (1988), and *Rationality: An Essay toward an Analysis* (1989).

In this article Bennett considers the moral consciences of Huckleberry Finn, the Nazi officer Heinrich Himmler, and the Calvinist theologian Jonathan Edwards. He is interested in how each, in his own way, resolves the conflict between his human sympathies and the moral doctrine he is following that requires him to override those sympathies. Huck Finn develops a deep attachment to Jim, the runaway slave, but the official morality of his community does not allow for fellow feelings towards slaves. When forced to choose between his kindly feelings and the official morality, Huck gives up on morality. Himmler set his sympathies aside. Jonathan Edwards's case represents a third way out: he allowed himself no sympathies at all. Bennett finds Edwards's solution to be as bad as Himmler's, if not worse. Bennett concludes that while we should not give our sympathies a "blank check," we must always give them great weight and be wary of acting on any principle that conflicts with them.

I

In this paper, I shall present not just the conscience of Huckleberry Finn but two others as well. One of them is the conscience of

THE CONSCIENCE OF HUCKLEBERRY FINN From *Philosophy* 49 (1974), pp. 123–134. Reprinted by permission of Cambridge University Press.

Heinrich Himmler. He became a Nazi in 1923; he served drably and quietly, but well, and was rewarded with increasing responsibility and power. At the peak of his career he held many offices and commands, of which the most powerful was that of leader of the SS— the principal police force of the Nazi regime. In this capacity, Himmler commanded the whole concentration-camp system, and was responsible for the execution of the so-called "final solution of the Jewish problem." It is important for my purposes that this piece of social engineering should be thought of not abstractly but in concrete terms of Jewish families being marched to what they think are bathhouses, to the accompaniment of loud-speaker renditions of extracts from *The Merry Widow* and *Tales of Hoffmann,* there to be choked to death by poisonous gases. Altogether, Himmler succeeded in murdering about four and a half million of them, as well as several million gentiles, mainly Poles and Russians.

The other conscience to be discussed is that of the Calvinist theologian and philosopher Jonathan Edwards. He lived in the first half of the eighteenth century, and has a good claim to be considered America's first serious and considerable philosophical thinker. He was for many years a widely renowned preacher and Congregationalist minister in New England; in 1748 a dispute with his congregation led him to resign (he couldn't accept their view that unbelievers should be admitted to the Lord's Supper in the hope that it would convert them); for some years after that he worked as a missionary, preaching to Indians through an interpreter; then in 1758 he accepted the presidency of what is now Princeton University, and within two months died from a smallpox inoculation. Along the way he wrote some first-rate philosophy; his book attacking the notion of free will is still sometimes read. Why I should be interested in Edwards's *conscience* will be explained in due course.

I shall use Heinrich Himmler, Jonathan Edwards, and Huckleberry Finn to illustrate different aspects of a single theme, namely the relationship between *sympathy* on the one hand and *bad morality* on the other.

II

All that I can mean by a "bad morality" is a morality whose principles I deeply disapprove of. When I call a morality bad, I cannot prove that mine is better; but when I here call any morality bad, I think you will agree with me that it is bad; and that is all I need.

There could be dispute as to whether the springs of someone's actions constitute a *morality*. I think, though, that we must admit that someone who acts in ways which conflict grossly with our morality may nevertheless have a morality of his own—a set of principles of action which he sincerely assents to, so that for him the problem of acting well or rightly or in obedience to conscience is the problem of conforming to *those* principles. The problem of conscientiousness can arise as acutely for a bad morality as for any other: Rotten principles may be as difficult to keep as decent ones.

As for "sympathy" I use this term to cover every sort of fellow-feeling, as when one feels pity over someone's loneliness, or horrified compassion over his pain, or when one feels a shrinking reluctance to act in a way which will bring misfortune to someone else. These *feelings* must not be confused with *moral judgments*. My sympathy for someone in distress may lead me to help him, or even to think that I ought to help him; but in itself it is not a judgment about what I ought to do but just a *feeling* for him in his plight. We shall get some light on the difference between feelings and moral judgments when we consider Huckleberry Finn.

Obviously, feelings can impel one to action, and so can moral judgments; and in a particular case sympathy and morality may pull in opposite directions. This can happen not just with bad moralities, but also with good ones like yours and mine. For example, a small child, sick and miserable, clings tightly to his mother and screams in terror when she tries to pass him over to the doctor to be examined. If the mother gave way to her sympathy, that is to her feeling for the child's misery and fright, she would hold it close and not let the doctor come near; but don't we agree that it might be wrong for her to act on such a feeling? Quite generally, then, anyone's moral principles may apply to a particular situation in a way which runs contrary to the particular thrusts of fellow-feeling that he has in that situation. My immediate concern is with sympathy in relation to bad morality, but not because such conflicts occur only when the morality is bad.

Now, suppose that someone who accepts a bad morality is struggling to make himself act in accordance with it in a particular situation where his sympathies pull him another way. He sees the struggle as one between doing the right, conscientious thing, and acting wrongly and weakly, like the mother who won't let the doctor come near her sick, frightened baby. Since we don't accept this person's morality, we may see the situation very differently, thoroughly disapproving of the action he regards as the right one, and endorsing the action which from his point of view constitutes weakness and backsliding.

Conflicts between sympathy and bad morality won't always be like this, for we won't disagree with every single dictate of a bad morality. Still, it can happen in the way I have described, with the agent's right action being our wrong one, and vice versa. That is just what happens in a certain episode in Chapter 16 of *The Adventures of Huckleberry Finn,* an episode which brilliantly illustrates how fiction can be instructive about real life.

III

Huck Finn has been helping his slave friend Jim to run away from Miss Watson, who is Jim's owner. In their raft-journey down the Mississippi River, they are near to the place at which Jim will become legally free. Now let Huck take over the story:

> Jim said it made him all over trembly and feverish to be so close to freedom. Well I can tell you it made me all over trembly and feverish, too, to hear him, because I begun to get it through my head that he *was* most free—and who was to blame for it? Why, *me.* I couldn't get that out of my conscience, no how nor no way. . . . It hadn't ever come home to me, before, what this thing was that I was doing. But now it did; and it stayed with me, and scorched me more and more. I tried to make out to myself that *I* warn't to blame, because *I* didn't run Jim off from his rightful owner; but it warn't no use, conscience up and say, every time: "But you knowed he was running for his freedom, and you could a paddled ashore and told somebody." That was so—I couldn't get around that, no way. That was where it pinched. Conscience says to me: "What had poor Miss Watson done to you, that you could see her nigger go off right under your eyes and never say one single word? What did that poor old woman do to you, that you could treat her so mean? . . ." I got to feeling so mean and miserable I most wished I was dead.

Jim speaks his plan to save up to buy his wife, and then his children, out of slavery; and he adds that if the children cannot be bought he will arrange to steal them. Huck is horrified:

> Thinks I, this is what comes of my not thinking. Here was this nigger which I had as good as helped to run away, coming right out flat-footed and saying he would steal his children—children that belonged to a man I didn't even know; a man that hadn't ever done me no harm.
>
> I was sorry to hear Jim say that, it was such a lowering of him. My conscience got to stirring me up hotter than ever, until at last I says to it: "Let up on me—it ain't too late, yet—I'll paddle ashore at first light, and tell." I felt easy, and happy, and light as a feather, right off. All my troubles was gone.

This is bad morality all right. In his earliest years Huck wasn't taught any principles, and the only one he has encountered since then are those of rural Missouri, in which slave-owning is just one kind of ownership and is not subject to critical pressure. It hasn't occurred to Huck to question those principles. So the action, to us abhorrent, of turning Jim in to the authorities presents itself *clearly* to Huck as the right thing to do.

For us, morality and sympathy would both dictate helping Jim to escape. If we felt any conflict, it would have both these on one side and something else on the other—greed for a reward, or fear of punishment. But Huck's morality conflicts with his sympathy, that is, with his unargued, natural feeling for his friend. The conflict starts when Huck sets off in the canoe towards the shore, pretending that he is going to reconnoiter, but really planning to turn Jim in:

> As I shoved off, [Jim] says: "Pooty soon I'll be a-shout'n for joy, en I'll say, it's all on accounts o' Huck I's a free man . . . Jim won't ever forgit you, Huck; you's de bes' fren' Jim's ever had; en you's de *only* fren' old Jim's got now."
>
> I was paddling off, all in a sweat to tell on him; but when he says this, it seemed to kind of take the tuck all out of me. I went along slow then, and I warn't right down certain whether I was glad I started or whether I warn't. When I was fifty yards off, Jim says:
>
> "Dah you goes, de ole true Huck; de on'y white genlman dat ever kep' his promise to ole Jim." Well, I just felt sick. But I says, I *got* to do it—I can't get *out* of it.

29

In the upshot, sympathy wins over morality. Huck hasn't the strength of will to do what he sincerely thinks he ought to do. Two men hunting for runaway slaves ask him whether the man on his raft is black or white:

> I didn't answer up prompt. I tried to, but the words wouldn't come. I tried, for a second or two, to brace up and out with it, but I warn't man enough—hadn't the spunk of a rabbit. I see I was weakening; so I just give up trying, and up and says: "He's white."

So Huck enables Jim to escape, thus acting weakly and wickedly— he thinks. In this conflict between sympathy and morality, sympathy wins.

One critic has cited this episode in support of the statement that Huck suffers "excruciating moments of wavering between honesty and respectability." That is hopelessly wrong, and I agree with the perceptive comment on it by another critic, who says:

> The conflict waged in Huck is much more serious: He scarcely cares for respectability and never hesitates to relinquish it, but he does care for honesty and gratitude—and both honesty and gratitude require that he should give Jim up. It is not, in Huck, honesty at war with respectability but love and compassion for Jim struggling against his conscience. His decision is for Jim and hell: a right decision made in the mental chains that Huck never breaks. His concern for Jim is and remains *irrational*. Huck finds many reasons for giving Jim up and none for stealing him. To the end Huck sees his compassion for Jim as a weak, ignorant, and wicked felony.[1]

That is precisely correct—and it can have that virtue only because Mark Twain wrote the episode with such unerring precision. The crucial point concerns *reasons,* which all occur on one side of the conflict. On the side of conscience we have principles, arguments, considerations, ways of looking at things:

> "It hadn't ever come home to me before what I was doing"
> "I tried to make out that I warn't to blame"
> "Conscience said 'But you knowed . . .'—I couldn't get around that"
> "What had poor Miss Watson done to you?"

---

[1] M.J. Sidnell, "Huck Finn and Jim," *The Cambridge Quarterly*, vol. 2, pp. 205–206.

"This is what comes of my not thinking"

". . . children that belonged to a man I didn't even know."

On the other side, the side of feeling, we get nothing like that. When Jim rejoices in Huck, as his only friend, Huck doesn't consider the claims of friendship or have the situation "come home" to him in a different light. All that happens is: "When he says this, it seemed to kind of take the tuck all out of me. I went along slow then, and I warn't right down certain whether I was glad I started or whether I warn't." Again, Jim's words about Huck's "promise" to him don't give Huck any *reason* for changing his plan: In his morality promises to slaves probably don't count. Their effect on him is of a different kind: "Well, I just felt sick." And when the moment for final decision comes, Huck doesn't weigh up pros and cons: he simply *fails* to do what he believes to be right—he isn't strong enough, hasn't "the spunk of a rabbit." This passage in the novel is notable not just for its finely wrought irony, with Huck's weakness of will leading him to do the right thing, but also for its masterly handling of the difference between general moral principles and particular unreasoned emotional pulls.

IV

Consider now another case of bad morality in conflict with human sympathy: the case of the odious Himmler. Here, from a speech he made to some SS generals, is an indication of the content of his morality:

> What happens to a Russian, to a Czech, does not interest me in the slightest. What the nations can offer in the way of good blood of our type, we will take, if necessary by kidnapping their children and raising them here with us. Whether nations live in prosperity or starve to death like cattle interests me only in so far as we need them as slaves to our *Kultur;* otherwise it is of no interest to me. Whether 10,000 Russian females fall down from exhaustion while digging an antitank ditch interests me only in so far as the antitank ditch for Germany is finished.[2]

---

[2]Quoted in William L. Shirer, *The Rise and Fall of the Third Reich* (New York, 1960), pp. 937–938. Next quotation: ibid., p. 966. All further quotations relating to Himmler are from Roger Manwell and Heinrich Fraenkel, *Heinrich Himmler* (London, 1965), pp. 132, 197, 184 (twice), 187.

But has this a moral basis at all? And if it has, was there in Himmler's own mind any conflict between morality and sympathy? Yes there was. Here is more from the same speech:

> I also want to talk to you quite frankly on a very grave matter . . . I mean . . . the extermination of the Jewish race. . . . Most of you must know what it means when 100 corpses are lying side by side, or 500, or 1,000. To have stuck it out and at the same time—apart from exceptions caused by human weakness—to have remained decent fellows, that is what has made us hard. This is a page of glory in our history which has never been written and is never to be written.

Himmler saw his policies as being hard to implement while still retaining one's human sympathies—while still remaining a "decent fellow." He is saying that only the weak take the easy way out and just squelch their sympathies, and is praising the stronger and more glorious course of retaining one's sympathies while acting in violation of them. In the same spirit, he ordered that when executions were carried out in concentration camps, those responsible "are to be influenced in such a way as to suffer no ill effect in their character and mental attitude." A year later he boasted that the SS had wiped out the Jews

> without our leaders and their men suffering any damage in their minds and souls. The danger was considerable, for there was only a narrow path between the Scylla of their becoming heartless ruffians unable any longer to treasure life, and the Charybdis of their becoming soft and suffering nervous breakdowns.

And there really can't be any doubt that the basis of Himmler's policies was a set of principles which constituted his morality—a sick, bad, wicked *morality*. He described himself as caught in "the old tragic conflict between will and obligation." And when his physician Kersten protested at the intention to destroy the Jews, saying that the suffering involved was "not to be contemplated," Kersten reports that Himmler replied:

> He knew that it would mean much suffering for the Jews. . . . "It is the curse of greatness that it must step over dead bodies to create new life. Yet we must . . . cleanse the soil or it will never bear fruit. It will be a great burden for me to bear."

This, I submit, is the language of morality.

So in this case, tragically, bad morality won out over sympathy. I am sure that many of Himmler's killers did extinguish their sympathies, becoming "heartless ruffians" rather than "decent fellows"; but not Himmler himself. Although his policies ran against the human grain to a horrible degree, he did not sandpaper down his emotional surfaces so that there was no grain there, allowing his actions to slide along smoothly and easily. He did, after all, bear his hideous burden, and even paid a price for it. He suffered a variety of nervous and physical disabilities, including nausea and stomach-convulsions, and Kersten was doubtless right in saying that these were "the expression of a psychic division which extended over his whole life."

This same division must have been present in some of those officials of the Church who ordered heretics to be tortured so as to change their theological opinions. Along with the brutes and the cold careerists, there must have been some who cared, and who suffered from the conflict between their sympathies and their bad morality.

V

In the conflict between sympathy and bad morality, then, the victory may go to sympathy as in the case of Huck Finn, or to morality as in the case of Himmler.

Another possibility is that the conflict may be avoided by giving up, or not ever having, those sympathies which might interfere with one's principles. That seems to have been the case with Jonathan Edwards. I am afraid that I shall be doing an injustice to Edwards's many virtues, and to his great intellectual energy and inventiveness; for my concern is only with the worst thing about him—namely his morality, which was worse than Himmler's.

According to Edwards, God condemns some men to an eternity of unimaginably awful pain, though he arbitrarily spares others—"arbitrarily" because none deserve to be spared:

> Natural men are held in the hand of God over the pit of hell; they have deserved the fiery pit, and are already sentenced to it; and God is dreadfully provoked, his anger is as great toward them as to those that are actually suffering the executions of the fierceness of his wrath in hell . . . ; the devil is waiting for them, hell is gaping for them, the flames gather and flash about them, and would fain lay hold on

them . . . ; and . . . there are no means within reach that can be any
security to them. . . . All that preserves them is the mere arbitrary
will, and unconvenanted unobliged forebearance of an incensed God.[3]

Notice that he says "they have deserved the fiery pit." Edwards insists
that men *ought* to be condemned to eternal pain; and his position isn't
that this is right because God wants it, but rather that God wants it
because it is right. For him, moral standards exist independently of
God, and God can be assessed in the light of them (and of course
found to be perfect). For example, he says:

> They deserve to be cast into hell; so that . . . justice never stands in
> the way, it makes no objection against God's using his power at any
> moment to destroy them. Yea, on the contrary, justice calls aloud for
> an infinite punishment of their sins.

Elsewhere, he gives elaborate arguments to show that God is acting
justly in damning sinners. For example, he argues that a punishment
should be exactly as bad as the crime being punished; God is infinitely excellent; so any crime against him is infinitely bad; and so
eternal damnation is exactly right as a punishment—it is infinite,
but, as Edwards is careful also to say, it is "no more than infinite."

Of course, Edwards himself didn't torment the damned; but the
question still arises of whether his sympathies didn't conflict with his
approval of eternal torment. Didn't he find it painful to contemplate
any fellow-human's being tortured for ever? Apparently not:

> The God that holds you over the pit of hell, much as one holds a
> spider or some loathsome insect over the fire, abhors you, and is
> dreadfully provoked . . . he is of purer eyes than to bear to have you
> in his sight; you are ten thousand times so abominable in his eyes as
> the most hateful venomous serpent is in ours.

When God is presented as being as misanthropic as that, one suspects
misanthropy in the theologian. This suspicion is increased when
Edwards claims that "the saints in glory will . . . understand how
terrible the sufferings of the damned are; yet . . . will not be sorry

---

[3]Vergilius Ferm (ed.), *Puritan Sage: Collected Writings of Jonathan Edwards* (New York,
1953), p. 370. Next three quotations: ibid., p. 366, p. 294 ("no more than infinite"),
p. 372.

for [them]."[4] He bases this partly on a view of human nature whose ugliness he seems not to notice:

> The seeing of the calamities of others tends to heighten the sense of our own enjoyments. When the saints in glory, therefore, shall see the doleful state of the damned, how will this heighten their sense of the blessedness of their own state. . . . When they shall see how miserable others of their fellow-creatures are . . . when they shall see the smoke of their torment . . . and hear their dolorous shrieks and cries, and consider that they in the mean time are in the most blissful state, and shall surely be in it to all eternity; how they will rejoice!

I hope this is less than the whole truth! His other main point about why the saints will rejoice to see the torments of the damned is that it is *right* that they should do so:

> The heavenly inhabitants . . . will have no love nor pity to the damned. . . . [This will not show] a want of spirit of love in them . . . for the heavenly inhabitants will know that it is not fit that they should love [the damned] because they will know then, that God has no love to them, nor pity for them.

The implication that *of course* one can adjust one's feelings of pity so that they conform to the dictates of some authority—doesn't this suggest that ordinary human sympathies played only a small part in Edwards's life?

VI

Huck Finn, whose sympathies are wide and deep, could never avoid the conflict in that way; but he is determined to avoid it, and so he opts for the only other alternative he can see—to give up morality altogether. After he has tricked the slave-hunters, he returns to the raft and undergoes a peculiar crisis:

> I got aboard the raft, feeling bad and low, because I knowed very well I had done wrong, and I see it warn't no use for me to try to learn to do right; a body that don't get *started* right when he's little, ain't got

---

[4]This and the next two quotations are from "The End of the Wicked Contemplated by the Righteous: Or, The Torments of the Wicked in Hell, No Occasion of Grief to the Saints in Heaven," from *The Works of President Edwards* (London, 1817), vol. 4, pp. 507–508, 511–512, and 509 respectively.

> no show—when the pinch comes there ain't nothing to back him up and keep him to his work, and so he gets beat. Then I thought a minute, and says to myself, hold on—s'pose you'd a done right and give Jim up; would you feel better than what you do now? No, says I, I'd feel bad—I'd feel just the same way I do now. Well, then, says I, what's the use you learning to do right, when it's troublesome to do right and ain't no trouble to do wrong, and the wages is just the same? I was stuck. I couldn't answer that. So I reckoned I wouldn't bother no more about it, but after this always do whichever come handiest at the time.

Huck clearly cannot conceive of having any morality except the one he has learned—too late, he thinks—from his society. He is not entirely a prisoner of that morality, because he does after all reject it; but for him that is a decision to relinquish morality as such; he cannot envisage revising his morality, altering its content in face of the various pressures to which it is subject, including pressures from his sympathies. For example, he does not begin to approach the thought that slavery should be rejected on moral grounds, or the thought that what he is doing is not theft because a person cannot be owned and therefore cannot be stolen.

The basic trouble is that he cannot or will not engage in abstract intellectual operations of any sort. In Chapter 33 he finds himself "feeling to blame, somehow" for something he knows he had no hand in; he assumes that this feeling is a deliverance of conscience; and this confirms him in his belief that conscience shouldn't be listened to:

> It don't make no difference whether you do right or wrong, a person's conscience ain't got no sense, and just goes for him *anyway*. If I had a yaller dog that didn't know no more than a person's conscience does, I would poison him. It takes up more than all of a person's insides, and yet ain't no good, nohow.

That brisk, incurious dismissiveness fits well with the comprehensive rejection of morality back on the raft. But this is a digression.

On the raft, Huck decides not to live by principles, but just to do whatever "comes handiest at the time"—always acting according to the mood of the moment. Since the morality he is rejecting is narrow and cruel, and his sympathies are broad and kind, the results will be good. But moral principles are good to have, because they help to protect one from acting badly at moments when one's sympathies happen to be in abeyance. On the highest possible estimate of the role one's sympathies should have, one can still allow for principles as embodiments of one's best feelings, one's broadest and keenest sympathies. On that view, principles can help one across intervals when one's feelings are at less than their best, i.e. through periods of misanthropy or meanness or self-centeredness or depression or anger.

What Huck didn't see is that one can live by principles and yet have ultimate control over their content. And one way such control can be exercised is by checking one's principles in the light of one's sympathies. This is sometimes a pretty straightforward matter. It can happen that a certain moral principle becomes untenable—meaning literally that one cannot hold it any longer—because it conflicts intolerably with the pity or revulsion or whatever that one feels when one sees what the principle leads to. One's experience may play a large part here: Experiences evoke feelings, and feelings force one to modify principles. Something like this happened to the English poet Wilfred Owen, whose experiences in the First World War transformed him from an enthusiastic soldier into a virtual pacifist. I can't document his change of conscience in detail; but I want to present something which he wrote about the way experience can put pressure on morality.

The Latin poet Horace wrote that it is sweet and fitting (or right) to die for one's country—*dulce et decorum est pro patria mori*—and Owen wrote a fine poem about how experience could lead one to relinquish that particular moral principle.[5] He describes a man who is too slow donning his gas mask during a gas attack—"As under a green sea I saw him drowning," Owen says. The poem ends like this:

> In all my dreams before my helpless sight
> He plunges at me, guttering, choking, drowning.
> If in some smothering dreams, you too could pace
> Behind the wagon that we flung him in,
> And watch the white eyes writhing in his face,
> His hanging face, like a devil's sick of sin;

---

[5]We are grateful to the Executors of the Estate of Harold Owen, and to Chatto and Windus Ltd. for permission to quote from Wilfred Owen's "Dulce et Decorum Est" and "Insensibility."

If you could hear, at every jolt, the blood
Come gargling from the froth-corrupted lungs,
Bitter as the cud
Of vile, incurable sores on innocent tongues,—
My friend, you would not tell with such high zest
To children ardent for some desperate glory,
The old Lie: Dulce et decorum est
Pro patria mori.

There is a difficulty about drawing from all this a moral for ourselves. I imagine that we agree in our rejection of slavery, eternal damnation, genocide, and uncritical patriotic self-abnegation; so we shall agree that Huck Finn, Jonathan Edwards, Heinrich Himmler, and the poet Horace would all have done well to bring certain of their principles under severe pressure from ordinary human sympathies. But then we can say this because we can say that all those are bad moralities, whereas we cannot look at our own moralities and declare them bad. This is not arrogance: It is obviously incoherent for someone to declare the system of moral principles that he *accepts* to be *bad,* just as one cannot coherently say of anything that one *believes* it but it is *false.*

Still, although I can't point to any of my beliefs and say "That is false," I don't doubt that some of my beliefs *are* false; and so I should try to remain open to correction. Similarly, I accept every single item in my morality—that is inevitable—but I am sure that my morality could be improved, which is to say that it could undergo changes which I should be glad of once I had made them. So I must try to keep my morality open to revision, exposing it to whatever valid pressures there are—including pressures from my sympathies.

I don't give my sympathies a blank check in advance. In a conflict between principle and sympathy, principles ought sometimes to win. For example, I think it was right to take part in the Second World War on the allied side; there were many ghastly individual incidents which might have led someone to doubt the rightness of his participation in that war; and I think it would have been right for such a person to keep his sympathies in a subordinate place on those occasions, not allowing them to modify his principles in such a way as to make a pacifist of him.

Still, one's sympathies should be kept as sharp and sensitive and aware as possible, and not only because they can sometimes affect one's principles or one's conduct or both. Owen, at any rate, says that feelings and sympathies are vital even when they can do nothing but bring pain and distress. In another poem he speaks of the blessings of being numb in one's feelings: "Happy are the men who yet before they are killed/Can let their veins run cold," he says. These are the ones who do not suffer from any compassion which, as Owen puts it, "makes their feet/Sore on the alleys cobbled with their brothers." He contrasts these "happy" ones, who "lose all imagination," with himself and others "who with a thought besmirch/Blood over all our soul." Yet the poem's verdict goes against the "happy" ones. Owen does not say that they will act worse than the others whose souls are besmirched with blood because of their keen awareness of human suffering. He merely says that they are the losers because they have cut themselves off from the human condition:

> By choice they made themselves immune
> To pity and whatever moans in man
> Before the last sea and the hapless stars;
> Whatever mourns when many leave these shores;
> Whatever shares
> The eternal reciprocity of tears.[6]

STUDY QUESTIONS

1. What does Bennett mean by a "bad morality"?
2. Does Bennett think principles play an important role in moral life? Can you suggest occasions where one's principles *should* overrule one's sympathies?
3. What are the consequences of Bennett's arguments for ethical relativism?
4. Why does Bennett claim that Jonathan Edwards's morality was even worse than Himmler's? Do you agree?
5. What are the implications of Bennett's position for the view that we must always follow our conscience?

---

[6]This paper began life as the Potter Memorial Lecture, given at Washington State University in Pullman, Washington, in 1972.

The Evil That Men Think—And Do

PHILIP HALLIE

A biographical sketch of Philip Hallie is found on page 9.

Philip Hallie summarizes and criticizes several recent theories of evil. In particular he objects to the views of Jonathan Bennett in "The Conscience of Huckleberry Finn," where Bennett claims that eighteenth-century theologian Jonathan Edwards, who killed no one, has a "worse morality" than Heinrich Himmler, who sent millions to their deaths but who appears to have suffered somewhat because occasionally he sympathized with those he tormented.

Hallie believes that Bennett can reach this odd conclusion only by perversely overlooking the truly horrific aspect of evil—its victims. On the contrary, it matters greatly that Edwards never actually killed or meant to kill anyone, and that Himmler tortured and killed millions. "Victims are as essential to morality as the presence or absence of sympathy. . . ."

Hallie claims that Bennett and others trivialize the notion of evil by concentrating too heavily on the psychology of evildoers and by paying scant attention to the fate of their victims. Hallie concludes with an excerpt from the official transcripts of the Nuremberg Trials, an excerpt he believes exemplifies the "wholeness of evil": it

THE EVIL THAT MEN THINK—AND DO From *Hastings Center Report*, December 1985. Reprinted by permission of the author.

reveals not only what a Nazi war criminal says he thought but, more significantly, it details what he did and the suffering it caused.

In a cartoon by Edward Kliban, a mechanic is waving his tools and pointing at what he has discovered under the hood of his customer's car. There, where the motor should be, squats a massive monster, a wicked grin revealing his terrible teeth. The mechanic is triumphantly proclaiming to his customer: "Well, *there's* your problem."

In her book, *Wickedness*, Mary Midgley writes that evil must not be seen as "something positive" or demonic like Kliban's monster. If evil were a demon we could only exorcise it, not understand it. To do so, she writes, one must see the various types of wickedness as *mixtures* of motives, some of which can be life-enhancing in themselves but are destructive in certain combinations. For instance, a rapist-murderer can be motivated by power and sex, but his way of combining these often healthy drives is destructive. For Midgley wickedness is "essentially destructive," not the way a terrible-toothed monster can be destructive but the way a person acting under various motives can fail to care about the feelings or even the lives of others. For her, evil is an absence of such caring, "an emptiness at the core of the individual. . . ." It is a negative, not a positive, demon.

This is a sensitive analysis, but the demon Wickedness is a straw demon: very few, if any, modern thinkers on the subject believe in the demonic. For most of them another cartoon would be more apt. A mechanic is waving his tools triumphantly before a customer and is pointing to what he has found under the hood of the car. There, where Kliban's demon was, is a mass of intricately intertwined pipes, and the mechanic is pointing to *this* and announcing, "Well, *there's* your problem." And the customer is as bewildered by this phenomenon as Kliban's customer was.

Many of the people who are writing about wickedness (or immorality or evil, call it what you will) are making it a very complicated matter, like those twisted pipes. Judith Shklar in her quite often brilliant book *Ordinary Vices* is more concerned with various ethical and political puzzles than she is with the ordinary vices she promises to talk about in her introduction and in her title. Usually the unique perplexities of unique people like Robert E. Lee, Richard II, Socrates, and Colonel Count Claus von Stauffenberg interest her more than any single idea of vice does. Her skeptical, energetic mind seeks out mine-fields, not highways: contradictions, not a monster.

My version of Kliban's cartoon applies also to the lucid, careful book *Immorality* by the philosopher Ronald D. Milo. Milo takes Aristotle's all-too-pat distinction between moral weakness and moral baseness, and refines it into a range of kinds and degrees of blameworthiness. In the seventh book of his *Nichomachean Ethics*, Aristotle said that the weak (or "incontinent") person is like a city that has good laws, but that does not live by them; the vicious (or "base" person) is like a city that has bad laws by which it *does* live. The zealous mass murderer is vicious without remorse; while the weak, penitent adulterer or drunkard knows he is doing wrong, but does nothing about it. Milo refines and develops this rather crude distinction, so that Aristotle's baseness is no longer a simple contrast between two kinds of cities. Like Shklar, Milo is too perceptive and too circumspect to join the simplifiers that Midgley deplores.

And yet, despite their perceptiveness and circumspection, many of our analyzers of evil have grossly simplified the idea of immorality. In their scrupulous examinations of complexities they have left out much of the ferocious ugliness of Kliban's monster. They too are negligent simplifiers.

For instance, Jonathan Bennett has written an essay entitled "The Conscience of Huckleberry Finn," in which he proves to his satisfaction that the morality of the eighteenth-century American theologian Jonathan Edwards was "worse than Himmler's." He insists that Heinrich Himmler, head of the SS and of all the police systems of Nazi Germany, and responsible for all of the tortures and the deaths perpetrated upon noncombatants by Nazi Germany, was not as wicked as Jonathan Edwards, who never killed or meant to kill anyone.

Why? Because Jonathan Edwards had no pity for the damned, and Himmler did have sympathy for the millions of people he tortured and destroyed. Bennett contends that there are two forces at work in the consciences of human beings: general moral principles and unreasoned "emotional pulls." One such "pull" is sympathy, and Jonathan Edwards's sermons showed no sympathy for the sinners who were in the hands of an angry God, while Himmler's speeches to his Nazi subordinates did express the emotional pull of sympathy. In the mind, the only place where "morality" dwells for Bennett, Himmler is no heartless ruffian, but a decent fellow who had a wrong-headed set of principles and who felt the pangs of sympathy for human beings he was crushing and grinding into death and worse.

The Central Role of the Victim

In Lewis Carroll's *Alice's Adventures in Wonderland* Tweedledee recites to Alice "The Walrus and the Carpenter." In the poem, the Walrus and the Carpenter come across some oysters while they are strolling on the beach. They manage to persuade the younger oysters to join them in

> A pleasant walk, a pleasant talk
> Along the briny beach

After a while they rest on a rock that is "conveniently low," so that the two of them can keep an eye on the oysters and can reach them easily. After a little chat, the Carpenter and the Walrus start eating the oysters.

The Walrus is a sympathetic creature, given to crying readily, who thanks the oysters for joining them, while the Carpenter is interested only in eating:

> "It seems a shame," the Walrus said
> "To play them such a trick.
> After we've brought them out so far
> And made them trot so quick!"
> The Carpenter said nothing but
> "The butter's spread too thick."

Then the Walrus, out of the goodness of his heart, bursts forth:

> "I weep for you," the Walrus said:
> "I deeply sympathize."
> With sobs and tears he sorted out
> Those of the largest size,
> Holding his pocket-handkerchief
> Before his streaming eyes.

And they finish off all the oysters.

Bennett, with his concern for the saving grace of sympathy, might find the "morality" of the Walrus better than the morality of the cold-blooded Carpenter, but Lewis Carroll, or rather Tweedledee and Tweedledum, are not so simple-minded:

> "I like the Walrus best," said Alice: "because he was a *little* sorry for the poor oysters."
>
> "He ate more than the Carpenter, though," said Tweedledee. "You see he held his handkerchief in front, so that the Carpenter couldn't count how many he took: contrariwise."
>
> "That was mean!" Alice said indignantly. "Then I like the Carpenter best—if he didn't eat so many as the Walrus."
>
> "But he ate as many as he could get," said Tweedledum.

Then Alice gives up trying to rank the Walrus and the Carpenter and gives voice to a wisdom that is as sound as it is obvious:

> "Well! They were both very unpleasant characters. . . ."

What Lewis Carroll saw, and what Bennett apparently does not, is that the victims are as essential in morality as the presence or absence of sympathy inside the head of the moral agent. And he also sees that sympathy, or rather expressions of sympathy, can be a device for eating more oysters by hiding your mouth behind a handkerchief—it certainly needn't slow your eating down.

Milo never violates the morally obvious as boldly as Bennett does, but when he ranks immoralities he too disregards the essential role of the victim in evil. His conclusions contradict Bennett's. For Milo, apparently, Himmler's would be "the most evil" kind of wrong-doing, just because of his scruples:

> . . . we think that the most evil or reprehensible kind of wrongdoing consists in willingly and intentionally doing something that one believes to be morally wrong, either because one simply does not care that it is morally wrong or because one prefers the pursuit of some other end to the avoidance of moral wrongdoing. . . .

This is a more subtle analysis of evil than Bennett's, but it too ranks evils without the wisdom of Tweedledum and Tweedledee. It too flattens out or ignores the central role of victims in the dance of evil.

Where Eichmann's Evil Lay

The most distinguished modern philosophic treatment of evil is Hannah Arendt's *Eichmann in Jerusalem, A Report on the Banality of Evil*. Like most of the philosophers who came after her she believed that the evil person is not necessarily a monster. In her report on the Eichmann trial as she witnessed it in Jerusalem in 1961 she shows us a man who did not act out of evil motives. She shows us a man, Adolf Eichmann, whose main trait was to have no interesting traits, except perhaps his "remoteness from reality." His banality resides in his never having *realized* what he was doing to particular human beings. Hannah Arendt tells us that, except for personal advancement, "He had no motives at all." He was an unimaginative bureaucrat who lived in the clichés of his office. He was no Iago, no Richard III, no person who wished "to prove a villain."

There is truth in this position. Eichmann was a commonplace, trite man if you look at him only in the dock and if you do not see that his boring clichés are directly linked with millions of tortures and murders. If you see the victims of Eichmann and of the office he held, then—and only then—do you see the evil of this man. Evil does not happen only in people's heads. Eichmann's evil happened in his head (and here Arendt is not only right but brilliantly perceptive) *and* (and the "and" makes a tight, essential linkage) in the freight cars and in the camps of Central Europe. His evil is the sum-total of his unimaginative head and his unimaginable tortures and murders. And this sum-total is not banal, not flat, not common-place. It is horrific.

As one of the most powerful philosophers of our time, Arendt was conscious of leaving something out by concentrating her attention upon the internal workings of the mind of a bureaucrat. Early in her book she wrote: "On trial are his deeds, not the sufferings of the Jews."

As if "his deeds" could be neatly peeled away from what he did to the Jews! *Her separation* of the mental activity of Eichmann from the pain-racked deaths of millions that this mental activity brought about made Eichmann's evil banal. Without these actual murders and tortures Eichmann was not evil; his maunderings were those of a pitiable, not a culpable man. His evil lay in his deeds, as Arendt says, but not only in his mental "deeds": it lay in all that he intended and all that he carried out, in his mind and in the world around him.

The Morality of Seeing

In Saul Bellow's novel *The Dean's December*, the narrator, Dean Albert Corde, makes a plea for seeing what there is to be seen:

> In the American moral crisis, the first requirement was to experience what was happening and to see what must be seen. The facts were covered from our perception. . . . The increase of theories and discourse, itself a cause of new, strange forms of blindness, the false representations of "communication," led to horrible distortions of public consciousness. Therefore the first act of morality was to disinter the reality, retrieve reality, dig it out from the trash, represent it anew as art would represent it. . . .
>
> We were no longer talking about anything. The language of discourse had shut out experience altogether. . . . I tried to make myself the moralist of seeing. . . .

The dynamic of passions, moral principles, and perceptions within the heads of moral agents is a dynamic that is part of evil, but those of us who want to face and to understand evil as best we can must, it seems to me, try to live up to Corde's "morality of seeing." We must do our best to see not only what is happening in the inward polities of the doers of evil but *also* what is happening in the lives of the sufferers of evil.

For instance, to write about Himmler requires not only the reading of a few carefully crafted speeches; it also demands learning about the context of these speeches. It is true that at least once Himmler looked as if he felt queasy at an execution, and it is also true that he wrote about this queasiness in terms not entirely unlike those of the Walrus. But even a superficial study of what was actually happening within Fortress Europe in those days makes quite clear that he was coping with a particular problem by talking about "damage in . . . minds and souls" and "human weakness."

Look at almost any volume of the record of the 1947 Nuremberg Trials—for example Volume IV, especially pages 311–355—and it will become plain that the efficient murdering of children as well as other defenseless human beings was being hindered by the depression and even the nervous breakdowns of the people who were herding together and executing these people. Himmler, in order to minimize inefficiency, needed to prepare his followers to deal with such scruples. At least he needed to do this to carry out the project of exterminating the Jews of Europe as well as the majority of the Slavs.

Talking about these scruples was not a *cri du coeur*. He was not opening his heart to his subordinates, as Bennett suggests: he was preparing them for dealing with the psychological problems of the executioners. He was holding up a handkerchief before his eyes, to go back to the imagery of Tweedledee's poem, so that he and his followers could murder more and more helpless human beings.

A Monster in Action

Even such vigorously human books as *Ordinary Vices* by Judith Shklar and *Wickedness* by Mary Midgley do not meet the obligations laid upon us by a morality of seeing. Shklar provides lurid and deep insights into the implications of making cruelty *summum malum*, the most indefensible and unforgivable evil, and into many other subjects, but she hastens into perplexities and puzzles before she carefully observes the factual contexts of her examples.

Midgley is memorably illuminating in her efforts to clear away the obstacles that keep us from taking wickedness seriously. For instance, very few readers of her book, if they are attentive, will ever describe a mass-murderer and a mass-rapist as "sick" after reading her truly remarkable analysis in the chapter entitled "The Elusiveness of Responsibility." One of her key arguments against replacing the words "wicked" and "evil" by the words "sick" and "ill" is that doing so *distances* us from the destruction that has been done. It removes the "sick" destroyers from blame and from anger (how dare you blame a person for being ill?). It "flattens out," to use her powerful phrase, the distinctions between murderers and kleptomaniacs, between those who make us defensibly angry, when we see what they have *done,* and those who engage only our compassion and help.

Still, so scrupulous is she in removing the obstacles to an awareness of wickedness that she does not reveal much about what evil is. Her description of wickedness as "negative" like darkness and cold (an absence of caring being like an absence of light or heat) is useful but difficult to understand in terms of examples, especially when she tells us that "evil in the quiet supporters [of, for example, a Hitler] is negative," and then tells us that what they do is "positive action." This is a confusing use of metaphysical terms that do not have a plain cash value in relation to observable facts. These terms bring us close

47

to the medieval soup and its casuistical arguments about whether evil is a "privation of good" or something "positive."

Milo's *Immorality* offers a scrupulously lucid and sustained argument about the types and blameworthiness of immorality. It is especially adroit at understanding the relationships between moral weakness and deep wickedness. But he, like these other recent writers on evil, is reluctant to face the full force of evil. He, like them, does not look deeply and carefully at examples, at the terrible details in history and the arts.

These writers are, perhaps, too timid to look hard at Kliban's monster and say, "Well, *there's* your problem." Evil is thick with fact and as ugly as that grinning monster. It is no worse to see it this way than it is to see it as an internal dynamic in a moral agent's head, or a set of carefully honed distinctions, or an array of puzzles and perplexities (as Shklar seems to see it). Many of the insights of these writers are useful for understanding the monster, or rather the many monsters that embody evil, but there is no substitute for seeing the harshness and ugliness of fact.

Here is a monster in action: He is Otto Ohlendorf who was, among other roles, head of Group D of the Action Groups assigned to exterminate Jews and Soviet political leaders in parts of Eastern Europe. To learn more about him, read pages 311–355 of Volume IV of the transcript of the Nuremberg trials of the major war criminals. Here is part of his testimony:

COLONEL POKROVSKY (for the Tribunal):	Why did they (the execution squads) prefer execution by shooting to killing in the gas vans?
OHLENDORF:	Because . . . in the opinion of the leader of the Einsatzkommandos [Action Groups], the unloading of the corpses was an unnecessary mental strain.
COL. POKROVSKY:	What do you mean by "an unnecessary mental strain?"
OHLENDORF:	As far as I can remember the conditions at the time—the picture presented by the corpses and probably because certain functions of the body had taken place, leaving the corpses lying in filth.

COL. POKROVSKY:	You mean to say that the sufferings endured prior to death were clearly visible on the victims? Did I understand you correctly?
OHLENDORF:	I don't understand the question; do you mean during the killing in the van?
COL. POKROVSKY:	Yes.
OHLENDORF:	I can only repeat what the doctor told me, that the victims were not conscious of their death in the van.
COL. POKROVSKY:	In that case your reply to my previous question, that the unloading of the bodies made a very terrible impression on the members of the execution squad, becomes entirely incomprehensible.
OHLENDORF:	And, as I said, the terrible impression created by the position of the corpses themselves, and by the state of the vans which had probably been dirtied and so on.
COL. POKROVSKY:	I have no further questions to put to this witness at the present stage of the Trial (p. 334).
COLONEL AMEN (for the Tribunal):	Referring to the gas vans which you said you received in the spring of 1942, what order did you receive with respect to the use of these vans?
OHLENDORF:	These gas vans were in future to be used for the killing of women and children.
COL. AMEN:	Will you explain to the Tribunal the construction of these vans and their appearance?
OHLENDORF:	The actual purpose of these vans could not be seen from the outside. They looked like closed trucks, and were so constructed that at the start of the motor, gas was conducted into the van, causing death in 10 to 15 minutes.
COL. AMEN:	Explain in detail just how one of these vans was used for an execution.
OHLENDORF:	The vans were loaded with the victims and driven to the place of burial, which was usually the same as that used for the mass executions. The time needed for transportation was sufficient to insure the death of the victims.

COL. AMEN:	How were the victims induced to enter the vans?
OHLENDORF:	They were told that they were to be transported to another locality.
COL. AMEN:	How was the gas turned on?
OHLENDORF:	I am not familiar with the technical details.
COL. AMEN:	How long did it take to kill the victims ordinarily?
OHLENDORF:	About 10 to 15 minutes; the victims were not conscious of what was happening to them (p. 322).
OHLENDORF:	I led the Einsatzgruppe, and therefore I had the task of seeing how the Einsatzkommandos executed the orders received.
HERR BABEL (for the Tribunal):	But did you have no scruples in regard to the execution of these orders?
OHLENDORF:	Yes, of course.
HERR BABEL:	And how is it that they were carried out regardless of these scruples?
OHLENDORF:	Because to me it is inconceivable that a subordinate leader should not carry out orders given by the leaders of the state (pp. 353–354).

I urge you to read the above extracts more than once. The wholeness of evil is there, and if Ohlendorf is not monstrous to you, you are the problem.

STUDY QUESTIONS

1. Do you agree with Hallie's critique of Bennett? In particular, do you think Hallie is right in saying that Heinrich Himmler's attitude does not exculpate him and that Jonathan Edwards's attitude counts for less than Himmler's deeds?

2. Explain Hallie's reference to Lewis Carroll's *Alice's Adventure in Wonderland*. Do you find the morality of the walrus better than the morality of the carpenter? Do you agree with Alice's assessment? Explain.

3. Explain Hannah Arendt's phrase "the banality of evil." How does Hallie criticize Arendt's view?

4. In what respect does the testimony of Nazi war criminal Ohlendorf exemplify the "wholeness of evil"? Explain.

38 Who Saw Murder Didn't Call Police

MARTIN GANSBERG

Martin Gansberg (b. 1920) is on the staff of the *New York Times*. He taught journalism at Fairleigh Dickinson University from 1947 to 1973.

In 1964, the American public was stunned by reports from Kew Gardens, Queens: Kitty Genovese was brutally stabbed while her neighbors passively witnessed the murder. Gansberg describes the incident in detail without overtly judging the bystanders.

For more than half an hour 38 respectable, law-abiding citizens in Queens watched a killer stalk and stab a woman in three separate attacks in Kew Gardens.

Twice their chatter and the sudden glow of their bedroom lights interrupted him and frightened him off. Each time he returned, sought her out, and stabbed her again. Not one person telephoned the police during the assault; one witness called after the woman was dead.

That was two weeks ago today.

Still shocked is Assistant Chief Inspector Frederick M. Lussen, in charge of the borough's detectives and a veteran of 25 years of homicide investigations. He can give a matter-of-fact recitation on many murders. But the Kew Gardens slaying baffles him—not because it is a murder, but because the "good people" failed to call the police.

"As we have reconstructed the crime," he said, "the assailant had three chances to kill this woman during a 35-minute period. He returned twice to complete the job. If we had been called when he first attacked, the woman might not be dead now."

This is what the police say happened beginning at 3:20 A.M. in the staid, middle-class, tree-lined Austin Street area:

Twenty-eight-year-old Catherine Genovese, who was called Kitty by almost everyone in the neighborhood, was returning home from her job as manager of a bar in Hollis. She parked her red Fiat in a lot adjacent to the Kew Gardens Long Island Rail Road Station, facing Mowbray Place. Like many residents of the neighborhood, she had parked there day after day since her arrival in Connecticut a year ago, although the railroad frowns on the practice.

She turned off the lights of her car, locked the door, and started to walk the 100 feet to the entrance of her apartment at 82–70 Austin Street, which is in a Tudor building, with stores on the first floor and apartments on the second.

The entrance to the apartment is in the rear of the building because the front is rented to retail stores. At night the quiet neighborhood is shrouded in the slumbering darkness that marks most residential areas.

Miss Genovese noticed a man at the far end of the lot, near a seven-story apartment house at 82–40 Austin Street. She halted. Then, nervously, she headed up Austin Street toward Lefferts Boulevard, where there is a call box to the 102nd Police Precinct in nearby Richmond Hill.

She got as far as a street light in front of a bookstore before the man grabbed her. She screamed. Lights went on in the 10-story apartment house at 82–67 Austin Street, which faces the bookstore. Windows slid open and voices punctuated the early-morning stillness.

Miss Genovese screamed: "Oh, my God, he stabbed me! Please help me! Please help me!"

From one of the upper windows in the apartment house, a man called down: "Let that girl alone!"

The assailant looked up at him, shrugged, and walked down Austin Street toward a white sedan parked a short distance away. Miss Genovese struggled to her feet.

Lights went out. The killer returned to Miss Genovese, now trying to make her way around the side of the building by the parking lot to get to her apartment. The assailant stabbed her again.

"I'm dying!" she shrieked. "I'm dying!"

Windows were opened again, and lights went on in many apartments. The assailant got into his car and drove away. Miss Genovese staggered to her feet. A city bus, 0–10, the Lefferts Boulevard line to Kennedy International Airport, passed. It was 3:35 A.M.

The assailant returned. By then, Miss Genovese had crawled to the back of the building, where the freshly painted brown doors to the apartment house held out hope for safety. The killer tried the first door; she wasn't there. At the second door, 82–62 Austin Street, he saw her slumped on the floor at the foot of the stairs. He stabbed her a third time—fatally.

It was 3:50 by the time the police received their first call, from a man who was a neighbor of Miss Genovese. In two minutes they were at the scene. The neighbor, a 70-year-old woman, and another woman were the only persons on the street. Nobody else came forward.

The man explained that he had called the police after much deliberation. He had phoned a friend in Nassau County for advice and then he had crossed the roof of the building to the apartment of the elderly woman to get her to make the call.

"I didn't want to get involved," he sheepishly told the police.

Six days later, the police arrested Winston Moseley, a 29-year-old business-machine operator, and charged him with the homicide. Moseley had no previous record. He is married, has two children and owns a home at 133–19 Sutter Avenue, South Ozone Park, Queens. On Wednesday, a court committed him to Kings County Hospital for psychiatric observation.

When questioned by the police, Moseley also said that he had slain Mrs. Annie May Johnson, 24, of 146–12 133d Avenue, Jamaica, on Feb. 29 and Barbara Kralik, 15, of 174–17 140th Avenue, Springfield Gardens, last July. In the Kralik case, the police are holding Alvin L. Mitchell, who is said to have confessed that slaying.

The police stressed how simple it would have been to have gotten in touch with them. "A phone call," said one of the detectives, "would have done it." The police may be reached by dialing "O" for operator or SPring 7–3100.

Today witnesses from the neighborhood, which is made up of one-family homes in the $35,000 to $60,000 range with the exception of the two apartment houses near the railroad station, find it difficult to explain why they didn't call the police.

A housewife, knowingly if quite casual, said, "We thought it was a lover's quarrel." A husband and wife both said, "Frankly, we were afraid." They seemed aware of the fact that events might have been different. A distraught woman, wiping her hands in her apron, said, "I didn't want my husband to get involved."

One couple, now willing to talk about that night, said they heard the first screams. The husband looked thoughtfully at the bookstore where the killer first grabbed Miss Genovese.

"We went to the window to see what was happening," he said, "but the light from our bedroom made it difficult to see the street." The wife, still apprehensive, added: "I put out the light and we were able to see better."

Asked why they hadn't called the police, she shrugged and replied: "I don't know."

A man peeked out from a slight opening in the doorway to his apartment and rattled off an account of the killer's second attack. Why hadn't he called the police at the time? "I was tired," he said without emotion. "I went back to bed."

It was 4:25 A.M. when the ambulance arrived to take the body of Miss Genovese. It drove off. "Then," a solemn police detective said, "the people came out."

STUDY QUESTIONS

1. Two professors at the Princeton Theological Seminary designed an experiment to find out why bystanders often ignore people in distress. They told several seminary students to report to the studio to record a Biblical text. The professors arranged that, on their way to the studio, the students would pass another student lying on the ground writhing and gasping. The researchers found that the only significant factor in determining who stopped was how much time students thought they had: Of those rushed for time, only 10 percent stopped; of those who had plenty of time, 63 percent. It seemed to make no statistical difference that half the students had been assigned to read the parable of the good Samaritan. Do these findings surprise you? Despite their poor showing, do you think the seminarians did better than a randomly selected group would have? Can we do anything as a society to increase the proportion of people who will stop?

2. Do you think more states should adopt a statute like the one in Vermont that legally requires bystanders to aid those in critical need when they can safely do so?
3. Do you agree with those who say that the thirty-eight witnesses to Kitty Genovese's death are accessories to murder?

The Moral Insight

JOSIAH ROYCE

Josiah Royce (1855–1916), a professor of philosophy at Harvard University, was a colleague of William James and a teacher of George Santayana during what are known as the "golden years" of Harvard philosophy. Royce wrote in almost every area of philosophy, but is principally known as a proponent of idealism. His best known work in ethics is *The Philosophy of Loyalty* (1908).

For Royce the key to moral understanding lies in the realization that our neighbor is a center of experience and desire just as we are. Royce asks that we look upon that neighbor in much the same way we look upon our *future* selves—as a distant and somewhat unreal center of experience, but nevertheless of great concern. Sympathy and pity for another are not enough. Fellow feeling must also bring us to the point of what Royce calls the moral insight: "Such as that is for me, so is it for him, nothing less."

. . . [The following] is our reflective account of the process that, in some form, must come to every one under the proper conditions. In this process we see the beginning of the real knowledge of duty to

THE MORAL INSIGHT From *The Religious Aspects of Philosophy* (Boston: Houghton Mifflin Co., 1885).

55

others. The process is one that any child can and does, under proper guidance, occasionally accomplish. It is the process by which we all are accustomed to try to teach humane behavior in concrete cases. We try to get people to realize what they are doing when they injure others. But to distinguish this process from the mere tender emotion of sympathy, with all its illusions, is what moralists have not carefully enough done. Our exposition [tries] to take this universally recognized process, to distinguish it from sympathy as such, and to set it up before the gates of ethical doctrine as the great producer of insight.

But when we say that to this insight common sense must come, under the given conditions, we do not mean to say: "So the man, once having attained insight, must act thenceforth." The realization of one's neighbor, in the full sense of the word realization, is indeed the resolution to treat him as if he were real, that is, to treat him unselfishly. But this resolution expresses and belongs to the moment of insight. Passion may cloud the insight in the very next moment. It always does cloud the insight after no very long time. It is as impossible for us to avoid the illusion of selfishness in our daily lives, as to escape seeing through the illusion at the moment of insight. We see the reality of our neighbor, that is, we determine to treat him as we do ourselves. But then we go back to daily action, and we feel the heat of hereditary passions, and we straightway forget what we have seen. Our neighbor becomes obscured. He is once more a foreign power. He is unreal. We are again deluded and selfish. This conflict goes on and will go on as long as we live after the manner of men. Moments of insight, with their accompanying resolutions; long stretches of delusion and selfishness: That is our life.

To bring home this view . . . to the reader, we ask him to consider carefully just what experience he has when he tries to realize his neighbor in the full sense that we have insisted upon. Not pity as such is what we desire him to feel. For whether or not pity happens to work in him as selfishly and blindly as we have found that it often does work, still not the emotion, but its consequences, must in the most favorable case give us what we seek. All the forms of sympathy are mere impulses. It is the insight to which they bring us that has moral value. And again, the realization of our neighbor's existence is not at all the discovery that he is more or less useful to us personally. All that would contribute to selfishness. In an entirely different way we must realize his existence, if we are to be really altruistic. What then is our neighbor?

We find that out by treating him in thought just as we do ourselves. What art thou? Thou art now just a present state, with its experiences, thoughts, and desires. But what is thy future Self? Simply future states, future experiences, future thoughts and desires, that, although not now existing for thee, are postulated by thee as certain to come, and as in some real relation to thy present Self. What then is thy neighbor? He too is a mass of states, of experiences, thoughts, and desires, just as real as thou art, no more but yet no less present to thy experience now than is thy future Self. He is not that face that frowns or smiles at thee, although often thou thinkest of him as only that. He is not the arm that strikes or defends thee, not the voice that speaks to thee, not that machine that gives thee what thou desirest when thou movest it with the offer of money. To be sure, thou dost often think of him as if he were that automaton yonder, that answers thee when thou speakest to it. But no, thy neighbor is as actual, as concrete, as thou art. Just as thy future is real, though not now thine, so thy neighbor is real, though his thoughts never are thy thoughts. Dost thou believe this? Art thou sure what it means? This is for thee the turning-point of thy whole conduct towards him. What we now ask of thee is no sentiment, no gush of pity, no tremulous weakness of sympathy, but a calm, clear insight. . . .

If he is real like thee, then is his life as bright a light, as warm a fire, to him, as thine to thee; his will is as full of struggling desires, of hard problems, of fateful decisions; his pains are as hateful, his joys as dear. Take whatever thou knowest of desire and of striving, of burning love and of fierce hatred, realize as fully as thou canst what that means, and then with clear certainty add: *Such as that is for me, so is it for him, nothing less.* If thou dost that, can he remain to thee what he has been, a picture, a plaything, a comedy, or a tragedy, in brief a mere Show? Behind all that show thou hast indeed dimly felt that there is something. Know that truth thoroughly. Thou hast regarded his thought, his feeling, as somehow different in sort from thine. Thou hast said: "A pain in him is not like a pain in me, but something far easier to bear." Thou hast made of him a ghost, as the imprudent man makes of his future self a ghost. Even when thou hast feared his scorn, his hate, his contempt, thou hast not fully made him for thee as real as thyself. His laughter at thee has made thy face feel hot, his frowns and clenched fists have cowed thee, his sneers have made thy throat feel choked. But that was only the social instinct in thee. It was not a full sense of his reality. Even so the little baby smiles back at one that smiles at it, but not because it realizes the approving joy of the other, only because it by instinct enjoys a smiling face; and even so the baby is frightened at harsh speech, but not because it realizes the other's anger. So, dimly and by instinct, thou hast lived with thy neighbor, and hast known him not, being blind. Thou hast even desired his pain, but thou hast not fully realized the pain that thou gavest. It has been to thee, not pain in itself, but the sight of his submission, of his tears, or of his pale terror. Of thy neighbor thou hast made a thing, no Self at all.

When thou hast loved, hast pitied, or hast reverenced thy neighbor, then thy feeling has possibly raised for a moment the veil of illusion. Then thou hast known what he truly is, a Self like thy present Self. But thy selfish feeling is too strong for thee. Thou hast forgotten soon again what thou hadst seen, and hast made even of thy beloved one only the instrument of thy own pleasure. Even out of thy power to pity thou hast made an object of thy vainglory. Thy reverence has turned again to pride. Thou hast accepted the illusion once more. No wonder that in his darkness thou findest selfishness the only rule of any meaning for thy conduct. Thou forgottest that without realization of thy future and as yet unreal self, even selfishness means nothing. Thou forgottest that if thou gavest thy present thought even so to the task of realizing thy neighbor's life, selfishness would seem no more plain to thee than the love of thy neighbor.

Have done then with this illusion that thy Self is all in all. Intuition tells thee no more about thy future Self than it tells thee about thy neighbors. Desire, bred in thee by generations of struggle for existence, emphasizes the expectation of thy own bodily future, the love for thy own bodily welfare, and makes thy body's life seem alone real. But simply try to know the truth. The truth is that all this world of life about thee is as real as thou art. All conscious life is conscious in its own measure. Pain is pain, joy is joy, everywhere even as in thee. The result of thy insight will be inevitable. The illusion vanishing, the glorious prospect opens before thy vision. Seeing the oneness of this life everywhere, the equal reality of all its moments, thou wilt be ready to treat it all with the reverence that prudence would have thee show to thy own little bit of future life. What prudence in its narrow respectability counseled, thou wilt be ready to do universally. As the prudent man, seeing the reality of his future self, inevitably works for it; so the enlightened man, seeing the reality of all conscious life, realizing that it is no shadow, but fact, at once and inevitably desires, if only for that one moment of insight, to enter into the service of the whole of it. . . . Lift up thy eyes, behold that life, and then turn away and forget it as thou canst; but if thou hast known that, thou hast begun to know thy duty.

STUDY QUESTIONS

1. Some people call Royce's "Moral Insight" a description of the moral point of view. Do you agree?
2. Is Royce's Insight really another version of the Golden Rule?
3. Royce recommends that we look upon our neighbor in the same way we look upon our future selves. Are you morally considerate of your future self? Should this be a basic moral precept: Do unto others as you would do unto your future self?

Billy Budd

HERMAN MELVILLE

Herman Melville (1819–1891) is considered one of the great American literary masters. *Billy Budd,* his last novel, was written the year of his death.

Billy Budd takes place in 1797 on the British naval ship *Bellipotent,* just following two notorious mutinies at Spithead and Nore. Billy Budd, a sailor on the *Bellipotent,* is gentle and trusting and well loved by the crew. He is also uneducated and has difficulty speaking when he is upset. John Claggart, Billy's superior officer, is a malicious and cruel man who deeply resents Billy's kindly nature and popularity among the men. Billy is unaware of Claggart's

BILLY BUDD From *Billy Budd: Sailor,* eds. Harrison Hayford and Merton M. Sealts, Jr. Reprinted by permission of The University of Chicago Press.

hatred until the moment he brings Billy before the ship's master, Captain Vere, and falsely accuses Billy of plotting a mutiny. Billy, stunned by Claggart's vicious lies and unable to speak, strikes out at him, accidentally killing him by the blow.

Everyone sympathizes with Billy. But Captain Vere (a good man who has been acting strange of late) sets up a military tribunal and, to everyone's surprise, testifies against Billy. In his testimony, Captain Vere acknowledges that Claggart was an evil man, but reminds the tribunal that they are a military court empowered only to judge Billy's deed—not his motives. According to military law, the punishment for striking a superior officer is death by hanging. Just as sailors must obey their superiors and not take the law into their own hands, so the tribunal has an absolute duty to obey the law. Moreover, because there had been several mutinies recently, it was all the more important that military law be enforced. Captain Vere says to the court: "Let not warm hearts betray heads that should be cool." Billy is convicted and hanged.

Critics disagree about the moral implications of Billy Budd. Some see Captain Vere as an evil man whose abstract notion of duty blinded him to true justice and compassion. For others, Vere is a moral hero who rises above sentiment to meet the need for order, authority, and law in human affairs.

Who in the rainbow can draw the line where the violet tint ends and the orange tint begins? Distinctly we see the difference of the colors, but where exactly does the one first blendingly enter into the other? So with sanity and insanity. In pronounced cases there is no question about them. But in some supposed cases, in various degrees supposedly less pronounced, to draw the exact line of demarcation few will undertake, though for a fee becoming considerate some professional experts will. There is nothing namable but that some men will, or undertake to, do it for pay.

Whether Captain Vere, as the surgeon professionally and privately surmised, was really the sudden victim of any degree of aberration, every one must determine for himself by such light as this narrative may afford.

That the unhappy event which has been narrated could not have happened at a worse juncture was but too true. For it was close on the heel of the suppressed insurrections, an aftertime very critical to naval authority, demanding from every English sea commander two qualities not readily interfusable—prudence and rigor. Moreover, there was something crucial in the case.

In the jugglery of circumstances preceding and attending the event on board the *Bellipotent,* and in the light of that martial code whereby it was formally to be judged, innocence and guilt personified in Claggart and Budd in effect changed places. In a legal view the apparent victim of the tragedy was he who had sought to victimize a man blameless; and the indisputable deed of the latter, navally regarded, constituted the most heinous of military crimes. Yet more. The essential right and wrong involved in the matter, the clearer that might be, so much the worse for the responsibility of a loyal sea commander, inasmuch as he was not authorized to determine the matter on that primitive basis.

Small wonder then that the *Bellipotent's* captain, though in general a man of rapid decision, felt that circumspectness not less than promptitude was necessary. Until he could decide upon his course, and in each detail; and not only so, but until the concluding measure was upon the point of being enacted, he deemed it advisable, in view of all the circumstances, to guard as much as possible against publicity. Here he may or may not have erred. Certain it is, however, that subsequently in the confidential talk of more than one or two gun rooms and cabins he was not a little criticized by some officers, a fact imputed by his friends and vehemently by his cousin Jack Denton to professional jealousy of Starry Vere. Some imaginative ground for invidious comment there was. The maintenance of secrecy in the matter, the confining all knowledge of it for a time to the place where the homicide occurred, the quarterdeck cabin; in these particulars lurked some resemblance to the policy adopted in those tragedies of the palace which have occurred more than once in the capital founded by Peter the Barbarian.

The case indeed was such that fain would the *Bellipotent's* captain have deferred taking any action whatever respecting it further than to keep the foretopman a close prisoner till the ship rejoined the squadron and then submitting the matter to the judgment of his admiral.

But a true military officer is in one particular like a true monk. Not with more of self-abnegation will the latter keep his vows of monastic obedience than the former his vows of allegiance to martial duty.

Feeling that unless quick action was taken on it, the deed of the foretopman, so soon as it should be known on the gun decks, would tend to awaken any slumbering embers of the Nore among the crew, a sense of the urgency of the case overruled in Captain Vere every other consideration. But though a conscientious disciplinarian, he was no lover of authority for mere authority's sake. Very far was he from embracing opportunities for monopolizing to himself the perils of moral responsibility, none at least that could properly be referred to an official superior or shared with him by his official equals or even subordinates. So thinking, he was glad it would not be at variance with usage to turn the matter over to a summary court of his own officers, reserving to himself, as the one on whom the ultimate accountability would rest, the right of maintaining a supervision of it, or formally or informally interposing at need. Accordingly a drumhead court was summarily convened, he electing the individuals composing it: the first lieutenant, the captain of marines, and the sailing master.

In associating an officer of marines with the sea lieutenant and the sailing master in a case having to do with a sailor, the commander perhaps deviated from general custom. He was prompted thereto by the circumstance that he took that soldier to be a judicious person, thoughtful, and not altogether incapable of grappling with a difficult case unprecedented in his prior experience. Yet even as to him he was not without some latent misgiving, for withal he was an extremely good-natured man, an enjoyer of his dinner, a sound sleeper, and inclined to obesity—a man who though he would always maintain his manhood in battle might not prove altogether reliable in a moral dilemma involving aught of the tragic. As to the first lieutenant and the sailing master, Captain Vere could not but be aware that though honest natures, of approved gallantry upon occasion, their intelligence was mostly confined to the matter of active seamanship and the fighting demands of their profession.

The court was held in the same cabin where the unfortunate affair had taken place. This cabin, the commander's, embraced the entire area under the poop deck. Aft, and on either side, was a small state-room, the one now temporarily a jail and the other a dead-house, and a yet smaller compartment, leaving a space between expanding forward into a goodly oblong of length coinciding with the ship's beam. A skylight of moderate dimension was overhead, and at each end of the oblong space were two sashed porthole windows easily convertible back into embrasures for short carronades.

All being quickly in readiness, Billy Budd was arraigned, Captain Vere necessarily appearing as the sole witness in the case, and as such temporarily sinking his rank, though singularly maintaining it in a matter apparently trivial, namely, that he testified from the ship's weather side, with that object having caused the court to sit on the lee side. Concisely he narrated all that had led up to the catastrophe, omitting nothing in Claggart's accusation and deposing as to the manner in which the prisoner had received it. At this testimony the three officers glanced with no little surprise at Billy Budd, the last man they would have suspected either of the mutinous design alleged by Claggart or the undeniable deed he himself had done. The first lieutenant, taking judicial primacy and turning toward the prisoner, said, "Captain Vere has spoken. Is it or is it not as Captain Vere says?"

In response came syllables not so much impeded in the utterance as might have been anticipated. They were these: "Captain Vere tells the truth. It is just as Captain Vere says, but it is not as the master-at-arms said. I have eaten the King's bread and I am true to the King."

"I believe you, my man," said the witness, his voice indicating a suppressed emotion not otherwise betrayed.

"God will bless you for that, your honor!" not without stammering said Billy, and all but broke down. But immediately he was recalled to self-control by another question, to which with the same emotional difficulty of utterance he said, "No, there was no malice between us. I never bore malice against the master-at-arms. I am sorry that he is dead. I did not mean to kill him. Could I have used my tongue I would not have struck him. But he foully lied to my face and in presence of my captain, and I had to say something, and I could only say it with a blow, God help me!"

In the impulsive aboveboard manner of the frank one the court saw confirmed all that was implied in words that just previously had perplexed them, coming as they did from the testifier to the tragedy and promptly following Billy's impassioned disclaimer of mutinous intent—Captain Vere's words, "I believe you, my man."

Next it was asked of him whether he knew of or suspected aught savoring of incipient trouble (meaning mutiny, though the explicit term was avoided) going on in any section of the ship's company.

The reply lingered. This was naturally imputed by the court to the same vocal embarrassment which had retarded or obstructed previous answers. But in main it was otherwise here, the question immediately recalling to Billy's mind the interview with the afterguardsman in the forechains. But an innate repugnance to playing a part at all approaching that of an informer against one's own shipmates—the same erring sense of uninstructed honor which had stood in the way of his reporting the matter at the time, though as a loyal man-of-war's man it was incumbent on him, and failure so to do, if charged against him and proven, would have subjected him to the heaviest of penalties; this, with the blind feeling now his that nothing really was being hatched, prevailed with him. When the answer came it was a negative.

"One question more," said the officer of marines, now first speaking and with a troubled earnestness. "You tell us that what the master-at-arms said against you was a lie. Now why should he have so lied, so maliciously lied, since you declare there was no malice between you?"

At that question, unintentionally touching on a spiritual sphere wholly obscure to Billy's thoughts, he was nonplused, evincing a confusion indeed that some observers, such as can readily be imagined, would have construed into involuntary evidence of hidden guilt. Nevertheless, he strove some way to answer, but all at once relinquished the vain endeavor, at the same time turning an appealing glance toward Captain Vere as deeming him his best helper and friend. Captain Vere, who had been seated for a time, rose to his feet, addressing the interrogator. "The question you put to him comes naturally enough. But how can he rightly answer it?—or anybody else, unless indeed it be he who lies within there," designating the compartment where lay the corpse. "But the prone one there will not rise to our summons. In effect, though, as it seems to me, the point you make is hardly material. Quite aside from any conceivable motive actuating the master-at-arms, and irrespective of the provocation to the blow, a martial court must needs in the present case confine its attention to the blow's consequence, which consequence justly is to be deemed not otherwise than as the striker's deed."

This utterance, the full significance of which it was not at all likely that Billy took in, nevertheless caused him to turn a wistful interrogative look toward the speaker, a look in its dumb expressiveness not unlike that which a dog of generous breed might turn upon his master, seeking in his face some elucidation of a previous gesture ambiguous to the canine intelligence. Nor was the same utterance without marked effect upon the three officers, more especially the soldier. Couched in it seemed to them a meaning unanticipated, involving a prejudgment on the speaker's part. It served to augment a mental disturbance previously evident enough.

The soldier once more spoke, in a tone of suggestive dubiety addressing at once his associates and Captain Vere: "Nobody is present—none of the ship's company, I mean—who might shed lateral light, if any is to be had, upon what remains mysterious in this matter."

"That is thoughtfully put," said Captain Vere; "I see your drift. Ay, there is a mystery; but, to use a scriptural phrase, it is a 'mystery of iniquity,' a matter for psychologic theologians to discuss. But what has a military court to do with it? Not to add that for us any possible investigation of it is cut off by the lasting tongue-tie of—him—in yonder," again designating the mortuary stateroom. "The prisoner's deed—with that alone we have to do."

To this, and particularly the closing reiteration, the marine soldier, knowing not how aptly to reply, sadly abstained from saying aught. The first lieutenant, who at the outset had not unnaturally assumed primacy in the court, now overrulingly instructed by a glance from Captain Vere, a glance more effective than words, resumed that primacy. Turning to the prisoner, "Budd," he said, and scarce in equable tones, "Budd, if you have aught further to say for yourself, say it now."

Upon this the young sailor turned another quick glance toward Captain Vere; then, as taking a hint from that aspect, a hint confirming his own instinct that silence was now best, replied to the lieutenant, "I have said all, sir."

The marine—the same who had been the sentinel without the cabin door at the time that the foretopman, followed by the master-at-arms, entered it—he, standing by the sailor throughout these judicial proceedings, was now directed to take him back to the after compartment originally assigned to the prisoner and his custodian. As the twain disappeared from view, the three officers, as partially liberated from some inward constraint associated with Billy's mere presence, simultaneously stirred in their seats. They exchanged looks of troubled indecision, yet feeling that decide they must and without long delay. For Captain Vere, he for the time stood—unconsciously with his back toward them, apparently in one of his absent fits— gazing out from a sashed porthole to windward upon the monotonous blank of the twilight sea. But the court's silence continuing, broken only at moments by brief consultations, in low earnest tones, this served to arouse him and energize him. Turning, he to-and-fro paced the cabin athwart; in the returning ascent to windward climbing the slant deck in the ship's lee roll, without knowing it symbolizing thus in his action a mind resolute to surmount difficulties even if against primitive instincts strong as the wind and the sea. Presently he came to a stand before the three. After scanning their faces he stood less as mustering his thoughts for expression than as one only deliberating how best to put them to well-meaning men not intellectually mature, men with whom it was necessary to demonstrate certain principles that were axioms to himself. Similar impatience as to talking is perhaps one reason that deters some minds from addressing any popular assemblies.

When speak he did, something, both in the substance of what he said and his manner of saying it, showed the influence of unshared studies modifying and tempering the practical training of an active career. This, along with his phraseology, now and then was suggestive of the grounds whereon rested that imputation of a certain pedantry socially alleged against him by certain naval men of wholly practical cast, captains who nevertheless would frankly concede that His Majesty's navy mustered no more efficient officer of their grade than Starry Vere.

What he said was to this effect: "Hitherto I have been but the witness, little more; and I should hardly think now to take another tone, that of your coadjutor for the time, did I not perceive in you— at the crisis too—a troubled hesitancy, proceeding, I doubt not, from the clash of military duty with moral scruple—scruple vitalized by compassion. For the compassion, how can I otherwise than share it? But, mindful of paramount obligations, I strive against scruples that may tend to enervate decision. Not, gentlemen, that I hide from myself that the case is an exceptional one. Speculatively regarded, it well might be referred to a jury of casuists. But for us here, acting not as casuists or moralists, it is a case practical, and under martial law practically to be dealt with.

"But your scruples: do they move as in a dusk? Challenge them. Make them advance and declare themselves. Come now; do they import something like this: If, mindless of palliating circumstances, we are bound to regard the death of the master-at-arms as the prisoner's deed, then does that deed constitute a capital crime whereof the penalty is a mortal one. But in natural justice is nothing but the prisoner's overt act to be considered? How can we adjudge to summary and shameful death a fellow creature innocent before God, and whom we feel to be so?—Does that state it aright? You sign sad assent. Well, I too feel that, the full force of that. It is Nature. But do these buttons that we wear attest that our allegiance is to Nature? No, to the King. Though the ocean, which is inviolate Nature primeval, though this be the element where we move and have our being as sailors, yet as the King's officers lies our duty in a sphere correspondingly natural? So little is that true, that in receiving our commissions we in the most important regards ceased to be natural free agents. When war is declared are we the commissioned fighters previously consulted? We fight at command. If our judgments approve the war, that is but coincidence. So in other particulars. So now. For suppose condemnation to follow these present proceedings. Would it be so much we ourselves that would condemn as it would be martial law operating through us? For that law and the rigor of it, we are not responsible. Our vowed responsibility is in this: That however pitilessly that law may operate in any instances, we nevertheless adhere to it and administer it.

"But the exceptional in the matter moves the hearts within you. Even so too is mine moved. But let not warm hearts betray heads that should be cool. Ashore in a criminal case, will an upright judge allow himself off the bench to be waylaid by some tender kinswoman of the accused seeking to touch him with her tearful plea? Well, the heart here, sometimes the feminine in man, is as that piteous woman, and hard though it be, she must here be ruled out."

He paused, earnestly studying them for a moment; then resumed.

"But something in your aspect seems to urge that it is not solely the heart that moves in you, but also the conscience, the private conscience. But tell me whether or not, occupying the position we do, private conscience should not yield to that imperial one formulated in the mode under which alone we officially proceed?"

Here the three men moved in their seats, less convinced than agitated by the course of an argument troubling but the more the spontaneous conflict within.

Perceiving which, the speaker paused for a moment; then abruptly changing his tone, went on.

"To steady us a bit, let us recur to the facts.—In wartime at sea a man-of-war's man strikes his superior in grade, and the blow kills. Apart from its effect the blow itself is, according to the Articles of War, a capital crime, Furthermore————"

"Ay, sir," emotionally broke in the officer of marines, "in one sense it was. But surely Budd purposed neither mutiny nor homicide."

"Surely not, my good man. And before a court less arbitrary and more merciful than a martial one, that plea would largely extenuate. At the Last Assizes it shall acquit. But how here? We proceed under the law of the Mutiny Act. In feature no child can resemble his father more than that Act resembles in spirit the thing from which it derives—War. In His Majesty's service—in this ship, indeed—there are Englishmen forced to fight for the King against their will. Against their conscience, for aught we know. Though as their fellow creatures some of us may appreciate their position, yet as navy officers what reck we of it? Still less recks the enemy. Our impressed men he would fain cut down in the same swath with our volunteers. As regards the enemy's naval conscripts, some of whom may even share our own abhorrence of the regicidal French Directory, it is the same on our side. War looks but to the frontage, the appearance. And the Mutiny Act, War's child, takes after the father. Budd's intent or non-intent is nothing to the purpose.

"But while, put to it by those anxieties in you which I cannot but respect, I only repeat myself—while thus strangely we prolong proceedings that should be summary—the enemy may be sighted and an engagement result. We must do; and one of two things must we do—condemn or let go."

"Can we not convict and yet mitigate the penalty?" asked the sailing master, here speaking, and falteringly, for the first.

"Gentlemen, were that clearly lawful for us under the circumstances, consider the consequences of such clemency. The people" (meaning the ship's company) "have native sense; most of them are familiar with our naval usage and tradition; and how would they take it? Even could you explain to them—which our official position forbids—they, long molded by arbitrary discipline, have not that kind of intelligent responsiveness that might qualify them to comprehend and discriminate. No, to the people the foretopman's deed, however it be worded in the announcement, will be plain homicide committed in a flagrant act of mutiny. What penalty for that should follow, they know. But it does not follow. *Why?* they will ruminate. You know what sailors are. Will they not revert to the recent outbreak at the Nore? Ay. They know the well-founded alarm—the panic it struck throughout England. Your clement sentence they would account pusillanimous. They would think that we flinch, that we are afraid of them—afraid of practicing a lawful rigor singularly demanded at this juncture, lest it should provoke new troubles. What shame to us such a conjecture on their part, and how deadly to discipline. You see then, whither, prompted by duty and the law, I steadfastly drive. But I beseech you, my friends, do not take me amiss. I feel as you do for this unfortunate boy. But did he know our hearts, I take him to be of that generous nature that he would feel even for us on whom this military necessity so heavy a compulsion is laid."

With that, crossing the deck he resumed his place by the sashed porthole, tacitly leaving the three to come to a decision. On the cabin's opposite side the troubled court sat silent. Loyal lieges, plain and practical, though at bottom they dissented from some points Captain Vere had put to them, they were without the faculty, hardly had the inclination, to gainsay one whom they felt to be an earnest man, one too not less their superior in mind than in naval rank. But it is not improbable that even such of his words as were not without influence over them, less came home to them than his closing appeal to their instinct as sea officers: in the forethought he threw out as to the practical consequences to discipline, considering the unconfirmed tone of the fleet at the time, should a man-of-war's man's violent killing at sea of a superior in grade be allowed to pass for aught else than a capital crime demanding prompt infliction of the penalty.

Not unlikely they were brought to something more or less akin to that harassed frame of mind which in the year 1842 actuated the commander of the U.S. brig-of-war *Somers* to resolve, under the so-called Articles of War, Articles modeled upon the English Mutiny

Act, to resolve upon the execution at sea of a midshipman and two sailors as mutineers designing the seizure of the brig. Which resolution was carried out though in a time of peace and within not many days' sail of home. An act vindicated by a naval court of inquiry subsequently convened ashore. History, and here cited without comment. True, the circumstances on board the *Somers* were different from those on board the *Bellipotent*. But the urgency felt, well-warranted or otherwise, was much the same.

Says a writer whom few know, "Forty years after a battle it is easy for a noncombatant to reason about how it ought to have been fought. It is another thing personally and under fire to have to direct the fighting while involved in the obscuring smoke of it. Much so with respect to other emergencies involving considerations both practical and moral, and when it is imperative promptly to act. The greater the fog the more it imperils the steamer, and speed is put on though at the hazard of running somebody down. Little ween the snug card players in the cabin of the responsibilities of the sleepless man on the bridge."

In brief, Billy Budd was formally convicted and sentenced to be hung at the yardarm in the early morning watch, it being now night. Otherwise, as is customary in such cases, the sentence would forthwith have been carried out. In wartime on the field or in the fleet, a mortal punishment decreed by a drumhead court—on the field sometimes decreed by but a nod from the general—follows without delay on the heel of conviction, without appeal.

STUDY QUESTIONS

1. Billy never intended to kill Claggart. Is it fair to hold people responsible for the unforeseen consequences of their acts?
2. Write a defense of Captain Vere's decision to argue for Billy's conviction. Next write a critique of the decision. Which do you find more convincing?
3. Apply Jonathan Bennett's analysis of duty and sympathy (in "The Conscience of Huckleberry Finn") to *Billy Budd*. Do you agree with Bennett's analysis?
4. Do you agree with Captain Vere that news of Billy's acquittal really could undermine military discipline throughout the

British navy? Wouldn't other British sailors understand that Billy Budd's was an exceptional case?
5. Vere distinguishes between military duty and moral duty. Should the latter always take priority?

Beyond Good and Evil

FRIEDRICH NIETZSCHE

Friedrich Nietzsche (1844–1900) was as much a poet as he was a philosopher. His precocious intelligence and learning led to his being appointed to a full professorship at the University of Basel at age twenty-six, a post he held all his productive life. His influence on modern continental thought was revolutionary. He is hailed as a forerunner of such twentieth century movements as Existentialism and Deconstructionism. Some consider Nietzsche's influence harmful, but this may be due to widespread misuse of his ideas by both the right and the left. Among his many works are *The Birth of Tragedy* (1872), *The Gay Science* (1882), *Beyond Good and Evil* (1886), and *Thus Spake Zarathustra* (1891).

Friedrich Nietzsche was contemptuous of the Judeo-Christian ethic, an ethic he thought suitable for the lowliest classes of mankind—"the cowardly, the timid and the insignificant." Although in an aristocratic society made up entirely of superior beings the ideal of equality might work, in an ordinary world it bestowed power on the weak and diminished the strong. A dynamic and healthy society must allow its superior and noble individuals to prevail; it must give full expression to the "will to

BEYOND GOOD AND EVIL Translated by Helen Zimmern. Reprinted by permission of George Allen & Unwin (Publishers) Ltd.

power"—Nietzsche's famous phrase that describes an innate drive in all living things toward domination and exploitation. Nietzsche deplores the "slave morality" that defines good and evil in terms of what alleviates the misery of inferior beings—a morality that favors patience, humility, sympathy, and friendliness. Nietzsche defends the "master morality" that honors pride, vanity, power, and "dreadfulness."

To refrain mutually from injury, from violence, from exploitation, and put one's will on a par with that of others: this may result in a certain rough sense in good conduct among individuals when the necessary conditions are given (namely, the actual similarity of the individuals in amount of force and degree of worth, and their co-relation within one organisation). As soon, however, as one wished to take this principle more generally, and if possible even as *the fundamental principle of society,* it would immediately disclose what it really is—namely, a Will to the *denial* of life, a principle of dissolution and decay. Here one must think profoundly to the very basis and resist all sentimental weakness: life itself is *essentially* appropriation, injury, conquest of the strange and weak, suppression, severity, obtrusion of peculiar forms, incorporation, and at the least, putting it mildest, exploitation;—but why should one for ever use precisely these words on which for ages a disparaging purpose has been stamped? Even the organisation within which, as was previously supposed, the individuals treat each other as equal—it takes place in every healthy aristocracy—must itself, if it be a living and not a dying organisation, do all that towards other bodies, which the individuals within it refrain from doing to each other: it will have to be the incarnated Will to Power, it will endeavour to grow, to gain ground, attract to itself and acquire ascendency—not owing to any morality or immorality, but because it *lives,* and because life *is* precisely Will to Power. On no point, however, is the ordinary consciousness of Europeans more unwilling to be corrected than on this matter; people now rave everywhere, even under the guise of science, about coming conditions of society in which "the exploiting character" is to be absent:—that sounds to my ears as if they promised to invent a mode of life which should refrain from all organic functions. "Exploitation" does not belong to a depraved, or imperfect and primitive society: it belongs to the *nature* of the living being as a primary organic function; it is a consequence of the intrinsic Will to Power, which is precisely the Will to Life.—Granting that as a theory this is a novelty—as a reality it is the *fundamental fact* of all history: let us be so far honest towards ourselves!

In a tour through the many finer and coarser moralities which have hitherto prevailed or still prevail on the earth, I found certain traits recurring regularly together, and connected with one another, until finally two primary types revealed themselves to me, and a radical distinction was brought to light. There is *master-morality* and *slave-morality;*—I would at once add, however, that in all higher and mixed civilisations, there are also attempts at the reconciliation of the two moralities; but one finds still oftener the confusion and mutual mis-understanding of them, indeed, sometimes their close juxtaposi-tion—even in the same man, within one soul. The distinctions of moral values have either originated in a ruling caste, pleasantly con-scious of being different from the ruled—or among the ruled class, the slaves and dependents of all sorts. In the first case, when it is the rulers who determine the conception "good," it is the exalted, proud disposition which is regarded as the distinguishing feature, and that which determines the order of rank. The noble type of man separates from himself the beings in whom the opposite of this exalted, proud disposition displays itself: he despises them. Let it at once be noted that in this first kind of morality the antithesis "good" and "bad" means practically the same as "noble" and "despicable";—the antith-esis "good" and *"evil"* is of a different origin. The cowardly, the timid, the insignificant, and those thinking merely of narrow utility are despised; moreover, also, the distrustful, with their constrained glances, the self-abasing, the dog-like kind of men who let them-selves be abused, the mendicant flatterers and above all the liars:—it is a fundamental belief of all aristocrats that the common people are untruthful. "We truthful ones"—the nobility in ancient Greece called themselves. It is obvious that everywhere the designations of moral value were at first applied to *men,* and were only derivatively and at a later period applied to *actions;* it is a gross mistake, therefore, when historians of morals start with questions like, "Why have sym-pathetic actions been praised?" The noble type of man regards *himself* as a determiner of values; he does not require to be approved of; he passes the judgment: "What is injurious to me is injurious in itself"; he knows that it is he himself only who confers honour on things; he is a *creator of values*. He honours whatever he recognises in himself: such morality is self-glorification. In the foreground there is the feeling of plenitude, of power, which seeks to overflow, the happiness of high tension, the consciousness of a wealth which would fain give and bestow:—the noble man also helps the unfortunate, but not—or scarcely—out of pity, but rather from an impulse generated by the super-abundance of power. The noble man honours in himself the powerful one, him also who has power over himself, who knows how to speak and how to keep silence, who takes pleasure in subjecting himself to severity and hardness, and has reverence for all that is severe and hard. "Wotan placed a hard heart in my breast," says an old Scandinavian Saga: it is thus rightly expressed from the soul of a proud Viking. Such a type of man is even proud of *not* being made for sympathy; the hero of the Saga therefore adds warningly: "He who has not a hard heart when young, will never have one." The noble and brave who think thus are the furthest removed from the morality which sees precisely in sympathy, or in acting for the good of others, or in disinterestedness, the characteristic of the moral; faith in oneself, pride in oneself, a radical enmity and irony towards "selflessness," belong as definitely to noble morality, as do a careless scorn and precaution in presence of sympathy and the "warm heart."—It is the powerful who *know* how to honour, it is their art, their domain for invention. The profound reverence for age and for tradition—all law rests on this double reverence,—the belief and prejudice in favour of ancestors and unfavourable to newcomers, is typical in the morality of the powerful; and if, reversely, men of "modern ideas" believe almost instinctively in "progress" and the "future," and are more and more lacking in respect for old age, the ignoble origin of these "ideas" has complacently betrayed itself thereby. A morality of the ruling class, however, is more especially foreign and irritating to present-day taste in the sternness of its principle that one has duties only to one's equals; that one may act towards beings of a lower rank, towards all that is foreign, just as seems good to one, or "as the heart desires," and in any case "beyond good and evil": it is here that sympathy and similar sentiments can have a place. The ability and obligation to exercise prolonged gratitude and prolonged revenge—both only within the circle of equals,—artfulness in retaliation, effete refinement of the idea in friendship, a certain necessity to have enemies (as outlets for the emotions of envy, quarrelsomeness, arrogance—in fact, in order to be a good *friend*): all these are typical characteristics of the noble morality, which, as has been pointed out, is not the morality of "modern ideas," and is therefore at present difficult to realise, and also to unearth and disclose.—It is otherwise with the second type of morality, *slave-morality*. Supposing that the abused, the oppressed, the suffering, the unemancipated, the weary, and those uncertain of themselves, should moralise, what will be the common element in their moral estimates? Probably a pessimistic suspicion with regard to the entire situation of man will find expression, perhaps a condemnation of man, together with his situation. The slave has an unfavourable eye for the virtues of the powerful; he has a scepticism and distrust, a *refinement* of distrust of everything "good" that is there honoured—he would fain persuade himself that the very happiness there is not genuine. On the other hand, *those* qualities which serve to alleviate the existence of sufferers are brought into prominence and flooded with light; it is here that sympathy, the kind, helping hand, the warm heart, patience, diligence, humility, and friendliness attain to honour; for here these are the most useful qualities, and almost the only means of supporting the burden of existence. Slave-morality is essentially the morality of utility. Here is the seat of the origin of the famous antithesis "good" and "evil":—power and dangerousness are assumed to reside in the evil, a certain dreadfulness, subtlety, and strength, which do not admit of being despised. According to slave-morality, therefore, the "evil" man arouses fear; according to master-morality, it is precisely the "good" man who arouses fear and seeks to arouse it, while the bad man is regarded as the despicable being. The contrast attains its maximum when, in accordance with the logical consequences of slave-morality, a shade of depreciation—it may be slight and well-intentioned—at last attaches itself to the "good" man of this morality; because, according to the servile mode of thought, the good man must in any case be the *safe* man: he is good-natured, easily deceived, perhaps a little stupid, *un bonhomme.*

. . .

I regard Christianity as the most fatal and seductive lie that has ever yet existed—as the greatest and most *impious lie:* I can discern the last sprouts and branches of its ideal beneath every form of disguise, I decline to enter into any compromise or false position in reference to it—I urge people to declare open war with it.

The *morality of paltry people* as the measure of all things: this is the most repugnant kind of degeneracy that civilisation has ever yet brought into existence. And this *kind of ideal* is hanging still, under the name of "God," over men's heads!!

However modest one's demands may be concerning intellectual cleanliness, when one touches the New Testament one cannot help experiencing a sort of inexpressible feeling of discomfort; for the unbounded cheek with which the least qualified people will have their say in its pages, in regard to the greatest problems of existence, and claim to sit in judgment on such matters, exceeds all limits. The impudent levity with which the most unwieldy problems are spoken of here (life, the world, God, the purpose of life), as if they were not problems at all, but the most simple things which these little bigots *know all about!!!* . . .

The *law,* which is the fundamentally realistic formula of certain self-preservative measures of a community, forbids certain actions that have a definite tendency to jeopardise the welfare of that community: it does *not* forbid the attitude of mind which gives rise to these actions—for in the pursuit of other ends the community requires these forbidden actions, namely, when it is a matter of opposing its *enemies.* The moral idealist now steps forward and says: "God sees into men's hearts: the action itself counts for nothing; the reprehensible attitude of mind from which it proceeds must be extirpated . . ." In normal conditions men laugh at such things; it is only in exceptional cases, when a community lives *quite* beyond the need of waging war in order to maintain itself, that an ear is lent to such things. Any attitude of mind is abandoned, the utility of which cannot be conceived.

This was the case, for example, when Buddha appeared among a people that was both peacable and afflicted with great intellectual weariness.

This was also the case in regard to the first Christian community (as also the Jewish), the primary condition of which was the absolutely *unpolitical* Jewish society. Christianity could grow only upon the soil of Judaism—that is to say, among a people that had already renounced the political life, and which led a sort of parasitic existence within the Roman sphere of government. Christianity goes a step *further:* it allows men to "emasculate" themselves even more; the circumstances actually favour their doing so.—*Nature* is *expelled* from morality when it is said, "Love ye your enemies": for *Nature's* injunction, "Ye shall *love* your neighbour and *hate* your enemy," has now become senseless in the law (in instinct); now, even *the love a man feels for his neighbour* must first be based upon something (*a sort of love of God*). *God* is introduced everywhere, and *utility* is withdrawn; the natural *origin* of morality is denied everywhere: the *veneration of Nature,* which lies in *acknowledging a natural morality,* is *destroyed* to the roots . . .

What is it I protest against? That people should regard this paltry and peaceful mediocrity, this spiritual equilibrium which knows nothing of the fine impulses of great accumulations of strength, as something high, or possibly as the standard of all things.

STUDY QUESTIONS

1. In your own words characterize what Nietzsche calls the "slave morality" and the "master morality."
2. Nietzsche believes that exploitation and domination of the weak by the strong is a "fundamental fact of all history." Assuming this belief is true, would you consider this an argument for the validity of the master morality? Might one not argue instead that we should curb our aggressive impulses and protect the weak?
3. How much truth do you find in Nietzsche's characterization of the Judeo-Christian ethic as a slave morality? Is he right when he says that it is "the morality of paltry people"?
4. Organize a debate between Josiah Royce and Friedrich Nietzsche on the validity of the Golden Rule.
5. Nietzsche has sometimes been accused of inspiring Nazism. Does anything in the selection support such an accusation?
6. How would Nietzsche react to Hallie's account of what transpired in Le Chambon during World War II?

SUGGESTED READINGS

Arendt, Hannah. *Eichmann in Jerusalem: A Report on the Banality of Evil.* New York: Viking Press, 1965.

Douglass, Frederick. *Life and Times of Frederick Douglass: Written by Himself.* New York: Collier Press, 1962.

Hallie, Philip. *Lest Innocent Blood Be Shed.* New York: Harper and Row, 1979.

Midgley, Mary. *Wickedness: A Philosophical Essay*. Boston: Routledge and Kegan Paul, 1984.

Milo, Richard D. *Immorality*. Princeton: Princeton University Press, 1984.

Nietzsche, Friedrich. *Beyond Good and Evil*. Chicago: Henry Regnery, 1965.

Noddings, Nell. *Women and Evil*. Berkeley: University of California, 1991.

Rosenthal, Abigail. *A Good Look at Evil*. Philadelphia: Temple University Press, 1988.

Taylor, Richard. *Good and Evil*. Buffalo, NY: Prometheus Press, 1970.

Tiger, Lionel. *The Manufacture of Evil*. New York: Harper and Row, 1987.

Chapter Two

MORAL DOCTRINES AND MORAL THEORIES

In this chapter we begin by presenting several sacred texts of the Judeo-Christian tradition that are central to the moral heritage of the Western world. The Biblical account of the genesis of the world, the revelation of moral laws in Exodus, the Psalms, the Sermon on the Mount, and the Parable of the Good Samaritan have inspired and guided people for centuries. The view that our moral obligations come directly from God is known as the Divine Command theory of morality. A number of philosophers have sought alternative accounts of morality. Some are atheists and, of course, reject out of hand any theory that presupposes a deity; others, though believers, look for an account of right and wrong that does not rely on revelation. Plato, in his dialogue *The Euthyphro*, first asked a question that often arises in connection with the Divine Command theory: Are the actions that God decrees good only because God approves of them, or does He approve of them because they are good? Might God just as easily decree that we be cruel and refrain from kindness, or do the divine decrees conform to independently valid criteria of good and evil? Perhaps the majority of moral philosophers believe that morality is independently valid. And some theologians move between the horns of the dilemma, maintaining that God's will and objective good are coincident. Much of moral philosophy since Plato consists of attempts to formulate objective criteria for what is right and good.

Two of the most influential alternatives to the Divine Command theory are utilitarianism and Kantianism. Utilitarianism was developed by British philosophers Jeremy Bentham (1748–1832) and John Stuart Mill (1806–1873). For the utilitarian, morally good actions are actions that increase the happiness of conscious beings. According to Mill's Greatest Happiness Principle, "Actions are right in proportion as they tend to promote happiness, wrong as they tend to produce the reverse of happiness." (And, says Mill, God's decrees are good precisely because obedience to them increases happiness; that is *why* God decreed them.) Mill and Bentham thought of the principle of utility as a moral yardstick. Just as two people who disagree over the height of a ceiling can settle the matter with a ruler, so two people who disagree over the rightness of an action need only subject it to the test of utility: Will it increase or diminish happiness?

Though many contemporary philosophers favor utilitarianism over other moral theories (indeed, one philosopher recently remarked that utilitarians constitute a silent majority among professional philosophers), they generally acknowledge it to be seriously flawed. Suppose we could greatly increase human happiness and diminish misery by occasionally, and perhaps secretly, abducting derelicts from city streets for use in fatal but urgent medical experiments. If utilitarian considerations were decisive, this practice might well be justifiable, even desirable. Yet it is surely wrong. Such a case suggests that we cannot always explain good and bad simply in terms of increasing or decreasing overall happiness.

Many philosophers reject utilitarianism in favor of Kantianism. Eighteenth-century philosopher Immanuel Kant (1724–1804) sought the foundations of morality in the human capacity to act rationally. A rational being is free to act out of principle and to refrain from acting from mere impulse or the desire for pleasure. According to Kant, the proper exercise of reason reveals to us our moral duties. It is not, he says, the *consequences* of an action (its "utility" as Bentham claims) that determine its moral character, but the principle on which the action is based. As rational creatures we must be consistent and objective. So, says Kant, we must always ask ourselves whether or not we base an action on a principle (Kant calls it a "maxim") that we consistently want to see adopted as a universal law governing the behavior of all rational beings. A utilitarian might justify an occasional lie that has pleasant consequences. For Kant this is unacceptable: Reason dictates honesty as a *universal* principle. Any deception, however one might try to justify it, is for Kant an affront to the dignity of the deceived. Principled behavior invariably respects oneself and others; it brooks no exceptions.

Kantianism is attractive for its emphasis on conscientiousness and human dignity, but, like utilitarianism, it faces difficulties. Acting on principle without regard for the consequences does not always seem right. According to Kant, if a murderer comes to your door demanding to know the whereabouts of an intended victim who is hiding in your house, you must not lie to him no matter what the consequences. Utilitarians criticize Kantians for their readiness to sacrifice human happiness for the sake of principles; on their side, Kantians object to utilitarians for failing to give moral principle a central place.

The Kantian willingness to sacrifice utility when a question of personal dignity is at stake shows up in Bernard Williams' criticism of J. J. C. Smart's contemporary version of utilitarianism. Williams is impatient with a doctrine that judges the moral worth of an action by referring to an impersonal calculus of pleasures and pains. On the other hand, others criticize Kant for dismissing consequences whenever a question of principle is at stake. Ursula Le Guin's story implicitly reproaches utilitarianism for callousness in justifying individual suffering when such suffering serves the general happiness. R. M. Hare's defense rejects such charges, pointing out that the utilitarian is very concerned to foster a community of considerate and kind people as the best way of promoting the general happiness.

Because Kant and Bentham differ in important ways, their fundamental similarities are easy to ignore. Both hold that morality is the same for everyone everywhere; thus both Bentham and Kant are prepared to judge exotic practices in other cultures by the same standards they judge practices of their own societies. In particular, both would condemn the practice that Mary Midgley cites in her essay "Trying Out One's New Sword," in which a Samurai warrior determines the effectiveness of his sword by seeing how cleanly it slices in two an unsuspecting passerby. And both theories are in keeping with the spirit of the sacred texts that begin this chapter. Indeed, both Kantians and utilitarians claim that their theories merely elaborate the Golden Rule.

Kantianism and utilitarianism are mainstream ethical theories whose influence today is undiminished in the Anglo-Saxon world. A third ethical theory, more popular in the community at large than among moral theorists, is known as ethical relativism. The ethical relativist claims that there are no objective criteria or standards for determining right and wrong. Each society has its own ethic, just as it has its own rules of etiquette and style of dress. Ethical relativism became popular in the nineteenth century when social scientists traveled to exotic regions and discovered a wide variety of moral practices. According to the ethical relativist, the moral precepts found in the Bible are no more or less correct than the quite different moral precepts found in the sacred texts of other societies. Anthropologist Ruth Benedict (1887–1948) argues this position in "A Defense of Moral Relativism"; personal experiences as a field anthropologist convinced her that morals, like rules of etiquette, are just a matter of group practice. Thus, Benedict says, "Mankind has always preferred to say, 'It is morally good,' rather than 'It is habitual' . . . But historically the two phrases are synonymous."

Ethical relativism is a tempting doctrine because it appeals to our desire to be tolerant of other societies. But it has not found much favor among professional philosophers. John Hospers' article, "The Problem with Relativism," crisply presents many of the objections that can be raised against ethical relativism. Mary Midgley makes the interesting point in "Trying Out One's New Sword" that if each society is a distinct unit and not to be judged except on its own terms, then not only are we unable to criticize another society for practices we as outsiders find morally objectionable, but we are, by the same token, unable to praise that society for those things that we find admirable.

Several philosophers point out that those who adopt ethical relativism because they wish to be respectful of other cultures cannot be selective in what they choose to tolerate. For example, they must not only tolerate the Aztecs, who practiced human sacrifice in their religious service, but also the mercenaries and colonialists whose moral code permitted them to exterminate or enslave such "heathens." Tolerance of exotic practices is double-edged in another respect as well. On one hand, it is a manifestation of a sophisticated appreciation of difference; on the other hand, our tolerance of violence or cruelty in other cultures verges on callousness toward the sufferings of the unfortunate victims. And, generally, as long as the perpetrators of what we look upon as a crime can point out that their behavior is acceptable and customary on "their own island," we cannot say clearly that an honest and consistent ethical relativist has grounds to condemn them.

The problem of whether moralists are in a position to pass judgment on the moral character of whole societies is poignantly raised by Jane Perlez's account of the social arrangements in some areas of Uganda that allow husbands relative freedom and urban leisure while their wives are consigned to primitive rural lives of hard and unremitting labor in the fields. V. S. Naipaul, championing the principles of a "universal civilization," does not hesitate to condemn all unjust social arrangements, even those sanctioned by religious traditions.

Finally, as the United Nations Declaration on Human Rights makes plain, ethical relativism is not a doctrine believed in by the majority of nations. The Declaration firmly asserts that all persons, regardless of cultural background or social status, have a number of the same rights. And while its provisions are not enforced, their acceptance by the United Nations General Assembly attests to the entrenched popularity of the belief that some fundamental ethical principles do apply universally.

The Judeo-Christian Tradition

Genesis and Exodus and the Psalms are from the Old Testament; the Sermon on the Mount (Luke 6:17–49) and the parable of the good Samaritan (Luke 10:25–37) are from the New Testament. The two Testaments comprehend more than 1,000 years of Judeo-Christian history.

Human beings are the highest creatures, but the biblical account does not say they were created first. Instead, the account is "evolutionary," proceeding from the creation of the physical world to the lower and higher life forms and culminating in the creation of human beings. Nature itself is good. Immorality entered the picture when human beings exercised choice in ways that defied God's will. Then they were expelled from Eden and fell from grace.

The more specific biblical moral codes are revealed in the Old and New Testaments, the first of which was revealed at Sinai to the Jewish people, who, under the leadership of Moses, had fled Egyptian enslavement. The Old Testament code is encapsulated in the Ten Commandments, some of which are theological in content, enjoining the worship of God and the observance of the Sabbath. Others are more purely moral in a secular sense, prohibiting crimes such as murder and theft, commanding filial respect and the avoidance of greed and covetousness.

Much common law is founded on biblical principles governing tort and commerce. Even our laws for dealing with political refugees are biblically prefigured in the demand that we are to behave respectfully to aliens. Indeed, much of what we count as human decency is traceable to what the two

Testaments command in regard to how one must treat the weak and unfortunate, including animals. The injunction to be compassionate is beautifully expressed in the Sermon on the Mount.

The two Testaments comprehend the classical period of Judeo-Christian history. They do not constitute a single ethical system. But they powerfully embody moral ideals of incalculable authority and influence.

Genesis

1

First Story of Creation

In the beginning, when God created the heavens and the earth, ²the earth was a formless wasteland, and darkness covered the abyss, while a mighty wind swept over the waters.

³Then God said, "Let there be light," and there was light. ⁴God saw how good the light was. God then separated the light from the darkness. ⁵God called the light "day," and the darkness he called "night." Thus evening came, and morning followed—the first day.

⁶Then God said, "Let there be a dome in the middle of the waters, to separate one body of water from the other." And so it happened: ⁷God made the dome, and it separated the water above the dome from the water below it. ⁸God called the dome "the sky." Evening came, and morning followed—the second day.

⁹Then God said, "Let the water under the sky be gathered into a single basin, so that the dry land may appear." And so it happened: the water under the sky was gathered into its basin, and the dry land appeared. ¹⁰God called the dry land "the earth," and the basin of the water he called "the sea." God saw how good it was. ¹¹Then God said, "Let the earth bring forth vegetation: every kind of plant that bears seed and every kind of fruit tree on earth that bears fruit with its seed in it." And so it happened: ¹²the earth brought forth every kind of plant that bears seed and every kind of fruit tree on earth that bears fruit with its seed in it. God saw how good it was. ¹³Evening came, and morning followed—the third day.

¹⁴Then God said: "Let there be lights in the dome of the sky, to separate day from night. Let them mark the fixed times, the days and the years, ¹⁵and serve as luminaries in the dome of the sky, to shed light upon the earth." And so it happened: ¹⁶God made the two great

85

lights, the greater one to govern the day, and the lesser one to govern the night; and he made the stars. [17] God set them in the dome of the sky, to shed light upon the earth, [18] to govern the day and the night, and to separate the light from the darkness. God saw how good it was. [19] Evening came, and morning followed—the fourth day.

[20] Then God said, "Let the water teem with an abundance of living creatures, and on the earth let birds fly beneath the dome of the sky." And so it happened: [21] God created the great sea monsters and all kinds of swimming creatures with which the water teems, and all kinds of winged birds. God saw how good it was [22] and God blessed them, saying, "Be fertile, multiply, and fill the water of the seas; and let the birds multiply on the earth." [23] Evening came, and morning followed—the fifth day.

[24] Then God said, "Let the earth bring forth all kinds of living creatures: cattle, creeping things, and wild animals of all kinds." And so it happened: [25] God made all kinds of wild animals, all kinds of cattle, and all kinds of creeping things of the earth. God saw how good it was. [26] Then God said: "Let us make man in our image, after our likeness. Let them have dominion over the fish of the sea, the birds of the air, and the cattle, and over all the wild animals and all the creatures that crawl on the ground."

[27] God created man in his image;
    in the divine image he created him;
    male and female he created them.

[28] God blessed them, saying: "Be fertile and multiply; fill the earth and subdue it.

Have dominion over the fish of the sea, the birds of the air, and all the living things that move on the earth." [29] God also said: "See, I give you every seed-bearing plant all over the earth and every tree that has seed-bearing fruit on it to be your food; [30] and to all animals of the land, all the birds of the air, and all the living creatures that crawl on the ground, I give all the green plants for food." And so it happened. [31] God looked at everything he had made, and he found it very good. Evening came, and morning followed—the sixth day.

2

[1] Thus the heavens and the earth and all their array were completed. [2] Since on the seventh day God was finished with the work he had

been doing, he rested on the seventh day from all the work he had undertaken. [3] So God blessed the seventh day and made it holy, because on it he rested from all the work he had done in creation.

[4] Such is the story of the heavens and the earth at their creation. . . .

[8] Then the LORD God planted a garden in Eden, in the east, and he placed there the man whom he had formed. [9] Out of the ground the LORD God made various trees grow that were delightful to look at and good for food, with the tree of life in the middle of the garden and the tree of the knowledge of good and bad. . . .

[15] The LORD God then took the man and settled him in the garden of Eden, to cultivate and care for it. [16] The LORD God gave man this order: "You are free to eat from any of the trees of the garden [17] except the tree of the knowledge of good and bad. From that tree you shall not eat; the moment you eat from it you are surely doomed to die."

[18] The LORD God said: "It is not good for the man to be alone. I will make a suitable partner for him." [19] So the LORD God formed out of the ground various wild animals and various birds of the air, and he brought them to the man to see what he would call them; whatever the man called each of them would be its name. [20] The man gave names to all the cattle, all the birds of the air, and all the wild animals; but none proved to be the suitable partner for the man.

[21] So the LORD God cast a deep sleep on the man, and while he was asleep, he took out one of his ribs and closed up its place with flesh. [22] The LORD God then built up into a woman the rib that he had taken from the man. When he brought her to the man, [23]the man said:

> "This one, at last, is bone of my bones
>   and flesh of my flesh;
> This one shall be called 'woman,'
>   for out of 'her man' this one has been taken."

[24] That is why a man leaves his father and mother and clings to his wife, and the two of them become one body.

[25] The man and his wife were both naked, yet they felt no shame.

3

The Fall of Man

[1] Now the serpent was the most cunning of all the animals that the LORD God had made. The serpent asked the woman, "Did God really tell you not to eat from any of the trees in the garden?" [2] The woman

answered the serpent: "We may eat of the fruit of the trees in the garden; ³it is only about the fruit of the tree in the middle of the garden that God said, 'You shall not eat it or even touch it, lest you die.'" ⁴But the serpent said to the woman: "You certainly will not die! ⁵No, God knows well that the moment you eat of it your eyes will be opened and you will be like gods who know what is good and what is bad." ⁶The woman saw that the tree was good for food, pleasing to the eyes, and desirable for gaining wisdom. So she took some of its fruit and ate it; and she also gave some to her husband, who was with her, and he ate it. ⁷Then the eyes of both of them were opened, and they realized that they were naked; so they sewed fig leaves together and made loincloths for themselves.

⁸When they heard the sound of the LORD God moving about in the garden at the breezy time of the day, the man and his wife hid themselves from the LORD God among the trees of the garden. ⁹The LORD God then called to the man and asked him, "Where are you?" ¹⁰He answered, "I heard you in the garden; but I was afraid, because I was naked, so I hid myself." ¹¹Then he asked, "Who told you that you were naked? You have eaten, then, from the tree of which I had forbidden you to eat!" ¹²The man replied, "The woman whom you put here with me—she gave me fruit from the tree, and so I ate it." ¹³The LORD God then asked the woman, "Why did you do such a thing?" The woman answered, "The serpent tricked me into it, so I ate it."

¹⁴Then the LORD God said to the serpent:

> "Because you have done this, you shall be banned
> from all the animals
> and from all the wild creatures;
> On your belly shall you crawl,
> and dirt shall you eat
> all the days of your life.
> ¹⁵I will put enmity between you and the woman,
> and between your offspring and hers;
> He will strike at your head,
> while you strike at his heel."

¹⁶To the woman he said:

> "I will intensify the pangs of your childbearing;
> in pain shall you bring forth children.

Yet your urge shall be for your husband,
and he shall be your master."

¹⁷ To the man he said: "Because you listened to your wife and ate from the tree of which I had forbidden you to eat,

"Cursed be the ground because of you!
In toil shall you eat its yield
all the days of your life.
¹⁸Thorns and thistles shall it bring forth to you,
as you eat of the plants of the field.
¹⁹By the sweat of your face
shall you get bread to eat,
Until you return to the ground,
from which you were taken;
For you are dirt,
and to dirt you shall return."

²⁰ The man called his wife Eve, because she became the mother of all the living.

²¹ For the man and his wife the LORD God made leather garments, with which he clothed them. ²² Then the LORD God said: "See! The man has become like one of us, knowing what is good and what is bad! Therefore, he must not be allowed to put out his hand to take fruit from the tree of life also, and thus eat of it and live forever." ²³ The LORD God therefore banished him from the garden of Eden, to till the ground from which he had been taken. ²⁴ When he expelled the man, he settled him east of the garden of Eden; and he stationed the cherubim and the fiery revolving sword, to guard the way to the tree of life.

Exodus

19

Arrival at Sinai

¹ In the third month after their departure from the land of Egypt, on its first day, the Israelites came to the desert of Sinai. ²After the journey from Rephidim to the desert of Sinai, they pitched camp.

While Israel was encamped here in front of the mountain, ³Moses went up the mountain to God. Then the LORD called to him and said, "Thus shall you say to the house of Jacob; tell the Israelites: ⁴You have seen for yourselves how I treated the Egyptians and how I bore you up on eagle wings and brought you here to myself. ⁵Therefore, if you hearken to my voice and keep my covenant, you shall be my special possession, dearer to me than all other people, though all the earth is mine. ⁶You shall be to me a kingdom of priests, a holy nation. That is what you must tell the Israelites." ⁷So Moses went and summoned the elders of the people. When he set before them all that the LORD had ordered him to tell them, ⁸the people all answered together, "Everything the LORD has said, we will do." Then Moses brought back to the LORD the response of the people.

⁹The LORD also told him, "I am coming to you in a dense cloud, so that when the people hear me speaking with you, they may always have faith in you also." When Moses, then, had reported to the LORD the response of the people, ¹⁰the LORD added, "Go to the people and have them sanctify themselves today and tomorrow. Make them wash their garments ¹¹and be ready for the third day; for on the third day the LORD will come down on Mount Sinai before the eyes of all the people. ¹²Set limits for the people all around the mountain, and tell them. Take care not to go up the mountain, or even to touch its base. If anyone touches the mountain he must be put to death. ¹³No hand shall touch him; he must be stoned to death or killed with arrows. Such a one, man or beast, must not be allowed to live. Only when the ram's horn resounds may they go up to the mountain." ¹⁴Then Moses came down from the mountain to the people and had them sanctify themselves and wash their garments. ¹⁵He warned them, "Be ready for the third day. Have no intercourse with any woman."

The Great Theophany

¹⁶On the morning of the third day there were peals of thunder and lightning, and a heavy cloud over the mountain, and a very loud trumpet blast, so that all the people in the camp trembled. ¹⁷But Moses led the people out of the camp to meet God, and they stationed themselves at the foot of the mountain. ¹⁸Mount Sinai was all wrapped in smoke, for the LORD came down upon it in fire. The smoke rose from it as though from a furnace, and the whole mountain trembled violently. ¹⁹The trumpet blast grew louder and louder, while Moses was speaking and God answering him with thunder.

²⁰When the LORD came down to the top of Mount Sinai, he summoned Moses to the top of the mountain, and Moses went up to

him. ¹²Then the LORD told Moses, "Go down and warn the people not to break through toward the LORD in order to see him; otherwise many of them will be struck down. ²²The priests, too, who approach the Lord must sanctify themselves; else he will vent his anger upon them." ²³Moses said to the LORD, "The people cannot go up to Mount Sinai, for you yourself warned us to set limits around the mountain to make it sacred." ²⁴The LORD repeated, "Go down now! Then come up again along with Aaron. But the priests and the people must not break through to come up to the LORD; else he will vent his anger upon them." ²⁵So Moses went down to the people and told them this.

20

The Ten Commandments

¹Then God delivered all these commandments:

²I, the LORD, am your God, who brought you out of the land of Egypt, that place of slavery. ³You shall not have other gods besides me. ⁴You shall not carve idols for yourselves in the shape of anything in the sky above or on the earth below or in the waters beneath the earth; ⁵you shall not bow down before them or worship them. For I, the LORD, your God, am a jealous God, inflicting punishment for their fathers' wickedness on the children of those who hate me, down to the third and fourth generation; ⁶but bestowing mercy down to the thousandth generation, on the children of those who love me and keep my commandments.

⁷"You shall not take the name of the LORD, your God, in vain. For the LORD will not leave unpunished him who takes his name in vain.

⁸"Remember to keep holy the sabbath day. ⁹Six days you may labor and do all your work, ¹⁰but the seventh day is the sabbath of the LORD, your God. No work may be done then either by you, or your son or daughter, or your male or female slave, or your beast, or by the alien who lives with you. ¹¹In six days the LORD made the heavens and the earth, the sea and all that is in them; but on the seventh day he rested. That is why the LORD has blessed the sabbath day and made it holy.

¹²"Honor your father and your mother, that you may have a long life in the land which the LORD, your God, is giving you.

¹³"You shall not kill.

¹⁴"You shall not commit adultery.

¹⁵"You shall not steal.

[16] "You shall not bear false witness against your neighbor.

[17] "You shall not covet your neighbor's house. You shall not covet your neighbor's wife, nor his male or female slave, nor his ox or ass, nor anything else that belongs to him."

The Fear of God

[18] When the people witnessed the thunder and lightning, the trumpet blast and the mountain smoking, they all feared and trembled. So they took up a position much farther away [19] and said to Moses, "You speak to us, and we will listen; but let not God speak to us, or we shall die." [20] Moses answered the people, "Do not be afraid, for God has come to you only to test you and put his fear upon you, lest you should sin." [21] Still the people remained at a distance, while Moses approached the cloud where God was.

[22] The LORD told Moses, "Thus shall you speak to the Israelites: You have seen for yourselves that I have spoken to you from heaven. [23] Do not make anything to rank with me; neither gods of silver nor gods of gold shall you make for yourselves. . . .

21

Personal Injury

[12] "Whoever strikes a man a mortal blow must be put to death. [13] He, however, who did not hunt a man down, but caused his death by an act of God, may flee to a place which I will set apart for this purpose. [14] But when a man kills another after maliciously scheming to do so, you must take him even from my altar and put him to death. [15] Whoever strikes his father or mother shall be put to death.

[16] "A kidnaper, whether he sells his victim or still has him when caught, shall be put to death.

[17] "Whoever curses his father or mother shall be put to death.

[18] "When men quarrel and one strikes the other with a stone or with his fist, not mortally, but enough to put him in bed, [19] the one who struck the blow shall be acquitted, provided the other can get up and walk around with the help of his staff. Still, he must compensate him for his enforced idleness and provide for his complete cure.

[20] "When a man strikes his male or female slave with a rod so hard that the slave dies under his hand, he shall be punished. [21] If, however, the slave survives for a day or two, he is not to be punished, since the slave is his own property.

²² "When men have a fight and hurt a pregnant woman, so that she suffers a miscarriage, but no further injury, the guilty one shall be fined as much as the woman's husband demands of him, and he shall pay in the presence of the judges. ²³ But if injury ensues, you shall give life for life, ²⁴ eye for eye, tooth for tooth, hand for hand, foot for foot, ²⁵ burn for burn, wound for wound, stripe for stripe.

²⁶ "When a man strikes his male or female slave in the eye and destroys the use of the eye, he shall let the slave go free in compensation for the eye. ²⁷ If he knocks out a tooth of his male or female slave, he shall let the slave go free in compensation for the tooth. . . .

Property Damage

³³ "When a man uncovers or digs a cistern and does not cover it over again, should an ox or an ass fall into it, ³⁴ the owner of the cistern must make good by restoring the value of the animal to its owner; the dead animal, however, he may keep.

³⁵ "When one man's ox hurts another's ox so badly that it dies, they shall sell the live ox and divide this money as well as the dead animal equally between them. ³⁶ But if it was known that the ox was previously in the habit of goring and its owner would not keep it in, he must make full restitution, an ox for an ox; but the dead animal he may keep.

³⁷ "When a man steals an ox or a sheep and slaughters or sells it, he shall restore five oxen for the one ox, and four sheep for the one sheep.

22

¹ [If a thief is caught in the act of housebreaking and beaten to death, there is no bloodguilt involved. ² But if after sunrise he is thus beaten, there is bloodguilt.] He must make full restitution. If he has nothing, he shall be sold to pay for his theft. ³ If what he stole is found alive in his possession, be it an ox, an ass or a sheep, he shall restore two animals for each one stolen.

⁴ "When a man is burning over a field or a vineyard, if he lets the fire spread so that it burns in another's field, he must make restitution with the best produce of his own field or vineyard. ⁵ If the fire spreads further, and catches on to thorn bushes, so that shocked grain or standing grain or the field itself is burned up, the one who started the fire must make full restitution.

Trusts and Loans

⁶ "When a man gives money or any article to another for safekeeping and it is stolen from the latter's house, the thief, if caught, must make twofold restitution. ⁷ If the thief is not caught, the owner of the house shall be brought to God, to swear that he himself did not lay hands on his neighbor's property. ⁸ In every question of dishonest appropriation, whether it be about an ox, or an ass, or a sheep, or a garment, or anything else that has disappeared, where another claims that the thing is his, both parties shall present their case before God; the one whom God convicts must make twofold restitution to the other.

⁹ "When a man gives an ass, or an ox, or a sheep, or any other animal to another for safekeeping, if it dies, or is maimed or snatched away, without anyone witnessing the fact, ¹⁰ the custodian shall swear by the LORD that he did not lay hands on his neighbor's property; the owner must accept the oath, and no restitution is to be made. ¹¹ But if the custodian is really guilty of theft, he must make restitution to the owner. ¹² If it has been killed by a wild beast, let him bring it as evidence, and he need not make restitution for the mangled animal.

¹³ "When a man borrows an animal from his neighbor, if it is maimed or dies while the owner is not present, the man must make restitution. ¹⁴ But if the owner is present, he need not make restitution. If it was hired, this was covered by the price of its hire.

Social Laws

¹⁵ "When a man seduces a virgin who is not betrothed, and lies with her, he shall pay her marriage price and marry her. ¹⁶ If her father refuses to give her to him, he must still pay him the customary marriage price for virgins.

¹⁷ "You shall not let a sorceress live.

¹⁸ "Anyone who lies with an animal shall be put to death.

¹⁹ "Whoever sacrifices to any god, except to the LORD alone, shall be doomed.

²⁰ "You shall not molest or oppress an alien, for you were once aliens yourselves in the land of Egypt. ²¹ You shall not wrong any widow or orphan. ²² If ever you wrong them and they cry out to me, I will surely hear their cry. ²³ My wrath will flare up, and I will kill you with the sword; then your own wives will be widows, and your children orphans.

[24] "If you lend money to one of your poor neighbors among my people, you shall not act like an extortioner toward him by demanding interest from him. [25] If you take your neighbor's cloak as a pledge, you shall return it to him before sunset; [26] for this cloak of his is the only covering he has for his body. What else has he to sleep in? If he cries out to me, I will hear him; for I am compassionate. . . .

23

[1] "You shall not repeat a false report. Do not join the wicked in putting your hand, as an unjust witness, upon anyone. [2] Neither shall you allege the example of the many as an excuse for doing wrong, nor shall you, when testifying in a lawsuit, side with the many in perverting justice. [3] You shall not favor a poor man in his lawsuit.

[4] "When you come upon your enemy's ox or ass going astray, see to it that it is returned to him. [5] When you notice the ass of one who hates you lying prostrate under its burden, by no means desert him; help him, rather, to raise it up.

[6] "You shall not deny one of your needy fellow men his rights in his lawsuit. [7] You shall keep away from anything dishonest. The innocent and the just you shall not put to death, nor shall you acquit the guilty. [8] Never take a bribe, for a bribe blinds even the most clearsighted and twists the words even of the just. [9] You shall not oppress an alien; you well know how it feels to be an alien, since you were once aliens yourselves in the land of Egypt.

Psalm 1

True Happiness

I

Happy the man who follows not
    the counsel of the wicked
Nor walks in the way of sinners,
    nor sits in the company of the
        insolent,
But delights in the law of the Lord
    and meditates on his law day and
        night.

He is like a tree
   planted near running water,
That yields its fruit in due season,
   and whose leaves never fade.
   [Whatever he does, prospers.]

II

Not so the wicked, not so;
   they are like chaff which the wind
     drives away.
Therefore in judgment the wicked
     shall not stand,
   nor shall sinners, in the assembly of
     the just.
For the LORD watches over the way
     of the just,
   but the way of the wicked vanishes.

Psalm 15

The Guest of God

A psalm of David.

I

O LORD, who shall sojourn in your
     tent?
Who shall dwell on your holy
     mountain?

II

He who walks blamelessly and does
     justice;
   who thinks the truth in his heart
   and slanders not with his tongue;
Who harms not his fellow man,
     nor takes up a reproach against his
     neighbor;

By whom the reprobate is despised,
  while he honors those who fear the
    LORD;
Who, though it be to his loss, changes
    not his pledged word;
  who lends not his money at usury
  and accepts not bribe against the
    innocent.

Psalm 23

The Lord, Shepherd and Host

A psalm of David.

I

The LORD is my shepherd; I shall not
    want
  In verdant pastures he gives me
    repose;
Beside restful waters he leads me;
  he refreshes my soul.
He guides me in right paths
  for his name's sake.
Even though I walk in the dark valley
  I fear no evil; for you are at my
    side
With your rod and your staff
  that give me courage.

II

You spread the table before me
  in the sight of my foes;
You anoint my head with oil;
  my cup overflows.
Only goodness and kindness follow
    me
  all the days of my life;
And I shall dwell in the house of the
    LORD
  for years to come.

The Sermon on the Mount

Coming down the mountain with them, he stopped at a level stretch where there were many of his disciples; a large crowd of people was with them from all Judea and Jerusalem and the coast of Tyre and Sidon, people who came to hear him and be healed of their diseases. Those who were troubled with unclean spirits were cured; indeed, the whole crowd was trying to touch him because power went out from him which cured all.

Then, raising his eyes to his disciples, he said:

> "Blest are you poor; the reign of God is yours.
> Blest are you who hunger; you shall be filled.
> Blest are you who are weeping; you shall laugh.

Blest shall you be when men hate you, when they ostracize you and insult you and proscribe your name as evil because of the Son of Man. On the day they do so, rejoice and exult, for your reward shall be great in heaven. Thus it was that their fathers treated the prophets.

> "But woe to you rich, for your consolation is now.
> Woe to you who are full; you shall go hungry.
> Woe to you who laugh now; you shall weep in your grief.

"Woe to you when all speak well of you. Their fathers treated the false prophets in just this way.

Love of One's Enemy

"To you who hear me, I say: Love your enemies, do good to those who hate you; bless those who curse you and pray for those who maltreat you. When someone slaps you on one cheek, turn and give him the other; when someone takes your coat, let him have your shirt as well. Give to all who beg from you. When a man takes what is yours, do not demand it back. Do to others what you would have them do to you. If you love those who love you, what credit is that to you? Even sinners love those who love them. If you do good to those who do good to you, how can you claim any credit? Sinners do as much. If you lend to those from whom you expect repayment, what merit is there in it for you? Even sinners lend to sinners, expecting to be repaid in full.

"Love your enemy and do good; lend without expecting repayment. Then will your recompense be great. You will rightly be called sons of the Most High, since he himself is good to the ungrateful and the wicked.

"Be compassionate, as your Father is compassionate. Do not judge, and you will not be judged. Do not condemn, and you will not be condemned. Pardon, and you shall be pardoned. Give, and it shall be given to you. Good measure pressed down, shaken together, running over, will they pour into the fold of your garment. For the measure you measure with will be measured back to you."

He also used images in speaking to them: "Can a blind man act as guide to a blind man? Will they not both fall into a ditch? A student is not above his teacher; but every student when he has finished his studies will be on a par with his teacher.

"Why look at the speck in your brother's eye when you miss the plank in your own? How can you say to your brother, 'Brother, let me remove the speck from your eye,' yet fail yourself to see the plank lodged in your own? Hypocrite, remove the plank from your own eye first; then you will see clearly enough to remove the speck from your brother's eye.

"A good tree does not produce decayed fruit any more than a decayed tree produces good fruit. Each tree is known by its yield. Figs are not taken from thornbushes, nor grapes picked from brambles. A good man produces goodness from the good in his heart; an evil man produces evil out of his store of evil. Each man speaks from his heart's abundance. Why do you call me 'Lord, Lord,' and not put into practice what I teach you? Any man who desires to come to me will hear my words and put them into practice. I will show you with whom he is to be compared. He may be likened to the man who, in building a house, dug deeply and laid the foundation on a rock. When the floods came the torrent rushed in on that house, but failed to shake it because of its solid foundation. On the other hand, anyone who has heard my words but not put them into practice is like the man who built his house on the ground without any foundation. When the torrent rushed upon it, it immediately fell in and was completely destroyed."

The Good Samaritan

On one occasion a lawyer stood up to pose him this problem: "Teacher, what must I do to inherit everlasting life?"

Jesus answered him: "What is written in the law? How do you read it?" He replied:

> "You shall love the Lord your God
> with all your heart,
> with all your soul,
> with all your strength,
> and with all your mind;
> and your neighbor as yourself."

Jesus said, "You have answered correctly. Do this and you shall live." But because he wished to justify himself he said to Jesus, "And who is my neighbor?" Jesus replied: "There was a man going down from Jerusalem to Jericho who fell prey to robbers. They stripped him, beat him, and then went off leaving him half-dead. A priest happened to be going down the same road; he saw him but continued on. Likewise there was a Levite who came the same way; he saw him and went on. But a Samaritan who was journeying along came on him and was moved to pity at the sight. He approached him and dressed his wounds, pouring in oil and wine. He then hoisted him on his own beast and brought him to an inn, where he cared for him. The next day he took out two silver pieces and gave them to the innkeeper with the request: 'Look after him, and if there is any further expense I will repay you on my way back.'

"Which of these three, in your opinion, was neighbor to the man who fell in with the robbers?" The answer came. "The one who treated him with compassion." Jesus said to him, "Then go and do the same."

STUDY QUESTIONS

1. Show how some common laws embody principles that one finds in the Bible. Apply your findings in a general discussion of how law and morality are related.
2. The story of Adam and Eve is interpreted by some theologians to be the story of "original sin." Try to give both a religious and a philosophical interpretation of the doctrine of original sin.
3. What moral ideals do Psalms 1, 15 and 23 express? What rewards does one get for living in accordance with them? Do you think that Psalm 1 accurately reflects reality? If not, does this vitiate its message?

4. A sermon often involes hyperbole. Do you believe that the in-junction to love one's enemy and to do good to those who hate us is seriously and literally intended? The moral teachings of Jesus are sometimes criticized for setting too high a standard for human behavior. Do you think the criticism is justified?

5. The Sermon on the Mount exhorts us to be compassionate "as your [heavenly] Father is compassionate." We also find this theme of *imitatio dei* in the Old Testament. This suggests that one ap-proach to the moral life is to conceive of ourselves as striving to imitate a morally perfect being. Do you think that this is a helpful way to think about the moral life?

The Principle of Utility

JEREMY BENTHAM

Jeremy Bentham (1748–1832) is the father of modern Utilitarianism. He was one of the leading political phi-losophers of his time, and his book *The Principles of Morals and Legislation* is a classic of moral and political philosophy.

According to Bentham's "principle of utility," actions are right when they increase happiness and diminish misery, wrong when they have the opposite effect. By "utility" he means the property of producing pleasure or happiness in conscious beings. Thus we should always do those acts that tend to increase overall happiness. Bentham is known as a "hedonistic utilitarian": pleasure is to be pur-sued, pain is to be avoided. A legislator, for example, should

THE PRINCIPLE OF UTILITY Excerpted from Jeremy Bentham, *The Principles of Morals and Legislation* (1789).

calculate the pleasure/pain ratio of each prospective law. Bentham proposes that we evaluate pleasures according to their intensity, duration, certainty, propinquity (nearness), fecundity (tendency to lead to other pleasures), purity (tendency *not* to be followed by pain), and, finally, extent (the number of persons to whom the pleasure extends). Bentham concedes that he cannot *prove* the truth of the principle of utility; but he claims that most of us implicitly accept it and act on it every day. And he suspects that any alternative principle will be "despotical, and hostile to all the rest of the human race."

The principle of utility is the foundation of the present work: it will be proper therefore at the outset to give an explicit and determinate account of what is meant by it. By the principle of utility is meant that principle which approves or disapproves of every action whatsoever, according to the tendency which it appears to have to augment or diminish the happiness of the party whose interest is in question: or, what is the same thing in other words, to promote or to oppose that happiness. I say of every action whatsoever; and therefore not only of every action of a private individual, but of every measure of government.

By utility is meant that property in any object, whereby it tends to produce benefit, advantage, pleasure, good, or happiness (all this in the present case comes to the same thing), or (what comes again to the same thing) to prevent the happening of mischief, pain, evil, or unhappiness to the party whose interest is considered: if that party be the community in general, then the happiness of the community: if a particular individual, then the happiness of that individual.

The interest of the community is one of the most general expressions that can occur in the phraseology of morals: no wonder that the meaning of it is often lost. When it has a meaning, it is this. The community is a fictitious *body*, composed of the individual persons who are considered as constituting as it were its *members*. The interest of the community then is, what?—the sum of the interests of the several members who compose it.

It is in vain to talk of the interests of the community, without understanding what is the interest of the individual. A thing is said to promote the interest, or to be *for* the interest, of an individual, when it tends to add to the sum total of his pleasures: or, what comes to the same thing, to diminish the sum total of his pains.

An action then may be said to be conformable to the principle of utility, or, for shortness sake, to utility (meaning with respect to the community at large), when the tendency it has to augment the happiness of the community is greater than any it has to diminish it.

A measure of government (which is but a particular kind of action, performed by a particular person or persons) may be said to be conformable to or dictated by the principle of utility, when in like manner the tendency which it has to augment the happiness of the community is greater than any which it has to diminish it.

When an action, or in particular a measure of government, is supposed by a man to be conformable to the principle of utility, it may be convenient, for the purposes of discourse, to imagine a kind of law or dictate, called a law or dictate of utility: and to speak of the action in question, as being conformable to such law or dictate.

A man may be said to be a partizan of the principle of utility, when the approbation or disapprobation he annexes to any action, or to any measure, is determined by and proportioned to the tendency which he conceives it to have to augment or to diminish the happiness of the community: or in other words, to its conformity or unconformity to the laws or dictates of utility.

Of an action that is conformable to the principle of utility one may always say either that it is one that ought to be done, or at least that it is not one that ought not to be done. One may say also, that it is right it should be done; at least that it is not wrong it should be done: that it is a right action; at least that it is not a wrong action. When thus interpreted, the words *ought,* and *right* and *wrong,* and others of that stamp, have a meaning: when otherwise, they have none.

Has the rectitude of this principle been ever formally contested? It should seem that it had, by those who have not known what they have been meaning. Is it susceptible of any direct proof? it should seem not: for that which is used to prove every thing else, cannot itself be proved: a chain of proofs must have their commencement somewhere. To give such proof is as impossible as it is needless.

Not that there is or ever has been that human creature breathing, however stupid or perverse, who has not on many, perhaps on most occasions of his life, deferred to it. By the natural constitution of the human frame, on most occasions of their lives men in general embrace this principle, without thinking of it: if not for the ordering of their own actions, yet for the trying of their own actions, as well as of those of other men. There have been, at the same time, not many, perhaps, even of the most intelligent, who have been disposed to embrace it purely and without reserve. There are even few who have not taken some occasion or other to quarrel with it, either on account of their not understanding always how to apply it, or on account of some prejudice or other which they were afraid to examine into, or could not bear to part with. For such is the stuff that man is made of: in principle and in practice, in a right track and in a wrong one, the rarest of all human qualities is consistency.

When a man attempts to combat the principle of utility, it is with reasons drawn, without his being aware of it, from that very principle itself. His arguments, if they prove any thing, prove not that the principle is *wrong,* but that, according to the applications he supposes to be made of it, it is *misapplied.* Is it possible for a man to move the earth? Yes; but he must first find out another earth to stand upon.

To disprove the propriety of it by arguments is impossible; but, from the causes that have been mentioned, or from some confused or partial view of it, a man may happen to be disposed not to relish it. Where this is the case, if he thinks the settling of his opinions on such a subject worth the trouble, let him take the following steps, and at length, perhaps, he may come to reconcile himself to it.

Let him settle with himself, whether he would wish to discard this principle altogether; if so, let him consider what it is that all his reasonings (in matters of politics especially) can amount to?

If he would, let him settle with himself, whether he would judge and act without any principle, or whether there is any other he would judge and act by?

If there be, let him examine and satisfy himself whether the principle he thinks he has found is really any separate intelligible principle; or whether it be not a mere principle in words, a kind of phrase, which at bottom expresses neither more nor less than the mere averment of his own unfounded sentiments; that is, what in another person he might be apt to call caprice?

If he is inclined to think that his own approbation or disapprobation, annexed to the idea of an act, without any regard to its consequences, is a sufficient foundation for him to judge and act upon, let him ask himself whether his sentiment is to be a standard of right and wrong, with respect to every other man, or whether every man's sentiment has the same privilege of being a standard to itself?

In the first case, let him ask himself whether his principle is not despotical, and hostile to all the rest of human race?

In the second case, whether it is not anarchial, and whether at this rate there are not as many different standards of right and wrong as there are men? and whether even to the same man, the same thing, which is right to-day, may not (without the least change in its nature) be wrong to-morrow? and whether the same thing is not right and wrong in the same place at the same time? and in either case, whether all argument is not at an end? and whether, when two men have said, "I like this," and "I don't like it," they can (upon such a principle) have any thing more to say?

If he should have said to himself, no: for that the sentiment which he proposes as a standard must be grounded on reflection, let him say on what particulars the reflection is to turn? if on particulars having relation to the utility of the act, then let him say whether this is not deserting his own principle and borrowing assistance from that very one in opposition to which he sets it up: or if not on those particulars, on what other particulars?

If he should be for compounding the matter, and adopting his own principle in part, and the principle of utility in part, let him say how far he will adopt it?

When he has settled with himself where he will stop, then let him ask himself how he justifies to himself the adopting it so far? and why he will not adopt it any farther?

Admitting any other principle than the principle of utility to be a right principle, a principle that it is right for a man to pursue; admitting (what is not true) that the word *right* can have a meaning without reference to utility, let him say whether there is any such thing as a *motive* that a man can have to pursue the dictates of it: if there is, let him say what that motive is, and how it is to be distinguished from those which enforce the dictates of utility: if not, then lastly let him say what it is this other principle can be good for?

Pleasures then, and the avoidance of pains, are the *ends* which the legislator has in view: it behoves him therefore to understand their *value*. Pleasures and pains are the *instruments* he has to work with: it behoves him therefore to understand their force, which is again, in other words, their value.

To a person considered *by himself,* the value of a pleasure or pain considered *by itself,* will be greater or less, according to the four following circumstances:

1. Its *intensity.*
2. Its *duration.*
3. Its *certainty* or *uncertainty.*
4. Its *propinquity* or *remoteness.*

These are the circumstances which are to be considered in estimating a pleasure or a pain considered each of them by itself. But when the value of any pleasure or pain is considered for the purpose of estimating the tendency of any *act* by which it is produced, there are two other circumstances to be taken into the account; these are,

5. Its *fecundity,* or the chance it has of being followed by sensations of the *same* kind: that is, pleasures, if it be a pleasure: pains, if it be a pain.
6. Its *purity,* or the chance it has of *not* being followed by sensations of the *opposite* kind: that is, pains, if it be a pleasure: pleasures, if it be a pain.

These two last, however, are in strictness scarcely to be deemed properties of the pleasure or the pain itself; they are not, therefore, in strictness to be taken into the account of the value of that pleasure or that pain. They are in strictness to be deemed properties only of the act, or other event, by which such pleasure or pain has been produced; and accordingly are only to be taken into the account of the tendency of such act or such event.

To a *number* of persons, with reference to each of whom the value of a pleasure or a pain is considered, it will be greater or less, according to seven circumstances: to wit, the six preceding ones; *viz.*

1. Its *intensity.*
2. Its *duration.*
3. Its *certainty* or *uncertainty.*
4. Its *propinquity* or *remoteness.*
5. Its *fecundity.*
6. Its *purity.*

And one other; to wit:

7. Its *extent;* that is, the number of persons to whom it
    extends; or (in other words) who are affected by it.

To take an exact account then of the general tendency of any act,
by which the interests of a community are affected, proceed as follows. Begin with any one person of those whose interests seem most
immediately to be affected by it: and take an account,

1. Of the value of each distinguishable *pleasure* which
    appears to be produced by it in the *first* instance.
2. Of the value of each *pain* which appears to be produced
    by it in the *first* instance.
3. Of the value of each pleasure which appears to be
    produced by it *after* the first. This constitutes the *fecundity*
    of the first *pleasure* and the *impurity* of the first *pain*.
4. Of the value of each *pain* which appears to be produced
    by it after the first. This constitutes the *fecundity* of the
    first *pain,* and the *impurity* of the first pleasure.
5. Sum up all the values of all the *pleasures* on the one side,
    and those of all the pains on the other. The balance, if it be
    on the side of pleasure, will give the *good* tendency of the
    act upon the whole, with respect to the interests of that
    individual person; if on the side of pain, the *bad* tendency
    of it upon the whole.
6. Take an account of the *number* of persons whose interests
    appear to be concerned; and repeat the above process with
    respect to each. *Sum* up the numbers expressive of the
    degrees of *good* tendency, which the act has, with respect
    to each individual, in regard to whom the tendency of it is
    good upon the whole: do this again with respect to each
    individual, in regard to whom the tendency of it is *bad*
    upon the whole. Take the *balance;* which, if on the side of
    pleasure, will give the general *good tendency* of the act, with
    respect to the total number or community of individuals
    concerned; if on the side of pain, the general *evil tendency,*
    with respect to the same community.

It is not to be expected that this process should be strictly pursued
previously to every moral judgment, or to every legislative or judicial
operation. It may, however, be always kept in view: and as near as the

process actually pursued on these occasions approaches to it, so near will such process approach to the character of an exact one.

The same process is alike applicable to pleasure and pain, in whatever shape they appear: and by whatever denomination they are distinguished: to pleasure, whether it be called *good* (which is properly the cause or instrument of pleasure) or *profit* (which is distant pleasure, or the cause or instrument of distant pleasure), or *convenience,* or *advantage, benefit, emolument, happiness,* and so forth; to pain, whether it be called *evil* (which corresponds to *good*), or *mischief,* or *inconvenience,* or *disadvantage,* or *loss,* or *unhappiness,* and so forth.

Nor is this a novel and unwarranted, any more than it is a useless theory. In all this there is nothing but what the practice of mankind, whatsoever they have a clear view of their own interest, is perfectly conformable to. An article of property, an estate in land, for instance, is valuable, on what account? On account of the pleasures of all kinds which it enables a man to produce, and what comes to the same thing the pains of all kinds which it enables him to avert. But the value of such an article of property is universally understood to rise or fall according to the length or shortness of the time which a man has in it: the certainty or uncertainty of its coming into possession: and the nearness or remoteness of the time at which, if at all, it is to come into possession. As to the *intensity* of the pleasures which a man may derive from it, this is never thought of, because it depends upon the use which each particular person may come to make of it; which cannot be estimated till the particular pleasures he may come to derive from it, or the particular pains he may come to exclude by means of it, are brought to view. For the same reason, neither does he think of the *fecundity* or *purity* of those pleasures.

STUDY QUESTIONS

1. What does Bentham mean by the interest of the community? How does the interest of the community determine the rightness or wrongness of a proposed course of action?

2. What does Bentham think about the possibility of proving the principle of utility?

3. How does Bentham assess the value to be assigned to a given pleasure or pain when evaluating a course of action?

4. How are the values of pleasures and pains related to the value of other things such as houses and symphonies?
5. Debate the question:
Bentham's moral philosophy is essentially at odds with the morality of the Judeo-Christian tradition.

Utilitarianism

J. J. C. SMART

J. J. C. Smart (b. 1920) is professor emeritus of the University of Adelaide and of the Australian National University. He is the author of several books, including *Philosophy and Scientific Realism* and *Ethics, Persuasion and Truth*.

Act-utiliarians tell us to choose *actions* that inc rease happiness and diminish misery. Rule-utilitarainism, on the other hand, tells us to act according to *rules* that tend to increase happiness and diminish misery. Thus an act-utilitarian might break a promise whenever the principle of utility favored doing so; according to the rule-utilitarianism, it is better all around if everyone follows the rules ("Keep your promises"; "Tell the truth") even when, in a particular case, adherence to the rule does not increase utility. Smart is an act-utilitarian, and he criticizes rule-utilitarians for being "rule worshippers." Why, he asks, should someone follow a rule in cases in which there is greater utility in breaking it? Smart also considers the problem of the "higher" and "lower" pleasures. It may well be that a dog gets more pleasure chasing a rat than a philosopher does contemplating the mysteries of the universe.

UTILITARIANISM From "An Outline of a System of Utilitarian Ethics" in *Utilitarianism: For and Against*, edited by J. J. C. Smart and Bernard Williams. Reprinted by permission of Cambridge University Press.

Should we then try to reduce the number of discontented philosophers and fill the world with happy dogs? Smart answers that it is inaccurate to describe dogs as happy. To call human beings happy, however, is not merely to describe them as contented, but to express approval for their form of contentness. Developing an idea of Bentham, Smart argues that the higher pleasures of poetry, philosophy, and science tend to be more "fecund" (that is, conducive to other pleasures) than the lower pleasures, such as drunkeness, chasing rats, or playing bingo. Smart addresses a number of other problems facing Utilitarianism: Should we try to increase the *average* happiness of human beings or should we try to increase the *total* amount of happiness in the world? Must we consider the remote consequences of our actions? Is there a place for rules in act-utilitarianism? Smart believes that act-utilitarianism is a simple and natural doctrine that will eventually appeal to all who care about the happiness of humankind.

The system of normative ethics which I am here concerned to defend is . . . *act*-utilitarianism. Act-utilitarianism is to be contrasted with rule-utilitarianism. Act-utilitarianism is the view that the rightness or wrongness of an action is to be judged by the consequences, good or bad, of the action itself. Rule-utilitarianism is the view that the rightness or wrongness of an action is to be judged by the goodness and badness of the consequences of a rule that everyone should perform the action in like circumstances. . . .

I have argued elsewhere[1] the objections to rule-utilitarianism as compared with act-utilitarianism. Briefly they boil down to the accusation of rule worship: the rule-utilitarian presumably advocates

---

[1] In my article "Extreme and restricted utilitarianism," *Philosophical Quarterly* 6 (1956) 334–354. This contains bad errors and a better version of the article will be found in Philippa Foot (ed.), *Theories of Ethics* (London: Oxford University Press, 1967) or Michael D. Bayles (ed.), *Contemporary Utilitarianism* (New York: Doubleday, 1968). In this article I used the terms "extreme" and "restricted" instead of Brandt's more felicitous "act" and "rule" which I now prefer.

his principle because he is ultimately concerned with human happiness: why then should he advocate abiding by a rule when he knows that it will not in the present case be most beneficial to abide by it? The reply that in most cases it is most beneficial to abide by the rule seems irrelevant. And so is the reply that it would be better that everybody should abide by the rule than that nobody should. This is to suppose that the only alternative to "everybody does *A*" is "no one does *A*." But clearly we have the possibility "some people do *A* and some don't." Hence to refuse to break a generally beneficial rule in those cases in which it is not most beneficial to obey it seems irrational and to be a case of rule worship.

The type of utilitarianism which I shall advocate will, then, be act-utilitarianism, not rule-utilitarianism. . . .

An act-utilitarian judges the rightness or wrongness of actions by the goodness and badness of their consequences. But is he to judge the goodness and badness of the consequences of an action solely by their pleasantness and unpleasantness? Bentham, who thought that quantity of pleasure being equal, the experience of playing pushpin was as good as that of reading poetry, could be classified as a hedonistic act-utilitarian. Moore, who believed that some states of mind, such as those of acquiring knowledge, had intrinsic value quite independent of their pleasantness, can be called an ideal utilitarian. Mill seemed to occupy an intermediate position. He held that there are higher and lower pleasures. This seems to imply that pleasure is a necessary condition for goodness but that goodness depends on other qualities of experience than pleasantness and unpleasantness. I propose to call Mill a quasi-ideal utilitarian. . . .

What Bentham, Mill and Moore are all agreed on is that the rightness of an action is to be judged solely by consequences, states of affairs brought about by the action. Of course we shall have to be careful here not to construe "state of affairs" so widely that any ethical doctrine becomes utilitarian. For if we did so we would not be saying anything at all in advocating utilitarianism. If, for example, we allowed "the state of having just kept a promise," then a deontologist who said we should keep promises simply because they are promises would be a utilitarian. And we do not wish to allow this. . . . Let us consider Mill's contention that it is "better to be Socrates dissatisfied than a fool satisfied." Mill holds that pleasure is not to be our sole criterion for evaluating consequences: the state of mind of Socrates might be less pleasurable than that of the fool, but, according to Mill, Socrates would be happier than the fool.

It is necessary to observe, first of all, that a purely hedonistic utilitarian, like Bentham, might agree with Mill in preferring the experiences of discontented philosophers to those of contented fools. His preference for the philosopher's state of mind, however, would not be an *intrinsic* one. He would say that the discontented philosopher is a useful agent in society and that the existence of Socrates is responsible for an improvement in the lot of humanity generally. Consider two brothers. One may be of a docile and easy temperament: he may lead a supremely contented and unambitious life, enjoying himself hugely. The other brother may be ambitious, may stretch his talents to the full, may strive for scientific success and academic honours, and may discover some invention or some remedy for disease or improvement in agriculture which will enable innumerable men of easy temperament to lead a contented life, whereas otherwise they would have been thwarted by poverty, disease or hunger. Or he may make some advance in pure science which will later have beneficial practical applications. Or, again, he may write poetry which will solace the leisure hours and stimulate the brains of practical men or scientists, thus indirectly leading to an improvement in society. That is, the pleasures of poetry or mathematics may be *extrinsically* valuable in a way in which those of pushpin or sunbathing may not be. Though the poet or mathematician may be discontented, society as a whole may be the more contented for his presence. . . .

Maybe we have gone wrong in talking of pleasure as though it were no more than contentment. Contentment consists roughly in relative absence of unsatisfied desires; pleasure is perhaps something more positive and consists in a balance between absence of unsatisfied desires and presence of satisfied desires. We might put the difference in this way: pure unconsciousness would be a limiting case of contentment, but not of pleasure. A stone has no unsatisfied desires, but then it just has no desires. Nevertheless, this consideration will not resolve the disagreement between Bentham and Mill. No doubt a dog has as intense a desire to discover rats as the philosopher has to discover the mysteries of the universe. Mill would wish to say that the pleasures of the philosopher were more valuable intrinsically than those of the dog, however intense these last might be. . . .

It is worth while enquiring how much practical ethics is likely to be affected by the possibility of disagreement over the question of Socrates dissatisfied versus the fool satisfied.

'Not very much,' one feels like saying at first. We noted that the most complex and intellectual pleasures are also the most fecund. Poetry elevates the mind, makes one more sensitive, and so harmonizes with various intellectual pursuits, some of which are of practical value. Delight in mathematics is even more obviously, on Benthamite views, a pleasure worth encouraging, for on the progress of mathematics depends the progress of mankind. Even the most hedonistic schoolmaster would prefer to see his boys enjoying poetry and mathematics rather than neglecting these arts for the pleasures of marbles or the tuckshop. Indeed many of the brutish pleasures not only lack fecundity but are actually the reverse of fecund. To enjoy food too much is to end up fat, unhealthy and without zest or vigour. To enjoy drink too much is even worse. In most circumstances of ordinary life the pure hedonist will agree in his practical recommendations with the quasi-ideal utilitarian.

This need not always be so. Some years ago two psychologists, Olds and Milner, carried out some experiments with rats. Through the skull of each rat they inserted an electrode. These electrodes penetrated to various regions of the brain. In the case of some of these regions the rat showed behaviour characteristics of pleasure when a current was passed from the electrode, in others they seemed to show pain, and in others the stimulus seemed neutral. That a stimulus was pleasure-giving was shown by the fact that the rat would learn to pass the current himself by pressing a lever. He would neglect food and make straight for this lever and start stimulating himself. In some cases he would sit there pressing the lever every few seconds for hours on end. This calls up a pleasant picture of the voluptuary of the future, a bald-headed man with a number of electrodes protruding from his skull, one to give the physical pleasure of sex, one for that of eating, one for that of drinking, and so on. Now is this the sort of life that all our ethical planning should culminate in? A few hours' work a week, automatic factories, comfort and security from disease, and hours spent at a switch, continually electrifying various regions of one's brain? Surely not. Men were made for higher things, one can't help wanting to say, even though one knows that men weren't made for anything, but are the product of evolution by natural selection.

It might be said that the objection to continual sensual stimulation of the above sort is that though it would be pleasant in itself it would be infecund of future pleasures. This is often so with the ordinary sensual pleasures. Excessive indulgence in the physical pleasures of sex may possibly have a debilitating effect and may perhaps interfere with the deeper feelings of romantic love. But whether stimulation by the electrode method would have this weakening effect and whether it would impair the possibility of future pleasures of the same sort is another matter. For example, there would be no excessive secretion of hormones. The whole biochemical mechanism would, almost literally, be short-circuited. Maybe, however, a person who stimulated himself by the electrode method would find it so enjoyable that he would neglect all other pursuits. Maybe if everyone became an electrode operator people would lose interest in everything else and the human race would die out.

Suppose, however, that the facts turned out otherwise: that a man could (and would) do his full share of work in the office or the factory and come back in the evening to a few hours' contented electrode work, without bad after-effects. This would be his greatest pleasure, and the pleasure would be so great intrinsically and so easily repeatable that its lack of fecundity would not matter. Indeed perhaps by this time human arts, such as medicine, engineering, agriculture, and architecture will have been brought to a pitch of perfection sufficient to enable most of the human race to spend most of its time electrode operating, without compensating pains of starvation, disease and squalor. Would this be a satisfactory state of society? Would this be the millennium towards which we have been striving? Surely the pure hedonist would have to say that it was.

It is time, therefore, that we had another look at the concept of happiness. Should we say that the electrode operator was really happy? This is a difficult question to be clear about, because the concept of happiness is a tricky one. But whether we should call the electrode operator "happy" or not, there is no doubt (a) that he would be *contented* and (b) that he would be *enjoying himself*. . . .

. . . To call a person "happy" is to say more than that he is contented for most of the time, or even that he frequently enjoys himself and is rarely discontented or in pain. It is, I think, in part to express a favourable attitude to the idea of such a form of contentment and enjoyment. That is, for A to call B "happy," A must be contented at the prospect of *B* being in his present state of mind and at the prospect of *A* himself, should the opportunity arise, enjoying that sort of state of mind. That is, "happy" is a word which is mainly descriptive (tied to the concepts of contentment and enjoyment) but which is also partly evaluative. It is because Mill approves of the "higher" pleasures, e.g., intellectual pleasures, so much more than he approves of the more simple and brutish pleasures, that, quite apart from consequences and side effects, he can pronounce the man who enjoys the pleasures of philosophical discourse as "more happy" than the man who gets enjoyment from pushpin or beer drinking.

The word "happy" is not wholly evaluative, for there would be something absurd, as opposed to merely unusual, in calling a man who was in pain, or who was not enjoying himself, or who hardly ever enjoyed himself, or who was in a more or less permanent state of intense dissatisfaction, a "happy" man. For a man to be happy he must, as a minimal condition, be fairly contented and moderately enjoying himself for much of the time. Once this minimal condition is satisfied we can go on to evaluate various types of contentment and enjoyment and to grade them in terms of happiness. . . .

To sum up so far, happiness is partly an evaluative concept, and so the utilitarian maxim "You ought to maximize happiness" is doubly evaluative. There is the possibility of an ultimate disagreement between two utilitarians who differ over the question of pushpin versus poetry, or Socrates dissatisfied versus the fool satisfied. . . .

Leaving these more remote possibilities out of account, however, and considering the decisions we have to make at present, the question of whether the "higher" pleasures should be preferred to the "lower" ones does seem to be of slight practical importance. There are already perfectly good hedonistic arguments for poetry as against pushpin. As has been pointed out, the more complex pleasures are incomparably more fecund than the less complex ones: not only are they enjoyable in themselves but they are a means to further enjoyment. Still less, on the whole, do they lead to disillusionment, physical deterioration or social disharmony. The connoisseur of poetry may enjoy himself no more than the connoisseur of whisky, but he runs no danger of a headache on the following morning. Moreover the question of whether the general happiness would be increased by replacing most of the human population by a bigger population of contented sheep and pigs is not one which by any stretch of the imagination could become a live issue. Even if we thought, on abstract grounds, that such a replacement would be desirable, we should not have the slightest chance of having our ideas generally adopted. . . .

Another type of ultimate disagreement between utilitarians, whether hedonistic or ideal, can arise over whether we should try to maximize the *average* happiness of human beings (or the average goodness of their states of mind) or whether we should try to maximize the *total* happiness or goodness. . . . I have not yet elucidated the concept of total happiness, and you may regard it as a suspect notion. But for present purposes I shall put it in this way: Would you be quite indifferent between (a) a universe containing only one million happy sentient beings, all equally happy, and (b) a universe containing two million happy beings, each neither more nor less happy than any in the first universe? Or would you, as a humane and sympathetic person, give a preference to the second universe? I myself cannot help feeling a preference for the second universe. But if someone feels the other way I do not know how to argue with him. It looks as though we have yet another possibility of disagreement within a general utilitarian framework.

This type of disagreement might have practical relevance. It might be important in discussions of the ethics of birth control. This is not to say that the utilitarian who values total, rather than average, happiness may not have potent arguments in favour of birth control. But he will need more arguments to convince himself than will the other type of utilitarian.

In most cases the difference between the two types of utilitarianism will not lead to disagreement in practice. For in most cases the most effective way to increase the total happiness is to increase the average happiness, and vice versa. . . .

I shall now state the act-utilitarian doctrine. . . .

Let us say, then, that the only reason for performing an action *A* rather than an alternative action *B* is that doing *A* will make mankind (or, perhaps, all sentient beings) happier than will doing *B*. . . . This is so simple and natural a doctrine that we can surely expect that many of my readers will have at least some propensity to agree. For I am talking . . . to sympathetic and benevolent men, that is, to men who desire the happiness of mankind. Since they have a favourable attitude to the general happiness, surely they will have a tendency to submit to an ultimate moral principle which does no more than express this attitude. It is true that these men, being human, will also have purely selfish attitudes. Either these attitudes will be in harmony with the general happiness (in cases where everyone's looking after his own interests promotes the maximum general happiness) or they will not be in harmony with the general happiness, in which case they will largely cancel one another out, and so could not be made the basis of an interpersonal discussion anyway. It is possible, then, that many sympathetic and benevolent people depart from or fail to attain a utilitarian ethical principle only under the stress of tradition, of superstition, or of unsound philosophical reasoning. If this hypothesis should turn out to be correct, at least as far as these readers are concerned, then the utilitarian may contend that there is no need for him to defend his position directly, save by stating it in a consistent manner, and by showing that common objections to it are unsound. After all, it expresses an ultimate attitude, not a liking for something merely as a means to something else. Save for attempting to remove confusions and discredit superstitions which may get in the way of clear moral thinking, he cannot, of course, appeal to argument and must rest his hopes on the good feeling of his readers. If any reader is not a sympathetic and benevolent man, then of course it cannot be expected that he will have an ultimate pro-attitude to human happiness in general. Also some good-hearted readers may reject the utilitarian position because of certain considerations relating to justice. . . .

The utilitarian's ultimate moral principle, let it be remembered, expresses the sentiment not of altruism but of benevolence, the agent counting himself neither more nor less than any other person. Pure altruism cannot be made the basis of a universal moral discussion in that it would lead different people to different and perhaps incompatible courses of action, even though the circumstances were identical. When two men each try to let the other through a door first a deadlock results. Altruism could hardly commend itself to those of a scientific, and hence universalistic, frame of mind. If you count in my calculations why should I not count in your calculations? And why should I pay more attention to my calculations than to yours? Of course we often tend to praise and honour altruism even more than generalized benevolence. This is because people too often err on the side of selfishness, and so altruism is a fault on the right side. If we can make a man try to be an altruist he may succeed as far as acquiring a generalized benevolence.

Suppose we could predict the future consequences of actions with certainty. Then it would be possible to say that the total future consequences of action *A* are such-and-such and that the total future consequences of action *B* are so-and-so. In order to help someone to decide whether to do *A* or to do *B* we could say to him: "Envisage the total consequences of *A*, and think them over carefully and imaginatively. Now envisage the total consequences of *B*, and think them over carefully. As a benevolent and humane man, and thinking of yourself just as one man among others, would you prefer the consequences of *A* or those of *B*?" That is, we are asking for a comparison of one (present and future) *total* situation with another (present and future) *total* situation. So far we are not asking for a *summation* or *calculation* of pleasures or happiness. We are asking only for a comparison of total situations. And it seems clear that we can frequently make such a comparison and say that one total situation is better than another. For example few people would not prefer a total situation in which a million people are well-fed, well-clothed, free of pain, doing interesting and enjoyable work, and enjoying the pleasures of conversation, study, business, art, humour, and so on, to a total situation where there are ten thousand such people only, or perhaps 999,999 such people plus one man with toothache, or neurotic, or shivering with cold. In general, we can sum things up by saying that if we are humane, kindly, benevolent people, we want as many people as possible now and in the future to be as happy as possible. Someone might object that we cannot envisage the total future situation, because this stretches into infinity. In reply to this we may say that it does not stretch into infinity, as all sentient life on earth will ultimately be extinguished, and furthermore we do not normally in practice need to consider very remote consequences, as these in the end approximate rapidly to zero like the furthermost ripples on a pond after a stone has been dropped into it.

But do the remote consequences of an action diminish to zero? Suppose that two people decide whether to have a child or remain childless. Let us suppose that they decide to have the child, and that they have a limitless succession of happy descendants. The remote consequences do not seem to get less. Not at any rate if these people are Adam and Eve. The difference would be between the end of the human race and a limitless accretion of human happiness, generation by generation. The Adam and Eve example shows that the "ripples on the pond" postulate is not needed in every case for a rational utilitarian decision. If we had some reason for thinking that every generation would be more happy than not we would not (in the Adam and Eve sort of case) need to be worried that the remote consequences of our action would be in detail unknown. The necessity for the "ripples in the pond" postulate comes from the fact that usually we do not know whether remote consequences will be good or bad. Therefore we cannot know what to do unless we can assume that remote consequences can be left out of account. This can often be done. Thus if we consider two actual parents, instead of Adam and Eve, then they need not worry about thousands of years hence. Not, at least, if we assume that there will be ecological forces determining the future population of the world. If these parents do not have remote descendants, then other people will presumably have more than they would otherwise. And there is no reason to suppose that my descendants would be more or less happy than yours. We must note, then, that unless we are dealing with "all or nothing" situations (such as the Adam and Eve one, or that of someone in a position to end human life altogether) we need some sort of "ripples in the pond" postulate to make utilitarianism workable in practice. I do not know how to prove such a postulate, though it seems plausible enough. If it is not accepted, not only utilitarianism, but also deontological systems like that of Sir David Ross, who at least admits beneficence as one *prima facie* duty among the others, will be fatally affected.

Sometimes, of course, more needs to be said. For example one course of action may make some people very happy and leave the rest as they are or perhaps slightly less happy. Another course of action may make all men rather more happy than before but no one very happy. Which course of action makes mankind happier on the whole? Again, one course of action may make it highly probable that everyone will be made a little happier whereas another course of action may give us a much smaller probability that everyone will be made very much happier. In the third place, one course of action may make everyone happy in a pig-like way, whereas another course of action may make a few people happy in a highly complex and intellectual way.

It seems therefore that we have to weigh the maximizing of happiness against equitable distribution, to weigh probabilities with happiness, and to weigh the intellectual and other qualities of states of mind with their pleasurableness. Are we not therefore driven back to the necessity of some calculus of happiness? Can we just say: "Envisage two total situations and tell me which you prefer"? If this were possible, of course there would be no need to talk of summing happiness or of a calculus. All we should have to do would be to put total situations in an order of preference.

Let us now consider the question of equity. Suppose that we have the choice of sending four equally worthy and intelligent boys to a medium-grade public school or of leaving three in an adequate but uninspiring grammar school and sending one to Eton. (For sake of the example I am making the almost certainly incorrect assumption that Etonians are happier than other public-school boys and that these other public-school boys are happier than grammar-school boys.) Which course of action makes the most for the happiness of the four boys? Let us suppose that we can neglect complicating factors, such as that the superior Etonian education might lead one boy to develop his talents so much that he will have an extraordinary influence on the well-being of mankind, or that the unequal treatment of the boys might cause jealousy and rift in the family. Let us suppose that the Etonian will be as happy as (we may hope) Etonians usually are, and similarly for the other boys, and let us suppose that remote effects can be neglected. Should we prefer the greater happiness of one boy to the moderate happiness of all four? Clearly one parent may prefer one total situation (one boy at Eton and three at the grammar school) while another may prefer the other total situation (all four at the medium-grade public school). Surely both parents have an equal claim to being sympathetic and benevolent, and yet their difference of opinion here is not founded on an empirical disagreement about facts. I suggest, however, that there are not in fact many cases in which such a disagreement could arise. Probably the parent who wished to send one son to Eton would draw the line at sending one son to Eton plus giving him expensive private tuition during the holidays plus giving his other sons no secondary education at all. It is only within rather small limits that this sort of disagreement about equity can arise. Furthermore the cases in which we can make one person *very* much happier without increasing *general* happiness are rare ones. The law of diminishing returns comes in here. So, in most practical cases, a disagreement about what should be done will be an empirical disagreement about what total situation is likely to be brought about by an action, and will not be a disagreement about which total situation is preferable. For example the inequalitarian parent might get the other to agree with him if he could convince him that there was a much higher probability of an Etonian benefiting the human race, such as by inventing a valuable drug or opening up the mineral riches of Antarctica, than there is of a non-Etonian doing so. (Once more I should like to say that I do not myself take such a possibility very seriously!) I must again stress that since disagreement about what causes produce what effects is in practice so much the most important sort of disagreement, to have intelligent moral discussion with a person we do not in fact need complete agreement with him about ultimate ends: an approximate agreement is sufficient. . . .

According to the act-utilitarian, then, the rational way to decide what to do is to decide to perform that one of those alternative actions open to us (including the null-action, the doing of nothing) which is likely to maximize the probable happiness or well-being of humanity as a whole, or more accurately, of all sentient beings. The utilitarian position is here put forward as a criterion of rational choice. It is true that we may choose to habituate ourselves to behave in accordance with certain rules, such as to keep promises, in the belief that behaving in accordance with these rules is generally optimific, and in the knowledge that we most often just do not have time to work out individual pros and cons. When we act in such an habitual fashion we do not of course deliberate or make a choice. The act-utilitarian will, however, regard these rules as mere rules of thumb, and will use them only as rough guides. Normally he will act in accordance with them when he has no time for considering probable consequences or when the advantages of such a consideration of consequences are likely to be outweighed by the disadvantage of the waste of time involved. He acts in accordance with rules, in short, when there is no time to think, and since he does not think, the actions which he does habitually are not the outcome of moral thinking. When he has to think what to do, then there is a question of deliberation or choice, and it is precisely for such situations that the utilitarian criterion is intended.

It is, moreover, important to realize that there is no inconsistency whatever in an act-utilitarian's schooling himself to act, in normal circumstances, habitually and in accordance with stereotyped rules.

He knows that a man about to save a drowning person has no time to consider various possibilities, such as that the drowning person is a dangerous criminal who will cause death and destruction, or that he is suffering from a painful and incapacitating disease from which death would be a merciful release, or that various timid people, watching from the bank, will suffer a heart attack if they see anyone else in the water. No, he knows that it is almost always right to save a drowning man, and in he goes. Again, he knows that we would go mad if we went in detail into the probable consequences of keeping or not keeping every trivial promise: we will do most good and reserve our mental energies for more important matters if we simply habituate ourselves to keep promises in all normal situations. Moreover he may suspect that on some occasions personal bias may prevent him from reasoning in a correct utilitarian fashion. . . .

Though even the act–utilitarian may on occasion act habitually and in accordance with particular rules, his criterion is, as we have said, *applied* in cases in which he does not act habitually but in which he deliberates and chooses what to do.

STUDY QUESTIONS

1. Those who assess the moral value of an act in terms of its consequences must have ways to judge a consequence as good or bad. Discuss the views of Bentham, Mill, and G. E. Moore on evaluating consequences.

2. What do you think of Mill's famous remark: "Better to be Socrates dissatisfied than a fool satisfied"?

3. What is act utilitarianism? What is rule utilitarianism? Discuss Smart's objections to rule utilitarianism. Why do some utilitarians favor it?

4. What do utilitarians like Bentham and Smart mean by characterizing some pleasures as "fecund"? Why are the pleasures of poetry said to be more fecund than the pleasures of playing pushpin?

5. The utilitarian is sometimes accused of overlooking issues of equity. According to Smart, "The cases in which one can make one person very much happier without increasing the general

happiness are rare ones." Assuming that this is true, how does it bear on the question of equity. *Is* it true?

6. How does Smart deal with the objection that someone made euphorically happy through electronic means is a utilitarian success? Do you find Smart's answer plausible? Do you think his answer is true to the spirit of utilitarianism?

A Critique of Utilitarianism

BERNARD WILLIAMS

Bernard Williams (b. 1929) is Deutsch Professor of Philosophy at the University of California, Berkeley. His books include *Morality, Problems of the Self, Moral Luck,* and *Ethics and the Limits of Philosophy.*

Bernard Williams's critique of consequentialism takes off from Smart's version of act utilitarianism. If the consequences are decisive in determining the right/wrongness of an action, Williams says, then it will often be right to do what is *prima facie* wrong. He presents two cases in which, on utilitarian grounds, one would be forced to act in a way that violated one's intuitive moral feelings. In each case, "if the agent does not do a certain disagreeable thing, someone else will," and with much worse consequences. The utilitarian holds that the agent must then overcome his squeamishness and do the lesser evil. In one

A CRITIQUE OF UTILITARIANISM From "A Critique of Utilitarianism" in *Utilitarianism: For and Against,* edited by J. J. C. Smart and Bernard Williams. Reprinted by permission of Cambridge University Press.

of Williams's examples, a soldier, Pedro, will shoot twenty innocent people unless a tourist, Jim, shoots one of them. If Jim agrees, the remaining nineteen will go free. So far as the utilitarian is concerned, for Jim to refrain from the murder is consequentially as bad as the positive act of killing nineteen more people. This position, Williams argues, shows that utilitarianism has a confused notion of responsibility and a totally inadequate notion of personal integrity. Williams argues that our deepest convictions, projects, and attitudes "do not compute" in the utilitarian calculus.

. . . [L]et us look . . . at two examples to see what utilitarianism might say about them, what we might say about utilitarianism and, most importantly of all, what would be implied by certain ways of thinking about the situations. . . .

(1) George, who has just taken his Ph.D. in chemistry, finds it extremely difficult to get a job. He is not very robust in health, which cuts down the number of jobs he might be able to do satisfactorily. His wife has to go out to work to keep them, which itself causes a great deal of strain, since they have small children and there are severe problems about looking after them. The results of all this, especially on the children, are damaging. An older chemist, who knows about this situation, says that he can get George a decently paid job in a certain laboratory, which pursues research into chemical and biological warfare. George says that he cannot accept this, since he is opposed to chemical and biological warfare. The older man replies that he is not too keen on it himself, come to that, but after all George's refusal is not going to make the job or the laboratory go away; what is more, he happens to know that if George refuses the job, it will certainly go to a contemporary of George's who is not inhibited by any such scruples and is likely if appointed to push along the research with greater zeal than George would. Indeed, it is not merely concern for George and his family, but (to speak frankly and in confidence) some alarm about this other man's excess of zeal, which has led the older man to offer to use his influence to get George the job . . . George's wife, to whom he is deeply attached, has views (the details of which need not concern us) from which it follows that at least

there is nothing particularly wrong with research into CBW. What should he do?

(2) Jim finds himself in the central square of a small South American town. Tied up against the wall are a row of twenty Indians, most terrified, a few defiant, in front of them several armed men in uniform. A heavy man in a sweat-stained khaki shirt turns out to be the captain in charge and, after a good deal of questioning of Jim which establishes that he got there by accident while on a botanical expedition, explains that the Indians are a random group of the inhabitants who, after recent acts of protest against the government, are just about to be killed to remind other possible protestors of the advantages of not protesting. However, since Jim is an honoured visitor from another land, the captain is happy to offer him a guest's privilege of killing one of the Indians himself. If Jim accepts, then as a special mark of the occasion, the other Indians will be let off. Of course, if Jim refuses, then there is no special occasion, and Pedro here will do what he was about to do when Jim arrived, and kill them all. Jim, with some desperate recollection of schoolboy fiction, wonders whether if he got hold of a gun, he could hold the captain, Pedro and the rest of the soldiers to threat, but it is quite clear from the set-up that nothing of that kind is going to work: any attempt at that sort of thing will mean that all the Indians will be killed, and himself. The men against the wall, and the other villagers, understand the situation, and are obviously begging him to accept. What should he do?

To these dilemmas, it seems to me that utilitarianism replies, in the first case, that George should accept the job, and in the second, that Jim should kill the Indian. Not only does utilitarianism give these answers but, if the situations are essentially as described and there are no further special factors, it regards them, it seems to me, as *obviously* the right answers. But many of us would certainly wonder whether, in (1), that could possibly be the right answer at all; and in the case of (2), even one who came to think that perhaps that was the answer, might well wonder whether it was obviously the answer. Nor is it just a question of the rightness or obviousness of these answers. It is also a question of what sort of considerations come into finding the answer. A feature of utilitarianism is that it cuts out a kind of consideration which for some others makes a difference to what they feel about such cases: a consideration involving the idea, as we might first and very simply put it, that each of us is specially responsible for what *he* does, rather than for what other people do. This is an idea closely connected with the value of integrity. It is often suspected that utilitarianism, at least in its direct forms, makes integrity as a value more or less unintelligible. I shall try to show that this suspicion is correct. . . .

. . . I want to consider now two types of effect that are often invoked by utilitarians, and which might be invoked in connexion with these imaginary cases. The attitude or tone involved in invoking these effects may sometimes seem peculiar; but that sort of peculiarity soon becomes familiar in utilitarian discussions, and indeed it can be something of an achievement to retain a sense of it.

First, there is the psychological effect on the agent. Our descriptions of these situations have not so far taken account of how George or Jim will be after they have taken the one course or the other; and it might be said that if they take the course which seemed at first the utilitarian one, the effects on them will be in fact bad enough and extensive enough to cancel out the initial utilitarian advantages of that course. Now there is one version of this effect in which, for a utilitarian, some confusion must be involved, namely that in which the agent feels bad, his subsequent conduct and relations are crippled and so on, *because he thinks that he has done the wrong thing*—for if the balance of outcomes was as it appeared to be *before* invoking this effect, then he has not (from the utilitarian point of view) done the wrong thing. So that version of the effect, for a rational and utilitarian agent, could not possibly make any difference to the assessment of right and wrong. However, perhaps he is not a thoroughly rational agent, and is disposed to have bad feelings, whichever he decided to do. Now such feelings, which are from a strictly utilitarian point of view irrational—nothing, a utilitarian can point out, is advanced by having them—cannot, consistently, have any great weight in a utilitarian calculation. I shall consider in a moment an argument to suggest that they should have no weight at all in it. But short of that, the utilitarian could reasonably say that such feelings should not be encouraged, even if we accept their existence, and that to give them a lot of weight is to encourage them. Or, at the very best, even if they are straightforwardly and without any discount to be put into the calculation, their weight must be small: they are after all (and at best) one man's feelings.

That consideration might seem to have particular force in Jim's case. In George's case, his feelings represent a larger proportion of what is to be weighed, and are more commensurate in character with other items in the calculation. In Jim's case, however, his feelings might seem to be of very little weight compared with other things that are at stake. There is a powerful and recognizable appeal that can be made on this point: as that a refusal by Jim to do what he has been invited to do would be a kind of self-indulgent squeamishness. That is an appeal which can be made by other than utilitarians—indeed, there are some uses of it which cannot be consistently made by utilitarians, as when it essentially involves the idea that there is something dishonourable about such self-indulgence. But in some versions it is a familiar, and it must be said a powerful, weapon of utilitarianism. One must be clear, though, about what it can and cannot accomplish. The most it can do, so far as I can see, is to invite one to consider how seriously, and for what reasons, one feels that what one is invited to do is (in these circumstances) wrong, and in particular, to consider that question from the utilitarian point of view. When the agent is not seeing the situation from a utilitarian point of view, the appeal cannot force him to do so; and if he does come round to seeing it from a utilitarian point of view, there is virtually nothing left for the appeal to do. If he does not see it from a utilitarian point of view, he will not see his resistance to the invitation, and the unpleasant feelings he associates with accepting it, *just* as disagreeable experiences of his; they figure rather as emotional expressions of a thought that to accept would be wrong. He may be asked, as by the appeal, to consider whether he is right, and indeed whether he is fully serious, in thinking that. But the assertion of the appeal, that he is being self-indulgently squeamish, will not itself answer that question, or even help to answer it, since it essentially tells him to regard his feelings just as unpleasant experiences of his, and he cannot, by doing that, answer the question they pose when they are precisely not so regarded, but are regarded as indications of what he thinks is right and wrong. If he does come round fully to the utilitarian point of view then of course he will regard these feelings just as unpleasant experiences of his. And once Jim—at least—has come to see them in that light, there is nothing left for the appeal to do, since *of course* his feelings, so regarded, are of virtually no weight at all in relation to the other things at stake. The "squeamishness" appeal is not an argument which adds in a hitherto neglected consideration. Rather, it is an invitation to consider the situation, and one's own feelings, from a utilitarian point of view.

The reason why the squeamishness appeal can be very unsettling, and one can be unnerved by the suggestion of self-indulgence in going against utilitarian considerations, is not that we are utilitarians who are uncertain what utilitarian value to attach to our moral feelings, but that we are partially at least not utilitarians, and cannot regard our moral feelings merely as objects of utilitarian value. Because our moral relation to the world is partly given by such feelings, and by a sense of what we can or cannot "live with," to come to regard those feelings from a purely utilitarian point of view, that is to say, as happenings outside one's moral self, is to lose a sense of one's moral identity; to lose, in the most literal way, one's integrity. . . .

Integrity

The [two] situations have in common that if the agent does not do a certain disagreeable thing, someone else will, and in Jim's situation at least the result, the state of affairs after the other man has acted, if he does, will be worse than after Jim has acted, if Jim does. The same, on a smaller scale, is true of George's case. I have already suggested that it is inherent in consequentialism that it offers a strong doctrine of negative responsibility: if I know that if I do X, O_1 will eventuate, and if I refrain from doing X, O_2 will, and that O_2 is worse than O_1, then I am responsible for O_2 if I refrain voluntarily from doing X. "You could have prevented it," as will be said, and truly, to Jim, if he refuses, by the relatives of the other Indians. . . . [But] what occurs if Jim refrains from action is not solely twenty Indians dead, but *Pedro's killing twenty Indians*. . . . That may be enough for us to speak, in some sense, of Jim's responsibility for that outcome, if it occurs; but it is certainly not enough, it is worth noticing, for us to speak of Jim's *making* those things happen. For granted this way of their coming about, he could have made them happen only by making Pedro shoot, and there is no acceptable sense in which his refusal makes Pedro shoot. If the captain had said on Jim's refusal, "you leave me with no alternative," he would have been lying, like most who use that phrase. While the deaths, and the killing, may be the outcome of Jim's refusal, it is misleading to think, in such a case, of Jim having an *effect* on the world through the medium (as it happens) of Pedro's acts; for this is to leave Pedro out of the picture in his essential role of one who has intentions and projects, projects for realizing which Jim's refusal would leave an opportunity. Instead of thinking in terms of supposed effects of Jim's projects on Pedro, it is more revealing to think in terms of the effects of Pedro's projects on Jim's decision. . . .

Utilitarianism would do well . . . to acknowledge the evident fact that among the things that make people happy is not only making other people happy, but being taken up or involved in any of a vast range of projects, or—if we waive the evangelical and moralizing associations of the word—commitments. One can be committed to such things as a person, a cause, an institution, a career, one's own genius, or the pursuit of danger.

Now none of these is itself the *pursuit of happiness:* by an exceedingly ancient platitude, it is not at all clear that there could be anything which was just that, or at least anything that had the slightest chance of being successful. Happiness, rather, requires being involved in, or at least content with, something else. It is not impossible for utilitarianism to accept that point: it does not have to be saddled with a naïve and absurd philosophy of mind about the relation between desire and happiness. What it does have to say is that if such commitments are worth while, then pursuing the projects that flow from them, and realizing some of those projects, will make the person for whom they are worth while, happy. It may be that to claim that is still wrong: it may well be that a commitment can make sense to a man (can make sense of his life) without his supposing that it will make him *happy*. But that is not the present point; let us grant to utilitarianism that all worthwhile human projects must conduce, one way or another, to happiness. The point is that even if that is true, it does not follow, nor could it possibly be true, that those projects are themselves projects of pursuing happiness. One has to believe in, or at least want, or quite minimally, be content with, other things, for there to be anywhere that happiness can come from.

Utilitarianism, then, should be willing to agree that its general aim of maximizing happiness does not imply that what everyone is doing is just pursuing happiness. On the contrary, people have to be pursuing other things. What those other things may be, utilitarianism, sticking to its professed empirical stance, should be prepared just to find out. No doubt some possible projects it will want to discourage, on the grounds that their being pursued involves a negative balance of happiness to others: though even there, the unblinking accountant's eye of the strict utilitarian will have something to put in the positive column, the satisfactions of the destructive agent. Beyond that, there will be a vast variety of generally beneficent or at least harmless projects; and some no doubt, will take the form not just of tastes or fancies, but of what I have called "commitments." It may even be that the utilitarian researcher will find that many of those with commitments, who have really identified themselves with objects outside themselves, who are thoroughly involved with other persons, or institutions, or activities or causes, are actually happier than those whose projects and wants are not like that. If so, that is an important piece of utilitarian empirical lore.

When I say "happier" here, I have in mind the sort of consideration which any utilitarian would be committed to accepting: as for instance that such people are less likely to have a break-down or commit suicide. Of course that is not all that is actually involved, but the point in this argument is to use to the maximum degree utilitarian notions, in order to locate a breaking point in utilitarian thought. In appealing to this strictly utilitarian notion, I am being more consistent with utilitarianism than Smart is. In his struggles with the problem of the brain-electrode man, Smart . . . commends the idea that "happy" is a partly evaluative term, in the sense that we call "happiness" those kinds of satisfaction which, as things are, we approve of. But *by what standard* is this surplus element of approval supposed, from a utilitarian point of view, to be allocated? There is no source for it, on a strictly utilitarian view, except further degrees of satisfaction, but there are none of those available, or the problem would not arise. Nor does it help to appeal to the fact that we dislike in prospect things which we like when we get there, for from a utilitarian point of view it would seem that the original dislike was merely irrational or based on an error. Smart's argument at this point seems to be embarrassed by a well-known utilitarian uneasiness, which comes from a feeling that it is not respectable to ignore the "deep," while not having anywhere left in human life to locate it.

On a utilitarian view . . . [t]he determination to an indefinite degree of my decisions by other people's projects is just another aspect of my unlimited responsibility to act for the best in a causal framework formed to a considerable extent by their projects.

The decision so determined is, for utilitarianism, the right decision. But what if it conflicts with some project of mine? This, the utilitarian will say, has already been dealt with: the satisfaction to you of fulfilling your project, and any satisfaction to others of your so doing, have already been through the calculating device and have been found inadequate. Now in the case of many sorts of projects, that is a perfectly reasonable sort of answer. But in the case of projects of the sort I have called "commitments," those with which one is more deeply and extensively involved and identified, this cannot just by itself be an adequate answer, and there may be no adequate answer at all. For, to take the extreme sort of case, how can a man, as a utilitarian agent, come to regard as one satisfaction among others, and a dispensable one, a project or attitude round which he has built his life, just because someone else's projects have so structured the causal scene that that is how the utilitarian sum comes out?

The point here is not, as utilitarians may hasten to say, that if the project or attitude is that central to his life, then to abandon it will be very disagreeable to him and great loss of utility will be involved. . . . On the contrary, once he is prepared to look at it like that, the argument in any serious case is over anyway. The point is that he is identified with his actions as flowing from projects and attitudes which in some cases he takes seriously at the deepest level, as what his life is about (or, in some cases, this section of his life— seriousness is not necessarily the same as persistence). It is absurd to demand of such a man, when the sums come in from the utility network which the projects of others have in part determined, that he should just step aside from his own project and decision and acknowledge the decision which utilitarian calculation requires. It is to alienate him in a real sense from his actions and the source of his action in his own convictions. It is to make him into a channel between the input of everyone's projects, including his own, and an output of optimific decision; but this is to neglect the extent to which *his* actions and *his* decisions have to be seen as the actions and decisions which flow from the projects and attitudes with which he is most closely identified. It is thus, in the most literal sense, an attack on his integrity.

[T]he immediate point of all this is to draw one particular contrast with utilitarianism: that to reach a grounded decision . . . should not be regarded as a matter of just discontinuing one's reactions, impulses and deeply held projects in the face of the pattern of utilities, nor yet merely adding them in—but in the first instance of trying to understand them.

Of course, time and circumstances are unlikely to make a grounded decision, in Jim's case at least, possible. Very often, we just act, as a possibly confused result of the situation in which we are engaged. That, I suspect, is very often an exceedingly good thing.

STUDY QUESTIONS

1. What are Williams's main objections to consequentialism? Do these objections apply more to act utilitarianism than to rule utilitarianism?
2. Williams brings two cases that pose difficulties for the consequentialists. Discuss both cases. Do you think George's refusal to take the job is right? Could it be construed as right on utilitarian grounds?
3. What does Williams mean by "deeply held projects"? Why should they count for more than utility?
4. What difference does Williams see between acting in ways that result in twenty people being killed and acting directly by killing one of them. Evidently the actual killing is worse. But why? Do his arguments persuade you? (What is so wonderful about having clean hands and avoiding direct responsibility for a death when they are gained at the expense of twenty lives?)
5. You are J. J. C. Smart and have just read Williams' essay. Write a short rejoinder to it.

The Ones Who Walk Away from Omelas

URSULA LE GUIN

Ursula Le Guin (b. 1929) is the author of numerous short stories and novels. These include the fantasy fiction novels *The Left Hand of Darkness* (1969) and *The Word for World in Forest* (1976). Among her most recent works is a collection of essays on writing, *The Language of Night: Essays on Fantasy and Science Fiction* (1979).

Ursula Le Guin tells of a highly civilized place called Omelas. Its inhabitants are sophisticated and, by most standards, they are happy. Moreover, they are considerate and decent to one another—with one exception. That exception is a necessary condition for the general welfare. But some citizens cannot reconcile themselves to it. These walk away from Omelas never to return. Le Guin's parable bears on fundamental ethical dilemmas, but most particularly it raises serious questions about the adequacy of utilitarianism as an ethical philosophy.

With a clamor of bells that set the swallows soaring, the Festival of Summer came to the city. Omelas, bright-towered by the sea. The rigging of the boats in harbor sparkled with flags. In the streets between houses with red roofs and painted walls, between old moss-grown gardens and under avenues of trees, past great parks and public buildings, processions moved. Some were decorous: old people in long stiff robes of mauve and grey, grave master workmen,

THE ONES WHO WALK AWAY FROM OMELAS copyright © 1973 by Ursula K. Le Guin; first appeared in *New Dimensions 3*; reprinted by permission of the author and the author's agent, Virginia Kidd.

133

quiet, merry women carrying their babies and chatting as they walked. In other streets the music beat faster, a shimmering of gong and tambourine, and the people went dancing, the procession was a dance. Children dodged in and out, their high calls rising like the swallows' crossing flights over the music and the singing. All the processions wound towards the north side of the city, where on the great water-meadow called the Green Fields boys and girls, naked in the bright air, with mud-stained feet and ankles and long, lithe arms, exercised their restive horses before the race. The horses wore no gear at all but a halter without bit. Their manes were braided with streamers of silver, gold, and green. They flared their nostrils and pranced and boasted to one another; they were vastly excited, the horse being the only animal who has adopted our ceremonies as his own. Far off to the north and west the mountains stood up half encircling Omelas on her bay. The air of morning was so clear that the snow still crowning the Eighteen Peaks burned with white-gold fire across the miles of sunlit air, under the dark blue of the sky. There was just enough wind to make the banners that marked the racecourse snap and flutter now and then. In the silence of the broad green meadows one could hear the music winding through the city streets, farther and nearer and ever approaching, a cheerful faint sweetness of the air that from time to time trembled and gathered together and broke out into the great joyous clanging of the bells.

Joyous! How is one to tell about joy? How describe the citizens of Omelas?

They were not simple folk, you see, though they were happy. But we do not say the words of cheer much any more. All smiles have become archaic. Given a description such as this one tends to make certain assumptions. Given a description such as this one tends to look next for the King, mounted on a splendid stallion and surrounded by his noble knights, or perhaps in a golden litter borne by great-muscled slaves. But there was no king. They did not use swords, or keep slaves. They were not barbarians. I do not know the rules and laws of their society, but I suspect that they were singularly few. As they did without monarchy and slavery, so they also got on without the stock exchange, the advertisement, the secret police, and the bomb. Yet I repeat that these were not simple folk, not dulcet shepherds, noble savages, bland utopians. They were not less complex than us. The trouble is that we have a bad habit, encouraged by pedants and sophisticates, of considering happiness as something rather stupid. Only pain is intellectual, only evil interesting. This is the treason of the artist: a refusal to admit the banality of evil and the terrible boredom of pain. If you can't lick 'em, join 'em. If it hurts, repeat it. But to praise despair is to condemn delight, to embrace violence is to lose hold of everything else. We have almost lost hold; we can no longer describe a happy man, nor make any celebration of joy. How can I tell you about the people of Omelas? They were not naïve and happy children—though their children were, in fact, happy. They were mature, intelligent, passionate adults whose lives were not wretched. O miracle! But I wish I could describe it better. I wish I could convince you. Omelas sounds in my words like a city in a fairy tale, long ago and far away, once upon a time. Perhaps it would be best if you imagined it as your own fancy bids, assuming it will rise to the occasion, for certainly I cannot suit you all. For instance, how about technology? I think that there would be no cars or helicopters in and above the streets; this follows from the fact that the people of Omelas are happy people. Happiness is based on a just discrimination of what is necessary, what is neither necessary nor destructive, and what is destructive. In the middle category, how-ever—that of the unnecessary but undestructive, that of comfort, luxury, exuberance, etc.—they could perfectly well have central heating, subway trains, washing machines, and all kinds of marvel-ous devices not yet invented here, floating light-sources, fuelless power, a cure for the common cold. Or they could have none of that: it doesn't matter. As you like it. I incline to think that people from towns up and down the coast have been coming in to Omelas during the last days before the Festival on very fast little trains and double-decked trams and that the train station of Omelas is actually the handsomest building in town, though plainer than the magnificent Farmers' Market. But even granted trains, I fear that Omelas so far strikes some of you as goody-goody. Smiles, bells, parades, horses, bleh. If so, please add an orgy. If an orgy would help, don't hesitate. Let us not, however, have temples from which issue beautiful nude priests and priestesses already half in ecstasy and ready to copulate with any man or woman, lover or stranger, who desires union with the deep godhead of the blood, although that was my first idea. But really it would be better not to have any temples in Omelas—at least, not manned temples. Religion yes, clergy no. Surely the beautiful nudes can just wander about, offering themselves like divine soufflés to the hunger of the needy and the rapture of the flesh. Let them join the processions. Let tambourines be struck above the copulations, and the glory of desire be proclaimed upon the gongs, and (a not unimportant point) let the offspring of these delightful rituals be beloved and looked after by all. One thing I know there is none of in Omelas is guilt. But what else should there be? I thought at first there were no drugs, but that is puritanical. For those who like it, the faint insistent sweetness of *drooz* may perfume the ways of the city, *drooz*, which first brings a great lightness and brilliance to the mind and limbs, and then after some hours a dreamy languor, and wonderful visions at last of the very arcana and inmost secrets of the Universe, as well as exciting the pleasure of sex beyond all belief; and it is not habit-forming. For more modest tastes I think there ought to be beer. What else, what else belongs in the joyous city? The sense of victory, surely, the celebration of courage. But as we did without clergy, let us do without soldiers. The joy built upon successful slaughter is not the right kind of joy; it will not do; it is fearful and it is trivial. A boundless and generous contentment, a magnanimous triumph felt not against some outer enemy but in communion with the finest and fairest in the souls of all men everywhere and the splendor of the world's summer: this is what swells the hearts of the people of Omelas, and the victory they celebrate is that of life. I really don't think many of them need to take *drooz*.

Most of the processions have reached the Green Fields by now. A marvelous smell of cooking goes forth from the red and blue tents of the provisioners. The faces of small children are amiably sticky; in the benign grey beard of a man a couple of crumbs of rich pastry are entangled. The youths and girls have mounted their horses and are beginning to group around the starting line of the course. An old woman, small, fat, and laughing, is passing out flowers from a basket, and tall young men wear her flowers in their shining hair. A child of nine or ten sits at the edge of the crowd, alone, playing on a wooden flute. People pause to listen, and they smile, but they do not speak to him, for he never ceases playing and never sees them, his dark eyes wholly rapt in the sweet, thin magic of the tune.

He finishes, and slowly lowers his hands holding the wooden flute.

As if that little private silence were the signal, all at once a trumpet sounds from the pavillion near the starting line: imperious, melancholy, piercing. The horses rear on their slender legs, and some of them neigh in answer. Sober-faced, the young riders stroke the horses' necks and soothe them, whispering, "Quiet, quiet, there my beauty, my hope. . . ." They begin to form in rank along the starting line. The crowds along the racecourse are like a field of grass and flowers in the wind. The Festival of Summer has begun.

Do you believe? Do you accept the festival, the city, the joy? No? Then let me describe one more thing.

In a basement under one of the beautiful public buildings of Omelas, or perhaps in the cellar of one of its spacious private homes, there is a room. It has one locked door, and no window. A little light seeps in dustily between cracks in the boards, secondhand from a cobwebbed window somewhere across the cellar. In one corner of the little room a couple of mops, with stiff, clotted, foul-smelling heads, stand near a rusty bucket. The floor is dirt, a little damp to the touch, as cellar dirt usually is. The room is about three paces long and two wide: a mere broom closet or disused tool room. In the room a child is sitting. It could be a boy or a girl. It looks about six, but actually is nearly ten. It is feeble-minded. Perhaps it was born defective, or perhaps it has become imbecile through fear, malnutrition, and neglect. It picks its nose and occasionally fumbles vaguely with its toes or genitals, as it sits hunched in the corner farthest from the bucket and the two mops. It is afraid of the mops. It finds them horrible. It shuts its eyes, but it knows the mops are still standing there; and the door is locked; and nobody will come. The door is always locked; and nobody ever comes, except that sometimes—the child has no understanding of time or interval—sometimes the door rattles terribly and opens, and a person, or several people, are there. One of them may come in and kick the child to make it stand up. The others never come close, but peer in at it with frightened, disgusted eyes. The food bowl and the water jug are hastily filled, the door is locked, the eyes disappear. The people at the door never say anything, but the child, who has not always lived in the tool room, and can remember sunlight and its mother's voice, sometimes speaks. "I will be good," it says. "Please let me out. I will be good!" They never answer. The child used to scream for help at night, and cry a good deal, but now it only makes a kind of whining, "eh-haa, eh-haa," and it speaks less and less often. It is so thin there are no calves to its legs; its belly protrudes; it lives on a half-bowl of corn meal and grease a day. It is naked. Its buttocks and thighs are a mass of festered sores, as it sits in its own excrement continually.

They all know it is there, all the people of Omelas. Some of them have come to see it, others are content merely to know it is there. They all know that it has to be there. Some of them understand why, and some do not, but they all understand that their happiness, the beauty of their city, the tenderness of their friendships, the health of their children, the wisdom of their scholars, the skill of their makers, even the abundance of their harvest and the kindly weathers of their skies, depend wholly on this child's abominable misery.

This is usually explained when they are between eight and twelve, whenever they seem capable of understanding; and most of those who come to see the child are young people, though often enough an adult comes, or comes back, to see the child. No matter how well the matter has been explained to them, these young spectators are always shocked and sickened at the sight. They feel disgust, which they had thought themselves superior to. They feel anger, outrage, impotence, despite all the explanations. They would like to do something for the child. But there is nothing they can do. If the child were brought up into the sunlight out of that vile place, if it were cleaned and fed and comforted, that would be a good thing, indeed; but if it were done, in that day and hour all the prosperity and beauty and delight of Omelas would wither and be destroyed. Those are the terms. To exchange all the goodness and grace of every life in Omelas for that single, small improvement: to throw away the happiness of thousands for the chance of the happiness of one: that would be to let guilt within the walls indeed.

The terms are strict and absolute; there may not even be a kind word spoken to the child.

Often the young people go home in tears, or in a tearless rage, when they have seen the child and faced this terrible paradox. They may brood over it for weeks or years. But as time goes on they begin to realize that even if the child could be released, it would not get much good of its freedom: a little vague pleasure of warmth and food, no doubt, but little more. It is too degraded and imbecile to know any real joy. It has been afraid too long ever to be free of fear. Its habits are too uncouth for it to respond to humane treatment. Indeed, after so long it would probably be wretched without walls about it to protect it, and darkness for its eyes, and its own excrement to sit in. Their tears at the bitter injustice dry when they begin to perceive the terrible justice of reality and to accept it. Yet it is their tears and anger, the trying of their generosity and the acceptance of their helplessness, which are perhaps the true source of the splendor of their lives. Theirs is no vapid, irresponsible happiness. They know that they, like the child, are not free. They know compassion. It is the existence of the child, and their knowledge of its existence, that makes possible the nobility of their architecture, the poignancy of their music, the profundity of their science. It is because of the child that they are so gentle with children. They know that if the wretched one were not there snivelling in the dark, the other one, the flute-player, could make no joyful music as the young riders line up in their beauty for the race in the sunlight of the first morning of summer.

Now do you believe in them? Are they not more credible? But there is one more thing to tell, and this is quite incredible.

At times one of the adolescent girls or boys who go to see the child does not go home to weep or rage, does not, in fact, go home at all. Sometimes also a man or woman much older falls silent for a day or two, and then leaves home. These people go out into the street, and walk down the street alone. They keep walking, and walk straight out of the city of Omelas, through the beautiful gates. They keep walking across the farmlands of Omelas. Each one goes alone, youth or girl, man or woman. Night falls; the traveler must pass down village streets, between the houses with yellow-lit windows, and on out into the darkness of the fields. Each alone, they go west or north, toward the mountains. They go on. They leave Omelas, they walk ahead into the darkness, and they do not come back. The place they go towards is a place even less imaginable to most of us than the city of happiness. I cannot describe it at all. It is possible that it does not exist. But they seem to know where they are going, the ones who walk away from Omelas.

[1976]

STUDY QUESTIONS

1. Ursula Le Guin makes a point of saying that the terms of Ome-las' happiness is the misery of one child. Some social theorists believe that the fortunate existence of those who live in the more

developed nations is achieved at the cost of much misery in undeveloped nations. If so, Le Guin's Omelas is a parable to our own situation. To what extent is the analogy apt, if at all?

2. Le Guin tells us that the citizens of Omelas are fully aware of the suffering of the child, but she makes a point of saying that those who stay in Omelas do not feel guilty. Is it possible to constantly feel guilty about the misery others? Explain and give examples.

3. If you were a citizen of Omelas would you stay or walk? Explain and justify your decision.

4. You are J. J. C. Smart or R. M. Hare and have just read Le Guin's story. How would you react to it? How do you defend against the implied objection to utilitarian ethics?

Loyalty and Evil Desires

R. M. HARE

R. M. Hare (b. 1919) is White's Professor of Moral Philosophy at Corpus Christi College, Oxford University. His books include *The Language of Morals* (1952), *Freedom and Reason* (1963), *Moral Theories* (1972), and *Essays in Ethical Theory* (1989).

Hare distinguishes between two levels of moral thinking. In our everyday lives we operate at the "intuitive level": we instinctively respond to situations

LOYALTY AND EVIL DESIRES, from *Moral Thinking* by R. M. Hare (1981) reprinted by permission of Oxford University Press.

without carefully thinking them through. In more reflective moments—the "critical level"—we carefully determine which intuitions and loyalties are worth preserving and fostering in people. Some intuitions—that parents should prefer the interests of their children to those of strangers, for example—are worth inculcating because of their long-run utility. Others, such as patriotism, appear questionable. Deploying this distinction, Hare defends utilitarianism from critics who claim it justifies evil acts, such as punishing the innocent or killing derelicts in order to use their hearts and kidneys for transplant surgery. Hare argues that such cases, which seem to shake our intuitive commitments, are almost always trumped up and artificial. In the very rare case in which a utilitarian judgment would actually call for killing someone, that act *would* be justified but it would then *not* be counterintuitive. Hare does not give an example of such a case, but presumably he would find it intuitively right to kill someone if it were sure that that was the only way to save many people from a horrible death. Intuitions are themselves subject to utilitarian calculus.

1. Suppose then that you are in a disputation with a utilitarian. Your object should be to enlist the sympathies of your audience on your side by showing that the utilitarian is committed to views which nearly everybody finds counterintuitive. What you have to do, therefore, is to find some moral opinion which nearly everybody will agree with, and bring utilitarianism into conflict with it. It is not necessary to choose for this purpose an opinion that can be defended by argument; any widely held prejudice will do. I have heard this kind of objection based on premises like 'Surely any theory is absurd which makes cruelty to animals as wicked as the same degree of cruelty to humans;' and no doubt in earlier centuries 'blacks' and 'whites' would have done as well. But obviously it is better if the opinion is a defensible one; the objection will then seem even more plausible.

Having selected your favoured received opinion, you can then proceed to bring utilitarianism into conflict with it in the following way. You find some example, rather simply described, in which, on an obvious interpretation of utilitarianism (and nearly all the versions of it can be made susceptible to this treatment, except for some versions of rule-utilitarianism which are highly implausible on other grounds) the utilitarian is committed to prescribing an act which almost everybody will agree is wrong. Give your case as much verisimilitude as you can. Professional opponents of utilitarianism are not always as careful as they should be about this. Sometimes they use extremely jejune examples, thinking the game to be a push-over, so that they need not take too much trouble with them. But it is better if the case is something which your audience can be got to believe really could happen. Thus you will seem to have established a knock-down counterinstance to the utilitarian theory; it will have been shown to require us to say some act is right when we all know it to be wrong.

2. Now suppose by contrast that you are on the opposite side in the disputation. . . .

. . . suppose that your opponent's case is the following: there are in a hospital two patients, one needing for survival a new heart and the other new kidneys; a down-and-out who is known to nobody and who happens to have the same tissue-type as both the patients strays in out of the cold. Ought they not to kill him, give his heart and kidneys to the patients, and thus save two lives at the expense of one? The utilitarian is supposed to have to say that they ought; the audience is supposed to say that they ought not, because it would be murder. Let us suppose that your opponent manages to get the audience to treat murder as a descriptive, not a secondarily evaluative, word . . . , and thus to call the statement that it would be murder a purely factual one, which can be established prior to any judgment that it would be wrong. I have simplified the case a little from the way it has sometimes been presented in the literature . . . , because the complications will not affect the moves we shall be making.

On this example you have to mount a two-pronged attack. If we are to do intuitive thinking, the matter is fairly simple. It *is* murder, and *would* therefore be wrong. A utilitarian does not have to dissent from this verdict at the intuitive level. If he has been well brought up (and in particular if he has been brought up by a sound critical utilitarian thinker) he will have that intuition, and it is a very good thing, from the utilitarian point of view, that he will have it. For just think what would be the consequences of a moral education which contained no prohibition on murder!

Your opponent will now object that although on the utilitarian view it is a good thing for people to have these intuitions or feelings, it also follows from that view that they ought to overcome and act contrary to them in cases like this, in which, *ex hypothesi*, it is for the best to do so. Let us ask, then, whether the doctors in the hospital ought to do this if they are utilitarians. It will turn upon their estimate of the *probability* of hitting off the act which is for the best by so doing. The crucial words are, of course, '*ex hypothesi;*' for your opponent has constructed his example with the express purpose of making the murder the act which will have the best consequences. You must not allow him simply to *assume* that this is so; he has to convince the audience, not just that it really could be so in a real-life situation, but that it could be known to be so by the doctors with a high degree of probability. For utilitarianism, as a method of choosing the most rational action (the best bet for a utilitarian) in a moral dilemma of this sort, requires them to maximize the *expectation* of utility (i.e. preference-satisfaction); and since, if they get it wrong, the consequences will be pretty catastrophic, the doctors have to be very sure that they are not getting it wrong. There is perhaps no need to go into any technicalities of games-theory to establish this point, though a full account would need to contain a method of weighing combinations of probabilities with utilities against one another, by asking which combination one would prefer, after exposure to logic and the facts.

It is fairly obvious that this high degree of probability will not be forthcoming in many actual situations, if any at all. Have the doctors checked on the down-and-out's connexions or lack of them? (How? By consulting the police records, perhaps! But a colleague of my psychiatrist sister once wrote in his notes, about a dishevelled individual brought in off the streets very late at night by the police, 'Has delusion that he is a high-ranking civil servant,' and it turned out that he was in fact a *very* high-ranking civil servant.) Have they absolute confidence in the discretion and support of all the nurses, porters, mortuarists, etc., who will know what has happened? Add to this the extreme unlikelihood of there being no other way of saving these patients, if they can be saved at all, and it will be evident that your opponent is not going to get much help out of this example, once it is insisted that it has to be fleshed out and given verisimilitude.

But perhaps that was not his intention. Perhaps, that is to say, he all along intended the example to be a dummy. Is he not allowed, after a brief introduction of the example to give its general shape, to skip the details and simply *posit* that it is a case where murder would be for the best? The audience, which is probably prejudiced against utilitarians anyway, will have no difficulty in imagining that the details could be filled in in a way that would suit his case and damage yours. But you must not let him get away with this. If we are talking about intuitive thinking in a real-life sort of situation, the example needs to be a real-life sort of example.

. . .

Your opponent may say 'Are there not some cases occurring in real life, albeit rarely, in which murder is justified on utilitarian grounds?' To which you should reply that he has not produced any, but that if he really did find one, we should have to do some critical thinking on it because it would be clearly so unusual as to be beyond the range of our intuitions. If we then found that murder really was justified in that case, we still should not have shown that the rational moral agent would commit the murder; for he would be unlikely to have sufficient evidential grounds for saying that it was the right act. But, giving your opponent everything that he asks for, if he did actually have sufficient evidence (a very unlikely contingency), murder would *in that case* be justified; though even then the agent in question, if he had been well brought up, might not do it, because it would go so much against all his moral feelings, which in a good man are powerful. So, owing to being a good man, he might fail to do the right act. If he did bring himself to do it, it would haunt him for the rest of his life. But until your opponent produces actual cases, you should not let yourself be troubled overmuch with fictional ones. If the actual cases are produced, you will probably find that the critical discussion of them will leave you and the audience at one, provided that the discussion is serious.

3. We are now in a position to apply the same technique to some more genuine problems. Let us take first the objection commonly made to utilitarianism that it does not allow us to give any weight to the duties usually thought to exist towards particular persons, or to ties of affection and loyalty which bind us to them but not to mankind in general. . . .For example, it is usually held that we have special duties to our spouses and children, and ought to have greater affection and loyalty to them than to total strangers, and so seek their good more earnestly. Similar things are said about the relation between a doctor and his patient, or a teacher and his pupil. And similar things *used* to be universally, and are still quite widely, accepted about that between a citizen and his country. I have heard the same argued about the loyalty of a worker to his union.

These last two instances might make us pause before proceeding on the assumption that all commonly upheld loyalties can be used as a stick to beat utilitarians with. They show how palpable, and how dubious, is the appeal to intuition when people say that utilitarianism treats everybody's preferences as of equal weight (e.g. those of my children and other people's children), and therefore has to be rejected as giving no weight to these feelings of special affection which we all think it a good thing to encourage. We have first to be sure that, in a particular example, it *is* a good thing to encourage these feelings. Even family loyalties provide examples of extremely various intuitions. In some countries it is considered wrong if someone who has obtained a position of power does not use it to advance the interests of the members of his family; in others this is called nepotism and thought corrupt. And even in Britain there is dispute about whether
• it is right for a well endowed father to try to get the best possible education for his children by sending them to expensive schools which others cannot afford.

This should warn us that even where intuitions are all in agreement, they should not be taken for granted; it needs to be established by critical thought which of them ought, in our present circumstances, to be fostered. Anybody who asks himself whether, and in what sense, he ought to bring up his children to be patriotic will see the force of this question. So let us proceed as before and ask our anti-utilitarian objector what level of thinking he is talking about, intuitive or critical. In order to make it easy for him, let us allow him to choose an example in which nearly everybody will agree that the loyalty in question is a good thing. A mother, say, has a new-born child and her maternal feelings make her provide for this child, but they do not, or not to anything like the same degree, impel her to provide for other people's children. Ought a utilitarian to condemn this partiality?

At the intuitive level we all think that the mother is to be praised, in all normal circumstances (barring a few extreme radical advocates of communes, and Plato). Given our two-level structure, there is nothing in this that a utilitarian need object to. *If* the intuition is one that ought to be inculcated (and this cannot be determined without critical thinking), the most likely way of doing the right thing in normal circumstances will be to follow the intuition. If this were not

so, then the intuition would not be the one which ought to be inculcated. If we ascend to the critical level and ask why it ought to be,
the answer is fairly obvious. If mothers had the propensity to care
equally for all the children in the world, it is unlikely that children
would be as well provided for even as they are. The dilution of the
responsibility would weaken it out of existence. Our traditional upbringing has taken account of this. And evidently Evolution (if we
may personify her) has had the same idea; there are, we are told, a
great many of these particular loyalties and affections which are genetically transmitted, and have no doubt favoured the survival of the
genes which transmit them. . . .

4. The general lines of the utilitarian answer to this objection
should by now be clear. *In so far* as the intuitions are desirable ones,
they can be defended on utilitarian grounds by critical thinking, as
having a high acceptance-utility; if they can be so defended, the best
bet, even for an act-utilitarian, will be to cultivate them and follow
them in all normal cases; if he cultivates them seriously, or has had
them cultivated for him by those who brought him up, all the associated moral feelings will be present, but will provide no argument
whatever against utilitarianism. Unlike intuitionism, it is actually
able to *justify* the intuitions, where they can be justified.

Faced with this argument the anti-utilitarian will produce examples in which we would all have the intuitions, but in which, he asks
us to suppose, the utilitarian would have to prescribe that we acted
contrary to them. This would be because in the particular cases sufficient information is assumed to be available to show that the intuitively right act would not be for the best. To take a pasteboard
example with which I was once confronted by Professor Bernard
Williams on television: You are in an air crash and the aircraft catches
fire, but you have managed to get out; in the burning plane are,
among others, your son and a distinguished surgeon who could, if
rescued, save many injured passengers' lives, to say nothing of those
whose lives he would save in his subsequent career. You have time to
rescue only one person.

It is hard to make Williams' example realistic. How do you know
he is so distinguished a surgeon—perhaps he was only shooting a
line when you struck up an acquaintance in the departure lounge?
Has he got his tools with him, and can he do any more for the injured
people than the first aid which the crew are trained to give (which

probably prescribes keeping them warm and immobile and giving some common drugs which, we hope, they managed to extract from the aircraft)? How promising is your son's future (he can probably look forward to a greater span of it than the surgeon)? However, setting aside all these minor points, we find that you have a very strong feeling that you ought to rescue your son and let the surgeon burn. But what does this show?

It would take a very hardened intuitionist to think that it shows that to rescue your son is your undoubted duty. You almost certainly will rescue your son. But that is because you have (rightly from the critical utilitarian point of view) been brought up to attach dominant importance to these family loyalties. Of course no upbringing takes into account such rare cases as this (they are not what those who influenced you were preparing you for, nor would evolution be affected by them). To be in an air crash of any sort is, fortunately, a statistically very rare experience; to be in one in which one has the opportunity to rescue anybody is rarer still; to be in one in which one can rescue precisely one person and no more is hardly to be expected. So you come to this unhappy experience entirely unprepared for it. Your intuitions were simply not designed to cope with it. However, you do have the strong moral feelings and will probably act on them in the split second, which is all you have in which to decide. And who is to blame you? Probably in a situation of complete uncertainty and panic it is the rational thing to do. The fraudulence of the example consists in suggesting that you can at one and the same time be in this emergency situation, and do the leisured critical thinking which would be necessary in order to justify you in going against your intuitions.

Undoubtedly critics of utilitarianism will go on trying to produce examples which are both fleshed out and reasonably likely to occur, and also support their argument. I am prepared to bet, however, that the nearer they get to realism and specificity, and the further from playing trains—a sport which has had such a fascination for them— the more likely the audience is, on reflection, to accept the utilitarian solution. I am thinking of their examples in which trolleys hurtling down the line out of control have to be shunted into various alternative groups of unfortunate people. I have myself, when helping to build a railway, seen trolleys run out of control, and therefore find the unrealism of the examples very obvious. The point is that one has not time to think what to do, and so relies on one's immediate intuitive reactions; but these give no guide to what critical thinking would prescribe if there were time for it. But, personal experience aside, I have done quite a lot of work on serious practical problems in medicine, war, politics, urban planning and the like, and have never come across any actual example in which this kind of anti-utilitarian argument was in the least convincing.

STUDY QUESTIONS

1. Explain R. M. Hare's distinction between "critical" and "intuitive" moral thinking.
2. You are R. M. Hare and you have just read Bernard Williams's argument against utilitarianism. Write a short rejoinder to it.
3. Hare is a utilitarian, but he does not believe that a morally good person should always act like a utilitarian. Explain.

Good Will, Duty, and the Categorical Imperative

IMMANUEL KANT

TRANSLATED BY T. K. ABBOTT

Immanuel Kant (1724–1804) is considered to be one of the greatest philosophers of all time. He lived in Königsberg, in East Prussia, and was a professor at the University there. Kant made significant and highly original contributions to esthetics, jurisprudence, and the philosophy of religion as well as to ethics and epistemology. His best known works are the *Critique of Pure Reason* (1781) and the *Foundations of the Metaphysics of Morals* (1785).

Human beings have desires and appetites. They are also rational, capable of knowing what is right, and capable of willing to do it. They can therefore exercise their wills in the rational control of desire for the purpose of right action. This is what persons of moral worth do. According to Kant, to possess moral worth is more important than to possess intelligence, humor, strength, or any other talent of the mind or body. These talents are valuable but moral worth has *absolute* value, commanding not mere admiration but reverence and respect. Human beings who do right merely because it pleases them are not yet intrinsically moral. For had it pleased them they would have done wrong. To act morally is to act from no other

GOOD WILL, DUTY, AND THE CATEGORICAL IMPERATIVE From *Fundamental Principles of the Metaphysics of Morals,* by Immanuel Kant. Translated by T. K. Abbott (1898).

motive than the motive of doing what is right. This kind of motive has nothing to do with anything as subjective as pleasure. To do right out of principle is to recognize an objective right that imposes an obligation on any rational being. Moral persons act in such a way that they could will that the principles of their actions should be universal laws for everyone else as well. This is one test of a moral act: Is it the kind of act that everyone should perform? Kant illustrates how this test can be applied to determine whether a given principle is moral and objective or merely subjective. For example, I may wish to break a promise, but that cannot be moral since I cannot will that promise-breaking be a universal practice.

Universal principles impose *categorical* imperatives. An imperative is a demand that I act in a certain fashion. For example, if I want to buy a house, it is imperative that I learn something about houses. But "Learn about houses!" is a *hypothetical* imperative since it is *conditional* on my wanting to buy a house. A *categorical* imperative is unconditional. An example is "Keep your promises." Thus an imperative is not preceded by any condition such as "if you want a good reputation." Hypothetical imperatives are "prudential": "If you want security, buy theft insurance." Categorical imperatives are moral: "Do not lie!" Kant argues that the categorical imperative presupposes the absolute worth of all rational beings as ends in themselves. Thus another formulation of the categorical imperative is, "So act as to treat humanity . . . as an end withal, never as a means only." Kant calls the domain of beings that are to be treated in this way the "kingdom of ends."

Nothing can possibly be conceived in the world, or even out of it, which can be called good, without qualification, except a Good Will. Intelligence, wit, judgment, and the other *talents* of the mind, however they may be named, or courage, resolution, perseverance, as qualities of temperament, are undoubtedly good and desirable in many respects; but these gifts of nature may also become extremely bad and mischievous if the will which is to make use of them, and which, therefore, constitutes what is called *character,* is not good. It is the same with the *gifts of fortune.* Power, riches, honour, even health, and the general well-being and contentment with one's condition which is called *happiness,* inspire pride, and often presumption, if there is not a good will to correct the influence of these on the mind, and with this also to rectify the whole principle of acting, and adapt it to its end. The sight of a being who is not adorned with a single feature of a pure and good will, enjoying unbroken prosperity, can never give pleasure to an impartial rational spectator. Thus a good will appears to constitute the indispensable condition even of being worthy of happiness.

There are even some qualities which are of service to this good will itself, and may facilitate its action, yet which have no intrinsic unconditional value, but always presuppose a good will, and this qualifies the esteem that we justly have for them, and does not permit us to regard them as absolutely good. Moderation in the affections and passions, self-control, and calm deliberation are not only good in many respects, but even seem to constitute part of the intrinsic worth of the person; but they are far from deserving to be called good without qualification, although they have been so unconditionally praised by the ancients. For without the principles of a good will, they may become extremely bad; and the coolness of a villain not only makes him far more dangerous, but also directly makes him more abominable in our eyes than he would have been without it.

A good will is good not because of what it performs or effects, not by its aptness for the attainment of some proposed end, but simply by virtue of the volition, that is, it is good in itself, and considered by itself is to be esteemed much higher than all that can be brought about by it in favour of any inclination, nay, even of the sum-total of all inclinations. Even if it should happen that, owing to special disfavour of fortune, or the niggardly provision of a step-motherly nature, this will should wholly lack power to accomplish its purpose, if with its greatest efforts it should yet achieve nothing, and there should remain only the good will (not, to be sure, a mere wish, but the summoning of all means in our power), then, like a jewel, it would still shine by its own light, as a thing which has its whole value in itself. Its usefulness or fruitlessness can neither add to nor take away anything from this value.

Thus the moral worth of an action does not lie in the effect expected from it, nor in any principle of action which requires to borrow its motive from this expected effect. For all these effects—agreeableness of one's condition, and even the promotion of the happiness of others—could have been also brought about by other causes, so that for this there would have been no need of the will of a rational being; whereas it is in this alone that the supreme and unconditional good can be found. The pre-eminent good which we call moral can therefore consist in nothing else than *the conception of law* in itself, *which certainly is only possible in a rational being,* in so far as this conception, and not the expected effect, determines the will. This is a good which is already present in the person who acts accordingly, and we have not to wait for it to appear first in the result.

But what sort of law can that be, the conception of which must determine the will, even without paying any regard to the effect expected from it, in order that this will may be called good absolutely and without qualification? As I have deprived the will of every impulse which could arise to it from obedience to any law, there remains nothing but the universal conformity of its actions to law in general, which alone is to serve the will as a principle, *i.e.* I am never to act otherwise than *so that I could also will that my maxim should become a universal law.* Here, now, it is the simple conformity to law in general, without assuming any particular law applicable to certain actions, that serves the will as its principle, and must so serve it, if duty is not to be a vain delusion and a chimerical notion. The common reason of men in its practical judgments perfectly coincides with this and always has in view the principle here suggested. Let the question be, for example: May I when in distress make a promise with the intention not to keep it? I readily distinguish here between the two significations which the question may have: Whether it is prudent, or whether it is right, to make a false promise? The former may undoubtedly often be the case. I see clearly indeed that it is not enough to extricate myself from a present difficulty by means of this subterfuge, but it must be well considered whether there may not hereafter spring from this lie much greater inconvenience than that from which I now free myself, and as, with all my supposed *cunning,* the consequences cannot be so easily foreseen but that credit once lost may be much more injurious to me than any mischief which I seek to avoid at present, it should be considered whether it would not be more *prudent* to act herein according to a universal maxim, and to make it a habit to promise nothing except with the intention of keeping it. But it is soon clear to me that such a maxim will still only be based on the fear of consequences. Now it is a wholly different thing to be truthful from duty, and to be so from apprehension of injurious consequences. In the first case, the very notion of the action already implies a law for me; in the second case, I must first look about elsewhere to see what results may be combined with it which would affect myself. For to deviate from the principle of duty is beyond all doubt wicked; but to be unfaithful to my maxim of prudence may often be very advantageous to me, although to abide by it is certainly safer. The shortest way, however, and an unerring one, to discover the answer to this question whether a lying promise is consistent with duty, is to ask myself, Should I be content that my maxim (to extricate myself from difficulty by a false promise) should hold good as a universal law, for myself as well as for others? And should I be able to say to myself, "Everyone may make a deceitful promise when he finds himself in a difficulty from which he cannot otherwise extricate himself"? Then I presently become aware that while I can will the lie, I can by no means will that lying should be a universal law. For with such a law there would be no promises at all, since it would be in vain to allege my intention in regard to my future actions to those who would not believe this allegation, or if they over-hastily did so, would pay me back in my own coin. Hence my maxim, as soon as it should be made a universal law, would necessarily destroy itself.

I do not, therefore, need any far-reaching penetration to discern what I have to do in order that my will be morally good. Inexperienced in the course of the world, incapable of being prepared for all its contingencies, I only ask myself: Canst thou also will that thy maxim should be a universal law? If not, then it must be rejected, and that not because of a disadvantage accruing from it to myself or even to others, but because it cannot enter as a principle into a possible universal legislation, and reason extorts from me immediate respect for such legislation. I do not indeed as yet *discern* on what this respect is based (this the philosopher may inquire), but at least I understand this, that it is an estimation of the worth which far outweighs all worth of what is recommended by inclination, and that the necessity of acting from *pure* respect for the practical law is what constitutes duty, to which every other motive must give place, because it is the condition of a will being good *in itself,* and the worth of such a will is above everything. . . .

. . . Everything in nature works according to laws. Rational beings alone have the faculty of acting according *to the conception* of laws, that is according to principles, *i.e.* have a *will.* Since the deduction of actions from principles requires *reason,* the will is nothing but practical reason. If reason infallibly determines the will, then the actions of such a being which are recognized as objectively necessary are subjectively necessary also, *i.e.* the will is a faculty to choose *that only* which reason independent on inclination recognizes as practically necessary, *i.e.* as good. But if reason of itself does not sufficiently determine the will, if the latter is subject also to subjective conditions (particular impulses) which do not always coincide with the objective conditions; in a word, if the will does not *in itself* completely accord with reason (which is actually the case with men), then the actions which objectively are recognized as necessary are subjectively contingent, and the determination of such a will according to objective laws is *obligation,* that is to say, the relation of the objective laws to a will that is not thoroughly good is conceived as the determination of the will of a rational being by principles of reason, but which the will from its nature does not of necessity follow.

The conception of an objective principle, in so far as it is obligatory for a will, is called a command (of reason), and the formula of the command is called an Imperative. . . .

Now all *imperatives* command either *hypothetically* or *categorically.* The former represent the practical necessity of a possible action as means to something else that is willed (or at least which one might possibly will). The categorical imperative would be that which represented an action as necessary of itself without reference to another end, *i.e.* as objectively necessary.

Since every practical law represents a possible action as good, and on this account, for a subject who is practically determinable by reason, necessary, all imperatives are formulae determining an action which is necessary according to the principle of a will good in some respects. If now the action is good only as a means *to something else,* then the imperative is *hypothetical;* if it is conceived as good *in itself* and consequently as being necessarily the principle of a will which of itself conforms to reason, then it is *categorical.* . . .

When I conceive a hypothetical imperative, in general I do not know beforehand what it will contain until I am given the condition. But when I conceive a categorical imperative, I know at once what it contains. For as the imperative contains besides the law only the necessity that the maxims shall conform to this law, while the law contains no conditions restricting it, there remains nothing but the general statement that the maxim of the action should conform to a universal law, and it is this conformity alone that the imperative properly represents as necessary.

There is . . . but one categorical imperative, namely, this: *Act only on that maxim whereby thou canst at the same time will that it should become a universal law.*

Now if all imperatives of duty can be deduced from this one imperative as from their principle, then, although it should remain undecided whether what is called duty is not merely a vain notion, yet at least we shall be able to show what we understand by it and what this notion means.

Since the universality of the law according to which effects are produced constitutes what is properly called *nature* in the most general sense (as to form), that is the existence of things so far as it is determined by general laws, the imperative of duty may be expressed thus: *Act as if the maxim of thy action were to become by thy will a universal law of nature.*

We will now enumerate a few duties, adopting the usual division of them into duties to ourselves and to others, and into perfect and imperfect duties.

1. A man reduced to despair by a series of misfortunes feels wearied of life, but is still so far in possession of his reason that he can ask himself whether it would not be contrary to his duty to himself to take his own life. Now he inquires whether the maxim of his action could become a universal law of nature. His maxim is: From self-love I adopt it as a principle to shorten my life when its longer duration is likely to bring more evil than satisfaction. It is asked then simply whether this principle founded on self-love can become a universal law of nature. Now we see at once that a system of nature of which it should be a law to destroy life by means of the very feeling whose special nature it is to impel to the improvement of life would contradict itself, and therefore could not exist as a system of nature; hence that maxim cannot possibly exist as a universal law of

nature, and consequently would be wholly inconsistent with the supreme principle of all duty.

2. Another finds himself forced by necessity to borrow money. He knows that he will not be able to repay it, but sees also that nothing will be lent to him, unless he promises stoutly to repay it in a definite time. He desires to make this promise, but he has still so much conscience as to ask himself: Is it not unlawful and inconsistent with duty to get out of a difficulty in this way? Suppose, however, that he resolves to do so, then the maxim of his action would be expressed thus: When I think myself in want of money, I will borrow money and promise to repay it, although I know that I never can do so. Now this principle of self-love or of one's own advantage may perhaps be consistent with my whole future welfare; but the question now is: Is it right? I change then the suggestion of self-love into a universal law, and state the question thus: How would it be if my maxim were a universal law? Then I see at once that it could never hold as a universal law of nature, but would necessarily contradict itself. For supposing it to be a universal law that everyone when he thinks himself in a difficulty should be able to promise whatever he pleases, with the purpose of not keeping his promise, the promise itself would become impossible, as well as the end that one might have in view in it, since no one would consider that anything was promised to him, but would ridicule all such statements as vain pretences.

3. A third finds in himself a talent which with the help of some culture might make him a useful man in many respects. But he finds himself in comfortable circumstances, and prefers to indulge in pleasure rather than to take pains in enlarging and improving his happy natural capacities. He asks, however, whether his maxim of neglect of his natural gifts, besides agreeing with his inclination to indulgence, agrees also with what is called duty. He sees then that a system of nature could indeed subsist with such a universal law although men (like the South Sea islanders) should let their talents rest, and resolve to devote their lives merely to idleness, amusement, and propagation of their species—in a word, to enjoyment; but he cannot possibly *will* that this should be a universal law of nature, or be implanted in us as such by a natural instinct. For, as a rational being, he necessarily wills that his faculties be developed, since they serve him, and have been given him, for all sorts of possible purposes.

4. A fourth, who is in prosperity, while he sees that others have to contend with great wretchedness and that he could help them, thinks: What concern is it of mine? Let everyone be as happy as Heaven pleases, or as he can make himself; I will take nothing from him nor even envy him, only I do not wish to contribute anything to his welfare or to his assistance in distress! Now no doubt if such a mode of thinking were a universal law, the human race might very well subsist, and doubtless even better than in a state in which everyone talks of sympathy and good-will, or even takes care occasionally to put it into practice, but, on the other side, also cheats when he can, betrays the rights of men, or otherwise violates them. But although it is possible that a universal law of nature might exist in accordance with that maxim, it is impossible to *will* that such a principle should have the universal validity of a law of nature. For a will which resolved this would contradict itself, inasmuch as many cases might occur in which one would have need of the love and sympathy of others, and in which, by such a law of nature, sprung from his own will, he would deprive himself of all hope of the aid he desires. . . .

We have thus established at least this much, that if duty is a conception which is to have any import and real legislative authority for our actions, it can only be expressed in categorical, and not at all in hypothetical imperatives. We have also, which is of great importance, exhibited clearly and definitely for every practical application the content of the categorical imperative, which must contain the principle of all duty if there is such a thing at all. We have not yet, however, advanced so far as to prove *à priori* that there actually is such an imperative, that there is a practical law which commands absolutely of itself, and without any other impulse, and that the following of this law is duty. . . .

Now I say: man and generally any rational being *exists* as an end in himself, *not merely as a means* to be arbitrarily used by this or that will, but in all his actions, whether they concern himself or other rational beings, must be always regarded at the same time as an end. All objects of the inclinations have only a conditional worth; for if the inclinations and the wants founded on them did not exist, then their object would be without value. But the inclinations themselves being sources of want are so far from having an absolute worth for which they should be desired, that, on the contrary, it must be the universal wish of every rational being to be wholly free from them.

Thus the worth of any object which is *to be acquired* by our action is always conditional. Beings whose existence depends not on our will but on nature's, have nevertheless, if they are non-rational beings, only a relative value as means, and are therefore called *things;* rational beings, on the contrary, are called *persons,* because their very nature points them out as ends in themselves, that is as something which must not be used merely as means, and so far therefore restricts freedom of action (and is an object of respect). These, therefore, are not merely subjective ends whose existence has a worth *for us* as an effort of our action, but *objective ends,* that is things whose existence is an end in itself: an end moreover for which no other can be substituted, which they should subserve *merely* as means, for otherwise nothing whatever would possess *absolute worth;* but if all worth were conditioned and therefore contingent, then there would be no supreme practical principle of reason whatever.

If then there is a supreme practical principle or, in respect of the human will, a categorical imperative, it must be one which, being drawn from the conception of that which is necessarily an end for everyone because it is an *an end in itself,* constitutes an *objective* principle of will, and can therefore serve as a universal practical law. The foundation of this principle is: *rational nature exists as an end in itself.* Man necessarily conceives his own existence as being so: so far then this is a *subjective* principle of human actions. But every other rational being regards its existence similarly, just on the same rational principle, that holds for me: so that it is at the same time an objective principle, from which as a supreme practical law all laws of the will must be capable of being deduced. Accordingly the practical imperative will be as follows: *So act as to treat humanity, whether in thine own person or in that of any other, in every case as an end withal, never as means only. . . .*

The conception of every rational being as one which must consider itself as giving all the maxims of its will universal laws, so as to judge itself and its actions from this point of view—this conception leads to another which depends on it and is very fruitful, namely, that of a *kingdom of ends.*

By a *kingdom* I understand the union of different rational beings in a system by common laws. Now since it is by laws that ends are determined as regards their universal validity, hence, if we abstract from the personal differences of rational beings, and likewise from all the content of their private ends, we shall be able to conceive all ends combined in a systematic whole (including both rational beings as ends in themselves, and also the special ends which each may propose of himself), that is to say, we can conceive a kingdom of ends, which on the preceding principles is possible.

For all rational beings come under the *law* that each of them must treat itself and all others *never merely as means,* but in every case *at the same time as ends in themselves.* Hence results a systematic union of rational beings by common objective laws, *i.e.* a kingdom which may be called a kingdom of ends. . . .

STUDY QUESTIONS

1. Why does Kant say that the good will is good without qualification?
2. For Kant, animals are not ends in themselves because they cannot reason. So, says Kant, they have no moral rights. Does this seem right to you?
3. How does Kant distinguish between hypothetical and categorical imperatives? What kind of imperatives do "prudential" concerns enjoin?
4. Describe an imaginary moral dilemma. Formulate a maxim for each alternative course of action and subject them to the test of universality. Which course of action do you think Kant would support?
5. What in your opinion is Kant's greatest contribution to moral philosophy? What are two of the most serious objections that can be raised against his position?

A Defense of Moral Relativism

RUTH BENEDICT

Ruth Benedict (1887–1948) was one of America's fore-most anthropologists. Her *Patterns of Culture* (1935) is considered a classic of comparative anthropology.

Morality, says Benedict, is a convenient term for socially approved customs (mores). What one society approves may be disgraceful and unacceptable to another. Moral rules, like rules of etiquette or styles of dress, vary from society to society. Morality is culturally relative. Values are shaped by culture. As Benedict points out, trances are highly regarded in India, so in India many people have trances. Some ancient societies praised homosexual love, so there homosexuality was a norm. Where material possessions are highly valued, people amass property. "Most individuals are plastic to the moulding force of the society into which they are born."

Modern social anthropology has become more and more a study of the varieties and common elements of cultural environment and the consequences of these in human behavior. For such a study of diverse

A DEFENSE OF MORAL RELATIVISM From "Anthropology and the Abnormal," by Ruth Benedict, in *The Journal of General Psychology* 10 (1934): 59–82. Reprinted by permission of Clark University Press.

social orders primitive peoples fortunately provide a laboratory not yet entirely vitiated by the spread of a standardized worldwide civilization. Dyaks and Hopis, Fijians and Yakuts are significant for psychological and sociological study because only among these simpler peoples has there been sufficient isolation to give opportunity for the development of localized social forms. In the higher cultures the standardization of custom and belief over a couple of continents has given a false sense of the inevitability of the particular forms that have gained currency, and we need to turn to a wider survey in order to check the conclusions we hastily base upon this near-universality of familiar customs. Most of the simpler cultures did not gain the wide currency of the one which, out of our experience, we identify with human nature, but this was for various historical reasons, and certainly not for any that gives us as its carriers a monopoly of social good or of social sanity. Modern civilization, from this point of view, becomes not a necessary pinnacle of human achievement but one entry in a long series of possible adjustments.

These adjustments, whether they are in mannerisms like the ways of showing anger, or joy, or grief in any society, or in major human drives like those of sex, prove to be far more variable than experience in any one culture would suggest. In certain fields, such as that of religion or of formal marriage arrangements, these wide limits of variability are well known and can be fairly described. In others it is not yet possible to give a generalized account, but that does not absolve us of the task of indicating the significance of the work that has been done and of the problems that have arisen.

One of these problems relates to the customary modern normal-abnormal categories and our conclusions regarding them. In how far are such categories culturally determined, or in how far can we with assurance regard them as absolute? In how far can we regard inability to function socially as diagnostic of abnormality, or in how far is it necessary to regard this as a function of the culture?

As a matter of fact, one of the most striking facts that emerge from a study of widely varying cultures is the ease with which our abnormals function in other cultures. It does not matter what kind of "abnormality" we choose for illustration, those which indicate extreme instability, or those which are more in the nature of character traits like sadism or delusions of grandeur or of persecution, there are well-described cultures in which these abnormals function at ease and with honor, and apparently without danger or difficulty to the society.

The most notorious of these is trance and catalepsy. Even a very mild mystic is aberrant in our culture. But most peoples have regarded even extreme psychic manifestations not only as normal and desirable, but even as characteristic of highly valued and gifted individuals. This was true even in our own cultural background in that period when Catholicism made the ecstatic experience the mark of sainthood. It is hard for us, born and brought up in a culture that makes no use of the experience, to realize how important a role it may play and how many individuals are capable of it, once it has been given an honorable place in any society. . . .

Cataleptic and trance phenomena are, of course, only one illustration of the fact that those whom we regard as abnormals may function adequately in other cultures. Many of our culturally discarded traits are selected for elaboration in different societies. Homosexuality is an excellent example, for in this case our attention is not constantly diverted, as in the consideration of trance, to the interruption of routine activity which it implies. Homosexuality poses the problem very simply. A tendency toward this trait in our culture exposes an individual to all the conflicts to which all aberrants are always exposed, and we tend to identify the consequences of this conflict with homosexuality. But these consequences are obviously local and cultural. Homosexuals in many societies are not incompetent, but they may be such if the culture asks adjustments of them that would strain any man's vitality. Wherever homosexuality has been given an honorable place in any society, those to whom it is congenial have filled adequately the honorable roles society assigns to them. Plato's *Republic* is, of course, the most convincing statement of such a reading of homosexuality. It is presented as one of the major means to the good life, and it was generally so regarded in Greece at that time.

The cultural attitude toward homosexuals has not always been on such a high ethical plane, but it has been very varied. Among many American Indian tribes there exists the institution of the berdache, as the French called them. These men-women were men who at puberty or thereafter took the dress and the occupations of women. Sometimes they married other men and lived with them. Sometimes they were men with no inversion, persons of weak sexual endowment who chose this rôle to avoid the jeers of the women. The berdaches were never regarded as of first-rate super-natural power, as similar men-women were in Siberia, but rather as leaders in women's occupations, good healers in certain diseases, or, among certain tribes, as the genial organizers of social affairs. In any case, they were socially placed. They were not left exposed to the conflicts that visit the deviant who is excluded from participation in the recognized patterns of his society.

The most spectacular illustrations of the extent to which normality may be culturally defined are those cultures where an abnormality of our culture is the cornerstone of their social structure. It is not possible to do justice to these possibilities in a short discussion. A recent study of an island of northwest Melanesia by Fortune describes a society built upon traits which we regard as beyond the border of paranoia. In this tribe the exogamic groups look upon each other as prime manipulators of black magic, so that one marries always into an enemy group which remains for life one's deadly and unappeasable foes. They look upon a good garden crop as a confession of theft, for everyone is engaged in making magic to induce into his garden the productiveness of his neighbors'; therefore no secrecy in the island is so rigidly insisted upon as the secrecy of a man's harvesting of his yams. Their polite phrase at the acceptance of a gift is, "And if you now poison me, how shall I repay you this present?" Their preoccupation with poisoning is constant; no woman ever leaves her cooking pot for a moment untended. Even the great affinal economic exchanges that are characteristic of this Melanesian culture area are quite altered in Dobu since they are incompatible with this fear and distrust that pervades the culture. They go farther and people the whole world outside their own quarters with such malignant spirits that all-night feasts and ceremonials simply do not occur here. They have even rigorous religiously enforced customs that forbid the sharing of seed even in one family group. Anyone else's food is deadly poison to you, so that communality of stores is out of the question. For some months before harvest the whole society is on the verge of starvation, but if one falls to the temptation and eats up one's seed yams, one is an outcast and a beachcomber for life. There is no coming back. It involves, as a matter of course, divorce and the breaking of all social ties.

Now in this society where no one may work with another and no one may share with another, Fortune describes the individual who was regarded by all his fellows as crazy. He was not one of those who periodically ran amok and, beside himself and frothing at the mouth, fell with a knife upon anyone he could reach. Such behavior they did not regard as putting anyone outside the pale. They did not even put the individuals who were known to be liable to these attacks under any kind of control. They merely fled when they saw the attack coming on and kept out of the way. "He would be all right tomorrow." But there was one man of sunny, kindly disposition who liked work and liked to be helpful. The compulsion was too strong for him to repress it in favor of the opposite tendencies of his culture. Men and women never spoke of him without laughing; he was silly and simple and definitely crazy. Nevertheless, to the ethnologist used to a culture that has, in Christianity, made his type the model of all virtue, he seemed a pleasant fellow. . . .

. . . Among the Kwakiutl it did not matter whether a relative had died in bed of disease, or by the hand of an enemy, in either case death was an affront to be wiped out by the death of another person. The fact that one had been caused to mourn was proof that one had been put upon. A chief's sister and her daughter had gone up to Victoria, and either because they drank bad whiskey or because their boat capsized they never came back. The chief called together his warriors. "Now I ask you, tribes, who shall wail? Shall I do it or shall another?" The spokesman answered, of course, "Not you, Chief. Let some other of the tribes." Immediately they set up the war pole to announce their intention of wiping out the injury, and gathered a war party. They set out, and found seven men and two children asleep and killed them. Then they felt good when they arrived at Sebaa in the evening.

The point which is of interest to us is that in our society those who on that occasion would feel good when they arrived at Sebaa that evening would be the definitely abnormal. There would be some, even in our society, but it is not a recognized and approved mood under the circumstances. On the Northwest Coast those are favored and fortunate to whom that mood under those circumstances is congenial, and those to whom it is repugnant are unlucky. This latter minority can register in their own culture only by doing violence to their congenial responses and acquiring others that are difficult for them. The person, for instance, who, like a Plains Indian whose wife has been taken from him, is too proud to fight, can deal with the Northwest Coast civilization only by ignoring its strongest bents. If he cannot achieve it, he is the deviant in that culture, their instance of abnormality.

This head-hunting that takes place on the Northwest Coast after a death is no matter of blood revenge or of organized vengeance. There is no effort to tie up the subsequent killing with any responsibility on the part of the victim for the death of the person who is being mourned. A chief whose son has died goes visiting wherever his fancy dictates, and he says to his host, "My prince has died today, and you go with him." Then he kills him. In this, according to their interpretation, he acts nobly because he has not been downed. He has thrust back in return. The whole procedure is meaningless without the fundamental paranoid reading of bereavement. Death, like all the other untoward accidents of existence, confounds man's pride and can only be handled in the category of insults.

Behavior honored upon the Northwest Coast is one which is recognized as abnormal in our civilization, and yet it is sufficiently close to the attitudes of our own culure to be intelligible to us and to have a definite vocabulary with which we may discuss it. The megalomaniac paranoid trend is a definite danger in our society. It is encouraged by some of our major preoccupations, and it confronts us with a choice of two possible attitudes. One is to brand it as abnormal and reprehensible, and is the attitude we have chosen in our civilization. The other is to make it an essential attribute we have chosen in our civilization. The other is to make it an essential attribute of ideal man, and this is the solution in the culture of the Northwest Coast.

These illustrations, which it has been possible to indicate only in the briefest manner, force upon us the fact that normality is culturally defined. An adult shaped to the drives and standards of either of these cultures, if he were transported into our civilization, would fall into our categories of abnormality. He would be faced with the psychic dilemmas of the socially unavailable. In his own culture, however, he is the pillar of society, the end result of socially inculcated mores, and the problem of personal instability in his case simply does not arise.

No one civilization can possibly utilize in its mores the whole potential range of human behavior. Just as there are great numbers of possible phonetic articulations, and the possibility of language depends on a selection and standardization of a few of these in order that speech communication may be possible at all, so the possibility of organized behavior of every sort, from the fashions of local dress and houses to the dicta of a people's ethics and religion, depends upon a similar selection among the possible behavior traits. In the field of recognized economic obligations or sex tabus this selection is as non-rational and subconscious a process as it is in the field of phonetics. It is a process which goes on in the group for long periods of time and is historically conditioned by innumerable accidents of isolation or of contact of peoples. In any comprehensive study of psychology, the selection that different cultures have made in the course of history within the great circumference of potential behavior is of great significance.

Every society, beginning with some slight inclination in one direction or another, carries its preference farther and farther, integrating itself more and more completely upon its chosen basis, and discarding those types of behavior that are uncongenial. Most of those organizations of personality that seem to us most uncontrovertibly abnormal have been used by different civilizations in the very foundations of their institutional life. Conversely the most valued traits of normal individuals have been looked on in differently organized cultures as aberrant. Normality, in short, within a very wide range, is culturally defined. It is primarily a term for the socially elaborated segment of human behavior in any culture; and abnormality, a term for the segment that that particular civilization does not use. The very eyes with which we see the problem are conditioned by the long traditional habits of our own society.

It is a point that has been made more often in relation to ethics than in relation to psychiatry. We do not any longer make the mistake of deriving the morality of our locality and decade directly from the inevitable constitution of human nature. We do not elevate it to the dignity of a first principle. We recognize that morality differs in every society, and is a convenient term for socially approved habits. Mankind has always preferred to say, "It is morally good," rather than "It is habitual," and the fact of this preference is matter enough for a critical science of ethics. But historically the two phrases are synonymous.

The concept of the normal is properly a variant of the concept of the good. It is that which society has approved. A normal action is one which falls well within the limits of expected behavior for a particular society. Its variability among different peoples is essentially a function of the variability of the behavior patterns that different societies have created for themselves, and can never be wholly divorced from a consideration of culturally institutionalized types of behavior.

Each culture is a more or less elaborate working-out of the potentialities of the segment it has chosen. In so far as a civilization is well integrated and consistent within itself, it will tend to carry farther and farther, according to its nature, its initial impulse toward a particular type of action, and from the point of view of any other culture those elaborations will include more and more extreme and aberrant traits.

Each of these traits, in proportion as it reinforces the chosen behavior patterns of that culture, is for that culture normal. Those individuals to whom it is congenial either congenitally, or as the result of childhood sets, are accorded prestige in that culture, and are not visited with the social contempt or disapproval which their traits would call down upon them in a society that was differently organized. On the other hand, those individuals whose characteristics are not congenial to the selected type of human behavior in that community are the deviants, no matter how valued their personality traits may be in a contrasted civilization.

The Dobuan who is not easily susceptible to fear of treachery, who enjoys work and likes to be helpful, is their neurotic and regarded as silly. On the Northwest Coast the person who finds it difficult to read life in terms of an insult contest will be the person upon whom fall all the difficulties of the culturally unprovided for. The person who does not find it easy to humiliate a neighbor, nor to see humiliation in his own experience, who is genial and loving, may, of course, find some unstandardized way of achieving satisfactions in his society, but not in the major patterned responses that his culture requires of him. If he is born to play an important rôle in a family with many hereditary privileges, he can succeed only by doing violence to his whole personality. If he does not succeed, he has betrayed his culture; that is, he is abnormal.

I have spoken of individuals as having sets toward certain types of behavior, and of these sets as running sometimes counter to the types of behavior which are institutionalized in the culture to which they belong. From all that we know of contrasting cultures it seems clear that differences of temperament occur in every society. The matter has never been made the subject of investigation, but from the available material it would appear that these temperament types are very likely of universal recurrence. That is, there is an ascertainable range of human behavior that is found wherever a sufficiently large series of individuals is observed. But the proportion in which behavior types stand to one another in different societies is not universal. The vast majority of the individuals in any group are shaped to the fashion of that culture. In other words, most individuals are plastic to the moulding force of the society into which they are born. In a society that values trance, as in India, they will have supernormal experience. In a society that institutionalizes homosexuality, they will be homosexual. In a society that sets the gathering of possessions as the chief human objective, they will amass property. The deviants, whatever the type of behavior the culture has institutionalized, will remain few in number, and there seems no more difficulty in moulding that vast malleable majority to the "normality" of what we consider an aberrant trait, such as delusions of reference, than to the normality of such accepted behavior patterns as acquisitiveness. The small proportion of the number of the deviants in any culture is not a function of the sure instinct with which that society has built itself upon the fundamental sanities, but of the universal fact that, happily, the majority of mankind quite readily take any shape that is presented to them. . . .

STUDY QUESTIONS

1. Do you think that the fact of cultural diversity is itself an argument for ethical relativism?
2. If Benedict's defense of ethical relativism is correct, then the correct way to resolve a personal dilemma might be to take a survey or poll to see what the majority in your society thinks is right. If the majority favors capital punishment and opposes abortion, for example, then capital punishment is right and abortion is wrong. Can you defend Benedict against this odd consequence?
3. Do you think that certain types of behavior (for example, executing children or beating animals to death) are wrong wherever they occur, despite attitudes prevailing in the societies that practice them? What makes these acts wrong?
4. How could Benedict account for notions of moral enlightenment and moral progress?

The Problem with Relativism

JOHN HOSPERS

John Hospers (b. 1918) is director of the School of Philosophy at the University of Southern California. He is the author of several books, including *Libertarianism: A Political Philosophy for Tomorrow* (1971) and *Understanding the Arts* (1982).

John Hospers distinguishes between two kinds of relativism. *Sociological Relativism* makes the empirical claim that many acts considered wrong in some societies are considered right in others. Although surely correct, this empirical claim carries no ethical implications.

Ethical Relativism (focusing on the diversity of ethical beliefs in different groups) asserts that "right" and "wrong" are defined sociologically. X is "right" means that X is right in group G. The same act or practice (X) may be wrong in another group.

Hospers gives several reasons for rejecting ethical relativism, among which are:

1. "What's right in one group is wrong in another." But no one belongs to one group only. [So] which group counts? My family? My country? Suppose my family believes one thing and my country enjoins another?

THE PROBLEM WITH RELATIVISM Excerpted selection from "Moral Problems," in *Human Conduct* by John Hospers. Copyright © 1961 by Harcourt Brace Jovanovich, Inc. Reprinted by permission of the publisher.

2. How many of the groups should count? A majority? Is there any reason to hold that what the majority of one group wants should be morally decisive?

3. Ethical error would be impossible if ethical relativism were true. By definition the (majority of the) group cannot be wrong. That is implausible.

Hospers holds the view that most people who think of themselves as ethical relativists simply are unaware of the unacceptable implications of this doctrine.

Relativism, when analyzed, breaks down into several different views.

1. *Sociological relativism* is simply the view that different groups of people—different tribes, different cultures, different civilizations—have different moral standards for evaluating acts as right or wrong. For example, in our society we believe that it is better to be caught for stealing than to escape capture; but the Spartan youth who allowed the fox to gnaw at his vital organs rather than be caught for stealing . . . reflected a popular belief that being caught was bad but stealing was not. The Dobu tribesmen of New Guinea believe that growing your own vegetables is honorable but stealing your neighbor's vegetables is still more honorable. The ancient Romans, unlike the Christians, had more respect for honor than for pity. They could be forgiving if they could gain some advantage from being so; otherwise they had virtually no feeling for victims, such as prisoners of war. Courage was prized; mercy and humility were not. Some desert tribes think it a sacred obligation, when one of their number has been killed or captured by an opposing tribe, to capture and kill (by slow torture) a member of that tribe, even if he is not the same man who committed the offense—a perfectly innocent man will do just as well. The Eskimos think it right to kill their parents after the parents have reached a certain age—indeed, the parents expect this—rather than take them along on their hazardous journeys. . . .

No one is likely to deny relativism in this sense. It would ill become the moral philosopher to say, "You sociologists and anthropologists are all wrong in the alleged facts which you report. It is all a tissue of lies!" Those who are best qualified to know what the Dobu tribes-men believe are those who have lived among the Dobu and seen for themselves.

Even so, the term "sociological relativism" is ambiguous. If the term merely means that there are moral beliefs held by one group which are not held by another, this is obviously true—an empirical fact. But if the term means that different groups have different *basic* moral principles, the statement is not obviously true and may even be false. Different groups *may* be using the same basic moral princi-ples but applying them in different ways to different situations. Imagine two tribes, each believing that they should do what is most conducive to the survival of as many people as possible within the tribe. One of the tribes lives in the desert, and the other where there is plenty of water. In the first tribe wasting even a small amount of water is considered a grave moral offense, perhaps even a capital offense; in the second tribe there are no rules at all about wasting water. This is an example of sociological relativism in the first sense; the one believes that wasting water is wrong and the other does not. But it is not an example of sociological relativism in the second sense, for both moral rules equally illustrate one basic moral principle, that what is right is what promotes survival. On this assumption they do not differ at all; what differs is the application of this one principle to different circumstances.

2. Sociological relativism is not an ethical doctrine at all; it tries to describe what people's moral beliefs *are;* it says nothing about whether any of them are preferable to others. *Ethical relativism,* how-ever, goes further; it has a definite view about right and wrong, and thus it enters the domain of ethics. According to ethical relativism, if there are two tribes or societies, and in one of them it is believed that acts of a certain kind are wrong while in the other it is believed that acts of that same kind are right, *both beliefs* are true: in the first society acts of that kind *are* wrong and in the other society they *are* right. Polygamy is right in polygamous societies but not in monog-amous societies. Thus there is no overall standard of right and wrong—what is right and what is wrong depends on the society of which you are a member.

Here at once we have an ambiguity. Let us suppose, for the mo-ment, that slavery is right in one society and wrong in another—not just that it is thought to be so, which would be sociological relativ-ism, but that it really is so, as ethical relativism says. But a person who holds this belief need not be a relativist at all. He may believe in some one overall standard of right, such as the maximum happiness of the people concerned. . . . And if so, since he has one standard of rightness, he is no relativist. A certain practice might make for the happiness of one society but not of another, and in that event it would be right in the one society but not in the other; only the application of the moral principle differs from one society to another, not the principle itself. Probably most people who call themselves ethical relativists are not so at all, for they believe in one moral standard which applies in different ways to different societies because of the various conditions in which they live. One might as well talk about gravitational relativism because a stone falls and a balloon rises; yet both events are equally instances of one law of universal gravitation.

But suppose that the person believes that there *is* no one overall standard and that what is right and what is wrong varies from one society to another without reference to any one overall moral principle. A person might believe that what is right for one group may be wrong for another and what is right for one individual may be wrong for another, though *not* because there is one overall moral principle of which these are different applications. The relativist will be hard put to it to give any reason *why* he believes this to be so, but he may state the position without any attempt to give reasons. In that event he can truly be called a relativist. But now he must face certain problems:

a. If we ask him *why* a practice that is right in one society is wrong in another, he will have no reason to present. There seems to be no general principle from which his position follows. This weakness, to put it mildly, will leave many people dissatisfied.

b. "What is right in one group is wrong in another," he says. But what exactly is a group? and which group is one to select? Every person is a member of many different groups—his nation, his state, his city, his club, his school, church, fraternity, or athletic association. Suppose that most of the people in his club think that a certain kind of act is wrong and that most of the people in his nation think it is right; what then?

c. How many of the group—whatever group it turns out to be— must think it is wrong before it really is wrong? The usual answer is, "The majority." Presumably this means anything over 50 percent. If 51 percent of his countrymen think adultery is wrong, then it is wrong for the people in that country; but if only 49 percent of them think it wrong, then it isn't. This conclusion is strange, to say the least. Can't a majority be mistaken? A minority view may sometimes spread and become a majority view later; in that event, was the act wrong before and right now? It is very easy to say, "Head hunting is right in a headhunting society, and if most of the people in the United States became headhunters, then headhunting would be right for us," and the same with such practices as polygamy, witchburning, conviction without a trial, cannibalism. But is there any reason why what most people believe should be true?

d. If what the majority of a society or group approves is *ipso facto* right in that society, how can there be any such thing as moral improvement? If someone in a headhunting society were convinced that headhunting was cruel, barbarous, and wrong and proceeded to share these sentiments with his chieftain, the relativistic chieftain would reply, "But the majority in our tribe considers it right, so it *is* right." In a society in which most people cheated the government on their income tax, it would be right to do so, though it would no longer be right once the percentage of cheaters dropped below 50. If ethical relativism is correct, it is clearly impossible for the moral beliefs of a society to be mistaken because the certainty of the majority that its beliefs were right would prove that those beliefs *were* right for that society at that time. The minority view would therefore be mistaken, no matter what it was. Needless to say, most people who state that "in morals everything is relative" and who proceed to call themselves ethical relativists are unaware of these implications of their theory.

STUDY QUESTIONS

1. Discuss the distinction between sociological relativism and ethical relativism. In what sense is the former not an ethical doctrine?
2. According to Hospers, one could believe that slavery is right in some societies and yet not be an ethical relativist. What *would* make one an ethical relativist?
3. Discuss two of Hospers' objections to ethical relativism that seem especially convincing to you. Do the objections persuade you to reject the doctrine?

4. Hospers says that most people who call themselves ethical relativists are not aware of the objections to it. Do you think they are aware but discount the objections? What, if anything, would it take to dislodge hard-line relativists from their position?

Trying Out One's New Sword

————————————————————————————————— 🙠

MARY MIDGLEY

Mary Midgley is a senior Lecturer at the University of Newcastle-upon-Tyne, England. She is the author of several books, including *Beast and Man* (1978), *Heart and Mind* (1981), *Evolution as a Religion: Strange Hopes and Stranger Fears* (1986), and *Wisdom, Information and Wonder* (1991).

Midgley criticizes "moral isolationalists" who disapprove of those who morally judge other cultures. She notes that moral isolationists disapprove less when someone from another culture passes moral judgment on *our* culture. Also, moral isolationists are inconsistent: They do not oppose *praising* an exotic culture. Moral judgment, says Midgley, is a human necessity: Why ban it interculturally? She points out that such a ban would not permit us to express disapproval of the Samurai custom of trying out a new sword by cleanly slicing an innocent passerby in two.

All of us are, more or less, in trouble today about trying to understand cultures strange to us. We hear constantly of alien customs. We see changes in our lifetime which would have astonished our parents. I want to discuss here one very short way of dealing with this difficulty, a drastic way which many people now theoretically favour. It

TRYING OUT ONE'S NEW SWORD From *Heart and Mind* by Mary Midgley. © by M. Midgley, to be used with permission from St. Martin's Press, Inc.

consists in simply denying that we can ever understand any culture except our own well enough to make judgments about it. Those who recommend this hold that the world is sharply divided into separate societies, sealed units, each with its own system of thought. They feel that the respect and tolerance due from one system to another forbids us ever to take up a critical position to any other culture. Moral judgment, they suggest, is a kind of coinage valid only in its country of origin.

I shall call this position "moral isolationism." I shall suggest that it is certainly not forced upon us, and indeed that it makes no sense at all. People usually take it up because they think it is a respectful attitude to other cultures. In fact, however, it is not respectful. Nobody can respect what is entirely unintelligible to them. To respect someone, we have to know enough about him to make a *favorable* judgment, however general and tentative. And we do understand people in other cultures to this extent. Otherwise a great mass of our most valuable thinking would be paralysed.

To show this, I shall take a remote example, because we shall probably find it easier to think calmly about it than we should with a contemporary one, such as female circumcision in Africa or the Chinese Cultural Revolution. The principles involved will still be the same. My example is this. There is, it seems, a verb in classical Japanese which means "to try out one's new sword on a chance wayfarer." (The word is *tsujigiri*, literally "crossroads-cut.") A samurai sword had to be tried out because, if it was to work properly, it had to slice through someone at a single blow, from the shoulder to the opposite flank. Otherwise, the warrior bungled his stroke. This could injure his honour, offend his ancestors, and even let down his emperor. So tests were needed, and wayfarers had to be expended. Any wayfarer would do—provided, of course, that he was not another Samurai. Scientists will recognize a familiar problem about the rights of experimental subjects.

Now when we hear of a custom like this, we may well reflect that we simply do not understand it; and therefore are not qualified to criticize it at all, because we are not members of that culture. But we are not members of any other culture either, except our own. So we extend the principle to cover all extraneous cultures, and we seem therefore to be moral isolationists. But this is, as we shall see, an impossible position. Let us ask what it would involve.

We must ask first: Does the isolating barrier work both ways? Are people in other cultures equally unable to criticize *us?* This question struck me sharply when I read a remark in *The Guardian* by an anthropologist about a South American Indian who had been taken into a Brazilian town for an operation, which saved his life. When he came back to his village, he made several highly critical remarks about the white Brazilians' way of life. They may very well have been justified. But the interesting point was that the anthropologist called these remarks "a damning indictment of Western civilization." Now the Indian had been in that town about two weeks. Was he in a position to deliver a damning indictment? Would we ourselves be qualified to deliver such an indictment on the Samurai, provided we could spend two weeks in ancient Japan? What do we really think about this?

My own impression is that we believe that outsiders can, in principle, deliver perfectly good indictments—only, it usually takes more than two weeks to make them damning. Understanding has degrees. It is not a slapdash yes-or-no matter. Intelligent outsiders can progress in it, and in some ways will be at an advantage over the locals. But if this is so, it must clearly apply to ourselves as much as anybody else.

Our next question is this: Does the isolating barrier between cultures block praise as well as blame? If I want to say that the Samurai culture has many virtues, or to praise the South American Indians, am I prevented from doing *that* by my outside status? Now, we certainly do need to praise other societies in this way. But it is hardly possible that we could praise them effectively if we could not, in principle, criticize them. Our praise would be worthless if it rested on definite grounds, if it did not flow from some understanding. Certainly we may need to praise things which we do not *fully* understand. We say "there's something very good here, but I can't quite make out what it is yet." This happens when we want to learn from strangers. And we can learn from strangers. But to do this we have to distinguish between those strangers who are worth learning from and those who are not. Can we then judge which is which?

This brings us to our third question: What is involved in judging? Now plainly there is no question here of sitting on a bench in a red robe and sentencing people. Judging simply means forming an opinion, and expressing it if it is called for. Is there anything wrong about this? Naturally, we ought to avoid forming—and expressing—*crude* opinions, like that of a simple-minded missionary, who might dismiss the whole Samurai culture as entirely bad, because non-Christian. But this is a different objection. The trouble with crude opinions is that they are crude, whoever forms them, not that they are formed by the wrong people. Anthropologists, after all, are outsiders quite as much as missionaries. Moral isolationism forbids us to form *any* opinions on these matters. Its ground for doing so is that we don't understand them. But there is much that we don't understand in our own culture too. This brings us to our last question: If we can't judge other cultures, can we really judge our own? Our efforts to do so will be much damaged if we are really deprived of our opinions about other societies, because these provide the range of comparison, the spectrum of alternatives against which we set what we want to understand. We would have to stop using the mirror which anthropology so helpfully holds up to us.

In short, moral isolationism would lay down a general ban on moral reasoning. Essentially, this is the programme of immoralism, and it carries a distressing logical difficulty. Immoralists like Nietzsche are actually just a rather specialized sect of moralists. They can no more afford to put moralizing out of business than smugglers can afford to abolish customs regulations. The power of moral judgment is, in fact, not a luxury, not a perverse indulgence of the self-righteous. It is a necessity. When we judge something to be bad or good, better or worse than something else, we are taking it as an example to aim at or avoid. Without opinions of this sort, we would have no framework of comparison for our own policy, no chance of profiting by other people's insights or mistakes. In this vacuum, we could form no judgments on our own actions.

Now it would be odd if Homo sapiens had really got himself into a position as bad as this—a position where his main evolutionary asset, his brain, was so little use to him. None of us is going to accept this sceptical diagnosis. We cannot do so, because our involvement in moral isolationism does not flow from apathy, but from a rather acute concern about human hypocrisy and other forms of wickedness. But we polarize that concern around a few selected moral truths. We are rightly angry with those who despise, oppress or steamroll other cultures. We think that doing these things is actually *wrong*. But this is itself a moral judgment. We could not condemn oppression and insolence if we thought that all our condemnations were just a trivial local quirk of our own culture. We could still less do it if we tried to stop judging altogether.

Real moral scepticism, in fact, could lead only to inaction, to our losing all interest in moral questions, most of all in those which concern other societies. When we discuss these things, it becomes instantly clear how far we are from doing this. Suppose, for instance, that I criticize the bisecting Samurai, that I say his behavior is brutal. What will usually happen next is that someone will protest, will say that I have no right to make criticisms like that of another culture. But it is most unlikely that he will use this move to end the discussion of the subject. Instead, he will justify the Samurai. He will try to fill in the background, to make me understand the custom, by explaining the exalted ideals of discipline and devotion which produced it. He will probably talk of the lower value which the ancient Japanese placed on individual life generally. He may well suggest that this is a healthier attitude than our own obsession with security. He may add, too, that the wayfarers did not seriously mind being bisected, that in principle they accepted the whole arrangement.

Now an objector who talks like this is implying that it *is* possible to understand alien customs. That is just what he is trying to make me do. And he implies, too, that if I do succeed in understanding them, I shall do something better than giving up judging them. He expects me to change my present judgment to a truer one—namely, one that is favourable. And the standards I must use to do this cannot just be Samurai standards. They have to be ones current in my own culture. Ideals like discipline and devotion will not move anybody unless he himself accepts them. As it happens, neither discipline nor devotion is very popular in the West at present. Anyone who appeals to them may well have to do some more arguing to make *them* acceptable, before he can use them to explain the Samurai. But if he does succeed here, he will have persuaded us, not just that there was something to be said for them in ancient Japan, but that there would be here as well.

Isolating barriers simply cannot arise here. If we accept something as a serious moral truth about one culture, we can't refuse to apply it—in however different an outward form—to other cultures as well, wherever circumstance admit it. If we refuse to do this, we just are not taking the other culture seriously. This becomes clear if we look at the last argument used by my objector—that of justification by consent of the victim. It is suggested that sudden bisection is quite in order, *provided* that it takes place between consenting adults. I cannot now discuss how conclusive this justification is. What I am pointing out is simply that it can only work if we believe that *consent* can make such a transaction respectable—and this is a thoroughly modern and Western idea. It would probably never occur to a Samurai; if it did, it would surprise him very much. It is *our* standard. In applying it, too, we are likely to make another typically Western demand. We shall ask for good factual evidence that the wayfarers actually do have this rather surprising taste—that they are really willing to be bi-sected. In applying Western standards in this way, we are not being confused or irrelevant. We are asking the questions which arise *from where we stand,* questions which we can see the sense of. We do this because asking questions which you can't see the sense of is humbug. Certainly we can extend our questioning by imaginative effort. We can come to understand other societies better. By doing so, we may make their questions our own, or we may see that they are really forms of the questions which we are asking already. This is not impossible. It is just very hard work. The obstacles which often prevent it are simply those of ordinary ignorance, laziness and prejudice.

If there were really an isolating barrier, of course, our own culture could never have been formed. It is no sealed box, but a fertile jungle of different influences—Greek, Jewish, Roman, Norse, Celtic and so forth, into which further influences are still pouring—American, Indian, Japanese, Jamaican, you name it. The moral isolationist's picture of separate, unmixable cultures is quite unreal. People who talk about British history usually stress the value of this fertilizing mix, no doubt rightly. But this is not just an odd fact about Britain. Except for the very smallest and most remote, all cultures are formed out of many streams. All have the problem of digesting and assimilating things which, at the start, they do not understand. All have the choice of learning something from this challenge, or, alternatively, of refusing to learn, and fighting it mindlessly instead.

This universal predicament has been obscured by the fact that anthropologists used to concentrate largely on very small and remote cultures, which did not seem to have this problem. These tiny societies, which had often forgotten their own history, made neat, self-contained subjects for study. No doubt it was valuable to emphasize their remoteness, their extreme strangeness, their independence of our cultural tradition. This emphasis was, I think, the root of moral isolationism. But, as the tribal studies themselves showed, even there the anthropologists were able to interpret what they saw and make judgments—often favourable—about the tribesmen. And the tribes-men, too, were quite equal to making judgments about the anthro-pologists—and about the tourists and Coca-Cola salesmen who followed them. Both sets of judgments, no doubt, were somewhat hasty, both have been refined in the light of further experience. A similar transaction between us and the Samurai might take even longer. But that is no reason at all for deeming it impossible. Morally as well as physically, there is only one world, and we all have to live in it.

STUDY QUESTIONS

1. How would a philosophical Samurai defend the practice of trying out a new sword? Does this defense have any merit? Ex-plain your answer.

2. The word "mores" usually connotes a variety of social practices. Yet Midgley says, "Morally as well as physically, there is only one world." If you believe she is right about this, then defend her view that we can judge the social practices and traditions of exotic cultures. If you disagree, show where she goes wrong.

3. Someone else might call Midgley's "moral isolationism" a "so-phisticated tolerance of cultural difference." Argue the case against Midgley and for "tolerance" to see whether you end up convincing yourself that she is wrong.

Uganda's Women: Children, Drudgery, and Pain

JANE PERLEZ

Jane Perlez (b. 1947) is a journalist at the *New York Times*.
She is currently bureau chief in Nairobi, Kenya.

The life of Safuyati Kawuda is like that of many rural African women. These
women, who produce almost three-quarters of Africa's food, lead lives of
hard and unceasing labor not shared by their husbands. The men, who may
visit their villages only occasionally, live urban lives while their wives work
and care for the children in dwellings that lack such amenities as running
water or electricity. Mrs. Kawuda's husband has several wives, including a
town wife. Mrs. Kawuda is not convinced that he stays faithful to the town
wife, and she fears that his promiscuity may result in AIDS. As a reporter,
Perlez makes no value judgments. But to many readers it will seem obvious
that the social system that condemns Mrs. Kawuda to a lifetime of unremitting and punishing labor is unfair to her.

NAMUTUMBA, Uganda—When 28-year-old Safuyati Kawuda
married the man she remembers as "handsome and elegant," her husband scraped together the bride price: five goats and three chickens.
The animals represented a centuries-old custom intended to compensate Mrs. Kawuda's father for losing the labor of his daughter.

In the decade since, Mrs. Kawuda has rarely seen her husband,
who long ago left this hot and dusty village for a town 70 miles away.

She has accepted her husband's acquisition of two other wives and has given birth to five of his 13 children.

Instead of laboring for her father she has toiled for her husband instead—hauling firewood, fetching water, digging in the fields, producing the food the family eats, and bearing and caring for the children.

Like Mrs. Kawuda, women in rural Africa are the subsistence farmers. They produce, without tractors, oxen, or even plows, more than 70 percent of the continent's food, according to the World Bank. Back-breaking hand cultivation is a job that African men consider to be demeaning "women's work." The male responsibility is generally to sell the food the women produce. But as urbanization has stepped up, men have gone to the cities in search of other jobs, leaving women like Mrs. Kawuda alone.

Many Inequalities

The discrepancy between the physical labor of women and men is accompanied by other pervasive inequalities. In the vast majority of African countries, women do not own or inherit land. Within families, boys are encouraged to go to school, girls are not. In many places, women treat wife-beating as an accepted practice. The Uganda Women's Lawyers Association recently embarked on a campaign to convince women that wife-battering is not a sign of a man's love.

Recent surveys in Africa show other significant disparities between men and women. In ten African countries, according to the United Nations Children's Fund, women and children together make up 77 percent of the population. Yet in only 16 percent of the households in those countries do the women have the legal right to own property.

Despite calls by the United Nations for the improvement of the lives of African women and efforts by the World Bank to finance projects focused on women, little has been done to improve the dismal status of rural women, African and Western experts say. With the continent's worsening economics in the 1980s, women suffered even more.

"The poor, the majority of whom are women, have had to take on additional work burdens in order to cope with cutbacks in social services and the increasing cost of living," the *Weekly Review*, a magazine in Kenya, reported last year.

No Expectations

Mrs. Kawuda has never attended school. She cannot read or write, although her husband can. She has no radio. The farthest she has been from home is Jinja, 70 miles away. She has no expectations of a better life because she has known nothing else. But her ignorance of the outside world does not stop her from knowing her life is unrelentingly tough. She knows that in her bones.

"Everything is difficult," Mrs. Kawuda said, as she bent over to hoe cassava, her bare, rough feet splattered with dark dirt. "It's more of a problem than it used to be to find firewood. If you can't find wood on the ground, you have to cut it and there is no one to help you. Digging in the fields is the most difficult. I don't like it."

Mrs. Kawuda shares her world of perpetual fatigue with her five children; her husband's second wife, Zainabu Kasoga, 27, and her four children. Her husband's third wife—"the town wife"—lives in Jinja, where the husband, 31-year-old Kadiri Mpyanku, a tea packer, spends most of his time.

When the husband visited Mrs. Kawuda on a recent weekend, he brought enough sugar for three days and a packet of beans. Mrs. Kawuda said she was dependent on him for clothes and other essentials, and money that she said he did not always have. In most households in the area, the men also live most of the time in either Jinja or Kampala, the capital.

Here in the village, 120 miles northeast of Kampala, Mrs. Kawuda and Mrs. Kasoga run a household with another woman, the wife of their husband's brother, Sayeda Naigaga, 20, and her three children.

Village Life

The women live without running water or electricity in three small, mud-wall structures. In the outdoor courtyard, life grinds on: the peeling and chopping of food, eating by adults and feeding of infants, washing, bathing, weaving and the receiving of guests all take place on the orange clay ground, packed smooth by the passage of bare feet.

In the old days, Ugandan men built separate houses for each wife, but such luxuries disappeared with the collapse of the economy. Mrs. Kawuda and her five children sleep in one room of the main shelter and Mrs. Kasoga and her four children in another. When their husband is around, he shuttles between the two bedrooms.

Mrs. Kawuda is of the Bisoga tribe, the second largest in Uganda and one where polygamy is common. Sexual and marriage mores differ in various parts of Africa. The Uganda Women's Lawyers Association estimates that 50 percent of marriages in Uganda are polygamous and, according to United Nations figures, a similar percentage exists in West Africa.

In Kenya, the Government's Women's Bureau estimates that about 30 percent of the marriages are polygamous. However, because of the economic burden of keeping several wives and families, the practice is declining, the bureau says.

Wives Often Hostile

Often the wives in a polygamous marriage are hostile toward each other. But perhaps as a survival instinct, Mrs. Kawuda and Mrs. Kasoga are friendly, taking turns with Mrs. Naigaga to cook for the 15-member household.

Days start with the morning ritual of collecting water. For these Ugandan women, the journey to the nearest pond takes half an hour. The six-gallon cans, when full of water, are heavy on the trip home.

Digging in the fields is the most loathed of the chores, but also the one the women feel most obliged to do since the family's food supply comes from what they grow. As they work under the sun, the women drape old pieces of clothing on their heads for protection. The youngest child, two-year-old Suniya, clings to her mother's back while Mrs. Kawuda hunches over, swinging a hoe, a sight as pervasive in rural Africa as an American mother gliding a cart along the aisles of a supermarket. "Having a baby on your back is easy," Mrs. Kawuda said. "When you are eight months pregnant and digging, it is more difficult."

There was no possibility the husband would help in the fields. It was his job to "supervise," said Mrs. Kawuda, ridiculing a suggestion that he might pitch in.

When he arrived late on a recent Saturday night, Mr. Mpyanku was treated as the imperious ruler by the children, some of whom tentatively came to greet him. He was barely acknowledged by the women, who seemed a little fearful and immediately served tea.

By early Sunday morning, he had disappeared to the nearby trading post to be with his male friends. "He has gone to discuss business with his friends," Mrs. Kawuda said. "What business can I discuss with him? Will we talk to him about digging cassava?"

Mrs. Kawuda said her husband had promised not to take any more wives. "But you never know what he thinks," she said. "I can't interfere in his affairs. If I did, he would say: 'Why is she poking her nose into my affairs?' "

Fertility and children remain at the center of rural marriage in Africa. Large numbers of children improve a household's labor pool and provide built-in security for parents in old age.

Mrs. Kawuda said she wanted one more child, in the hopes of its being another boy. After that, she said, she would use an injectible form of contraceptive. It is a method popular among African rural women because it can be used without their husband's knowledge. But in reality, contraception was an abstraction to Mrs. Kawuda since she had no idea where to get it. She has never heard of condoms.

A recent concern for African women is AIDS, which like much else in their lives they seem powerless to control. Unconvinced by her husband's assurances that he is faithful to his town wife, Mrs. Kawuda said: "He can say it's all right, we need not worry. But you never know what he does in town. He fears AIDS, too. But he messes around too much."

A worldly person compared to his wives, Mr. Mpyanku speaks reasonable English and has traveled to Kenya.

He described himself as the provider of cash for the rural family. But Mr. Mpyanku's emphasis is on his own livelihood and his urban life.

He rode the most comfortable form of transportation home, a nonstop mini bus from Jinja that cost about $1.50, instead of the cheaper taxi at $1. He would do the same on his return.

Yet his oldest child, a daughter, Maliyamu, ten, missed much of her schooling last year. Her report card said the $7 in school fees had not been paid. It was a cheerless sign that Mrs. Kawuda's daughter would, like her mother, remain uneducated and repeat for another generation the cycle of female poverty and punishing physical labor.

STUDY QUESTIONS

1. Of the three moral theories—utilitarianism, Kantianism and relativism—which do you think provides the best approach to Mrs. Kawuda's predicament?

2. What do you think V. S. Naipaul would say about the plight of Mrs. Kawuda? (See next essay.)
3. Using Mrs. Kawuda's situation as an example of a putatively immoral arrangement, stage a debate on the following proposition: "There are universal moral principles that apply to all societies."

Our Universal Civilization

V. S. NAIPAUL

V. S. Naipaul (b. 1932) is a novelist and writer. He was born in Trinidad where his grandfather had immigrated from India. He attended Oxford University. He is the author of more than twenty books and has won numerous literary prizes. Among his books are *A House for Mr. Biswas* (1961), *A Bend in the River* (1979) and *The Enigma of Arrival* (1987).

Naipaul contrasts a "universal civilization" that cherishes individual freedom with more rigid and repressive traditional cultures. The former, he believes, transcends national and religious boundaries and is tolerant of a variety of civilizations and histories. The latter are fearful and intolerant of modern achievements, even while they depend on them and make use of them. Naipaul argues that in particular those countries that have been colonized by the Arab faith are intolerant of universal ideals and have even shut out their own pre-Islamic histories and cultures. In some fundamentalist societies

(Iran, for example), Western societies are abominated and feared, but the ancient ancestor societies are equally perceived as a threat. Islam itself is to suffice as a "complete way of life."

Naipaul singles out and extols societies that accept the Christian ideal of doing unto others as you would have others do unto you—"[a] simple idea which was and is dazzling to me." Naipaul considers this precept to be one of the defining precepts of a truly universal civilization. The other is the "beautiful idea" that happiness is to be pursued and that its pursuit is a universal right. "It is an elastic idea; it fits all men." It contains other fundamental ideas: choice, individual responsibility, the life of the intellect. Naipaul describes his own personal odyssey, moving from his childhood in Trinidad to England where he was permitted to develop himself as a writer of world renown. Having traveled all over the world, Naipaul now believes that the closed cultures will not, in the end, be able to survive contact with the liberating ideals of a universal civilization. "[O]ther more rigid systems [will] in the end blow away."

I've given this talk the title of Our Universal Civilization. It is a rather big title, and I am a little embarrassed by it. I feel I should explain how it came about. I have no unifying theory of things. To me situations and people are always specific, always of themselves. That is why one travels and writes: to find out. To work in the other way would be to know the answers before one knew the problems. That is a recognized way of working, I know, especially if one is a political or religious or racial missionary. But I would have found it hard.

That was why I thought, when this invitation to talk came, that it would be better for me to find out what kind of issues members of the Institute were interested in. Myron Magnet, a senior fellow of the Institute, was in England at the time. We talked on the telephone; and then, some days later, he sent me a handwritten list of questions. They were very serious questions, very important. Are we—are communities—as strong only as our beliefs? Is it enough for beliefs or an ethical view to be passionately held? Does the passion give validity to the ethics? Are beliefs or ethical views arbitrary, or do they represent something essential in the cultures where they flourish?

It was easy to read through to some of the anxieties that lay behind the questions. There was a clear worry about certain fanaticisms "out there." At the same time there was a certain philosophical diffidence about how that anxiety could be expressed, since no one wants to use words or concepts that might boomerang on himself. You know how words can be used: I am civilized and steadfast; you are barbarian and fanatical; he is primitive and blind. Of course, I was on the side of the questioner, and understood his drift. But I got to feel, over the next few days, and perhaps from my somewhat removed position, that I couldn't share the pessimism implied by the questions. I felt that the very pessimism of the questions, and their philosophical diffidence, defined the strength of the civilization out of which it issued. And so the theme of my talk, Our Universal Civilization, was given me.

I am not going to attempt to define this civilization. I will only speak of it in a personal way. It is the civilization, first of all, which gave me the idea of the writing vocation. It is the civilization in which I have been able to practice my vocation as a writer. To be a writer, you need—to start with—a certain kind of sensibility. The sensibility itself is created, or given direction, by an intellectual atmosphere.

Sometimes an atmosphere can be too refined, a civilization too achieved, too ritualized. Eleven years ago, when I was traveling in Java, I met a young man who wanted above everything else to be a poet and to live the life of the mind. This ambition had been given him by his modern education; but it was hard for the young man to explain to his mother exactly what he was up to. This mother was a person of culture and elegance; that should be stressed. She was elegant in visage and dress and speech; her manners were like art; they were Javanese court manners.

So I asked the young man—bearing in mind that we were in Java, where ancient epics live on in the popular art of puppet plays—"But isn't your mother secretly proud that you are a poet?" He said in English—I mention this to give a further measure of his education in his far-off Javanese town—"She wouldn't have even a sense of what being a poet is."

And the poet's friend and mentor, a teacher at the local university, amplified this. The friend said, "The only way he would have of making his mother understand what he is trying to do would be to suggest that he is being a poet in the classical tradition. And she would find this absurd. She would reject it as an impossibility." It would be rejected as an impossibility, because for the poet's mother the epics of her country—and to her they would have been like sacred texts—already existed, had already been written. They had only to be learned or consulted.

For the mother, all poetry had already been written. That particular book, it might be said, was closed: it was part of the perfection of her culture. To be told by her son, who was twenty-eight, not all that young, that he was hoping to be a poet would be like a devout mother in another culture asking her writer-son what he intended to write next, and getting the reply, "I am thinking of adding a book to the Bible." Or, to attempt another comparison, the young man would be like the character in the story by Borges who had taken on himself the task of rewriting Don Quixote. Not just retelling the story, or copying out the Cervantes original; but seeking, by an extraordinary process of mind-clearing and re-creation, to arrive—without copying or falsity, and purely through original thought—at a narrative coinciding word by word with the Cervantes book.

I understood the predicament of the young man in central Java. His background, after all, was not far removed from the Hindu aspect of my own Trinidad background. We were an agricultural immigrant community from India. The ambition to become a writer, the introduction to writing and ideas about writing, had been given me by my father. He was born in 1906, the grandson of someone who had come to Trinidad as a baby. And somehow, in spite of all the discouragements of the society of that small agricultural colony, the wish to be a writer had come to my father; and he had made himself into a journalist, even with the limited opportunities for journalism that existed in that colony.

We were a people of ritual and sacred texts. We also had our epics—and they were the very epics of Java; we heard them constantly sung or chanted. But it couldn't be said that we were a literary people. Our literature, our texts, didn't commit us to an exploration of our world; rather, they were cultural markers, giving us a sense of the wholeness of our world, and the alienness of what lay outside. I don't believe that, in his family, anyone before my father would have thought of original literary composition. That idea came to my father in Trinidad with the English language; somehow, in spite of the colonial discouragements of the place, an idea of the high civilization connected with the language came to my father; and he was given some knowledge of literary forms. Sensibility is not enough if you are going to be a writer. You need to arrive at the forms that can contain or carry your sensibility; and literary forms—whether in poetry or drama, or prose fiction—are artificial, and ever-changing.

This was a part of what was passed on to me at a very early age. At a very early age—in all the poverty and bareness of Trinidad, far away, with a population of half a million—I was given the ambition to write books, and specifically to write novels, which my father had presented to me as the highest form. But books are not created just in the mind. Books are physical objects. To write them, you need a certain kind of sensibility; you need a language, and a certain gift of language; and you need to possess a particular literary form. To get your name on the spine of the created physical object, you need a vast apparatus outside yourself. You need publishers, editors, designers, printers, binders; booksellers, critics, newspapers, and magazines and television where the critics can say what they think of the book; and, of course, buyers and readers.

I want to stress this mundane side of things, because it is easy to take it for granted; it is easy to think of writing only in its personal, romantic aspect. Writing is a private act; but the published book, when it starts to live, speaks of the cooperation of a particular kind of society. The society has a certain degree of commercial organization. It also has certain cultural or imaginative needs. It doesn't believe that all poetry has already been written. It needs new stimuli, new writing; and it has the means of judging the new things that are offered.

This kind of society didn't exist in Trinidad. It was necessary, therefore, if I was going to be a writer, and live by my books, to travel out to that kind of society where the writing life was possible. This meant, for me at that time, going to England. I was traveling from the periphery, the margin, to what to me was the center; and it was my hope that, at the center, room would be made for me. I was asking a lot, asking, in fact, more of the center than of my own society. The center, after all, had its own interests, its own world view, its own ideas of what it wanted in novels. And it still does. My subjects were far-off: but a little room was made for me in the England of the 1950s. I was able to become a writer, and to grow in the profession. It took time; I was forty—and had been publishing in England for fifteen years—before a book of mine was seriously published in the United States.

But I always recognized, in England in the 1950s, that as someone with a writing vocation there was nowhere else for me to go. And if I have to describe the universal civilization I would say it is the civilization that both gave the prompting and the idea of the literary vocation; and also gave the means to fulfill that prompting; the civilization that enabled me to make that journey from the periphery to the center; the civilization that links me not only to this audience but also to that now not-so-young man in Java whose background was as ritualized as my own, and on whom—as on me—the outer world had worked, and given the ambition to write.

It is easier today for someone setting out to be a writer from a place like Java or Trinidad; subjects once far-off are no longer so. But I have never been able to take my career for granted. I know that there are still large tracts of the world where the cultural or economic conditions I described a while ago do not obtain, and someone like myself would not have been able to become a writer. I couldn't have become a writer in the Mohammedan world; in China; in Japan—the Japanese make room for the literary culture only of the countries they see themselves competing against. I couldn't have become the kind of writer I am in Eastern Europe or the Soviet Union or black Africa. I don't think I could have taken my gifts even to India.

You will understand, then, how important it was to me to know when I was young that I could make this journey from the margin to the center, from Trinidad to London. The ambition to be a writer assumed that this was possible. So, in fact, I was taking it for granted, in spite of my ancestry and Trinidad background, that with another, equally important part of myself I was part of a larger civilization. I suppose the same could be said of my father, though he was closer to the ritual ways of our Hindu and Indian past.

But I never formulated the idea of the universal civilization until quite recently—until eleven years ago, when I traveled for many months in a number of non-Arab Muslim countries to try to understand what had driven them to their rage. That Muslim rage was just beginning to be apparent. "Fundamentalism"—in connection with the Mohammedan world—was not a word often used by the newspapers in 1979; they hadn't yet worked through to that concept. What they spoke of more was "the revival of Islam." And that, indeed, to anyone contemplating it from a distance, was a puzzle. Islam, which had apparently so little to offer its adherents in the last century and in the first half of this—What did it have to offer to an infinitely more educated, infinitely faster world in the later years of the century?

The adaptation of my own family and Trinidad Indian community to the colonial Trinidad and, through that, to the twentieth century hadn't been easy. It had been painful for us, an Asian people, living instinctive, ritualized lives to awaken to an idea of our history and to learn to live with the idea of our political helplessness. There had been very difficult social adjustments as well. For example; in our culture marriages had always been arranged; it took some time, and many damaged lives, for us to arrive at the other way. All of this went with the personal intellectual growth I have described.

And I thought, when I began to travel in the Muslim world, that I would be traveling among people who would be like the people of my own community. A large portion of Indians were Muslims; we had both had a similar nineteenth-century imperial or colonial history. I thought that religion was an accidental difference. I thought, as people said, that faith was faith; that people living at a certain time in history would have felt the same urges.

But it wasn't like that. The Muslims said that their religion was fundamental to them. And it was: it made for an immense difference. I have to stress that I was traveling in the non-Arab Muslim world. Islam began as an Arab religion; it spread as an Arab empire. In Iran, Pakistan, Malaysia, Indonesia—the countries of my itinerary—I was traveling, therefore, among people who had been converted to what was an alien faith. I was traveling among people who had to make a double adjustment—an adjustment to the European empires of the nineteenth and twentieth centuries; and an earlier adjustment to the Arab faith. You might almost say that I was among people who had been doubly colonized, doubly removed from themselves.

Because I was soon to discover that no colonization had been so thorough as the colonization that had come with the Arab faith. Colonized or defeated peoples can begin to distrust themselves. In the Muslim countries I am talking about this distrust had all the force of religion. It was an article of the Arab faith that everything before the faith was wrong, misguided, heretical; there was no room in the heart or mind of these believers for their pre-Mohammedan past. So ideas of history were quite different from ideas of history elsewhere; there was no wish here to go back as far as possible into the past, and to learn as much as possible about the past.

Persia had a great past; it had been the rival in classical times of Greece and Rome. But you wouldn't have believed it in Iran in 1979; for the Iranians the glory and the truth had begun with the coming of Islam. Pakistan was a very new Muslim state. But the land was very old. In Pakistan were the ruins of the very old cities of Mohenjo-Daro and Harappa. Fabulous ruins, the discovery of which earlier this century had given a new idea of the history of the subcontinent. Not only pre-Islamic ruins; but possibly also pre-Hindu. There was an archaeological department, inherited from British days, that looked after the sites. But there was, especially with the growth of fundamentalism, a contrary current. This was expressed in a letter to a newspaper while I was there. The ruins of the cities, the writer said, should be hung with quotations from the Koran, saying that this was what befell unbelievers.

The faith abolished the past. And when the past was abolished like this, more than an idea of history suffered. Human behavior, and ideals of good behavior, could suffer. When I was in Pakistan the newspapers were running articles to mark the anniversary of the Arab conquest of Sind. This was the first part of the Indian subcontinent to be conquered by the Arabs. It occurred at the beginning of the eighth century. The kingdom of Sind—an enormous area: the southern half of Afghanistan, the southern half of Pakistan—at that time was a Hindu-Buddhist kingdom. The brahmins didn't really understand the outside world; the Buddhists didn't believe in taking life. It was a kingdom waiting to be conquered, you might say. But it took a long time for Sind to be conquered; it was very far away from the Arab heartland, across immense deserts. Six or seven Arab expeditions foundered.

At one time the third caliph himself, the third successor to the Prophet, called one of his lieutenants and said, "O Hakim, have you seen Hindustan and learnt all about it?" Hakim said, "Yes, O commander of the faithful." The caliph said, "Give us a description of it." And all Hakim's frustration and bitterness came out in his reply. "Its

193

water is dark and dirty," Hakim said. "Its fruit is bitter and poisonous. Its land is stony and its earth is salt. A small army will soon be annihilated, and a large one will soon die of hunger."

This should have been enough for the caliph. But, looking still for some little encouragement, he asked Hakim, "What about the people? Are they faithful, or do they break their word?" Clearly, faithful people would have been easier to subdue, easier to lighten of their money. But Hakim almost spat out his reply. "The people are treacherous and deceitful," Hakim said. And at that the caliph did take fright—the people of Sind sounded quite an enemy—and he ordered that the conquest of Sind to be attempted no more.

But Sind was too tempting. The Arabs tried again and again. The organization and the drive and the attitudes of the Arabs, fortified by their new faith, in a world still tribal and disorganized, easy to conquer, the drive of the Arabs was remarkably like that of the Spaniards in the New World eight hundred years later—and this was not surprising, since the Spaniards themselves had been conquered and ruled by the Arabs for some centuries. Spain, in fact, fell to the Arabs at about the same time as Sind did.

The final conquest of Sind was set on foot from Iraq, and was superintended from the town of Kufa by Hajjaj, the governor of Iraq. The topicality is fortuitous, I assure you. The aim of the Arab conquest of Sind—and this conquest had been thought about almost as soon as the faith had been established—the aim of the conquest had always been the acquiring of slaves and plunder, rather than the spreading of the faith. And when finally Hajjaj, the governor of Iraq, received the head of the king of Sind, together with 60,000 slaves from Sind, and the royal one-fifth of the loot of Sind, that one-fifth decreed by the religious law, he

> placed his forehead on the ground and offered prayers of thanksgiving, by two genuflections to God, and praised him, saying: "Now I have got all the treasures, whether open or buried, as well as other wealth, and the kingdom of the world."

There was a famous mosque in the town of Kufa. Hajjaj called the people there, and from the pulpit he told them: "Good news and good luck to the people of Syria and Arabia, whom I congratulate on

the conquest of Sind and on the possession of immense wealth . . .
which the great and omnipotent God has kindly bestowed on them."

I am quoting from a translation of a thirteenth-century Persian
text, the *Chachnama*. It is the main source for the story of the conquest of Sind. It is a surprisingly modern piece of writing, a good
fast narrative, with catching detail and dialogue. It tells a terrible
story of plunder and killing—the Arab army was allowed to kill for
days after the fall of every town in Sind; and then the plunder was
assessed and distributed to the soldiers, after one-fifth had been set
aside for the caliph. But to the Persian writer, the story—written
five hundred years after the conquest—is only "a pleasant tale of
conquest." It is Arab or Muslim imperial genre writing. After
five hundred years—and though the Mongols are about to break
through—the faith still holds; there is no new moral angle on the
destruction of the kingdom of Sind.

This was the event that was being commemorated by articles in
the newspapers when I was in Pakistan in 1979. There was an article
by a military man about the successful Arab general. The article tried
to be fair, in a military way, to the armies of both sides. It drew a
rebuke from the chairman of the National Commission of Historical
and Cultural Research.

This is what the chairman said. "Employment of appropriate
phraseology is necessary when one is projecting the image of a hero.
Expressions such as 'invader' and 'defenders' and 'the Indian army'
fighting bravely but not being quick enough to 'fall upon the withdrawing enemy' loom large in the article. It is further marred by
some imbalanced statements such as follows: 'Had Raja Dahar defended the Indus heroically, and stopped Qasim from crossing it, the
history of this subcontinent would have been quite different.' One
fails to understand"—this is the chairman of the Commission of
Historical and Cultural Research—"whether the writer is applaud-
ing the defeat of the hero or lamenting the defeat of his rival." After
1,200 years, the holy war is still being fought. The hero is the Arab
invader, bringer of the faith. The rival whose defeat is to be ap-
plauded—and I was reading this in Sind—is the man of Sind.

To possess the faith was to possess the only truth; and possession
of this truth set many things on its head. To believe that the time

before the coming of the faith was a time was to be judged in one way; what lay outside it was to be judged in another. The faith altered values, ideas of good behavior, human judgments.

So I not only began to understand what people in Pakistan meant when they told me that Islam was a complete way of life, affecting everything; I began to understand that—though it might be said that we had shared a common subcontinental origin—I had traveled a different way. I began to formulate the idea of the universal civilization—which, growing up in Trinidad, I had lived in or been part of without quite knowing that I did so.

Starting with the Hindu background of the instinctive, ritualized life; growing up in the unpromising conditions of colonial Trinidad; I had—through the process I have tried to describe earlier—gone through many stages of knowledge and self-knowledge. I had a better idea of Indian history and Indian art than my grandparents had. They possessed rituals, epics, myth; their identity lay within that light; beyond that light there was darkness, which they wouldn't have been able to penetrate. I didn't possess the rituals and the myths; I saw them at a distance. But I had in exchange been granted the ideas of inquiry and the tools of scholarship. Identity for me was a more complicated matter. Many things had gone to make me. But there was no problem for me there. Whole accumulations of scholarship were mine, in the sense that I had access to them. I could carry four or five or six different cultural ideas in my head. I knew about my ancestry and my ancestral culture; I knew about the history of India and its political status; I knew where I was born, and I knew the history of the place; I had a sense of the New World. I knew about the literary forms I was interested in; and I knew about the journey I would have to make to the center in order to exercise the vocation I had given myself.

Now, traveling among non-Arab Muslims, I found myself among a colonized people who had been stripped by their faith of all that expanding intellectual life, all the varied life of the mind and senses, the expanding cultural and historical knowledge of the world, that I had been growing into on the other side of the world. I was among people whose identity was more or less contained in the faith. I was among people who wished to be pure.

In Malaysia they were desperate to rid themselves of their past, desperate to cleanse their people of tribal or animist practices, all the subconscious life, freighted with the past, that links people to the earth on which they walk, all the rich folk life that awakened people elsewhere cultivate and dredge for its poetry. They wished, the more earnest of these Malay Muslims, to be nothing but their imported Arab faith; I got the impression that they would have liked, ideally, to make their minds and souls a blank, an emptiness, so that they could be nothing but their faith. Such effort; such self-imposed tyranny. No colonization could have been greater than this colonization by the faith.

While the faith held, while it appeared to be unchallenged, the world perhaps held together. But when there appeared this powerful, encompassing civilization from outside, men didn't know what to do. They could do only what they were capable of doing; they could only become more assiduous in the faith, more self-wounding, more ready to turn away from what they didn't feel they could master.

Muslim fundamentalism in places like Malaysia and Indonesia seems new. But Europe has been in the East for a long time, and there has been Muslim anxiety there for almost all of this time. This anxiety, this meeting of the two opposed worlds, the outgoing world of Europe and the closed world of the faith, was spotted a hundred years ago by the writer Joseph Conrad who with his remote Polish background, his wish as a traveler to render exactly what he saw, was able at time of high imperialism to go far beyond the imperialistic, surface ways of writing about the East and native peoples.

To Conrad the world he traveled in was new; he looked hard at it. There is a quotation I would like to read from Conrad's second book, published in 1896, nearly one hundred years ago, in which he catches something of the Muslim hysteria of that time—the hysteria which a hundred years later, with greater education and wealth of the native peoples, and the withdrawing of empires, was to turn into the fundamentalism we hear about.

> A half-naked, betel-chewing pessimist stood upon the bank of the tropical river, on the edge of the still and immense forests; a man angry, powerless, empty-handed, with a cry of bitter discontent ready on his lips; a cry that, had it come out, would have rung through the virgin solitudes of the woods as true, as great, as profound, as any

> philosophical shriek that ever came from the depths of an easy-chair
> to disturb the impure wilderness of chimneys and roofs.

Philosophical hysteria—those were the words I wanted to give to you, and I think they still apply. They bring me back to the list of questions and issues that the senior fellow of the Institute, Myron Magnet, sent to me when he was in England last summer. Why, he asked, are certain societies or groups content to enjoy the fruits of progress, while affecting to despise the conditions that promote progress? What belief system do they oppose to it? And then, more specifically: Why is Islam held up in opposition to Western values? The answer, I believe, is that philosophical hysteria. It is not an easy thing to define or understand, and the Muslim spokesmen do not really help. They speak clichés, but that might only be because they perhaps have no way of expressing what they feel. And some have overriding political causes; and others are really religious missionaries rather than scholars.

But years ago, while the Shah still ruled, there appeared in the United States a small novel by a young Iranian woman that in its subdued, unpolitical way foreshadowed the hysteria that was to come. The novel was called *Foreigner*; the author was Nahid Rachlin. Perhaps it was as well that the novel appeared while the Shah ruled, and had to avoid politics; it is just possible that the delicate feeling of this novel might have been made trivial or ordinary if it had run into political protest.

The central figure of the book is a young Iranian woman who does research work in Boston as a biologist. She is married to an American, and she might seem to be all right, well-adapted. But when she goes back on a holiday to Teheran she loses her balance. She has some trouble with the bureaucracy. She can't get an exit visa; she begins to feel lost. She is disturbed by memories of her crowded, oppressive Iranian childhood, with its prurient sexual intimations; disturbed by what remains of her old family life; disturbed by the overgrown, thuggish city, full of "Western" buildings. And that is interesting, that use of "Western" rather than big: it is as though the strangeness of the outside world has come to Teheran itself.

Disturbed in this way, the young woman reflects on her time in the

United States. It is not the time of clarity, as it might have once appeared. She sees it now to be a time of emptiness. She can't say why she has lived the American life. Sexually and socially—in spite of her apparent success—she has never been in control; and she cannot say, either, why she has been doing the research work she has been doing. All this is very subtly and effectively done; we can see that the young woman was not prepared for the movement between civilizations, the movement out of the shut-in Iranian world; where the faith was the complete way, filled everything, left no spare corner of the mind or will or soul, to the other world where it was necessary to be an individual and responsible; where people developed vocations, and were stirred by ambition and achievement, and believed in perfectibility. Once we understand or have an intimation of that, we see, with the central figure of the novel, what a torment and emptiness that automatic, imitative life in Boston has been for her.

Now, in her distress, she falls ill. She goes to a hospital. The doctor there understands her unhappiness. He too has spent some time in the United States; when he came back, he said, he soothed himself by visiting mosques and shrines for a month. He tells the young woman that her pain comes from an old ulcer. "What you have," he says, in his melancholy, seductive way, "is a Western disease." And the research biologist eventually arrives at a decision. She will give up that Boston-imposed life of the intellect and meaningless work; she will turn her back on the American emptiness; she will stay in Iran and put on the veil. She will do as the doctor did; she will visit shrines and mosques. Having decided that, she becomes happier than she has ever been.

Immensely satisfying, that renunciation. But it is intellectually flawed: it assumes that there will continue to be people striving out there, in the stressed world, making drugs and medical equipment, to keep the Iranian doctor's hospital going.

Again and again, on my Islamic journey in 1979, I found a similar unconscious contradiction in people's attitudes. I remember especially a newspaper editor in Teheran. His paper had been at the heart of the revolution. In the middle of 1979 it was busy, in a state of glory. Seven months later, when I went back to Teheran, it had lost its heart; the once busy main room was empty; all but two of the staff had disappeared. The American embassy had been seized; a financial crisis had followed; many foreign firms had closed down; advertising had dried up; the newspaper editor could hardly see his way ahead; every issue of the paper lost money; waiting for the crisis to end, the editor, it might be said, had become as much a hostage as the diplomats. He also, as I now learned, had two sons of university age. One was studying in the United States; the other had applied for a visa, but then the hostage crisis had occurred. This was news to me—that the United States should have been so important to the sons of one of the spokesmen of the Islamic revolution. I told the editor I was surprised. He said, speaking especially of the son waiting for the visa, "It's his future."

Emotional satisfaction on one hand; thought for the future on the other. The editor was as divided as nearly everyone else. One of Joseph Conrad's earliest stories of the East Indies, from the 1890s, was about a local raja or chieftain, a murderous man, a Muslim (though it is never explicitly said), who in a crisis, having lost his magical counselor, swims out one night to one of the English merchant ships in the harbor to ask the sailors, representatives of the immense power that had come from the other end of the world, for an amulet, a magical charm. The sailors are at a loss but then someone among them gives the raja a British coin, a sixpence commemorating Queen Victoria's jubilee; and the raja is well pleased. Conrad didn't treat the story as a joke; he loaded it with philosophical implications for both sides, and I feel now that he saw truly.

In the one hundred years since that story, the wealth of the world has grown, power has grown, education has spread; the disturbance, the philosophical shriek, has been amplified. The division in the revolutionary editor's spirit, and the renunciation of the fictional biologist, both contain a tribute—unacknowledged, but all the more profound—to the universal civilization. Simple charms alone cannot be acquired from it; other, difficult things come with it as well: ambition, endeavor, individuality.

The universal civilization has been a long time in the making. It wasn't always universal; it wasn't always as attractive as it is today. The expansion of Europe gave it for at least three centuries a racial tint, which still causes pain. In Trinidad I grew up in the last days of that kind of racialism. And that, perhaps, has given me a greater appreciation of the immense changes that have taken place since the end of the war, the extraordinary attempt of this civilization to accommodate the rest of the world, and all the currents of that world's thought.

I come back now to the first questions Myron Magnet put to me earlier this year. Are we only as strong as our beliefs? Is it sufficient merely to hold a world view, an ethical view, intensely? You will understand the anxieties behind the questions. The questions, of course, for all their apparent pessimism, are loaded; they contain their own answers. But they are also genuinely double-edged. For that reason they can also be seen as a reaching out to a far-off and sometimes hostile system of fixed belief; they can be seen as an aspect of the universality of our civilization at this period. Philosophical diffidence meets philosophical hysteria; and the diffident man is, at the end, the more in control.

Because my movement within this civilization has been from the periphery to the center, I may have seen or felt certain things more freshly than people to whom those things were everyday. One such thing was my discovery, as a child, a child worried about pain and cruelty, my discovery of the Christian precept, Do unto others as you would have others do unto you. There was no such human consolation in the Hinduism I grew up with, and—although I have never had any religious faith—the simple idea was, and is, dazzling to me, perfect as a guide to human behavior.

A later realization—I suppose I have sensed it most of my life, but I have understood it philosophically only during the preparation of this talk—has been the beauty of the idea of the pursuit of happiness. Familiar words, easy to take for granted; easy to misconstrue. This idea of the pursuit of happiness is at the heart of the attractiveness of the civilization to so many outside it or on its periphery. I find it marvelous to contemplate to what an extent, after two centuries, and after the terrible history of the earlier part of this century, the idea has come to a kind of fruition. It is an elastic idea; it fits all men. It implies a certain kind of society, a certain kind of awakened spirit. I don't imagine my father's parents would have been able to under-stand the idea. So much is contained in it: the idea of the individual, responsibility, choice, the life of the intellect, the idea of vocation and perfectibility and achievement. It is an immense human idea. It can-not be reduced to a fixed system. It cannot generate fanaticism. But it is known to exist; and because of that, other more rigid systems in the end blow away.

201

STUDY QUESTIONS

1. What precisely does Naipaul mean by a "universal civilization." Do you agree there is one?

2. Some say it is ethnocentric and elitist for members of free societies (England or America, for example) to judge other traditional cultures (Iran or Indonesia, say) by Western standards; others say it is callous to deny that people all over the world have a right to the same freedoms and liberties we enjoy in the West. With whom are you most in agreement?

3. You are V. S. Naipaul and you have just read Ruth Benedict's defense of ethical relativism. Write a short rejoinder to it.

4. Naipaul speaks very favorably of the "universal civilization," and very harshly of the traditional cultures. But is this fair? After all, the so-called universal culture which gives great latitude to the individual has begotten many well-known problems: crime, breakdown of families, drugs, alienation. Traditional cultures may have a poor record on human rights, but they often offer certain compensating goods: stability, safety, community, strong families, spiritual values. Are severe social problems the inevitable price to be paid for tolerance and individual freedom? Discuss.

The United Nations Charter: The Universal Declaration of Human Rights

The Universal Declaration of Human Rights was adopted by the United Nations General Assembly on December 10, 1948. The Declaration was characterized as "a common standard of achievement for all peoples and all nations." The first twenty-one articles of the Declaration of Human Rights are similar to the first ten amendments of the U.S. Constitution, the Bill of Rights. Articles twenty-two through twenty-seven, which assert rights to economic and social benefits, reflect specific articles in the Soviet constitution.

The Declaration was condemned by the American Association of Anthropology as "a statement of rights conceived only in terms of the values prevalent in Western Europe and America." Calling it "ethnocentric," the association suggested that the Declaration betrayed a lack of respect for cultural differences.

The articles of the Universal Declaration of Human Rights declare that all human beings have the right to a dignified and secure existence. They prohibit torture and slavery. They enjoin equality before the law and prohibit arbitrary arrest in any country. They prohibit limitations of movement within national borders.

The Articles assert the right of political asylum; the right to citizenship in some country; the right of adults to marry and have families; the right to one's property; the right to freedom of thought, conscience, and religion; the right to social security; the right to belong to unions; the right to a decent standard of living and access to health; the right to an education. The Articles assert the principle of freedom of assembly—the freedom to take part in the government of one's country.

Finally, the Articles assure that no state may engage in any activity aimed at the restriction of any of the rights and liberties set forth in the declaration.

It should be noted that the members of the United Nations General Assembly, in thus proclaiming universal standards of social ethics for all societies, are not ethical relativists.

Preamble

Whereas recognition of the inherent dignity and of the equal and inalienable rights of all members of the human family is the foundation of freedom, justice and peace in the world,

Whereas disregard and contempt for human rights have resulted in barbarous acts which have outraged the conscience of mankind, and the advent of a world in which human beings shall enjoy freedom of speech and belief and freedom from fear and want has been proclaimed as the highest aspiration of the common people,

Whereas it is essential, if man is not to be compelled to have recourse, as a last resort, to rebellion against tyranny and oppression, that human rights should be protected by the rule of law,

Whereas it is essential to promote the development of friendly relations between nations,

Whereas the people of the United Nations have in the Charter reaffirmed their faith in fundamental human rights, in the dignity and worth of the human person and in the equal rights of men and women and have determined to promote social progress and better standards of life in larger freedom,

Whereas Member States have pledged themselves to achieve, in cooperation with the United Nations, the promotion of universal respect for and observance of human rights and fundamental freedoms,

Whereas a common understanding of these rights and freedoms is of the greatest importance for the full realization of this pledge,

Now, Therefore,

The General Assembly Proclaims

This Universal Declaration of Human Rights as a common standard of achievement for all peoples and all nations, to the end that every individual and every organ of society, keeping this Declaration constantly in mind, shall strive by teaching and education to promote respect for these rights and freedoms and by progressive measures, national and international, to secure their universal and effective recognition and observance, both among the peoples of Member States themselves and among the peoples of territories under their jurisdiction.

Article 1   All human beings are born free and equal in dignity and rights. They are endowed with reason and conscience and should act towards one another in a spirit of brotherhood.

Article 2   Everyone is entitled to all the rights and freedoms set forth in this Declaration, without distinction of any kind, such as race, colour, sex, language, religion, political or other opinion, national or social origin, property, birth or other status.

Furthermore, no distinction shall be made on the basis of the political, jurisdictional or international status of the country or territory to which a person belongs, whether it be independent, trust, non-self-governing or under any other limitation of sovereignty.

Article 3   Everyone has the right to life, liberty and security of person.

Article 4   No one shall be held in slavery or servitude; slavery and the slave trade shall be prohibited in all their forms.

Article 5   No one shall be subjected to torture or to cruel, inhuman or degrading treatment or punishment.

Article 6   Everyone has the right to recognition everywhere as a person before the law.

Article 7   All are equal before the law and are entitled without any discrimination to equal protection of the law. All are entitled to equal protection against any discrimination in violation of this Declaration and against any incitement to such discrimination.

Article 8   Everyone has the right to an effective remedy by the competent national tribunals for acts violating the fundamental rights granted him by the constitution or by law.

Article 9   No one shall be subjected to arbitrary arrest, detention or exile.

Article 10   Everyone is entitled in full equality to a fair and public hearing by an independent and impartial tribunal, in the determination of his rights and obligations and of any criminal charge against him.

Article 11   (1) Everyone charged with a penal offence has the right to be presumed innocent until proved guilty according to law in a public trial at which he has had all the guarantees necessary for his defence.

(2) No one shall be held guilty of any penal offence on account of any act or omission which did not constitute a penal offence, under national or international law, at the time when it was committed. Nor shall a heavier penalty be imposed than the one that was applicable at the time the penal offence was committed.

Article 12   No one shall be subjected to arbitrary interference with his privacy, family, home or correspondence, nor to attacks upon his honour and reputation. Everyone has the right to the protection of the law against such interference or attacks.

Article 13   (1) Everyone has the right to freedom of movement and residence within the borders of each state.

(2) Everyone has the right to leave any country, including his own, and to return to his country.

Article 14   (1) Everyone has the right to seek and to enjoy in other countries asylum from persecution.

(2) This right may not be invoked in the case of prosecutions

genuinely arising from non-political crimes or from acts contrary to the purposes and principles of the United Nations.

Article 15   (1) Everyone has the right to a nationality.

(2) No one shall be arbitrarily deprived of his nationality nor denied the right to change his nationality.

Article 16   (1) Men and women of full age, without any limitation due to race, nationality or religion, have the right to marry and to found a family. They are entitled to equal rights as to marriage, during marriage and at its dissolution.

(2) Marriage shall be entered into only with the free and full consent of the intending spouses.

(3) The family is the natural and fundamental group unity of society and is entitled to protection by society and the State.

Article 17   (1) Everyone has the right to own property alone as well as in association with others.

(2) No one shall be arbitrarily deprived of his property.

Article 18   Everyone has the right to freedom of thought, conscience and religion; this right includes freedom to change his religion or belief, and freedom, either alone or in community with others and in public or private, to manifest his religion or belief in teaching, practice, worship and observance.

Article 19   Everyone has the right to freedom of opinion and expression; this right includes freedom to hold opinions without interference and to seek, receive and impart information and ideas through any media and regardless of frontiers.

Article 20   (1) Everyone has the right to freedom of peaceful assembly and association.

(2) No one may be compelled to belong to an association.

Article 21   (1) Everyone has the right to take part in the government of his country, directly or through freely chosen representatives.

(2) Everyone has the right of equal access to public service in his country.

(3) The will of the people shall be the basis of the authority of government; this will shall be expressed in periodic and genuine

elections which shall be by universal and equal suffrage and shall be held by secret vote or by equivalent free voting procedures.

Article 22 Everyone, as a member of society, has the right to social security and is entitled to realization, through national effort and international co-operation and in accordance with the organization and resources of each State, of the economic, social and cultural rights indispensable for his dignity and the free development of his personality.

Article 23 (1) Everyone has the right to work, to free choice of employment, to just and favourable conditions of work and to protection against unemployment.

(2) Everyone, without any discrimination, has the right to equal pay for equal work.

(3) Everyone who works has the right to just and favourable remuneration ensuring for himself and his family an existence worthy of human dignity, and supplemented, if necessary, by other means of social protection.

(4) Everyone has the right to form and to join trade unions for the protection of his interests.

Article 24 Everyone has the right to rest and leisure, including reasonable limitation of working hours and periodic holidays with pay.

Article 25 (1) Everyone has the right to a standard of living adequate for the health and well-being of himself and of his family, including food, clothing, housing and medical care and necessary social services, and the right to security in the event of unemployment, sickness, disability, widowhood, old age or other lack of livelihood in circumstances beyond his control.

(2) Motherhood and childhood are entitled to special care and assistance. All children, whether born in or out of wedlock, shall enjoy the same social protection.

Article 26 (1) Everyone has the right to education. Education shall be free, at least in the elementary and fundamental stages. Elementary education shall be compulsory. Technical and professional education shall be made generally available and higher education shall be equally accessible to all on the basis of merit.

(2) Education shall be directed to the full development of the

human personality and to the strengthening of respect for human rights and fundamental freedoms. It shall promote understanding, tolerance and friendship among all nations, racial or religious groups, and shall further the activities of the United Nations for the maintenance of peace.

(3) Parents have a prior right to choose the kind of education that shall be given to their children.

Article 27   (1) Everyone has the right freely to participate in the cultural life of the community, to enjoy the arts and to share in scientific advancement and its benefits.

(2) Everyone has the right to the protection of the moral and material interests resulting from any scientific, literary or artistic production of which he is the author.

Article 28   Everyone is entitled to a social and international order in which the rights and freedoms set forth in this Declaration can be fully realized.

Article 29   (1) Everyone has duties to the community in which alone the free and full development of his personality is possible.

(2) In the exercise of his rights and freedoms, everyone shall be subject only to such limitations as are determined by law solely for the purpose of securing due recognition and respect for the rights and freedoms of others and of meeting the just requirements of morality, public order and the general welfare in a democratic society.

(3) These rights and freedoms may in no case be exercised contrary to the purposes and principles of the United Nations.

Article 30   Nothing in this Declaration may be interpreted as implying for any State, group or person any right to engage in any activity or to perform any act aimed at the destruction of any of the rights and freedoms set forth herein.

STUDY QUESTIONS

1. The Declaration contains thirty articles. Discuss three that you consider very important and defend their fundamental character.
2. Obviously the Declaration has not been enforced. What then is its value, if any? Discuss.

3. Do you agree that all human beings throughout the world have the rights and liberties outlined in the articles? How would you argue in their defense if someone challenged some or all of the articles?

4. The first twenty-one articles assert *negative* rights of freedom from governmental interference. Later articles (21–28) assert positive rights that require a government to ensure such basic benefits as work, housing, and medical care. Many conservatives object to the inclusion of positive rights as endorsing socialism. On the other hand, many socialists maintain that exclusive rights of liberty merely give everyone the right to starve. Critically discuss this issue.

5. The American Anthropological Association objected to the Universal Declaration of Human Rights being "ethnocentric." Critically discuss. Do you agree with the Association that the lack of moral consensus in the world "validates" ethical relativism?

SUGGESTED READINGS

Baier, Kurt. *The Moral Point of View*. Ithaca, NY: Cornell University Press, 1958.

Benedict, Ruth. *Patterns of Culture*. Boston: Houghton Mifflin Company, 1934.

Blum, Lawrence C. *Friendship, Altruism and Morality*. Boston: Routledge and Kegan Paul, 1980.

Bonevac, Daniel; Boon, William; and Phillips, Stephen, Eds. *Beyond the Western Tradition: Readings in Moral and Political Philosophy*. Mountain View, CA: Mayfield Press, 1992.

Butler, Joseph. *Fifteen Sermons Upon Human Nature*. 1726.

Frankena, William. *Ethics*. Englewood Cliffs, NJ: Prentice-Hall, 1973.

Gert, Bernard. *The Moral Rules: A New Rational Foundation for Morality*. New York: Harper and Row, 1970.

Harman, Gilbert. *The Nature of Morality: An Introduction to Ethics*. New York: Oxford University Press, 1977.

Hospers, John. *Human Conduct*. New York: Harcourt, Brace and World, 1961.

Kittay, Eva Feder, and Diana T. Meyers, eds. *Women and Moral Theory*. Totowa, NJ: Littlefield, Adams and Company, 1987.

Ladd, John, ed. *Ethical Relativism*. Belmont, CA: Wadsworth Books, 1973.

Mackie, J. L. *Ethics: Inventing Right and Wrong*. New York: Penguin Books, 1977.

Margolis, Joseph. *The Truth about Relativism*. Cambridge, MA: Blackwell, 1991.

Midgley, Mary. *Heart and Mind*. New York: St. Martin's Press, 1981.

Singer, Marcus. *Generalization in Ethics*. New York: Alfred A. Knopf, 1961.

Smart, J. J. C., and Bernard Williams. *Utilitarianism: For and Against*. Cambridge: Cambridge University Press, 1973.

Sumner, W. G. *Folkways*. Boston: Ginn Press, 1907.

Warnock, G. J. *The Object of Morality*. London: Methuen and Company, 1971.

Williams, Bernard. *Ethics and the Limits of Philosophy*. Cambridge: Harvard University Press, 1985.

Wong, David. *Moral Relativity*. Los Angeles: University of California Press, 1984.

Chapter Three

VIRTUE

Several acorns fall from a tree. One is eaten by a squirrel. Another decays on the ground. A third grows into an oak tree. We say that the third acorn's fate is appropriate to it, that it succeeds where the other two fail. In our view, the acorn's goal or purpose is to become an oak tree, as if its self-fulfillment depends on achieving this goal. Yet we are aware that to speak of a goal here is grossly anthropomorphic. The acorn is not a conscious being trying to achieve the happy outcome of development. Nor do we feel that this happy outcome is really more natural than the outcome of rotting or being eaten. Indeed, since only a tiny minority of acorns become oak trees, the unhappy outcomes are more natural than the happy one.

All the same, our intuition that becoming an oak tree is the appropriate career for an acorn is sound. Any organic matter, a leaf, for example, can rot on the ground; any nut can serve as squirrel fodder. But only the acorn can grow into an oak tree. The Greeks defined the function or natural purpose of a thing as an activity that is specific to it—an activity that it alone performs or one that it performs better than anything else can. In this sense we think that the third acorn's career is the "happy" or proper one. The metaphor of a happy outcome for the acorn leans heavily on the Greek meaning of happiness (*eudaimonia*) as well-functioning, self-fulfilling activity.

212

A biologist could tell us quite a bit about the special characteristics that enable the acorn to perform its function. The Greeks called such characteristics "excellences" or "virtues." In the broad sense a virtue is any trait or capacity that enables an object to perform its appropriate function. More commonly, "virtue" refers to a special kind of excellence that only human beings possess or lack. In this narrow sense the virtues are *moral* excellences that contribute to a life of human fulfillment. And in this sense we speak of the virtues in contrast to vices. A question now arises: What goal is appropriate for human beings? There are in fact rival conceptions of human fulfillment; some of them are represented by the selections in this chapter.

The Greeks confronted this question with their characteristic simplicity and boldness. Human beings, says Aristotle, are rational animals. They are also social animals. They naturally fulfill themselves in functioning as rational and social beings. Given such conceptions of human purpose, such virtues as temperance, magnanimity, and courage come to the fore as traits that allow people to lead graceful lives in a political community.

Saint Augustine conceives of the life appropriate to a human being rather differently. Human beings are rational and social beings, but that they are creatures of God is even more important: Human purpose and happiness are found in following God. While the Greeks—with their secular conception of the good life—primarily emphasize such "cardinal virtues" as wisdom, courage, and temperance. Augustine—with his Christian conception of the good life—gives priority to such other virtues as charity, humility, and faith. The modern philosopher is less ready to state a conception of the good life for all human beings at all times. Alasdair MacIntyre's conception of human fulfillment is historical. He argues that social context and tradition are always crucial in defining moral obligations: "There is no way to possess the virtues except as part of a tradition in which we inherit them. . . ."

Several articles presented in Chapter Three give a good idea of the sort of investigation into particular virtues the contemporary philosopher pursues. In his article on generosity, James D. Wallace distinguishes economic generosity from generous-mindedness. Wallace formulates characteristics of generosity, one of which is that the generous person gives more than duty requires. Here we touch on an important difference between a morality of duty and a morality of virtue. Godlovitch's topic is wisdom, which he finds less well understood than other virtues, despite its status as a cardinal virtue. Taylor flouts the tradition that pride is a vice. Distinguishing pride from conceit, Taylor argues it is a virtuous trait, necessary for self-respect and a sense of moral worth.

Most modern philosophers believe that no one universally acceptable conception of human fulfillment exists, and largely have dropped the effort to formulate one. They do not do so because they generally disagree with Aristotle's conception of humans as rational and social beings. That conception is, after all, a truism. But philosophers by now recognize it as a very general truism from which they cannot deduce an interesting set of particular virtues. In fact, some argue that Aristotle himself does not proceed in a teleological way when he specifies the particular virtues. In any case, most current philosophers of virtue proceed without conceiving of human happiness as neatly tied to certain moral traits that contribute to the good life. Reading Philippa Foot or Robert C. Roberts, we see a careful attempt to clarify the virtues by isolating the features that distinguish them from other excellences. They do not justify the virtues by some teleological deduction, although in a general way we are brought to recognize that the virtues are beneficial to their possessor. The contemporary philosopher's hardest work comes in understanding the virtues not through the contribution they make to human happiness, but as qualities, in themselves, of a good and decent person. In effect, the virtues themselves define the good life.

The Moral Virtues

ARISTOTLE

TRANSLATED BY J. A. K. THOMSON

Aristotle (384–322 B.C.) is one of the greatest philosophers of all time. He was the son of a Macedonian physician, the personal tutor of Alexander the Great, and a
student of Plato. He wrote on a wide range of subjects,
including logic (which he founded as a science), metaphysics, biology, ethics, politics, and literature. During
the Middle Ages, the authority of his teachings in all
matters of secular philosophy was undisputed. It would
be difficult to exaggerate his influence on the development of Western culture.

Aristotle defines happiness as functioning well. The function of a thing is its special kind of activity, what it can
do better than anything else. Thus, the function of human beings is the exercise of their capacity to reason. A
capacity that enables a thing or a being to function well is
a virtue. Aristotle defines happiness (well-functioning) as
an activity in accordance with virtue. Reason plays a part
in all of the specified human virtues. Courageous persons, for example, use reason to control fear; temperate
persons use it to control their appetites. Properly employed, reason directs us to a course of moderation between extremes (for example, between the excesses of fear
and folly, or gluttony and abstemiousness). Aristotle gives
some general rules for pursuing the course of virtuous

THE MORAL VIRTUES From *The Ethics of Aristotle*. Translated by J. A. K. Thomson. Reprinted with
permission of George Allen & Unwin (Publishers) Ltd.

moderation: (i) avoid the extreme that more strongly opposes the virtue, (ii) guard against excessive hedonism, and (iii) attend to your characteristic faults. These are not hard and fast rules, but rough and ready guides.

Aristotle worked out in detail the means, excesses, and deficiencies for all the moral virtues that he recognized. W. T. Jones, a historian of philosophy, conveniently summarizes Aristotle's views in the following table:

Activity	Vice (excess)	Virtue (mean)	Vice (deficit)
Facing death	Too much fear (i.e., cowardice)	Right amount of fear (i.e., courage)	Too little fear (i.e., foolhardiness)
Bodily actions (eating, drinking, sex, etc.)	Profligacy	Temperance	No name for this state, but it may be called "insensitivity"
Giving money	Prodigality	Liberality	Illiberality
Large-scale giving	Vulgarity	Magnificence	Meanness
Claiming honors	Vanity	Pride	Humility
Social intercourse	Obsequiousness	Friendliness	Sulkiness
According honors	Injustice	Justice	Injustice
Retribution for wrongdoing	Injustice	Justice	Injustice

Source: W. T. Jones, *The Classical Mind* (New York: Harcourt, Brace, & World, 1952, 1969), p. 268.

No doubt people will say, "To call happiness the highest good is a truism. We want a more distinct account of what it is." We might arrive at this if we could grasp what is meant by the "function" of a human being. If we take a flautist or a sculptor or any craftsman—in fact any class of men at all who have some special job or profession—we find that his special talent and excellence comes out in that job, and this is his function. The same thing will be true of man simply as man—that is of course if "man" does have a function. But is it likely that joiners and shoemakers have certain functions or specialized activities, while man as such has none but has been left by Nature a functionless being? Seeing that eye and hand and foot and every one of our members has some obvious function, must we not believe that in like manner a human being has a function over and above these particular functions? Then what exactly is it? The mere act of living is not peculiar to man—we find it even in the vegetable kingdom—and what we are looking for is something peculiar to him. We must therefore exclude from our definition the life that manifests itself in mere nurture and growth. A step higher should come the life that is confined to experiencing sensations. But that we see is shared by horses, cows, and the brute creation as a whole. We are left, then, with a life concerning which we can make two statements. First, it belongs to the rational part of man. Secondly, it finds expression in actions. The rational part may be either active or passive: passive in so far as it follows the dictates of reason, active in so far as it possesses and exercises the power of reasoning. A similar distinction can be drawn within the rational life; that is to say, the reasonable element in it may be active or passive. Let us take it that what we are concerned with here is the reasoning power in action, for it will be generally allowed that when we speak of "reasoning" we really mean *exercising* our reasoning faculties. (This seems the more correct use of the word.) Now let us assume for the moment the truth of the following propositions. (a) The function of a man is the exercise of his non-corporeal faculties or "soul" in accordance with, or at least not divorced from, a rational principle. (b) The function of an individual and of a *good* individual in the same class— a harp player, for example, and a good harp player, and so through the classes—is generically the same, except that we must add superiority in accomplishment to the function, the function of the harp player being merely to play on the harp, while the function of the good harp player is to play on it well. (c) The function of man is a certain form of life, namely an activity of the soul exercised in combination with a rational principle or reasonable ground of action. (d) The function of a good man is to exert such activity well. (e) A function is performed well when performed in accordance with the excellence proper to it.—If these assumptions are granted, we conclude that the good for man is "an activity of soul in accordance with goodness" or (on the supposition that there may be more than one form of goodness) "in accordance with the best and most complete form of goodness."

. . . Let us begin, then, with this proposition. Excellence of whatever kind affects that of which it is the excellence in two ways. (1) It produces a good state in it. (2) It enables it to perform its function well. Take eyesight. The goodness of your eye is not only that which makes your eye good, it is also that which makes it function well. Or take the case of a horse. The goodness of a horse makes him a good horse, but it also makes him good at running, carrying a rider, and facing the enemy. Our proposition, then, seems to be true, and it enables us to say that virtue in a man will be the disposition which (a) makes him a good man, (b) enables him to perform his function well. We have already touched on this point, but more light will be thrown upon it if we consider what is the specific nature of virtue.

Every form, then, of applied knowledge, when it performs its function well, looks to the mean and works to the standard set by that. It is because people feel this that they apply the *cliché*, "You couldn't add anything to it or take anything from it" to an artistic masterpiece, the implication being that too much and too little alike destroy perfection, while the mean preserves it. Now if this be so, and if it be true, as we say, that good craftsmen work to the standard of the mean, then, since goodness like Nature is more exact and of a higher character than any art, it follows that goodness is the quality that hits the mean. By "goodness" I mean goodness of moral character, since it is moral goodness that deals with feelings and actions, and it is in them that we find excess, deficiency, and a mean. It is possible, for example, to experience fear, boldness, desire, anger, pity, and pleasures and pains generally, too much or too little or to the right amount. If we feel them too much or too little, we are wrong. But to have these feelings at the right times on the right occasions towards the right people for the right motive and in the right way is to have them in the right measure, that is, somewhere between the extremes; and this is what characterizes goodness. The same may be said of the mean and extremes in actions. Now it is in the field of actions and feelings that goodness operates; in them we find excess, deficiency, and, between them, the mean, the first two being wrong, the mean right and praised as such. Goodness, then, is a mean condition in the sense that it aims at and hits the mean.

Consider, too, that it is possible to go wrong in more ways than one. (In Pythagorean terminology evil is a form of the Unlimited, good of the Limited.) But there is only one way of being right. That is why going wrong is easy, and going right is difficult; it is easy to miss the bull's-eye and difficult to hit it. Here, then, is another explanation of why the too much and the too little are connected with evil and the mean with good. As the poet says,

Goodness is one, evil is multiform.

We may now define virtue as a disposition of the soul in which, when it has to choose among actions and feelings, it observes the mean relative to us, this being determined by such a rule or principle as would take shape in the mind of a man of sense or practical wisdom. We call it a mean condition as lying between two forms of badness, one being excess and the other deficiency; and also for this reason, that, whereas badness either falls short of or exceeds the right measure in feelings and actions, virtue discovers the mean and deliberately chooses it. Thus, looked at from the point of view of its essence as embodied in its definition, virtue no doubt is a mean; judged by the standard of what is right and best, it is an extreme.

Aristotle enters a caution. Though we have said that virtue observes the mean in actions and passions, we do not say this of all acts and all feelings. Some are essentially evil and, when these are involved, our rule of applying the mean cannot be brought into operation.[1]

But choice of a mean is not possible in every action or every feeling. The very names of some have an immediate connotation of evil. Such are malice, shamelessness, envy among feelings, and among actions adultery, theft, murder. All these and more like them have a bad name as being evil in themselves; it is not merely the excess or deficiency of them that we censure. In their case, then, it is impossible to act rightly; whatever we do is wrong. Nor do circumstances make any difference in the rightness or wrongness of them. When a man commits adultery there is no point in asking whether it is with the right woman or at the right time or in the right way, for to do anything like that is simply wrong. It would amount to claiming that there is a mean and excess and defect in unjust or cowardly or intemperate actions. If such a thing were possible, we should find ourselves with a mean quantity of excess, a mean of deficiency, an excess of excess and a deficiency of deficiency. But just as in temperance and justice there can be no mean or excess or deficiency, because the mean

---

[1] The italicized interpolations in this selection are the translator's.

in a sense *is* an extreme, so there can be no mean or excess or deficiency in those vicious actions—however done, they are wrong. Putting the matter into general language, we may say that there is no
mean in the extremes, and no extreme in the mean, to be observed
by anybody.

*After the definition comes its application to the particular virtues. In these
it is always possible to discover a mean—at which the virtue aims—between
an excess and a deficiency. Here Aristotle found that a table or diagram of
the virtues between their corresponding vices would be useful, and we are to
imagine him referring to this in the course of his lectures.*

But a generalization of this kind is not enough; we must show that
our definition fits particular cases. When we are discussing actions
particular statements come nearer the heart of the matter, though
general statements cover a wider field. The reason is that human
behaviour consists in the performance of particular acts, and our
theories must be brought into harmony with them.

You see here a diagram of the virtues. Let us take our particular
instances from that. In the section confined to the feelings inspired
by danger you will observe that the mean state is "courage." Of
those who go to extremes in one direction or the other the man who
shows an excess of fearlessness has no name to describe him, the man
who exceeds in confidence or daring is called "rash" or "foolhardy,"
the man who shows an excess of fear and a deficiency of confidence
is called a "coward." In the pleasures and pains—though not all
pleasures and pains, especially pains—the virtue which observes the
mean is "temperance," the excess is the vice of "intemperance." Persons defective in the power to enjoy pleasures are a somewhat rare
class, and so have not had a name assigned to them: suppose we call
them "unimpressionable." Coming to the giving and acquiring of
money, we find that the mean is "liberality," the excess "prodigality,"
the deficiency "meanness." But here we meet a complication. The
prodigal man and the mean man exceed and fall short in opposite
ways. The prodigal exceeds in giving and falls short in getting
money, whereas the mean man exceeds in getting and falls short in
giving it away. Of course this is but a summary account of the
matter—a bare outline. But it meets our immediate requirements.
Later on these types of character will be more accurately delineated.

But there are other dispositions which declare themselves in the way they deal with money. One is "lordliness" or "magnificence," which differs from liberality in that the lordly man deals in large sums, the liberal man is small. Magnificence is the mean state here, the excess is "bad taste" or "vulgarity," the defect is "shabbiness." These are not the same as the excess and defect on either side of liberality. How they differ is a point which will be discussed later. In the matter of honour the mean is "proper pride," the excess "vanity," the defect "poor-spiritedness." And just as liberality differs, as I said, from magnificence in being concerned with small sums of money, so there is a state related to proper pride in the same way, being concerned with small honours, while pride is concerned with great. For it is possible to aspire to small honours in the right way, or to a greater or less extent than is right. The man who has this aspiration to excess is called "ambitious;" if he does not cherish it enough, he is "unambitious;" but the man who has it to the right extent—that is, strikes the mean—has no special designation. This is true also of corresponding dispositions with one exception, that of the ambitious man, which is called "ambitiousness." This will explain why each of the extreme characters stakes out a claim in the middle region. Indeed we ourselves call the character between the extremes sometimes "ambitious" and sometimes "unambitious." That is proved by our sometimes praising a man for being ambitious and sometimes for being unambitious. The reason will appear later. In the meantime let us continue our discussion of the remaining virtues and vices, following the method already laid down.

Let us next take anger. Here too we find excess, deficiency, and the mean. Hardly one of the states of mind involved has a special name; but, since we call the man who attains the mean in this sphere "gentle," we may call his disposition "gentleness." Of the extremes the man who is angry over-much may be called "irascible," and his vice "irascibility;" while the man who reacts too feebly to anger may be called "poor-spirited" and his disposition "poor-spiritedness."

. . . As regards veracity, the character who aims at the mean may be called "truthful" and what he aims at "truthfulness." Pretending, when it goes too far, is "boastfulness" and the man who shows it is a "boaster" or "braggart." If it takes the form of understatement, the pretence is called "irony" and the man who shows it "ironical." In agreeableness in social amusement the man who hits the mean is "witty" and what characterizes him is "wittiness." The excess is "buffoonery" and the man who exhibits that is a "buffoon." The opposite of the buffoon is the "boor" and his characteristic is "boor-ishness." In the other sphere of the agreeable—the general business of life—the person who is agreeable in the right way is "friendly" and his disposition "friendliness." The man who makes himself too agreeable, supposing him to have no ulterior object, is "obsequious;" if he has such an object, he is a "flatterer." The man who is deficient in this quality and takes every opportunity of making himself dis-agreeable may be called "peevish" or "sulky" or "surly."

But it is not only in settled dispositions that a mean may be observed in passing states of emotion.

Even when feelings and emotional states are involved one notes that mean conditions exist. And here also, it would be agreed, we may find one man observing the mean and another going beyond it, for instance, the "shamefaced" man, who is put out of countenance by anything. Or a man may fall short here of the due mean. Thus any one who is deficient in a sense of shame, or has none at all, is called "shameless." The man who avoids both extremes is "modest," and him we praise. For, while modesty is not a form of goodness, it is praised; it and the modest man. Then there is "righteous indigna-tion." This is felt by any one who strikes the mean between "envy" and "malice," by which last word I mean a pleased feeling at the misfortunes of other people. These are emotions concerned with the pains and pleasures we feel at the fortunes of our neighbours. The man who feels righteous indignation is pained by undeserved good fortune; but the envious man goes beyond that and is pained at any-body's success. The malicious man, on the other hand, is so far from being pained by the misfortunes of another that he is actually tickled by them.

However, a fitting opportunity of discussing these matters will present itself in another place. And after that we shall treat of justice. In that connexion we shall have to distinguish between the various kinds of justice—for the word is used in more senses than one—and show in what way each of them is a mean.

But after all, proceeds Aristotle, the true determinant of the mean is not the geometer's rod but the guiding principle in the good man's soul. The diagram of the virtues and vices, then, is just an arrangement and, as Aristotle goes on to show, an unimportant one at that.

Thus there are three dispositions, two of them taking a vicious form (one in the direction of excess, the other of defect) and one a good form, namely, the observance of the mean. They are all opposed to one another, though not all in the same way. The extreme states are opposed both to the mean and one another, and the mean is opposed to both extremes. For just as the equal is greater compared with the less, and less compared with the greater, so the mean states (whether in feelings or actions) are in excess if compared with the deficient, and deficient if compared with the excessive, states. Thus a brave man appears rash when set beside a coward, and cowardly when set beside a rash man; a temperate man appears intemperate beside a man of dull sensibilities, and dull if contrasted with an intemperate man. This is the reason why each extreme character tries to push the mean nearer the other. The coward calls the brave man rash, the rash man calls him a coward. And so in the other cases. But, while all the dispositions are opposed to one another in this way, the greatest degree of opposition is that which is found between the two extremes. For they are separated by a greater interval from one another than from the mean, as the great is more widely removed from the small, and the small from the great, than either from the equal. It may be added that sometimes an extreme bears a certain resemblance to a mean. For example, rashness resembles courage, and prodigality resembles liberality. But between the extremes there is always the maximum dissimilarity. Now opposites are by definition things as far removed as possible from one another. Hence the farther apart things are, the more opposite they will be. Sometimes it is the deficiency, in other instances it is the excess, that is more directly opposed to the mean. Thus cowardice, a deficiency, is more opposed to courage than is rashness, an excess. And it is not insensibility, the deficiency, that is more opposed to temperance but intemperance, the excess. This arises from one or other of two causes. One lies in the nature of the thing itself and may be explained as follows. When one extreme is nearer to the mean and resembles it more, it is not that extreme but the other which we tend to oppose to the mean. For instance, since rashness is held to be nearer and liker to courage than is cowardice, it is cowardice which we tend to oppose to courage on the principle that the extremes which are remoter from the mean strike us as more opposite to it. The other cause lies in ourselves. It is the things to which we are naturally inclined that appear to us more opposed to the mean. For example, we have a natural inclination to pleasure, which makes us prone to fall into intemperance. Accordingly we tend to describe as opposite to the mean those things towards which we have an instinctive inclination. For this reason intemperance, the excess, is more opposed to temperance than is insensibility to pleasure, the deficiency.

I have said enough to show that moral excellence is a mean, and I have shown in what sense it is so. It is, namely, a mean between two forms of badness, one of excess and the other of defect, and is so described because it aims at hitting the mean point in feelings and in actions. This makes virtue hard of achievement, because finding the middle point is never easy. It is not everybody, for instance, who can find the centre of a circle—that calls for a geometrician. Thus, too, it is easy to fly into a passion—anybody can do that—but to be angry with the right person and to the right extent and at the right time and with the right object and in the right way—that is not easy, and it is not everyone who can do it. This is equally true of giving or spending money. Hence we infer that to do these things properly is rare, laudable, and fine.

Aristotle now suggests some rules for our guidance.

In view of this we shall find it useful when aiming at the mean to observe these rules. (1) *Keep away from that extreme which is the more opposed to the mean.* It is Calypso's advice:

Swing around the ship clear of this surf and surge.

For one of the extremes is always a more dangerous error than the other; and—since it is hard to hit the bull's-eye—we must take the next best course and choose the least of the evils. And it will be easiest for us to do this if we follow the rule I have suggested. (2) *Note the errors into which we personally are most liable to fall.* (Each of us has his natural bias in one direction or another.) We shall find out what ours are by noting what gives us pleasure and pain. After that we must drag ourselves in the opposite direction. For our best way of reaching the middle is by giving a wide berth to our darling sin. It is the method used by a carpenter when he is straightening a warped board. (3) *Always be particularly on your guard against pleasure and pleasant things.* When Pleasure is at the bar the jury is not impartial. So it will be best for us if we feel towards her as the Trojan elders felt towards Helen, and regularly apply their words to her. If we are for packing her off, as they were with Helen, we shall be the less likely to go wrong.

To sum up. These are the rules by observation of which we have the best chance of hitting the mean. But of course difficulties spring up, especially when we are confronted with an exceptional case. For example, it is not easy to say precisely what is the right way to be angry and with whom and on what grounds and for how long. In fact, we are inconsistent on this point, sometimes praising people who are deficient in the capacity for anger and calling them "gentle," sometimes praising the choleric and calling them "stout fellows." To be sure we are not hard on a man who goes off the straight path in the direction of too much or too little, if he goes off only a little way. We reserve our censure for the man who swerves widely from the course, because then we are bound to notice it. Yet it is not easy to find a formula by which we may determine how far and up to what point a man may go wrong before he incurs blame. But this difficulty of definition is inherent in every object of perception; such questions of degree are bound up with the circumstances of the individual case, where our only criterion *is* the perception.

So much, then, has become clear. In all our conduct it is the mean state that is to be praised. But one should lean sometimes in the direction of the more, sometimes in that of the less, because that is the readiest way of attaining to goodness and the mean.

STUDY QUESTIONS

1. How, according to Aristotle, does reason determine right action? How does this connect with the general principle that virtuous action is a mean between extremes?
2. In Aristotle's view, what is happiness and how does it relate to virtue?
3. Of two extremes, one is usually worse, being "more opposed to the mean." Aristotle proposes that we take special care to avoid that extreme. Give an example (not found in Aristotle) of a person in a situation that falls under Aristotle's rule. Be concrete in showing how to apply the rule.
4. In the typical situation where we must choose an action guided by Aristotle's principles, do we have several choices, all falling within the range of the mean between two extremes, or does the

principle of the mean uniquely determine a particular course of action? Answer this question, supplying a concrete example of your own.

Of the Morals of the Catholic Church

SAINT AUGUSTINE

Saint Augustine (A.D. 354–420), born in North Africa, is recognized as one of the very greatest Christian philosophers. His best known works are his *Confessions* (A.D. 400) and *The City of God* (A.D. 427).

Augustine defines happiness as the enjoyment of the highest good. The highest good is not something that can be lost by accident or misfortune, for 'hen we cannot enjoy it confidently. Such a good must therefore be of the soul and not the body. Augustine concludes that the chief good is the possession of virtue. The virtuous Christian follows God, avoiding sin and obeying His will.

Happiness is in the enjoyment of man's chief good. Two conditions of the chief good: 1st, Nothing is better than it; 2nd, it cannot be lost against the will.

How then, according to reason, ought man to live? We all certainly desire to live happily; and there is no human being but assents to this statement almost before it is made. But the title happy cannot, in my

OF THE MORALS OF THE CATHOLIC CHURCH From *The Works of Aurelius Augustine.* Edited by M. Dods (T. & T. Clark, Edinburgh, 1892). Reprinted with permission from T. & T. Clark Ltd., Edinburgh, Scotland.

opinion, belong either to him who has not what he loves, whatever it may be, or to him who has what he loves if it is hurtful, or to him who does not love what he has, although it is good in perfection. For one who seeks what he cannot obtain suffers torture, and one who has got what is not desirable is cheated, and one who does not seek for what is worth seeking for is diseased. Now in all these cases the mind cannot but be unhappy, and happiness and unhappiness cannot reside at the same time in one man; so in none of these cases can the man be happy. I find, then, a fourth case, where the happy life exists,—when that which is man's chief good is both loved and possessed. For what do we call enjoyment but having at hand the object of love? And no one can be happy who does not enjoy what is man's chief good, nor is there any one who enjoys this who is not happy. We must then have at hand our chief good, if we think of living happily.

We must now inquire what is man's chief good, which of course cannot be anything inferior to man himself. For whoever follows after what is inferior to himself, becomes himself inferior. But every man is bound to follow what is best. Wherefore man's chief good is not inferior to man. Is it then something similar to man himself? It must be so, if there is nothing above man which he is capable of enjoying. But if we find something which is both superior to man, and can be possessed by the man who loves it, who can doubt that in seeking for happiness man should endeavour to reach that which is more excellent than the being who makes the endeavour? For if happiness consists in the enjoyment of a good than which there is nothing better, which we call the chief good, how can a man be properly called happy who has not yet attained to his chief good? or how can that be the chief good beyond which something better remains for us to arrive at? Such, then, being the chief good, it must be something which cannot be lost against the will. For no one can feel confident regarding a good which he knows can be taken from him, although he wishes to keep and cherish it. But if a man feels no confidence regarding the good which he enjoys, how can he be happy while in such fear of losing it?

Man—what?

Let us then see what is better than man. This must necessarily be hard to find, unless we first ask and examine what man is. I am not now called upon to give a definition of man. The question here seems to me to be,—since almost all agree, or at least, which is enough, those I have now to do with are of the same opinion with me, that we are made up of soul and body,—What is man? Is he both of these? or is he the body only, or the soul only? For although the things are two, soul and body, and although neither without the other could be called man (for the body would not be man without the soul, nor again would the soul be man if there were not a body animated by it), still it is possible that one of these may be held to be man, and may be called so. What then do we call man? Is he soul and body, as in a double harness, or like a centaur? Or do we mean the body only, as being in the service of the soul which rules it, as the word lamp denotes not the light and the case together, but only the case, though on account of the light? Or do we mean only mind, and that on account of the body which it rules, as horseman means not the man and the horse, but the man only, and that as employed in ruling the horse? This dispute is not easy to settle; or, if the proof is plain, the statement requires time. This is an expenditure of time and strength which we need not incur. For whether the name man belongs to both, or only to the soul, the chief good of man is not the chief good of the body; but what is the chief good either of both soul and body, or of the soul only, that is man's chief good.

Man's chief good is not the chief good of the body only, but the chief good of the soul.

Now if we ask what is the chief good of the body, reason obliges us to admit that it is that by means of which the body comes to be in its best state. But of all the things which invigorate the body, there is nothing better or greater than the soul. The chief good of the body, then, is not bodily pleasure, not absence of pain, not strength, not beauty, not swiftness, or whatever else is usually reckoned among the goods of the body, but simply the soul. For all the things mentioned the soul supplies to the body by its presence, and, what is above them all, life. Hence I conclude that the soul is not the chief good of man, whether we give the name of man to soul and body together, or to the soul alone. For as, according to reason, the chief good of the body is that which is better than the body, and from which the body receives vigour and life, so whether the soul itself is man, or soul and body both, we must discover whether there is anything which goes before the soul itself, in following which the soul comes to the perfection of good of which it is capable in its own kind. If such a thing can be found, all uncertainty must be at an end, and we must pronounce this to be really and truly the chief good of man.

If, again, the body is man, it must be admitted that the soul is the chief good of man. But clearly, when we treat of morals—when we inquire what manner of life must be held in order to obtain happiness—it is not the body to which the precepts are addressed, it is not bodily discipline which we discuss. In short, the observance of good customs belongs to that part of us which inquires and learns, which are the prerogatives of the soul; so, when we speak of attaining to virtue, the question does not regard the body. But if it follows, as it does, that the body which is ruled over by a soul possessed of virtue is ruled both better and more honourably, and is in its greatest perfection in consequence of the perfection of the soul which rightfully governs it, that which gives perfection to the soul will be man's chief good, though we call the body man. For if my coachman, in obedience to me, feeds and drives the horses he has charge of in the most satisfactory manner, himself enjoying the more of my bounty in proportion to his good conduct, can any one deny that the good condition of the horses, as well as that of the coachman, is due to me? So the question seems to me to be not, whether soul and body is man, or the soul only, or body only, but what gives perfection to the soul; for when this is obtained, a man cannot but be either perfect, or at least much better than in the absence of this one thing.

Virtue gives perfection to the soul; the soul obtains virtue by following God; following God is the happy life.

No one will question that virtue gives perfection to the soul. But it is a very proper subject of inquiry whether this virtue can exist by itself or only in the soul. Here again arises a profound discussion, needing lengthy treatment; but perhaps my summary will serve the purpose. God will, I trust, assist me, so that, notwithstanding our feebleness, we may give instruction on these great matters briefly as well as intelligibly. In either case, whether virtue can exist by itself without the soul, or can exist only in the soul, undoubtedly in the pursuit of virtue the soul follows after something, and this must be either the soul itself, or virtue, or something else. But if the soul follows after itself in the pursuit of virtue, it follows after a foolish thing; for before obtaining virtue it is foolish. Now the height of a follower's desire is to reach that which he follows after. So the soul must either not wish to reach what it follows after, which is utterly absurd and unreasonable, or, in following after itself while foolish, it reaches the folly which it flees from. But if it follows after virtue in the desire to reach it, how can it follow what does not exist? or how can it desire to reach what it already possesses? Either, therefore, virtue exists beyond the soul, or if we are not allowed to give the name of virtue except to the habit and disposition of the wise soul, which can exist only in the soul, we must allow that the soul follows after something else in order that virtue may be produced in itself; for neither by following after nothing, nor by following after folly, can the soul, according to my reasoning, attain to wisdom.

This something else, then, by following after which the soul becomes possessed of virtue and wisdom, is either a wise man or God. But we have said already that it must be something that we cannot lose against our will. No one can think it necessary to ask whether a wise man, supposing we are content to follow after him, can be taken from us in spite of our unwillingness or our persistence. God then remains, in following after whom we live well, and in reaching whom we live both well and happily.

STUDY QUESTIONS

1. What does Augustine mean by happiness? How does this conception of happiness differ from others with which you are acquainted?
2. What does Augustine mean by "following God"? How does he argue that happiness consists in following God?
3. What does the idea of virtue as primarily theological imply for morality in general?

Virtue or Duty?

BERNARD MAYO

Bernard Mayo (b. 1920) is an English philosopher. He is the author of *Ethics and the Moral Life* (1958) and *The Philosophy of Right and Wrong* (1986).

Mayo points out that the classical philosophers did not lay down principles of moral behavior but concentrated instead on the character of the moral person. He claims that classical moral theory is superior to a modern (Kantian) ethics of duty. "The basic moral question, for Aristotle, is not, What shall I do? but, What shall I be?" The morality of "doing" is logically simple: We determine what we ought to do by seeing whether it maximizes happiness (utilitarianism) or is universalizable (Kantianism). The morality of "being" has another kind of simplicity, which Mayo calls the unity of character. Persons of character, heroes or saints, do not merely give us principles to follow; more importantly, they provide an example for us to follow. An ethics of character is more flexible than an ethics of rules. We can find more than one good way to follow a good personal example.

The philosophy of moral principles, which is characteristic of Kant and the post-Kantian era, is something of which hardly a trace exists in Plato. . . . Plato says nothing about rules or principles or laws, except when he is talking politics. Instead he talks about virtues and vices, and about certain types of human character. The key word in

VIRTUE OR DUTY? From *Ethics and the Moral Life* by Bernard Mayo. Reprinted by permission of Macmillan Accounts and Administration Ltd., London and Basingstoke.

Platonic ethics is Virtue; the key word in Kantian ethics is Duty. And modern ethics is a set of footnotes, not to Plato, but to Kant. . . .

Attention to the novelists can be a welcome correction to a tendency of philosophical ethics of the last generation or two to lose contact with the ordinary life of man which is just what the novelists, in their own way, are concerned with. Of course there are writers who can be called in to illustrate problems about Duty (Graham Greene is a good example). But there are more who perhaps never mention the words duty, obligation or principle. Yet they are all concerned—Jane Austen, for instance, entirely and absolutely—with the moral qualities or defects of their heroes and heroines and other characters. This points to a radical one-sidedness in the philosophers' account of morality in terms of principles: it takes little or no account of qualities, of what people *are*. It is just here that the old-fashioned word Virtue used to have a place; and it is just here that the work of Plato and Aristotle can be instructive. Justice, for Plato, though it is closely connected with acting according to law, does not *mean* acting according to law: it is a quality of character, and a just action is one such as a just man would do. Telling the truth, for Aristotle, is not, as it was for Kant, fulfilling an obligation; again it is a quality of character, or, rather, a whole range of qualities of character, some of which may actually be defects, such as tactlessness, boastfulness, and so on—a point which can be brought out, in terms of principles, only with the greatest complexity and artificiality, but quite simply and naturally in terms of character.

If we wish to enquire about Aristotle's moral views, it is no use looking for a set of principles. Of course we can find *some* principles to which he must have subscribed—for instance, that one ought not to commit adultery. But what we find much more prominently is a set of character-traits, a list of certain types of person—the courageous man, and the niggardly man, the boaster, the lavish spender and so on. The basic moral question, for Aristotle, is not, What shall I do? but, What shall I be?

These contrasts between doing and being, negative and positive, and modern as against Greek morality were noted by John Stuart Mill; I quote from the *Essay on Liberty:*

> Christian morality (so-called) has all the characters of a reaction; it
> is, in great part, a protest against Paganism. Its ideal is negative rather

than positive, passive rather than active; Innocence rather than Nobleness; Abstinence from Evil, rather than energetic Pursuit of the Good; in its precepts (as has been well said) "Thou shalt not" predominates unduly over "Thou shalt . . ." Whatever exists of magnanimity, highmindedness, personal dignity, even the sense of honour, is derived from the purely human, not the religious part of our education, and never could have grown out of a standard of ethics in which the only worth, professedly recognised, is that of obedience.

Of course, there are connections between being and doing. It is obvious that a man cannot just *be;* he can only be what he is by doing what he does; his moral qualities are ascribed to him because of his actions, which are said to manifest those qualities. But the point is that an ethics of Being must include this obvious fact, that Being involves Doing; whereas an ethics of Doing, such as I have been examining, may easily overlook it. As I have suggested, a morality of principles is concerned only with what people do or fail to do, since that is what rules are for. And as far as this sort of ethics goes, people might well have no moral qualities at all except the possession of principles and the will (and capacity) to act accordingly.

When we speak of a moral quality such as courage, and say that a certain action was courageous, we are not merely saying something about the action. We are referring, not so much to what is done, as to the kind of person by whom we take it to have been done. We connect, by means of imputed motives and intentions, with the character of the agent as courageous. This explains, incidentally, why both Kantians and Utilitarians encounter, in their different ways, such difficulties in dealing with motives, which their principles, on the face of it, have no room for. A Utilitarian, for example, can only praise a courageous action in some such way as this: the action is of a sort such as a person of courage is likely to perform, and courage is a quality of character the cultivation of which is likely to increase rather than diminish the sum total of human happiness. But Aristotelians have no need of such circumlocution. For them a courageous action just is one which proceeds from and manifests a certain type of character, and is praised because such a character trait is good, or better than others, or is a virtue. An evaluative criterion is sufficient: there is no need to look for an imperative criterion as well, or rather instead, according to which it is not the character which is good, but the cultivation of the character which is right. . . .

No doubt the fundamental moral question is just "What ought I to do?" And according to the philosophy of moral principles, the answer (which must be an imperative "Do this") must be derived from a conjunction of premisses consisting (in the simplest case) firstly of a rule, or universal imperative, enjoining (or forbidding) all actions of a certain type in situations of a certain type, and, secondly, a statement to the effect that this is a situation of that type, falling under that rule. In practice the emphasis may be on supplying only one of these premisses, the other being assumed or taken for granted: one may answer the question "What ought I to do?" either by quoting a rule which I am to adopt, or by showing that my case is legislated for by a rule which I do adopt. To take a previous example of moral perplexity, if I am in doubt whether to tell the truth about his condition to a dying man, my doubt may be resolved by showing that the case comes under a rule about the avoidance of unnecessary suffering, which I am assumed to accept. But if the case is without precedent in my moral career, my problem may be soluble only by adopting a new principle about what I am to do now and in the future about cases of this kind.

This second possibility offers a connection with moral ideas. Suppose my perplexity is not merely an unprecedented situation which I could cope with by adopting a new rule. Suppose the new rule is thoroughly inconsistent with my existing moral code. This may happen, for instance, if the moral code is one to which I only pay lip-service; if . . . its authority is not yet internalised, or if it has ceased to be so; it is ready for rejection, but its final rejection awaits a moral crisis such as we are assuming to occur. What I now need is not a rule for deciding how to act in this situation and others of its kind. I need a whole set of rules, a complete morality, new principles to live by.

Now according to the philosophy of moral character, there is another way of answering the fundamental question "What ought I to do?" Instead of quoting a rule, we quote a quality of character, a virtue: we say "Be brave," or "Be patient" or "Be lenient." We may even say "Be a man": if I am in doubt, say, whether to take a risk, and someone says "Be a man," meaning a morally sound man, in this case a man of sufficient courage. (Compare the very different ideal invoked in "Be a gentleman." I shall not discuss whether this is a *moral* ideal.) Here, too, we have the extreme cases, where a man's moral perplexity extends not merely to a particular situation but to his whole way of living. And now the question "What ought I to do?" turns into the question "What ought I to be?"—as, indeed, it was treated in the first place. ("Be brave.") It is answered, not by quoting a rule or a set of rules, but by describing a quality of character or a type of person. And here the ethics of character gains a practical simplicity which offsets the greater logical simplicity of the ethics of principles. We do not have to give a list of characteristics or virtues, as we might list a set of principles. We can give a unity to our answer.

Of course we can in theory give a unity to our principles: this is implied by speaking of a *set* of principles. But if such a set is to be a system and not merely aggregate, the unity we are looking for is a logical one, namely the possibility that some principles are deductible from others, and ultimately from one. But the attempt to construct a deductive moral system is notoriously difficult, and in any case ill-founded. Why should we expect that all rules of conduct should be ultimately reducible to a few?

Saints and Heroes

But when we are asked "What shall I be?" we can readily give a unity to our answer, though not a logical unity. It is the unity of character. A person's character is not merely a list of dispositions; it has the organic unity of something that is more than the sum of its parts. And we can say, in answer to our morally perplexed questioner, not only "Be this" and "Be that," but also "Be like So-and-So"—where So-and-So is either an ideal type of character, or else an actual person taken as representative of the ideal, an exemplar. Examples of the first are Plato's "just man" in the Republic; Aristotle's man of practical wisdom, in the Nicomachean Ethics; Augustine's citizen of the City of God; the good Communist; the American way of life (which is a collective expression for a type of character). Examples of the second kind, the exemplar, are Socrates, Christ, Buddha, St. Francis, the heroes of epic writers and of novelists. Indeed the idea of the Hero, as well as the idea of the Saint, are very much the expression of this attitude to morality. Heroes and saints are not merely people who did things. They are people whom we are expected, and expect ourselves, to imitate. And imitating them means not merely doing what they did; it means being like them. Their status is not in the least like that of legislators whose laws we admire; for the character of a legislator is irrelevant to our judgment about his legislation. The

235

heroes and saints did not merely give us principles to live by (though some of them did that as well): they gave us examples to follow.

Kant, as we should expect, emphatically rejects this attitude as "fatal to morality." According to him, examples serve only to render *visible* an instance of the moral principle, and thereby to demonstrate its practical feasibility. But every exemplar, such as Christ himself, must be judged by the independent criterion of the moral law, before we are entitled to recognize him as worthy of imitation. I am not suggesting that the subordination of exemplars to principles is incorrect, but that it is one-sided and fails to do justice to a large area of moral experience.

Imitation can be more or less successful. And this suggests another defect of the ethics of principles. It has no room for ideals, except the ideal of a perfect set of principles (which, as a matter of fact, is intelligible only in terms of an ideal character or way of life), and the ideal of perfect conscientiousness (which is itself a character-trait). This results, of course, from the "black-or-white" nature of moral verdicts based on rules. There are no degrees by which we approach or recede from the attainment of a certain quality or virtue; if there were not, the word "ideal" would have no meaning. Heroes and saints are not people whom we try to be *just* like, since we know that is impossible. It is precisely because it is impossible for ordinary human beings to achieve the same qualities as the saints, and in the same degree, that we do set them apart from the rest of humanity. It is enough if we try to be a little like them. . . .

STUDY QUESTIONS

1. Morality, says Mayo, involves "being" as well as "doing." What does he mean by "being" and "doing" in this context? What sort of moral theory concentrates on doing? On being?

2. Philosophers of virtue or moral character tell us how to develop ourselves as moral persons. They answer the question "What ought I to do?" by telling us what to be. How does that work?

3. Mayo says that the moral content of literature emphasizes character and virtue more than duty and obligation. Is he right about this? If he is, then is a moral philosophy of duty necessarily inadequate?

Tradition and the Virtues

ALASDAIR MACINTYRE

Alasdair MacIntyre (b. 1929) is professor of philosophy at Vanderbilt University. He has authored many books, including *After Virtue* (1981) and *Whose Justice? Which Rationality?* (1988).

Alasdair MacIntyre's perspective on virtue is historical and "particularist." "[We] all approach our own circumstances as bearers of a particular social identity." Each of us "inhabits a role" in our social environment. (We are citizens of a country; a son, daughter, parent, aunt, and so forth, in a family.) Such roles provide our "moral starting points." What is good for a person also must be good for one who inhabits the particular role. "As such I inherit from the past of my family, my city, my tribe, my nation, a variety of debts, inheritances, rightful expectations and obligations."

Ideally, each human life is a unity. The meaning and ethical worth of any person's act can be understood only as a part of the life story of that person. But a person's history only makes sense in terms of the social and historical contexts that define his or her roles, expectations, and obligations.

Because virtue is best understood in terms of the way one lives one's roles in a narrative the background of which is richly historical and traditional, the *teaching* of virtue is best accomplished through stories. "Man is essentially a story telling animal," and moral education is realized primarily through narrative means. "Deprive children of stories and you leave them unscripted, anxious stutterers in their actions as in their words."

MacIntyre criticizes most modern approaches to ethics for neglecting history and tradition by attending exclusively to principles that apply universally to all individuals regardless of social role. He warns that the insistence on evaluating all acts and projects in terms of abstract universal principles is dangerous. On the other hand, a virtuous respect for particular traditions is conducive to a decent and balanced life. MacIntyre therefore urges that we should recognize and promote a special virtue: "the virtue of having an adequate sense of the traditions to which one belongs or which confront one."

Any contemporary attempt to envisage each human life as a whole, as a unity, whose character provides the virtues with an adequate *telos* encounters two different kinds of obstacle, one social and one philosophical. The social obstacles derive from the way in which modernity partitions each human life into a variety of segments, each with its own norms and modes of behavior. So work is divided from leisure, private life from public, the corporate from the personal. So both childhood and old age have been wrenched away from the rest of human life and made over into distinct realms. And all these separations have been achieved so that it is the distinctiveness of each and not the unity of the life of the individual who passes through those parts in terms of which we are taught to think and to feel.

The philosophical obstacles derive from two distinct tendencies, one chiefly, though not only, domesticated in analytical philosophy and one at home in both sociological theory and in existentialism. The former is the tendency to think atomistically about human action and to analyze complex actions and transactions in terms of simple components. Hence the recurrence in more than one context of the notion of a "basic action." That particular actions derive their character as parts of larger wholes is a point of view alien to our dominant ways of thinking and yet one which it is necessary at least to consider if we are to begin to understand how a life may be more than a sequence of individual actions and episodes.

Equally the unity of a human life becomes invisible to us when a sharp separation is made either between the individual and the roles he or she plays . . . or between the different role . . . enactments of an individual life so that the life comes to appear as nothing but a series of unconnected episodes—a liquidation of the self. . . .

[T]he liquidation of the self into a set of demarcated areas of role-playing allows no scope for the exercise of dispositions which could genuinely be accounted virtues in any sense remotely Aristotelian. For a virtue is not a disposition that makes for success only in some one particular type of situation. What are spoken of as the virtues of a good committee man or of a good administrator or of a gambler or a pool hustler are professional skills professionally deployed in those situations where they can be effective, not virtues. Someone who genuinely possesses a virtue can be expected to manifest it in very different types of situation, many of them situations where the practice of a virtue cannot be expected to be effective in the way that we expect a professional skill to be. Hector exhibited one and the same courage in his parting from Andromache and on the battlefield with Achilles; Eleanor Marx exhibited one and the same compassion in her relationship with her father, in her work with trade unionists and in her entanglement with Aveling. And the unity of a virtue in someone's life is intelligible only as a characteristic of a unitary life, a life that can be conceived and evaluated as a whole. Hence just as in the discussion of the changes in and fragmentation of morality which accompanied the rise of modernity in the earlier parts of this book, each stage in the emergence of the characteristically modern views of the moral judgment was accompanied by a corresponding stage in the emergence of the characteristically modern conceptions of self-hood; so now, in defining the particular pre-modern concept of the virtues with which I have been preoccupied, it has become necessary to say something of the concomitant concept of selfhood, a concept of a self whose unity resides in the unity of a narrative which links birth to life to death as narrative beginning to middle to end.

Such a conception of the self is perhaps less unfamiliar than it may appear at first sight. Just because it has played a key part in the cultures which are historically predecessors of our own, it would not be surprising if it turned out to be still an unacknowledged presence in many of our ways of thinking and acting. Hence it is not inappropriate to begin by scrutinizing some of our most taken-for-granted, but clearly correct conceptual insights about human actions and selfhood in order to show how natural it is to think of the self in a narrative mode.

It is a conceptual commonplace, both for philosophers and for ordinary agents, that one and the same segment of human behavior may be correctly characterized in a number of different ways. To the question "What is he doing?" the answers may with equal truth and appropriateness be "Digging," "Gardening," "Taking exercise," "Preparing for winter" or "Pleasing his wife." Some of these answers will characterize the agent's intentions, other unintended consequences of his actions, and of these unintended consequences some may be such that the agent is aware of them and others not. What is important to notice immediately is that any answer to the questions of how we are to understand or to explain a given segment of behavior will presuppose some prior answer to the question of how these different correct answers to the question "What is he doing?" are related to each other. For if someone's primary intention is to put the garden in order before the winter and it is only incidentally the case that in so doing he is taking exercise and pleasing his wife, we have one type of behavior to be explained; but if the agent's primary intention is to please his wife by taking exercise, we have quite another type of behavior to be explained and we will have to look in a different direction for understanding and explanation.

In the first place the episode has been situated in an annual cycle of domestic activity, and the behavior embodies an intention which presupposes a particular type of household-cum-garden setting with the peculiar narrative history of that setting in which this segment of behavior now becomes an episode. In the second instance the episode has been situated in the narrative history of a marriage, a very different, even if related, social setting. We cannot, that is to say, characterize behavior independently of intentions, and we cannot characterize intentions independently of the settings which make those intentions intelligible both to agents themselves and to others.

I use the word "setting" here as a relatively inclusive term. A social setting may be an institution, it may be what I have called a practice, or it may be a milieu of some other human kind. But it is central to the notion of a setting as I am going to understand it that a setting has a history, a history within which the histories of individual agents not only are, but have to be, situated, just because without the setting and its changes through time the history of the individual agent and his changes through time will be unintelligible. Of course one and the same piece of behavior may belong to more than one setting. There are at least two different ways in which this may be so.

In my earlier example the agent's activity may be part of the history both of the cycle of household activity and of his marriage, two histories which have happened to intersect. The household may have its own history stretching back through hundreds of years, as do the histories of some European farms, where the farm has had a life of its own, even though different families have in different periods inhabited it; and the marriage will certainly have its own history, a history which itself presupposes that a particular point has been reached in the history of the institution of marriage. If we are to relate some particular segment of behavior in any precise way to an agent's intentions and thus to the settings which that agent inhabits, we shall have to understand in a precise way how the variety of correct characterizations of the agent's behavior relate to each other first by identifying which characteristics refer us to an intention and which do not and then by classifying further the items in both categories.

Where intentions are concerned, we need to know which intention or intentions were primary, that is to say, of which it is the case that, had the agent intended otherwise, he would not have performed that action. Thus if we know that a man is gardening with the self-avowed purposes of healthful exercise and of pleasing his wife, we do not yet know how to understand what he is doing until we know the answer to such questions as whether he would continue gardening if he continued to believe that gardening was healthful exercise, but discovered that his gardening no longer pleased his wife, *and* whether he would continue gardening, if he ceased to believe that gardening was healthful exercise, but continued to believe that it pleased his wife, *and* whether he would continue gardening if he changed his beliefs on both points. That is to say, we need to know both what certain of his beliefs are and which of them are causally effective; and, that is to say, we need to know whether certain contrary-to-fact hypothetical statements are true or false. And until we know this, we shall not know how to characterize correctly what the agent is doing. . . .

Consider what the argument so far implies about the interrelationships of the intentional, the social and the historical. We identify a particular action only by invoking two kinds of context, implicitly if not explicitly. We place the agent's intentions, I have suggested, in causal and temporal order with reference to their role in his or her history; and we also place them with reference to their role in the history of the setting or settings to which they belong. In doing this, in determining what causal efficacy the agent's intentions had in one or more directions, and how his short-term intentions succeeded or failed to be constitutive of long-term intentions, we ourselves write a further part of these histories. Narrative history of a certain kind turns out to be the basic and essential genre for the characterization of human action. . . .

At the beginning of this chapter I argued that in successfully identifying and understanding what someone else is doing we always move towards having a particular episode in the context of a set of narrative histories, histories both of the individuals concerned and of the settings in which they act and suffer. It is now becoming clear that we render the actions of others intelligible in this way because action itself has a basically historical character. It is because we all live out narratives in our lives and because we understand our own lives in terms of the narratives that we live out that the form of narrative is appropriate for understanding the actions of others. Stories are lived before they are told—except in the case of fiction. . . .

A central thesis then begins to emerge: man is in his actions and practice, as well as in his fictions, essentially a story-telling animal. He is not essentially, but becomes through his history, a teller of stories that aspire to truth. But the key question for men is not about their own authorship; I can only answer the question "What am I to do?" if I can answer the prior question "Of what story or stories do I find myself a part?" We enter human society, that is, with one or more imputed characters—roles into which we have been drafted—and we have to learn what they are in order to be able to understand how others respond to us and how our responses to them are apt to be construed. It is through hearing stories about wicked stepmothers, lost children, good but misguided kings, wolves that suckle twin boys, youngest sons who receive no inheritance but must make their own way in the world and eldest sons who waste their inheritance on riotous living and go into exile to live with the swine, that children learn or mislearn both what a child and what a parent is, what the cast of characters may be in the drama into which they have been born and what the ways of the world are. Deprive children of stories and you leave them unscripted, anxious stutterers in their actions as in their words. Hence there is no way to give us an understanding of any society, including our own, except through the stock of stories which constitute its initial dramatic resources. Mythology, in its original sense, is at the heart of things. Vico was right and so was Joyce. And so too of course is that moral tradition from heroic society to its medieval heirs according to which the telling of stories has a key part in educating us into the virtues.

To be the subject of a narrative that runs from one's birth to one's death is, I remarked earlier, to be accountable for the actions and experiences which compose a narratable life. It is, that is, to be open to being asked to give a certain kind of account of what one did or what happened to one or what one witnessed at any earlier point in one's life than the time at which the question is posed. Of course someone may have forgotten or suffered brain damage or simply not attended sufficiently at the relevant time to be able to give the relevant account. But to say of someone under some one description ("The prisoner of the Chateau d'If") that he is the same person as someone characterized quite differently ("The Count of Monte Cristo") is precisely to say that it makes sense to ask him to give an intelligible narrative account enabling us to understand how he could at different times and different places be one and the same person and yet be so differently characterized. Thus personal identity is just that identity presupposed by the unity of the character which the unity of a narrative requires. Without such unity there would not be subjects of whom stories could be told.

The other aspect of narrative selfhood is correlative: I am not only accountable, I am one who can always ask others for an account, who can put others to the question. I am part of their story, as they are part of mine. The narrative of any one life is part of an interlocking set of narratives. Moreover this asking for and giving of accounts itself plays an important part in constituting narratives. Asking you what you did and why, saying what I did and why, pondering the differences between your account of what I did and my account of what I did, and *vice versa,* these are essential constituents of all but the very simplest and barest of narratives. Thus without the account-ability of the self those trains of events that constitute all but the simplest and barest of narratives could not occur; and without that same accountability narratives would lack that continuity required to make both them and the actions that constitute them intelligible. . . .

It is now possible to return to the question from which this enquiry into the nature of human action and identity started: In what does the unity of an individual life consist? The answer is that its unity is the unity of a narrative embodied in a single life. To ask "What is the good for me?" is to ask how best I might live out that unity and bring it to completion. To ask "What is the good for man?" is to ask what all answers to the former question must have in common. But now it is important to emphasize that it is the systematic asking of these two questions and the attempt to answer them in deed as well as in word which provide the moral life with its unity. The unity of a human life is the unity of a narrative quest. Quests sometimes fail, are frustrated, abandoned or dissipated into distractions; and human lives may in all these ways also fail. But the only criteria for success or failure in a human life as a whole are the criteria of success or failure in a narrated or to-be-narrated quest. A quest for what?

Two key features of the medieval conception of a quest need to be recalled. The first is that without some at least partly determinate conception of the final *telos* there could not be any beginning to a quest. Some conception of the good for man is required. Whence is such a conception to be drawn? Precisely from those questions which led us to attempt to transcend that limited conception of the virtues which is available in and through practices. It is in looking for a conception of *the* good which will enable us to order other goods, for a conception of *the* good which will enable us to extend our understanding of the purpose and content of the virtues, for a conception of *the* good which will enable us to understand the place of integrity and constancy in life, that we initially define the kind of life which is a quest for the good. But secondly it is clear the medieval conception of a quest is not at all that of a search for something already adequately characterized, as miners search for gold or geologists for oil. It is in the course of the quest and only through encountering and coping with the various particular harms, dangers, temptations and distractions which provide any quest with its episodes and incidents that the goal of the quest is finally to be understood. A quest is always an education both as to the character of that which is sought and in self-knowledge.

The virtues therefore are to be understood as those dispositions which will not only sustain practices and enable us to achieve the goods internal to practices, but which will also sustain us in the relevant kind of quest for the good, by enabling us to overcome the harms, dangers, temptations and distractions which we encounter, and which will furnish us with increasing self-knowledge and increasing knowledge of the good. The catalogue of the virtues will therefore include the virtues required to sustain the kind of households and the kind of political communities in which men and women can seek for the good together and the virtues necessary for philosophical enquiry about the character of the good. We have then arrived at a provisional conclusion about the good life for man: the good life for man is the life spent in seeking for the good life for man, and the virtues necessary for the seeking are those which will enable us to understand what more and what else the good life for man is. We have also completed the second stage in our account of the virtues, by situating them in relation to the good life for man and not only in relation to practices. But our enquiry requires a third stage.

For I am never able to seek for the good or exercise the virtues only *qua* individual. This is partly because what it is to live the good life concretely varies from circumstance to circumstance even when it is one and the same conception of the good life and one and the same set of virtues which are being embodied in a human life. What the good life is for a fifth-century Athenian general will not be the same as what it was for a medieval nun or a seventeenth-century farmer. But it is not just that different individuals live in different social circumstances; it is also that we all approach our own circumstances as bearers of a particular social identity. I am someone's son or daughter, someone else's cousin or uncle; I am a citizen of this or that city, a member of this or that guild or profession; I belong to this clan, that tribe, this nation. Hence what is good for me has to be the good for one who inhabits these roles. As such, I inherit from the past of my family, my city, my tribe, my nation, a variety of debts, inheritances, rightful expectations and obligations. These constitute the given of my life, my moral starting point. This is in part what gives my life its own moral particularity.

This thought is likely to appear alien and even surprising from the standpoint of modern individualism. From the standpoint of individualism I am what I myself choose to be. I can always, if I wish to, put in question what are taken to be the merely contingent social features of my existence. I may biologically be my father's son; but I cannot be held responsible for what he did unless I choose implicitly or explicitly to assume such responsibility. I may legally be a citizen of a certain country; but I cannot be held responsible for what my country does or has done unless I choose implicitly or explicitly to assume such responsibility. Such individualism is expressed by those modern Americans who deny any responsibility for the effects of slavery upon black Americans, saying "I never owned any slaves." It is more subtly the standpoint of those other modern Americans who accept a nicely calculated responsibility for such effects measured precisely by the benefits they themselves as individuals have indirectly received from slavery. In both cases "being an American" is not in itself taken to be part of the moral identity of the individual. And of course there is nothing peculiar to modern Americans in this attitude: the Englishman who says, "*I* never did any wrong to Ireland; why bring up that old history as though it had something to do with *me?*" or the young German who believes that being born after 1945 means that what Nazis did to Jews has no moral relevance to his relationship to his Jewish contemporaries, exhibit the same attitude, that according to which the self is detachable from its social and historical roles and statuses. And the self so detached is of course a self very much at home in either Sartre's or Goffman's perspective, a self that can have no history. The contrast with the narrative view of the self is clear. For the story of my life is always embedded in the story of those communities from which I derive my identity. I am born with a past; and to try to cut myself off from that past, in the individualist mode, is to deform my present relationships. The possession of an historical identity and the possession of a social identity coincide. Notice that rebellion against my identity is always one possible mode of expressing it.

Notice also that the fact that the self has to find its moral identity in and through its membership in communities such as those of the family, the neighborhood, the city and the tribe does not entail that the self has to accept the moral *limitations* of the particularity of those forms of community. Without those moral particularities to begin from there would never be anywhere to begin; but it is in moving forward from such particularity that the search for the good, for the universal, consists. Yet particularity can never be simply left behind or obliterated. The notion of escaping from it into a realm of entirely universal maxims which belong to man as such, whether in its eighteenth-century Kantian form or in the presentation of some modern analytical moral philosophies, is an illusion and an illusion with painful consequences. When men and women identify what are in fact their partial and particular causes too easily and too completely with the cause of some universal principle, they usually behave worse than they would otherwise do.

What I am, therefore, is in key part what I inherit, a specific past that is present to some degree in my present. I find myself part of a history and that is generally to say, whether I like it or not, whether I recognize it or not, one of the bearers of a tradition. It was important when I characterized the concept of a practice to notice that practices always have histories and that at any given moment what a practice is depends on a mode of understanding it which has been transmitted often through many generations. And thus; insofar as the virtues sustain the relationships required for practices, they have to sustain relationships to the past—and to the future—as well as in the present. But the traditions through which particular practices are transmitted and reshaped never exist in isolation for larger social traditions. What constitutes such traditions?

We are apt to be misled here by the ideological uses to which the concept of a tradition has been put by conservative political theorists. Characteristically such theorists have followed Burke in contrasting tradition with reason and the stability of tradition with conflict. Both contrasts obfuscate. For all reasoning takes place within the context of some traditional mode of thought, transcending through criticism and invention the limitations of what had hitherto been reasoned in that tradition; this is as true of modern physics as of medieval logic. Moreover when a tradition is in good order it is always partially constituted by an argument about the goods the pursuit of which gives to that tradition its particular point and purpose.

So when an institution—a university, say, or a farm, or a hospital—is the bearer of a tradition of practice or practices, its common life will be partly, but in a centrally important way, constituted by a continuous argument as to what a university is and ought to be or what good farming is or what good medicine is. Traditions, when vital, embody continuities of conflict. Indeed when a tradition becomes Burkean, it is always dying or dead. . . .

A living tradition then is an historically extended, socially embodied argument, and an argument precisely in part about the goods which constitute that tradition. Within a tradition the pursuit of goods extends through generations, sometimes through many generations. Hence the individual's search for his or her good is generally and characteristically conducted within a context defined by those traditions of which the individual's life is a part, and this is true both of those goods which are internal to practices and of the goods of a single life. Once again the narrative phenomenon of embedding is crucial: the history of a practice in our time is generally and characteristically embedded in and made intelligible in terms of the larger and longer history of the tradition through which the practice in its present form was conveyed to us; the history of each of our own lives is generally and characteristically embedded in and made intelligible in terms of the larger and longer histories of a number of traditions. I have to say "generally and characteristically" rather than "always," for traditions decay, disintegrate and disappear. What then sustains and strengthens traditions? What weakens and destroys them?

The answer in key part is: the exercise or the lack of exercise of the relevant virtues. The virtues find their point and purpose not only in sustaining those relationships necessary if the variety of goods internal to practices are to be achieved and not only in sustaining the form of an individual life in which that individual may seek out his or her good as the good of his or her whole life, but also in sustaining those traditions which provide both practices and individual lives with their necessary historical context. Lack of justice, lack of truthfulness, lack of courage, lack of the relevant intellectual virtues—these corrupt traditions, just as they do those institutions and practices which derive their life from the traditions of which they are the contemporary embodiments. To recognize this is of course also to recognize the existence of an additional virtue, one whose importance is perhaps most obvious when it is least present, the virtue of having an adequate sense of the traditions to which one belongs or which confront one. . . .

STUDY QUESTIONS

1. What roles do history and tradition play in MacIntyre's moral philosophy? Choose a specific moral question and describe how MacIntyre approaches it. Then choose another moral philosopher whom you have studied and illustrate the difference in approach.
2. Discuss and explain: "I can only answer the question 'What am I to do?' if I can answer the question 'Of what story or stories am I a part?'"
3. "I am someone's son or daughter . . . I belong to this clan, that tribe, this nation. Hence, what is good for me must be good for one who inhabits these roles." Critically discuss the concept of the virtues implied by the way in which they are related to one's role and to one's place in the community.
4. What does MacIntyre find wrong with "modern individualism"? How is individualism at odds with a life of virtue? How does it conflict with tradition? In what ways is individualism morally irresponsible?
5. What does MacIntyre mean by a "living tradition"? How do the virtues sustain traditions? How do traditions and practices help give content to the virtues?

Virtues and Vices

PHILIPPA FOOT

Philippa Foot (b. 1920) is a Senior Research Fellow of Somerville College, Oxford, and Griffin Professor Emeritus at the University of California at Los Angeles. She is the author of *Theories of Ethics* (1967) and *Virtues and Vices* (1978).

Foot distinguishes the virtues from other beneficial human traits such as health or good memory. These latter are not virtues since they do not engage a person's will and character. A generous or courageous person is virtuous in wanting the good fortune or safety of others and in having the strength of character to act. Wisdom presents a difficulty: How can knowledge or wisdom be a matter of intention or desire? Foot replies that a wise person values (wants) the proper ends; such valuation engages the will. The virtues are also "corrective" in inhibiting the tendency to yield to temptation. Foot addresses a special problem: Can anyone with evil purpose exercise a virtue, for example, show courage in murdering someone? Her answer is no.

I

. . . It seems clear that virtues are, in some general way, beneficial. Human beings do not get on well without them. Nobody can get on well if he lacks courage, and does not have some measure of temperance and wisdom, while communities where justice and charity are lacking are apt to be wretched places to live, as Russia was under the

VIRTUES AND VICES From *Virtues and Vices* by Philippa Foot. Reprinted by permission of the publisher, University of California Press.

Stalinist terror, or Sicily under the Mafia. But now we must ask to whom the benefit goes, whether to the man who has the virtue or rather to those who have to do with him? In the case of some of the virtues the answer seems clear. Courage, temperance and wisdom benefit both the man who has these dispositions and other people as well; and moral failings such as pride, vanity, worldliness, and avarice harm both their possessor and others, though chiefly perhaps the former. But what about the virtues of charity and justice? These are directly concerned with the welfare of others, and with what is owed to them; and since each may require sacrifice of interest on the part of the virtuous man both may seem to be deleterious to their possessor and beneficial to others. Whether in fact it is so has, of course, been a matter of controversy since Plato's time or earlier. It is a reasonable opinion that on the whole man is better off for being charitable and just, but this is not to say that circumstances may not arise in which he will have to sacrifice everything for charity or justice.

Nor is this the only problem about the relation between virtue and human good. For one very difficult question concerns the relation between justice and the common good. Justice, in the wide sense in which it is understood in discussions of the cardinal virtues, and in this paper, has to do with that to which someone has a right—that which he is owed in respect of non-interference and positive service—and rights may stand in the way of the pursuit of the common good. Or so at least it seems to those who reject utilitarian doctrines. This dispute cannot be settled here, but I shall treat justice as a virtue independent of charity, and standing as a possible limit on the scope of that virtue.

Let us say then, leaving unsolved problems behind us, that virtues are in general beneficial characteristics, and indeed ones that a human being needs to have, for his own sake and that of his fellows. This will not, however, take us far towards a definition of a virtue, since there are many other qualities of a man that may be similarly beneficial, as for instance bodily characteristics such as health and physical strength, and mental powers such as those of memory and concentration. What is it, we must ask, that differentiates virtues from such things?

As a first approximation to an answer we might say that while health and strength are excellences of the body, and memory and concentration of the mind, it is the will that is good in a man of virtue. But this suggestion is worth only as much as the explanation that follows it. What might we mean by saying that virtue belongs to the will?

In the first place we observe that it is primarily by his intentions that a man's moral dispositions are judged. If he does something unintentionally this is usually irrelevant to our estimate of his virtue. But of course this thesis must be qualified, because failures in performance rather than intention may show a lack of virtue. This will be so when, for instance, one man brings harm to another without realising he is doing it, but where his ignorance is itself culpable. Sometimes in such cases there will be a previous act or omission to which we can point as the source of the ignorance. Charity requires that we take care to find out how to render assistance where we are likely to be called on to do so, and thus, for example, it is contrary to charity to fail to find out about elementary first aid. But in an interesting class of cases in which it seems again to be performance rather than intention that counts in judging a man's virtue there is no possibility of shifting the judgment to previous intentions. For sometimes one man succeeds where another fails not because there is some specific difference in their previous conduct but rather because his heart lies in a different place; and the disposition of the heart is part of virtue.

Thus it seems right to attribute a kind of moral failing to some deeply discouraging and debilitating people who say, without lying, that they mean to be helpful; and on the other side to see virtue *par excellence* in one who is prompt and resourceful in doing good. In his novel *A Single Pebble* John Hersey describes such a man, speaking of a rescue in a swift flowing river.

> It was the head tracker's marvellous swift response that captured my admiration at first, his split second solicitousness when he heard a cry of pain, his finding in mid-air, as it were, the only way to save the injured boy. But there was more to it than that. His action, which could not have been mulled over in his mind, showed a deep, instinctive love of life, a compassion, an optimism, which made me feel very good . . .

What this suggests is that a man's virtue may be judged by his innermost desires as well as by his intentions and this fits with our idea that a virtue such as generosity lies as much in someone's attitudes as in his actions. Pleasure in the good fortune of others is, one thinks, the sign of a generous spirit; and small reactions of pleasure and displeasure often the surest signs of a man's moral disposition.

None of this shows that it is wrong to think of virtues as belonging to the will; what it does show is that "will" must here be understood in its widest sense, to cover what is wished for as well as what is sought.

A different set of considerations will, however, force us to give up any simple statement about the relation between virtue and will, and these considerations have to do with the virtue of wisdom. Practical wisdom, we said, was counted by Aristotle among the intellectual virtues, and while our *wisdom* is not quite the same as *phronēsis* or *prudentia* it too might seem to belong to the intellect rather than the will. Is not wisdom a matter of knowledge, and how can knowledge be a matter of intention or desire? The answer is that it isn't, so that there is good reason for thinking of wisdom as an intellectual virtue. But on the other hand wisdom has special connexions with the will, meeting it at more than one point.

In order to get this rather complex picture in focus we must pause for a little and ask what it is that we ourselves understand by wisdom: what the wise man knows and what he does. Wisdom, as I see it, has two parts. In the first place the wise man knows the means to certain good ends; and secondly he knows how much particular ends are worth. Wisdom in its first part is relatively easy to understand. It seems that there are some ends belonging to human life in general rather than to particular skills such as medicine or boatbuilding, ends having to do with such matters as friendship, marriage, the bringing up of children, or the choice of ways of life; and it seems that knowledge of how to act well in these matters belongs to some people but not to others. We call those who have this knowledge wise, while those who do not have it are seen as lacking wisdom. So, as both Aristotle and Aquinas insisted, wisdom is to be contrasted with cleverness because cleverness is the ability to take the right steps to any end, whereas wisdom is related only to good ends, and to human life in general rather than to the ends of particular arts.

Moreover, we should add, there belongs to wisdom only that part of knowledge which is within the reach of any ordinary adult human being: knowledge that can be acquired only by someone who is clever or who has access to special training is not counted as part of wisdom, and would not be so counted even if it could serve the ends that wisdom serves. It is therefore quite wrong to suggest that wisdom cannot be a moral virtue because virtue must be within the reach of anyone who really wants it and some people are too stupid to be anything but ignorant even about the most fundamental matters of human life. Some people are wise without being at all clever or well informed: they make good decisions and they know, as we say, "what's what."

In short wisdom, in what we called its first part, is connected with the will in the following ways. To begin with it presupposes good ends: the man who is wise does not merely know *how* to do good things such as looking after his children well, or strengthening someone in trouble, but must also want to do them. And then wisdom, in so far as it consists of knowledge which anyone can gain in the course of an ordinary life, is available to anyone who really wants it. As Aquinas put it, it belongs "to a power under the direction of the will."[1]

The second part of wisdom, which has to do with values, is much harder to describe, because here we meet ideas which are curiously elusive, such as the thought that some pursuits are more worthwhile than others, and some matters trivial and some important in human life. Since it makes good sense to say that most men waste a lot of their lives in ardent pursuit of what is trivial and unimportant it is not possible to explain the important and the trivial in terms of the amount of attention given to different subjects by the average man. But I have never seen, or been able to think out, a true account of this matter, and I believe that a complete account of wisdom, and of certain other virtues and vices must wait until this gap can be filled. What we can see is that one of the things a wise man knows and a foolish man does not is that such things as social position, and wealth, and the good opinion of the world, are too dearly bought at the cost of health or friendship or family ties. So we may say that a man who lacks wisdom "has false values," and that vices such as vanity and worldliness and avarice are contrary to wisdom in a special way. There is always an element of false judgment about these vices, since the man who is vain for instance sees admiration as more important than it is, while the worldly man is apt to see the good life as one of wealth and power. Adapting Aristotle's distinction between the weak-willed man (the akratēs) who follows pleasure though he

---

[1]Aquinas, *Summa Theologica*, 1a2ae Q.56 a.3.

knows, in some sense, that he should not, and the licentious man (the akolastos) who sees the life of pleasure as the good life,[2] we may say that moral failings such as these are never purely "akratic." It is true that a man may criticise himself or his worldliness or vanity or love of money, but then it is his values that are the subject of his criticism.

Wisdom in this second part is, therefore, partly to be described in terms of apprehension, and even judgment, but since it has to do with a man's attachments it also characterises his will.

The idea that virtues belong to the will, and that this helps to distinguish them from such things as bodily strength or intellectual ability has, then, survived the consideration of the virtue of wisdom, albeit in a fairly complex and slightly attenuated form. And we shall find this idea useful again if we turn to another important distinction that must be made, namely that between virtues and other practical excellences such as arts and skills.

Aristotle has sometimes been accused, for instance by von Wright, of failing to see how different virtues are from arts or skills,[3] but in fact one finds, among the many things that Aristotle and Aquinas say about this difference, the observation that seems to go to the heart of the matter. In the matter of arts and skills, they say, voluntary error is preferable to involuntary error, while in the matter of virtues (what we call virtues) it is the reverse.[4] The last part of the thesis is actually rather hard to interpret, because it is not clear what is meant by the idea of involuntary viciousness. But we can leave this aside and still have all we need in order to distinguish arts or skills from virtues. If we think, for instance, of someone who deliberately makes a spelling mistake (perhaps when writing on the blackboard in order to explain this particular point) we see that this does not in any way count against his skill as a speller: "I did it deliberately" rebuts an accusation of this kind. And what we can say without running into any difficulties is that there is no comparable rebuttal in the case of an accusation relating to lack of virtue. If a man acts unjustly or uncharitably, or in a cowardly or intemperate manner, "I did it deliberately" cannot on any interpretation lead to exculpation. So, we may say, a virtue is not, like a skill or an art, a mere capacity: it must actually engage the will.

---

[2]Aristotle, *Nicomachean Ethics*, especially bk. VII.

[3]G. H. von Wright, *The Varieties of Goodness* (London, 1963), chapter VIII.

[4]Aristotle op. cit. 1140 b. 22–25. Aquinas op. cit. 1a2ae Q.57 a.4.

II

I shall now turn to another thesis about the virtues, which I might express by saying that they are *corrective,* each one standing at a point at which there is some temptation to be resisted or deficiency of motivation to be made good. As Aristotle put it, virtues are about what is difficult for men, and I want to see in what sense this is true, and then to consider a problem in Kant's moral philosophy in the light of what has been said.

Let us first think about coverage and temperance. Aristotle and Aquinas contrasted these virtues with justice in the following respect. Justice was concerned with operations and courage and temperance with passions.[5] What they meant by this seems to have been, primarily, that the man of courage does not fear immoderately nor the man of temperance have immoderate desires for pleasure, and that there was no corresponding moderation of a passion implied in the idea of justice. This particular account of courage and temperance might be disputed on the ground that a man's courage is measured by his action and not by anything as uncontrollable as fear; and similarly that the temperate man who must on occasion refuse pleasures need not *desire* them any less than the intemperate man. Be that as it may (and something will be said about it later) it is obviously true that courage and temperance have to do with particular springs of action as justice does not. Almost any desire can lead a man to act unjustly, not even excluding the desire to help a friend or to save a life, whereas a cowardly act must be motivated by fear or a desire for safety, and an act of intemperance by a desire for pleasure, perhaps even for a particular range of pleasures such as those of eating or drinking or sex. And now, going back to the idea of virtues as correctives one may say that it is only because fear and the desire for pleasure often operate as temptations that courage and temperance exist as virtues at all. As things are we often want to run away not only where that is the right thing to do but also where we should stand firm; and we want pleasure not only where we should seek pleasure but also where we should not. If human nature had been different there would have been no need of a corrective disposition in either place, as fear and pleasure would have been good guides to conduct throughout life. So Aquinas says, about the passions,

---

[5]Aristotle op. cit. 1106 b. 15 and 1129 a.4 have this implication; but Aquinas is more explicit in op. cit. 1a2ae Q.60 a.2.

> They may incite us to something against reason, and so we need a curb, which we name *temperance*. Or they may make us shirk a course of action dictated by reason, through fear of dangers or hardships. Then a person needs to be steadfast and not run away from what is right; and for this *courage* is named.[6]

As with courage and temperance so with many other virtues: there is, for instance, a virtue of industriousness only because idleness is a temptation; and of humility only because men tend to think too well of themselves. Hope is a virtue because despair too is a temptation; it might have been that no one cried that all was lost except where he could really see it to be so, and in this case there would have been no virtue of hope.

With virtues such as justice and charity it is a little different, because they correspond not to any particular desire or tendency that has to be kept in check but rather to a deficiency of motivation; and it is this that they must make good. If people were as much attached to the good of others as they are to their own good there would no more be a general virtue of benevolence than there is a general virtue of self-love. And if people cared about the rights of others as they care about their own rights no virtue of justice would be needed to look after the matter, and rules about such things as contracts and promises would only need to be made public, like the rules of a game that everyone was eager to play.

On this view of the virtues and vices everything is seen to depend on what human nature is like, and the traditional catalogue of the two kinds of dispositions is not hard to understand. Nevertheless it may be defective, and anyone who accepts the thesis that I am putting forward will feel free to ask himself where the temptations and deficiencies that need correcting are really to be found. It is possible, for example, that the theory of human nature lying behind the traditional list of virtues and vices puts too much emphasis on hedonistic and sensual impulses, and does not sufficiently take account of less straightforward inclinations such as the desire to be put upon and dissatisfied, or the unwillingness to accept good things as they come along.

It should now be clear why I said that virtues should be seen as

---

[6]Aquinas op. cit. 1a2ae Q.61 a.3.

correctives; and part of what is meant by saying that virtue is about things that are difficult for men should also have appeared. The further application of this idea is, however, controversial, and the following difficulty presents itself: that we both are and are not inclined to think that the harder a man finds it to act virtuously the more virtue is needed where it is particularly hard to act virtuously; yet on the other it could be argued that difficulty in acting virtuously shows that the agent is imperfect in virtue: according to Aristotle, to take pleasure in virtuous action is the mark of true virtue, with the self-mastery of the one who finds virtue difficult only a second best. How then is this conflict to be decided? Who shows most courage, the one who wants to run away but does not, or the one who does not even want to run away? Who shows most charity, the one who finds it easy to make the good of others his object, or the one who finds it hard?

What is certain is that the thought that virtues are corrective does not constrain us to relate virtue to difficulty in each individual man. Since men in general find it hard to face great dangers or evils, and even small ones, we may count as courageous those few who without blindness or indifference are nevertheless fearless even in terrible circumstances. And when someone has a natural charity or generosity it is, at least part of the virtue that he has; if natural virtue cannot be the whole of virtue this is because a kindly or fearless disposition could be disastrous without justice and wisdom, and these virtues have to be learned, not because natural virtue is too easily acquired. I have argued that the virtues can be seen as correctives in relation to human nature in general but not that each virtue must present a difficulty to each and every man.

Nevertheless many people feel strongly inclined to say that it is for moral effort that moral praise is to be bestowed, and that in proportion as a man finds it easy to be virtuous so much the less is he to be morally admired for his good actions. The dilemma can be resolved only when we stop talking about difficulties standing in the way of virtuous action as if they were of only one kind. The fact is that some kinds of difficulties do indeed provide an occasion for much virtue, but that others rather show that virtue is incomplete.

To illustrate this point I shall first consider an example of honest action. We may suppose for instance that a man has an opportunity to steal, in circumstances where stealing is not morally permissible, but that he refrains. And now let us ask our old question. For one man it is hard to refrain from stealing and for another man it is not: which shows the greater virtue in acting as he should? It is not difficult to see in this case that it makes all the difference whether the difficulty comes from circumstances, as that a man is poor, or that his theft is unlikely to be detected, or whether it comes from something that belongs to his own character. The fact that a man is *tempted* to steal is something about him that shows a certain lack of honesty: of the thoroughly honest man we say that it "never entered his head," meaning that it was never a real possibility for him. But the fact that he is poor is something that makes the occasion more *tempting,* and difficulties of this kind make honest action all the more virtuous.

A similar distinction can be made between different obstacles standing in the way of charitable action. Some circumstances, as that great sacrifice is needed, or that the one to be helped is a rival, give an occasion on which a man's charity is severely tested. Yet in given circumstances of this kind it is the man who acts easily rather than the one who finds it hard who shows the most charity. Charity is a virtue of attachment, and that sympathy for others which makes it easier to help them is part of the virtue itself.

These are fairly simple cases, but I am not supposing that it is always easy to say where the relevant distinction is to be drawn. What, for instance, should we say about the emotion of fear as an obstacle to action? Is a man more courageous if he fears much and nevertheless acts, or if he is relatively fearless? Several things must be said about this. In the first place it seems that the emotion of fear is not a necessary condition for the display of courage; in face of a great evil such as death or injury a man may show courage even if he does not tremble. On the other hand even irrational fears may give an occasion for courage: if someone suffers from claustrophobia or a dread of heights he may require courage to do that which would not be a courageous action for others. But not all fears belong from this point of view to the circumstances rather than to a man's character. For while we do not think of claustrophobia or a dread of heights as features of character, a general timorousness may be. Thus, although pathological fears are not the result of a man's choices and values some fears may be. The fears that count against a man's courage are those that we think he could overcome, and among them, in a special class, those that reflect the fact that he values safety too much.

In spite of problems such as these, which have certainly not all been solved, both the distinction between different kinds of obstacles to virtuous action, and the general idea that virtues are correctives, will be useful in resolving a difficulty in Kant's moral philosophy closely related to the issues discussed in the preceding paragraphs. In a passage in the first section of the *Groundwork of the Metaphysics of Morals* Kant notoriously tied himself into a knot in trying to give an account of those actions which have as he put it "positive moral worth." Arguing that only actions done out of a sense of duty have this worth he contrasts a philanthropist who "takes pleasure in spreading happiness around him" with one who acts out of respect for duty, saying that the actions of the latter but not the former have moral worth. Much scorn has been poured on Kant for this curious doctrine, and indeed it does seem that something has gone wrong, but perhaps we are not in a position to scoff unless we can give our own account of the idea on which Kant is working. After all it does seem that he is right in saying that some actions are in accordance with duty, and even required by duty, without being the subjects of moral praise, like those of the honest trader who deals honestly in a situation in which it is in his interest to do so.

It was this kind of example that drove Kant to his strange conclusion. He added another example, however, in discussing acts of self-preservation; these he said, while they normally have no positive moral worth, have it when a man preserves his life not from inclination but without inclination and from a sense of duty. Is he not right in saying that acts of self-preservation normally have no moral significance but that they may have it, and how do we ourselves explain this fact?

To anyone who approaches this topic from a consideration of the virtues the solution readily suggests itself. Some actions are in accordance with virtue without requiring virtue for their performance, whereas others are both in accordance with virtue and such as to show possession of a virtue. So Kant's trader was dealing honestly in a situation in which the virtue of honesty is not required for honest dealing, and it is for this reason that his action did not have "positive moral worth." Similarly, the care that one ordinarily takes for one's life, as for instance on some ordinary morning in eating one's breakfast and keeping out of the way of a car on the road, is something for which no virtue is required. As we said earlier there is no general virtue of self-love as there is a virtue of benevolence or charity, because men are generally attached sufficiently to their own good. Nevertheless in special circumstances virtues such as temperance, courage, fortitude, and hope may be needed if someone is to preserve his life. Are these circumstances in which the preservation of one's own life is a duty? Sometimes it is so, for sometimes it is what is owed to others that should keep a man from destroying himself, and then he may act out of a sense of duty. But not all cases in which acts of self-preservation show virtue are like this. For a man may display each of the virtues just listed even where he does not do any harm to others if he kills himself or fails to preserve his life. And it is this that explains why there may be a moral aspect to suicide which does not depend on possible injury to other people. It is not that suicide is "always wrong," whatever that would mean, but that suicide is *sometimes* contrary to virtues such as courage and hope.

Let us now return to Kant's philanthropists, with the thought that it is action that is in accordance with virtue and also displays a virtue that has moral worth. We see at once that Kant's difficulties are avoided, and the happy philanthropist reinstated in the position which belongs to him. For charity is, as we said, a virtue of attachment as well as action, and the sympathy that makes it easier to act with charity is part of the virtue. The man who acts charitably out of a sense of duty is not to be undervalued, but it is the other who most shows virtue and therefore to the other that most moral worth is attributed. Only a detail of Kant's presentation of the case of the dutiful philanthropist tells on the other side. For what he actually said was that this man felt no sympathy and took no pleasure in the good of others because "his mind was clouded by some sorrow of his own," and this is the kind of circumstance that increases the virtue that is needed if a man is to act well.

III

It was suggested above that an action with "positive moral worth," or as we might say a positively good action, was to be seen as one which was in accordance with virtue, by which I mean contrary to no virtue, and moreover one for which a virtue was required. Nothing has so far been said about another case, excluded by the formula, in which it might seem that an act displaying one virtue was nevertheless contrary to another. In giving this last description I am thinking not of two virtues with competing claims, as if what were required by justice could nevertheless be demanded by charity, or something of that kind, but rather of the possibility that a virtue such as courage or temperance or industry which overcomes a special temptation, might be displayed in an act of folly or villainy. Is this something that we must allow for, or is it only good or innocent actions which can be acts of these virtues? Aquinas, in his definition of virtue, said that virtues can produce only good actions, and that they are dispositions "of which no one can make bad use,"[7] except when they are treated as objects, as in being the subject of hatred or pride. The common opinion nowadays is, however, quite different. With the notable exception of Peter Geach hardly anyone sees any difficulty in the thought that virtues may sometimes be displayed in bad actions. Von Wright, for instance, speaks of the courage of the villain as if this were a quite unproblematic idea, and most people take it for granted that the virtues of courage and temperance may aid a bad man in his evil work. It is also supposed that charity may lead a man to act badly, as when someone does what he has no right to do, but does it for the sake of a friend.

There are, however, reasons for thinking that the matter is not as simple as this. If a man who is willing to do an act of injustice to help a friend, or for the common good, is supposed to act out of charity, and he so acts where a just man will not, it should be said that the unjust man has more charity than the just man. But do we not think that someone not ready to act unjustly may yet be perfect in charity, the virtue having done its whole work in prompting a man to do the acts that are permissible? And is there not more difficulty than might appear in the idea of an act of injustice which is nevertheless an act of courage? Suppose for instance that a sordid murder were in question, say a murder done for gain or to get an inconvenient person out of the way, but that this murder had to be done in alarming circumstances or in the face of real danger; should we be happy to say that such an action was an act of courage or a courageous act? Did the murderer, who certainly acted boldly, or with intrepidity, if he did the murder, also act courageously? Some people insist that they are ready to say this, but I have noticed that they like to move over to a murder for the sake of conscience, or to some other act done in the course of a villainous enterprise but whose immediate end is innocent or positively good. On their hypothesis, which is that bad acts can

---

[7] Aquinas op. cit. 1a2ae Q.56 a.5.

easily be seen as courageous acts or acts of courage, my original example should be just as good.

What are we to say about this difficult matter? There is no doubt that the murderer who murdered for gain was *not a coward:* he did not have a second moral defect which another villain might have had. There is no difficulty about this because it is clear that one defect may neutralise another. As Aquinas remarked, it is better for a blind horse if it is slow.[8] It does not follow, however, that an act of villainy can be courageous; we are inclined to say that it "took courage," and yet it seems wrong to think of courage as equally connected with good actions and bad.

One way out of this difficulty might be to say that the man who is ready to pursue bad ends does indeed have courage, and shows courage in his action, but that in him courage is not a virtue. Later I shall consider some cases in which this might be the right thing to say, but in this instance it does not seem to be. For unless the murderer consistently pursues bad ends his courage will often result in good; it may enable him to do many innocent or positively good things for himself or for his family and friends. On the strength of an individual bad action we can hardly say that in him courage is not a virtue. Nevertheless there is something to be said even about the individual action to distinguish it from one that would readily be called an act of courage or a courageous act. Perhaps the following analogy may help us to see what it is. We might think of words such as "courage" as naming characteristics of human beings in respect of a certain power, as words such as "poison" and "solvent" and "corrosive" so name the properties of physical things. The power to which virtue-words are so related is the power of producing good action, and good desires. But just as poisons, solvents and corrosives do not always operate characteristically, so it could be with virtues. If P (say arsenic) is a poison it does not follow that P acts as a poison wherever it is found. It is quite natural to say on occasion "P does not act as a poison here" though P is a poison and it is P that is acting here. Similarly courage is not operating as a virtue when the murderer turns his courage, which is a virtue to bad ends. Not surprisingly the resistance that some of us registered was not to the expression "the courage of the murderer" or to the assertion that what he did "took courage" but rather to the description of that action as an

---

[8]Aquinas op. cit. 1a2ae Q.58 a.4.

act of courage or a courageous act. It is not that the action *could* not be so described, but that the fact that courage does not here have its characteristic operation is a reason for finding the description strange.

In this example we were considering an action in which courage was not operating as a virtue, without suggesting that in that agent it generally failed to do so. But the latter is also a possibility. If someone is both wicked and foolhardy this may be the case with courage, and it is even easier to find examples of a general connexion with evil rather than good in the case of some other virtues. Suppose, for instance, that we think of someone who is overindustrious, or too ready to refuse pleasure, and this is characteristic of him rather than something we find on one particular occasion. In this case the virtue of industry, or the virtue of temperance, has a systematic connexion with defective action rather than good action; and it might be said in either case that the virtue did not operate as a virtue in this man. Just as we might say in a certain setting "P is not a poison here" though P is a poison and P is here, so we might say that industriousness, or temperance, is not a virtue in some. Similarly in a man habitually given to wishful thinking, who clings to false hopes, hope does not operate as a virtue and we may say that it is not a virtue in him.

The thought developed in the last paragraph, to the effect that not every man who has a virtue has something that is a virtue in him, may help to explain a certain discomfort that one may feel when discussing the virtues. It is not easy to put one's finger on what is wrong, but it has something to do with a disparity between the moral ideas that may seem to be implied in our talk about the virtues, and the moral judgments that we actually make. Someone reading the foregoing pages might, for instance, think that the author of this paper always admired most those people who had all the virtues, being wise and temperate as well as courageous, charitable, and just. And indeed it is sometimes so. There are some people who do possess all these virtues and who are loved and admired by all the world, as Pope John XXIII was loved and admired. Yet the fact is that many of us look up to some people whose chaotic lives contain rather little of wisdom or temperance, rather than to some others who possess these virtues. And while it may be that this is just romantic nonsense I suspect that it is not. For while wisdom always operates as a virtue, its close relation prudence does not, and it is prudence rather than wisdom that inspires many a careful life. Prudence is not a virtue in everyone, any more than industriousness is, for in some it is rather an overanxious concern for safety and propriety, and a determination to keep away from people or situations which are apt to bring trouble with them; and by such defensiveness much good is lost. It is the same with temperance. Intemperance can be an appalling thing, as it was with Henry VIII of whom Wolsey remarked that

> rather than he will either miss or want any part of his will or appetite, he will put the loss of one half of his realm in danger.

Nevertheless in some people temperance is not a virtue, but is rather connected with timidity or with a grudging attitude to the acceptance of good things. Of course what is best is to live boldly yet without imprudence or intemperance, but the fact is that rather few can manage that.

STUDY QUESTIONS

1. What does Foot mean by saying "Virtue belongs to the will"?
2. How do the virtues benefit their possessors? What special features must a beneficial trait possess to be counted as a virtue?
3. What is wisdom's relation to the will? To all of the other virtues?
4. Foot argues that what appears to be courage in a murder really is not. Do you agree with her?
5. Do you agree with Foot that wise persons know the means to good ends *and* want those ends? Can wise persons not desire the ends they judge to be worthwhile?
6. In what sense are the virtues "corrective"? What significance does Foot give to this feature of virtue?

Will Power and the Virtues

ROBERT C. ROBERTS

Robert C. Roberts (b. 1942) is a professor of philosophy and psychological studies at Wheaton College. He has written numerous articles on psychology, theology, and ethics.

Robert C. Roberts distinguishes between motivated virtues and virtues of the will, the former characterized by some desire or motive to behave in a morally correct manner. Here the presence of the right desire (e.g., to tell the truth, to help the needy) is a condition for possessing the virtue (e.g., of honesty, of compassion). Virtues of the will are not grounded in desire, but grounded in the capacity to *resist* desire (e.g., courage resists the desire to flee; self-control and perseverance resist the desire to relax and enjoy oneself).

The two kinds of virtues complement each other. One who possesses only the virtues of the will could be a moral monster (having great powers of self-control and patience in the service of evil). On the other hand, a weak-willed person who possesses the passionate virtues will be at the mercy of nonmoral passions. Such a person will be unable to resist temptation.

The second half of Roberts' paper is devoted to arguments for the thesis that virtues of the will have the char-

FROM WILL POWER AND THE VIRTUES First appeared in *Philosophical Review* (April 1984), pp. 227–247. Extensively revised by author for this edition. Revision reprinted by permission of the author.

acter of personal skills or techniques. The person who can control his impulses possesses certain skills of self-mastery. Although such skills are in part innate, they are learnable, and a weak-willed person can learn techniques for strengthening will. "The virtue of will power is the athletic side of the moral life."

I

Since Elizabeth Anscombe's challenge to modern moral philosophy in 1958[1], a number of authors have tried to answer the general question "What is a virtue?" or as G. H. von Wright says, to "shape a concept of a virtue." This project has thrown light on the nature of the virtues, but has sometimes raised the expectation that they must all be the same kind of trait.[2] One broad consensus has been that virtues are not skill-like dispositions or powers. I shall argue here that one group of virtues, which I call the moral strengths or virtues of will power, are largely skill-like.

Some theorists have proposed that moral virtues are all determinations of the good will, but a broad-ranging list of traits having moral relevance will probably include some that are not easily corralled into this pen. For example, foresight and psychological insight are characteristics of an ideally moral person, yet it seems wrong to call them determinations of the will. Gentleness, politeness, and friendliness, in some people at least, are styles of behavioral demeanor that may be neither characteristics of the will nor willed into being by their possessors. So probably not all morally relevant traits are matters of the will. Yet it is clear why philosophers might make this mistake, for many of the virtues most central to the moral life, such as truthfulness, courage, justice, compassion, and self-control, *are* determinations of the will.

---

[1] "Modern Moral Philosophy," *Philosophy*, vol. 33 (1958), pp. 1–19.

[2] Important essays in which the tendency is evident are chapter 7 of von Wright's *The Varieties of Goodness* (London: Routledge, 1963); R. B. Brandt's "Traits of Character: A Conceptual Analysis," *American Philosophical Quarterly*, vol. 7 (1970), pp. 23–37; Philippa Foot's "Virtues and Vices" in *Virtues and Vices* (Berkeley: University of California Press, 1978); and John McDowell's "Virtue and Reason," *Monist*, vol. 62 (1979), pp. 331–350.

But this observation won't get us very far unless we know what will is. Broadly, we employ "will" and its cognates in two ways. In the first kind of case we designate inclinations and disinclinations, desires and aversions, motivations. If I go willingly to a horse race, I go gladly or at least with minimal distaste. A willful person does just whatever he wants to, without regard for the rights or concerns of others. To lose the will to live is no longer to care much about living. In the second kind of case "will" designates not motivations, but a family of capacities for resisting adverse inclinations. When we say someone has a "strong will" we are often referring to the presence in her of such virtues as perseverance, resoluteness, courage, patience, and self-control. When we speak of "efforts of will," we refer to the acts or activities corresponding to such virtues: fighting boredom, controlling one's emotions, resisting temptation, persevering in the face of discouragement, overcoming the impulse to flee, fighting anxiety, forcing oneself to the magnanimous gesture, and the like.[3] That this use of "will" is distinct from its use to designate motivation is suggested by the oddity of the expression "an effort of wanting."

Where people make efforts, there exist human capacities. A person can make a muscular effort because in general he has muscular powers, and an effort to pay attention because he can pay attention. (Obviously, it doesn't follow that he has the power to do the particular act he tries to do; efforts can fail in many ways, and some of these involve a failure to possess, or to possess enough of, the relevant capacity.) So if people do make efforts of will—that is, efforts to resist adverse inclinations—then there exist human capacities by which to resist adverse inclinations. I contend in this paper that the virtues of will power are indeed largely capacities, and that these are best thought of as skills. But first I want to discuss the relation between the virtues of will power and some other virtues.

---

[3]When I call a virtue a "virtue of will power," I do not suggest that every action exemplifying it is an exercise of will power. There are acts of courage and patience and perseverance (I do not say this about self-control) that do not require will power, much less an effort of will. I use this name to indicate a salient, but not necessary, feature of these virtues. Also, will power is probably, as a matter of psychological fact, always needed in the *acquisition* of these virtues.

II

Virtues can be classified in different ways for different purposes. A broad division that throws light on the psychology of the moral life is the distinction between the virtues of will power and those that are substantive and motivational. I call virtues like truthfulness, compassion, justice, generosity, promise-keeping, and gratitude "substantive" because they are the psychological embodiment of ethical rules—the substance of the ethical patterns of behavior and judgment and emotion. To be truthful is to be disposed to tell the truth in appropriate situations, to judge well which situations demand telling the truth, to be "alive" to dishonesty in oneself and others, and to feel uneasiness, guilt, indignation, sadness, and other emotions upon encountering dishonesty in oneself and others. Compassion is the disposition to help others who are suffering, to notice and recognize sufferers as sufferers, to see them as in some fundamental way similar to oneself, and to be sad to see suffering and glad to see it relieved.

By contrast, patience does not imply any characteristically ethical patterns of behavior, judgment, or emotion. Racists, cheats, sadists, and thieves may well be persevering, resolute, and self-controlled; and indeed will be more likely to succeed in their several callings if they are. Whether courage is equally lacking in moral substance has been questioned.[4] Philippa Foot has noted that we are disinclined to call particularly heinous acts, such as "a murder done for gain or to get an inconvenient person out of the way"[5] courageous, even if they are done in circumstances which would require courage. But our disinclination here can be accounted for by the *associations* that "courage" has for us: we do associate courage with the substantive moral virtues, and there are important ethical and anthropological reasons

---

[4]Lester Hunt has argued that all virtues are dispositions to act on principles. See his "Character and Thought," *American Philosophical Quarterly,* vol. 15 (1978), pp. 177–86 and his "Generosity and the Diversity of the Virtues," in R. B. Kruschwitz and R. C. Roberts (eds.) *The Virtues* (Belmont, CA: Wadsworth, 1986). He has thus sought the principle on which courage is the disposition to act. He comes up with the following: courageous acts "are the ones which are done from the principle that one's own safety, in general, has no more than a certain measure of importance." "Courage and Principle," *Canadian Journal of Philosophy,* vol. 10 (1980) p. 289. But this principle does not seem to me a moral one; to act morally one needs to know *what* is worth risking one's safety for, and it is the principles embodied in the substantive virtues that tell one that.

[5]Foot, "Virtues and Vices," p. 15.

for this association, which in turn give courage its moral importance. And Foot admits that it is only the attribution of courage to the *act* that troubles us; we find no difficulty in calling a murderer courageous, nor in saying that his act "took courage."

By saying the substantive virtues are "motivational," I mean what I think Aristotle is talking about when he says

> We may even go so far as to state that the man who does not enjoy performing noble actions is not a good man at all. Nobody would call a man just who does not enjoy acting justly, nor generous who does not enjoy generous actions, and so on (*Nicomachean Ethics* 1099a).

To be just is to want just states of affairs to prevail and consequently, in the appropriate circumstances, to want to do what will bring about such states of affairs. Thus the just person takes satisfaction ("pleasure") in the performance and beholding of such actions, and feels frustration ("pain") at failure in them. But Aristotle seems to be less than lucid about the distinction between kinds of virtues that I am pointing out. For he says that "A man who endures danger with joy, or at least without pain, is courageous; if he endures it with pain, he is a coward (*Nicomachean Ethics* 1104b)."[6] But enjoying facing dangers is surely not a criterion of courage. There may be a psychological connection between a person's achieving self-mastery and his taking pleasure either in some aspects of the activity itself or in the fruits of it. But the quality of a person's self-mastery cannot be called into question on the account of his failing to enjoy it. Whereas the idea of a just person who nevertheless hates doing just actions, or is indifferent to their fruits, is a contradiction.

A person who enjoys enduring dangers is better called daredevilish than brave. A particularly bizarre illustration of one way for courage to be a motivational virtue has been collected by William James.[7]

---

[6]But compare 1117b.

[7]*The Varieties of Religious Experience* (Garden City, NY: Doubleday, 1978), pp. 266–67, note. H. A. Prichard finds another way of making courage a passional virtue: for him it is not an enjoyment of dangers, but "the desire to conquer one's feelings of terror arising from the sense of shame which they arouse." *Moral Obligation* (New York: Oxford University Press, 1950), p. 13. Although some courageous actions are motivated by shame of fear, the most typical moral examples are motivated in other ways (see[8]). I hold that there is *no* motive characteristic of courageous actions as a class.

I believe, says General Skobeleff, that my bravery is simply the passion for and at the same time the contempt of danger. The risk of life fills me with an exaggerated rapture. The fewer there are to share it, the more I like it . . . a meeting of man to man, a duel, a danger into which I can throw myself head-foremost, attracts me, moves me, intoxicates me. I am crazy for it, I love it, I adore it. I run after danger as one runs after women . . . my entire nature runs to meet the peril with an impetus that my will would in vain try to resist.

If joy in enduring danger were a mark of courage, General Skobeleff would appear to be an exceptually courageous man. And no doubt a casual observer of his exploits might call him courageous. But this peek at the General's interiority shows that his disposition is not courage. For whatever else courage may be, it is a virtue; but the disposition he describes is a vice. Even the courage of the thief elicits our admiration; for though his disregard for property rights is despicable, still he possesses a capacity without which one leads a crippled life. But there is nothing admirable about the General's lust for dangers; and we can guess that people who possess it tend to be a menace both to society and to themselves. For positions of leadership we want courageous persons, but not daredevils. We do not want our generals to be enthusiasts for military exploits.

Unlike justice, compassion, generosity, and friendship, courage and self-control do not in themselves supply motives. A person can feed the poor out of compassion, struggle on behalf of the oppressed out of concern for justice (i.e., out of concern for people who are being treated unjustly), and perform sacrifices out of friendship. But actions exhibiting courage and self-control are not done *out of* courage and self-control.[8] Actions done out of moral motives may, however, be done *in virtue of* courage and self-control and patience, if

---

[8] Though they are sometimes done for the sake of courage and self-control, as when you "do every day or two something for no other reason than that you would rather not do it, so that when the hour of dire need draws nigh, it may find you not unnerved and untrained to stand the test." William James, *Principles of Psychology*, vol. 1 (Cambridge, MA: Harvard University Press, 1981), p. 126. Or as when, like G. Gordon Liddy, you eat a rat as an exercise in mastering your fear of rats. *Will: The Autobiography of G. Gordon Liddy* (New York: St. Martin's Press, 1981), p. 24. But this kind of case is untypical, the typical case being that of acting courageously or self-controlledly for the sake of some other end. If someone always acted courageously only to exhibit courage or train herself in it, and never out of friendship, justice, compassion, and so forth, her action would not be moral. And to the extent that acting courageously out of the desire to be courageous is morally praiseworthy, this is because courage is in aid of the actions characteristic of the substantive and motivational virtues.

the circumstances, psychological and environmental, demand such virtues.[9]

I think Plato is on the right track when he calls courage a "preservative."[10] A preservative is in the service of something other than itself that is cherished, and needed because this cherished thing is in some way threatened. Courage, self-control, and patience are in the service of the moral and prudential life, and needed because this life is beset with trials. These trials, which are part of the everyday context in which we exercise the virtues, are functions of our desires and aversions. The virtues of will power are the capacities by which a person copes with these trials in the interests of the moral and prudential life.

Philippa Foot has noticed this "corrective" character of the virtues of will power:[11]

> As things are we often want to run away not only where that is the right thing to do but also where we should stand firm; and we want pleasure not only where we should seek pleasure but also where we should not. If human nature had been different there would have been no need of a corrective disposition in either place. . . .

But she mistakenly generalizes this characteristic to all the virtues:

> There is . . . a virtue of industriousness only because idleness is a temptation; and of humility only because men tend to think too well of themselves. Hope is a virtue because despair is a temptation. . . .

Her mistake is that of confusing the existence of something with the existence of its name or concept. If people were never led astray by

---

[9]Aquinas seems to be aware of the distinction to which I point when he says, "By its nature virtue is concerned with the good rather than the difficult" and "A man exposes himself to mortal danger only to preserve justice. Therefore the praise accorded to courage derives in a sense from justice" (*Summa Theologiae* 2a2ae 123.12). But Aquinas is not consistent in this observation that courage and similar virtues do not supply a motive, for he assimilates courage and charity by saying, "Charity does prompt the act of martyrdom as its first and most important moving force by being the virtue commanding it, but courage does so as the directly engaged moving force, being the virtue which brings out the act" (2a2ae 124.2). But unless the martyr is acting not just courageously but for the sake of courage (which is not the typical case and certainly not necessary for martyrdom), it seems wrong to say that courage "prompts" the act in any sense. Courage *facilitates* the act, but only motives *prompt* it.

[10]*Republic* 429c–e.

[11]"Virtues and Vices," p. 9.

fears and pleasures, it is plausible that courage and self-control themselves would not arise. For courage and self-control are the capacities to manage our inclinations, when they are wayward, to flee dangers and seek pleasures. But industriousness is needed not basically because people are prone to laziness, but because work is a good thing. Industriousness could exist in a world in which no one suffered from laziness, and hope in a world where no one ever despaired, and honesty in a world where no one lied—though it is likely that in such a world these virtues would not be named or much noticed. The substantive virtues are "corrective" in the trivial sense that there are vices which correspond to them; the virtues of will power are corrective in the significant sense that, in our present psychological condition but not in every imaginable one, they are needed to keep us on the path of virtue and our higher self-interest.

III

But this is not the whole story. In assessing the degree to which an action reflects moral credit on its agent, we often feel two contrary tendencies. On the one side, like Kant, we are inclined to give greater credit for actions (or character traits) that result from moral struggle. We might call this the hero assessment: just as running a mile in under four minutes is praised not as a speedy mode of transportation, but as an extraordinary feat for legs and lungs and spirit, so some acts are morally praised not just because they are good, but also because they are difficult. Why do we tend to think a moral achievement greater if more difficult? Not, I think, just because we have confused morality with athletics. One obvious reason is that morally difficult actions display some virtues—namely the virtues of will power. But I think a deeper basis for our feeling here is that the greater the moral obstacles a person has overcome in doing something the more her action seems to be her own *achievement*, her own *choice*, and thus to reflect credit on her as an *agent*. It seems to show that her action is *hers* in a special way.

But the moment we make the hero assessment we may have some doubts and think: The very fact that somebody *has* those fears and lusts and countermoral impulses which make right action difficult for him reflects discredit on him; an action is the more praiseworthy the more it is done purely out of moral inclinations and in the absence of contrary inclinations—that is, the more it is done *without* moral

273

struggle. This we might call the purity of heart assessment. Here the emphasis is not on the agent as an achiever, but rather, I should almost say, as a personal *artifact*. Here we assess the individual not with respect to how he brought off the act or how he got to be the kind of person he is, but just with respect to what he *is* in the sense of the configuration of his cares and uncares. The ideally moral person is one who is concerned about important things and relatively unconcerned about relatively unimportant things, and so he does not have to struggle with himself to do what is right.

These kinds of assessments correspond to the kinds of virtues I have distinguished. When we make the hero assessment, we are asking of an action or trait that its accomplishment require one or more of the virtues of will power. If we make the purity of heart assessment, we are laying emphasis on the motivational virtues. The virtues of will power are needed on the road to purity of heart because in most of us the moral inclinations are so weak and the road so strewn with psychological obstacles. But unlike the motivational virtues, these are not the substance of the moral life, and their "corrective" function is no longer needed when full sainthood has been attained.

As I have suggested, however, the virtues of will power are needed not only for their "corrective" function, but also because they are essential to the development of the agent's agenthood. Struggles are an important part of the way we become centers of initiation of actions and passions. They are the contexts in which the shape of our personality takes on that toughness and independence that we call "autonomy," and that seems to be a basic feature of mature personhood. Could a person gain autonomy without struggle, and thus without the capacities necessary to win in struggles? In a famous letter John Keats wrote,[12]

> The common cognomen of this world among the misguided and superstitious is "a vale of tears" from which we are to be redeemed by a certain arbitrary interposition of God and taken to Heaven—What a little circumscribe [d] straightened notion! Call the world if you Please "The vale of Soul-making." Then you will find out the use of the world . . . I say "Soul making." Soul as distinguished from an Intel-

---

[12] *The Letters of Keats*, vol. 2 (Cambridge, MA: Harvard University Press, 1958) pp. 101 f.

ligence—There may be intelligences or sparks of the divinity in millions—but they are not Souls . . . till they acquire identities, till each one is personally itself . . . Do you not see how necessary a World of Pains and troubles is to school an intelligence and make it a soul?

We might generalize Keats' "World of Pains and troubles" to "a World of temptations" (psychological adversities). We can guess that it will never be possible to give a person a moral "identity"—a tough and abiding passion for justice or a stable and focused desire to relieve suffering—by injecting him with a drug or giving him a brain operation or fiddling with his genes. But the impossibility of giving somebody moral character in this way seems to be more than psychological. For even if we could in this way produce a being who was indistinguishable, in terms of his present dispositions, from a saint, still I think we would have no inclination whatsoever to canonize him. For the praise for his saintliness, and thus for his deeds, would not be due *him*. If it were due anyone, the pharmacologist or brain surgeon would seem more likely candidates. So the idea of somebody acquiring moral character without struggle seems not only psychologically, but logically amiss. Such a person does not have an appropriate moral history. Thus, if powers of will are those powers by which moral struggles are prosecuted, they are more than just "corrective." They are a logically and psychologically necessary part of our development as persons.

The relation, then, between the virtues of will power and the substantive virtues is mutual need: neither kind can exist as moral virtues without the other kind. Without the virtues of will power, the moral motives would too often be sabotaged by counter-moral impulses and the relative weakness of the substantive virtues; nor would these latter be gained in a morally appropriate way. On the other hand, the character of a person who had only the virtues of will power would be empty of moral content.

IV

I want now to consider the view of the virtues of will power that I take to be the strongest alternative to my suggestion that they are capacities. Richard Brandt has argued[13] that moral character traits

---

[13]"Traits of Character: A Conceptual Analysis," *American Philosophical Quarterly*, vol. 7 (1970), pp. 23–37.

are "the kind of dispositions that wants and aversions are." They are inclinations that can be called into activity by features of a subject's environment or thoughts and which, when they have become active, issue in behavior of a type corresponding to the inclination. Thus a person with the trait of sympathy, if he sees a child in distress from falling off his bicycle, will go to the child and help or comfort him, if some other, competing and stronger, inclination is not presently active in him. For example, if what knocked the child from his bike is a bag of $100 bills falling off a truck, which are now floating up the street in the wind, the active trait of sympathy may start to be challenged by that of avarice. Assuming the sympathetic and avaricious individual judges the wind strong enough to render the fulfillment of the one desire incompatible with that of the other, then his behavior at that moment will be determined by the relative strength of these two inclinations. Brandt generalizes:

> The motivation theory of character traits holds that, under conditions not fully understood, they become active and generate "force vectors" in the psychological field of the person, their direction and degree depending partly on the person's beliefs; what the person actually does is a function of the force vectors in his psychological field at the moment of action.

This account, like Aristotle's, begins to fidget when virtues of will power are mentioned. Unlike Aristotle and Prichard, Brandt does not treat courage as though it is a motivational virtue; but he does treat it as nothing but a function of motivations, among which are to be found some moral ones. Such virtues, though not themselves tendencies of the desire/aversion sort, must be understood as the relative weakness of desires/aversions that stand in opposition to virtuous behavior. Thus the courage of the rat-phobic who crawls under the house after a child is simply the weakness, relative to his desire to free the child, of his desire to avoid the company of rats. On this analysis a generally courageous or self-controlled person is just one who has sufficiently intense moral and prudential desires and aversions that they override, usually, his morally and prudentially aversive motivations.

Some cases of courage, and the like, fit Brandt's analysis. We do sometimes ascribe courage to a person whose impulse to act virtuously is strong enough, by itself, to override his impulse to flee. Maybe this is typical of the courage of the saints: in them the motivational virtues are so strong that in a sense they do not need courage. That is, in them courage is not a function of will power. But most of us would not have much courage or patience if we didn't have will power, so we are led, like James D. Wallace, to feel that Brandt's analysis has neglected something. These virtues are not just "privative states," but some kind of "positive capacity."[14]

V

If desires and aversions (duly shaped by our beliefs) were the only kind of element contributing to our psychological "force vectors," the virtues of will power would not be capacities or powers, but only patterns of relative strength among our desires and aversions. However, our desires and aversions are not the only psychological factors contributing to our actions and the course of our lives; for there is also such a thing as our *management* of our desires and aversions. People are capacitated in numerous ways. We have bodily powers like food and oxygen assimilation, physical strengths (muscles and bones), faculties (sight, hearing, smell), and aptitudes (mathematics, music, linguistics). The capacities to resist adverse inclinations seem to be learned. Since learned capacities are called skills, I propose that powers of will are skills of self-management.

Skills may be more or less completely mental, like the ability to focus attention at will, or motor, like riding a bicycle. But most skills have both motor and mental aspects. Riding a bike in traffic requires a combination of motor skill and knowledge of rules of the road, attentiveness to events occurring in the traffic, judgment about the speed of cars relative to their distance from oneself and one another and one's own speed or potential for speed, and so forth. It is characteristic of skills in both their mental and motor aspects that they become in large part "automatic" and unnoticed by their practitioners. Many skills combine procedures governed by rules which can be

---

[14]*Virtues and Vices* (Ithaca, NY: Cornell University Press, 1978), p. 61. Wallace suggests that the "positiveness" of virtues like courage is their capacity to preserve us in the course of practical reason. But as Amélie Rorty has pointed out, the *akrates* need not consider the course which he fails to take to be the more rational of the choices which conflict in him. "Where Does the Akratic Break Take Place?" *Australasian Journal of Philosophy*, vol. 58 (1980), pp. 336f. Just as *akrasia* cannot be defined as a form of irrationality, so courage and other virtues that are the opposites of *akrasia* cannot be defined as capacities to preserve rationality. Their "positiveness" lies not here, but in their being capacities.

(though by no means always are) formulated, patterns of such "automatic" physical and mental behavior, and a certain element of creativity in the application of the rules and the "automatic" behaviors to new challenges. Most sports and games, and activities such as weaving, portrait photography, algebra, speaking a language, cooking, getting dressed, and cabinet building would be skills falling under this last description.

People can be more or less skilled in the management of their own inclinations, and these skills are an important part of the virtues of will power. We can be more or less good at breaking bad habits and forming new ones, at deferring gratification, at resisting cravings and impulses; we can be trained and/or train ourselves in the control of emotions like anxiety, fear, disappointment, anger, and hatred. I want to illustrate and partially analyze these truths in a moment. But before I do, let me consider four *a priori* objections to the proposal that virtues can be skills.

Three such arguments are found in James D. Wallace's book *Virtues and Vices*, pp. 44–47. The first argument is this:

1. Courage and patience are capacities to overcome difficulties arising from inclinations contrary to right action.
2. Inclinations contrary to right action are not technical difficulties, but skills are always capacities to overcome technical difficulties.

So courage and patience are not skills.

The crux of the argument is the word "technical." It sounds right to say that of the various kinds of difficulties standing in the way of acting compassionately toward a rebellious and abusive teenage son, the difficulty of overcoming one's feelings of resentment toward him (which might be met by possessing patience) is not a *technical* one. (We might say, "Not technical, but *moral!*") "Technical" difficulties in this situation might be questions of psychological strategy: What is in the son's best interest? Confront him and have it out? Assert some authority over him? Use benign neglect? Shower him with affection? Or some combination of these? To answer a "technical" question like this, one might consult a professional, thus perhaps increasing one's skill in handling rebellious sons. But one would not (so suggests Wallace's argument) seek such "technical" guidance as to, or training in, how to handle one's *own* feelings of resentment toward the son. *That* is a matter not of "technique," but of morality.

But why not seek such "technical" help in handling one's own emotions? One reason we are inclined to accept the "not technical, but moral" disjunction is a failure to distinguish virtues like courage and patience from the substantive moral virtues like caring for one's children. But if somebody already has a moral motive, and then finds that bad habits and adverse emotions are getting in the way of acting lovingly, the psychologist has a potential role. And though we would not normally call this role "technical," what she may supply here is precisely information and training of a "how to" sort. I suggest that when this "how to" knowledge has become assimilated, the person will have gained in the virtue of patience.

Here is Wallace's second argument:

> 1. If any trait is a skill, then it can be inculcated through instruction in techniques and by practice that leads to proficiency.
> 2. But no virtue can be so inculcated.
> So no virtue is a skill.

But the second premise is false. As Aristotle points out,

> By being habituated to despise things that are terrible and to stand our ground against them we become brave, and it is when we have become so that we shall be most able to stand our ground against them (1104b).

In the next section I shall illustrate how the virtues of will power can be inculcated through instruction and practice.

Wallace next adapts an insight from Gilbert Ryle, namely that it is logically amiss to say someone has forgotten the difference between right and wrong. Wallace's third argument is this:

> 1. If any trait is a skill, it can be forgotten
> 2. But courage, self-control, and patience cannot be forgotten.
> So these traits are not skills.

Both premises are questionable. In general it is only more complicated skills that are forgettable, and even here it is unlikely that a skill, well-learned, will be completely forgotten. Someone who has played the piano well, and then lets twenty years elapse without practicing, will get rusty indeed. But that she has not lost all her skill will be evident from how quickly the skill returns with practice. A total loss of the skill would require more than forgetting; it would take some kind of injury or illness or aging process resulting in neurological or muscular deterioration. But simple skills are virtually unforgettable: one does not forget how to swim, or ride a bike, or walk. It is possible that courage and self-control are simple enough to be as unforgettable as bike riding. (Though perhaps like bike riding they are susceptible of considerable development and sophistication.)

It seems to me that courage, and the like, cannot be flat forgotten; but if we allow that getting "rusty" is a sort of forgetting or partial forgetting, it is not so obvious that one cannot forget courage. Consider the autobiography of Gordon Liddy, who in prison felt it necessary to exercise himself in withstanding pain, to make sure that he hadn't gone soft.

Unlike Wallace, Ryle nowhere claims it is logically amiss to say someone has forgotten a virtue, but only to say that someone has forgotten the difference between right and wrong.[15] Ryle explains this impossibility by the fact that to know the difference between right and wrong is a matter of caring about right and wrong, and ceasing to care is not a sort of forgetting. In my terms, Ryle is only claiming the impossibility of forgetting the motivational virtues—because only these "tell us" the difference between right and wrong.

Wallace is clear enough about the difference between the substantive virtues and the virtues of will power not to explain the supposed unforgettability of self-control and patience by the supposition that they are modes of caring.

> The reason is not that there is a motivational component to these things that cannot be lost by forgetting. The reason why one cannot forget how to be brave or honest is like the reason why one cannot forget how to see or how to be strong: there is no "how to" to these things.

But as we shall see in the next section, this supposition too is false.

A fourth argument that no virtue is a skill has been presented by Philippa Foot. Following Aristotle and Aquinas she notes that when a person's action bespeaks a lack of a skill (let us say he misspells a word), he can defend himself against the implication by saying "I did it intentionally." But when his action bespeaks a lack of virtue (let us

[15]Gilbert Ryle, *Collected Papers*, vol. 2 (London: Hutchinson, 1971), pp. 381*ff.*

say he tells a lie), he does not exculpate himself by saying "I did it intentionally." Thus no virtue is a skill.[16]

Foot's argument overlooks that virtues relate in more than one way to morality. It is of course true that an action does not become any the less immoral by being intentional; and so when doing the moral thing (say, being compassionate) requires the exercise of a skill virtue (say, patience), the fact that one's failure of patience was intentional is no *moral* exculpation. But claiming that the failure to exercise patience was intentional *would* defend against the accusation of lacking patience. If patience is a virtue, then one can defend against the implication of failure to possess a virtue by claiming that failure to exercise it was intentional.

VI

I shall now indicate sketchily some ways people manage their adverse inclinations, and draw attention to the skill-likeness of these ways. Like other skills, some of these ways are strategic, like the duck hunter's knowledge of the precise moment to rise in the blind, while others are more basic, like his ability to squeeze the trigger without disrupting his aim. My argument is not that because there are strategies for developing courage, courage must be a skill. One might develop compassion by the strategy of meditating on the lives of compassionate people. It is rather that being courageous is *in itself* (often subtly and subconsciously) in part strategic, and so is formally like those many skills that have strategic dimensions. Nor is my argument that merely because the exercise of these virtues can develop them, they must be skills. Performing compassionate actions can perhaps cause a person to become more compassionate. Instead, I shall try to describe the specific similarities between these exercises and ones which issue in skills. I shall speak first of the management of cravings and impulses, then of emotions.

Cravings and Impulses Søren Kierkegaard depicts a gambler struggling against his compulsion:[17]

> Imagine that he . . . said to himself in the morning, "So I solemnly vow by all that is holy that I shall nevermore have anything to do with

---

[16]See Foot, "Virtues and Vices," pp. 7*f.*

[17]*For Self-Examination and Judge For Yourselves!* trans. Walter Lowrie (Princeton, NJ: Princeton University Press, 1968), p. 69.

gambling, nevermore—tonight shall be the last time." Ah, my friend, he is lost! Strange as it may seem I should venture to bet rather on the opposite, supposing that there was a gambler who at such a moment said to himself, "Very well, thou shalt be allowed to gamble all the rest of thy life, every blessed day—but tonight thou shalt let it alone," and so he did . . . For the resolution of the first man was a knavish trick of lust, but that of the other is a way of hoaxing lust . . . Lust is strong merely in the instant. . . .

The more normal development of this aspect of self-control might occur as follows: parents teaching their children to defer gratification would begin with small stretches of time. They would say not, "Here is your Easter basket, and you may eat your chocolate bunny the day after tomorrow," but instead, "After dinner, you may bite off his ear." (And, by the way, they will not set the temptation out of the child's reach until the appointed time, nor keep a nervous eagle eye out so as to slap the hand that reaches for the bunny, but will let the child develop her own ability to resist the impulses she may feel.) If the parents are wise in engineering settings for gratification-deferment that are manageable for the child, she may, with some trial-and-error of her own, grow up with a nearly unreflective tendency to pick for herself deferment goals that are realistic given her own powers of resistance, and thus put herself in for a minimum of discouragement. It is imaginable that this skill of self-management might develop without any explicit discussion of its rules or reflection on them, and might be as natural as speaking one's native language. This is not to say that the tougher cases of urge-control would be without struggle.

A cabinet builder follows a dictum that might be expressed, "He who starts a project square and level has less need of compensating exercises in ensuing stages." When he was a novice his teacher perhaps had to voice the dictum a few times, but after he had built some cabinets himself the dictum became integrated into the practice, sinking to the status of a mentally unrehearsed policy or rule of skill founded on the ineluctable geometric properties of cabinets, floors, and walls. The remark that "Lust is strong merely in the instant" is an easily accessible piece of psychological wisdom, one that can become as integral a part of a person's dealings with himself as the carpenter's dictum is of his dealings with boards and nails. The more self-mastering person knows, either intuitively or perhaps expressly, such things as that committing oneself to long-term abstention from the fulfilment of a strong impulse is probably either self-deceptive or likely to overwhelm and discourage. (I am told that "one day at a time" is one of the basic tenets of Alcoholics Anonymous.) Skill at the management of impulses and cravings must take this fact of human nature into consideration, just as carpentry must take geometric truths into consideration.

We can imagine that at first, upon hearing or formulating for himself this dictum, the weak-willed gambler might succeed in "hoaxing his lust" by explicitly telling himself that he is not promising to abstain for life, after all, but only for the next twenty-four hours. Then when the next day comes he renews his commitment, assuring himself that it is only for the day, and so on. But after the rule has been applied successfully a few times, the "hoaxing" may change gradually to a habit, a subconscious policy of choosing manageable time-parameters for one's choices of self-denial. When this happens, the individual is beginning to gain a stronger will.

The way of mastering impulses that I have just discussed is strategic: In its more self-conscious (though not in its deeper and more usual) forms it involves considering what one is up against and then, in the light of this, figuring out a way to meet the challenge. But there may also be an aspect of impulse-mastery that is more basic. Boyd Barrett[18] proposes a number of exercises by which a person can increase his ability to resist impulses. These involve doing such "useless" things as standing on a chair for ten consecutive minutes and trying to do so contentedly; listening to the ticking of a clock and making some definite movements at every fifth tick; and replacing in a box, slowly and deliberately, one hundred matches. In all such activities one is almost certain to get impulses to quit: boredom, physical discomfort, thoughts of things one would rather be doing. We might speculate that here one does not necessarily resist the impulse by some "method" such as hoaxing the lust or reconstruing the impulse. Maybe one resists the impulse to discontinue the activity by simply continuing the activity. If this interpretation is correct,

---

[18]In a book called *Strength of Will and How to Develop It*, discussed in Robert Assagioli, *The Act of Will* (New York: Viking Press, 1973), pp. 39 *ff.*

then there would seem to be a power to resist impulses that is a basic ability—basic not in the sense that it is unlearned, but in the sense that one does not exercise it by exercising some other ability. It would be like some people's ability to look cross-eyed or wiggle their ears.

Emotions Some impulses are emotions, as when fear is the impulse to flee or boredom the impulse to quit an activity. But other impulses are not emotions: for example, physical pain, and lusts for sex, money, gambling, and philosophical discussion. Conversely, not all adverse emotions are impulses. An impulse, it seems, must be directed at *doing* something, and when I experience an adverse emotion such as malicious joy, I may not be inclined to do anything at all except continue dwelling on whatever it is I am maliciously joyful about. In such cases the emotion is adverse not because of what it may lead to but because it is itself unfitting, morally or from the point of view of psychological health or happiness.

There are two senses in which we may control an emotion. If it is an impulse to some undesirable behavior such as fleeing a situation that should be faced or emitting some angry behavior that will have untoward consequences, then controlling it may just mean resisting the act to which it is an impulse. But it may also mean the reshaping of the emotion itself: mitigating the anger or fear, or eliminating them altogether, or mutating them into some less offensive cousin. For the sake of brevity I shall focus here on the control of emotions in the second sense.

Any of the virtues of will power may be directed upon emotions. Self-control can be, among other things, a mastery of anger, resentment, malicious joy, envy, contempt, and boredom. Where patience is directed to a task, emotions with which it typically must deal are boredom and frustration. (A related virtue is tenaciousness or perseverance, whose primary emotional adversary seems to be discouragement or some degree of hopelessness.) Where patience is used in dealing with people, typically mastered emotions are anger and resentment and boredom. The emotions to which courage relates are fear and anxiety.

In some cases anger diminishes with oblique behavioral "expression." Thus a worker may diminish anger at an oppressive superior by kicking pasteboard boxes around in the privacy of a garage and cursing loudly. It may help to imagine the superior's face or backside in the boxes and to go through the procedure in a somewhat ritualisic and comical[19] manner. Similar activities may have the effect of increasing one's anger at the superior, so knowing when this sort of thing will work and prescribing to oneself and carrying out appropriate rituals is clearly a skill-like ability, a kind of self-directed practical wisdom.

One can often alter an emotion by behaving in a way that conflicts with it. Thus if I am afraid of someone, one way to handle the fear is to stand up straight, look him in the eye, and speak clearly in a strong and even voice. Although the fear may not disappear entirely, it will certainly be less than if I shrink back, speak in a weak mumble, and generally present myself to myself as one who is in an oppressive situation.[20] I think that courageous people typically are aware, intuitively, of the influence that their bodily dispositions and voice and speech have on their anxiety and fear, and practice this kind of self-management. It is far from obvious that courageous people typically feel fears and anxieties less intensely than cowardly people. But through practice in facing up to threatening situations, they have learned how to manage and mitigate their fears.

Skillful self-talk is another way of controlling emotion. I am becoming impatient with my four-year-old's bedtime delaying tactics, and verging on anger; so I talk to myself: "I did the same when I was four," or "Notice how ingenious her tactics are—bright little gal, huh?" or "Just relax and bear with it a moment longer; it *will* soon be over." Such self-talk often mitigates or even dispels the welling anger, along with the urges to be abrupt, to behave punishingly, and generally to lose my cool. Perseverance may also involve self-talk, making use of "the power of positive thinking," as well as the tactics of reading encouraging literature (e.g., to help one persevere in a diet or a language-learning program) and associating with encouraging people. But self-talk and these more external self-management tactics are crude forms of this aspect of self-control: the experienced self-controller just flashes the strategic thoughts across her mind at the appropriate moments, the way a basketball player moves intelligently but without deliberation in the split-second of court action.

---

[19]For an account of how comical representations, and the capacity to appreciate them, can be connected with moral virtues, see my essay "Humor and the Virtues," *Inquiry*, vol. 31 (1988), p. 2.

[20]For an explanation of why techniques like this work, see my "Solomon on the Control of Emotions," *Philosophy and Phenomenological Research* (March 1984) and "What An Emotion Is: A Sketch," *Philosophical Review* (April 1988).

VII

Before I end, I must put the thesis of this paper in perspective.[21] I have argued that the virtues of will power are in an important aspect skills or skill-like powers. But I have nowhere claimed that this is the whole story of these virtues.

There may be saints whose patience and courage do not involve any exercise of will power, in the form either of efforts of will or of an effortless mastery of adverse impulses and emotions. The reason their goodness involves no exercise of will power is what makes them saints: they don't have any adverse impulses or emotions to which will power might be applied. Whether there are any saints in this sense I don't know; but there are certainly particular acts of courage and perseverence that involve no exercise of will power. Some acts of heroic courage are performed so spontaneously that there can be no question of the individual overcoming his fears; he just doesn't have any fears at the moment.

But even when skills of self-mastery are still needed, there are two other features typical of people with the virtues of will power. First, they *care* intensely about something. I have argued that the virtues of will power, when they are moral, derive their moral import from the concerns in the interest of which they are exercised. But the virtues of will power are never exercised apart from any motivation whatsoever; and generally speaking, the more intense the concerns, the more likely that the skills of self-mastery will be exercised and their power increased. So where courage does have moral import, it generally will be true that the deeper the courage the more powerful the

---

[21]Another kind of perspective is the diversity of the moralities in which virtues of will power appear. In this paper I have tried to characterize these virtues in a generic way. But within a given moral tradition they will also have nongeneric features. Stoic courage and Christian courage, though both capacities for managing fear and anxiety, are different enough to be considered different virtues. The traditions provide distinctive resources for dealing with these adverse emotions, and the resources get incorporated in the skills. Thus a major resource in the stoic repertoire is the characteristically stoic thought that "harms" are unavoidable anyway; resignation, then, becomes part of the strategy for reducing fear. Christian courage, by contrast, trades heavily on the thought of the presence and trustworthiness of God, and it is these that the developed Christian brings to bear on fearsome situations. In both traditions something like meditation on the respective resources is essential to the cultivation of the virtue.

For an elaboration of three virtues of will power (self-control, patience, and perseverance) in a distinctively Christian form, see my *The Strengths of a Christian* (Philadelphia: Westminster Press, 1984).

moral concerns of the individual. Not all morally passionate people are courageous, but it is typical of courageous people that they are passionate.

The second feature typical of people with the virtues of will power is self-confidence. There is a correlation between people's ability to handle their adverse inclinations and their confidence in their ability to determine their own destiny. Of course, it is generally typical of skilled people that they are confident of themselves respecting the skill in question. And so, since self-mastery is so fundamental to the successful conduct of a human life, it might seem that self-confidence is a by-product of the virtues of will power rather than an element of them. But while self-mastering skills clearly cause self-confidence, it is equally true that self-confidence grounds the exercise of self-mastery skills. When an athlete loses her self-confidence, she loses some of her ability to exercise her skill, even though her skill *per se* is not at all diminished. Similarly, in a situation of testing the individual who has ceased to believe that she can persevere will show herself as weak even though she possesses all the necessary skills to see her through her difficulty. An athlete needs three things for success: the requisite skills, an enthusiasm for the game, and a belief in her own powers. And the virtues of will power are the athletic side of the moral life.

STUDY QUESTIONS

1. Courage, says Roberts, is not a motivational virtue—so no courageous act is "done out of courage." What does Roberts mean by a "motivational virtue"? List some examples.
2. What is a substantive virtue? Why does Roberts think that someone who exercises a substantive virtue must enjoy exercising it?
3. What are "virtues of will-power," and how do these virtues perform "corrective functions"? How do they help us develop our "moral agency"?
4. According to Roberts, the application of the will in managing our inclination to do wrong requires skill. Give an example of the skill required to master anger, temptation, or envy. How does "practice" in such self-mastery help make us more proficient?

5. Roberts notes that some people are so good by nature as not to be tempted to do wrong. Such people have no need of the virtues of will power. Roberts suggests that such people may be the true moral saints. Do you think this is true of some ordinary people with respect to particular virtues? For example, some people seem not to "know the meaning of fear"; these are naturally courageous people. Others are never tempted to sexual sin or excess; these are naturally chaste people. And so forth. Are people more virtuous when they have to overcome temptations to do wrong? Or does the very temptation to do wrong detract somewhat from the goodness of that person? Is someone who "wouldn't hurt a fly" more virtuous than another who successfully curbs a violent temper? (Here the medieval moralists are helpful; the student may, for example, wish to look at Abelard's essay in Chapter Four.)

Generosity

JAMES D. WALLACE

James D. Wallace (b. 1937) is a professor of philosophy at the University of Illinois in Urbana. He is the author of *Virtues and Vices* (1978) and *Moral Relevance and Moral Conflict* (1988).

Generosity is a virtue concerned with giving. Wallace distinguishes between economic generosity, where the object one gives has a market value, and generosity of the heart or mind, where one gives intangible things such as kindness or encouragement. In primary generosity, agents directly concern themselves with the good of others rather than being inadvertently helpful. Normally, generosity exceeds what is expected or required by cus-

GENEROSITY From *Virtues and Vices* by James D. Wallace. Reprinted by permission of the author and Cornell University Press.

tom. The distinguishing features of economic generosity are (1) giving with the intention to benefit, (2) giving what has market value, and (3) giving more than is normally required. In the case of generous-mindedness, what one gives has no market value but the other criteria apply. The virtue of generosity illustrates that morality is sometimes a matter of acting beyond the call of duty.

Economic Generosity

Generosity is concerned with giving, and different kinds of generosity can be distinguished according to the kind of things given. Aristotle said that generosity (*eleutheriotēs*) has to do with giving and taking of things whose value is measured in money.[1] There is a virtue called generosity, the actions fully characteristic of which are meritorious, which has to do with freely giving things that have a *market value*—freely giving goods and services of a type that normally are exchanged on the open market. This sort of generosity I call "economic generosity" to distinguish it from other varieties. One can be generous in the judgments one makes about the merits and demerits of others, and one can be generous in forgiving those who trespass against one. "Generous-mindedness" and "generous-heartedness," as these other kinds of generosity might be called, do not involve being generous with things whose value is measured in money. These are like economic generosity in certain ways, but they also differ in important respects, as I shall try subsequently to show. Unless otherwise indicated, however, by generosity I mean economic generosity.

A generous person is one who has a certain attitude toward his own things, the value of which is measured in money, and who also has a certain attitude toward other people. Generosity, like other forms of benevolence, in its primary occurrence, involves as one of its constitutents a concern for the happiness and well-being of others. The actions fully characteristic of generosity have as their goal promoting someone else's well-being, comfort, happiness, or pleasure— someone else's good. In *primary generosity,* the agent is concerned

---

[1]*Nicomachean Ethics*, IV, 1, 1119b21–27.

directly about the good of another. Thus, an action fully characteristic of generosity might be done to please someone or to help someone, with no further end in view beyond pleasing or helping. "I just wanted to do something nice for them" or "I just wanted her to have it" are typical explanations of generous acts.

That an act fully characteristic of *the virtue,* generosity, is motivated in this way by a direct concern for the good of another is not immediately obvious, because we sometimes call giving "generous" and mean only that the giver is giving more than someone in his situation normally gives. Thus, the host is being generous with the mashed potatoes when he unthinkingly heaps unusually large portions on the plates. Or perhaps he does not do it unthinkingly. It might be that he is giving such generous portions because he wants to use up all the potatoes to prevent them from spoiling. Being generous in this way—giving a lot for reasons such as these—would not tend to show that the host is a *generous person,* even if he did so frequently. If we restrict ourselves to the kind of generous action that is fully characteristic of a generous person, then in every case, the agent's giving will be motivated by a direct concern for the good (in the broad sense) of another. I shall say in such cases that the agent intends to *benefit* the recipient.

There is a further complication. The virtue generosity, in its *primary occurrence,* I have said, involves a sort of direct concern for the good of others, as do other forms of benevolence. Someone who is deficient in such concern or who lacks it altogether might admire generous people for their generosity and want as far as he can to be like them. He might then want to do in certain situations what a generous person would do. Acting as a generous person would act because one regards generosity as a virtue, and wants, therefore, to emulate the generous person is meritorious, and it reflects credit upon the agent. It is, however, a secondary sort of generosity. It depends, for its merit, upon the fact that primary generosity *is* a virtue and is thus a worthy ideal at which to aim. I will concentrate, therefore, upon primary generosity, which does involve a direct concern for the good of another. An account of why this is a virtue is easily extended to explain why a generous person is worthy of emulation.

A certain sort of attitude on the part of the agent toward what he gives is also a feature of actions fully characteristic of the virtue generosity. In acting generously, one must give something that one values—something that one, therefore, has some reason to keep rather than discard or abandon. If, for example, one is about to throw away an article of clothing, and on the way to the trash barrel one meets someone who would like to have it, it would not be *generous* of one to give it to him. What disqualifies such giving from being generous is neither the giver's motive nor the nature of what is given but rather the fact that the giver himself does not value the object enough. Similarly, when we do favors for one another, giving matches or coins for parking meters, often what is given is too insignificant for the giving of it to be generous. One may be being kind in giving things that one does not particularly value, but for the giving to be generous, one must value the thing given for some reason. I may have acquired a particularly repulsive piece of primitive art that I have no desire to keep. Still, I might generously give it to a museum if it were a valuable piece—one I could sell or exchange for something I really want. How *generous* one is being in giving something generally depends upon how much one values the thing given, how much one is giving up.

Usually, the giver must give in excess of what he is required to give by morality or custom, if his giving is to be generous. Where there exists a generally recognized moral obligation to give, or where giving is customary, then normally one's giving is not generous even though it is prompted by a direct concern for the good of the recipient. If one were certain of a more than ample and continuing supply of food, so that it would clearly be wrong not to give some food to a neighbor who would otherwise go hungry, giving the neighbor a portion of food would not be generous. Similarly, to give a person a gift when one is expected to do so, because it is customary to exchange gifts (for example birthdays, Christmas, weddings, etc.), is normally not a matter of generosity, even though one aims to please the recipient. If one gives *more* than what is expected in such cases, then the giving might be generous. A generous person is one who exceeds normal expectations in giving, and one who gives no more than what is generally expected in the circumstances is not apt to be cited for generosity.

A special problem arises in cases of the following sort. Although it would clearly be wrong for a certain person *not* to give, he does not see this. Nevertheless, he does give on a generous impulse. Suppose, for example, that a certain person is a social Darwinist, convinced that it is wrong to give the necessities of life to people in need, because this enables the weak to survive, thus weakening the species.

She encounters a starving family, and touched by their plight, she provides food for them, though not without a twinge of social Darwinist guilt. Assuming that what she gives is not insignificant to her, but that it is no more than what the family needs to keep them alive, is her giving generous? On the one hand, she is really doing no more than the minimum required of her by the duty to help people in distress, and this makes one hesitate to say that she is being generous. On the other hand, *she* does not recognize any moral obligation here, and it is the kind and generous side of her nature that overcomes her cruel principles and leads her to give. This seems to support the view that she is being generous.

An act fully characteristic of generosity will normally have the following features.

1. The agent, because of his direct concern for the good of the recipient, gives something with the intention of benefiting the recipient.
2. The agent gives up something of his that has a market value and that he has some reason to value and, therefore, to keep.
3. The agent gives more than one is generally expected, because of moral requirements or custom, to give in such circumstances.

In normal cases, an act that meets these three conditions will be a generous act, and a generous act will have these three features. There are, however, abnormal cases—cases in which the agent has, concerning the circumstances mentioned in the three conditions, a false belief or an unusual or eccentric attitude. The case of the social Darwinist is such a case. She thinks she is morally required *not* to give, when in fact she is required to give. If one accepts *her* view of the situation, her act is generous. In fact, however, the third condition is not satisfied. In another sort of abnormal case, the agent values what he gives, but in fact the gift is utterly worthless—it is literally trash. Here it is not clear that the second condition is fulfilled, but from the agent's odd point of view, the act is generous. The very rich often give to charity sums of money that are large in comparison with what others give, and their gifts seem generous. These sums, however, which are substantial, may be relatively insignificant to the donors, and one may wonder whether condition (2) is satisfied in such a case. Does the donor, who has so much, in fact have reason to value and keep what he gives, or is his "gift" analogous to an ordinary person's giving away a book of matches? In a rather different sort of case, someone might be convinced that he is morally required to give away nearly all he has to the poor. For this reason, he divests himself of a substantial fortune. In such cases, it may be that condition (1) is not satisfied. The agent believes, in effect, that condition (3) is not satisfied, since he believes that he is required to do this. These circumstances will make one hesitate to call his giving generous, although other features of the case incline one toward the view that he is being generous.

In these cases involving unusual beliefs or attitudes, one is pulled simultaneously in two different directions. The way the agent sees the situation and the way one expects him to see the situation diverge. Crucial conditions are satisfied from one way of regarding the case and unsatisfied from the other. It is not surprising that one is reluctant to say simply that the act is (or is not) fully characteristic of the virtue generosity. Any such statement must be qualified, and the actual consequences of the qualification may or may not be important, depending upon the case. Normally, of course, the agent's beliefs about the features in (1)–(3) will not be grossly mistaken nor will his attitudes toward those things be unusual or eccentric. In such cases, if the three conditions are satisfied, the act is unqualifiedly generous, and vice versa.

A generous person is one who has a tendency to perform actions that meet these conditions. The stronger the tendency, the more generous the person.

Generous-Mindedness

The conditions in the preceding section are meant as an account of actions that are fully characteristic of *economic generosity*—generosity that involves giving things whose value is measured in money. Another kind of generosity, however, has to do with making judgments about the merits and failings of other people. This too is a virtue, which sometimes is called *generous-mindedness*.[2] I will try briefly to

---

[2] I am indebted to David Shwayder for bringing this topic to my attention.

indicate some similarities and differences between this virtue and economic generosity.

Generous-mindedness is shown by seeing someone else's merit (technical, moral, etc.) in cases where it is difficult to see because the facts of the case admit of other, not unreasonable interpretations, or because the situation is complex and the merit is not immediately apparent. Generous-mindedness is also shown by seeing that a derogatory judgment is not called for in cases where the facts might not unreasonably be taken to indicate a derogatory judgment. Many of us actually dislike to find that others are as good or better than we are, so that we have some desire to find grounds for derogatory judgments. It is plausible to think that people of otherwise fair judgment are sometimes led to think less of others than they should because they do not want to think well of them or because they want to think ill of them. They do not purposely close their eyes to merit; rather because they do not wish to find it, they do not try hard enough to find it. This may involve a certain amount of self-deception, but I suspect that in many cases the matter is more straightforward. If someone wants to find another inferior to himself in some respect, then where he sees some (prima facie) grounds for such a judgment, he is apt to be quick to seize upon it and regard the matter as settled. A generous-minded person is one who wants to think well of other people, so that in such cases he will look and find the merit that might otherwise go overlooked. Of course, it is possible to be too generous-minded—to overlook demerit because one does not want to find it.

If someone exhibits generous-mindedness in his judgment on a particular occasion, his act of judgment will not fulfill the conditions for an act of economic generosity. It will have features, however, that can be seen as analogous to the features characteristic of economic generosity. If an individual is well-disposed toward other people, then besides wanting to benefit them by giving them things, he will wish them well. He will tend to want their undertakings to succeed and to reflect well on them. If he wants to think well of others, he will be apt to look harder for merit, and he will, therefore, be more likely to find it. Generous-mindedness seems properly regarded as a manifestation of good will toward others that shows a direct concern for the well-being of others.

Economic generosity generally involves giving more than is

required or customary, and there is a counterpart to this in generous-mindedness. The generous-minded person sees merit where a competent evaluator might miss it, where it would be reasonable (though incorrect) to find that there is no such merit. In this way, one might say that generous-mindedness leads a person to go beyond what is required of an evaluator. . . .

For generous-mindedness not to distort one's judgment—for it not to lead one to incorrect evaluations—an individual must be a competent evaluator and be conscientious about reaching a correct judgment. Also, it does seem that if one has sufficiently good judgment and is sufficiently concerned to make the right judgment, then this by itself should lead one to see merit when it is present just as well as would the desire to *find merit*. The strong desire to make favorable judgments, moreover, *may* distort one's judgment. It may lead one to overlook defects and to find merit where it is not. A strong desire to make *the correct evaluation* cannot distort one's judgment in this way. Generous-mindedness should not be regarded as a primary virtue of evaluators. It can counteract an inclination to build oneself up by tearing others down, but so too can a strong desire to evaluate correctly. Generous-mindedness is a manifestation of the sort of concern for others that is characteristic of all forms of benevolence. It derives the greatest part of its merit from this concern. . . .

STUDY QUESTIONS

1. How would you measure the extent of generosity when (a) the person is mean-spirited but forces himself to give out of a sense of moral obligation; or (b) the person is innately kind and gives effortlessly?
2. What does Wallace mean by generous-mindedness? Do you believe that a stingy person who lacks economic generosity can be generous-minded? Conversely, can a mean-spirited person be economically generous?
3. Do we have a duty to be generous? Would not that be like having a duty to do more than our duty?

On Wisdom

STANLEY GODLOVITCH

Stanley Godlovitch (b. 1947) teaches at Mount Royal College in Calgary, Canada. He is a frequent writer of articles on ethics.

Stanley Godlovitch says that philosophers, despite all their protestations about its importance and all their praise of it, show little interest in wisdom. He tries to give an account of wisdom that will explain why wisdom is so neglected, why it is so difficult to understand, and why, as a virtue, wisdom is so rare.

Godlovitch considers and rejects several popular conceptions of wisdom that identify wisdom with age or experience, or with prudential competence. He then turns to Socrates' definition of wisdom as knowledge and critical understanding. However, using Socrates as the paradigm of a wise person creates puzzles. For one of Socrates' themes is that most people do not know what they think they know: Socratic wisdom consists in knowing that we do not know. Yet, this is not the entire story. For Socrates also points to a stage in human understanding when a person comes into "contact with the unchanging . . . and this state of the soul is called wisdom." Among the unchanging truths whose grasp makes us wise are that we shall all die and that immediate triumphs are evanescent. Such truisms enable us to assess our experience by giving it its true worth, and one reason we associate wisdom with age is that older persons are in a

ON WISDOM First appeared in *Canadian Journal of Philosophy* (March 1981). Reprinted by permission of the author.

better position psychologically to appreciate the significance of the eternal verities and to apply them in evaluating the significance of a particular act or event. Wisdom is a virtue of perspective. Unlike courage, it is not episodic. Godlovitch puts wisdom alongside such nonutilitarian personal characteristics as dignity, self-respect, and decency.

Wisdom is so rare precisely because it demands of us a perspective that is psychologically difficult to achieve and live by. In many ways wisdom is an unpopular and embarrassing virtue, quite at odds with the lives that most of us choose to lead. The wise person—by his or her life or his or her teaching—tends to expose us, debunking our lives as somewhat pointless. This is not easy to accept, and so we may react to this perspective with hostility. Socrates' fate stands as a warning to those who too zealously advertise the value of wisdom.

When I first began to study philosophy I was introduced to the discipline in that magically traditional way by being assured that what lay before me was the love of wisdom. Why this had any adolescent appeal still puzzles me, but, like many others, I joined in as spectator to and occasionally as a removed participant in all the rough and tumble of a Socratic sparring match in the Athenian marketplace. There was some talk of wisdom, to be sure, which seemed to link it with a humble admission of ignorance or a pitch against yielding to temptation, but neither was ever deeply revealing. I waited for more. My next encounter a few years later turned up little more than the surname of an English disciple of Wittgenstein. Somehow the trail had gone to brush, despite the apparent health and energy of philosophy.

I'm not sure whether or not philosophy has anything to do with wisdom. If it does, then it seems to pursue it with no more success than any of a number of other branches of learning. Tradition, however, and sentiment prod me to try to understand a little better what wisdom is and what it's not if only to discover why philosophers are so disinterested in it.

The idea of wisdom certainly invades much of the folklore of our own and of other cultures. Wise men, literally so called, appear in much religious literature. We live with the wisdom of the ancients, the wisdom of the elderly, and even transplant this quality metaphorically to time or nature or the body. And philosophy, of course, began putatively as a method for seeking it out.

We appear to see wisdom as a human feature associated with age and experience. It carries much positive moral force in being regarded as a rare and noble virtue, one which we would all wish to have. It has an epistemic quality, and is linked with some special variety of knowledge the acquisition of which is reserved for the privileged. There are, further, connections it has with behaviour, with the way things are done and with the nature of decisions and choices. This is no transient visitor to our discourse, nor has it gone so dated as to rank with such relics as chivalry and gallantry. The more we extend the catalogue of its appearances, the more apparent it becomes that we are dealing with a wide range of notions, some of which lack the dignity we give to whatever wisdom the Wise have. Moreover, as will become apparent, that mystical variety of wisdom, the one mention of which is the most familiar of all, seems less clear than many of the others.

Consider, for example, the most humdrum of cases. A man is seized with a powerful temptation to hop a plane to Bermuda. He books his seat and makes a reservation at a hotel. A few days before departure he begins to regard his plans as silly and recognizes that there are quite a few things he really should see to at home. So he cancels the trip. A day after his would-be departure he learns that the hotel he was to have been in has been struck by a tidal wave with great loss of life. His relief, needless to say, is immense. A friend, having heard the story, drops by and compliments him on the wisdom of his having stayed at home. Here, the decision to refrain from a holiday is wise only because it is lucky. True, in the light of undesirable consequences, the man has certainly avoided what he would have shunned had he known in advance. But his choice was deprived of that information, and so its so-called wisdom is not his as such. This is a very minimal sense of wisdom, perhaps one common to all other senses. We can formulate it as follows: a given choice or decision or action is a wise one provided that our making it avoids the undesirable consequences that would have arisen had we chosen some other considered alternative. The paradigm of the wise choice (though shot through with irony) is the beloved gun-to-the-head offer-he-couldn't-refuse case.

There are two disappointing features about this species of wisdom. It certainly doesn't make wise men of us, and it doesn't even seem to rise above sheer coincidence. Surely, wisdom ought to draw more out of us than a sigh of relief. So, let us strengthen the brew. Another man is offered a job at a very attractive salary by a competitor of the firm he works for. He is, naturally, flattered and very gripped with the prospect. However, before betraying his parent firm, he undertakes a little research and discovers that the firm about to snatch him up has a rather shaky financial record, that it has undergone an epidemic of high-level resignations, that its sales forecasts are not healthy, and so on. He weighs up the risks, and declines the offer. Sure enough, within a year the company has gone into receivership and many of its executives are out looking for employment. Our man does not sigh and thankfully mop his brow. He knew this would happen. He confides the tale to a colleague who replies robustly: "Good thinking. Wise decision. Stick with Acme and you'll never want."

We have here the minimal element but we have something else as well. The factors that go into making the decision reflect directly upon the likelihood of certain consequences. The decision itself is one which is unequivocally grounded in a careful prediction about its beneficial outcome. This takes in a concern for foresight, and has the smell of plans, and plots and calculation about it. The mere desire for monetary gain has been but one considered feature, and has been shelved in the light of overriding discoveries. This type of case gets quite close to Plato's view of wisdom as the supremacy of reason over the passions. Because the choice is guided by a learned appraisal of its consequences, the choice is a rational one. From that it inherits its wisdom. We rise to the next level. A given choice is a wise one provided that the choice calculatedly avoids the undesirable consequences that would otherwise have arisen.

The disappointments do not vanish. No one will deny that our executive is cautious and clever. His good fortune is very much due to his own effort. But the wisdom of his ways comes a little too cheaply. Though we have rid ourselves of accident and luck, we've got little more than prudence and craft as replacements. Insofar as any of us chooses carefully, the prize for which is the maximal satisfaction of our desires, we become wise in this sense. Merely being self-interestedly sensible, however, does not usher us into the elite class of the Wise. There are besides, the usual worries about the extent to which we wish to press the notion. A man who calculatedly and successfully commits mass murder and escapes punishment may indeed be cunning and, as it happens, act in his own best interest but I, for one, would gag a little on the words: "There is wisdom in what he has done." Not all prudent choices display wisdom; though, in this slightly supra-minimal sense, all may be wise. The trouble is that we expect something special in the epistemic content of wisdom, something out of the ordinary; and we also expect some presence of value beyond the mean triviality of self-interest. We need not fare any better if we conceive of cases where the calculated decision relates to actions which are designed to benefit others. In the first place, such benefit need not rank particularly high on a moral scale even if the act is in some way altruistic. If I plan, by weighing strategies, to secure for my family a monopoly on the North American heroin traffic, and succeed, my moves may well be considered as having been wise ones by my successors, but the context somehow forbids my entry to sainthood. Secondly, even if my intentions are of supreme worthiness, my wisdom will certainly be in doubt (if considered at all) should my calculations backfire.

Whatever the wisdom philosophers used to seek is, it does not shine forth in these considerations of the "the wise thing to do." In this regard, the strictures on any lofty variety of wisdom are more stringent than they are on moral goodness. Good men and good deeds seem to travel together. Though choices, when praised for their goodness might still smack of prudence and self-interest (the virtues of the sensible man), the goodness of an action hangs heavy with the moral stature of the agent. Very few individuals who manage usually to do the wise thing make the grade of the wise man.

The reason for this impasse is that the special and important notion of wisdom we admire has very little, if anything, to do with practical action and its antecedents. We should, then, turn to more profitable ground wherein the more refined epistemic and moral connotations may be located.

One starting point might be the emphasis we place on the connection between wisdom and age. It is not uncommon for us to deny the possibility of wisdom to a young, though mature, person. Again, following Plato's lead in the *Republic,* Socrates first seeks out revelation not from the sharp-witted ambitious youngsters on the make, but from the retired and successful business man, Cephalus. For Plato and his mentor, it is painfully obvious that, though wisdom may come with age, it need not. Cephalus is superficial, uncritical, a little bored by this line of inquiry, and probably quite absorbed by clipping stock coupons. However biting this portrayal might be, Plato himself does not forsake the line between wisdom and age when he gives us his hero on trial. So, we may ask, what is the attraction?

It may just contingently happen that all those who have been deemed to have been wise have been old at the time. This, though possible, is not convincing. The number of societies that have reserved an honoured place for their councils of elders is too large. In our own society, the wisdom of a politician or statesman seems to be correlated with age. From the young we're supposed to reap dynamism, daring, and efficiency; from the old, judiciousness, selflessness, and wisdom. Empirically we discover these connections to be shattered hourly. It's the expectation, however, which survives disconfirmation.

Though few would say that age as such imparts wisdom without accepting liberal exceptions—for age also may bring senility or dogmatism—some see it as necessary. Why? The aged have lived longer and so have more experience of life, may be one reply. This might be a pattern of thought which claims that, given hindsight and retrospect, we are better equipped to judge ourselves after the fact. This view is, of course, best captured by Shaw's lament that youth is wasted on the young.

The link between wisdom and age must be grounded not in the number of years as such but the quantity and quality of experience long life has provided. Simple quantity will not suffice because a lifetime of unending repetition of experience could hardly be said to contribute to a stockpile of wisdom. I suppose that many societies, some of the lifestyles of which are very elemental, will nevertheless attribute wisdom to their elders. If we consider a simple agrarian society, the vast extent of all expected experiential variety may well be had before a life is half over. What might count in such cases is not the assortment of experiences had by any individual, but some presumption about changes in the assessment of that experience. These changes are themselves part of experience and so provide the life with reflective if not physical variety.

This approach sounds persuasive but for a few awkward comparisons. Let us say I faithfully attend a showing of *Citizen Kane* every year for years. Further, suppose that each time I see the film differently so that the differences in my viewing history go well beyond the ritual repetition of the same visual input. This might stand as a stripped-down model of the wisdom of the elders. Although it may be true that each experience is distinct and distinctly revealing, it may nevertheless be pressing matters to say that, in some sense, each viewing is more perceptive or profoundly comprehended than its predecessor. Difference of experience in no way assures superiority of experience. Furthermore, any given later collection of such experiences is not guaranteed superiority of insight (or whatever is valuable about them) over any one earlier experience. At least, I see no special reason for saying they are. After all, it is certainly possible that any one viewing should be seen as the best one. Merely re-considering the sameness of experience over time from slightly different perspectives each time does not give the quantity of such reviews or the latest of them special significance.

It would seem most sensible to say that the attribute of wisdom lies in the nature of the assessment of experience rather than in the stage of life at which such assessment is made. But this does damage to the link between age and wisdom. If such an alliance exists, it must be founded on stronger stuff. There must in other words, be something about the experience and assessment of experience of the old that gives it majesty. What may it be?

There is a frequent temptation to say that the acquisition of wisdom may be complete as is humanly possible near the end of life but that, nevertheless, the very process of living is one accompanied by greater and greater wisdom. If it's true that "as one gets older, one gets wiser" we must be able to say that at any one point in our lives we possess more wisdom than we had at any earlier point. The only factor that distinguishes the elderly is that they've acquired as much as can be acquired given our mortality. I think it would be very hard to make this guarantee stick. My attitudes about and evaluations of life may remain substantially unchanged despite the growing conflagration on my birthday cake. Many people just happen to be conservative in this way. If we persist in loyalty to our motto, then we seem to have made it a matter of definition and not one subject to meaningful confirmation or disconfirmation in any given case. I hope there is more to it than this because, otherwise, it is just reminiscent of the fake profundity playfully satirized by Henry Reed in "Chard Whitlow":

> As we get older we do not get any younger.
> Seasons return, and to-day I am fifty-five
> And this time last year I was fifty-four,
> And this time next year I shall be sixty-two.

So, we might admit, though hesitantly, that as one gets older, sometimes all that happens is that one gets older. Wisdom oughtn't to come quite so effortlessly.

Let's grant the existence of a case where wisdom has increased with age. (Perhaps we should also grant that it can decrease as well if we insist upon the empirical way). How can we characterize greater wisdom? We know that something must have changed with time, something in the perspective of the aging individual. For this perspective to be a wiser one it must also be an improvement of some sort. The later experience must be superior in quality. What would count in its favour? It cannot merely be the evaluation of the person himself. We may chronically fancy our latest insights to be our best ones, but that just shows that human vanity is always freshest in its most recent phase. Nor can we trust entirely the judgment of others about this individual because they may merely be paying tribute to something they've not yet thought of. We have to have a conception of greater wisdom which, in the weak sense, couldn't have been had by this person at any earlier stage in his life, and more strongly, perhaps, in the light of the greatest wisdom being the prize of the elderly, couldn't have been had by anyone else who happened to be younger.

We must avoid the triviality of the definitional sense of "greater age, greater wisdom" as well. In a sublimely unimportant sense, given the life I have led, the uniqueness of perspective I now have couldn't have been mine earlier if I never had it before. There seems, however, nothing to dissuade me from saying that I could possibly have led a different life such that what I now know about experience I could have known while twenty years younger. Indeed, if the elderly can impart wisdom, if wisdom is a variety of knowledge or perspective, then the very young have the opportunity to short-cut the cost of aging in order to get where the aged are.

This hits a few snags. Providing we persist in attributing greater wisdom to the old, either wisdom cannot be imparted, or the young cannot understand what is imparted. If the former is the case, then we certainly have no grounds for calling the wisdom of the aged greater because, we the younger, have not, *ex hypothesi,* been given anything with which to compare it. Should the latter be advocated, it seems the wise can only communicate with the wise in which case, given that final wisdom comes complete and consistent, they'd have rather little to say to one another, and certainly no cause for chatting with youngsters. Neither is satisfactory because wisdom is characteristically sought out and appreciated by those who think they've less of it than others. Many great wise men of our culture are revered as teachers. Who has ever thought much of a circumstance where the teacher couldn't teach or the student couldn't hack the course?

What this amounts to is, I think, a serious erosion of the age-wisdom axis. If it makes any sense at all to say that wisdom can be imparted then no particular supremacy can conceivably go to the wisdom of the elders other than that they may be the first ones to spread it round. But once it is in circulation, age, the deposit of experience, will not matter very much. It all becomes very like the syndrome which has it, with great truth, that any decent freshman in physics knows far more about matter in motion than did Galileo.

This last adage may, however, provide a reprieve. What the freshman cannot be said to have under his belt are more discoveries about mechanics than the son of the famous Florentine lute composer. Learning about experience and acquiring that experience through living are powerfully distinct. Just as the freshman's impressive knowledge of physics does not make him a genius, so the young Plato is not made wise by taking to heart the message of his teacher. So it goes for the individual case. The greater wisdom I may now feel I have is derived not only from the conclusions of experience but from the struggle through it. Though this last route seems hopeful, the issue is not at all settled. It's unavoidably true that the older I become the more experience I will have had. It's quite another thing to say that the mere having of it need do anything to boost my sagacity. Further experience can just as easily dull my perception of life as it can improve it. Nor is there anything to dismiss my saying that my later experience was in large part moulded by my earlier contact with someone who had wisdom.

We like to believe that, having lived through some momentous experience, the insight we have about it is greater, more intense, or clearer than that of those we may have imparted it to. We may fancy that our contacts with love or sorrow, fame or failure, have given us something which of necessity just cannot be had by those who learn by our stories without having played the parts. Academics, for example, are not commonly attributed with more than infancy in the down-in-the-gutter disquisitions on "the real world out there" generously supplied by their mercantile brethren. It must be something like this which we generalize about when we twist together age and wisdom.

I'm uneasy about all of this. What we take to be greater clarity and so greater wisdom may be somewhat exaggerated. Such experiences are certainly more personal and strikingly so. They are also more memorable. But these of themselves do not reward the conclusions we draw with any greater virtue they have on their own. That someone may have lived through insightful experience is often a matter of chance unless one sought it out in the first place. We would be oddly beneficent to credit anyone for simply having had certain experiences which, contingently, led to those insights we call wise. For those reasons, the argument "I've lived longer, so I know more about life" does not shed any blinding light on wisdom. If wisdom lies anywhere, it must rest at least with the ability to draw certain types of conclusion from experience, and not from mere persistence through life. Having that ability cannot merely rest with a high score in years.

Age as such then is not a sure guide to wisdom nor is wisdom something we can all look forward to in our later years as we might our pensions or retirement. The Shavian retort that we can when older more fully appreciate what we couldn't have appreciated when younger fails at least on two counts to gain much ground. If the quantity of experience is necessary for the appreciation of experience, then a young man with an older man's appreciation of his youth is an impossibility. Knowing Shaw, this might indeed have been precisely what he meant. Secondly, if appreciation is not so dependent, then there is nothing in the reflections of maturity as such that give them superiority over the reflections of youth no matter how mistaken, rash, and unreflective they may seem in retrospect. Remarks like Shaw's are akin to regrets at not having done earlier what one cannot do now. Regrets may be frequent episodes in later life and they may command our fullest sympathy, but the most regretful of men cannot as such compel us to venerate his wisdom.

One last comment on the theme of age. Though now considered a little old-fashioned, there have been common references to the wisdom of the ancients or the wisdom of the fathers or some such reference to folkloric heroes of the past. These seem extensions of the links between wisdom and old age except they are spread over entire cultural histories. The frailty of such views is readily visible. The culture of the present is necessarily older than the culture of the past. Its accumulated experience and opportunity for hindsight are therefore greater. Greater wisdom attributed to members of younger and probably more primitive societies seems more nostalgic than consistent. Perhaps the confusion lies in a temptation to think of "the good old days" as historically older rather than historically former. When I reflect on my own past I remember the activities of a younger man. Odd, isn't it, that we conceive our cultural present as youthful in relation to the earlier stages it has passed through. However we take birthdays, Beethoven is not two hundred and ten years old. He died at fifty-seven in a society with a musically youthful culture that had not yet amassed enough knowledge and experience to fit him up with a passable hearing aid.

Perhaps the ideas we have considered have been incidental. It certainly does not seem as though too much store is to be placed in the relationship between wisdom and action, and that between wisdom and old age. Though both are decidedly part of our framework of thought, the former deals with little more than enlightened egoism and the latter with peculiar analogies we draw between increasing wealth as a result of continual savings and growing wisdom ensured by continual experience. What positive gains we have made have been slight; namely, that wisdom is somehow linked to the avoidance of the undesirable and that it has something to do with the assessment of and the capacity to reflect upon experience.

Another Platonic theme, the relation between wisdom and knowledge, might prove more helpful. The Wise are customarily taken to be endowed with a variety of knowledge and understanding quite out of the ordinary. If anything shows up the inadequacy of the avenues we have already travelled on, this does. The wise thing to do does not constitute wisdom if it's simply a sensible and well-planned course of action. No saying of an elder counts as wise if it's just platitudinous.

The account Plato gives of Socrates' finest hour is fraught with irony, replete with the paradoxical ways of the world's greatest sophist:

> And I am called wise for my hearers always imagine that I myself possess the wisdom which I find wanting in others: but the truth is, O men of Athens, that God only is wise; and by his answer he intends to show that the wisdom of men is worth little or nothing: he is not speaking of Socrates, he is only using my name by way of illustration, as if he said, He, O men, is the wisest who, like Socrates, knows that his wisdom is in truth worth nothing.[1]

We can take this in at least two ways. The first is that there is no body of knowledge which can go by the name of wisdom, but only specific bodies of knowledge pertinent only to very particular matters. This is a favourite Socratic strategy, the moral of which is; do not seek wisdom because all you're ever going to find is musicianship, or salesmanship, or statesmanship, and so on. The second is the ploy of the collapsing ladder which once climbed, deposits you where you started. Wisdom is the knowledge that one knows nothing, a revelation with a built-in-self-destruct device. Either way there is no human wisdom.

Though the message here seems unrepentently pessimistic, I think we can soften it somewhat and give it some hope. If taken at his word, Socrates would have to be denying the possibility of his own chosen vocation. At the very least he would have to be admitting that the journey has no destination. Besides, the perennial recognition of wisdom cannot be so easily dismissed. Let us suppose this milder message; namely, that whatever knowledge the wise have it is not the sort of knowledge bound by the particularities of expertise. No matter how thorough a knowledge of a craft, trade, or profession a man might have, none of this counts one whit towards his pretension to wisdom. Needless to say, this does away with virtually all varieties of knowledge. It certainly rids us of role-related knowledge, i.e., the knowledge that comes with being a chemist or violin maker or historian and so on. When we seek clarification of what remains we are left, whatever the case, with knowledge at a level of generality which seems to be neutral with respect to whatever other knowledge of the world we happen to have via other domains of learning.

---

[1]Plato, *Apology* (trans. B. Jowett), 23a–b.

One typical Socratic candidate emerges from the *Phaedo:*

> But when returning into herself (the soul) reflects, then she passes into the other world, the region of purity, and eternity, and immortality, and unchangeableness . . . then she ceases from her wandering, and being in contact with things unchanging is unchanging in relation to them. And this state of the soul is called wisdom?[2]

If we can make any contemporary mileage out of this lyricism, the most we can say is that wisdom consists of knowledge of necessary truth, truth no matter what. There is no doubt that this has a warming effect if only because a recognition of wisdom carries with it a variety of complete faith in the soundness of the judgment no matter what culture or time we happen to inhabit. This is to say, the knowledge of the wise is knowledge which fits whatever world it happens to emerge in.

Not every candidate fulfilling the formal requirement is going to do. All those necessary truths we see in tautologies will scarcely impress, nor will we be moved by Pythagorean excesses about number and shapes. Logic and mathematics have no claim to wisdom, no more than do the quasi-Aristotelian appeals to natural essences and necessary *a posteriori* truth. What we want are claims blazened with undying truth about human life and experience which stand outside the incidental changes in the range of that experience and the culturally tied attitudes about it.

Suddenly we appear to have some prospect for success, but the optimism is perhaps premature. There are numerous claims which fit as well as do any the restrictions we have placed on wise sayings, yet which somehow lack the grandeur and mystery they ought to have. If we require such unhesitating truths, we seem free to consult the class of judgments about the necessities of existence. Judgments like "All men must die" or "All men must eat and sleep," no matter how ponderously and pontifically uttered, are scarcely gems of wisdom. They're true to be sure, and possibly even true of all of us no matter when and where we live, but they fall flat, and that is because they're so obvious and trivial we would scarcely appreciate let alone revere their utterance. Furthermore, they fail to secure uncompromising conviction because we can easily anticipate their being falsified by some future innovation in bio-medical research.

---

[2]Plato, *Phaedo* (trans B. Jowett), 79d.

Even if we search in other directions such as the Socratic discovery that we are all inevitably and hopelessly ignorant in that grand sense which prods us to recognize our unavoidable limitations, we may still question why that revelation deserves the title of wisdom. The reason for this is simply that no one would deny such claims. They are so broad as to be platitudinous, at least as truths about the human condition. After all, how seriously could a man resist the imputation that he will never know everything, and why indeed should he? Such claims which dodge the fallibility of the empirical, claims about the limitations of the individual or those vast hazy truths like "this too will pass," are not in themselves deeply profound because they fail almost stunningly to tell us anything about ourselves which we might possibly have missed. Their cosmic generality is won only through their seemingly banal immunity from question. Though they are not formally empty as are tautologies, they are, as truths, just as hollow. The flight to the pure, eternal, and unchangeable seems scheduled to land at the mundane and mouldy. Wisdom still awaits clearance.

There is always room at this juncture for a return match. I have suggested that although we may understand wisdom as a unique variety of knowledge, that very uniqueness is suspect. The necessity and generality it must carry merely disguise its actual poverty of content. What seems to be missed is any sense of revelation or profundity which, surely, must be the gift of the wise. However, it is not clear whether these supposed truisms are quite as uninteresting as they appear.

Those who see in wisdom a variety of knowledge may quite pertinently say that the general truisms of the wise take on an entirely different tinge when cast in the perspective of the ways men are prone to regard their own experience. It may just be a fact of our existence that we live and think of our lives as though such universal truths had no substance. We may indeed bathe in the illusions of arrogant omniscience, or immortality, and fashion our activities as though these were genuinely to be counted on. The wisdom of the Stoic, for example, cuts deeply into our expectations and deceptions, and persists in the reminder that our individual affairs are not quite nearly so magnificent in their triumph or grief as we care to imagine them. What the wise have is not a secret repository of knowledge unavailable to the masses, but rather the good sense to take seriously the unquestionable truth of the truism.

Wisdom becomes then a variety of knowledge not by virtue of its inscrutable depth, but rather by virtue of a suspicion that such knowledge should have priority in our assessment of experience. This, however, changes the picture considerably. For the advice of the wise becomes, on this interpretation, more like a reminder and perhaps even an admonition rather than the transmission of exotic information. The previous attempts at linking wisdom with action and with age take on a new perspective. If we couple consistently the necessary truth of the wise with our behavior we move considerably farther than the achievement of good solid sense. That calculating aspect must be ruled out because it is simply too particular, too specific, to yield anything more than expertise. The reliance upon age gains importance not because of the years of experience the aged have, but because there is a sense in which the aged no longer care about the plans and prospects they once had and so are psychologically in the best position to be freed of the forgetfulness of unchanging truths, a forgetfulness which helps feed the fires of those whose future is still largely a product of hopeful imagination.

What now emerges is not a vital link between wisdom and knowledge, because I think it fair to insist that the actual content of that knowledge is not special and mysterious in the way, say, that a layman may find the latest esoteric discoveries of physics. It certainly is not knowledge requiring expertise of any kind, nor need we prepare in any way to be privy to it. The knowledge involved is, however, universal, unchanging, and whatever else one may need to characterize its necessity. Where the wise emerge amidst this apparent banality of content is in their taking such knowledge seriously, recognizing how very stably true it is in the midst of passing deception so easily winning its victims.

The emphasis alters because it is not the knowledge of the wise we acknowledge to be special but the value they place and invite us to place on it. In some sense, the recognition of wisdom is the recognition of that which we, the unwise, not only have known but should have known all along. This last feature draws closer the connection between wisdom and virtue, perhaps the most recurrent bond to be established between the two.

In this regard, a number of matters come to light. The truisms of the wise gain respect not only because we are prone to accept their truth, but because the nature of that truth renders insignificant whatever screen of revealed illusions we have used to shield ourselves from it. The sayings of the wise are thus subtle provocations directed at our tendency to illusion. Were this tendency absent, were we naturally inclined to gauge our experience in the light of those features which, in the end, we cannot deny, there would be no virtue of wisdom in our conception of things. That there is, and that it is one we value without hesitation can only point to the confession that we see ourselves as unmindful at heart.

What are we doing when we call a given human feature a virtue? Amongst other things, we draw attention to a quality which would, if found in all men, improve life. We also point to something which is, under the title of virtue, in fact not very common amongst men nor on the whole eagerly accepted by them. Wisdom appears to be a virtue we give an honoured place. However, unlike other more modest virtues like honesty or courage, loyalty or charitableness, wisdom is not generally regarded as something which manifests itself episodically. The others attach to persons because they distinguish the behavior of such persons. We know quite well enough what brave or loyal people do to earn their stripes. As we discovered, however, "the wise thing to do" does not in any way confer wisdom upon an agent the way doing the courageous thing might encourage the attribute of bravery. Wisdom is not that tidily dispositional, nor do the wise perform as identifiable a service to their fellows as do the honest.

This raises an interesting peculiarity about wisdom. It is as if it is deliberately hidden from view quite in contrast to the public advertisement of numerous other virtues. A man may spend his entire life tending a flower garden and yet be wise nonetheless. Wisdom is not a virtue revealed by display, and seems, indeed, to grow more gracious with retirement.

This might easily cause us to ask wherein the virtue of wisdom lies. It is not as if our history were punctuated by the actions of the wise which have demonstrably made matters better than they might otherwise have been. We do not stand on firm ground if we try to exhort others to wisdom in the way we might encourage generosity or patience. We need not even feel comfortable with the thought of modelling our lives after those of the wise, and so their existence cannot be counted on as an example for all of us to follow.

What has this virtue of wisdom to offer? Why should we applaud it and wish it one of our features? Here the history of philosophy can provide a few tentative answers. The repository of wisdom has been rooted in a conception of human nature which is other-worldly. If we consider Plato and Aristotle's philosopher, Spinoza's free man, or Kant's moral agent much becomes clear, for in all cases do we have ideals of character severed utterly from the continual impact of all those events and states of mind which draw us toward that very special status we seek for ourselves. Whereas the brave man is attended to for his personal accomplishment, the wise man may boast no such individuating traits. What on the contrary is in common amongst the models of wisdom given to us through Greek and European philosophy is an image lacking all personality. Plato and Aristotle sought their release from the individual through conceptions of serenity detached from concern for all those items like possessions or social station which carve boundaries around individuals. Spinoza yielded himself up to a universal determinism so fierce as to leave freedom little more extravagance than the recognition by an atom of consciousness of determinisms's ubiquity. Kant submerged all particularity into the anonymity of reason alone. There is no question that, for these philosophers, the state of wisdom lay locked in these conceptions. It is no wonder then that the wise, though thought so grand, should appear at the vanishing point of human business. It is also no surprise that we seem unable to locate any cultural display of public commendation for wisdom. In the end this can only be because this puzzling virtue is antagonistic to all that is public.

The prize of wisdom, its unlikely appeal, must lie in a recognition that, relative to the truisms about life, it is the only rational response possible. Its rarity as a virtue is, in a way, a tribute to the value we place on such rationality and also a helpless realization that the type of life it demands is not psychologically compatible with the lives we generally choose to lead.

The consideration of typical virtues throws wisdom into a class of its own. This is because a typical virtue is merely one the possession of which is typically achievable without overstepping the bounds of psychological plausibility. There are whole hosts of virtues which are simply not all that difficult to acquire. One need only consider the characteristic lists so beloved by the civilized gentlemen of the eighteenth century. Hume, for example, is no exception when he wishes us to be openly warm to the following constituents of the good man: justice, fidelity, honour, allegiance, chastity, humanity, generosity, charity, affability, lenity, mercy, moderation, public spirit, discretion, caution, enterprise, industry, assiduity, frugality, economy, good-sense, prudence, discernment, temperance, sobriety, patience, constancy, perseverance, forethought, considerateness, secrecy, order, insinuation, address, presence of mind, quickness of conception, facility of expression. "These and a thousand more of the same kind, no man will ever deny to be excellencies and perfections."[3] Nor must we forget Wit and Manners. These are all distinguished by at least two features. We can, all of us, aspire (without condemnation to sainthood) to develop these characteristics in ourselves without too much fuss; and, all of these virtues reflect directly upon our successful dealings with others. The common virtue is notably a social feature and is directed largely to smoothing out the rougher edges of human association. Further, such virtues can be deliberately acquired. They can be groomed and cultivated and, in the end, made to work for us.

Wisdom sits alone. We cannot rehearse or practice it. We cannot be prompted to assume it—whether for our sake or for the sake of others. We cannot expect, should we be in possession of it, to win friends and influence people. Wisdom calls into prominence a state of mind rather than a readiness to act in specified ways. As such, its status as a virtue must remain rather aloof.

I asked at the outset why it was that modern philosophers appear so uninterested in wisdom and think, now, I might be able to provide some answer. If wisdom deserves any mention at all, it seems to fit naturally, though superficially, into talk about morality. Indeed, there appears to be no other role it is fit to play in a philosophical environment which no longer accepts that the function of philosophy is to furnish a guide for the perplexed. But the study of morality, if it is at all an investigation into virtue, must centre round the complex of issues that deal with our public lives, our responses and reactions to others. Needless to say, the grip of utilitarianism holds such concerns strongly. In such a light, whatever wisdom is, it scarcely is fashionable as a *moral* virtue because those are seen of necessity to be social. Wisdom cannot even be made to look like those darlings of Hume's, i.e. "qualities useful to ourselves" or "qualities immediately agreeable to others," simply because in our tradition the release sought by Plato as the ultimate moral end is considered best buried in the ascetic fanaticism of the past. Hume again:

---

[3]David Hume, *Inquiry Concerning the Principles of Morals*, Section VI, part I.

> Celibacy, fasting, penance, mortification, self-denial, humility, si-
> lence, solitude, and the whole train of monkish virtues; for what
> reason are they everywhere rejected by men of sense, but because they
> serve no manner of purpose; neither qualify him for the entertainment
> of company, nor increase his power of self-enjoyment?[4]

Whether or not this represents a mindless castigation of the virtue
of wisdom I am not in a position to say. What does seem unavoidable
is that the absence of talk about wisdom seems linked to a belief that
it is associated with the "monkish virtues" and so has no power of
benefit in discussions of morality. This surely derives from the inherent privacy of wisdom and its abrasive separation from the demands
of a gregarious species. It also stems from a split between the attainment of wisdom and the value placed on self-love. A tradition of
struggle to liberate and justify self-concern as morally acceptable
cannot do much business with a conception of virtue which presses
to blast "the dear self" out of existence. The history of the search for
wisdom reveals attitudes which confess that, as a whole, we're not
quite as important as we think we are, and that, as individuals, we're
not really important at all. If morality is seen as one sphere in which
the conflict and cooperation between me and others is manifested,
the grand and possibly ineffable vanishing act of the Wise is not likely
to be asked in for a guest appearance.

What this means, of course, is that wisdom cannot comfortably
assume a role within moral philosophy. It cannot even be used as a
target in attacks on such awkward remainders as supererogation because, though other virtues may be seen as casting obligations on us,
no one has ever suggested that we have a duty to be wise. Indeed,
within the entire sphere of what is now taken to be moral concern,
the moral field populated by rights, duties, the valuation of acts and
men, intentions, motives, and consequences there is no cause to
speak of wisdom at all. It might even be unintelligible to conceive it
as a moral virtue lacking as it does all pretence to refashion human
affairs in the name of universal benefit.

Though this might explain the neglect of the concept of wisdom,
it certainly fails to warrant it. Thought about wisdom calls to mind
many thematically related notions few of which have themselves seen

---

[4]David Hume, *op. cit.,* Section IX, part I.

extensive contemporary treatment. For, if we look at wisdom as it was looked at we detect a concern with a conception of human virtue which, though only marginally geared toward happiness or well-being, seems nevertheless to survive in the darker corners of morality. I refer with a deliberate sense of the old-fashioned to the notion of human excellence, that itself reflecting on certain exceptional qualities of members of our species which are distinct in force from the social utility of altruism. Examples would be notions like dignity, integrity, decency, self-respect, rationality, serenity, or wisdom. Some of these are occasionally used to counter the supposed evils within moral theories—notably utilitarianism—and that can only be because some of those theories are clearly felt to belittle or, worse, manipulate aspects of life which cannot be sacrificed at any costs. But these reminders about human excellence do not themselves constitute an alternative moral picture; not, that is, one dedicated to the guidance of decision. This is because we do not really know what it is if anything these peculiar virtues do for human life, nor do we know what precisely would count as restoring them should they be abused. Perhaps some understanding of these universally respected features might account for the growing frustration with ethical theory, and also prepare the way for its future development. Whatever the case, some room need be made for these, even if it means recasting our current rather mercantile models of moral behavior.

I have throughout this paper attempted to clarify some features of wisdom against a backdrop of general philosophical neglect. What has emerged is by no means an uninteresting concept, but one which, for some of the reasons outlined, falls outside contemporary philosophical concern. In examining wisdom in its epistemic and moral dimensions I have tried to show that it fails to rouse any special puzzles about some inscrutable sense of profundity as far as content is concerned, and also that it gains its title to virtue only at the expense of moving clear of our conception of typical virtues. I have, despite this, urged that a notion like wisdom points relevantly beyond our customary views about moral thought in much the same way as do attributes like dignity or self-respect. That is to say that such qualities belong to our moral schemes even though they slip past the usual emphasis upon the interaction of humans and the moral mechanisms of rights, obligations, moral strategies, and the like, which govern such interaction. Because of this I would argue that modern moral philosophy cannot afford to dismiss an approach to morality in the spirit of the Athenians or the rationalists of the enlightenment as dated.

Before closing, there is another small matter that need be discussed; namely, the features supposed to contrast with wisdom. These will illuminate, I think, some of the less accessible characteristics of wisdom. I have, so far, hedged round the question of the nature of the other-than-wise. At times I have allowed the young to fill the role, at others the unmindful, and sometimes have merely smeared the class round with the epithet "unwise." The traditional account is not nearly so courteous, for it is here that the fool rises to prominence. Just as wisdom is held to ride higher than the wise thing to do, so the fool is not merely one who happens unwittingly to do foolish deeds. The fault of the fool is far more brutally base than that.

What is interesting is that there is hardly a denunciation of a person so cutting and dismissive as that of calling someone a fool. What is even more fascinating is that we tend not to invoke moral derision in the customary sense when branding someone as a fool. There is, though, a strange uneasiness about such attributions, one which leaves them not quite as contrary to wisdom as might first appear. People are called fools when, for example, they stubbornly and almost naively act against their own best interest. Some are seen to be fools in contrast to pragmatic and 'realistic' agents. Here there is no question that the fool is a character somehow devoid of expertise, perhaps hopelessly so. Such fools, to our disgrace, might nevertheless have wisdom. There is another species of fool closely related to the first. Those are people whose manner and demeanour fail grotesquely to meet accepted standards. Such fools are born at formal dinner parties and august gatherings. These fools, too, are not antithetical to the wise. Where all fools join ranks, however, is in lacking something like an appropriate and expected level of intelligent perspective. The fool cast apart from wisdom must be as empty of the recognition of necessity as the wise are deeply involved with it. The fool, then, is not merely one lacking manipulative skill or elegant poise. His defects are far less redeemable because unlike his colleagues, he cannot be cured by any training program. Unfortunately, the fool turns out to be one whose entire life is misconceived. Further, and more damaging, the wise give us to understand that the fool is no passing stranger to the world. Indeed, he is present in all of us lacking wisdom. Here perhaps is the least acceptable aspect of those virtue theories in which wisdom is given extreme importance. Whatever wisdom is, it is very rare. If it is necessary as a component of the properly moral man, then it must be that the vast majority of us cannot make the grade. The numerous charges of elitism brought against Plato or of iciness lodged against Kant are the reactions of moral democrats all of whom fashion morality as a system accessible to everyone. In these liberal conceptions, the only requirement (and even this is not very pressing) is that one learn to temper one's unfortunate but forgiveable selfishness on those occasions when others might happen to be affected by one's actions. The achievement of wisdom has clearly never been viewed as so relatively minor an effort. This too might explain the neglect and also account for reactions such as Hume's which would brand such conceptions of human ineptitude as pointlessly negative and hardly worth the anguish. The wise, then, are tarred with the same brush used to silence the chronic tradition of fanatical harangue directed at the sorry state of our souls.

Of course, this assimilation is unfair because it has never been the tradition of the wise to pummel us with our limitations, let alone threaten us with their mortal danger. The aftershock is rather more subtly damaging. By contrast to the wise, we are enjoined in the end to see ourselves as pathetic. This is far harder to swallow and yet is gracefully easy to ignore. The one philosopher who bothered passionately about this matter got himself into a great deal of trouble. Perhaps we've learned a professional lesson. One is always wise to avoid litigation.

STUDY QUESTIONS

1. Why does the popular identification of wisdom with age and experience give an inadequate concept of wisdom?
2. Why is the identification of wisdom with prudential understanding and skill inadequate?
3. In what sense is wisdom a knowledge of truisms? How does wisdom enable us to remove the illusion and deceptions that hide the truisms from us?
4. Discuss the relation of wisdom to serenity.
5. Godlovitch suggests that, unlike the other virtues, wisdom cannot be cultivated deliberately. For this reason, no one has a duty

to be wise. Also, wisdom is rare. Is there anything paradoxical about a virtue that is not enjoined on us as a duty and that is inaccessible to all but a few?

6. Everyone thinks well of wisdom, yet wise people are often scorned. What is there about wisdom that renders it unpopular and suspect?

The Virtue of Pride

RICHARD TAYLOR

Richard Taylor (b. 1919) is the Leavitt-Spencer Professor of Philosophy at Union College. Previously he taught at the University of Rochester. Among Taylor's many books are *Good and Evil* (1971), *With Heart and Mind* (1973), and *Ethics, Faith and Reason* (1985).

Richard Taylor defines "pride" as *justified* love of oneself, as distinguished from conceit, vanity, and egoism. Proud persons may be unjustified in feeling proud; if so, they are merely "conceited." The vain person delights in the admiration of others, regardless of the qualities in themselves that arouse the admiration. Egoism is characterized by excessive absorption in oneself. Conceit, vanity, and egoism usually are not compatible with the virtue of pride. For Taylor, pride is a general virtue that presupposes other virtues such as courage, honor, and discipline.

The Nature of Pride

Pride is not a matter of manners or demeanor. One does not become proud simply by affecting certain behavior or projecting an impression that has been formed in the mind. It is a personal excellence

THE VIRTUE OF PRIDE From *Ethics, Faith and Reason* by Richard Taylor. Copyright © 1985 by Prentice-Hall. Reprinted by permission of the publisher.

much deeper than this. In fact, it is the summation of most of the other virtues, since it presupposes them.

Pride is the justified love for oneself. The qualification "justified" is crucial. Simpletons can love themselves and are, in fact, very apt to do so; but they are not proud, for there are no qualities of excellence to justify that love. They have not pride but mere conceit, which is something different altogether. Conceit is the simpleton's unwarranted sense of self-importance. Conceited persons thus imagine themselves as possessed of great worth, when in fact they have little or none; and that is why they are simple, as well as being very tiresome to others and of little worth in the eyes of those who are genuinely proud.

Genuinely proud people perceive themselves as better than others, and their pride is justified because their perception is correct. Thus they love themselves, not as children and ordinary people do, for these do not possess the kind of worth that justifies such self-esteem, but because they really are, in the classical sense of the term, good. Their virtues are not assimilated ones, nor do they consist merely in the kind of innocence that wins the approbation of others. Instead, they are their own in the truest sense: that they come from within themselves and win the approbation of the only judge who counts—oneself.

Arrogance, Vanity, and Egoism

Pride is not arrogance, and a proud person would never be overbearing towards others. While conceit is an attitude towards oneself, which in that respect resembles pride, arrogance is a way of behaving, a mannerism, and one that is profoundly offensive. One is arrogant only towards other persons. Arrogance cannot be exhibited in solitude, although conceit can—in vainglorious fantasy, for example, or at the other extreme, in solitary weeping.

Arrogance implies a belittling of the opinions, conduct, or personal qualities of another person in an effort to draw attention to one's own presumed superiority. It is, therefore, most easily exhibited towards persons who stand in an inferior position, such as waiters or other servants, employees, clerks, and so on. Police officers, particularly those who are vulgar or otherwise lacking in personal excellence, are very prone to arrogance, for one's inferior position cannot be more manifest than in the presence of a police officer's gun. It is for this same reason that cowards, given suitable circumstances, are likely to be arrogant. Since the fault that cancels their personal worth, namely cowardice, is so grave and ineradicable, they attempt to compensate with arrogance and browbeating or, given the opportunity, outright cruelty.

Vanity and egoism, too, must be distinguished from pride, for they have little in common with it. Vanity is the delight people derive from praise or flattering allusions to themselves, from whatever source, and with respect to whatever things are alluded to, whether significant or not. Thus vain people delight in flattering comment from inferior persons, such as from children, or even from total strangers, whereas a truly proud person would be quite oblivious to this. Vain people can even be seen trying to elicit attention and admiring comment in public places, and from persons entirely unknown to them, by their loud and excessive laughter, for example, or their swaggering gait, or by their attire, or by the importance or beauty of their companions. Thus a man sometimes enjoys entering a restaurant with a beautiful companion on his arm, even though he may never have been there before and may know no one in the room. Similarly, a woman is sometimes pleased to draw looks, even from strangers, to her tasteful clothing. Such are familiar examples of vanity, and they could be multiplied at length. It is something to which every normal person is prone, for who can fail to be pleasantly aware of the admiring attention of others? A vain person, however, seeks that attention, sometimes going to great length to get it, while a proud person tries to ignore it, and would be ashamed to actually set about trying to elicit it. This would be especially true with respect to such things as clothing, or the influence one has over other people or external things, in other words, things having no connection with one's true nature or excellence.

Egoism is similar to vanity, though perhaps some distinctions between the two are useful. Egoism is a certain cast of mind, characterized by excessive absorption in oneself, to the extent that one's awareness of others is clouded. Vanity, as noted, is the delight evoked by the favorable attention of others, quite regardless of what qualities elicit such attention. Thus egoism may be more characteristic of men, and vanity of women, though of course such broad generalizations are not without many exceptions. Men do often tend to be absorbed in themselves to the detriment of their awareness of others, seeing these others as instruments to the pursuit of their own goals. This is perhaps an expression of the male concern for power and influence. Women, on the other hand, are sometimes more concerned to be "attractive," something which has very much to do with appearance. And the lesser self-absorption on the part of women may explain, to some extent at least, their sometimes greater awareness of the feelings of others; these others might include children and animals, and this awareness sometimes rises to genuine compassion. To be sure, men are also capable of this, but there seem to be differences of degree.

Neither vanity nor egoism is very compatible with genuine pride, even though no one can hope or pretend to be entirely without them. While vain people delight in others' admiration for things they *have*—possessions, for instance—proud people have little interest in the admiration of others except for what they *are;* and even that admiration must come only from such persons, always relatively few, who are themselves proud people, in the truest sense, and hence better. Thus, while no one would want to be poor, a proud person does not mind being erroneously thought to be poor. A person of excessive vanity or egoism, on the other hand, tries very hard to create the impression of affluence even when that is a false impression, something a proud person would not think of doing. Vain or self-centered persons live beyond their means, or spend what limited resources they have on things that will be seen by others—cars, house furnishings, clothing, and so on. Such persons thus try to compensate for their limitations as persons by augmenting those things that are external to themselves and their characters. One who is quite stupid, for example, tries to compensate with a showy car or house; or one who fears danger or dreads death tries to compensate with excessive but insincere affability. They try, in other words, to be *thought* good, in the original, nonmoral sense of that term, when in fact they are not.

Pride and Self-Approbation

Proud people are not much concerned with what others think of them and care nothing at all for the opinions of insignificant persons, but are instead concerned with what they think of themselves. Others know you for what you appear to be, which can be misleading, but you know yourself for what you are—at least, you are in a privileged position to. If it is you who are ignorant, or silly, or weak-willed, or fearful, or vain, then, however well you may succeed in concealing these faults from others, you cannot entirely conceal them from yourself unless you are very stupid. And for this reason proud people would not try to conceal themselves from themselves nor have any reason to, regardless of how little they care about the opinions of others. For proud people, as noted, are those who *justifiably* love themselves, that is, who have a high *and correct* opinion of their real worth. They therefore do not compare themselves with others with respect to things that are extraneous to themselves. For example, they do not compare their possessions with those of their neighbors or associates, or if they happen to be aware that what they own far exceeds what their neighbors own, they do not let on to this. Instead, they compare themselves only with the best. They are properly ashamed if others are wiser than they, or if others conduct their lives with better order and rationality, or if others have greater courage and self-discipline. Similarly, their envy is reserved, not for those who are praised by the multitude, for whatever reason, but for those whose honor is deserved and is bestowed only by the best.

Proud people do not bow to any others, except in such purely ceremonious ways as tipping their hats; nor are they deferential to persons of special status or rank, such as those holding high offices, or persons who are wealthy, or persons of a special and conspicuous class, such as priests—with the exception, once again, of purely ceremonious gestures of deference, such as the use of "sir" and "ma'm" in addressing them. The most conspicuous exception to these generalizations is old people who have grown wise with their years. Such persons are truly venerable, and pride is never compromised by treating them as such. The experience of years, quite by itself, may confer wisdom, and nothing is more deserving of honor than this; so it is not inappropriate that others, aspiring to wisdom, should bow to those who have won it.

The Marks of Pride

Pride is seen in things both great and small. One of the great tests, for example, is the individual's response to acute danger, or his or her reaction to a life-threatening disease or to humiliation at the hands of enemies. One type of person bears these things with a natural, unpracticed fortitude and nobility while, at the other extreme, some collapse into whimpering and self-pity. With respect to death, a proud person knows that even his or her own life is not worth clinging to at the cost of pride or honor; would never want it prolonged beyond the point where the virtues upon which pride rests have become debilitated; and would, for this reason, prefer to die ten years too soon than ten days too late.

And there are other great tests, such as one's reaction to the death of a son or daughter who was intelligent, and strong, and filled with promise of great achievement.

But such things as these are negative, being tests of strength in adversity. There are great positive tests as well; the power one displays in writing and speech, sensitivity to music and other things of great beauty, and perhaps above all else, one's own creative power. Whether you follow experience and reason to form your beliefs on either great or petty matters, or whether, on the other hand, you simply embrace whatever opinions answer to your fondest desires, this, as well as any other test, distinguishes a wise and proud person from a vain and foolish one. Thus people who are given to ideologies and faiths, that is, to large and untested claims that they find satisfying and reassuring, are not wise and cannot therefore be proud; for whatever love they may have for themselves can hardly be justified. On the other hand, those who accept even unpleasant facts because they are facts, or do not shrink from drawing appropriate inferences from what they observe, even when these facts or observations may run counter to everything they have been taught and everything they desperately hope is true, such persons are wise, whether learned or not, and have at least that one correct basis for self-approbation. If, in addition, they are learned, then they have still another. And if, in addition to those qualities, they are creative, self-disciplined, and courageous, then they have still others; and there comes a point where external things which contribute nothing to those qualities are clearly seen by them to be worth very little, however much they may delight simple people.

But there are also, as noted, lesser marks of pride, easily recognized by other proud persons, though not understood by the meek and the foolish. A proud person is, for example, serious, but not solemn, whereas a meek person's effort to be serious results only in a laughable solemnity. Such a person puts on a grave face and a reserved manner and imagines that he or she has become serious. Hearty laughter and the enjoyment of life are compatible with seriousness, which is positive and affirmative, but not with mere solemnity, which is negative and withdrawn. Again, a proud person is not garrulous and does not speak merely for the sake of "making conversation" or of hearing words flow. On matters not worthy of comment—such as weather, minor political issues, or things in the immediate surroundings—proud people normally say nothing at all. They do not mind long periods of dead silence, feel no embarrassment or anxiety at this, nor any need to break such silence with idle observations except when silence would be interpreted as rudeness. Proud people delight in the company of other proud and worthwhile persons, and seek above all to discover and appreciate their strengths and virtues. Their awareness of these is not clouded by self-absorption, nor by any desire to project a good impression of themselves; for they know that their own excellences will be recognized by others of similar excellence and do not care if they are not seen by those who lack this.

One category of behavior which is sometimes erroneously associated with pride is the fastidious observance of what is called etiquette. Etiquette comprises the many rules of social intercourse, often petty in nature, which enable people to associate comfortably in special circumstances such as social gatherings. These rules are often important in preventing embarrassment and awkwardness, but they have almost nothing to do with pride and can sometimes even work against it. Thus, proud people are not ashamed to whistle in public places where such behavior is harmless though uncommon, nor do they mind wearing old or baggy clothing, for example, if that is their taste. Etiquette, by its very nature, encourages a kind of mindless conformity, whereas those who are proud conform their behavior to standards which are their own.

A proud person does not pretend to an insincere equality with others who are inferior, that is, who are meek, foolish, or silly. A person is not worthy of esteem just by the fact of being a person but, rather, by the fact of being a person of outstanding worth, which is something quite rare.

The Place of Externals

Among the lesser marks of pride are also those things that moralists once referred to as "externals," meaning by this all those things that are extraneous to what a person inherently is. Dress, for instance, is an external thing, as are one's reputation and standing in the popular mind, the praise or honors one receives from small-minded people, and so on.

Thus, with respect to dress, proud people do not ask what others expect of them, or how they wish them to look, and the least consideration in their minds is how *others* dress. They ask instead what will please themselves. It is compatible with perfect and beautiful pride never to wear a suit or necktie, to dress in baggy trousers and sweat shirt and cheap shoes. This description fits the appearance of one of the proudest persons of our century, Albert Einstein, whose almost superhuman virtues were combined with a boundless compassion and sweetness. But let it be added that affectation in dress, or the deliberate attempt to be outlandish and garish and to attract the attention of others, is not pride but, as noted before, vanity. For again, the good opinion that one should seek is one's own, not others', and certainly not that of strangers.

Pride and Morality

With respect to what is popularly called "morality," a proud person is in the best sense the creator of his or her own. Nothing is done *merely* because it is recommended and done by others. Rather, something is done because *he* or *she* sees it as worthy of being done, and especially because it is worthy of himself or herself. Thus a proud person would not injure or betray a friend, not because it would be "wrong," or would violate vulgar morality, but because it would be shameful. Nor would a proud person cheat or take dishonest advantage of anyone, again, not because it would be wrong, but because it would be incompatible with his or her own worth. To act otherwise would imply that there are external things that are of greater importance than one's own excellence, which would be totally inconsistent with pride. But perhaps the clearest indication of the ethics of pride is found in those situations for which popular morality has no clear rules. Consider, for example, the finding of things whose ownership is uncertain, or for which no owner can be determined at all. Thus, for example, if money or other valuables are found on the ground, a proud person does not hesitate to take them; but such a person could not be imagined seeing someone drop these things and then picking them up unless, of course, to restore them to the person who dropped them. The reason for such behavior does not rest upon any common notion of theft but on one's own clear notion of honor. But perhaps the best illustration of all is found in the opportunity to take money or other valuables from a corpse. These things, in the nature of the case, do not belong to anyone (assuming no surviving kin) and are thus, for all practical purposes, simply found. There is no clear rule of popular morality covering such a situation, for it is of rare occurrence, never occurring at all in the lives of most people. Yet a proud person would not have the slightest inclination to do such a thing, and for a reason that is overwhelming and conclusive, namely that such an act would be shameful. It is not shameful in the sense that we have been taught to regard it as such, for little has ever been said on such infrequent things. Rather, it is shameful in the true sense of the word, as being incompatible with one's own worth as a person, a worth that is possessed only by the proud. To be sure, this does leave humble persons with little incentive for personal honor, but that is not an ontoward consequence, for such persons have little of this incentive anyway. They can be cajoled to decency by others, or compelled by laws and morality, but a genuinely proud person is cajoled to nothing at all by others, and is law-abiding and moral only as a condition of civilized life. Someone possessed of personal excellence requires more than morality for a life that is, in its true and original sense, good.

Such (in outline and with much omitted) is the virtue of pride. It is not the only virtue, nor even the highest, that being, without doubt, wisdom; but it is nevertheless, in the sense that was explained, a kind of summation of the virtues.

It is also a specimen of aspiration, which cannot be proved to be worth having. But in this area little can be proved anyway. We are dealing not with things that are true, in the usual sense, but with things that are good, in the philosophical sense. And as to the question whether this or any other virtue is worth having and worth giving a great deal to have, one has, of course, to find the answer within oneself. Conduct can sometimes be forced upon one, but virtue can only be discovered.

STUDY QUESTIONS

1. Taylor says that genuinely proud people perceive themselves as better than others and that their pride is justified because their perception is correct. Do you agree?

2. Does Taylor's justifiably proud individual appear to be a likable person? A moral person?
3. Taylor says that egoism may be more characteristic of men and vanity of women. Do you think he is right?
4. What does Taylor mean when he says pride is "justified" self-love? How does one know when one's self-love is justified?
5. Is Taylor a Nietzschean?

Ideals of Human Excellence and Preserving Natural Environments

―――――――――――――――――――――――――――――――――――

THOMAS E. HILL, JR.

Thomas E. Hill, (b. 1937) is professor of philosophy at the University of North Carolina, Chapel Hill. He has published numerous articles on contemporary moral issues and is the author of *Autonomy and Self-Respect* (1991).

Thomas Hill's essay investigates the relationship between a regard for the environment and a regard for persons. He seeks to articulate the grounds for the widespread feeling that, utility aside, there is something very wrong with the person who treats nonsentient nature as a mere resource to be exploited. Some environmentalists have argued that plants and trees have rights of their own. Hill rejects this as too controversial.

Other philosophers argue that a world in which trees and plants exist is a better world than one that lacks such

IDEALS OF HUMAN EXCELLENCE AND PRESERVING NATURAL ENVIRONMENTS Excerpted from an article of the same name that first appeared in *Environmental Ethics*, vol. 5, 1983. Reprinted by permission of The University of Georgia and the author.

things. But the idea of the intrinsic goodness of nature abstracted from all human preferences is also dismissed by Hill as too controversial. For similar reasons, Hill finds religious answers inadequate.

Hill then suggests that we turn away from attempts to characterize nature itself as having rights or being intrinsically good to look at what may be morally wrong with the person who looks upon nature as a mere resource. What sort of person can be indifferent to the destruction of a forest? According to Hill, the destroyer of a forest tends to value all things instrumentally and narrowly; the attitude of such a person betrays a lack of humility. "If a person views all nonsentient nature merely as a resource, then it seems unlikely that he has developed the capacity needed to overcome self-importance."

Hill holds that those who tend to be ungrateful and insensitive to what nature gives us tend to be ungrateful and insensitive to their fellow human beings. Conversely, those who value such traits as humility, gratitude, and sensitivity have reason to promote the love of nature.

I

A wealthy eccentric bought a house in a neighborhood I know. The house was surrounded by a beautiful display of grass, plants, and flowers, and it was shaded by a huge old avocado tree. But the grass required cutting, the flowers needed tending, and the man wanted more sun. So he cut the whole lot down and covered the yard with asphalt. After all it was his property and he was not fond of plants.

It was a small operation, but it reminded me of the strip mining of large sections of the Appalachians. In both cases, of course, there were reasons for the destruction, and property rights could be cited as justification. But I could not help but wonder, "What sort of person would do a thing like that?"

Many Californians had a similar reaction when a recent governor defended the leveling of ancient redwood groves, reportedly saying, "If you have seen one redwood, you have seen them all."

Incidents like these arouse the indignation of ardent environmentalists and leave even apolitical observers with some degree of moral discomfort. The reasons for these reactions are mostly obvious. Uprooting the natural environment robs both present and future generations of much potential use and enjoyment. Animals too depend on the environment; and even if one does not value animals for their own sakes, their potential utility for us is incalculable. Plants are needed, of course, to replenish the atmosphere quite aside from their aesthetic value. These reasons for hesitating to destroy forests and gardens are not only the most obvious ones, but also the most persuasive for practical purposes. But, one wonders, is there nothing more behind our discomfort? Are we concerned solely about the potential use and enjoyment of the forests, etc., for ourselves, later generations, and perhaps animals? Is there not something else which disturbs us when we witness the destruction or even listen to those who would defend it in terms of cost/benefit analysis?

Imagine that in each of our examples those who would destroy the environment argue elaborately that, even considering future generations of human beings and animals, there are benefits in "replacing" the natural environment which outweigh the negative utilities which environmentalists cite.[1] No doubt we could press the argument on the facts, trying to show that the destruction is shortsighted and that its defenders have underestimated its potential harm or ignored some pertinent rights or interests. But is this all we could say? Suppose we grant, for a moment, that the utility of destroying the redwoods, forests, and gardens is equal to their potential for use and enjoyment by nature lovers and animals. Suppose, further, that we even grant that the pertinent human rights and animal rights, if any, are evenly divided for and against destruction. Imagine that we also concede, for argument's sake, that the forests contain no potentially useful endangered species of animals and plants. Must we then conclude that there is no further cause for moral concern? Should we then feel morally indifferent when we see the natural environment uprooted?

---

[1]When I use the expression "the natural environment," I have in mind the sort of examples with which I began. For some purposes it is important to distinguish cultivated gardens from forests, virgin forests from replenished ones, irreplaceable natural phenomena from the replaceable, and so on; but these distinctions, I think, do not affect my main points here. There is also a broad sense, as Hume and Mill noted, in which all that occurs, miracles aside, is "natural." In this sense, of course, strip mining is as natural as a beaver cutting trees for his dam, and, as parts of nature, we cannot destroy the "natural" environment but only alter it. As will be evident, I shall use *natural* in a narrower, more familiar sense.

II

Suppose we feel that the answer to these questions should be negative. Suppose, in other words, we feel that our moral discomfort when we confront the destroyers of nature is not fully explained by our belief that they have miscalculated the best use of natural resources or violated rights in exploiting them. Suppose, in particular, we sense that part of the problem is that the natural environment is being viewed exclusively as a natural *resource*. What could be the ground of such a feeling? That is, what is there in our system of normative principles and values that could account for our remaining moral dissatisfaction?[2]

Some may be tempted to seek an explanation by appeal to the interests, or even the rights, of plants. After all, they may argue, we only gradually came to acknowledge the moral importance of all human beings, and it is even more recently that consciences have been aroused to give full weight to the welfare (and rights?) of animals. The next logical step, it may be argued, is to acknowledge a moral requirement to take into account the interests (and rights?) of plants. The problem with the strip miners, redwood cutters, and the like, on this view, is not just that they ignore the welfare and rights of people and animals; they also fail to give due weight to the survival and health of the plants themselves.

The temptation to make such a reply is understandable if one assumes that all moral questions are exclusively concerned with whether *acts* are right or wrong, and that this, in turn, is determined entirely by how the acts impinge on the rights and interests of those directly affected. On this assumption, if there is cause for moral concern, some right or interest has been neglected; and if the rights and interests of human beings and animals have already been taken into account, then there must be some other pertinent interests, for example those of plants. A little reflection will show that the assumption is mistaken; but, in any case, the conclusion that plants have

---

[2]This paper is intended as a preliminary discussion in *normative* ethical theory (as opposed to *metaethics*). The task, accordingly, is the limited, though still difficult, one of articulating the possible basis in our beliefs and values for certain particular moral judgments. Questions of ultimate justification are set aside. What makes the task difficult and challenging is not that conclusive proofs from the foundation of morality are attempted; it is rather that the particular judgments to be explained seem at first not to fall under the most familiar moral principles (e.g., utilitarianism, respect for rights).

rights or morally relevant interests is surely untenable. We do speak of what is "good for" plants, and they can "thrive" and also be "killed." But this does not imply that they have "interests" in any morally relevant sense. Some people apparently believe that plants grow better if we talk to them, but the idea that the plants suffer and enjoy, desire and dislike, etc., is clearly outside the range of both common sense and scientific belief. The notion that the forests should be preserved to avoid *hurting* the trees or because they have a *right* to life is not part of a widely shared moral consciousness, and for good reason.[3]

Another way of trying to explain our moral discomfort is to appeal to certain religious beliefs. If one believes that all living things were created by a God who cares for them and entrusted us with the use of plants and animals only for limited purposes, then one has a reason to avoid careless destruction of the forests, etc., quite aside from their future utility. Again, if one believes that a divine force is immanent in all nature, then too one might have reason to care for more than sentient things. But such arguments require strong and controversial premises, and, I suspect, they will always have a restricted audience.

Early in this century, due largely to the influence of G. E. Moore, another point of view developed which some may find promising.[4] Moore introduced, or at least made popular, the idea that certain states of affairs are intrinsically valuable—not just valued, but valuable, and not necessarily because of their effects on sentient beings. Admittedly Moore came to believe that in fact the only intrinsically valuable things were conscious experiences of various sorts,[5] but this

---

[3] I assume here that having a right presupposes having interests in a sense which in turn presupposes a capacity to desire, suffer, etc. Since my main concern lies in another direction, I do not argue the point, but merely note that some regard it as debatable. See, for example, W. Murray Hunt, "Are *Mere Things* Morally Considerable?" *Environmental Ethics* 2 (1980): 59–65; Kenneth E. Goodpaster, "On Stopping at Everything," *Environmental Ethics* 2 (1980): 288–94; Joel Feinberg, "The Rights of Animals and Unborn Generations," in William Blackstone, ed., *Philosophy and Environmental Crisis* (Athens: University of Georgia Press, 1974), pp. 43–68; Tom Regan, "Feinberg on What Sorts of Beings Can Have Rights," *Southern Journal of Philosophy* (1976): 485–98; Robert Elliot, "Regan on the Sort of Beings that Can Have Rights," *Southern Journal of Philosophy* (1978): 701–05; Scott Lehmann, "Do Wildernesses Have Rights?" *Environmental Ethics* 2 (1981): 129–46.

[4] G. E. Moore, *Principia Ethica* (Cambridge: Cambridge University Press, 1903); *Ethics* (London: H. Holt, 1912).

[5] G. E. Moore, "Is Goodness a Quality?" *Philosophical Papers* (London: George Allen and Unwin, 1959), pp. 95–97.

restriction was not inherent in the idea of intrinsic value. The intrinsic goodness of something, he thought, was an objective, nonrelational property of the thing, like its texture or color, but not a property perceivable by sense perception or detectable by scientific instruments. In theory at least, a single tree thriving alone in a universe without sentient beings, and even without God, could be intrinsically valuable. Since, according to Moore, our duty is to maximize intrinsic value, his theory could obviously be used to argue that we have reason not to destroy natural environments independently of how they affect human beings and animals. The survival of a forest might have worth beyond its worth *to* sentient beings.

This approach, like the religious one, may appeal to some but is infested with problems. There are, first, the familiar objections to intuitionism, on which the theory depends. Metaphysical and epistemological doubts about nonnatural, intuited properties are hard to suppress, and many have argued that the theory rests on a misunderstanding of the words *good, valuable,* and the like.[6] Second, even if we try to set aside these objections and think in Moore's terms, it is far from obvious that everyone would agree that the existence of forests, etc., is intrinsically valuable. The test, says Moore, is what we would say when we imagine a universe with just the thing in question, without any effects or accompaniments, and then we ask, "Would its existence be better than its nonexistence?" Be careful, Moore would remind us, not to construe this question as, "Would you *prefer* the existence of that universe to its nonexistence?" The question is, "Would its existence have the objective, nonrelational property, intrinsic goodness?"

Now even among those who have no worries about whether this really makes sense, we might well get a diversity of answers. Those prone to destroy natural environments will doubtless give one answer, and nature lovers will likely give another. When an issue is as controversial as the one at hand, intuition is a poor arbiter.

The problem, then, is this. We want to understand what underlies our moral uneasiness at the destruction of the redwoods, forests, etc., even apart from the loss of these as resources for human beings and animals. But I find no adequate answer by pursuing the questions, "Are rights or interests of plants neglected?" "What is God's will on the matter?" and "What is the intrinsic value of the existence of a tree

---

[6]See, for example, P. H. Nowell-Smith, *Ethics* (New York: Penguin Books, 1954).

or forest?" My suggestion, which is in fact the main point of this paper, is that we look at the problem from a different perspective. That is, let us turn for a while from the effort to find reasons why certain *acts* destructive of natural environments are morally wrong to the ancient task of articulating our ideals of human excellence. Rather than argue directly with destroyers of the environment who say, "Show me why what I am doing is *immoral*," I want to ask, "What sort of person would want to do what they propose?" The point is not to skirt the issue with an *ad hominem*, but to raise a different moral question, for even if there is no convincing way to show that the destructive acts are wrong (independently of human and animal use and enjoyment), we may find that the willingness to indulge in them reflects the absence of human traits that we admire and regard morally important.

This strategy of shifting questions may seem more promising if one reflects on certain analogous situations. Consider, for example, the Nazi who asks, in all seriousness, "Why is it wrong for me to make lampshades out of human skin—provided, of course, I did not myself kill the victims to get the skins?" We would react more with shock and disgust than with indignation, I suspect, because it is even more evident that the question reveals a defect in the questioner than that the proposed act is itself immoral. Sometimes we may not regard an act wrong at all though we see it as reflecting something objectionable about the person who does it. Imagine, for example, one who laughs spontaneously to himself when he reads a newspaper account of a plane crash that kills hundreds. Or, again, consider an obsequious grandson who, having waited for his grandmother's inheritance with mock devotion, then secretly spits on her grave when at last she dies. Spitting on the grave may have no adverse consequences and perhaps it violates no rights. The moral uneasiness which it arouses is explained more by our view of the agent than by any conviction that what he did was immoral. Had he hesitated and asked, "Why shouldn't I spit on her grave?" it seems more fitting to ask him to reflect on the sort of person he is than to try to offer reasons why he should refrain from spitting.

III

What sort of person, then, would cover his garden with asphalt, strip mine a wooded mountain, or level an irreplaceable redwood grove? Two sorts of answers, though initially appealing, must be ruled out. The first is that persons who would destroy the environment in these ways are either shortsighted, underestimating the harm they do, or else are too little concerned for the well-being of other people. Perhaps too they have insufficient regard for animal life. But these considerations have been set aside in order to refine the controversy. Another tempting response might be that we count it a moral virtue, or at least a human ideal, to love nature. Those who value the environment only for its utility must not really love nature and so in this way fall short of an ideal. But such an answer is hardly satisfying in the present context, for what is at issue is *why* we feel moral discomfort at the activities of those who admittedly value nature only for its utility. That it is ideal to care for nonsentient nature beyond its possible use is really just another way of expressing the general point which is under controversy.

What is needed is some way of showing that this ideal is connected with other virtues, or human excellences, not in question. To do so is difficult and my suggestions, accordingly, will be tentative and subject to qualification. The main idea is that, though indifference to nonsentient nature does not *necessarily* reflect the absence of virtues, it often signals the absence of certain traits which we want to encourage because they are, in most cases, a natural basis for the development of certain virtues. It is often thought, for example, that those who would destroy the natural environment must lack a proper appreciation of their place in the natural order, and so must either be ignorant or have too little humility. Though I would argue that this is not necessarily so, I suggest that, given certain plausible empirical assumptions, their attitude may well be rooted in ignorance, a narrow perspective, inability to see things as important apart from themselves and the limited groups they associate with, or reluctance to accept themselves as natural beings. Overcoming these deficiencies will not guarantee a proper moral humility, but for most of us it is probably an important psychological preliminary. Later I suggest, more briefly, that indifference to nonsentient nature typically reveals absence of either aesthetic sensibility or a disposition to cherish what has enriched one's life and that these, though not themselves moral virtues, are a natural basis for appreciation of the good in others and gratitude.[7]

---

[7]The issues I raise here, though perhaps not the details of my remarks, are in line with Aristotle's view of moral philosophy, a view revitalized recently by Philippa Foot's

Consider first the suggestion that destroyers of the environment lack an appreciation of their place in the universe.[8] Their attention, it seems, must be focused on parochial matters, on what is, relatively speaking, close in space and time. They seem not to understand that we are a speck on the cosmic scene, a brief stage in the evolutionary process, only one among millions of species on Earth, and an episode in the course of human history. Of course, they know that there are stars, fossils, insects, and ancient ruins; but do they have any idea of the complexity of the processes that led to the natural world as we find it? Are they aware how much the forces at work within their own bodies are like those which govern all living things and even how much they have in common with inanimate bodies? Admittedly scientific knowledge is limited and no one can master it all; but could one who had a broad and deep understanding of his place in nature really be indifferent to the destruction of the natural environment?

This first suggestion, however, may well provoke a protest from a sophisticated anti-environmentalist.[9] "Perhaps *some* may be indifferent to nature from ignorance," the critic may object, "but *I* have studied astronomy, geology, biology, and biochemistry, and I still unashamedly regard the nonsentient environment as simply a resource for our use. It should not be wasted, of course, but what should be preserved is decidable by weighing longterm costs and benefits." "Besides," our critic may continue, "as philosophers you

<hr>

Virtue and Vice (Berkeley: University of California Press, 1979), Alasdair MacIntyre's *After Virtue* (Notre Dame: Notre Dame Press, 1981), and James Wallace's *Virtues and Vices* (Ithaca and London: Cornell University Press, 1978), and other works. For other reflections on relationships between character and natural environments, see John Rodman, "The Liberation of Nature," *Inquiry* (1976):83–131 and L. Reinhardt, "Some Gaps in Moral Space: Reflections on Forests and Feelings," in Mannison, McRobbie, and Routley, eds., *Environmental Philosophy* (Canberra: Australian National University Research School of Social Sciences, 1980).

[8]Though for simplicity I focus upon those who do strip mining, etc., the argument is also applicable to those whose utilitarian calculations lead them to preserve the redwoods, mountains, etc., but who care for only sentient nature for its own sake. Similarly the phrase "indifferent to nature" is meant to encompass those who are indifferent *except* when considering its benefits to people and animals.

[9]For convenience I use the labels *environmentalist* and *anti-environmentalist* (or *critic*) for the opposing sides in the rather special controversy I have raised. Thus, for example, my "environmentalist" not only favors conserving the forests, etc., but finds something objectionable in wanting to destroy them even aside from the costs to human beings and animals. My "anti-environmentalist" is not simply one who wants to destroy the environment; he is a person who has no qualms about doing so independent of the adverse effects on human beings and animals.

should know the old Humean formula, 'You cannot derive an *ought* from an *is*.' All the facts of biology, biochemistry, etc., do not entail that I ought to love nature or want to preserve it. What one understands is one thing; what one values is something else. Just as nature lovers are not necessarily scientists, those indifferent to nature are not necessarily ignorant."

Although the environmentalist may concede the critic's logical point, he may well argue that, as a matter of fact, increased understanding of nature tends to heighten people's concern for its preservation. If so, despite the objection, the suspicion that the destroyers of the environment lack deep understanding of nature is not, in most cases, unwarranted, but the argument need not rest here.

The environmentalist might amplify his original idea as follows: "When I said that the destroyers of nature do not appreciate their place in the universe, I was not speaking of intellectual understanding alone, for, after all, a person can *know* a catalog of facts without ever putting them together and seeing vividly the whole picture which they form. To see oneself as just one part of nature is to look at oneself and the world from a certain perspective which is quite different from being able to recite detailed information from the natural sciences. What the destroyers of nature lack is this perspective, not particular information."

Again our critic may object, though only after making some concessions: "All right," he may say, "*some* who are indifferent to nature may lack the cosmic perspective of which you speak, but again there is no *necessary* connection between this failing, if it is one, and any particular evaluative attitude toward nature. In fact, different people respond quite differently when they move to a wider perspective. When *I* try to picture myself vividly as a brief, transitory episode in the course of nature, I simply get depressed. Far from inspiring me with a love of nature, the exercise makes me sad and hostile. You romantics think only of poets like Wordsworth and artists like Turner, but you should consider how differently Omar Khayyam responded when he took your wider perspective. His reaction, when looking at his life from a cosmic viewpoint, was 'Drink up, for tomorrow we die.' Others respond in an almost opposite manner with a joyless Stoic resignation, exemplified by the poet who pictures the wise man, at the height of personal triumph, being served a magnificent banquet, and then consummating his marriage to his beloved, all the while reminding himself, 'Even this shall pass away.'"[10] In sum, the critic may object, "Even if one should try to see oneself as one small transitory part of nature, doing so does not dictate any particular normative attitude. Some may come to love nature, but others are moved to live for the moment; some sink into sad resignation; others get depressed or angry. So indifference to nature is not necessarily a sign that a person fails to look at himself from the larger perspective."

The environmentalist might respond to this objection in several ways. He might, for example, argue that even though some people who see themselves as part of the natural order remain indifferent to nonsentient nature, this is not a common reaction. Typically, it may be argued, as we become more and more aware that we are parts of the larger whole we come to value the whole independently of its effect on ourselves. Thus, despite the possibilities the critic raises, indifference to nonsentient nature is still in most cases a sign that a person fails to see himself as part of the natural order.

If someone challenges the empirical assumption here, the environmentalist might develop the argument along a quite different line. The initial idea, he may remind us, was that those who would destroy the natural environment fail to *appreciate* their place in the natural order. "Appreciating one's place" is not simply an intellectual appreciation. It is also an attitude, reflecting what one values as well as what one knows. When we say, for example, that both the servile and the arrogant person fail to *appreciate* their place in a society of equals, we do not mean simply that they are ignorant of certain empirical facts, but rather that they have certain objectionable attitudes about their importance relative to other people. Similarly, to fail to appreciate one's place in nature is not merely to lack knowledge or breadth of perspective, but to take a certain attitude about what matters. A person who *understands* his place in nature but still views nonsentient nature merely as a resource takes the attitude that nothing is *important* but human beings and animals. Despite first appearances, he is not so much like the pre-Copernican astronomers who made the intellectual error of treating the Earth as the "center of the universe" when they made their calculations. He is more like the

---

[10]"Even this shall pass away," by Theodore Tildon, in *The Best Loved Poems of the American People*, ed. Hazel Felleman (Garden City, N.Y.: Doubleday & Co., 1936).

337

racist who, though well aware of other races, treats all races but his own as insignificant.

So construed, the argument appeals to the common idea that awareness of nature typically has, and should have, a humbling effect. The Alps, a storm at sea, the Grand Canyon, towering redwoods, and "the starry heavens above" move many a person to remark on the comparative insignificance of our daily concerns and even of our species, and this is generally taken to be a quite fitting response.[11] What seems to be missing, then, in those who understand nature but remain unmoved is a proper humility.[12] Absence of proper humility is not the same as selfishness or egoism, for one can be devoted to self-interest while still viewing one's own pleasures and projects as trivial and unimportant.[13] And one can have an exaggerated view of one's own importance while grandly sacrificing for those one views as inferior. Nor is the lack of humility identical with belief that one has power and influence, for a person can be quite puffed up about himself while believing that the foolish world will never acknowledge him. The humility we miss seems not so much a belief about one's relative effectiveness and recognition as an attitude which measures the importance of things independently of their relation to oneself or to some narrow group with which one identifies. A paradigm of a person who lacks humility is the self-important emperor who grants status to his family because it is *his,* to his subordinates because *he* appointed them, and to his country because *he* chooses to glorify it. Less extreme but still lacking proper humility is the elitist who counts events significant solely in proportion to how they affect his class. The suspicion about those who would destroy the environment, then, is that what they count important is too narrowly confined insofar as it encompasses only what affects beings who, like us, are capable of feeling.

This idea that proper humility requires recognition of the importance of nonsentient nature is similar to the thought of those who

---

[11]An exception, apparently, was Kant, who thought "the starry heavens" sublime and compared them with "the moral law within," but did not for all that see our species as comparatively insignificant.

[12]By "*proper* humility" I mean that sort and degree of humility that is a morally admirable character trait. How precisely to define this is, of course, a controversial matter; but the point for present purposes is just to set aside obsequiousness, false modesty, underestimation of one's abilities, and the like.

[13]I take this point from some of Philippa Foot's remarks.

charge meat eaters with "species-ism." In both cases it is felt that people too narrowly confine their concerns to the sorts of beings that are most like them. But, however intuitively appealing, the idea will surely arouse objections from our nonenvironmentalist critic. "Why," he will ask, "do you suppose that the sort of humility I *should* have requires me to acknowledge the importance of nonsentient nature aside from its utility? You cannot, by your own admission, argue that nonsentient nature *is* important, appealing to religious or intuitionist grounds. And simply to assert, without further argument, that an ideal humility requires us to view nonsentient nature as important for its own sake begs the question at issue. If proper humility is acknowledging the relative importance of things as one should, then to show that I must lack this you must first establish that one *should* acknowledge the importance of nonsentient nature."

Though some may wish to accept this challenge, there are other ways to pursue the connection between humility and response to nonsentient nature. For example, suppose we grant that proper humility requires only acknowledging a due status to sentient beings. We must admit, then, that it is logically possible for a person to be properly humble even though he viewed all nonsentient nature simply as a resource. But this logical possibility may be a psychological rarity. It may be that, given the sort of beings we are, we would never learn humility before persons without developing the general capacity to cherish, and regard important, many things for their own sakes. The major obstacle to humility before persons is self-importance, a tendency to measure the significance of everything by its relation to oneself and those with whom one identifies. The processes by which we overcome self-importance are doubtless many and complex, but it seems unlikely that they are exclusively concerned with how we relate to other people and animals. Learning humility requires learning to feel that something matters besides what will affect oneself and one's circle of associates. What leads a child to care about what happens to a lost hamster or a stray dog he will not see again is likely also to generate concern for a lost toy or a favorite tree where he used to live.[14] Learning to value things for their own sake, and to count

---

[14]The causal history of this concern may well depend upon the object (tree, toy) having given the child pleasure, but this does not mean that the object is then valued only for further pleasure it may bring.

what affects them important aside from their utility, is not the same as judging them to have some intuited objective property, but it is necessary to the development of humility and it seems likely to take place in experiences with nonsentient nature as well as with people and animals. If a person views all nonsentient nature merely as a resource, then it seems unlikely that he has developed the capacity needed to overcome self-importance.

IV

This last argument, unfortunately, has its limits. It presupposes an empirical connection between experiencing nature and overcoming self-importance, and this may be challenged. Even if experiencing nature promotes humility before others, there may be other ways people can develop such humility in a world of concrete, glass, and plastic. If not, perhaps all that is needed is limited experience of nature in one's early, developing years; mature adults, having overcome youthful self-importance, may lie well enough in artificial surroundings. More importantly, the argument does not fully capture the spirit of the intuition that an ideal person stands humbly before nature. That idea is not simply that experiencing nature tends to foster proper humility before other people; it is, in part, that natural surroundings encourage and are appropriate to an ideal sense of oneself as part of the natural world. Standing alone in the forest, after months in the city, is not merely good as a means of curbing one's arrogance before others; it reinforces and fittingly expresses one's acceptance of oneself as a natural being.

Previously we considered only one aspect of proper humility, namely, a sense of one's relative importance with respect to other human beings. Another aspect, I think, is a kind of *self-acceptance*. This involves acknowledging, in more than a merely intellectual way, that we are the sort of creatures that we are. Whether one is self-accepting is not so much a matter of how one attributes *importance* comparatively to oneself, other people, animals, plants, and other things as it is a matter of understanding, facing squarely, and responding appropriately to who and what one is, e.g., one's powers and limits, one's affinities with other beings and differences from them, one's unalterable nature and one's freedom to change. Self-acceptance is not merely intellectual awareness, for one can be intellectually aware that one is growing old and will eventually die while nevertheless behaving in a thousand foolish ways that reflect a refusal to acknowledge these facts. On the other hand, self-acceptance is not passive resignation, for refusal to pursue what one truly wants within one's limits is a failure to accept the freedom and power one has. Particular behaviors, like dyeing one's gray hair and dressing like those twenty years younger, do not *necessarily* imply lack of self-acceptance, for there could be reasons for acting in these ways other than the wish to hide from oneself what one really is. One fails to accept oneself when the patterns of behavior and emotion are rooted in a desire to disown and deny features of oneself, to pretend to oneself that they are not there. This is not to say that a self-accepting person makes no value judgments about himself, that he likes all facts about himself, wants equally to develop and display them; he can, and should feel remorse for his past misdeeds and strive to change his current vices. The point is that he does not disown them, pretend that they do not exist or are facts about something other than himself. Such pretense is incompatible with proper humility because it is seeing oneself as better than one is.

Self-acceptance of this sort has long been considered a human excellence, under various names, but what has it to do with preserving nature? There is, I think, the following connection. As human beings we are part of nature, living, growing, declining, and dying by natural laws similar to those governing other living beings; despite our awesomely distinctive human powers, we share many of the needs, limits, and liabilities of animals and plants. These facts are neither good nor bad in themselves, aside from personal preference and varying conventional values. To say this is to utter a truism which few will deny, but to accept these facts, as facts about one-self, is not so easy—or so common. Much of what naturalists deplore about our increasingly artificial world reflects, and encourages, a denial of these facts, an unwillingness to avow them with equanimity.

Like the Victorian lady who refuses to look at her own nude body, some would like to create a world of less transitory stuff, reminding us only of our intellectual and social nature, never calling to mind our affinities with "lower" living creatures. The "denial of death," to which psychiatrists call attention,[15] reveals an attitude incompatible with the sort of self-acceptance which philosophers, from the

---

[15]See, for example, Ernest Becker, *The Denial of Death* (New York: Free Press, 1973).

ancients to Spinoza and on, have admired as a human excellence. My suggestion is not merely that experiencing nature causally promotes such self-acceptance, but also that those who fully accept themselves as part of the natural world lack the common drive to disassociate themselves from nature by replacing natural environments with artificial ones. A storm in the wilds helps us to appreciate our animal vulnerability, but, equally important, the reluctance to experience it may *reflect* an unwillingness to accept this aspect of ourselves. The person who is too ready to destroy the ancient redwoods may lack humility, not so much in the sense that he exaggerates his importance relative to others, but rather in the sense that he tries to avoid seeing himself as one among many natural creatures.

V

My suggestion so far has been that, though indifference to nonsentient nature is not itself a moral vice, it is likely to reflect either ignorance, a self-importance, or a lack of self-acceptance which we must overcome to have proper humility. A similar idea might be developed connecting attitudes toward nonsentient nature with other human excellences. For example, one might argue that indifference to nature reveals a lack of either an aesthetic sense or some of the natural roots of gratitude.

When we see a hillside that has been gutted by strip miners or the garden replaced by asphalt, our first reaction is probably, "How ugly!" The scenes assault our aesthetic sensibilities. We suspect that no one with a keen sense of beauty could have left such a sight. Admittedly not everything in nature strikes us as beautiful, or even aesthetically interesting, and sometimes a natural scene is replaced with a more impressive architectural masterpiece. But this is not usually the situation in the problem cases which environmentalists are most concerned about. More often beauty is replaced with ugliness.

At this point our critic may well object that, even if he does lack a sense of beauty, this is no moral vice. His cost/benefit calculations take into account the pleasure others may derive from seeing the forests, etc., and so why should he be faulted?

Some might reply that, despite contrary philosophical traditions, aesthetics and morality are not so distinct as commonly supposed. Appreciation of beauty, they may argue, is a human excellence which morally ideal persons should try to develop. But, setting aside this controversial position, there still may be cause for moral concern about those who have no aesthetic response to nature. Even if aesthetic sensibility is not itself a moral virtue, many of the capacities of mind and heart which it presupposes may be ones which are also needed for an appreciation of other people. Consider, for example, curiosity, a mind open to novelty, the ability to look at things from unfamiliar perspectives, empathetic imagination, interest in details, variety, and order, and emotional freedom from the immediate and the practical. All these, and more, seem necessary to aesthetic sensibility, but they are also traits which a person needs to be fully sensitive to people of all sorts. The point is not that a moral person must be able to distinguish beautiful from ugly people; the point is rather that unresponsiveness to what is beautiful, awesome, dainty, dumpy, and otherwise aesthetically interesting in nature probably reflects a lack of the openness of mind and spirit necessary to appreciate the best in human beings.

The anti-environmentalist, however, may refuse to accept the charge that he lacks aesthetic sensibility. If he claims to appreciate seventeenth-century miniature portraits, but to abhor natural wildernesses, he will hardly be convincing. Tastes vary, but aesthetic sense is not *that* selective. He may, instead, insist that he *does* appreciate natural beauty. He spends his vacations, let us suppose, hiking in the Sierras, photographing wildflowers, and so on. He might press his argument as follows: "I enjoy natural beauty as much as anyone, but I fail to see what this has to do with preserving the environment independently of human enjoyment and use. Nonsentient nature is a resource, but one of its best uses is to give us pleasure. I take this into account when I calculate the costs and benefits of preserving a park, planting a garden, and so on. But the problem you raised explicitly set aside the desire to preserve nature as a means to enjoyment. I say, let us enjoy nature fully while we can, but if all sentient beings were to die tomorrow, we might as well blow up all plant life as well. A redwood grove that no one can use or enjoy is utterly worthless."

The attitude expressed here, I suspect, is not a common one, but it represents a philosophical challenge. The beginnings of a reply may be found in the following. When a person takes joy in something, it

343

is a common (and perhaps natural) response to come to cherish it. To cherish something is not simply to be happy with it at the moment, but to care for it for its own sake. This is not to say that one necessarily sees it as having feelings and so wants it to feel good; nor does it imply that one judges the thing to have Moore's intrinsic value. One simply wants the thing to survive and (when appropriate) to thrive, and not simply for its utility. We see this attitude repeatedly regarding mementos. They are not simply valued as a means to remind us of happy occasions; they come to be valued for their own sake. Thus, if someone really took joy in the natural environment, but was prepared to blow it up as soon as sentient life ended, he would lack this common human tendency to cherish what enriches our lives. While this response is not itself a moral virtue, it may be a natural basis of the virtue we call "gratitude." People who have no tendency to cherish things that give them pleasure may be poorly disposed to respond gratefully to persons who are good to them. Again the connection is not one of logical necessity, but it may nevertheless be important. A nonreligious person unable to "thank" anyone for the beauties of nature may nevertheless feel "grateful" in a sense; and I suspect that the person who feels no such "gratitude" toward nature is unlikely to show proper gratitude toward people.

Suppose these conjectures prove to be true. One may wonder what is the point of considering them. Is it to disparage all those who view nature merely as a resource? To do so, it seems, would be unfair, for, even if this attitude typically stems from deficiencies which affect one's attitudes toward sentient beings, there may be exceptions and we have not shown that their view of nonsentient nature is itself blameworthy. But when we set aside questions of blame and inquire what sorts of human traits we want to encourage, our reflections become relevant in a more positive way. The point is not to insinuate that all anti-environmentalists are defective, but to see that those who value such traits as humility, gratitude, and sensitivity to others have reason to promote the love of nature.

STUDY QUESTIONS

1. Hill is looking for moral reasons to be respectful of nature. Can

one reasonably maintain that nonsentient nature is, in no sense, something that one must "respect"?

2. Why, in Hill's view, are utilitarian considerations inadequate as grounds for an environmental ethic?

3. Discuss the attempts to ground environmental ethics in a religious belief or attitude. Discuss G. E. Moore's idea of "intrinsically valuable states of affairs."

4. What do you think of Hill's contention that treating nature as a mere resource is morally insensitive?

5. Kant maintained that animals and nonsentient beings are outside the moral domain; nevertheless, he held that people should not be cruel to animals because of the effect on their own characters. Is Hill's position somewhat similar to Kant's?

SUGGESTED READINGS

Aristotle. *Nichomachean Ethics.*

Aquinas, Saint Thomas. *Treatise on the Virtues,* Translated and edited by John Oesterle. Englewood Cliffs, NJ: Prentice-Hall, 1966.

Cooper, John M. *Reason and the Human Good in Aristotle.* Cambridge, MA: Harvard University Press, 1975.

Dent, N. J. H. *The Moral Psychology of the Virtues.* Cambridge, England: Cambridge University Press, 1984.

Feinberg, Joel. *Moral Concepts.* Oxford University Press, 1969.

Fried, Charles. *Right and Wrong.* Cambridge, MA: Harvard University Press, 1978.

Geach, Peter. *The Virtues.* Cambridge, MA: Cambridge University Press, 1977.

Hauerwas, Stanley. *A Community of Character.* Notre Dame, IN: University of Notre Dame Press, 1981.

Kraut, Richard. *Aristotle and the Human Good.* Princeton, NJ: Princeton University Press, 1991.

MacIntyre, Alasdair. *After Virtue.* Notre Dame, IN: University of Notre Dame Press, 1981.

MacIntyre, Alasdair. *Whose Justice? Which Rationality?* Notre Dame, IN: University of Notre Dame Press, 1988.

Mayo, Bernard. *Ethics and the Moral Life.* New York: Saint Martin's Press, 1958.

Murdoch, Iris. *The Sovereignty of the Good*. New York: Schocken Books, 1971.

Norton, David L. *Democracy and Moral Development: A Politics of Virtue*. Berkeley, CA: University of California Press, 1992.

Pieper, Joseph. *The Four Cardinal Virtues*. Notre Dame, IN: University of Notre Dame Press, 1966.

Plato, *The Republic*.

Rescher, Nicholas. *Unselfishness*. Pittsburgh, PA: University of Pittsburgh Press, 1975.

Slote, Michael. *Goods and Virtues*. Oxford University Press, 1983.

Von Wright, G. H. *The Varieties of Goodness*. London: Humanities' Press, 1963.

Wallace, J. D. *Virtues and Vices*. Ithaca, NY: Cornell University Press, 1978.

Warnock, G. J. *The Object of Morality*. Princeton, NJ: Princeton University Press, 1969.

Chapter Four

VICE

What is vice? The question has both Christian and pagan answers. The philosophers of antiquity, from Plato to Plutarch, saw vice as a defect that we may overcome by education and discipline, including self-discipline. Virtuous persons are free of vice; their lives are ordered and rational. Plutarch's analysis of vice and virtue is fairly representative of the views of most educated thinkers in the pre-Christian era. Base persons are not controlled by reason; they are prone to impulse, discontented, ridden with anxiety. Plutarch was influenced as much by the Stoic and Epicurean philosophers as he was by Plato and Aristotle. The popular connotations of the word "epicurean" distort the doctrine; the Epicureans were far more concerned with the problem of avoiding pain and frustration than with the pursuit of pleasure and satisfaction. For both Stoics and Epicureans, contentment and inner tranquility, not pleasure, is the essence of the good life. Conversely, a vice is a character defect that promotes inner tensions and chaos as well as outer deeds that are base or ignoble.

Why are some people so susceptible to vice? The pagans attribute vice to improper development. Aristotle and Plato, in somewhat different ways, stress the *learned* character of the virtues. Virtue is a product of an education that includes self-discipline as well as discipline by parents and teachers. Persons of vice, then, have failed to shape a better character for themselves and are responsible for what they are.

The great pagan philosophers thought of virtue as the disposition to do what is right and the developed disinclination to do what is wrong. The Christian philosophers did not disagree with this, but their conception of vice is more highly seasoned. For Augustine and Abelard, to do wrong is to *sin,* to rebel against God: The sinner defies God by transgressing His law. Augustine argues that the impulse to sin is not simply a drive to satisfy desires. As he sees it, sin needs no motive beyond the perverse desire to sin. The desire to do evil is an endowment of Adam and Eve, the original sinners: Since the Fall, man has loved sin for its own sake; sin is, as it were, its own reward. According to Augustine, the pagan view that humans are fully able to control vice and develop the virtues by education and self-discipline is unduly optimistic. He maintains that we cannot achieve salvation or happiness without God's grace.

The question of human perfectability is important whether or not one views it in theological terms. Is it altogether utopian to hope for a day when cruelty and gratuitous malice are things of the past? If Augustine is right, this change will take a miracle.

Sin construed as defiance and rebellion against the powers of good is a more dramatic affair than character defect due to improper education. Augustine and Abelard locate the moment of sin at the moment one consents to do wrong. The act itself is anticlimactic. If, for example, I decide to murder someone, then the moment I *intend* to do this is the moment of sin. Even if I subsequently fail to carry out my intention, my sin is already complete. Kant's deontological ethic of the good will ("nothing is absolutely good except the good will") is a later variant of the Christian doctrine that locates the moment of doing right or wrong in the consent rather than in the act itself.

We should note that Abelard's view of sin is somewhat more complimentary to humanity than Augustine's. Abelard does not emphasize perversity, stressing instead the natural pleasure we achieve by sinning. The inclination to sin is natural and not blameworthy, but we are obligated to resist temptation; in failing to resist we "consent" to wrong and sin. Thus Christian philosophers differ on the nature of vice: Are we vicious because we succumb to natural desire (Abelard), or are we somewhat diabolical (Augustine)?

Recognizing a strong tendency to evil in humans, the Christian philosophers consider persons who have base desires to be virtuous provided they do not "consent" to those desires. The pagan philosophers would have found this odd. Philippa Foot echoes their view (see her "Virtues and Vices" in Chapter 3) when she points out that we feel something is not quite right about the idea of a virtuous person beset by base desires and constantly overcoming them. Both viewpoints have strengths. Surely the pagans were not realistic in thinking of virtue as freedom from even the temptation to do wrong. And surely, as Abelard says, the very merit of doing what is right is due at least in part to the existence of a temptation to do what is wrong, a temptation we resist. If the temptation to vice is absent altogether, we are less praiseworthy for remaining virtuous. On the other hand, we do think of people as virtuous if they are not even tempted to do what is base. The two intuitions conflict, yet each is persuasive. This usually shows that more analysis is needed. The interested reader may wish to go back to Foot's article and proceed from there.

Modern philosophers tend to reject the Augustinian thesis that something in man is ineradicably corrupt. Kant and Butler do so explicitly. Butler argues that all vice is due to self-deception stemming from a false regard for oneself. He denies that anyone loves sin.

> Vice in general consists in having an unreasonable and too great regard for ourselves, in comparison of others. Robbery and murder is never from the love of injustice or cruelty, but to gratify some other passion, to gain some supposed advantage: and it is false selfishness alone, whether cool or passionate, which makes a man resolutely pursue that end, be it ever so much to the injury of another.

Kant, too, denies the existence of any impulse to evil that is not connected with a desire to satisfy oneself in some way. "We have . . . no direct inclination towards evil as evil, but only an indirect one." If Kant and Butler are right, the evil we do is always inadvertent: It is not what we are after.

Most traditional philosophers agree that we need a uniform account of vice and virtue. We have already seen that Augustine and Abelard find the common denominator of the vices in the consent to wrongdoing in defiance of God. Butler finds it in the element of self-deception that permits people to do what they want without admitting to themselves that an action is wrong and self-debasing. Kant, we saw, finds the unity of virtue in the will. The very first philosopher to propose a unified theory of the virtues and vices was Plato, who identified virtue with knowledge and vice with ignorance. Ever since then, philosophers have been hard at work trying to give meaningful substance to what seems right about these identifications.

Though contemporary philosophers (and some novelists) are still in the business of praising virtue and condemning vice, the atmosphere in which this is done has changed. Nowadays writers on virtue will take pains to show that what they are praising really is a virtue and beneficial, or, if they are condemning a particular vice, will be at some pains to show that it really is a vice and harmful. Susan Jacoby's essay argues against those, who while generally condemning revenge, make an exception of sexual revenge. Farrell presents reasons for reversing the common view that envy is a more pardonable vice than jealousy. Charles Fried sees the need to argue that the liar is indeed a bad character. And where the Christian philosopher confidently assumed that greed or promiscuity are vices, the contemporary philosopher is more hesitant.

Vice

PLUTARCH

TRANSLATED BY FRANK COLE BABBITT

Plutarch (A.D. 46–120) was a Greek moralist and biographer. His *Lives* is a classic in the genre of short biography. Plutarch's philosophy was neo-Platonic and he was a sharp critic of Epicureanism.

Plutarch contrasts persons of virtue with persons of vice, claiming that the former can achieve equanimity even in poverty. He depicts the latter as ill and peevish, incapable of truly enjoying even the external things they covet. Plutarch points out that we cannot rid ourselves of vice the way we rid ourselves of bad company. Vicious persons must live in constant proximity to their unpleasant selves.

1. Clothes are supposed to make a man warm, not of course by warming him themselves in the sense of adding their warmth to him, because each garment by itself is cold, and for this reason very often persons who feel hot and feverish keep changing from one set of clothes to another; but the warmth which a man gives off from his own person the clothing, closely applied to the body, confines and enwraps, and does not allow it, when thus imprisoned in the body, to be dissipated again. Now the same condition existing in human affairs deceives most people, who think that, if they surround themselves with vast houses, and get together a mass of slaves and money, they shall live pleasantly. But a pleasant and happy life comes not

VICE Reprinted by permission of the publishers and the Loeb Classical Library from Plutarch's *Moralia*, trans. by Frank Cole Babbitt (Cambridge, MA: Harvard University Press, 1928, 1956, 1962).

from external things, but, on the contrary, man draws on his own character as a source from which to add the element of pleasure and joy to the things which surround him.

> Bright with a blazing fire a house looks far more cheerful,

and wealth is pleasanter, and repute and power more resplendent, if with them goes the gladness which springs from the heart; and so too men bear poverty, exile, and old age lightly and gently in proportion to the serenity and mildness of their character.

2. As perfumes make coarse and ragged garments fragrant, but the body of Anchises gave off a noisome exudation,

> Damping the linen robe adown his back,

so every occupation and manner of life, if attended by virtue, is untroubled and delightful, while, on the other hand, any admixture of vice renders those things which to others seem splendid, precious, and imposing, only troublesome, sickening, and unwelcome to their possessors.

> This man is happy deemed 'mid public throng,
> But when he opens his door he's thrice a wretch;
> His wife controls, commands, and always fights.

Yet it is not difficult for any man to get rid of a bad wife if he be a real man and not a slave; but against his own vice it is not possible to draw up a writing of divorcement and forthwith to be rid of troubles and to be at peace, having arranged to be by himself. No, his vice, a settled tenant of his very vitals always, both at night and by day,

> Burns, but without e'er a brand, and consigns to an eld all untimely.

For in travelling vice is a troublesome companion because of arrogance, at dinner an expensive companion owing to gluttony, and a distressing bedfellow, since by anxieties, cares and jealousies it drives out and destroys sleep. For what slumber there may be is a sleep and repose for the body only, but for the soul terrors, dreams, and agitations, because of superstition.

> When grief o'ertakes me as I close my eyes,
> I'm murdered by my dreams.

says one man. In such a state do envy, fear, temper, and licentiousness put a man. For by day vice, looking outside of itself and conforming its attitude to others, is abashed and veils its emotions, and does not give itself up completely to its impulses, but oftentimes resists them and struggles against them; but in the hours of slumber, when it has escaped from opinion and law, and got away as far as possible from feeling fear or shame, it sets every desire stirring, and awakens its depravity and licentiousness. It "attempts incest," as Plato says, partakes of forbidden meats, abstains from nothing which it wishes to do, but revels in lawlessness so far as it can, with images and visions which end in no pleasure or accomplishment of desire, but have only the power to stir to fierce activity the emotional and morbid propensities.

3. Where, then, is the pleasure in vice, if in no part of it is to be found freedom from care and grief, or contentment or tranquillity or calm? For a well-balanced and healthy condition of the body gives room for engendering the pleasures of the flesh; but in the soul lasting joy and gladness cannot possibly be engendered, unless it provide itself first with cheerfulness, fearlessness, and courageousness as a basis to rest upon, or as a calm tranquillity that no billows disturb; otherwise, even though some hope or delectation lure us with a smile, anxiety suddenly breaks forth, like a hidden rock appearing in fair weather, and the soul is overwhelmed and confounded.

4. Heap up gold, amass silver, build stately promenades, fill your house with slaves and the city with your debtors; unless you lay level the emotions of your soul, put a stop to your insatiate desires, and quit yourself of fears and anxieties, you are but decanting wine for a man in a fever, offering honey to a bilious man, and preparing tidbits and dainties for sufferers from colic or dysentery, who cannot retain them or be strengthened by them, but are only brought nearer to death thereby. Does not your observation of sick persons teach you that they dislike and reject and decline the finest and costliest viands which their attendants offer and try to force upon them; and then later, when their whole condition has changed, and good breathing, wholesome blood, and normal temperature have returned to their bodies, they get up and have joy and satisfaction in eating plain bread with cheese and cress? It is such a condition that reason creates in the soul. You will be contented with your lot if you learn what the honourable and good is. You will be luxurious in poverty, and live like a king, and you will find no less satisfaction in the care-free life of a private citizen than in the life connected with high military or civic office. If you become a philosopher, you will live not

353

unpleasantly, but you will learn to subsist pleasantly anywhere and with any resources. Wealth will give your gladness for the good you will do to many, poverty for your freedom from many cares, repute for the honours you will enjoy, and obscurity for the certainty that you shall not be envied.

STUDY QUESTIONS

1. Plutarch seems to deny that vice contains any real pleasure or satisfaction. Do you agree?
2. Do you agree with his claim that persons given over to vice are "poor company" for everyone, including themselves?
3. Plutarch associates vice with a troubled nature, and virtue with a contented, serene nature. Are these correlations realistic?
4. Plutarch claims that the person of vice is subject to the ills of poverty, while the person of virtue transcends them. Does this claim have merit? In your opinion, what effect does economic circumstance have on a virtuous or a vicious nature?

The Depths of Vice

SAINT AUGUSTINE

TRANSLATED BY JOHN K. RYAN

A biographical sketch of Saint Augustine is found on page 192.

Augustine, writing about his sixteenth year, describes the time he and his friends stole some pears for which they had no use. He ponders the motive and concludes that the perverse desire to defy God's will, an expression of man's corrupted nature, was itself the motive. Augustine is now

THE DEPTHS OF VICE From *The Confessions of St. Augustine*. Translated by John K. Ryan. Copyright © 1960 by Doubleday and Company, Inc. Reprinted by permission of the publisher.

disgusted with his past self, but confesses that he was once ready to sin whenever someone urged, "Let's go! Let's do it!"

I wish to bring back to mind my past foulness and the carnal corruptions of my soul. This is not because I love them, but that I may love you, my God. Out of love for your love I do this. In the bitterness of my remembrance, I tread again my most evil ways, so that you may grow sweet to me, O sweetness that never fails, O sweetness happy and enduring, which gathers me together again from that disordered state in which I lay in shattered pieces, wherein, turned away from you, the one, I spent myself upon the many. For in my youth, I burned to get my fill of hellish things. I dared to run wild in different darksome ways of love. My comeliness wasted away. I stank in your eyes, but I was pleasing to myself and I desired to be pleasing to the eyes of men. . . .

The Stolen Fruit

Surely, Lord, your law punishes theft, as does that law written on the hearts of men, which not even iniquity itself blots out. What thief puts up with another thief with a calm mind? Not even a rich thief will pardon one who steals from him because of want. But I willed to commit theft, and I did so, not because I was driven to it by any need, unless it were by poverty of justice, and dislike of it, and by a glut of evildoing. For I stole a thing of which I had plenty of my own and of much better quality. Nor did I wish to enjoy that thing which I desired to gain by theft, but rather to enjoy the actual theft and the sin of theft.

In a garden nearby to our vineyard there was a pear tree, loaded with fruit that was desirable neither in appearance nor in taste. Late one night—to which hour, according to our pestilential custom, we had kept our street games—a group of very bad youngsters set out to shake down and rob this tree. We took great loads of fruit from it, not for our own eating, but rather to throw it to the pigs; even if we did eat a little of it, we did this to do what pleased us for the reason that it was forbidden. . . .

When there is discussion concerning a crime and why it was committed, it is usually held that there appeared possibility that the appetites would obtain some of these goods, which we have termed lower, or there was fear of losing them. These things are beautiful and fitting, but in comparison with the higher goods, which bring happiness, they are mean and base. A man commits murder: why did he do so? He coveted his victim's wife or his property; or he wanted to rob him to get money to live on; or he feared to be deprived of some such thing by the other; or he had been injured, and burned for revenge. Would anyone commit murder without reason and out of delight in murder itself? Who can believe such a thing? Of a certain senseless and utterly cruel man it was said that he was evil and cruel without reason. Nevertheless, a reason has been given, for he himself said, "I don't want to let my hand or will get out of practice through disuse." Why did he want that? Why so? It was to the end that after he had seized the city by the practice of crime, he would attain to honors, power, and wealth, and be free from fear of the law and from trouble due to lack of wealth or from a guilty conscience. Therefore, not even Catiline himself loved his crimes, but something else, for sake of which he committed them.

The Anatomy of Evil

What was it that I, a wretch, loved in you, my act of theft, my deed of crime done by night, done in the sixteenth year of my age? You were not beautiful, for you were but an act of thievery. In truth, are you anything at all, that I may speak to you? The fruit we stole was beautiful, for it was your creation, O most beautiful of all beings, creator of all things, God the good, God the supreme good and my true good. Beautiful was the fruit, but it was not what my unhappy soul desired. I had an abundance of better pears, but those pears I gathered solely that I might steal. The fruit I gathered I threw away, devouring in it only iniquity, and that I rejoiced to enjoy. For if I put any of that fruit into my mouth, my sin was its seasoning. But now, O Lord my God, I seek out what was in that theft to give me delight, and lo, there is no loveliness in it. I do not say such loveliness as there is in justice and prudence, or in man's mind, and memory, and senses, and vigorous life, nor that with which the stars are beautiful and glorious in their courses, or the land and the sea filled with their living kinds, which by new births replace those that die, nor even that flawed and shadowy beauty found in the vices that deceive us.

For pride imitates loftiness of mind, while you are the one God, highest above all things. What does ambition seek, except honor and glory, while you alone are to be honored above all else and are glorious forever? The cruelty of the mighty desires to be feared: but who is to be feared except the one God, and from his power what can be seized and stolen away, and when, or where, or how, or by whom? The caresses of the wanton call for love; but there is naught more caressing than your charity, nor is anything to be loved more wholesomely than your truth, which is beautiful and bright above all things. Curiosity pretends to be a desire for knowledge, while you know all things in the highest degree. Ignorance itself and folly are cloaked over the names of simplicity and innocence, because nothing more simple than you can be found. What is more innocent than you, whereas to evil men their own works are hostile? Sloth seeks rest as it were, but what sure rest is there apart from the Lord? Luxury of life desires to be called plenty and abundance; you are the fullness and the unfailing plenty of incorruptible pleasure. Prodigality casts but the shadow of liberality, while you are the most affluent giver of all good things. Avarice desires to possess many things, and you possess all things. Envy contends for excellence: what is more excellent than you? Anger seeks vengeance: who takes vengeance with more justice than you? Fear shrinks back at sudden and unusual things threatening what it loves, and is on watch for its own safety. But for you what is unusual or what is sudden? Or who can separate you from what you love? Where, except with you, is there firm security? Sadness wastes away over things now lost in which desire once took delight. It did not want this to happen, whereas from you nothing can be taken away.

Thus the soul commits fornication when it is turned away from you and, apart from you, seeks such pure, clean things as it does not find except when it returns to you. In a perverse way, all men imitate you who put themselves far from you, and rise up in rebellion against you. Even by such imitation of you they prove that you are the creator of all nature, and that therefore there is no place where they can depart entirely from you.

What, therefore did I love in that theft of mine, in what manner did I perversely or viciously imitate my Lord? Did it please me to go against your law, at least by trickery, for I could not do so with might? Did it please me that as a captive I should imitate a deformed liberty, by doing with impunity things illicit bearing a shadowy likeness of your omnipotence? Behold, your servant flees from his Lord and follows after a shadow! O rottenness! O monstrous life and deepest death! Could a thing give pleasure which could not be done lawfully, and which was done for no other reason but because it was unlawful? . . .

Evil Communications

What was my state of mind? Truly and clearly, it was most base, and woe was it to me who had it. Yet, what was it? Who understands his sins? It was like a thing of laughter, which reached down as it were into our hearts, that we were tricking those who did not know what we were doing and would most strenuously resent it. Why, then, did even the fact that I did not do it alone give me pleasure? Is it because no one can laugh readily when he is alone? No one indeed does laugh readily when alone. However, individual men, when alone and when no one else is about, are sometimes overcome by laughter if something very funny affects their senses or strikes their mind. But that deed I would not have done alone; alone I would never have done it.

Behold, the living record of my soul lies before you, my God. By myself I would not have committed that theft in which what pleased me was not what I stole but the fact that I stole. This would have pleased me not at all if I had done it alone; nor by myself would I have done it at all. O friendship too unfriendly! Unfathomable seducer of the mind, greed to do harm for fun and sport, desire for another's injury, arising not from desire for my own gain or for vengeance, but merely when someone says, "Let's go! Let's do it!" and it is shameful not to be shameless!

A Soul in Waste

Who can untie this most twisted and intricate mass of knots? It is a filthy thing: I do not wish to think about it; I do not wish to look upon it. I desire you, O justice and innocence, beautiful and comely to all virtuous eyes, and I desire this unto a satiety that can never be satiated. With you there is true rest and life untroubled. He who enters into you enters into the joy of his Lord, and he shall have no fear, and he shall possess his soul most happily in him who is the supreme good. I fell away from you, my God, and I went astray, too far astray from you, the support of my youth, and I became to myself a land of want.

STUDY QUESTIONS

1. Do you agree with Augustine that we often pursue vice for its own sake?

2. Explain what Augustine means when he says that, "in a perverse way, all men imitate [God] who put themselves far from [Him], and rise up in rebellion against [Him]."

3. Do you agree with Augustine's implicit claim that a crime such as theft is worse when committed for the thrill of it rather than for personal material gain?

4. People sometimes say that evil will be greatly mitigated when human nature changes for the better. Do you believe that human beings have evolved morally? Can we reasonably expect that they may become significantly more moral than they now are? What would Augustine say?

Desire and Sin

PETER ABELARD

TRANSLATED BY R. MCCALLUM

Peter Abelard (1079–1142) was the foremost logician of his age and one of the greatest philosophers of the Middle Ages. He is best known, however, for his tragic love affair with Heloise. He wrote influential treatises on theology, metaphysics, logic, and ethics.

Abelard distinguishes moral defects from other "defects of the mind" such as poor memory or dullwittedness. Moral defects dispose us to bad actions; morally defective individuals have characters that lead them or allow them to do the evil they want to do. In actually sinning they consent to an evil impulse: Instead of resisting it, they

DESIRE AND SIN From *Abelard's Ethics*. Translated by R. McCallum. Reprinted by permission of the publisher, Basil Blackwell Publisher Limited.

359

will it and act on it. Abelard denies that the truly virtuous person is free of evil impulses. To be virtuous is precisely to have the capacity or disposition to control the evil impulses that even the good person possesses, by not consenting to act on those impulses. By emphasizing the active will to do right in the face of a natural desire to do wrong, Abelard is a forerunner of Kant.

Prologue

In the study of morals we deal with the defects or qualities of the mind which dispose us to bad or good actions. Defects and qualities are not only mental, but also physical. There is bodily weakness; there is also the endurance which we call strength. There is sluggishness or speed; blindness or sight. When we now speak of defects, therefore, we pre-suppose defects of the mind, so as to distinguish them from the physical ones. The defects of the mind are opposed to the qualities; injustice to justice; cowardice to constancy; intemperance to temperance.

Chapter I. The Defect of Mind Bearing upon Conduct

Certain defects or merits of mind have no connection with morals. They do not make human life a matter of praise or blame. Such are dull wits or quick insight; a good or a bad memory; ignorance or knowledge. Each of these features is found in good and bad alike. They have nothing to do with the system of morals, nor with making life base or honourable. To exclude these we safeguarded above the phrase "defects of mind" by adding "which dispose to bad actions," that is, those defects which incline the will to what least of all either should be done or should be left undone.

Chapter II. How Does Sin Differ from a Disposition to Evil?

Defect of this mental kind is not the same thing as sin. Sin, too, is not the same as a bad action. For example, to be irascible, that is, prone or easily roused to the agitation of anger is a defect and moves the mind to unpleasantly impetuous and irrational action. This defect, however, is in the mind so that the mind is liable to wrath, even when it is not actually roused to it. Similarly, lameness, by reason of which a man is said to be lame, is in the man himself even when he does not walk and reveal his lameness. For the defect is there though action be lacking. So, also, nature or constitution renders many liable to luxury. Yet they do not sin because they are like this, but from this very fact they have the material of a struggle whereby they may, in the virtue of temperance, triumph over themselves and win the crown. As Solomon says: "Better a patient than a strong man; and the Lord of his soul than he that taketh a city." (Prov. xvi, 32.) For religion does not think it degrading to be beaten by man; but it is degrading to be beaten by one's lower self. The former defeat has been the fate of good men. But, in the latter, we fall below ourselves. The Apostle commends victory of this sort; "No one shall be crowned who has not truly striven." (2 Tim. ii, 5.) This striving, I repeat, means standing less against men than against myself, so that defects may not lure me into base consent. Though men cease to oppose us, our defects do not cease. The fight with them is the more dangerous because of its repetition. And as it is the more difficult, so victory is the more glorious. Men, however much they prevail over us, do not force baseness upon us, unless by their practice of vice they turn us also to it and overcome us through our own wretched consent. They may dominate our body; but while our mind is free, there is no danger to true freedom. We run no risk of base servitude. Subservience to vice, not to man, is degradation. It is the overlordship of defects and not physical serfdom which debases the soul.

Chapter III. Definition of "Defect" and of Sin

Defect, then, is that whereby we are disposed to sin. We are, that is, inclined to consent to what we ought not to do, or to leave undone what we ought to do. Consent of this kind we rightly call sin. Here is the reproach of the soul meriting damnation or being declared guilty by God. What is that consent but to despise God and to violate His laws? God cannot be set at enmity by injury, but by contempt. He is the highest power, and is not diminished by any injury, but He avenges contempt of Himself. Our sin, therefore, is contempt of the Creator. To sin is to despise the Creator; that is, not to do for Him what we believe we should do for Him, or, not to renounce what we think should be renounced on His behalf. We have defined sin

361

negatively by saying that it means not doing or not renouncing what we ought to do or renounce. Clearly, then, we have shown that sin has no reality. It exists rather in *not being* than in *being*. Similarly we could define shadows by saying: The absence of light where light usually is.

Perhaps you object that sin is the desire or will to do an evil deed, and that this will or desire condemns us before God in the same way as the will to do a good deed justifies us. There is as much quality, you suggest, in the good will as there is sin in the evil will; and it is no less "in being" in the latter than in the former. By willing to do what we believe to be pleasing to God we please Him. Equally, by willing to do what we believe to be displeasing to God, we displease Him and seem either to violate or despise His nature.

But diligent attention will show that we must think far otherwise of this point. We frequently err, and from no evil will at all. Indeed, the evil will itself, when restrained, though it may not be quenched, procures the palm-wreath for those who resist it. It provides, not merely the materials for combat, but also the crown of glory. It should be spoken of rather as a certain inevitable weakness than as sin. Take, for example, the case of an innocent servant whose harsh master is moved with fury against him. He pursues the servant, drawing his sword with intent to kill him. For a while the servant flees and avoids death as best he can. At last, forced all unwillingly to it, he kills his master so as not to be killed by him. Let anyone say what sort of evil will there was in this deed. His will was only to flee from death and preserve his own life. Was this an evil will? You reply: "I do not think this was an evil will. But the will that he had to kill the master who was pursuing him was evil." Your answer would be admirable and acute if you could show that the servant really willed what you say that he did. But, as I insisted, he was unwillingly forced to his deed. He protracted his master's life as long as he could, knowing that danger also threatened his own life from such a crime. How, then was a deed done voluntarily by which he incurred danger to his own life? . . .

Sin, therefore, is sometimes committed without an evil will. Thus sin cannot be defined as "will." True, you will say, when we sin under constraint, but not when we sin willingly, for instance, when we will to do something which we know ought not to be done by us. There the evil will and sin seem to be the same thing. For example, a man sees a woman; his concupiscence is aroused; his mind is enticed by fleshly lust and stirred to base desire. This wish, this lascivious longing, what else can it be, you say, than sin?

I reply: What if that wish may be bridled by the power of temperance? What if its nature is never to be entirely extinguished but to persist in struggle and not fully fail even in defeat? For where is the battle if the antagonist is away? Whence the great reward without grave endurance? When the fight is over nothing remains but to reap the reward. Here we strive in contest in order elsewhere to obtain as victors a crown. Now, for a contest, an opponent is needed who will resist, not one who simply submits. This opponent is our evil will over which we triumph when we subjugate it to the divine will. But we do not entirely destroy it. For we need ever expect to encounter our enemy. What achievement before God is it if we undergo nothing contrary to our own will, but merely practice what we please? Who will be grateful to us if in what we say we do for him we merely satisfy our own fancy?

You will say, what merit have we with God in acting willingly or unwillingly? Certainly none: I reply. He weighs the intention rather than the deed in his recompense. Nor does the deed, whether it proceed from a good or an evil will, add anything to the merit, as we shall show shortly. But when we set His will before our own so as to follow His and not ours, our merit with God is magnified, in accordance with that perfect word of Truth: "I came not to do mine own will, but the will of Him that sent me." (John vi, 38.) To this end He exhorts us: "If anyone comes to me, and does not hate father, and mother . . . yea his own soul also, he is not worthy of me." (Luke xiv, 26.) That is to say, "unless a man renounces his parents' influence and his own will and submits himself to my teaching, he is not worthy of me." Thus we are bidden to hate our father, not to destroy him. Similarly with our own will. We must not be led by it; at the same time, we are not asked to root it out altogether.

When the Scripture says: "Go not after your own desires" (Eccles. xviii, 30) . . . I think that it is plain that no natural physical delight can be set down as sin, nor can it be called guilt for men to delight in what, when it is done, must involve the feeling of delight.

For example, if anyone obliged a monk, bound in chains, to lie among women, and the monk by the softness of the couch and by contact with his fair flatterers is allured into delight, though not into consent, who shall presume to designate guilt the delight which is naturally awakened?

You may urge, with some thinkers, that the carnal pleasure, even in lawful intercourse, involves sin. Thus David says: "Behold in sin was I conceived." (Ps. 1, 7.) And the Apostle, when he had said: "Ye return to it again" (I Cor. vii, 5), adds nevertheless, "This I say by way of concession, not of command." (ibid., v, 6.) Yet authority rather than reason, seems to dictate the view that we should allow simple physical delight to be sin. For, assuredly, David was conceived not in fornication, but in matrimony: and concession, that is forgiveness, does not, as this standpoint avers, condone when there is no guilt to forgive. As for what David meant when he says that he had been conceived "in iniquity" or "in sin" and does not say "whose" sin, he referred to the general curse of original sin, wherein from the guilt of our first parents each is subject to damnation, as it is elsewhere stated: "None are pure of stain, not the infant a day old, if he has life on this earth." As the blessed Jerome reminds us and as manifest reason teaches, the soul of a young child is without sin. If, then, it is pure of sin, how is it also impure by sinful corruption? We must understand the infant's purity from sin in reference to its personal guilt. But its contact with sinful corruption, its "stain," is in reference to penalty owed by mankind because of Adam's sin. He who has not yet perceived by reason what he ought to do cannot be guilty of contempt of God. Yet he is not free from the contamination of the sin of his first parents, from which he contracts the penalty, though not the guilt, and bears in penalty what they committed in guilt. When, therefore, David says that he was conceived in iniquity or sin, he sees himself subject to the general sentence of damnation from the guilt of his racial parents, and he assigns the sins, not to his father and mother but to his first parents. . . .

We come, then, to this conclusion, that no one who sets out to assert that all fleshly desire is sin may say that the sin itself is increased by the doing of it. For this would mean extending the consent of the soul into the exercise of the action. In short, one would be stained not only by consent to baseness, but also by the mire of the deed, as if what happens externally in the body could possibly soil the soul. Sin is not, therefore, increased by the doing of an action: and nothing mars the soul except what is of its own nature, namely consent. This we affirmed was alone sin, preceding action in will, or subsequent to the performance of action. Although we wish for, or do, what is unseemly, we do not therefore sin. For such deeds not uncommonly occur without there being any sin. On the other hand, there may be consent without the external effects, as we have indicated. There was wish without consent in the case of the man who was attracted by a woman whom he caught sight of, or who was tempted by his neighbour's fruit, but who was not enticed into consent. There was evil consent without evil desire in the servant who unwillingly killed his master.

Certain acts which ought not to be done often are done, and without any sin, when, for instance, they are commited under force or ignorance. No one, I think, ignores this fact. A woman under constraint of violence, lies with another's husband. A man, taken by some trick, sleeps with one whom he supposed to be his wife, or kills a man, in the belief that he himself has the right to be both judge and executioner. Thus to desire the wife of another or actually lie with her is not sin. But to consent to that desire or to that action is sin. This consent to covetousness the law calls covetousness in saying: "Thou shalt not covet." (Deut. v, 21.) Yet that which we cannot avoid ought not to be forbidden, nor that wherein, as we said, we do not sin. But we should be cautioned about the consent to covetousness. So, too, the saying of the Lord must be understood: "Whosoever shall look upon a woman to desire her." (Matt. v, 28.) That is, whosoever shall so look upon her as a slip into consent to covetousness, "has already committed adultery with her in his heart" (Matt. v, 28), even though he may not have committed adultery in deed. He is guilty of sin, though there be no sequel to his intention. . . .

Blessed Augustine, in his careful view of this question, reduces every sin or command to terms of charity and covetousness, and not to works. "The law," he says, "inculcates nothing but charity, and forbids nothing but covetousness." The Apostle, also, asserts: "All the law is contained in one word: thou shalt love thy neighbour as thyself," (Rom. xiii, 8, 10), and again, "Love is the fulfilling of the law." (ibid.)

Whether you actually give alms to a needy person, or charity makes you ready to give, makes no difference to the merit of the deed. The will may be there when the opportunity is not. Nor does it rest entirely with you to deal with every case of need which you encounter. Actions which are right and actions which are far from right are done by good and bad men alike. The intention alone separates the two classes of men. . . .

Briefly to summarize the above argument: Four things were postulated which might be carefully distinguished from one another.

1. Imperfection of soul, making us liable to sin.
2. Sin itself, which we decided is consent to evil or contempt of God.
3. The will or desire of evil.
4. The evil deed.

To wish is not the same thing as to fulfil a wish. Equally, to sin is not the same as to carry out a sin. In the first case, we sin by consent of the soul: the second is a matter of the external effect of an action, namely, when we fulfil in deed that whereunto we have previously consented. When, therefore, temptation is said to proceed through three stages, suggestion, delight, consent, it must be understood that, like our first parents, we are frequently led along these three paths to the commission of sin. The devil's persuasion comes *first* promising from the taste of the forbidden fruit immortality. Delight follows. When the woman sees the beautiful tree, and perceives that the fruit is good, her appetite is whetted by the anticipated pleasure of tasting. This desire she ought to have repressed, so as to obey God's command. But in consenting to it, she was drawn *secondly* into sin. By penitence she should have put right this fault, and obtained pardon. Instead, she *thirdly* consummated the sin by the deed. Eve thus passed through the three stages to the commission of sin.

By the same avenues we also arrive not at sin, but at the action of sin, namely, the doing of an unseemly deed through the suggestion or prompting of something within us. If we already know that such a deed will be pleasant, our imagination is held by anticipatory delight and we are tempted thereby in thought. So long as we give consent to such delight, we sin. Lastly, we pass to the third stage, and actually commit the sin.

It is agreed by some thinkers that carnal suggestion, even though the person causing the suggestion be not present, should be included under sinful suggestion. For example, a man having seen a woman falls into a sensual desire for her. But it seems that this kind of suggestion should simply be called delight. This delight, and other delights of the like kind, arise naturally and, as we said above, they are not sinful. The Apostle calls them "human temptations." No temptation has taken you yet which was not common to men. God is faithful, and will not suffer you to be tempted above what you are able; but will, with the temptation make a way of escape, that you may be able to bear it. By temptation is meant, in general, any movement of the soul to do something unseemly, whether in wish or consent. We speak of human temptation without which it is hardly or never possible for human weakness to exist. Such are sexual desire, or the pleasures of the table. From these the Psalmist asks to be delivered when he says: "Deliver me from my wants, O Lord" (Ps. xxiv, 17); that is, from the temptations of natural and necessary appetites that they may not influence him into sinful consent. Or, he may mean: "When this life is over, grant me to be without those temptations of which life has been full."

When the Apostle says: "No temptation has taken you but what is human," his statement amounts to this: Even if the soul be stirred by that delight which is, as we said, human temptation, yet God would not lead the soul into that consent wherein sin consists. Someone may object: But by what power of our own are we able to resist those desires? We may reply: "God is faithful, who will not allow you to resist those desires?" We may reply: "God is faithful, who will not allow you to be tempted," as the Scripture says. In other words: We should rather trust him than rely upon ourselves. He promises help, and is true to His promises. He is faithful, so that we should have complete faith in Him. Out of pity God diminishes the degree of human temptation, does not suffer us to be tempted above what we are able, in order that it may not drive us to sin at a pace we cannot endure, when, that is, we strive to resist it. Then, too, God turns the temptation to our advantage: for He trains us thereby so that the recurrence of temptation causes us less care, and we fear less the onset of a foe over whom we have already triumphed, and whom we know how to meet. . . .

STUDY QUESTIONS

1. Abelard maintains that persons who will to murder others but are externally prevented from carrying out their purpose have sinned as completely as those who actually murder. Do you agree? What are the implications of this for moral philosophy?

367

2. The moral report card has one grade for accomplishment and another for effort. Which grade counts more for Abelard? How does he argue for giving it more weight?
3. What does Abelard mean by "consent to baseness"? How does "consent" differ from "desire"? Can consent to baseness occur without base desire?
4. How does Abelard's Christian conception of vice differ from one that is not grounded in a religious doctrine? Is the difference significant?

The Hypocrites

DANTE ALIGHIERI

TRANSLATED BY JOHN CIARDI

Dante Alighieri (1265–1321) is the Florentine author of the *Divine Comedy,* which is regarded as one of the supreme literary works of all time. It recounts the poet's journey through Hell (the *Inferno*), Purgatory (the *Purgatorio*), and finally Heaven (the *Paradiso*), and describes the fate of human souls after death.

Dante intended the *Divine Comedy* as an allegory. In a letter to his patron he wrote, "[I]ts subject is: 'Man, as by good or ill deserts, in the exercise of his free choice, becomes liable to rewarding or punishing justice.'" The *Inferno* is also meant as an allegorical description of the state of sinners' souls while they are still alive. Thus, hypocrites, even while alive, may appear to be "all dazzle, golden and fair," but on the inside they are heavy, leaden, and tormented. For Dante, the internal effects of sin are as punishing as the torments of Hell.

THE HYPOCRITES From the *Inferno* by Dante Alighieri. Translated by John Ciardi. Copyright 1954, 1982 by John Ciardi. Reprinted by arrangement with the New American Library.

About us now in the depth of the pit we found
   a painted people, weary and defeated.
   Slowly, in pain, they paced it round and round.

All wore great cloaks cut to as ample a size
   as those worn by the Benedictines of Cluny.[1]
   The enormous hoods were drawn over their eyes.

The outside is all dazzle, golden and fair;
   the inside, lead, so heavy that Frederick's capes,[2]
   compared to these, would seem as light as air.

O weary mantle for eternity!
   We turned to the left again along their course,
   listening to their moans of misery,

but they moved so slowly down that barren strip,
   tired by their burden, that our company
   was changed at every movement of the hip.[3]

And walking thus, I said: "As we go on,
   may it please you to look about among these people
   for any whose name or history may be known."

And one who understood Tuscan cried to us there
   as we hurried past: "I pray you check your speed,
   you who run so fast through the sick air:

it may be I am one who will fit your case."
   And at his words my Master turned and said:
   "Wait now, then go with him at his own pace."

I waited there, and saw along that track
   two souls who seemed in haste to be with me;
   but the narrow way and their burden held them back.

---

[1]*the Benedictines of Cluny:* The habit of these monks was especially ample and elegant. St. Bernard once wrote ironically to a nephew who had entered this monastery: "If length of sleeves and amplitude of hood made for holiness, what could hold me back from following [your lead]."

[2]*Frederick's capes:* Frederick II executed persons found guilty of treason by fastening them into a sort of leaden shell. The doomed man was then placed in a cauldron over a fire and the lead was melted around him.

[3]*our company was changed, etc.:* Another tremendous Dantean figure. Sense: "They moved so slowly that at every step (movement of the hip) we found ourselves beside new sinners."

When they had reached me down that narrow way
    they stared at me in silence and amazement,
    then turned to one another. I heard one say:

"This one seems, by the motion of his throat,
    to be alive; and if they are dead, how is it
    they are allowed to shed the leaden coat?"

And then to me "O Tuscan, come so far
    to the college of the sorry hypocrites,
    do not disdain to tell us who you are."

And I: "I was born and raised a Florentine
    on the green and lovely banks of Arno's waters,
    I go with the body that was always mine.

But who are *you,* who sighing as you go
    distill in floods of tears that drown your cheeks?
    What punishment is this that glitters so?"

"These burnished robes are of thick lead," said one,
    "and are hung on us like counterweights, so heavy
    that we, their weary fulcrums, creak and groan.

Jovial Friars and Bolognese were we.[4]
    We were chosen jointly by your Florentines[5]
    to keep the peace, an office usually

held by a single man; near the Gardingo[6]
    one still may see the sort of peace we kept.
    I was called Catalano, he, Loderingo."

---

[4]*Jovial Friars:* A nickname given to the military monks of the order of the Glorious Virgin Mary founded at Bologna in 1261. Their original aim was to serve as peacemakers, enforcers of order, and protectors of the weak, but their observance of their rules became so scandalously lax, and their management of worldly affairs so self-seeking, that the order was disbanded by Papal decree.

[5]*We were chosen jointly . . . to keep the peace:* Catalano del Malavolti (c. 1210–1285), a Guelph, and Loderingo degli Andolo (c. 1210–1293), a Ghibelline, were both Bolognese and, as brothers of the Jovial Friars, both had served as *podestà* (the chief officer charged with keeping the peace) of many cities for varying terms. In 1266 they were jointly appointed to the office of *podestà* of Florence on the theory that a bipartisan administration by men of God would bring peace to the city. Their tenure of office was marked by great violence, however; and they were forced to leave in a matter of months. Modern scholarship has established the fact that they served as instruments of Clement IV's policy in Florence, working at his orders to overthrow the Ghibellines under the guise of an impartial administration.

I began: "O Friars, your evil . . ."—and then I saw
 a figure crucified upon the ground[7]
 by three great stakes, and I fell still in awe.

When he saw me there, he began to puff great sighs
 into his beard, convulsing all his body;
 and Friar Catalano, following my eyes,

said to me: "That one nailed across the road
 counselled the Pharisees that it was fitting
 one man be tortured for the public good.

Naked he lies fixed there, as you see,
 in the path of all who pass; there he must feel
 the weight of all through all eternity.

His father-in-law and the others of the Council[8]
 which was a seed of wrath to all the Jews,
 are similarly staked for the same evil."

Then I saw Virgil marvel for a while[9]
 over that soul so ignominiously
 stretched on the cross in Hell's eternal exile.

Then, turning, he asked the Friar: "If your law permit,
 can you tell us if somewhere along the right
 there is some gap in the stone wall of the pit

through which we two may climb to the next brink
 without the need of summoning the Black Angels
 and forcing them to raise us from this sink?"

He: "Nearer than you hope, there is a bridge
 that runs from the great circle of the scarp
 and crosses every ditch from ridge to ridge,

---

[6]*Gardingo:* The site of the palace of the Ghibelline family degli Uberti. In the riots resulting from the maladministration of the two Jovial Friars, the Ghibellines were forced out of the city and the Uberti palace was razed.

[7]*a figure crucified upon the ground:* Caiaphas. His words were: "It is expedient that one man shall die for the people and that the whole nation perish not." (*John* xi, 50.)

[8]*his father-in-law and the others:* Annas, father-in-law of Caiaphas, was the first before whom Jesus was led upon his arrest. (*John* xviii, 13.) He had Jesus bound and delivered to Caiaphas.

[9]*I saw Virgil marvel:* Caiaphas had not been there on Virgil's first descent into Hell.

except that in this it is broken; but with care
    you can mount the ruins which lie along the slope
    and make a heap on the bottom." My Guide stood
                        there

motionless for a while with a dark look.
    At last he said: "He lied about this business,
    who spears the sinners yonder with his hook."[10]

And the Friar: "Once at Bologna I heard the wise
    discussing the Devil's sins; among them I heard
    that he is a liar and the father of lies."

When the sinner had finished speaking, I saw the face
    of my sweet Master darken a bit with anger:[11]
    he set off at a great stride from that place,

and I turned from that weighted hypocrite
    to follow in the prints of his dear feet.

STUDY QUESTIONS

1.   Why is hypocrisy a vice?
2.   What forms of hypocrisy are most damaging?
3.   Do hypocrites deceive themselves as well as others?
4.   Is Dante right about the psychological and spiritual effects of hypocrisy? Does hypocrisy weigh people down and make them "weary and defeated"?
5.   Can a hypocrite be happy?

---

[10]*he lied . . . who spears the sinners yonder:* Malacoda.

[11]*darken a bit:* The original is *turbato un poco d'ira.* A bit of anger befits the righteous indignation of Human Reason, but immoderate anger would be out of character. One of the sublimities of Dante's writing is the way in which even the smallest details reinforce the great concepts.

Self-deception

SAMUEL JOHNSON

Samuel Johnson (1709–1784), immortalized by his famous biographer, Boswell, was one of the most prominent figures of eighteenth-century English intellectual life. He wrote essays, novels, biographies, political tracts, a dictionary, and poetry, all in a scintillating style.

Johnson examines the devices of self-deceivers. One device they use is to congratulate themselves on a single act of generosity, thereby conferring on themselves the attribute "compassionate" or "generous," even though the vast majority of their actions are mean and self-serving. Or they may praise goodness verbally, and thereby deceive themselves into thinking they are good. Still another device is to appear virtuous by dwelling on the evils of others. Self-deceivers will try to keep their distance from people who truly know what they are like, preferring the company of those who won't expose them to themselves. And they avoid "self-communion."

One sophism by which men persuade themselves that they have those virtues which they really want, is formed by the substitution of single acts for habits. A miser who once relieved a friend from the danger of a prison, suffers his imagination to dwell for ever upon his own heroick generosity; he yields his heart up to indignation at those who are blind to merit, or insensible to misery, and who can please themselves with the enjoyment of that wealth, which they never permit others to partake. From any censures of the world, or reproaches of his conscience, he has an appeal to action and to knowledge; and though his whole life is a course of rapacity and avarice, he concludes himself to be tender and liberal, because he has once performed an act of liberality and tenderness.

As a glass which magnifies objects by the approach of one end to the eye, lessens them by the application of the other, so vices are extenuated by the inversion of that fallacy, by which virtues are augmented. Those faults which we cannot conceal from our own notice, are considered, however frequent, not as habitual corruptions, or settled practices, but as casual failures, and single lapses. A man who has, from year to year, set his country to sale, either for the gratification of his ambition or resentment, confesses that the heat of party now and then betrays the severest virtue to measures that cannot be seriously defended. He that spends his days and nights in riot and debauchery, owns that his passions oftentimes overpower his resolution. But each comforts himself that his faults are not without precedent, for the best and the wisest men have given way to the violence of sudden temptations.

There are men who always confound the praise of goodness with the practice, and who believe themselves mild and moderate, charitable and faithful, because they have exerted their eloquence in commendation of mildness, fidelity, and other virtues. This is an error almost universal among those that converse much with dependents, with such whose fear or interest disposes them to a seeming reverence for any declamation, however enthusiastick, and submission to any boast, however arrogant. Having none to recall their attention to their lives, they rate themselves by the goodness of their opinions, and forget how much more easily men may shew their virtue in their talk than in their actions.

The tribe is likewise very numerous of those who regulate their lives, not by the standard of religion, but the measure of other men's virtue; who lull their own remorse with the remembrance of crimes more atrocious than their own, and seem to believe that they are not bad while another can be found worse.

For escaping these and a thousand other deceits, many expedients have been proposed. Some have recommended the frequent consultation of a wise friend, admitted to intimacy, and encouraged to sincerity. But this appears a remedy by no means adapted to general use: for in order to secure the virtue of one, it presupposes more virtue in two than will generally be found. In the first, such a desire of rectitude and amendment, as may incline him to hear his own accusation from the mouth of him whom he esteems, and by whom, therefore, he will always hope that his faults are not discovered; and in the second such zeal and honesty, as will make him content for his friend's advantage to lose his kindness.

A long life may be passed without finding a friend in whose understanding and virtue we can equally confide, and whose opinion we can value at once for its justness and sincerity. A weak man, however honest, is not qualified to judge. A man of the world, however penetrating, is not fit to counsel. Friends are often chosen for similitude of manners, and therefore each palliates the other's failings, because they are his own. Friends are tender and unwilling to give pain, or they are interested, and fearful to offend.

These objections have inclined others to advise, that he who would know himself, should consult his enemies, remember the reproaches that are vented to his face, and listen for the censures that are uttered in private. For his great business is to know his faults, and those malignity will discover, and resentment will reveal. But this precept may be often frustrated; for it seldom happens that rivals or opponents are suffered to come near enough to know our conduct with so much exactness as that conscience should allow and reflect the accusation. The charge of an enemy is often totally false, and commonly so mingled with falsehood, that the mind takes advantage from the failure of one part to discredit the rest, and never suffers any disturbance afterward from such partial reports.

Yet it seems that enemies have been always found by experience the most faithful monitors; for adversity has ever been considered as the state in which a man most easily becomes acquainted with himself, and this effect it must produce by withdrawing flatterers, whose business it is to hide our weaknesses from us, or by giving loose to malice, and licence to reproach; or at least by cutting of those pleasures which called us away from meditation on our conduct, and repressing that pride which too easily persuades us, that we merit whatever we enjoy.

Part of these benefits it is in every man's power to procure himself, by assigning proper portions of his life to the examination of the rest, and by putting himself frequently in such a situation by retirement and abstraction, as may weaken the influence of external objects. By this practice he may obtain the solitude of adversity without its melancholy, its instructions without its censures, and its sensibility without its perturbations.

The necessity of setting the world at a distance from us, when we are to take a survey of ourselves, has sent many from high stations to the severities of a monastick life; and indeed, every man deeply engaged in business, if all regard to another state be not extinguished, must have the conviction, tho', perhaps, not the resolution of Valdesso, who, when he solicited Charles the Fifth to dismiss him, being asked, whether he retired upon disgust, answered that he laid down his commission, for no other reason but because "there ought to be some time for sober reflection between the life of a soldier and his death."

There are few conditions which do not entangle us with sublunary hopes and fears, from which it is necessary to be at intervals disencumbered, that we may place ourselves in his presence who views effects in their causes, and actions in their motives; that we may, as Chillingworth expresses it, consider things as if there were no other beings in the world but God and ourselves; or, to use language yet more awful, "may commune with our own hearts, and be still."

STUDY QUESTIONS

1. Self-deceivers are sometimes virtuous. How, in Johnson's opinion, does this aid in self-deception?
2. What part does self-deception play in our choice of friends?
3. Why does Johnson say that we should consult not our friends but our enemies if we want to learn about ourselves? Do you think he is right?
4. What techniques of self-deception does Johnson mention? Can you think of others?

Upon Self-deceit

BISHOP BUTLER

Joseph Butler (1692–1752) was an English moral philosopher and theologian. In 1738, he was made a bishop of the Church of England. Butler's *Fifteen Sermons*, from which the present selection is taken, are still admired for their style, acumen, and good sense.

Butler cites the example of King David to show how easily even good persons can deceive themselves. King David commited an injustice without condemning himself, but was morally outraged on hearing that someone else had done a similar thing. Butler points out the difficulty of living by the ancient dictum "Know thyself." Self-deception often works in the service of self-regard. We want something and make ourselves believe we do right in acquiring it when, in fact, we do wrong. Moreover, we retain a good opinion of ourselves by avoiding the company of those who would condemn us. Self-deceit is especially prevalent in the undefined areas of moral behavior where moral duties are not *explicit*. There self-deceivers can be ungenerous and spiteful, and still remain within the letter of the law, comfortably at peace with their conscience. Butler argues that self-deception is a very grave moral defect because it enables us to do evil in a self-righteous manner. Self-deception "undermines the whole principle of good" and so is worse than open, unhypocritical wickedness.

UPON SELF-DECEIT From *Fifteen Sermons upon Human Nature* by Joseph Butler (1726).

> And Nathan said to David, Thou art the man. *2 Samuel 12.7*

These words are the application of Nathan's parable to David, upon occasion of his adultery with Bathsheba, and the murder of Uriah her husband. The parable, which is related in the most beautiful simplicity, is this: *There were two men in one city; the one rich, and the other poor. The rich man had exceeding many flocks and herds: but the poor man had nothing, save one little ewe lamb, which he had bought and nourished up: and it grew up together with him, and with his children: it did eat of his own meat, and drank of his own cup, and lay in his bosom, and was unto him as a daughter. And there came a traveller unto the rich man, and he spared to take of his own flock and of his own herd, to dress for the wayfaring man that was come unto him; but took the poor man's lamb, and dressed it for the man that was come to him. And David's anger was greatly kindled against the man; and he said to Nathan, As the Lord liveth, the man that hath done this thing shall surely die: and he shall restore the lamb fourfold, because he did this thing, and because he had not pity.* David passes sentence, not only that there should be a fourfold restitution made; but he proceeds to the rigour of justice, *the man that hath done this thing shall die:* and this judgment is pronounced with the utmost indignation against such an act of inhumanity; *As the Lord liveth, he shall surely die: and his anger was greatly kindled against the man.* And the Prophet answered, *Thou art the man.* He had been guilty of much greater inhumanity, with the utmost deliberation, thought, and contrivance. Near a year must have passed, between the time of the commission of his crimes, and the time of the Prophet's coming to him; and it does not appear from the story, that he had in all this while the least remorse or contrition.

Nothing is more strange than our self-partiality.

There is not any thing, relating to men and characters, more surprising and unaccountable, than this partiality to themselves, which is observable in many; as there is nothing of more melancholy reflection, respecting morality, virtue, and religion. Hence it is that many men seem perfect strangers to their own characters. They think, and reason, and judge quite differently upon any matter relating to themselves, from what they do in cases of others where they are not interested. Hence it is one hears people exposing follies, which they themselves are eminent for; and talking with great severity against particular vices, which, if all the world be not mistaken, they themselves are notoriously guilty of. This self-ignorance and self-partiality may be in all different degrees. It is a lower degree of it which David himself refers to in these words, *Who can tell how oft he offendeth? O cleanse thou me from my secret faults.* This is the ground of that advice of Elihu to Job: *Surely it is meet to be said unto God,— That which I see not, teach thou me; if I have done iniquity, I will do no more.* And Solomon saw this thing in a very strong light, when he said, *He that trusteth his own heart is a fool.*

Hence the 'Know thyself' of the ancients.

This likewise was the reason why that precept, *Know thyself,* was so frequently inculcated by the philosophers of old. For if it were not for that partial and fond regard to ourselves, it would certainly be no great difficulty to know our own character, what passes within, the bent and bias of our mind; much less would there be any difficulty in judging rightly of our own actions. But from this partiality it frequently comes to pass, that the observation of many men's being themselves last of all acquainted with what falls out in their own families, may be applied to a nearer home, to what passes within their own breasts.

Usual temper: (a) absence of mistrust: (b) assumption that all is right: (c) disregard of precept, when against ourselves.

There is plainly, in the generality of mankind, an absence of doubt or distrust, in a very great measure, as to their moral character and behaviour; and likewise a disposition to take for granted, that all is right and well with them in these respects. The former is owing to their not reflecting, not exercising their judgment upon themselves; the latter, to self-love. I am not speaking of that extravagance, which is sometimes to met with; instances of persons declaring in words at length, that they never were in the wrong, nor had ever any diffidence to the justness of their conduct, in their whole lives. No, these people are too far gone to have anything said to them. The thing before us is indeed of this kind, but in a lower degree, and confined to the moral character; somewhat of which we almost all of us have, without reflecting upon it. Now consider how long, and how grossly, a person of the best understanding might be imposed upon by one of whom he had not any suspicion, and in whom he placed an entire confidence; especially if there were friendship and real kindness in the case: surely this holds even stronger with respect to that self we are all so fond of. Hence arises in men a disregard of reproof and instruction, rules of conduct and moral discipline, which occasionally come in their way: a disregard, I say, of these; not in every respect, but in this single one, namely, as what may be of service to them in particular towards mending their own hearts and tempers, and making them better men. It never in earnest comes into their thoughts, whether such admonitions may not relate, and be of service to themselves; and this quite distinct from a positive persuasion to the contrary, a persuasion from reflection that they are innocent and blameless in those respects. Thus we may invert the observation which is somewhere made upon Brutus, that he never read, but in order to make himself a better man. It scarce comes into the thoughts of the generality of mankind, that this use is to be made of moral reflections which they meet with; that this use, I say, is to be made of them by themselves, for every body observes and wonders that it is not done by others.

Also exclusive self-interest.

Further, there are instances of persons having so fixed and steady an eye upon their own interest, whatever they place it in, and the interest of those whom they consider as themselves, as in a manner to regard nothing else; their views are almost confined to this alone. Now we cannot be acquainted with, or in any propriety of speech be said to know any thing, but what we attend to. If therefore they attend only to one side, they really will not, cannot see or know what is to be alleged on the other. Though a man hath the best eyes in the world, he cannot see any way but that which he turns them. Thus these persons, without passing over the least, the most minute thing, which can possibly be urged in favour of themselves, shall overlook entirely the plainest and most obvious things on the other side.

They inquire only to justify.

And whilst they are under the power of this temper, thought and consideration upon the matter before them has scarce any tendency to set them right: because they are engaged; and their deliberation concerning an action to be done, or reflection upon it afterwards, is not to see whether it be right, but to find out reasons to justify or palliate it; palliate it, not to others, but to themselves.

With self-ignorance, perhaps, only in the favourite propensity.

In some there is to be observed a general ignorance of themselves, and wrong way of thinking and judging in every thing relating to themselves; their fortune, reputation, every thing in which self can come in: and this perhaps attended with the rightest judgment in all other matters. In others this partiality is not so general, has not taken hold of the whole man, but is confined to some particular favourite passion, interest, or pursuit; suppose ambition, covetousness, or any other. And these persons may probably judge and determine what is perfectly just and proper, even in things in which they themselves are concerned, if these things have no relation to their particular favourite passion or pursuit. Hence arises that amazing incongruity, and seeming inconsistency of character, from whence slight observers take it for granted, that the whole is hypocritical and false; not being able otherwise to reconcile the several parts: whereas in truth there is real honesty, so far as it goes. There is such a thing as men's being honest to such a degree, and in such respects, but no further. And this, as it is true, so it is absolutely necessary to be taken notice of, and allowed them; such general and undistinguishing censure of their whole character, as designing and false, being one main thing which confirms them in their self-deceit. They know that the whole censure is not true; and so take for granted that no part of it is.

The judgment is perverted through the passions.

But to go on with the explanation of the thing itself: Vice in general consists in having an unreasonable and too great regard to ourselves, in comparison of others. Robbery and murder is never from the love of injustice or cruelty, but to gratify some other passion, to gain some supposed advantage: and it is false selfishness alone, whether cool or passionate, which makes a man resolutely pursue that end, be it ever so much to the injury of another. But whereas, in common and ordinary wickedness, this unreasonableness, this partiality and selfishness, relates only, or chiefly, to the temper and passions in the characters we are now considering, it reaches to the understanding, and influences the very judgment. And, besides that general want of distrust and diffidence concerning our own character, there are, you see, two things, which may thus prejudice and darken the understanding itself: that overfondness for ourselves, which we are all so liable to; and also being under the power of any particular passion or appetite, or engaged in any particular pursuit. And these, especially the last of the two, may be in so great a degree, as to influence our judgment, even of other persons and their behaviour. Thus a man, whose temper is former to ambition or covetousness, shall even approve of them sometimes in others. . . .

Frequent difficulty of defining: enhanced by vice.

It is to be observed then, that as there are express determinate acts of wickedness, such as murder, adultery, theft: so, on the other hand, there are numberless cases in which the vice and wickedness cannot be exactly defined; but consists in a certain general temper and course of action, or in the neglect of some duty, suppose charity or any other, whose bounds and degrees are not fixed. This is the very province of self-deceit and self-partiality: here it governs without check or control. For what commandment is there broken? Is there a transgression where there is no law? A vice which cannot be defined?

Whoever will consider the whole commerce of human life, will see that a great part, perhaps the greatest part, of the intercourse amongst mankind, cannot be reduced to fixed determinate rules. Yet in these cases there is a right and a wrong: a merciful, a liberal, a kind and compassionate behaviour, which surely is our duty; and an unmerciful contracted spirit, an hard and oppressive course of behaviour, which is most certainly immoral and vicious. But who can define precisely, wherein that contracted spirit and hard usage of others consist, as murder and theft may be defined? There is not a word in our language, which expresses more detestable wickedness than *oppression:* yet the nature of this vice cannot be so exactly stated, nor the bounds of it so determinately marked, as that we shall be able to say in all instances, where rigid right and justice ends, and oppression begins. In these cases there is great latitude left, for every one to determine for, and consequently to deceive himself. It is chiefly in these cases that self-deceit comes in; as every one must see that there is much larger scope for it here, than in express, single, determinate acts of wickedness. . . .

It is safer to be wicked in the ordinary way, than from this corruption lying at the root.

Upon the whole it is manifest, that there is such a thing as this self-partiality and self-deceit: that in some persons it is to a degree which would be thought incredible, were not the instances before our eyes; of which the behaviour of David is perhaps the highest possible one, in a single particular case; for there is not the least appearance, that it reached his general character: that we are almost all of us influenced by it in some degree, and in some respects: that therefore every one ought to have an eye to and beware of it. And all that I have further to add upon this subject is, that either there is a difference between right and wrong, or there is not: religion is true, or it is not. If it be not, there is no reason for any concern about it: but if it be true, it requires real fairness of mind and honesty of heart. And, if people will be wicked, they had better of the two be so from the common vicious passions without such refinements, than from this deep and calm source of delusion; which undermines the whole principle of good; darkens that light, that *candle of the Lord within,* which is to direct our steps; and corrupts conscience, which is the guide of life.

STUDY QUESTIONS

1. What does Butler mean when he says that many people are strangers to their own character? How far is he right in believing that we succeed in deceiving ourselves? Is there not a part of us that knows the truth?
2. Do you agree that the injunction "Know thyself" should be a fundamental moral rule?
3. According to Butler, vice results from having an unreasonably high regard for ourselves in comparison with others. Do you think he is right?
4. What does Butler mean when he tells us that being wicked in "ordinary ways" is safer than being deeply self-deluded?
5. Why is self-deception most prevalent where the vice is undefined?

Jealousy, Envy, and Spite

IMMANUEL KANT

TRANSLATED BY LOUIS ENFIELD

A biographical sketch of Immanuel Kant is found on page 149.

In this selection, excerpted from his lectures on ethics, Kant gives readers an account of the vices of jealousy, envy, spite, ingratitude, and malice. When we compare ourselves with others who are morally or materially better than us, we may become jealous of what they possess; then we may either attempt to depreciate that possession or try to emulate them by acquiring those same moral qualities or material objects. *Grudge* is the displeasure we feel when someone else has what we lack. Grudge becomes *envy* when we begrudge others their happiness. If we possess a good we do not need, but take pleasure in refusing to give it to someone who needs it, then we are *spiteful*. Another vice, *ingratitude,* has its origin in the resentment of another's superiority. In the extreme, ungrateful persons hate their benefactors. Kant calls the extremes of envy and ingratitude "devilish vices." A third devilish vice is *malice*—the gratuitous desire to see others fail. Malicious persons enjoy the misery of others. Kant denies that people are directly inclined to be "devilish." In this respect he differs from Augustine.

JEALOUSY, ENVY, AND SPITE From "Jealousy, Envy, and Grudge" from *Lectures on Ethics* by Immanuel Kant. Translated by Louis Enfield (Harper & Row, 1963). Reprinted by permission of Methuen and Company Ltd.

There are two methods by which men arrive at an opinion of their worth: by comparing themselves with the idea of perfection and by comparing themselves with others. The first of these methods is sound; the second is not, and it frequently even leads to a result diametrically opposed to the first. The idea of perfection is a proper standard, and if we measure our worth by it, we find that we fall short of it and feel that we must exert ourselves to come nearer to it; but if we compare ourselves with others, much depends upon who those others are and how they are constituted, and we can easily believe ourselves to be of great worth if those with whom we set up comparison are rogues. Men love to compare themselves with others, for by that method they can always arrive at a result favourable to themselves. They choose as a rule the worst and not the best of the class with which they set up comparison; in this way their own excellence shines out. If they choose those of greater worth the result of the comparison is, of course, unfavourable to them.

When I compare myself with another who is better than I, there are but two ways by which I can bridge the gap between us. I can either do my best to attain to his perfections, or else I can seek to depreciate his good qualities. I either increase my own worth, or else I diminish his so that I can always regard myself as superior to him. It is easier to depreciate another than to emulate him, and men prefer the easier course. They adopt it, and this is the origin of jealousy. When a man compares himself with another and finds that the other has many more good points, he becomes jealous of each and every good point he discovers in the other, and tries to depreciate it so that his own good points may stand out. This kind of jealousy may be called grudging. The other species of the genus jealousy, which makes us try to add to our good points so as to compare well with another, may be called emulating jealousy. The jealousy of emulation is, as we have stated, more difficult than the jealousy of grudge and so is much the less frequent of the two.

Parents ought not, therefore, when teaching their children to be good, to urge them to model themselves on other children and try to emulate them, for by so doing they simply make them jealous. If I tell my son, "Look, how good and industrious John is," the result will be that my son will bear John a grudge. He will think to himself that, but for John, he himself would be the best, because there would be no comparison. By setting up John as a pattern for imitation I anger my son, make him feel a grudge against this so-called paragon,

385

and I instil jealousy in him. My son might, of course, try to emulate John, but not finding it easy, he will bear John ill-will. Besides, just as I can say to my son, "Look, how good John is," so can he reply: "Yes, he is better than I, but are there not many who are far worse? Why do you compare me with those who are better? Why not with those who are worse than I?" Goodness must, therefore, be commended to children in and for itself. Whether other children are better or worse has no bearing on the point. If the comparison were in the child's favour, he would lose all ground of impulse to improve his own conduct. To ask our children to model themselves on others is to adopt a faulty method of upbringing, and as time goes on the fault will strike its roots deep. It is jealousy that parents are training and presupposing in their children when they set other children before them as patterns. Otherwise, the children would be quite indifferent to the qualities of others. They will find it easier to belittle the good qualities of their patterns than to emulate them, so they will choose the easier path and learn to show a grudging disposition. It is true that jealousy is natural, but that is no excuse for cultivating it. It is only a motive, a reserve in case of need. While the maxims of reason are still undeveloped in us, the proper course is to use reason to keep it within bounds. For jealousy is only one of the many motives, such as ambition, which are implanted in us because we are designed for a life of activity. But so soon as reason is enthroned, we must cease to seek perfection in emulation of others and must covet it in and for itself. Motives must abdicate and let reason bear rule in their place.

Persons of the same station and occupation in life are particularly prone to be jealous of each other. Many business-men are jealous of each other; so are many scholars, particularly in the same line of scholarship; and women are liable to be jealous of each other regarding men.

Grudge is the displeasure we feel when another has an advantage; his advantage makes us feel unduly small and we grudge it him. But to grudge a man his share of happiness is envy. To be envious is to desire the failure and unhappiness of another not for the purpose of advancing our own success and happiness but because we might then ourselves be perfect and happy as we are. An envious man is not happy unless all around him are unhappy; his aim is to stand alone in the enjoyment of his happiness. Such is envy, and we shall learn below that it is satanic. Grudge, although it too should not be countenanced, is natural. Even a good-natured person may at times be grudging. Such a one may, for instance, begrudge those around him their jollity when he himself happens to be sorrowful; for it is hard to bear one's sorrow when all around are joyful. When I see every-body enjoying a good meal and I alone must content myself with inferior fare, it upsets me and I feel a grudge; but if we are all in the same boat I am content. We find the thought of death bearable, because we know that all must die; but if everybody were immortal and I alone had to die, I should feel aggrieved. It is not things them-selves that affect us, but things in their relation to ourselves. We are grudging because others are happier than we. But when a good-natured man feels happy and cheerful, he wishes that every one else in the world were as happy as he and shared his joy; he begrudges no one his happiness.

When a man would not grant to another even that for which he himself has no need, he is spiteful. Spite is a maliciousness of spirit which is not the same thing as envy. I may not feel inclined to give to another something which belongs to me, even though I myself have no use for it, but it does not follow that I grudge him his own possessions, that I want to be the only one who has anything and wish him to have nothing at all. There is a deal of grudge in human nature which could develop into envy but which is not itself envy. We feel pleasure in gossiping about the minor misadventures of other people; we are not averse, although we may express no pleasure thereat, to hearing of the fall of some rich man; we may enjoy in stormy weather, when comfortably seated in our warm, cosy par-lour, speaking of those at sea, for it heightens our own feeling of comfort and happiness; there is grudge in all this, but it is not envy.

The three vices which are the essence of vileness and wickedness are ingratitude, envy, and malice. When these reach their full degree they are devilish.

Men are shamed by favours. If I receive a favour, I am placed under an obligation to the giver; he has a call upon me because I am indebted to him. We all blush to be obliged. Noble-minded men accordingly refuse to accept favours in order not to put themselves under an obligation. But this attitude predisposes the mind to ingratitude. If the man who adopts it is noble-minded, well and good; but if he be proud and selfish and has perchance received a favour, the feeling that he is beholden to his benefactor hurts his pride and, being selfish, he cannot accommodate himself to the idea that he owes his benefac-tor anything. He becomes defiant and ungrateful. His ingratitude might even conceivably assume such dimensions that he cannot bear his benefactor and becomes his enemy. Such ingratitude is of the devil; it is out of all keeping with human nature. It is inhuman to hate and persecute one from whom we have reaped a benefit, and if such conduct were the rule it would cause untold harm. Men would then be afraid to do good to anyone lest they should receive evil in return for their good. They would become misanthropic.

The second devilish vice is envy. Envy is in the highest degree detestable. The envious man does not merely want to be happy; he wants to be the only happy person in the world; he is really contented only when he sees nothing but misery around him. Such an intolerable creature would gladly destroy every source of joy and happiness in the world.

Malice is the third kind of viciousness which is of the devil. It consists in taking a direct pleasure in the misfortunes of others. Men prone to this vice will seek, for instance, to make mischief between husband and wife, or between friends, and then enjoy the misery they have produced. In these matters we should make it a rule never to repeat to a person anything that we may have heard to his disadvantage from another, unless our silence would injure him. Otherwise we start an enmity and disturb his peace of mind, which our silence would have avoided, and in addition we break faith with our informant. The defence against such mischief-makers is upright conduct. Not by words but by our lives we should confute them. As Socrates said: We ought so to conduct ourselves that people will not credit anything spoken in disparagement of us.

These three vices—ingratitude (*ingratitudo qualificata*), envy, and malice—are devilish because they imply a direct inclination to evil. There are in man certain indirect tendencies to wickedness which are human and not unnatural. The miser wants everything for himself, but it is no satisfaction to him to see that his neighbour is destitute. The evilness of a vice may thus be either direct or indirect. In these three vices it is direct.

We may ask whether there is in the human mind an immediate inclination to wickedness, an inclination to the devilish vices. Heaven stands for the acme of happiness, hell for all that is bad, and the earth stands midway between these two extremes; and just as goodness which transcends anything which might be expected of a human being is spoken of as being angelic, so also do we speak of devilish wickedness when the wickedness oversteps the limits of human nature and becomes inhuman. We may take it for granted that the human mind has no immediate inclination to wickedness, but is only indirectly wicked. Man cannot be so ungrateful that he simply must hate his neighbour; he may be too proud to show his gratitude and so avoid him, but he wishes him well. Again, our pleasure in the misfortune of another is not direct. We may rejoice, for example, in a man's misfortunes, because he was haughty, rich and selfish; for man loves to preserve equality. We have thus no direct inclination towards evil as evil, but only an indirect one. But how are we to explain the fact that even young children have the spirit of mischief strongly developed? For a joke, a boy will stick a pin in an unsuspecting playmate, but it is only for fun. He has no thought of the pain the other must feel on all such occasions. In the same spirit he will torture animals; twisting the cat's tail or the dog's. Such tendencies must be nipped in the bud, for it is easy to see where they will lead. They are, in fact, something animal, something of the beast of prey which is in us all, which we cannot overcome, and the source of which we cannot explain. There certainly are in human nature characteristics for which we can assign no reason. There are animals too who steal anything that comes their way, though it is quite useless to them; and it seems as if man has retained this animal tendency in his nature.

Ingratitude calls for some further observations here. To help a man in distress is charity; to help him in less urgent needs is benevolence; to help him in the amenities of life is courtesy. We may be the recipients of a charity which has not cost the giver much and our gratitude is commensurate with the degree of good-will which moved him to the action. We are grateful not only for what we have received but also for the good intention which prompted it, and the greater the effort it has cost our benefactor, the greater our gratitude.

Gratitude may be either from duty or from inclination. If an act of kindness does not greatly move us, but if we nevertheless feel that it is right and proper that we should show gratitude, our gratitude is merely prompted by a sense of duty. Our heart is not grateful, but we have principles of gratitude. If however, our heart goes out to our benefactor, we are grateful from inclination. There is a weakness of the understanding which we often have cause to recognize. It consists in taking the conditions of our understanding as conditions of the thing understood. We can estimate force only in terms of the obstacles it overcomes. Similarly, we can only estimate the degree of goodwill in terms of the obstacles it has to surmount. In consequence we cannot comprehend the love and goodwill of a being for whom there are no obstacles. If God has been good to me, I am liable to think that after all it has cost God no trouble, and that gratitude to God would be mere fawning on my part. Such thoughts are not at all unnatural. It is easy to fear God, but not nearly so easy to love God from inclination because of our consciousness that God is a being whose goodness is unbounded but to whom it is no trouble to shower kindness upon us. This is not to say that such should be our mental attitude; merely that when we examine our hearts, we find that this is how we actually think. It also explains why to many races God appeared to be a jealous God, seeing that it cost Him nothing to be more bountiful with His goodness; it explains why many nations thought that their gods were sparing of their benefits and that they required propitiating with prayers and sacrifices. This is the attitude of man's heart; but when we call reason to our aid we see that God's goodness must be of a high order if He is to be good to a being so unworthy of His goodness. This solves our difficulty. The gratitude we owe to God is not gratitude from inclination, but from duty, for God is not a creature like ourselves, and can be no object of our inclinations.

We ought not to accept favours unless we are either forced to do so by dire necessity or have implicit confidence in our benefactor (for he ceases to be our friend and becomes our benefactor) that he will not regard it as placing us under an obligation to him. To accept favours indiscriminately and to be constantly seeking them is ignoble and the sign of a mean soul which does not mind placing itself under obligations. Unless we are driven by such dire necessity that it compels us to sacrifice our own worth, or unless we are convinced that our benefactor will not account it to us as a debt, we ought rather to suffer deprivation than accept favours, for a favour is a debt which can never be extinguished. For even if I repay my benefactor tenfold, I am still not even with him, because he has done me a kindness which he did not owe. He was the first in the field, and even if I return his gift tenfold I do so only as repayment. He will always be the one who was the first to show kindness and I can never be beforehand with him.

The man who bestows favours can do so either in order to make the recipient indebted to him or as an expression of his duty. If he makes the recipient feel a sense of indebtedness, he wounds his pride and diminishes his sense of gratitude. If he wishes to avoid this he must regard the favours he bestows as the discharge of a duty he owes to mankind, and he must not give the recipient the impression that it is a debt to be repaid. On the other hand, the recipient of the favour must still consider himself under an obligation to his benefactor and must be grateful to him. Under these conditions there can be benefactors and beneficiaries. A right-thinking man will not accept kindnesses, let alone favours. A grateful disposition is a touching thing and brings tears to our eyes on the stage, but a generous disposition is lovelier still. Ingratitude we detest to a surprising degree; even though we are not ourselves the victims of it, it angers us to such an extent that we feel inclined to intervene. But this is due to the fact that ingratitude decreases generosity.

Envy does not consist in wishing to be more happy than others—that is grudge—but in wishing to be the only one to be happy. It is this feeling which makes envy so evil. Why should not others be happy along with me? Envy shows itself also in relation to things which are scarce. Thus the Dutch, who as a nation are rather envious, once valued tulips at several hundreds of florins apiece. A rich merchant, who had one of the finest and rarest specimens, heard that another had a similar specimen. He thereupon bought it from him for 2,000 florins and trampled it underfoot, saying that he had no use for it, as he already possessed a specimen, and that he only wished that no one else should share that distinction with him. So it is also in the matter of happiness.

Malice is different. A malicious man is pleased when others suffer, he can laugh when others weep. An act which willfully brings unhappiness is cruel; when it produces physical pain it is bloodthirsty. Inhumanity is all these together, just as humanity consists in sympathy and pity, since these differentiate man from the beasts. It is difficult to explain what gives rise to a cruel disposition. It may arise when a man considers another so evilly disposed that he hates him. A man who believes himself hated by another, hates him in return, although the former may have good reason to hate him. For if a man is hated because he is selfish and has other vices, and he knows that he is hated for these reasons, he hates those who hate him although these latter do him no injustice. Thus kings who know that they are hated by their subjects become even more cruel. Equally, when a man has done a good deed to another, he knows that the other loves him, and so he loves him in return, knowing that he himself is loved. Just as love is reciprocated, so also is hate. We must for our own sakes guard against being hated by others lest we be affected by that hatred and reciprocate it. The hater is more disturbed by his hatred than is the hated.

STUDY QUESTIONS

1. How does Kant distinguish spite from envy? Why is the extreme of envy "devilish"?
2. We sometimes say to a friend, "I envy you." Can we envy people without begrudging their happiness? How does Kant view this?
3. Why does Kant advise us to compare ourselves with the ideal of perfection? What vices are associated with comparing ourselves with others?
4. What are the three devilish vices and what is devilish about them? Does Kant believe that the devilish vices are natural? What is their origin in people?
5. What does Kant think is wrong about accepting favors? Do you think Kant demands too much of the average person? Is his doctrine too austere?

Of Jealousy and Envy

DANIEL FARRELL

Daniel Farrell (b. 1943) is an associate professor of philosophy at Ohio State University. He is the author of numerous articles in the area of ethics and public policy.

Farrell's essay challenges the traditional attitudes toward the vices of jealousy and envy. Unlike envy, which generally involves two parties, jealousy involves three. For example, *A* may be jealous of *B* because the affections of *B* are turning to *C*, or because the honors that have hitherto been bestowed on *A* by *B* are now being bestowed on *C*. In envy, *A* covets what *B* has and begrudges *B*'s having it. Traditionally, envy is said to be less indicative of vice or deficiency of character than jealousy. But, argues Farrell, while jealousy is a natural reaction to the loss of favor, envy seems to reveal a meanness of spirit—a displeasure at the good fortune of others.

If Farrell is right, jealousy deserves a better press than envy. It should be noted that Farrell's argument tends to sustain an older biblical view in which the Ten Commandments condemn covetousness, but do not mention jealousy except to say that God is a jealous God who insists on having the exclusive regard of mankind.

Few emotions are looked upon with more opprobrium in our society than jealousy and envy. And few emotions cause more trouble in interpersonal relationships: jealousy (typically, but not exclusively, as we shall see) in sexual and romantic relationships, envy in these as well as in relationships of other sorts. Particularly significant in this connection is the fact that we are so often told that it is wrong to be jealous or envious of others, or that the fact that we sometimes

OF JEALOUSY AND ENVY by Daniel M. Farrell. From *Philosophical Review* 100 (1991). Copyright 1991 Cornell University. Reprinted by permission of the publisher and author.

experience these emotions reveals something bad or objectionable about our character.

In what follows I try to determine why it is that we think of these emotions in the way we do and how plausible it is to so regard them. I proceed by saying, first, roughly what I think each of these emotions involves—that is, roughly what it is to be jealous and roughly what it is to feel envy. I then show how an understanding of what each of these emotions is can help us to get clear on what attitudes it might be reasonable to have toward someone who is feeling one or the other of them in a given situation. In connection with this latter task, I am particularly concerned with evaluating certain common claims about what each of these emotions shows about the person who is experiencing it. And, very roughly, what I suggest is that envy is decidedly deserving, at least in its full-bodied form, of its ill-repute, but that jealousy is in fact not as objectionable as it is generally made out to be.

I

Let us begin with jealousy. Suppose I'm at a party with my friend Linda and I happen to see her chatting with a particularly good-looking man on the other side of the room. He tells a long and evidently very funny story, she laughs appreciatively and tells a story of her own, and eventually they walk off to the kitchen for more drinks. A bit later I notice that Linda and her new friend are dancing and that he cuts a considerably better figure on the dance floor than I. Finally, when the time comes to leave, Linda suggests we stay a while longer. The night is young, she says, and she's having a particularly good time. I continue talking to friends, while Linda wanders off to spend more time with Prince Charming.

It certainly would not be surprising if I felt a twinge of jealousy under these circumstances. I might not be jealous, of course, and if I am jealous, this may show something awful about me. Nonetheless, I have felt just a bit jealous in situations like this in the past, and I suspect that I am likely to suffer mild recurrences in similar situations in the future. More important, whether or not I would be jealous in a situation like this, it is certainly the sort of case in which it is plausible to talk about the possibility of jealousy. An ordinary person will have no difficulty, in other words, in seeing it as a case in which one might be jealous.

Consider next a case of what I call *professional* jealousy. Suppose I am a professional tennis player and one important source of gratification for me is the fact that I am considered one of the best players on the pro circuit. Surely if some younger player suddenly begins to attract a lot of attention, and people gradually seem to be coming to the conclusion that he is a better player than I, it is possible that I will start to feel something akin to what we imagined I was feeling in the case just described. No doubt it will not be exactly like what I felt in that case, and the differences may turn out to be more important than the similarities. Nonetheless, it is interesting, I think, that we can imagine an old pro acting in ways which in some very straightforward sense suggest that he is jealous because of the attention a younger pro is starting to receive. He talks about the latter's bad days a little too much, let us suppose, and about his own good days a little too often. My point, as before, is not that the one player *must* experience feelings of jealousy when beginning to see what people think of the other player, but that the one player *might* be jealous of the other in a case like this and that we certainly have no trouble imagining such a case.

What sort of general truths do cases like these suggest? Notice first that in each of these cases jealousy occurs in a very similar and rather special context: In each case our protagonist is jealous because some third party seems to be getting from some second party something that the first party (our protagonist) wants. This fact about jealousy—that it seems always to occur in a context involving three or more independent parties—is important in distinguishing jealousy from envy, as we shall see.[1]

Notice second, though, that cases like these suggest another, quite important general point; namely, that jealousy presupposes a certain kind of desire, on the part of the jealous individual, and a certain kind of *belief*. In a typical case of sexual jealousy, for example, one person, A, is desirous of retaining the (perhaps exclusive) affection of another person, B, but is fearful that B is beginning to feel more

---

[1] The party of whom I am jealous need not actually exist, of course, nor need she be (imagined to be) some *one* person or group (see note 4 in this connection). What is important is that I think I have a rival (or a set of rivals). Notice, too, that the party of whom I am jealous doesn't have to be a *person*; nor, for that matter, does the jealous party or the party whose affections the jealous party wants. I might be jealous because of your interest in some animal or in a hobby; and my dog might be jealous because of my interest in you, just as *I* might be jealous because of *his* interest in you.

affection (or whatever) for some third person, C. Similarly, in a typical case of professional jealousy we find one person, A, who wants something—esteem or admiration, for example—from some other person (or group of persons), B, and who is fearful that B is beginning to feel more esteem (or whatever) for some other person, C. As we shall see, even in cases that don't involve three people—as when we speak of an animal feeling jealous—something like a belief that it is not favored in some way in which it wants or desires to be favored seems to be necessary if the concept of jealousy is to apply.[2]

Suppose we try to generalize these remarks, putting them in the form of a two-part thesis about what I call the conceptual presuppositions of jealousy. We would then want to say, first, that jealousy is, necessarily, an emotion that arises only in what we may call a three-party context: A is jealous of C because B seems to be favoring C (in respect R) rather than A. We would also want to say, second, that jealousy is, again necessarily, something that one feels only when one has a desire to be favored by some other person (or by some group), in some respect R, to some third person (or whatever), and only when one believes—or at any rate suspects—that one is not so favored. As we shall see, thinking of jealousy in this way enables us both to understand and to assess some of the many things that are said about this emotion and what it tells us about the jealous person.[3] Before pursuing these matters, though, we need to pause in order to consider an important objection to what has just been said, an objection that centers on the fact that there seem to be cases where we find jealousy in two-party contexts and, what's more, in contexts that do not involve the sorts of desires and beliefs that our present analysis requires. Consideration of this objection enables us to introduce the

---

[2]Notice, by the way, that the clearest cases of jealousy are cases where A not only *wants* to be favored in some way over C, but also believes that until now he or she *has* been so favored. It is more problematic, I think, to speak of jealousy in cases where A wants to be favored by someone in some way but has never *been* favored in that way by the person by whom he or she wants to be favored. Nonetheless, for simplicity's sake I refer in what follows to A's desire to be favored rather than—as would no doubt be more accurate, at least for most cases—to A's desire to *continue* to be favored.

[3]Unless otherwise indicated, when I say "the jealous person" or "the jealous individual," I am referring to someone who is *occurrently* jealous, as we might say: someone who is actually experiencing this emotion in some specific situation. I do not mean to refer, as these locations might be thought to suggest, to the person who is *prone* to jealousy.

other object of our attention in this essay—envy—and helps us to indicate exactly how it is that jealousy and envy differ.

II

We can begin with the undeniable fact that we sometimes talk about jealousy in two- rather than three-party contexts. For instance, when you learn that I have just gotten a year's sabbatical you might say, "That's terrific! I'm really jealous!" Or, painfully aware of how difficult it is for me to do, when I see how easy it is for you to write up your ideas I might say, "I'm really jealous. I wish I could write as easily as you." These are perfectly ordinary uses of the word "jealous," it seems to me, and yet they do not conform at all to the three-party paradigm just suggested.

Now, what I want to say here, despite the apparent propriety of speaking in the ways just described, is that in cases like these we are really talking about *envy* rather than jealousy. In saying this, of course, I am implicitly suggesting that common usage is to some extent misleading in this connection, since we do indeed use the word "jealous" in just these ways. This is certainly not a fatal objection to my contention, however—or so it seems to me—since it often happens that common usage fails to honor distinctions that themselves emerge only from an analysis of common usage.

Let us begin, then, by asking when the concept of envy is most appropriately and least controversially used in ordinary discourse. The clearest sort of case, it seems to me, is a two-party case where one person has something—some thing, literally, or some trait or capacity, say—that another person doesn't have but would very much like to have, and where the one person is somehow *bothered* by the fact that the second person has the relevant good while the first does not. Thus I can be envious of your wealth, your good looks, or your physical prowess, and I will be envious of you in these respects if, in contemplating the fact that you have them while I do not, I experience a certain negative affect because this is so. To be sure, we sometimes say the one party is jealous of the other in cases like this, and that is the point with which we are now concerned. But leaving aside for a moment exactly what we would say in such cases, notice that there are important differences between cases like these and the paradigms of jealousy mentioned earlier. To begin with, notice that in these new cases it is not literally your money or good looks or physical prowess that I want, nor is it necessarily the case that I want you to have any less money or to be any less handsome or physically adept. I just want more money—as much, at least, as you have—and it may very well be a matter of complete indifference to me whether or not you retain yours. In the earlier cases, by contrast, you have something that I want and that we cannot both have. For example, in the sexual case I want Linda's primary affections and I don't want you to have them. Similarly, in the tennis-pro case I want the attention that you are getting; *ex hypothesi* we can't both have that attention, and I want for me rather than you to have it.

What is perhaps even more significant than the difference just mentioned, however, is what I call the difference in focus between the two sorts of cases. In the latter cases I'm upset because you have something I want—money, good looks, or whatever—and don't have (or at any rate don't think I have). In the cases of sexual and professional jealousy, by contrast, I am upset not just because of what the person of whom I'm jealous *has*—namely, the affection or esteem of someone else who matters to me—but also because the subject of my jealousy has been given that affection or esteem, freely, by that other party. Of course, in both sorts of cases I am upset because, among other things, in some sense you have something I want. What bothers me in the case of jealousy, however, is not just that you have something I want—namely, a certain person's or group's esteem— but that you have been given that affection or esteem by someone who is important to me and from whom I want that esteem or affection. And herein lies the difference in focus to which I wish to call attention. In cases of envy, there are just you and I, so to speak, and what you have and I don't. In genuine cases of jealousy, on the other hand, there are you and I *and* the person who is giving *you* what I want *that person* to give *me*.[4]

---

[4]For the sake of simplicity, I am writing as though *you* always exist, in cases of jealousy, and are some one specific person. However, this is not really accurate, since you may *not* exist (being a mere figment of my imagination, for example), or you may exist but without my really knowing you (I just know or suspect that there's someone competing with me). Or I may be jealous not of any particular person but of any and all of a whole series of real or imaginary rivals. I ignore these complications here for ease of expression, though they should of course be borne in mind.

III

We can summarize our conclusions thus far as follows. Jealousy is an essentially three-party emotion, in which one party, A, is bothered by the fact that some other party, B, seems to favor some third party, C, in some respect in which A desires to be favored by B instead.[5] Envy, by contrast, while sometimes occurring in three-party contexts, is in essence a two-party emotion, in which one party is bothered by the fact that another party has something that the first party wants but does not seem to have.[6]

Obviously, there are plenty of questions one might want to raise at this point, just as there are plenty of problems one might want to urge against the claims that have just been made. Here, however, I want to focus on just one of the many questions that might be thought to need attention; namely, the question of exactly what is meant when we say that, in the case of each of these emotions, we are dealing with a situation where someone is bothered by the perception that something or other is or is not the case. What, we want to ask, is the nature of the botherment in each case? And why, for that matter, should we suppose that we must *be* bothered or pained in such cases in order to be either envious or jealous? Is it not enough, for jealousy, to believe we are not favored in some way in which we want to be favored? And, similarly, are we not already envious on noticing that another has something that we want for ourselves but do not have? Unless we can answer these and a number of related questions, we can hardly claim to have said what it is to be envious or jealous, much less to have put ourselves into a position to be able to address the many claims we hear made about what these emotions show about the person who is feeling them.

Let us begin with jealousy. And let us note at once that we actually

---

[5]Note that while one's desire to be favored over another party, in the relevant sorts of cases, is usually a desire to be *preferred* over that party in some respect, it is possible for this desire to be thought just as highly of, or to be treated in the same way as the other party or parties.

[6]Note that I am speaking somewhat loosely here, for the sake of simplicity when I say that in the case of envy A wants something that B has. It may be that A wants that very thing and they cannot both have it. Typically, though, what A wants is the *kind* of thing B has; for example, money or good looks. For more on this, see section V.

have two questions before us rather than just one. The first is the question of why we must suppose we need to be bothered or pained by something—that is, by one of our beliefs or perceptions—if we are plausibly going to be said to be jealous. The second is the question of what, supposing we must be bothered or pained in order to be jealous, is the nature of the botherment or pain in question.

Now, the first of these is a question I am afraid I simply cannot answer at the present time. If you say you believe I can plausibly be said to be jealous, once I begin to suspect I am not being favored in some way in which I want to be favored, and can plausibly be said to be jealous in such a case even though I am not the least bit bothered by the fact that I am not favored as I want to be favored, I have no argument to show you are mistaken. Indeed, it may be that common usage occasionally supports such a way of speaking. However, I think that many of us would say, upon reflection, that if I really am not bothered by the fact that I am not favored as I want to be favored, then I really am not jealous. After all, if this were not so, how would we distinguish between the people who are jealous when they believe they are not favored in some way in which they want to be favored and the people who, discovering this, just don't care?

Far more interesting, it seems to me, is the question of just what it means to say that jealousy consists in being bothered by the fact that we are not (as we believe) favored in some way in which we want to be favored. What exactly do we mean by "bothered" here, we want to ask, and what exactly is the difference between someone who *is* bothered (or pained) by the fact of not being favored in some way and someone who is not (someone, say, who just doesn't care)?

One answer, of course, would be to say that we are bothered or pained by the fact that we are not favored by another in some way just in case we *feel bad*—that is, just in case we are consciously experiencing a certain negative affect—as a result of our belief. Aside from being intolerably vague, however, this answer is unacceptable because it fails to account for cases in which, consciously at any rate, we are utterly unaware of being jealous, but where we certainly are jealous and where everyone else around can see that this is so. No doubt, we typically do feel something when we are jealous, something very painful. But we can evidently be jealous without realizing it, and indeed without feeling it, and our account must somehow make sense of the fact that this is so.

Our account must be able to explain, therefore, not only what it is to be bothered by the fact that we are not favored in some way, in cases where our being bothered is something we are quite well aware of, but also what it is to be bothered by this sort of thing in cases where we are *not* aware of being bothered by it. And for this, it seems to me, we need a very general notion. Indeed, it seems to me we need a notion that is not necessarily *experiential* at all. We need to be able to say, in other words, that a person can be bothered by something, in the sense of the term that interests us, even though we are not strictly speaking *feeling* anything at all in connection with the object of our concern.

What sense of bothered, then, is available to us? One possibility is that the quasi-mechanical notion of disruption: We might say that we are bothered by the thought that something is or is not the case, just in case our normal pattern of thoughts or actions or feelings is some-how disrupted by the thought that such and such is or is not the case. This is, of course, a rather vague way of speaking, and, unfortu-nately, we cannot at present afford the time and space to make it any less vague. Still, I think it is clear enough for present purposes: We are bothered or pained by the thought that we are not favored in some way in which we admittedly want to be favored, on this view, just in case the thought that this is so disrupts in some way the regular flow of our thoughts, feelings, or actions.

Now, with just two qualifications, I think this account is right. The first qualification is this. In order to capture the fact that jealousy is a painful emotion, at least when consciously felt, I think we need to say that the disruption caused by the relevant belief must be of a kind that would be experienced as painful, if it were consciously experienced, or at least as otherwise negative rather than as pleasur-able or somehow positive. Thus the woman who is delighted at the fact that (as she believes) her lover has been unfaithful cannot be said to be jealous because of what she is experiencing, even if her delight is so intense as to disrupt her normal pattern of thoughts, feelings, or actions.[7]

---

[7]This, of course, is arguably already entailed by the fact that, for jealousy, the jealous party must *want* the favoring that she believes (or suspects) she is not now getting.

The second qualification we need to add to the foregoing (disruption) account of jealousy is this: We need to say something about what the *object* of our state of mind has to be if that state of mind, supposing all the other conditions have been met, is plausibly to be said to warrant saying we are jealous. To see this, it will suffice to note that we can become *angry*, say, or *fearful*, as a result of coming to believe we are not favored in some way in which we want to be favored, and thus can become bothered as a result of coming to have this belief, without its following that we are jealous. For suppose we are angry and our anger is focused entirely on the fact that we believe our partner's choice of the third party is stupid. Or suppose we are afraid, as a result of what we have come to believe, but our fear is focused entirely on the fact that we will be at grave risk of contracting some venereal disease as a result of our partner's depredations. In such cases, it seems implausible to me to say we are jealous, supposing conditions are just as we have imagined, even though it is true that we are bothered by the fact that we are not favored in some way in which we want to be favored. What we need, I think, is to suppose that, whatever else we feel, we are bothered not simply by some special aspect or consequence of the fact that we are not favored as we want to be favored but, rather, that we are bothered by the very fact that we are not favored as we want to be favored. Given this— for example, given that we are angry not because of our partner's *stupidity* in choosing another, but because of the very fact that another has been chosen—I think we have enough to say that we are jealous and to say this regardless of whether our jealousy is experienced, phenomenologically, as anger, fear, or whatever.[8]

We can now take up the case of envy. We argued that to be envious of another is to be bothered by the fact that (as we believe) you have something (or some kind of thing) that I want for myself but believe I do not have. Our current question, then, is this: What can we say about how I must be bothered in the relevant sorts of circumstances

---

[8] One important consequence of my view is that there is no special phenomenological feeling that is the feeling of jealousy. Provided all our other conditions are met, what the jealous person feels may be phenomenologically indistinguishable from what the person who is merely angry or afraid is feeling. The *objects* of their respective emotions, however, will differ and will be what accounts for the fact that their emotions are different.

in order for my botherment to qualify as envy rather than, say, anger, indignation, irritation, or whatever?

One answer to this question, of course, is analogous to the first answer we considered when we raised this same sort of question about jealousy. This answer, which is supported to some extent by ordinary usage, holds that I do not in fact have to be bothered by my perception of your advantages in order to be envious of you for having those advantages. Recall, in this connection, the sorts of cases mentioned in our discussion of the difference between jealousy and envy. We said that people sometimes say they are jealous of someone else when, in our terms, what they really mean to say is that they are envious of them. What's relevant about these sorts of cases here, of course— supposing for a moment that what the parties in question are reporting is in fact envy rather than jealousy—is this: When you say to me, "I envy you your ability to [do such and such]," it's not at all clear that what you are saying would be falsified if we were to discover that in fact you were not the least bit bothered or pained by the fact that (as you believe) I can do such and such while you cannot. It is not at all clear, that is to say, when we are thinking about cases of this sort, that you really do have to be bothered by your perception of another's advantages in order for you plausibly to say that you are envious of those advantages.

Let us call cases of the sort we are imagining here cases of apparently friendly envy. Does the existence of such cases show what the argument just sketched suggests—namely, that it is possible to envy others because of some good they have without at the same time being bothered, in any way, by our realization that they have that good while we do not? I think not. Rather, I think that what such cases show is that we sometimes attribute envy to ourselves in what I shall call a "purely formal" way. On such occasions, it seems to me, we are not really attributing envy to ourselves at all. Instead, we are simply indicating to our interlocutor that she has something that we admire and would very much like to have ourselves. We do say on such occasions, of course, that we envy the individual in question. It does not follow from this, however, that we are actually envious of her, much less that we are in fact feeling—or have in fact felt—the emotion that currently interests us. And to the degree that we are not feeling something in such cases—or, at any rate, are not in some sense bothered by our perception that the other person has what she has—it seems to me to be reasonable to say we are not really feeling envy.[9]

Suppose this is right. Suppose, that is to say, we cannot be said to be feeling, or to have felt, envy unless we are feeling, or at some point have felt, some generally negative affect because of what we believe about what others have and we lack. This, of course, leaves entirely untouched the question with which we began; namely, the question of exactly what that generally negative affect has to be if, given the other circumstances we have associated with envy, the party who is so affected is rightly to be said to be feeling envy as opposed to mere anger, say, or indignation, or whatever.

Now here, I think, it will be useful to turn away from polite or friendly contexts for a moment and look, instead, at a somewhat more dramatic example of someone who we would all agree is clearly feeling envy: an actor, say, who, witnessing the consummate skill of one of his fellows, is green with envy, as we might say. I think it's obvious that we would say that such an individual's envy is *constituted*, in part, by the fact that he is indeed bothered or pained by what he perceives as the other actor's superior skills. But what more can we say about the nature of this botherment and about how being thus bothered in cases of envy differs from being similarly bothered, in other cases, but not envious?

One answer is suggested by most dictionaries and by the etymology of "envy": To be envious of another is to look askance at that person because of what the person has and one does not. The *Oxford English Dictionary*, for example, tells us that to envy is, among other things, to "look maliciously upon. The feeling of mortification or ill will occasioned by the contemplation of superior advantages possessed by another."[10] The suggestion here that envy involves malice

---

[9] I am not suggesting here that any case of apparently friendly envy is a case in which one is attributing envy to oneself in a "purely formal" way. My point is merely that one can attribute envy to oneself in this way without actually feeling envy and that this will be so precisely when one attributes envy to oneself in these kinds of circumstances without at the same time feeling at all bothered by the fact that the other party has what one wants but doesn't have.

[10] This definition fails to make it clear that for envy we have to suppose that the person in question *wants* the superior advantages in question. Without this assumption, it is possible that we will have, not envy, but what we might call *Freudenschadde*, or sorrow at another's good fortune, which is the obverse of the familiar *Schaddenfreude*.

or ill will is one that has to bear considerable scrutiny. Notice, though, that the idea that envy involves something like malice or ill will is supported, to some degree at least, by certain strains in popular thinking about this emotion. For if we did not think that envy involves some such feeling, why would we think of it as something objectionable and, in its extreme forms, even sinful?

One problem with this line of thought has to do with cases of apparently friendly envy like those described earlier. To be sure, if our previous remarks are right, many cases of this sort are not really cases of *envy* and hence do not pose a problem for the view that envy presupposes something like ill will or malice toward the ones of whom we are envious. I think it is clear, however, that in some cases of apparently friendly envy, we are in fact envious—not because we say we are but because we are in fact *bothered*, however mildly, by the fact that they have what we want but do not have. And cases like these, it seems to me, which are quite possible even if our earlier remarks are right, do indeed pose a problem for definitions of envy like the one that we have culled from the O.E.D. For it would be quite implausible, I think, to suppose that in these sorts of cases one's botherment takes the form of anything even remotely resembling malice or ill will.

What, then, shall we say the affective side of envy involves, if we are not to say that it involves anything quite so strong as malice or ill will? As in the case of jealousy, I want to suggest what some may consider a surprising answer to this question: I want to suggest that there is no *one* feeling or inner experience that we all undergo when we are feeling envy. Rather, I think that any of a number of different affects will qualify as envy provided that they occur in circumstances of the sort that we have sketched and are directed at the very fact that another has what we want but do not ourselves have.

The proof of this claim, it seems to me, is exactly analogous to our earlier line of argument, where we showed that unless we are bothered by the very fact that we are not favored as we want to be favored, we will not be feeling jealousy. Thus suppose that I am situated in a two-party case where I see that you have something I want—a huge amount of money, let's say—and suppose that, upon perceiving that this is so, I begin to feel anger or ill will toward you. Does it follow that I am feeling envious of you? It seems to me that it does not. For suppose I believe you have gotten this money unfairly—indeed, suppose I believe that the money is rightfully mine, having been cunningly embezzled from me by you. In such a case, I might well feel ill will, anger, or whatever, toward you without at the same time feeling envy. My anger is perfectly understandable, that is to say, as an expression of indignation over the fact that, as I believe, I have been wronged by you. And we can imagine ourselves feeling anger (or whatever) in exactly the same circumstances without feeling envy at all.

Of course, as in the case of our discussion of jealousy, it is tempting to suppose that what the preceding argument shows is that botherment in the sorts of cases that interest us is envy only when it has a certain unique feel—for example, that mere anger in such circumstances differs from envy, or from envy and anger, by virtue of being some special and quite possibly unique feeling that the relevant person has. As I said, however, I think that this conclusion is unwarranted. For I think that what makes our pain or botherment envy, as distinct from any of the other things we might be feeling in such a situation, is not some special qualitative tone but, rather, the fact that the pain is occasioned by the mere fact that (as we believe) they have the money and we do not. Thus if we suppose, in the case imagined, not only that I am bothered by the fact that you have money that belongs to me, but also that I am bothered simply because you have money while I do not, we can say that I am both indignant over the fact that you have money that does not belong to you and envious of the money that you have and I want.

We may now return to the phenomenon of so-called "friendly" envy and the problem it appeared to pose for the conception of envy that presupposes that this emotion involves something like malice or ill will. If our remarks are right, we can now resolve this problem quite straightforwardly, and we can do so without invoking the possibility that what we have here are importantly distinct kinds of envy. For if our remarks are right, neither malice nor ill will nor anything like these feelings is *required* for a person's emotional state to qualify—in the sorts of circumstances that interest us—as envy. I *may* feel ill will toward you as a result of my belief that you have what I want but do not have, just as I may feel anger, without ill will, or a mild form of annoyance, or whatever. But no one of these affective states is essential, on our analysis, for my feeling to qualify as envy. Rather, what's essential, as we have seen, is that my negative feelings, whatever precisely they involve, be focused on the very fact that you have what I want but apparently do not have. Thus whenever we have any negative affect in a two-party context of the sort we have described, we will have envy, on our view, provided that the object of that affect is the *very fact* that the one party apparently has something or some kind of thing that the other party wants.

IV

Let us assume that our remarks thus far are right: To be jealous is to be bothered or pained by the fact that, as we believe, we are not favored by others in some way in which we want to be favored (some other party apparently being so favored by those other people instead); to be envious is to be bothered or pained by the fact that (as we believe) someone else has something that we want but do have.[11] The question I want to raise now is this: In light of our analyses of what they are, what can we say about these emotions and what they do and do not show about the person who is experiencing them?

We can begin with the case of jealousy. And we can note at once that in at least one respect it is easy to see how our analysis can help us to advance the discussion over what this emotion does and does not show about the jealous person. For inasmuch as our analysis enables us to distinguish the various components of jealousy, it enables us to examine the various claims that are made about this emotion in a rather more systematic way than would otherwise have been possible. Consider in this connection the rather common claim that jealousy is a particularly *childish* emotion or, alternatively, that it is an emotion that only emotionally immature people would be likely to feel. On our analysis this has to come down either to the claim that only immature people could want to be favored in any of the various ways the jealous people necessarily want to be favored on our account, or to the claim that only immature people would be bothered by the fact that they are apparently not favored in some way in

---

[11]For the sake of simplicity I am speaking loosely here. One needn't, on our view, want the very thing the other person has in order to be envious. One merely needs to want it *or* something that is like it in relavent respects. See note 6 in this connection.

which they want to be favored. For on our account, to be jealous is just to be bothered by the fact that (as we believe) we are not favored in some way in which we want to be favored, and hence what's objectionable about jealousy must either be the desire to be so favored or the botherment that constitutes the affective part of the jealous response.[12]

Now, I do not wish to pursue this particular allegation here—I mean the allegation that jealousy is necessarily a sign of childishness or immaturity—since it's not clear to me exactly how one is to settle arguments about whether something is or is not a mark of immaturity. I do, however, want to note two points in passing. First, it seems to me that it would be quite implausible to suppose that it is the jealous people's *affective response*, given the apparent frustration of their presumed desire, that shows them to be somehow childish or immature. For given a desire to be favored in a certain way, it seems quite natural to imagine people being pained or bothered by the fact that (as they believe) this desire is not being met. To be sure, we can imagine someone's affective response being out of all proportion to what we would expect of an adult individual. This, however, is an independent point. For here we are concerned only with the question of whether the mere fact that someone is bothered in the relevant circumstances is itself enough to convict that person of childishness or immaturity. And, offhand at any rate, it seems to me to be clear that it is not.

The second point I want to make in this connection concerns the evaluation of the sort of desire that our analysis shows is involved whenever we feel jealousy in a given set of circumstances. Is the fact that we want to be favored in some respect—favored with sexual exclusivity, for example, or favored by our professional colleagues in some way—necessarily a mark of childishness or immaturity? As I have already indicated, it seems to me that answers to questions of this sort are virtually impossible to defend. However, I do think it is hard to see, offhand, why we should suppose that there is anything necessarily immature about wanting to be favored in some way by

---

[12]Of course, another thing that might be wrong or objectionable about a person's jealousy on our account is this: The belief that one is not favored in the relevant way may be unfounded—perhaps ludicrously so. I ignore this problem here only for the sake of brevity.

some particular person or group. There certainly seems to be nothing intrinsically objectionable, or childish, about wanting to be favored in some way *professionally*, nor is it clear—again, offhand—why it should be thought to be odd or otherwise objectionable to want to be favored sexually in certain ways: to want you, for example, to share your sexual favors only with me.[13]

The charges made against the jealous person, though, do not always amount to charges of childishness or immaturity. Sometimes it is said, instead, that jealousy is a sign of possessiveness, or of insecurity, or of a belief in what we might call the limited-commodity view of love and affection, according to which each of us has only a limited amount of love and affection to give to others and hence according to which it would perhaps make sense to want you to limit your affections to me (the fault in this last instance, of course, lying not in having this desire, given one's belief in the limited commodity view, but in actually accepting that view in the first place). These are much more serious and much more interesting charges, it seems to me, quite independently of the fact that, if proven, they might or might not tend to suggest that there is something childish or immature about wanting to be favored in the ways that, on our account, a jealous person necessarily wants to be favored. Before leaving the subject of jealousy, therefore, and what it does and does not show about the jealous person, I want to consider some of these other charges, at least in a brief and programmatic way.

Consider first the claim that jealousy is a sign of insecurity. If the account developed earlier is right, there is of course at least one respect in which this claim is trivially true: The jealous people[14] are—*ex hypothesi*, on our account—people who believe or suspect that

---

[13]Notice, though, that if it were made clear that a person wanted to be favored by another in every respect imaginable, we would be inclined to think there was something wrong with the person. One virtue of our analysis, it seems to me, is precisely that it enables us to distinguish this sort of case from the less immoderate sorts of cases imagined earlier.

[14]I mean, of course, someone who is experiencing jealousy at a given time, not someone who is prone to jealousy and in *that* sense a jealous person. (See note 3.) People who are prone to jealousy may well tend to be insecure in the sense—described later—which I argue is not necessarily connected with jealousy (as an occurrent emotion, that is). This is one of the many very interesting questions that space prohibits us from taking up in the present paper.

they are not favored in some respect in which they desire to be favored; hence jealousy is indeed a sign of insecurity, in this sense, inasmuch as it occurs, necessarily, only when we doubt that we are desired or favored in some relevant respect. Surely this, however, is not what people mean to say when they say that jealousy is a sign of insecurity. Presumably, at least some people who make this kind of claim mean to make a far more radical claim about the interconnections between jealousy and insecurity. I assume, in particular, that they mean to say that jealousy somehow betokens a kind of insecurity that is independent, logically, of our doubts about whether we are favored as we want to be favored, and that is merely signaled, as we might say, by our concern with whether or not we are favored.

What is this insecurity, then, that jealousy supposedly betokens, and how plausible is it to suppose that in fact jealousy does betoken it? As for the first of these questions, I think what people have in mind is something like the following. Jealous individuals are pictured as being unable to stand on their own; they have a bad self-image, as we might say, and need—to an unhealthy degree—reassurances of some sort in order to feel good about themselves. Since one kind of reassurance would be the thought that other people—at least certain other people—think more highly of these individuals than they do of others, such people will want to be thought more highly of—their insecurity thus explaining their desire—and will understandably be disturbed when they are not.

Now, I think it is reasonable to suppose that we have here a good explanation of why some people care about whether they are favored in the ways in which we have shown a jealous person will necessarily want to be favored. However, the question we need to ask here is whether this is the only possible explanation—that is, whether, as we often hear, the jealous person is *necessarily* an insecure person. And in order to see that this is not the only possible explanation, it seems to me we simply have to ask why—feelings of insecurity aside—people do in fact care about whether they are favored in any of the various possible respects. Why does it matter to them, if it is not because they are insecure in the sense explained?

Consider first the case of an animal or a young child. Obviously, animals and children sometimes care in the relevant way. Is it plausible to suppose that this concern is always based on insecurity in the sense explained? It seems obvious to me that it is not. For one thing, it *feels good* to be favored, or to be treated as though one is somehow special, and hence it should not surprise us that humans and non-humans alike sometimes seem to want to be so treated, independently of whether or not they suffer from the sort of personal insecurity discussed. For another thing, it is not at all clear that nonhuman animals and very young children are capable of the rather sophisticated process of forming—consciously or unconsciously—a bad self-image in the sense our account requires. Again, it is far simpler, and much closer to the facts, it seems to me, to say that these creatures just like being favored—they find it intrinsically pleasurable, as we might say—and hence want to be favored for the pleasure that's in it.[15]

Of course, someone might claim that mature adults would want to be treated as special in these ways only if they were insecure or only if they were afraid of a loss and wanted reassurance. But without further argument, and some convincing evidence, this would seem to be either ad hoc or unwarrantably dogmatic. After all, if it is plausible to suppose that being favored is pleasurable, in and of itself, for children and animals, it seems plausible to suppose that it is similarly pleasurable for adults. And if this is so, I think we can conclude that the likely truth of the matter is that some people have the relevant sorts of desires because they are pathologically insecure, others because they are—perhaps understandably—fearful of loss and hence want or need reassurance, and still others simply because it feels good to be treated as special. On this account there turn out to be all sorts of reasons—and very different reasons in different cases—for why people desire to be favored in the relevant ways. The point is simply that no one of these explanations—for example, the insecurity explanation—is necessarily implicated in any one case.

---

[15]Perhaps it would be more accurate to say that they find it pleasurable—in and of itself—for reasons that we haven't explained. This removes the perhaps objectionable notion of intrinsic desirability and leaves it open to behavioral scientists to determine why a given person desires to be favored in a given way. The answer to the advocate of the insecurity analysis would then be that it seems terribly implausible to suppose that we will find the same explanation in every case; namely, personal insecurity.

Consider next the claim that jealousy is a sign of an objectionable kind of possessiveness: When we feel jealous because people we care about show that they care about someone else, we are revealing that we think of them as ours, it is sometimes said, or as somehow bound to us in ways that make it inappropriate for them to share their love with others. But, then, to admit to jealousy, this argument continues, is surely to admit to an ugly and very objectionable view of our standing vis-à-vis the relevant person or persons. For no one belongs to another in the way jealousy shows we think another belongs to us, and to think otherwise is to show that we don't appreciate this elementary truth.

Now, before we can assess this line of thought, it will be useful to begin by asking what we generally mean by possessiveness, independently of cases where jealousy is involved, and why it is that we generally think of possessiveness as wrong. One very obvious answer, it seems to me, is this: We picture a possessive man as a man who is excessively concerned about his possessions and who makes too much of the fact that they are his—that is, of the fact that it is he who has the say, so to speak, about who uses them or about what shall or shall not be done with them. It's not so much that the possessive man literally won't let go of his possessions as that he insists on the importance of the fact that they are his—his as objects he owns and thereby his to regulate and control.

Now imagine the case of the man for whom it is very important that his wife have sexual relations with only him. One would think that if the idea of possessiveness has anything at all to do with jealousy, it is in just this sort of case that it does. And in fact I think there is something like possessiveness, in the sense just described, in at least some cases of this sort. For the man for whom it is important to be the only person with whom his wife has sexual relations may—and probably often does—think of his wife in something like the way he thinks about his car or his favorite fishing rod: "That's mine," he might say; "leave it alone." Moreover, and perhaps even more important, such a man's possessiveness—his feeling that a thing is his—itself suggests some of the other sins that are commonly laid at the jealous person's door. For in trying to say a moment ago wherein his possessiveness resides, we were driven to talk about the possessive man as a man who is much concerned about the things he owns—

thus introducing the possibility that our exclusionist really thinks about his wife as a mere thing or object rather than as a person—and in reflecting on the notion of ownership we were in turn driven to talk about the notion of control: His possessions are his, among other things, only insofar as it is he who gets to say who uses them and when; in other words, only if he controls them in some sense.

Despite the fact that there are these similarities, however, between the notions of possessiveness, control, and treating another person as an object rather than a person, on the one hand, and some cases of sexual jealousy, on the other (cases, that is, in which the jealousy presupposes a desire for sexual exclusivity), it is far from clear that these notions are necessarily connected with the possibility of jealousy. For one thing, of course, it is not clear how any of the points we have just been making is relevant to professional jealousy. How is my wanting to be considered a better teacher than Professor K, for example, a sign of possessiveness or a sign that I think of my students as mere objects or that somehow I am concerned with controlling them or their likes and dislikes? For another thing, it is not clear how these sorts of considerations are relevant to all the other sorts of cases of sexual jealousy, the cases where we are concerned not about sexual exclusivity, in and of itself, but about our lovers' opinions of us—as lovers, say, or as thinkers, charmers, or whatever. In these cases, one is certainly not thinking of one's lover as a mere object; indeed, it is hard to see how even possessiveness and a need to control others are relevant here, except in trivial ways.

Perhaps, though, the point intended here is that, these sorts of cases aside—professional cases, that is, and nonexclusivist sexual cases—in cases where jealousy *is* connected with a desire for sexual exclusivity, the jealous people are necessarily possessive and controlling or control-seeking people and also people who, inasmuch as they want what they want, think of their mates more as objects than as people. To see that even this is not so, let us begin with the charge that inasmuch as the sexual exclusivist seems to think of his partner in some sense as one of his possessions, he treats her more as an object than as a person. Is this really an accurate characterization of what's going on in such cases?

It seems to me that it is not. A man who thought of his wife strictly as an object wouldn't in fact feel jealousy, it seems to me, when he suspected her of infidelity (or, rather, of having been bedded by another, as we would have to say). On the contrary, I should think he would feel something more like indignation, say, or some similar emotion, in the way that we feel indignant or somehow wronged when someone uses something of ours without our permission or against our will. To the degree that a man does feel jealous when he suspects his wife of infidelity, on the other hand, it seems to me it's precisely because he is thinking of her as a person, in at least this respect: What bothers him is that she *chose* to sleep with the other man (assuming that she did sleep with another man). If we think of choosers as necessarily people, then we must say that to be jealous presupposes that one thinks of the other as—to that extent at least— a person.[16]

It will be clear by now how I think we should approach the problem of interpreting and evaluating the various things that people are inclined to say about jealousy and what it shows about the jealous person. For if I am right, jealousy can be thought of as a rather special kind of threat-response—a response, that is, to the possibility that one's status as a favored individual is in jeopardy. And if this is right, one way to approach the claims that interest us is to ask, of any given claim that jealousy shows this or that, why the fact that you care about your status in the relevant ways should be thought to suggest this or that. Unfortunately, because of limitations of time and space, further illustration of this way of analyzing the various claims made about jealousy must be left as an exercise for readers to perform on their own.

---

[16]Notice in this connection how odd it would be for a man to react to the fact that his wife has been raped by another man by being jealous of the rapist. Of course, some husbands *may* experience feelings of jealousy in such cases. It seems to me that their jealousy is intelligible, however, only if we assume that they suspect the woman *wanted* sex with the rapist or possibly enjoyed it. (Unfortunately, there is some reason to believe that many husbands are in fact inclined in such cases to just such suspicions.) Notice, too, that if I am jealous because my dog Poldy seems to prefer Linda's company to mine, this is no counterexample to the claim, advanced earlier that if A is jealous of C, then A is necessarily thinking of B as having freely *chosen* C and hence, to that extent at least, is necessarily thinking of B as a person. For my jealousy would be crazy if it weren't for the fact that at such times I *am* thinking of Poldy as a chooser and in that sense as a person.

V

If the argument of the preceding section is right, jealousy does not deserve the unqualified opprobrium with which it is often regarded. I have not, of course, defended jealousy, in any positive sense. I have merely tried to show that many of the charges that are commonly made against it will not withstand scrutiny, at least when they are understood as general claims about what jealousy necessarily shows us about the jealous person.

What about envy, though? What is the received wisdom about this emotion, and what can we say about it in light of the foregoing remarks?

Notice first of all that envy does not, in our own culture, come in for anything like the abuse that jealousy tends to receive. To be sure, to give in to envy is generally thought to be a fault, and a proneness or general disposition to experience this emotion would presumably be thought to be a serious defect of character. Still, in contrast to the case of jealousy, envy is not generally thought to be suggestive, in and of itself, of any other (further) vices or deficiencies of character. [17]

Now, this, I think, is actually rather odd. For if our remarks are right, there is at least this to be said against envy: It shows a kind of meanness, at least in one somewhat old-fashioned sense of the term. For while envy is not displeasure felt *simply* because of another's good fortune—this would be meanness of an even worse sort—it is nonetheless displeasure at another's good fortune *given that the person enjoys the good fortune and one does not (also) enjoy it oneself*. The displeasure or negative affect we have identified with envy, that is to say, is not simply the displeasure consequent upon my realization that I do not have something I want to have. Rather, it is a displeasure generated by my perception or belief that you have what I want but do not have

---

[17]This has not always been the case. In the Middle Ages, for example, Roman Catholic theology counted envy a capital sin. And in Dante's *Purgatorio*, those who had been guilty of this sin remained on the Second Terrace until they were purged of it. (See especially Cantos XIII and XIV and the very interesting remarks that Dante makes about this emotion.) The remarks that follow can be thought of, in signficant part, as an attempt to determine why envy was thought to be, if not the most serious of sins, a fairly serious sin nonetheless.

myself. And this, it seems to me, is a rather suspect state of mind, since it suggests that your good fortune does indeed offend me, not in and of itself, but in the context of my realization that my own desire is unfulfilled while yours is not.

It might be objected to this, of course, that in cases of what we called apparently friendly envy, we do not find displeasure—at another's good fortune—of the sort we are discussing here. And this much, at least, is true: For those cases where, as we said, the verbal expression of envy is playing a purely formal role, there is indeed no displeasure at another's good fortune. But, of course, in such cases, as we also said, we are not really dealing with envy: The speaker is not describing emotional feelings in such cases, but simply pointing out the desirability of what the interlocutor has. Thus cases like these, at any rate, do not undermine our claim, according to which the actual occurrence of envy suggests a certain meanness or smallness of spirit.

What about cases of apparently friendly envy, though, where I really am feeling at least slightly envious but where, as we granted earlier, it would be unreasonable to say the feeling is ill will? In what sense is the fact that I am experiencing negative affect in these circumstances a sign of meanness or of anything else that might plausibly be thought to render me something less than wholly admirable?

Here, I think, we need to recognize two related points. First, we must note that the negative feelings that constitute the affective side of envy will tend to vary enormously from case to case. Thus in a case of the sort alluded to earlier, it may be that I am pained—and hence actually feeling envy—only slightly and only for a moment or so. And while it might be said to be undesirable, morally, to be the sort of person who is even slightly and very briefly pained in such circumstances—we would admire people who were not even momentarily pained at the thought that others have what they don't have but want—one would hardly want to inveigh at length against the character of someone who was susceptible to such brief and superficial feelings of displeasure at another's good fortune. In other cases, by contrast, we can imagine a man who is consumed with anguish because of the fact that, as he believes, another has something—some thing, literally, or some trait or capacity—that he lacks but very much wants to have. And here, I think, we would see fit to make a strong negative judgment about this man's character: not because of his displeasure at not having the thing he wants to have, but because of the presence of the super-added displeasure that constitutes his feelings of envy—the displeasure generated, that is, not by his perception that he lacks something he wants but by his perception that he lacks it while someone else has it.

So the first point we need to note in connection with the problem posed by genuine cases of apparently friendly envy is that there is nothing surprising in the fact that the negative feelings that constitute the affective side of envy will tend to vary in intensity in different sorts of cases. The second point we need to note is this. The relevant feelings will indeed vary in intensity in the way just described. It nonetheless remains true that they are negative feelings—feelings of displeasure or discontent, if not of resentment and ill will—and that they are negative feelings occasioned by our perception (or, at any rate, belief) that someone else has something that we (also) want for ourselves but don't have (or, at any rate, don't believe we have). Thus if I am right in supposing that to be thus discomfited by the fact that another has what one wants but doesn't have is to be less virtuous than, ideally, one ought to be, we can say even if one's degree of meanness or viciousness is small in certain cases, one is nonetheless always somewhat mean when one experiences the feeling that is the feeling of envy.

My argument here presupposes, of course, among other things, that it is mean or vicious—inconsistent with ideal moral virtue, that is to say—to be susceptible to displeasure at the thought that another has something that one wants but does not have. And someone might deny this. It might be argued that it is only human or perfectly natural to be susceptible to, and then to feel, this sort of displeasure in the relevant circumstances, and hence that it is unreasonable to think less of someone for being so disposed, much less to hold that person liable to change these dispositions to the degree that they can be changed.[18]

---

[18] Another objection would hold that the relevant dispositions are not something over which we have any control and hence are not something one can in any sense hold against us, even as regards our virtue in the sense suggested. (See Adams, 1985, for useful reflections.)

Now, answering this objection adequately would take more space than is in fact available to us here. For one thing, we would have to work out in a great deal more detail the implications of the fact that feelings of the sort that interest us vary enormously in their intensity and hence, presumably, in the degree in which, even on our account, they detract from a person's virtue. And, for another thing, we would have to say much more about the sense in which feeling displeasure at another's good fortune, even in the sorts of circumstances we have in mind, is arguably vicious or mean. In the absence of this fuller account, however, it is reasonable to assume, it seems to me, that the burden is on anyone who would defend envy against the charges made earlier. For we do ordinarily think less of me for begrudging you such good as I happen to enjoy. And, as we have seen, if our analysis of envy is correct, something very much like this is going on when one person actually *feels* envy because of the advantages that another person enjoys.

VI

I have certainly not *proved* here that envy is somehow more objectionable than jealousy, even supposing what we are comparing are cases of each emotion that are in most respects roughly on a par (in intensity, for example, or extent, or duration). Indeed, it is not clear to me exactly what a proof of such a proposition would involve. Still, I have tried to establish, to the best of my ability, at least this much: Many of the things that are frequently said against jealousy do not in fact appear to be things we can actually say against this emotion, once we reflect on what jealousy is and on what the charges against it are; in the case of envy, by contrast, while little is typically said against it, there do in fact appear to be a number of things that *can* be said against it and that, so far as I can see, do not disappear once we are clear on what it is to feel envy and what the charges against it, thus conceived, really are. Barring a deeper account of these matters, therefore—which account I hope the present remarks can be said to serve—I think we can conclude that, first appearances notwithstanding, envy really is, morally at least, rather more objectionable than jealousy.

REFERENCES

Adams, Robert M. 1985. "Involuntary Sins." *Philosophical Review*, 94, 1, 3–31. *Oxford English Dictionary*. 1933. Oxford: Clarendon Press.

STUDY QUESTIONS

1. How does Farrell distinguish envy from jealousy?
2. Can you think of specific cases where jealousy is definitely worse than envy? If so, does your example count against Farrell's argument?
3. On Farrell's account, could an absence of jealousy indicate a character failing? In your own view could *A*'s lack of jealousy with respect to *B*'s attentions to *C* indicate that *A* does not "really love" *B*?
4. Compare Farrell's analysis of jealousy and envy with Kant's. With whom are you most in agreement?

Sexual Revenge

SUSAN JACOBY

Susan Jacoby is a journalist and essayist. Among her works are *Wild Justice* (1983) and two books on the Soviet Union.

Revenge seems to be the most pardonable vice. Our tolerance of this vice extends even to law. Jacoby's essay focuses on sexual revenge where an "unwritten law" tolerates violence by a jealous husband against an unfaithful wife. A similar latitude has been customary in the murder of a rapist by the husband or brother of the violated woman. Jacoby's account of sexual revenge traces changes in the attitude of the public, which once considered such revenge to be the exclusive province of men, to the present day, when it sometimes recognizes that women have the right to take private vengeance on abusive husbands. Jacoby shows that acts of private retribution promote more misery than satisfaction. If she is right, the legal exoneration of vengeance, whether by men or by women, should not be tolerated.

. . . A history of passion or "love" is repeatedly offered as a mitigating factor when a crime involves intimates or former intimates. On June 4, 1980, a young Chicago man named Wayne Birch shot and killed his former girlfriend, Venira Curtis, who was pregnant by and about to marry another man. Both victim and killer were black, and Curtis was a secretary. There was nothing glamorous about the case—no millionaire diet doctor to attract the attention of the national and international press. But the crime was both brutal and calculated. Birch had repeatedly threatened Curtis after she left him; he had broken her car windows and pulled a gun on her and her fiancé, promising to kill her if she brought charges against him. She and her father, who had urged her to testify, were on their way to court for the trial when Birch appeared at their house and shot his "true love" through the head.

The State of Illinois permits the death penalty in cases where the assailant has killed someone who planned to testify against him in a criminal trial. But the judge did not even hand down a life sentence; he sentenced Birch to twenty-five years, with eligibility for parole after eleven years, when he will still be a young man. Why? Not because the judge opposed life sentences but because the victim and the killer had once been romantically involved. The judge concluded that Birch killed his former girlfriend because he wanted her back and she was in love with another man—not to prevent her from testifying against him. In his view, the killing was a crime of the heart rather than an act of calculated vengeance—and his sentence reflected the social consensus that crimes of the heart and crimes of the head are to be judged by different standards.

The use of psychiatry to exculpate those who attack their intimates is a modern twist on the ancient unwritten law that grants a certain legitimacy to the impassioned cry "If I can't have you, no one will." In the past, that legitimacy was enjoyed only by men. Today, as a result of the changing balance of sexual power, some women have also been able to invoke the protection of a legal custom dictated by passion rather than reason.

The unwritten law: It does not belong within quotation marks, with their implications of skepticism, thoughtful consideration, distance. By definition, the unwritten law was engraved on no stone tablets; it originated in the deepest, most destructive human passions and was upheld by the strength and social authority of men. A simple tableau comes to mind—a cowboy returning early to his home on the range, surprising his wife with another man, pumping them both full of bullets. Although this surely is the classic example of socially sanctioned vengeance—one that survived well into the twentieth century in many cultures, including the Italian and American South—the unwritten law is best understood as a broad code covering many aspects of social, sexual, and familial relations between women and men.

These include the traditional patriarchal powers of husbands and fathers, which, as the continued prevalence of wife beating and sexual child abuse suggests, are extremely difficult to limit through written laws; seduction and its consequences, inside and outside of marriage; rape, inside and outside of marriage, and the vengeance exacted for rape by the male relatives of a violated woman. The historic difficulty, or absolute inability, of women to exact their own retribution for rape cannot be overestimated as a factor in the development of the tangled laws, written and unwritten, linking sex and revenge. It is hardly surprising that some women today are claiming an "equal right" to vengeance outside the law; the extra-legal rights long accorded to men—both as instigators and avengers of crimes of passion—laid the groundwork for the regressive and legally illegitimate invocation of the unwritten law as women's "right." . . .

Christine de Pizan, writing at the end of the fourteenth and the beginning of the fifteenth centuries, became the first literary woman to take up her pen in defense of rape victims. Drawing on the mixture of pagan myth and Christian allegory that was the *métier* of scholars in her era, she recounted the tribulations of the queen of the Galatians, who was taken hostage during the Roman conquest of her land and raped by a Roman officer.

> He entreated and coaxed her with fine presents, but after he saw that pleading would not work, he violently raped her. The lady suffered terrible sorrow over this outrage and could not stop thinking of a way to avenge herself, biding her time until she saw her chance. When the ransom was brought to deliver her husband and herself, the lady said that the money should be turned over in her presence to the officer who was holding them. She told him to weigh the gold to have a better count, so that he would not be deceived. When she saw that he intended to weigh the ransom and that none of his men would be there, the lady, who had a knife, stabbed him in the neck and killed him. She took his head and without difficulty brought it to her husband and told him the entire story and how she had taken vengeance.

Christine relates this tale with great relish and approval, and she speaks with equal admiration of Roman and Christian women who took their own lives to demonstrate their detestation of rape. Christine, who may well have been the first woman in the Western world to earn her living by writing (she was a widely known lyric poet and official biographer to the French King Charles V), wrote her *Book of the City of Ladies* (*Le Livre de la Cité des Dames*, which appeared in 1405) in direct response to the male epic poems of the age of chivalry, which on the one hand idealized the purity and beauty of women and on the other portrayed them as the seductive, deceitful, and vindictive sex. For Christine, tales of women who killed their rapists or committed suicide to mitigate their disgrace were the logical answers to the male vision of the woman who "was asking for it." The scope of her learning did not extend to law. As a devout Christian writing at the close of the Middle Ages, she would hardly have been aware of the changes in Jewish law providing women with the tentative legal basis to demand retribution for rape. As an artist who was educated in Italy and spent her adult life in France, she would have been equally uninformed about English statutes that gave raped women legal standing before the king's courts—a weapon that would ultimately prove more useful to the victim than a knife turned upon her rapist in rage or herself in shame. Private vengeance is the preferred weapon of those who have no access to public retribution.

In the eleventh and twelfth centuries, talmudists took the first steps toward a Jewish view of rape as an injury to the woman herself rather than as a form of property damage inflicted on her husband or father. The changes in rabbinical interpretation appear, from a modern perspective, as picayune, grudging, even ludicrous modifications of a fundamentally unjust legal concept of women as property; nevertheless, they were genuine advances for Jewish women at the time. Ordinarily, the damages for rape were paid to a virgin's father. The problem that perplexed the rabbis of the Middle Ages was what to do about the rape of an "independent" virgin—one whose father was dead and who was unbetrothed. (The cyclical violence visited upon European Jews during the Crusades must have left a considerable number of fatherless virgins. Rabbinical law was, of course, enforced only when both the assailant and the victim were Jews; the talmudists could do nothing about rapes of Jews by Christians in the name of their God.) . . . A "semi-independent" virgin was one whose father was still alive but who was betrothed (and had not yet celebrated her nuptials). As one Jewish scholar notes, there are opposing traditions concerning the question of whether a semi-independent virgin is entitled to collect the fine herself. Some wildly progressive rabbis even argued that indemnity for the mental and physical anguish of rape should always be paid to the virgin herself, even if she was totally dependent on her father, but that view did not prevail. . . .

In England, the twelfth and thirteenth centuries greatly expanded the *theoretical* power of women to demand retribution for rape. As Brownmiller observes, a woman had little chance of bringing a successful suit against her rapist unless she was a propertied virgin or a wife of impeccable reputation. Nevertheless, it is impossible to overestimate the importance of a comprehensive set of laws stating unequivocally that the woman, not her husband or father, was the aggrieved party in a rape. . . .

It is a sad, ironic twist of history to hear the unwritten law—a concept that has done so much damage to women for millennia—invoked in defense of women who have, under admittedly serious provocation, taken their own violent revenge. Inez Garcia, testifying in her own defense, admitted she had killed the man who abetted her rape and said she was glad. "I feel anyone who has been raped has the right to kill back," she said, adding that she was sorry she had only killed the man who stood by and watched and had not gotten the actual rapist as well.

It is understandable that such assertions are unsettling to men—and not only to the rapists among them. From my feminist perspective, the claim of women's right to violent revenge is, for different reasons, equally disturbing. On the most practical level, the extension of social tolerance to a small number of women who carry out violent acts of sexual vengeance is of little use to the vast majority of women, who are neither physically nor emotionally equipped to select a weapon and pursue their rapists through the darkened streets. In a strictly legal sense, the tendency to place crimes of passion and intimacy outside the law can be turned against women—once again—as easily as it can be used to defend them. In the late 1970s, a few acquittals of battered wives who turned against their husbands and killed them generated enormous publicity; the exoneration of these women represented a reversal of the standards normally applied to wives and mothers. At the same time, other battered wives were being convicted of manslaughter or committed to mental institutions for taking action against their brutal husbands. These cases—being dog-bites-woman rather than woman-bites-dog stories—attracted no attention at all.

Meanwhile, there has been no diminution of the traditional leniency accorded men who commit crimes of passion. Wayne Birch escaped a life sentence because he and his victim had once been romantically involved. Richard Herrin, after hammering Bonnie Garland to death, was convicted of manslaughter rather than murder because the killing took place a day after Bonnie told him she wanted to be free to date other men. John Hinckley's obsession with the actress Jodie Foster certainly played a role in his successful insanity defense. All of the controversy surrounding the Hinckley verdict has focused on the role of psychiatrists in the courtroom; however, the romantic, sexual nature of Hinckley's primary obsession was from the beginning tailor-made for a psychiatric defense. Given the federal stipulation that the burden of proving sanity rests with the prosecution, it is probable that Hinckley would have been acquitted in any event. Nevertheless, it is interesting to speculate on the question of whether a jury would have been as convinced of Hinckley's insanity under the law if his main fantasy had been one of conquering the world instead of proving his love for a teenaged actress. "I don't know why love has to hurt so much," Hinckley declared in several bizarre telephone interviews with newspaper reporters. As a basis for rationalizing violence and revenge, references to "love" and "honor" have served men much more often than they have served women.

In utilitarian and legal terms, the claim of a female right to violent revenge is an ineffectual tool for righting the wrongs of women. In terms of female self-esteem, the assertion is a true disaster. Woman as uncontrolled avenger is the mirror image of woman as a prisoner of man. In both instances, her life is beyond her control.

Twentieth-century judges and jurors do not assume the existence of daughterly devotion, but they can be just as uneasy as their nineteenth-century counterparts in the face of openly expressed female violence and revenge. On March 9, 1977, Francine Hughes, a mother of four in a small town in central Michigan, poured gasoline around the bed of her husband and set fire to him as he slept in an alcoholic stupor. She drove away from the house with her children as the bed was engulfed in flames and immediately turned herself in to the police. No woman ever had more reason to kill a man than Francine Hughes did, and her case became a feminist cause célèbre.

The slain man was, in fact, Hughes's former husband, although newspaper accounts generally referred to him as her husband. She had divorced him in 1971 after seven years of marriage, mainly because she found his physical abuse unbearable. But it is understand-

425

able that the newspapers described James Hughes as her husband, because she continued to behave like a wife even after the bitter divorce. From her testimony at the trial, it was clear that she remained bound to him emotionally, on some occasions sexually, and always as a target for abuse.

He was living in the same house with his former wife at the time of his death because she had agreed, at his mother's urging, to nurse him back to health after a serious automobile accident. He had made a good enough recovery from his injuries to beat her up repeatedly. Hughes's continuing sense of obligation to a man who had systematically abused her is a striking example of the victimization that some women are bred to accept. It is impossible to imagine a man returning with concern to the bedside of a wife who had subjected him to physical torture. Unlike many battered wives, Francine Hughes had summoned up the courage to divorce her husband, but she was unable to sever the emotional tie.

On the day James Hughes was killed, he had already beaten Francine and forced her to have sexual relations with him; there was nothing unusual about that. He had also made a bonfire in the back yard of her school textbooks. Francine, who had dropped out of high school to marry, was taking business courses at a local community college; she wanted to be able to support her children, get off welfare, and move away from the small community where she had grown up. James had already threatened to kill her if she continued with her business classes.

And so Francine poured the gasoline around the bed and lit it. Her murder trial was held in Lansing, the nearby state capital, where a jury acquitted her on the basis of temporary insanity. After a short period of psychiatric testing, she was declared sane and released from custody. Many feminists were indignant because Hughes's lawyer had chosen the safer plea of temporary insanity in preference to a plea of self-defense. This view is expressed by Ann Jones, who argues that "the notion of the 'preventative strike,' so widely used in international conflicts, seems downright cowardly when applied to a battered woman who sneaks up on a man. Thus, Hughes's attorney, taking no chances, hedged on the self-defense principle so clear to feminists and argued instead, much like the attorneys of the seduced-and-abandoned maidens a century ago, that the woman was temporarily insane."

Of course, this interpretation of self-defense is not at all clear to all feminists—any more than the idea of a preventive nuclear strike is acceptable to those who are not affiliated with the Dr. Strangelove School of International Relations. I believe Francine Hughes was fortunate to have a lawyer who was more interested in obtaining his client's acquittal than in making an ideological point. One can easily imagine a self-defense plea exonerating a woman who picked up a knife or gun to protect herself against a charging two-hundred-pound man—even if he was unarmed—since the male body, by virtue of its superior strength and physical training, is usually weapon enough to overcome an ordinary woman. But it would be extremely difficult for any jury, mindful of the traditional definition of self-defense as a response to imminent deadly force, to acquit a woman who set fire to a sleeping man—however brutal the man may have been in the preceding years or hours. Some lawyers and judges have argued that the traditional boundaries of self-defense should be broadened to recognize the special condition of a woman who has been terrorized by a man for years. But where does the broadening process stop? Inez Garcia, who was acquitted at her second trial after an initial conviction was overturned, killed an accomplice to her rape twenty minutes after her assailants had left the house. Would a self-defense plea have been recognized if she had "only" been beaten rather than raped? Would it have been accepted if she had killed the man the following day? The following week? . . .

Reason is a particularly fragile barrier against vengeance when the latter is motivated by familial or erotic passion. Vindictive impulses between husband and wife, parent and child, lover and lover are truly beyond the law, but many vindictive acts are not—or ought not to be. Legislation cannot produce morality, kindness, decency, love, or the slightest measure of empathy—but it can promote restraint. Law is most necessary where inner restraints are most likely to fail. Within the context of intimacy gone wrong—when sexual desire and protectiveness are transmuted into rage and possessiveness—internal controls are at their weakest.

No law, it is frequently argued, can ever deter an individual man or woman from committing a crime of passion and sexual revenge: the brutal husband will continue to beat his wife; the battered woman will wait for the moment when she can avenge herself upon a violent man; Othello will murder Desdemona; Medea will slaughter her children. But this argument ignores the extent to which individual actions are influenced by social expectations; the popular and legal distinction between acts of sexual violence and revenge committed within a family and the same acts committed within a more impersonal context cannot fail to affect the frequency of such incidents. One can neither prove nor disprove the hypothesis that fewer men would beat their wives if husbands were hauled off to prison with some regularity for the offense, because retribution is almost never imposed on men who assault "their" women. But the absence of such retribution conveys an unmistakable social judgment—a judgment that a man may, by virtue of his intimate relationship with a woman, inflict violence that would be punished if it were directed toward anyone else. And the corollary to the treatment of sexual violence by the powerful as a "special case" is the responsive vengeance that may be elicited in the weak.

Public safety demands abandonment of the special status that custom and law have long accorded acts of sexual vengeance and violence. As human beings, we may sympathize with the rejected lover who, in an agony of disappointment, kills the object of his or her frustrated passion; with the mother or father who, having been beaten as a child, abuses his or her own child in turn; with the rape victim who stalks her attacker in the night. As citizens, we cannot afford to exempt these acts from the normal process of crime and punishment. . . .

We can understand the emotions of a distraught lover as we cannot understand the emotions of a thug who kills a man for the five dollars in his wallet, but that identification should not be allowed to obscure the fact that the result is the same in both cases: an innocent victim is dead. In an emotional or psychoanalytic sense, true innocence is nonexistent, but victims are innocent under the law unless they are attacked while in the act of attacking another. Psychological or emotional rationalizations should carry no more weight in cases of sexual violence than in cases of bank robbery or drunken driving.

It ought not to be necessary to stress that public regulation of sexual revenge should extend equal protection to, and demand equal accountability from, both sexes. Centuries of rationalizing male vengeance have, however, bred entirely predictable modern rationalizations for female vengeance. I believe it is outrageous to extend the definition of self-defense to exonerate a woman who kills a rapist a half hour, or a day, or a week after he leaves her house—just as I believe it is, and always has been, outrageous to suggest that women "ask for it." Insistence on a gender-blind attitude toward sexual revenge should not be construed to imply acceptance of the nonsensical charge of "reverse discrimination," sometimes used to describe recent changes in laws concerning rape and wife beating. I feel obliged to point out, once again, that women are generally the victims rather than the instigators of sexual violence.

The special position of sexual revenge in law is merely an outgrowth of the mythicization of erotic violence that has always played, and continues to play, such an important role in our culture. Sexual vengeance and violence (and I believe the latter is almost always motivated by the former) become symbols for atavistic notions of, on the one hand, civilized honor and, on the other, release from the normal constraints of civilization. . . .

For both men and women, the unwritten law dies hard. And the revenge exacted in its name, however glorified in myth, is seldom sweet.

STUDY QUESTIONS

1. Jacoby does not approve of private vengeance. "Public safety demands abandonment of the special status that custom and law have long accorded acts of sexual vengeance and violence . . . As citizens we cannot afford to exempt these acts from the normal process of crime and punishment." Do you agree?
2. Do you agree that psychological and emotional rationalizations should carry more weight in cases of "crimes of passion" than in cases of bank robbery or drunk driving?
3. Argue the case for or against taking revenge.
4. Is there any moral justification for giving *sexual* revenge a special status among acts of revenge?

The Evil of Lying

CHARLES FRIED

Charles Fried (b. 1935) is a professor of law at the Harvard University School of Law. He has written several books and articles in the area of ethics; his most recent books are *Right and Wrong* (1978), *Contract as Promise: A Theory of Contractual Obligation* (1981), and *Order and Law: Arguing the Reagan Revolution* (1992).

Fried distinguishes between acts that are merely bad and acts that are wrong. He cites Bentham's belief that lying is not wrong and not always bad. He discusses the views of Kant and Augustine, who hold that lying is wrong even when the effects are good. We lie, says Fried, when we intentionally induce a false belief. He asks, If that effect is not bad, how can lying be wrong? He answers that lying is wrong because the effect of lying is *always* bad; lies tamper with the judgment of the persons lied to, thereby interfering with them in a fundamentally disrespectful way. If you could intentionally induce a false belief in yourself, that too would be wrong.

Lying is wrong because it violates the integrity of another's mind, and because it violates trust. In breaking that trust—here Fried quotes Kant—one does wrong to men in general, not only to the gullible victims. Fried compares lying to passing a counterfeit bill.

The evil of lying is as hard to pin down as it is strongly felt. Is lying wrong or is it merely something bad? If it is bad, why is it bad—is it

THE EVIL OF LYING Reprinted by permission of the author and publisher from *Right and Wrong* by Charles Fried (Cambridge, MA) Harvard University Press. Copyright © 1978 by the President and Fellows of Harvard College.

bad in itself or because of some tendency associated with it? Compare lying to physical harm. Harm is a state of the world and so it can only be classified as bad; the wrong I argued for was the *intentional doing* of harm. Lying, on the other hand, can be wrong, since it is an action. But the fact that lying is an action does not mean that it *must* be wrong rather than bad. It might be that the action of lying should be judged as just another state of the world—a time-extended state, to be sure, but there is no problem about that—and as such it would count as a negative element in any set of circumstances in which it occurred. Furthermore, if lying is judged to be bad it can be bad in itself, like something ugly or painful, or it can be bad only because of its tendency to produce results that are bad in themselves.

If lying were bad, not wrong, this would mean only that, other things being equal, we should avoid lies. And if lying were bad not in itself but merely because of its tendencies, we would have to avoid lies only when those tendencies were in fact likely to be realized. In either case lying would be permissible to produce a net benefit, including the prevention of more or worse lies. By contrast the categorical norm "Do not lie" does not evaluate states of affairs but is addressed to moral agents, forbidding lies. Now if lying is wrong it is also bad in itself, for the category of the intrinsically bad is weaker and more inclusive than the category of the wrong. And accordingly, many states of the world are intrinsically bad (such as destruction of valuable property) but intentional acts bringing them about are not necessarily wrong.

Bentham plainly believed that lying is neither wrong nor even intrinsically bad: "Falsehood, take it by itself, consider it as not being accompanied by any other material circumstances, nor therefore productive of any material effects, can never, upon the principle of utility, constitute any offense at all" (*An Introduction to the Principles of Morals and Legislation,* ch. 16, sec. 24). By contrast, Kant and Augustine argued at length that lying is wrong. Indeed, they held that lying is not only wrong *unless* excused or justified in defined ways (which is my view) but that lying is always wrong. Augustine sees lying as a kind of defilement, the liar being tainted by the lie, quite apart from any consequences of the lie. Kant's views are more complex. He argues at one point that lying undermines confidence and trust among men generally: "Although by making a false statement I do no wrong to him who unjustly compels me to speak, yet I do wrong to men in general . . . I cause that declarations in general

431

find no credit, and hence all rights founded on contract should lose their force; and this is a wrong to mankind" ("On a Supposed Right to Tell Lies from Benevolent Motives," in *Kant's Critique of Practical Reason and Other Works,* translated by T. K. Abbott [London: Longmans, Green, 1973]). This would seem to be a consequentialist argument, according to which lying is bad only insofar as it produces these bad results. But elsewhere he makes plain that he believes these bad consequences to be necessarily, perhaps even conceptually linked to lying. In this more rigoristic vein, he asserts that lying is a perversion of one's uniquely human capacities irrespective of any consequences of the lie, and thus lying is not only intrinsically bad but wrong.[1]

Finally, a number of writers have taken what looks like an intermediate position: the evil of lying is indeed identified with its consequences, but the connection between lying and those consequences, while not a necessary connection, is close and persistent, and the consequences themselves are pervasive and profound. Consider this passage from a recent work by G. F. Warnock:

> I do not necessarily do you any harm at all by deed or word if I induce you to believe what is not in fact the case; I may even do you good, possibly by way, for example, of consolation or flattery. Never-

---

[1] "The greatest violation of man's duty to himself merely as a moral being (to humanity in his own person) is . . . the lie. In the doctrine of Law an intentional wrong is called a lie only if it infringes on another's right. But . . . in ethics . . . every deliberate untruth deserves this harsh name. By a lie a man makes himself contemptible . . . and violates the dignity of humanity in his own person. And so, since the harm that can come to others from it is not the characteristic property of this vice (for if it were, the vice would consist only in violating one's duty to others), we do not take this harm into account here . . . By a lie man throws away and, as it were, annihilates his dignity as a man. A man [who lies] . . . has even less worth than if he were a mere thing. For a thing, as something real and given, has the property of being serviceable . . . But the man who communicates his thoughts to someone in words which yet (intentionally) contain the contrary of what he thinks on the subject has a purpose directly opposed to the natural purposiveness of the power of communicating one's thoughts and therefore renounces his personality and makes himself a mere deceptive appearance of man, not man himself.

"A lie (in the ethical sense of the term), as an intentional untruth as such, need not be harmful to others in order to be pronounced reprehensible; for then it would be a violation of the rights of others . . . A lie requires a second person whom one intends to deceive, and intentionally to deceive oneself seems to contain a contradiction.

"Man as a moral being (*homo noumenon*), cannot use his natural being (*homo phaenomenon*) as a mere means (a speaking machine), as if it were not bound to its intrinsic end (the communication of thought)." (*Tugendlehre* [428–430], translated by Mary J. Gregor, *The Doctrine of Virtue,* Philadelphia: University of Pennsylvania Press, 1964.)

theless, though deception is not thus necessarily directly damaging it is easy to see how crucially important it is that the natural inclination to have recourse to it should be counteracted. It is, one might say, not the implanting of false beliefs that is damaging, but rather the generation of the suspicion that they may be being implanted. For this undermines trust; and, to the extent that trust is undermined, all cooperative undertakings, in which what one person can do or has reason to do is dependent on what others have done, are doing, or are going to do, must tend to break down. . . . There is no sense in my asking you for your opinion on some point, if I do not suppose that your answer will actually express your opinion (verbal communication is doubtless the most important of all our co-operative undertakings). (*The Object of Morality* [London: Methuen, 1971], p. 84.)

Warnock does not quite say that truth-telling is good in itself or that lying is wrong, yet the moral quality of truth-telling and lying is not so simply instrumental as it is, for instance, for Bentham. Rather, truth-telling seems to bear a fundamental, pervasive relation to the human enterprise, just as lying appears to be fundamentally subversive of that enterprise. What exactly is the nature of this relation? How does truth-telling bear to human goods a relation which is more than instrumental but less than necessary?

The very definition of lying makes plain that consequences are crucial, for lying is intentional and the intent is an intent to produce a consequence: false belief. But how can I then resist the consequentialist analysis of lying? Lying is an attempt to produce a certain effect on another, and if that effect (consequence) is not bad, now can lying be wrong? I shall have to argue, therefore, that to lie is to intend to produce an effect which always has something bad about it, an effect moreover of the special sort that it is wrong to produce it intentionally. To lay that groundwork for my argument about lying, I must consider first the moral value of truth.

Truth and Rationality

A statement is true when the world is the way the statement says it is.[2] Utilitarians insist (as in the quotation from Bentham above) that

---

[2]This definition is derived from Alfred Tarski via Donald Davidson, "Meaning and Truth," in Jay F. Rosenberg and Charles Travis, eds., *Reading in the Philosophy of Language* (Englewood Cliffs, NJ: Prentice-Hall, 1971). See also Gottlob Frege,

truth, like everything else, has value just exactly as it produces value—pleasure, pain, the satisfaction or frustration of desire. And of course it is easy to show that truth (like keeping faith, not harming the innocent, respecting rights) does not always lead to the net satisfactions of desire, to the production of utility. It may *tend* to do so, but that tendency explains only why we should discriminate between occasions when truth does and when it does not have value—an old story. It is an old story, for truth—like justice, respect, and self-respect—has a value which consequentialist analyses (utilitarian or any other) do not capture. Truth, like respect, is a foundational value.

The morality of right and wrong does not count the satisfaction of desire as the overriding value. Rather, the integrity of persons, as agents and as the objects of the intentional agency of others, has priority over the attainment of the goals which agents choose to attain. I have sought to show how respect for physical integrity is related to respect for the person. The person, I argued, is not just a locus of potential pleasure and pain but an entity with determinate characteristics. The person is, among other things, necessarily an incorporated, a physical, not an abstract entity. In relation to truth we touch another necessary aspect of moral personality: the capacity for judgment, and thus for choice. It is that aspect which Kant used to ground his moral theory, arguing that freedom and rationality are the basis for moral personality. John Rawls makes the same point, arguing that "moral personality and not the capacity for pleasure and pain . . . [is] the fundamental aspect of the self . . . The essential unity of the self is . . . provided by the concept of right" (*A Theory of Justice* [Cambridge, Mass.: Harvard University Press, 1971], p. 563). The concept of the self is prior to the goods which the self chooses, and these goods gather their moral significance from the fact that they have been chosen by moral beings—beings capable of understanding and acting on moral principles.

In this view freedom and rationality are complementary capacities, or aspects of the same capacity, which is moral capacity. A man is free insofar as he is able to act on a judgment because he perceives it

---

"The Thought: A Logical Inquiry," and Michael Dummett, "Truth," both in Peter Strawson, ed., *Philosophical Logic* (Oxford: Oxford University Press, 1967). The difficulties in arriving at a satisfactory conception of truth do not touch the moral issues that I discuss in this chapter. Indeed, I suppose that any of a large class of definitions might be substituted for the one I used in the text and my substantive argument would go through without a hitch.

to be correct; he is free insofar as he may be moved to action by the judgments his reason offers to him. This is the very opposite of the Humean conception of reason as the slave of the passions. There is no slavery here. The man who follows the steps of a mathematical argument to its conclusion because he judges them to be correct is free indeed. To the extent that we choose our ends we are free; and as to objectively valuable ends which we choose because we see their value, we are still free.

Now, rational judgment is true judgment, and so the moral capacity for rational choice implies the capacity to recognize the matter on which choice is to act and to recognize the kind of result our choices will produce. This applies to judgments about other selves and to judgments in which one locates himself as a person among persons, a self among selves. These judgments are not just arbitrary suppositions: *they are judged to be true of the world.* For consider what the self would be like if these judgments were not supposed to be true. Maybe one might be content to be happy in the manner of the fool of Athens who believed all the ships in the harbor to be his. But what of our perceptions of other people? Would we be content to have those whom we love and trust the mere figments of our imaginations? The foundational values of freedom and rationality imply the foundational value of truth, for the rational man is the one who judges aright, that is, truly. Truth is not the same as judgment, as rationality; it is rather the proper subject of judgment. If we did not seek to judge truly, and if we did not believe we could judge truly, the act of judgment would not be what we know it to be at all.

Judgment and thus truth are *part* of a structure which as a whole makes up the concept of self. A person's relation to his body and the fact of being an incorporated self are another part of that structure. These two parts are related. The bodily senses provide matter for judgments of truth, and the body includes the physical organs of judgment.

The Wrong of Lying

So our capacity for judgment is foundational and truth is the proper object of that capacity, but how do we get to the badness of lying, much less its categorical wrongness? The crucial step to be supplied has to do not with the value of truth but with the evil of lying. We must show that to lie to someone is to injure him in a way that particularly touches his moral personality. From that, the passage is indeed easy to the conclusion that to inflict such injury intentionally (remember that all lying is by hypothesis intentional) is not only bad but wrong. It is this first, crucial step which is difficult. After all, a person's capacity for true judgment is not necessarily impaired by inducing in him a particular false belief. Nor would it seem that a person suffers a greater injury in respect to that capacity when he is induced to believe a falsity than when we intentionally prevent him from discovering the truth, yet only in the first case do we lie. Do we really do injury to a person's moral personality when we persuade him falsely that it rained yesterday in Bangkok—a fact in which he has no interest? And do we do him more injury than when we fail to answer his request for yesterday's football scores, in which he is mildly interested? Must we not calculate the injury by the *other* harm it does: disappointed expectations, lost property, missed opportunities, physical harm? In this view, lying would be a way of injuring a person in his various substantive interests—a way of stealing from him, hurting his feelings, perhaps poisoning him—but then the evil of lying would be purely instrumental, not wrong at all.

All truth, however irrelevant or trivial, has value, even though we may cheerfully ignore most truths, forget them, erase them as encumbrances from our memories. The value of every truth is shown just in the judgment that the only thing we must not do is falsify truth. Truths are like other people's property, which we can care nothing about but may not use for our own purposes. It is as if the truth were not ours (even truth we have discovered and which is known only to us), and so we may not exercise an unlimited dominion over it. Our relations to other people have a similar structure: we may perhaps have no duty to them, we may be free to put them out of our minds to make room for others whom we care about more, but we may not harm them. And so we may not falsify truth. But enough of metaphors—what does it mean to say that the truth is not ours?

The capacity for true judgment is the capacity to arrive at judgments which are in fact true of the world as it exists apart from our desires, our choices, our values. It is the world presented to us by true judgments—including true judgments about ourselves—which we then make the subject of our choices, our valuation. Now, if we treat the truth as our own, it must be according to desire or valuation. But for rational beings these activities are supposed to depend on truth; we are supposed to desire and choose according to the world as it is. To choose that something not be the case when it is in fact the case is very nearly self-contradictory—for choice is not *of* truth but *on the basis of* truth. To deliberate about whether to believe a truth (not whether it is indeed true—another story altogether) is like deciding whether to cheat at solitaire. All this is obvious. In fact I suppose one cannot even coherently talk about choosing to believe something one believes to be false. And this holds equally for all truths—big and little, useful, useless, and downright inconvenient. But we do and must calculate *about* (and not just *with*) truths all the time as we decide what truths to acquire, what to forget. We decide all the time not to pursue some inquiry because it is not worth it. Such calculations surely must go forward on the basis of what truths are useful, given one's plans and desires. Even when we pursue truth for its own sake, we distinguish between interesting and boring truths.

Considering what truth to acquire or retain differs, however, from deliberately acquiring false beliefs. All truths are acquired as propositions correctly (truly) corresponding to the world, and in this respect, all truths are equal. A lie, however, has the form and occupies the role of truth in that it too purports to be a proposition about the world; only the world does not correspond to it. So the choice of a lie is not like a choice among truths, for the choice of a lie is a choice to affirm as the basis for judgment a proposition which does not correspond to the world. So, when I say that truth is foundational, that truth precedes choice, what I mean is *not* that this or that truth is foundational but that judging according to the facts is foundational to judging at all. A scientist may deliberate about which subject to study and, having chosen his subject, about the data worth acquiring, but he cannot even deliberate as a scientist about whether to acquire false data. Clearly, then, there is something funny (wrong?) about lying to oneself, but how do we go from there to the proposition that it is wrong to lie to someone else? After all, much of the peculiarity about lying to oneself consists in the fact that it seems not so much bad as downright self-contradictory, logically impossible, but that does not support the judgment that it is wrong to lie to another. I cannot marry myself, but that hardly makes it wrong to marry someone else.

Let us imagine a case in which you come as close as you can to lying to yourself: You arrange some operation, some fiddling with your brain that has no effect other than to cause you to believe a proposition you know to be false and also to forget entirely the prior history of how you came to believe that proposition. It seems to me that you do indeed harm yourself in such an operation. This is because a free and rational person wishes to have a certain relation to reality: as nearly perfect as possible. He wishes to build his conception of himself and the world and his conception of the good on the basis of truth. Now if he affirms that the truth is available for fiddling in order to accommodate either his picture of the world or his conception of the good, then this affirms that reality is dependent on what one wants, rather than what one wants being fundamentally constrained by what there is. Rationality is the respect for this fundamental constraint of truth. This is just another way of saying that the truth is prior to our plans and prospects and must be respected whatever our plans might be. What if the truth we "destroy" by this operation is a very trivial and irrelevant truth—the state of the weather in Bangkok on some particular day? There is still an injury to self, because the fiddler must have some purpose in his fiddling. If it is a substantive purpose, then the truth is in fact relevant to that purpose, and my argument holds. If it is just to show it can be done, then he is only trying to show he can do violence to his rationality— a kind of moral blasphemy. Well, what if it is a very *little* truth? Why, then, it is a very little injury he does himself—but that does not undermine my point.[3]

Now, when I lie to you, I do to you what you cannot actually do to yourself—brain-fiddling being only an approximation. The nature of the injury I would do to myself, if I could, explains why lying to you is to do you harm, indeed why it is wrong. The lie is an injury because it produces an effect (or seeks to) which a person as a moral agent should not wish to have produced in him, and thus it is as much an injury as any other effect which a moral agent would not wish to have produced upon his person. To be sure, some people may want to be lied to. That is a special problem; they are like people who want to suffer (not just are willing to risk) physical injury. In

---

[3]Distinguish from this the frequent and important instances where one refuses to receive certain truths: the man of honor who will not read scandalous accusations about another's private life, the judge who will not receive unauthorized information about a matter before him. These do not involve deliberate espousals of falsity. There is, after all, a proper domain of secret, private truths and of things which are none of our business.

general, then, I do not want you to lie to me in the same way that as a rational man I would not lie to myself if I could. But why does this make lying wrong and not merely bad?[4]

Lying is wrong because when I lie I set up a relation which is essentially exploitative. It violates the principle of respect, for I must affirm that the mind of another person is available to me in a way in which I cannot agree my mind would be available to him—for if I do so agree, then I would not expect my lie to be believed. When I lie, I am like a counterfeiter: I do not want the market flooded with counterfeit currency; I do not want to get back my own counterfeit bill. Moreover, in lying to you, I affirm such an unfairly unilateral principle in respect to an interest and capacity which is crucial, as crucial as physical integrity: your freedom and your rationality. When I do intentional physical harm, I say that your body, your person, is available for my purposes. When I lie, I lay claim to your mind.

Lying violates respect and is wrong, as is any breach of trust. Every lie is a broken promise, and the only reason this seems strained is that in lying the promise is made and broken at the same moment. Every lie necessarily implies—as does every assertion—an assurance, a warranty of its truth. The fact that the breach accompanies the making should, however, only strengthen the conclusion that this is wrong. If promise-breaking is wrong, then a lie must be wrong, since there cannot be the supervening factor of changed circumstances which may excuse breaches of promises to perform in the future.

The final one of the convergent strands that make up the wrong of lying is the shared, communal nature of language. This is what I think Kant had in mind when he argued that a lie does wrong "to men in general." If whether people stood behind their statements depended wholly on the particular circumstances of the utterance, then the whole point of communication would be undermined. For every utterance would simply be the occasion for an analysis of the total circumstances (speaker's and hearer's) in order to determine what, if anything, to make of the utterance. And though we do often

---

[4]It may be the case that every instance of any intentional injury to another person constitutes a wrongful relation (is wrong), but I am not prepared to argue that. I would rather examine the circumstances of this one kind of injury, lying, and show how that is wrong.

wonder and calculate whether a person is telling the truth, we do so from a baseline, a presumption that people do stand behind their statements. After all, the speaker surely depends on such a baseline. He wants us to think that he is telling the truth. Speech is a paradigm of communication, and all human relations are based on some form of communication. Our very ability to think, to conceptualize, is related to speech. Speech allows the social to penetrate the intimately personal. Perhaps that is why Kant's dicta seem to vacillate between two positions: lying as a social offense, and lying as an offense against oneself; the requirement of an intent to deceive another, and the insistence that the essence of the wrong is not injury to another but to humanity. Every lie violates the basic commitment to truth which stands behind the social fact of language.

I have already argued that bodily integrity bears a necessary relation to moral integrity, so that an attack upon bodily integrity is wrong, not just bad. The intimate *and* social nature of truth make the argument about lying stronger. For not only is the target aspect of the victim crucial to him as a moral agent but, by lying, we attack that target by a means which itself offends his moral nature; the means of attack are social means which can be said to belong as much to the victim as to his assailant. There is not only the attack at his moral vitals, but an attack with a weapon which belongs to him. Lying is, thus, a kind of treachery. (*Kind of* treachery? Why not treachery pure and simple?) It is as if we not only robbed a man of his treasure but in doing so used his own servants or family as our agents. That speech is our *common* property, that it belongs to the liar, his victim and all of us makes the matter if anything far worse.

So this is why lying is not only bad (a hurt), but wrong, why lying is wrong apart from or in addition to any other injury it does, and why lying seems at once an offense against the victim and against mankind in general, an offense against the liar himself, and against the abstract entity, truth. Whom do you injure when you pass a counterfeit bill?

What about little pointless lies? Do I really mean they are wrong? Well, yes, even a little lie is wrong, *if* it is a true piece of communication, an assertion of its own truth and not just a conventional way of asserting nothing at all or something else (as in the case of polite or diplomatic formulas). A little lie is a little wrong, but it is still something you must not do.

STUDY QUESTIONS

1. Why does Fried think that lying is both wrong and bad?
2. What does Fried mean when he says, "Truth, like respect, is a foundational value"? What does this imply for the nature of lying?
3. Lying must be deliberate. Can you lie to yourself? Could that be wrong? What is Fried's view?
4. What, precisely, is the effect of a lie on the person lied to? What is wrong with this effect? Give your own arguments in defense of the view that a serious lie is sometimes (never) justified.

SUGGESTED READINGS

Alighieri, Dante. *Inferno*.

Bloomfield, Morton. *The Seven Deadly Sins*. East Lansing, MI: Michigan State University Press, 1967.

Burton, Robert. *The Anatomy of Melancholy* (originally published 1621). New York: Vintage Press, 1977.

Freud, Sigmund. *Civilization and Its Discontents*. Edited and translated by James Strachey. New York: Norton, 1962.

Jacoby, Susan. *Wild Justice: The Evolution of Revenge*. New York: Harper and Row, 1983.

Ross, Edward Alsworth. *Sin and Society: An Analysis of Latter Day Iniquity* (originally published 1907). New York: Harper Torchbooks, 1973.

Chapter Five

WHY BE MORAL?

Philosophers have long affirmed the need for moral rules. But it is one thing to recognize the value of living in a community that acknowledges and enforces some rules of conduct, and quite another to answer the question, "Why should I be moral?" Here the stress is on *I*. Why should *I* not take advantage of the fact that most people respect the rules? One answer is that crime is risky, that it does not pay. But that is a dubious proposition. And what if I can disobey the moral law with impunity? Why should I not then selfishly ignore the moral rules that most people obey?

One doctrine recognizes the force of this question by affirming that there is indeed nothing wrong in being selfish and egoistic. The *locus classicus* for ethical egoism (as this doctrine is called) is the story, told by Plato, of Gyges, the shepherd who finds a ring that can render him invisible. Gyges uses the ring to murder the King and take over the government. The ethical egoist might well approve of Gyges' behavior. But Plato is sharply opposed to this doctrine; Plato believes he has refuted it in *The Republic* by showing that the selfish and unjust human being is flawed and unhappy.

A contemporary version of ethical egoism is here represented by Harry Browne's essay. Unsurprisingly, most moral philosophers reject ethical egoism. James Rachels argues that it is a morally perverse theory and seeks to expose its logical errors. Once the constraints of morality are thrown off, there seem to be no limits to what egoists may do, short of harming themselves in some way. As Rachels puts it, the ethical egoist who enjoys watching fires could consistently hold that burning down department stores full of people is "right for him."

Peter Singer tackles the question by arguing, as Plato did, that being moral is essential to happiness. Plato sought to persuade his readers that human well-functioning included moral behavior: To live immorally is to live an inferior existence that shuts out all light and health. Singer argues that amoral people (such as psychopaths) and selfish people (prudent egoists) lead dreary, boring, and meaningless lives.

The amoralist is a negative ideal type. The opposed ideal is the supermoralist or *Moral Saint*. The life of the moral saint is, in Susan Wolf's words, "dominated by the commitment to improving the welfare of others or of society as a whole." Wolf rejects the ideal of moral sainthood; the supermoralist has no time for art, amusements, and other "frivolities." Such people may be worthy, but they are undeveloped in important ways, and may well be dull and boring companions. Robert Adams sees them differently: Moral saints are fascinating, exciting people of great religious passion. He denies that they are totally committed to good works; on the contrary, the moral saint overflows with goodness and does not begrudge time spent on fun. A more concrete picture of moral sainthood is given by George Orwell's description of Mahatma Gandhi. Orwell's portrait is more closely in accord with Adams. But Orwell too has reservations about the ideal of moral sainthood—at least as Gandhi embodied it. Unquestionably, Gandhi was an extraordinary human being; he was inspirational and original. (Gandhi was the first to appreciate the political force of nonviolent resistance.) Yet, says Orwell, there was something inhuman and unattractive about Gandhi's sainthood.

Both the amoralist and the supermoralist are looked upon with suspicion by the majority of moral philosophers concerned with the bread-and-butter questions of what it means to live morally and decently. Such suspicion is perhaps a tribute to the powerful influence of Aristotle on moral philosophy. Aristotle thought of the ideally moral person as one who avoids extremes: the ideal is a moderate mode of behavior available to all well-meaning persons of good sense. That perspective on morality occupies the moral center; it is not easily put aside for long.

The Ring of Gyges

PLATO

Plato [*ca* 428–348 (or 347) B.C.], considered by many to be the greatest philosopher who ever lived, is the author of *The Republic* and other great dialogues. Plato's influence on Western culture is incalculable.

In *The Republic,* Plato describes the ideal society where justice reigns supreme. It opens with a scene in which Socrates confronts powerful arguments that disparage justice. We find Glaucon summarizing the views of those who think that justice is merely a compromise between the freedom to do wrong with impunity and to suffer wrong without redress. Because we would risk punitive action by doing wrong, we accept a limitation on our freedom. So justice is a kind of arrangement (like a system of traffic lights) that is not in itself valuable or desirable, but is put in place (to prevent accidents) to prevent our suffering wrong from others.

   The Ring of Gyges rendered the wearer invisible, enabling the shepherd Gyges to do as he pleased without fear of reprisal—and he used it to murder the King of Lydia. But did Gyges behave unnaturally? Glaucon argues that anyone in Gyges' situation would be a fool not to take full advantage of the power to do wrong with impunity. This suggests that justice is nothing more than a preventive device—only we lack the power that Gyges possessed.

THE RING OF GYGES From *The Republic* by Plato. Translated by G. M. A. Grube (Indianapolis, IN: Hackett, 1974), pp. 31–33. Reprinted by permission of the publisher.

In the remainder of *The Republic,* Socrates argues that the citizens of an ideal society would be just because they loved justice and not (merely) because they feared the consequences of suffering injustice.

GLAUCON (TO SOCRATES):
I have never heard from anyone the sort of defence of justice that I want to hear, proving that it is better than injustice. I want to hear it praised for itself, and I think I am most likely to hear this from you. Therefore I am going to speak at length in praise of the unjust life and in doing so I will show you the way I want to hear you denouncing injustice and praising justice. See whether you want to hear what I suggest.

SOCRATES:
I want it more than anything else. Indeed, what subject would a man of sense talk and hear about more often with enjoyment?

GLAUCON:
Splendid, then listen while I deal with the first subject I mentioned: the nature and origin of justice.

They say that to do wrong is naturally good, to be wronged is bad, but the suffering of injury so far exceeds in badness the good of inflicting it that when men have done wrong to each other and suffered it, and have had a taste of both, those who are unable to avoid the latter and practise the former decide that it is profitable to come to an agreement with each other neither to inflict injury nor to suffer it. As a result they begin to make laws and covenants, and the law's command they call lawful and just. This, they say, is the origin and essence of justice; it stands between the best and the worst, the best being to do wrong without paying the penalty and the worst to be wronged without the power of revenge. The just then is a mean between two extremes; it is welcomed and honoured because of men's lack of the power to do wrong. The man who has that power, the real man, would not make a compact with anyone not to inflict injury or suffer it. For him that would be madness. This then,

Socrates, is, according to their argument, the nature and origin of justice.

Even those who practise justice do so against their will because they lack the power to do wrong. This we could realize very clearly if we imagined ourselves granting to both the just and the unjust the freedom to do whatever they liked. We could then follow both of them and observe where their desires led them, and we would catch the just man redhanded travelling the same road as the unjust. The reason is the desire for undue gain which every organism by nature pursues as a good, but the law forcibly sidetracks him to honour equality. The freedom I just mentioned would most easily occur if these men had the power which they say the ancestor of the Lydian Gyges possessed. The story is that he was a shepherd in the service of the ruler of Lydia. There was a violent rainstorm and an earthquake which broke open the ground and created a chasm at the place where he was tending sheep. Seeing this and marvelling, he went down into it. He saw, besides many other wonders of which we are told, a hollow bronze horse. There were window-like openings in it; he climbed through them and caught sight of a corpse which seemed of more than human stature, wearing nothing but a ring of gold on its finger. This ring the shepherd put on and came out. He arrived at the usual monthly meeting which reported to the king on the state of the flocks, wearing the ring. As he was sitting among the others he happened to twist the hoop of the ring towards himself, to the inside of his hand, and as he did this he became invisible to those sitting near him and they went on talking as if he had gone. He marvelled at this and, fingering the ring, he turned the hoop outward again and became visible. Perceiving this he tested whether the ring had this power and so it happened: if he turned the hoop inwards he became invisible, but was visible when he turned it outwards. When he realized this, he at once arranged to become one of the messengers to the king. He went, committed adultery with the king's wife, attacked the king with her help, killed him, and took over the kingdom.

Now if there were two such rings, one worn by the just man, the other by the unjust, no one, as these people think, would be so incorruptible that he would stay on the path of justice or bring himself to keep away from other people's property and not touch it, when he could with impunity take whatever he wanted from the market, go into houses and have sexual relations with anyone he wanted, kill anyone, free all those he wished from prison, and do the other things which would make him like a god among men. His actions would be in no way different from those of the other and they would both follow the same path. This, some would say, is a great proof that no one is just willingly[1] but under compulsion, so that justice is not one's private good, since wherever either thought he could do wrong with impunity he would do so. Every man believes that injustice is much more profitable to himself than justice, and any exponent of this argument will say that he is right. The man who did not wish to do wrong with that opportunity, and did not touch other people's property, would be thought by those who knew it to be very foolish and miserable. They would praise him in public, thus deceiving one another, for fear of being wronged. So much for my second topic.

As for the choice between the lives we are discussing, we shall be able to make a correct judgment about it only if we put the most just man and

---

[1]This of course directly contradicts the famous Socratic paradox that no one is willingly bad and that people do wrong because they have not the knowledge to do right, which is virtue.

the most unjust man face to face; otherwise we cannot do so. By face to face I mean this: let us grant to the unjust the fullest degree of injustice and to the just the fullest justice, each being perfect in his own pursuit. First, the unjust man will act as clever craftsmen do—a top navigator for example or physician distinguishes what his craft can do and what it cannot; the former he will undertake, the latter he will pass by, and when he slips he can put things right. So the unjust man's correct attempts at wrongdoing must remain secret; the one who is caught must be considered a poor performer, for the extreme of injustice is to have a reputation for justice, and our perfectly unjust man must be granted perfection in injustice. We must not take this from him, but we must allow that, while committing the greatest crimes, he has provided himself with the greatest reputation for justice; if he makes a slip he must be able to put it right; he must be a sufficiently persuasive speaker if some wrongdoing of his is made public; he must be able to use force, where force is needed, with the help of his courage, his strength, and the friends and wealth with which he has provided himself.

Having described such a man, let us now in our argument put beside him the just man, simple as he is and noble, who, as Aeschylus put it, does not wish to appear just but to be so. We must take away his reputation, for a reputation for justice would bring him honour and rewards, and it would then not be clear whether he is what he is for justice's sake or for the sake of rewards and honour. We must strip him of everything except justice and make him the complete opposite of the other. Though he does no wrong, he must have the greatest reputation for wrongdoing so that he may be tested for justice by not weakening under ill repute and its consequences. Let him go his incorruptible way until death with a reputation for injustice throughout his

	life, just though he is, so that our two men may reach the extremes, one of justice, the other of injustice, and let them be judged as to which of the two is the happier.
SOCRATES:	Whew! My dear Glaucon, what a mighty scouring you have given those two characters, as if they were statues in a competition.

STUDY QUESTIONS

1. Glaucon presents a popular conception of the origin of justice as an agreement by each individual to refrain from doing wrong on condition that one is protected from wrongdoing by others. What does this "social contract theory" imply about the nature of justice?

2. Glaucon notes that the person who appears just to others but who is not just seems happier than one who appears unjust to others but who in fact is just. What challenge does this present to Socrates?

3. Gyges can do wrong with impunity. But we cannot. We are told that crime does not pay. But is this true? Suppose it is false. Can we still make out a case for being just and refraining from crime?

4. Glaucon's arguments seem to present Socrates with an insuperable problem since justice seems to be for "losers." How would you set about resolving the problem?

The Unselfishness Trap

HARRY BROWNE

Harry Browne is a journalist and lives in New York City. He is the author of *How I Found Freedom in an Unfree World* (1973).

Harry Browne objects to the view of many moralists that we should put others' happiness ahead of our own. If we were all to sacrifice our own happiness for the sake of others, eventually no one would be happy. "The unselfishness concept is a merry-go-round that has no ultimate purpose." Gift-givers and favor-doers presuppose that they know what will make others happy. Spending money on yourself is much more efficient (you know what makes you happy) and creates more happiness all around. Browne recommends "prudential generosity": Be sensitive to the needs and desires of those who might in turn benefit you. He grounds his views on psychological egoism, the doctrine that human beings act from a single motive—self-love. "Why should you feel guilty for seeking your own happiness when that's what everyone else is doing too?"

The Unselfishness Trap is the belief that you must put the happiness of others ahead of your own.

Unselfishness is a very popular ideal, one that's been honored

THE UNSELFISHNESS TRAP From *How I Found Freedom in an Unfree World* by Harry Browne. Reprinted by permission of Macmillan Publishing Company. Copyright © 1973 by Harry Browne.

throughout recorded history. Wherever you turn, you find encouragement to put the happiness of others ahead of your own—to do what's best for the world, not for yourself.

If the ideal is sound, there must be something unworthy in seeking to live your life as you want to live it.

So perhaps we should look more closely at the subject—to see if the ideal *is* sound. For if you attempt to be free, we can assume that someone's going to consider that to be selfish.

We saw in Chapter 2 that each person always acts in ways he believes will make him feel good or will remove discomfort from his life. Because everyone is different from everyone else, each individual goes about it in his own way.

One man devotes his life to helping the poor. Another one lies and steals. Still another person tries to create better products and services for which he hopes to be paid handsomely. One woman devotes herself to her husband and children. Another one seeks a career as a singer.

In every case, the ultimate motivation has been the same. Each person is doing what *he* believes will assure his happiness. What varies between them is the *means* each has chosen to gain his happiness.

We could divide them into two groups labeled "selfish" and "unselfish," but I don't think that would prove anything. For the thief and the humanitarian each have the same motive—to do what he believes will make him feel good.

In fact, we can't avoid a very significant conclusion: *Everyone is selfish*. Selfishness isn't really an issue, because everyone selfishly seeks his own happiness.

What we need to examine, however, are the means various people choose to achieve their happiness. Unfortunately, some people oversimplify the matter by assuming that there are only two basic means; sacrifice yourself for others or make them sacrifice for you. Happily, there's a third way that can produce better consequences than either of those two.

A Better World?

Let's look first at the ideal of living for the benefit of others. It's often said that it would be a better world if everyone were unselfish. But would it be?

If it were somehow possible for everyone to give up his own happiness, what would be the result? Let's carry it to its logical conclusion and see what we find.

To visualize it, let's imagine that happiness is symbolized by a big red rubber ball. I have the ball in my hands—meaning that I hold the ability to be happy. But since I'm not going to be selfish, I quickly pass the ball to you. I've given up my happiness for you.

What will you do? Since you're not selfish either, you won't keep the ball; you'll quickly pass it on to your next-door neighbor. But he doesn't want to be selfish either, so he passes it to his wife, who likewise gives it to her children.

The children have been taught the virtue of unselfishness, so they pass it to playmates, who pass it to parents, who pass it to neighbors, and on and on and on.

I think we can stop the analogy at this point and ask what's been accomplished by all this effort. Who's better off for these demonstrations of pure unselfishness?

How would it be a better world if everyone acted that way? Whom would we be unselfish for? There would have to be a selfish person who would receive, accept, and enjoy the benefits of our unselfishness for there to be any purpose to it. But that selfish person (the object of our generosity) would be living by lower standards than we do.

For a more practical example, what is achieved by the parent who "sacrifices" himself for his children, who in turn are expected to sacrifice themselves for *their* children, etc.? The unselfishness concept is a merry-go-round that has no ultimate purpose. No one's self-interest is enhanced by the continual relaying of gifts from one person to another to another.

Perhaps most people have never carried the concept of unselfishness to this logical conclusion. If they did, they might reconsider their pleas for an unselfish world.

Negative Choices

But, unfortunately, the pleas continue, and they're a very real part of your life. In seeking your own freedom and happiness, you have to deal with those who tell you that you shouldn't put yourself first. That creates a situation in which you're pressured to act negatively—

to put aside your plans and desires in order to avoid the condemnation of others.

As I've said before, one of the characteristics of a free man is that he's usually choosing positively—deciding which of several alternatives would make him the happiest; while the average person, most of the time, is choosing which of two or three alternatives will cause him the least discomfort.

When the reason for your actions is to avoid being called "selfish" you're making a negative decision and thereby restricting the possibilities for your own happiness.

You're in the Unselfishness Trap if you regretfully pay for your aunt's surgery with the money you'd saved for a new car, or if you sadly give up the vacation you'd looked forward to in order to help a sick neighbor.

You're in the trap if you feel you're *required* to give part of your income to the poor, or if you think that your country, community, or family has first claim on your time, energy, or money.

You're in the Unselfishness Trap any time you make negative choices that are designed to avoid being called "selfish."

It isn't that no one else is important. You might have a self-interest in someone's well-being, and giving a gift can be a gratifying expression of the affection you feel for him. But you're in the trap if you do such things in order to appear unselfish.

Helping Others

There *is* an understandable urge to give to those who are important and close to you. However, that leads many people to think that indiscriminate giving is the key to one's own happiness. They say that the way to be happy is to make others happy; get your glow by basking in the glow you've created for someone else.

It's important to identify that as a personal opinion. If someone says that giving is the key to happiness, isn't he saying that's the key to *his* happiness?

I think we can carry the question further, however, and determine how efficient such a policy might be. The suggestion to be a giver presupposes that you're able to judge what will make someone else happy. And experience has taught me to be a bit humble about assuming what makes others happy.

My landlady once brought me a piece of her freshly baked cake because she wanted to do me a favor. Unfortunately, it happened to be a kind of cake that was distasteful to me. I won't try to describe the various ways I tried to get the cake plate back to her without being confronted with a request for my judgment of her cake. It's sufficient to say that her well-intentioned favor interfered with my own plans.

And now, whenever I'm sure I know what someone else "needs," I remember that incident and back off a little. There's no way that one person can read the mind of another to know all his plans, goals, and tastes.

You may know a great deal about the desires of your intimate friends. But *indiscriminate* gift-giving and favor-doing is usually a waste of resources—or, worse, it can upset the well-laid plans of the receiver.

When you give to someone else, you might provide something he values—but probably not the thing he considers most important. If you expend those resources for *yourself,* you automatically devote them to what you consider to be most important. The time or money you've spent will most likely create more happiness that way.

If your purpose is to make someone happy, you're most apt to succeed if you make yourself the object. You'll never know another person more than a fraction as well as you can know yourself.

Do you want to make someone happy? Go to it—use your talents and your insight and benevolence to bestow riches of happiness upon the one person you understand well enough to do it efficiently— yourself. I guarantee that you'll get more genuine appreciation from yourself than from anyone else.

Give to you.

Support your local self.

Alternatives

As I indicated earlier in this chapter, it's too often assumed that there are only two alternatives: (1) sacrifice your interests for the benefit of others; or (2) make others sacrifice their interests for you. If nothing else were possible, it would indeed be a grim world.

Fortunately, there's more to the world than that. Because desires vary from person to person, it's possible to create exchanges between individuals in which both parties benefit.

For example, if you buy a house, you do so because you'd rather

455

have the house than the money involved. But the seller's desire is different—he'd rather have the money than the house. When the sale is completed, each of you has received something of greater value than what you gave up—otherwise you wouldn't have entered the exchange. Who, then, has had to sacrifice for the other?

In the same way, your daily life is made up of dozens of such exchanges—small and large transactions in which each party gets something he values more than what he gives up. The exchange doesn't have to involve money; you may be spending time, attention, or effort in exchange for something you value.

Mutually beneficial relationships are possible when desires are compatible. Sometimes the desires are the same—like going to a movie together. Sometimes the desires are different—like trading your money for someone's house. In either case, it's the *compatibility* of the desires that makes the exchange possible.

No sacrifice is necessary when desires are compatible. So it makes sense to seek out people with whom you can have mutually beneficial relationships.

Often the "unselfishness" issue arises only because two people with nothing in common are trying to get along together—such as a man who likes bowling and hates opera married to a woman whose tastes are the opposite. If they're to do things together, one must "sacrifice" his pleasure for the other. So each might try to encourage the other to be "unselfish."

If they were compatible, the issue wouldn't arise because each would be pleasing the other by doing what was in his own self-interest.

An efficiently selfish person *is* sensitive to the needs and desires of others. But he doesn't consider those desires to be demands upon him. Rather, he sees them as *opportunities*—potential exchanges that might be beneficial to him. He identifies desires in others so that he can decide if exchanges with them will help him get what he wants.

He doesn't sacrifice himself for others, nor does he expect others to be sacrificed for him. He takes the third alternative—he finds relationships that are mutually beneficial so that no sacrifice is required.

Please Yourself

Everyone is selfish; everyone is doing what he believes will make himself happier. The recognition of that can take most of the sting out of accusations that you're being "selfish." Why should you feel guilty for seeking your own happiness when that's what everyone else is doing, too?

The demand that you be unselfish can be motivated by any number of reasons: that you'd help create a better world, that you have a moral obligation to be unselfish, that you give up your happiness to the selfishness of someone else, or that the person demanding it has just never thought it out.

Whatever the reason, you're not likely to convince such a person to stop his demands. But it will create much less pressure on you if you realize that it's *his* selfish reason. And you can eliminate the problem entirely by looking for more compatible companions.

To find constant, profound happiness requires that you be free to seek the gratification of your own desires. It means making positive choices.

If you slip into the Unselfishness Trap, you'll spend a good part of your time making negative choices—trying to avoid the censure of those who tell you not to think of yourself. You won't have time to be free.

If someone finds happiness by doing "good works" for others, let him. That doesn't mean that's the best way for you to find happiness.

And when someone accuses you of being selfish, just remember that he's only upset because you aren't doing what *he* selfishly wants you to do.

STUDY QUESTIONS

1. Browne claims that when we behave unselfishly we, more often than not, sacrifice our own happiness. Do you agree?
2. Browne says that everyone is selfish because we all do what we believe will make us feel good. Critics of egoism such as James Rachels claim that what makes an act selfish or unselfish is its *object*, not simply that it makes you feel good. If you are the sort of person who feels good *when you help others*, then you are unselfish. If you feel good only *when helping yourself*, then you are selfish. Critically discuss the issue that divides Rachels and Browne and assess their respective positions.
3. Medical researchers appear to have discovered some astonishing correlations between behaving unselfishly and a higher

resistance to some major diseases. What implications might such a finding have for ethical egoism?

Egoism and Moral Skepticism

JAMES RACHELS

James Rachels (b. 1941) is Dean of the School of Humanities at the University of Alabama. He is editor of several books, including *Understanding Moral Philosophy* (1976) and *Moral Problems: A Collection of Philosophical Essays* (1979).

Psychological egoism is the view that human beings always act from a single motive: self-love. Ethical egoism is the moral theory that says we *ought* to act only from self-love. Rachels tries to expose the logical and moral weaknesses of both theories. For example, he challenges the view often proffered by defenders of psychological egoism: We are selfish because we *always do what we want to do.* One person *wants* to visit and cheer up a lonely elderly neighbor; another wants to rob and terrorize his neighbor. Both do what they want; both are selfish. Rachels points out that what makes an act selfish is its *object,* not that you want to do it. If the object of most of your actions is to please yourself, then you are selfish; if you often want to please others, you are kind. If you want to harm them, you are malicious. Rachels also argues that both psychological and ethical egoisms rest upon a distorted view of human nature. Most of us are sympathetic

EGOISM AND MORAL SKEPTICISM From *A New Introduction to Philosophy* by James Rachels. Edited by Steven M. Cahn. Copyright © 1971 by Steven M. Cahn. Reprinted by permission of Steven M. Cahn.

and care about the well-being of others. The reason we do not burn down a department store is not because it might not be in our long-range best interest to do so, but because "people might be burned to death."

I

Our ordinary thinking about morality is full of assumptions that we almost never question. We assume, for example, that we have an obligation to consider the welfare of other people when we decide what actions to perform or what rules to obey; we think that we must refrain from acting in ways harmful to others, and that we must respect their rights and interests as well as our own. We also assume that people are in fact capable of being motivated by such considerations, that is, that people are not wholly selfish and that they do sometimes act in the interests of others.

Both of these assumptions have come under attack by moral skeptics, as long ago as by Glaucon in Book II of Plato's *Republic*. Glaucon recalls the legend of Gyges, a shepherd who was said to have found a magic ring in a fissure opened by an earthquake. The ring would make its wearer invisible and thus would enable him to go anywhere and do anything undetected. Gyges used the power of the ring to gain entry to the Royal Palace where he seduced the Queen, murdered the King, and subsequently seized the throne. Now Glaucon asks us to determine that there are two such rings, one given to a man of virtue and one given to a rogue. The rogue, of course, will use his ring unscrupulously and do anything necessary to increase his own wealth and power. He will recognize no moral constraints on his conduct, and, since the cloak of invisibility will protect him from discovery, he can do anything he pleases without fear of reprisal. So there will be no end to the mischief he will do. But how will the so-called virtuous man behave? Glaucon suggests that he will behave no better than the rogue: "No one, it is commonly believed, would have such iron strength of mind as to stand fast in doing right or keep his hands off other men's goods, when he could go to the market-place and fearlessly help himself to anything he wanted, enter houses and sleep with any woman he chose, set prisoners free and kill men at his pleasure, and in a word go about among men with the powers of a god. He would behave no better than the other; both would take the same course."[1] Moreover, why shouldn't he? Once he is freed from the fear of reprisal, why shouldn't a man simply do what he pleases, or what he thinks is best for himself? What reason is there for him to continue being "moral" when it is clearly not to his own advantage to do so?

These skeptical views suggested by Glaucon have come to be known as *psychological egoism* and *ethical egoism* respectively. Psychological egoism is the view that all men are selfish in everything that they do, that is, that the only motive from which anyone ever acts is self-interest. On this view, even when men are acting in ways apparently calculated to benefit others, they are actually motivated by the belief that acting in this way is to their own advantage, and if they did not believe this, they would not be doing that action. Ethical egoism is, by contrast, a normative view about how men *ought* to act. It is the view that, regardless of how men do in fact behave, they have no obligation to do anything except what is in their own interests. According to the ethical egoist, a person is always justified in doing whatever is in his own interest, regardless of the effect on others.

Clearly, if either of these views is correct, then "the moral institution of life" (to use Butler's well-turned phrase) is very different than what we normally think. The majority of mankind is grossly deceived about what is, or ought to be, the case, where morals are concerned.

II

Psychological egoism seems to fly in the face of the facts. We are tempted to say, "Of course people act unselfishly all the time. For example, Smith gives up a trip to the country, which he would have enjoyed very much, in order to stay behind and help a friend with his studies, which is a miserable way to pass the time. This is a perfectly clear case of unselfish behavior, and if the psychological egoist thinks that such cases do not occur, then he is just mistaken." Given such obvious instances of "unselfish behavior," what reply can the egoist make? There are two general arguments by which he might try to show that all actions, including those such as the one just outlined, are in fact motivated by self-interest. Let us examine these in turn:

---

[1] *The Republic of Plato,* trans. F. M. Cornford (Oxford, 1941), p. 45.

A. The first argument goes as follows. If we describe one person's action as selfish, and another person's action as unselfish, we are overlooking the crucial fact that in both cases, assuming that the action is done voluntarily, *the agent is merely doing what he most wants to do.* If Smith stays behind to help his friend, that only shows that he wanted to help his friend more than he wanted to go to the country. And why should he be praised for his "unselfishness" when he is only doing what he wants to do? He cannot be said to be acting unselfishly.

This argument is so bad that it would not deserve to be taken seriously except for the fact that so many otherwise intelligent people have been taken in by it. First, the argument rests on the premise that people never voluntarily do anything except what they want to do. But this is patently false; there are at least two classes of actions that are exceptions to this generalization. One is the set of actions which we may not want to do, but which we do anyway as a means to an end which we want to achieve; for example, going to the dentist in order to stop a toothache, or going to work every day in order to be able to draw our pay at the end of the month. These cases may be regarded as consistent with the spirit of the egoist argument, however, since the ends mentioned are wanted by the agent. But the other set of actions are those which we do, not because we want to, nor even because there is an end which we want to achieve, but because we feel ourselves *under an obligation* to do them. For example, someone may do something because he has promised to do it, and thus feels obligated, even though he does not want to do it. It is sometimes suggested that in such cases we do the action, because, after all, we want to keep our promises; so, even here, we are doing what we want. However, this dodge will not work: If I have promised to do something, and if I do not want to do it, then it is simply false to say that I want to keep my promise. In such cases we feel a conflict precisely because we do not want to do what we feel obligated to do. It is reasonable to think that Smith's action falls roughly into this second category: He might stay behind, not because he wants to, but because he feels that his friend needs help.

But suppose we were to concede, for the sake of the argument, that all voluntary action is motivated by the agent's wants, or at least that Smith is so motivated. Even if these were granted, it would not follow that Smith is acting selfishly or from self-interest. For if Smith wants to do something that will help his friend, even when it means forgoing his own enjoyments, that is precisely what makes him *un-selfish*. What else could unselfishness be, if not wanting to help others? Another way to put the same point is to say that it is the *object* of a want that determines whether it is selfish or not. The mere fact that I am acting on *my* wants does not mean that I am acting selfishly; that depends on *what it is* that I want. If I want only my own good, and care nothing for others, then I am selfish; but if I also want other people to be well-off and happy, and if I act on *that* desire, then my action is not selfish. So much for this argument.

B. The second argument for psychological egoism is this. Since so-called unselfish actions always produce a sense of self-satisfaction in the agent,[2] and since this sense of satisfaction is a pleasant state of consciousness, it follows that the point of the action is really to achieve a pleasant state of consciousness, rather than bring about any good for othe.s. Therefore, the action is "unselfish" only at a superficial level of analysis. Smith will feel much better with himself for having stayed to help his friend—if he had gone to the country, he would have felt terrible about it—and that is the real point of the action. According to a well-known story, this argument was once expressed by Abraham Lincoln:

> Mr. Lincoln once remarked to a fellow-passenger on an old-time mud-coach that all men were prompted by selfishness in doing good. His fellow-passenger was antagonizing this position when they were passing over a corduroy bridge that spanned a slough. As they crossed this bridge they espied an old razor-backed sow on the bank making a terrible noise because her pigs had got into the slough and were in danger of drowning. As the old coach began to climb the hill, Mr. Lincoln called out, "Driver, can't you stop just a moment?" Then Mr. Lincoln jumped out, ran back, and lifted the little pigs out of the mud and water and placed them on the bank. When he returned, his companion remarked: "Now, Abe, where does selfishness come in on this little episode?" "Why, bless your soul, Ed, that was the very essence of selfishness. I should have had no peace of mind all day had I gone on and left that suffering old sow worrying over those pigs. I did it to get peace of mind, don't you see?"[3]

---

[2]Or, as it is sometimes said, "It gives him a clear conscience," or "He couldn't sleep at night if he had done otherwise," or "He would have been ashamed of himself for not doing it," and so on.

This argument suffers from defects similar to the previous one. Why should we think that merely because someone derives satisfaction from helping others this makes him selfish? Isn't the unselfish man precisely the one who *does* derive satisfaction from helping others, while the selfish man does not? If Lincoln "got peace of mind" from rescuing the piglets, does this show him to be selfish, or, on the contrary, doesn't it show him to be compassionate and good-hearted? (If a man were truly selfish, why should it bother his conscience that *others* suffer—much less pigs?) Similarly, it is nothing more than shabby sophistry to say, because Smith takes satisfaction in helping his friend, that he is behaving selfishly. If we say this rapidly, while thinking about something else, perhaps it will sound all right; but if we speak slowly, and pay attention to what we are saying, it sounds plain silly.

Moreover, suppose we ask *why* Smith derives satisfaction from helping his friend. The answer will be, it is because Smith cares for him and wants him to succeed. If Smith did not have these concerns, then he would take no pleasure in assisting him; and these concerns, as we have already seen, are the marks of unselfishness, not selfishness. To put the point more generally: If we have a positive attitude toward the attainment of some goal, then we may derive satisfaction from attaining that goal. But the *object* of our attitude is *the attainment of that goal;* and we must want to attain the goal *before* we can find any satisfaction in it. We do not, in other words, desire some sort of "pleasurable consciousness" and then try to figure out how to achieve it; rather, we desire all sorts of different things—money, a new fishing-boat, to be a better chessplayer, to get a promotion in our work, etc.—and because we desire these things, we derive satisfaction from attaining them. And so, if someone desires the welfare and happiness of another person, he will derive satisfaction from that; but this does not mean that this satisfaction is the object of his desire, or that he is in any way selfish on account of it.

It is a measure of the weakness of psychological egoism that these insupportable arguments are the ones most often advanced in its favor. Why, then, should anyone ever have thought it a true view? Perhaps because of a desire for theoretical simplicity: In thinking

---

[3]Frank C. Sharp, *Ethics* (New York, 1928), pp. 74–75. Quoted from the Springfield (Ill.) *Monitor* in the *Outlook*, vol. 56, p. 1059.

about human conduct, it would be nice if there were some simple formula that would unite the diverse phenomena of human behavior under a single explanatory principle, just as simple formulae in physics bring together a great many apparently different phenomena. And since it is obvious that self-regard is an overwhelmingly important factor in motivation, it is only natural to wonder whether all motivation might not be explained in these terms. But the answer is clearly no; while a great many human actions are motivated entirely or in part by self-interest, only by a deliberate distortion of the facts can we say that all conduct is so motivated. This will be clear, I think, if we correct three confusions which are commonplace. The exposure of these confusions will remove the last traces of plausibility from the psychological egoist thesis.

The first is the confusion of selfishness with self-interest. The two are clearly not the same. If I see a physician when I am feeling poorly, I am acting in my own interest but no one would think of calling me "selfish" on account of it. Similarly, brushing my teeth, working hard at my job, and obeying the law are all in my self-interest but none of these are examples of selfish conduct. This is because selfish behavior is behavior that ignores the interests of others, in circumstances in which their interests ought not to be ignored. This concept has a definite evaluative flavor; to call someone "selfish" is not just to describe his action but to condemn it. Thus, you would not call me selfish for eating a normal meal in normal circumstances (although it may surely be in my self-interest); but you would call me selfish for hoarding food while others about are starving.

The second confusion is the assumption that every action is done *either* from self-interest or from other-regarding motives. Thus, the egoist concludes that if there is no such thing as genuine altruism then all actions must be done from self-interest. But this is certainly a false dichotomy. The man who continues to smoke cigarettes, even after learning about the connection between smoking and cancer, is surely not acting from self-interest, not even by his own standards—self-interest would dictate that he quit smoking at once—and he is not acting altruistically either. He *is,* no doubt, smoking for the pleasure of it, but all that this shows is that undisciplined pleasure-seeking and acting from self-interest are very different. This is what led Butler to remark that "The thing to be lamented is, not that men have so great regard to their own good or interest in the present world, for they have not enough."[4]

464

The last two paragraphs show (*a*) that it is false that all actions are selfish, and (*b*) that it is false that all actions are done out of self-interest. And it should be noted that these two points can be made, and were, without any appeal to putative examples of altruism.

The third confusion is the common but false assumption that a concern for one's own welfare is incompatible with any genuine concern for the welfare of others. Thus, since it is obvious that everyone (or very nearly everyone) does desire his own well-being, it might be thought that no one can really be concerned with others. But again, this is false. There is no inconsistency in desiring that everyone, including oneself *and* others, be well-off and happy. To be sure, it may happen on occasion that our own interests conflict with the interests of others, and in these cases we will have to make hard choices. But even in these cases we might sometimes opt for the interests of others, especially when the others involved are our family or friends. But more importantly, not all cases are like this: Sometimes we are able to promote the welfare of others when our own interests are not involved at all. In these cases not even the strongest self-regard need prevent us from acting considerately toward others.

Once these confusions are cleared away, it seems to me obvious enough that there is no reason whatever to accept psychological egoism. On the contrary, if we simply observe people's behavior with an open mind, we may find that a great deal of it is motivated by self-regard, but by no means all of it; and that there is no reason to deny that "the moral institution of life" can include a place for the virtue of beneficence.[5]

III

The ethical egoist would say at this point, "Of course it is possible for people to act altruistically, and perhaps many people do act that way—but there is no reason why they *should* do so. A person is under no obligation to do anything except what is in his own interests."[6]

---

[4]*The Works of Joseph Butler*, ed. W. E. Gladstone (Oxford, 1896), vol. 2, p. 26.

[5]The capacity for altruistic behavior is not unique to human beings. Some interesting experiments with rhesus monkeys have shown that these animals will refrain from operating a device for securing food if this causes other animals to suffer pain. See Masserman, Wechkin, and Terris, "'Altruistic Behavior in Rhesus Monkeys," *The American Journal of Psychiatry*, vol. 121 (1964), 584–585.

[6]I take this to be the view of Ayn Rand, insofar as I understand her confusing doctrine.

This is really quite a radical doctrine. Suppose I have an urge to set fire to some public building (say, a department store) just for the fascination of watching the spectacular blaze: According to this view, the fact that several people might be burned to death provides no reason whatever why I should not do it. After all, this only concerns *their* welfare, not my own, and according to the ethical egoist the only person I need think of is myself.

Some might deny that ethical egoism has any such monstrous consequences. They would point out that it is really to my own advantage not to set the fire—for, if I do that I may be caught and put into prison (unlike Gyges, I have no magic ring for protection). Moreover, even if I could avoid being caught it is still to my advantage to respect the rights and interests of others, for it is to my advantage to live in a society in which people's rights and interests are respected. Only in such a society can I live a happy and secure life; so, in acting kindly toward others, I would merely be doing my part to create and maintain the sort of society which it is to my advantage to have.[7] Therefore, it is said, the egoist would not be such a bad man; he would be as kindly and considerate as anyone else, because he would see that it is to his own advantage to be kindly and considerate.

This is a seductive line of thought, but it seems to me mistaken. Certainly it is to everyone's advantage (including the egoist's) to preserve a stable society where people's interests are generally protected. But there is no reason for the egoist to think that merely because *he* will not honor the rules of the social game, decent society will collapse. For the vast majority of people are not egoists, and there is no reason to think that they will be converted by his example—especially if he is discreet and does not unduly flaunt his style of life. What this line of reasoning shows is not that the egoist himself must act benevolently, but that he must encourage *others* to do so. He must take care to conceal from public view his own self-centered method of decision-making, and urge others to act on precepts very different from those on which he is willing to act.

The rational egoist, then, cannot advocate that egoism be universally adopted by everyone. For he wants a world in which his own interests are maximized; and if other people adopted the egoistic

---

[7]*Cf.* Thomas Hobbes, *Leviathan* (London, 1651), chap. 17.

policy of pursuing their own interests to the exclusion of his interest, as he pursues his interest to the exclusion of theirs, then such a world would be impossible. So he himself will be an egoist, but he will want others to be altruists.

This brings us to what is perhaps the most popular "refutation" of ethical egoism current among philosophical writers—the argument that ethical egoism is at bottom inconsistent because it cannot be universalized.[8] The argument goes like this:

To say that any action or policy of action is *right* (or that it *ought* to be adopted) entails that it is right for *anyone* in the same sort of circumstances. I cannot, for example, say that it is right for me to lie to you, and yet object when you lie to me (provided, of course, that the circumstances are the same). I cannot hold that it is all right for me to drink your beer and then complain when you drink mine. This is just the requirement that we be consistent in our evaluations; it is a requirement of logic. Now it is said that ethical egoism cannot meet this requirement because, as we have already seen, the egoist would not want others to act in the same way that he acts. Moreover, suppose he *did* advocate the universal adoption of egoistic policies: he would be saying to Peter, "You ought to pursue your own interests even if it means destroying Paul"; and he would be saying to Paul, "You ought to pursue your own interests even if it means destroying Peter." The attitudes expressed in these two recommendations seem clearly inconsistent—he is urging the advancement of Peter's interest at one moment, and countenancing their defeat at the next. Therefore, the argument goes, there is no way to maintain the doctrine of ethical egoism as a consistent view about how we ought to act. We will fall into inconsistency whenever we try.

What are we to make of this argument? Are we to conclude that ethical egoism has been refuted? Such a conclusion, I think, would be unwarranted; for I think that we can show, contrary to this argument, how ethical egoism can be maintained consistently. We need only to interpret the egoist's position in a sympathetic way: We should say that he has in mind a certain kind of world which he would prefer over all others; it would be a world in which his own interests were maximized, regardless of the effects on other people.

8See, for example, Brian Medlin, "Ultimate Principles and Ethical Egoism," *Australasian Journal of Philosophy,* vol. 35 (1957), 111–118; and D. H. Monro, *Empiricism and Ethics* (Cambridge, 1967), chap. 16.

The egoist's primary policy of action, then, would be to act in such a way as to bring about, as nearly as possible, this sort of world. Regardless of however morally reprehensible we might find it, there is nothing *inconsistent* in someone's adopting this as his ideal and acting in a way calculated to bring it about. And if someone did adopt this as his ideal, then he would advocate universal altruism; as we have already seen, he would want other people to be altruists. So if he advocates any principles of conduct for the general public, they will be altruistic principles. This would not be inconsistent; on the contrary, it would be perfectly consistent with his goal of creating a world in which his own interests are maximized. To be sure, he would have to be deceitful; in order to secure the good will of others, and a favorable hearing for his exhortations to altruism, he would have to pretend that he was himself prepared to accept altruistic principles. But again, that would be all right; from the egoist's point of view, this would merely be a matter of adopting the necessary means to the achievement of his goal—and while we might not approve of this, there is nothing inconsistent about it. Again, it might be said, "He advocates one thing, but does another. Surely *that's* inconsistent." But it is not; for what he advocates and what he does are both calculated as means to an end (the *same* end, we might note); and as such, he is doing what is rationally required in each case. Therefore, contrary to the previous argument, there is nothing inconsistent in the ethical egoist's view. He cannot be refuted by the claim that he contradicts himself.

Is there, then, no way to refute the ethical egoist? If by "refute" we mean show that he has made some *logical* error, the answer is that there is not. However, there is something more that can be said. The egoist challenge to our ordinary moral convictions amounts to a demand for an explanation of why we should adopt certain policies of action, namely policies in which the good of others is given importance. We can give an answer to this demand, albeit an indirect one. The reason one ought not to do actions that would hurt other people is: Other people would be hurt. The reason one ought to do actions that would benefit other people is: Other people would be benefited. This may at first seem like a piece of philosophical sleight-of-hand, but it is not. The point is that the welfare of human beings is something that most of us value *for its own sake,* and not merely for the sake of something else. Therefore, when *further* reasons are demanded for valuing the welfare of human beings, we cannot point to anything further to satisfy this demand. It is not that we have no reason for pursuing these policies, but that our reason *is* that these policies are for the good of human beings.

So if we are asked, "Why shouldn't I set fire to this department store?" one answer would be, "Because if you do, people may be burned to death." This is a complete, sufficient reason which does not require qualification or supplementation of any sort. If someone seriously wants to know why this action shouldn't be done, that's the reason. If we are pressed further and asked the skeptical question, "But why shouldn't I do actions that will harm others?" we may not know what to say—but this is because the questioner has included in his question the very answer we would like to give: "Why shouldn't you do actions that will harm others? Because doing those actions would harm others." The egoist, no doubt, will not be happy with this. He will protest that *we* may accept this as a reason, but *he* does not. And here the argument stops: There are limits to what can be accomplished by argument, and if the egoist really doesn't care about other people—if he honestly doesn't care whether they are helped or hurt by his actions—then we have reached those limits. If we want to persuade him to act decently toward his fellow humans, we will have to make our appeal to such other attitudes as he does possess, by threats, bribes, or other cajolery. That is all that we can do.

Though some may find this situation distressing (we would like to be able to show that the egoist is just *wrong*), it holds no embarrassment for common morality. What we have come up against is simply a fundamental requirement of rational action, namely, that the existence of reasons for action always depends on the prior existence of certain attitudes in the agent. For example, the fact that a certain course of action would make the agent a lot of money is a reason for doing it only if the agent wants to make money; the fact that practicing at chess makes one a better player is a reason for practicing only if one wants to be a better player; and so on. Similarly, the fact that a certain action would help the agent is a reason for doing the action only if the agent cares about his own welfare, and the fact that an action would help others is a reason for doing it only if the agent cares about others. In this respect ethical egoism and what we might call ethical altruism are in exactly the same fix: Both require that the agent *care* about himself, or other people, before they can get started.

So a nonegoist will accept "It would harm another person" as a reason not to do an action simply because he cares about what happens to that other person. When the egoist says that he does *not* accept that as a reason, he is saying something quite extraordinary. He is saying that he has no affection for friends or family, that he never feels pity or compassion, that he is the sort of person who can look on scenes of human misery with complete indifference, so long as he is not the one suffering. Genuine egoists, people who really don't care at all about anyone than themselves, are rare. It is important to keep this in mind when thinking about ethical egoism; it is easy to forget just how fundamental to human psychological makeup the feeling of sympathy is. Indeed, a man without any sympathy at all would scarcely be recognizable as a man; and that is what makes ethical egoism such a disturbing doctrine in the first place.

IV

There are, of course, many different ways in which the skeptic might challenge the assumptions underlying our moral practice. In this essay I have discussed only two of them, the two put forward by Glaucon in the passage that I cited from Plato's *Republic*. It is important that the assumptions underlying our moral practice should not be confused with particular judgments made within that practice. To defend one is not to defend the other. We may assume—quite properly, if my analysis has been correct—that the virtue of beneficence does, and indeed should, occupy an important place in "the moral institution of life"; and yet we may make constant and miserable errors when it comes to judging when and in what ways this virtue is to be exercised. Even worse, we may often be able to make accurate moral judgments, and know what we ought to do, but not do it. For these ills, philosophy alone is not the cure.

.

STUDY QUESTIONS

1. The great Renaissance philosopher Thomas Hobbes was a proponent of psychological egoism. Someone once saw him giving money to a beggar and asked if this kindly gesture did not prove that psychological egoism was wrong. Hobbes replied that his

action was indeed self-interested because helping beggars made him feel good. Evaluate Hobbes's riposte in light of Rachels's discussion.

2. If you found the Ring of Gyges and no longer needed to appear to abide by moral rules, do you think you would behave as Gyges did? Do you think that other controls would prevent you from becoming amoral?

3. What is Rachels's strongest argument against psychological egoism? Against ethical egoism? Are Rachels's arguments persuasive?

4. The psychological egoist says that self-love motivates all human action. A number of philosophers have argued that self-hate, altruism, and malice also motivate human beings. Who do you think is right?

Why Not Murder?

FYODOR DOSTOYEVSKI

Fyodor Dostoyevski (1821–1881) was one of the greatest Russian novelists. His stories are both dramatic and philosophical. Among his most famous works are *The House of the Dead* (1860), *Crime and Punishment* (1866), *The Idiot* (1867), and *The Brothers Karamazov* (1879).

The "criminal mind" fascinated Fyodor Dostoyevski. The crime in *Crime and Punishment* is murder. The victim is a wealthy and heartless old woman who "deserves to die." Raskolnikov is not so much interested in getting her money as he is in righting the injustice of the fact that she possesses it while so many other people suffer want. Dostoyevski suggests that Raskolnikov may even distribute the money once he gets it. Of course murder is a

WHY NOT MURDER? From *Crime and Punishment* by Fyodor Dostoyevski. Translated by Jessie Coulson (Oxford University Press, 1953). Reprinted by permission of the publisher.

471

crime, but is it *morally* wrong to rid the world of this woman? Raskolnikov convinces himself that this evil woman does not deserve the protection of the law. She is "not human." Why not murder her and put her money to good use? Raskolnikov decides to kill her after he overhears others arguing that killing this evil and miserly old woman would be right. Raskolnikov believes there would be general agreement that the world would be better without her. In any case, she would hardly be an "innocent victim." Yet in the course of the crime, Raskolnikov finds himself killing a second victim, one who is altogether innocent. Now Raskolnikov sees himself to be morally as well as legally culpable. Dostoyevski's novel is an implicit argument against putting oneself above the moral law.

Later Raskolnikov learnt, by some chance, why the dealer and his wife had asked Lizaveta to come and see them. It was a perfectly usual transaction, with nothing out of the ordinary about it. An impoverished family, lately come to St. Petersburg, wished to dispose of some articles of women's clothing and similar things. It would not have paid them to sell in the market and so they were looking for a dealer. Lizaveta undertook such transactions, selling on commission, and going round arranging business deals, and she had a large clientele because she was honest and never haggled, but named her price and stuck to it. She did not talk much and, as we have said, was timid and meek . . .

Raskolnikov had recently become superstitious. Traces of this superstition remained in him long afterwards, almost ineradicable. And in after years he was always inclined to see something strange and mysterious in all the happenings of this time, as if special coincidences and influences were at work. As long before as the previous winter a fellow student, Pokorev, who was leaving for Kharkov, had mentioned Alëna Ivanovna's address to him in conversation, in case he ever needed to pawn anything. For a long time he did not go near her, since he had his lessons and was managing to get along somehow, but six weeks earlier he had remembered the address. He had two things suitable for pawning: his father's old silver watch and a gold ring set with three little red stones, given to him as a keepsake by his sister when they parted. He decided to take the ring, and sought out the old woman; at first sight, before he knew anything about her, he felt an irresistible dislike of her. He took her two rouble notes and on his way home stopped at a miserable little tavern and asked for tea. He sat down, deep in thought; a strange idea seemed to be pecking away in his head, like a chicken emerging from the shell, and all his attention was fixed on it.

At another table near by, a student, who was unknown to him and whom he did not remember ever seeing, was sitting with a young officer. They had been playing billiards and were drinking tea. Suddenly he heard the student talking about the moneylender Alëna Ivanovna, giving the officer her address. This struck Raskolnikov as rather odd: he had just left her, and here they were talking about her. Of course, it was the merest chance, but exactly when he was finding it impossible to rid himself of an extraordinary impression, here was somebody reinforcing it, for the student was beginning to tell his friend some details about this Alëna Ivanovna.

"She's quite famous," he said; "she always has money to lay out. She's as rich as a Jew, she can put her hands on five thousand roubles at once, and yet she doesn't turn up her nose at the interest on a rouble. A lot of our fellows have been to her. But she's an old bitch . . ."

And he began to recount how spiteful and cranky she was, and how, if payment was only one day overdue, the pledge would be lost. She would lend only a quarter as much as things were worth, she would demand five or even seven per cent a month, and so on. The student's tongue had run away with him, and, among other things, he informed his hearer that the old woman had a sister, Lizaveta, whom the vicious little thing was always beating and whom she kept in complete subjection and treated as if she were a child, although Lizaveta stood at least five foot ten . . .

"She's another extraordinary creature, you know!" cried the student, and burst out laughing.

They began to talk about Lizaveta. The student seemed greatly to enjoy this and kept on laughing, and the officer listened with great interest and asked the student to send this Lizaveta to do his mending. Raskolnikov also learned all about her, not missing one word. Lizaveta was the old woman's younger step-sister (they had different mothers) and was about thirty-five. She worked for her sister day in and day out, did all the cooking and washing in the house, and in addition took in sewing and even went out scrubbing floors, and everything she earned she handed over to her sister. She dared not accept any orders or undertake any work without the old woman's permission. As Lizaveta knew, the old woman had already made her will, leaving to the younger sister only furniture and other chattels, while all the money went to a monastery in N—— Province for masses for the eternal repose of her soul. Lizaveta was a woman of the working-class, not educated, and unmarried; she was remarkably tall and extremely ungainly, with big, long, splay feet, shod with down-at-heel goat-skin shoes, and she always kept herself very clean. But what the student found the most surprising and amusing was that Lizaveta was pregnant . . .

"But I thought you said she was monstrously ugly," remarked the officer.

"Well, she's very dark-skinned, and looks like a guardsman in disguise, but, you know, she's no monster. She has a nice kind face and eyes—she's even very attractive. The proof is, a lot of people like her. She is so quiet and gentle and mild, and will consent to anything. And she's really got a very nice smile."

"You like her yourself, don't you?" laughed the officer.

"Because she's an oddity. But I'll tell you what: I swear I could kill that damned old woman and rob her, without a single twinge of conscience," exclaimed the student hotly.

The officer laughed again, but Raskolnikov found this so strange that he shuddered.

"Let me ask you a serious question," went on the student, even more heatedly. "I was joking just now, of course, but look here: on the one hand you have a stupid, silly, utterly unimportant, vicious, sickly old woman, no good to anybody, but in fact quite the opposite, who doesn't know herself why she goes on living, and will probably die tomorrow without any assistance. Do you understand what I am saying?"

"Oh, I follow you," answered the officer, earnestly studying his companion's vehemence.

"Listen, then. On the other hand you have new, young forces running to waste for want of backing, and there are thousands of them, all over the place. A hundred, a thousand, good actions and promising beginnings might be forwarded and directed aright by the

474

money that old woman destines for a monastery; hundreds, perhaps thousands, of existences might be set on the right path, scores of families saved from beggary, from decay, from ruin and corruption, from the lock hospitals—and all with her money! Kill her, take her money, on condition that you dedicate yourself with its help to the service of humanity and the common good: don't you think that thousands of good deeds will wipe out one little, insignificant transgression? For one life taken, thousands saved from corruption and decay! One death, and a hundred lives in exchange—why, it's simple arithmetic! What is the life of that stupid, spiteful, consumptive old woman weighed against the common good? No more than the life of a louse or a cockroach—less, indeed, because she is actively harmful. She battens on other people's lives, she is evil; not long since she bit Lizaveta's finger, out of sheer malice, and it almost had to be amputated!"

"She doesn't deserve to live, certainly," remarked the officer, "but there you are, that's nature."

"But don't you see, man, nature must be guided and corrected, or else we should all be swamped with prejudices. Otherwise there could never be one great man. They talk of 'duty, conscience'—I've got nothing to say against duty and conscience—but what are we to understand by them? Stop, I will put another question to you. Listen!"

"No, you stop; I will ask you a question. Listen!"

"Well?"

"Here you've been holding forth and making a regular speech, but tell me this: would you kill the old woman with your own hands, or not?"

"Of course not! For the sake of justice, I . . . This is not a question of me at all!"

"Well, if you ask me, so long as you won't, justice doesn't come into it. Let's have another game!"

Raskolnikov was deeply disturbed. No doubt there was nothing in all this but the most usual and ordinary youthful talk and ideas, such as he had heard often enough in other forms and about other subjects. But why must he listen at this particular moment to that particular talk and those particular ideas when there had just been born in his own brain *exactly the same ideas?* And why, at the very moment when he was carrying away from the old woman's flat the germ of his idea, should he chance upon a conversation about that same old woman? . . . This always seemed to him a strange coincidence. This casual public-house conversation had an extraordinary influence on the subsequent development of the matter, as if there were indeed something fateful and fore-ordained about it.

When he returned home from the Haymarket he threw himself on the sofa and sat there without moving for an hour. It grew dark, and he had no candles, not that it would have entered his head to light one if he had. Afterwards he was never able to remember whether he had been thinking of anything definite during that hour. At length he felt his recent chills and fever return, and realized with pleasure that he could lie down where he was. Soon a heavy leaden sleep weighed him down.

He slept unusually long and dreamlessly. Nastasya, coming into his room next morning at ten o'clock, could hardly shake him awake. She had brought him some tea and bread. The tea was once again what remained in her own teapot.

"Goodness, he's still asleep!" she exclaimed indignantly, "he's always asleep!"

He raised himself with an effort. His head ached; he stood up, took a few steps, and fell back on the sofa again.

"Are you going to sleep again?" exclaimed Nastasya. "Are you ill, or what?"

He did not answer.

"Do you want any tea?"

"Afterwards," he said with an effort, closing his eyes again and turning to the wall. Nastasya stood over him.

"Perhaps he really *is* ill," she said, turned on her heel and went out.

She came back at two o'clock with some soup. He was lying there as before. The tea was untouched. Nastasya was quite offended and began to shake him roughly.

"Why ever do you still go on sleeping?" she exclaimed, looking at him with positive dislike. He sat up and remained gazing at the floor without a word to her.

"Are you ill or aren't you?" asked Nastasya, and again received no answer.

"You want to go out for a bit," she said, after a short silence, "and get a bit of a blow. Are you going to have anything to eat, eh?"

"Later," he said feebly. "Clear out!" He waved her away.

476

She stood there a little longer, looking at him pityingly, and then went out.

After a few minutes he raised his eyes and stared at the tea and soup. Then he took up some bread and a spoon and began to eat.

He ate a little—two or three spoonfuls—but without appetite, and quite mechanically. His head no longer ached so much. When he had eaten, he stretched out once more on the sofa, but he could not go to sleep again and lay without stirring, face downwards, with his head buried in the pillow. He lost himself in a maze of waking dreams, and very strange ones they were; in the one that recurred most often he was in Africa, in Egypt, at some oasis. A caravan was resting, the camels lying peacefully and the men eating their evening meal; all around, the palms stood in a great circle. He was drinking the water from a stream which flowed babbling beside him, clear and cool, running marvellously bright and blue over the coloured stones and the clean sand with its gleams of gold . . . All at once he distinctly heard a clock strike. He roused himself with a start, raised his head and looked at the window, trying to estimate the time, and then, suddenly wide awake, sprang up as if he had been catapulted from the sofa. He crept to the door on tiptoe, quietly eased it open, and stood listening for sounds from the staircase. His heart was beat-ing wildly. But the staircase was quiet, as though everyone were asleep . . . It seemed to him incredibly strange that he could have gone on sleeping in such utter forgetfulness ever since the previous night, without having made the least preparation . . . And it might have been six o'clock that struck just now . . . An extraordinarily confused and feverish bustle had now replaced his sleepy torpor. He had not many preparations to make. He was straining every nerve to take everything into consideration and let nothing slip his memory, and his heart thumped so heavily that he could scarcely breathe. First of all he must make a loop and sew it into his overcoat, the work of a moment. He groped under his pillow and drew out from among the linen stuffed under it an old unwashed shirt that was falling to pieces. From among its tatters he ripped out a strip about an inch and a half wide and twelve long. He folded this strip in two, took off his only outer garment, a loose summer overcoat of thick stout cotton mate-rial, and sewed the two ends of the strip together to the inside, under the left armhole. His hands shook as he sewed, but he controlled them, and when he put the coat on again nothing showed from the outside. He had got the needle and thread ready long before, and had kept them on the little table, pinned into a piece of paper. As for the loop, that was an ingenious device of his own; it was meant to hold the axe. He could hardly carry an axe in his hands through the streets. And even if he had hidden it under his coat, he would still have had to support it with his hand, which would be noticeable. But now he need only lay the axe-head in the loop and it would hang peacefully under his arm all the way. With his hand in his pocket he could support the end of the shaft so that it would not swing; and as the coat was very wide and hung like a sack, nobody could possibly notice that he was holding something through the pocket. He had thought of this loop at least two weeks before.

Having finished this task, he thrust his fingers into the narrow crevice between the bottom of his "Turkish" divan and the floor, groping under the left-hand corner for the *pledge* he had prepared and hidden there. It was not really a pledge at all, however, but simply a piece of smoothly-planed board, about the size and thickness of a silver cigarette-case. He had found it by chance, on one of his walks, in a yard where there was some sort of workshop in an out-building. On the same occasion he picked up in the street, a little later, a smooth thin iron plate, rather smaller than the wood, apparently broken off something. Laying the two together, he had tied them securely with thread and then wrapped them neatly and carefully in clean white paper and made them into a parcel with thin string tied in a compli-cated knot that would need a great deal of skill to undo. This was done in order to distract the old woman's attention for a time while she dealt with the knot, and thus enable him to choose his moment. The iron plate had been added to increase the weight, so that she should not immediately recognize that the "pledge" was made of wood. He had hidden the whole thing under the sofa until he needed it. He had just got it out when he heard someone shouting in the courtyard.

"It went six ages ago."

"Ages ago! Oh God!"

He flung himself towards the door, listened, seized his hat, and crept as stealthily as a cat down his thirteen stairs. The most impor-tant step still lay before him—stealing an axe from the kitchen. He had long since come to the conclusion that he needed an axe to accomplish his purpose. He did possess a folding garden-knife, but he could not rely on a knife, or on his own strength in wielding it, and therefore finally settled on an axe. One noticeable peculiarity

478

characterized all the final decisions he arrived at in this affair: the more settled they were, the more hideous and absurd they appeared in his eyes. In spite of his agonizing internal struggles he could never throughout the whole time believe for one instant in the practicability of his schemes.

If it had somehow come about that the whole project had been analysed and finally decided down to the last detail, and no further doubts remained, he would very likely have renounced the whole idea for its absurdity, enormity, and impossibility. But there were in fact innumerable doubts and unsettled details. As for where he would obtain the axe, this trifle did not disturb him in the slightest, for nothing could be easier. The fact was that Nastasya was often out of the house, especially in the evening; she was always calling on the neighbours or running out to the shops, and the door was always left wide open; this was the landlady's only quarrel with her. Thus it would only be necessary to slip quietly into the kitchen, when the time came, take the axe, and then an hour later (when *it* was all over), put it back again. One doubt still remained, however: suppose he came back after an hour to return the axe, and found Nastasya back at home? It would, of course, be necessary to go straight past and wait until she went out again, but what if meanwhile she remembered the axe and looked for it, and raised an outcry? That would create suspicion, or at least give grounds for it.

But all these were trifles, about which he had not even begun to think, and there was no time for them now. He had thought about the main point, but he had put the details aside until *he had convinced himself.* This last, however, appeared definitely unrealizable. So at least it seemed to him. He could not, for example, picture himself ceasing at a given moment to think about it, getting up and—simply going there . . . Even his recent *rehearsal* (that is, his visit for a final survey of the scene) had been no more than a *test,* and far from a serious one, as though he had said to himself: "Very well, let us go and try whether it's just an idle fancy!"—and then immediately failed in the test, spat, and run away, exasperated with himself. And yet it would seem that his analysis, in the sense of a moral solution of the question, was concluded; his casuistry had the cutting edge of a razor, and he could no longer find any conscious objections in his own mind. But in the last resort he simply did not believe himself and obstinately, slavishly groped for objections on all sides, as if he were driven by some compulsion. His reactions during this last day, which had come upon him so unexpectedly and settled everything at one stroke, were almost completely mechanical, as though someone had taken his hand and pulled him along irresistibly, blindly, with supernatural strength and without objection. It was as if a part of his clothing had been caught in the wheel of a machine and he was being dragged into it.

The first question he had been concerned with—a long time ago now—was why most crimes were so easily discovered and solved, and why nearly every criminal left so clear a trail. He arrived by degrees at a variety of curious conclusions, and, in his opinion, the chief cause lay not so much in the material impossibility of concealing the crime as in the criminal himself; nearly every criminal, at the moment of the crime, was subject to a collapse of will-power and reason, exchanging them for an extraordinarily childish heedlessness, and that just at the moment when judgement and caution were most indispensable. He was convinced that this eclipse of reason and failure of will attacked a man like an illness, developed gradually and reached their height shortly before the commission of the crime, continuing unchanged at the moment of commission and for some time, varying with the individual, afterwards; their subsequent course was that of any other disease. The further question whether the disease engenders the crime, or whether the nature of crime somehow results in its always being accompanied by some manifestation of disease, he did not feel competent to answer.

Having arrived at this conclusion, he decided that he personally would not be subject to any such morbid subversion, that his judgement and will would remain steadfast throughout the fulfilment of his plans, for the simple reason that what he contemplated was "no crime" . . . We omit the course of reasoning by which he arrived at this latter verdict, since we have already run too far ahead . . . We shall add only that the practical, material difficulties played only a very secondary role in his thinking. "It will suffice to concentrate my will and my judgement on them, and they will all be overcome, when the time comes, when I have to come to grips with all the details of the affair, down to the most minute . . ." But he made no progress towards action. He continued to have less and less faith in his final decisions, and when the hour struck, everything seemed to go awry, in a haphazard and almost completely unexpected way.

One small circumstance nonplussed him even before he reached the foot of the stairs. As he drew level with his landlady's kitchen door, which stood open as usual, he peered carefully round it to make sure beforehand that the landlady herself was not there in Nastasya's absence, and if she was not, that her door was firmly closed so that she would not happen to look out and see him when he went in for the axe. But what was his consternation at seeing that Nastasya was at home in her kitchen on this occasion, and busy taking linen from a basket and hanging it on a line. When she caught sight of him she ceased her occupation and turned towards him, watching him as he went past. He turned his eyes away and walked on as if he had not noticed her. But it was all over: he had no axe! It was a terrible blow.

"Where did I get the idea," he thought, going out through the gate, "where did I get the idea that she was certain to be out now? Why, why, why, was I so convinced of it?" He felt crushed, even humiliated, and ready to laugh spitefully at himself . . . He was seething with dull, brutal rage.

He had stopped uncertainly in the gateway. To go out now and walk about the steets for form's sake, and to return to his room, were both equally repugnant to him. "What an opportunity is lost for ever!" he muttered, standing aimlessly in the gateway, just opposite the porter's dark little room, which also stood open. Suddenly he started. Inside the little room, not two paces away, under a bench on the right-hand side, something shining caught his eye . . . He looked all round—nobody! On tiptoe he approached the porter's lodge, went down the two steps, and called the porter in a feeble voice. "Yes, he's out! but he must be somewhere near, in the courtyard, since the door is open." He threw himself headlong on the axe (it was an axe), drew it out from where it lay between two logs under the bench, hung it in the loop on the spot, thrust both hands into his pockets and went out. He had not been seen. "It was not my planning, but the devil, that accomplished that!" he thought, and laughed strangely, extraordinarily heartened by this stroke of luck.

He walked quietly and sedately, without hurrying, so as not to arouse suspicion. He paid little attention to the passers-by, and carefully avoided looking at their faces, trying to be unnoticed himself. Suddenly he remembered his hat. "My God! I had the money two days ago, and hadn't the sense to spend it on a cap!" and he cursed himself from the bottom of his heart.

Glancing casually into a shop, he saw from the clock that hung on the wall that it was already ten minutes past seven. He would have to hurry; he wanted to go round about, so as to approach the house from the other side.

Earlier, when he had tried to imagine what all this would be like, he had thought he would be very frightened. But he was not; indeed he was not frightened at all. His mind was even occupied, though not for long together, with irrelevant thoughts.

Passing the Yusupov Gardens, he began to consider the construction of tall fountains in all the squares, and how they would freshen the air. Following this train of thought he came to the conclusion that if the Summer Gardens could be extended right across the Champ de Mars and joined to those of the Mikhaylovsky Palace, it would add greatly to the beauty and amenities of the city. Then he suddenly began to wonder why, in big towns, people chose of their own free will to live where there were neither parks nor gardens, but only filth and squalor and evil smells. This reminded him of his own walks in the neighbourhood of the Haymarket, and brought him back to himself. "What rubbish!" he thought. "It would be better not to think at all!"

"So it is true that men going to execution are passionately interested in any object they chance to see on the way." The thought passed through his mind as briefly as a flash of lightning, for he suppressed it at once . . . But he had arrived; here was the house and the gate. Somewhere a clock struck, once. "What, can it possibly be half-past seven? Surely not; time is really flying!"

Luck was again with him as he turned in at the gate. At that very moment, as if by design, a huge load of hay also turned in, just in front of him, and completely screened him while he was passing through the archway. As soon as it had cleared the gateway and was in the courtyard, he slipped past it to the right. On the other side of the cart he could hear several voices shouting and quarrelling, but nobody noticed him and nobody passed him. Many of the windows opening on to the great courtyard stood open, but he could not find the strength to raise his head. The old woman's staircase was near, immediately to the right of the gate. Already he was on the stairs.

Drawing a deep breath and pressing his hand above his wildly beating heart, he once more felt for the axe and settled it in its loop, then began to mount the stairs carefully and quietly, listening at every step. But the staircase was empty at this hour; all the doors were closed and nobody was to be seen. On the second floor, it is true, the door of an empty flat was open, and painters were at work inside, but they did not even look up. He stopped for a moment, considering, and then went on. "Of course, it would be better if they were not there, but . . . there are two floors above them."

But here was the fourth floor, here was the door, here was the empty flat opposite. On the third floor the flat immediately below the old woman's also showed every sign of being empty: the visiting-card tacked to the door had been removed—they had left . . . He was out of breath. For a moment the thought stirred in his mind: "There is still time to go away." But he ignored it and began to listen at the old woman's door—dead silence! Then once more he listened down the stairs, long and attentively . . . Then he looked round for the last time, crept close to the door, straightened his clothes, and once again tried the axe in its loop. "I wonder if I look too pale," he thought, "and too agitated. She is mistrustful . . . Wouldn't it be better if I waited a little longer . . . until my heart stops thumping so? . . ."

But his heart did not stop. On the contrary, its throbbing grew more and more violent . . . He could stand it no longer, but stretched his hand slowly towards the bell, and rang it. After a few moments he rang again, louder.

There was no answer. There was no point in going on ringing in vain, and he was not in the mood to do so. The old woman was certainly at home, but she was suspicious and she was alone. He knew something of her habits . . . and he applied his ear to the door again. Either his hearing had grown strangely acute (which did not seem likely) or the sound was really distinctly audible, but at any rate he suddenly heard the careful placing of a hand on the handle of a lock and the rustle of clothing close to the door. Someone was standing silently just inside the door and listening, just as he was doing outside it, holding her breath and probably also with her ear to the door . . .

He purposely shifted his position and audibly muttered something, so as not to give the impression that he was being furtive; then he rang a third time, but quietly and firmly, without betraying any impatience. When he was afterwards able to recall everything clearly and plainly, that minute seemed stamped into his memory for ever; he could not understand whence he had acquired so much cunning, especially as his mind seemed momentarily to cloud over, and he lost all consciousness of his own body . . . A moment later, he heard the bolt being lifted.

As before, the door opened the merest crack, and again two sharp and mistrustful eyes peered at him from the darkness. Then Raskolnikov lost his head and made what might have been a serious mistake.

Apprehensive that the old woman might be alarmed at their being alone, and without any hope that his appearance would reassure her, he took hold of the door and pulled it towards him, so that she should not be tempted to lock herself in again. Although she did not pull the door shut again at this, she did not relinquish the handle, so that he almost pulled her out on the stairs. When he saw that she was standing across the doorway in such a way that he could not pass, he advanced straight upon her, and she stood aside startled. She seemed to be trying to say something but finding it impossible, and she kept her eyes fixed on him.

"Good evening, Alëna Ivanovna," he began, as easily as possible, but his voice refused to obey him, and was broken and trembling, "I have . . . brought you . . . something . . . but hadn't we better come in here . . . to the light? . . ." And without waiting for an invitation, he passed her and went into the room. The old woman hastened after him; her tongue seemed to have been loosened.

"God Lord! What are you doing? . . . Who are you? What do you want?"

"Excuse me, Alëna Ivanovna . . . You know me . . . Raskolnikov . . . See, I have brought the pledge I promised the other day," and he held it out to her.

The old woman threw a glance at it, but then immediately fixed her eyes on those of her uninvited guest. She looked at him attentively, ill-naturedly, and mistrustfully. A minute or so went by; he even thought he could see a glint of derision in her eyes, as if she had guessed everything. He felt that he was losing his nerve and was frightened, so frightened that he thought if she went on looking at him like that, without a word, for even half a minute longer, he would turn tail and run away.

"Why are you looking at me like that, as though you didn't recognize me?" he burst out angrily. "Do you want it, or don't you? I can take it somewhere else; it makes no difference to me."

He had not intended to say this, but it seemed to come of its own accord.

The old woman collected herself, and her visitor's resolute tone seemed to lull her mistrust.

"Why be so hasty, my friend? . . . What is it?" she asked, looking at the packet.

"A silver cigarette case; surely I told you that last time?"

She stretched out her hand.

"But what makes you so pale? And your hands are trembling. Are you ill or something?"

"Fever," he answered abruptly. "You can't help being pale . . . when you haven't anything to eat," he added, hardly able to articulate his words. His strength was failing again. But apparently the answer was plausible enough; the old woman took the packet.

"What is it?" she asked, weighing it in her hand and once again fixing her eyes on Raskolnikov.

"A thing . . . a cigarette-case . . . silver . . . look at it."

"It doesn't feel like silver. Lord, what a knot!" Trying to undo the string she turned for light towards the window (all her windows were closed, in spite of the oppressive heat), moved away from him and stood with her back to him. He unbuttoned his coat and freed the axe from the loop, but still kept it concealed, supporting it with his right hand under the garment. His arms seemed to have no strength in them; he felt them growing more and more numb and stiff with every moment. He was afraid of letting the axe slip and fall . . . His head was whirling.

"Why is it all wrapped up like this?" exclaimed the woman sharply, and turned towards him.

There was not a moment to lose. He pulled the axe out, swung it up with both hands, hardly conscious of what he was doing, and almost mechanically, without putting any force behind it, let the butt-end fall on her head. His strength seemed to have deserted him, but as soon as the axe descended it all returned to him.

The old woman was, as usual, bare-headed. Her thin fair hair, just turning grey, and thick with grease, was plaited into a rat's tail and fastened into a knot above her nape with a fragment of horn comb. Because she was so short the axe struck her full on the crown of the head. She cried out, but very feebly, and sank in a heap to the floor, still with enough strength left to raise both hands to her head. One of them still held the "pledge." Then he struck her again and yet again, with all his strength, always with the blunt side of the axe, and always on the crown of the head. Blood poured out as if from an overturned glass and the body toppled over on its back. He stepped away as it fell, and then stooped to see the face: she was dead. Her wide-open eyes looked ready to start out of their sockets, her forehead was wrinkled and her whole face convulsively distorted.

He laid the axe on the floor near the body and, taking care not to smear himself with the blood, felt in her pocket, the right-hand pocket, from which she had taken her keys last time. He was quite collected, his faculties were no longer clouded nor his head swimming, but his hands still shook. Later he remembered that he had been very painstakingly careful not to get bedaubed . . . He pulled out the keys; they were all together, as he remembered them, on a steel ring. He hurried straight into the bedroom with them. It was a very small room; on one wall was an enormous case of icons, and another was occupied by the big bed, very clean, covered with a silk patchwork quilt. The chest of drawers stood against the third wall. It was strange, but as soon as he began to try the keys in it, and heard their jingling, a convulsive shudder shook him; he longed suddenly to abandon the whole affair and go away. But this lasted only for a moment; it was too late now to retreat. He was even laughing at himself when another, most alarming, idea flashed into his mind, the idea that perhaps the old woman was still alive and might yet recover consciousness. He left the keys and the chest and ran back to the body, seized the axe and brandished it over the old woman again, but did not bring it down. There could be no doubt that she was dead. Stooping down again to examine the body more closely, he saw clearly that the skull was shattered. He stretched out his hand to touch her, but drew it back again; he could see plainly enough without that. By this time the blood had formed a pool on the floor. Then he noticed a cord round the old woman's neck and tugged at it, but it was too strong to snap, and besides, it was slippery with blood. He tried to draw it out from the bosom of her dress, but it seemed to be caught on something and would not come. Impatiently he raised the axe again, to sever the cord with a blow as it lay on the body, but he could not bring himself to do this, and finally, after struggling with it for two minutes, and getting the axe and his hands smeared with blood, he managed with some difficulty to cut the cord without touching the body with the axe; he took it off, and found, as he expected, a purse hanging there. There were two crosses on the cord, one of cypress-wood and the other of brass, as well as an enamelled religious medal, and beside them hung a small, soiled, chamois-leather purse, with a steel frame and clasp. It was crammed full;

Raskolnikov thrust it into his pocket without examining it and threw the crosses down on the old woman's breast; then, this time taking the axe with him, he hurried back into the bedroom.

With dreadful urgency he seized the keys and began to struggle with them once more. But all his efforts failed to force them into the locks, not so much because his hands were trembling as because his energy was misdirected; he would see, for example, that a key was the wrong one and would not fit, and yet go on thrusting at the lock with it. He pulled himself together and remembered that the big key with toothed wards, hanging with the other smaller ones, could not possibly belong to the chest of drawers, but must be for some trunk or other (as he had thought on the previous occasion), and that perhaps it was there that everything was hidden. He left the chest and looked first of all under the bed, knowing that old women usually keep their trunks there. He was right; there stood an important-looking steel-studded trunk of red leather, about thirty inches long, with a rounded lid. The toothed key fitted the lock and opened the trunk. On top, under a white sheet, lay a hare-skin coat with a red lining; under this were a silk dress, then a shawl, and then, at the bottom, what looked like a heap of rags. His first impulse was to wipe his bloody hands on the red lining of the fur coat. "It is red, so blood will not show on it," he reasoned, and then suddenly realized what he was doing and thought, with fear in his heart, "Good God, am I going out of my mind?"

But no sooner had he disturbed the rags than a gold watch slid out from under the coat. Hastily he began turning everything over, and found a number of gold articles thrust in among the rags, bracelets, chains, earrings, pins, and so forth, probably pledges, some of them perhaps unredeemed. Some were in cases, some simply wrapped in newspaper, but neatly and carefully, with the paper tidily folded and the packets tied with tape. He began to cram them hastily into the pockets of his overcoat and trousers, without opening the cases or undoing the parcels, but he did not manage to collect very many . . .

A footstep sounded in the room where the old woman lay. He stopped and remained motionless as the dead. But all was still; he must have imagined it. Then he distinctly heard a faint cry, or perhaps rather a feeble interrupted groaning, then dead silence again for a minute or two. He waited, crouching by the trunk, hardly daring to breathe; then he sprang up, seized the axe, and ran out of the room.

There in the middle of the floor, with a big bundle in her arms, stood Lizaveta, as white as a sheet, gazing in frozen horror at her murdered sister and apparently without the strength to cry out. When she saw him run in, she trembled like a leaf and her face twitched spasmodically; she raised her hand as if to cover her mouth, but no scream came and she backed slowly away from him towards the corner, with her eyes on him in a fixed stare, but still without a sound, as though she had no breath left to cry out. He flung himself forward with the axe; her lips writhed pitifully, like those of a young child when it is just beginning to be frightened and stands ready to scream, with its eyes fixed on the object of its fear. The wretched Lizaveta was so simple, brow-beaten, and utterly terrified that she did not even put up her arms to protect her face, natural and almost inevitable as the gesture would have been at this moment when the axe was brandished immediately above it. She only raised her free left hand a little and slowly stretched it out towards him as though she were trying to push him away. The blow fell on her skull, splitting it open from the top of the forehead almost to the crown of the head, and felling her instantly. Raskolnikov, completely beside himself, snatched up her bundle, threw it down again, and ran to the entrance.

The terror that possessed him had been growing greater and greater, especially after this second, unpremeditated murder. He wanted to get away as quickly as possible. If he had been in a condition to exercise a soberer judgment and see things more clearly, if he could only have recognized all the difficulty of his position and how desperate, hideous, and absurd it was, if he could have understood how many obstacles to surmount, perhaps even crimes to commit, still lay before him, before he could escape from the house and reach home—very probably he would have abandoned everything and given himself up, not out of fear for himself so much as from horror and repulsion for what he had done. Repulsion, indeed, was growing in his heart with every moment. Not for anything in the world would he have returned to the trunk, or even to the room.

But a growing distraction, that almost amounted to absentmindedness, had taken possession of him; at times he seemed to forget what he was doing, or rather to forget the important things and cling to trivialities. However, when he glanced into the kitchen and saw a pail half full of water on a bench, it gave him the idea of washing his hands and the axe. His hands were sticky with blood. He put the head of the axe in the water, then took a piece of soap that lay in a broken saucer on the window-sill, and began to wash his hands in the pail. When he had washed them he drew out the axe and washed the blade and then spent some three minutes trying to clean the part of the handle that was blood-stained, using soap to get the blood out. After this he wiped it with a cloth which was drying on a line stretched across the kitchen, and then spent a long time examining it carefully at the window. There were no stains left, but the handle was still damp. With great care he laid the axe in the loop under his coat. Then, as well as the dim light in the kitchen allowed, he examined his overcoat, trousers, and boots. At first glance there was nothing to give him away, except for some stains on his boots. He wiped them with a damp rag. He knew, however, that he had not been able to see very well, and might have failed to notice something quite conspicuous. He stood hesitating in the middle of the room. A dark and tormenting idea was beginning to rear its head, the idea that he was going out of his mind and that he was not capable of reasoning or of protecting himself. Perhaps what he was doing was not at all what ought to be done . . . "My God, I must run, I must run!" he muttered and hurried back to the entrance. Here there awaited him a more extreme terror than any he had yet experienced.

He stood still, staring, unable to believe his eyes; the door, the outer door leading to the staircase, the door at which he had rung a short time ago, and by which he had entered, was at least a hand's-breadth open; all this time it had been like that, neither locked nor bolted, all the time! The old woman had not locked it behind him, perhaps by way of precaution. But, good God, he had seen Lizaveta after that! And how could he have failed to realize that she had come from outside, and could certainly not have come through the wall?

He flung himself at the door and put up the bolt.

"But no, that's not right either! I must go, I must go . . ."

He lifted the bolt clear, opened the door, and stood listening on the landing.

He stood there a long time. Somewhere far below, probably under the gateway, two voices were raised loudly and shrilly in argument. "What are they doing?" He waited patiently. At last the voices fell silent, as though they had been cut off; "they" had gone away. He was preparing to descend when suddenly a door on the floor below opened noisily and somebody started down the stairs, humming a tune. "Why are they making so much noise?" he wondered for a moment. He closed the door again behind him and waited. At last all was quiet; there was not a sound. He was already setting his foot on the stairs when once more he heard footsteps.

When he first heard them, the steps were far away, at the very bottom of the staircase, but he afterwards remembered clearly and distinctly that from the very first sound he guessed that they were certainly coming *here,* to the fourth floor, to the old woman's flat. Why? Was there something special, something significant, about them? The steps were heavy, regular, unhurrying. Already they had reached the first floor, they were coming on, their sound was clearer and clearer. He could hear the newcomer's heavy breathing. Already the steps had passed the second floor . . . They were coming here! Suddenly he felt as if he had turned to stone, like a sleeper who dreams that he is being hotly pursued and threatened with death, and finds himself rooted to the spot, unable to stir a finger.

At length, when the footsteps had begun the last flight, he started to life, and just managed to slip swiftly and dextrously back from the landing into the flat and close the door behind him. Then he grasped the bolt and slid it gently, without a sound, into its socket. Instinct had come to his aid. When he had done, he stayed quiet, holding his breath, close to the door. The unknown visitor was also at the door. They were standing now, opposite one another, as he and the old woman had stood, with the door dividing them, when he had listened there a short time ago.

The visitor drew several heavy breaths. "He must be a big stout man," thought Raskolnikov, grasping the axe tightly. Everything seemed to be happening in a dream. The visitor seized the bell and rang it loudly.

As soon as its tinny sound had died, Raskolnikov imagined he heard movement inside the room, and for some seconds he listened as seriously as though it were possible. The unknown rang again, waited a little longer and then suddenly began to tug impatiently at the door-handle with all his might. Terrified, Raskolnikov watched the bolt rattling in its socket and waited in numb fear for it to jump clean out. This seemed likely to happen at any moment, so violently was the door shaken. He would have held the bar with his hand, except that *he* might discern it. His head was beginning to spin again. "I am going to faint!" he thought, but the unknown began to speak and he recovered himself immediately.

"Are they fast asleep in there, or dead, or what, confound them?"

the visitor boomed in a resounding voice. "Hey! Alëna Ivanovna, you old witch! Lizaveta Ivanovna, my peerless beauty! Open the door! Oh, confound it all, they must be asleep or something!"

Thoroughly annoyed, he tugged at the bell again with all his might, a dozen times in succession. He was plainly a person of imperious temper and familiar with the place.

At this moment light, hurrying footsteps sounded not very far down the stairs. Somebody else was approaching, whom Raskolnikov had not heard at first.

"Isn't anybody in?" cried the new arrival in loud and cheerful tones to the first visitor, who was still tugging at the bell. "How are you, Koch?"

"Judging by his voice, he must be very young," thought Raskolnikov.

"God only knows! I've nearly broken the door down," answered Koch. "But how is it that you know me?"

"Surely you remember? The day before yesterday, at Gambrinus's, I beat you three times running at billiards."

"O-o-oh . . ."

"Aren't they here then? That's strange. In fact, it's quite absurd. The old woman's got nowhere to go to. And I am here on business."

"So am I, old man."

"Well, what are we to do? Go back, I suppose. And I was expecting to get some money!" exclaimed the young man.

"Of course we must go back, but why make an appointment? The old witch fixed a time with me herself. It's a long way for me to come here, too. And where the devil she can have got to, I don't know. She sits here, day in and day out, the old witch, with her bad legs, and never lifts a finger, and now all at once she goes gallivanting off!"

"Hadn't we better ask the porter?"

"Ask him what?"

"Where she's gone and when she's coming back."

"Hm . . . the devil! . . . ask him . . . But she never goes anywhere . . ." and he pulled at the handle again. "The devil! There's nothing for it; we must go."

"Stop!" exclaimed the young man. "Look! Do you see how the door resists when you pull it?"

"Well?"

"That means it's bolted, not locked! Can you hear the bar rattling?"

"Well?"

"Don't you understand? That means one of them is at home. If everybody were out, they would have locked the door from outside, not bolted it from inside. But now—do you hear the bolt rattle? But to bolt the door from inside, somebody must be at home. Do you understand? They must be in, but they aren't opening the door."

"Tck! That's quite right!" exclaimed Koch, surprised. "Then what on earth are they doing?" And he shook the door again, in a rage.

"Stop!" cried the young man again, "leave the door alone! There's something very wrong here . . . After all, you rang, and shook the door, and they haven't opened it; so either they've both fainted, or . . ."

"What?"

"I'll tell you what; let's go to the porter and get him to rouse them."

"Done!" Both started downstairs.

"Stop! Why don't you stay here while I run down for the porter?"

"Why?"

"Well, one never knows!"

"All right . . ."

"You see, I am studying to be an examining magistrate. There is plainly, plai-ainly something wrong here!" cried the young man excitedly, as he ran down the stairs.

Koch, left alone, touched the bell again, so softly that it made only one tinkle; then, as though he were considering the matter and making tests to convince himself once more that the door was held only by the bolt, he began to move the handle, pulling it towards him and letting it go again. Then he stooped down, puffing, and looked through the keyhole, but the key was in it on the inside and consequently nothing could be seen.

Raskolnikov stood clutching his axe, in a sort of delirium. He was even prepared to fight them when they came in. While they were knocking at the door and arranging what they would do, he was more than once tempted to put an end to it all at once by calling out to them from behind the door. Several times he felt like railing and jeering at them, while the door remained closed. "If only they would be quick!" he thought.

"What the devil? . . ."

The time was passing—one minute, two minutes, and nobody came. Koch was getting restless.

"Oh, the devil! . . ." he exclaimed impatiently, abandoning his watch and starting to hurry downstairs, with his boots clattering on the steps. The sounds died away.

"Oh, God, what am I to do?"

Raskolnikov took off the bolt and opened the door a little. Since he could hear nothing, he walked out without stopping to consider, closed the door behind him as well as he could, and went downstairs.

He had gone down three flights when a great commotion broke out below him. Where could he go? There was nowhere to hide. He was on the point of running back to the flat.

"Hi, stop! You devil! Just wait!"

Down below someone tore out of a flat shouting and did not so much run as tumble down the stairs, yelling at the top of his voice:

"Mitka! Mitka! Mitka! Mitka! Blast your eyes!"

The shout rose to a shriek; its last echoes resounded from the courtyard; it died away. At the same instant several persons talking loudly and rapidly started noisily up the stairs. There were three or four of them. He could distinguish the young man's voice. "It's them!"

In complete desperation he went straight towards them: let come what might! If they stopped him, all was lost; if they let him pass, all was still lost: they would remember him. They were already close; only one flight still lay between them—and suddenly, salvation! A few steps below him on the right, the door of an empty flat was wide open; it was the second-floor flat in which painters had been work-ing, but now, most opportunely, they had gone. Probably it was they who had run out so noisily a few minutes before. The floors had just been painted, and in the middle of the room stood a tub and an earthenware crock of paint with a brush in it. In a trice he had slipped through the open door and hidden himself against the wall. It was none too soon; *they* had already reached the landing. They turned up the stairs and went on to the fourth floor, talking loudly. He waited a little, tiptoed out and ran downstairs.

There was nobody on the stairs, nobody in the gateway. He walked through quickly and turned to the left along the street.

He knew very well, he was terribly aware, that at this moment they were inside the flat, that they had been astonished to find the door unfastened when it had been closed against them so recently, that they had already seen the bodies and that no more than a minute would pass before they would begin to suspect, and then realize fully, that the murderer had only just left, and had managed to conceal himself somewhere, slip past them, and make his escape; perhaps they would even guess that he had been in the empty flat when they passed it on their way upstairs. All the same, he simply dared not increase his pace, even though it was still nearly a hundred yards to the first turning. "Hadn't I better slip into some gateway and wait on a staircase? No, that would be disastrous! Oughtn't I to get rid of the axe? What about taking a cab? . . . A fatal blunder!"

At last he reached a side-street and, half dead, turned into it; now he knew that he was already half-way to safety; his presence here was less suspicious, and besides there were very many people about and he could lose himself among them like one grain of sand on the sea-shore. But his racking anxieties had taken so much out of him that he could hardly move. Sweat poured out of him; his neck was quite wet. "You've had a drop too much!" someone called after him as he came out on the canal.

He no longer knew quite what he was doing, and the farther he went the worse his condition became. Afterwards he remembered, however, that he had been afraid, coming to the canal bank, because there were fewer people about, which made him more conspicuous, and he nearly turned back into the street he had just left. Although he could hardly stand he took a roundabout way and arrived home from an entirely different direction.

Even when he entered his own gateway he had hardly recovered control of himself; at least, he was already on the stairs before he remembered the axe. Now he had to face a very important task—returning it without being seen. He was certainly in no condition to realize that perhaps it would be much better if he did not restore the axe to its former place but threw it away, perhaps later, in some other courtyard.

Everything, however, went without a hitch. The porter's door was closed but not locked, which meant that he was probably at home. But Raskolnikov had so completely lost his powers of reasoning that he went straight to the door of the lodge and opened it. If the porter had asked him what he wanted, he might quite possibly have simply handed him the axe. But the porter was again out and he put the axe in its former place under the bench; he even partly covered it with logs as before. Afterwards, on his way to his room, he met no one, not a soul; even the landlady's door was closed. He went in and flung himself down on the sofa just as he was. He did not sleep, but lay there in a stupor. If anybody had entered the room he would have sprung up at once with a cry. Disjointed scraps and fragments of ideas floated through his mind, but he could not seize one of them, or dwell upon any, in spite of all his efforts . . .

STUDY QUESTIONS

1. Raskolnikov thinks that those who spread misery do not deserve the protection of the law. Discuss this proposition.
2. Raskolnikov's act defies conventional morality. Does it do so in the name of some higher morality? Is Raskolnikov a kind of Nietzschean who cannot make the grade?
3. What, in your view, is Dostoyevski's moral position? How does *he* see Raskolnikov?
4. There is the hint that Raskolnikov might have had in mind distributing the money to others far more worthy than the evil old moneylender. Discuss the morality of robbing the rich to give to the poor. Can such conduct be justified on utilitarian grounds? (In this connection look again at the distinction between "act utilitarianism" and "rule utilitarianism" in the J. J. C. Smart selection.)

Why Act Morally?

PETER SINGER

Peter Singer (b. 1946) teaches philosophy at La Trobe University in Victoria, Australia. His books include *Aninal Liberation* (1975), *Practical Ethics* (1979), *The Expanding Circle* (1981), *Applied Ethics* (1986), and *Embryo Experimentation* (1990).

Singer examines the link between vice and unhappiness from a utilitarian standpoint. Psychopaths have a character type that enables them to pursue pleasure with indifference to the suffering they cause others. The existence of psychopaths untroubled by conscience and apparently enjoying themselves seems to count against the thesis that immorality leads to unhappiness. Singer counters this by arguing that psychopaths and others who completely lack such virtues as benevolence and compassion are unable to do more than pursue short-range objectives. All they can do is continue their selfish pursuit of more pleasure. But their satisfactions are short-lived and their capacity for enjoyment soon becomes jaded. Even prudent egoists whose selfish goals are long-range end up desperately bored and without the resources to relieve that boredom. If Singer is right, the utilitarian, too, can consistently maintain that a virtuous character is needed for an interesting and meaningful life.

It might be said that since philosophers are not empirical scientists,

WHY ACT MORALLY? From *Practical Ethics* by Peter Singer. Reprinted by permission of the publisher, Cambridge University Press.

discussion of the connection between acting ethically and living a fulfilled and happy life should be left to psychologists, sociologists and other appropriate experts. The question is not, however, dealt with by any other single discipline and its relevance to practical ethics is reason enough for our looking into it.

What facts about human nature could show that ethics and self-interest coincide? One theory is that we all have benevolent or sympathetic inclinations which make us concerned about the welfare of others. Another relies on a natural conscience which gives rise to guilt feelings when we do what we know to be wrong. But how strong are these benevolent desires or feelings of guilt? Is it possible to suppress them? If so, isn't it possible that in a world in which humans and other animals are suffering in great numbers, suppressing one's conscience and sympathy for others is the surest way to happiness?

To meet this objection those who would link ethics and happiness must assert that we cannot be happy if these elements of our nature are suppressed. Benevolence and sympathy, they might argue, are tied up with the capacity to take part in friendly or loving relations with others, and there can be no real happiness without such relationships. For the same reason it is necessary to take at least some ethical standards seriously, and to be open and honest in living by them— for a life of deception and dishonesty is a furtive life, in which the possibility of discovery always clouds the horizon. Genuine acceptance of ethical standards is likely to mean that we feel some guilt— or at least that we are less pleased with ourselves than we otherwise would be—when we do not live up to them.

These claims about the connection between our character and our prospects of happiness are no more than hypotheses. Attempts to confirm them by detailed research are sparse and inadequate. A. H. Maslow, an American psychologist, asserts that human beings have a need for self-actualization, which involves growing towards courage, kindness, knowledge, love, honesty, and unselfishness. When we fulfil this need we feel serene, joyful, filled with zest, sometimes euphoric, and generally happy. When we act contrary to our need for self-actualization we experience anxiety, despair, boredom, shame, emptiness and are generally unable to enjoy ourselves. It would be nice if Maslow should turn out to be right; unfortunately the data Maslow produces in support of his theory consist of very limited studies of selected people. The theory must await confirmation or falsification from larger, more rigorous and more representative studies.

Human nature is so diverse that one may doubt if any generalization about the kind of character that leads to happiness could hold for all human beings. What, for instance, of those we call "psychopaths"? Psychiatrists use this term as a label for a person who is asocial, impulsive, egocentric, unemotional, lacking in feelings of remorse, shame or guilt, and apparently unable to form deep and enduring personal relationships. Psychopaths are certainly abnormal, but whether it is proper to say that they are mentally ill is another matter. At least on the surface, they do not *suffer* from their condition, and it is not obvious that it is in their interest to be "cured." Hervey Cleckley, the author of a classic study of psychopathy entitled *The Mask of Sanity,* notes that since his book was first published he has received countless letters from people desperate for help—but they are from the parents, spouses and other relatives of psychopaths, almost never from the psychopaths themselves. This is not surprising, for while psychopaths are asocial and indifferent to the welfare of others, they seem to enjoy life. Psychopaths often appear to be charming, intelligent people, with no delusions or other signs of irrational thinking. When interviewed they say things like:

> A lot has happened to me, a lot more will happen. But I enjoy living and I am always looking forward to each day. I like laughing and I've done a lot. I am essentially a clown at heart—but a happy one. I always take the bad with the good.

There is no effective therapy for psychopathy, which may be explained by the fact that psychopaths see nothing wrong with their behaviour and often find it extremely rewarding, at least in the short term. Of course their impulsive nature and lack of a sense of shame or guilt means that some psychopaths end up in prison, though it is hard to tell how many do not, since those who avoid prison are also more likely to avoid contact with psychiatrists. Studies have shown that a surprisingly large number of psychopaths are able to avoid prison despite grossly antisocial behaviour, probably because of their well-known ability to convince others that they are truly repentant, that it will never happen again, that they deserve another chance, etc., etc.

The existence of psychopathic people counts against the contention that benevolence, sympathy and feelings of guilt are present in everyone. It also appears to count against attempts to link happiness with the possession of these inclinations. But let us pause before we accept this latter conclusion. Must we accept psychopaths' own evaluations of their happiness? They are, after all, notoriously persuasive liars. Moreover, even if they are telling the truth as they see it, are they qualified to say that they are really happy, when they seem unable to experience the emotional states that play such a large part in the happiness and fulfilment of more normal people? Admittedly, a psychopath could use the same argument against us: how can we say that we are truly happy when we have not experienced the excitement and freedom that comes from complete irresponsibility? Since we cannot enter into the subjective states of psychopathic people, nor they into ours, the dispute is not easy to resolve.

Cleckley suggests that the psychopaths' behaviour can be explained as a response to the meaninglessness of their lives. It is characteristic of psychopaths to work for a while at a job and then just when their ability and charm have taken them to the crest of success, commit some petty and easily detectable crime. A similar pattern occurs in their personal relationships. (There is support to be found here for Thomas Nagel's account of imprudence as rational only if one fails to see oneself as a person existing over time, with the present merely one among other times one will live through. Certainly psychopathic people live largely in the present and lack any coherent life plan.)

Cleckley explains this erratic and to us inadequately motivated behaviour by likening the psychopath's life to that of children forced to sit through a performance of *King Lear*. Children are restless and misbehave under these conditions because they cannot enjoy the play as adults do. They act to relieve boredom. Similarly, Cleckley says, psychopaths are bored because their emotional poverty means that they cannot take interest in, or gain satisfaction from, what for others are the most important things in life: love, family, success in business or professional life, etc. These things simply do not matter to them. Their unpredictable and anti-social behaviour is an attempt to relieve what would otherwise be a tedious existence.

These claims are speculative and Cleckley admits that they may not be possible to establish scientifically. They do suggest, however, an aspect of the psychopath's life that undermines the otherwise attractive nature of the psychopath's free-wheeling life. Most reflective people, at some time or other, want their life to have some kind of meaning. Few of us could deliberately choose a way of life which we regarded as utterly meaningless. For this reason most of us would not choose to live a psychopathic life, however enjoyable it might be.

Yet there is something paradoxical about criticizing the psychopath's life for its meaninglessness. Don't we have to accept, in the absence of religious belief, that life really is meaningless, not just for the psychopath but for all of us? And if this is so, why should we not choose—if it were in our powers to choose our personality—the life of a psychopath? But is it true that, religion aside, life is meaningless? Now our pursuit of reasons for acting morally has led us to what is often regarded as the ultimate philosophical question.

Has Life a Meaning?

In what sense does rejection of belief in a god imply rejection of the view that life has any meaning? If this world had been created by some divine being with a particular goal in mind, it could be said to have a meaning, at least for that divine being. If we could know what the divine being's purpose in creating us was, we could then know what the meaning of our life was for our creator. If we accepted our creator's purpose (though why we should do that would need to be explained) we could claim to know the meaning of life.

When we reject belief in a god we must give up the idea that life on this planet has some preordained meaning. Life *as a whole* has no meaning. Life began, as the best available theories tell us, in a chance combination of gases; it then evolved through random mutations and natural selection. All this just happened; it did not happen for any overall purpose. Now that it has resulted in the existence of beings who prefer some states of affairs to others, however, it may be possible for particular lives to be meaningful. In this sense atheists can find meaning in life.

Let us return to the comparison between the life of a psychopath and that of a more normal person. Why should the psychopath's life not be meaningful? We have seen that psychopaths are egocentric to an extreme: neither other people, nor worldly success, nor anything else really matters to them. But why is their own enjoyment of life not sufficient to give meaning to their lives?

Most of us would not be able to find happiness by deliberately setting out to enjoy ourselves without caring about anyone or anything else. The pleasures we obtained in that way would seem empty, and soon pall. We seek a meaning for our lives beyond our own pleasures, and find fulfilment and happiness in doing what we see to be meaningful. If our life has no meaning other than our own happiness, we are likely to find that when we have obtained what we think we need to be happy, happiness itself still eludes us.

That those who aim at happiness for happiness's sake often fail to find it, while others find happiness in pursuing altogether different goals, has been called "the paradox of hedonism." It is not, of course, a logical paradox but a claim about the way in which we come to be happy. Like other generalizations on this subject it lacks empirical confirmation. Yet it matches our everyday observations, and is consistent with our nature as evolved, purposive beings. Human beings survive and reproduce themselves through purposive action. We obtain happiness and fulfilment by working towards and achieving our goals. In evolutionary terms we could say that happiness functions as an internal reward for our achievements. Subjectively, we regard achieving the goal (or progressing towards it) as a reason for happiness. Our own happiness, therefore, is a by-product of aiming at something else, and not to be obtained by setting our sights on happiness alone.

The psychopath's life can now be seen to be meaningless in a way that a normal life is not. It is meaningless because it looks inward to the pleasures of the present moment and not outward to anything more long-term or far-reaching. More normal lives have meaning because they are lived to some larger purpose.

All this is speculative. You may accept or reject it to the extent that it agrees with your own observation and introspection. My next—and final—suggestion is more speculative still. It is that to find an enduring meaning in our lives it is not enough to go beyond psychopaths who have no long-term commitments or life-plans; we must also go beyond more prudent egoists who have long-term plans concerned only with their own interests. The prudent egoists may find meaning in their lives for a time, for they have the purpose of furthering their own interests; but what, in the end, does that amount to? When everything in our interests has been achieved, do we just sit back and be happy? Could we be happy in this way? Or would we decide that we had still not quite reached our target, that there was something else we needed before we could sit back and

501

enjoy it all? Most materially successful egoists take the latter route, thus escaping the necessity of admitting that they cannot find happiness in permanent holidaying. People who slaved to establish small businesses, telling themselves they would do it only until they had made enough to live comfortably, keep working long after they have passed their original target. Their material "needs" expand just fast enough to keep ahead of their income. Retirement is a problem for many because they cannot enjoy themselves without a purpose in life. The recommended solution is, of course, to find a new purpose, whether it be stamp collecting or voluntary work for a charity.

Now we begin to see where ethics comes into the problem of living a meaningful life. If we are looking for a purpose broader than our own interests, something which will allow us to see our lives as possessing significance beyond the narrow confines of our own conscious states, one obvious solution is to take up the ethical point of view. The ethical point of view does, as we have seen, require us to go beyond a personal point of view to the standpoint of an impartial spectator. Thus looking at things ethically is a way of transcending our inward-looking concerns and identifying ourselves with the most objective point of view possible—with, as Sidgwick put it, "the point of view of the universe."

The point of view of the universe is a lofty standpoint. In the rarefied air that surrounds it we may get carried away into talking, as Kant does, of the moral point of view "inevitably" humbling all who compare their own limited nature with it. I do not want to suggest anything as sweeping as this. Earlier in this chapter, in rejecting Thomas Nagel's argument for the rationality of altruism, I said that there is nothing irrational about being concerned with the quality of one's own existence in a way that one is not concerned with the quality of existence of other individuals. Without going back on this, I am now suggesting that rationality, in the broad sense which includes self-awareness and reflection on the nature and point of our own existence, may push us towards concerns broader than the quality of our own existence; but the process is not a necessary one and those who do not take part in it—or, in taking part, do not follow it all the way to the ethical point of view—are not irrational or in error. Psychopaths, for all I know, may simply be unable to obtain as much happiness through caring about others as they obtain by antisocial acts. Other people find collecting stamps an entirely adequate way of giving purpose to their lives. There is nothing irrational about that; but others again grow out of stamp collecting as they become more aware of their situation in the world and more reflective about their purposes. To this third group the ethical point of view offers a meaning and purpose in life that one does not grow out of.

(At least, one cannot grow out of the ethical point of view until all ethical tasks have been accomplished. If that utopia were ever achieved, our purposive nature might well leave us dissatisfied, much as the egoist is dissatisfied when he has everything he needs to be happy. There is nothing paradoxical about this, for we should not expect evolution to have equipped us, in advance, with the ability to enjoy a situation that has never previously occurred. Nor is this going to be a practical problem in the near future.)

"Why act morally?" cannot be given an answer that will provide everyone with overwhelming reasons for acting morally. Ethically indefensible behaviour is not always irrational. We will probably always need the sanctions of the law and social pressure to provide additional reasons against serious violations of ethical standards. On the other hand, those reflective enough to ask the question we have been discussing in this chapter are also those most likely to appreciate the reasons that can be offered for taking the ethical point of view.

STUDY QUESTIONS

1.   Do you think ethics and self-interest coincide? Compare Singer's defense of this general proposition with that of some classical philosophers who also believe that the virtuous person is happy.
2.   Should we accept the psychopaths' claim that they are actually happy when they appear to be enjoying themselves?
3.   Singer believes that the lives of psychopaths and rational egoists are meaningless and boring, perhaps even despairingly so. Has he made a persuasive case for this conclusion?
4.   What does Singer mean by the ethical point of view and why does he recommend it to us?

Moral Saints

SUSAN WOLF

Susan Wolf (b. 1952) is an associate professor of philosophy at the University of Maryland. She has published numerous essays in ethics and metaphysics.

Susan Wolf critically examines the assumption that we ought to be as morally good as possible, that is, that we ought to strive to be moral saints. She finds the idea of moral sainthood to be wanting because it discourages the development of desirable personal traits and styles that are at odds with "a life dominated by a commitment to improving the welfare of others or society as a whole." Two kinds of moral saints are distinguished. The Loving Saint enjoys total commitment: "His happiness lies in the happiness of others." The Rational Saint is dominated by duty: "This person sacrifices his own interest to others and feels the sacrifice as such."

The moral saint abjures such morally profitless activities as playing games or reading novels. Moreover, it goes against the grain for him to enjoy cynical wit. "[He] might well enjoy a good episode of *Father Knows Best* [but] he may not in good conscience be able to laugh at a Marx Brothers movie . . ." In short, the moral saint is dull. The idea of moral sainthood disturbs us because it demands that we sacrifice many things we rightly hold dear or amusing.

MORAL SAINTS By Susan Wolf. Reprinted from *The Journal of Philosophy*, August 1982, pp. 419–439. By permission of the publisher and author.

Wolf concludes that no moral theory that takes morality itself to be the overriding guide to human conduct can
be satisfactory. Some persons may choose to be moral
saints, and that is legitimate. But it is wrong to treat
moral perfection as something that all should strive for.
"[A] person may be perfectly wonderful without being
perfectly moral."

I don't know whether there are any moral saints. But if there are, I
am glad that neither I nor those about whom I care most are among
them. By *moral saint* I mean a person whose every action is as morally
good as possible, a person, that is, who is as morally worthy as can
be. Though I shall in a moment acknowledge the variety of types of
person that might be thought to satisfy this description, it seems to
me that none of these types serve as unequivocally compelling personal ideals. In other words, I believe that moral perfection, in the
sense of moral saintliness, does not constitute a model of personal
well-being toward which it would be particularly rational or good or
desirable for a human being to strive.

Outside the context of moral discussion, this will strike many as
an obvious point. But, within that context, the point, if it be granted,
will be granted with some discomfort. For within that context it is
generally assumed that one ought to be as morally good as possible
and that what limits there are to morality's hold on us are set by
features of human nature of which we ought not to be proud. If, as I
believe, the ideals that are derivable from common sense and philosophically popular moral theories do not support these assumptions,
then something has to change. Either we must change our moral
theories in ways that will make them yield more palatable ideals, or,
as I shall argue, we must change our conception of what is involved
in affirming a moral theory.

In this paper, I wish to examine the notion of a moral saint, first,
to understand what a moral saint would be like and why such a being
would be unattractive, and, second, to raise some questions about the
significance of this paradoxical figure for moral philosophy. I shall
look first at the model(s) of moral sainthood that might be extrapolated from the morality or moralities of common sense. Then I shall

consider what relations these have to conclusions that can be drawn from utilitarian and Kantian moral theories. Finally, I shall speculate on the implications of these considerations for moral philosophy.

Moral Saints and Common Sense

Consider first what, pretheoretically, would count for us—contemporary members of Western culture—as a moral saint. A necessary condition of moral sainthood would be that one's life be dominated by a commitment to improving the welfare of others or of society as a whole. As to what role this commitment must play in the individual's motivational system, two contrasting accounts suggest themselves to me which might equally be thought to qualify a person for moral sainthood.

First, a moral saint might be someone whose concern for others plays the role that is played in most of our lives by more selfish, or, at any rate, less morally worthy concerns. For the moral saint, the promotion of the welfare of others might play the role that is played for most of us by the enjoyment of material comforts, the opportunity to engage in the intellectual and physical activities of our choice, and the love, respect, and companionship of people whom we love, respect, and enjoy. The happiness of the moral saint, then, would truly lie in the happiness of others, and so he would devote himself to others gladly, and with a whole and open heart.

On the other hand, a moral saint might be someone for whom the basic ingredients of happiness are not unlike those of most of the rest of us. What makes him a moral saint is rather that he pays little or no attention to his own happiness in light of the overriding importance he gives to the wider concerns of morality. In other words, this person sacrifices his own interests to the interests of others, and feels the sacrifice as such.

Roughly, these two models may be distinguished according to whether one thinks of the moral saint as being a saint out of love or one thinks of the moral saint as being a saint out of duty (or some other intellectual appreciation and recognition of moral principles). We may refer to the first model as the model of the Loving Saint; to the second, as the model of the Rational Saint.

[A]bove all, a moral saint must have and cultivate those qualities which are apt to allow him to treat others as justly and kindly as possible. He will have the standard moral virtues to a nonstandard degree. He will be patient, considerate, even-tempered, hospitable, charitable in thought as well as in deed. He will be very reluctant to make negative judgments of other people. He will be careful not to favor some people over others on the basis of properties they could not help but have.

Perhaps what I have already said is enough to make some people begin to regard the absence of moral saints in their lives as a blessing. For there comes a point in the listing of virtues that a moral saint is likely to have where one might naturally begin to wonder whether the moral saint isn't, after all, too good—if not too good for his own good, at least too good for his own well-being. For the moral virtues, given that they are, by hypothesis, *all* present in the same individual, and to an extreme degree, are apt to crowd out the nonmoral virtues, as well as many of the interests and personal characteristics that we generally think contribute to a healthy, well-rounded, richly developed character.

In other words, if the moral saint is devoting all his time to feeding the hungry or healing the sick or raising money for Oxfam, then necessarily he is not reading Victorian novels, playing the oboe, or improving his backhand. Although no one of the interests or tastes in the category containing these latter activities could be claimed to be a necessary element in a life well lived, a life in which *none* of these possible aspects of character are developed may seem to be a life strangely barren.

The reasons why a moral saint cannot, in general, encourage the discovery and development of significant nonmoral interests and skills are not logical but practical reasons. There are, in addition, a class of nonmoral characteristics that a moral saint cannot encourage in himself for reasons that are not just practical. There is a more substantial tension between having any of these qualities unashamedly and being a moral saint. These qualities might be described as going against the moral grain. For example, a cynical or sarcastic wit, or a sense of humor that appreciates this kind of wit in others, requires that one take an attitude of resignation and pessimism toward the flaws and vices to be found in the world. A moral saint, on the other hand, has reason to take an attitude in opposition to this—he should try to look for the best in people, give them the benefit of the doubt as long as possible, try to improve regrettable situations as long as there is any hope of success. This suggests that, although a moral saint might well enjoy a good episode of *Father Knows Best,* he may not in good conscience be able to laugh at a Marx Brothers movie or enjoy a play by George Bernard Shaw.

An interest in something like gourmet cooking will be, for different reasons, difficult for a moral saint to rest easy with. For it seems to me that no plausible argument can justify the use of human resources involved in producing a *paté de canard en croute* against possible alternative beneficent ends to which these resources might be put. If there is a justification for the institution of haute cuisine, it is one which rests on the decision *not* to justify every activity against morally beneficial alternatives, and this is a decision a moral saint will never make. Presumably, an interest in high fashion or interior design will fare much the same, as will, very possibly, a cultivation of the finer arts as well.

A moral saint will have to be very, very nice. It is important that he not be offensive. The worry is that, as a result, he will have to be dull-witted or humorless or bland.

This worry is confirmed when we consider what sorts of characters, taken and refined both from life and from fiction, typically form our ideals. One would hope they would be figures who are morally good—and by this I mean more than just not morally bad—but one would hope, too, that they are not just morally good, but talented or accomplished or attractive in nonmoral ways as well. We may make ideals out of athletes, scholars, artists—more frivolously, out of cowboys, private eyes, and rock stars. We may strive for Katherine Hepburn's grace, Paul Newman's "cool"; we are attracted to the high-spirited passionate nature of Natasha Rostov; we admire the keen perceptiveness of Lambert Strether. Though there is certainly nothing immoral about the ideal characters or traits I have in mind, they cannot be superimposed upon the ideal of a moral saint. For although it is a part of many of these ideals that the characters set high, and not merely acceptable, moral standards for themselves, it is also essential to their power and attractiveness that the moral strengths go, so to speak, alongside of specific, independently admirable, nonmoral ground projects and dominant personal traits.

When one does finally turn one's eyes toward lives that are dominated by explicitly moral commitments, moreover, one finds oneself relieved at the discovery of idiosyncrasies or eccentricities not quite in line with the picture of moral perfection. One prefers the blunt, tactless, and opinionated Betsy Trotwood to the unfailingly kind and patient Agnes Copperfield; one prefers the mischievousness and the sense of irony in Chesterton's Father Brown to the innocence and undiscriminating love of St. Francis.

It seems that, as we look in our ideals for people who achieve nonmoral varieties of personal excellence in conjunction with or colored by some version of high moral tone, we look in our paragons of moral excellence for people whose moral achievements occur in conjunction with or colored by some interests or traits that have low moral tone. In other words, there seems to be a limit to how much morality we can stand. . . .

Moreover, there is something odd about the idea of morality itself, or moral goodness, serving as the object of a dominant passion in the way that a more concrete and specific vision of a goal (even a concrete *moral* goal) might be imagined to serve. Morality itself does not seem to be a suitable object of passion. Thus, when one reflects, for example, on the Loving Saint easily and gladly giving up his fishing trip or his stereo or his hot fudge sundae at the drop of the moral hat, one is apt to wonder not at how much he loves morality, but at how little he loves these other things. One thinks that, if he can give these up so easily, he does not know what it *is* to truly love them. There seems, in other words, to be a kind of joy which the Loving Saint, either by nature or by practice, is incapable of experiencing. The Rational Saint, on the other hand, might retain strong nonmoral and concrete desires—he simply denies himself the opportunity to act on them. But this is no less troubling. The Loving Saint one might suspect of missing a piece of perceptual machinery, of being blind to some of what the world has to offer. The Rational Saint, who sees it but foregoes it, one suspects of having a different problem—a pathological fear of damnation, perhaps, or an extreme form of self-hatred that interferes with his ability to enjoy the enjoyable in life.

In other words, the ideal of a life of moral sainthood disturbs not simply because it is an ideal of a life in which morality unduly dominates. The normal person's direct and specific desires for objects, activities, and events that conflict with the attainment of moral perfection are not simply sacrificed but removed, suppressed, or subsumed. The way in which morality, unlike other possible goals, is apt to dominate is particularly disturbing, for it seems to require either the lack or the denial of the existence of an identifiable, personal self.

This distinctively troubling feature is not, I think, absolutely unique to the ideal of the moral saint, as I have been using that phrase. It is shared by the conception of the pure aesthete, by a certain kind of religious ideal, and, somewhat paradoxically, by the model of the thorough-going, self-conscious egoist. It is not a coincidence that the ways of comprehending the world of which these ideals are the extreme embodiments are sometimes described as "moralities" themselves. At any rate, they compete with what we ordinarily mean by "morality." Nor is it a coincidence that these ideals are naturally described as fanatical. But it is easy to see that these other types of perfection cannot serve as satisfactory personal ideals; for the realization of these ideals would be straightforwardly immoral. It may come as a surprise to some that there may in addition be such a thing as a *moral* fanatic.

Some will object that I am being unfair to "common-sense morality"—that it does not really require a moral saint to be either a disgusting goody-goody or an obsessive ascetic. Admittedly, there is no logical inconsistency between having any of the personal characteristics I have mentioned and being a moral saint. It is not morally wrong to notice the faults and shortcomings of others or to recognize and appreciate nonmoral talents and skills. Nor is it immoral to be an avid Celtics fan or to have a passion for caviar or to be an excellent cellist. With enough imagination, we can always contrive a suitable history and set of circumstances that will embrace such characteristics in one or another specific fictional story of a perfect moral saint.

If one turned onto the path of moral sainthood relatively late in life, one may have already developed interests that can be turned to moral purposes. It may be that a good golf game is just what is needed to secure that big donation to Oxfam. Perhaps the cultivation of one's exceptional artistic talent will turn out to be the way one can make one's greatest contribution to society. Furthermore, one might stumble upon joys and skills in the very service of morality. If, because the children are short a ninth player for the team, one's generous offer to serve reveals a natural fielding arm or if one's part in the campaign against nuclear power requires accepting a lobbyist's invitation to lunch at Le Lion d'Or, there is no moral gain in denying the satisfaction one gets from these activities. The moral saint, then, may, by happy accident, find himself with nonmoral virtues on which he can capitalize morally or which make psychological demands to which he has no choice but to attend. The point is that, for a moral saint, the existence of these interests and skills can be given at best the status of happy accidents—they cannot be encouraged for their own sakes as distinct, independent aspects of the realization of human good.

It must be remembered that from the fact that there is a tension between having any of these qualities and being a moral saint it does not follow that having any of these qualities is immoral. For it is not part of common-sense morality that one ought to be a moral saint. Still, if someone just happened to want to be a moral saint, he or she would not have or encourage these qualities, and, on the basis of our common-sense values, this counts as a reason not to want to be a moral saint. . . .

The fact that the moral saint would be without qualities which we have and which, indeed, we like to have, does not in itself provide reason to condemn the ideal of the moral saint. The fact that some of these qualities are good qualities, however, and that they are qualities we *ought* to like, does provide reason to discourage this ideal and to offer other ideals in its place. In other words, some of the qualities the moral saint necessarily lacks are virtues, albeit nonmoral virtues, in the unsaintly characters who have them. The feats of Groucho Marx, Reggie Jackson, and the head chef at Lutèce are impressive accomplishments that it is not only permissible but positively appropriate to recognize as such. In general, the admiration of and striving toward achieving any of a great variety of forms of personal excellence are character traits it is valuable and desirable for people to have. In advocating the development of these varieties of excellence, we advocate nonmoral reasons for acting, and in thinking that it is good for a person to strive for an ideal that gives a substantial role to the interests and values that correspond to these virtues, we implicitly acknowledge the goodness of ideals incompatible with that of the moral saint. Finally, if we think that it is *as* good, or even better for a person to strive for one of these ideals than it is for him or her to strive for and realize the ideal of the moral saint, we express a conviction that it is good not to be a moral saint.

Moral Saints and Moral Theories

I have tried so far to paint a picture—or, rather, two pictures—of what a moral saint might be like, drawing on what I take to be the attitudes and beliefs about morality prevalent in contemporary, common-sense thought. To my suggestion that common-sense morality generates conceptions of moral saints that are unattractive or otherwise unacceptable, it is open to someone to reply, "so much the worse for common-sense morality." After all, it is often claimed that the goal of moral philosophy is to correct and improve upon common-sense morality, and I have as yet given no attention to the question of what conceptions of moral sainthood, if any, are generated from the leading moral theories of our time.

A quick, breezy reading of utilitarian and Kantian writings will suggest the images, respectively, of the Loving Saint and the Rational Saint. A utilitarian, with his emphasis on happiness, will certainly prefer the Loving Saint to the Rational one, since the Loving Saint will himself be a happier person than the Rational Saint. A Kantian, with his emphasis on reason, on the other hand, will find at least as much to praise in the latter as in the former. Still, both models, drawn as they are from common sense, appeal to an impure mixture of utilitarian and Kantian intuitions. A more careful examination of these moral theories raises questions about whether either model of moral sainthood would really be advocated by a believer in the explicit doctrines associated with either of these views.

Certainly, the utilitarian in no way denies the value of self-realization. He in no way disparages the development of interests, talents, and other personally attractive traits that I have claimed the moral saint would be without. Indeed, since just these features enhance the happiness both of the individuals who possess them and of those with whom they associate, the ability to promote these features both in oneself and in others will have considerable positive weight in utilitarian calculations.

This implies that the utilitarian would not support moral

sainthood as a universal ideal. A world in which everyone, or even a large number of people, achieved moral sainthood—even a world in which they *strove* to achieve it—would probably contain less happiness than a world in which people realized a diversity of ideals involving a variety of personal and perfectionist values. More pragmatic considerations also suggest that, if the utilitarian wants to influence more people to achieve more good, then he would do better to encourage them to pursue happiness-producing goals that are more attractive and more within a normal person's reach.

These considerations still leave open, however, the question of what kind of an ideal the committed utilitarian should privately aspire to himself. Utilitarianism requires him to want to achieve the greatest general happiness, and this would seem to commit him to the ideal of the moral saint.

One might try to use the claims I made earlier as a basis for an argument that a utilitarian should choose to give up utilitarianism. If, as I have said, a moral saint would be a less happy person both to be and to be around than many other possible ideals, perhaps one could create more total happiness by not trying too hard to promote the total happiness. But this argument is simply unconvincing in light of the empirical circumstances of our world. The gain in happiness that would accrue to oneself and one's neighbors by a more well-rounded, richer life than that of the moral saint would be pathetically small in comparison to the amount by which one could increase the general happiness if one devoted oneself explicitly to the care of the sick, the downtrodden, the starving, and the homeless. Of course, there may be psychological limits to the extent to which a person can devote himself to such things without going crazy. But the utilitarian's individual limitations would not thereby become a positive feature of his personal ideals.

The unattractiveness of the moral saint, then, ought not rationally convince the utilitarian to abandon his utilitarianism. It may, however, convince him to take efforts not to wear his saintly moral aspirations on his sleeve. If it is not too difficult, the utilitarian will try not to make those around him uncomfortable. He will not want to appear "holier than thou"; he will not want to inhibit others' ability to enjoy themselves. In practice, this might make the perfect utilitarian a less nauseating companion than the moral saint I earlier portrayed. But insofar as this kind of reasoning produces a more bearable public personality, it is at the cost of giving him a personality that must be evaluated as hypocritical and condescending when his private thoughts and attitudes are taken into account.

Still, the criticisms I have raised against the saint of common-sense morality should make some difference to the utilitarian's conception of an ideal which neither requires him to abandon his utilitarian principles nor forces him to fake an interest he does not have or a judgment he does not make. For it may be that a limited and carefully monitored allotment of time and energy to be devoted to the pursuit of some nonmoral interests or to the development of some nonmoral talents would make a person a better contributor to the general welfare than he would be if he allowed himself no indulgences of this sort. The enjoyment of such activities in no way compromises a commitment to utilitarian principles as long as the involvement with these activities is conditioned by a willingness to give them up whenever it is recognized that they cease to be in the general interest.

This will go some way in mitigating the picture of the Loving Saint that an understanding of utilitarianism will on first impression suggest. But I think it will not go very far. For the limitations on time and energy will have to be rather severe, and the need to monitor will restrict not only the extent but also the quality of one's attachment to these interests and traits. They are only weak and somewhat peculiar sorts of passions to which one can consciously remain so conditionally committed. Moreover, the way in which the utilitarian can enjoy these "extra-curricular" aspects of his life is simply not the way in which these aspects are to be enjoyed insofar as they figure into our less saintly ideals.

The problem is not exactly that the utilitarian values these aspects of his life only as a means to an end, for the enjoyment he and others get from these aspects are not a means to, but a part of, the general happiness. Nonetheless, he values these things only because of and insofar as they *are* a part of the general happiness. He values them, as it were, under the description "a contribution to the general happiness." This is to be contrasted with the various ways in which these aspects of life may be valued by nonutilitarians. A person might love literature because of the insights into human nature literature affords. Another might love the cultivation of roses because roses are things of great beauty and delicacy. It may be true that these features of the respective activities also explain why these activities are happiness-producing. But, to the nonutilitarian, this may not be to the point.

For if one values these activities in these more direct ways, one may not be willing to exchange them for others that produce an equal, or even a greater amount of happiness. From that point of view, it is not because they produce happiness that these activities are valuable; it is because these activities are valuable in more direct and specific ways that they produce happiness.

To adopt a phrase of Bernard Williams', the utilitarian's manner of valuing the not explicitly moral aspects of his life "provides (him) with one thought too many."[1] The requirement that the utilitarian have this thought—periodically, at least—is indicative of not only a weakness but a shallowness in his appreciation of the aspects in question. Thus, the ideals toward which a utilitarian could acceptably strive would remain too close to the model of the common-sense moral saint to escape the criticisms of that model which I earlier suggested. Whether a Kantian would be similarly committed to so restrictive and unattractive a range of possible ideals is a somewhat more difficult question.

The Kantian believes that being morally worthy consists in always acting from maxims that one could will to be universal law, and doing this not out of any pathological desire but out of reverence for the moral law as such. Or, to take a different formulation of the categorical imperative, the Kantian believes that moral action consists in treating other persons always as ends and never as means only. Presumably, and according to Kant himself, the Kantian thereby commits himself to some degree of benevolence as well as to the rules of fair play. But we surely would not will that *every* person become a moral saint, and treating others as ends hardly requires bending over backwards to protect and promote their interests. On one interpretation of Kantian doctrine, then, moral perfection would be achieved simply by unerring obedience to a limited set of side-constraints. On this interpretation, Kantian theory simply does not yield an ideal conception of a person of any fullness comparable to that of the moral saints I have so far been portraying.

On the other hand, Kant does say explicitly that we have a duty of benevolence, a duty not only to allow others to pursue their ends, but to take up their ends as our own. In addition, we have positive duties to ourselves, duties to increase our natural as well as our moral

---

[1]"Persons, Character and Morality" in Amelie Rorty, ed., *The Identities of Persons* (Berkeley: University of California Press, 1976), 214.

perfection. These duties are unlimited in the degree to which they *may* dominate a life. If action in accordance with and motivated by the thought of these duties is considered virtuous, it is natural to assume that the more one performs such actions, the more virtuous one is. Moreover, of virtue in general Kant says, "it is an ideal which is unattainable while yet our duty is constantly to approximate to it."[2] On this interpretation, then, the Kantian moral saint, like the other moral saints I have been considering, is dominated by the motivation to be moral.

Which of these interpretations of Kant one prefers will depend on the interpretation and the importance one gives to the role of the imperfect duties in Kant's over-all system. Rather than choose between them here, I shall consider each briefly in turn.

On the second interpretation of Kant, the Kantian moral saint is, not surprisingly, subject to many of the same objections I have been raising against other versions of moral sainthood. Though the Kantian saint may differ from the utilitarian saint as to *which* actions he is bound to perform and which he is bound to refrain from performing, I suspect that the range of activities acceptable to the Kantian saint will remain objectionably restrictive. Moreover, the manner in which the Kantian saint must think about and justify the activities he pursues and the character traits he develops will strike us, as it did with the utilitarian saint, as containing "one thought too many." As the utilitarian could value his activities and character traits only insofar as they fell under the description of "contributions to the general happiness," the Kantian would have to value his activities and character traits insofar as they were manifestations of respect for the moral law. If the development of our powers to achieve physical, intellectual, or artistic excellence, or the activities directed toward making others happy are to have any moral worth, they must arise from a reverence for the dignity that members of our species have as a result of being endowed with pure practical reason. This is a good and noble motivation, to be sure. But it is hardly what one expects to be dominantly behind a person's aspirations to dance as well as Fred Astaire, to paint as well as Picasso, or to solve some outstanding

---

[2]Immanuel Kant, *The Doctrine of Virtue*, trans. Mary J. Gregor (New York: Harper and Row, 1964), 71.

problem in abstract algebra, and it is hardly what one hopes to find lying dominantly behind a father's action on behalf of his son or a lover's on behalf of her beloved.

Since the basic problem with any of the models of moral sainthood we have been considering is that they are dominated by a single, all-important value under which all other possible values must be subsumed, it may seem that the alternative interpretation of Kant, as providing a stringent but finite set of obligations and constraints, might provide a more acceptable morality. According to this interpretation of Kant, one is as morally good as can be so long as one devotes some limited portion of one's energies toward altruism and the maintenance of one's physical and spiritual health, and otherwise pursues one's independently motivated interests and values in such a way as to avoid overstepping certain bounds. Certainly, if it be a requirement of an acceptable moral theory that perfect obedience to its laws and maximal devotion to its interests and concerns be something we can wholeheartedly strive for in ourselves and wish for in those around us, it will count in favor of this brand of Kantianism that its commands can be fulfilled without swallowing up the perfect moral agent's entire personality.

Even this more limited understanding of morality, if its connection to Kant's views is to be taken at all seriously, is not likely to give an unqualified seal of approval to the nonmorally directed ideals I have been advocating. For Kant is explicit about what he calls "duties of apathy and self-mastery"—duties to ensure that our passions are never so strong as to interfere with calm, practical deliberation, or so deep as to wrest control from the more disinterested, rational part of ourselves. The tight and self-conscious rein we are thus obliged to keep on our commitments to specific individuals and causes will doubtless restrict our value in these things, assigning them a necessarily attenuated place.

A more interesting objection to this brand of Kantianism, however, comes when we consider the implications of placing the kind of upper bound on moral worthiness which seemed to count in favor of this conception of morality. For to put such a limit on one's capacity to be moral is effectively to deny, not just the moral necessity, but the moral goodness of a devotion to benevolence and the maintenance of justice that passes beyond a certain, required point. It is to deny the possibility of going morally above and beyond the call of a restricted set of duties. Despite my claim that all-consuming moral saintliness is not a particularly healthy and desirable ideal, it seems perverse to insist that, were moral saints to exist, they would not, in their way, be remarkably noble and admirable figures. Despite my conviction that it is as rational and as good for a person to take Katharine Hepburn or Jane Austen as her role model instead of Mother Teresa, it would be absurd to deny that Mother Teresa is a morally better person.

I can think of two ways of viewing morality as having an upper bound. First, we can think that altruism and impartiality are indeed positive moral interests, but that they are moral only if the degree to which these interests are actively pursued remains within certain fixed limits. Second, we can think that these positive interests are only incidentally related to morality and that the essence of morality lies elsewhere, in, say, an implicit social contract or in the recognition of our own dignified rationality. According to the first conception of morality, there is a cut-off line to the amount of altruism or to the extent of devotion to justice and fairness that is worthy of moral praise. But to draw this line earlier than the line that brings the altruist in question into a worse-off position than all those to whom he devotes himself seems unacceptably artificial and gratuitous. According to the second conception, these positive interests are not essentially related to morality at all. But then we are unable to regard a more affectionate and generous expression of good will toward others as a natural and reasonable extension of morality, and we encourage a cold and unduly self-centered approach to the development and evaluation of our motivations and concerns.

A moral theory that does not contain the seeds of an all-consuming ideal of moral sainthood thus seems to place false and unnatural limits on our opportunity to do moral good and our potential to deserve moral praise. Yet the main thrust of the arguments of this paper has been leading to the conclusion that, when such ideals are present, they are not ideals to which it is particularly reasonable or healthy or desirable for human beings to aspire. These claims, taken together, have the appearance of a dilemma from which there is no obvious escape. In a moment, I shall argue that, despite appearances, these claims should not be understood as constituting a dilemma. But, before I do, let me briefly describe another path which those who are convinced by my above remarks may feel inclined to take.

If the above remarks are understood to be implicitly critical of the views on the content of morality which seem most popular today, an alternative that naturally suggests itself is that we revise our views about the content of morality. More specifically, my remarks may be taken to support a more Aristotelian, or even a more Nietzschean, approach to moral philosophy. Such a change in approach involves substantially broadening or replacing our contemporary intuitions about which character traits constitute moral virtues and vices and which interests constitute moral interests. If, for example, we include personal bearing, or creativity, or sense of style, as features that contribute to one's *moral* personality, then we can create moral ideals which are incompatible with and probably more attractive than the Kantian and utilitarian ideals I have discussed. Given such an alteration of our conception of morality, the figures with which I have been concerned above might, far from being considered to be moral saints, be seen as morally inferior to other more appealing or more interesting models of individuals.

This approach seems unlikely to succeed, if for no other reason, because it is doubtful that any single, or even any reasonably small number of substantial personal ideals could capture the full range of possible ways of realizing human potential or achieving human good which deserve encouragement and praise. Even if we could provide a sufficiently broad characterization of the range of positive ways for human beings to live, however, I think there are strong reasons not to want to incorporate such a characterization more centrally into the framework of morality itself. For, in claiming that a character trait or activity is morally good, one claims that there is a certain kind of reason for developing that trait or engaging in that activity. Yet, lying behind our criticism of more conventional conceptions of moral sainthood, there seems to be a recognition that among the immensely valuable traits and activities that a human life might positively embrace are some of which we hope that, if a person does embrace them, he does so *not* for moral reasons. In other words, no matter how flexible we make the guide to conduct which we choose to label "morality," no matter how rich we make the life in which perfect obedience to this guide would result, we will have reason to hope that a person does not wholly rule and direct his life by the abstract and impersonal consideration that such a life would be morally good.

Once it is recognized that morality itself should not serve as a comprehensive guide to conduct, moreover, we can see reasons to retain the admittedly vague contemporary intuitions about what the classification of moral and nonmoral virtues, interests, and the like should be. That is, there seem to be important differences between the aspects of a person's life which are currently considered appropriate objects of moral evaluation and the aspects that might be included under the altered conception of morality we are now considering, which the latter approach would tend wrongly to blur or to neglect. Moral evaluation now is focused primarily on features of a person's life over which that person has control; it is largely restricted to aspects of his life which are likely to have considerable effect on other people. These restrictions seem as they should be. Even if responsible people could reach agreement as to what constituted good taste or a healthy degree of well-roundedness, for example, it seems wrong to insist that everyone try to achieve these things or to blame someone who fails or refuses to conform.

If we are not to respond to the unattractiveness of the moral ideals that contemporary theories yield either by offering alternative theories with more palatable ideals or by understanding these theories in such a way as to prevent them from yielding ideals at all, how, then, are we to respond? Simply, I think, by admitting that moral ideals do not, and need not, make the best personal ideals. Earlier, I mentioned one of the consequences of regarding as a test of an adequate moral theory that perfect obedience to its laws and maximal devotion to its interests be something we can wholeheartedly strive for in ourselves and wish for in those around us. Drawing out the consequences somewhat further should, I think, make us more doubtful of the proposed test than of the theories which, on this test, would fail. Given the empirical circumstances of our world, it seems to be an ethical fact that we have unlimited potential to be morally good, and endless opportunity to promote moral interests. But this is not incompatible with the not-so-ethical fact that we have sound, compelling, and not particularly selfish reasons to choose not to devote ourselves univocally to realizing this potential or to taking up this opportunity.

Thus, in one sense at least, I am not really criticizing either Kantianism or utilitarianism. Insofar as the point of view I am offering bears directly on recent work in moral philosophy, in fact, it bears on critics of these theories who, in a spirit not unlike the spirit of most of this paper, point out that the perfect utilitarian would be flawed in this way or the perfect Kantian flawed in that.[3] The assumption lying behind these claims, implicitly or explicitly, has been that the recognition of these flaws shows us something wrong with utilitarianism as opposed to Kantianism, or something wrong with Kantianism as opposed to utilitarianism, or something wrong with both of these theories as opposed to some nameless third alternative. The claims of this paper suggest, however, that this assumption is unwarranted. The flaws of a perfect master of a moral theory need not reflect flaws in the intramoral content of the theory itself.

Moral Saints and Moral Philosophy

In pointing out the regrettable features and the necessary absence of some desirable features in a moral saint, I have not meant to condemn the moral saint or the person who aspires to become one. Rather, I have meant to insist that the ideal of moral sainthood should not be held as a standard against which any other ideal must be judged or justified, and that the posture we take in response to the recognition that our lives are not as morally good as they might be need not be defensive.[4] It is misleading to insist that one is *permitted* to live a life in which the goals, relationships, activities, and interests that one pursues are not maximally morally good. For our lives are not so comprehensively subject to the requirement that we apply for permission, and our nonmoral reasons for the goals we set ourselves are not excuses, but may rather be positive, good reasons which do not exist *despite* any reasons that might threaten to outweigh them. In other words, a person may be *perfectly wonderful* without being *perfectly moral*.[5]

---

[3]See, e.g., Williams, "Persons, Character," and J. J. C. Smart and Bernard Williams, *Utilitarianism: For and Against* (New York: Cambridge, 1973). Also, Michael Stocker, "The Schizophrenia of Modern Ethical Theories," *Journal of Philosophy* 63, 14 (August 12, 1976): 453–66.

[4]George Orwell makes a similar point in "Reflections on Gandhi," in *A Collection of Essays by George Orwell* (New York: Harcourt Brace Jovanovich, 1945), 176: "sainthood is . . . a thing that human beings must avoid. . . . It is too readily assumed that . . . the ordinary man only rejects it because it is too difficult; in other words, that the average human being is a failed saint. It is doubtful whether this is true. Many people genuinely do not wish to be saints, and it is probable that some who achieve or aspire to sainthood have never felt much temptation to be human beings."

[5]I have benefited from the comments of many people who have heard or read an earlier draft of this paper. I wish particularly to thank Douglas MacLean, Robert Nozick, Martha Nussbaum, and the Society for Ethics and Legal Philosophy.

STUDY QUESTIONS

1. Discuss Wolf's thematic remark that morality does not seem to be a suitable object of passion. Is this why she sees the moral saint as a dull personality? What is wrong with being worthy and right without being very interesting? (Is it necessary to be "interesting"?)

2. What specifically does Wolf find unattractive about the Loving Saint? The Rational Saint? Do you share her reactions?

3. Morality seems by its very nature to invite a total dedication, one that has no upper limit. It would seem that there is nothing wrong with those who exclusively dedicate themselves to being moral, even at the expense of other ways of living. Yet Wolf finds that the ideal of total dedication is unattractive and not universally worthy of pursuit. How does Wolf deal with the fact that morality seems to call for extreme dedication?

Saints

ROBERT M. ADAMS

Robert M. Adams (b. 1937) is professor of philosophy at the University of California at Los Angeles. He has published articles on topics in ethics, metaphysics, and the history of modern philosophy. Oxford University Press has recently published a collection of Adams' papers entitled *The Virtue of Faith and Other Essays in Philosophical Theology*.

Robert Adams defends sainthood from the charge of dullness. He first points out that Wolf's unattractive picture of the moral saint as "so very, very nice" and as lacking the "ability to enjoy the enjoyable in life" is not true to life. Real saints are not bland. Adams argues that Wolf arrived at her unsympathetic picture by adopting a conception of saints as persons who maximize moral value in every one of their actions. According to Adams, Wolf errs in seeing value only in those actions that improve the lot of others. While real saints certainly have been devoted to others, such devotion has not been exclusive. Saints perceive their goodness as overflowing from a boundless divine source. They are not obsessed with being perfect; nor do we think any the less of them for this. In characterizing the saint as a moral perfectionist, Wolf gets it wrong.

SAINTS By Robert M. Adams. Reprinted from *The Journal of Philosophy*, July 1984, pp. 392–401. By permission of the publisher and author.

Adams agrees with Wolf that maximal devotion to morality is not the sole ideal of perfection. But because Adams's conception of sainthood differs from Wolf's, Adams does not accept Wolf's view that not everyone should aspire to sainthood. For Adams sees nothing wrong in the attempt to tap the source of divine inspiration in the pursuit of perfection in art or philosophy, or in any of the fields that take time away from a life exclusively devoted to good moral works. Adams agrees with Wolf that morality can be exaggerated when he says, "we ought not to make a religion of morality." Indeed, from a religious point of view, the kind of narrow and exclusive preoccupation with morality that Wolf rightly criticizes as unworthy of maximal devotion is a kind of idolatry. Saints are not exclusively moral. Since God is a lover of beauty, the divinely inspired artist could also be saintly.

Wolf looks with disfavor on a life of maximal devotion to any ideal, but Adams justifies maximal devotion to God as a way of living a variegated life of excellence. Adams notes that, historically, moral concepts have their origin in religion, and ends his essay by raising the question whether a satisfactory conception of morality can be detached from all reference to a divine source.

One of the merits of Susan Wolf's fascinating and disturbing essay on "Moral Saints"[1] is that it brings out very sharply a fundamental problem in modern moral philosophy. On the one hand, we want to say that morality is of supreme value, always taking precedence over other grounds of choice, and that what is morally best must be absolutely best. On the other hand, if we consider what it would be like really to live in accordance with that complete priority of the moral, the ideal of life that emerges is apt to seem dismally grey and unattractive, as Wolf persuasively argues. I want to present a diagnosis of the problem that differs from Wolf's. Replies to Wolf might be

---

[1]Originally published in *The Journal of Philosophy* 79, 8 (August 1982): 419–439.

offered on behalf of the utilitarian and Kantian moral theories that she discusses, but of them I shall have little to say. My concern here is to see that sainthood, not Kant or utilitarianism, receives its due.

What Are Saints Like?

The first thing to be said is that there *are* saints—people like St. Francis of Assisi and Gandhi and Mother Teresa—and they are quite different from what Wolf thinks a moral saint would be. In the end I will conclude that they are not exactly *moral* saints in Wolf's sense. But she writes about some of them as if they were, and discussions of moral sainthood surely owe to the real saints much of their grip on our attention. So it will be to the point to contrast the actuality of sainthood with Wolf's picture of the moral saint.

Wolf argues that moral saints will be "unattractive" because they will be lacking in individuality and in the "ability to enjoy the enjoyable in life," and will be so "very, very nice" and inoffensive that they "will have to be dull-witted or humorless or bland." But the real saints are not like that. It is easier to think of St. Francis as eccentric than as lacking in individuality. And saints are not bland. Many have been offended at them for being very, very truthful instead of very, very nice. (Think of Gandhi—or Jesus.) Saints may not enjoy all the same things as other people, and perhaps a few of them have been melancholy; but an exceptional capacity for joy is more characteristic of them. (For all his asceticism, one thinks again of St. Francis.) There are joys (and not minor ones) that only saints can know. And as for attractiveness, the people we think of first as saints were plainly people who were intensely interesting to almost everyone who had anything to do with them, and immensely attractive to at least a large proportion of those people. They have sometimes been controversial, but rarely dull; and their charisma has inspired many to leave everything else in order to follow them.

Wolf may have set herself up, to some extent, for such contrasts, by conceiving of moral sainthood purely in terms of commitment or devotion to moral ends or principles. There are other, less voluntary virtues that are essential equipment for a saint—humility, for instance, and perceptiveness, courage, and a mind unswayed by the voices of the crowd. The last of these is part of what keeps saints from being bland or lacking in individuality.

In order to understand how Wolf arrives at her unflattering picture of the moral saint, however, we must examine her stated conception of moral sainthood.

Wolf's Argument

Wolf states three criteria for moral sainthood; and they are not equivalent. (1) In her third sentence she says, "By *moral saint* I mean a person whose every action is as morally good as possible." (2) Immediately she adds: "a person, that is, who is as morally worthy as can be." Her words imply that these two characterizations amount to the same thing, but it seems to me that the first expresses at most a very questionable test for the satisfaction of the second. The idea that only a morally imperfect person would spend half an hour doing something morally indifferent, like taking a nap, when she could have done something morally praiseworthy instead, like spending the time in moral self-examination, is at odds with our usual judgments and ought not to be assumed at the outset. The assumption that the perfection of a person, in at least the moral type of value, depends on the maximization of that type of value in every single action of the person lies behind much that is unattractive in Wolf's picture of moral sainthood; but I believe it is a fundamental error.

(3) On the next page we get a third criterion: "A necessary condition of moral sainthood would be that one's life be dominated by a commitment to improving the welfare of others or of society as a whole." Here again, while it might be claimed that this is a necessary condition of a person's, or her acts', being as morally worthy as possible, the claim is controversial. It has been held as a moral thesis that the pursuit of our own perfection ought sometimes to take precedence for us over the welfare of others. The utilitarian, likewise, will presumably think that many people ought to devote their greatest efforts to their own happiness and perfection, because that is what will maximize utility. Given a utilitarian conception of moral rightness as doing what will maximize utility, why shouldn't a utilitarian say that such people, and their acts, can be as morally worthy as possible (and thus can satisfy Wolf's first two criteria of moral sainthood) when they pursue their own happiness and perfection? Presumably, therefore, Wolf is relying heavily on her third criterion, as an independent test, when she says that such cases imply "that the

utilitarian would not support moral sainthood as a universal idea."

This third criterion is obviously related to Wolf's conception of morality. Later in her paper she contrasts the moral point of view with "the point of view of individual perfection," which is "the point of view from which we consider what kinds of lives are good lives, and what kinds of persons it would be good for ourselves and others to be." "The moral point of view . . . is the point of view one takes up insofar as one takes the recognition of the fact that one is just one person among others equally real and deserving of the good things in life as a fact with practical consequences, a fact the recognition of which demands expression in one's actions and in the form of one's practical deliberations." And moral theories are theories that offer "answers to the question of what the most correct or the best way to express this fact is."

This account of moral theory and the moral point of view is in clear agreement with Wolf's third criterion of moral sainthood on one central issue: morality, for her, has exclusively to do with one's regard for the good (and perhaps she would add, the rights) of other persons. One's own dignity or courage or sexuality pose *moral* issues for Wolf only to the extent that they impinge on the interests of other people. Otherwise they can be evaluated from the point of view of individual perfection (and she obviously takes that evaluation very seriously) but not from the moral point of view. This limitation of the realm of the moral is controversial, but (without wishing to be committed to it in other contexts) I shall use "moral" and "morality" here in accordance with Wolf's conception.

It might still be doubted whether her third criterion of moral sainthood follows from her definition of the moral point of view. A utilitarian, for reasons indicated above, might argue that for many people a life not "dominated by a commitment to improving the welfare of others or of society as a whole" could perfectly express "recognition of the fact that one is just one person among others equally real and deserving of the good things of life." Dedication to the good of others is not the same as weighing their good equally with one's own. But if the former is not implied by the latter, it is the altruistic dedication that constitutes Wolf's operative criterion of moral excellence (though I suspect she looks to the equal weighing for a criterion of the morally obligatory). I do not wish to quibble about this; for what interests me most in Wolf's paper is what she says about moral devotion, and weighing one's own good equally with the good of others (demanding as that may be) is something less than devotion.

Thus Wolf's three criteria of moral sainthood seem to me to be separable. The second (maximal moral worthiness of the person, rather than the act) probably comes the closest to expressing an intuitive idea of moral sainthood in its most general form. But the other two seem to be her working criteria. I take all three to be incorporated as necessary conditions in Wolf's conception of moral sainthood.

The center of Wolf's argument can now be stated quite simply. It is that in a life perfectly "dominated by a commitment to improving the welfare of others or of society as a whole" there will not be room for other interests. In particular there will not be time or energy or attention for other good interests, such as the pursuit of aesthetic or athletic excellence. The moral saint will not be able to pursue these interests, or encourage them in others, unless "by happy accident" they have an unusual humanitarian payoff. But from the point of view of individual perfection we have to say that some of the qualities that the moral saint is thus prevented from fostering in herself or others are very desirable, and there are commendable ideals in which they have a central place. So "if we think that it is *as* good, or even better for a person to strive for one of these ideals than it is for him or her to strive for and realize the ideal of the moral saint, we express a conviction that it is good not to be a moral saint."

Sainthood and Religion

While those actual saints whom I have mentioned have indeed been exceptionally devoted to improving the lives and circumstances of other people, it would be misleading to say that their lives have been "dominated by a commitment to improving the welfare of others or of society as a whole." For sainthood is an essentially religious phenomenon, and even so political a saint as Gandhi saw his powerful humanitarian concern in the context of a more comprehensive devotion to God. This touches the center of Wolf's argument, and helps to explain why actual saints are so unlike her picture of the moral saint. Wolf's moral saint sees limited resources for satisfying immense human needs and unlimited human desires, and devotes himself wholly to satisfying them as fully (and perhaps as fairly) as possible. This leaves him no time or energy for anything that does not *have* to be done. Not so the saints. The substance of sainthood is not sheer will power striving like Sisyphus (or like Wolf's Rational Saint) to accomplish a boundless task, but goodness overflowing from a boundless source. Or so, at least, the saints perceive it.

They commonly have time for things that do not *have* to be done, because their vision is not of needs that exceed any possible means of satisfying them, but of a divine goodness that is more than adequate to every need. They are not in general even trying to make their *every action* as good as possible, and thus they diverge from Wolf's first criterion of moral sainthood. The humility of the saint may even require that she spend considerable stretches of time doing nothing of any great importance or excellence. Saintliness is not perfectionism, though some saints have been perfectionistic in various ways. There is an unusual moral goodness in the saints, but we shall not grasp it by asking whether any of their actions could have been morally worthier. What makes us think of a Gandhi, for example, as a saint is something more positive, which I would express by saying that goodness was present in him in exceptional power.

Many saints have felt the tensions on which Wolf's argument turns. Albert Schweitzer, whom many have honored as a twentieth-century saint, was one who felt keenly the tension between artistic and intellectual achievement on the one hand and a higher claim of humanitarian commitment on the other. Yet in the midst of his humanitarian activities in Africa, he kept a piano and spent some time playing it— even before he realized that keeping up this skill would help him raise money for his mission. Very likely that time could have been employed in actions that would have been morally worthier, but that fact by itself surely has no tendency to disqualify Schweitzer from sainthood, in the sense in which people are actually counted as saints. We do not demand as a necessary condition of sainthood that the saint's every act be the morally worthiest possible in the circumstances, nor that he try to make it so.

The religious character of sainthood also helps to explain how the saint can be so self-giving without lacking (as Wolf suggests the Loving Saint must) an interest in his own condition as a determinant of his own happiness. In fact saints have typically been intensely and frankly interested in their own condition, their own perfection, and their own happiness. Without this interest they would hardly have been fitted to lead others for whom they desired perfection and happiness. What enables them to give of themselves unstintedly is not a lack of interest in their own persons, but a trust in God to provide for their growth and happiness.

Should Everyone Be a Saint?

Even if it can be shown that the life of a Gandhi or a St. Francis is happier and more attractive than Wolf claims that the life of a moral saint would be, we still face questions analogous to some of those she presses. Would it be good if everyone were a saint? Should we all aspire to be saints?

Not everybody *could* be a Gandhi. He himself thought otherwise. "Whatever is possible for me is possible even for a child," he wrote.[2] This is a point on which we may venture to disagree with him. A life like his involves, in religious terms, a vocation that is not given to everyone. Or to put the matter in more secular terms, not all who set themselves to do it will accomplish as much good by humanitarian endeavor as Wolf seems to assume that any utilitarian can. But perhaps some of us assume too easily that we could not be a Gandhi. In all probability there could be more Gandhis than there are, and it would be a very good thing if there were.

Wolf, however, will want to press the question whether there are not human excellences that could not be realized by a Gandhi, or even by someone who seriously aspired to be one, and whether it would not be good for some people to aspire to these excellences instead of aspiring to sainthood. My answer to these questions is affirmative, except for the "instead of aspiring to sainthood." Given the limits of human time and energy, it is hard to see how a Gandhi or a Martin Luther King, Jr., could at the same time have been a great painter or a world-class violinist. Such saints may indeed attain and employ great mastery in the arts of speaking and writing. But there are demanding forms of excellence, in the arts and in science, for example, and also in philosophy, which probably are not compatible with their vocation (and even less compatible with the vocation of a

---

[2]M. K. Gandhi, *Gandhi's Autobiography: The Story of My Experiments with Truth*, trans. Mahadev Desai (Washington, D.C.: Public Affairs Press, 1948), 7.

St. Francis, for reasons of life-style rather than time and energy). And I agree that it is good that some people aspire to those excellences and attain them.

But if it is right to conclude that not everyone should aspire to be a Gandhi or a Martin Luther King or a St. Francis, it may still be too hasty to infer that not everyone should aspire to sainthood. Perhaps there are other ways of being a saint. That will depend, of course, on what is meant by "saint"; so it is time to offer a definition.

If sainthood is an essentially religious phenomenon, as I claim, it is reasonable to seek its central feature (at least for theistic religions) in the saint's relation to God. "Saint" means "holy"—indeed they are the same word in most European languages. Saints are people in whom the holy or divine can be seen. In a religious view they are people who submit themselves, in faith, to God, not only loving Him but also letting His love possess them, so that it works through them and shines through them to other people. What interests a saint may have will then depend on what interests God has, for sainthood is a participation in God's interests. And God need not be conceived as what Wolf would call a "moral fanatic." He is not so limited that His moral concerns could leave Him without time or attention or energy for other interests. As the author of all things and of all human capacities, He may be regarded as interested in many forms of human excellence, for their own sake and not just for the sake of their connection with what would be classified as *moral* concerns in any narrow sense. This confirms the suggestion that Gandhi and Martin Luther King and St. Francis exemplify only certain types of sainthood, and that other types may be compatible with quite different human excellences—and in particular, with a great variety of demanding artistic and intellectual excellences. I do not see why a Fra Angelico or a Johann Sebastian Bach or a Thomas Aquinas could not have been a saint in this wider sense.

Now I suspect that Wolf will not be satisfied with the conclusion that a saint could be an Angelico or a Bach or an Aquinas. And I do not think that the sticking point here will be that the three figures mentioned all dealt with religious subjects. After all, much of Bach's and Aquinas's work is not explicitly religious, and it would be easy to make a case that a saint could have done most of Cézanne's work. The trouble, I rather expect Wolf to say, is that the forms of artistic and intellectual excellence typified by these figures are too sweet or too nice or too wholesome to be the only ones allowed us. There are darker triumphs of human creativity that we also admire; could a saint have produced them?

Not all of them. I admire the art of Edvard Munch, but I certainly grant that most of his work would not have been produced by a saint. I do not think that is a point against the aspiration to sainthood, however, nor even against a desire for universal sainthood. Who knows? Perhaps Munch would have painted even greater things of another sort if he had been a saint. But that is not the crucial point. Perhaps he would have given up painting and done something entirely different. The crucial point is that although I might aspire to Munch's artistic talent and skill, I certainly would not aspire to be a person who would use it to express what he did, nor would I wish that on anyone I cared about. In view not merely of the intensity of unhappiness, but also of the kind of unhappiness that comes to expression in Munch's art, it would be perverse to aspire to it, nobly as Munch expressed it. The lesson to be learned from such cases is that our ethical or religious view of life ought to allow for some ambivalence, and particularly for the appreciation of some things that we ought not to desire.

Van Gogh provides an interesting example of a different sort. There is much in his life to which one would not aspire, and his canvases sometimes express terror, even madness, rather than peace. Yet I would hesitate to say that a saint could not have painted them. The saints have not been strangers to terror, pain, and sadness; and if in Van Gogh's pictures we often see the finite broken by too close an approach of the transcendent, that is one of the ways in which the holy can show itself in human life. Certainly Van Gogh wanted to be a saint; and perhaps, in an unorthodox and sometimes despairing way, he was one.

Is Morality a Suitable Object of Maximal Devotion?

Wolf's arguments lead her to reject an important received opinion about the nature of morality and about what it means to accept a moral theory—the opinion, namely, that it is "a test of an adequate moral theory that perfect obedience to its laws and maximal devotion to its interests be something we can whole-heartedly strive for in ourselves and wish for in those around us." There are two parts to the received opinion, as it has to do with perfect obedience and with maximal devotion. I cannot see that Wolf's arguments call in question the desirability of perfect obedience to the laws of morality, unless those laws make all good deeds obligatory (as in a rigorous act utilitarianism). Wolf seems on the whole to prefer the view that even nonmoral ideals to which it would be good to aspire ought not to involve the infringement of moral *requirements;* and so she concludes that if (as she has argued) "we have reason to want people to live lives that are not morally perfect, then any plausible moral theory must make use of some conception of supererogation." What she clearly rejects in the received opinion, then, is the desirability of maximal devotion to the interests of morality.

In this I agree with her. We ought not to make a religion of morality. Without proposing, like Kierkegaard and Tillich, to define religion as maximal devotion, I would say that maximal devotion (like sainthood) is essentially religious, or at least that it has its proper place only in religion. Wolf is going too far when she says that "morality itself does not seem to be a suitable object of passion." But maximal devotion is much more than passion. And morality, as Wolf conceives of it, is too narrow to be a suitable object of maximal or religious devotion. Her reason (and one good reason) for thinking this is that a demand for universal maximal devotion to morality excludes too many human excellences.

Religion is richer than morality, because its divine object is so rich. He is not too narrow to be a suitable object of maximal devotion. Since He is lover of beauty, for instance, as well as commander of morals, maximal submission of one's life to Him may in some cases (as I have argued) encompass an intense pursuit of artistic excellence in a way that maximal devotion to the interests of morality, narrowly understood, cannot. Many saints and other religious people, to be sure, have been quite hostile to some of the forms of human endeavor and achievement that I agree with Wolf in prizing. What I have argued is that the breadth of the Creator's interests makes possible a conception of sainthood that does not require this hostility.

There is for many (and not the least admirable) among us a strong temptation to make morality into a substitute for religion, and in so doing to make morality the object of a devotion that is maximal, at least in aspiration, and virtually religious in character. Such a devotion to morality, conceived as narrowly as Wolf conceives of it, would be, from a religious point of view, idolatry. The conclusion to which Wolf's arguments tend is that it would also be, from what she calls "the point of view of individual perfection," oppressive.

On the other hand, the loss of the possibility of sainthood, and of maximal devotion, would be a great loss. Wolf says, "A moral theory that does not contain the seeds of an all-consuming ideal of moral sainthood . . . seems to place false and unnatural limits on our opportunity to do moral good and our potential to deserve moral praise." This seems right, but I do not think it is just our indefinite (not infinite) opportunities and capacities that generate the all-consuming ideal. There are other departments of human life (such as memorization) in which our potential to deserve praise is indefinite but in which it would be bizarre to adopt an all-consuming ideal. The fact is that many of the concepts that we use in morality were developed in a religious tradition; and to tear them loose entirely from a context in which something (distinct perhaps from morality but including it) claims maximal devotion seems to threaten something that is important for the seriousness of morality.

It may not, in other words, be so easy to have a satisfactory conception of morality without religion—that is, without belief in an appropriate object of maximal devotion, an object that is larger than morality but embraces it.[3]

STUDY QUESTIONS

1. Adams is accusing Wolf of having caricatured the Moral Saint. Real saints are not like that. What might be Wolf's reply? What do you think of moral saints? What do you think of sainthood as an ideal to be pursued?
2. According to Adams, Wolf has erred in thinking of moral saints as those whose perfection consists in maximizing value in all of their actions. Why is this characterization of the moral saint erroneous?
3. Adams sees the saint as essentially religious. "The religious character of the saint . . . [explains] how the saint can be so self-giving without lacking (as Wolf suggests) an interest in . . . his

---
[3]I wish to thank the Center of Theological Inquiry for fellowship support during the writing of this paper, and Marilyn McCord Adams, for helpful comments on an earlier version.

own happiness." How, in Adams's view, does the religious element make the saint more human and attractive?

4. Many, like Adams, hold that religion is a suitable object of maximal devotion. Adams goes further when he suggests that we cannot have a satisfactory conception of morality that is not grounded in religion. Discuss this contention, and discuss the related contention that anyone maximally devoted to a cause is at bottom "religious."

5. According to Adams, Wolf errs in thinking that the saint must be maximally devoted to being morally perfect. Indeed, Adams says one may be saintly as an artist. Does Adams use the term sainthood too loosely? What is your conception of a saint? Is it closer to Wolf's or to Adams's?

Reflections on Gandhi

GEORGE ORWELL

George Orwell (1903–1950), British novelist and journalist, was an influential social critic and political analyst. Like Hemingway, Orwell fought in the Spanish Civil War. His best-known novels are *Animal Farm* (1945) and *1984* (1949).

George Orwell reviews Mahatma Gandhi's autobiography, using the occasion to appraise Gandhi's saintly nature. Among Gandhi's qualities are physical courage, lack of envy or feeling of superiority, willingness to believe the best of people, freedom from all forms of prejudice. "I believe," says Orwell, "that even Gandhi's worst enemies would admit that he . . . enriched the world simply

REFLECTIONS ON GANDHI From *Shooting an Elephant and Other Essays* by George Orwell. Copyright 1949 by *Partisan Review;* renewed 1977 by Sonia Orwell. Reprinted by permission of Harcourt Brace Jovanovich, Inc.

by being alive." Yet Orwell finds Gandhi not altogether lovable. Orwell rejects the idea that Gandhi was concerned with human welfare in a Western sense. "Gandhi's teachings cannot be squared with the belief . . . that our job is to make life worth living on this Earth. . . . They make sense only on the assumption that the world of solid objects is an illusion to be escaped from."

Gandhi's abstentions were no animal food, no spices, no tobacco, no sexual intercourse, and no close friendships. Orwell notes that the latter is entailed by Gandhi's mission: "To love humanity as a whole, one cannot give one's preference to any individual person."

Orwell believes that Gandhi's abstentions mark the point at which his religious attitudes conflict with ordinary human concerns. Gandhi was prepared even to allow his sick child to die rather than allow the child to transgress vegetarian strictures. Orwell: "There must be some limit to what we will do, and [for Gandhi] the limit is well on this side of chicken broth." This attitude, says Orwell, may be noble, but "it is inhuman."

Yet Orwell finds Gandhi's unrelenting pacifism, his courage, his doctrine of nonviolent resistance altogether admirable. Gandhi's pacifist methods worked well when directed against a society that had a free press and that gave him respectful publicity. Gandhi earns the chief credit for a peaceful end to British rule in India. "[O]ne may reject sainthood as an ideal and therefore feel that Gandhi's basic aims were anti-human . . . but compared with other leading political figures of our time, how clean a smell he has managed to leave behind!"

Saints should always be judged guilty until they are proved innocent, but the tests that have to be applied to them are not, of course, the same in all cases. In Gandhi's case the questions one feels inclined to ask are: to what extent was Gandhi moved by vanity—by the consciousness of himself as a humble, naked old man, sitting on a praying mat and shaking empires by sheer spiritual power—and to what extent did he compromise his own principles by entering politics, which of their nature are inseparable from coercion and fraud? To give a definite answer one would have to study Gandhi's acts and writings in immense detail, for his whole life was a sort of pilgrimage in which every act was significant. But this partial autobiography,[1] which ends in the nineteen-twenties, is strong evidence in his favor, all the more because it covers what he would have called the unregenerate part of his life and reminds one that inside the saint, or near-saint, there was a very shrewd, able person who could, if he had chosen, have been a brilliant success as a lawyer, an administrator, or perhaps even a businessman.

At about the time when the autobiography first appeared I remember reading its opening chapters in the ill-printed pages of some Indian newspaper. They made a good impression on me, which Gandhi himself at that time, did not. The things that one associated with him—home-spun cloth, "soul forces," and vegetarianism—were unappealing, and his medievalist program was obviously not viable in a backward, starving, overpopulated country. It was also apparent that the British were making use of him, or thought they were making use of him. Strictly speaking, as a Nationalist, he was an enemy, but since in every crisis he would exert himself to prevent violence— which, from the British point of view, meant preventing any effective action whatever—he could be regarded as "our man." In private this was sometimes cynically admitted. The attitude of the Indian millionaires was similar. Gandhi called upon them to repent, and naturally they preferred him to the Socialists and Communists who, given the chance, would actually have taken their money away. How reliable such calculations are in the long run is doubtful; as Gandhi himself says, "in the end deceivers deceive only themselves"; but at any rate the gentleness with which he was nearly always handled was due partly to the feeling that he was useful. The British Conservatives only became really angry with him when, as in 1942, he was in effect turning his non-violence against a different conqueror.

But I could see even then that the British officials who spoke of him with a mixture of amusement and disapproval also genuinely liked and admired him, after a fashion. Nobody ever suggested that

---

[1] *The Story of my Experiments with Truth.* By M. K. Gandhi. Translated from the Gujarati by Mahadex Desai. Public Affairs Press.

he was corrupt, or ambitious in any vulgar way, or that anything he did was actuated by fear or malice. In judging a man like Gandhi one seems instinctively to apply high standards, so that some of his virtues have passed almost unnoticed. For instance, it is clear even from the autobiography that his natural physical courage was quite outstanding: the manner of his death was a later illustration of this, for a public man who attached any value to his own skin would have been more adequately guarded. Again, he seems to have been quite free from that maniacal suspiciousness which, as E. M. Forster rightly says in *A Passage to India,* is the besetting Indian vice, as hypocrisy is the British vice. Although no doubt he was shrewd enough in detecting dishonesty, he seems wherever possible to have believed that other people were acting in good faith and had a better nature through which they could be approached. And though he came of a poor middle-class family, started life rather unfavorably, and was probably of unimpressive physical appearance, he was not afflicted by envy or by the feeling of inferiority. Color feeling when he first met it in its worst form in South Africa, seems rather to have astonished him. Even when he was fighting what was in effect a color war, he did not think of people in terms of race or status. The governor of a province, a cotton millionaire, a half-starved Dravidian coolie, a British private soldier were all equally human beings, to be approached in much the same way. It is noticeable that even in the worst possible circumstances, as in South Africa when he was making himself unpopular as the champion of the Indian community, he did not lack European friends.

Written in short lengths for newspaper serialization, the autobiography is not a literary masterpiece, but it is the more impressive because of the commonplaceness of much of its material. It is well to be reminded that Gandhi started out with the normal ambitions of a young Indian student and only adopted his extremist opinions by degrees and, in some cases, rather unwillingly. There was a time, it is interesting to learn, when he wore a top hat, took dancing lessons, studied French and Latin, went up the Eiffel Tower, and even tried to learn the violin—all this was the idea of assimilating European civilization as thoroughly as possible. He was not one of those saints who are marked out by their phenomenal piety from childhood onward, nor one of the other kind who forsake the world after sensational debaucheries. He makes full confession of the misdeeds of his youth, but in fact there is not much to confess. As a frontispiece to the book there is a photograph of Gandhi's possessions at the time of his death. The whole outfit could be purchased for about £5, and Gandhi's sins, at least his fleshly sins, would make the same sort of appearance if placed all in one heap. A few cigarettes, a few mouthfuls of meat, a few annas pilfered in childhood from the maidservant, two visits to a brothel (on each occasion he got away without "doing anything"), one narrowly escaped lapse with his landlady in Plymouth, one outburst of temper—that is about the whole collection. Almost from childhood onward he had a deep earnestness, an attitude ethical rather than religious, but, until he was about thirty, no very definite sense of direction. His first entry into anything describable as public life was made by way of vegetarianism. Underneath his less ordinary qualities one feels all the time the solid middle-class businessmen who were his ancestors. One feels that even after he had abandoned personal ambition he must have been a resourceful, energetic lawyer and a hardheaded political organizer, careful in keeping down expenses, an adroit handler of committees and an indefatigable chaser of subscriptions. His character was an extraordinarily mixed one, but there was almost nothing in it that you can put your finger on and call bad, and I believe that even Gandhi's worse enemies would admit that he was an interesting and unusual man who enriched the world simply by being alive. Whether he was also a lovable man, and whether his teachings can have much value for those who do not accept the religious beliefs on which they are founded, I have never felt fully certain.

Of late years it has been the fashion to talk about Gandhi as though he were not only sympathetic to the Western left-wing movement, but were integrally part of it. Anarchists and pacifists, in particular, have claimed him for their own, noticing only that he was opposed to centralism and State violence and ignoring the other-worldly, antihumanist tendency of his doctrines. But one should, I think, realize that Gandhi's teachings cannot be squared with the belief that Man is the measure of all things and that our job is to make life worth living on this earth, which is the only earth we have. They make sense only on the assumption that God exists and that the world of solid objects is an illusion to be escaped from. It is worth considering the disciplines which Gandhi imposed on himself and which—though he might not insist on every one of his followers observing every detail—he considered indispensable if one wanted to serve either God or humanity. First of all, no meat-eating, and if possible no animal food in any form. (Gandhi himself, for the sake of his health, had to compromise on milk, but seems to have felt this to be a backsliding.) No alcohol or tobacco, and no spices or condiments even of a vegetable kind, since food should be taken not for its own sake but solely in order to preserve one's strength. Secondly, if possible, no sexual intercourse. If sexual intercourse must happen, then it should be for the sole purpose of begetting children and presumably at long intervals. Gandhi himself, in his middle thirties, took the vow of *brahmacharya,* which means not only complete chastity but the elimination of sexual desire. This condition, it seems, is difficult to attain without a special diet and frequent fasting. One of the dangers of milk-drinking is that it is apt to arouse sexual desire. And finally—this is the cardinal point—for the seeker after goodness there must be no close friendships and no exclusive loves whatever.

Close friendships, Gandhi says, are dangerous, because "friends react on one another" and through loyalty to a friend one can be led into wrong-doing. This is unquestionably true. Moreover, if one is to love God, or to love humanity as a whole, one cannot give one's preference to any individual person. This again is true, and it marks the point at which the humanistic and the religious attitude cease to be reconcilable. To an ordinary human being, love means nothing if it does not mean loving some people more than others. The autobiography leaves it uncertain whether Gandhi behaved in an inconsiderate way to his wife and children, but at any rate it makes clear that on three occasions he was willing to let his wife or a child die rather than administer the animal food prescribed by the doctor. It is true that the threatened death never actually occurred, and also that Gandhi—with, one gathers, a good deal of moral pressure in the opposite direction—always gave the patient the choice of staying alive at the price of committing a sin: still, if the decision had been solely his own, he would have forbidden the animal food, whatever the risks might be. There must, he says, be some limit to what we will do in order to remain alive, and the limit is well on this side of chicken broth. This attitude is perhaps a noble one, but, in the sense which— I think—most people would give to the word, it is inhuman. The essence of being human is that one does not seek perfection, that one *is* sometimes willing to commit sins for the sake of loyalty, that one

does not push asceticism to the point where it makes friendly intercourse impossible, and that one is prepared in the end to be defeated
and broken up by life, which is the inevitable price of fastening one's
love upon other human individuals. No doubt alcohol, tobacco, and
so forth, are things that a saint must avoid, but sainthood is also a
thing that human beings must avoid. There is an obvious retort to
this, but one should be wary about making it. In this yogi-ridden
age, it is too readily assumed that "non-attachment" is not only better
than a full acceptance of earthly life, but that the ordinary man only
rejects it because it is too difficult: in other words, that the average
human being is a failed saint. It is doubtful whether this is true.
Many people genuinely do not wish to be saints, and it is probable
that some who achieve or aspire to sainthood have never felt much
temptation to be human beings. If one could follow it to its psychological roots, one would, I believe, find that the main motive for
"non-attachment" is a desire to escape from the pain of living, and
above all from love, which, sexual or non-sexual, is hard work. But
it is not necessary here to argue whether the other-worldly or the
humanistic ideal is "higher." The point is that they are incompatible.
One must choose between God and Man, and all "radicals" and
"progressives," from the mildest liberal to the most extreme anar-
chist, have in effect chosen Man.

However, Gandhi's pacifism can be separated to some extent from
his other teachings. Its motive was religious, but he claimed also for
it that it was a definite technique, a method, capable of producing
desired political results. Gandhi's attitude was not that of most Western pacifists. *Satyagraha,* first evolved in South Africa, was a sort of
non-violent warfare, a way of defeating the enemy without hurting
him and without feeling or arousing hatred. It entailed such things
as civil disobedience, strikes, lying down in front of railway trains,
enduring police charges without running away and without hitting
back, and the like. Gandhi objected to "passive resistance" as a translation of *Satyagraha:* in Gujarati, it seems, the word means "firmness
in the truth." In his early days Gandhi served as a stretcher-bearer on
the British side in the Boer War, and he was prepared to do the same
again in the war of 1914–18. Even after he had completely abjured
violence he was honest enough to see that in war it is usually necessary to take sides. He did not—indeed, since his whole political life
centered round a struggle for national independence, he could not—

take the sterile and dishonest line of pretending that in every war both sides are exactly the same and it makes no difference who wins. Nor did he, like most Western pacifists, specialize in avoiding awkward questions. In relation to the late war, one question that every pacifist had a clear obligation to answer was: "What about the Jews? Are you prepared to see them exterminated? If not, how do you propose to save them without resorting to war?" I must say that I have never heard, from any Western pacifist, an honest answer to this question, though I have heard plenty of evasions, usually of the "you're another" type. But it so happens that Gandhi was asked a somewhat similar question in 1938 and that his answer is on record in Mr. Louis Fischer's *Gandhi and Stalin*. According to Mr. Fischer, Gandhi's view was that the German Jews ought to commit collective suicide, which "would have aroused the world and the people of Germany to Hitler's violence." After the war he justified himself: the Jews had been killed anyway, and might as well have died significantly. One has the impression that this attitude staggered even so warm an admirer as Mr. Fischer, but Gandhi was merely being honest. If you are not prepared to take life, you must often be prepared for lives to be lost in some other way. When, in 1942, he urged nonviolent resistance against a Japanese invasion, he was ready to admit that it might cost several million deaths.

At the same time there is reason to think that Gandhi, who after all was born in 1869, did not understand the nature of totalitarianism and saw everything in terms of his own struggle against the British government. The important point here is not so much that the British treated him forbearingly as that he was always able to command publicity. As can be seen from the phrase quoted above, he believed in "arousing the world," which is only possible if the world gets a chance to hear what you are doing. It is difficult to see how Gandhi's methods could be applied in a country where opponents of the régime disappear in the middle of the night and are never heard of again. Without a free press and the right of assembly, it is impossible not merely to appeal to outside opinion, but to bring a mass movement into being, or even to make your intentions known to your adversary. Is there a Gandhi in Russia at this moment? And if there is, what is he accomplishing? The Russian masses could only practice civil disobedience if the same idea happened to occur to all of them simultaneously, and even then, to judge by the history of the Ukraine famine, it would make no difference. But let it be granted that non-violent resistance can be effective against one's own government, or against an occupying power: even so, how does one put it into practice internationally? Gandhi's various conflicting statements on the late war seem to show that he felt the difficulty of this. Applied to foreign politics, pacifism either stops being pacifist or becomes appeasement. Moreover the assumption, which served Gandhi so well in dealing with individuals, that all human beings are more or less approachable and will respond to a generous gesture, needs to be seriously questioned. It is not necessarily true, for example, when you are dealing with lunatics. Then the question becomes: Who is sane? Was Hitler sane? And is it not possible for one whole culture to be insane by the standards of another? And, so far as one can gauge the feelings of whole nations, is there any apparent connection between a generous deed and a friendly response? Is gratitude a factor in international politics?

These and kindred questions need discussion, and need it urgently, in the few years left to us before somebody presses the button and the rockets begin to fly. It seems doubtful whether civilization can stand another major war, and it is at least thinkable that the way out lies through non-violence. It is Gandhi's virtue that he would have been ready to give honest consideration to the kind of question that I have raised above; and, indeed, he probably did discuss most of these questions somewhere or other in his innumerable newspaper articles. One feels of him that there was much that he did not understand, but not that there was anything that he was frightened of saying or thinking. I have never been able to feel much liking for Gandhi, but I do not feel sure that as a political thinker he was wrong in the main, nor do I believe that his life was a failure. It is curious that when he was assassinated, many of his warmest admirers exclaimed sorrowfully that he had lived just long enough to see his life work in ruins, because India was engaged in a civil war which had always been foreseen as one of the by-products of the transfer of power. But it was not in trying to smooth down Hindu-Moslem rivalry that Gandhi had spent his life. His main political objective, the peaceful ending of British rule, had after all been attained. As usual the relevant facts cut across one another. On the other hand, the British did get out of India without fighting, an event which very few observers indeed would have predicted until about a year before it happened. On the other hand, this was done by a Labor government, and it is certain that a Conservative government, especially a government

543

headed by Churchill, would have acted differently. But if, by 1945, there had grown up in Britain a large body of opinion sympathetic to Indian independence, how far was this due to Gandhi's personal influence? And if, as may happen, India and Britain finally settle down into a decent and friendly relationship, will this be partly because Gandhi, by keeping up his struggle obstinately and without hatred, disinfected the political air? That one even thinks of asking such questions indicates his stature. One may feel, as I do, a sort of aesthetic distaste for Gandhi, one may reject the claims of sainthood made on his behalf (he never made any such claim himself, by the way), one may also reject sainthood as an ideal and therefore feel that Gandhi's basic aims were anti-human and reactionary: but regarded simply as a politician, and compared with the other leading political figures of our time, how clean a smell he has managed to leave behind!

STUDY QUESTIONS

1. Orwell: "Gandhi enriched the world simply by being alive." Why do you think he made people feel this way? Are you acquainted with anyone whose life enriches the *world*?
2. What light does the example of Gandhi cast on the Wolf-Adams controversy? Does it favor either view? Does it favor a third characterization of saintliness?
3. Orwell calls Gandhi "inhuman." In what ways was he inhuman? Are most saints inhuman in those ways? Why, despite that, was Gandhi lovable? Is Gandhi someone to emulate?
4. What is the idea behind nonviolent resistance? Is it always a feasible method? If not, why not?
5. Orwell notes that some have found Gandhi "aesthetically distasteful," that some have rejected sainthood as an ideal, and that some liberal critics have considered Gandhi's basic aims as "antihuman and reactionary." Do you react to Gandhi in any of these ways? If you do, explain and justify your reactions. If you don't, explain why you don't.

SUGGESTED READINGS

Butler, Joseph. *Five Sermons*, Stuart Brown, Jr., ed. Indianapolis, IN: Bobbs-Merrill, 1950.

MacIntyre, Alasdair. "Egoism and Altruism," Paul Edwards, ed. In *The Encyclopedia of Philosophy*. New York: Macmillan and Free Press, 1967, vol. 2, pp. 462–466.

Nagel, Thomas. *The Possibility of Altruism*. Oxford University Press, 1970.

Nietzsche, Friedrich. *Thus Spake Zarathustra*, Walter Kaufmann, ed. In *The Portable Nietzsche*. New York: Viking Press, 1954.

Olson, Robert. *The Morality of Self-Interest*. New York: Harcourt, Brace and World, 1965.

Rand, Ayn. *The Virtue of Selfishness*. New York: Signet, 1964.

Singer, Peter. *The Expanding Circle: Ethics and Sociobiology*. New York: Farrer, Straus and Giroux, 1981.

Chapter Six

MORAL EDUCATION

Sooner or later most of us face the problem of what and how to teach a child about moral behavior. Teachers of earlier generations felt free to pass on to children a set of moral precepts and prohibitions; they did not worry about compromising the child's autonomy.

Many teachers today lack confidence in their knowledge of right and wrong. How can one teach what one is not sure of? Even the ethical principles that teachers are prepared to defend are believed by them to be culturally determined. Contemporary teachers see themselves as children of Western culture; they are aware that many of the values they hold dear are not held dear in other cultures. Moreover, they recognize that social norms shift rapidly; behavior deemed wrong in one generation is tolerated and even praised in the next. In this prevailing climate of ethical relativism, moral training appears arbitrary and even presumptuous.

A related problem is the compunction the comtemporary teacher feels in doing anything that smacks of "indoctrination"—a word redolent of the thought conrol and social manipulation that one associates with totalitarian states. Finally, the need to teach *tolerance* of the opinions of others makes the job of teaching values even more difficult; teachers cannot put themselves completely behind the values they are trying to inculcate if they must at the same time show themselves to be tolerant of those who may disapprove heartily of them, or even jeer at them.

The articles of this chapter should be read with such contemporary issues and problems in mind. The first selection presents the classical Aristotelian doctrine on moral education that unself-consciously and unabashedly insists children be trained, habituated, and guided to virtuous behavior. Moral education in the Aristotelian tradition is directed to specific goals. Good behavior is rewarded and reinforced. Vice is punished and discouraged. The character is molded carefully. Tolerance of several points of view and of diversity in moral attitudes was not unknown in Ancient Greece, yet tolerance is not one of the classical virtues. Indeed, tolerance could not be thought of as a primary virtue by anyone who aims to instill a sense of indignation and revulsion at the sight of vice.

Lawrence Kohlberg, a moral psychologist, argues that directive moral education interferes with a child's autonomy and moral development. Kohlberg rejects the Aristotelian tradition in moral education, disparaging it as the old "bag of virtues" approach. He himself avoids ethical relativism by a kind of Platonic insistence that all children are innately moral. Their cognitive and social development consists in an unfolding of their moral potential in a series of stages that ideally culminates in the highest stage of moral understanding: an appreciation of one's duty as a rational moral agent.

George Sher and William J. Bennett reject Kohlberg's arguments against teaching the virtues. They point out that *all* good teaching inculcates belief; in a sense, indoctrination is an inescapable responsibility of the teacher. Sher and Bennett's critique of Kohlberg is, in part, a defense of the traditional Aristotelian approach. Other critics of Kohlberg find him insensitive to different *styles* of moral development. Carol Gilligan, for example, claims that men and women develop morally in different ways. Men tend to adopt a "rights perspective" and women a "caring perspective." The former is more abstract, detached, and impartial; the latter is more concrete, emotional, and personal. Gilligan criticizes Kohlberg for neglecting and undervaluing the moral experience of women. Sher finds Gilligan's claims excessive and unsubstantiated. He points out that the tension between an emphasis on mercy and care and an emphasis on justice and rights is an old one that is much discussed by moral philoso-phers. And he suggests that this tension does not necessarily corre-spond to a gender difference in moral style.

Allan Bloom ascribes the present malaise in moral education to the pervasive influence of ethical relativism—a doctrine that disparages the idea that any moral principles are objective and universal. The complete ("unprincipled") tolerance of moral diversity is inhospita-ble to a moral education that could train the student to defend uni-versal and inalienable human rights. In the current relativistic climate, inalienable rights are seen as "Western values"; their rejec-tion by other cultures is tolerantly accommodated. Like Bloom, Christina Sommers believes that the current climate of moral opin-ion—its relativism, its overvaluing of tolerance—breeds moral apa-thy and with it, the hope that the government will somehow compensate for the loss of individual moral initiative.

Some recent thinkers believe that the best moral education is a classical education. Ronald Duska argues that the study of great lit-erature helps students find meaning in their lives. Literature trains the passions and the sensibilities. And, *contra* Kohlberg, Duska views moral progress more as an affair of greater passion and sensibility than an affair of greater understanding and wisdom.

James Stockdale tells how his knowledge of history and philosophy helped him survive with dignity eight years of captivity. Any perusal of contemporary essays on moral education immediately suggests that the old question, "Can virtue be taught?" has not gone away. Stockdale's story shows at least that virtue can be learned.

Habit and Virtue

ARISTOTLE

A biographical sketch of Aristotle is found on page 215.

How does one become virtuous? According to Aristotle, although we are endowed by nature with the capacity to acquire virtue, we are not virtuous by nature. We become virtuous by performing virtuous acts repeatedly until such acts become "second nature." Legislators, too, seek to promote virtue in citizens by a moral education that habituates citizens to virtuous behavior. This goal is achieved by exposing young people to situations where they may exhibit courage or temperance and by reinforcing such behavior through repetition and reward for creditable performance. Right acts demonstrate moderation. For example, courageous acts avoid the extremes of cowardice on the one side and foolhardiness on the other.

Moral education is compared to training for strength. We become strong by *doing* things that require strength. Similarly, we become virtuous by behaving virtuously until such behavior "stands firm" in us. Pains and pleasures are used as incentives to virtuous behavior during moral training. Later, virtuous behavior becomes pleasurable to us as an end in itself.

Aristotle considers an objection to his view that we become virtuous by behaving virtuously: that it seems we must have been virtuous to begin with. Aristotle replies that our earliest virtuous activity may be somewhat random; the educator identifies the virtuous activity and

HABIT AND VIRTUE From *Nicomachean Ethics* by Aristotle. Translated by Terence Irwin (Indianapolis, IN: Hackett, 1985), pp. 33–40. Reprinted by permission of the publisher.

reinforces it. After the right behavior is reinforced and the wrong behavior is rejected and rendered undesirable, the student has learned to be virtuous automatically. The virtue is internalized; it is no longer a virtue of deed, but of character. Virtuous behavior that stems from character is not random at all, but consists of acts done in the manner that a just or temperate person would do them.

Virtues of Character in General

How a Virtue of Character is Acquired

Virtue, then, is of two sorts, virtue of thought and virtue of character. Virtue of thought arises and grows mostly from teaching, and hence needs experience and time. Virtue of character [i.e. of *ēthos*] results from habit [*ethos*]; hence its name "ethical," slightly varied from "*ethos.*"

Virtue comes about, not by a process of nature, but by habituation

Hence it is also clear that none of the virtues of character arises in us naturally.

(1) What is natural cannot be changed by habituation

For if something is by nature [in one condition], habituation cannot bring it into another condition. A stone, e.g., by nature moves downwards, and habituation could not make it move upwards, not even if you threw it up ten thousand times to habituate it; nor could habituation make fire move downwards, or bring anything that is by nature in one condition into another condition.

Thus the virtues arise in us neither by nature nor against nature, but we are by nature able to acquire them, and reach our complete perfection through habit.

(2) Natural capacities are not acquired by habituation

Further, if something arises in us by nature, we first have the capacity for it, and later display the activity. This is clear in the case of the senses; for we did not acquire them by frequent seeing or hearing, but already had them when we exercised them, and did not get them by exercising them.

Virtues, by contrast, we acquire, just as we acquire crafts, by having previously activated them. For we learn a craft by producing the same product that we must produce when we have learned it, becoming builders, e.g., by building and harpists by playing the harp; so also, then, we become just by doing just actions, temperate by doing temperate actions, brave by doing brave actions.

(3) Legislators concentrate on habituation

What goes on in cities is evidence for this also. For the legislator makes the citizens good by habituating them, and this is the wish of every legislator; if he fails to do it well he misses his goal. [The right] habituation is what makes the difference between a good political system and a bad one.

(4) Virtue and vice are formed by good and bad actions

Further, just as in the case of a craft, the sources and means that develop each virtue also ruin it. For playing the harp makes both good and bad harpists, and it is analogous in the case of builders and all the rest; for building well makes good builders, building badly, bad ones. If it were not so, no teacher would be needed, but everyone would be born a good or a bad craftsman.

It is the same, then, with the virtues. For actions in dealings with [other] human beings make some people just, some unjust; actions in terrifying situations and the acquired habit of fear or confidence make some brave and others cowardly. The same is true of situations involving appetites and anger; for one or another sort of conduct in these situations makes some people temperate and gentle, others intemperate and irascible.

Conclusion: The importance of habituation

To sum up, then, in a single account: A state [of character] arises from [the repetition of] similar activities. Hence we must display the right activities, since differences in these imply corresponding differences in the states. It is not unimportant, then, to acquire one sort of habit or another, right from our youth; rather, it is very important, indeed all-important.

What is the right sort of habituation?

This is an appropriate question, for the aim of ethical theory is practical

Our present inquiry does not aim, as our others do, at study; for the purpose of our examination is not to know what virtue is, but to become good, since otherwise the inquiry would be of no benefit to us. Hence we must examine the right way to act, since, as we have said, the actions also control the character of the states we acquire.

First, then, actions should express correct reason. That is a common [belief], and let us assume it; later we will say what correct reason is and how it is related to the other virtues.

But let us take it as agreed in advance that every account of the actions we must do has to be stated in outline, not exactly. As we also said at the start, the type of accounts we demand should reflect the subject-matter; and questions about actions and expediency, like questions about health, have no fixed [and invariable answers].

And when our general account is so inexact, the account of particular cases is all the more inexact. For these fall under no craft or profession, and the agents themselves must consider in each case what the opportune action is, as doctors and navigators do.

The account we offer, then, in our present inquiry is of this inexact sort; still, we must try to offer help.

The right sort of habituation must avoid excess and deficiency

First, then, we should observe that these sorts of states naturally tend to be ruined by excess and deficiency. We see this happen with strength and health, which we mention because we must use what is evident as a witness to what is not. For both excessive and deficient exercises ruin strength; and likewise, too much or too little eating or drinking ruins health, while the proportionate amount produces, increases and preserves it.

The same is true, then, of temperance, bravery and the other virtues. For if, e.g., someone avoids and is afraid of everything, standing firm against nothing, he becomes cowardly, but if he is afraid of nothing at all and goes to face everything, he becomes rash. Similarly, if he gratifies himself with every pleasure and refrains from none, he becomes intemperate, but if he avoids them all, as boors do, he becomes some sort of insensible person. Temperance and bravery, then, are ruined by excess and deficiency but preserved by the mean.

The same actions, then, are the sources and causes both of the emergence and growth of virtues and of their ruin; but further, the activities of the virtues will be found in these same actions. For this is also true of more evident cases, e.g. strength, which arises from eating a lot and from withstanding much hard labour, and it is the strong person who is most able to do these very things. It is the same with the virtues. Refraining from pleasures makes us become temperate, and when we have become temperate we are most able to refrain from pleasures. And it is similar with bravery; habituation in disdaining what is fearful and in standing firm against it makes us become brave, and when we have become brave we shall be most able to stand firm.

Pleasure and pain are important in habituation

But [actions are not enough]; we must take as a sign of someone's state his pleasure or pain in consequence of his action. For if someone who abstains from bodily pleasures enjoys the abstinence itself, then he is temperate, but if he is grieved by it, he is intemperate. Again, if he stands firm against terrifying situations and enjoys it, or at least does not find it painful, then he is brave, and if he finds it painful, he is cowardly.

[Pleasures and pains are appropriately taken as signs] because virtue of character is concerned with pleasures and pains.

Virtue is concerned with pleasure and pain

(1) For it is pleasure that causes us to do base actions, and pain that causes us to abstain from fine ones. Hence we need to have had the appropriate upbringing—right from early youth, as Plato says—to

make us find enjoyment or pain in the right things; for this is the correct education.

(2) Further, virtues are concerned with actions and feelings; but every feeling and every action implies pleasure or pain; hence, for this reason too, virtue is concerned with pleasures and pains.

(3) Corrective treatment [for vicious actions] also indicates [the relevance of pleasure and pain], since it uses pleasures and pains; it uses them because such correction is a form of medical treatment, and medical treatment naturally operates through contraries.

(4) Further, as we said earlier, every state of soul is naturally related to and concerned with whatever naturally makes it better or worse; and pleasures and pains make people worse, from pursuing and avoiding the wrong ones, at the wrong time, in the wrong ways, or whatever other distinctions of that sort are needed in an account.

These [bad effects of pleasure and pain] are the reason why people actually define the virtues as ways of being unaffected and undisturbed [by pleasures and pains]. They are wrong, however, because they speak [of being unaffected] unconditionally, not of being unaffected in the right or wrong way, at the right or wrong time, and the added specifications.

We assume, then, that virtue is the sort of state [with the appropriate specifications] that does the best actions concerned with pleasures and pains, and that vice is the contrary. The following points will also make it evident that virtue and vice are concerned with the same things.

(5) There are three objects of choice—fine, expedient and pleasant—and three objects of avoidance—their contraries, shameful, harmful and painful. About all these, then, the good person is correct and the bad person is in error, and especially about pleasure. For pleasure is shared with animals, and implied by every object of choice, since what is fine and what is expedient appear pleasant as well.

(6) Further, since pleasure grows up with all of us from infancy on, it is hard to rub out this feeling that is dyed into our lives; and we estimate actions as well [as feelings], some of us more, some less, by pleasure and pain. Hence, our whole inquiry must be about these, since good or bad enjoyment or pain is very important for our actions.

(7) Moreover, it is harder to fight pleasure than to fight emotion,

[though that is hard enough], as Heracleitus says. Now both craft and virtue are concerned in every case with what is harder, since a good result is even better when it is harder. Hence, for this reason also, the whole inquiry, for virtue and political science alike, must consider pleasures and pains; for if we use these well, we shall be good, and if badly, bad.

In short, virtue is concerned with pleasures and pains; the actions that are its sources also increase it or, if they are done differently, ruin it; and its activity is concerned with the same actions that are its sources.

But our claims about habituation raise a puzzle: How can we become good without being good already?

However, someone might raise this puzzle: "What do you mean by saying that to become just we must first do just actions and to become temperate we must first do temperate actions? For if we do what is grammatical or musical, we must already be grammarians or musicians. In the same way, then, if we do what is just or temperate, we must already be just or temperate."

First reply: Conformity versus understanding

But surely this is not so even with the crafts, for it is possible to produce something grammatical by chance or by following someone else's instructions. To be a grammarian, then, we must both produce something grammatical and produce it in the way in which the grammarian produces it, i.e. expressing grammatical knowledge that is in us.

Second reply: Crafts versus virtues

Moreover, in any case what is true of crafts is not true of virtues. For the products of a craft determine by their own character whether they have been produced well; and so it suffices that they are in the right state when they have been produced. But for actions expressing virtue to be done temperately or justly [and hence well] it does not suffice that they are themselves in the right state. Rather, the agent must also be in the right state when he does them. First, he must know [that he is doing virtuous actions]; second, he must decide on

555

them, and decide on them for themselves; and, third, he must also do them from a firm and unchanging state.

As conditions for having a craft these three do not count, except for the knowing itself. As a condition for having a virtue, however, the knowing counts for nothing, or [rather] for only a little, whereas the other two conditions are very important, indeed all-important. And these other two conditions are achieved by the frequent doing of just and temperate actions.

Hence actions are called just or temperate when they are the sort that a just or temperate person would do. But the just and temperate person is not the one who [merely] does these actions, but the one who also does them in the way in which just or temperate people do them.

It is right, then, to say that a person comes to be just from doing just actions and temperate from doing temperate actions; for no one has even a prospect of becoming good from failing to do them.

Virtue requires habituation, and therefore requires practice, not just theory

The many, however, do not do these actions but take refuge in arguments, thinking that they are doing philosophy, and that this is the way to become excellent people. In this they are like a sick person who listens attentively to the doctor, but acts on none of his instructions. Such a course of treatment will not improve the state of his body; any more than will the many's way of doing philosophy improve the state of their souls.

STUDY QUESTIONS

1. Aristotle denies that the virtues are in us by nature. What is there in us that makes it possible for us to acquire the virtues? How do we acquire them?
2. What does Aristotle mean by saying that actions determine the character of the states that we acquire?
3. According to Aristotle, the virtues are "preserved by the mean." For example, we become temperate by refraining from extreme pleasures. Explain Aristotle's remark and discuss several other examples of preserving the mean.

4.   Is Aristotle open to the charge that in training a child to be virtuous by habituating it to certain modes of behavior, he is interfering with its autonomy? If not, what *would* constitute an illegitimate interference?
5.   If behaving temperately makes one temperate, it would seem to follow that one must be temperate in order to become temperate. How does Aristotle avoid this paradox?

The Child as a Moral Philosopher

LAWRENCE KOHLBERG

Lawrence Kohlberg (1927–1987) was professor of education and social psychology at Harvard University. He wrote numerous articles on cognitive moral development and was director of the Harvard University Center for Moral Development and Education.

The psychologist Lawrence Kohlberg was interested in moral development. Like several other thinkers (see especially Allan Bloom in this chapter), he was concerned with the problems that arise in a relativistic approach to the teaching of values. In this essay Kohlberg says he will "demonstrate that moral education can be free from the charge of cultural relativity and arbitrary indoctrination." The problem of indoctrination cannot be dismissed by insisting that in teaching values the teacher need not indoctrinate students but merely "socialize" them. Nor can the problem of indoctrination be mitigated by confining teachers to the inculcation of "positive" values: for who is to say which values are to be called positive? Kohlberg

THE CHILD AS A MORAL PHILOSOPHER From "Indoctrination v. Relativity in Value Education" in *The Philosophy of Moral Development*, Vol. 1, by Lawrence Kohlberg (New York: Harper & Row/ Chicago: University of Chicago Press, joint publication, 1971). Reprinted by permission of the Estate of Lawrence Kohlberg.

also objects to values clarification, which avoids indoctrination by allowing the teacher to present a smorgasborg of values for the child to choose from. This only confuses the student and renders teachers ineffective as moral educators. (They cannot, for example, persuasively condemn cheating.)

With this background Kohlberg introduces his three-level (six-stage) theory of transcultural moral development. According to Kohlberg all children begin with a preconventional first level in which morality is determined largely by expected punishment and reward, move on to a conventional second level where social norms and need for approval dominate, and eventually proceed to a third level where the individual is self-motivated to adhere to universal moral principles. Good teachers do not indoctrinate; they merely assist students in moving from one stage to the next stage by helping them become conscious of where they currently are and by showing them where they might go next. Such forward movement is brought about by discussing problematic moral situations. For example, children are presented with the Heinz dilemma in which Heinz, who lacks the money to buy a lifesaving drug, obtains it by robbing the druggist. Children are asked whether Heinz did the right thing. Such discussion sharpens children's moral sensibility and also helps move children to a more sophisticated level of moral development.

Thus, Kohlberg's answer to relativism is to argue that in all societies individuals go through the very *same* stages of moral development—though in some cultures the majority of the population are fixed at a conventional level of moral development and have not reached the stage of universal justice. The ideal development goes beyond conventional morality to recognize universal principles of justice and equality.

Although *moral education* has a forbidding sound to teachers, they constantly practice it. They tell children what to do, make evaluations of children's behavior, and direct children's relations in the classrooms. Sometimes teachers do these things without being aware that they are engaging in moral education, but the children are aware of it. For example, my second-grade son told me that he did not want to be one of the bad boys. Asked "Who were the bad boys?" he replied, "The ones who don't put their books back where they belong and get yelled at." His teacher would have been surprised to know that her concerns with classroom management defined for her children what she and her school thought were basic moral values or that she was engaged in value indoctrination.

Most teachers are aware that they are teaching values, like it or not, and are very concerned as to whether this teaching is unjustified indoctrination. In particular, they are uncertain as to whether their own moral opinions should be presented as "moral truths," whether they should be expressed merely as personal opinion or should be omitted from classroom discussion entirely. As an example, an experienced junior high school teacher told us,

> My class deals with morality and right and wrong quite a bit. I don't expect all of them to agree with me; each has to satisfy himself according to his own convictions, as long as he is sincere and thinks he is pursuing what is right. I often discuss cheating this way but I always get *defeated,* because they still argue cheating is all right. After you accept the idea that kids have the right to build a position with logical arguments, you have to accept what they come out with, even though you drive at it ten times a year and they still come out with the same conclusion.

This teacher's confusion is apparent. She believes everyone should "have his own ideas," and yet she is most unhappy if this leads to a point where some of these ideas include the notion that "it's all right to cheat." In other words, she is smack up against the problem of relativity of values in moral education. Using this teacher as an example, I will attempt to demonstrate that moral education can be free from the charge of cultural relativity and arbitrary indoctrination that inhibits her when she talks about cheating.

Cop-Out Solutions to the Relativity Problem

To begin with, I want to reject a few cop-outs or false solutions sometimes suggested as solving the relativity problem. One is to call moral education *socialization*. Sociologists have sometimes claimed that moralization in the interests of classroom management and maintenance of the school as a social system is a hidden curriculum; that it performs hidden services in helping children adapt to society (Jackson, 1968). They have argued that, since praise and blame on the part of teachers is a necessary aspect of the socialization process, the teacher does not have to consider the psychological and philosophic issues of moral education. In learning to conform to the teacher's expectations and the school rules, children are becoming socialized, they are internalizing the norms and standards of society. I argue in Chapter 2 why this approach is a cop-out. In practice, it means that we call the teacher's yelling at her students for not putting their books away *socialization*. To label it *socialization* does not legitimate it as valid education, nor does it remove the charge of arbitrary indoctrination from it. Basically, this sociological argument implies that respect for social authority is a moral good in itself. Stated in different terms, the notion that it is valid for the teacher to have an unreflective hidden curriculum is based on the notion that the teacher is the agent of the state, the church, or the social system, rather than being a free moral agent dealing with children who are free moral agents. The notion that the teacher is the agent of the state is taken for granted in some educational systems, such as that of the Soviets. However, the moral curriculum is not hidden in Soviet education; it is done explicitly and well as straight indoctrination (Bronfenbrenner, 1968). For the moment, I will not argue what is wrong with indoctrination but will assume that it is incompatible with the conceptions of civil liberties that are central not only to American democracy but to any just social system.

Let us turn now to the second cop-out. This is to rely on vaguely positive and honorific-sounding terms such as "moral values" or "moral and spiritual values." We can see in the following statements how a program called "Teaching Children Values in the Upper Elementary School" (Carr and Wellenberg, 1966) relies on a vague usage of "moral and spiritual values":

> Many of our national leaders have expressed anxiety about an increasing lack of concern for personal moral and spiritual values. Throughout history, nations have sought value systems to help people live congenially. The Golden Rule and the Ten Commandments are examples of such value systems. Each pupil needs to acquire a

foundation of sound values to help him act correctly and make proper choices between right and wrong, truth and untruth. The teacher can develop a sound value system in the following ways:

1. Be a good example.
2. Help young people to assess conflict situations and to gain insight into the development of constructive values and attitudes. Situations arise daily in which pupils can receive praise that will reinforce behavior that exemplified desired values.
3. Show young people how to make generalizations concerning experience through evaluation and expression of desirable values.
4. Help students acquire an understanding of the importance of values that society considers worthwhile.
5. Aid children to uphold and use positive values when confronted by adverse pressure from peers. [p. 11]

The problem, however, is to define these "positive values." We may agree that "positive values" are desirable, but the term conceals the fact that teachers, children, and societies have different ideas as to what constitutes "positive values." Although Carr and Wellenberg cite the Ten Commandments and the Golden Rule as "value systems sought by nations," they also could have used the code of Hitler or of the communist youth as examples of "value systems sought by nations."

I raise the issue of the "relativity of values" in this context because the words *moral, positive,* and *values* are interpreted by each teacher in a different way, depending on the teacher's own values and standards.

This becomes clear when we consider our third cop-out. This is the cop-out of defining moral values in terms of what I call a "bag of virtues." By a "bag of virtues," I mean a set of personality traits generally considered to be positive. Defining the aims of moral education in terms of a set of "virtues" is as old as Aristotle, who said, "Virtue . . . [is] of two kinds, intellectual and moral. . . . [The moral] virtues we get by first exercising them . . . we become just by doing just acts, temperate by doing temperate acts, brave by doing brave acts."

The attraction of such an approach is evident. Although it is true that people often cannot agree on details of right and wrong or even on fundamental moral principles, we all think such "traits" as honesty and responsibility are good things. By adding enough traits to the virtue bag, we eventually get a list that contains something to suit everyone.

This approach to moral education was widely prevalent in the public schools in the 1920s and 1930s and was called "character education." The educators and psychologists, such as Havighurst and Taba (1949), who developed these approaches defined character as the sum total of a set of "those traits of personality which are subject to the moral sanctions of society."

One difficulty with this approach to moral character is that everyone has his own bag. However, the problem runs deeper than the composition of a given list of virtues and vices. Although it may be true that the notion of teaching virtues, such as honesty or integrity, arouses little controversy, it is also true that a vague consensus on the goodness of these virtues conceals a great deal of actual disagreement over their definitions. What is one person's "integrity" is another person's "stubbornness," what is one person's honesty in "expressing your true feelings" is another person's insensitivity to the feelings of others. This is evident in controversial fields of adult behavior. Student protestors view their behavior as reflecting the virtues of altruism, idealism, awareness, and courage. Those in opposition regard the same behavior as reflecting the vices of irresponsibility and disrespect for "law and order." Although this difficulty can be recognized clearly in college education, it is easier for teachers of younger children to think that their judgments in terms of the bag of virtues are objective and independent of their own value biases. However, a parent will not agree that a child's specific failure to obey an "unreasonable" request by the teacher was wrong, even if the teacher calls the act "uncooperative," as some teachers are prone to do.

I have summarized three cop-outs from the relativity problem and rejected them. Socialization, teaching positive values, and developing a bag of virtues all leave the teacher where she was—stuck with her own personal value standards and biases to be imposed on her students. There is one last cop-out to the relativity problem. That is to lie back and enjoy it or encourage it. In the new social studies, this is called *value clarification*.

As summarized by Engel (in Simon, 1971, p. 902), this position holds that

In the consideration of values, there is no single correct answer, but value clarification is supremely important. One must contrast value clarification and value inculcation. Inculcation suggests that the learner has limited control and hence limited responsibility in the development of his own values. He needs to be told what values are or what he should value.

This is not to suggest, however, that nothing is ever inculcated. As a matter of fact, in order to clarify values, at least one principle needs to be adopted by all concerned. Perhaps the only way the principle can be adopted is through some procedure which might best be termed *inculcation*. That principle might be stated as follows: in the consideration of values there is no single correct answer. More specifically it might be said that the adequate posture both for students and teachers in clarifying values is openness.

Although the basic premise of this value clarification approach is that "everyone has his own values," it is further advocated that children can and should learn (1) to be more aware of their own values and how they relate to their decisions, (2) to make their values consistent and to order them in hierarchies for decisions, (3) to be more aware of the divergencies between their value hierarchies and those of others, and (4) to tolerate these divergencies. In other words, although values are regarded as arbitrary and relative, there may be universal, rational strategies for making decisions that maximize these values. Part of this rational strategy is to recognize that values are relative. Within this set of premises, it is quite logical to teach that values are relative as part of the overall program.

An elaboration of this approach can be found in *Decision Making: A Guide for Teachers Who Would Help Preadolescent Children Become Imaginative and Responsible Decision Makers* (Dodder and Dodder, 1968). In a portion of this book, modern social scientific perspectives are used to develop a curriculum unit entitled "Why Don't We All Make the Same Decisions?" A set of classroom materials and activities are then presented to demonstrate to children the following propositions: (1) we don't all make the same decisions because our values are different; (2) our values tend to originate outside ourselves; (3) our values are different because each of us has been influenced by different important others; and (4) our values are different because each of us has been influenced by a different cultural environment.

The teacher is told to have the children discuss moral dilemmas in such a way as to reveal those different values. As an example, one child might make a moral decision in terms of avoiding punishment, another in terms of the welfare of other people, another in terms of certain rules, another in terms of getting the most for himself. The children are then to be encouraged to discuss their values with each other and to recognize that everyone has different values. Whether or not "the welfare of others" is a more adequate value than "avoiding punishment" is not an issue to be raised by the teacher. Rather, the teacher is instructed to teach only that "our values are different."

Indeed, acceptance of the idea that *all* values are relative does, logically, lead to the conclusion that the teacher should not attempt to teach *any* particular moral values. This leaves the teacher in the quandary of our teacher who could not successfully argue against cheating. The students of a teacher who has been successful in communicating moral relativism will believe, like the teacher, that "everyone has his own bag" and that "everyone should keep doing his thing." If one of these students has learned his relativity lesson, when he is caught cheating he will argue that he did nothing wrong. The basis of his argument will be that his own hierarchy of values, which may be different from that of the teacher, made it right for him to cheat. Although recognizing that other people believe that cheating is wrong, he himself holds the "value" that one should cheat when the opportunity presents itself. If teachers want to be consistent and retain their relativistic beliefs, they would have to concede.

Now I am not criticizing the value clarification approach itself. It is a basic and valuable component of the new social studies curricula, as I have discussed (1973). My point is, rather, that value clarification is not a sufficient solution to the relativity problem. Furthermore, the actual teaching of relativism is itself an indoctrination or teaching of a fixed belief, a belief that we are going to show is not true scientifically or philosophically. . . .

A Typological Scheme on the Stages of Moral Thought

In other words, I am happy to report that I can propose a solution to the relativity problem that has plagued philosophers for three thousand years. I can say this with due modesty because it did not depend on being smart. It only happened that my colleagues and I were the first people in history to do detailed cross-cultural studies on the development of moral thinking.

The following dilemma should clarify the issue:

The Heinz Dilemma

> In Europe, a woman was near death from a very bad disease, a special kind of cancer. There was one drug that the doctors thought might save her. It was a form of radium that a druggist in the same town had recently discovered. The drug was expensive to make, but the druggist was charging ten times what the drug cost him to make. He paid $200 for the radium and charged $2,000 for a small dose of the drug. The sick woman's husband, Heinz, went to everyone he knew to borrow the money, but he could get together only about $1,000, which was half of what it cost. He told the druggist that his wife was dying and asked him to sell it cheaper or let him pay later. But the druggist said, "No, I discovered the drug and I'm going to make money from it." Heinz got desperate and broke into the man's store to steal the drug for his wife.

Should the husband have done that? Was it right or wrong? Is your decision that it is right (or wrong) objectively right, is it morally universal, or is it your personal opinion? If you think it is morally right to steal the drug, you must face the fact that it is legally wrong. What is the basis of your view that it is morally right, then, more than your personal opinion? Is it anything that can be agreed on? If you think so, let me report the results of a National Opinion Research Survey on the question, asked of a representative sample of adult Americans. Seventy-five percent said it was wrong to steal, though most said they might do it.

Can one take anything but a relativist position on the question? By a relativist position, I mean a position like that of Bob, a high school senior. He said, "There's a million ways to look at it. Heinz had a moral decision to make. Was it worse to steal or let his wife die? In my mind, I can either condemn him or condone him. In this case, I think it was fine. But possibly the druggist was working on a capitalist morality of supply and demand."

I went on to ask Bob, "Would it be wrong if he didn't steal it?"

Bob replied, "It depends on how he is oriented morally. If he thinks it's worse to steal than to let his wife die, then it would be

565

wrong what he did. It's all relative; what I would do is steal the drug. I can't say that's right or wrong or that it's what everyone should do."

But even if you agree with Bob's relativism you may not want to go as far as he did. He started the interview by wondering if he could answer because he "questioned the whole terminology, the whole moral bag." He continued, "But then I'm also an incredible moralist, a real puritan in some sense and moods. My moral judgment and the way I perceive things morally changes very much when my mood changes. When I'm in a cynical mood, I take a cynical view of morals, but still, whether I like it or not, I'm terribly moral in the way I look at things. But I'm not too comfortable with it." Bob's moral perspective was well expressed in the late Joe Gould's poem called "My Religion." Brief and to the point, the poem said, "In winter I'm a Buddhist, in the summer I'm a nudist."

Now, Bob's relativism rests on a confusion. The confusion is that between relativity as the social science fact that different people *do* have different moral values and relativity as the philosophic claim that people *ought* to have different moral values, that no moral values are justified for all people.

To illustrate, I quote a not atypical response of one of my graduate students to the same moral dilemma. She said, "I think he should steal it because if there is any such thing as a universal human value, it is the value of life, and that would justify it."

I then asked her, "Is there any such thing as a universal human value?" and she answered, "No, all values are relative to your culture."

She began by claiming that one ought to act in terms of the universal value of human life, implying that human life is a universal value in the sense that it is logical and desirable for all people to respect all human life, that one can demonstrate to other people that it is logical and desirable to act in this way. If she were clear in her thinking, she would see that the fact that all people do not always act in terms of this value does not contradict the claim that all people ought to always act in accordance with it. Because she made this confusion, she ended in total confusion.

What I am going to claim is that if we distinguish the issues of universality as fact and the possibility of universal moral ideals we get a positive answer to both questions. As far as facts go, I claim just the opposite of what Dodder and Dodder (1968) claimed to be basic social science truths. I claim that

1. We often make different decisions and yet have the same basic moral values.

2. Our values tend to originate inside ourselves as we process our social experience.

3. In every culture and subculture of the world, both the same basic moral values and the same steps toward moral maturity are found. Although social environments directly produce different specific beliefs (for example, smoking is wrong, eating pork is wrong), they do not engender different basic moral principles (for example, "consider the welfare of others," "treat other people equally," and so on).

4. Basic values are different largely because we are at different levels of maturity in thinking about basic moral and social issues and concepts. Exposure to others more mature than ourselves helps stimulate maturity in our own value process.

All parents know that the basic values of their children do not come from the outside, from the parents, although many wish they did. For example, at the age of four my son joined the pacifist and vegetarian movement and refused to eat meat because, he said, it is bad to kill animals. In spite of his parents' attempts to dissuade him by arguing about the difference between justified and unjustified killing, he remained a vegetarian for six months. However, he did recognize that some forms of killing were "legitimate." One night I read to him from a book about Eskimo life that included a description of a seal-killing expedition. While listening to the story, he became very angry and said, "You know, there is one kind of meat I would eat, Eskimo meat. It's bad to kill animals so it's all right to eat Eskimos."

This episode illustrates (1) that children often generate their own moral values and maintain them in the face of cultural training, and (2) that these values have universal roots. Every child believes it is bad to kill because regard for the lives of others or pain at death is a natural empathic response, although it is not necessarily universally and consistently maintained. In this example, the value of life led both to vegetarianism and to the desire to kill Eskimos. This latter desire comes also from a universal value tendency: a belief in justice or reciprocity here expressed in terms of revenge or punishment (at higher levels, the belief that those who infringe on the rights of others cannot expect their own rights to be respected).

I quoted my son's response because it is shockingly different from the way you think and yet it has universal elements you will recognize. What is the shocking difference between my son's way of thinking and your own? If you are a psychoanalyst, you will start thinking about oral cannibalistic fantasies and defenses against them and all that. However, that is not really what the difference is at all. You do not have to be cannibalistic to wonder why it is right for humans to kill and eat animals but it is not right for animals or humans to kill and eat humans. The response really shows that my son was a philosopher, like every young child: he wondered about things that most grown-ups take for granted. If you want to study children, however, you have to be a bit of a philosopher yourself and ask the moral philosopher's question: "Why is it all right to kill and eat animals but not humans?" I wonder how many of you can give a good answer. In any case, Piaget started the modern study of child development by recognizing that the child, like the adult philosopher, was puzzled by the basic questions of life: by the meaning of space, time, causality, life, death, right and wrong, and so on. What he found was that the child asked all the great philosophic questions but answered them in a very different way from the adults. This way was so different that Piaget called the difference a difference in stage or quality of thinking, rather than a difference in amount of knowledge or accuracy of thinking. The difference in thinking between you and my son, then, is basically a difference in stage.

My own work on morality started from Piaget's notions of stages and Piaget's notion that the child was a philosopher. Inspired by Jean Piaget's (1948) pioneering effort to apply a structural approach to moral development, I have gradually elaborated over the years a typological scheme describing general stages of moral thought that can be defined independently of the specific content of particular moral decisions or actions. We studied seventy-five American boys from early adolescence on. These youths were continually presented with hypothetical moral dilemmas, all deliberately philosophical, some found in medieval works of casuistry. On the basis of their reasoning about these dilemmas at a given age, we constructed the typology of definite and universal levels of development in moral thought.

The typology contains three distinct levels of moral thinking, and within each of these levels are two related stages. These levels and stages may be considered separate moral philosophies, distinct views of the social-moral world.

We can speak of the children as having their own morality or series of moralities. Adults seldom listen to children's moralizing. If children throw back a few adult clichés and behave themselves, most parents—and many anthropologists and psychologists as well—think that the children have adopted or internalized the appropriate parental standards.

Actually, as soon as we talk with children about morality we find that they have many ways of making judgments that are not "internalized" from the outside and that do not come in any direct and obvious way from parents, teachers, or even peers.

The preconventional level is the first of three levels of moral thinking; the second level is conventional; and the third is postconventional or autonomous. Although preconventional children are often "well behaved" and responsive to cultural labels of good and bad, they interpret these labels in terms of their physical consequences (punishment, reward, exchange of favors) or in terms of the physical power of those who enunciate the rules and labels of good and bad.

This level is usually occupied by children aged four to ten, a fact well known to sensitive observers of children. The capacity of "properly behaved" children of this age to engage in cruel behavior when there are holes in the power structure is sometimes noted as tragic (*Lord of the Flies* and *High Wind in Jamaica*), sometimes as comic (Lucy in *Peanuts*).

The second or conventional level also can be described as *conformist*—but that is perhaps too smug a term. Maintaining the expectations and rules of the individual's family, group, or nation is perceived as valuable in its own right. There is a concern not only with conforming to the individual's social order but in maintaining, supporting, and justifying this order.

The postconventional level is characterized by a major thrust toward autonomous moral principles that have validity and application apart from authority of the groups or people who hold them and apart from the individual's identification with those people or groups.

Within each of these three levels, there are two discernible stages. The following paragraphs explain the dual moral stages of each level just described.

569

Definition of Moral Stages

Preconventional Level

At this level, the child is responsive to cultural rules and labels of good and bad, right or wrong, but interprets these labels in terms of either the physical or the hedonistic consequences of action (punishment, reward, exchange of favors) or in terms of the physical power of those who enunciate the rules and labels. The level is divided into the following two stages:

Stage 1. *The Punishment and Obedience Orientation*

The physical consequences of action determine its goodness or badness regardless of the human meaning or value of these consequences. Avoidance of punishment and unquestioning deference to power are valued in their own right.

Stage 2. *The Instrumental Relativist Orientation*

Right action consists of that which instrumentally satisfies one's needs and occasionally the needs of others. Human relations are viewed in terms like those of the marketplace. Elements of fairness, reciprocity, and equal sharing are present, but they are always interpreted in a physical, pragmatic way. Reciprocity is a matter of "You scratch my back and I'll scratch yours."

Conventional Level

At this level, maintaining the expectations of the individual's family, group, or nation is perceived as valuable in its own right, regardless of immediate and obvious consequences. The attitude is not only one of conformity to personal expectations and social order, but of loyalty to it, of actively maintaining, supporting, and justifying the order and of identifying with the people or group involved in it. At this level, there are the following two stages:

Stage 3. *The Interpersonal Concordance or "Good Boy–Nice Girl" Orientation*

Good behavior is that which pleases or helps others and is approved by them. There is much conformity to stereotypical images of what is majority or "natural" behavior. Behavior is frequently judged by intention—the judgment "he means well" becomes important for the first time. One earns approval by being "nice."

570

Stage 4. *Society Maintaining Orientation*

There is an orientation toward authority, fixed rules, and the maintenance of the social order. Right behavior consists of doing one's duty, showing respect for authority, and maintaining the given social order for its own sake.

Postconventional, Autonomous, or Principled Level

At this level, there is a clear effort to define moral values and principles that have validity and application apart from the authority of the groups or people holding these principles and apart from the individual's own identification with these groups. This level again has two stages:

Stage 5. *The Social Contract Orientation*

Right action tends to be defined in terms of general individual rights and in terms of standards that have been critically examined and agreed on by the whole society. There is a clear awareness of the relativism of personal values and opinions and a corresponding emphasis on procedural rules for reaching consensus. Aside from what is constitutionally and democratically agreed on, the right is a matter of personal "values" and "opinion." The result is an emphasis on the "legal point of view," but with an emphasis on the possibility of changing law in terms of rational considerations of social utility (rather than freezing it in terms of Stage 4 "law and order"). Outside the legal realm, free agreement and contract are the binding elements of obligation. This is the "official" morality of the American government and Constitution.

Stage 6. *The Universal Ethical Principle Orientation*

Right is defined by the decision of conscience in accord with self-chosen ethical principles appealing to logical comprehensiveness, universality, and consistency. These principles are abstract and ethical (the Golden Rule, the categorical imperative); they are not concrete moral rules such as the Ten Commandments. At heart, these are universal principles of justice, of the reciprocity and equality of human rights, and of respect for the dignity of human beings as individuals.

To understand what these stages mean concretely, let us look at them with regard to two of twenty-five basic moral concepts or

571

aspects used to form the dilemmas we used in our research. One such aspect, for instance, is "motive given for rule obedience or moral action." In this instance, the six stages look like this:

1. Obey rules to avoid punishment.
2. Conform to obtain rewards, have favors returned, and so on.
3. Conform to avoid disapproval and dislike by others.
4. Conform to avoid censure by legitimate authorities and resultant guilt.
5. Conform to maintain the respect of the impartial spectator judging in terms of community welfare.
6. Conform to avoid self-condemnation.

In another of these twenty-five moral aspects, the value of human life, the six stages can be defined thus:

1. The value of human life is confused with the value of physical objects and is based on the social status or physical attributes of the possessor.
2. The value of human life is seen as instrumental to the satisfaction of the needs of its possessor or of other people.
3. The value of human life is based on the empathy and affection of family members and others toward its possessor.
4. Life is conceived as sacred in terms of its place in a categorical moral or religious order of rights and duties.
5. Life is valued both in terms of its relation to community welfare and in terms of life being a universal human right.
6. Human life is sacred—a universal human value of respect for the individual.

I have called this scheme a *typology*. This is because about 67 percent of most people's thinking is at a single stage, regardless of the moral dilemma involved. We call our types *stages* because they seem to represent an invariant development sequence. "True" stages come one at a time and always in the same order.

In our stages, all movement is forward in sequence and does not skip steps. Children may move through these stages at varying

speeds, of course, and may be found half in and half out of a particular stage. Individuals may stop at any given stage and at any age,
but if they continue to move, they must move in accord with these
steps. Moral reasoning of the conventional kind or Stages 3–4, never
occurs before the preconventional Stage 1 and Stage 2 thought has
taken place. No adult in Stage 4 has gone through Stage 5, but all
Stage 5 adults have gone through Stage 4.

Although the evidence is not complete, my study strongly suggests that moral change fits the stage pattern just described.

As a single example of our findings of stage sequence, take the
progress of two boys on the aspect "the value of human life." The
first boy, Tommy, who had suggested that one should perhaps steal
for an important person, is asked, "Is it better to save the life of one
important person or a lot of unimportant people?" At age ten, he
answers, "All the people that aren't important because one man just
has one house, maybe a lot of furniture, but a whole bunch of people
have an awful lot of furniture, and some of these poor people might
have a lot of money and it doesn't look it."

Clearly Tommy is Stage 1: he confuses the value of a human being
with the value of the property he possesses. Three years later (age
thirteen), Tommy's conceptions of life's values are most clearly elicited by the question "Should the doctor 'mercy kill' a fatally ill
woman requesting death because of her pain?" He answers, "Maybe
it would be good to put her out of pain, she'd be better off that way.
But the husband wouldn't want it, it's not like an animal. If a pet dies
you can get along without it—it isn't something you really need.
Well, you can get a new wife, but it's not really the same."

Here his answer is Stage 2: the value of the woman's life is partly
contingent on its instrumental value to her husband, who cannot
replace her as easily as he can a pet.

Three years later still (age sixteen), Tommy's conception of life's
value is elicited by the same question, to which he replies, "It might
be best for her, but her husband—it's human life—not like an animal;
it just doesn't have the same relationship that a human being does to
a family. You can become attached to a dog, but nothing like a human, you know."

Now Tommy has moved from a Stage 2 instrumental view of the
woman's value to a Stage 3 view based on the husband's distinctively
human empathy and love for someone in his family. Equally clearly,

it lacks any basis for a universal human value of the woman's life, which would hold if she had no husband or if her husband did not love her. Tommy, then, has moved step by step through three stages during the age ten to sixteen. Although bright (IQ 120), he is a slow developer in moral judgment.

Let us take another boy, Richard, to show us sequential movement through the remaining three steps. At age thirteen, Richard said about the mercy killing, "If she requests it, it's really up to her. She is in such terrible pain, just the same as people are always putting animals out of their pain," and in general showed a mixture of Stage 2 and Stage 3 responses concerning the value of life. At sixteen, he said, "I don't know. In one way, it's murder, it's not right or privilege of man to decide who shall live and who should die. God put life into everybody on earth and you're taking away something from that person that came directly from God, and you're destroying something that is very sacred, it's in a way part of God and it's almost destroying a part of God when you kill a person. There's something of God in everyone."

Here Richard clearly displays a Stage 4 concept of life as sacred in terms of its place in a categorical moral or religious order. The value of human life is universal; it is true for all humans. It still, however, depends on something else—on respect for God and God's authority; it is not an autonomous human value. Presumably if God told Richard to murder, as God commanded Abraham to murder Isaac, he would do so.

At age twenty, Richard said to the same question, "There are more and more people in the medical profession who think it is a hardship on everyone, the person, the family, when you know they are going to die. When a person is kept alive by an artificial lung or kidney, it's more like being a vegetable than being a human. If it's her own choice, I think there are certain rights and privileges that go along with being a human being. I am a human being, and I have certain desires for life, and I think everybody else does too. You have a world of which you are the center, and everybody else does too, and in that sense we're all equal."

Richard's response is clearly Stage 5, in that the value of life is defined in terms of equal and universal human rights in a context of relativity ("You have a world of which you are the center, and in that sense we're all equal") and of concern for utility or welfare consequences.

At twenty-four, Richard says, "A human life, whoever it is, takes precedence over any other moral or legal value. A human life has inherent value whether or not it is valued by a particular individual. The worth of the individual human being is central where the principles of justice and love are normative for all human relationships."

This young man is at Stage 6 in seeing the value of human life as absolute in representing a universal and equal respect for the human as an individual. He has moved step by step through a sequence culminating in a definition of human life as centrally valuable rather than derived from or dependent on social or divine authority.

In a genuine and culturally universal sense, these steps lead toward an increased morality of value judgment, where morality is considered as a form of judging, as it has been in a philosophic tradition running from the analyses of Kant to those of the modern analytic or "ordinary language" philosophers. At Stage 6 people have disentangled judgments of—or language about—human life from status and property values (Stage 1); from its uses to others (Stage 2); from interpersonal affection (Stage 3); and so on; they have a means of moral judgment that is universal and impersonal. Stage 6 people answer in moral words such as *duty* or *morally right* and use them in a way implying universality, ideals and impersonality. They think and speak in phrases such as "regardless of who it was" or "I would do it in spite of punishment."

Universal Invariant Sequence of Moral Development

When I first decided to explore moral development in other cultures, I was told by anthropologist friends that I would have to throw away my culture-bound moral concepts and stories and start from scratch learning a whole new set of values for each new culture. My first try consisted of a brace of villages, one Atayal (Malaysian aboriginal) and the other Taiwanese.

My guide was a young Chinese ethnographer who had written an account of the moral and religious patterns of the Atayal and Taiwanese villages. Taiwanese boys in the ten to thirteen age group were asked about a story involving theft of food: A man's wife is starving to death but the store owner would not give the man any food unless he could pay, and he cannot. Should he break in and steal some food? Why? Many of the boys said, "He should steal the food for his

575

wife because if she dies he'll have to pay for her funeral, and that costs a lot."

My guide was amused by these responses, but I was relieved: they were, of course, "classic" Stage 2 responses. In the Atayal village, funerals were not such a big thing, so the Stage 2 boys said, "He should steal the food because he needs his wife to cook for him."

This means that we have to consult our anthropologists to know what content Stage 2 children will include in instrumental exchange calculations, or what Stage 4 adults will identify as the proper social order. But one certainly does not have to start from scratch. What made my guide laugh was the difference in form between the children's Stage 2 thought and his own, a difference definable independently of particular cultures.

Figures 1.1 and 1.2 indicate the cultural universality of the sequence of stages we have found. Figure 1.1 presents the age trends for middle-class urban boys in the United States, Taiwan, and Mexico. At age ten in each country, the order of use of each stage is the same as the order of its difficulty or maturity.

In the United States, by age sixteen the order is the reverse, from the highest to the lowest, except that Stage 6 is still little used. At age thirteen, the good-boy middle stage (Stage 3) is most used.

The results in Mexico and Taiwan are the same, except that development is a little slower. The most conspicuous feature is that, at the age of sixteen, Stage 5 thinking is much more salient in the United States than in Mexico or Taiwan. Nevertheless, it is present in the other countries, so we know that this is not purely an American democratic construct.

Figure 1.2 shows strikingly similar results from two isolated villages, one in Yucatan, one in Turkey. Although conventional moral thought increases steadily from ages ten to sixteen, it still has not achieved a clear ascendancy over preconventional thought.

Trends for lower-class urban groups are intermediate in the rate of development between those for the middle-class and for the village boys. In the three divergent cultures that I studied, middle-class children were found to be more advanced in moral judgment than matched lower-class children. This was not due to the fact that the middle-class children heavily favored some one type of thought that could be seen as corresponding to the prevailing middle-class pattern. Instead, middle-class and working-class children move

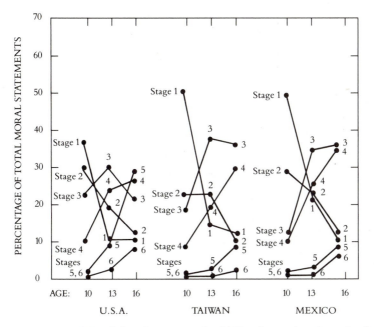

FIGURE 1.1   Moral development of middle-class urban boys in the United States, Taiwan, and Mexico. At age ten, the stages are used according to difficulty. At age thirteen, Stage 3 is most used by all three groups. At age sixteen, U.S. boys have reversed the order of age ten stages (with the exception of 6). In Taiwan and Mexico, conventional (3–4) stages prevail at age sixteen, with Stage 5 also little used (Kohlberg, 1968a).

through the same sequences, but the middle-class children move faster and farther.

This sequence is not dependent on a particular religion or on any religion at all in the usual sense. I found no important differences in the development of moral thinking among Catholics, Protestants, Jews, Buddhists, Moslems, and atheists.

In summary, the nature of our sequence is not significantly affected by widely varying social, cultural, or religious conditions. The only thing that is affected is the rate at which individuals progress through this sequence.

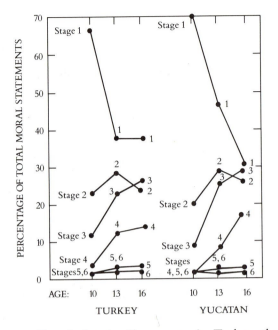

FIGURE 1.2   Two isolated villages, one in Turkey, the other in Yucatan, show similar patterns in moral thinking. There is no reversal of order, and conventional (stages 3–4) thought does not gain in a clear ascendancy over preconventional stages at age sixteen (Kohlberg, 1968a).

Why should there be such a universal invariant sequence of development? In answering this question, we need first to analyze these developing social concepts in terms of their internal logical structure. At each stage, the same basic moral concept or aspect is defined, but at each higher stage this definition is more differentiated, more integrated, and more general or universal. When one's concept of human life moves from Stage 1 to Stage 2, the value of life becomes more differentiated from the value of property, more integrated (the value of life enters an organizational hierarchy where it is "higher" than property so that one steals property in order to save life), and more universalized (the life of any sentient being is valuable regardless of status or property). The same advance is true at each stage in the hierarchy. Each step of development, then, is a better cognitive organization than the one before it, one that takes account of every-thing present in the previous stage but making new distinctions and organizes them into a more comprehensive or more equilibrated structure. The fact that this is the case has been demonstrated by a series of studies indicating that children and adolescents comprehend all stages up to their own, but not more than one stage beyond their own (Rest, 1973). And, importantly, they prefer this next stage.

Moral thought, then, seems to behave like all other kinds of thought. Progress through the moral levels and stages is character-ized by increasing differentiation and increasing integration, and hence is the same kind of progress that scientific theory represents. Like acceptable scientific theory—or like any theory or structure of knowledge—moral thought may be considered partially to generate its own data as it goes along, or at least to expand so as to contain in a balanced, self-consistent way a wider and wider experiential field. The raw data in the case of our ethical philosophies may be consid-ered as conflicts between roles, or values, or as the social order in which people live.

The social worlds of all people seem to contain the same basic structures. All the societies we have studied have the same basic institutions—family, economy, law, government. In addition, how-ever, all societies are alike because they are societies—systems of defined complementary roles. In order to play a social role in the family, school, or society, children must implicitly take the role of others toward themselves and toward others in the group. These role-taking tendencies form the basis of all social institutions. They rep-resent various patternings of shared or complementary expectations.

In the preconventional and conventional levels (Stages 1–4), moral content or value is largely accidental or culture bound. Anything from "honesty" to "courage in battle" can be the central value. But in the higher postconventional levels, Socrates, Lincoln, Thoreau, and Martin Luther King tend to speak without confusion of tongues, as it were. This is because the ideal principles of any social structure are basically alike, if only because there simply are not that many principles that are articulate, comprehensive, and integrated enough to be satisfying to the human intellect. And most of these principles have gone by the name of justice.

I have discussed at some length the culturally universal sequences of stages of moral judgment. I have not entirely clarified how such a sequence helps to resolve relativistic questioning of moral principles, a task taken up in our Chapter 4, "From *Is* to *Ought*." It is easier to clarify how such a sequence helps resolve the dilemma of relativity versus indoctrination in values education. The sequence provides us with a concept of moral development that can be stimulated by education without indoctrination and yet that helps to move student judgment toward more adequate principles.

The way to stimulate stage growth is to pose real or hypothetical dilemmas to students in such a way as to arouse disagreement and uncertainty as to what is right. The teacher's primary role is to present such dilemmas and to ask Socratic questions that arouse student reasoning and focus student listening on one another's reasons.

I noted research by Rest (1973) showing that students prefer the highest stage of reasoning they comprehend but that they do not comprehend more than one stage above their own. As a result, assimilation of reasoning occurs primarily when it is the next stage up from the student's level. Developmental moral discussion thus arouses cognitive-moral conflict and exposes students to reasoning by other students at the next stage above their own.

Using this approach, Blatt and Kohlberg (1975) were able to stimulate one-third of experimental classes of students to advance one stage in a time period in which control classes remained unchanged in moral stage. One year later, the experimental classes retained their relative advance over the control classes.

The developmental approach, first experimentally elaborated by Blatt, is one that any thoughtful classroom teacher may practice. Unlike values clarification, its assumptions are not relativistic but, rather, are based on universal goals and principles. It asks the student for reasons, on the assumption that some reasons are more adequate than others.

The approach differs from indoctrinative approaches because it tries to move student's thinking in a direction that is natural for the student rather than moving the student in the direction of accepting the teacher's moral assumptions. It avoids preaching or didacticism linked to the teacher's authority. . . .

STUDY QUESTIONS

1. Examine the evidence for Kohlberg's claim that moral development is fundamentally the same in all cultures. Does this amount

to much more than adopting liberal ideas of justice and equality as "the highest stage" and then noting that individuals in some societies do (or aspire to) live by them?

2. Kohlberg claims that no one skips a "stage." Can this be confirmed empirically? How does Kohlberg support his argument for this claim?

3. Kohlberg's highest stages are termed "postconventional." Yet a great deal of morality is conventional and parochial (patriotism, filial and other kinship loyalties), being determined by social position and role and cultural norms. Does Kohlberg escape cultural relativism at the price of downgrading much of the bread-and-butter morality of our conventional daily lives?

4. Kohlberg seems opposed to the usual practices in moral education (e.g., parental and teacher threats, behavior codes, parental/ teacher encouragement to cultivate virtues and abjure vice, morally inspiring literature and biographies, a thorough knowledge of the moral traditions of American society). Yet, doesn't a child need just such an "old-fashioned" moral education in order to progress through the first four stages? Discuss.

REFERENCES

Blatt, M., and L. Kohlberg. "The Effects of Classroom Moral Discussion upon Children's Level of Moral Judgment." *Journal of Moral Education* 4 (1975): 129–61.

Bronfenbrenner, U. "Soviet Methods of Upbringing and Their Effects: A Social-Psychological Analysis." Paper read at conference on Studies of the Acquisition and Development of Values, National Institute of Child Health and Human Development, Washington, D.C., May 23, 1968.

Carr, D. B., and E. P. Wellenberg. *Teaching Children Values.* (Freeport, CA: Honor Your Partner Records, 1966).

Dodder, C., and B. Dodder. *Decision Making: A Guide for Teachers Who Would Help Preadolescent Children Become Imaginative and Responsible Decision Makers.* (Boston: Beacon Press, 1968).

Havighurst, R. J., and H. Taba. *Adolescent Character and Personality.* (New York: Wiley, 1949).

Jackson, P. W. *Life in the Classroom*. (New York: Holt, Rinehart and Winston, 1968).

Kohlberg, L. "Moral Development and the New Social Studies." *Social Education* 37 (1973): 368–75.

Piaget, J. *The Moral Judgment of the Child*. New York: Free Press, 1948. (Originally published 1932.)

Rest, J. "The Hierarchical Nature of Moral Judgment." *Journal of Personality* 41 (1973): 86–109.

Simon, S. "Value-Clarification vs. Indoctrination." *Social Education* 35 (1971): 902.

Moral Education and Indoctrination

GEORGE SHER and WILLIAM J. BENNETT

George Sher (b. 1942) is professor of philosophy at the University of Vermont. He has written many articles on moral philosophy and metaphysics, and is the author of *Desert* (1987).

William J. Bennett (b. 1943), formally chairman of the National Endowment for the Humanities, most recently was Secretary of Education in the Reagan Administration. (He coauthored this selection prior to being named Secretary of Education.) Bennett has, in addition, taught philosophy at the University of Texas.

George Sher and William Bennett advocate "directive moral education" in which students are explicitly encouraged to accept and to behave in accordance with specific

MORAL EDUCATION AND INDOCTRINATION By George Sher and William J. Bennett. Reprinted from *The Journal of Philosophy*, November 1982, pp. 665–677. Reprinted by permission of the publisher and authors.

principles (e.g., respect for democratic values, treat others as you would like to be treated), and to develop certain traits (e.g., honesty, courage, and self-discipline).

To the objection that directive moral education violates autonomy, Sher and Bennett reply that what really matters is the autonomy of the adult the child will become. Most children cannot be motivated by reason alone. They need such other motives as fear of punishment, parental/teacher approval, desire to imitate a respected model. As mature adults we are capable of understanding the reasons behind a moral principle, and these reasons alone are often sufficient to motivate us. But why, ask Sher and Bennett, should the fact that we are also partly conditioned by childhood training detract from our autonomy? Indeed, moral education helps us to become autonomous. If children develop good moral habits such as truth telling and fairness to others, it will be easier for them to act in accordance with a reasoned morality. "When [good] habits exist in persons who do not appreciate moral reasons, they may be mere facsimiles of virtue. However, when they exist in conjunction *with* an appreciation of reasons, they surely do contribute to moral autonomy."

Sher and Bennett consider the objection that directive moral education violates the American social ideals of tolerance and pluralism. They admit the danger that fanatics might misuse the system, but believe the problem can be avoided if teachers are encouraged to teach only those values that satisfy "high standards of justification," such as fairness, honesty, and consideration for others.

Sher and Bennett also point to a fallacy in pluralism: the pluralist cannot demand that teachers be neutral toward *all* values since pluralism itself is based on the value of tolerance. "If we . . . value toleration, then we must also value the general acceptance of principles that support and further it."

It is now widely agreed that educators have no business inculcating moral views in the classroom. According to many philosophers and educational theorists, all attempts to influence students' moral behavior through exhortation and personal example are indoctrinative and should give way to more discursive efforts to guide children in developing their own values.[1] Yet although the nondirective approach to moral education has become the new orthodoxy, its philosophical underpinnings remain largely unexplored. In particular, the familiar charge that all directive moral education is indoctrinative has not been carefully defended. In this paper, we will argue that no plausible version of it *can* be defended and that adequate moral education must include both directive *and* discursive elements. Because the charge of indoctrination is so unclear, we will not confront it directly. Instead, we will address two closely related claims: that directive moral education (1) violates a student's autonomy, and (2) involves sectarian teaching inappropriate to a pluralistic society. If these complaints can be shown to lack substance, then the charge of indoctrination will carry little weight.

I

Before discussing the major objections to directive moral education, we must make clearer what such education involves. In particular, we must specify (a) the traits and principles to be taught, and (b) the relevant methods of teaching them, and (c) the positive reasons for adopting such methods.

The traits and principles we have in mind are best illustrated by example. In Talawanda, Ohio, the local school district recently took

---

[1] Thus, for example: "[I]t is . . . wrong to teach ethics by presenting and attempting to inculcate a number of rules or precepts of conduct so as to improve, or at least to alter character, dispositions, or responses. The most effective means for altering responses, and possibly character as well, are those of advertising, propaganda (is there any difference?), indoctrination and brainwashing. These are all objectionable on moral grounds, so one cannot possibly improve character by these means" [Marcus Singer, "The Teaching of Introductory Ethics," *The Monist*, LVIII, 4 (October 1974), p. 617]. "If moral education promotes a definite moral perspective, it tends to be toward indoctrination and the denial of moral autonomy. . . . The problem and the challenge of moral education in our age is to find a middle way which neither indoctrinates young people into one set of moral rules nor gives them the impression that decision making is all a matter of personal opinion" [Robert Hall, "Moral Education Today: Progress, Prospects and Problems of a Field Come of Age," *The Humanist* (November/December 1978), p. 12].

the position that "the schools should help students realize the importance" of principles and traits including:

- Achieving self-discipline, defined as the strength to do what we believe we should do, even when we would rather not do it.
- Being trustworthy, so that when we say we will or will not do something, we can be believed.
- Telling the truth, especially when it hurts us to do so.
- Having the courage to resist group pressures to do what we believe, when alone, that we should not do.
- Using honorable means, those that respect the rights of others, in seeking our individual and collective ends.
- Conducting ourselves, where significant moral behavior is involved, in a manner which does not fear exposure.
- Having the courage to say, "I'm sorry, I was wrong."
- Treating others as we would wish to be treated; recognizing that this principle applies to persons of every class, race, nationality, and religion.
- Doing work well, whatever that work may be.
- Respecting the democratic values of free speech, a free press, freedom of assembly, freedom of religion, and due process of law. Recognizing that this principle applies to speech we abhor, groups we dislike, persons we despise.

Later, we will discuss the degree to which the Talawanda list embodies moral or ideological bias. For now, it suffices to note that the items just listed are close to noncontroversial within our society. They illustrate, but do not exhaust, the traits and principles whose directive teaching we will discuss.

What, exactly, does such teaching involve? Although a full account is again impossible, certain elements stand out. Of these, perhaps the most important is a teacher or administrator's willingness to demonstrate that he himself endorses certain principles—that he accepts them as guides in his own conduct and expects his students to do likewise. This requires that he act as an intentional model of behavior in accordance with the favored principles. It also requires that he explicitly urge his students to develop habits of acting in similar ways and that he express his disapproval, both verbally and through punishment, when his expectations are not met. It is often desirable to explain *why* one should act in the relevant ways, but efforts to influence behavior should not be confined to such explanations. Both encouragement and expressions of disapproval may persist when the proffered reasons are not grasped.

Why should morality be taught in these ways? Quite obviously, any rationale for adopting directive methods must be an instrumental one. The claim must be that, at elementary levels of development, such methods are effective ways of getting children to internalize desirable habits and behave in desirable ways and that, at more advanced levels, the previous application of these methods is necessary for the success of more discursive methods. We believe these claims are supported by recent studies of child and adolescent development and "moral psychology."[2] However, even if all empirical issues remained open, the permissibility of directive moral education would still be worth ascertaining. Even those who are not convinced that such methods work must be interested in learning whether we would be morally permitted to employ them if they did.

II

Consider, first, the objection that directive moral education violates autonomy. At the core of this objection is a distinction between actions produced by nonrational causes and actions motivated by an awareness of the reasons for performing them. When a child acts to imitate a respected model or in response to exhortation or threat, he is said to be motivated only in the former way. Even if there are good reasons for his action, the very same techniques that have motivated his act could just as well have been used to motivate behavior unsupported by such reasons. Thus, his behavior is evidently *not* produced simply by his appreciation of the reasons for it. Hence, it is said to be neither fully his own nor an appropriate object of moral appraisal.

There is plainly something right about this objection. On any plausible account, an adequate moral education must produce not

---

[2]See especially Norman T. Feather, "Values in Adolescence," and Martin L. Hoffman, "Moral Development in Adolescence," in Joseph Adelson, ed., *The Handbook of Adolescent Psychology* (New York: Wiley, 1980), pp. 247–344.

only a tendency to act rightly, but also a tendency to do so for the right reasons. But, despite its superficial clarity, the objection as stated is both ambiguous and incomplete. It is ambiguous because it does not specify whether the person whose autonomy is violated is the child to whom directive education is administered or the adult whom the child will later become. It is incomplete because it does not explain *how* autonomy is violated in either case.

Whose autonomy is violated by directive moral education? Of the two possible answers, the more straightforward is "the child's." But to this answer, there is a quick rejoinder. However desirable it is to appeal to a person's appreciation of reasons, it surely need not be wrong to influence his behavior in other ways when he cannot respond to reasons alone. But this is manifestly true of young children. With them, appeals to principle simply fail. We must ascend the developmental scale quite far before such appeals promise much success. According to the leading proponent of nondirective moral education, Lawrence Kohlberg, the most common motive for moral action among 13-year-olds is still a desire to avoid disapproval and dislike by others.[3] In Kohlberg's typology, this motive is three full stages away from conscientious aversion to self-reproach. Moreover, in Kohlberg's view, one cannot reach a given stage of moral development without first traversing all the lower stages. Thus, even Kohlberg must acknowledge that, before middle adolescence, most children cannot respond to unadorned appeals to moral reasons. But if so, we do not violate their autonomy when we supplement such appeals with more efficacious influences.

This reply may appear inconclusive; for the opponent of directive moral education can respond by weakening his requirements for autonomy. Instead of contending that moral autonomy requires that one act from moral reasons, he can assert that it requires only that one's motives be those of the highest Kohlbergian level available to one. If so, even a child who acts to satisfy an impersonally construed authority (Kohlberg's level 4) may act significantly more autonomously than one who seeks to imitate a respected elder or to avoid punishment. However, considered by itself, such denatured "autonomy" has little value. Its main significance is pretty clearly to

---

[3]For elaboration, see Kohlberg, *The Philosophy of Moral Development* (New York: Harper & Row, 1981).

pave the way for further moral development. Thus, the response does not really save the claim that directive techniques violate a child's autonomy. If anything, it reinforces the claim that what is violated is the autonomy of the adult whom the child will become.

Put in this second form, the objection no longer presupposes an obviously impossible ideal of autonomy. Unlike children, mature adults often do seem to respond to moral reasons. But why should the previous application of directive techniques be thought to prevent this? It is true that directive techniques use nonrational means to produce desires and character traits that will eventually influence one's adult actions. However, even if an adult *is* motivated by a desire that was originally produced by nonrational means, it still seems possible for his action to be done for good moral reasons. In particular, this still seems possible if his nonrationally produced desire is precisely to act *in accordance with* such reasons. But it is surely just this desire which the sensitive practitioner of directive moral education seeks to instill.

If moral autonomy required only action in accordance with moral reasons, this response would be decisive. However, another strain of thought construes the requirements for autonomy more strictly. On this view, genuine moral autonomy requires not only that an agent act *in accordance with* moral reasons, but also that he *be motivated by* his awareness of them. In Kantian terms, the autonomous agent must be "self-legislating." On this expanded account the effectiveness of a past directive education may again seem threatening to current autonomy. If without his past directive education the agent would not now act as he does, then it is apparently just the desires produced by that education which supply the motivational energy for his current act. But if so, that motivational energy is evidently *not* supplied by his recognition of reasons themselves. His recognition of reasons may *trigger* the motivational energy for his act; but what is triggered is still energy with an independent source. Hence, the requirements for moral autonomy still seem unsatisfied.

With this refinement, we approach the heart of the objection that directive moral education violates autonomy. But although the refinement is familiar, the resulting argument is problematical. Most obviously, it rests on both the obscure metaphor of motivational energy and the undefended requirement that autonomous acts must draw such energy from reasons themselves. But the difficulty goes deeper. Even if its premises were both intelligible and defensible, the argument would be a non sequitur. Although it purports to demonstrate that directive moral education *violates* moral autonomy, it really shows only that such education does not *contribute* to moral autonomy. Far from establishing that directive techniques are pernicious, it at best establishes that they are morally neutral.

For why *should* desires produced by nonrational techniques be thought to prevent one from being motivated by an appreciation of reasons? Is the point merely that anyone subject to nonrationally produced desires would perform his act even if he were *not* motivated by an appreciation of the moral reasons for it? If so, then the most that follows is that his act is motivationally overdetermined. Since this does not negate the motivating force of his appreciation of reasons, it does not undermine his autonomy. Is the point rather that, if one's directively induced desires are required to produce one's action, then the motivation supplied by one's appreciation of reasons is too *weak* to produce it—that the latter motivation requires supplementation? If so, then, without his directive moral education, the agent would not have performed the act at all, and so *a fortiori* would not have performed it autonomously. Here again, nothing suggests that his directive moral education has reduced or violated his autonomy.

Given these considerations, even the strengthened analysis of autonomy does not establish that directive moral education violates one's later autonomy. To show this, one would need two yet stronger premises: that (1) a single act cannot simultaneously be motivated by both the agent's recognition of reasons and a nonrationally induced desire, and (2) when motivation from both sources converges, the motivational energy supplied by the nonrationally induced desire always excludes that supplied by an appreciation of reasons. But although these premises would indeed save the argument, there is little independent basis for them. In ordinary contexts, energy from any number of sources can combine to produce a single result. Hence, given our working metaphor, we must also presume that *motivational* energy from different sources can combine. The presumption must be that the motivating force of reasons does *not* give way when other factors motivate the same act. Moreover, these presumptions are not defeated by any independent theoretical considerations; for no adequate theory of how reasons motivate has yet been proposed.

III

So far, we have argued that directive moral education need not violate anyone's present or future moral autonomy. This conclusion, if correct, suffices to rebut the first objection to directive education. But more can be said here. Even if autonomy does require motivation by moral reasons, one's past directive education may actually help such autonomy to develop and flourish.

To see how directive education can have this result, recall first that, even if one's grasp of a moral reason does supply one with some impulse to do the right thing, that impulse may be too weak to issue in action. Because of this, its effect may depend on other factors. In particular, that effect may well be increased by one's past directive education. Of course, the desires produced by such education will not contribute to one's moral autonomy if they merely add their weight to the motivation supplied by one's appreciation of reasons. However, and crucially, a past directive education may also augment one's appreciation of reasons in another way. It may neutralize or eliminate what would otherwise be a competing motive, and so may enable one's appreciation of reasons to affect one more strongly. If directive education works this way, it will indeed render the agent more autonomous. Put in terms of our guiding metaphor, its function will be not to provide an additional source of motivational energy, but rather to clear away obstacles so that the energy supplied by reasons can suffice.

How likely is it that directive moral education actually does work in this way? It is not likely to do so always or exclusively. That directive education does not *always* work by eliminating obstacles to moral reasons is shown by the fact that it motivates even very young children and can motivate adults to act immorally. That it rarely works *only* by eliminating such obstacles is suggested by the fact that one's prerational desires seem likely to persist as one matures. But even if a past directive education often affects adults in ways that do not enhance their autonomy, it may simultaneously affect them in other ways as well. Thus, the question is not whether our model is exclusively correct, but only whether it accurately reflects *one* way in which directive moral education often works.

When the question is put this way, we think its answer is clearly yes. It is a psychological commonplace that one's ability to respond to any reason depends on various external considerations. Hunger, anxiety, pain, and fear can all reduce the effect of reasons by diminishing attention to them and by supplying other motives. Thus, eliminating these distractions plainly does increase the motivating force of reasons. But if so, then eliminating other distractions seems likely to serve a similar function. Two considerations which most often distract us from moral obligations are preoccupation with our own interests and concern for our own comfort. Hence, one very natural way of increasing the motivating force of moral reasons is to reduce the impact of such distractions. But how better to prevent someone from being unduly distracted by self-interest than by causing him to acquire settled habits of honesty, fair play, and concern for others? Given these habits, one will automatically discount one's selfish interests when they conflict with one's duty. Hence, one will attach proper weight to one's moral obligations as a matter of course. Moreover, how better to ensure that someone will follow his decisions through than by causing him to acquire further habits of diligence, perseverance, and conscientiousness? Given *these* habits, one will not be sidetracked by the blandishments of comfort or inertia. Hence, one's appreciation of reasons will again be rendered more effective.

Given all of this, the traditional content of directive moral education acquires new significance. As the Talawanda list suggests, such education has long aimed at producing the habits just mentioned. These habits are often criticized as poor substitutes for self-conscious and reasoned morality, but we can now see that this criticism misses the point. Far from being alternatives to self-conscious morality, the habits are best understood as indispensible auxiliaries to it. They increase the impact of moral reasons by reducing one's tendency to be diverted. When the habits exist in persons who do not appreciate moral reasons, they may be mere facsimilies of virtue. However, when they exist in conjunction *with* an appreciation of reasons, they surely do contribute to moral autonomy.

IV

Until now, we have considered only the objection that directive moral education violates the ideal of the morally autonomous agent. However, one may also argue that it violates a related *social* ideal. There is wide agreement that our society should be both tolerant and plural-istic. Instead of stifling disagreements, it should accept and encour-age diversity of opinion and should protect unpopular attitudes and beliefs. But a society that officially practices directive moral educa-tion seems not to do this. Instead of encouraging diversity, it instills in all children a single "approved" set of values. Far from being neutral, it is unabashedly partisan. Thus, such education may seem flatly incompatible with pluralism and tolerance.

This argument is narrower in scope than its predecessor; for it tells only against the use of directive techniques in public schools. Still, it does seem to animate many charges of indoctrination, and so we must examine it. To see the problems it raises, consider first the premise that society should tolerate and protect diverse values. This premise may mean either that (1) society should not coerce or perse-cute those who already hold unorthodox values, or (2) society should not try to induce people to acquire (or prevent people from acquiring) any values they do not yet hold. Whenever society coerces or perse-cutes those with unpopular values, it provides a disincentive for others to acquire those values. Hence, any violation of (1) is likely to violate (2). However, society may tolerate dissenters while trying to prevent others from acquiring their values. Hence, a violation of (2) does not necessarily violate (1).

Directive moral education neither persecutes anyone nor coerces any adults. When its techniques include punishment, it may be said to coerce children. However, (1) is generally not taken to apply to children, and punishment is in any case theoretically dispensable. Thus, directive moral education need not violate (1). It does violate (2); but that counts against it only if (2) is a proper interpretation of the pluralistic ideal. At first glance, (2) may appear to follow from a more general requirement that unorthodox views should receive a fair hearing. However, this would imply that we owe fair treatment to values as well as persons; and, as John Rawls has noted, such an obligation is highly unlikely.[4] Thus, the more promising strategy is to defend (2) less directly. To do that, one might appeal either to a societal obligation to allow persons to choose their own values or else to the undesirable consequences of inculcating official values. We will argue that neither defense succeeds.

The claim that societal attempts to inculcate values would violate

---

[4]"Fairness to Goodness," *Philosophical Review*, LXXXIV, 4 (October 1975): p. 554.

an obligation to allow people to choose their own values is inherently problematical. In standard cases, people's choices are guided by their values, but here it is precisely one's basic values that are said to *be* chosen. Hence, the relevant choices cannot be grounded in any deeper values. But how, then, *are* such choices grounded? Shall we say they have no grounding, but are simply arbitrary? If so, they hardly warrant society's protection. Are they grounded in considerations outside the agent's value system, such as his recognition of independent moral reasons? If so, the complaint against inculcating values must be that it prevents people from *responding* to such reasons. But we already know this is false. The desires and habits produced by directive moral education need not diminish, but may actually enhance, the motivating force of moral reasons. Is the claim, finally, that societally induced desires and habits do allow rational choice of values when they coincide with moral reasons, but prevent it in cases of conflict? If so, the argument is not that it is wrong to inculcate values, but only that society may inculcate the wrong values. Thus construed, the argument appeals to consequences. Hence, having come this far, we may abandon the rubric of choice, and confront the consequentialist approach directly.

The *locus classicus* of consequentialist arguments for tolerance is John Stuart Mill's *On Liberty*.[5] It is true that Mill's main target is not the inculcation of values, but rather intolerance involving coercion and persecution. However, there are also passages where Mill suggests that his arguments *do* extend to education, and presumably *a fortiori* to directive education. Moreover, whatever Mill's own views, any convincing consequentialist argument for (2) is likely to rest on precisely the familiar claims that society is fallible, that genuine challenges to belief enhance understanding, and that diverse practices provide people with a variety of models and "experiments of living." Thus, it is essentially the Millian arguments that we must now consider. Do they show that society should refrain from using nonrational techniques to instill values in its citizens?

We think not. Mill is right to insist that neither anyone's subjective feeling of certainty nor the agreement of society can guarantee the truth of an opinion or the utility of its adoption. However, the warrant for accepting the values of fairness, honesty, and consideration of others is no mere feeling of conviction. Instead, there is good

---

[5]*On Liberty* (Indianapolis: Hackett, 1978).

independent reason to believe that, if any moral propositions are true, propositions enjoining such behavior are among them. Moreover, if the issue turns on social utility, then the warrant for inculcating these values is still more obvious. There is of course a danger that, once any inculcation of values is admitted, dogmatists and fanatics will seek to inculcate values that are *not* well-grounded or useful. However, this danger, though real, is far from decisive. If we can avoid the slippery slope of insisting that *no* values be inculcated, then we can also do so by insisting that society inculcate only values that satisfy high standards of justifiability. This will of course require some exercise of judgment; but that seems unavoidable in any case. As Mill himself remarks, "there is no difficulty in proving any ethical standard whatever to work ill, if we suppose universal idiocy to be conjoined with it."[6]

In view of this, (2) cannot be supported by appealing to human fallibility. But the consequentialist arguments are no better. A person's comprehension of his beliefs and values may indeed be deepened by challenges posed by dissenters, but such challenges are generally not needed to promote either adequate comprehension or tenacious acceptance of moral values. The suggestion that they are is contradicted by common experience. Moreover, even if wide-spread challenges to moral values did bring real benefits, these would be trivial compared to the mischief done by large numbers of people uncommitted to honesty, integrity, or concern for others. Nor, similarly, is it likely that exposure to cruelty, dishonesty, and insensitivity will promote personal development or bring out traits beneficial to others.

These considerations show that directive moral education need not be condemned as incompatible with pluralism. But that point can also be made in another way. It would be self-defeating for pluralists to demand that society be completely neutral toward all values; for the general acceptance of some values is required by pluralism itself. This holds most obviously for the value of toleration, but it is no less true of other values on the Talawanda list. If people were not committed to fairness, cooperation, and trustworthiness, they could hardly maintain a framework within which the rights of the weak

---

[6]*Utilitarianism* (Indianapolis: Hackett, 1979), p. 23.

and unpopular were protected. This may or may not justify the coercive suppression of some views—intolerance in the name of tolerance remains a disputed question of liberalism—but it surely does call for something beyond mere neutrality. If we as a society value toleration, then we must also value the general acceptance of principles that support and further it. Hence, if there is an effective method of advancing such principles which is not otherwise objectionable, we must acknowledge a strong case for adopting it. But precisely this is true of directive moral education. Thus, at least some forms of it seem justified by our commitment to toleration itself.

V

We have now rejected several familiar arguments against directive moral education. However, in endorsing such education, we do not mean that it should be used to teach every widely accepted moral belief or that it should utilize every effective method of procuring assent. Despite the strong moral component in many issues of economic distribution, foreign policy, and religion, we believe that normative propositions about these matters should generally not be taught directively. And although we believe that fairness and honesty *should* be taught directively, we believe their teaching should not involve immoderate humiliation or pain. But if we are to make such distinctions, we face a difficult further question: why are some forms of directive moral education permissible but others not?

This question is too large for us to answer fully, but some considerations are obviously relevant. To warrant directive teaching, a moral principle must first be clearly and firmly grounded. In addition, it should be simple enough to be comprehended at an early developmental stage, general enough to apply in a variety of situations, and central rather than peripheral to our moral corpus. To be acceptable as a *method* of directive teaching, a practice must neither impair a child's later ability to respond to moral reasons nor violate his rights. In many instances, the satisfaction of these requirements is undisputed. However, if an otherwise eligible principle or method is unacceptable to a conscientious minority, then respect for that minority may itself dictate restraint in directive teaching.

With this we can confront a final objection. It is sometimes said that because directive moral education reflects the prevailing moral climate, it inevitably favors existing practices and institutions. Because it grows out of entrenched attitudes, it is said objectionably to perpetuate the status quo. But we can now see that such worries are overblown. If the principles and habits that are directively taught are strongly justified, central to our evaluative scheme, and of more than parochial application, they are not likely to ratify all aspects of the status quo. Instead, they may well generate considerable dissatisfaction with existing realities. If someone is fair, considers others' interests, and respects democratic values, then he will be highly critical of many existing practices. If he is unmoved by group pressures, he will press his criticism even when it is unpopular. If he respects the truth and disdains dishonorable means, he will abjure self-interested silence. All in all, such a person is unlikely to be passive and indiscriminately accepting. Instead, he is apt vigorously to oppose various existing practices.

This shows that directive moral education need not favor the status quo. But should it ever be used to teach principles that *do* have this effect? To see the problem here, consider some further Talawanda entries:

- Practicing good sportsmanship. Recognizing that although the will to win is important, winning is not all-important.
- Showing respect for the property of others—school property, business property, government property, everyone's property.
- Abstaining from premature sexual experience and developing sexual attitudes compatible with the values of family life.

We believe there is much to be said for each of these. However, each is closely associated with a contested social institution. The first presupposes the legitimacy of competition, the second assumes an economic system which distributes wealth unequally, and the third overtly favors marriage and the family. Alternatives to each institution have been proposed. Does this imply that these principles should not be directively taught?

We believe this question has no simple answer. To decide whether association with an existing institution disqualifies a principle, one must first clarify the nature of the association. Does the principle merely apply *only in the context of* the institution? Or does it, in addition, require that one *accept* it? If acceptance of (say) property or the family is required, must one accept only some form of the institution, or all its current details? If the details need not be accepted, the argument amounts to little. But even if a principle does require full acceptance of an existing institution, the question of its directive teaching is not settled. The main reasons for not directively teaching such principles are to permit full evaluation of alternative institutions and to display respect for persons proposing them. However, despite their relevance, these factors are not always decisive. We saw above that a major determinant of whether a principle should be directively taught is its degree of justification. But if so, then when a principle requires acceptance of a contested institution, we cannot avoid asking how reasonable it is to oppose that institution and how plausible the alternatives are. If these questions are asked, their answers may tip the balance. Hence, directive teaching of principles favoring existing institutions cannot be ruled out.

This of course says little of substance. To evaluate directive teaching about property, sexual behavior, or other matters of controversy, one must say more about a whole range of issues. But that much more must be said is precisely our point. Where directive moral education is concerned, we begin to make progress only when we abandon as sterile the notion of indoctrination and its cognates.

STUDY QUESTIONS

1. How do Sher and Bennett reply to the objection that directive moral education violates autonomy? Evaluate their response.

2. What reasons do Sher and Bennett give for their contention that a directive moral education enhances one's moral autonomy? Do you agree?

3. Do you agree with some critics of Sher and Bennett who say that directive moral education violates American social ideals of pluralism and tolerance? Discuss.

4. Sher and Bennett claim that it is self-defeating for pluralists to demand that society be completely neutral toward all values. Do you find their arguments convincing?

In a Different Voice

CAROL GILLIGAN

Carol Gilligan (b. 1936) is professor of education in the Graduate School of Education at Harvard University. She has written numerous articles on moral psychology and is the author of *In a Different Voice* (1982).

Carol Gilligan discusses "different ideas about human development, different ways of imagining the human condition, different notions of what is of value in life." She notes that developmental theories in psychology project an ideal that views individual development and maturation as moving away from emotional perspectives toward a stage of impersonal justice in dealing with others. According to Sigmund Freud, this moral ideal is more accessible to men than to women because women are "more often influenced in their judgments by feelings of affection and hostility." But Nancy Chodorow argues that women are *naturally* more attuned to others and that their moral ideals are defined through (emotional) attachment, rather than impersonal separation. Gilligan develops this theme by arguing that development itself should be redefined to give care and attachment an importance that is lacking in the standard (male) ideal of justice and autonomy.

The neglect of a woman's perspective has given a male bias to the findings of recent research in the psychology of moral education. Gilligan claims that Lawrence

IN A DIFFERENT VOICE Excerpted by permission of the author and publisher from *In a Different Voice* by Carol Gilligan (Cambridge, MA: Harvard University Press). Copyright © 1982 by Carol Gilligan.

Kohlberg's six stages of moral development assume the impersonal male "justice perspective," thereby assuring the result that women are morally deficient because of their tendency to understand moral issues in emotional and personal ways. Kohlberg's research, which concentrates on male subjects, concludes that in the highest stages of moral development the individual uses universal impartial ethical principles to justify moral rights. Gilligan argues that this developmental ideal that emphasizes the "rights" perspective over the "care perspective" is biased against women. And indeed Kohlberg "finds" that women are fixed in the earlier stages of moral development as he defines them. A perspective that is sensitive to the ideal of responsibility and caring would do more justice to women and their particular life cycles. "Only when life cycle theorists divide their attention and begin to live with women as they have lived with men will their vision encompass both sexes and their theories become correspondingly more fertile."

In the second act of *The Cherry Orchard,* Lopahin, a young merchant, describes his life of hard work and success. Failing to convince Madame Ranevskaya to cut down the cherry orchard to save her estate, he will go on in the next act to buy it himself. He is the self-made man who, in purchasing the estate where his father and grandfather were slaves, seeks to eradicate the "awkward, unhappy life" of the past, replacing the cherry orchard with summer cottages where coming generations "will see a new life." In elaborating this developmental vision, he reveals the image of man that underlies and supports his activity: "At times when I can't go to sleep, I think: Lord, thou gavest us immense forests, unbounded fields and the widest horizons, and living in the midst of them we should indeed be giants"—at which point, Madame Ranevskaya interrupts him, saying, "You feel the need for giants—They are good only in fairy tales, anywhere else they only frighten us."

Conceptions of the human life cycle represent attempts to order and make coherent the unfolding experiences and perceptions, the changing wishes and realities of everyday life. But the nature of such conceptions depends in part on the position of the observer. The brief excerpt from Chekhov's play suggests that when the observer is a woman, the perspective may be of a different sort. Different judgments of the image of man as giant imply different ideas about human development, different ways of imagining the human condition, different notions of what is of value in life.

At a time when efforts are being made to eradicate discrimination between the sexes in the search for social equality and justice, the differences between the sexes are being rediscovered in the social sciences. This discovery occurs when theories formerly considered to be sexually neutral in their scientific objectivity are found instead to reflect a consistent observational and evaluative bias. Then the presumed neutrality of science, like that of language itself, gives way to the recognition that the categories of knowledge are human constructions. The fascination with point of view that has informed the fiction of the twentieth century and the corresponding recognition of the relativity of judgment infuse our scientific understanding as well when we begin to notice how accustomed we have become to seeing life through men's eyes.

A recent discovery of this sort pertains to the apparently innocent classic *The Elements of Style* by William Strunk and E. B. White. The Supreme Court ruling on the subject of discrimination in classroom texts led one teacher of English to notice that the elementary rules of English usage were being taught through examples which counterposed the birth of Napoleon, the writings of Coleridge, and statements such as "He was an interesting talker. A man who had traveled all over the world and lived in half a dozen countries," with "Well, Susan, this is a fine mess you are in" or, less drastically, "He saw a woman, accompanied by two children, walking slowly down the road."

Psychological theorists have fallen as innocently as Strunk and White into the same observational bias. Implicitly adopting the male life as the norm, they have tried to fashion women out of a masculine cloth. It all goes back, of course, to Adam and Eve—a story which shows, among other things, that if you make woman out of a man, you are bound to get into trouble. In the life cycle, as in the Garden of Eden, the woman has been the deviant.

The penchant of developmental theorists to project a masculine image, and one that appears frightening to women, goes back at least to Freud who built his theory of psychosexual development around the experiences of the male child that culminate in the Oedipus complex. In the 1920s, Freud struggled to resolve the contradictions posed for his theory by the differences in female anatomy and the different configuration of the young girl's early family relationships. After trying to fit women into his masculine conception, seeing them as envying that which they missed, he came instead to acknowledge, in the strength and persistence of women's pre-Oedipal attachments to their mothers, a developmental difference. He considered this difference in women's development to be responsible for what he saw as women's developmental failure.

Having tied the formation of the superego or conscience to castration anxiety, Freud considered women to be deprived by nature of the impetus for a clear-cut Oedipal resolution. Consequently, women's superego—the heir to the Oedipus complex—was compromised: it was never "so inexorable, so impersonal, so independent of its emotional origins as we require it to be in men." From this observation of difference, that "for women the level of what is ethically normal is different from what it is in men," Freud concluded that women "show less sense of justice than men, that they are less ready to submit to the great exigencies of life, that they are more often influenced in their judgements by feelings of affection or hostility."

Thus a problem in theory became cast as a problem in women's development, and the problem in women's development was located in their experience of relationships. Nancy Chodorow, attempting to account for "the reproduction within each generation of certain general and nearly universal differences that characterize masculine and feminine personality and roles," attributes these differences between the sexes not to anatomy but rather to "the fact that women, universally, are largely responsible for early child care." Because this early social environment differs for and is experienced differently by male and female children, basic sex differences recur in personality development. As a result, "in any given society, feminine personality comes to define itself in relation and connection to other people more than masculine personality does."

In her analysis, Chodorow relies primarily on Robert Stoller's studies which indicate that gender identity, the unchanging core of personality formation, is "with rare exception firmly and irreversibly established for both sexes by the time a child is around three." Given that for both sexes the primary caretaker in the first three years of life is typically female, the interpersonal dynamics of gender identity formation are different for boys and girls. Female identity formation

601

takes place in a context of ongoing relationship since "mothers tend to experience their daughters as more like, and continuous with, themselves." Correspondingly, girls, in identifying themselves as female, experience themselves as like their mothers, thus fusing the experience of attachment with the process of identity formation. In contrast, "mothers experience their sons as a male opposite," and boys, in defining themselves as masculine, separate their mothers from themselves, thus curtailing "their primary love and sense of empathic tie." Consequently, male development entails a "more emphatic individuation and a more defensive firming of experienced ego boundaries." For boys, but not girls, "issues of differentiation have become intertwined with sexual issues."

Writing against the masculine bias of psychoanalytic theory, Chodorow argues that the existence of sex differences in the early experiences of individuation and relationship "does not mean that women have 'weaker' ego boundaries than men or are more prone to psychosis." It means instead that "girls emerge from this period with a basis for 'empathy' built into their primary definition of self in a way that boys do not." Chodorow thus replaces Freud's negative and derivative description of female psychology with a positive and direct account of her own: "Girls emerge with a stronger basis for experiencing another's needs or feelings as one's own (or of thinking that one is so experiencing another's needs and feelings). Furthermore, girls do not define themselves in terms of the denial of preoedipal relational modes to the same extent as do boys. Therefore, regression to these modes tends not to feel as much a basic threat to their ego. From very early, then, because they are parented by a person of the same gender . . . girls come to experience themselves as less differentiated than boys, as more continuous with and related to the external object-world, and as differently oriented to their inner object-world as well."

Consequently, relationships, and particularly issues of dependency, are experienced differently by women and men. For boys and men, separation and individuation are critically tied to gender identity since separation from the mother is essential for the development of masculinity. For girls and women, issues of femininity or feminine identity do not depend on the achievement of separation from the mother or on the progress of individuation. Since masculinity is defined through separation while feminity is defined through attachment, male gender identity is threatened by intimacy while female gender identity is threatened by separation. Thus males tend to have difficulty with relationships, while females tend to have problems with individuation. The quality of embeddedness in social interaction and personal relationships that characterizes women's lives in contrast to men's, however, becomes not only a descriptive difference but also a developmental liability when the milestones of childhood and adolescent development in the psychological literature are markers of increasing separation. Women's failure to separate then becomes by definition a failure to develop.

The sex differences in personality formation that Chodorow describes in early childhood appear during the middle childhood years in studies of children's games. Children's games are considered by George Herbert Mead and Jean Piaget as the crucible of social development during the school years. In games, children learn to take the role of the other and come to see themselves through another's eyes. In games, they learn respect for rules and come to understand the ways rules can be made and changed.

Janet Lever, considering the peer group to be the agent of socialization during the elementary school years and play to be a major activity of socialization at that time, set out to discover whether there are sex differences in the games that children play. Studying 181 fifth-grade, white, middle-class children, ages ten and eleven, she observed the organization and structure of their playtime activities. She watched the children as they played at school during recess and in physical education class, and in addition kept diaries of their accounts as to how they spent their out-of-school time. From this study, Lever reports sex differences: boys play out of doors more often than girls do; boys play more often in large and age-heterogeneous groups; they play competitive games more often, and their games last longer than girls' games. The last is in some ways the most interesting finding. Boys' games appeared to last longer not only because they required a higher level of skill and were thus less likely to become boring, but also because, when disputes arose in the course of a game, boys were able to resolve the disputes more effectively than girls: "During the course of this study, boys were seen quarrelling all the time, but not once was a game terminated because of a quarrel and no game was interrupted for more than seven minutes. In the gravest debates, the final word was always, to 'repeat the play,' generally followed by a chorus of 'cheater's proof.'" In fact, it seemed that the boys enjoyed the legal debates as much as they did the game itself, and even marginal players of lesser size or skill participated equally in these recurrent squabbles. In contrast, the eruption of disputes among girls tended to end the game.

Thus Lever extends and corroborates the observations of Piaget in his study of the rules of the game, where he finds boys becoming through childhood increasingly fascinated with the legal elaboration of rules and the development of fair procedures for adjudicating conflicts, a fascination that, he notes, does not hold for girls. Girls, Piaget observes, have a more "pragmatic" attitude toward rules, "regarding a rule as good as long as the game repaid it."

Girls are more tolerant in their attitudes toward rules, more willing to make exceptions, and more easily reconciled to innovations. As a result, the legal sense, which Piaget considers essential to moral development, "is far less developed in little girls than in boys."

The bias that leads Piaget to equate male development with child development also colors Lever's work. The assumption that shapes her discussion of results is that the male model is the better one since it fits the requirements for modern corporate success. In contrast, the sensitivity and care for the feelings of others that girls develop through their play have little market value and can even impede professional success. Lever implies that, given the realities of adult life, if a girl does not want to be left dependent on men, she will have to learn to play like a boy.

To Piaget's argument that children learn the respect for rules necessary for moral development ·by playing rule-bound games, Lawrence Kohlberg adds that these lessons are most effectively learned through the opportunities for role-taking that arise in the course of resolving disputes. Consequently, the moral lessons inherent in girls' play appear to be fewer than in boys'. Traditional girls' games like jump rope and hopscotch are turn-taking games, where competition is indirect since one person's success does not necessarily signify another's failure. Consequently, disputes requiring adjudication are less likely to occur. In fact, most of the girls whom Lever interviewed claimed that when a quarrel broke out, they ended the game. Rather than elaborating a system of rules for resolving disputes, girls subordinated the continuation of the game to the continuation of relationships.

Lever concludes that from the games they play, boys learn both the independence and the organizational skills necessary for coordinating the activities of large and diverse groups of people. By participating in controlled and socially approved competitive situations, they learn to deal with competition in a relatively forthright manner—to play with their enemies and to compete with their friends—all in accordance with the rules of the game. In contrast, girls' play tends to occur in smaller, more intimate groups, often the best-friend dyad, and in private places. This play replicates the social pattern of primary human relationships in that its organization is more cooperative. Thus, it points less, in Mead's terms, toward learning to take the role of "the generalized other," less toward the abstraction of human relationships. But it fosters the development of the empathy and sensitivity necessary for taking the role of "the particular other" and points more toward knowing the other as different from the self.

The sex differences in personality formation in early childhood that Chodorow derives from her analysis of the mother-child relationship are thus extended by Lever's observations of sex differences in the play activities of middle childhood. Together these accounts suggest that boys and girls arrive at puberty with a different interpersonal orientation and a different range of social experiences.

. . .

"It is obvious," Virginia Woolf says, "that the values of women differ very often from the values which have been made by the other sex." Yet, she adds, "it is the masculine values that prevail." As a result, women come to question the normality of their feelings and to alter their judgments in deference to the opinion of others. In the nineteenth-century novels written by women, Woolf sees at work "a mind which was slightly pulled from the straight and made to alter its clear vision in deference to external authority." The same deference to the values and opinions of others can be seen in the judgments of twentieth-century women. The difficulty women experience in finding or speaking publicly in their own voices emerges repeatedly in the form of qualification and self-doubt, but also in intimations of a divided judgment, a public assessment and private assessment which are fundamentally at odds.

Yet the deference and confusion that Woolf criticizes in women derive from the values she sees as their strength. Women's deference is rooted not only in their social subordination but also in the substance of their moral concern. Sensitivity to the needs of others and the assumption of responsibility for taking care lead women to attend to voices other than their own and to include in their judgment other points of view. Women's moral weakness, manifest in an apparent diffusion and confusion of judgment, is thus inseparable from women's moral strength, an overriding concern with relationships and responsibilities. The reluctance to judge may itself be indicative of the care and concern for others that infuse the psychology of women's development and are responsible for what is generally seen as problematic in its nature.

Thus women not only define themselves in a context of human relationship but also judge themselves in terms of their ability to care. Women's place in man's life cycle has been that of nurturer, caretaker, and helpmate, the weaver of those networks of relationships on which she in turn relies. But while women have thus taken care of men, men have, in their theories of psychological development, as in their economic arrangements, tended to assume or devalue that care. When the focus on individuation and individual achievement extends into adulthood and maturity is equated with personal autonomy, concern with relationships appears as a weakness of women rather than as a human strength.

The discrepancy between womanhood and adulthood is nowhere more evident than in the studies on sex-role stereotypes reported by Broverman, Vogel, Broverman, Clarkson, and Rosenkrantz. The repeated finding of these studies is that the qualities deemed necessary for adulthood—the capacity for autonomous thinking, clear decision-making, and responsible action—are those associated with masculinity and considered undesirable as attributes of the feminine self. The stereotypes suggest a splitting of love and work that relegates expressive capacities to women while placing instrumental abilities in the masculine domain. Yet looked at from a different perspective, these stereotypes reflect a conception of adulthood that is itself out of balance, favoring the separateness of the individual self over connection to others, and leaning more toward an autonomous life of work than toward the interdependence of love and care.

The discovery now being celebrated by men in mid-life of the importance of intimacy, relationships, and care is something that women have known from the beginning. However, because that knowledge in women has been considered "intuitive" or "instinctive," a function of anatomy coupled with destiny, psychologists have neglected to describe its development. In my research, I have found that women's moral development centers on the elaboration of that knowledge and thus delineates a critical line of psychological development in the lives of both of the sexes. The subject of moral development not only provides the final illustration of the reiterative pattern in the observation and assessment of sex differences in the literature on human development, but also indicates more particularly why the nature and significance of women's development has been for so long obscured and shrouded in mystery.

The criticism that Freud makes of women's sense of justice, seeing it as compromised in its refusal of blind impartiality, reappears not only in the work of Piaget but also in that of Kohlberg. While in Piaget's account of the moral judgment of the child, girls are an aside, a curiosity to whom he devotes four brief entries in an index that omits "boys" altogether because "the child" is assumed to be male, in the research from which Kohlberg derives his theory, females simply do not exist. Kohlberg's six stages that describe the development of moral judgment from childhood to adulthood are based empirically on a study of eighty-four boys whose development Kohlberg has followed for a period of over twenty years. Although Kohlberg claims universality for his stage sequence, those groups not included in his original sample rarely reach his higher stages.

Prominent among those who thus appear to be deficient in moral development when measured by Kohlberg's scale are women, whose judgments seem to exemplify the third stage of his six-stage sequence. At this stage morality is conceived in interpersonal terms and goodness is equated with helping and pleasing others. This conception of goodness is considered by Kohlberg and Kramer to be functional in the lives of mature women insofar as their lives take place in the home. Kohlberg and Kramer imply that only if women enter the traditional arena of male activity will they recognize the inadequacy of this moral perspective and progress like men toward higher stages where relationships are subordinated to rules (stage four) and rules to universal principles of justice (stages five and six).

Yet herein lies a paradox, for the very traits that traditionally have defined the "goodness" of women, their care for and sensitivity to the needs of others, are those that mark them as deficient in moral development. In this version of moral development, however, the conception of maturity is derived from the study of men's lives and reflects the importance of individuation in their development. Piaget, challenging the common impression that a developmental theory is

607

built like a pyramid from its base in infancy, points out that a conception of development instead hangs from its vertex of maturity, the point toward which progress is traced. Thus, a change in the definition of maturity does not simply alter the description of the highest stage but recasts the understanding of development, changing the entire account.

When one begins with the study of women and derives developmental constructs from their lives, the outline of a moral conception different from that described by Freud, Piaget, or Kohlberg begins to emerge and informs a different description of development. In this conception, the moral problem arises from conflicting responsibilities rather than from competing rights and requires for its resolution a mode of thinking that is contextual and narrative rather than formal and abstract. This conception of morality as concerned with the activity of care centers moral development around the understanding of responsibility and relationships, just as the conception of morality as fairness ties moral development to the understanding of rights and rules.

This different construction of the moral problem by women may be seen as the critical reason for their failure to develop within the constraints of Kohlberg's system. Regarding all constructions of responsibility as evidence of a conventional moral understanding, Kohlberg defines the highest stages of moral development as deriving from a reflective understanding of human rights. That the morality of rights differs from the morality of responsibility in its emphasis on separation rather than connection, in its consideration of the individual rather than the relationship as primary, is illustrated by two responses to interview questions about the nature of morality. The first comes from a twenty-five-year-old man, one of the participants in Kohlberg's study:

> [*What does the word morality mean to you?*] Nobody in the world knows the answer. I think it is recognizing the right of the individual, the rights of other individuals, not interfering with those rights. Act as fairly as you would have them treat you. I think it is basically to preserve the human being's right to existence. I think that is the most important. Secondly, the human being's right to do as he pleases, again without interfering with somebody else's rights.
>
> [*How have your views on morality changed since the last interview?*] I think I am more aware of an individual's rights now. I used to be

looking at it strictly from my point of view, just for me. Now I think I am more aware of what the individual has a right to.

Kohlberg cites this man's response as illustrative of the principled conception of human rights that exemplifies his fifth and sixth stages. Commenting on the response, Kohlberg says. "Moving to a perspective outside of that of his society, he identifies morality with justice (fairness, rights, the Golden Rule), with recognition of the rights of others as these are defined naturally or intrinsically. The human being's right to do as he pleases without interfering with somebody else's rights is a formula defining rights prior to social legislation."

The second response comes from a woman who participated in the rights and responsibilities study. She also was twenty-five and, at the time, a third-year law student:

> [*Is there really some correct solution to moral problems, or is everybody's opinion equally right?*] No, I don't think everybody's opinion is equally right. I think that in some situations there may be opinions that are equally valid, and one could conscientiously adopt one of several courses of action. But there are other situations in which I think there are right and wrong answers, that sort of inhere in the nature of existence, of all individuals here who need to live with each other to live. We need to depend on each other, and hopefully it is not only a physical need but a need of fulfillment in ourselves, that a person's life is enriched by cooperating with other people and striving to live in harmony with everybody else, and to that end, there are right and wrong, there are things which promote that end and that move away from it, and in that way it is possible to choose in certain cases among different courses of action that obviously promote or harm that goal.
>
> [*Is there a time in the past when you would have thought about these things differently?*] Oh, yeah, I think that I went through a time when I thought that things were pretty relative, that I can't tell you what to do and you can't tell me what to do, because you've got your conscience and I've got mine.
>
> [*When was that?*] When I was in high school. I guess that it just sort of dawned on me that my own ideas changed, and because my own judgment changed, I felt I couldn't judge another person's judgment. But now I think even when it is only the person himself who is going to be affected, I say it is wrong to the extent it doesn't cohere with what I know about human nature and what I know about you, and

just from what I think is true about the operation of the universe, I could say I think you are making a mistake.

[*What led you to change, do you think?*] Just seeing more of life, just recognizing that there are an awful lot of things that are common among people. There are certain things that you come to learn promote a better life and better relationships and more personal fulfillment than other things that in general tend to do the opposite, and the things that promote these things, you would call morally right.

This response also represents a personal reconstruction of morality following a period of questioning and doubt, but the reconstruction of moral understanding is based not on the primacy and universality of individual rights, but rather on what she describes as a "very strong sense of being responsible to the world." Within this construction, the moral dilemma changes from how to exercise one's rights without interfering with the rights of others to how "to lead a moral life which includes obligations to myself and my family and people in general." The problem then becomes one of limiting responsibilities without abandoning moral concern. When asked to describe herself, this woman says that she values "having other people that I am tied to, and also having people that I am responsible to. I have a very strong sense of being responsible to the world, that I can't just live for my enjoyment, but just the fact of being in the world gives me an obligation to do what I can to make the world a better place to live in, no matter how small a scale that may be on." Thus while Kohlberg's subject worries about people interfering with each other's rights, this woman worries about "the possibility of omission, of your not helping others when you could help them."

The issue that this woman raises is addressed by Jane Loevinger's fifth "autonomous" stage of ego development, where autonomy, placed in the context of relationships, is defined as modulating an excessive sense of responsibility through the recognition that other people have responsibility for their own destiny. The autonomous stage in Loevinger's account witnesses a relinquishing of moral dichotomies and their replacement with "a feeling for the complexity and multifaceted character of real people and real situations." Whereas the rights conception of morality that informs Kohlberg's principled level (stages five and six) is geared to arriving at an objectively fair or just resolution to moral dilemmas upon which all rational persons could agree, the responsibility conception focuses instead on the limitations of any particular resolution and describes the conflicts that remain.

Thus it becomes clear why a morality of rights and noninterference may appear frightening to women in its potential justification of indifference and unconcern. At the same time, it becomes clear why, from a male perspective, a morality of responsibility appears inconclusive and diffuse, given its insistent contextual relativism. Women's moral judgments thus elucidate the pattern observed in the description of the developmental differences between the sexes, but they also provide an alternative conception of maturity by which these differences can be assessed and their implications traced. The psychology of women that has consistently been described as distinctive in its greater orientation toward relationships and interdependence implies a more contextual mode of judgment and a different moral understanding. Given the differences in women's conceptions of self and morality, women bring to the life cycle a different point of view and order human experience in terms of different priorities.

The myth of Demeter and Persephone, which McClelland cites as exemplifying the feminine attitude toward power, was associated with the Eleusinian Mysteries celebrated in ancient Greece for over two thousand years. As told in the Homeric *Hymn to Demeter,* the story of Persephone indicates the strengths of interdependence, building up resources and giving, that McClelland found in his research on power motivation to characterize the mature feminine style. Although, McClelland says, "it is fashionable to conclude that no one knows what went on in the Mysteries, it is known that they were probably the most important religious ceremonies, even partly on the historical record, which were organized by and for women, especially at the onset before men by means of the cult of Dionysos began to take them over." Thus McClelland regards the myth as "a special presentation of femine psychology." It is, as well, a life-cycle story par excellence.

Persephone, the daughter of Demeter, while playing in a meadow with her girlfriends, sees a beautiful narcissus which she runs to pick. As she does so, the earth opens and she is snatched away by Hades, who takes her to his underworld kingdom. Demeter, goddess of the earth, so mourns the loss of her daughter that she refuses to allow anything to grow. The crops that sustain life on earth shrivel up, killing men and animals alike, until Zeus takes pity on man's suffering and persuades his brother to return Persephone to her mother.

But before she leaves, Persephone eats some pomegranate seeds, which ensures that she will spend part of every year with Hades in the underworld.

The elusive mystery of women's development lies in its recognition of the continuing importance of attachment in the human life cycle. Woman's place in man's life cycle is to protect this recognition while the developmental litany intones the celebration of separation, autonomy, individuation, and natural rights. The myth of Persephone speaks directly to the distortion in this view by reminding us that narcissism leads to death, that the fertility of the earth is in some mysterious way tied to the continuation of the mother-daughter relationship, and that the life cycle itself arises from an alternation between the world of women and that of men. Only when life-cycle theorists divide their attention and begin to live with women as they have lived with men will their vision encompass the experience of both sexes and their theories become correspondingly more fertile.

STUDY QUESTIONS

1. Gilligan speaks of "a consistent observational and evaluative bias" in the way women are viewed. How is this bias manifested in the social and psychological sciences? How is it manifested in general?

2. What is negative about Sigmund Freud's account of women's development? How does Nancy Chodorow correct Freud in a positive way?

3. How do girls and boys characteristically handle disputes? Rules? What general bearing does this have on their individual perspective on morality?

4. What, according to Gilligan, are the peculiar moral strengths of women? What is the distinction between "a morality of rights" and a "morality of responsibility"? How does Gilligan deploy this distinction in criticizing Lawrence Kohlberg?

5. Some feminists have attributed to Gilligan the view that women are by nature morally superior to men. Do you find this to be a reasonable reading of Gilligan's point of view? (Does Gilligan's approach lead to a kind of reverse sexism?)

6. Gilligan sees the male ethic, with its formal emphasis on obli-

gation, as inadequate. Can a similar criticism be reasonably made of an ethic that elevates care and personal commitment over formal obligation?

Other Voices, Other Rooms? Women's Psychology and Moral Theory

rr~

GEORGE SHER

George Sher (b. 1942) is Herbert S. Autrey professor of philosophy at Rice University. He has written many articles on moral philosphy and metaphysics, and is the author of *Desert* (1987).

George Sher examines Carol Gilligan's thesis that women have a distinctive moral "voice." According to Gilligan, women's morality tends to be more contextual and personal than men's. Women are motivated more by feeling, care, and responsibility than by impartial and abstract moral principles about duty. Gilligan concludes that existing moral theories embody a male bias and fail to take specific account of women's moral orientation.

George Sher challenges the originality of Gilligan's contentions, pointing out that the tensions between care and duty, between the personal and the impersonal, between abstract principle and contextual reality are old and well-known themes in moral philosophy. All of the standard theories (Rawls's social contractarianism, for

OTHER VOICES, OTHER ROOMS? WOMEN'S PSYCHOLOGY AND MORAL THEORY, by George Sher. Reprinted from *Women and Moral Theory* eds. E. Kittay and Diana Meyers. Reprinted by permission of Rowman & Littlefield.

example) must assign proper places to care and duty, balancing, for example, considerations of justice with considerations of mercy. Sher acknowledges that Gilligan may have suggested a better way to deal with the familiar tensions between care and duty, and partiality and impartiality. He concedes that she may have shown that women are more sensitive to certain aspects of these familiar oppositions than men are. But he disputes the claim that she has discovered anything new or uncovered any serious inadequacies in existing moral theories.

Of all the reasons for the recent surge of interest in Carol Gilligan's work, not the least is the idea that her findings may have important implications for moral theory. Although this idea is not always made explicit, its overall thrust is clear enough. By showing that women and men construe moral problems differently, and by demonstrating that their moral development traverses different stages, Gilligan is thought to have uncovered an imbalance in existing moral theories. She is thought to have shown that their standard categories and questions embody a subtle bias—a male bias—and thus to have opened our eyes to alternative possibilities.[1] Here I want to register some skepticism about this idea. Despite their undeniable importance, I believe Gilligan's findings open few new doors for moral theory. Women's moral judgments may be expressed in a different voice, but that voice echoes through some quite familiar rooms.

For an initial sense of what is at stake, let us briefly review Gilligan's reconstruction of women's moral thought. Her conception of the prevailing paradigms, and her views about how women deviate from them, are interwoven with her discussion of the three empirical studies around which her book[2] is built. Thus, I shall begin by citing a few representative passages:

---

[1]Thus, for example, Linda J. Nicholson writes, in an issue of *Social Research* devoted to Gilligan's work, that "many feminists have responded that the masculinity of the authors has affected the very content of the theory itself . . . I agree with the feminist argument" (Linda J. Nicholson, "Women, Morality and History," *Social Research*, 50, 3 (Autumn 1983), p. 514). I do not mean to imply that either Nicholson or the other contributors to that issue subscribe to the specific views I criticize below.

[2]Carol Gilligan, *In a Different Voice* (Cambridge: Harvard University Press, 1982). All pages references in the text are to this volume.

Claire's inability to articulate her moral position stems in part from the fact that hers is a contextual judgment, bound to the particulars of time and place, contingent always on "that mother" and that "unborn child" and thus resisting a categorical formulation. To her the possibilities of imagination outstrip the capacity for generalization [pp. 58–59].

Hypothetical dilemmas, in the abstraction of their presentation, divest moral actors from the history and psychology of their individual lives and separate the moral problem from the social contingencies of its possible occurrence. In doing so, these dilemmas are useful for the distillation and refinement of objective principles of justice and for measuring the formal logic of equality and reciprocity. However, the reconstruction of the dilemma in its contextual particularity allows the understanding of cause and consequence which engages the compassion and tolerance repeatedly noted to distinguish the moral judgments of women [p. 100].

Seeing in the dilemma not a math problem with humans but a narrative of relationships that extends over time, Amy envisions the wife's continuing need for her husband and the husband's continuing concern for his wife and seeks to respond to the druggist's need in a way that would sustain rather than sever connection. Just as she ties the wife's survival to the preservation of relationships, so she considers the value of the wife's life in a context of relationships [p. 28].

Women's construction of the moral problem as a problem of care and responsibility in relationships rather than as one of rights and rules ties the development of their moral thinking to changes in their understanding of responsibility and relationships, just as the conception of morality as justice ties development to the logic of equality and reciprocity [p. 73].

Thus it becomes clear why a morality of rights and noninterference may appear frightening to women in its potential justification of indifference and unconcern. At the same time, it becomes clear why, from a male perspective, a morality of responsibility appears inconclusive and diffuse given its insistent contextual relativism [p. 22].

In these and many similar passages, Gilligan elaborates her conception of women's distinctive moral "voice" through a series of oppositions. She can be read as saying that women's morality is concrete and contextual rather than abstract; that it is nonprincipled rather than principled; that it is personal rather than impersonal; that it motivates through care rather than through awareness of duty; and that it is structured around responsibilities rather than rights. There is room for debate over which of these claims Gilligan regards as fundamental, and, indeed, over which she is committed to at all. But if our question is whether any aspect (or plausible extension) of Gilligan's findings can lead to a recasting of moral theory, then we will do well to examine each opposition.

Thus, consider first the suggestion that women's moral decisions are concrete and contextual rather than abstract. Taken literally, the opposition here seems spurious, for at least *prima facie*, it is hard to see either how all contextual features could ever be *irrelevant* to a moral decision, or how they all could be *relevant* to it. Even the most unbending absolutist, who believes that (say) no promises should ever be broken, must allow moral agents to pay enough attention to context to ascertain whether a particular act *would* break a promise; and additional attention to context is required by the notorious problem of conflict of duty. Yet, on the other hand, even the most ardent proponent of "situation ethics" must acknowledge that moral decision-making requires some selectivity of attention, and thus too, some abstraction from total context. The woman who agonizes over an abortion may be influenced by a myriad of "particulars of time and place"; but given the uncountable number of such particulars, she plainly cannot consider them all. *A fortiori*, she cannot assign them all weight. Thus, the proper question is not so much *whether* context is relevant, but rather how many, and which aspects of it are pertinent to our moral decisions, and how these interact to generate moral duties. But when the role of context is thus tamed,[3] it no longer represents a new discovery for moral theory. Instead, the questions it raises are the very stuff of orthodox normative ethics.[4]

---

[3] That it must be so tamed is one of the few points of agreement between Owen Flanagan and Lawrence Kohlberg in their interchange on moral development. See Owen J. Flanagan, "Virtue, Sex, and Gender: Some Philosophical Reflections on the Moral Psychology Debate," *Ethics* 92 (April 1982), pp. 499–512; and Lawrence Kohlberg, "A Reply to Owen Flanagan and Some Comments on the Puka-Goodpaster Exchange," *Ethics*, 92 (April 1982), pp. 513–28.

[4] Moral philosophers have proposed a variety of approaches to the question of which aspects of one's context are morally relevant. Some focus exclusively on a single factor, such as the happiness or preference-satisfaction that available acts would produce. See, for instance, John Stuart Mill, *Utilitarianism* (Indianapolis: Hackett Publishing Company, 1979). Others hold that more than one factor is relevant, but that some factors

Not surprisingly, these *a priori* remarks are borne out by the reports of Gilligan's own subjects. Despite Gilligan's claim that these women make moral decisions contextually and concretely, their words often evidence a well developed sense of differential relevance. Moreover, this sense emerges not only in their responses to Kohlberg's hypothetical dilemmas, but also in their formulations of dilemmas from their actual lives. Thus, for example, Claire, whose doubts about her activities as an abortion counselor were the occasion for the first passage quoted, remarks that "yes, life is sacred, but the quality of life is also important, and it has to be the determining thing in this particular case" [p. 58]. One might quarrel with Claire's characterization of life as "sacred" when she takes its value to be overridden by other considerations; but she is undeniably trying both to isolate the relevant features of her situation and to impose an order upon them.

This is, of course, not to deny that women may in general be more attuned than men to context; nor is it to deny that such receptivity may be extremely important in shaping women's moral assessments. Certainly genetic or environmental factors may have conspired to make women especially sensitive to what their acts really mean to the persons they affect. It is also conceivable that women may care more than men about this. Indeed, given Gilligan's data, such differences seem far more than mere possibilities. Furthermore, any reasonable theory will acknowledge that both the rightness of one's acts and one's moral goodness are heavily influenced by how accurately and full one assesses one's situation and the possibilities for action within it. For a deontologist, one's attentiveness to context determines how well one appreciates the nature, and so too the right-making characteristics of the available acts; for a consequentialist, it determines how well one appreciates those acts' potential consequences. Yet even taken together, these concessions imply at most that women may be

---

take priority over others. This approach is exemplified by John Rawls' "lexical ordering" of his principles of justice; see his *A Theory of Justice* (Cambridge: Harvard University Press, 1971). Still others say that more than one factor is relevant, and that there are no priority rules to adjudicate conflicts. See, for example, W. D. Ross, *The Right and the Good* (Oxford: Oxford University Press, 1973), and William Frankena, *Ethics*, 2nd Edition (Englewood Cliffs: Prentice-Hall, 1973). Again, R. M. Hare has argued that a factor's moral relevance for an agent depends on his willingness to universalize a principle in which it appears; see his *Freedom and Reason* (Oxford: Oxford University Press, 1963).

better than men at one aspect of a multifaceted common enterprise. They surely do not imply that women operate within a "morality of context" while men do not. If Kohlberg's "masculine" stage-sequence construes moral development only as movement toward greater abstraction, and ignores the possibility that persons may also develop in sensitivity to context, then so much the worse for its pretensions to measure all aspects of moral progress. So much the worse, too, for its claim to capture all that is importantly common among traditional competing theories.

This way of dismissing the contextual/abstract distinction may seem too quick. Even if we agree that every moral decision requires both sensitivity to context and abstraction from it, we need not agree about the form such abstraction must take. More specifically, even if persons cannot make moral decisions without selectively focusing on some features of their situations, there remains a question about whether the selected features can license decisions all by themselves, or whether they can do so only in concert with more general moral principles. It is a commonplace of most moral theories that if a given constellation of facts is to be a good reason for a person X to do A, then a similar constellation must be equally good reason for another person Y, or for the same person X at a different time.[5] Putting the point slightly differently, most theories agree that all moral justification involves at least tacit appeal to principle. Yet Gilligan can be read as taking her findings to show that women's decisions are often *not* backed by universal principles.[6] Hence, her results may seem to point the way to a new view of what constitutes a moral reason.

With this, we have shifted from the first to the second of our contrasts. Underlying the opposition between the contextual and the abstract, we have found a further opposition between the principled and the nonprincipled. This second opposition is, for us, the more

---

[5]For two of the many statements of this view, see Henry Sidgwick, *Methods of Ethics*, 7th Ed. (London: Macmillin, 1922), Book III, Chap. I; and J.L. Mackie, *Ethics: Inventing Right and Wrong* (Harmondsworth, England: Penguin, 1977), chap. 4.

[6]As the editors of this volume have suggested to me, Gilligan's point may be not that women's decisions are nonprincipled, but only that their principles tend not to be couched in such terms as fairness and justice. I agree that this interpretation is available, but continue to regard the stronger interpretation as at least as plausible. More importantly, even if Gilligan herself does not hold the stronger view, the questions of its tenability and relation to her data remain worth discussing.

interesting; for the role of principle in moral thought is far less clear than the mere need for abstraction. There have, of course, been many attempts to show that nonprincipled decisions are irrational, or in other ways deficient. But when pitted against these, Gilligan's findings may seem to carry considerable weight. For if women commonly do make nonprincipled decisions, then to reject such decisions as unacceptable would be to dismiss the standard moral *modus operandi* of half the world's population.

It is, in fact, a nice question of metatheory how heavily such empirical findings should weigh against other, more nearly *a priori* arguments about standards of rationality. To philosophers sympathetic to naturalism, who operate in the spirit of Nelson Goodman's suggestion that "[t]he process of justification is the delicate one of making mutual adjustments between rules and accepted inferences,"[7] the empirical findings will presumably matter a lot. To others, more a prioristically inclined, they will presumably matter less. But in fact, and fortunately, we need not resolve the general problem of method here. For, despite appearances to the contrary, Gilligan's results show very little about the role of principle in women's decisions.

To see why, we must keep our attention firmly fixed on what acting on principle is. As we saw, to act on principle is just to act for reasons that one takes (or perhaps: would take) to apply with similar force to any others who were similarly situated. But, given the counterfactual element of this formulation, the mere fact that women's responses are rarely *couched* in terms of principle provides little evidence about the underlying structure of their decisions. Even persons who fail to mention principles in reconstructing their deliberations, and indeed even persons who explicitly disavow them, may well have decided on principled grounds. Their omissions or disavowals may reflect, not a lack of commitment to principles, but rather an imperfect appreciation of what such commitment amounts to. Whether one acts on principle depends not just on what one says about principles, but rather on what one does or would say (or do) about a variety of other matters. There are, of course, difficult problems here—problems about which questions would best elicit a person's considered views, about what distinguishes deviations from

---

[7]Nelson Goodman, *Fact, Fiction, and Forecast* (Indianapolis: Bobbs-Merrill, 1965), p. 64.

principles from lack of commitment to them, and about which acts or assertions would best show that persons regard their reasons as fully general. However, given our purposes, we need not resolve these problems. Instead, we need only note that *whatever* resolution one adopts, no one can establish the role of principle in a subject's deliberations without some focused and directive counterfactual inquiry. Since Gilligan's questions do not take this form, the responses she elicits do not show that women's decisions are generally nonprincipled (or even that they are less often principled than men's).

This is, I think, not quite to say that Gilligan's data provide *no* evidence for such a conclusion. Since that conclusion is one possible explanation of women's reluctance to appeal explicitly to principles, it does draw some confirmation from Gilligan's data. But because the same data can be explained in many other ways, the degree of confirmation is minimal. Of the plausible competing explanations, one— that Gilligan's subjects lack the somewhat recondite understanding of principled action that figures in philosophical debates—has already been noted. But there are also others. Women's principles may be hedged with more qualifications than men's, and so may be more difficult to articulate, and thus less ready at hand. Women, being more attuned to the need for qualification, may be more aware of the inadequacies of the principles that first come to mind, and so more hesitant to assert them. Women may attach comparatively less importance to the generality of their reasons, and comparatively more to the reasons' complete specification. Given these and other possibilities, the fact that women seldom explicitly invoke moral principles implies little about whether their actual decisions are principled.

This is still not the end of the story. A further aspect of Gilligan's account is that women's moral decisions tend in two ways to be more personal than men's. For one thing, her female subjects often represent moral dilemmas as problems in balancing the needs of specific individuals (who sometimes, but not always, include themselves). For another, they often represent the proper resolutions to these dilemmas as stemming not from impersonal duty, but rather from personal sympathy and care. Since there is at least a *prima facie* tension between the duty to implement an impersonal principle and the concern that stems from a personal relationship, these findings may seem to lend further (if indirect) support to the view that women's decisions are nonprincipled. In addition, they may seem to add further dimension to the claim that women approach problems of conflicting interests differently than men. If these things are true, then our earlier question of how heavily to count actual practice in establishing standards of moral reasonableness will return with a vengeance.

Yet before concluding this, we must look more closely at the tension between personal relationship and impersonal principle, and at the prospects for resolving it within something like the traditional framework. Let us begin by asking why that tension should be thought to exist at all. Although there are surely many contributing factors, one obvious reason is the unique and unrepeatable nature of personal relationships. Because such relationships are rooted in particular histories of transactions between particular persons, any demands they impose must apply to those persons alone. Even if other persons are similarly situated, their different histories will insure that they are not subject to similar demands. Moreover, if personal relationships do impose demands, then those demands must apparently not just differ from, but also sometimes conflict with, the demands of impersonal principle. In particular, such conflict must arise whenever relationship and principle call for incompatible acts.

Thus interpreted, the opposition between the personal and the impersonal is at least *prima facie* plausible. Yet on this account, its challenge to the familiar body of theory invites at least two objections. Most obviously, even if historically rooted relationships do raise questions about the hegemony of a morality of principle, they cannot possibly provide a comprehensive alternative to it; for many pressing moral choices affect only persons with whom the agent *has* no personal relationship. This may be obscured by the prominence of parents, husbands, and lovers in the reports of Gilligan's subjects; but it emerges as soon as we scrutinize the "relationships" between newly pregnant women and the fetuses they carry. It emerges yet more clearly when we consider such cases as that of Hilary, who as a trial lawyer has discovered that the opposing counsel has

> overlooked a document that provided critical support for his client's "meritorious claim." Deliberating whether or not to tell her opponent . . . Hilary realized that the adversary system of justice impedes not only "the supposed search for truth" but also the expression of

concern for the person on the other side. Choosing in the end to adhere to the system, in part because of the vulnerability of her own professional position, she sees herself as having failed to live up to her standard of personal integrity as well as to her moral ideal of self-sacrifice [p. 135].

Whatever Hilary's compromised ideal amounts to, it is plainly *not* an ideal of responsiveness to personal relationships; for no such relationships here exist.[8]

Of course, even if decisions like Hilary's cannot be guided by the demands of personal relationships, they may still be motivated and guided by care and sympathy for all the affected parties. That this is part of what Gilligan takes Hilary to have sacrificed is suggested by her observation that the adversary system impedes "the expression of concern for the person on the other side." Yet as soon as care and concern are detached from the demands of unique and historically rooted relationships—as soon as they are said to be elicited merely by the affected parties' common humanity, or by the fact that those parties all have interests, or all can suffer—the care and concern are once again viewed as appropriate responses to shared and repeatable characteristics. By so regarding them, we completely lose the contrast between the particularity of relationship and the generality of principle. Having lost it, we seem to be left with an approach that seeks to resolve moral dilemmas through sympathetic identification with all the affected parties. Yet far from being novel, this approach—which is at least closely related to that of the familiar impartial and benevolent observer—is central to the existing tradition.[9]

---

[8]In a recent public presentation, Gilligan has distinguished between the view that care rests on attachment, and the view that care rests on knowledge gained through attachment. If she holds that personal relationships are important primarily because they provide a sort of knowledge that can guide and inform our dealings even with strangers, her view is of course not vulnerable to the objections just mounted. It is, however, then vulnerable to the objection to follow.

[9]Two classical representatives of this approach are: David Hume, *Treatise of Human Nature*, L. A. Selby-Bigge, ed. (Oxford: Oxford University Press, 1960), bk. III, pt. III, sec. 1; and Adam Smith, *The Theory of Moral Sentiments*, in L.A. Selby-Bigge, *The British Moralists* Vol. 1 (Oxford: Oxford University Press, 1897), pp. 257–77. For a more recent treatment, see R. M. Hare, *Moral Thinking* (Oxford: Oxford University Press, 1981), part II.

There is also a deeper difficulty with the suggestion that a morality that is sensitive to the demands of relationship must be incompatible with a morality of duty and principle. As I have reconstructed it, the incompatibility arises when the demands of relationship and principle conflict. Yet the assumption that such conflict is inevitable should itself not go unquestioned. Even if we concede that relationships impose demands which *differ* from the demands of moral principles—and I think we ought to concede this—it remains possible that each set of demands might be adjusted to, and might be bounded by, the other. It is, on the one hand, not at all farfetched that friendship might never demand that one betray the trust of another, or that one do anything else that is seriously wrong. It is also not farfetched that the demands of some impersonal moral principles might be contingent on the prior demands of personal relationships. For one thing, we may sometimes be morally permitted, or even required, to give our friends and loved ones preference over others. For another, even where we are not forced to choose whom to help, we may be morally required to produce just the responses that our relationships demand. Such a convergence of demands upon a single action would be no more anomalous than the convergence that occurs when a given act is demanded both by (say) an obligation one has incurred by undertaking a public position and one's natural duty to support just institutions. In general, the demands of relationship and principle may be so interwoven that there is no theoretical bar to our being fully responsive to both.

Needless to say, there are many questions here. It is one thing to suggest that the demands of relationship and impersonal principle might be reconciled, and quite another to tell a plausible detailed story about how this would work. Of all the problems facing such an account, perhaps the most familiar is the objection that the motive of duty is in some sense alienating, and that persons who act merely on principle are *ipso facto* not displaying the affection and care appropriate to personal relationships. Bernard Williams has put this worry well in his influential discussion of the suggestion that a moral principle might license a decision to save one's wife rather than a stranger when only one can be saved. Williams remarks that "this construction provides the agent with one thought too many: it might have been hoped by some (for instance, by his wife) that his motivating thought, fully spelled out, would be the thought that it was his wife, not that it was his wife and, that in situations of this kind, it is permissible to save one's wife."[10] Yet Williams' worry, though provocative, is far from decisive. In an interesting recent essay, Marcia Baron has argued that the worry draws its apparent force partly from our tendency to associate acting from duty with motives that really are inimical to care and affection, but that have no intrinsic connection with duty, and partly from a failure to see that moral principles may operate not as independent sources of motivating force, but rather as filters through which other motives must pass.[11] Since I find Baron's diagnosis convincing, I shall not discuss this problem further. Instead, I shall briefly take up another, less familiar problem that the reconciliationist project faces.

In a nutshell, the further problem is that of justification. It is the problem of finding, within the standard repertoire of justificatory approaches, resources sufficient to ground not merely principles of impartial morality, but also principles licensing the sort of partiality that reconciliationism requires. Put (too) briefly, the difficulty here is that both deontologists and consequentialists have standardly tried to justify their favored principles from some abstract and general perspective. For this reason, the impersonality of their starting points may itself seem to guarantee the rejection of any principles which acknowledge the demands of personal relationships. As Williams notes, this point seems to obtain

> even when the moral point of view is itself explained under conditions of ignorance of some abstractly conceived contracting parties . . . For while the contracting parties are pictured as making some kind of self-interested or prudential choice of a set of rules, they are entirely abstract persons making this choice in ignorance of their own particular properties, tastes, and so forth.[12]

---

[10]Bernard Williams, "Persons, Character, and Morality," in Amelie Rorty, ed., *The Identities of Persons* (Berkeley: University of California Press, 1976), pp. 214–15.

[11]Marcia Baron, "The Alleged Moral Repugnance of Acting from Duty," *The Journal of Philosophy* LXXXI, 4 (April 1984), pp. 197–220. For related discussion, see Peter Railton, "Alienation, Consequentialism, and the Demands of Morality," *Philosophy and Public Affairs*, 13, 2 (Spring 1984), pp. 134–171.

[12]Williams, "Persons, Character, and Morality," pp. 198–99. The approach to which Williams alludes is of course that developed by Rawls in *A Theory of Justice*.

If this is right, and if Gilligan is right to say that women often resolve dilemmas precisely by responding to the demands of personal relationships, then we will indeed be forced to choose between denying that women's decisions are made on moral grounds and radically altering our conceptions of what counts as well grounded morality.

But *does* the impersonality of the familiar justificatory approaches rule out the justification of principles that accommodate the demands of personal relationships? Although we obviously cannot examine all the possibilities, it will be worth our while to look more closely at one familiar strategy. Since the Rawlsian approach has already been mentioned, I shall stick with it. In this approach, a principle is justified if it would be chosen by rational and self-interested persons who were ignorant of the particulars of their situations, and thus were prevented from making biased choices. Although I am no particular friend of hypothetical contractarianism, I cannot see that its difficulties lie where Williams says they do. It is true that Rawls himself says little about personal relationships, and true also that Richards' adaptation of his framework leads to such "righteous absurdities" as that persons should not base their relationships on "arbitrary physical characteristics alone."[13] But none of this implies that Rawlsian contractors could not, in fact, agree on more sensible principles concerning relationships. It does not imply that they could not agree on principles that prescribe compliance with the demands of personal relationships under certain conditions, or that permit or require some partiality to friends and loved ones. In particular, the choice of such principles seems plainly *not* to be ruled out merely by the ignorance of the contracting parties. The contractors' ignorance does rule out the choice of principles that name either specific agents who are allowed or required to be partial or the specific recipients of their partiality. However, this is irrelevant; for the question is not whether any *given* person may or should display partiality to any other, but rather whether *all* persons may or should be partial to their wives, husbands, or friends. The relevant principles, even if licensing or dictating partiality, must do so impartially. Hence, there is no ob-

---

[13]David A. J. Richards, *A Theory of Reasons for Action* (Oxford: Oxford University Press, 1971), p. 94. The apt phrase "righteous absurdity" is used by Williams in "Persons, Character, and Morality," p. 212.

vious reason why such principles could not be chosen even by contractors ignorant of the particulars of their lives.

Can we go further? Is there any positive reason for rational, self-
interested, but ignorant Rawlsian contractors to opt for principles
that adjust duties and obligations to the demands of personal relationships? To answer this question fully, we would have to say far
more about the demands of relationships than can be said here. But
given present purposes, which are merely dialectical, there is indeed
something to be said. Our question about the Rawlsian contractors
has arisen because their failure to choose principles adjusted to the
demands of relationships would support the broader claim that *all*
impersonal justificatory strategies yield principles that sometimes
conflict with the demands of relationships. This, in turn, would
combine with Gilligan's findings to suggest a reconceptualization of
the moral point of view in more personal and relationship-oriented
terms. But this last move will only be plausible if the demands of
personal relationships are in themselves sufficiently compelling to
warrant description as moral demands. Hence, for us, the question is
not what the Rawlsian contractors would choose *simpliciter*, but
rather what they would choose *on the assumption that the demands of
relationships are this compelling.*

When the issue is framed in these terms, I think the Rawlsian
contractors might well have good reason to choose principles that
conflicted as little as possible with the demands of personal relationships. To see why, consider what the demands of relationships would
have to be like to be compelling enough to qualify as moral demands.
At a minimum, they would have to be so urgent that persons could
not violate them without at the same time violating their own integrity. The demands would have to grow out of the kind of deep
personal commitment that, as Williams put it, "compels . . . allegiance to life itself."[14] In addition, when viewed from the perspective
of the other parties to relationships, the demands would have to
dictate responses that were not merely optional, but were in some
sense owed. The demands' nonfulfillment would have to be real
grounds for complaint. Just how relationships can generate such de-

---

[14]Williams, "Persons, Character, and Morality," p. 215.

mands is of course a large part of the mystery about them. But if they can—and I believe they not only can but often do—then the satisfaction of those demands, when they arise, must itself be a good that transcends mere personal preference. Like liberty and other Rawlsian primary goods, a general ability both to give and to receive such satisfaction must be something it is rational to want whatever else one wants. But if so, then rational contractors endowed with full general information about human psychology could hardly avoid wanting to protect this ability. Since protecting it requires choosing principles whose prescriptions are adjusted to the demands of important relationships, I conclude that they would indeed be motivated to choose such principles.

This conclusion might be challenged through appeal to the last of Gilligan's oppositions. As derived, the conclusion rests on the premise that morality is fundamentally a matter of what persons owe to others. It thus appears to presuppose that any genuinely moral principle must specify people's *rights*. Yet one of Gilligan's most persistent themes is that a preoccupation with rights rather than responsibilities is itself a typically male construction. As she often notes, her female subjects think less about what they are entitled to than about what they are responsible for providing. Thus, it may seem illegitimate for us to say that only demands that specify responses that are owed can qualify as moral. For, if we do say this, we may seem to beg the question against those who see Gilligan's work as prefiguring a new vision of morality.

Yet, here again, the worry is overdrawn. Let us simply grant that women, at least in the earlier stages of their development, think more readily of what they are responsible for providing than of what they are entitled to receive. Even so, nothing follows about the status of the responsibilities they acknowledge. Indeed, one very reasonable suggestion is that they regard themselves as responsible for providing sympathy, care, and help to others precisely *because* they regard themselves as owing these things. Putting the point in terms of rights, and ignoring the complexities and differing interpretations of that notion, we can say that nothing rules out the possibility that women regard others as having a *right* to their sympathy, care, and help. To suppose otherwise would be to conflate the well supported claim that women are less concerned than men with the protection of *their*

627

rights with the quite different claim that women are less inclined than men to think that people *have* rights (or to hold views functionally equivalent to this).

All things considered, Gilligan's findings seem neither to undermine nor decisively to adjudicate among the familiar options of moral theory. They may edge us in certain theoretical directions, but the movement they compel takes us nowhere near the boundaries of the known territories. This is not to deny that the findings suggest that women are, in some respects, better equipped than men to reach morally adequate decisions; but it is to deny that that result requires any exotic recasting of our familiar understanding of "morally adequate." To all of this, the still-hopeful revisionist might finally complain that I have interpreted the received body of theory so broadly that it is not clear what *could* show that it needs radical revision. But this, though true, is precisely the point I want to make. The oppositions of concrete and abstract, personal and impersonal, duty and care are not recent empirical discoveries, but generic determinants of the moral problematic. We have always known that an adequate theory must assign each its proper place. What we have not known, and what Gilligan's findings bring us little closer to knowing, is what those places are.

STUDY QUESTIONS

1. What contribution, if any, does Sher think Gilligan has made to ethical theory? Do you agree with Sher's estimate of the value of Gilligan's contribution?

2. How does Sher argue against Gilligan's claim that women's moral decisions are non-principled rather than principled? Personal rather than impersonal? What does Sher find wrong with the contention that women's moral decisions are concrete and contextual rather than abstract? Do you find Sher's arguments convincing?

3. Explain Sher's defense of Rawlsian contractarianism against the objection that it is indifferent to the demands of personal relationships. What is the relevance of this defense to Gilligan's argument?

4. In novels such as *Les Miserables* or *Huckleberry Finn*, we find the theme of conflict between an ethic of abstract principle and an ethic of care and compassion presented in a genderless way. Does this support Sher's criticism of Gilligan?

Literature and Moral Education

๛

RONALD DUSKA

Ronald Duska (b. 1937) is professor of philosophy at Rosemont College in Pennsylvania. He has published numerous articles in ethics and is the author of *Moral Development: A Guide to Piaget and Kohlberg* (1973).

Ronald Duska criticizes current moral philosophy, including "applied ethics," charging it with being too formal. The application of formal rules to concrete problems very often does not lead to definitive solutions and even when it does, we are still faced with the question: "Why be moral?"

Duska notes that even formal philosophers implicitly appeal to some ideal of happiness in arriving at solutions to ethical questions. But happiness is not a clearly defined good that we set and pursue. Rather, happiness *accompanies* our activities when we are passionately doing the best we can do "with the hand that has been dealt us."

Passion gives meaning and point to our lives. "No one deeply in love ever asks whether life has meaning." But passion can go wrong. (Witness the tragic consequences of Othello's governing passion, jealousy.) Literature is the

LITERATURE AND MORAL EDUCATION From "What Is Literature to Ethics or Ethics to Literature?" in *Listening: Journal of Religion and Culture*, Winter 1982, by Ronald Duska. Reprinted by permission of the publisher.

primary source for studying the relationship of the passions to happiness and unhappiness. Literature is relevant to ethics in several ways. First and foremost, it shows us how the meaning of our lives is bound up with our passions. Second, it helps to develop our empathy toward others, thereby helping us to become more sensitive, open, and caring persons. Great literature also provides insight into fictional characters: fiction reveals moral truths. Morality has to do with the heart; immorality has to do with insensitivity and lack of care. Thus, literature helps us toward a concrete understanding of "the passionate human being."

Quarry the granite rock with razors, or moor the vessel with a thread of silk; then may you hope with such keen and delicate instruments as human knowledge and human reason to contend against those giants, the passion and pride of man.

John Henry Newman

One can always learn from literature.[1] That statement might offend some purists among contemporary aestheticians who would want to claim that the function of literature as art is to delight and that to use literature for didactic purposes is to abuse it. But the fact remains that literature, good literature, has always been a marvelous teacher. It humanizes us as perhaps nothing else can. Hence the topic of this paper. I want to examine a few ways in which literature aids us in dealing with ethical matters. My conviction, which may appear perverse to some is that in many ways literature contributes more to the clarification of values and the development of morals than ethical theory as it is done today.

I will claim that contemporary ethical theory is inadequate because it rests on an unrealistic picture of human life which largely ignores or misconstrues the role of the passions[2] in constituting a meaningful

---

[1] Under the word "literature" I mean to include for the most part, novels, poems, stories and dramas. I also have in mind good literature, classics if you will, and not things like drugstore novels. I am of course assuming there is a difference between run of the mill literature and good or significant literature.

[2] In this paper I am using the word "passions" rather indiscriminately in a generic sense to include a whole host of areas which would be placed under what psychologists call

human life. Literature, however, expresses or represents in a unique way the passionate sources of human action and consequently shows us what a meaningful human life is in a way that ethics does not. In short, it provides us with what ethical theory does not, content for what has become the formally stringent but largely vacuous enterprise of contemporary ethical theory. I begin with a defense of that claim.

A generation ago, G. E. M. Anscombe requested a moratorium on ethical theory. Since then, Philippa Foot expressed a desire to quit talking about "morality." Rather than acceding to the wishes of these two esteemed philosophers, ethicists have talked and written even more about ethical issues. However, rather than dry as dust discussions of ethical theory or meta-ethics, the talk now revolves around pertinent and substantive ethical issues, often under the name of applied ethics. For my part, instead of teaching about naturalistic fallacies, I now find myself engaged in medical and business ethics, talking about abortion, genetic engineering, corporate responsibility, preferential hiring and a host of other topics. Nevertheless, periodically I ask myself "Why?" Is the kind of discussion carried on about these issues relevant? The topics certainly are relevant, but can this be said of our treatment of them?

The standard move of most "applied ethicists" is to take one of the two canonized ethical theories, either the deontological principles of Kant or Ross, possibly updated by his contemporary disciples and apply them/it to either a class of actions like suicide and abortion or to a particular ethical dilemma. For example, if we address euthanasia or suicide, two problems of the same stripe: either we begin by talking about the duty to oneself or others and the contradictoriness of the taking of a human life to preserve the values of life; or we begin by talking of the rationality of euthanasia or suicide in terms of the consequences of this type of action, and determine whether it is right by deciding whether it will maximize happiness.

One must grant that both of these methods have something to be

---

the affective side of man, i.e., feelings, emotions, attitudes, dispositions, etc. Much of the sorting out of what I have in mind can be found in Robert Solomon's excellent book, *The Passions*, (Doubleday, 1973). The book is partly responsible for some of the directions of this paper, although I would not claim that the paper intentionally follows it, nor would I hold the book responsible for the shortcomings of my thoughts.

said in their favor, for they do show that if certain principles are accepted, certain actions logically follow as appropriate or inappropriate. Nevertheless, for anyone who has ever taught courses in applied ethics, this procedure leaves much to be desired.

What is the problem? First, it seems to be that the application of formal rules to materially concrete problems never leads to definitive solutions. For every answer there is a counter objection and a kind of skepticism is encouraged. Second, even if a definitive solution would be arrived at, a highly unlikely possibility, the question, why do what is prescribed would still remain, i.e., we could still ask, "Why be moral?" "Why do what we have determined that we should?"

There are defenses of these procedures. In a remarkably well written textbook called *Moral Reasoning,* Victor Grassian offers a defense of the study of ethics. According to Grassian, even though the study of ethics will not make us into a good person, it can serve to help us better understand and classify our own moral principles, even refine and change them (one hesitates to ask whether for the better or worse); and it can lead us to a consistent set of principles. Grassian states, at the end of the defense:

> By studying the arguments that philosophers give for their ethical positions and the objections they pose to the view of others, a person's ability to defend his own positions and recognize their shortcomings will itself be sharpened. This is by far the *most important* thing that the study of ethics has to offer.[3]

Marvelous! But with all the sharpening, changing and elimination of shortcomings, something is still missing. What is the good of all this eristic ability if it leads to the sharpening of misguided principles which can be used by a despot or tyrant to justify his behavior? Further, what is the good if it cannot lead to a good person behaving well? What Grassian offers is vaguely reminiscent of what the Sophists offered, is it not?

To give my point more substance let us examine a dilemma found in Grassian's text and demonstrate what ethical theorists are likely to do with it.

---

[3]Victor Grassian, *Moral Reasoning* (Englewood Cliffs, NJ: Prentice Hall, 1981), p. 5.

A Poisonous Cup of Coffee

> Tom, hates his wife and wanting her dead, puts poison in her coffee, thereby killing her. Joe also hates his wife and would like her dead. One day, Joe's wife accidentally puts poison in her coffee, thinking it's cream. Joe, who happens to be a chemist, has the antidote, but he does not give it to her. Knowing that he is the only one who can save her, he lets her die. Is Joe's failure to act as bad as Tom's action? Why or why not?

It seems fairly obvious that Grassian is using this dilemma to provoke a discussion of the difference (if there is any) between killing and letting die (a distinction that is quite useful in contrasting active and passive euthanasia, among other issues). For that, the dilemma might be pertinent. However, when we look at the questions asked, we cannot help but be frustrated. "Is Joe's failure to act *as bad as* Tom's action?" How would students, confronted with this question, answer it? It requires some sort of calculus to determine quantitatively the relative merits of two reprehensible actions. Presumably the answer would look something like this: From a utilitarian perspective the consequences for the woman are the same. However, Tom is liable to prosecution for homicide whereas it is unlikely that Joe is, and thus it would seem that Tom's action is worse than Joe's because it brings worse consequences. A possible answer from a deontological perspective might be that both actions are equally wrong because they use another person as a means, except that if one distinguishes between killing and letting die, one might say that Joe did not *use* his wife, if using must be an act of commission rather than an omission.

Note what happens. We begin with two obviously immoral acts and then are asked for reasons why one is worse than the other. The reasons are expected to be based on a very general principle, either deontological or consequentialist. The principles quite often conflict, as in cases where good consequences are brought about by immoral means. In that case neither set of reasons is persuasive.

Surely this sort of intellectual rumination is sterile. How, though, did this sort of procedure become so predominant? I suspect that ethicists, under the influence of, or in response to positivism, got locked into a quasi-scientific mode of proceeding, or perhaps more accurately into using an engineering model. If I want to achieve a certain end, I need to perform certain appropriate operations. Given an end, my only problem is to discover acceptable means. Acceptable paths are those which fall within permissible procedures—in ethics the deontological requirements of justice and fairness determine what is acceptable. Thus, we have a goal, find acceptable means, and "Voila!" arrive rigorously at an answer. Unfortunately, deontology does not tell us what to do, only to do it with equity and fairness, while utilitarianism has yet to get clear about what the appropriate ends of man are. However, wouldn't the engineering model work if we could get clear about the ends of man?

If we could find the ends of man and get agreement on them wouldn't my objections lose their force? It is quite fashionable in searching for an end to appeal to a picture or way of life which is held forth as an ideal. In appealing to such an ideal, one attempts to show how one's position on a certain moral issue can be understood in the light of that picture of the ideal life. This sort of appeal is supposed to serve as a justification of one's ethical judgments. We see this in the theory of R. M. Hare when he says, "If pressed to justify a decision completely, we have to give a complete specification of the way of life of which it is a part."[4] Or it can be seen in the theory of P. H. Nowell-Smith, when he says, "Moral philosophy is a practical science; its aim is to answer questions in the form, 'What shall I do?'" But no general answer can be given to this type of question. The most a moral philosopher can do is to paint a picture of various types of life in the manner of Plato and ask which type of life you really want to lead."[5]

It would make the task of this paper quite easy if I were to settle for either of these approaches and say, "Yes. Quite right. Except literature, or fiction if you prefer, is much better at painting pictures than philosophy. Thus, rather than depending on philosophers, let us go to novels and plays and perhaps biographies where we get presentations of specific lives and choose the ones that appeal to us." But there is something amiss. Hare speaks of deciding on a type of life that is completely specified. Who makes choices in that way?

---

[4]R. M. Hare, *The Language of Morals* (Cambridge, MA: Oxford University Press, 1960), p. 79.

[5]P. H. Nowell-Smith, *Ethics*, (Middlesex: Penguin Books Ltd., 1954), p. 319.

That is simply not what we do.[6] Nowell-Smith speaks of asking what type of life we want, but that is probably not what we do either.[7] Hare and Nowell-Smith attack the problem from the engineer's model. Give me a picture of your goal, (chosen with Hare, and wanted with Nowell-Smith) and then we will figure out what needs to be done to get there. Hare and Nowell-Smith are not the only people who approach ethics in this way. It is a common way of proceeding in ethics. Generally, though, the goal was given the name "Happiness." Suppose, however, we raise some seemingly outrageous questions. Is happiness really the ultimate end of life? Or, if there is an ultimate end, is it the kind philosophers look for?

Happiness is quite often construed as some goal to be pursued or some state to be accomplished as in, "the pursuit of happiness." Often, too, it is thought to be reducible to pleasure or at least the avoidance of pain. It is seen as the goal, the *terminus ad quem* of life. This, however, is precisely the engineering view of life we discussed above.

However, happiness, thus construed, rarely serves as a real goal in life, except according to the anemic views of our engineering friends, the utilitarians. Aristotle's view of happiness, although quite vague and empty in terms of content, seems correct to the extent that he asserts that it is not an end in the sense of a product or a *terminus ad quem* of an activity. Rather it is something that accompanies activity.

---

[6]I am well aware of the dogmatic appearance of this remark. However, even though the point of this section is critical, I am more concerned with presenting an alternative view to this type of approach which Hare and Nowell-Smith offer, than with getting bogged down in what would be important, but nonetheless tedious refutations of their approach. If I would develop an argument, though, it would be to the effect that Hare forgets that human beings make decisions in an historical environmental context and that they have been conditioned by that environment. This results in our having habits and dispositions which partly constitute what we are and limit what we decide upon. We simply do not stand back from our context and make decisions without factors influencing us. A hint of such an argument can be found on pp. 7–9.

[7]As with the claim against Hare, I will not interrupt the presentation of the main point of the paper to develop a sustained argument against Nowell-Smith. However, he ought to recognize that we do not always know what we want and that occurs because our imagination is needed to intend new goals. Sartre makes an argument to this effect in his defense of freedom in *Being and Nothingness*. Note that literature, by giving us imaginative views of new possibilities of living can furnish many new options. It seems it was this sort of thing that Oscar Wilde had in mind when he asserted that "Nature imitates Art."

Anyone who has been disappointed when he has gone out for a good time ought to recognize that one does not seem to be able to "pursue" happiness successfully. This is the hedonistic paradox: those who strive for happiness rarely achieve it, whereas those who pursue other things might find it. Happiness accompanies a life process, but it is not the goal of life in the engineering sense of a goal.

If, however, life is not to be construed as the pursuit of a predetermined goal, how is it to be construed? R. G. Collingwood[8] in writing on art makes a distinction between art and craft that may be helpful. A craft for him is an enterprise where we have a clear goal in mind and where specific steps can be taken to achieve that goal. Collingwood's notion of a craftsman parallels our notion of an engineer. But art is not craft. The true artist does not know his end: he discovers it as he works it out. He works it out through the expressing of his emotions. I would like to suggest that human life is also the working out of our emotions or passions, without a clear notion of where the end is. Thus if ethics or morality concerns itself with the art of living it should do this viewing life as art in Collingwood's sense and not in the sense of art as a craft.

But let us see if the living out of life is really like the working out of an artpiece as Collingwood describes it. When a painter puts a line on the canvas he thereby limits the next line. It can be an indefinite number of lines, but it cannot be just any old line and be appropriate. When an author sketches his character, the character can develop in any number of ways but not just willy-nilly. By page two of *Catcher in the Rye* there are things that Salinger can do with Holden Caulfield, but there are also things he cannot do. To complete the work he must be creative, but creative within the limits set by the opening lines. Just as Salinger creates Caulfield without fully forseeing possible outcomes, we create our lives without fully forseeing possible outcomes. In sum, we do not know where we will end up, but a large part of the working out will depend on where we are. We need to creatively respond to where we are to make our life a finished whole.

There is a contemporary song, "The Gambler," which can also be seen as analogous to human life. One of the verses runs, "No hand's a winner and no hand's a loser" while another runs, "You never count

---

[8]Robin G. Collingwood, *Principles of Art* (London: Oxford University Press, 1938), esp. pp. 128–135.

your money while you're sittin at the table. There'll be plenty time for countin, when the dealin's done." In the game of life, the cards one is dealt and the attitudes one has dictate what one does to be successful. One can fold with bad cards, or one can bluff. One can lose with good cards or see it through and perhaps win. It depends on what one does with what one gets, and yet there are no guarantees. The point is that in most people's lived existence, the best laid plans go astray. Thus, to view the living of a human life as analogous to the process of an engineer building a bridge or a craftsman making a product is to misconstrue what is involved.

Very well, then, what is involved? To get at that I would like to turn to Camus' treatment of a classical literary figure, Sisyphus. Let us examine the closing lines of Camus' *Myth of Sisyphus*.

> I leave Sisyphus at the foot of the mountain! One always finds one's burden again. But Sisyphus teaches the higher fidelity that negates the gods and raises rocks. He too concludes that *all is well*. This universe henceforth without a master seems to him neither sterile nor futile. Each atom of that stone, each mineral flake of that night filled mountain, in itself form a world. The struggle itself toward the heights is enough to fill a man's heart. One must imagine Sisyphus happy.[9]

Incredible as it sounds, Camus suggests that Sisyphus is happy. This however is in no way the happiness associated with pleasure, but rather a happiness coming from a life that is full. Note that Camus asserts, "The struggle . . . is enough to *fill* a man's heart." Obviously, if we wish to call Sisyphus "happy" in Camus' sense we need to revise our meaning of the concept, since it does not accord with our common understanding of happiness. But let us leave that and recognize that what Camus is doing is approving of Sisyphus because he has made his life *full*. Could we not say that in the midst of a meaningless existence Sisyphus has carved out a meaningful life?

Note further that Sisyphus does not choose his life. His lot is given. "One always finds one's burden again." Further Sisyphus does not get what he wants. He, like the gambler, makes the best of what he gets. Nowell-Smith's "wants" and Hare's "choice" are wrong because life does not proceed the way they imagine. Their

---

[9]Albert Camus, *The Myth of Sisyphus*, translated by Justin O'Brien (New York: Alfred A. Knopf, Inc., 1955).

637

quasi-scientific engineering model has led them astray, and to the extent that happiness is construed as an end to be pursued it can serve as a goal for only the most shallow kinds of lives.

But if the craft—engineering model won't do, what will? The clue to this can be found in Sisyphus. Making one's life full seems to be the answer. But if we look at what makes Sisyphus' life full, it seems to be his determination and disposition, those things I would wish to include under the rubric of the passions.

If then the meaningful life is the passionate life, where do we go to find out about it? The best portraits of human passion are found in literature. They are not found in Ethics and some would argue that they are not found in Psychology either. Be that as it may, literature is surely a primary source. Let us claim then that passions are a necessary condition for a full human life, and turn to a piece of literature which not only shows this, but simultaneously depicts the struggle of a person with her passions. I have in mind Amy Lowell's *Patterns*. What this poem teaches us or at least shows us is that we are not automata hooked up to a conveyor belt leading us down the road to happiness. We are individuals in a situation with our passions and we must try to make the best of it. Recall the closing lines.

> In Summer and in Winter I shall walk
> Up and down
> The patterned garden paths
> In my stiff, brocaded gown.
> The Squills and daffodils
> Will give place to pillared roses, and to asters, and to snow.
> I shall go
> Up and down,
> In my gown.
> Gorgeously arrayed,
> Boned and stayed.
> And the softness of my body will be guarded from embrace
> By each button, hook, and lace.
> For the man who should loose me is dead,
> Fighting with the Duke in Flanders,
> In a pattern called a war.
> Christ! What are patterns for?[10]

---

[10]Amy Lowell, *Patterns*, as found in *Best Loved Poems of all Time* (Hallmark, 1971), p. 27.

This is a picture of life, but it is not full. It is empty because it has lost its passion. Lowell's heroine does not stand back objectively and put forth models of the good life. One cannot do that with her own life. She is in the middle of it. Her wants and her passions are removed. What is to be done? The answer is fairly clear . . . new passions must develop. Patterns, rules if you will, are not enough. Could we not also suggest that empty moral rules are also not enough? We learn two things from Lowell. Patterns are not enough to live life. We need to be passionate. No one deeply in love ever asks whether life has meaning. No one passionately engaged in a task asks the question either.

But will just any passions do? Passions may be a necessary condition for a full life, but are they sufficient? Is not something else necessary?

To examine that question I wish to cite some lines from *Othello*. Note his final speech:

> Soft you; a word or two before you go.
> I have done the state some service, and they know't.
> No more of that. I pray you, in your letters,
> When you shall these unlucky deeds relate,
> Speak of me as I am; nothing extenuate,
> Nor set down aught in malice: then must you speak
> Of one that loved not wisely but too well;
> Of one not easily jealous, but being wrought
> Perplex'd in the extreme; of one whose hand,
> Like the base Indian, threw a pearl away
> Richer than all his tribe; one of whose subdued eyes
> Albeit unused to the melting mood,
> Drops tears as fast as the Arabian trees
> Their medicinal gum. Set you down this;
> And say besides, that in Aleppo once,
> Where a malignant and a turban'd Turk
> Beat a Venetian and traduced the state,
> I took by the throat the circumcised dog,
> And smote him, thus. (Stabs himself.)[11]

Here is without doubt a man living out his passions. Here is a life certainly not seeking happiness. But it is a tragic life. Consequently

---

[11]*Othello*, Act V, scene 2.

it is apparent that passions, though they make life full do not necessarily make for the best life. The passions must be evaluated.

But the evaluation of passions is by no means impossible. Certain passions are appropriate, others not. For example, there are times my anger is inappropriate. There are passions that are destructive. Lowell's heroine's life is empty. We see that. Othello's life is tragic. Why? Because jealousy is a destructive passion, just as is hate. One could even argue that Sisyphus' obstinancy is not the best of passions. Even though it gets him through his burdens it does not allow a life to flower as it might.

We make value judgments about passions easily. Lowell's heroine *needs* a new passion to make her life full. Othello on the other hand does not need more passion; he needs better ones. In some situations passion itself is required and in others some passion *should* have been checked.

The surprising thing is that literature seems to have the ability to show the deficiencies and strengths of the passions. I am not sure I can solve the epistemological question of how this is possible, but it does seem to be a fact. One thought comes to mind though as worth pursuing. If living human life is like doing art in Collingwood's sense, and if there are ways of evaluating art, perhaps we can find some clues for evaluating life in aesthetics. This is not a new suggestion. It was made by Wittgenstein when he said that ethical reasons may well be like aesthetic reasons. Unfortunately, we are not able to develop this theme at this time, not so much for lack of space as for lack of knowing how. Consequently, I leave that as a topic to be pursued at a later time and make some final comments about what I have tried to show.

First, if ethics is irrelevant it is irrelevant because it misconstrues what life is really like, and its procedures for determining what to do fail to take into account the psychology of the passions and the passions' role in making life meaningful. To the extent that literature portrays, imitates or represents human life it shows us that most lives are problematic and, rather than being lives in pursuit of happiness, they are attempts to live out life, perhaps with a hope that we can eke out a bit of happiness along the way, but more importantly in a meaningful way. And, literature shows clearly that the meaning most often comes from the passions.

It should be noted that the encounter with literature can have other benefits. Literature, in allowing us to identify with others, allows us to develop empathy, a requisite for developing our ability to care. It also *shows* us ways of coping *with certain problems* and perhaps even *shows* the shortcomings and flaws of certain lives. All of these contributions are important. Still, the main point of this paper was to claim that literature is relevant to moral considerations because it deals with human beings' inner lives as they are, even if the characters are fictional, whereas ethics deals mainly with rules and maxims that seem so formal that they hardly touch human lives.

If this is so, it is clear that a task needs to be done by ethicists or at least philosophers. We need to begin[12] to deal with the psychology of the passions. Literature, to the extent that it portrays them faithfully, can teach us a great deal about them. Next we need to begin to evaluate them in terms of their potential for making a life good or bad. Literature again provides models. If we do this, we might begin to give our ethical considerations a content they desperately need, and talk about good men in a way that has force.

Let me conclude with a short comment on a few lines written by Stephen King: "If we say that morality proceeds simply from a good heart—which has little to do with ridiculous posturings and happily-ever-afterings—and immorality proceeds from a lack of care, from shoddy observation . . . we may realize we have arrived at a critical stance, one both workable and humane. Fiction is the truth inside the lie."[13]

If morality has to do with the heart, the passionate side of man and immorality with a lack of care, then is it not obvious that we ethicists need to investigate these areas with much more concern? And is it not also obvious that one of the best places to start to understand and experience the passionate human being is in literature?

STUDY QUESTIONS

1. What in particular does Duska find wrong with a mainstream theory such as utilitarianism? Compare Duska's criticism of utilitarianism with Bernard Williams's critique (see Chapter Two).

---

[12]"Begin" may not be the correct word. As I have indicated Robert Solomon has begun the type of enterprise I have in mind. What we need to do is expand on such work.

[13]Stephen King, "Notes on Horror," *Quest*, June 1981, vol. 5, no. 5, p. 31.

2. What view of happiness does Duska endorse? How is his conception of happiness related to the proposition that the meaningful life is the passionate life?

3. Duska finds contemporary morality wanting because it ignores the passions. MacIntyre finds it wanting because it ignores traditions, roles, and historical context. Are they both right? Are these critiques of contemporary morality complementary? Or would each critic say that the other's views totally miss the point of what is wrong with current ethics? What is your own view of these two perspectives?

4. What are the implications of Duska's views for the teaching of ethics? Is morality better taught in classes on literature than in classes on moral philosophy? How would you devise a curriculum of moral education that reflected Duska's insights?

The Closing of the American Mind

ALLAN BLOOM

Allan Bloom (b. 1930) is a professor on the faculty of the Committee of Social Thought at the University of Chicago. He is the translator and editor of Plato's *Republic* and Rousseau's *Emile,* and the author of *Shakespeare's Politics* and *The Closing of the American Mind.*

Allan Bloom is highly critical of the turn taken by American higher education. According to Bloom, the contemporary student enters college equipped with the dogma that truth is culturally relative. The dogma gives primacy to tolerance and openness as the most important moral virtue. The student believes that any claim to absolute

THE CLOSING OF THE AMERICAN MIND From *The Closing of the American Mind* by Allan Bloom (New York: Simon & Schuster, 1987). Copyright © 1987 by Allan Bloom. Reprinted by permission of the publisher.

truth can lead to intolerance. Bloom says that this view rejects and undercuts the old ideal that postulated a set of universal truths and inalienable rights for all, regardless of culture. According to the old doctrine, all people have certain rights. According to the new doctrine, this is a Western value judgment that does not have the status of a fact. The fact-value distinction (along with relativism) belongs to the popular philosophy that Bloom inveighs against. Bloom observes that history and the social sciences are deployed to further the new passion for tolerance and relativism. The indiscriminate openness to other cultures goes hand in hand with a growing contempt for our own. We go to the "bazaar of cultures" and find our own wanting. Teachers of openness often are "actively hostile to the Declaration of Independence and the Constitution."

Bloom argues that the new openness and relativism result in a drab conformism. Having no faith in the objective search for a universal good, we drearily create all the lifestyles we want but without any belief in them as truly valuable. Nor is there hope that there are great or wise human beings anywhere who can reveal the truth about life. "Thus what is advertised as a great opening is a great closing."

The ideal is to get along. No one has the truth. No culture is morally superior. "Why fight?" Yet Bloom points out that other cultures do believe in their own superiority and will fight for them. Such ethnocentrism is almost universal, and can be countered only by a belief in universal reason and in natural inalienable rights for all. "Openness used to be the virtue that permitted us to seek the good by using reason. It now means accepting everything."

There is one thing a professor can be absolutely certain of: almost every student entering the university believes, or says he believes, that truth is relative. If this belief is put to the test, one can count on the students' reaction: they will be uncomprehending. That anyone

643

should regard the proposition as not self-evident astonishes them, as though he were calling into question 2 + 2 = 4. These are things you don't think about. The students' backgrounds are as various as America can provide. Some are religious, some atheists; some are to the Left, some to the Right; some intend to be scientists, some humanists or professionals or businessmen; some are poor, some rich. They are unified only in their relativism and in their allegiance to equality. And the two are related in a moral intention. The relativity of truth is not a theoretical insight but a moral postulate, the condition of a free society, or so they see it. They have all been equipped with this framework early on, and it is the modern replacement for the inalienable natural rights that used to be the traditional American grounds for a free society. That it is a moral issue for students is revealed by the character of their response when challenged—a combination of disbelief and indignation: "Are you an absolutist?," the only alternative they know, uttered in the same tone as "Are you a monarchist?" or "Do you really believe in witches?" This latter leads into the indignation, for someone who believes in witches might well be a witchhunter or a Salem judge. The danger they have been taught to fear from absolutism is not error but intolerance. Relativism is necessary to openness; and this is the virtue, the only virtue, which all primary education for more than fifty years has dedicated itself to inculcating. Openness—and the relativism that makes it the only plausible stance in the face of various claims to truth and various ways of life and kinds of human beings—is the great insight of our times. The true believer is the real danger. The study of history and of culture teaches that all the world was mad in the past; men always thought they were right, and that led to wars, persecutions, slavery, xenophobia, racism, and chauvinism. The point is not to correct the mistakes and really be right; rather it is not to think you are right at all.

The students, of course, cannot defend their opinion. It is something with which they have been indoctrinated. The best they can do is point out all the opinions and cultures there are and have been. What right, they ask, do I or anyone else have to say one is better than the others? If I pose the routine questions designed to confute them and make them think, such as, "If you had been a British administrator in India, would you have let the natives under your governance burn the widow at the funeral of a man who had died?," they either remain silent or reply that the British should never have been there in the first place. It is not that they know very much about other nations, or about their own. The purpose of their education is not to make them scholars but to provide them with a moral virtue— openness. . . .

The old view was that, by recognizing and accepting man's natural rights, men found a fundamental basis of unity and sameness. Class, race, religion, national origin or culture all disappear or become dim when bathed in the light of natural rights, which give men common interests and make them truly brothers. The immigrant had to put behind him the claims of the Old World in favor of a new and easily acquired education. This did not necessarily mean abandoning old daily habits or religions, but it did mean subordinating them to new principles. There was a tendency, if not a necessity, to homogenize nature itself.

The recent education of openness has rejected all that. It pays no attention to natural rights or the historical origins of our regime, which are now thought to have been essentially flawed and regressive. It is progressive and forward-looking. It does not demand fundamental agreement or the abandonment of old or new beliefs in favor of the natural ones. It is open to all kinds of men, all kinds of lifestyles, all ideologies. There is no enemy other than the man who is not open to everything. . . .

Liberalism . . . the kind that we knew from John Stuart Mill and John Dewey, taught us that the only danger confronting us is being closed to the emergent, the new, the manifestations of progress. No attention had to be paid to the fundamental principles or the moral virtues that inclined men to live according to them. To use language now popular, civic culture was neglected. And this turn in liberalism is what prepared us for cultural relativism and the fact-value distinction, which seemed to carry that viewpoint further and give it greater intellectual weight.

History and social science are used in a variety of ways to overcome prejudice. We should not be ethnocentric, a term drawn from anthropology, which tells us more about the meaning of openness. We should not think our way is better than others. The intention is not so much to teach the students about other times and places as to make them aware of the fact that their preferences are only that— accidents of their time and place. Their beliefs do not entitle them as individuals, or collectively as a nation, to think they are superior to anyone else. John Rawls is almost a parody of this tendency, writing hundreds of pages to persuade men, and proposing a scheme of government that would force them, not to despise anyone. In *A Theory of Justice,* he writes that the physicist or the poet should not look down on the man who spends his life counting blades of grass or performing any other frivolous or corrupt activity. Indeed, he should be esteemed, since esteem from others, as opposed to self-esteem, is a basic need of all men. So indiscriminateness is a moral imperative because its opposite is discrimination. . . .

Sexual adventurers like Margaret Mead and others who found America too narrow told us that not only must we know other cultures and learn to respect them, but we could also profit from them. We could follow their lead and loosen up, liberating ourselves from the opinion that our taboos are anything other than social constraints. We could go to the bazaar of cultures and find reinforcement for inclinations that are repressed by puritanical guilt feelings. All such teachers of openness had either no interest in or were actively hostile to the Declaration of Independence and the Constitution.

The civil rights movement provides a good example of this change in thought. In its early days almost all the significant leaders, in spite of tactical and temperamental differences, relied on the Declaration of Independence and the Constitution. They could charge whites not only with the most monstrous injustices but also with contradicting their own most sacred principles. The blacks were the true Americans in demanding the equality that belongs to them as human beings by natural and political right. This stance implied a firm conviction of the truth of the principles of natural right and of their fundamental efficacy within the Constitutional tradition, which, although tarnished, tends in the long run toward fulfilling those principles. They therefore worked through Congress, the Presidency, and, above all, the Judiciary. By contrast, the Black Power movement that supplanted the older civil rights movement—leaving aside both its excesses and its very understandable emphasis on self-respect and refusal to beg for acceptance—had at its core the view that the Constitutional tradition was always corrupt and was constructed as a defense of slavery. Its demand was for black identity, not universal rights. Not rights but power counted. It insisted on respect for blacks as blacks, not as human beings simply.

Yet the Constitution does not promise respect for blacks, whites, yellows, Catholics, Protestants, or Jews. It guarantees the protection of the rights of individual human beings. This has not proved to be enough, however, to what is perhaps by now a majority of Americans.

The upshot of all this for the education of young Americans is that they know much less about American history and those who were held to be its heroes. This was one of the few things that they used to come to college with that had something to do with their lives. Nothing has taken its place except a smattering of facts learned about other nations or cultures and a few social science formulas. None of this means much, partly because little attention has been paid to what is required in order truly to convey the spirit of other places and other times to young people, or for that matter to anyone, partly because the students see no relevance in any of it to the lives they are going to lead or to their prevailing passions. It is the rarest of occurrences to find a youngster who has been infused by this education with a longing to know all about China or the Romans or the Jews.

All to the contrary. There is an indifference to such things, for relativism has extinguished the real motive of education, the search for a good life. Young Amnericans have less and less knowledge of and interest in foreign places. In the past there were many students who actually knew something about and loved England, France, Germany, or Italy, for they dreamed of living there or thought their lives would be made more interesting by assimilating their languages and literatures. Such students have almost disappeared, replaced at most by students who are interested in the political problems of Third World countries and in helping them to modernize, with due respect to their old cultures, of course. This is not learning from others but condescension and a disguised form of a new imperialism. It is the Peace Corps mentality, which is not a spur to learning but to a secularized version of doing good works.

Actually openness results in American conformism—out there in the rest of the world is a drab diversity that teaches only that values are relative, whereas here we can create all the life-styles we want. Our openness means we do not need others. Thus what is advertised as a great opening is a great closing. No longer is there a hope that there are great wise men in other places and times who can reveal the truth about life—except for the few remaining young people who look for a quick fix from a guru. Gone is the real historical sense of a Machiavelli who wrested a few hours from each busy day in which "to don regal and courtly garments, enter the courts of the ancients and speak with them."

None of this concerns those who promote the new curriculum. The point is to propagandize acceptance of different ways, and indifference to their real content is as good a means as any. It was not necessarily the best of times in America when Catholics and Protestants were suspicious of and hated one another; but at least they were taking their beliefs seriously, and the more or less satisfactory accommodations they worked out were not simply the result of apathy about the state of their souls. Practically all that young Americans have today is an insubstantial awareness that there are many cultures, accompanied by a saccharine moral drawn from that awareness: We should all get along. Why fight? . . .

One of the techniques of opening young people up is to require a college course in a non-Western culture. Although many of the persons teaching such courses are real scholars and lovers of the areas they study, in every case I have seen this requirement—when there are so many other things that can and should be learned but are not required, when philosophy and religion are no longer required—has a demagogic intention. The point is to force students to recognize that there are other ways of thinking and that Western ways are not better. It is again not the content that counts but the lesson to be drawn. Such requirements are part of the effort to establish a world community and train its member—the person devoid of prejudice. But if the students were really to learn something of the minds of any of these non-Western cultures—which they do not—they would find that each and every one of these cultures is ethnocentric. All of them think their way is the best way, and all others are inferior. Herodotus tells us that the Persians thought that they were the best, that those nations bordering on them were next best, that those nations bordering on the nations bordering on them were third best, and so on, their worth declining as the concentric circles were farther from the Persian center. This is the very definition of ethnocentrism. Something like this is as ubiquitous as the prohibition against incest between mother and son.

Only in the Western nations, i.e., those influenced by Greek philosophy, is there some willingness to doubt the identification of the good with one's own way. One should conclude from the study of non-Western cultures that not only to prefer one's own way but to believe it best, superior to all others, is primary and even natural—exactly the opposite of what is intended by requiring students to study these cultures. What we are really doing is applying a Western prejudice—which we covertly take to indicate the superiority of our culture—and deforming the evidence of those other cultures to attest to its validity. The scientific study of other cultures is almost exclusively a Western phenomenon, and in its origin was obviously connected with the search for new and better ways, or at least for validation of the hope that our own culture really is the better way, a validation for which there is no felt need in other cultures. If we are to learn from those cultures, we must wonder whether such scientific study is a good idea. Consistency would seem to require professors of openness to respect the ethnocentrism or closedness they find everywhere else. However, in attacking ethnocentrism, what they actually do is to assert unawares the superiority of their scientific understanding and the inferiority of the other cultures which do not recognize it at the same time they reject all such claims to superiority. They both affirm and deny the goodness of their science. They face a problem akin to that faced by Pascal in the conflict between reason and revelation, without the intellectual intransigence that forced him to abandon science in favor of faith.

The reason for the non-Western closedness, or ethnocentrism, is clear. Men must love and be loyal to their families and their peoples in order to preserve them. Only if they think their own things are good can they rest content with them. A father must prefer his child to other children, a citizen his country to others. That is why there are myths—to justify these attachments. And a man needs a place and opinions by which to orient himself. This is strongly asserted by those who talk about the importance of roots. The problem of getting along with outsiders is secondary to, and sometimes in conflict with, having an inside, a people, a culture, a way of life. A very great narrowness is not incompatible with the health of an individual or a people, whereas with great openness it is hard to avoid decomposition. The firm binding of the good with one's own, the refusal to see a distinction between the two, a vision of the cosmos that has a special place for one's people, seem to be conditions of culture. This is what really follows from the study of non-Western cultures proposed for undergraduates. It points them back to passionate attachment to their own and away from the science which liberates them from it. Science now appears as a threat to culture and a dangerous uprooting charm. In short, they are lost in a no-man's-land between the goodness of knowing and the goodness of culture, where they have been placed by their teachers who no longer have the resources to guide them. Help must be sought elsewhere.

Greek philosophers were the first men we know to address the problem of ethnocentrism. Distinctions between the good and one's own, between nature and convention, between the just and the legal are the signs of this movement of thought. They related the good to the fulfillment of the whole natural human potential and were aware that few, if any, of the nations of men had ways that allowed such fulfillment. They were open to the good. They had to use the good, which was not their own, to judge their own. This was a dangerous business because it tended to weaken wholehearted attachment to their own, hence to weaken their peoples as well as to expose themselves to the anger of family, friends, and countrymen. Loyalty versus quest for the good introduced an unresolvable tension into life. But the awareness of the good as such and the desire to possess it are priceless humanizing acquisitions.

This is the sound motive contained, along with many other less sound ones, in openness as we understand it. Men cannot remain content with what is given them by their culture if they are to be fully human. This is what Plato meant to show by the image of the cave in the *Republic* and by representing us as prisoners in it. A culture is a cave. He did not suggest going around to other cultures as a solution to the limitations of the cave. Nature should be the standard by which we judge our own lives and the lives of peoples. That is why philosophy, not history or anthropology, is the most important human science. Only dogmatic assurance that thought is culture-bound, that there is no nature, is what makes our educators so certain that the only way to escape the limitations of our time and place is to study other cultures. History and anthropology were understood by the Greeks to be useful only in discovering what the past and other peoples had to contribute to the discovery of nature. Historians and anthropologists were to put peoples and their conventions to the test, as Socrates did individuals, and go beyond them.

These scientists were superior to their subjects because they saw a problem where others refused to see one, and they were engaged in the quest to solve it. They wanted to be able to evaluate themselves and others.

This point of view, particularly the need to know nature in order to have a standard, is uncomfortably buried beneath our human sciences, whether they like it or not, and accounts for the ambiguities and contradictions I have been pointing out. They want to make us culture-beings with the instruments that were invented to liberate us from culture. Openness used to be the virtue that permitted us to seek the good by using reason. It now means accepting everything and denying reason's power. The unrestrained and thoughtless pursuit of openness, without recognizing the inherent political, social, or cultural problem of openness as the goal of nature, has rendered openness meaningless. Cultural relativism destroys both one's own and the good. What is most characteristic of the West is science, particularly understood as the quest to know nature and the consequent denigration of convention—i.e., culture or the West understood as a culture—in favor of what is accessible to all men as men through their common and distinctive faculty, reason. Science's latest attempts to grasp the human situation—cultural relativism, historicism, the fact-value distinction—are the suicide of science. Culture, hence closedness, reigns supreme. Openness to closedness is what we teach. . . .

It was always known that there were many and conflicting opinions about the good, and nations embodying each of them. Herodotus was at least as aware as we are of the rich diversity of cultures. But he took that observation to be an invitation to investigate all of them to see what was good and bad about each and find out what he could learn about good and bad from them. Modern relativists take that same observation as proof that such investigation is impossible and that we must be respectful of them all. Thus students, and the rest of us, are deprived of the primary excitement derived from the discovery of diversity, the impulse of Odysseus, who, according to Dante, traveled the world to see the virtues and vices of men. History and anthropology cannot provide the answers, but they can provide the material on which judgment can work.

I know that men are likely to bring what are only their prejudices to the judgment of alien peoples. Avoiding that is one of the main purposes of education. But trying to prevent it by removing the authority of men's reason is to render ineffective the instrument that can correct their prejudices. True openness is the accompaniment of the desire to know, hence of the awareness of ignorance. To deny the possibility of knowing good and bad is to suppress true openness. . . .

Error is indeed our enemy, but it alone points to the truth and therefore deserves our respectful treatment. The mind that has no prejudices at the outset is empty. It can only have been constituted by a method that is unaware of how difficult it is to recognize that a prejudice is a prejudice. Only Socrates knew, after a lifetime of unceasing labor, that he was ignorant. Now every high-school student knows that. How did it become so easy? What accounts for our amazing progress? Could it be that our experience has been so impoverished by our various methods, of which openness is only the latest, that there is nothing substantial enough left there to resist criticism, and we therefore have no world left of which to be really ignorant? Have we so simplified the soul that it is no longer difficult to explain? To an eye of dogmatic skepticism, nature herself, in all her lush profusion of expressions, might appear to be a prejudice. In her place we put a gray network of critical concepts, which were invented to interpret nature's phenomena but which strangled them and therewith destroyed their own *raison d'être*. Perhaps it is our first task to resuscitate those phenomena so that we may again have a world to which we can put our questions and be able to philosophize. This seems to me to be our educational challenge.

STUDY QUESTIONS

1. Explain what Bloom means when he says that to deny the possibility of knowing good and bad is to suppress true openness.
2. According to Bloom, recent education tends to reject natural rights. How?
3. Bloom points out that most cultures are ethnocentric. What conclusion does Bloom draw from this?
4. Bloom blames the popularity of ethical relativism and the fact–value distinction for much of what is wrong about current education. What harm does Bloom see in these doctrines? Do you agree that their popularity is pernicious?

5. What are the most significant differences between the older style of education favored by Bloom and the newer style that he is criticizing? If you agree that something is badly awry with contemporary education, what do you think should be done? Can one return to the old teaching of the "eternal verities"?

6. The American Anthropological Association criticized the U.N. Universal Declaration of Human Rights for being "ethnocentric," saying that "Respect for differences between cultures is validated by the scientific fact that no technique of qualitatively evaluating cultures has been discovered." Bloom criticizes this point of view, saying that it undermines the concept of inalienable rights. Bloom and the A.A.A. are diametrically opposed on this issue. Critically examine both positions and state your own conclusions.

Where Have All the Good Deeds Gone?

CHRISTINA SOMMERS

Christina Sommers (b. 1950) teaches philosophy at Clark University in Worcester, Massachusetts. She has written a number of articles on ethics, feminist philosophy, and moral education.

Sommers contends that social morality is replacing private moral initiative: The modern individual delegates too much moral responsibility to institutions. The literature of the applied ethics movement reflects this change from concern with private morality to concern with public policy by emphasizing public policy issues, such

WHERE HAVE ALL THE GOOD DEEDS GONE? From *Hastings Center Report*, August 1982. © Institute of Society, Ethics and the Life Sciences, 360 Broadway, Hastings-on-Hudson, NY 10706.

as capital punishment and recombinant DNA research, and neglecting normative ethics in the private sphere. Sommers maintains that social solutions are not sufficient. We badly need the individual "moral amateur."

Miller House is an old-age home in a well-to-do Boston suburb. As in many other homes for the elderly, conditions are grim. No matter how cold it is outside, old men sit downcast on the front porch. Sometimes one of them wanders over to a nearby fast-food restaurant where he will sit alone at a table for hours. One resident, Mr. Kelly, recently slipped out the front door and did not stop walking for three days. The police picked him up forty miles away, dazed from lack of sleep and still clutching his cardboard suitcase, and brought him back.

Mr. Richards, age eighty-four, sleeps more than twenty hours a day, waking only for meals and cigarette breaks. He hates Miller House. "I don't like fish cakes," he says. "We have them all the time and the director makes me eat them."

For the past seven years Miss Pickins, who is ninety-one, has lived in Miller House. Last year her doctor ordered her to stop smoking. This upset a daily routine she had enjoyed—coffee and cigarettes in the lounge downstairs with the men. She became depressed, lost interest in leaving her room, and now spends most of her time there alone. The woman who runs the home makes Miss Pickins keep the sound of her radio so low that she cannot hear it. Once she did not finish her dessert, and as punishment she no longer gets any. These little injustices keep her in a constant rage.

Simone de Beauvoir has said, "By the fate it allots to its members who can no longer work, society gives itself away." Who is to blame for the fate that has been allotted to Miss Pickins, Mr. Kelly, and Mr. Richards? It is fashionable to condemn civic agencies and the government. But government agencies are responsible for enforcing standards of cleanliness and safety: should we also require that they meet standards of good-heartedness and neighborliness? What the Miller residents need is kindly attention: someone to talk to them, to take an interest in them, and to mitigate the little cruelties that seem always to tempt those in charge of helpless people. Should the state pay a social worker twenty dollars to make sure Miss Pickins gets her dessert? A few concerned neighbors could transform the residence into a much happier place. But that is not going to happen.

One reason, no doubt, is that a lot of people are uncaring and irresponsible, but far more important is the attitude of the responsible private individuals who no longer see themselves as the seat of moral initiative. Good deeds have been given over to experts: the acts that constitute the social morality of our time are being performed by paid professionals in large public agencies. Helping the needy, the sick, and the aged has become an operation whose scale and character leave little room for the virtuous private person. Our ancestors in their idiosyncratic charitable endeavors look like moral amateurs.

Professionals who do use volunteers see them as incipient professionals. The assistant manager of the Greater Boston Red Cross observes: "Volunteers are there but you have to offer them something . . . career benefits and resumé experience." The Children's Museum of Boston offers the potential volunteer entries for a curriculum vitae—a volunteer fund raiser is called a "corporate membership marketing specialist"; someone who helps paint walls, a "maintenance assistant." Since professionals look down on amateurs, executives of social institutions feel forced to counter the stigma of amateurism by conferring on the volunteer a quasi-professional status. The loss of confidence in private moral initiative is part of a general derogation of amateurism, a phenomenon that Christopher Lasch has called the "atrophy of competence."

Is it excessive to say that our society has become more morally passive? After all, the past few decades have seen the growth of liberal ideals and their realization in social programs that have benefited great numbers of people. Also, private moral initiative is not sufficient to guarantee a decent life to citizens in a complex society like our own. Without social security, Medicaid, and board of health regulations, the Miller residents would be much worse off.

The political diversion of moral energies, however, has given rise to a new kind of hypocrisy. It is now possible to consider ourselves morally exemplary simply because we adhere to an enlightened set of social principles. We may vote in accordance with these principles, but they require nothing of us personally: we need never lift a finger to help anyone and we need take no active part in social reform movements. We can even permit ourselves to be ruthless in relations with other people. Because morality has been sublimated into ideology, great numbers of people, the young and educated especially, feel they have an adequate moral identity merely because they hold the "right" views on such matters as ecology, feminism, socialism, and nuclear energy. They may lead narrow, self-indulgent lives, obsessed with their physical health, material comforts, and personal growth, yet still feel a moral advantage over those who actively work to help the needy but who are, in their eyes, ideologically unsound.

The problems that arise from the imbalance of private morality and public policy transcend questions of liberal left versus conservative right. Where the left is directly responsible for the false and the unworkable doctrine that ethics is reducible to public policy, the right wishes to dismantle crucial institutions that protect people's rights to a sustainable existence. Conservatives too believe that one may discharge moral duties by holding and advocating "correct" views on public policy (against busing and gun control, for prayers in the school and the death penalty). If the extreme right proves effective, the indigent will have lost such protection as public policy now provides—and this in a society whose members have lost the will and the way to be their brothers' keeper. Moreover, in any number of situations direct action is simply inappropriate (housing for the elderly or disaster relief are prime examples) and the need for concerted social effort and sound public policy is clear. But being right and effective in social ethics is only half of the moral life; and the growing belief that it is more than half should be combated and dispelled. Courses in ethics might be one place to begin.

A glance at a typical anthology of a college course in ethics reveals that most of what the student will read is directed toward analyzing and criticizing policies on such issues as punishment, recombinant DNA research, abortion, and euthanasia. Since the student is not likely to be personally involved in, say, inflicting the death penalty on anyone, the point is to learn how to form responsible opinions. Inevitably the student gets the idea that applying ethics to modern life is mainly a matter of being for or against some social policy. And since many of the articles read like briefs written for a judge or legislator, before long the student loses sight of him- or herself as a moral agent and begins to think like a proto-jurist or legislator.

The net effect of identifying normative ethics with public policy is to justify the moral passivity of the individual. But private benevolence continues to be badly needed in all areas of social concern. The paid functionaries who have virtually excluded the unpaid, well-meaning person are in no position to replace or repair the bonds that have been weakened by the atrophy of private moral initiative. Intellectuals, too, have lost their nerve. Consider the following, from Simone de Beauvoir's *The Coming of Age:*

> Once we have understood what the state of the aged really is, we cannot satisfy ourselves with calling for a more generous "old age policy," higher pensions, decent housing, and organized leisure. It is the whole system that is at issue and our claim cannot be otherwise than radical—change life itself.

Here is the mysterious and ultimately despairing demand of the contemporary social philosopher who has lost sight of the morally concerned citizen. The concrete need is not for revolutionizing society, perhaps not even for reforming it, but for finding a way to reach people like Miss Pickins and the other residents of Miller House.

STUDY QUESTIONS

1. Sommers assumes that private persons have a moral responsibility to do something about lonely, needy, elderly people in their community. Do you agree?
2. Isn't it excessive to say that our society has become morally passive? After all, in the past few decades we have seen the implementation of enlightened social policies that have helped unprecedented numbers of people. Is Sommers asking us to return to "the good old days" that were not really all that good?
3. What does Sommers mean by the "moral amateur"?
4. Does Sommers exaggerate the shift from private to social morality? Does she exaggerate the need for more private activity?

The World of Epictetus

VICE ADMIRAL JAMES BOND STOCKDALE, USN

James Stockdale (b. 1923) spent ten years in Vietnam, two as a combat naval aviator and eight as a prisoner of war (four years in solitary confinement). He received the Congressional Medal of Honor and, since retiring from the Navy as President of the War College, has pursued the scholarly life. Stockdale has ten honorary degrees, and is currently a Senior Fellow at the Hoover Institution on War, Revolution and Peace. His most recent books are *In Love and War* (1984) and *A Vietnam Experience: Ten Years of Reflection* (1985).

James Stockdale was a senior naval wing commander when he was shot down over North Vietnam in 1965. The article tells of the resources Stockdale found in himself in order to survive the ordeal with his sense of self-respect intact. Not all his fellow prisoners were as internally resourceful. Stockdale reports that he owed a great deal to a classical education that gave him an invaluable perspective on his situation. He learned from literature and from the Bible (*Job* especially) that life is not fair. The *Enchiridion* of Epictetus taught him to concern himself only with what was within his power. As a prisoner he was physically powerless, and had to learn to control and strengthen his will. He learned that integrity was far more valuable than sleep or food if the latter were

THE WORLD OF EPICTETUS By Vice Admiral James Bond Stockdale, USN. Reprinted from the *Atlantic Monthly*, April 1978. By permission of the author.

obtained from his captors at the price of loss of self-respect. He learned that persons of little learning or philosophy were more vulnerable to brainwashing and the weakness that leads to treasonable betrayal of fellow prisoners. As a result, Stockdale recommends training in history and philosophy for professional soldiers. "In stress situations, the fundamental, the hardcore classical subjects, are what serve best."

In 1965 I was a forty-one-year-old commander, the senior pilot of Air Wing 16, flying combat missions in the area just south of Hanoi from the aircraft carrier *Oriskany*. By September of that year I had grown quite accustomed to briefing dozens of pilots and leading them on daily air strikes; I had flown nearly 200 missions myself and knew the countryside of North Vietnam like the back of my hand. On the ninth of that month I led about thirty-five airplanes to the Thanh Hoa Bridge, just west of that city. That bridge was tough; we had been bouncing 500-pounders off it for weeks.

The September 9 raid held special meaning for *Oriskany* pilots because of a special bomb load we had improvised; we were going in with our biggest, the 2000-pounders, hung not only on our attack planes but on our F-8 fighter-bombers as well. This increase in bridge-busting capability came from the innovative brain of a major flying with my Marine fighter squadron. He had figured out how we could jury-rig some switches, hang the big bombs, pump out some of the fuel to stay within takeoff weight limits, and then top off our tanks from our airborne refuelers while en route to the target. Although the pilot had to throw several switches in sequence to get rid of his bombs, a procedure requiring above-average cockpit agility, we routinely operated on the premise that all pilots of Air Wing 16 were above average. I test-flew the new load on a mission, thought it over, and approved it; that's the way we did business.

Our spirit was up. That morning, the *Oriskany* Air Wing was finally going to drop the bridge that was becoming a North Vietnamese symbol of resistance. You can imagine our dismay when we crossed the coast and the weather scout I had sent on ahead radioed back that ceiling and visibility were zero-zero in the bridge area. In the tiny cockpit of my A-4 at the front of the pack, I pushed the

659

button on the throttle, spoke into the radio mike in my oxygen mask, and told the formation to split up and proceed in pairs to the secondary targets I had specified in my contingency briefing. What a letdown.

The adrenaline stopped flowing as my wingman and I broke left and down and started sauntering along toward our "milk run" target: boxcars on a railroad siding between Vinh and Thanh Hoa, where the flak was light. Descending through 10,000 feet, I unsnapped my oxygen mask and let it dangle, giving my pinched face a rest—no reason to stay uncomfortable on this run.

As I glided toward that easy target, I'm sure I felt totally self-satisfied. I had the top combat job that a Navy commander can hold and I was in tune with my environment. I was confident—I knew airplanes and flying inside out. I was comfortable with the people I worked with and I knew the trade so well that I often improvised variations in accepted procedures and encouraged others to do so under my watchful eye. I was on top. I thought I had found every key to success and had no doubt that my Academy and test-pilot schooling had provided me with everything I needed in life.

I passed down the middle of those boxcars and smiled as I saw the results of my instinctive timing. A neat pattern—perfection. I was just pulling out of my dive low to the ground when I heard a noise I hadn't expected—the *boom boom boom* of a 57-millimeter gun—and then I saw it just behind my wingtip. I was hit—all the red lights came on, my control system was going out—and I could barely keep that plane from flying into the ground while I got that damned oxygen mask up to my mouth so I could tell my wingman that I was about to eject. What rotten luck. And on a "milk run"!

The descent in the chute was quiet except for occasional rifle shots from the streets below. My mind was clear, and I said to myself, "five years." I knew we were making a mess of the war in Southeast Asia, but I didn't think it would last longer than that; I was also naive about the resources I would need in order to survive a lengthy period of captivity.

The Durants have said that culture is a thin and fragile veneer that superimposes itself on mankind. For the first time I was on my own, without the veneer. I was to spend years searching through and refining my bag of memories, looking for useful tools, things of

660

value. The values were there, but they were all mixed up with technology, bureaucracy, and expediency, and had to be brought up into the open.

Education should take care to illuminate values, not bury them amongst the trivia. Are our students getting the message that without personal integrity intellectual skills are worthless?

Integrity is one of those words which many people keep in that desk drawer labeled "too hard." It's not a topic for the dinner table or the cocktail party. You can't buy or sell it. When supported with education, a person's integrity can give him something to rely on when his perspective seems to blur, when rules and principles seem to waver, and when he's faced with hard choices of right or wrong. It's something to keep him on the right track, something to keep him afloat when he's drowning; if only for practical reasons, it is an attribute that should be kept at the very top of a young person's consciousness.

The importance of the latter point is highlighted in prison camps, where everyday human nature, stripped bare, can be studied under a magnifying glass in accelerated time. Lessons spotlighted and absorbed in that laboratory sharpen one's eye for their abstruse but highly relevant applications in the "real time" world of now.

In the five years since I've been out of prison, I've participated several times in the process of selecting senior naval officers for promotion or important command assignments. I doubt that the experience is significantly different from that of executives who sit on "selection boards" in any large hierarchy. The system must be formal, objective, and fair; if you've seen one, you've probably seen them all. Navy selection board proceedings go something like this.

The first time you know the identity of the other members of the board is when you walk into a boardroom at eight o'clock on an appointed morning. The first order of business is to stand, raise your right hand, put your left hand on the Bible, and swear to make the best judgment you can, on the basis of merit, without prejudice. You're sworn to confidentiality regarding all board members' remarks during the proceedings. Board members are chosen for their experience and understanding; they often have knowledge of the particular individuals under consideration. They must feel free to speak their minds. They read and grade dozens of dossiers, and each candidate is discussed extensively. At voting time, a member casts his vote by selecting and pushing a "percent confidence" button, visible only to himself, on a console attached to his chair. When the last member pushes his button, a totalizer displays the numerical average "confidence" of the board. No one knows who voted what.

I'm always impressed by the fact that every effort is made to be fair to the candidate. Some are clearly out, some are clearly in; the borderline cases are the tough ones. You go over and over those in the "middle pile" and usually you vote and revote until late at night. In all the boards I've sat on, no inference or statement in a "jacket" is as sure to portend a low confidence score on the vote as evidence of a lack of directness or rectitude of a candidate in his dealings with others. Any hint of moral turpitude really turns people off. When the crunch comes, they prefer to work with forthright plodders rather than with devious geniuses. I don't believe that this preference is unique to the military. In any hierarchy where people's fates are decided by committees or boards, those who lose credibility with their peers and who cause their superiors to doubt their directness, honesty, or integrity are dead. Recovery isn't possible.

The linkage of men's ethics, reputations, and fates can be studied in even more vivid detail in prison camp. In that brutally controlled environment a perceptive enemy can get his hooks into the slightest chink in a man's ethical armor and accelerate his downfall. Given the right opening, the right moral weakness, a certain susceptibility on the part of the prisoner, a clever extortionist can drive his victim into a downhill slide that will ruin his image, self-respect, and life in a very short time.

There are some uncharted aspects to this, some traits of susceptibility which I don't think psychologists yet have words for. I am thinking of the tragedy that can befall a person who has such a need for love or attention that he will sell his soul for it. I use tragedy with the rigorous definition Aristotle applied to it: the story of a good man with a flaw who comes to an unjustified bad end. This is a rather delicate point and one that I want to emphasize. We had very very few collaborators in prison, and comparatively few Aristotelian tragedies, but the story and fate of one of these good men with a flaw might be instructive.

He was handsome, smart, articulate, and smooth. He was almost sincere. He was obsessed with success. When the going got tough, he decided expediency was preferable to principle.

This man was a classical opportunist. He befriended and worked for the enemy to the detriment of his fellow Americans. He made a tacit deal; moreover, he accepted favors (a violation of the code of conduct). In time, out of fear and shame, he withdrew; we could not get him to communicate with the American prisoner organization.

I couldn't learn what made the man tick. One of my best friends in prison, one of the wisest persons I have ever known, had once been in a squadron with this fellow. In prisoners' code I tapped a question to my philosophical friend: "What in the world is going on with that fink?"

"You're going to be surprised at what I have to say," he meticulously tapped back. "In a squadron he pushes himself forward and dominates the scene. He's a continual fountain of information. He's the person everybody relies on for inside dope. He works like mad; often flies more hops than others. It drives him crazy if he's not liked. He tends to grovel and ingratiate himself before others. I didn't realize he was really pathetic until I was sitting around with him and his wife one night when he was spinning his yarns of delusions of grandeur, telling of his great successes and his pending ascension to the top. His wife knew him better than anybody else; she shook her head with genuine sympathy and said to him: 'Gee, you're just a phony.'"

In prison, this man had somehow reached the point where he was willing to sell his soul just to satisfy this need, this immaturity. The only way he could get the attention that he demanded from authority was to grovel and ingratiate himself before the enemy. As a soldier he was a miserable failure, but he had not crossed the boundary of willful treason; he was not written off as an irrevocable loss, as were the two patent collaborators with whom the Vietnamese soon arranged that he live.

As we American POWs built our civilization, and wrote our own laws (which we leaders obliged all to memorize), we also codified certain principles which formed the backbone of our policies and attitudes. I codified the principles of compassion, rehabilitation, and forgiveness with the slogan: "It is neither American nor Christian to nag a repentant sinner to his grave." (Some didn't like it, thought it seemed soft on finks.) And so, we really gave this man a chance.

663

Over time, our efforts worked. After five years of self-indulgence he got himself together and started to communicate with the prisoner organization. I sent the message "Are you on the team or not?"; he replied, "Yes," and came back. He told the Vietnamese that he didn't want to play their dirty games anymore. He wanted to get away from those willful collaborators and he came back and he was accepted, after a fashion.

I wish that were the end of the story. Although he came back, joined us, and even became a leader of sorts, he never totally won himself back. No matter how forgiving we were, he was conscious that many resented him—not so much because he was weak but because he had broken what we might call a gentleman's code. In all of those years when he, a senior officer, had willingly participated in making tape recordings of anti-American material, he had deeply offended the sensibilities of the American prisoners who were forced to listen to him. To most of us it wasn't the rhetoric of the war or the goodness or the badness of this or that issue that counted. The object of our highest value was the well-being of our fellow prisoners. He had broken that code and hurt some of those people. Some thought that as an informer he had indirectly hurt them physically. I don't believe that. What indisputably hurt them was his not having the sensitivity to realize the damage his opportunistic conduct would do to the morale of a bunch of Middle American guys with Middle American attitudes which they naturally cherished. He should have known that in those solitary cells where his tapes were piped were idealistic, direct, patriotic fellows who would be crushed and embarrassed to have him, a senior man in excellent physical shape, so obviously not under torture, telling the world that the war was wrong. Even if he believed what he said, which he did not, he should have had the common decency to keep his mouth shut. You can sit and think anything you want, but when you insensitively cut down those who want to love and help you, you cross a line. He seemed to sense that he could never truly be one of us.

And yet he was likable—particularly back in civilization after release—when tension was off, and making a deal did not seem so important. He exuded charm and "hail fellow" sophistication. He wanted so to be liked by all those men he had once discarded in his search for new friends, new deals, new fields to conquer in Hanoi. The tragedy of his life was obvious to us all. Tears were shed by some of his old prison mates when he was killed in an accident that strongly resembled suicide some months later. The Greek drama had run its course. He was right out of Aristotle's book, a good man with a flaw who had come to an unjustified bad end. The flaw was insecurity: the need to ingratiate himself, the need for love and adulation at any price.

He reminded me of Paul Newman in *The Hustler*. Newman couldn't stand success. He knew how to make a deal. He was handsome, he was smart, he was attractive to everybody; but he had to have adulation, and therein lay the seed of tragedy. Playing high-stakes pool against old Minnesota Fats (Jackie Gleason), Newman was well in the lead, and getting more full of himself by the hour. George C. Scott, the pool bettor, whispered to his partner: "I'm going to keep betting on Minnesota Fats; this other guy [Newman] is a born loser—he's all skill and no character." And he was right, a born loser—I think that's the message.

How can we educate to avoid these casualties? Can we by means of education prevent this kind of tragedy? What we prisoners were in was a one-way leverage game in which the other side had all the mechanical advantage. I suppose you could say that we all live in a leverage world to some degree; we all experience people trying to use us in one way or another. The difference in Hanoi was the degradation of the ends (to be used as propaganda agents of an enemy, or as informers on your fellow Americans), and the power of the means (total environmental control including solitary confinement, restraint by means of leg-irons and handcuffs, and torture). Extortionists always go down the same track: the imposition of guilt and fear for having disobeyed their rules, followed in turn by punishment, apology, confession, and atonement (their payoff). Our captors would go to great lengths to get a man to compromise his own code, even if only slightly, and then they would hold that in their bag, and the next time get him to go a little further.

Some people are psychologically, if not physically, at home in extortion environments. They are tough people who instinctively avoid getting sucked into the undertows. They never kid themselves or their friends; if they miss the mark they admit it. But there's another category of person who gets tripped up. He makes a small compromise, perhaps rationalizes it, and then makes another one; and then he gets depressed, full of shame, lonesome, loses his willpower and self-respect, and comes to a tragic end. Somewhere along the line he realizes that he has turned a corner that he didn't mean to turn. All too late he realizes that he has been worshiping the wrong gods and discovers the wisdom of the ages: life is not fair.

In sorting out the story after our release, we found that most of us had come to combat constant mental and physical pressure in much the same way. We discovered that when a person is alone in a cell and sees the door open only once or twice a day for a bowl of soup, he realizes after a period of weeks in isolation and darkness that he has to build some sort of ritual into his life if he wants to avoid becoming an animal. Ritual fills a need in a hard life and it's easy to see how formal church ritual grew. For almost all of us, this ritual was built around prayer, exercise, and clandestine communication. The prayers I said during those days were prayers of quality with ideas of substance. We found that over the course of time our minds had a tremendous capacity for invention and introspection, but had the weakness of being an integral part of our bodies. I remembered Descartes and how in his philosophy he separated mind and body. One time I cursed my body for the way it decayed my mind. I had decided that I would become a Gandhi. I would have to be carried around on a pallet and in that state I could not be used by my captors for propaganda purposes. After about ten days of fasting, I found that I had become so depressed that soon I would risk going into interrogation ready to spill my guts just looking for a friend. I tapped to the guy next door and I said, "Gosh, how I wish Descartes could have been right, but he's wrong." He was a little slow to reply; I reviewed Descartes's deduction with him and explained how I had discovered that body and mind are inseparable.

On the positive side, I discovered the tremendous file-cabinet volume of the human mind. You can memorize an incredible amount of material and you can draw the past out of your memory with remarkable recall by easing slowly toward the event you seek and not crowding the mind too closely. You'll try to remember who was at your birthday party when you were five years old, and you can get it, but only after months of effort. You can break the locks and find the answers, but you need time and solitude to learn how to use this marvelous device in your head which is the greatest computer on earth.

Of course many of the things we recalled from the past were utterly useless as sources of strength or practicality. For instance, events brought back from cocktail parties or insincere social contacts were almost repugnant because of their emptiness, their utter lack of value. More often than not, the locks worth picking had been on old schoolroom doors. School days can be thought of as a time when one is filling the important stacks of one's memory library. For me, the golden doors were labeled history and the classics. The historical perspective which enabled a man to take himself away from all the agitation, not necessarily to see a rosy lining, but to see the real nature of the situation he faced, was truly a thing of value.

Here's how this historical perspective helped me see the reality of my own situation and thus cope better with it. I learned from a Vietnamese prisoner that the same cells we occupied had in years before been lived in by many of the leaders of the Hanoi government. From my history lessons I recalled that when metropolitan France permitted communists in the government in 1936, the communists who occupied cells in Vietnam were set free. I marveled at the cycle of history, all within my memory, which prompted Hitler's rise in Germany, then led to the rise of the Popular Front in France, and finally vacated this cell of mine halfway around the world ("Perhaps Pham Van Dong lived here"). I came to understand what tough people these were. I was willing to fight them to the death, but I grew to realize that hatred was an indulgence, a very inefficient emotion. I remember thinking, "If you were committed to beating the dealer in a gambling casino, would *hating* him help your game?" In a pidgin English propaganda book the guard gave me, speeches by these old communists about their prison experiences stressed how they learned to beat down the enemy by being united. It seemed comforting to know that we were united against the communist administration of Hoa Lo prison just as the Vietnamese communists had united against the French administration of Hoa Lo in the thirties. Prisoners are prisoners, and there's only one way to beat administrations. We resolved to do it better in the sixties than they had in the thirties. You don't base system-beating on any thought of political idealism; you do it as a competitive thing, as an expression of self-respect.

Education in the classics teaches you that all organizations since the beginning of time have used the power of guilt; that cycles are repetitive; and that this is the way of the world. It's a naive person who comes in and says, "Let's see, what's good and what's bad?" That's a quagmire. You can get out of that quagmire only by recalling how wise men before you accommodated the same dilemmas. And I believe a good classical education and an understanding of history can best determine the rules you should live by. They also give you the power to analyze reasons for these rules and guide you as to how to apply them to your own situation. In a broader sense, all my education helped me. Naval Academy discipline and body contact sports helped me. But the education which I found myself using most was what I got in graduate school. The messages of history and philosophy I used were simple.

The first one is this business about life not being fair. That is a very important lesson and I learned it from a wonderful man named Philip Rhinelander. As a lieutenant commander in the Navy studying political science at Stanford University in 1961, I went over to philosophy corner one day and an older gentleman said, "Can I help you?" I said, "Yes, I'd like to take some courses in philosophy." I told him I'd been in college for six years and had never had a course in philosophy. He couldn't believe it. I told him that I was a naval officer and he said, "Well, I used to be in the Navy. Sit down." Philip Rhinelander became a great influence in my life.

He had been a Harvard lawyer and had pleaded cases before the Supreme Court and then gone to war as a reserve officer. When he came back he took his doctorate at Harvard. He was also a music composer, had been director of general education at Harvard, dean of the School of Humanities and Sciences at Stanford, and by the time I met him had by choice returned to teaching in the classroom. He said, "The course I'm teaching is my personal two-term favorite—The Problem of Good and Evil—and we're starting our second term." He said the message of his course was from the Book of Job. The number one problem in this world is that people are not able to accommodate the lesson in the book.

He recounted the story of Job. It starts out by establishing that Job was the most honorable of men. Then he lost all his goods. He also lost his reputation, which is what really hurt. His wife was badgering him to admit his sins, but he knew he had made no errors. He was not a patient man and demanded to speak to the Lord. When the Lord appeared in the whirlwind, he said, "Now, Job, you have to shape up! Life is not fair." That's my interpretation and that's the way the book ended for hundreds of years. I agree with those of the opinion that the happy ending was spliced on many years later. If you read it, you'll note that the meter changes. People couldn't live with the original message. Here was a good man who came to unexplained grief, and the Lord told him: "That's the way it is. Don't challenge me. This is my world and you either live in it as I designed it or get out."

This was a great comfort to me in prison. It answered the question "Why me?" It cast aside any thoughts of being punished for past actions. Sometimes I shared the message with fellow prisoners as I tapped through the walls to them, but I learned to be selective. It's a strong message which upsets some people.

Rhinelander also passed on to me another piece of classical information which I found of great value. On the day of our last session together he said, "You're a military man, let me give you a book to remember me by. It's a book of military ethics." He handed it to me, and I bade him goodbye with great emotion. I took the book home and that night started to read it. It was the *Enchiridion* of the philosopher Epictetus, his "manual" for the Roman field soldier.

As I began to read, I thought to myself in disbelief, "Does Rhinelander think I'm going to draw lessons for my life from this thing? I'm a fighter pilot. I'm a technical man. I'm a test pilot. I know how to get people to do technical work. I play golf; I drink martinis. I know how to get ahead in my profession. And what does he hand me? A book that says in part, 'It's better to die in hunger, exempt from guilt and fear, than to live in affluence and with perturbation.'" I remembered this later in prison because perturbation was what I was living with. When I ejected from the airplane on that September morn in 1965, I had left the land of technology. I had entered the world of Epictetus, and it's a world that few of us, whether we know it or not, are ever far away from.

In Palo Alto, I had read this book, not with contentment, but with annoyance. Statement after statement: "Men are disturbed not by things, but by the view that they take of them." "Do not be concerned with things which are beyond your power." "Demand not that events should happen as you wish, but wish them to happen as they do happen and you will go on well." This is stoicism. It's not the last word, but it's a viewpoint that comes in handy in many circumstances, and it surely did for me. Particularly this line:

"Lameness is an impediment to the body but not to the will." That was significant for me because I wasn't able to stand up and support myself on my badly broken leg for the first couple of years I was in solitary confinement.

Other statements of Epictetus took on added meaning in the light of extortions which often began with our captors' callous pleas: "If you are just reasonable with us we will compensate you. You get your meals, you get to sleep, you won't be pestered, you might even get a cellmate." The catch was that by being "reasonable with us" our enemies meant being their informers, their propagandists. The old stoic had said, "If I can get the things I need with the preservation of my honor and fidelity and self-respect, show me the way and I will get them. But, if you require me to lose my own proper good, that you may gain what is no good, consider how unreasonable and foolish you are." To love our fellow prisoners was within our power. To betray, to propagandize, to disillusion conscientious and patriotic shipmates and destroy their morale so that they in turn would be destroyed was to lose one's proper good.

What attributes serve you well in the extortion environment? We learned there, above all else, that the best defense is to keep your conscience clean. When we did something we were ashamed of, and our captors realized we were ashamed of it, we were in trouble. A little white lie is where extortion and ultimately blackmail start. In 1965, I was crippled and I was alone. I realized that they had all the power. I couldn't see how I was ever going to get out with my honor and self-respect. The one thing I came to realize was that if you don't lose integrity you can't be had and you can't be hurt. Compromises multiply and build up when you're working against a skilled extortionist or a good manipulator. You can't be had if you don't take that first shortcut, or "meet them halfway," as they say, or look for that tacit "deal," or make that first compromise.

Bob North, a political science professor at Stanford, taught me a course called Comparative Marxist Thought. This was not an anti-communist course. It was the study of dogma and thought patterns. We read no criticisms of Marxism, only primary sources. All year we read the works of Marx and Lenin. In Hanoi, I understood more about Marxist theory than my interrogator did. I was able to say to that interrogator, "That's not what Lenin said; you're a deviationist."

One of the things North talked about was brainwashing. A psychologist who studied the Korean prisoner situation, which somewhat paralleled ours, concluded that three categories of prisoners were involved there. The first was the redneck Marine sergeant from Tennessee who had an eighth-grade education. He would get in that interrogation room and they would say that the Spanish-American War was started by the bomb within the *Maine,* which might be true, and he would answer, "B.S." They would show him something about racial unrest in Detroit. "B.S." There was no way they could get to him; his mind was made up. He was a straight guy, red, white, and blue, and everything else was B.S.! He didn't give it a second thought. Not much of a historian, perhaps, but a good security risk.

In the next category were the sophisticates. They were the fellows who could be told these same things about the horrors of American history and our social problems, but had heard it all before, knew both sides of every story, and thought we were on the right track. They weren't ashamed that we had robber barons at a certain time in our history; they were aware of the skeletons in most civilizations' closets. They could not be emotionally involved and so they were good security risks.

The ones who were in trouble were the high school graduates who had enough sense to pick up the innuendo, and yet not enough education to accommodate it properly. Not many of them fell, but most of the men that got entangled started from that background.

The psychologist's point is possibly oversimplistic, but I think his message has some validity. A little knowledge is a dangerous thing.

Generally speaking, I think education is a tremendous defense; the broader, the better. After I was shot down my wife, Sybil, found a clipping glued in the front of my collegiate dictionary: "Education is an ornament in prosperity and a refuge in adversity." She certainly agrees with me on that. Most of us prisoners found that the so-called practical academic exercises in how to do things, which I'm told are proliferating, were useless. I'm not saying that we should base education on training people to be in prison, but I am saying that in stress situations, the fundamentals, the hardcore classical subjects, are what serve best.

Theatrics also helped sustain me. My mother had been a drama coach when I was young and I was in many of her plays. In prison I learned how to manufacture a personality and live it, crawl into it, and hold that role without deviation. During interrogations, I'd check the responses I got to different kinds of behavior. They'd get worried when I did things irrationally. And so, every so often, I would play that "irrational" role and come completely unglued. When I could tell that pressure to make a public exhibition of me was building, I'd stand up, tip the table over, attempt to throw the chair through the window, and say, "No way, Goddammit! I'm not doing that! Now, come over here and fight!" This was a risky ploy, because if they thought you were acting, they would slam you into the ropes and make you scream in pain like a baby. You could watch their faces and read their minds. They had expected me to behave like a stoic. But a man would be a fool to make their job easy by being conventional and predictable. I could feel the tide turn in my favor at that magic moment when their anger turned to pleading: "Calm down, now calm down." The payoff would come when they decided that the risk of my going haywire in front of some touring American professor on a "fact-finding" mission was too great. More important, they had reason to believe that I would tell the truth—namely, that I had been in solitary confinement for four years and tortured fifteen times—without fear of future consequences. So theatrical training proved helpful to me.

Can you educate for leadership? I think you can, but the communists would probably say no. One day in an argument with an interrogator, I said, "You are so proud of being a party member, what are the criteria?" He said in a flurry of anger, "There are only four: you have to be seventeen years old, you have to be selfless, you have to be smart enough to understand the theory, and you've got to be a person who innately influences others." He stressed that fourth one. I think psychologists would say that leadership is innate, and there is truth in that. But, I also think you can learn some leadership traits that naturally accrue from a good education: compassion is a necessity for leaders, as are spontaneity, bravery, self-discipline, honesty, and above all, integrity.

I remember being disappointed about a month after I was back when one of my young friends, a prison mate, came running up after a reunion at the Naval Academy. He said with glee, "This is really great, you won't believe how this country has advanced. They've practically done away with plebe year at the Academy, and they've got computers in the basement of Bancroft Hall." I thought, "My God, if there was anything that helped us get through those eight years, it was plebe year, and if anything screwed up that war, it was computers!"

STUDY QUESTIONS

1. In his years of confinement and torment, Stockdale reverted to the stoic philosophy of Epictetus. Is stoicism primarily a philosophy for critical and extreme situations? If not, how does it apply in ordinary life?

2. How does Stockdale define personal integrity? Does this conform to your idea of personal integrity? How did readings in history and philosophy help Stockdale retain his dignity and integrity under great stress?

3. Discuss the case of the officer who betrayed his fellow prisoners. Stockdale attributes this to a character fault. Could a proper moral education of the kind Stockdale advocates have prevented it?

4. What does Stockdale's article tell us about the importance or unimportance of a formal training in ethics? Is great fiction more valuable for moral development? Compare Stockdale's views on moral education with Duska's.

SUGGESTED READINGS

Damon, William. *The Moral Child*. New York: Macmillan, 1988.

Dykstra, Craig. *Vision and Character*. New York: Paulist Press, 1981.

Gilligan, Carol. *In a Different Voice*. Cambridge, MA: Harvard University Press, 1982.

Grimshaw, Jean. *Philosophy and Feminist Thinking*. Minneapolis: University of Minnesota Press, 1986.

Joy, Donald. *Moral Development Foundations*. Nashville: Abingdon Press, 1983.

Kagan, Jerome, ed. *The Emergence of Morality in Children*. Chicago: University of Chicago Press, 1986.

Kohlberg, Lawrence. *Essays on Moral Development*, vols. I and II. San Francisco: Harper and Row, 1981, 1984.

Noddings, Nel. *Caring: A Feminine Approach to Ethics and Moral Education*. Berkeley: University of California Press, 1984.

Parr, Susan Resneck. *The Moral of the Story: Literature, Values, and American Education*. New York: Columbia University Press, 1982.

Sichel, Betty. *Moral Education: Character, Community and Ideals*. Philadelphia: Temple University Press, 1988.

Chapter Seven

CHARACTER, DIGNITY, AND SELF-RESPECT

A being capable of wronging another being is a moral agent. A being capable of being wronged by a moral agent is a moral patient. A moral agent has duties; a moral patient has rights.

Any person is at once a moral agent and a moral patient. Consider the notion of self-respect. Respect for oneself as a moral patient is one meaning of self-respect. So understood, to respect oneself is to fulfill the duties one owes to oneself. What does one owe to oneself? Christopher Lasch calls attention to the currently popular assumption—reflected in television commercials that urge us to indulge in certain expensive luxuries because "you owe it to yourself"—that we owe ourselves gratification and pleasure. Lasch is probably right to claim that many people today see self-indulgence as a *moral* duty. All the same, we recognize something slightly ludicrous about refusing to wear or eat something inferior "because I have too much respect for myself."

Contrast this narcissistic idea of self-respect with Kant's idea that the primary self-duty is "the universal duty which devolves upon man of so ordering his life as to be fit for the performance of all moral duties." Kant is still talking of duties to one's ("patient") self. But he claims that morally we owe that self *not* happiness or gratification but self-development as a moral agent. This older ideal of self-obligation is entirely consistent with the concept of virtue-based ethics. The imperative is to become virtuous, to "build character." For Kant, as for the philosophers of virtue, human beings are, in the last analysis, responsible for the kind of person they are (selfish or kind, courageous or cowardly, temperate or self-indulgent). Since virtue is not given to us, we must develop it. Virtue-based ethics' answer to the question "What do we owe to ourselves?" thus (roughly) coincides with Kant's answer: We owe it to ourselves to develop ourselves as moral agents.

Respect for the self as moral patient is one aspect of self-respect. But the self has two aspects and "self-respect" has a second meaning: respect for oneself as moral agent. Persons who consistently behave in an honorable way (discharging their obligations to themselves and others) justifiably can view themselves as moral beings worthy of commendation. Their track record as moral agents is evidence of character, and indeed, respect for one's "agent" self is respect for oneself as a "person of character." Conversely, persons of weak character necessarily lack this form of self-respect. In effect, persons who respect themselves and others as moral patients also will come to respect themselves as moral agents. Kant speaks of this as "noble pride" or "proper self-esteem." Thomas Hill applies the Kantian idea of duty to oneself in finding moral fault with those who defer servilely to others. According to Hill, excessive deference at the expense of oneself betrays a lack of self-respect and an insufficient understanding of what one owes oneself as an autonomous moral agent.

Joan Didion's concept of self-respect also is agent oriented. To have self-respect is to be a person of character with a better-than-average record of acting in accordance with one's principles. Didion stresses that people with the strength of character to achieve this record also are people who accept responsibility for their actions. Thus the tendency to find excuses for oneself indicates a lack of self-respect.

Anthony Quinton's article surveys the vicissitudes of virtue-based ethics in the past few centuries and the changes in conceptions of self-respect and character. Quinton finds that the Victorian emphasis on strength of character is a thing of the past. The transformation Quinton describes can be characterized as a shift of emphasis from the self as an active moral agent to the patient self as a repository of rights, with a corresponding shift in the notion of self-respect. According to Quinton, persons of "character" are persons with the consistent strength of will to apply reason to achieve a long-range gain in situations where they are tempted strongly to forego that gain in favor of immediate satisfactions. Quinton's person of character is the very antithesis of the person Christopher Lasch calls "the new narcissist," a type Lasch finds alarmingly prevalent today.

Lasch, Coles, Didion, and Quinton all deal with the same general phenomenon: Morally speaking, modern men and women see themselves primarily as centers of needs and rights, and only secondarily as centers of obligations and duties. Lasch and Quinton find that a weakening of tradition and social roles accompanies the shift of emphasis to the self as moral patient. Quinton recognizes character, honor, and self-abnegation as currently unfashionable. He believes that each of us must work to reverse this trend. For Coles and Lasch, the new narcissism is socially and morally regressive. Coles is hopeful that character still predominates. Lasch is rather more pessimistic. Robert Coles's "field study" mitigates some of Lasch's negative judgments on the current state of American character. Coles offers much anecdotal evidence that children have an innate sense of dignity and self-respect. Far from being narcissistic, the children Coles observes are unselfish and morally brave.

Dignity and Self-respect

IMMANUEL KANT

TRANSLATED BY LOUIS ENFIELD

A biographical sketch of Immanuel Kant is found on page 149.

Moral persons do their duty to themselves as well as others; such persons deserve respect and will rightfully respect themselves. Self-respect is essential to self-worth. For example, says Kant, drunkards fail in their duty to themselves; the result is self-contempt. Similarly, weak persons who constantly find excuses for their moral lapses are contemptible in their own eyes as well as in the eyes of others. Suicide violates self-duty most seriously, since in suicide people use their own free will to destroy themselves as moral agents, thereby using themselves as a means (to avoid pain) and not as an end. Kant denies that we owe ourselves happiness: "Not self-favour but self-esteem" is the principle of self-duty. For Kant, self-respect comes to those who earn it by living a principled life.

I

By way of introduction it is to be noted that there is no question in moral philosophy which has received more defective treatment than

DIGNITY AND SELF-RESPECT From "Proper Self-respect," and "Duties to Oneself," from *Lectures on Ethics* by Immanuel Kant. Translated by Louis Enfield (New York: Harper & Row, 1963). Reprinted by permission of Methuen and Company Ltd.

that of the individual's duty towards himself. No one has framed a proper concept of self-regarding duty. It has been regarded as a detail and considered by way of an afterthought, as an appendix to moral philosophy, on the view that man should give a thought to himself only after he has completely fulfilled his duty towards others. . . . It was taken for granted that a man's duty towards himself consisted . . . in promoting his own happiness. In that case everything would depend on how an individual determined his own happiness; for our self-regarding duties would consist in the universal rule to satisfy all our inclinations in order to further our happiness. This would, however, militate seriously against doing our duty towards others. In fact, the principle of self-regarding duties is a very different one, which has no connexion with our well-being or earthly happiness. Far from ranking lowest in the scale of precedence, our duties towards ourselves are of primary importance and should have pride of place; for (deferring for the moment the definition of what constitutes this duty) it is obvious that nothing can be expected from a man who dishonours his own person. He who transgresses against himself loses his manliness and becomes incapable of doing his duty towards his fellows. A man who performed his duty to others badly, who lacked generosity, kindness and sympathy, but who nevertheless did his duty to himself by leading a proper life, might yet possess a certain inner worth; but he who has transgressed his duty towards himself, can have no inner worth whatever. Thus a man who fails in his duty to himself loses worth absolutely; while a man who fails in his duty to others loses worth only relatively. It follows that the prior condition of our duty to others is our duty to ourselves; we can fulfil the former only in so far as we first fulfil the latter. Let us illustrate our meaning by a few examples of failure in one's duty to oneself. A drunkard does no harm to another, and if he has a strong constitution he does no harm to himself, yet he is an object of contempt. We are not indifferent to cringing servility; man should not cringe and fawn; by so doing he degrades his person and loses his manhood. If a man for gain or profit submits to all indignities and makes himself the plaything of another, he casts away the worth of his manhood. Again, a lie is more a violation of one's duty to oneself than of one's duty to others. A liar, even though by his lies he does no harm to any one, yet becomes an object of contempt, he throws away his personality; his behaviour is vile, he has transgressed his duty towards himself. We can carry the argument further and say that to accept favours and benefits is also a breach of one's duty to oneself. If I accept favours, I contract debts which I can never repay, for I can never get on equal terms with him who has conferred the favours upon me; he has stolen a march upon me, and if I do him a favour I am only returning a *quid pro quo;* I shall always owe him a debt of gratitude, and who will accept such a debt? For to be indebted is to be subject to an unending constraint. I must for ever be courteous and flattering towards my benefactor, and if I fail to be so he will very soon make me conscious of my failure; I may even be forced to using subterfuge so as to avoid meeting him. But he who pays promptly for everything is under no constraint; he is free to act as he please; none will hinder him. Again, the faint-hearted who complain about their luck and sigh and weep about their misfortunes are despicable in our eyes; instead of sympathizing with them we do our best to keep away from them. But if a man shows a steadfast courage in his misfortune, and though greatly suffering, does not cringe and complain but puts a bold face upon things, to such a one our sympathy goes out. Moreover, if a man gives up his freedom and barters it away for money, he violates his manhood. Life itself ought not to be rated so highly as to warrant our being prepared, in order only not to lose it, to live otherwise than as a man should, i.e. not a life of ease, but so that we do not degrade our manhood. We must also be worthy of our manhood; whatsoever makes us unworthy of it makes us unfit for anything, and we cease to be men. Moreover, if a man offers his body for profit for the sport of others—if, for instance, he agrees in return for a few pints of beer to be knocked about—he throws himself away, and the perpetrators who pay him for it are acting as vilely as he. Neither can we without destroying our person abandon ourselves to others in order to satisfy their desires, even though it be done to save parents and friends from death; still less can this be done for money. If done in order to satisfy one's own desires, it is very immodest and immoral, but yet not so unnatural; but if it be done for money, or for some other reason, a person allows himself to be treated as a thing, and so throws away the worth of his manhood. It is the same with the vices of the flesh (*crimina carnis*), which for that reason are not spoken of. They do no damage to anyone, but dishonour and degrade a man's own person; they are an offence against the dignity of manhood in one's own person. The most serious offence against the duty one owes to oneself is suicide. But why should suicide be so abominable? It is no answer

to say "because God forbids it." Suicide is not an abomination because God has forbidden it; it is forbidden by God because it is
abominable. If it were the other way about, suicide would not be
abominable if it were not forbidden; and I should not know why God
had forbidden it, if it were not abominable in itself. The ground,
therefore, for regarding suicide and other transgressions as abominable and punishable must not be found in the divine will, but in
their inherent heinousness. Suicide is an abomination because it implies the abuse of man's freedom of action: he uses his freedom to
destroy himself. His freedom should be employed to enable him to
live as a man. He is free to dispose as he pleases of things appertaining
to his person, but not of his person; he may not use his freedom
against himself. For a man to recognize what his duty is towards
himself in this respect is far from easy: because although man has
indeed a natural horror of suicide, yet we can argue and quibble
ourselves into believing that, in order to rid himself of trouble and
misery, a man may destroy himself. The argument makes a strong
appeal; and in terms of the rule of prudence suicide may often be the
surest and best course; none the less suicide is in itself revolting. The
rule of morality, which takes precedence of all rules of reflective
prudence, commands apodeictically and categorically that we must
observe our duties to ourselves; and in committing suicide and reducing himself to a carcase, man uses his powers and his liberty
against himself. Man is free to dispose of his condition but not of his
person; he himself is an end and not a means; all else in the world is
of value only as a means, but man is a person and not a thing and
therefore not a means. It is absurd that a reasonable being, an end for
the sake of which all else is means, should use himself as a means. It
is true that a person can serve as a means for others (e.g. by his
work), but only in a way whereby he does not cease to be a person
and an end. Whoever acts in such a way that he cannot be an end,
uses himself as a means and treats his person as a thing. . . .

The duties we owe to ourselves do not depend on the relation of
the action to the ends of happiness. If they did, they would depend
on our inclinations and so be governed by rules of prudence. Such
rules are not moral, since they indicate only the necessity of the means
for the satisfaction of inclinations, and cannot therefore bind us. The
basis of such obligation is not to be found in the advantages we
reap from doing our duty towards ourselves, but in the worth of

manhood. This principle does not allow us an unlimited freedom in respect of our own persons. It insists that we must reverence humanity in our own person, because apart from this man becomes an object of contempt, worthless in the eyes of his fellows and worthless in himself. Such faultiness is absolute. Our duties towards ourselves constitute the supreme condition and the principle of all morality; for moral worth is the worth of the person as such; our capacities have a value only in regard to the circumstances in which we find ourselves. Socrates lived in a state of wretchedness; his circumstances were worthless; but though his circumstances were so ill-conditioned, yet he himself was of the highest value. Even though we sacrifice all life's amenities we can make up for their loss and sustain approval by maintaining the worth of our humanity. We may have lost everything else, and yet still retain our inherent worth. Only if our worth as human beings is intact can we perform our other duties; for it is the foundation stone of all other duties. A man who has destroyed and cast away his personality, has no intrinsic worth, and can no longer perform any manner of duty.

Let us next consider the basis of the principle of all self-regarding duties.

Freedom is, on the one hand, that faculty which gives unlimited usefulness to all other faculties. It is the highest order of life, which serves as the foundation of all perfections and is their necessary condition. All animals have the faculty of using their powers according to will. But this will is not free. It is necessitated through the incitement of *stimuli,* and the actions of animals involve a *bruta necessitas.* If the will of all beings were so bound to sensuous impulse, the world would possess no value. The inherent value of the world, the *summum bonum,* is freedom in accordance with a will which is not necessitated to action. Freedom is thus the inner value of the world. But on the other hand, freedom unrestrained by rules of its conditional employment is the most terrible of all things. The actions of animals are regular; they are performed in accordance with rules which necessitate them subjectively. Mankind apart, nature is not free; through it all there runs a subjectively necessitating principle in accordance with which everything happens regularly. Man alone is free; his actions are not regulated by any such subjectively necessitating principle; if they were, he would not be free. And what then? If the freedom of man were not kept within bounds by objective rules, the result would be the completest savage disorder. There could then be no certainty that man might not use his powers to destroy himself, his fellows, and the whole of nature. I can conceive freedom as the complete absence of orderliness, if it is not subject to an objective determination. The grounds of this objective determination must lie in the understanding, and constitute the restrictions to freedom. Therefore the proper use of freedom is the supreme rule. What then is the condition under which freedom is restricted? It is the law. The universal law is therefore as follows: Let thy procedure be such that in all thine actions regularity prevails. What does this restraint imply when applied to the individual? That he should not follow his inclinations. The fundamental rule, in terms of which I ought to restrain my freedom, is the conformity of free behaviour to the essential ends of humanity. I shall not then follow my inclinations, but bring them under a rule. He who subjects his person to his inclinations, acts contrary to the essential end of humanity; for as a free being he must not be subjected to inclinations, but ought to determine them in the exercise of his freedom; and being a free agent he must have a rule, which is the essential end of humanity. In the case of animals inclinations are already determined by subjectively compelling factors; in their case, therefore, disorderliness is impossible. But if man gives free rein to his inclinations, he sinks lower than an animal because he then lives in a state of disorder which does not exist among animals. A man is then in contradiction with the essential ends of humanity in his own person, and so with himself. All evil in the world springs from freedom. Animals, not being free, live according to rules. But free beings can only act regularly, if they restrict their freedom by rules. Let us reflect upon the actions of man which refer to himself, and consider freedom in them. These spring from impulse and inclinations or from maxims and principles. It is essential, therefore, that man should take his stand upon maxims and restrain by rules the free actions which relate to himself. These are the rules of his self-regarding duties. For if we consider man in respect of his inclinations and instincts, he is loosed from them and determined by neither. In all nature there is nothing to injure man in the satisfaction of his desires; all injurious things are his own invention, the outcome of his freedom. We need only instance strong drink and the many dishes concocted to tickle his palate. In the unregulated pursuit of an inclination of his own devising, man becomes an object of utter contempt, because his freedom makes it possible for him to turn nature inside out in order to satisfy himself. Let him devise what he pleases

683

for satisfying his desires, so long as he regulates the use of his devices; if he does not, his freedom is his greatest misfortune. It must therefore be restricted, though not by other properties or faculties, but by itself. The supreme rule is that in all the actions which affect himself a man should so conduct himself that every exercise of his power is compatible with the fullest employment of them. Let us illustrate our meaning by examples. If I have drunk too much I am incapable of using my freedom and my powers. Again, if I kill myself, I use my powers to deprive myself of the faculty of using them. That freedom, the principle of the highest order of life, should annul itself and abrogate the use of itself conflicts with the fullest use of freedom. But freedom can only be in harmony with itself under certain conditions; otherwise it comes into collision with itself. If there were no established order in Nature, everything would come to an end, and so it is with unbridled freedom. Evils are to be found, no doubt, in Nature, but the true moral evil, vice, only in freedom. We pity the fortunate, but we hate the vicious and rejoice at their punishment. The conditions under which alone the fullest use of freedom is possible, and can be in harmony with itself, are the essential ends of humanity. It must conform with these. The principle of all duties is that the use of freedom must be in keeping with the essential ends of humanity. Thus, for instance, a human being is not entitled to sell his limbs for money, even if he were offered ten thousand thalers for a single finger. If he were so entitled, he could sell all his limbs. We can dispose of things which have no freedom but not of a being which has free will. A man who sells himself makes himself a thing and, as he has jettisoned his person, it is open to anyone to deal with him as he pleases. Another instance of this kind is where a human being makes himself a thing by making himself an object of enjoyment for some one's sexual desire. It degrades humanity, and that is why those guilty of it feel ashamed. We see, therefore, that just as freedom is the source of virtue which ennobles mankind, so is it also the root of the most dreadful vices—such as, for instance, a *crimen carnis contra naturam,* since it can devise all manner of means to satisfy its inclinations. Some crimes and vices, the result of freedom (e.g. suicide), make us shudder, others are nauseating; the mere mention of them is loathsome; we are ashamed of them because they degrade us below the level of beasts; they are grosser even than suicide, for the mention of suicide makes us shudder, but those other crimes and vices cannot be mentioned without producing nausea. Suicide is the most abominable of the vices which inspire dread and hate, but nausea and contempt indicate a lower level still.

Not self-favour but self-esteem should be the principle of our duties towards ourselves. This means that our actions must be in keeping with the worth of man. There are in us two grounds of action; inclinations, which belong to our animal nature, and humanity, to which the inclinations must be subjected. Our duties to ourselves are negative; they restrict our freedom in respect of our inclinations, which aim at our own welfare. Just as law restricts our freedom in our relations with other men, so do our duties to ourselves restrict our freedom in dealing with ourselves. All such duties are grounded in a certain love of honour consisting in self-esteem; man must not appear unworthy in his own eyes; his actions must be in keeping with humanity itself if he is to appear in his own eyes worthy of inner respect. . . .

II

Humility, on the one hand, and true, noble pride on the other, are elements of proper self-respect; shamelessness is its opposite. We have reason to have but a low opinion of ourselves as individuals, but as representatives of mankind we ought to hold ourselves in high esteem. In the light of the law of morality, which is holy and perfect, our defects stand out with glaring distinctness and on comparing ourselves with this standard of perfection we have sufficient cause to feel humble. But if we compare ourselves with others, there is no reason to have a low opinion of ourselves; we have a right to consider ourselves as valuable as another. This self-respect in comparison with others constitutes noble pride. A low opinion of oneself in relation to others is no humility; it is a sign of a little spirit and of a servile character. To flatter oneself that this is virtue is to mistake an imitation for the genuine article; it is monk's virtue and not at all natural; this form of humility is in fact a form of pride. There is nothing unjust or unreasonable in self-esteem; we do no harm to another if we consider ourselves equal to him in our estimation. But if we are to pass judgment upon ourselves we must draw a comparison between ourselves and the purity of the moral law, and we then have cause to feel humble. We should not compare ourselves with other righteous men who, like ourselves, model themselves on the moral law. The Gospel does not teach humility, but it makes us humble.

Our self-esteem may arise from self-love and then it is favour and partiality towards ourselves. This pragmatic self-respect in accordance with rules of prudence is reasonable and possible inasmuch as it keeps us in confidence. No one can demand of me that I should humiliate myself and value myself less than others; but we all have the right to demand of a man that he should not think himself superior. Moral self-esteem, however, which is grounded in the worth of humanity, should not be derived from comparison with others, but from comparison with the moral law. Men are greatly inclined to take others as the measure of their own moral worth, and if they find that there are some whom they surpass it gives them a feeling of moral pride; but it is much more than pride if a man believes himself perfect as measured by the standard of the moral law. I can consider myself better than some others; but it is not very much only to be better than the worst, and there is really not much moral pride in that. Moral humility, regarded as the curbing of our self-conceit in face of the moral law, can thus never rest upon a comparison of ourselves with others, but with the moral law. Humility is therefore the limitation of the high opinion we have of our moral worth by comparison of our actions with the moral law. The comparison of our actions with the moral law makes us humble. Man has reason to have but a low opinion of himself because his actions not only contravene the moral law but are also lacking in purity. His frailty causes him to transgress the law, and his weakness makes his actions fall short of its purity. If an individual takes a lenient view of the moral law, he may well have a high opinion of himself and be conceited, because he judges himself by a false standard. The conceptions which the ancients had of humility and all moral virtues were impure and not in keeping with the moral law. The Gospel first presented morality in its purity, and there is nothing in history to compare with it. But if this humility is wrongly construed, harm may result; for it does not bring courage, but the reverse. Conscious of his shortcomings, a man may feel that his actions can never attain to the level of the moral law and he may give up trying, and simply do nothing. Self-conceit and dejection are the two rocks on which man is wrecked if he deviates, in the one direction or the other, from the moral law. On the one hand, man should not despair, but should believe himself strong enough to follow the moral law, even though he himself is not conformable to it. On the other hand, he ought to avoid self-conceit and an exaggerated notion of his powers; the purity of the moral law should prevent him from falling into this pitfall, for no one who has the law explained to him in its absolute purity can be so foolish as to imagine that it is within his powers fully to comply with it. The existence of this safeguard makes the danger of self-conceit less than that of inertia grounded in faith. It is only the lazy, those who have no wish to do anything themselves but to leave it all to God, who interpret their religion thus. The remedy against such dejection and inertia is to be found in our being able to hope that our weakness and infirmity will be supplemented by the help of God if we but do the utmost that the consciousness of our capacity tells us we are able to do. This is the one and indispensable condition on which we can be worthy of God's help, and have a right to hope for it. In order to convince man of his weakness, make him humble and induce him to pray to God for help, some writers have tried to deny to man any good disposition. This can do no good. It is certainly right and proper that man should recognize how weak he is, but not by the sacrifice of his good dispositions, for if he is to receive God's help he must at least be worthy of it. If we depreciate the value of human virtues we do harm, because if we deny good intentions to the man who lives aright, where is the difference between him and the evildoer? Each of us feels that at some time or other we have done a good action from a good disposition and that we are capable of doing so again. Though our actions are all very imperfect, and though we can never hope that they will attain to the standard of the moral law, yet they may approach ever nearer and nearer to it.

STUDY QUESTIONS

1. Do you agree with Kant that you have moral duties to yourself? If so, in your opinion, what are they?
2. Do you find Kant's arguments against suicide convincing? Do you agree that suicide is "the most abominable of the vices"?
3. Kant says, "The duties we owe to ourselves do not depend on the relation of the action to the ends of happiness." Is our duty,

then, to make *others* happy? No one happy? What does Kant see
our duty to be?

4. A United States Congressman who was found guilty of accepting "Abscam" bribes pleaded before the judge, "Alcoholism
made me lose my judgment." What would Kant say about this
man's self-respect? In which ways, according to Kant, has this
man failed in his duties to himself?

5. What does Kant mean by "worth"? By self-worth? Why does
our human worth demand reverence? What follows when we
lack a sense of self-worth?

Character and Culture

ANTHONY QUINTON

Anthony Quinton (b. 1925) is President of Trinity College, Oxford. He is the author of a number of books
including *The Nature of Things* (1973), *Utilitarian Ethics*
(1973), and *Thoughts and Thinkers* (1982).

Quinton describes the decline of the concepts of character
and will over the past hundred years. The person of character "pursues purposes without being distracted by
passing impulses." Character and will are measured by
strength; thus, persons of very weak character are said to
have "no character." As Quinton understands it, character is very much like self-control. He argues that character is the essence of virtue in the classical sense, since
virtuous persons are those persons of reason who pursue
their principled aims without letting passion interfere.
Character in this sense was recently undermined, says
Quinton, by several historical attacks. One came with the
new sexual liberation espoused by some late Victorians

CHARACTER AND CULTURE Reprinted by permission of *The New Republic,* © 1983, The New
Republic, Inc.

and early twentieth-century rationalists (George Bernard Shaw and Bertrand Russell, for example). Another was initiated by estheticists such as Ruskin and Pater. The result is the current permissive morality in both its passive and ecstatic forms (the latter calling for active indulgence of instincts and drives). Both styles are hostile to character and will. The decline of religion is the third factor in the rise of the "characterless self." The religious impulse is transformed into "radical agitation in the interests of various species of underdog." Yet another concern is the current fear of total extinction that creates a climate of living for the moment, "for tomorrow we die." Quinton notes that the literature of modern moral philosophy has neglected character and will, paying far more attention to what people have a right to than to what sort of person they should be. Quinton calls on moral philosophy to redress the imbalance by attending once again to virtue.

In 1973, in "Art, Will and Necessity," Lionel Trilling wrote:

> The concept of the will no longer figures significantly in the systematic psychology of our day. Those of us who are old enough to have been brought up in the shadow of the nineteenth century can recall how important the will was once thought to be in the conduct of the personal life, how confidently our parents and teachers pointed to the practical as well as the moral advantages of having a will of developed strength and discipline. Nothing could be more alien to the contemporary style of rearing and teaching the young. In the nineteenth century the will was a central and controlling topic in psychological and ethical theory—as how could it not be, given an economic system in which the unshakeable resolve of the industrial entrepreneur was of the essence, and given the temperaments of its great cultural figures?

I would like to reopen this question, to inquire what character and will actually are; and then, mindful of the fact that the word "ethics" means different things in the two main English-speaking countries—moral practice here, moral theory in England—I shall consider the declining presence of character and will in actual moral life and their distinctly marginal, even furtive, role in organized thinking about morality.

Character is different from personality. Personality is the style or form of a person's presentation of himself, typically in more or less short-lived encounters. It is, therefore, something that can be put on and taken off more or less at will, like clothing or makeup, the device which makes it possible to be all things to all men for those who want to be so. The derivation of the word from *persona,* a mask, is not evidence, but it is surely symptomatic. Character, by contrast, is something more deeply rooted, not innate or unalterable, but at least a fairly hard-won achievement; character is the reality of which personality is the appearance. I am treating personality here in the sense which it usually has in colloquial speech. Psychologists engaged in the study of what they call personality apply the word much more widely to cover the whole range of a person's dispositions, character and personality colloquially understood being among those dispositions but not exhausting them.

Character is essential or fundamental and not, like personality, a matter of the surface. It is modifiable by teaching and, in a way, by effort, unlike such innate and constitutional things as temperament, tastes, and intellectual power. It is comparatively unspecific, unlike abilities and skills. My main claim is that it is in essence resolution, determination, a matter of pursuing purposes without being distracted by passing impulses. It is something that is measured in terms of its strength. Its strength, indeed, is its existence, for the weaker it is the closer it comes to nonexistence. In that respect it is like the will, as we ordinarily conceive it. To have a will is to have a fairly strong one. To have a very weak will is the next best thing to having no will at all.

Is this a peculiar, idiosyncratic notion of character? It comprises, at any rate, three of the four virtues that Plato took to be most important: prudence, courage, moderation. Insofar as his fourth virtue, justice, is taken to be impartiality or fairness—the power, that is, to resist the promptings of immediate affection or favor—it is also a quality of character. The qualities of character I have mentioned are all dispositions to resist the immediate solicitations of impulse. Prudence is a settled resistance to whim, courage to fear, temperance to greed, justice or selfishness or particular affections. One could add industriousness as resistance to laziness, reliability as resistance to taking the easiest way. They are, generally speaking, ways of deferring gratification, of protecting the achievement of some valued object in the future from being undermined by the pull of lesser objects near at hand.

In the light of these considerations I propose that the idea of character is procedural rather than substantive. It is not a matter of having a particular set of desires alongside the instinctive, impulsive desires we share with other animals. It is the disposition or habit of controlling one's immediate, impulsive desires, so that we do not let them issue in action until we have considered the bearing of that action on the achievement of other, remoter objects of desire. Understood this way, character is much the same thing as self-control or strength of will. Like them it may be used for bad purposes. But one may suspect that only those of the most delightful innate temperament and preferences can achieve much morally without it, and then only if their circumstances are very safe and easy—that is, if all that is required of a moral agent is kindliness.

The cognitive distinguishing mark of the human species is its reasoning power, the ability that we have, conferred by language, to think about what is outside the immediate zone of perception and to work out what to do to produce or prevent future possibilities, contingent on our action, that we find attractive or repellent. Strength of character, by holding in check impulses excited by what is immediately present, allows the cognitive harvest of our reasoning powers to have an effect on what we do. To conceive character in this way is to give an acceptable sense to the idea that reason can and should control the passions.

In the English-speaking world we live and move amid the ruins of Victorian morality, in which character and will occupied an important place. Its central theme was one of strenuous self-discipline. It was itself a reaction against the consciously nonstrenuous morality of the eighteenth century which preceded it, and which was, in its turn, a reversal of the gloomy fanaticism of the seventeenth century and the epoch of the wars of religion. Character and strength of will were not repudiated by the secular good sense of the Augustans. Long-term aims were essential for the rational management of life and for morality, which was seen as an indispensable part of that code of rational living. But the aims now approved were secular and

691

terrestrial, to be pursued by steady and prudent application, not with guilty fanatical enthusiasm. Hume's words for morally desirable qualities of character are representative: they are, he maintained, those that are "agreeable or useful," the properties, we might feel, more of an ideal weekend guest than of a collaborator in some risky and ambitious undertaking.

The morality of the eighteenth century was a relaxed and elegant version of the ideal of life of the Protestant commercial middle class, which had been progressively reconciled to life on this sinful earth by the worldly success that had accrued to its hard work and foresight. It was such sober and prudent people who established the first European settlement in North America, people of such moderate outlook as to be capable of using turkey for purposes of celebration. Acquiescing in their own good fortune, they found an emblem, after a century and a half, in Benjamin Franklin, a believer in only the most judicious and economical repression of instinct. By the middle of the nineteenth century an altogether more severe and ascetic ideal of life had replaced his genial accommodation of long-term goals and short-term needs.

The main ingredients of Victorianism are nearly all aspects of an ideal of self-reliance. At the top is industry, in which effort is accompanied by scrupulous workmanship. Honesty and fidelity to promises, so advantageous in the nineteenth-century business world of small enterprises, are seen as required in all people's activities. Waste is deplored, so that opportunity should not be let slip and so that provision is made against ill fortune. Sexuality is narrowly confined within the limits of monogamy. Benevolence is confined to the unfortunate; the merely pitiable do not as such deserve it, since they may be simply failures. Decorum must be maintained, serving as a kind of fireproof matting to keep down smoldering impulses to passion and extravagance.

This morality was overcome by two main lines of attack. The first of them is the rationalism of a group of late nineteenth- and early twentieth-century thinkers who sought to revive the Enlightenment, notably Samuel Butler, George Bernard Shaw, and Bertrand Russell. They attacked Victorian ideas about sex, property, the relations of men to women, and of adults to children; and, consequentially, the decorum that they saw as preserving the moral errors they attacked at one level and the religion they saw as sanctifying them at another. They hoped that a new, more rational morality would free people to perfect themselves. These late-Victorian and Edwardian moral reformers were themselves people of strong character, richly endowed with will. Shaw and Russell were very hard workers; Shaw was physically ascetic above and beyond the call of Victorianism, undefiled by drink, meat, or sexuality.

The other line of attack on Victorianism was, as far as England and no doubt the English-speaking world in general is concerned, an import from continental Europe, particularly France. What I have in mind is a sequence of hedonisms, by no means closely related or sympathetic to each other. To start with, there is the decadence of the 1890s, which, in its politer form, was aestheticism, the Paterian life of intense private sensation. After 1918 the sensations pursued become rougher and more primordial, but there is the same desire to shock and to ridicule older pieties. Vulgar Freudianism, the idea that all inhibition is bad, unhealthy, the cause of neurosis, helped to fill the sails of this pleasure-boat. Just as aestheticism had a kind of rural correlate in the sandal-wearing communities of admirers of Ruskin, given to free love or the drinking of fruit juice, so the rural arm of the hedonism of the 1920s was the instinctualism of D. H. Lawrence, who recruited Freud for his own special uses as did the heroines of Scott Fitzgerald and the early Evelyn Waugh.

In our time everyday morality, emancipated from Victorianism, takes two principal forms, corresponding in their rough and popular way to the two lines of moral reform I have described. The first is the negatively permissive morality whose ideal of life is one of passive consumption, of the more or less inert enjoyment of material and, one might say, recreational satisfactions. An important feature is the unloading onto something called "society" of the duty of ensuring that the means of satisfaction are available at minimal cost and effort, and also of the responsibility for the failures and crimes of individuals. The quality most admired is amiability, a sort of uncritical endorsement of the wants and acts of others, free from all trace of censoriousness.

The second is the ecstatic morality that enjoins the unrestricted indulgence of instinct up to, and even beyond, the limits of ordinary self-preservation. It is less widespread than permissiveness, being largely confined to the young. On this view all frustration or inhibition is bad and unhealthy. Older ideas of the natural goodness of mankind are reanimated, often with the qualification that innocence can survive only in communities sequestered from the corrupting influences of the urban, industrial world. [In this system of thought the freaked-out adolescent takes over the role of Wordsworth's baby as "mighty prophet, seer blest."]

Both moral styles are, even at their best, hostile to character and will. For the permissive, strength of character is tiresome and embarrassing, a source of unnecessary trouble, spoiling things by its imposition of disagreeable restraints, souring the enjoyment of life with irrational guilt. For the ecstatic, strength of character is more like a disease, a neurotic deformation of personality fostered by individualism and to be helped by immersion in a collectivity in which selfhood is dismantled. From a point of view which neither would accept, both are juvenile: permissiveness in its idealization of the style of life of the pampered child, receiving presents and having fun; ecstaticism in its idealization of the wholly uncontrolled or runaway child, living wildly with a gang.

There is a great deal of social commentary and description in which the decline of character and will has been recorded, with and without implied attitudes of welcome or distaste. There is also a great deal of explanatory material at hand, ranging from the influence of theories at one extreme to that of new modes of social organization at the other. Of theories the most relevant are those that affirm the motivation of human conduct by forces that agents are not aware of, above all Freudian psychoanalysis. In particular, the Freudian account of the conscience or superego as the product of aggression turned by the individual against himself through fear of the withdrawal of parental love suggests that obedience to its commands is some sort of self-mutilation. Perhaps Freud did not intend his theory of the superego to have the comprehensively undermining effect that it has had. To argue that conscientiousness or a sense of guilt can be pathologically exaggerated need not show that conscientiousness in general is a sickness, let alone that character or strength of will is. Freud himself was the unashamed possessor of a will of great strength. There is an instructive aspect to his account of conscience in what he says about civilization. Although he sees it as having some qualities of a collective neurosis, he takes the renunciation of instinct it requires to be preferable to the alternative of uncontrolled aggressiveness.

Another factor in the emergence of the characterless self is the decline of religion, or at least its transformation into radical agitation in the interests of various species of underdog. Other features of our times that might be cited in an explanatory way are the prospect of total extinction by nuclear war; the relapse to seventeenth-century levels of brutality in politics, intensified by improved technology; the general disappointment of enlightened liberal expectations as crime has increased at home and despotism abroad, particularly in those parts of the world that have secured political independence from the West. But more to the point, I believe, is the enlargement of the institutions in which people work or with which they are otherwise involved. In the first place, that instills feelings of powerlessness and dependence and so contracts the sphere of action of character and will. Secondly, conscientiousness diminishes when the actions to which it prompts us concern our relations to remote, impersonal organizations rather than concrete individuals.

Whatever the correct explanation may be, there can be no doubt of the fact that a large moral change has taken place in the Western, or at any rate English-speaking, world in the twentieth century. Many would see it as primarily a change in the content of morality, in our conceptions of what actions are right and wrong and of what states of affairs our actions should be morally applied to produce or prevent: specifically that hitherto dominant adult males are on the same footing with women and children, and that the supposed rights of those who earn and own should be subordinated to the claims of those who want and need.

What I am suggesting is that such an account of what has happened does not go far enough—that these changes of content or substance are less fundamental than changes of form which have accompanied them and have altered the whole conception of the moral agent. The liberal or progressive proposers of the changes in moral content that have taken place hoped they would provide conditions in which the dominated or unfortunate would be free to express their strength of character in achievement previously impossible for them. Instead we have witnessed the pervasive decline of character.

Character and will have been very much neglected in modern moral philosophy as well as in life. In fact, philosophers have neglected the subjects far longer—ever since philosophical reflection on morality began to be conducted in an independently rational manner, abstracted from, although not necessarily in conflict with, the morality of religion, in the seventeenth century. In the century that followed,

Butler, Hume, and Kant all still concerned themselves with the topic of virtue, which is closely connected with character, since it is partly constitutive of it. But their prime interest was in rightness or duty, which is a property of actions, and only secondarily with the dispositions in agents from which right actions flow.

Since Hume and Kant the topic of virtue has been largely of marginal concern to moral philosophers. Their main concern has been with the question of whether the rightness of acts is intrinsic to them, as Kant and other rationalists like Samuel Clarke supposed, or is a function of the goodness of the consequences which actions of the kind in question can be reasonably expected to produce. Agreeing in general that virtue is the disposition to right action, they have divided into those who see as virtuous only the Kantian motive, which is more or less guaranteed to lead to right action, and those less rigorous thinkers who admit as virtuous any disposition of agents which tends to right action in most cases.

I used to be satisfied with the Humean view. What I now reject in it is the assimilation it makes of virtues in particular and, by implication, of qualities of character in general, to desires, conceived either as settled preferences or as qualities of temperament. Virtues and qualities of character are, I am now convinced, not just given elements in an agent's appetitive constitution, but cultivated and disciplined modes of choice, by which passive appetites are held in check and so brought into contention with longer term purposes. The distinction can be conveniently illuminated by contrasting two ways in which the slightly archaic word "benevolence" can be taken. On the one hand it can be used to refer to a direct appetite or preference for the happiness of others or, again, to settled amiability of temperament. On the other, it can be taken as something more in the nature of a policy, or a principle of giving weight in one's decisions to others' happiness or well-being.

The emphasis was once very different in philosophical reflection on morality. In the classical world the notion of virtue was the primary or fundamental moral notion. The chief question for the moral philosopher, according to Plato and Aristotle, was not so much "what should I do?" asked at some specific juncture, but "how should I live?" or, more exactly, "what sort of person should I be?" Since the early modern period and the resecularization of philosophy the question has become "how am I to find out what I should do?" It is not that that question did not arise for the classical moral thinkers. But the Thrasymachus with whom Socrates argues in the early part of Plato's *Republic* is more a man who does not see that he has a motive for acting justly or rightly than one who is skeptical of conventional beliefs about what it is right or just to do.

Modern moral philosophy, like the rest of philosophy, is inveterately epistemological. And from that point of view, the picking out of certain human dispositions as virtues or morally good qualities of character is secondary. Both Hume and Kant determine the virtuousness of benevolence and fidelity in the one case and conscientiousness in the other by their relation to the independently established moral qualities of actions, that is by their rightness. Cognitively speaking, then, the moral quality of agents is derived from the moral quality of actions. For consequentialists the moral quality of actions is derived in its turn from the value of the states of affairs to which those actions can be reasonably expected to lead.

I have argued that the cognitive pre-occupations of moral philosophers in recent times have led them to ignore virtue, and character generally. It is as if they had seen their task as that of considering the activities of the moral agent in the thick of choice, of the moral critic hoping for some ratification of his critical authority, of the moral disputant involved in disagreement with someone who rejects his moral convictions. There is another perspective from which virtue and character bulk larger. This is the perspective of the moral educator. You have to have some confident idea about what is morally right before you can set about getting people to do it. But it is little use knowing what should be done unless you can get people to do it.

In general outline it seems clear enough that two factors operate in the moral development of the normally brought-up child. The first is simple imitation, the second that pursuit of parental approval which Freud painted in such funereal colors. The fact that virtue and character have such humble beginnings does not undermine or invalidate them. Since we start as minute savages it is inevitable that all our higher achievements should start in some more or less deplorable or undignified Yeatsian rag and bone shop. The fallacy involved in denying that is a curious survival of the pre-Darwinian superstition that the greater cannot come out of the lesser.

Not all development or improvement of character is externally induced. There is such an activity as self-examination; it was a habit for our pious forebears, but we are more likely to be pushed into it by some conspicuous occasion for disgust with ourselves. Morally mature human beings ordinarily acquire certain moral preferences, for courage over cowardice, for equability over petulance. There is no paradox in saying that one can be led by these preferences into the effort of seeking to improve one's character. The fact that in such self-improvement one will need to draw on qualities of character such as determination still does not generate the paradox of using a trait of character to bring itself into existence. The man who says to himself "I really must cultivate more resolution" is in a bit of a fix if he has none whatever. You cannot enter the game with nothing at all or develop the muscle in a missing limb.

There is a weird piece of argument in the ethics of Kant which I always used to ridicule. He said that if nature had intended men to make happiness their overriding end, they would have been fitted out with instincts that led them automatically to it. But, since we have reason, our proper purpose must be something different. I am not yet ready to swallow this whole, but I do now have some sympathy for it. Our instincts are not enough; evolution has organized and modified them, and provided us with a long infancy in which the formation of character can take place. If for no more dignified reason, we should hang on to character for self-defense, as the porcupine does to his prickles or the lobster to his shell.

STUDY QUESTIONS

1. Why does Quinton think of character as a hard-won achievement?

2. Character, says Quinton, is a disposition or habit of controlling one's immediate impulsive desires. Does this commit Quinton to the view that even a very immoral person may have a strong character? Do you see a difference between having a strong character and having a good character? Is having a strong character a necessary condition for being a morally good person?

3. What does Quinton mean when he calls the character a "procedural" rather than a "substantive" concept?

4. Quinton criticizes contemporary society for ignoring the traditional virtues by making a cardinal virtue of "amiability"—"a sort of uncritical endorsement of the wants and acts of others." Do you think his criticism is fair?
5. How and why, according to Quinton, has modern philosophy as a discipline neglected character and will?

On the Nature of Character: Field Notes

ROBERT COLES

Robert Coles (b. 1929) has been at Harvard University for many years, both as clinician and teacher. He is the author of numerous books including *Children in Crisis* (1967), *The Political Life of Children* (1986), and *The Moral Life of Children* (1986).

Robert Coles's discussion of moral character is anecdotal, consisting primarily of what many students and teachers reported about character and character development. Coles "went into the field" seeking insight into the nature of character. He had grown impatient with the psychologist's approach to character and personality, an approach that focuses mainly on disorders and pathology, and that casts little light on "character building" in the moral sense.

Talking to Ruby Bridges—one of the first black children to challenge school segregation in the deep South by daily facing up to the wrath of those who lined up to jeer and curse as she entered the school—Coles was convinced further that the "professional" description of

ON THE NATURE OF CHARACTER: FIELD NOTES By Robert Coles. Reprinted from "America's Schools: Portraits and Perspectives," in *Daedalus,* Journal of the American Academy of Arts and Sciences, Fall 1981. By permission of the publisher.

Ruby as culturally deprived and disadvantaged did scant justice to her bravery and strength of character. His contact with children like Ruby Bridges led Coles to distinguish between character and the capacity for moral *thinking*. The latter, for someone like Lawrence Kohlberg, is central to being moral.

In other field studies, Coles spoke to students and teachers in private schools in New England. Here the students were more articulate, but again Coles was pleased to find that they were "not anxious to have all human behavior [reduced to] psychology or psychopathology." Some of those to whom Coles spoke maintained that the study of literature was an important source for the understanding and the building of character. Returning to the South, Coles spoke to teachers and principals of the more disadvantaged schools. Some told him that they helped their students by insisting on responsibility. "Let these kids work hard and better themselves, and be good members of their families . . . and they'll show character . . . But to me character means an active person who is ready to face the world and make a mark on it." Coles was impressed by the importance of religion in the lives of the more disadvantaged children, and he characterizes the Church as "a lifeline that rescues [some] from the culture of narcissism." Coles concludes by citing with approval Kierkegaard's dictum that "morality is character."

In the Harvard College of the decade after the Second World War, Gordon Allport was a significant figure indeed—interested always in connecting the newly influential social sciences to the ethical and religious concerns of earlier social and psychological scholars: William James, of course, and William McDougall, and farther back, J. S. Mill or John Locke. I still remember a lecture of Allport's in 1950 in which he stressed the distinction between character and personality. He was forever anxious to acknowledge Freud's perceptive, trenchant thrusts into the outer precincts of consciousness, while at the same time remind us what Freud could afford to ignore about himself and certain others: a moral center that was, quite simply, *there*. No amount of psychoanalysis, even an interminable stretch of it, Allport cautioned us—drawing on Freud's givens with respect to human development—can provide a strong conscience to a person who has grown up in such a fashion as to become chronically dishonest, mean-spirited, a liar. "Psychoanalysis can provide insight, can help us overcome inhibitions," we were told, "but it was not meant to be an instrument of 'character building.'" I found recently my old college notes, found that sentence. I had put a big question mark above the phrase "character building," as if to say: What is it, really? I had heard the expression often enough in the Boy Scouts, in Sunday School, and, not least, from my somewhat Puritanical parents. They set great store by virtues they referred to as self-discipline, responsibility, honesty (often described as "the best policy"), and not least, the one my mother most commonly mentioned, "good conduct." Could it be that a social *scientist,* in the middle of the twentieth century, was mentioning such qualities in a college lecture—was, in fact, asking us to consider how they might be evaluated in people, with some accuracy and consistency?[1]

At that time such efforts were still being made, notably by Robert Havighurst and Hilda Taba and their colleagues at the University of Chicago.[2] But as I got nearer and nearer to becoming a doctor, then a pediatrician, then a child psychiatrist, I heard less and less about "character" and more and more about "character disorders"—certain elements of psychopathology that many psychoanalysts today connect with the vicissitudes of what is called "psychosexual development."[3] In his early productive years, before he turned fanciful—if not deranged—Wilhelm Reich placed great emphasis on what he called "character reactions," the particular way each person works out his or her psychodynamic fate. "In the main," he once said, "character proves to be a narcissistic defense mechanism."[4] No doubt

---

[1] A good summary of Allport's sensitive moral and psychological writing is found in *Personality: A Psychological Interpretation* (New York: Holt, 1937).

[2] See R. J. Havighurst and H. Taba, *Adolescent Character and Personality* (New York: Wiley, 1949). Also, more recently, R. Havighurst and R. Peck, *The Psychology of Character Development* (New York: Wiley, 1960).

[3] See *Disorders of Character*, by Joseph Michaels (Springfield, Illinois: Thomas, 1955), for a suggestive discussion, with a first-rate bibliography.

[4] Wilhelm Reich, *Character Analysis*, 3d ed. (New York: Farrar, Straus & Giroux, 1972), p. 169.

such a generalization can be helpful; we are brought closer to the subliminal workings of the mind, and to its historic necessities of symbolic expression and self-protection, in the face of turmoil generated from within, never mind the stresses that "life" manages to bring. But at some point, even the most factual-minded or dispassionately "rational" of psychoanalytic observers, anxious to maintain a "value-free" posture, would be tempted to observe that there is more to the assessment of human beings than an analysis (even one "in-depth") of narcissistic defense mechanisms can provide.

Hitler's mechanisms, Stalin's, those of any number of murderers or thieves, surely offered what Reich called a "character armor"—as do, right now, the mechanisms employed by Mother Theresa's unconscious, and that belonging to Dom Helder of Brazil's Recife, or to such among us in America as Robert Penn Warren or Eudora Welty or, until her death recently, Dorothy Day. At some point the issue becomes decidedly moral—or, in today's flat, impoverished language, a "normative matter." If I may call upon Gordon Allport again, "character is personality evaluated," a descriptive notion that may make up, in its everyday usefulness, for whatever is lost so far as "psychodynamic relevance" goes.

How we go about doing that evaluation is a matter of great import. In recent years character has been of little concern for many of us whose interest is mental life, or the social and cultural life of human beings. The very word may suggest a prescientific age; may remind us of pietistic avowals or moralistic banalities many of us have tried to put behind us; may bring up the spectre of a word being used to protect the privileges of the well-born, the powerful—as if what is at issue is etiquette, polish, a certain appearance or manner of talking and carrying oneself. How much fairer, some say, to judge people through their academic performance, or through standardized tests: no risk of subjectivity, not to mention self-serving partiality. Still, it is not only Emerson, in another age, who suggested that "character is higher than intellect," and who observed that "a great soul will be strong to live, as well as strong to think."[5] Walker Percy today reminds us of those "who get all A's and flunk life."[6] And surely, a

---

[5]In his well-known oration, "The American Scholar," delivered before Harvard's Phi Beta Kappa Society on August 31, 1837.

century that has witnessed learned individuals like Jung and Heidegger embrace Nazism, not to mention any number of intellectuals preach uncritically the virtues of Stalinist totalitarianism, is not going to be completely uninterested in such distinctions as the age-old polarity of knowledge as against wisdom.

In my own working life the question of "character" came up in the early 1960s when my wife and I were getting to know the black children who initiated school desegregation in the South, often against high odds—mob violence, even—and the young men and women who made up the nonviolent sit-in movement. I remember the clinical appraisals, psychological histories, and socioeconomic comments I wrote then. I remember my continuing effort to *characterize* those children, those youths—as if one weighty, academically acceptable adjective after another would, in sum, do the job. Ruby was from a "culturally deprived," a "culturally disadvantaged," family. Tessie's grandmother was illiterate. Lawrence was counterphobic, suffering "deep down" from a mix of anxiety and depression. Martha "projected" a lot. George was prone to "reaction-formations." Jim seemed to have a "character disorder," even a "borderline personality." Fred might well become psychotic later on. Meanwhile, these youthful American citizens were walking past grown men and women who were calling them the foulest of names, who were even threatening to kill them—and such hecklers were escaping sociological and psychological scrutiny in the bargain, while any number of judges were ordering "evaluations" by my kind to be done on sit-in students who were violating the (segregationist) laws, and who were thought to be (and eventually declared by doctors to be) "sick" or "delinquent" or "troubled" or "sociopathic" or "psychopathic." A historic crisis had confronted a region politically, and in so doing, had ripped open the political, economic, racial aspects of our manner of judging others—the direct connection between what the Bible calls "principalities and powers," and what in our everyday life is "normal" or "proper" behavior. One day, as I mumbled some statements suffused with the words of psychiatric theory to "explain" a given child's behavior, my wife said, "You are making her sound as

---

[6]Walker Percy, *The Second Coming* (New York: Farrar, Straus & Giroux, 1980). See also his wonderful collection of essays, which take up the same theme again and again, *The Message in the Bottle* (New York: Farrar, Straus & Giroux, 1975).

if she ought to be on her way to a child guidance clinic, but she is walking into a school building—and no matter the threats, she is holding her head up high, even smiling at her obscene hecklers. Last night she even prayed for them!"

It was my wife's judgment that Ruby Bridges, aged six, was demonstrating to all the world *character*. Even if cognitive psychologists were to declare such a child not old enough to make certain recognitions or distinctions; even if other theorists were to find Ruby unable to do very much moral reasoning or analysis; even if still other social scientists or clinicians were to emphasize her severe "problems"— her imitative habits, her fearful responses, her Oedipal tensions, her moments of blind obedience or terror-struck submission; even if she were to demonstrate to any number of curious observers—armed with questions, tests, stories to be analyzed, crayons to be used on drawing paper—certain handicaps, developmental difficulties, emotional impasses or disorders, cognitive blocks, age-related blind spots; nevertheless, she was managing to face those mobs with a quiet, stoic dignity that impressed her teachers, newspaper reporters, and federal marshals (who escorted her each day to and from school). One of her teachers, as a matter of fact, said that she herself could never submit to such a daily scene—suggesting that moral *behavior* is not necessarily the same thing as a capacity for moral *thinking;* that character may not be something one ascertains through questionnaires or through experiments done on a university campus.

Against such vexing theoretical difficulties (which had become for me a matter of continuing astonishment, if not haunting confusion), a chance to talk again with young people in a variety of school situations was most welcome. My wife and I had spent years visiting a number of Atlanta's high schools, though not George Washington Carver School.[7] We had spent a season visiting a high school north of Chicago, though not Highland Park High School.[8] And we have children in the private schools of New England, though not St. Paul's School. I decided to keep trying to gain some sense of the variations

---

[7]See my *Children of Crisis: A Study of Courage and Fear*, vol. I (Boston: Atlantic-Little, Brown, 1967).

[8]See the section, "Schools" in volume 3 of *Children of Crisis: The South Goes North* (Boston: Atlantic-Little, Brown, 1967).

in the moral life of the young by emphasizing that subject in my planned visits to these three schools, in the hope that more and more of what Anna Freud calls "direct observation" (as opposed to eagerly speculative and all too inclusive and unqualified generalizations) will help us to understand where "personality" ends and "character" begins in the mind's life.

The "methodology" is thoroughly simple—a mere beginning in exploration, but perhaps not an altogether futile way to learn something about certain young people. I asked the principals of the two public high schools and the headmaster of the private school to "select two teachers qualified to judge character"; those teachers would, in turn, select four or so students who, they believe, possess "character" or "high character." When the principals of Highland Park and Carver asked what I meant by such a word, such an expression, I replied simply that I was trying to find out precisely *that*. I told each principal that I wanted to speak with all the students chosen together, rather than separately, and that I wanted to meet also with the two teachers together.

I went to St. Paul's School first. The headmaster had arranged for two teachers to select four students, and we met in a classroom a good distance from the headmaster's office. We were, in a sense, free—no classes, no one to interrupt or keep an eye on what was to be a full morning's discussion. I told the students, two young men and two young women, that I wanted to explore the meaning to them of "character," and we were, with no hesitation, off to a sustained inquiry.

The word was not a strange one for these students; they had heard it used repeatedly, they said, though none had ever really stopped to think about its meaning. Early on one of the young women said, "We talk about 'human nature' or 'personality' or 'identity'; I suppose in the past they talked about 'character.'" Yet these students were quite articulate as they sifted and sorted among themselves and their classmates in search of a definition, a way of looking at a particular subject. In no time a whole school was being morally scrutinized: the "jocks," the "beautiful people," the "social butterflies," the "freaks," the "party people," the "grinds," various teachers, and the "goodly heritage," a phrase many who have gone to St. Paul's have heard again and again.

Much time was spent struggling with the question of arrogance, with the temptation of self-importance and self-centeredness—a personal hazard these four were not loath to acknowledge. They were in a school known as one of the best in America. They were, in different ways, doing well there—one academically; one as a scholar-athlete; one for showing concern and compassion for others, near and afar; one as a person trusted and liked by a wide assortment of classmates. Yet they worried that their success was a temptation to "become stuck-up," as one put it. Self-righteousness and self-consciousness were additional hazards—elements likely to shut a person off, making that person less responsive to other people. Gradually, how one responds to others took on high importance. One of the young men put it this way: "I tend to be a private person. I like to take long walks by myself. At times I don't want company. I want to hold onto my individuality. But I like to be with others, too. I like to be a *friend*. I'd like to think that if someone were in trouble, he'd turn to me, and I'd be there, and I'd put that person's trouble above my needs, including taking a solitary walk!"

Other topics came up frequently: the tension between adjustment to the demands of various cliques and the private values a given individual feels to be important—or put differently, the tension between loyalty to one's friends and loyalty to one's own memories, habits, yearnings; the tension between one's competitive side and one's regard for others; and more crudely, the tension between one's wish to win and one's willingness to help others. The word "honesty" was mentioned over and over—an Augustinian examination, done with today's psychological panache: who is "really" honest, and for what "underlying" reasons? Moreover, does it "pay" in this society to be honest all the time? When do honesty and self-effacement turn into "masochism"? When does pride in one's convictions turn into a bullying egotism? If you really do have "a sense of yourself," are you not in danger of being smug, self-serving, all too sure of your own significance? When does popularity reduce one's individuality to the point that one belongs to a herd, has lost a mind of one's own?

Such questions were asked quite earnestly, and always with regard to the matter at hand: the characteristics of character. When pressed by one another (I ended up being, most of the time, a listener), the students offered lists: a person who sticks to a set of principles; a person who can risk unpopularity, yet is commanding enough to

gain the respect of others; a person who has the courage to be himself, herself; a person who is open-minded, who plays fair with
others, who doesn't lie and cheat and, interestingly enough, deceive
himself, herself. These were students who believed such qualities to
be only partially present. These were students, in fact, who had a
decidedly dialectical turn of mind: "You can try to be a better person,
but it's a struggle. You can be humble, and that way, intimidate
people. You can *use* humility. It's hard to know what's genuine in
people. Sometimes people pretend to be something, but they're really
just the opposite. They flip and they flop. I don't like people who are
sanctimonious. They lecture others, and people take it, but it's out
of fear, or there is guilt, and it's being exploited. Every once in a
while, I prefer someone who puts his cards on the table and shows
he's a real pain in the neck to these holier-than-thou types. Character
doesn't mean being a goody-goody person! If you're that kind of
person, there's a lot of meanness, probably, inside you, or competitiveness that you're not letting on about to others. Maybe you don't
know about it yourself!"

These were, obviously, what we would now call a psychologically
sophisticated breed of youth. Yet, they were (thank God!) not anxious to have all human behavior a matter of psychology or psychopathology—or sociology, either: "There are reasons we end up being
one kind of person or another kind of person, but when you actually
become that person (when you're nice to others most of the time), then
that's a true achievement. A lot of people *don't* become nice, and it's
no excuse to say you had a bad childhood or you never had the right
luck. I think you have to take your troubles and overcome them!"
The Puritan spirit lives still in the woods of southern New Hampshire, no matter the references—and they were many—to "adolescence," "identity," Sigmund Freud's ideas, the latest notions of what
"motivates" people, what makes us "anxious" or "strung out" or
"ambivalent."

More than anything else, these four youths grappled with what
used to be commonly called "the meaning of life" in philosophy
lectures (before the advent of logical positivism, computers, the li-
bido theory, and a strictly materialist view of life, liberty, the pursuit
of happiness). One of the young men said this toward the end of our
meeting time: "What matters—don't you think?—is what you *do*
with your life. I've tried to be independent, to have my own
thoughts, but to listen to others. I hope to live comfortably, but I

hope I won't be greedy and selfish. I don't know what our responsibilities are—to ourselves and our friends and family and neighbors, and to others in places abroad I'll never even see. Even today, this is a big world. What are we supposed to do? We're lucky to be here at St. Paul's. We have such a good life. What do we owe others? Isn't that 'character'—what you decide to do for others, not just yourself?"

The "great suck of self," Walker Percy calls it in *The Second Coming*—the inevitable pull toward our own thoughts, our own wishes, our navels. Adolescence is not the only period of self-absorption, these youths seemed already to know. For them, one is likely to be neither bad nor good. For them, character was no categorical trait. For them, character is not a possession, but something one searches for: a quality of mind and heart one struggles for, sometimes with a bit more success than at other times. Not one of these four wanted to spell out a definition, set down a compulsory series of attributes, offer a list of candidates. One heard from their mouths expressions of confusion, annoyance, vanity, self-satisfaction, self-criticism, self-doubt, self-assurance. One heard, maybe most of all, tentativeness—a reluctance to speak definitively about an aspect of human behavior one student kept describing as "hard to pin down," but also as "important to consider when you're thinking about someone."

The two teachers I met at St. Paul's school, a middle-aged man who taught math, a young woman who taught English, had met, discussed the subject of "character," and added to one another's notions, so that, in the end, there was a final written statement available:

- The aggregate of distinctive qualities belonging to an individual
- Moral vigor or firmness, especially as acquired through self-discipline
- The ability to respond to a setback
- The ability to form an attachment to ideals of a larger community or organization than oneself, and to exert one's influence for the good of the greater body
- The possession of a sense of humor that allows one to see that there is more to life than living
- The ability to be an *individual* in a crowd of *different* people
- A sense of self that has been found through experience
- The ability to allow others to be individuals, even though they may be different

- The ability to disagree with others without condemning (or losing respect for) the individual one disagrees with
- A sensitivity toward the feelings of others
- An understanding of the wholeness of other people's personalities or character (even when it is different from one's own)

These were two individuals who had thought long and hard about a vexing subject—whom to chose, and why? A very bright person, involved in many activities, able to speak coherently and easily, headed straight for Harvard, as against a quiet person who defers to the ideas of others in a classroom, does well, but "not all that well," yet in numerous moments seems to reach out for others, not to save them, or turn them into psychiatric cases, but simply "to do a good turn"? A marvelous athlete who also is a leader in many ways during the course of a school year, as against a hardworking youth who is most often self-effacing, yet managed to stand up once or twice on a matter of ethical principle, no matter the risks and the penalties? And surely a host of alternatives, because, as one teacher put it, "when you judge 'character,' you judge the overall person and compare him, or her, to others, and you do so over time, the school year."

In Highland Park, north of Chicago, a somewhat different arrangement had been made. The principal of this suburban high school had selected two teachers, as I requested, but they had picked four students each—seven girls and one boy, interestingly enough. We met in a room across the hall from the principal's office. Twice he asked how we were doing, offered water, tea, coffee—in general, showed a distinct, active interest in our discussions. He himself had thought about the word "character," and as with so many of us, found it a bit puzzling and elusive. So did the students I spent a winter morning with. Several of them said that character had a lot to do with personality; in fact, declared "a good personality" or a "well-rounded person" to be equivalent descriptions to "good character" or "high character." Two young women dissented, however: "Character has to do with honesty. You can be popular, and have a shrink's seal of approval, but not have character!"

We fairly quickly got into a discussion of ethnic and racial tensions—in the school, in our society as a whole. At St. Paul's the

709

cliques were enumerated, as if they threatened individuality, hence character, through the requirements of social cohesion; at Highland Park High School the dominant social divisions, at least for these students, had to do with class and race: Italians and Jews, "working people" and "wealthier people," blacks and whites.

I was given some outspoken lessons in how one's family life affects one's situation in school, and not least, one's character: "It all depends on who you are! Some kids want to go to an Ivy League school; that's all that's on their minds. They put up a good front, to show they have 'character'; they join clubs, and have all these hobbies and interests, so as to impress the teachers and the people who read college applications. Some kids have to work while going to school. They try to get a good deal, a job that pays well. They're making contacts even now for later on. It's built into their 'character' that the world is tough, and you have to know people to get ahead. A lot of the black kids are here because there's a military base in the school district. They come and then they go. It's hard to figure them out. It's in their 'character' to stay away from us whites. There's a lot of tension among us whites. Go into the johns, and you'll see a lot of writing! [I went, and I saw the ethnic slurs.] But a lot of the time we get along pretty well. We've got brainy ones here, headed for college since they were born, and don't get in their way, or else! We've got kids who will work in a store or a factory, and not be ashamed. They see the world different. They take different courses. They have their own code."

The speaker is a wry, outspoken, somewhat detached young woman, bound for college, but "not a fancy one." She is neither Italian nor Jewish, but Anglo-Irish. She had made a certain virtue out of marginality, and the others in the room seemed a bit deferential: "She isn't pushed around by anyone. She's her own person. She can mingle with anyone. She doesn't put on airs with anyone." The associations moved relentlessly from social situation to moral conduct—not the first time, or the last, such a progression would be made for me in the course of this study. "You have to know where the person is coming from," I was told several times. Explain! "Well, if you've got a lot going for you, then you can be more relaxed. True, you can be a tightwad and be rich; but it's easier to be generous if you've got a lot behind you!" On the other hand, one student insisted, "there's still room for being poor and good in this world!"

She persisted: "I know some kids, right in this school, and they're not here now, they weren't chosen to be here, and they're from pretty poor families, compared to others; their fathers just get by, make a living. And they would give you the shirt off their backs, those kids: that's character. And they wouldn't go talking about what they've done, bragging, and showing off—*that's* character! Some people, they know how to play up to the teachers, and they get a big reputation, but what's the *truth* about them? What are they like when no one is looking, and what are they like when no one is listening?"

We touched many bases. Class and character. Egotism and character. Psychology and character. Smartness and character. Motivation and character. Caring and character. Manners and character. To be stuck-up. To be considerate. To be a help when a person needs help—a flat tire, a car ride, a pencil or piece of paper, a loan of money, a sympathetic ear. To take risks, extend oneself to others, brave social pressures. Grade-mongers. Leaders and followers. Hypocrites. People who have one or another veneer. The "way-down-deep truth" of a person. A final test of character: sickness, financial straits, a disaster. Character and mental health.

Part of *Ordinary People* had been made in Highland Park. The students had watched the filming, and they wondered: If one is hurt, bewildered, "seeing a shrink," can one have the "mental peace" to demonstrate character? Consumerism, selfishness—can one defy them, develop "an ability not to be absorbed with objects." And at some interesting and suggestive length: literature as a means of understanding character, as in *To Kill a Mockingbird* (Atticus had character, he was open-minded, stood up for what he believed, no matter the risks and costs, and so was a "moral man"); or as in *Macbeth* (Lady Macbeth was a "bad person," a "bad character"). And politics: Lincoln and Eisenhower and Truman had character; Johnson lacked it, as do Nixon and Carter. "All politicians probably lie," one student observed, "and maybe all people do, but some just keep on lying, and you can't trust them, and you don't like them, and they're just no damn good, and you can tell, after awhile, even if they tell you they pray every other minute! The truth about a person's character eventually comes out, *eventually*."

Such faith was not universally shared. There was much talk of appearance as against reality: the way people present themselves to others, as opposed to some inner truth about each of us. In contrast

711

to the students at St. Paul's School, these students were distinctly more interested in the relationship between a person's social, economic, ethnic, or racial background—a person's circumstances—and that person's behavior, hence character. And it did come down to that, they all agreed at the end: "You are the way you act—in the long run." What did that qualification mean? Well, it goes like this: "Some people can put on an act. But if you keep your wits, and keep an eye on them, you find out the truth about them. If they're good people, kind to others, not just wrapped up in themselves, you'll find it out. If they're putting on a production, you'll find that out." No one, in that regard, seemed to have any doubts about his or her ultimate psychological acuity—or about the long-run dramatic capacities of one or another individual.

There was, as we were ending, a spirited, occasionally tense discussion of tests, grades, the criteria used by colleges and graduate schools to evaluate people. "I know kids who get all A's, and would murder their parents, their brothers and sisters, if they stood in their way," one youth offered. Yes, but there's plenty of nastiness to go around, others said, even among those who do poorly in school. What *should* various committees of admission do? How *does* one make a fairly accurate moral judgment about a person? Numbers may not tell enough. Multiple choice questions may not do justice to life's strangeness—the ironies and ambiguities, the complexities and inconsistencies and contradictions we all struggle with, though some with more decency and integrity and generosity of spirit than others. But how do we arrive at an estimate of a person's essential kindness with respect to others—in the face of thousands of importunate applicants, each putting on the very best face possible? Don't interviews have *their* hazards, the unpredictable variations of mood and temperament, the nuances of subjectivity which can, alas, of a sudden, amount to outright prejudice? We ended on an eclectic note—the desirability of taking a lot into consideration when accepting people for a job, a place in a college, and yes, when judging that elusive concept "character." The last person to leave the room, the young woman who spoke least, said that she thought "character meant being kind and good, even when there was no one to reward you for being kind and good."

These were students acutely aware of the divisions in this society—as Tillie Olsen put it in her story O Yes, the ways we "sort." The two

Highland Park High School teachers were similarly sensitive to issues of "class and caste," as the splits among us have sometimes been
described. Actually, the teachers were themselves a bit split. The
assistant principal, a man, is quite in touch with the more academic
students of the school; whereas the woman teacher is very much
involved with those students who are working at jobs while trying
to get through Highland Park—and who are headed, mostly, for
what many social scientists would call "service jobs," or membership
in the "working class," or the "lower-middle to middle-middle-
class," and on and on. The two did not argue, however; in fact, they
largely echoed the sentiments of their chosen students: "Grades aren't
the whole story, by any means"; and very emphatically, "Character
has something to do with moral life."

Both teachers worried about class—expressed concern, for instance, that "mere etiquette" can deceive, or insisted that human
scoundrels, like wolves, find sheepskins ("social veneer") aplenty to
wear. I heard practically nothing about class-connected deceit at St.
Paul's, a lot about it at Highland Park—and character seemed to
require, everyone agreed, an impressive absence of such a tendency.
Moreover, psychiatry and psychoanalysis were even more prominently mentioned than at St. Paul's—a way of getting to the "deeper
truth" about people, hence to a judgment of their character. (Fallout
from *Ordinary People?*) As already mentioned, disturbed people were
described as less likely to show high character. When I mentioned
Gandhi's personal eccentricities, if not moments of cruelty, vanity,
thoughtlessness, the students were ready, all too ready, to take the
clue, the hint, and write him off as sick. When I reminded them that
he was, yet, a rather impressive moral leader, the students worried
about the burdens placed on his family, and about his own psychiatric ones.

If I had a little trouble persuading this group of students and their
teachers that, neurosis or no neurosis, a person's moral motives can
affect his or her character, they had no trouble letting me know that
a neighborhood, a level of income, the possession of a given nationality, can all affect a person's character. The teachers especially emphasized the distinction between the quietly considerate person, as
against the demonstrative, if not flamboyant, doer of public good
deeds, a performer of sorts. "Some students want to get an A in character, too," one teacher said, as we broke off, a reminder that not

only can life be unfair, as one American president took pains to remind us, but virtue can be unfairly perceived—when, in truth, sins are being shrewdly masked. As Flannery O'Connor observed, through the comic irony of a title to one of her stories, a good man is hard to find—and maybe, when the pressures are high, almost impossible to take for granted.

At George Washington Carver High School, in Atlanta, Georgia, I had quite another discussion, with the principal ready to point out the extreme hazards to what he called "character formation" well before I saw (in a room that belonged, really, to his office suite) the four children (two boys and two girls) and two teachers (both women, one who teaches math, the other biology). "There is a problem with drugs," he explained. "There is a problem with poverty, with terrible poverty, with welfare homes, with absent fathers, with unemployment all over the place." He gave me a lively lecture of the school's history—once a "dumping ground for school failures," now a "place of hope," much connected to businesses that offer promising black youths a great variety of jobs, a chance "to enter the mainstream," in the principal's words. In time I was able to begin talking with the four selected youths, though not before being told emphatically: "Character is something you have to build, right here in this school, every day. You have to lay down the law, and see that it's enforced. Character means discipline and hard work and looking to the future and getting there!" Of the three school leaders, Carver's principal was the only one to volunteer (or hazard) such an explication.

The students were not averse to this line of reasoning. These were young people who were determined to find jobs, determined to be hard workers, strong parents—and not reluctant to explain why such a commitment was connected to a definition, in their minds, of the word "character": "A lot of us, even here, with the principal and the teachers bearing down every minute on us, have trouble reading and writing. We're not going to college, most of us. We're going to try to get a job and hold onto it! It takes character, I think, to do that— not take the easy way out and drink or use drugs or say the white man is on our backs, so what the devil can we do! To me, character is being stubborn. It's staying in there, it's getting out of a hole, and breathing the fresh air, and not falling down anymore."

My wife and I spent three years in Atlanta, talking with youths such as these—young black men and women trying, in the face of adversity, to forge a better life for themselves. These were more outspoken and self-assured individuals than the ones we got to know in the early 1960s. They were quick to describe themselves as "job-hungry" and as full of determination, willfulness, hopeful anticipation. They were not, though, uninterested in some of the refinements of psychology I had heard discussed in Illinois and New Hampshire: "There's success and success. It's not only getting there, it's how you get there. If you have character, that means you keep trying, no matter how hard it is, and you don't lose your soul while you're doing that. You have to say to yourself, 'I'll go so far and no farther.' You have to draw the line, and if you do, and you can hold to it, you've got character." Nods all around, followed by smiles of recognition as the temptations get mentioned: white devils and black devils who offer serious distractions in the form of drugs and booze, bribes and payoffs, an assortment of "tricks." These are street-smart kids, and they have lots of savvy about Atlanta politics, Atlanta vice, Atlanta hypocrisy, black and white alike. Their moralism and self-conscious, urgently stated rectitude is hard earned, if (they seem to know) not entirely invulnerable.

One pushes the word "character," gets responses connected to hardship, ambition, the requirements of people living on the edge, hence with little interest in metaphysical or metapsychological speculation. Character? Why, J. R. in *Dallas* lacks it, utterly; Dr. King had it, that's for sure. Character? A lot of big shots may seem to have it, but too bad more people don't know who is scratching whose back. On the other hand, there's a woman who works in a Howard Johnson's motel, and she lost her husband from cancer, and she has five kids, and she has two of them out of high school and in good jobs, and the other three are headed that way, and she doesn't stand for any foolishness, *none,* and she takes those kids to church every Sunday, and they pray hard and long, and she has character, in case anyone wants to know! The church—at long last it comes up in a talk about character! Not in a school that bears the name of St. Paul, no less; and not in a school where Catholics and Jews seem ready to square off at each other all day, every day; but in Carver, you bet. Each of these four high-school-age Americans (no fools about getting high or about the demands of the flesh or about the various shortcuts people take) goes to church on Sundays, and if there is reluctance sometimes (the joy of a late sleep), there is, after all, no real choice: "We have to go. Our mother says we have to go, and once we're there, I don't half mind! I like it there. I'll make my kids go, too."

Much talk of "uplift." Much reference to "building" oneself into "a stronger person," getting "on the map." How? There are auto repair shops. There are radio and TV repair shops. There are cosmetology shops. There are dry-cleaning places. There are tailoring and sewing and shoe repair places. There is a big airport, and people work there—on engines if they are on top, otherwise as cleaning people or doing errands, or driving buses and taxis, "lots of things." (No angst about capitalism at Carver!) If you get one of those jobs, and you hold onto it; if you get yourself a girlfriend or a boyfriend, and they become a wife or a husband, and you become a father or a mother, and you "stay with it," and be good to your family, earn them a living, take care of them; if you remain loyal to your church, and pray to God when you're weak; if you don't forget your people, and try to lend a hand to the ones who didn't make it, who stumbled and fell and are hurt and sad and wondering what the point of it all is, and maybe have done wrong, done it too many times—if all that is "inscribed on your soul," then, by God, you have character, and it's important to say "by God," because it's "His grace that does things."

"I'm not as small after church as I am before church," one of these four told me—a lifeline that rescues at least one American, temporarily, from "the culture of narcissism." As for "good manners," they aren't superficial at all; they tell of something very deep down, no matter what so-called depth psychologists have to say, not to mention those who make of them religious figures: "You can tell a person by how he speaks to you. If he's respectful, then he's good; if he gives you the shoulder, then he's bad. I don't care if someone has a lot of bad in him. If he keeps it a secret from the whole world, then he's way out front. If he shows his bad self to everyone, he's putting it on us, man, and it's hard enough without that—another hassle to deal with. My grandmother tells us: 'Keep your mouth shut if there's no good to come out of it. Keep your mischief to yourself. We've all got it—but some of us don't show it off.' She's right; she has character."

Some other virtues that bespeak character: punctuality; how you carry yourself; an ability to laugh, when there's a good excuse for crying or shouting or shaking your fists; how you speak—with clear enunciation of words, so that others may hear you; self-respect, as measured by neatness and choice of clothes, as well as respect for others, as measured by a smile, a please, a thank you; obedience—to your elders, to the law, to your own self-evident ideas of what is right and wrong. "We all stray," said one of the young women, "but if we try hard not to keep repeating ourselves, and if we're not afraid to learn from our mistakes, and if we're willing to work hard, and sacrifice, then we have character." Pieties, all those remarks, the skeptical, psychoanalyzed liberal Yankee muses—fighting off embarrassment, wonder, a touch of awe, and emotional memories of other youths in other Atlanta spots, youths similarly hard-pressed, who managed to "overcome," and youths similarly unwilling to be self-pitying in the face of the severe inequities of this life.

The two teachers—my wife got to know so many very much like these two: tough-minded, outspoken, a touch contemptuous of anyone who wants to offer sympathy, never mind condolences. They are demanding, insistent, forceful women: "Let these kids work hard, and better themselves, and be good members of their families, and they'll show character; that's how, the only way!" And candidly, bluntly, unapologetically: "We chose the best we have to talk with you. We chose the smart ones, the ones who could talk with you and get themselves across. We have others here who would tax your patience and understanding. Maybe they have 'character,' too. I don't think character is the property of the lucky and the smart and the successful, no sir. But to me, character means an active person, who is ready to face the world, and make a mark on it. That's why I chose these kids. They're ready, they're ready to turn their backs on all their troubles, our troubles, and be good—be full of action. 'Never be lazy,' I tell my kids at home, and here in school. There's that expression: going to meet 'the man.' Well, I say we can become 'the man' ourselves. We can take control of our own lives, be our own masters. It may be preachy of me to talk like this, but we've got to pep-talk ourselves, and then *get on with it!* I pray to God—we need His help badly—that more and more of these kids at Carver *will* get on with it."

On the way home, back North again, I took out my books and papers: notes to write, ideas to savor, comparisons to make. There it was, the wonderful message that Kierkegaard gave us over a century ago, the message I often wish a few of us theorists of moral development would keep in constant mind: "Morality is character, character is that which is engraved (χαράσσοω); but the sand and the sea have no character and neither has abstract intelligence, for character is really inwardness. Immorality, as energy, is also character; but to be neither moral nor immoral is merely ambiguous, and ambiguity enters into life when the qualitative distinctions are weakened by a gnawing reflection."[9]

He was a great one for leaps, that nineteenth century version of the melancholy (if spiritedly so) Dane. I wondered on my flight home whether he might somewhere in this universe be smiling, be assenting to the message, the slightly hectoring statement delivered by that mathematics teacher, and later by her tough, occasionally *very* tough, principal, who told me that he had "a lot of bad characters" to deal with, but damned if he couldn't "take them on," "turn them around," "convert their wasted energy into useful energy." It all sounded slightly like the noise of strained braggadocio: I'll talk big, and hope for the best. It all sounded exaggerated, romantic—like Kierkegaard. It all sounded pretty good, though, to those four young people and two of their teachers.

STUDY QUESTIONS

1. Coles notes that certain learned individuals (Carl Jung, Martin Heidegger among them) embraced Nazism. What moral does Coles draw about the relevant importance of character and intellect? Do you find his point of view persuasive?
2. What does Coles seem to mean by "character"? Explain how Ruby Bridges demonstrated character. Is Coles's notion of character naive? Profound? Discuss.
3. Contrast Coles and Kohlberg on moral development, and assess the relative merits of their approaches.
4. Look over the list of twelve character traits that emerge from the discussion of St. Paul. Choose three that you consider the most important and defend your choices.

---

[9]Søren Kierkegaard, *The Present Age*, translated by Alexander Dru (New York: Harper & Row, 1962), p. 43.

The New Narcissism

CHRISTOPHER LASCH

Christopher Lasch (b. 1932) is a professor of history at the University of Rochester. He is the author of a number of books, including *Haven in a Heartless World* (1977) and *The Culture of Narcissism* (1979).

Christopher Lasch describes a new personal ideal that emphasizes living for the moment, and being for oneself. The "new narcissists" feel free to abandon their social roles (for example, as parent or citizen) for the higher purpose of self-fulfillment by self-gratification. The goal of these new individuals is "personal well-being, health, and psychic security." Seeking this goal is incompatible with a direct concern for politics. Nevertheless, Lasch observes that narcissists are sometimes radical politically when the risks give them a sense of well-being and importance. Lasch distinguishes between the nineteenth-century ideal of the rugged individualist and the new individualist ideal. The former were outwardly oriented; they saw the world as a "wilderness to be shaped by [their] own design." Contemporary individualists are self-absorbed; for them, "the world is a mirror." Lasch warns that the new narcissists cannot succeed since the psychic equilibrium of any individual requires "submission to the rules of social intercourse." By denying themselves a social role, narcissists leave themselves open to a sense

THE NEW NARCISSISM Reprinted from *The Culture of Narcissism: American Life in an Age of Diminishing Expectations,* by Christopher Lasch, by permission of W. W. Norton & Company, Inc. Copyright ©1979 by W. W. Norton & Company, Inc.

of inner emptiness. By their self-absorption they live a life of self-gratification in which love plays no part.

The Waning of the Sense of Historical Time

As the twentieth century approaches its end, the conviction grows that many other things are ending too. Storm warnings, portents, hints of catastrophe haunt our times. The "sense of an ending," which has given shape to so much of twentieth-century literature, now pervades the popular imagination as well. The Nazi holocaust, the threat of nuclear annihilation, the depletion of natural resources, well-founded predictions of ecological disaster have fulfilled poetic prophecy, giving concrete historical substance to the nightmare, or death wish, that avant-garde artists were the first to express. The question of whether the world will end in fire or in ice, with a bang or a whimper, no longer interests artists alone. Impending disaster has become an everyday concern, so commonplace and familiar that nobody any longer gives much thought to how disaster might be averted. People busy themselves instead with survival strategies, measures designed to prolong their own lives, or programs guaranteed to ensure good health and peace of mind.

Those who dig bomb shelters hope to survive by surrounding themselves with the latest products of modern technology. Communards in the country adhere to an opposite plan: to free themselves from dependence on technology and thus to outlive its destruction or collapse. A visitor to a commune in North Carolina writes: "Everyone seems to share this sense of imminent doomsday." Stewart Brand, editor of the *Whole Earth Catalogue,* reports that "sales of the *Survival Book* are booming; it's one of our fastest moving items." Both strategies reflect the growing despair of changing society, even of understanding it, which also underlies the cult of expanded consciousness, health, and personal "growth" so prevalent today.

After the political turmoil of the sixties, Americans have retreated to purely personal preoccupations. Having no hope of improving their lives in any of the ways that matter, people have convinced themselves that what matters is psychic self-improvement: getting in touch with their feelings, eating health food, taking lessons in ballet or belly-dancing, immersing themselves in the wisdom of the East, jogging, learning how to "relate," overcoming the "fear of pleasure." Harmless in themselves, these pursuits, elevated to a program and wrapped in the rhetoric of authenticity and awareness, signify a retreat from politics and a repudiation of the recent past. Indeed Americans seem to wish to forget not only the sixties, the riots, the new left, the disruptions on college campuses, Vietnam, Watergate, and the Nixon presidency, but their entire collective past, even in the antiseptic form in which it was celebrated during the Bicentennial. Woody Allen's movie *Sleeper,* issued in 1973, accurately caught the mood of the seventies. Appropriately cast in the form of a parody of futuristic science fiction, the film finds a great many ways to convey the message that "political solutions don't work," as Allen flatly announces at one point. When asked what he believes in, Allen, having ruled out politics, religion, and science, declares: "I believe in sex and death—two experiences that come once in a lifetime."

To live for the moment is the prevailing passion—to live for yourself, not for your predecessors or posterity. We are fast losing the sense of historical continuity, the sense of belonging to a succession of generations originating in the past and stretching into the future. It is the waning of the sense of historical time—in particular, the erosion of any strong concern for posterity—that distinguishes the spiritual crisis of the seventies from earlier outbreaks of millenarian religion, to which it bears a superficial resemblance. Many commentators have seized on this resemblance as a means of understanding the contemporary "cultural revolution," ignoring the features that distinguish it from the religions of the past. A few years ago, Leslie Fiedler proclaimed a "New Age of Faith." More recently, Tom Wolfe has interpreted the new narcissism as a "third great awakening," an outbreak of orgiastic, ecstatic religiosity. Jim Hougan, in a book that seems to present itself simultaneously as a critique and a celebration of contemporary decadence, compares the current mood to the millennialism of the waning Middle Ages. "The anxieties of the Middle Ages are not much different from those of the present," he writes. Then as now, social upheaval gave rise to "millenarian sects."

Both Hougan and Wolfe inadvertently provide evidence, however, that undermines a religious interpretation of the "consciousness movement." Hougan notes that survival has become the "catchword of the seventies" and "collective narcissism" the dominant disposition. Since "the society" has no future, it makes sense to live only for

721

the moment, to fix our eyes on our own "private performance," to become connoisseurs of our own decadence, to cultivate a "transcendental self-attention." These are not the attitudes historically associated with millenarian outbreaks. Sixteenth-century Anabaptists awaited the apocalypse not with transcendental self-attention but with ill-concealed impatience for the golden age it was expected to inaugurate. Nor were they indifferent to the past. Ancient popular traditions of the "sleeping king"—the leader who will return to his people and restore a lost golden age—informed the millenarian movements of this period. The Revolutionary of the Upper Rhine, anonymous author of the *Book of a Hundred Chapters,* declared, "The Germans once held the whole world in their hands and they will do so again, and with more power than ever." He predicted that the resurrected Frederick II, "Emporer of the Last Days," would reinstate the primitive German religion, move the capital of Christendom from Rome to Trier, abolish private property, and level distinctions between rich and poor.

Such traditions, often associated with national resistance to foreign conquest, have flourished at many times and in many forms, including the Christian vision of the Last Judgment. Their egalitarian and pseudohistorical content suggests that even the most radically otherworldly religions of the past expressed a hope of social justice and a sense of continuity with earlier generations. The absence of these values characterizes the survivalist mentality of the seventies. The "world view emerging among us," writes Peter Marin, centers "solely on the self" and has "individual survival as its sole good." In an attempt to identify the peculiar features of contemporary religiosity, Tom Wolfe himself notes that "most people, historically, have *not* lived their lives as if thinking, 'I have only one life to live.' Instead they have lived as if they are living their ancestors' lives and their offspring's lives. . . ." These observations go very close to the heart of the matter, but they call into question his characterization of the new narcissism as a third great awakening.

The Therapeutic Sensibility

The contemporary climate is therapeutic, not religious. People today hunger not for personal salvation, let alone for the restoration of an earlier golden age, but for the feeling, the momentary illusion, of personal well-being, health, and psychic security. Even the radicalism of the sixties served, for many of those who embraced it for personal rather than political reasons, not as a substitute religion but as a form of therapy. Radical politics filled empty lives, provided a sense of meaning and purpose. In her memoir of the Weathermen, Susan Stern described their attraction in language that owes more to psychiatry and medicine than to religion. When she tried to evoke her state of mind during the 1968 demonstrations at the Democratic National Convention in Chicago, she wrote instead about the state of her health. "I felt good. I could feel my body supple and strong and slim, and ready to run miles, and my legs moving sure and swift under me." A few pages later, she says: "I felt real." Repeatedly she explains that association with important people made her feel important. "I felt I was part of a vast network of intense, exciting and brilliant people." When the leaders she idealized disappointed her, as they always did, she looked for new heroes to take their place, hoping to warm herself in their "brilliance" and to overcome her feeling of insignificance. In their presence, she occasionally felt "strong and solid"—only to find herself repelled, when disenchantment set in again, by the "arrogance" of those whom she had previously admired, by "their contempt for everyone around them."

Many of the details in Stern's account of the Weathermen would be familiar to students of the revolutionary mentality in earlier epochs: the fervor of her revolutionary commitment, the group's endless disputes about fine points of political dogma, the relentless "self-criticism" to which members of the sect were constantly exhorted, the attempt to remodel every facet of one's life in conformity with the revolutionary faith. But every revolutionary movement partakes of the culture of its time, and this one contained elements that immediately identified it as a product of American society in an age of diminishing expectations. The atmosphere in which the Weathermen lived—an atmosphere of violence, danger, drugs, sexual promiscuity, moral and psychic chaos—derived not so much from an older revolutionary tradition as from the turmoil and narcissistic anguish of contemporary America. Her preoccupation with the state of her psychic health, together with her dependence on others for a sense of selfhood, distinguish Susan Stern from the kind of religious seeker who turns to politics to find a secularized salvation. She needed to establish an identity, not to submerge her identity in a larger cause.

The narcissist differs also, in the tenuous quality of his selfhood, from an earlier type of American individualist, the "American Adam" analyzed by R. W. B. Lewis, Quentin Anderson, Michael Rogin, and by nineteenth-century observers like Tocqueville. The contemporary narcissist bears a superficial resemblance, in his self-absorption and delusions of grandeur, to the "imperial self" so often celebrated in nineteenth-century American literature. The American Adam, like his descendants today, sought to free himself from the past and to establish what Emerson called "an original relation to the universe." Nineteenth-century writers and orators re-stated again and again, in a great variety of forms, Jefferson's doctrine that the earth belongs to the living. The break with Europe, the abolition of primogeniture, and the looseness of family ties gave substance to their belief (even if it was finally an illusion) that Americans, alone among the people of the world, could escape the entangling influence of the past. They imagined, according to Tocqueville, that "their whole destiny is in their own hands." Social conditions in the United States, Tocqueville wrote, severed the tie that formerly united one generation to another. "The woof of time is every instant broken and the track of generations effaced. Those who went before are soon forgotten; of those who will come after, no one has any idea: the interest of man is confined to those in close propinquity to himself."

Some critics have described the narcissism of the 1970s in similar language. The new therapies spawned by the human potential movement, according to Peter Marin, teach that "the individual will is all powerful and totally determines one's fate"; thus they intensify the "isolation of the self." This line of argument belongs to a well-established American tradition of social thought. Marin's plea for recognition of "the immense middle ground of human community" recalls Van Wyck Brooks, who criticized the New England transcendentalists for ignoring "the genial middle ground of human tradition." Brooks himself, when he formulated his own indictment of American culture, drew on such earlier critics as Santayana, Henry James, Orestes Brownson, and Tocqueville. The critical tradition they established still has much to tell us about the evils of untrammeled individualism, but it needs to be restated to take account of the differences between nineteenth-century Adamism and the narcissism of our own time. The critique of "privatism," though it helps to keep alive the need for community, has become more and more misleading as the possibility of genuine privacy recedes. The contemporary American may have failed, like his predecessors, to establish any sort of common life, but the integrating tendencies of modern industrial society have at the same time undermined his "isolation." Having surrendered most of his technical skills to the corporation, he can no longer provide for his material needs. As the family loses not only its productive functions but many of its reproductive functions as well, men and women no longer manage even to raise their children without the help of certified experts. The atrophy of older traditions of self-help has eroded everyday competence, in one area after another, and has made the individual dependent on the state, the corporation, and other bureaucracies.

Narcissism represents the psychological dimension of this dependence. Notwithstanding his occasional illusions of omnipotence, the narcissist depends on others to validate his self-esteem. He cannot live without an admiring audience. His apparent freedom from family ties and institutional constraints does not free him to stand alone or to glory in his individuality. On the contrary, it contributes to his insecurity, which he can overcome only by seeing his "grandiose self" reflected in the attentions of others, or by attaching himself to those who radiate celebrity, power, and charisma. For the narcissist, the world is a mirror, whereas the rugged individualist saw it as an empty wilderness to be shaped to his own design.

In the nineteenth-century American imagination, the vast continent stretching westward symbolized both the promise and the menace of an escape from the past. The West represented an opportunity to build a new society unencumbered by feudal inhibitions, but it also tempted men to throw off civilization and to revert to savagery. Through compulsive industry and relentless sexual repression, nineteenth-century Americans achieved a fragile triumph over the id. The violence they turned against the Indians and against nature originated not in unrestrained impulse but in the white Anglo-Saxon superego, which feared the wildness of the West because it objectified the wildness within each individual. While celebrating the romance of the frontier in their popular literature, in practice Americans imposed on the wilderness a new order designed to keep impulse in check while giving free rein to acquisitiveness. Capital accumulation in its own right sublimated appetite and subordinated the pursuit of self-interest to the service of future generations. In the heat of the struggle to win the West, the American pioneer gave full vent to his rapacity and murderous cruelty, but he always envisioned the result—not without

725

misgivings, expressed in a nostalgic cult of lost innocence—as a peaceful, respectable, churchgoing community safe for his women and children. He imagined that his offspring, raised under the morally refining influence of feminine "culture," would grow up to be sober, law-abiding, domesticated American citizens, and the thought of the advantages they would inherit justified his toil and excused, he thought, his frequent lapses into brutality, sadism, and rape.

Today Americans are overcome not by the sense of endless possibility but by the banality of the social order they have erected against it. Having internalized the social restraints by means of which they formerly sought to keep possibility within civilized limits, they feel themselves overwhelmed by an annihilating boredom, like animals whose instincts have withered in captivity. A reversion to savagery threatens them so little that they long precisely for a more vigorous instinctual existence. People nowadays complain of an inability to feel. They cultivate more vivid experiences, seek to beat sluggish flesh to life, attempt to revive jaded appetites. They condemn the superego and exalt the lost life of the senses. Twentieth-century peoples have erected so many psychological barriers against strong emotion, and have invested those defenses with so much of the energy derived from forbidden impulse, that they can no longer remember what it feels like to be inundated by desire. They tend, rather, to be consumed with rage, which derives from defenses against desire and gives rise in turn to new defenses against rage itself. Outwardly bland, submissive, and sociable, they seethe with an inner anger for which a dense, over-populated, bureaucratic society can devise few legitimate outlets.

The growth of bureaucracy creates an intricate network of personal relations, puts a premium on social skills, and makes the unbridled egotism of the American Adam untenable. Yet at the same time it erodes all forms of patriarchal authority and thus weakens the social superego, formerly represented by fathers, teachers, and preachers. The decline of institutionalized authority in an ostensibly permissive society does not, however, lead to a "decline of the superego" in individuals. It encourages instead the development of a harsh, punitive superego that derives most of its psychic energy, in the absence of authoritative social prohibitions, from the destructive, aggressive impulses within the id. Unconscious, irrational elements in the superego come to dominate its operation. As authority figures in modern society lose their "credibility," the superego in individuals increasingly derives from the child's primitive fantasies about his parents—fantasies charged with sadistic rage—rather than from internalized ego ideals formed by later experience with loved and respected models of social conduct.

The struggle to maintain psychic equilibrium in a society that demands submission to the rules of social intercourse but refuses to ground those rules in a code of moral conduct encourages a form of self-absorption that has little in common with the primary narcissism of the imperial self. Archaic elements increasingly dominate personality structure, and "the self shrinks back," in the words of Morris Dickstein, "toward a passive and primeval state in which the world remains uncreated, unformed." The egomaniacal, experience-devouring, imperial self regresses into a grandiose, narcissistic, infantile, empty self: a "dark wet hole," as Rudolph Wurlitzer writes in *Nog,* "where everything finds its way sooner or later. I remain near the entrance, handling goods as they are shoved in, listening and nodding. I have been slowly dissolving into this cavity."

Plagued by anxiety, depression, vague discontents, sense of inner emptiness, the "psychological man" of the twentieth century seeks neither individual self-aggrandizement nor spiritual transcendence but peace of mind, under conditions that increasingly militate against it. Therapists, not priests or popular preachers of self-help or models of success like the captains of industry, become his principal allies in the struggle for composure; he turns to them in the hope of achieving the modern equivalent of salvation, "mental health." Therapy has established itself as the successor both to rugged individualism and to religion; but this does not mean that the "triumph of the therapeutic" has become a new religion in its own right. Therapy constitutes an antireligion, not always to be sure because it adheres to rational explanation or scientific methods of healing, as its practitioners would have us believe, but because modern society "has no future" and therefore gives no thought to anything beyond its immediate needs. Even when therapists speak of the need for "meaning" and "love," they define love and meaning simply as the fulfillment of the patient's emotional requirements. It hardly occurs to them—nor is there any reason why it should, given the nature of the therapeutic enterprise—to encourage the subject to subordinate his needs and interests to those of others, to someone or some cause or tradition outside himself. "Love" as self-sacrifice or self-abasement, "meaning" as submission to a higher loyalty—these sublimations strike the therapeutic sensibility as intolerably oppressive, offensive to common sense and injurious to personal health and well-being. To liberate humanity from such out-moded ideas of love and duty has become the mission of the post-Freudian therapies and particularly of their converts and popularizers, for whom mental health means the overthrow of inhibitions and the immediate gratification of every impulse.

STUDY QUESTIONS

1. How does the narcissistic self differ from Kant's noble self or Quinton's person of character?

2. In 1923, a study known as Middletown recorded the attitudes and practices of citizens in Muncie, Indiana. In 1977, researchers made another study in Muncie, called Middletown III, and were surprised to find that, despite more permissive views on divorce, marijuana, and pornography, students at Muncie High School answered a number of questions exactly the same way their grandparents did in 1923. The majority in both groups, for example, reported that they regarded the Bible as a "sufficient guide for modern life." Does this suggest that Lasch and other pessimistic social critics may be exaggerating the changes that have occurred in American society over the past two decades?

3. What, for Lasch, is the importance of a sense of tradition and a knowledge of history? What role does their presence or absence play in moral development?

On Self-respect

JOAN DIDION

Joan Didion (b. 1934) is a well-known novelist and essayist. Her published works include novels such as *Play It as It Lays* (1971) and *A Book of Common Prayer* (1977), and collections of essays titled *Slouching Towards Bethlehem* (1970) and *The White Album* (1979).

What is self-respect and how does one develop it? For Didion, self-respecting persons are persons of character who accept responsibility for their lives and actions. Self-respect requires discipline, the ability to forego immediate gratification, and the ability to take risks and stick to plans. Persons who have these characteristics respect themselves. Persons who lack them live with a certain self-contempt and a contempt for those who uncritically admire them.

Once, in a dry season, I wrote in large letters across two pages of a notebook that innocence ends when one is stripped of the delusion that one likes oneself. Although now, some years later, I marvel that a mind on the outs with itself should have nonetheless made painstaking record of its every tremor, I recall with embarrassing clarity the flavor of those particular ashes. It was a matter of misplaced self-respect.

I had not been elected to Phi Beta Kappa. This failure could scarcely have been more predictable or less ambiguous (I simply did

ON SELF-RESPECT Reprinted by permission of Farrar, Straus and Giroux, Inc. "On Self-Respect" from *Slouching Towards Bethlehem* by Joan Didion. Copyright ©1961, 1968 by Joan Didion.

not have the grades), but I was unnerved by it; I had somehow thought myself a kind of academic Raskolnikov, curiously exempt from the cause-effect relationships which hampered others. Although even the humorless nineteen-year-old that I was must have recognized that the situation lacked real tragic stature, the day that I did not make Phi Beta Kappa nonetheless marked the end of something, and innocence may well be the word for it. I lost the conviction that lights would always turn green for me, the pleasant certainty that those rather passive virtues which had won me approval as a child automatically guaranteed me not only Phi Beta Kappa keys but happiness, honor, and the love of a good man; lost a certain touching faith in the totem power of good manners, clean hair, and proven competence on the Stanford-Binet scale. To such doubtful amulets had my self-respect been pinned, and I faced myself that day with the nonplused apprehension of someone who has come across a vampire and has no crucifix at hand.

Although to be driven back upon oneself is an uneasy affair at best, rather like trying to cross a border with borrowed credentials, it seems to me now the one condition necessary to the beginnings of real self-respect. Most of our platitudes notwithstanding, self-deception remains the most difficult deception. The tricks that work on others count for nothing in that very well-lit back alley where one keeps assignations with oneself: no winning smiles will do here, no prettily drawn lists of good intentions. One shuffles flashily but in vain through one's marked cards—the kindness done for the wrong reason, the apparent triumph which involved no real effort, the seemingly heroic act into which one had been shamed. The dismal fact is that self-respect has nothing to do with the approval of others—who are, after all, deceived easily enough; has nothing to do with reputation, which, as Rhett Butler told Scarlett O'Hara, is something people with courage can do without.

To do without self-respect, on the other hand, is to be an unwilling audience of one to an interminable documentary that details one's failings, both real and imagined, with fresh footage spliced in for every screening. *There's the glass you broke in anger, there's the hurt on X's face; watch now, this next scene, the night Y came back from Houston, see how you muff this one.* To live without self-respect is to lie awake some night, beyond the reach of warm milk, phenobarbital, and the sleeping hand on the coverlet, counting up the sins of commission and omission, the trusts betrayed, the promises subtly broken, the gifts irrevocably wasted through sloth or cowardice or carelessness. However long we postpone it, we eventualy lie down alone in that notoriously uncomfortable bed, the one we make ourselves. Whether or not we sleep in it depends, of course, on whether or not we respect ourselves.

To protest that some fairly improbable people, some people who *could not possibly respect themselves,* seem to sleep easily enough is to miss the point entirely, as surely as those people miss it who think that self-respect has necessarily to do with not having safety pins in one's underwear. There is a common superstition that "self-respect" is a kind of charm against snakes, something that keeps those who have it locked in some unblighted Eden, out of strange beds, ambivalent conversations, and trouble in general. It does not at all. It has nothing to do with the face of things, but concerns instead a separate peace, a private reconciliation. Although the careless, suicidal Julian English in *Appointment in Samarra* and the careless, incurably dishonest Jordan Baker in *The Great Gatsby* seem equally improbable candidates for self-respect, Jordan Baker had it, Julian English did not. With that genius for accommodation more often seen in women than in men, Jordan took her own measure, made her own peace, avoided threats to that peace: "I hate careless people," she told Nick Carraway. "It takes two to make an accident."

Like Jordan Baker, people with self-respect have the courage of their mistakes. They know the price of things. If they choose to commit adultery, they do not then go running, in an access of bad conscience, to receive absolution from the wronged parties; nor do they complain unduly of the unfairness, the undeserved embarrassment, of being named co-respondent. In brief, people with self-respect exhibit a certain toughness, a kind of moral nerve; they display what was once called *character,* a quality which, although approved in the abstract, sometimes loses ground to other, more instantly negotiable virtues. The measure of its slipping prestige is that one tends to think of it only in connection with homely children and United States senators who have been defeated, preferably in the primary, for reelection. Nonetheless, character—the willingness to accept responsibility for one's own life—is the source from which self-respect springs.

Self-respect is something that our grandparents, whether or not they had it, knew all about. They had instilled in them, young, a certain discipline, the sense that one lives by doing things one does not particularly want to do, by putting fears and doubts to one side, by weighing immediate comforts against the possibility of larger, even intangible, comforts. It seemed to the nineteenth century admirable, but not remarkable, that Chinese Gordon put on a clean white suit and held Khartoum against the Mahdi; it did not seem unjust that the way to free land in California involved death and difficulty and dirt. In a diary kept during the winter of 1846, an emigrating twelve-year-old named Narcissa Cornwall noted coolly: "Father was busy reading and did not notice that the house was being filled with strange Indians until Mother spoke about it." Even lacking any clue as to what Mother said, one can scarcely fail to be impressed by the entire incident: the father reading, the Indians filing in, the mother choosing the words that would not alarm, the child duly recording the event and noting further that those particular Indians were not, "fortunately for us," hostile. Indians were simply part of the *donnée*.

In one guise or another, Indians always are. Again, it is a question of recognizing that anything worth having has its price. People who respect themselves are willing to accept the risk that the Indians will be hostile, that the venture will go bankrupt, that the liaison may not turn out to be one in which *every day is a holiday because you're married to me*. They are willing to invest something of themselves; they may not play at all, but when they do play, they know the odds.

That kind of self-respect is a discipline, a habit of mind that can never be faked but can be developed, trained, coaxed forth. It was once suggested to me that, as an antidote to crying, I put my head in a paper bag. As it happens, there is a sound physiological reason, something to do with oxygen, for doing exactly that, but the psychological effect alone is incalculable; it is difficult in the extreme to continue fancying oneself Cathy in *Wuthering Heights* with one's head in a Food Fair bag. There is a similar case for all the small disciplines, unimportant in themselves; imagine maintaining any kind of swoon, commiserative or carnal, in a cold shower.

But those small disciplines are valuable only insofar as they represent larger ones. To say that Waterloo was won on the playing fields of Eton is not to say that Napoleon might have been saved by a crash program in cricket; to give formal dinners in the rain forest would be pointless did not the candlelight flickering on the liana call forth deeper, stronger disciplines, values instilled long before. It is a kind of ritual, helping us to remember who and what we are. In order to remember it, one must have known it.

To have that sense of one's intrinsic worth which constitutes self-respect is potentially to have everything: the ability to discriminate, to love and to remain indifferent. To lack it is to be locked within oneself, paradoxically incapable of either love or indifference. If we do not respect ourselves, we are on the one hand forced to despise those who have so few resources as to consort with us, so little perception as to remain blind to our fatal weaknesses. On the other, we are peculiarly in thrall to everyone we see, curiously determined to live out—since our self-image is untenable—their false notions of us. We flatter ourselves by thinking this compulsion to please others an attractive trait: a gist for imaginative empathy, evidence of our willingness to give. Of *course* I will play Francesca to your Paolo, Helen Keller to anyone's Annie Sullivan: no expectation is too mis-placed, no role too ludicrous. At the mercy of those we cannot but hold in contempt, we play roles doomed to failure before they are begun, each defeat generating fresh despair at the urgency of divin-ing and meeting the next demand made upon us.

It is the phenomenon sometimes called "alienation from self." In its advanced stages, we no longer answer the telephone, because someone might want something; that we could say *no* without drowning in self-reproach is an idea alien to this game. Every en-counter demands too much, tears the nerves, drains the will, and the specter of something as small as an unanswered letter arouses such disproportionate guilt that answering it becomes out of the question. To assign unanswered letters their proper weight, to free us from the expectations of others, to give us back to ourselves—there lies the great, the singular power of self-respect. Without it, one eventually discovers the final turn of the screw: one runs away to find oneself, and finds no one at home.

STUDY QUESTIONS

1. Do you agree with Didion's claim that self-respect has nothing to do with the approval of others?

2. Didion defines character as willingness to accept responsibility

for your life. Can persons of character be self-righteous? Hypocritical? Self-excusers? Why does Didion think that being a self-
excuser is inconsistent with having self-respect? Can you imagine people, ruthless criminals, for example, who accept responsibility for their actions, but can nevertheless be said to have no
character or self-respect?

3. Didion says self-respect is a "discipline," or "a habit of mind that
   can never be faked, but can be developed [and] trained . . ." How
   might someone develop more self-respect?

4. What, according to Didion, is the cost of living without self-
   respect?

5. Do you think most people are more concerned about their good
   reputation or their self-respect? Which is harder to live without?

Servility and Self-respect

THOMAS E. HILL, JR.

A biographical sketch of Thomas E. Hill, Jr. is found on
page 327.

According to Thomas Hill, servility is a moral defect. He
discusses three servile types: the Uncle Tom, the Self-
deprecator, and the Deferential Wife.

The Uncle Tom is exploited by white people but "does
not feel he has the right to expect anything better." The
Self-deprecator is not oppressed externally, but constantly
shrinks from giving voice to his own preferences; his
self-contempt invites exploitation and humiliation by
others. The Deferential Wife tends to count her own interests as relatively unimportant. "No one is trampling

SERVILITY AND SELF-RESPECT By Thomas E. Hill, Jr. First published in *Monist,* Journal of the
Department of Philosophy, University of California at Los Angeles, vol. 57, no. 1. By permission
of the publisher.

on her rights, she says; for she is quite glad and proud to serve her husband as she does."

Each servile type is morally defective. But why is servility to be condemned? All are lacking self-respect; yet utilitarian grounds do not explain what is wrong with this. It may even be that the Uncle Tom's sufferings are balanced by the pleasures he gives to his master. The Deferential Wife may be taking perverse pleasure in her own submissiveness. The Self-deprecator may be masochistic and derive pleasure from humiliation.

According to Hill, the morally objectionable feature the three types share is their failure to acknowledge and to respect their personal rights. The Uncle Tom implicitly denies that he is the moral equal of those who exploit him. The Deferential Wife appears voluntarily to have waived her rights in consenting to defer to her husband's demands. It may be, says Hill, that "her consent has been coerced by her lack of viable options open to women in her society." Hill then argues for the following thesis: Disregard for one's own rights is objectionable on Kantian grounds, which require one to respect the moral law by respecting all persons including oneself. "The objection to the servile person . . . is that he does not satisfy the basic requirement to respect morality."

Several motives underlie this paper. In the first place, I am curious to see if there is a legitimate source for the increasingly common feeling that servility can be as much a vice as arrogance is. There seems to be something morally defective about the Uncle Tom and the submissive housewife; and yet, on the other hand, if the only interests they sacrifice are their own, it seems that we should have no right to complain. Secondly, I have some sympathy for the now unfashionable view that each person has duties to himself as well as to others. It does seem absurd to say that a person could literally violate his own rights or owe himself a debt to gratitude, but I suspect that the classic defenders to duties to oneself had something different in mind. If there are duties to oneself, it is natural to expect that a duty to avoid being servile would have a prominent place among them. . . .

I

Three examples may give a preliminary idea of what I mean by *servility*. Consider, first, an extremely deferential black, whom I shall call the *Uncle Tom*. He always steps aside for white men; he does not complain when less qualified whites take over his job; he gratefully accepts whatever benefits his all-white government and employers allot him, and he would not think of protesting its insufficiency. He displays the symbols of deference to whites, and of contempt towards blacks: he faces the former with bowed stance and a ready "Sir" and "Ma'am"; he reserves his strongest obscenities for the latter. Imagine, too, that he is not playing a game. He is not the shrewdly prudent calculator, who knows how to make the best of a bad lot and mocks his masters behind their backs. He accepts without question the idea that, as a black, he is owed less than whites. He may believe that blacks are mentally inferior and of less social utility, but that is not the crucial point. The attitude which he displays is that what he values, aspires for, and can demand is of less importance than what whites value, aspire for, and can demand. He is far from the picture book's carefree, happy servant, but he does not feel that he has a right to expect anything better.

Another pattern of servility is illustrated by a person I shall call the *Self-deprecator*. Like the Uncle Tom, he is reluctant to make demands. He says nothing when others take unfair advantage of him. When asked for his preferences or opinions, he tends to shrink away as if what he said should make no difference. His problem, however, is not a sense of racial inferiority but rather an acute awareness of his own inadequacies and failures as an individual. These defects are not imaginary: he has in fact done poorly by his own standards and others'. But, unlike many of us in the same situation, he acts as if his failings warrant quite unrelated maltreatment even by strangers. His sense of shame and self-contempt makes him content to be the instrument of others. He feels that nothing is owed him until he has earned it and that he has earned very little. He is not simply playing a masochist's game of winning sympathy by disparaging himself. On the contrary, he assesses his individual merits with painful accuracy.

A rather different case is that of the *Deferential Wife*. This is a woman who is utterly devoted to serving her husband. She buys the clothes *he* prefers, invites the guests *he* wants to entertain, and makes love whenever *he* is in the mood. She willingly moves to a new city in order for him to have a more attractive job, counting her own friendships and geographical preferences insignificant by comparison. She loves her husband, but her conduct is not simply an expression of love. She is happy, but she does not subordinate herself as a means to happiness. She does not simply defer to her husband in certain spheres as a trade-off for his deference in other spheres. On the contrary, she tends not to form her own interests, values, and ideals; and, when she does, she counts them as less important than her husband's. She readily responds to appeals from Women's Liberation that she agrees that women are mentally and physically equal, if not superior, to men. She just believes that the proper role for a woman is to serve her family. As a matter of fact, much of her happiness derives from her belief that she fulfills this role very well. No one is trampling on her rights, she says; for she is quite glad, and proud, to serve her husband as she does.

Each one of these cases reflects the attitude which I call servility.[1] It betrays the absence of a certain kind of self-respect. What I take this attitude to be, more specifically, will become clearer later on. It is important at the outset, however, not to confuse the three cases sketched above with other, superficially similar cases. In particular, the cases I have sketched are not simply cases in which someone refuses to press his rights, speaks disparagingly of himself, or devotes himself to another. A black, for example, is not necessarily servile because he does not demand a just wage; for, seeing that such a demand would result in his being fired, he might forbear for the sake of his children. A self-critical person is not necessarily servile by virtue of bemoaning his faults in public; for his behavior may be merely a complex way of satisfying his own inner needs quite independent of a willingness to accept abuse from others. A woman need not be servile whenever she works to make her husband happy and prosperous; for she might freely and knowingly choose to do so from love or from a desire to share the rewards of his success. If the effort

---

[1]Each of the cases is intended to represent only one possible pattern of servility. I make no claims about how often these patterns are exemplified, nor do I mean to imply that only these patterns could warrant the labels "Deferential Wife," "Uncle Tom," etc. All the more, I do not mean to imply any comparative judgments about the causes or relative magnitude of the problems of racial and sexual discrimination. One person, e.g. a self-contemptuous woman with a sense of racial inferiority, might exemplify features of several patterns at once; and, of course, a person might view her being a woman the way an Uncle Tom views his being black, etc.

did not require her to submit to humiliation or maltreatment, her choice would not mark her as servile. There may, of course, be grounds for objecting to the attitudes in these cases; but the defect is not servility of the sort I want to consider. It should also be noted that my cases of servility are not simply instances of deference to superior knowledge or judgment. To defer to an expert's judgment on matters of fact is not to be servile; to defer to his every wish and whim is. Similarly, the belief that one's talents and achievements are comparatively low does not, by itself, make one servile. It is no vice to acknowledge the truth, and one may in fact have achieved less, and have less ability, than others. To be servile is not simply to hold certain empirical beliefs but to have a certain attitude concerning one's rightful place in a moral community.

· · ·

II

Are there grounds for regarding the attitudes of the Uncle Tom, the Self-deprecator, and the Deferential Wife as morally objectionable? Are there moral arguments we could give them to show that they ought to have more self-respect? None of the more obvious replies is entirely satisfactory.

One might, in the first place, adduce utilitarian considerations. Typically the servile person will be less happy than he might be. Moreover, he may be less prone to make the best of his own socially useful abilities. He may become a nuisance to others by being overly dependent. He will, in any case, lose the special contentment that comes from standing up for one's rights. A submissive attitude encourages exploitation, and exploitation spreads misery in a variety of ways. These considerations provide a *prima facie* case against the atttitudes of the Uncle Tom, the Deferential Wife, and the Self-deprecator, but they are hardly conclusive. Other utilities tend to counterbalance the ones just mentioned. When people refuse to press their rights, there are usually others who profit. There are undeniable pleasures in associating with those who are devoted, understanding, and grateful for whatever we see fit to give them—as our fondness for dogs attests. Even the servile person may find his attitude a source of happiness, as the case of the Deferential Wife illustrates. There may be comfort and security in thinking that the hard choices must be made by others, that what I would say has little to do with what ought to be done. Self-condemnation may bring relief from the pangs of guilt even if it is not deliberately used for that purpose. On balance, then, utilitarian considerations may turn out to favor servility as much as they oppose it.

For those who share my moral intuitions, there is another sort of reason for not trying to rest a case against servility on utilitarian considerations. Certain utilities seem irrelevant to the issue. The utilitarian must weigh them along with others, but to do so seems morally inappropriate. Suppose, for example, that the submissive attitudes of the Uncle Tom and the Deferential Wife result in positive utilities for those who dominate and exploit them. Do we need to tabulate *these* utilities before conceding that servility is objectionable? The Uncle Tom, it seems, is making an error, a moral error, quite apart from consideration of how much others in fact profit from his attitude. The Deferential Wife may be quite happy; but if her happiness turns out to be contingent on her distorted view of her own rights and worth as a person, then it carries little moral weight against the contention that she ought to change that view. Suppose I could cause a woman to find her happiness in denying all her rights and serving my every wish. No doubt I could do so only by nonrational manipulative techniques, which I ought not to use. But is this the only objection? My efforts would be wrong, it seems, not only because of the techniques they require but also because the resultant attitude is itself objectionable. When a person's happiness stems from a morally objectionable attitude, it ought to be discounted. That a sadist gets pleasure from seeing others suffer should not count even as a partial justification for his attitude. That a servile person derives pleasure from denying her moral status, for similar reasons, cannot make her attitude acceptable. These brief intuitive remarks are not intended as a refutation of utilitarianism, with all its many varieties; but they do suggest that it is well to look elsewhere for adequate grounds for rejecting the attitudes of the Uncle Tom, the Self-deprecator, and the Deferential Wife.

. . .

III

Why, then, is servility a moral defect? There is, I think, another sort of answer which is worth exploring. The first part of this answer must be an attempt to isolate the objectionable features of the servile person; later we can ask why these features are objectionable. As a step in this direction, let us examine again our three paradigm cases. The moral defect in each case, I suggest, is a failure to understand and acknowledge one's own moral rights. I assume, without argument here, that each person has moral rights. Some of these rights may be basic human rights; that is, rights for which a person needs only to be human to qualify. Other rights will be derivative and contingent upon his special commitments, institutional affiliations, etc. Most rights will be *prima facie* ones; some may be absolute. Most can be waived under appropriate conditions; perhaps some cannot. Many rights can be forfeited; but some, presumably, cannot. The servile person does not, strictly speaking, violate his own rights. At least in our paradigm cases he fails to acknowledge fully his own moral status because he does not fully understand what his rights are, how they can be waived, and when they can be forfeited.

The defect of the Uncle Tom, for example, is that he displays an attitude that denies his moral equality with whites. He does not realize, or apprehend in an effective way, that he has as much right to a decent wage and a share of political power as any comparable white. His gratitude is misplaced; he accepts benefits which are his by right as if they were gifts. The Self-deprecator is servile in a more complex way. He acts as if he has forfeited many important rights which in fact he has not. He does not understand, or fully realize in his own case, that certain rights to fair and decent treatment do not have to be earned. He sees his merits clearly enough, but he fails to see that what he can expect from others is not merely a function of his merits. The Deferential Wife *says* that she understands her rights vis-à-vis her husband, but what she fails to appreciate is that her consent to serve him is a valid waiver of her rights only under certain conditions. If her consent is coerced, say, by the lack of viable options for women in her society, then her consent is worth little. If socially fostered ignorance of her own talents and alternatives is responsible for her consent, then her consent should not count as a fully legitimate waiver of her right to equal consideration within the marriage. All the more, her consent to defer constantly to her husband is not a legitimate setting aside of her rights if it results from her mistaken belief that she has a moral duty to do so. (Recall: "The *proper* role for a woman is to serve her family.") If she believes that she has a *duty* to defer to her husband, then, whatever she may say, she cannot fully understand that she has a *right* not to defer to him. When she says that she freely gives up such a right, she is confused. Her confusion is rather like that of a person who has been persuaded by an unscrupulous lawyer that it is legally incumbent on him to refuse a jury trial but who nevertheless tells the judge that he understands that he has a right to a jury trial and freely waives it. He does not really understand what it is to have and freely give up the right if he thinks that it would be an offense for him to exercise it.

Insofar as servility results from moral ignorance or confusion, it need not be something for which a person is to blame. . . . Suppose, however, that our servile persons come to know their rights but do not substantially alter their behavior. Are they not still servile in an objectionable way?

. . .

The answer, I think, should depend upon why the deferential role is played. If the motive is a morally commendable one, or a desire to avert dire consequences to oneself, or even an ambition to set an oppressor up for a later fall, then I would not count the role player as servile. The Uncle Tom, for instance, is not servile in my sense if he shuffles and bows to keep the Klan from killing his children, to save his own skin, or even to buy time while he plans the revolution. Similarly, the Deferential Wife is not servile if she tolerates an abusive husband because he is so ill that further strain would kill him, because protesting would deprive her of her only means of survival, or because she is collecting atrocity stories for her book against marriage. If there is fault in these situations, it seems inappropriate to call it *servility*. The story is quite different, however, if a person continues in his deferential role just from laziness, timidity, or a desire for some minor advantage. He shows too little concern for his moral status as a person, one is tempted to say, if he is willing to deny it for a small profit or simply because it requires some effort and courage to affirm it openly. A black who plays the Uncle Tom merely to gain an advantage over other blacks is harming them, of course; but he is also displaying disregard for his own moral position as an equal among human beings. Similarly, a woman throws away her rights too lightly if she continues to play the subservient role because she is used to it or is too timid to risk a change. A Self-deprecator who readily accepts what he knows are violations of his rights may be indulging his peculiar need for punishment at the expense of denying something more valuable. In these cases, I suggest, we have a kind of servility independent of any ignorance or confusion about one's rights. The person who has it may or may not be blameworthy, depending on many factors; and the line between servile and nonservile role playing will often be hard to draw. Nevertheless, the objectionable feature is perhaps clear enough for present purposes: it is a willingness to disavow one's moral status, publicly and systematically, in the absence of any strong reason to do so.

. . .

IV

The objectionable feature of the servile person, as I have described him, is his tendency to disavow his own moral rights either because he misunderstands them or because he cares little for them. The question remains: why should anyone regard this as a moral defect? After all, the rights which he denies are is own. He may be unfortunate, foolish, or even distasteful; but why *morally* deficient? One sort of answer, quite different from those reviewed earlier, is suggested by some of Kant's remarks. Kant held that servility is contrary to a perfect nonjuridical duty to oneself.[2] To say that the duty is perfect is roughly to say that it is stringent, never overridden by other considerations (e.g., beneficence). To say that the duty is nonjuridical is to say that a person cannot legitimately be coerced to comply. Although Kant did not develop an explicit argument for this view, an argument can easily be constructed from materials which reflect the spirit, if not the letter, of his moral theory. The argument which I have in mind is prompted by Kant's contention that respect for persons, strictly speaking, is respect for moral law.[3] If taken as a claim about

---

[2]See Immanuel Kant, *The Doctrine of Virtue*, Part II of *The Metaphysics of Morals*, ed. by M. J. Gregor (New York: Harper & Row, 1964), pp. 99–103; Prussian Academy edition, vol. VI, pp. 434–37.

[3]Immanuel Kant, *Groundwork of the Metaphysics of Morals*, ed. by H. J. Paton (New York: Harper & Row, 1964), p. 69; Prussian Academy edition, vol. IV, p. 401; *The Critique of Practical Reason*, ed. by Lewis W. Beck (New York: Bobbs-Merrill, 1956), pp. 81, 84; Prussian Academy edition, vol. V, pp. 78, 81. My purpose here is not to interpret what Kant meant but to give a sense to his remark.

all sorts of respect, this seems quite implausible. If it means that we respect persons only for their moral character, their capacity for moral conduct, or their status as "authors" of the moral law, then it seems unduly moralistic. My strategy is to construe the remark as saying that at least one sort of respect for persons is respect for the rights which the moral law accords them. If one respects the moral law, then one must respect one's own moral rights; and this amounts to having a kind of self-respect incompatible with servility.

The premises for the Kantian argument, which are all admittedly vague, can be sketched as follows:

First, let us assume, as Kant did, that all human beings have equal basic human rights. Specific rights vary with different conditions, but all must be justified from a point of view under which all are equal. Not all rights need to be earned, and some cannot be forfeited. Many rights can be waived but only under certain conditions of knowledge and freedom. These conditions are complex and difficult to state; but they include something like the condition that a person's consent releases others from obligation only if it is autonomously given, and consent resulting from underestimation of one's moral status is not autonomously given. Rights can be objects of knowledge, but also of ignorance, misunderstanding, deception, and the like.

Second, let us assume that my account of servility is correct; or, if one prefers, we can take it as a definition. That is, in brief, a servile person is one who tends to deny or disavow his own moral rights because he does not understand them or has little concern for the status they give him.

Third, we need one formal premise concerning moral duty, namely, that each person ought, as far as possible, to respect the moral law. In less Kantian language, the point is that everyone should approximate, to the extent that he can, the ideal of a person who fully adopts the moral point of view. Roughly, this means not only that each person ought to do what is morally required and refrain from what is morally wrong but also that each person should treat all the provisions of morality as valuable—worth preserving and prizing as well as obeying. One must, so to speak, take up the spirit of morality as well as meet the letter of its requirements. To keep one's promises, avoid hurting others, and the like, is not sufficient; one should also

743

take an attitude of respect towards the principles, ideals, and goals of morality. A respectful attitude towards a system of rights and duties consists of more than a disposition to conform to its definite rules of behavior; it also involves holding the system in esteem, being unwilling to ridicule it, and being reluctant to give up one's place in it. The essentially Kantian idea here is that morality, as a system of equal fundamental rights and duties, is worthy of respect, and hence a completely moral person would respect it in word and manner as well as in deed. And what a completely moral person would do, in Kant's view, is our duty to do so far as we can.

The assumptions here are, of course, strong ones, and I make no attempt to justify them. They are, I suspect, widely held though rarely articulated. In any case, my present purpose is not to evaluate them but to see how, if granted, they constitute a case against servility. The objection to the servile person, given our premises, is that he does not satisfy the basic requirement to respect morality. A person who fully respected a system of moral rights would be disposed to learn his proper place in it, to affirm it proudly, and not to tolerate abuses of it lightly. This is just the sort of disposition that the servile person lacks. If he does not understand the system, he is in no position to respect it adequately. This lack of respect may be no fault of his own, but it is still a way in which he falls short of a moral ideal. If, on the other hand, the servile person knowingly disavows his moral rights by pretending to approve of violations of them, then, barring special explanations, he shows an indifference to whether the provisions of morality are honored and publicly acknowledged. This avoidable display of indifference, by our Kantian premises, is contrary to the duty to respect morality. The disrespect in this second case is somewhat like the disrespect a religious believer might show towards his religion if, to avoid embarrassment, he laughed congenially while nonbelievers were mocking the beliefs which he secretly held. In any case, the servile person, as such, does not express disrespect for the system of moral rights in the obvious way by violating the rights of others. His lack of respect is more subtly manifested by his acting before others as if he did not know or care about his position of equality under that system.

The central idea here may be illustrated by an analogy. Imagine a club, say, an old German dueling fraternity. By the rules of the club, each member has certain rights and responsibilities. These are the same for each member regardless of what titles he may hold outside the club. Each has, for example, a right to be heard at meetings, a right not to be shouted down by the others. Some rights cannot be forfeited: for example, each may vote regardless of whether he has paid his dues and satisfied other rules. Some rights cannot be waived: for example, the right to be defended when attacked by several members of the rival fraternity. The members show respect for each other by respecting the status which the rules confer on each member. Now one new member is careful always to allow the others to speak at meetings; but when they shout him down, he does nothing. He just shrugs as if to say, "Who am I to complain?" When he fails to stand up in defense of a fellow member, he feels ashamed and refuses to vote. He does not deserve to vote, he says. As the only commoner among illustrious barons, he feels that it is his place to serve them and defer to their decisions. When attackers from the rival fraternity come at him with swords drawn, he tells his companions to run and save themselves. When they defend him, he expresses immense gratitude—as if they had done him a gratuitous favor. Now one might argue that our new member fails to show respect for the fraternity and its rules. He does not actually violate any of the rules by refusing to vote, asking others not to defend him, and deferring to the barons, but he symbolically disavows the equal status which the rules confer on him. If he ought to have respect for the fraternity, he ought to change his attitude. Our servile person, then, is like the new member of the dueling fraternity in having insufficient respect for a system of rules and ideals. The difference is that everyone ought to respect morality whereas there is no comparable moral requirement to respect the fraternity.

The conclusion here is, of course, a limited one. Self-sacrifice is not always a sign of servility. It is not a duty always to press one's rights. Whether a given act is evidence of servility will depend not only on the attitude of the agent but also on the specific nature of his moral rights, a matter not considered here. Moreover, the extent to which a person is responsible, or blameworthy, for his defect remains an open question. Nevertheless, the conclusion should not be minimized. In order to avoid servility, a person who gives up his rights must do so with a full appreciation for what they are. A woman, for example, may devote herself to her husband if she is uncoerced, knows what she is doing, and does not pretend that she has no decent alternative. A self-contemptuous person may decide not to press various unforfeited rights but only if he does not take the attitude that he is too rotten to deserve them. A black may demand less than is due to him provided he is prepared to acknowledge that no one has a right to expect this of him. Sacrifices of this sort, I suspect, are extremely rare. Most people, if they fully acknowledged their rights, would not autonomously refuse to press them.

An even stronger conclusion would emerge if we could assume that some basic rights cannot be waived. . . .

Even if there are no specific rights which cannot be waived, there might be at least one formal right of this sort. This is the right to some minimum degree of respect from others. No matter how willing a person is to submit to humiliation by others, they ought to show him some respect as a person. By analogy with self-respect, as presented here, this respect owed by others would consist of a willingness to acknowledge fully, in word as well as action, the person's basically equal moral status as defined by his other rights. To the extent that a person gives even tacit consent to humiliations incompatible with this respect, he will be acting as if he waives a right which he cannot in fact give up. To do this, barring special explanations, would mark one as servile.

. . .

Kant suggests that duties to oneself are a precondition of duties to others. On our account of servility, there is at least one sense in which this is so. Insofar as the servile person is ignorant of his own rights, he is not in an adequate position to appreciate the rights of others. Misunderstanding the moral basis for his equal status with others, he is necessarily liable to underestimate the rights of those with whom he classifies himself. On the other hand, if he plays the servile role knowingly, then, barring special explanation, he displays a lack of concern to see the principles of morality acknowledged and respected and thus the absence of one motive which can move a moral person to respect the rights of others. In either case, the servile person's lack of self-respect necessarily puts him in a less than ideal position to respect others. Failure to fulfill one's duty to oneself, then, renders a person liable to violate duties to others. This, however, is a consequence of our argument against servility, not a presupposition of it.

STUDY QUESTIONS

1. Hill considers servility to be a moral flaw. Yet, traditionally, meekness has been one of the Christian virtues. Is Hill at odds with this tradition? If so, do you find the traditional conception defective? Or is Hill missing something?

2. Hill suggests that the Deferential Wife who consents to being deferent may nevertheless have been coerced by the lack of viable options open to women. In that case, we may discount her consent as not freely given. Do social conditions coerce consent? And if they do, is it fair to consider the women so coerced to be morally defective?

3. The author of *Uncle Tom's Cabin* thought of Uncle Tom as a moral hero. So did the millions of her readers. Yet today we appear ready to think of Uncle Tom in an entirely different light. Are we morally more sophisticated than the people of the nineteenth century? (Consider also such "deferential wives" as Dorothea Casaubon in George Eliot's *Middlemarch* or Mrs. Ramsey in Virginia Woolf's *To the Lighthouse*.)

4. According to Hill, the servile person does not satisfy the basic requirement to respect morality. How does Hill arrive at this position?

5. Do you know of someone of superior moral character who, nevertheless, seems to fit Hill's descriptions of one who is excessively self-effacing and deferential? How do you square your perception of this person with the arguments presented here for thinking of him or her as someone who does not respect morality?

SUGGESTED READINGS

Bellah, Robert *et al.*, eds. *Individualism and Commitment in American Life*. New York: Harper & Row, 1984.

Goffman, Erving. *The Presentation of Self in Everyday Life*. New York: Doubleday, 1979.

Hochschild, Arlie. *The Managed Heart*. Los Angeles: University of California Press, 1984.

Kant, Immanuel. *Lectures on Ethics,* trans. Louis Enfield. New York: The Century Company, 1930.

Kupperman, Joel J. *Character*. New York: Oxford University Press, 1991.

Lasch, Christopher. *The Culture of Narcissism*. New York: Norton, 1979.

Rorty, Amelie. *The Identities of Persons*. Berkeley and Los Angeles: University of California Press, 1976.

Sennett, Richard. *The Fall of Public Man*. New York: Alfred A. Knopf, 1977.

Williams, Bernard. *Moral Luck*. Cambridge, MA: Cambridge University Press, 1981.

Yankelovich, Daniel. *New Rules: Searching for Fulfillment in a World Turned Upside Down*. New York: Random House, 1981.

Chapter Eight

MORALITY AND THE FAMILY

What is happening to the family? We can find the answer by looking at the change in attitudes and practices regarding filial relations, parental authority, the status of women, and divorce—changes that have destabilized traditional family ties.

Several authors in Chapter Eight see contemporary irreverence toward traditional family norms as socially pernicious. Rabbi Norman Lamm is concerned with the family as an institution that guarantees the survival of moral and religious traditions. Christina Sommers tries to show that many contemporary moral philosophers contribute to a climate of opinion that undermines the network of moral obligations that binds the members of a family. Rebecca West discusses the effect of divorce on children and considers whether prohibiting divorce would be wise. Implicit in the articles of Lamm, Sommers, and Lin Yutang is the conviction of a need to preserve the family's integrity as a social institution of great value for civilization. Thus they tend to subordinate such other moral considerations as the desirability of allowing family members a great deal of individual freedom to the wider concern of preserving the family itself.

In contrast, Jane English represents the many contemporary philosophers who aim to liberate individuals from family practices they view as oppressive. For example, according to English we only owe our parents those duties we owe to good friends in general. No friendship, no obligations.

Lin Yutang, following Confucius and Mencius, would find the views that English expresses altogether unacceptable and inhumane. In the Chinese tradition, feelings of gratitude and respect for one's parents rank highly among the moral virtues. Lin Yutang points out that filial regard for parents and grandparents does not come naturally; it must be "taught by culture." Yutang finds Western society sadly lacking in the kind of acculturation that assures its members a dignified old age.

Trebilcot and Wasserstrom are more directly concerned with the "gender system," which they consider "sexist" and unfair to women. They argue for replacing the basic institutions that reinforce gender differences by a new social arrangement in which sexual difference plays no social or legal role. In such an "androgynous" or "assimilationist" society, the family as we know it would have no legal status and would not necessarily be the primary social unit within which children are reared. Wasserstrom and Trebilcot are radical feminist philosophers. Sommers's critique of philosophers hostile to the family defends a more liberal and less radical feminism than is currently popular.

On Growing Old Gracefully

LIN YUTANG

Lin Yutang (1895–1976) was a novelist and a philosopher. He is the author of a number of books, including *The Importance of Living* (1937) and *The Wisdom of China and India* (1955).

Lin Yutang describes the Chinese family system's treatment of old people and contrasts it with Western norms and attitudes. He notes that we need strong cultural norms to assure respect for parents, grandparents, and older people in general. "A natural man loves his children, but a cultured man loves his parents." Chinese deference and respect for age contrasts sharply with Western attitudes, where we view growing old as almost disgraceful and expect old people not to "interfere" in the family's home life.

The Chinese family system, as I conceive it, is largely an arrangement of particular provision for the young and the old, for since childhood and youth and old age occupy half our life, it is important that the young and the old live a satisfactory life. It is true that the young are more helpless and can take less care of themselves, but on the other hand, they can get along better without material comforts than the old people. A child is often scarcely aware of material hardships,

ON GROWING OLD GRACEFULLY From *The Importance of Living* by Lin Yutang (William Heinemann Ltd., 1931). Reprinted with the permission of Mrs. Lin Yutang.

751

with the result that a poor child is often as happy as, if not happier than, a rich child. He may go barefooted, but that is a comfort, rather than a hardship to him, whereas going barefooted is often an intolerable hardship for old people. This comes from the child's greater vitality, the bounce of youth. He may have his temporary sorrows, but how easily he forgets them. He has no idea of money and no millionaire complex, as the old man has. At the worst, he collects only cigar coupons for buying a pop-gun, whereas the dowager collects Liberty Bonds. Between the fun of these two kinds of collection there is no comparison. The reason is the child is not yet intimidated by life as all grown-ups are. His personal habits are as yet unformed, and he is not a slave to a particular brand of coffee, and he takes whatever comes along. He has very little racial prejudice and absolutely no religious prejudice. His thoughts and ideas have not fallen into certain ruts. Therefore, strange as it may seem, old people are even more dependent than the young because their fears are more definite and their desires are more delimited.

Something of this tenderness toward old age existed already in the primeval consciousness of the Chinese people, a feeling that I can compare only to the Western chivalry and feeling of tenderness toward women. If the early Chinese people had any chivalry, it was manifested not toward women and children, but toward the old people. That feeling of chivalry found clear expression in Mencius in some such saying as, "The people with grey hair should not be seen carrying burdens on the street," which was expressed as the final goal of a good government. Mencius also described the four classes of the world's most helpless people as: "The widows, widowers, orphans, and old people without children." Of these four classes, the first two were to be taken care of by a political economy that should be so arranged that there would be no unmarried men and women. What was to be done about the orphans Mencius did not say, so far as we know, although orphanages have always existed throughout the ages, as well as pensions for old people. Every one realizes, however, that orphanages and old age pensions are poor substitutes for the home. The feeling is that the home alone can provide anything resembling a satisfactory arrangement for the old and the young. But for the young, it is to be taken for granted that not much need be said, since there is natural parental affection. "Water flows downwards and not upwards," the Chinese always say, and therefore the affection for parents and grandparents is something that stands more in need of being taught by culture. A natural man loves his children, but a cultured man loves his parents. In the end, the teaching of love and respect for old people became a generally accepted principle, and if we are to believe some of the writers, the desire to have the privilege of serving their parents in their old age actually became a consuming passion. The greatest regret a Chinese gentleman could have was the eternally lost opportunity of serving his old parents with medicine and soup on their deathbed, or not to be present when they died. For a high official in his fifties or sixties not to be able to invite his parents to come from their native village and stay with his family at the capital, "seeing them to bed every night and greeting them every morning," was to commit a moral sin of which he should be ashamed and for which he had constantly to offer excuses and explanations to his friends and colleagues. This regret was expressed in two lines by a man who returned too late to his home, when his parents had already died:

> The tree desires repose, but the wind will not stop;
> The son desires to serve, but his parents are already gone.

It is to be assumed that if man were to live his life like a poem, he would be able to look upon the sunset of his life as his happiest period, and instead of trying to postpone the much feared old age, be able actually to look forward to it, and gradually build up to it as the best and happiest period of his existence. In my efforts to compare and contrast Eastern and Western life, I have found no differences that are absolute except in this matter of the attitude towards age, which is sharp and clearcut and permits of no intermediate positions. The differences in our attitude towards sex, toward women, and toward work, play, and achievement are all relative. The relationship between husband and wife in China is not essentially different from that in the West, nor even the relationship between parent and child. Not even the ideas of individual liberty and democracy and the relationship between the people and their ruler are, after all, so very different. But in the matter of our attitude toward age, the difference is absolute, and the East and West take exactly opposite points of view. This is clearest in the matter of asking about a person's age or telling one's own. In China, the first question a person asks the other on an official call, after asking about his name and surname is, "What is your glorious age?" If the person replies apologetically that he is twenty-three or twenty-eight, the other party generally comforts him by saying that he has still a glorious future, and that one day he may become old. But if the person replies that he is thirty-five or thirty-eight, the other party immediately exclaims with deep respect, "Good luck!"; enthusiasm grows in proportion as the gentleman is able to report a higher and higher age, and if the person is anywhere over fifty, the inquirer immediately drops his voice in humility and respect. That is why all old people, if they can, should go and live in China, where even a beggar with a white beard is treated with extra kindness. People in middle age actually look forward to the time when they can celebrate their fifty-first birthday, and in the case of successful merchants or officials, they would celebrate even their forty-first birthday with great pomp and glory. But the fifty-first birthday, or the half-century mark, is an occasion of rejoicing for people of all classes. The sixty-first is a happier and grander occasion than the fifty-first and the seventy-first is still happier and grander, while a man able to celebrate his eighty-first birthday is actually looked upon as one specially favored by heaven. The wearing of a beard becomes the special prerogative of those who have become grandparents, and a man doing so without the necessary qualifications, either of being a grandfather or being on the other side of fifty, stands in danger of being sneered at behind his back. The result is that young men try to pass themselves off as older than they are by imitating the pose and dignity and point of view of the old people, and I have known young Chinese writers graduated from the middle schools, anywhere between twenty-one and twenty-five, writing articles in the magazines to advise what "the young men ought and ought not to read," and discussing the pitfalls of youth with a fatherly condescension.

This desire to grow old and in any case to appear old is understandable when one understands the premium generally placed upon old age in China. In the first place, it is a privilege of the old people to talk, while the young must listen and hold their tongue. "A young man is supposed to have ears and no mouth," as a Chinese saying goes. Men of twenty are supposed to listen when people of thirty are talking, and these in turn are supposed to listen when men of forty are talking. As the desire to talk and to be listened to is almost universal, it is evident that the further along one gets in years, the better chance he has to talk and to be listened to when he goes about in society. It is a game of life in which no one is favored, for everyone has a chance of becoming old in his time. Thus a father lecturing his son is obliged to stop suddenly and change his demeanor the moment the grandmother opens her mouth. Of course he wishes to be in the grandmother's place. And it is quite fair, for what right have the young to open their mouth when the old men can say, "I have crossed more bridges than you have crossed streets!" What right have the young got to talk?

In spite of my acquaintance with Western life and the Western attitude toward age, I am still continually shocked by certain expressions for which I am totally unprepared. Fresh illustrations of this attitude come up on every side. I have heard an old lady remarking that she has had several grandchildren, but, "It was the first one that hurt." With the full knowledge that American people hate to be thought of as old, one still doesn't quite expect to have it put that way. . . .

I have no doubt that the fact that the old men of America still insist on being so busy and active can be directly traced to individualism carried to a foolish extent. It is their pride and their love of independence and their shame of being dependent upon their children. But among the many human rights the American people have provided for in the Constitution, they have strangely forgotten about the right to be fed by their children, for it is a right and an obligation growing out of service. How can any one deny that parents who have toiled for their children in their youth, have lost many a good night's sleep when they were ill, have washed their diapers long before they could talk and have spent about a quarter of a century bringing them up and fitting them for life, have the right to be fed by them and loved and respected when they are old? Can one not forget the individual and his pride of self in a general scheme of home life in which men are justly taken care of by their parents and, having in turn taken care of their children, are also justly taken care of by the latter? The Chinese have not got the sense of individual independence because the whole conception of life is based upon mutual help within the home; hence there is no shame attached to the circumstance of one's being served by his children in the sunset of one's life. Rather it is considered good luck to have children who can take care of one. One lives for nothing else in China.

In the West, the old people efface themselves and prefer to live alone in some hotel with a restaurant on the ground floor, out of consideration for their children and an entirely unselfish desire not to interfere in their home life. But the old people have the right to

755

interfere, and if interference is unpleasant, it is nevertheless natural, for all life, particularly the domestic life, is a lesson in restraint. Parents interfere with their children anyway when they are young, and the logic of noninterference is already seen in the results of Behaviorists, who think that all children should be taken away from their parents. If one cannot tolerate one's own parents when they are old and comparatively helpless, parents who have done so much for us, whom else can one tolerate in the home? One has to learn self-restraint anyway, or even marriage will go on the rocks. And how can the personal service and devotion and adoration of loving children ever be replaced by the best hotel waiters?

The Chinese idea supporting this personal service to old parents is expressly defended on the sole ground of gratitude. The debts to one's friends may be numbered, but the debts to one's parents are beyond number. Again and again, Chinese essays on filial piety mention the fact of washing diapers, which takes on significance when one becomes a parent himself. In return, therefore, is it not right that in their old age, the parents should be served with the best food and have their favorite dishes placed before them? The duties of a son serving his parents are pretty hard, but it is sacrilege to make a comparison between nursing one's own parents and nursing a stranger in a hospital. For instance, the following are some of the duties of the junior at home, as prescribed by Tu Hsishih and incorporated in a book of moral instruction very popular as a text in the old schools:

> In the summer months, one should, while attending to his parents, stand by their side and fan them, to drive away the heat and the flies and mosquitoes. In winter, he should see that the bed quilts are warm enough and the stove fire is hot enough, and see that it is just right by attending to it constantly. He should also see if there are holes or crevices in the doors and windows, that there may be no draft, to the end that his parents are comfortable and happy.

> A child above ten should get up before his parents in the morning, and after the toilet go to their bed and ask if they have had a good night. If his parents have already gotten up, he should first curtsy to them before inquiring after their health, and should retire with another curtsy after the question. Before going to bed at night, he should prepare the bed, when the parents are going to sleep, and stand by

until he sees that they have fallen off to sleep and then pull down the bed curtain and retire himself.

Who, therefore, wouldn't want to be an old man or an old father or grandfather in China?

This sort of thing is being very much laughed at by the proletarian writers of China as "feudalistic," but there is a charm to it which makes many old gentlemen inland cling to it and think that modern China is going to the dogs. The important point is that every man grows old in time, if he lives long enough, as he certainly desires to. If one forgets this foolish individualism which seems to assume that an individual can exist in the abstract and be literally independent, one must admit that we must so plan our pattern of life that the golden period lies ahead in old age and not behind us in youth and innocence. For if we take the reverse attitude, we are committed without our knowing to a race with the merciless course of time, forever afraid of what lies ahead of us—a race, it is hardly necessary to point out, which is quite hopeless and in which we are eventually all defeated. No one can really stop growing old; he can only cheat himself by not admitting that he is growing old. And since there is no use fighting against nature, one might just as well grow old gracefully. The symphony of life should end with a grand finale of peace and serenity and material comfort and spiritual contentment, and not with the crash of a broken drum or cracked cymbals.

STUDY QUESTIONS

1. Describe Lin Yutang's account of how the West and the East treat their elderly people.
2. Yutang asks, "How can any one deny that parents who have toiled for their children . . . have lost many a good night's sleep when they were ill, have washed their diapers . . . and have spent about a quarter of a century bringing them up . . . have the right to be fed by them and loved and respected when they are old?" Do you agree with him? Do you feel a moral obligation to care for your parents when they are old?
3. How does Yutang distinguish between debts of friendship and debts to parents? Do you see a fundamental difference between the two?

4. Does Yutang criticize Western mores fairly? Or does he fail to understand the kind of individualism that characterizes human relations in our society? Some say the price for deference to the aged is a feeling of obligation that may interfere with our sense of independence. Do you agree with this?

What Do Grown Children Owe Their Parents?

JANE ENGLISH

Jane English (1947–1978), who taught philosophy at the University of North Carolina, Chapel Hill, wrote several articles and edited a number of books in the area of practical ethics. She died tragically at 31 in an expedition on the Matterhorn.

Jane English argues that grown children have no filial obligations. She distinguishes between relations based on reciprocal favors and relationships of friendship. Both involve duties, but English argues that friendship and its duties ought to be the norm governing the relationship of grown children and parents. Filial obligation is not required per se; it is the result of friendship rather than a debt owed for services rendered. Thus obligations to parents exist "just so long as friendship exists."

WHAT DO GROWN CHILDREN OWE THEIR PARENTS? © *Having Children: Philosophical and Legal Reflections on Parenthood,* edited by Onora O'Neill and William Ruddick (New York: Oxford University Press, 1979).

What do grown children owe their parents? I will contend that the answer is "nothing." Although I agree that there are many things that children *ought* to do for their parents, I will argue that it is inappropriate and misleading to describe them as things "owed." I will maintain that parents' voluntary sacrifices, rather than creating "debts" to be "repaid," tend to create love or "friendship." The duties of grown children are those of friends and result from love between them and their parents, rather than being things owed in repayment for the parents' earlier sacrifices. Thus, I will oppose those philosophers who use the word "owe" whenever a duty or obligation exists. Although the "debt" metaphor is appropriate in some moral circumstances, my argument is that a love relationship is not such a case.

Misunderstandings about the proper relationship between parents and their grown children have resulted from reliance on the "owing" terminology. For instance, we hear parents complain, "You owe it to us to write home (keep up your piano playing, not adopt a hippie lifestyle), because of all we sacrificed for you (paying for piano lessons, sending you to college)." The child is sometimes even heard to reply, "I didn't ask to be born (to be given piano lessons, to be sent to college)." This inappropriate idiom of ordinary language tends to be obscure, or even to undermine, the love that is the correct ground of filial obligation.

1. Favors Create Debts

There are some cases, other than literal debts, in which talk of "owing," though metaphorical, is apt. New to the neighborhood, Max barely knows his neighbor, Nina, but he asks her if she will take in his mail while he is gone for a month's vacation. She agrees. If, subsequently, Nina asks Max to do the same for her, it seems that Max has a moral obligation to agree (greater than the one he would have had if Nina had not done the same for him), unless for some reason it would be a burden far out of proportion to the one Nina bore for him. I will call this a *favor:* when A, at B's request, bears some burden for B, then B incurs an obligation to reciprocate. Here the metaphor of Max's "owing" Nina is appropriate. It is not literally a debt, of course, nor can Nina pass this IOU on to heirs, demand payment in the form of Max's taking out her garbage, or sue Max.

Nonetheless, since Max ought to perform one act of similar nature and amount of sacrifice in return, the term is suggestive. Once he reciprocates, the debt is "discharged"—that is, their obligations revert to the condition they were in before Max's initial request.

Contrast a situation in which Max simply goes on vacation and, to his surprise, finds upon his return that his neighbor has mowed his grass twice weekly in his absence. This is a voluntary sacrifice rather than a favor, and Max has no duty to reciprocate. It would be nice for him to volunteer to do so, but this would be supererogatory on his part. Rather than a favor, Nina's action is a friendly gesture. As a result, she might expect Max to chat over the back fence, help her catch her straying dog, or something similar—she might expect the development of a friendship. But Max would be chatting (or whatever) out of friendship, rather than in repayment for mown grass. If he did not return her gesture, she might feel rebuffed or miffed, but not unjustly treated or indignant, since Max has not failed to perform a duty. Talk of "owing" would be out of place in this case.

It is sometimes difficult to distinguish between favors and non-favors, because friends tend to do favors for each other, and those who exchange favors tend to become friends. But one test is to ask how Max is motivated. Is it "to be nice to Nina" or "because she did x for me"? Favors are frequently performed by total strangers without any friendship developing. Nevertheless, a temporary obligation is created, even if the chance for repayment never arises. For instance, suppose that Oscar and Matilda, total strangers, are waiting in a long checkout line at the supermarket. Oscar, having forgotten the oregano, asks Matilda to watch his cart for a second. She does. If Matilda now asks Oscar to return the favor while she picks up some tomato sauce, he is obligated to agree. Even if she had not watched his cart, it would be inconsiderate of him to refuse, claiming he was too busy reading the magazines. He may have had a duty to help others, but he would not "owe" it to her. But if she had done the same for him, he incurs an additional obligation to help, and talk of "owing" is apt. It suggests an agreement to perform equal, reciprocal, canceling sacrifices.

2. The Duties of Friendship

The terms "owe" and "repay" are helpful in the case of favors, because the sameness of the amount of sacrifice on the two sides is important; the monetary metaphor suggests equal quantities of sacrifice. But friendship ought to be characterized by *mutuality* rather than reciprocity: friends offer what they can give and accept what they need, without regard for the total amounts of benefits exchanged. And friends are motivated by love rather than by the prospect of repayment. Hence, talk of "owing" is singularly out of place in friendship.

For example, suppose Alfred takes Beatrice out for an expensive dinner and a movie. Beatrice incurs no obligation to "repay" him with a goodnight kiss or a return engagement. If Alfred complains that she "owes" him something, he is operating under the assumption that she should repay a favor, but on the contrary his was a generous gesture done in the hopes of developing a friendship. We hope that he would not want her repayment in the form of sex or attention if this was done to discharge a debt rather than from friendship. Since, if Alfred is prone to reasoning in this way, Beatrice may well decline the invitation or request to pay for her own dinner, his attitude of expecting a "return" on his "investment" could hinder the development of a friendship. Beatrice should return the gesture only if she is motivated by friendship.

Another common misuse of the "owing" idiom occurs when the Smiths have dined at the Joneses' four times, but the Joneses at the Smiths' only once. People often say, "We owe them three dinners." This line of thinking may be appropriate between business acquaintances, but not between friends. After all, the Joneses invited the Smiths not in order to feed them or to be fed in turn, but because of the friendly contact presumably enjoyed by all on such occasions. If the Smiths do not feel friendship toward the Joneses, they can decline future invitations and not invite the Joneses; they owe them nothing. Of course, between friends of equal resources and needs, roughly equal sacrifices (though not necessarily roughly equal dinners) will typically occur. If the sacrifices are highly out of proportion to the resources, the relationship is closer to servility than to friendship.[1]

Another difference between favors and friendship is that after a friendship ends, the duties of friendship end. The party that has sacrificed less owes the other nothing. For instance, suppose Elmer

---

[1] *Cf.* Thomas E. Hill, Jr., "Servility and Self-respect," *Monist* 57 (1973). Thus, during childhood, most of the sacrifices will come from the parents, since they have most of the resources and the child has most of the needs. When children are grown, the situation is usually reversed.

donated a pint of blood that his wife Doris needed during an operation. Years after their divorce, Elmer is in an accident and needs one pint of blood. His new wife, Cora, is also of the same blood type. It seems that Doris not only does not "owe" Elmer blood, but that she should actually refrain from coming forward if Cora has volunteered to donate. To insist on donating not only interferes with the newlyweds' friendship, but it belittles Doris and Elmer's former relationship by suggesting that Elmer gave blood in hopes of favors returned instead of simply out of love for Doris. It is one of the heart-rending features of divorce that it attends to quantity in a relationship previously characterized by mutuality. If Cora could not donate, Doris's obligation is the same as that for any former spouse in need of blood; it is not increased by the fact that Elmer similarly aided her. It *is* affected by the degree to which they are still friends, which in turn may (or may not) have been influenced by Elmer's donation.

In short, unlike the debts created by favors, the duties of friendship do not require equal quantities of sacrifice. Performing equal sacrifices does not cancel the duties of friendship, as it does the debts of favors. Unrequested sacrifices do not themselves create debts, but friends have duties regardless of whether they requested or initiated the friendship. Those who perform favors may be motivated by mutual gain, whereas friends should be motivated by affection. These characteristics of the friendship relation are distorted by talk of "owing."

3. Parents and Children

The relationship between children and their parents should be one of friendship characterized by mutuality rather than one of reciprocal favors. The quantity of parental sacrifice is not relevant in determining what duties the grown child has. The medical assistance grown children ought to offer their ill mothers in old age depends upon the mothers' need, not upon whether they endured a difficult pregnancy, for example. Nor do one's duties to one's parents cease once an equal quantity of sacrifice has been performed, as the phrase "discharging a debt" may lead us to think.

Rather, what children ought to do for their parents (and parents for children) depends upon (1) their respective needs, abilities, and resources and (2) the extent to which there is an ongoing friendship between them. Thus, regardless of the quantity of childhood sacrifices, an able, wealthy child has an obligation to help his needy parents more than does a needy child. To illustrate, suppose sisters Cecile and Dana are equally loved by their parents, even though Cecile was an easy child to care for, seldom ill, while Dana was often sick and caused some trouble as a juvenile delinquent. As adults, Dana is a struggling artist living far away, while Cecile is a wealthy lawyer living nearby. When the parents need visits and financial aid, Cecile has an obligation to bear a higher proportion of these burdens than her sister. This results from her abilities, rather than from the quantities of sacrifice made by the parents earlier.

Sacrifices have an important causal role in creating an ongoing friendship, which may lead us to assume incorrectly that it is the sacrifices that are the source of obligation. That the source is the friendship instead can be seen by examining cases in which the sacrifices occurred but the friendship, for some reason, did not develop or persist. For example, if a woman gives up her newborn child for adoption, and if no feelings of love ever develop on either side, it seems that the grown child does not have an obligation to "repay" her for her sacrifices in pregnancy. For that matter, if the adopted child has an unimpaired love relationship with the adoptive parents, he or she has the same obligations to help them as a natural child would have.

The filial obligations of grown children are a result of friendship, rather than owed for services rendered. Suppose that Vance married Lola despite his parents' strong wish that he marry within their religion, and that as a result, the parents refuse to speak to him again. As the years pass, the parents are unaware of Vance's problems, his accomplishments, the birth of his children. The love that once existed between them, let us suppose, has been completely destroyed by this event and thirty years of desuetude. At this point, it seems, Vance is under no obligation to pay his parents' medical bills in their old age, beyond his general duty to help those in need. An additional, filial obligation would only arise from whatever love he may still feel for them. It would be irrelevant for his parents to argue, "But look how much we sacrificed for you when you were young," for that sacrifice was not a favor but occurred as part of a friendship which existed at the time but is now, we have supposed, defunct. A more appropriate message would be, "We still love you, and we would like to renew our friendship."

I hope this helps to set the question of what children ought to do for their parents in a new light. The parental argument, "You ought to do *x* because we did *y* for you," should be replaced by, "We love you and you will be happier if you do *x*," or "We believe you love us, and anyone who loved us would do *x*." If the parents' sacrifice had been a favor, the child's reply, "I never asked you to do *y* for me," would have been relevant; to the revised parental remarks, this reply is clearly irrelevant. The child can either do *x* or dispute one of the parents' claims: by showing that a love relationship does not exist, or that love for someone does not motivate doing *x*, or that he or she will not be happier doing *x*.

Seen in this light, parental requests for children to write home, visit, and offer them a reasonable amount of emotional and financial support in life's crises are well founded, so long as a friendship still exists. Love for others does call for caring about and caring for them. Some other parental requests, such as for more sweeping changes in the child's lifestyle or life goals, can be seen to be insupportable, once we shift the justification from debts owed to love. The terminology of favors suggests the reasoning, "Since we paid for your college education, you owe it to us to make a career of engineering, rather than becoming a rock musician." This tends to alienate affection even further, since the tuition payments are depicted as investments for a return rather than done from love, as though the child's life goals could be "bought." Basing the argument on love leads to different reasoning patterns. The suppressed premise, "If A loves B, then A follows B's wishes as to A's lifelong career" is simply false. Love does not even dictate that the child adopt the parents' values as to the desirability of alternative life goals. So the parents' strongest available argument here is, "We love you, we are deeply concerned about your happiness, and in the long run you will be happier as an engineer." This makes it clear that an empirical claim is really the subject of the debate.

The function of these examples is to draw out our considered judgments as to the proper relation between parents and their grown children, and to show how poorly they fit the model of favors. What is relevant is the ongoing friendship that exists between parents and children. Although that relationship developed partly as a result of parental sacrifices for the child, the duties that grown children have to their parents result from the friendship rather than from the sacrifices. The idiom of owing favors to one's parents can actually be destructive if it undermines the role of mutuality and leads us to think in terms of quantitative reciprocal favors.

STUDY QUESTIONS

1. How does English distinguish between duties created by debts and duties created by friendship?
2. Do you agree with English that filial obligation is not owed for services rendered, but instead results from friendship? How would Lin Yutang react to this view?
3. In some states, law requires children of poor elderly people to contribute to their support. Do you think English would argue for or against this? Do you support legislation of this kind?
4. Can we criticize English for advocating a "minimalist ethic" according to which no duties of self-sacrifice or altruism apply outside one's small circle of friends—all people, even family members, are moral strangers unless one voluntarily "contracts" an obligation?
5. How might English account for the moral duty many people feel to take care of not only their own elderly parents, but needy elderly people in general?

Traditional Jewish Family Values

NORMAN LAMM

Rabbi Norman Lamm (b. 1927), president of Yeshiva University, is the author of *Faith and Doubt* (1971) and *The Good Society* (1974).

Lamm presents an idealized model of the traditional Jewish family and contrasts it with the average contemporary Jewish family. The traditional family is much more rigorously organized, its members' roles are strictly defined, and, consequently, the family itself is more important as an institution. This results in greater intimacy and a strong sense of mutual obligation, for example, to the elderly who are esteemed as authoritative. Members of the traditional family practice a great deal of restraint and forebearance, emphasizing duty, rather than rights. Finally, the family sees itself as part of a more general community of Jewish families that is, in turn, part of a continuous tradition and history. The traditional family is religious and committed to carrying on a Jewish tradition. This, says Lamm, gives it further cohesiveness.

Lamm argues for the importance of the "benevolent authority" that parents exercise, an authority all the more effective because the higher authority of God qualifies it. According to Lamm, a family that lacks a central authority cannot be cohesive. The children of such families tend

TRADITIONAL JEWISH FAMILY VALUES From *Jewish Consciousness-raising*. Edited by Norman Linzer. © 1973 by the Board of Jewish Education of Greater New York. Reprinted by permission of the copyright holder.

to be confused and disoriented. Lamm warns that we are losing our sense of commitment to tradition in a world without faith and cannot replace it simply by recognizing how badly we need it.

. . . I am going to set up a contrast between two arbitrarily designed models, one of a traditional and the other of a modern Jewish home. My excuse is that I am not aiming at sociological accuracy but at clarity of exposition. First, the idealized version of the traditional Jewish home is characterized by a high degree of intimacy, of love, of devotion, usually non–demonstrative. The husband normally is a monogamist and the wife is satisfied to be at home. As opposed to this, contemporary parents are more remote. They are encouraged to follow their own interests. The mother is told that she should not allow her life to be wrapped up entirely in her children and in her home, but should find outside interests. The father, when he comes back from the office, seeks out a peer group or other kinds of involvements. As a result, the parents seek their own particular levels of interest, or areas of interest, and are removed from the nexus of the home.

Second, in traditional Jewish homes there is a special esteem for age, which is cherished for its own sake. Of course, this goes back to the Biblical commandments of "Honor thy father and mother" and honor for the teacher and elder, but sociologically speaking, it is not so much a revealed norm as a lived value. The traditional home likely as not included an extended family larger than the nuclear family. Most Jewish children grew up in the presence of a grandfather or a grandmother, some kind of living relic of the past, and developed a natural respect and reverence for age not because of any specific function of the elderly, but because age itself was valued. Compare that now to the contemporary emphasis on youth and youthfulness, especially in America but all over the Western world as well. That the focus of our culture is the young is often revealed in some of the inanities of the Jewish community organizations and its press. We are so geared to the young that when we want to decide the great questions of the day, we send out a researcher to take a statistical analysis of what high school sophomores are thinking, because that represents "the wave of the future" which ought, by implication, to determine our stand, not only with regard to dress and speech but even with regard to policy, religion, etc. I am presenting a caricature, of course (although I have certain specific incidents in mind), but it does contain the kernel of a true reflection of the quality of life in America.

Third, in this idealized picture of the traditional Jewish home, there were more or less well defined roles for father and mother. Probably, this was not only true for the Jewish home: it was the case for general culture in which Jews found themselves in pre-modern or pre-contemporary times. A little boy knew what was expected of him when he became a big boy and a big man, and a little girl knew the role into which she was emerging and for which, therefore, she ought to be striving. This clear role definition is increasingly absent in the contemporary home, where there occurs a great deal of blurring and interchanging of roles, with consequent functional chaos when it comes to identifying the roles of father and mother as separate and distinct from each other.

Fourth, the traditional Jewish home emphasized the value of self-restraint, of renunciation, "Thou shalt not." The modern home, in our pop-culture, regards "Thou shalt not" as an excessive inhibition which can harm the emotions and mentality of the growing child. Morally, the modern home is characterized much more by permissiveness than by renunciation and restraint. Perhaps one can best describe the difference between the traditional Jewish home and the modern Jewish home by the polarity of duty and right. The traditional home emphasized duty. What am I supposed to do? What must I do? The modern Jewish home is more a matter of rights: the children's right, the wife's right, the mother's right, the father's right. Everyone has his or her rights, and in this competition of rights a balance has to be struck and a harmony established so that everyone gets his due. The emphasis is not on the contribution that I must make, but rather on what my fair share is, what my rights are.

Finally, in the traditional Jewish home there is understood and presupposed a commitment by all members of the family to a goal or a source that transcends the family. There is some kind of transcendent commitment which binds the members of the family. This transcendent commitment is usually some aspect of, or combination of aspects of, the Jewish tradition—the Jewish people, Jewish law, Jewish religion, God, Torah. The modern home lacks the axiological or ideological cohesiveness. If a religious or nationalistic commitment is present, it is not considered particularly important. It never really plays a central role in the life of the family. Again I ask you not to charge me with being unscientific. I am setting up models, and not insisting, of course, that every modern family follows one path or every traditional family the other.

The five elements, for the purpose of our discussion, may be reduced to three more basic issues: love, authority, and commitment.

Love

Let us begin with the first one, love. The traditional Jewish family structure is disintegrating. As time goes on and assimilation increases, you find that the whole pattern I have described as the paradigm of a Jewish family that we have inherited from the past, is falling apart. We are experiencing an accelerated decentralization of the family as a result of the various centrifugal forces which tend to pull the family apart. As it is wrenched out of the context of a stable, self-sufficient Jewish community life, the family begins to disintegrate at the edges. Eventually, the community as a whole follows suit. Furthermore, modern goals such as the desideratum of self-fulfillment and self-realization, which really are basic and important values for moderns, tend to polarize individuals in the family. They diminish the virtues of self-sacrifice, of loyalty, of restraint which had previously acted as centripetal forces in favor of the family unit. If I must seek my self-fulfillment and my self-realization, I will find that that often conflicts with what I might otherwise consider my specific duties to my parents, to my wife, to my children, to the family as a whole. . . .

Now, in the highly structured traditional Jewish family, especially the patriarchal one, where there is a clear source of authority (which we shall discuss in more detail later), the family enforces a practical conformity with its norms and its ideological commitment. Sometimes, however, the traditional Jewish family, in enforcing this ideological pattern, this whole routine of life for all its members, overuses its discipline which overwhelms the element of love. In this model we have set up the traditional Jewish family; love and devotion were ever-present, but so was discipline, which guaranteed family cohesion. But sometimes it happened that the discipline was too strong, so that it became rigid, thus diminishing the element of love, warmth, spontaneity, and the sense of intimacy. That is why you find sometimes that within Orthodox families—especially in the modern

769

or contemporary period—there is a rigidity and a defensiveness against the "outside world" that was not true when the entire community was more or less traditional. Often an Orthodox family in our days finds itself on the defensive as a cognitive minority and develops a kind of "man the ramparts" psychology, and even philosophy, that undergirds it. It is not always the healthiest thing for the development of a family's solidarity to feel that they are living in a beleagured fortress. Sometimes it helps, sometimes it doesn't. But because of it, parents in a truly Orthodox family will sometimes be harsh with children—overly harsh—neglecting, in this sense, some of the wisdom of their own tradition.

This wisdom can best be recapitulated in a famous story told of the founder of the Hasidic movement, the Besht (Rabbi Israel Baal Shem Tov). A father once came to him to complain that his son was going off on the wrong path and leaving Jewish morality and Jewish religious practice. He said to the Rabbi, "What can I do? He is destroying my life, he is destroying everything I've stood for." The Besht answered in three words: *"Love him more."* Instead of bearing down on him, love him more. And with love you probably can achieve a great deal more than by cracking the whip. If you are overly harsh, if you are overly insistent upon conformity to standards that you have inherited which you cherish, then this kind of strictness can be counter-productive.

Authority

The center of gravity in the family makes it a family and not just a group of biologically related people who happen to live under the same roof. The father is usually the source of authority in the traditional Jewish family, but not always. Sometimes it is the mother. In a number of very pious families today in this country, as in the *shtetl,* a young husband will spend several years of intensive study in a *Kollel,* a school of advanced Talmudic research. If he was a great or at least a good scholar, he usually was the source of authority. It sometimes happened that the father who went off to study was not quite that competent and never amounted to much. In that case, the mother, who had much less education and was sometimes illiterate, often was, by virtue of her own gut wisdom, the real and effective head of the family. (One can cite similar instances of a secularized version of this pattern. There are young men in modern, non-religious families who go off to graduate school with their fellowships and scholarships to earn their degrees, while the working wife is the one who really is the "smart" one and runs the family.) However, as a rule it is the father who represented the patriarchal communal authority for his particular family. In the discussion that is now to follow, if I use the term "father," you may easily substitute "mother" if the particular family circumstances call for it. He or she is the one person who above all other represents authority for the entire family. . . .

This father in the traditional Jewish family is an *authority*. He is not a "pal" to his children. He does not run the family along the lines of a participatory democracy where every important problem is taken to a vote with children possessing one-man, one-vote rights equally with father and mother. In this family you do not find the contemporary penchant for an unconscious divination of the future by a reverential observation of the "younger set." Here, then, is no assumption that, since the future is always an improvement over the present, a higher point in inevitable "progress," therefore, children possess some intuitive wisdom to which parents must make obeisance. Not here do you find the phenomenon of treating children as the brokers of the peer group, who actually inform parents how to be "with it" and run things. Often, as you are well aware, the failure of parents to exercise discipline is not really a sign of their love for their children, but rather a disguise for their fundamental lack of concern. If I don't genuinely care for my child, then I will act like a "pal," let him do as he wishes, and delude myself into thinking that in this manner he will think better of me. But with such an attitude, the role of the authority in the family is eroded. This liberal posture, and in radical circles, this conscious and deliberate egalitarianism, represents a frontal attack on the structure of the family by gutting its source and focus of authority.

One must bear in mind that the authority of parents in traditional Judaism was never considered absolute, even in Biblical days. The father was not acknowledged as a kind of petty tyrant who could do with his family as he liked. He was, to follow the metaphor, a constitutional monarch. . . . The father was not the absolute sovereign of that family. This Biblical and Rabbinic teaching must be compared to the then contemporary or even later cultures. In the Grecian and

Roman times, a father had the legal right to put a child to death for disobedience. In Greece, a child who was weak and therefore a drain on the family's finances could be taken up to a mountain and left to die. This was accepted as normal and legitimate practice by parents. Not so in Judaism, where *a* source of authority does not imply *absolute* authority. Only God is absolute authority. Parental direction had to be benevolent, and even loving, giving the family its reference point and its structure.

This description of the exercise of benevolent authority and discipline in the traditional Jewish family is, of course, idealized. It was not always so effective. There was apparently always present in Jewish life the phenomenon of Jewish overindulgence of children. Let me illustrate this with two interesting examples from Jewish literature and history. The universality of this proclivity for excessive forbearance by Jewish parents is given fascinating testimony in the following passage:

> There is yet one other evil disease regarding raising children that is not practiced by other people. A child sits at the table with his father and mother and he is the first to stretch forth his hand to partake of the food. He thus grows up arrogant, without fear or culture or refinement, acting as if his father and mother were friends or siblings. By the time he is 8 or 9 years old and his parents wish to correct their earlier mistakes, they no longer are able to, for his childish habits have already become second nature . . .

> Another bad and bitter practice: Parents take a child to school, and in front of the child, warn the teacher not to punish him. When the child hears this, he no longer pays attention to his school work and his disobedience grows worse. This was not the practice of our ancestors. In their days, if a child came crying to his father or mother and told of being punished by a teacher, they would send along the child a gift to the teacher and congratulate the teacher . . .

Modern though it sounds, this complaint comes from *Tzeror Hachayyim* by Rabbi Mosheh Hagiz, over 220 years ago. Two centuries ago, in the pre-modern period, Jewish parents were already indulgent, so this Jewish syndrome is older than the modern period.

Let us cite one more passage, this time advice by a German Jew on the desirable method of raising children.

A man should begin to train his children in the service of God and in good character when they are yet very young. He must be careful not to permit his love for them to indulge them and permit them to do whatever they wish. . . . However, he must be very careful not to frighten them unnecessarily, lest the child be driven to harm himself. . . . Every parent must judge his child's individual personality and treat him accordingly. Also, if a parent is always angry, the child will come to despise him and pay no more attention to his approach than to a barking dog.

This frank and intelligent advice comes from *Yosef Ometz* of 350 years ago. It is worth listening to him closely. It summarizes, in a way, 3,000 years of cumulative Jewish experience. It is the frequent absence of this combined love and authority, which equals intelligent discipline, that bedevils so many families today.

Commitment

After love and authority, our third and final element for discussion is: commitment. The father in this idealized Jewish traditional family is not only the visible and present focus of authority for the children, but he is also a symbol, the representative and refractor of a Higher Authority. . . . The father effectively acts as the psychological focus for the child of an authority greater than the father himself. He is a surrogate, a broker, of a kind of authority that is beyond the family itself. The father as authority is not self-contained and, in traditional Judaism, he is not self-authenticating. There is a higher authority which legitimates the role of the father. The father is only the broker of this higher authority of God, Torah, Judaism, tradition. The father grounds his authority in the sanction of the Transcendent to which father and son and mother and daughter are all mutually committed. This sanction of the father's authority (or, if you will, the authority of his authority) is the cement of commitment that helped bind the family and make of it a cohesive, well-structured unit. The child knows: if I am angry at my father and I want to rebel, I may hate him; I may even have a death wish for him. But I know all along that there is something beyond father; he is not the ultimate ground of authority, and some day I will be the continuation of my own family because all of us are bound to something much higher.

The focus of the commitment must be beyond the father or

773

whoever happens to be the authority in that family, in order for the family to be united by this commitment.

Thus, this religious commitment is a necessary but not sufficient condition for the reconstitution of family life. Most Jewish homes today are fundamentally non-Jewish. ("Ethnic Jewishness" is totally irrelevant in this respect.) Those Jewish values which do survive, however you want to describe them, are the fortuitous results of a cultural lag. When the fundamental commitment has spent itself, the accompanying phenomena tend to continue for a while: but you can't draw endlessly on that spent capital. Take a minor example: education. Most of us have or had parents whose formal education was less than the one that we possess. Why? The answer is: the Jewish drive for education. A Jewish boy and a Jewish girl must get an education. We, in turn, give this value to our children. But I don't know how much longer this is going to continue, not only because the counter-culture makes a virtue a nonachievement rather than achievement, but because our whole impulse for education—to take this one Jewish value—derives from a religious commitment. It is not primarily a sociological phenomenon—the way for the immigrants to get out of the sweatshops. The original inclination comes from the *Mitzvah* of *Talmud Torah,* the religious commandment to study the Torah. This purely religious norm later became secularized, turning from "Torah" to "education," and that meant how to be a doctor or a lawyer or a professor. But when you cut off the major commitment—the religious commitment—all its derivative Jewish values can continue only by virtue of a cultural lag. Alone, these values have only limited endurance and must soon vanish.

Prescription

So much for analysis. Let us now turn to prescription. Unfortunately, I believe I have a much better grasp of what's wrong than I have any ability to prescribe for it. But since the theme assigned to me requires prescription as well, I shall try my hand and hope the medicine I offer you is at least somewhat effective. I feel that the best approach is the indirect one. Let me follow my outline with a slight change, and discuss authority first.

For a family to be cohesive, to be healthy, there has to be a source— a focus of authority. A totally shared authority is inadequate because it is unfocused; it means that no one really knows what's going on. Children under such conditions become confused, not knowing whom to turn to. . . . When I say authority, I hope I will not be misunderstood. I am not speaking of the petty tyrant who pulls at his suspenders and says "I'm boss because I wear the pants in the family." I refer, rather, to an intelligent, enlightened attitude where there is, within rational psychological limits, a division of labor, a division of responsibility, and a division of authority, but where at least there is some kind of grouping around a center.

Of course, there are special problems with fatherless families. What does one do in a family made fatherless through death or divorce or separation or abandonment? Here I believe one ought to begin to search out a surrogate father. Either mother must learn how to assert authority or, if she is constitutionally unable to do so, there has to be some way for her children to find a father-model, whether it be a teacher or someone else who can firmly assert moral responsibility and moral authority. Granted, this is easier said than done.

Love. If it doesn't exist, the family situation seems almost hopeless, because of personal, psychological, and sociocultural reasons. Even the minimum effort that would be necessary to support it under such conditions appears to me to be heroic. The problem is complicated nowadays by the fact that the nuclear family in contemporary Jewish life is largely divorced from the extended family, and it is the extended family which tends to retain Judaism's social and moral norms longer than the solitary nuclear family. When a unit consisting of father and mother and children are pulled out of the context of the larger Jewish group, it will tend to lose any traditional values much more quickly than a continuing Jewish neighborhood will lose those same values even if they are already suffering the attrition of assimilation. The Jewish community as a whole has, of course, undergone assimilatory erosion, but I think that the great move to suburbia which came about during the '50s was the beginning of a precipitate abandonment of the whole Jewish nexus, which was a core of the residue of Jewish values. In other words, upper social mobility spelled for us a very sudden downward trend in psychological stability and religious continuity.

Finally, let us turn to the theme of commitment. In the absence of any genuine inner religious commitment in a Jewish family, we must seek some external idea or cause which can attract and centralize the commitment of the individual members of the family. I am a great believer in the fact that the focus of family cohesiveness must be transcendent and not immanent. It cannot be the family for the family's sake. It just doesn't work in the kind of society in which we live, with all its centrifugal pulls. It has got to be something beyond the family to which all members, or most members of the family, are mutually committed.

Conclusions

. . . You say: what can we do? My answer is: we are facing a terribly messy situation. It is the universal condition of man today—of man without God, of man without faith, without an awareness of transcendence, man who feels terribly endangered by the gaping existential void within him, by the threat of meaninglessness which is aggravated by the ubiquitous awareness of death. You just cannot fill the transcendental void by values which we sit down and artificially create. There is no way out. To be honest, either we choose the real thing, or we are in despair. We cannot in one hour or in one lifetime ever hope to devise an adequate substitute for religious faith; in any event, according to my own commitments, substitutes are called—idols.

The Jewish family was strong not when it discussed values but when it lived them. It began to disintegrate when it substituted cocktails for *kiddush* and tuxedo for *tallit*. Traditional Jewish wholesomeness was grounded in a spiritual commitment, in a sublime web of ritual acts invested with both metaphysical significance and nostalgic and historic recollection, so that individuals were both synchronically and diachronically part of a people—a people called a *mishpachah* (family) at its very founding by Abraham. These are not just disembodied "values" or artificial "rituals," but part of a living organism, which gave life and vitality to the family and a sense of validity to its members, despite the ubiquitous domestic problems to which Jews, like all humans, are heir.

STUDY QUESTIONS

1. Lamm gives several criteria of family integrity. In your opinion, are these specific to the traditional Jewish family or are they more

general? For example, would a cohesive Catholic or Protestant family satisfy *these* conditions or some others? Specify them.

2. According to Lamm, commitment to the authority of God is an important ingredient in the cohesive family. How, in your opinion, does such commitment contribute to a family's integrity? Is commitment to God an *essential* ingredient?

3. Assuming Lamm is right, how, if in any way, can we create the conditions necessary for stable families? Lamm himself points out that we cannot do this artificially. Are there natural ways?

4. If Lamm's criteria for the close-knit family are indeed too stringent for modern times, is the rapid decline of the family as an institution inevitable?

Divorce

REBECCA WEST

Rebecca West (1892–1982) was one of the foremost figures in twentieth-century Anglo-American intellectual life. Her work, which includes fiction, criticism, biography, history, and travel reporting, is admired for its wit, eloquence, and intellectual power.

In her essay on divorce, Rebecca West assumes that the family is a vital institution. This raises a question: Should we preserve the family by outlawing divorce even at the cost of individual happiness? West's answer is a qualified no. She describes the harmful effects of divorce on children, effects of a "radiating kind, likely to travel down and down through the generations, such as few would care to have on their consciences." Conversely, she notes that, sometimes, remaining with a brutal parent can be

DIVORCE From *The London Daily Express*, 1930. Reprinted by permission of A. D. Peters & Co. Ltd.

even more harmful. West also argues in favor of the right to divorce because countries that do not allow it are often oppressive and sexually hypocritical.

The way one looks at divorce depends on the way one looks at a much broader question.

Is the mental state of humanity so low that it is best to lay down invariable rules for it which have been found to lead to the greatest happiness of the greatest number, and insist that everyone keep them in spite of the hardship necessarily inflicted on certain special cases, thus dragooning the majority into compulsory happiness? Or is it so high that it is safe to lay down rules which will admit of variation for different people in different circumstances, when it seems to them these variations can secure their happiness?

If one agrees with the first view, then one is bound to disapprove altogether of divorce. If one agrees with the second, then one is bound to approve of legislation which enables unhappily married persons to separate and remarry.

Though I have the kind of temperament that hates to own failure and would never wish to break a marriage I had made, I regard divorce laws as a necessary part of the arrangements in a civilized State. This is the result of my experience of life in countries where there is practically no divorce, and in countries where divorce is permissible on grounds of varying latitude.

Superficially the case against divorce is overwhelming: and indeed it should never be forgotten, least of all by those who approve of divorce as a possibility. Getting a divorce is nearly always as cheerful and useful an occupation as breaking very valuable china. The divorce of married people with children is nearly always an unspeakable calamity. It is only just being understood, in the light of modern psychological research, how much a child depends for its healthy growth on the presence in the home of both its parents. This is not a matter of its attitude to morals; if divorce did nothing more than make it accustomed to the idea of divorce, then no great harm would be done. The point is that if a child is deprived of either its father or its mother it feels that it has been cheated out of a right. It cannot be reasoned out of this attitude, for children are illogical, especially where their affections are concerned, to an even greater degree than ourselves. A child who suffers from this resentment suffers much more than grief: he is liable to an obscuring of his vision, to a warping of his character. He may turn against the parent to whom the courts have given him, and regard him or her as responsible for the expulsion of the other from the home. He may try to compensate himself for what he misses by snatching everything else he can get out of life, and become selfish and even thievish. He may, through yearning for the unattainable parent, get himself into a permanent mood of discontent, which will last his life long and make him waste every opportunity of love and happiness that comes to him later.

If either parent remarries, the child may feel agonies of jealousy. What is this intruder coming in and taking affection when already there is not as much as there ought to be? This is an emotion that is felt by children even in the case of fathers and mothers who have lost their partners by death: as witness the innumerable cases of children who come up before the Juvenile Courts and prove on examination to have committed their offences as acts of defiance against perfectly inoffensive and kindly step-parents. It is felt far more acutely in the case of parents whose relationships have been voluntarily severed, who have no excuse of widowhood or widowerhood to justify the introduction of a new partner. This, of course, need not always happen. One of the happiest homes I can think of is the second venture of a man and a woman who both divorced their first partners as a result of conduct that poisoned not only their lives but their children's: it is one of the most cheerful sights I know to see their combined family of four children realizing with joy and surprise that actually they can have a family life like other people. But that man and that woman are not only kindly people, they are clever people. They handle the children with extreme sensitiveness to the issues involved. More commonly the situation for the child is not completely salved.

In fact, people with children who divorce husbands or wives because they are troublesome are likely to find themselves saddled with rather more discontent than they hoped to escape. And the new trouble is of a radiating kind, likely to travel down and down through the generations, such as few would care to have on their consciences.

As for the divorce of childless married couples, there is of course a matter of infinitely less social significance. If it is regarded too lightly it cheats a lot of them out of their one chance of happiness. A man and woman marry each other because they represent to each other the types they have always found attractive and about which they have spun innumerable romantic dreams. They then grow disappointed with each other because they insist on being themselves, the human beings they happened to be born, instead of the dreamed-of types. If they stay together it may in time penetrate to each that the other may not have the qualities of the imagined one, but may have real and valuable virtues which are much more useful; and a very kindly feeling of attachment may develop. But if a couple break up during the first shock of disappointment they are certain to go off and immediately find other people who resemble the dreamed-of types, marry them, and go through the same process of disillusionment, ending in another separation. Thus a whole group of people will be involved in sterile and inharmonious excitements which will waste the very short time we are given to establish ourselves in fruitful and harmonious relationships.

Against these considerations, of course, we have to reckon that although the consequences of being the child of divorced parents are heavy, they are sometimes not so heavy as the consequences of being a child brought up in close propinquity and at the mercy of a brutal and vicious parent. We have also to admit that in the case of a childless couple there may be reasons why a divorce may become as essential to a human being's continued existence as food or air. There is infidelity, there is drunkenness, there is, above all, cruelty, not only of the body but of the mind. No one who has not been through it can know the full horror of being tied to a man who craves war instead of peace, whose love is indistinguishable from hate. The day that is poisoned from its dawn by petty rages about nothing, by a deliberate destruction of everything pleasant: the night that is full of fear, because it is certain that no one can suffer all this without going mad, and if one goes mad there will be nobody to be kind; these are things to which no human being should have a life sentence.

But brutal and vicious parents are in a minority. Human nature is not so bad as all that. The opponents of divorce are therefore justified when they ask if it is not dangerous to give the victims of this minority the power to free themselves from these burdens that cannot be borne, when that power will inevitably be available to those who want to free themselves from burdens that they only think cannot be borne. For human beings are stupid; they do not know what is best for them, they certainly will not use that power wisely. If the majority is to suffer unnecessarily from these facilities for divorce, would it not be better to withdraw and let the minority fend for itself?

I do not think so. Because there is another element involved; and that is the general attitude of the community toward sex. That seems to be invariably less sane where there is no divorce than where there is. What makes humanity stupid is that it will act on certain mad fairy-tales about life which it refuses to outgrow, and its attitude to sex determines all these mad fairy-tales.

The lack of divorce corrupts the community's attitude to sex for several reasons. First of all, it deprives marriage of all standards. If one cannot be penalized for failure in an activity, and the prizes for success in it are of a highly rarefied and spiritual nature, the baser man will regard it as a go-as-you-please affair. The man who knows that he can commit adultery without the slightest check from society will have to be a very high type if he does not come to the conclusion that, since society is so indifferent to it, adultery must be a trivial matter. But his natural jealousy will not permit him to think like that of his wife's adultery. That he will punish in all of the very extensive ways which are open to him through his economic power.

Thus there starts the fictitious system of morality which, instead of regarding sexual conduct as a means to an end, and that end the continuance of the species in the most harmonious conditions, places purely arbitrary values on different sexual entities and plays a game with them like Mah-Jong. Since a man's adultery does not matter and a woman's adultery does, it follows that a man's whole sexual life is without moral significance, and a woman's sexual life is portentous with it. Whenever you have no divorce laws you must have the double standard of morality. Consequently a large part of the male sex, as much as is not controlled by idealism, roves about the world trying with complete impunity to persuade the female sex to a course of action which, should the female comply, leads them to disaster. The seducer, it must be noted, has an enormous advantage in countries where there is no divorce. Even in England, we sometimes come across a Don Juan who has the luck to have a wife who will not divorce him, and note how useful he finds this in persuading ladies that he loves them. He can so safely say that he would marry them if he could, without danger that his bluff will be called. Every

Don Juan enjoys this advantage in a country where there is no divorce. Illegitimate births follow which—because of the arbitrary distinction between the sexes—are not robbed of their sting as they are in the countries where divorce is possible by laws that guarantee the offspring its maintenance, but result in the persecution of mother and child.

In fact, sex is associated with cruelty in countries where there is no divorce, as it is in the institution of prostitution: this also flourishes wherever there is this double standard of morality. No illicit love affair, where both parties are exercising free choice, can possibly do the community as much harm as the traffic between the prostitute and her client. That a woman should be held in contempt for submitting to the same physical relationship that is the core of marriage degrades marriage, and all women, and all men; and the greater the contempt she is held in the more she becomes genuinely contemptible. For as she sinks lower she becomes more and more a source of disease, and more and more a brutalized machine. It is in countries where there is no divorce that the prostitute is most firmly established as the object of extra-marital adventures and is most deeply despised.

One can test this by its converse if one goes to a library and turns up old comic papers and plays, particularly farces. As the law and society began to sanction divorce, and impressed on the public a sense of moral obligation, this ceased to be the case.

It is one of the most important things in the world that people should have a sane and kindly outlook on sex; that it should not be associated with squalor and cruelty. Because divorce makes it clear to the ordinary man and woman that they must behave well in the married state or run the risk of losing its advantages, it does impress on them some rudiments of a sane attitude towards sex. It therefore lifts up the community to a level where happy marriages, in which the problem of our human disposition to cruelty and jealousy is satisfactorily solved, are much more likely to occur.

STUDY QUESTIONS

1. Rebecca West says that "people with children who divorce husbands or wives because they are troublesome are likely to find themselves saddled with rather more discontent than they hoped

to escape. And the new trouble is of a radiating kind, likely to travel down and down through the generations, such as few would care to have on their consciences." Can West be consistent in permitting divorce, given her views on its ill effects?

2. Why does West believe that lack of divorce has a corrupting effect on society? Do you agree that the human cost of permitting divorce is lower than the cost of outlawing it?

3. West notes that children suffer from the effects of divorce through several generations. If this is so, wouldn't prohibiting divorce be morally right in those cases where one or both parents do not brutalize the children? Why, after all, should parents be allowed to inflict a divorce on their innocent children?

Sex Roles and the Ideal Society

RICHARD WASSERSTROM

Richard Wasserstrom (b. 1936) is professor of philosophy at the University of California at Santa Cruz. He has served as President of the American Philosophical Association (Pacific Division), and is the author of numerous articles and books in ethics and social philosophy. Among his books are *War and Morality* (1970) and *Philosophy and Social Issues* (1980).

Richard Wasserstrom argues for a society that incorporates the "assimilationist ideal." In the assimilationist society, whether one is male or female signifies no more than whether one is blue-eyed or brown-eyed. "[N]o political rights or social institutions, practices and norms would mark the physiological differences between males

SEX ROLES AND THE IDEAL SOCIETY Excerpted from *Philosophy and Social Issues* by Richard Wasserstrom (Notre Dame, IN: University of Notre Dame Press, 1980), pp. 23–41.

and females as important. . . . Bisexuality, not hetero-sexuality or homosexuality would be the typical intimate, sexual relationship in the ideal society that was assimilationist in respect to sex."

Wasserstrom considers and rejects a number of popular arguments against assimilationism. To the objection that gender role differences are to some extent determined by biological differences, Wasserstrom replies that apart from childbearing, all major roles and functions are determined socially; for example, child rearing could be assigned without regard for sex. To the argument that this would be "unnatural," Wasserstrom replies that all social arrangements are in one sense unnatural, and that we are morally bound to institute arrangements that will give everyone, male or female, equality of opportunity and personal autonomy. The attempt to keep the status quo is conservative and illiberal. To the argument that the universality of gender roles suggests that they serve vital human purposes, Wasserstrom replies that no such purposes have ever been demonstrated and that the universality of sexual differentiation in respect to social roles is, anyway, morally irrelevant since such differentiation usually keeps women in subordinate positions; morally we should rectify this state of affairs by instituting the appropriate assimilationist reforms.

Wasserstrom considers the argument that children are better raised by women. Even if this is so, Wasserstrom argues that it is objectionable to assign to women an onerous burden that involves a disproportionate share of what is unpleasant, unsatisfying, unrewarding work.

Wasserstrom points out that many of the objections to assimilationism overlook the fact that one's sex is not a matter of choice, while the choice of social arrangements and reforms that we can institute is ours to make as moral and socially responsible beings. A nonassimilationist society cannot be viewed plausibly as a good or just society. So we must work for the assimilationist ideal.

. . . [O]ne conception of a nonracist society is that which is captured by what I shall call the assimilationist ideal: a nonracist society would be one in which the race of an individual would be the functional equivalent of the eye color of individuals in our society today. In our society no basic political rights and obligations are determined on the basis of eye color. No important institutional benefits and burdens are connected with eye color. Indeed, except for the mildest sort of aesthetic preferences, a person would be thought odd who even made private, social decisions by taking eye color into account. It would, of course, be unintelligible, and not just odd, were a person to say today that while he or she looked blue-eyed, he or she regarded himself or herself as really a brown-eyed person. Because eye color functions differently in our culture than does race, there is no analogue to passing for eye color. Were the assimilationist ideal to become a reality, the same would be true of one's race. In short, according to the assimilationist ideal, a nonracist society would be one in which an individual's race was of no more significance in any of these three areas than is eye color today.

What is a good deal less familiar is an analogous conception of the good society in respect to sexual differentiation—one in which an individual's sex were to become a comparably unimportant characteristic. An assimilationist society in respect to sex would be one in which an individual's sex was of no more significance in any of the three areas than is eye color today. There would be no analogue to transsexuality, and, while physiological or anatomical sex differences would remain, they would possess only the kind and degree of significance that today attaches to the physiologically distinct eye colors persons possess.

It is apparent that the assimilationist ideal in respect to sex does not seem to be as readily plausible and obviously attractive here as it is in the case of race. In fact, many persons invoke the possible realization of the assimilationist ideal as a reason for rejecting the Equal Rights Amendment and indeed the idea of women's liberation itself. The assimilationist ideal may be just as good and just as important an ideal in respect to sex as it is in respect to race, but it is important to realize at the outset that this appears to be a more far-reaching proposal when applied to sex rather than race and that many more persons think there are good reasons why an assimilationist society in respect to sex would not be desirable than is true for the comparable racial ideal. Before such a conception is assessed, however, it will be useful to provide a somewhat fuller characterization of its features.

To begin with, it must be acknowledged that to make the assimilationist ideal a reality in respect to sex would involve more profound and fundamental revisions of our institutions and our attitudes than would be the case in respect to race. On the institutional level we would, for instance, have to alter significantly our practices concerning marriage. If a nonsexist society is a society in which one's sex is no more significant than eye color in our society today, then laws which require the persons who are getting married to be of different sexes would clearly be sexist laws.

More importantly, given the significance of role differentiation and ideas about the psychological differences in temperament that are tied to sexual identity, the assimilationist ideal would be incompatible with all psychological and sex-role differentiation. That is to say, in such a society the ideology of the society would contain no proposition asserting the inevitable or essential attributes of masculinity or feminity; it would never encourage or discourage the ideas of sisterhood or brotherhood; and it would be unintelligible to talk about the virtues or the disabilities of being a woman or a man. In addition, such a society would not have any norms concerning the appropriateness of different social behavior depending upon whether one were male or female. There would be no conception of the existence of a set of social tasks that were more appropriately undertaken or performed by males or by females. And there would be no expectation that the family was composed of one adult male and one adult female, rather than, say, just two adults—if two adults seemed the appropriate number. To put it simply, in the assimilationist society in respect to sex, persons would not be socialized so as to see or understand themselves or others as essentially or significantly who they were or what their lives would be like because they were either male or female. And no political rights or social institutions, practices, and norms would mark the physiological differences between males and females as important.

Were sex like eye color, these kinds of distinctions would make no sense. Just as the normal, typical adult is virtually oblivious to the eye color of other persons for all significant interpersonal relationships, so, too, the normal, typical adult in this kind of nonsexist society would be equally as indifferent to the sexual, physiological differences of other persons for all significant interpersonal relationships. Bisexuality, not heterosexuality or homosexuality, would be the typical intimate, sexual relationship in the ideal society that was assimilationist in respect to sex. . . .

. . . [T]here appear to be very few, if any, respects in which the ineradicable, naturally occurring differences between males and females *must* be taken into account. The industrial revolution has certainly made any of the general differences in strength between the sexes capable of being ignored by the good society for virtually all significant human activities. And even if it were true that women are naturally better suited than men to care for and nurture children, it is also surely the case that men can be taught to care for and nurture children well. Indeed, the one natural or biological fact that seems *required* to be taken into account is the fact that reproduction of the human species requires that the fetus develop *in utero* for a period of months. Sexual intercourse is not necessary, for artificial insemination is available. Neither marriage nor the nuclear family is necessary either for conception or child rearing. Given the present state of medical knowledge and what might be termed the natural realities of female pregnancy, it is difficult to see why any important institutional or interpersonal arrangements are constrained to take the existing biological differences as to the phenomenon of *in utero* pregnancy into account.

But to say all this is still to leave it a wholly open question to what degree the good society *ought* to build upon any ineradicable biological differences, or to create ones in order to construct institutions and sex roles which would thereby maintain a substantial degree of sexual differentiation. . . .

The point that is involved here is a very general one that has application in contexts having nothing to do with the desirability or undesirability of maintaining substantial sexual differentiation. It has to do with the fact that humans possess the ability to alter their natural and social environment in distinctive, dramatic, and unique ways. An example from the nonsexual area can help bring out this too seldom recognized central feature. It is a fact that some persons born in human society are born with congenital features such that they cannot walk or walk well on their legs. They are born naturally crippled or lame. However, humans in our society certainly possess the capability to devise and construct mechanical devices and institutional arrangements which render this natural fact about some persons relatively unimportant in respect to the way they and others will

787

live together. We can bring it about, and in fact are in the process of bringing it about, that persons who are confined to wheelchairs can move down sidewalks and across streets because the curb stones at corners of intersections have been shaped so as to accommodate the passage of wheelchairs. And we can construct and arrange buildings and events so that persons in wheelchairs can ride elevators, park cars, and be seated at movies, lectures, meetings, and the like. Much of the environment in which humans live is the result of their intentional choices and actions concerning what that environment shall be like. They can elect to construct an environment in which the natural incapacity of some persons to walk or walk well is a major difference or a difference that will be effectively nullified vis-à-vis the lives that they, too, will live.

Nonhuman animals cannot do this in anything like the way humans can. A fox or an ape born lame is stuck with the fact of lameness and the degree to which that will affect the life it will lead. The other foxes or apes cannot change things. This capacity of humans to act intentionally and thereby continuously create and construct the world in which they and others will live is at the heart of what makes studies of nonhuman behavior essentially irrelevant to and for most if not all of the normative questions of social, political, and moral theory. Humans can become aware of the nature of their natural and social environment and then act intentionally to alter the environment so as to change its impact upon or consequences for the individuals living within it. Nonhuman animals cannot do so. This difference is, therefore, one of fundamental theoretical importance. At the risk of belaboring the obvious, what it is important to see is that the case against any picture of the good society of an assimilationist sort—if it is to be a defensible critique—ought to rest on arguments concerned to show why some other ideal would be preferable; it cannot plausibly rest in any significant respect upon the claim that the sorts of biological differences typically alluded to in contexts such as these require that the society not be assimilationist in character.

There are, though, several other arguments based upon nature, or the idea of the "natural" that also must be considered and assessed. First, it might be argued that if a way of doing something is natural, then it ought to be done that way. Here, what may be meant by "natural" is that this way of doing the thing is the way it would be done if culture did not direct or teach us to do it differently. It is not clear, however, that this sense of "natural" is wholly intelligible; it supposes that we can meaningfully talk about how humans would behave in the absence of culture. And few if any humans have ever lived in such a state. Moreover, even if this is an intelligible notion, the proposal that the natural way to behave is somehow the appropriate or desirable way to behave is strikingly implausible. It is, for example, almost surely natural, in this sense of "natural," that humans would eat their food with their hands, except for the fact that they are, almost always, socialized to eat food differently. Yet, the fact that humans would naturally eat this way, does not seem in any respect to be a reason for believing that that is thereby the desirable or appropriate way to eat food. And the same is equally true of any number of other distinctively human ways of behaving.

Second, someone might argue that substantial sexual differentiation is natural not in the sense that it is biologically determined nor in the sense that it would occur but for the effects of culture, but rather in the sense that substantial sexual differentiation is a virtually universal phenomenon in human culture. By itself, this claim of virtual universality, even if accurate, does not directly establish anything about the desirability or undesirability of any particular ideal. But it can be made into an argument by the addition of the proposition that where there is a widespread, virtually universal social practice or institution, there is probably some good or important purpose served by the practice or institution. Hence, given the fact of substantial sex-role differentiation in all, or almost all, cultures, there is on this view some reason to think that substantial sex-role differentiation serves some important purpose for and in human society.

This is an argument, but it is hard to see what is attractive about it. The premise which turns the fact of sex-role differentiation into any kind of a strong reason for sex-role differentiation is the premise of conservatism. And it is no more or less convincing here than elsewhere. There are any number of practices or institutions that are typical and yet upon reflection seem without significant social purpose. Slavery was once such an institution; war perhaps still is. . . .

To put it another way, the question that seems fundamentally to be at issue is whether it is desirable to have a society in which sex-role differences are to be retained in the way and to the degree they are today—or even at all. The straightforward way to think about the question is to ask what would be good and what would be bad about a society in which sex functioned like eye color does in our society;

or alternatively, what would be good and what would be bad about a society in which sex functioned in the way in which religious identity does today; or alternatively, what would be good and what would be bad about a society in which sex functioned in the way in which it does today. We can imagine what such societies would look like and how they might work. It is hard to see how thinking about answers to this question is substantially advanced by reference to what has typically or always been the case. If it is true, for instance, that the sex-role-differentiated societies that have existed have tended to concentrate power and authority in the hands of males, have developed institutions and ideologies that have perpetuated that concentration, and have restricted and prevented women from living the kinds of lives that persons ought to be able to live for themselves, then this, it seems to me, says far more about what may be wrong with any strongly nonassimilationist ideal than does the conservative premise say what may be right about any strongly nonassimilationist ideal. . . .

One strong, affirmative moral argument on behalf of the assimilationist ideal is that it does provide for a kind of individual autonomy that a substantially nonassimilationist society cannot provide. The reason is because any substantially nonassimilationist society will have sex roles, and sex roles interfere in basic ways with autonomy. The argument for these two propositions proceeds as follows.

Any nonassimilationist society must have some institutions and some ideology that distinguishes between individuals in virtue of their sexual physiology, and any such society will necessarily be committed to teaching the desirability of doing so. That is what is implied by saying it is nonassimilationist rather than assimilationist. And any substantially nonassimilationist society will make one's sexual identity an important characteristic so that there will be substantial psychological, role, and status differences between persons who are male and those who are female. That is what is implied by saying that it is substantially nonassimilationist. Any such society will necessarily have sex roles, a conception of the places, characteristics, behaviors, etc., that are appropriate to one sex or the other but not both. That is what makes it a *sex* role.

Now, sex roles are, I think, morally objectionable on two or three quite distinct grounds. One such ground is absolutely generic and applies to all sex roles. The other grounds are less generic and apply only to the kinds of sex roles with which we are familiar and which are a feature of patriarchal societies, such as our own. I begin with the more contingent, less generic objections.

We can certainly imagine, if we are not already familiar with, societies in which the sex roles will be such that the general place of women in that society can be described as that of the servers of men. In such a society individuals will be socialized in such a way that women will learn how properly to minister to the needs, desires, and interests of men; women and men will both be taught that it is right and proper that the concerns and affairs of men are more important than and take precedence over those of women; and the norms and supporting set of beliefs and attitudes will be such that this role will be deemed the basic and appropriate role for women to play and men to expect. Here, I submit, what is objectionable about the connected set of institutions, practices, and ideology—the structure of the prevailing sex role—is the role itself. It is analogous to a kind of human slavery. The fundamental moral defect—just as is the case with slavery—is not that women are being arbitrarily or capriciously assigned to the social role of server, but that such a role itself has no legitimate place in the decent or just society. As a result, just as in the case with slavery, the assignment on *any* basis of individuals to such a role is morally objectionable. A society arranged so that such a role is a prominent part of the structure of the social institutions can be properly characterized as an *oppressive* one. It consigns some individuals to lives which have no place in the good society, which restrict unduly the opportunities of these individuals, and which do so in order improperly to enhance the lives and opportunities of others.

But it may be thought possible to have sex roles and all that goes with them without having persons of either sex placed within a position of general, systemic dominance or subordination. Here, it would be claimed, the society would not be an oppressive one in this sense. Consider, for example, the kinds of sex roles with which we are familiar and which assign to women the primary responsibilities for child rearing and household maintenance. It might be argued first that the roles of child rearer and household maintainer are not in themselves roles that could readily or satisfactorily be eliminated from human society without the society itself being deficient in serious, unacceptable ways. It might be asserted, that is, that these are roles or tasks that simply must be filled if children are to be raised in a satisfactory way. Suppose this is correct, suppose it is granted that society would necessarily have it that these tasks would have to be done. Still, if it is also correct that, relatively speaking, these are unsatisfying and unfulfilling ways for humans to concentrate the bulk of their energies and talents, then, to the degree to which this is so, what is morally objectionable is that if this is to be a *sex* role, then women are unduly and unfairly allocated a disproportionate share of what is unpleasant, unsatisfying, unrewarding work. Here the objection is the degree to which the burden women are required to assume is excessive and unjustified vis-à-vis the rest of society, i.e., the men. Unsatisfactory roles and tasks, when they are substantial and pervasive, should surely be allocated and filled in the good society in a way which seeks to distribute the burdens involved in a roughly equal fashion.

Suppose, though, that even this feature were eliminated from sex roles, so that, for instance, men and women shared more equally in the dreary, unrewarding aspects of housework and child care, and that a society which maintained sex roles did not in any way have as a feature of that society the systemic dominance or superiority of one sex over the other, there would still be a generic moral defect that would remain. The defect would be that any set of sex roles would necessarily impair and retard an individual's ability to develop his or her own characteristics, talents, capacities, and potential life-plans to the extent to which he or she might desire and from which he or she might derive genuine satisfaction. Sex roles, by definition, constitute empirical and normative limits of varying degrees of strength—restrictions on what it is that one can expect to do, be, or become. As such, they are, I think, at least prima facie objectionable.

To some degree, all role-differentiated living is restrictive in this sense. Perhaps, therefore, all role differentiation in society is to some degree troublesome, and perhaps all strongly role-differentiated societies are objectionable. But the case against sex roles and the concomitant sexual differentiation they create and require need not rest upon this more controversial point. For one thing that distinguishes sex roles from many other roles is that they are wholly involuntarily assumed. One has no choice about whether one shall be born a male or female. And if it is a consequence of one's being born a male or a female that one's subsequent emotional, intellectual, and material development will be substantially controlled by this fact, then it is necessarily the case that substantial, permanent, and involuntarily assumed restraints have been imposed on some of the most central factors concerning the way one will shape and live one's life. The point to be emphasized is that this would necessarily be the case, even in the unlikely event that substantial sexual differentiation could be maintained without one sex or the other becoming dominant and developing oppressive institutions and an ideology to support that dominance and oppression. Absent some far stronger showing than seems either reasonable or possible that potential talents, abilities, interests, and the like are inevitably and irretrievably distributed between the sexes in such a way that the sex roles of the society are genuinely congruent with and facilitative of the development of those talents, abilities, interests, and the like that individuals can and do possess, sex roles are to this degree incompatible with the kind of respect which the good or the just society would accord to each of the individual persons living within it. It seems to me, therefore, that there are persuasive reasons to believe that no society which maintained what I have been describing as *substantial* sexual differentiation could plausibly be viewed as a good or just society.

STUDY QUESTIONS

1. What does Richard Wasserstrom mean by the "Assimilationist Ideal"? What reasons does he give for aspiring to it and for working to realize it?
2. Wasserstrom says that "bisexuality, not heterosexuality or homosexuality, would be the typical intimate, sexual relationship in the ideal society that was assimilationist in respect to sex." Why does bisexuality become the ideal form of sexual intimacy for Wasserstrom? If you disagree with him, where do you think his argument goes wrong?
3. How does Wasserstrom respond to the following arguments against assimilationism: (1) sexual differentiation is natural and (2) sexual differentiation is a universal phenomenon in human culture.
4. Wasserstrom claims that sex roles are harmful because they interfere with individual freedom and autonomy. Could it be argued that the sexual differentiation between men and women enriches people's lives and that an "assimilated" (fully androgynous) society would be alienating and demoralizing for most people?

Two Forms of Androgynism

JOYCE TREBILCOT

Joyce Trebilcot (b. 1933) is coordinator of Women's Studies at Washington University and is the editor of *Mothering: Essays in Feminist Theory* (1984).

Androgyny, the sharing of male and female characteristics, is a biological term that has been redefined by many feminist thinkers to apply to men and women who reject the assignment of masculine and feminine roles along sexual lines. Joyce Trebilcot distinguishes between sex ("biological difference") and gender ("psychosocial difference"). The androgynous person rejects the idea that gender roles should correspond to sexual difference.

Trebilcot distinguishes two kinds of androgyny and discusses the virtues of each. The *monoandrogynist* holds that males and females should cultivate the best characteristics of *both* sexes and that *both* sexes should perform masculine and feminine roles. Thus everyone should strive to be nurturant and assertive, and everyone should perform tasks that usually are associated with a given sex. If one is living with someone, then one will share the responsibility for, say, housework, child care, car repairs,

TWO FORMS OF ANDROGYNISM By Joyce Trebilcot. Reprinted from the *Journal of Social Philosophy*, January 1977. By permission of Villanova University and the author.

snow shoveling, and the like. By contrast, the *polyandrog-ynist* advocates a variety of options that would allow a man or a woman to adopt a purely feminine or masculine role. Both varieties of androgyny seek to break the connection between sex and gender as a social ideal, but the polyandrogynist argues that, as a matter of individual choice, one might still opt for a lifestyle that follows the conventional pattern. Trebilcot examines several arguments favoring monoandrogyny, but in the end concludes that polyandrogynism should be promoted as the ideal because it is freer and more flexible.

Traditional concepts of women and men, of what we are and should be as females and males, of the implications of sex for our relationships to one another and for our places in society, are not acceptable. But what models, if any, should we adopt to replace them? In this paper I consider just two of the alternatives discussed in recent literature—two versions of androgynism.

In discussing these two views I follow the convention of distinguishing between sex (female and male) and gender (feminine and masculine). Sex is biological, whereas gender is psychosocial. Thus, for example, a person who is biologically female may be—in terms of psychological characteristics or social roles—feminine or masculine, or both.

Although what counts as feminine and masculine varies among societies and over time, I use these terms here to refer to the gender concepts traditionally dominant in our own society. Femininity, on this traditional view, has nurturing as its core: it centers on the image of woman as mother, as provider of food, warmth, and emotional sustenance. Masculinity focuses on mastery: it comprises the notion of man struggling to overcome obstacles, to control nature, and also the notion of man as patriarch or leader in society and the family.

The first form of androgynism to be discussed here takes the word "androgyny" literally, so to speak. In this word the Greek roots for man (*andros*) and woman (*gynē*) exist side by side. According to the first form of androgynism, both feminine and masculine characteristics should exist "side by side" in every individual: each woman and man should develop personality traits and engage in activities traditionally assigned to only one sex. Because this view postulates a single ideal for everyone, I call it monoandrogynism, or, for brevity, *M*.

Monoandrogynism, insofar as it advocates shared roles, is now official policy in a number of countries. For example, the Swedish government presented a report to the United Nations in 1968 specifying that in Sweden, "every individual, regardless of sex, shall have the same practical opportunities not only for education and employment but also fundamentally the same responsibility for his or her own financial support as well as shared responsibility for child upbringing and housework."[1]

Closer to home, Jessie Bernard, in her discussion of women's roles, distinguishes the one-role view, according to which a woman's place is in the home; the two-role pattern, which prescribes a combination of the traditional housewife-mother functions and work outside the home; and what she calls the "shared-role ideology" which holds "that children should have the care of both parents, that all who benefit from the services supplied in the household should contribute to them, and that both partners should share in supporting the household."[2]

Caroline Bird in her chapter "The Androgynous Life" writes with approval of role-sharing. She also suggests that the ideal person "combines characteristics usually attributed to men with characteristics usually attributed to women."[3] The psychological dimension of *M* is stressed by Judith M. Bardwick. In her essay "Androgyny and Humanistic Goals, or Goodbye, Cardboard People," she discusses a view according to which the ideal or "healthy" person would have traits of both genders. "We would then expect," she says, "both nurturance and competence, openness and objectivity, compassion and competitiveness from both women and men, as individuals, according to what they were doing."[4]

---

[1]Official Report to the United Nations on the Status of Women in Sweden, 1968. Quoted in Rita Liljeström, "The Swedish Model," in Georgene H. Seward and Robert C. Williamson, eds., *Sex Roles in Changing Society* (New York: Random House, 1970), p. 200.

[2]Jessie Bernard, *Women and the Public Interest* (Chicago: Aldine, 1971); and idem, *The Future of Marriage* (New York: Bantam Books, 1972). The quotation is from the latter book, p. 279.

[3]Caroline Bird, *Born Female* (New York: Pocket Books, 1968), p. xi.

The work of these and other writers provides the basis for a normative theory, M, which prescribes a single ideal for everyone: the person who is, in both psychological characteristics and social roles, both feminine and masculine.

The second form of androgynism shares with the first the principle that biological sex should not be a basis for judgments about the appropriateness of gender characteristics. It differs from the first, however, in that it advocates not a single ideal but rather a variety of options including "pure" femininity and masculinity as well as any combination of the two. According to this view, all alternatives with respect to gender should be equally available to and equally approved for everyone, regardless of sex. Thus, for example, a female might acceptably develop as a completely feminine sort of person, as both feminine and masculine in any proportion, or as wholly masculine. Because this view prescribes a variety of acceptable models, I call it polyandrogynism, or P.[5]

Constantina Safilios-Rothschild supports P in her recent book *Women and Social Policy*. In this work she makes a variety of policy recommendations aimed at bringing about the liberation of both sexes. Liberation requires, she says, that individuals live "according to their wishes, inclinations, potentials, abilities, and needs rather than according to the prevailing stereotypes about sex roles and sex-appropriate modes of thought and behavior." Some persons, she adds, "might *choose* to behave according to their sex's stereotypic . . . patterns. But some women and some men may *choose,* if they are so inclined, to take options in some or all of the life sectors now limited to the opposite sex."[6]

Carolyn Heilbrun's work also suggests P. In *Toward a Recognition of Androgyny* she writes, "The ideal toward which I believe we should

---

[4]Judith M. Bardwick, "Androgyny and Humanistic Goals, or Goodbye, Cardboard People," in Mary Louise McBee and Kathryn A. Blake, eds., *The American Woman: Who Will She Be?* (Beverly Hills, CA: Glencoe Press, 1974), p. 61.

[5]"Monoandrogynism" and "polyandrogynism" are perhaps not very happy terms, but I have been unable to find alternatives which are both descriptive and non-question-begging. In an earlier version of this paper I used "A_1" and "A_2" but these labels are not as perspicuous as "M" and "P." Mary Anne Warren in "The Ideal of Androgyny" (unpublished) refers to "the strong thesis" and "the weak thesis," but this terminology tends to prejudice judgment as to which view is preferable. Hence, I use "M" and "P."

[6]Constantina Safilios-Rothschild, *Women and Social Policy* (Englewood Cliffs, NJ: Prentice-Hall 1974), p. 7; emphasis hers.

move is best described by the term 'androgyny.' This ancient Greek word . . . defines a condition under which the characteristics of the sexes, and the human impulses expressed by men and women, are not rigidly assigned. Androgyny seeks to liberate the individual from the confines of the appropriate." Androgyny suggests, Heilbrun says, "a full range of experience open to individuals who may, as women, be aggressive, as men, tender; it suggests a spectrum upon which human beings choose their places without regard to propriety or custom."[7]

This second form of androgynism focuses on a variety of options rather than on the single model of the part-woman/part-man (that is, of the androgyne in the classic sense). It is appropriate, however, to extend the term "androgynism" to apply to it; for, like *M*, it seeks to break the connection between sex and gender.

For both forms of androgynism, the postulated ideals are best construed so as to exclude aspects of traditional gender concepts which are morally objectionable. Femininity should not be taken to include, for example, weakness, foolishness, or incompetence. Similarly, tendencies such as those to authoritarianism and violence should be eliminated from the concept of masculinity. Most importantly, aspects of the gender concepts which prescribe female submissiveness and male domination (over women and over other men) must, on moral grounds, be excluded from both the single ideal advocated by *M* and the range of options recommended by *P*.

Either form of androgyny may, in the long run, lead to major changes in human attributes. It is often suggested that the androgyne is a person who is feminine part of the time and masculine part of the time. But such compartmentalization might be expected to break down, so that the feminine and masculine qualities would influence one another and be modified. Imagine a person who is at the same time and in the same respect both nurturant and mastery-oriented, emotional and rational, cooperative and competitive, and so on. I shall not undertake here to speculate on whether this is possible, or, if it is, on how such qualities might combine. The point is just that androgyny in the long run may lead to an integrating of femininity and masculinity that will yield new attributes, new kinds of

---

[7]Carolyn Heilbrun, *Toward a Recognition of Androgyny* (New York: Harper & Row, 1973), pp. 7–8.

personalities. The androgyne at this extreme would perhaps be not part feminine and part masculine, but neither feminine nor masculine, a person in whom the genders disappear.

I turn now to the question of which of these two forms of androgynism is more acceptable. I am not concerned here to evaluate these positions in relation to other alternatives (for example, to the traditional sexual constitution of society or to matriarchy).[8] For the sake of this discussion, I assume that either *M* or *P* is preferable to any alternative, and that the problem is only to decide between them. Let us first consider this problem not as abstract speculation, and not as a problem for some distant society, but rather as an immediate issue for our own society. The question is then: Which form of androgynism is preferable as a guide to action for us here and now?

Suppose we adopt *M*. Our task then is to provide opportunities, encouragement, and perhaps even incentives for those who are now feminine to be also masculine, and conversely. Suppose, on the other hand, that we adopt *P*. Our task is to create an environment in which, without reference to sex, people choose among all (moral) gender alternatives. How can this best be accomplished? What is required, clearly, is that the deeply-entrenched normative connection between sex and gender be severed. Virtually everyone now, in formulating preferences for the self and in judging the appropriateness of gender characteristics for others, at least on some occasions takes it, consciously or otherwise, that the sex of the individual in question is a relevant consideration: that one is female tends to count in favor of a feminine trait and against a masculine one, and conversely. In order to break this connection, it must be shown that masculinity is acceptable for females and femininity for males. There must, then, be opportunities, encouragement, and perhaps even incentives for gender-crossing. But this is what is required by *M*. Hence, under present conditions, the two forms of androgynism prescribe the same course of action—that is, the promotion of gender-crossing.

The question "Which form of androgynism is preferable here and

---

[8] My current view is that we should work for the universal realization of women's values; but that is another paper. (For some arguments against the use of the term "androgyny" in feminist theory, see, for example, Mary Daly, "The Qualitative Leap beyond Patriarchal Religion," *Quest: A Feminist Quarterly*, vol. 1, no. 4 [Spring 1975], pp. 29*ff*.; and Janice Raymond, "The Illusion of Androgyny," *Quest*, vol. 2, no. 1 [Summer 1975].)

now?" then, is misconstrued. If one is an androgynist of either sort, what one must do now is seek to break the normative connection between sex and gender by bringing about gender-crossing. However, once the habit of taking sex as a reason for gender evaluation is overcome, or is at least much weaker and less widespread than it is today, then the two forms of androgynism do prescribe different courses of action. In particular, on M "pure" gender is condemned, but on P it is accepted. Let us consider, then, which version of androgynism is preferable for a hypothetical future society in which femininity and masculinity are no longer normatively associated with sex.

The major argument in favor of P is, of course, that because it stipulates a variety of acceptable gender alternatives it provides greater gender freedom than M. Now, freedom is a very high priority value, so arguments for M must be strong indeed. Let us consider, then, two arguments used to support M over P—one psychological, one ethical.

The psychological argument holds that in a society which is open with respect to gender, many people are likely to experience anxiety when faced with the need, or opportunity, to choose among different but equally acceptable gender models. Consider the words of Judith M. Bardwick:

> People need guidelines, directions that are agreed upon because they help each individual to know where one ought to go, how one can get there, and how far one is from one's goal. It is easier to sustain frustration that comes from knowing how far you are from your objective or what barriers are in your way than it is to sustain the anxiety that comes from not being sure about what you want to do or what others want you to do. It will be necessary, then, to develop new formulations by which people will guide their lives.[9]

Bardwick says that anxiety "comes from not being sure about what you want to do or what others want you to do." But in a society of the sort proposed by P, the notion that one should seek to please others in deciding among gender models would be rejected; ideally "what others want you to do" in such a society is to make your own decisions. Of course there is still the problem of not being sure about what *you* want to do. Presumably, under P, people would provide

---

[9]Bardwick, *op. cit.*, p. 50.

one another with help and support in finding suitable life-styles. Nevertheless, it could be that for some, choosing among alternatives would be anxiety-producing. On the other hand, under M, the lack of approved alternatives could produce frustration. Hence, the argument from anxiety should be paired with an argument from frustration. In M, socialization is designed to make everyone androgynous (in ways similar, perhaps, to those which have traditionally produced exclusive femininity and masculinity in our own society), and frustration is part of the cost. In P, socialization is directed toward enabling people to perceive, evaluate, and choose among alternatives, and there is a risk of anxiety. We are not now in a position to decide whether the frustration or the anxiety is worse, for there are no data on the numbers of people likely to suffer these emotions nor on the extent of the harm that they are likely to do. Hence, neither the argument from anxiety nor the argument from frustration is of any help in deciding between the two forms of androgynism.

I turn now to a more persuasive argument for M, one which claims that androgyny has universal value. This argument supports M not, as the argument from anxiety does, because M prescribes some norm or other, but rather because of the content of the norm. The argument holds that both traditional genders include qualities that have human value, qualities that it would be good for everyone to have. Among the elements of femininity, candidates for universal value are openness and responsiveness to needs and feelings, and being gentle, tender, intuitive, sensitive, expressive, considerate, cooperative, compassionate. Masculine qualities appealed to in this connection include being logical, rational, objective, efficient, responsible, independent, courageous. It is claimed, then, that there are some aspects of both genders (not necessarily all or only the ones I have mentioned) which are desirable for everyone, which we should value both in ourselves and in one another. But if there are aspects of femininity and masculinity which are valuable in this way—which are, as we might call them, virtues—they are *human* virtues, and are desirable for everyone. If Smith is a better person for being compassionate or courageous, then so is Jones, and never mind the sex of Smith or Jones. Hence, the argument concludes, the world envisioned by M, in which everyone or nearly everyone is both feminine and masculine, is one in which life for everyone is more rewarding than the world advocated by P, in which some people are of only one gender; therefore we should undertake to bring about M.

The argument claims, then, that both genders embody traits that it would be valuable for everyone to have. But how is this claim to be tested? Let us adopt the view that to say that something is valuable for everyone is, roughly, to say that if everyone were unbiased, well-informed, and thinking and feeling clearly, everyone would, in fact, value it. As things are now, it is difficult or impossible to predict what everyone would value under such conditions. But there is an alternative. We can seek to establish conditions in which people do make unbiased, informed, etc., choices, and see whether they then value both feminine and masculine traits.

But this reminds us, of course, of the program of *P*. *P* does not guarantee clear thought and emotional sensitivity, but it does propose an environment in which people are informed about all gender options and are unbiased with respect to them. If, in this context, all or most people, when they are thinking clearly, etc., tend to prefer, for themselves and others, both feminine and masculine virtues, we will have evidence to support the claim that androgyny has universal value. (In this case, *P* is likely to change into *M*.) On the other hand, if "pure" gender is preferred by many, we should be skeptical of the claim that androgyny has universal value. (In this case we should probably seek to preserve *P*.) It appears, then, that in order to discover whether *M* is preferable to *P*, we should seek to bring about *P*.

In summary, we have noted the argument from freedom, which supports *P;* arguments from anxiety and frustration, which are indecisive; and the argument from universal value, whose analysis suggests the provisional adoption of *P*. As far as I know, there are no additional major arguments which can plausibly be presented now for either side of the issue. Given, then, the problem of deciding between *M* and *P* without reference to other alternatives, my tentative conclusion is that because of the great value of freedom, and because in an atmosphere of gender-freedom we will be in a good position to evaluate the major argument for *M* (that is, the argument from the universal value of androgyny), *P* is preferable to *M*.

Of course all we have assumed about the specific nature of the hypothetical society for which we are making this judgment is that the connection between sex and gender would be absent, as would be the unacceptable components of traditional gender concepts, particularly dominance and submission. It might be, then, that particular social conditions would constitute grounds for supporting M rather than P. For example, if the society in question were hierarchical with leadership roles tightly held by the predominantly masculine individuals, and if leaders with feminine characteristics were more likely to bring about changes of significant value (for example, eliminating war or oppression), it could reasonably be argued that M, in which everyone, including leaders, has both feminine and masculine characteristics, would be preferable to P. But such conditions are only speculative now.

STUDY QUESTIONS

1. What importance does the distinction between sexual difference and gender difference play in feminist thinking? To which difference is the recommendation for an androgynous lifestyle relevant?
2. Trebilcot believes that one should be free to choose one's gender "without regard to propriety or custom." Are there morally sound reasons that she may be overlooking for giving importance to propriety and custom in choosing a gender role? Is gender role really a matter of choice?
3. What moral arguments support the adoption of androgyny as a social ideal?
4. What is monoandrogyny? Polyandrogyny? What are the arguments for adopting the former as an individual ideal?
5. Is the ideal of androgyny distasteful to you? If it is, can you defend your aversion to it from the arguments that seem to show it to be an ideal that would mitigate sexist injustice?

Philosophers Against the Family*

CHRISTINA SOMMERS

A biographical sketch of Christina Sommers is found on page 653.

Christina Sommers points out that recent moral philosophy neglects the family and tends even to be actively hostile to it. Hostility to such a basic institution as the family is part of a radical social philosophy that seeks the reform of social arrangements that are seen to be unjust or inimical to individual freedom. Sommers distinguishes between direct and indirect criticisms of the family by social philosophers.

The direct criticisms are exemplified by many feminist thinkers who view the family as the bastion of a "gender system" that oppresses women. The more radical feminists argue for an androgynous or assimilationist social system that would do away with all institutions in which sex difference plays a role. Sommers criticizes these radical feminists for being ideologically inflexible and for paying little attention to what women actually want. And she points out that the feminist attack on the family is

*This paper is part of a project funded by an NEH Fellowship for College Teachers. Earlier versions were read at a conference at the University of Minnesota, "Ethics: The Personal Turn," and at the Philosopher's Forum at Long Island University. I received helpful criticism on both occasions. For the unabridged version of this paper, see Hugh LaFollette and George Graham, eds., *Person to Person* (Philadelphia, PA: Temple University Press), forthcoming.

irresponsible in not attending to the human costs of instituting the proposed ideal. Sommers suggests that what we need is a liberal feminism more in tune with the grassroots aspirations of women.

The indirect criticisms undermine the family by holding to a "volunteerist theory" of obligation that excludes the "special duties." According to most contemporary moral philosophers, no obligation is binding that is not grounded in a voluntary commitment. Since we do not choose our parents, brothers, sisters, and the like, and since we only rarely assume special responsibilities with respect to them in a voluntary or explicit way, it would follow that we have no special moral obligations to any of our kin. Sommers argues that this theory of obligation undermines the network of mutual obligations that characterizes the family and its members. She points out that philosophers accept the volunteerist theory and use it to deny a moral basis for filial and other obligations that have not been voluntarily assumed. According to Sommers, the volunteerist theory is a popular dogma that is altogether inadequate as a way of understanding our obligations to those close to us.

Much of what commonly counts as personal morality is measured by how well we behave within family relationships. We live our moral lives as son or daughter to this mother and that father, as brother or sister to this sister or brother, as father or mother, grandfather, granddaughter to this boy or girl or that man or woman. These relationships and the moral duties defined by them were once popular topics of moral casuistry; but when we turn to the literature of recent moral philosophy, we find little discussion of what it means to be a good son or daughter, a good mother or father, a good husband or wife, a good brother or sister.

Modern ethical theory concentrates on more general topics. Perhaps the majority of us who involve ourselves with ethics accept some version of Kantianism or utilitarianism, yet these mainstream doctrines are better designed for telling us about what we should do as persons in general than about our special duties as parents or children or siblings. We believe, perhaps, that such universal theories can account fully for the morality of special relations. In any case, modern ethics is singularly silent on the bread and butter issues of personal morality in everyday life. However, silence is only part of it. With the exception of marriage itself, family relationships are a biological given. The contemporary philosopher is, on the whole, actively unsympathetic to the idea that we have *any* duties defined by relationships into which we have not voluntarily entered. We do not, after all, choose our parents or siblings. And even if we do choose to have children, this is not the same as choosing, say, our friends. Because the special relationships that constitute the family as a social arrangement are, in this sense, not voluntarily assumed, many moralists feel bound in principle to dismiss them altogether. The practical result is that philosophers are to be found among those who are contributing to an ongoing disintegration of the traditional family. In what follows I shall expose some of the philosophical roots of the current hostility to family morality. My own view that the ethical theses underlying this hostility are bad philosophy will be made evident throughout the discussion.

1. The Moral Vantage

Social criticism is a heady pastime to which philosophers are professionally addicted. One approach, Aristotelian in method and temperament, is antiradical, though it may be liberal, and approaches the task of needed reform with a prima facie respect for the norms of established morality. It is conservationist and cautious in its recommendations for change. It is, therefore, not given to such proposals as abolishing the family or abolishing private property and, indeed, does not look kindly on such proposals from other philosophers. The antiradicals I am concerned about are not those who would be called Burkean. I shall call them liberal but this use of "liberal" is somewhat perverse since, in my stipulative use of the term, a liberal is a philosopher who advocates social reform but always in a conservative spirit. My liberals share with Aristotle the conviction that the traditional arrangements have great moral weight and that common opinion is a primary source of moral truth. A good modern example is Henry Sidgwick with his constant appeal to Common Sense. But philosophers like John Stuart Mill, William James, and Bertrand Russell also can be cited. On the other hand, because no radical can be called a liberal in my sense, many so-called liberals could be excluded perversely. Thus when John Rawls toys with the possibility of abolishing the family because kinship bias is a force inimical to equality of opportunity, he is no liberal.

The more exciting genre of social criticism is not liberal-Aristotelian but radical and Platonist in spirit. Its vantage is external or even supernal to the social institutions it has placed under moral scrutiny. Plato was as aware as anyone could be that what he called the cave was social reality. One reason for calling it a cave was to emphasize the need, as he saw it, for an external, objective perspective on established morality. Another consideration in calling it a cave was his conviction that common opinion was benighted, and that reform could not be accomplished except by substantial "consciousness raising" and enlightened social engineering. Plato's supernal vantage made it possible for him to look on social reality in somewhat the way the Army Corps of Engineers looks upon a river that must have its course changed and its waywardness tamed. In our own day much social criticism of a Marxist variety has taken this radical approach to social change. And, of course, much contemporary feminist philosophy is radical.

Some philosophers are easily classifiable as radical or liberal. John Locke is clearly a liberal, Leon Trotsky is clearly a radical. I remarked a moment ago that there is a radical strain in Rawls. But it is a strain only: Rawls's attitude to social reality is not, finally, condescending. On the other hand, much contemporary social criticism is radical in temper. In particular, I shall suggest that the prevailing attitude toward the family is radical and not liberal. And the inability of mainstream ethical theory to come to grips with the special obligations that family members bear to one another contributes to the current disregard of the commonsense morality of the family cave. We find, indeed, that family obligations are criticized and discounted precisely because they do not fit the standard theories of obligation. If I am right, contemporary ethics is at a loss when it comes to dealing with parochial morality; but few have acknowledged this as a defect to be repaired. Instead the common reaction has been: if the family does not fit my model of autonomy, rights, or obligations, then so much the worse for the family.

To illustrate this, I cite without comment recent views on some aspects of family morality.

1. Michael Slote[1] maintains that any child capable of supporting itself is "morally free to opt out of the family situation." To those who say that the child should be expected to help his needy parents for a year or two out of reciprocity or fair play, Slote responds:

   > The duty of fair play presumably exists only where past benefits are voluntarily accepted . . . and we can hardly suppose that a child has voluntarily accepted his role in family . . . life.[2]

2. Virgina Held[3] wants traditional family roles to be abolished and she recommends that husbands and wives think of themselves as roommates of the same sex in assigning household and parental tasks. (She calls this the "Roommate Test.") To the objection that such a restructuring might injure family life, she replies that similar objections were made when factory workers demanded overtime pay.

3. The late Jane English[4] defended the view that adult children owe their parents no more than they owe their good friends. "[A]fter friendship ends, the duties of friendship end." John Simmons[5] and Jeffrey Blustein[6] also look with suspicion upon the idea that there is a debt of gratitude to the parents for what, in any case, they were duty-bound to do.

4. Where Slote argues for the older child's right to leave, Howard Cohen[7] argues for granting that right to young children who still need parental care. He proposes that

---

[1]Michael Slote, "Obedience and Illusions," in Onora O'Neill and William Ruddick, eds., *Having Children* (New York: Oxford, 1979), p. 320.

[2]Slote, p. 230.

[3]Virginia Held, "The Obligations of Mothers and Fathers," in Joyce Trebilcot, ed., *Mothering: Essays in Feminist Theory* (Totowa, NJ: Rowman and Allanheld, 1983), pp. 7–20.

[4]Jane English, "What Do Grown Children Owe Their Parents?" in O'Neill and Ruddick, *op. cit.*, pp. 351–56.

[5]John Simmons, *Moral Principles and Political Obligation* (Princeton, NJ: Princeton University Press, 1979), p. 162.

[6]Jeffrey Blustein, *Parents and Children: The Ethics of the Family* (New York: Oxford, 1982), p. 182.

[7]Howard Cohen, *Equal Rights for Children* (Totowa, NJ: Rowman and Littlefield, 1980), p. 66.

every child be assigned a "trusted advisor" or agent. If the child wants to leave his parents, his agent will be charged with finding alternative caretakers for him.

The philosophers I have cited are not atypical in their dismissive attitude to commonsense morality or in their readiness to replace the parochial norms of the family cave with practices that would better approximate the ideals of human rights and equality. A theory of rights and obligations that applies generally to moral agents is, in this way, applied to the family with the predictable result that the family system of special relations and non-contractual special obligations is judged to be grossly unfair to its members.

2. Feminism and the Family

I have said that the morality of the family has been relatively neglected. The glaring exception to this is, of course, the feminist movement. Although the movement is complex, I am confined primarily to its moral philosophers, of whom the most influential is Simone de Beauvoir. For de Beauvoir, a social arrangement that does not allow all its participants full autonomy is to be condemned. De Beauvoir criticizes the family as an unacceptable arrangement since, for women, marriage and childbearing are essentially incompatible with their subjectivity and freedom:

> The tragedy of marriage is not that it fails to assure woman the promised happiness . . . but that it mutilates her; it dooms her to repetition and routine . . . At twenty or thereabouts mistress of a home, bound permanently to a man, a child in her arms, she stands with her life virtually finished forever.[8]

For de Beauvoir the tragedy goes deeper than marriage. The loss of subjectivity is unavoidable as long as human reproduction requires the woman's womb. De Beauvoir starkly describes the pregnant woman who ought to be a "free individual" as a "stockpile of colloids, an incubator, an egg."[9] And as recently as 1977 she compared childbearing and nurturing to slavery.[10]

---

[8]Simone de Beauvoir, *The Second Sex*, tr. H. M. Parshley (New York: Random House 1952), p. 534.
[9]De Beauvoir, p. 553.
[10]De Beauvoir, "Talking to De Beauvoir," *Spare Rib* (March 1977), p. 2.

It would be a mistake to say that de Beauvoir's criticism of the family is outside the mainstream of Anglo-American philosophy. Her criterion of moral adequacy may be formulated in continental existentialist terms, but its central contention is generally accepted: who would deny that an arrangement that systematically thwarts the freedom and autonomy of the individual is *eo ipso* defective? What is perhaps a bit odd to Anglo-American ears is that de Beauvoir makes such scant appeal to ideals of fairness and equality. For her, it is the loss of autonomy that is decisive.

De Beauvoir is more pessimistic than most feminists she has influenced about the prospects for technological and social solutions. But implicit in her critique is the ideal of a society in which sexual differences are minimal or nonexistent. This ideal is shared by many contemporary feminist philosophers. The views of Richard Wasserstrom, Ann Ferguson, Carol Gould, and Alison Jaggar are representative.

Wasserstrom's approach to social criticism is Platonist in its hypothetical use of a good society. The ideal society is nonsexist and "assimilationist."[11] Social reality is scrutinized for its approximation to this ideal and criticism is directed against all existing norms. Take the custom of having sexually segregated bathrooms: whether this is right or wrong "depends on what the good society would look like in respect to sexual differentiation." The key question in evaluating any law or arrangement in which sex difference figures is: "What would the good or just society make of (it)?"[12]

Thus the supernal light shines on the cave, revealing its moral defects. *There*, in the ideal society, gender in the choice of lover or spouse would be of no more significance than eye color. *There* the family would consist of adults but not necessarily of different sexes and not necessarily in pairs. *There* we find equality ensured by a kind of affirmative action which compensates for disabilities. If women are somewhat weaker than men, or if they are subject to lunar disabilities, then this must be compensated for. (Wasserstrom compares women to persons with congenital defects for whom the good society makes special arrangements.) Such male-dominated sports as

---

[11]Richard Wasserstrom, *Philosophy and Social Issues* (Notre Dame, IN: University of Notre Dame Press, 1980), p. 26.

[12]Wasserstrom, p. 23.

wrestling and football will there be eliminated and marriage, as we know it, will not exist. "Bisexuality, not heterosexuality or homosexuality, would be the typical intimate, sexual relationship in the ideal society that was assimilationist in respect to sex."[13]

Other feminist philosophers are equally confident about the need for sweeping change. Ann Ferguson wants a "radical reorganization of child rearing." She recommends communal living and a de-emphasis on biological parenting. In the ideal society "[l]ove relationships, and the sexual relationships developing out of them, would be based on the individual meshing-together of androgynous human beings."[14] Carol Gould argues for androgyny and for abolishing legal marriage. She favors single parenting, co-parenting and communal parenting. The only arrangement she opposes emphatically is the traditional one where the mother provides primary care for the children.[15] Alison Jaggar, arguing for a "socialist feminism," wants a society that is both classless and genderless. She looks to the day of a possible transformation of such biological functions as insemination, lactation, and gestation "so that one woman could inseminate another . . . and . . . fertilized ova could be transplanted into women's or even men's bodies." This idea is partly illustrated in a science fiction story that Jaggar praises in which "neither sex bears children, but both sexes, through hormone treatments, suckle them . . ."[16] To those of us who find this bizarre, Jaggar replies that this betrays the depth of our prejudice in favor of the "natural" family.

Though they differ in detail, the radical feminists hold to a common social ideal that is broadly assimilationist in character and inimical to the traditional family. Sometimes it seems as if the radical feminist simply takes the classical Marxist eschatology of the

---

[13]Wasserstrom, p. 26.

[14]Ann Ferguson, "Androgyny as an Ideal for Human Development," in *Feminism and Philosophy*, eds. M. Vetterling-Braggin, F. Elliston and J. English (Totowa, NJ: Rowman and Littlefield, 1977), pp. 45–69.

[15]Carol Gould, "Private Rights and Public Virtues: Woman, the Family and Democracy," in *Beyond Domination*, ed. Carol Gould (Totowa, NJ: Rowman and Allanheld, 1983), pp. 3–18.

[16]Alison Jaggar, "Human Biology in Feminist Theory: Sexual Equality Reconsidered," in Gould, *op. cit.*, p. 41. Jaggar is serious about the possibility and desirability of what she calls the "transformation of sexuality," which is elaborated in her book *Feminist Politics and Human Nature* (Totowa, NJ: Rowman and Allanheld, 1983), p. 132.

811

Communist Manifesto and substitutes "gender" for "class." Indeed, the feminist and the old-fashioned Marxist do have much in common. Both see their caves as politically divided into two warring factions: one oppressing, the other oppressed. Both see the need of raising the consciousness of the oppressed group to its predicament and to the possibility of removing its shackles. Both look forward to the day of a classless or genderless society. Both deny the value and naturalness of tradition. Both believe that people and the institutions they inhabit are as malleable as Silly Putty. And both groups are zealots, paying little attention to the tragic personal costs to be paid for the revolution they wish to bring about. The feminists tell us little about that side of things. To begin with, how will the benighted myriads in the cave who do not wish to "mesh together" with other androgynous beings be reeducated? And how are children to be brought up in the genderless society? Plato took great pains to explain his methods: would the new methods be as thoroughgoing? Unless these questions can be given plausible answers, the supernal attack on the family must always be irresponsible. The appeal to the just society justifies nothing until it can be shown that the radical proposals do not have monstrous consequences. That has not been shown. Indeed, given the perennially dubious state of the social sciences, it is precisely what *cannot* be shown.

Any social arrangement that falls short of the assimilationist ideal is labeled "sexist." It should be noted that this characteristically feminist use of the term "sexist" differs significantly from its popular or literal sense. Literally, and popularly, "sexism" connotes unfair discrimination. But in its extended philosophical use it connotes discrimination, period. Wasserstrom and many feminists trade on the popular pejorative connotations of sexism when they invite us to be antisexist. Most liberals are antisexist in the popular sense. But to be antisexist in the technical, radical philosophical sense is not merely to be opposed to discrimination against women; it is to be *for* what Wasserstrom calls the assimilationist ideal. The antisexist philosopher opposes any social policy that is nonandrogynous, objecting, for example, to legislation that allows for maternity leave. As Alison Jaggar remarks: "We do not, after all, elevate 'prostate leave' into a special right of men."[17] From being liberally opposed to sexism, one

---

[17]Alison Jaggar, "On Sex Equality," in *Sex Equality*, ed. Jane English (Englewood Cliffs, NJ: Prentice-Hall, 1977), p. 102.

may in this way be led insensibly to a radical critique of the family whose ideal is assimilationist and androgynous. For it is very clear that the realization of the androgynous ideal is incompatible with the survival of the family as we know it.

The neological extension of such labels as "sexism," "slavery," and "prostitution" is a feature of radical discourse. The liberal too sometimes calls for radical solutions to social problems. Some institutions are essentially unjust. To "reform" slavery or a totalitarian system of government is to eliminate them. Radicals trade on these extreme practices in characterizing other practices. They may, for example, characterize low wages as "slave" wages and the workers who are paid them as "slave" laborers. Taking these descriptions seriously may start one on the way to treating a free-labor market system as a "slave system" that, in simple justice, must be overthrown and replaced by an alternative system of production. The radical feminist typically explains that, "existentially," women, being treated by men as sex objects, are especially prone to bad faith and false consciousness. Marxist feminists see them as part of an unawakened and oppressed economic class. Clearly we cannot call on a deluded woman to cast off her bonds before we have made her aware of her bondage. So the first task of freeing the slave woman is dispelling the thrall of a false and deceptive consciousness. One must "raise" her consciousness to the "reality" of her situation. (Some feminists acknowledge that it may in fact be too late for many of the women who have fallen too far into the delusions of marriage and motherhood. But the educative process can save many from falling into the marriage and baby trap.)

In this sort of rhetorical climate nothing is what it seems. Prostitution is another term that has been subjected to a radical enlargement. Alison Jaggar believes that a feminist interpretation of the term "prostitution" is badly needed and asks for a "philosophical theory of prostitution." Observing that the average woman dresses for men, marries a man for protection, and so forth, she says: "For contemporary radical feminists, prostitution is the archetypal relationship of women to men."[18]

Of course, the housewife Jaggar has in mind might be offended at the suggestion that she herself is a prostitute, albeit less well paid and

---

[18]Alison Jaggar, "Prostitution," in Marilyn Pearsell, ed., *Women and Values: Reading in Recent Feminist Philosophy* (Belmont, CA: Wadsworth, 1986), pp. 108–121.

less aware of it than the professional street prostitute. To this the radical feminist reply is (quoting Jaggar):

> [I]ndividuals' intentions do not necessarily indicate the true nature of what is going on. Both men and women might be outraged at the description of their candlelit dinner as prostitution, but the radical feminist argues this outrage is due simply to the participants' failure or refusal to perceive the social context in which their dinner date occurs.[19]

Apparently, this failure or refusal to perceive affects most women. Thus we may even suppose that the majority of women who have been treated to a candlelit dinner by a man prefer it to other dining alternatives they have experienced. To say that these preferences are misguided is a hard and condescending doctrine. It would seem that most feminist philosophers are not overly impressed with Mill's principle that there can be no appeal from a majority verdict of those who have experienced two alternatives.

The dismissive feminist attitude to the widespread preferences of women takes its human toll. Most women, for example, prefer to have children and those who have them rarely regret having them. It is no more than sensible, from a utilitarian standpoint, to take note of such widespread preferences and to take it seriously in planning one's own life. But a significant number of women discount this general verdict as benighted, taking more seriously the idea that the reported joys of motherhood are exaggerated and fleeting, if not altogether illusory. These women tell themselves and others that having babies is a trap to be avoided. But for many women childlessness has become a trap of its own, somewhat lonelier than the more conventional traps of marriage and babies. Some come to find their childlessness regrettable; this sort of regret is common to those who flout Mill's reasonable maxim by putting the verdict of ideology over the verdict of human experience.

3. Feminists Against Femininity

It is a serious defect of American feminism that it concentrates its zeal on impugning femininity and feminine culture at the expense of the grass roots fight against economic and social injustices to which

---

[19]Jaggar, "Prostitution," p. 117.

women are subjected. As we have seen, the radical feminist attitude to the woman who enjoys her femininity is condescending or even contemptuous. Indeed, the contempt for femininity reminds one of misogynist biases in such philosophers as Kant, Rousseau, and Schopenhauer, who believed that femininity was charming but incompatible with full personhood and reasonableness. The feminists deny the charm, but they too accept the verdict that femininity is weakness. It goes without saying that an essential connection between femininity and powerlessness has not been established by *either* party.

By denigrating conventional feminine roles and holding to an assimilationist ideal in social policy, the feminist movement has lost its natural constituency. The actual concerns, beliefs, and aspirations of the majority of women are not taken seriously *except* as illustrations of bad faith, false consciousness, and successful brainwashing. What women actually want is discounted and reinterpreted as to what they (have been led to) *think* they want ("a man," "children"). What most women *enjoy* (male gallantry, candlelit dinners, sexy clothes, makeup) is treated as an obscenity (prostitution).

As the British feminist, Janet Radcliffe Richards, says:

> Most women still dream about beauty, dress, weddings, dashing lovers, domesticity and babies . . . but if feminists seem (as they do) to want to eliminate nearly all of these things—beauty, sex conventions, families and all—for most people that simply means the removal of everything in life which is worth living for.[20]

Radical feminism creates a false dichotomy between sexism and assimilation, as if there were nothing in between. This view ignores completely the middle ground in which a woman can be free of oppression and nevertheless feminine in the sense abhorred by many feminists. For women are simply not waiting to be freed from the particular chains the radical feminists are trying to sunder. The average woman enjoys her femininity. She wants a man, not a roommate. She wants children and the time to care for them. When she enters the work force, she wants fair opportunity and equal treatment. These are the goals that women actually have, and they are not easily attainable. But they will never be furthered by an elitist radical movement that views the actual aspirations of women as the product of a

---

[20]Janet Radcliffe Richards, *The Skeptical Feminist* (Middlesex, England: Penguin Books, 1980), pp. 341–42.

false consciousness. There is room for a liberal feminism that would work for reforms that would give women equal opportunity in the workplace and in politics, but would leave unimpugned the basic institutions that women want and support, i.e., marriage and motherhood. Such a feminism is already in operation in some European countries. But it has been obstructed here in the United States by the ideologues who now hold the seat of power in the feminist movement.[21]

In characterizing and criticizing American feminism, I have not taken into account the latest revisions and qualifications of a lively and variegated movement. There is a kind of "Feminism of the Week" that one cannot hope to keep abreast of short of divorcing all other concerns. The best one can do for present purposes is attend to central theses and arguments that bear on the feminist treatment of the family. Nevertheless, even for this limited purpose it would be wrong to omit discussion of an important turn taken by feminism in the past few years. I have in mind the recent literature on the theme that there is a specific female ethic that differs from the male ethic in being more "concrete," less rule oriented, more empathic and "caring," and more attentive to the demands of a particular context.[22] The kind of feminism that accepts the idea that women differ from men in approaching ethical dilemmas and social problems from a "care perspective" is not oriented to androgyny as a positive ideal. Rather it seeks to develop a special female ethic and to give it greater practical scope.

The stress on context might lead one to think that these feminists are more sympathetic to the family as the social arrangement that shapes the moral development of women since the family is the context for many of the moral dilemmas that women actually face. However, one sees as yet no attention being paid to the fact that feminism itself is a force working against the preservation of

---

[21]See Sylvia Ann Hewlett, *A Lesser Life: The Myth of Woman's Liberation in America* (New York: William Morrow, 1986).

[22]See, for example, Carol Gilligan, *In a Different Voice* (Cambridge, MA: Harvard University Press, 1982); Eva Kittay and Diana Meyers, eds., *Women and Moral Theory* (Totowa, NJ: Rowman and Littlefield, 1987); Lawrence Blum, *Friendship, Altruism and Morality* (London: Routledge & Kegan Paul, 1980); Jean Grimshaw, *Philosophy and Feminist Thinking* (Minneapolis, MN: University of Minnesota Press, 1986); Nel Noddings, *Caring: A Feminine Approach to Ethics and Moral Education* (Berkeley, CA: University of California Press, 1984).

the family. Psychologists like Carol Gilligan and philosophers like Lawrence Blum concentrate their attention on the moral quality of caring relationships, yet these relationships themselves are not viewed in their concrete embedment in any formal social or institutional arrangement.

It should also be said that some feminists are moving away from the earlier hostility to motherhood.[23] Here, too, one sees the weakening of the positive assimilationist ideal in the acknowledgment of a primary gender role. However, childrearing is not seen primarily within the context of the family but as a special relationship between mother and daughter or (more awkwardly) between mother and son, a relationship that effectively excludes the male parent. And the new celebration of motherhood remains largely hostile to traditional familial arrangements.

It is too early to say whether a new style of nonassimilationist feminism will lead to a mitigation of the feminist assault on the family or even on femininity. In any case, the recognition of a female ethic of care and responsibility is hardly inconsistent with a social ethic that values the family as a vital (perhaps indispensable) institution. And the recognition that women have their own moral style may well be followed by a more accepting attitude toward the kind of femininity that some feminists currently reject. One may even hope to see the "holier than thou" aspects of feminism fade into a relaxed recognition that both sexes have their distinctive graces and virtues. Such a feminism would not be radical but liberal.

4. The Indirect Attack

The philosophers I shall now discuss do not criticize the family directly; in some cases they do not even mention the family. However, each one holds a view that subverts, ignores, or denies the special moral relations that characterize the family and are responsible for its functioning. And if they are right, family morality is a vacuous subject.

Judith Thomson maintains that an abortion may be permissible even if the fetus is deemed a person from the moment of conception,[24]

---

[23]See, for example, Joyce Trebilcot, ed., *Mothering: Essays in Feminist Theory* (Totowa, NJ: Rowman and Allanheld, 1984).

[24]Judith Thomson, "A Defense of Abortion," in *Philosophy and Public Affairs*, vol. 1, no. 1, 1972.

for in that case being pregnant would be like having an adult surgically attached to one's body. And it is arguable that if one finds oneself attached to another person, one has the right to free oneself even if such freedom is obtained at the price of the other person's death by, say, kidney failure. I shall, for purposes of this discussion, refer to the fetus as a prenatal child. I myself do not think the fetus is a person from the moment of conception. Nor does Thomson. But here we are interested in her argument for the proposition that abortion of a prenatal child/person should be permissible.

Many have been repelled by Thomson's comparison of pregnancy to arbitrary attachment. Thomson herself is well aware that the comparison may be bizarre. She says:

> It may be said that what is important is not merely the fact that the fetus is a person, but that it is a person for whom the woman has a special kind of responsibility issuing from the fact that she is its mother.[25]

To this Thomson replies: "Surely we do not have any such 'special responsibility' for a person unless we have assumed it, explicitly or implicitly." If the mother does not try to prevent pregnancy, does not obtain an abortion, but instead gives birth to it and takes it home with her, then, at least implicitly, she has assumed responsibility for it.

One might object that although pregnancy is a state into which many women do not enter voluntarily, it is nevertheless a state in which one has some responsibility to care for the prenatal child. Many pregnant women do feel such a prenatal responsibility, and take measures to assure the prenatal child's survival and future health. But here one must be grateful to Professor Thomson for her clarity. A mother who has not sought pregnancy deliberately bears *no* special responsibility to her prenatal child. For she has neither implicitly nor explicitly taken on the responsibility of caring for it. For example, the act of taking the infant home from the hospital implies voluntary acceptance of such responsibility. By choosing to take it with her, the mother undertakes to care for the infant and no longer has the right to free herself of the burden of motherhood at the cost of the child's life.

---

[25]Thomson, p. 64.

The assumption, then, is that there are no noncontractual obligations or special duties defined by the kinship of mother to child. As
for social expectations, none are legitimate in the morally binding
sense unless they are underpinned by an implicit or explicit contract
freely entered into. If this assumption is correct, sociological arrangements and norms have no moral force unless they are voluntarily
accepted by the moral agent who is bound by them. I shall call this
the "volunteer theory of moral obligation." It is a thesis that is so
widely accepted today that Thomson saw no need to argue for it.

Michael Tooley's arguments in defense of infanticide provide another solid example of how a contemporary philosopher sidetracks
and ultimately subverts the special relations that bind the family.[26]
Tooley holds that being sentient confers the prima facie right not to
be treated cruelly, and that possession of those characteristics that
make one a person confers the *additional* right to life. Tooley then
argues that infants lack these characteristics and so may be painlessly
killed. In reaching this conclusion, Tooley's sole consideration is
whether the infant intrinsically possesses the relevant "right-to-life-
making characteristic" of personality—a consideration that abstracts
from any right to care and protection that the infant's relation to its
parents confers on it causally and institutionally. For Tooley, as for
Thomson, the relations of family or motherhood are morally irrelevant. So it is perhaps not surprising that one finds nothing in the
index under "family," "mother," or "father" in Tooley's book on
abortion and infanticide.

Howard Cohen is concerned strictly with the rights of persons
irrespective of the special relations they may bear to others.[27] Just as
Thomson holds that the mother's right to the free unencumbered use
of her body is not qualified by any special obligations to her child, so
Cohen holds that the child's right to a no-fault divorce from its
parents cannot be diminished because of the special relation it bears
to them. Where Thomson is concerned with the overriding right of
the mother, Cohen is concerned with the right of the child. Yet all
three philosophers agree that the right of a child is not less strong
than the right of any adult. Indeed, Thomson compares the unborn

---

[26]Michael Tooley, "Abortion and Infanticide," in *Philosophy and Public Affairs*, vol. 2,
no. 1, 1972.
[27]Howard Cohen, *Equal Rights for Children*, chs. V and VI.

child to a fully grown adult and Tooley holds that any person—be it child, adult, or sapient nonhuman—is equal in rights.

Our three philosophers are typical in holding that any moral requirement is either a general duty incumbent on everyone or else a specific obligation voluntarily assumed. Let us call a requirement a *duty* if it devolves on the moral agents whether or not they have voluntarily assumed it. (It is, for example, a duty to refrain from murder.) And let us call a requirement an *obligation* only if it devolves on certain moral agents but not necessarily on all moral agents. (One is, for example, morally obligated to keep a promise.) According to our three philosophers, all duties are general in the sense of being requirements on all moral agents. Any moral requirement that is *specific* to a given moral agent must be grounded in his or her voluntary commitment. Thus, there is no room for any special requirement on a moral agent that has not been assumed voluntarily by that agent. In other words, *there are no special duties.* This is what I am calling the volunteer theory of obligation. According to the voluntaristic thesis, all duties are general and only those who volunteer for them have any obligations toward them.

This thesis underlies Cohen's view that the child can divorce its parents. For it is unnecessary to consider whether the child has any special duties to the parents that could conflict with the exercise of its right to leave them. It underlies Thomson's view that the woman who had not sought pregnancy has no special responsibility to her unborn child and that any such responsibility that she may later have is assumed implicitly by her voluntary act of taking it home with her. In underlies Tooley's psychobiological method for answering the moral question of infanticide by determining the right-making characteristics of personhood: all we need to know about the neonate is whether or not it possesses the psychological characteristics of personhood. If it does, then it has a right to life. If it does not, then it is not a person and thus may be killed painlessly. It is unnecessary to consider the question of whether the child has a special relation to anyone who may have a "special responsibility" to see to the child's survival.

What I am calling the volunteer thesis is a confidently held thesis of many contemporary Anglo-American philosophers. It is easy to see that the thesis is contrary to what Sidgwick called Common Sense. For it means that there is no such thing as filial duty per se, no such thing as the special duty of mother to child, and generally no such thing as a morality of special family or kinship relations. All of which is contrary to what people think. For most people think that we do owe special debts to our parents even though we have not voluntarily assumed our obligations to them. Most people think that what we owe to our own children does not have its origin in any voluntary undertaking, explicit or implicit, that we have made to them. And, "preanalytically," many people believe that we owe special consideration to our siblings even at times when we may not *feel* very friendly to them. But if there are no special duties, then most of these prima facie requirements are misplaced and without moral force, and should be looked upon as archaic survivals to be ignored in assessing our moral obligations.

The idea that to be committed to an individual is to have made a voluntarily implicit or explicit commitment to that individual is generally fatal to family morality. For it looks upon the network of felt obligation and expectation that binds family members as a sociological phenomenon that is without presumptive moral force. The social critics who hold this view of family obligation usually are aware that promoting it in public policy must further the disintegration of the traditional family as an institution. But whether they deplore the disintegration or welcome it, they are bound in principle to abet it.

It may be that so many philosophers have accepted the voluntaristic dogma because of an uncritical use of the model of promises as the paradigm for obligations. If all obligations are like the obligation to keep a promise, then indeed they could not be incumbent on anyone who did not undertake to perform in a specified way. But there is no reason to take promises as paradigmatic of obligation. Indeed, the moral force of the norm of promise-keeping must itself be grounded in a theory of obligations that moral philosophers have yet to work out.

A better defense of the special duties would require considerably more space than I can give it here.[28] However, I believe the defense of special duties is far more plausible than rival theories that reject special duties. My primary objective has been to raise the strong suspicion that the volunteer theory of obligation is a dogma that is

---

[28]For a defense of the special duties not assumed voluntarily, see Christina Sommers, "Filial Morality," *The Journal of Philosophy*, no. 8, August 1986.

very probably wrong and misconceived, a view that is certainly at odds with common opinion.

Once we reject the doctrine that a voluntary act by the person concerned is a necessary condition of special obligation, we are free to respect the commonsense views that attribute moral force to many obligations associated with kinship and other family relationships. We may then accept the family as an institution that defines many special duties but that is nevertheless imperfect in numerous respects. Nevertheless, we still face the choice of how, as social philosophers, we are to deal with these imperfections. That is, we have the choice of being liberal or conservative in our attitude toward reform.

Burkean conservatives would change little or nothing, believing that the historical development of an institution has its own wisdom. They oppose utopian social engineering, considering it altogether immoral in the profound sense of destroying the very foundations of the special duties. But Burkeans also oppose what Karl Popper called "piecemeal social engineering," which seeks to remedy unjust practices without destroying the institution that harbors them. For Burkeans believe, on empirical grounds, that reform is always dangerous: that reform usually has unforseen consequences worse than the original injustices sought to be eliminated. Thus, conservatives are much like environmental conservationists in their attitude toward an ecological system: their general advice is extreme caution or hands off.

Liberals are more optimistic about the consequences of reform. Like conservatives, they believe that the norms of any tradition or institution not essentially unjust have prima facie moral force. All of which means we can rely on our commonsense beliefs that the system of expectations within the family is legitimate and should be respected. The liberal will acknowledge that a brother has the right to expect more help from a brother than from a stranger and not just because of what he has done for him lately. And the case is the same for all traditional expectations that characterize family members. On the other hand, there may be practices within the family that are systematically discriminatory and unfair to certain members. Unlike conservatives, liberals are prepared to do some piecemeal social engineering to eliminate injustice in the family.

It should be said that the appeal to common sense or common opinion is not final. For common sense often delivers conflicting verdicts on behavior. But a commonsense verdict is strongly presumptive. For example, there is the common belief that biological mothers have a special responsibility to care for their children, even their unwanted children. One *takes* this as presumptive evidence of an *objective* moral responsibility on the part of the mother. Note that the "verdict" of common sense is not really a verdict at all. Rather, it is evidence of a moral consideration that *must* enter into the final verdict on what to do and how to behave. Thomson ignores common sense when she asserts that the mother of a child, born or unborn, has no special responsibility to it unless she has in some way voluntarily assumed responsibility for it. Now, to say that a pregnant woman may have a moral responsibility to her unborn child does not entail that abortion is impermissible. For there are other common-sense considerations that enter here and other responsibilities that the mother may have (to her other children, to herself) that may conflict and override the responsibility to the fetus. So common sense is often not decisive. One may say that a commonsense opinion is symptomatic of a prima facie duty or liberty, as the case may be. Yet it still remains for the casuist to determine the *weight* of the duty in relation to other moral considerations that also may have the support of common sense. Politically and morally, lack of respect for common sense fosters illiberalism and elitism. Here we have the radical temper that often advocates actions and policies wildly at odds with common opinion—from infanticide to male lactation, from no-fault divorce on demand for children to the "roommate test" for marital relationships.

5. The Broken Family

In the final section we look at certain of the social consequences of applying radical theory to family obligation. I have suggested that, insofar as moral philosophers have any influence on the course of social history, their influence has recently been in aid of institutional disintegration. I shall now give some indication of how the principled philosophical disrespect for common sense in the area of family morality has weakened the family and how this affects the happiness of its members. Although much of what I say here is fairly well known, it is useful to say it in the context of an essay critical of the radical way of approaching moral philosophy. For there are periods in history when the radical way has great influence. And it is worth seeing what happens when Plato succeeds in Syracuse.

The most dramatic evidence of the progressive weakening of the family is found in the statistics on divorce. Almost all divorce is painful and most divorce affects children. Although divorce does not end but merely disrupts the life of a child, the life it disrupts is uncontroversially the life of a person who can be wronged directly by the actions of a moral agent. One might, therefore, expect that philosophers who carefully examine the morality of abortion also would carefully examine the moral ground for divorce. But here, too, the contemporary reluctance of philosophers to deal with the special casuistry of family relations is evidenced. For example, there are more articles on euthanasia or on recombinant DNA research than on divorce.

Each year there are another million and a quarter divorces in the United States affecting over one million children. The mother is granted custody in ninety percent of the cases, although legally it is no longer a matter of course. There is very persuasive evidence that children of divorced parents are affected seriously and adversely. Compared with children from intact families, they are referred more often to school psychologists, are more likely to have lower IQ and achievement test scores, are arrested more often, and need more remedial classes.[29] Moreover, these effects show little correlation to economic class. Children in the so-called latency period (between six and twelve) are the most seriously affected. In one study of children in this age group, one-half the subjects showed evidence of a "consolidation into troubled and conflicted depressive behavior patterns."[30] Their behavior patterns included "continuing depression and low self-esteem, combined with frequent school and peer difficulties."

One major cause for the difference between children from broken and intact families is the effective loss of the father. In the *majority* of cases the child has not seen the father within the past year. Only one child in six has seen his or her father in the past week; only 16 percent have seen their fathers in the past month; 15 percent see them once a year; the remaining 52 percent have had no contact at all for the past year. Although 57 percent of college educated fathers see their

---

[29]Lenore Weitzman, *The Divorce Revolution: The Unexpected Social and Economic Consequences for Women and Children in America* (New York: The Free Press, 1985).

[30]A. Skolnick and J. Skolnick, eds., *Family in Transition* (Boston: Little Brown, 1929), p. 452.

children at least once a month, their weekly contact is the same as for all other groups (one in six).[31]

It would be difficult to demonstrate that the dismissive attitude of most contemporary moral philosophers to the moral force of kinship ties and conventional family roles has been a serious factor in contributing to the growth in the divorce rate. But that is only because it is so difficult in general to demonstrate how much bread is baked by the dissemination of philosophical ideas. It is surely fair to say that the emphasis on autonomy and equality, when combined with the philosophical denigration of family ties, may have helped to make divorce both easy and respectable, thereby facilitating the rapid change from fault-based to no-fault divorce. If contemporary moralists have not caused the tide of family disintegration, they are avidly riding it. On the other side, it is not difficult to demonstrate that there is very little in recent moral philosophy that could be cited as possibly contributing to *stemming* the tide.

In the past two decades there has been a celebrated resurgence of interest in applied or practical ethics. It would appear, however, that the new enthusiasm for getting down to normative cases does not extend to topics of personal morality defined by family relationships. Accordingly, the children who are being victimized by the breakdown of the family have not benefited from this. Indeed, we find far more concern about the effect of divorce on children from philosophers a generation or two ago when divorce was relatively rare than we find today. Thus, Bertrand Russell writes:

> [H]usband and wife, if they have any love for their children, will so regulate their conduct as to give their children the best chance of a happy and healthy development. This may involve, at times, very considerable self-repression. And it certainly requires that both should realize the superiority of the claims of children to the claims of their own romantic emotions.[32]

And while Russell is not opposed to divorce, he believes that children place great contraints on it.

---

[31]Weitzman, p. 259.

[32]Bertrand Russell, *Marriage and Morals* (New York: Liveright, 1929), p. 236.

825

. . . parents who divorce each other, except for grave cause, appear to me to be failing their parental duty.[33]

Discerning and sensitive observers of a generation ago did not need masses of statistics to alert them to the effects of divorce on children. Nor did it take a professional philosopher (citing statistics gathered by a professional sociologist) to see that acting to dissolve a family must be evaluated morally primarily in terms of what such action means for the children.

Writing in the *London Daily Express* in 1930, Rebecca West says:

> The divorce of married people with children is nearly always an unspeakable calamity. It is only just being understood . . . how much a child depends for its healthy growth on the presence in the home of both its parents. . . . The point is that if a child is deprived of either its father or its mother it feels that it has been cheated out of a right.[34]

West describes the harmful effects of divorce on children as effects of "a radiating kind, likely to travel down and down through the generations, such as few would care to have on their consciences."

I have quoted West in some fullness because her remarks contrast sharply with what one typically finds in contemporary college texts. In a book called *Living Issues in Ethics,* the authors discuss unhappy parents and the moral questions they face in contemplating divorce.

> We believe that staying together for the sake of the children is worse than the feelings and adjustment of separation and divorce.[35]

Further on the authors give what they feel to be a decisive reason for this policy:

> Remaining together in an irreconcilable relationship violates the norm of interpersonal love.

One of the very few philosophers to discuss the question of divorce and its consequences for children is Jeffrey Blustein in his book, *Parents and Children.* Blustein looks with equanimity on the priority of personal commitment to parental responsibility, pointing out that

---

[33]Russell, p. 238.

[34]Rebecca West, *London Daily Express,* 1930

[35]R. Nolan and F. Kirkpatrick, eds., *Living Issues in Ethics* (Belmont, CA: Wadsworth, 1983), p. 147.

> The traditional view . . . that the central duties of husband and wife are the . . . duties of parenthood is giving way to a conception of marriage as essentially involving a serious commitment between two individuals as individuals.[36]

Blustein also tells us (without telling us how he knows it) that children whose parents are unhappily married are worse off than if their parents were divorced.

> Indeed it could be argued that precisely on account of the children the parents' unhappy marriage should be dissolved. . . .[37]

The suggestion that parents who are unhappy should get a divorce "for the sake of the children" is *very* contemporary.

To my knowledge, no reliable study has yet been made that compares children of divorced parents to children from intact families whose parents do not get on well together. So I have no way of knowing whether the claims of these authors are true or not. Moreover, because any such study would be compromised by certain arbitrary measures of parental incompatibility, one should probably place little reliance on them. It is, therefore, easy to see that contemporary philosophers are anxious to jump to conclusions that do not render implausible the interesting view that the overriding question in considering divorce is the compatibility of the parents, and that marital ties should be dissolved when they threaten or thwart the personal fulfillment of one or both the marital partners.

These philosophers set aside special duties and replace them with an emphasis on friendship, compatibility, and interpersonal love among family members. However, this has a disintegrative effect. That is to say, if what one owes to members of one's family is largely to be understood in terms of feelings of personal commitment, definite limits are placed on what one owes. For as feelings change, so may one's commitments. The result is a structure of responsibility within the family that is permanently unstable.

I have, in this final section, illustrated the indifference of contemporary philosophers to the family by dwelling on their indifference to the children affected by divorce. Nevertheless, I hope it is clear that nothing I have said is meant to convey that I oppose divorce. I

---

[36]Blustein, *Parents and Children*, p. 230.
[37]Blustein, p. 232.

do not. Neither Russell nor West nor any of the sane and compassionate liberal thinkers of the recent past opposed divorce. They simply did not play fast and loose with family mores, did not encourage divorce, and pointed out that moralists must insist that the system of family obligations is only partially severed by a divorce that cuts the marital tie. Morally, as well as legally, the obligations to the children remain as before. Legally, this is still recognized. But in a moral climate where the system of family obligation is given no more weight than can be justified in terms of popular theories of deontic volunteerism, the obligatory ties are too fragile to survive the personal estrangements that result from divorce. It is, therefore, to be expected that parents (especially fathers) will be off and away doing their own thing. And the law is largely helpless.

I have no special solutions to the tragedy of economic impoverishment and social deprivation that results from the weakening of family ties. I believe in the right of divorce and do not even oppose no-fault divorce. I do not know how to get back to the good old days when moral philosophers had the common sense to acknowledge the moral weight of special ties and the courage to condemn those who failed in them—the days when, in consequence, the *climate* of moral approval and disapproval was quite different from what it is today. I do not know how to make fathers ashamed of their neglect and inadvertent cruelty. What I do know is that moral philosophers should be paying far more attention to the social consequences of their views than they are. It is as concrete as taking care that what one says will not affect adversely the students whom one is addressing. If what students learn from us encourages social distintegration, then we are responsible for the effects this may have on their lives and on the lives of their children. This then is a grave responsibility, even graver than the responsibility we take in being for or against something as serious as euthanasia or capital punishment—since most of our students will never face these questions in a practical way.

I believe then that responsible moral philosophers are liberal or conservative but not radical. They respect human relationships and traditions and the social environment in which they live as much as they respect the natural environment and its ecology. They respect the family. William James saw the rejection of radicalism as central to the pragmatist way of confronting moral questions.

> [Experience] has proved that the laws and usages of the land are what yield the maximum of satisfaction. . . . The presumption in cases of

conflict must always be in favor of the conventionally recognized good. The philosopher must be a conservative, and in the construction of his casuistic scale must put things most in accordance with the customs of the community on top.[38]

A moral philosophy that does not give proper weight to the customs and opinions of the community is presumptuous in its attitude and pernicious in its consequences. In an important sense it is not a moral philosophy at all. For it is humanly irrelevant.

STUDY QUESTIONS

1. Briefly explain Sommers's distinction between Aristotelian and Platonic social criticism. What bearing does the distinction have on the feminist debate?
2. Is Sommers's suggestion that radical feminists are unsympathetic to "femininity" fair? Can *any* effective feminist movement accept standards of femininity that seem to view women as the "weaker vessel?"
3. Critically discuss Sommers's criticism of "consciousness raising."
4. How does Sommers characterize the moral philosophers' indirect attack on the family? Give examples of how the integrity of the family is undermined by the indirect attack.
5. Give arguments for and against the doctrine that an obligation to a particular person must be one that is assumed voluntarily. Do you accept the "volunteerist" theory? If not, why not?

SUGGESTED READINGS

Becker, Gary. *A Treatise on the Family*. Cambridge, MA: Harvard University Press, 1981.

Berger, Brigitte and Peter. *The War over the Family: Capturing the Middle Ground*. New York: Doubleday, 1983.

Bernard, Jessie. *The Future of Motherhood*. New York: Penguin, 1975.

---

[38]William James, "The Moral Philosopher and the Moral Life", in *Essays in Pragmatism* (New York: Hafner, 1948), p. 80.

Blustein, Jeffrey. *Parents and Children. The Ethics of the Family.* Oxford University Press, 1983.

Chodorow, Nancy. *The Reproduction of Mothering: Psychoanalysis and Sociology of Gender.* Los Angeles: University of California Press, 1978.

Daniels, Norman. *Am I My Parent's Keeper?: An Essay on Justice Between the Young and the Old.* Oxford University Press, 1987.

Lamm, Norman, ed. *The Good Society: Jewish Ethics in Action.* New York: Viking Press, 1974.

McKee, Patrick. *Philosophical Foundations of Gerontology.* New York: Human Sciences Press, 1982.

Nicholson, Linda. *Gender and History: The Limits of Social Theory in the Age of the Family.* New York: Columbia University Press, 1988.

O'Neil, Onora, and William Ruddick, eds. *Having Children: Philosophical and Legal Reflections on Parenthood.* New York: Oxford University Press, 1979.

Russell, Bertrand. *Marriage and Morals.* New York: Liveright Publishing Corp., 1929.

Scruton, Roger. *Sexual Desire: A Moral Philosophy of the Erotic.* New York: Macmillan, 1986.

Shils, Edward. *Tradition.* Chicago: University of Chicago Press, 1981.

Trebilcot, Joyce, ed. *Mothering: Essays in Feminist Theory.* Totowa, NJ: Rowman and Allanheld, 1984.

Vetterling-Braggin, Mary, ed. *"Femininity," "Masculinity," and "Androgyny": A Modern Philosophical Discussion.* Totowa, NJ: Rowman and Allanheld, 1982.

Chapter Nine

MORALITY AND SOCIETY

One striking development in contemporary moral philosophy is the increasing attention we pay to specific practical questions in social ethics. Is abortion right or wrong? Are physicians ever authorized to give lethal injections to dying, pain-ridden patients who request their own death? Do animals have moral rights? The practical ethics movement originated in the late sixties when philosophers began to participate in national debates on such issues as free speech, civil disobedience, capital punishment, euthanasia, and abortion. The recent interest in applying ethical theory to practical social problems is not a novel development, for philosophers since Plato and Aristotle continuously have concerned themselves with questions of everyday morality. The period between 1940 and 1970 is something of a historical exception. During those post–World War II decades, Western philosophy became increasingly analytical and methodologically rigorous. Clarification and theory were of primary concern; applied ethics was secondary. Although this interest in theory and method has not waned, in the past fifteen years philosophers have reentered the arena of applied ethics with a vengeance. Consider what social philosopher Michael Walzer says about the new popularity of applied ethics:

> . . . [W]hen in our books and college courses we argue about distributive justice, killing in war, deception in politics, medical ethics . . . we are . . . engaged in a common human activity . . . temporarily discontinued at American universities at some cost. Now it is apparently about to be resumed. . . . It presses us back toward older moralities, or forward to newer ones, in which personal choice and utilitarian calculation are subjected to the discipline of public philosophy.

The essays in Chapter Nine deal primarily with questions of social policy. Here morality is somewhat impersonal since, in the main, our actions are not directed to persons with whom we are acquainted. Nevertheless, as the controversy over abortion shows, the issues strike home in a very personal way. The controversy turns on how to interpret fundamental moral principles. Consider the argument offered by those who oppose abortion:

1. It is wrong to kill an innocent human being.
2. The fetus is an innocent human being.
. . . It is wrong to kill the fetus.

The conclusion follows logically from the two premises. The question then is whether to accept the premises, and that, in turn, depends on how we should interpret them. John Noonan and Stanley Hauerwas present arguments for accepting both premises. Most defenders of the women's right challenge (1) or (2). Mary Anne Warren offers criteria for being a *person*, and she argues that only those human beings who are also persons qualify for an overriding right to life. According to Warren, because fetuses and brain-dead human beings lack the attributes of personhood, the prohibition against the destruction of human life does not apply. Judith Jarvis Thomson goes further, contending that in circumstances where one's liberty is threatened, even persons may be destroyed to free oneself. Thomson argues that in an unwanted pregnancy the mother's liberty is compromised and she may take drastic measures to regain it.

Though arguments like these are made with the aim of influencing social policy, they demand of us a very personal response. Even the debate on whether and how much to sacrifice for famine relief shows that there is clearly a personal side to the ethical question of what to do about the multitudes whom we shall never know, but who need our help. Peter Singer maintains that readers themselves have a serious moral obligation to do all they can to fight world hunger. Garrett Hardin argues that international famine relief can be responsible for a cycle of increasing misery. In effect, Hardin argues, a well-meaning and good-hearted moralist like Singer may do far more harm than good.

John Arthur claims that even if Singer is right about the overall utility of famine relief, it still is not our duty to do without luxuries in order to help distant strangers. Common morality does not make such demands on ordinary human beings, and common morality is reasonable in this respect since "morality is not for angels." But Murdoch and Oaten do not agree that the demands are excessive. And they find serious fault with Hardin's empirical arguments that famine relief is counterproductive.

One broad area of social morality is political. In a democratic society, the views of the electorate often are decisive in the formation of policies regarding a host of questions of domestic and foreign policy. Policies on abortion, capital punishment, war, famine aid (by government action), human rights here and in foreign countries, all have their moral dimensions, and citizens are called upon to support policies they deem worthy. Here too, however, moral agency and responsibility is not society's; it resides with the individuals who choose to promote this or that social policy. And, of course, those of us who are in government or other positions of authority are personally required to implement policy in a humane manner.

Famine, Affluence, and Morality

PETER SINGER

A biographical sketch of Peter Singer is found on page 496.

Singer describes the mass starvation in many parts of the world and argues that affluent persons are morally obligated to contribute part of their time and income toward alleviating hunger. He assumes that passivity, when people are able to act to prevent evil, is morally wrong. Nowadays we can help people over great distances; instant communication and air travel have transformed the world into a "global village." If, says Singer, bystanders see a child drowning in a shallow pond, they ought to save that child even if it means muddying their clothes. Failure to do so is gross moral negligence. Singer compares the citizens of the affluent West to these bystanders.

As I write this, in November 1971, people are dying in East Bengal from lack of food, shelter, and medical care. The suffering and death that are occurring there now are not inevitable, not unavoidable in any fatalistic sense of the term. Constant poverty, a cyclone, and a civil war have turned at least nine million people into destitute refugees; nevertheless, it is not beyond the capacity of the richer nations

FAMINE, AFFLUENCE, AND MORALITY From *Philosophy and Public Affairs*, vol. 1, no. 3 (Spring 1972). Copyright © 1972 by Princeton University Press. Reprinted by permission of Princeton University Press.

to give enough assistance to reduce any further suffering to very small proportions. The decisions and actions of human beings can prevent this kind of suffering. Unfortunately, human beings have not made the necessary decisions. At the individual level, people have, with very few exceptions, not responded to the situation in any significant way. Generally speaking, people have not given large sums to relief funds; they have not written to their parliamentary representatives demanding increased government assistance; they have not demonstrated in the streets, held symbolic fasts, or done anything else directed toward providing the refugees with the means to satisfy their essential needs. At the government level, no government has given the sort of massive aid that would enable the refugees to survive for more than a few days. Britain, for instance, has given rather more than most countries. It has, to date, given £14,750,000. For comparative purposes, Britain's share of the nonrecoverable development costs of the Anglo-French Concorde project is already in excess of £275,000,000, and on present estimates will reach £400,000,000. The implication is that the British government values a supersonic transport more than thirty times as highly as it values the lives of the nine million refugees. Australia is another country which, on a per capita basis, is well up in the "aid to Bengal" table. Australia's aid, however, amounts to less than one-twelfth of the cost of Sydney's new opera house. The total amount given, from all sources, now stands at about £65,000,000. The estimated cost of keeping the refugees alive for one year is £464,000,000. Most of the refugees have now been in the camps for more than six months. The World Bank has said that India needs a minimum of £300,000,000 in assistance from other countries before the end of the year. It seems obvious that assistance on this scale will not be forthcoming. India will be forced to choose between letting the refugees starve or diverting funds from her own development program, which will mean that more of her own people will starve in the future.[1]

These are the essential facts about the present situation in Bengal. So far as it concerns us here, there is nothing unique about this situation except its magnitude. The Bengal emergency is just the

---

[1] There was also a third possibility: that India would go to war to enable the refugees to return to their lands. Since I wrote this paper, India has taken this way out. The situation is no longer that described above, but this does not affect my argument, as the next paragraph indicates.

latest and most acute of a series of major emergencies in various parts of the world, arising both from natural and from man-made causes. There are also many parts of the world in which people die from malnutrition and lack of food independent of any special emergency. I take Bengal as my example only because it is the present concern, and because the size of the problem has ensured that it has been given adequate publicity. Neither individuals nor governments can claim to be unaware of what is happening there.

What are the moral implications of a situation like this? In what follows, I shall argue that the way people in relatively affluent countries react to a situation like that in Bengal cannot be justified; indeed, the whole way we look at moral issues—our moral conceptual scheme—needs to be altered, and with it, the way of life that has come to be taken for granted in our society.

In arguing for this conclusion I will not, of course, claim to be morally neutral. I shall, however, try to argue for the moral position that I take, so that anyone who accepts certain assumptions, to be made explicit, will, I hope, accept my conclusion.

I begin with the assumption that suffering and death from lack of food, shelter, and medical care are bad. I think most people will agree about this, although one may reach the same view by different routes. I shall not argue for this view. People can hold all sorts of eccentric positions, and perhaps from some of them it would not follow that death by starvation is in itself bad. It is difficult, perhaps impossible, to refute such positions, and so for brevity I will henceforth take this assumption as accepted. Those who disagree need read no further.

My next point is this: if it is in our power to prevent something bad from happening, without thereby sacrificing anything of comparable moral importance, we ought, morally, to do it. By "without sacrificing anything of comparable moral importance" I mean without causing anything else comparably bad to happen, or doing something that is wrong in itself, or failing to promote some moral good, comparable in significance to the bad thing that we can prevent. This principle seems almost as uncontroversial as the last one. It requires us only to prevent what is bad, and not to promote what is good, and it requires this of us only when we can do it without sacrificing anything that is, from the moral point of view, comparably important. I could even, as far as the application of my argument to the Bengal emergency is concerned, qualify the point so as to make it: if it is in our power to prevent something very bad from happening, without thereby sacrificing anything morally significant, we ought, morally, to do it. An application of this principle would be as follows: if I am walking past a shallow pond and see a child drowning in it, I ought to wade in and pull the child out. This will mean getting my clothes muddy, but this is insignificant, while the death of the child would presumably be a very bad thing.

The uncontroversial appearance of the principle just stated is deceptive. If it were acted upon, even in its qualified form, our lives, our society, and our world would be fundamentally changed. For the principle takes, firstly, no account of proximity or distance. It makes no moral difference whether the person I can help is a neighbor's child ten yards from me or a Bengali whose name I shall never know, ten thousand miles away. Secondly, the principle makes no distinction between cases in which I am the only person who could possibly do anything and cases in which I am just one among millions in the same position.

I do not think I need to say much in defense of the refusal to take proximity and distance into account. The fact that a person is physically near to us, so that we have personal contact with him, may make it more likely that we *shall* assist him, but this does not show that we *ought* to help him rather than another who happens to be further away. If we accept any principle of impartiality, universalizability, equality, or whatever, we cannot discriminate against someone merely because he is far away from us (or we are far away from him). Admittedly, it is possible that we are in a better position to judge what needs to be done to help a person near to us than one far away, and perhaps also to provide the assistance we judge to be necessary. If this were the case, it would be a reason for helping those near to us first. This may once have been a justification for being more concerned with the poor in one's own town than with famine victims in India. Unfortunately for those who like to keep their moral responsibilities limited, instant communication and swift transportation have changed the situation. From the moral point of view, the development of the world into a "global village" has made an important, though still unrecognized, difference to our moral situation. Expert observers and supervisors, sent out by famine relief organizations or permanently stationed in the famine-prone areas, can direct our aid to a refugee in Bengal almost as effectively as we could get it to someone in our own block. There would seem, therefore, to be no possible justification for discriminating on geo-graphical grounds.

There may be a greater need to defend the second implication of my principle—that the fact that there are millions of other people in the same position, in respect to the Bengali refugees, as I am, does not make the situation significantly different from a situation in which I am the only person who can prevent something very bad from occurring. Again, of course, I admit that there is a psycholog-ical difference between the cases; one feels less guilty about doing nothing if one can point to others, similarly placed, who have also done nothing. Yet this can make no real difference to our moral obligations. Should I consider that I am less obliged to pull the drowning child out of the pond if on looking around I see other people, no further away than I am, who have also noticed the child but are doing nothing? One has only to ask this question to see the absurdity of the view that numbers lessen obligation. It is a view that is an ideal excuse for inactivity; unfortunately most of the major evils—poverty, overpopulation, pollution—are problems in which everyone is almost equally involved.

The view that numbers do make a difference can be made plausible if stated in this way: if everyone in circumstances like mine gave £5 to the Bengal Relief Fund, there would be enough to provide food, shelter, and medical care for the refugees; there is no reason why I should give more than anyone else in the same circumstances as I am; therefore I have no obligation to give more than £5. Each premise in this argument is true, and the argument looks sound. It may convince us, unless we notice that it is based on a hypothetical premise, al-though the conclusion is not stated hypothetically. The argument would be sound if the conclusion were: if everyone in circumstances like mine were to give £5, I would have no obligation to give more than £5. If the conclusion were so stated, however, it would be ob-vious that the argument has no bearing on a situation in which it is not the case that everyone else gives £5. This, of course, is the actual situation. It is more or less certain that not everyone in circumstances like mine will give £5. So there will not be enough to provide the needed food, shelter, and medical care. Therefore by giving more than £5 I will prevent more suffering than I would if I gave just £5.

It might be thought that this argument has an absurd consequence. Since the situation appears to be that very few people are likely to give substantial amounts, it follows that I and everyone else in similar circumstances ought to give as much as possible, that is, at least up to the point at which by giving more one would begin to cause serious suffering for oneself and one's dependents—perhaps even beyond this point to the point of marginal utility, at which by giving more one would cause oneself and one's dependents as much suffering as one would prevent in Bengal. If everyone does this, however, there will be more than can be used for the benefit of the refugees, and some of the sacrifice will have been unnecessary. Thus, if everyone does what he ought to do, the result will not be as good as it would be if everyone did a little less than he ought to do, or if only some do all that they ought to do.

The paradox here arises only if we assume that the actions in question—sending money to the relief funds—are performed more or less simultaneously, and are also unexpected. For if it is to be expected that everyone is going to contribute something, then clearly each is not obliged to give as much as he would have been obliged to had others not been giving too. And if everyone is not acting more or less simultaneously, then those giving later will know how much more is needed, and will have no obligation to give more than is necessary to reach this amount. To say this is not to deny the principle that people in the same circumstances have the same obligations, but to point out that the fact that others have given, or may be expected to give, is a relevant circumstance: those giving after it has become known that many others are giving and those giving before are not in the same circumstances. So the seemingly absurd consequence of the principle I have put forward can occur only if people are in error about the actual circumstances—that is, if they think they are giving when others are not, but in fact they are giving when others are. The result of everyone doing what he really ought to do cannot be worse than the result of everyone doing less than he ought to do, although the result of everyone doing what he reasonably believes he ought to do could be.

If my argument so far has been sound, neither our distance from a preventable evil nor the number of other people who, in respect to that evil, are in the same situation as we are, lessens our obligation to mitigate or prevent that evil. I shall therefore take as established the principle I asserted earlier. As I have already said, I need to assert it only in its qualified form: if it is in our power to prevent something very bad from happening, without thereby sacrificing anything else morally significant, we ought, morally, to do it.

The outcome of this argument is that our traditional moral categories are upset. The traditional distinction between duty and charity cannot be drawn, or at least, not in the place we normally draw it. Giving money to the Bengal Relief Fund is regarded as an act of charity in our society. The bodies which collect money are known as "charities." These organizations see themselves in this way—if you send them a check, you will be thanked for your "generosity." Because giving money is regarded as an act of charity, it is not thought that there is anything wrong with not giving. The charitable man may be praised, but the man who is not charitable is not condemned. People do not feel in any way ashamed or guilty about spending money on new clothes or a new car instead of giving it to famine relief. (Indeed, the alternative does not occur to them.) This way of looking at the matter cannot be justified. When we buy new clothes not to keep ourselves warm but to look "well-dressed" we are not providing for any important need. We would not be sacrificing anything significant if we were to continue to wear our old clothes, and give the money to famine relief. By doing so, we would be preventing another person from starving. It follows from what I have said earlier that we ought to give money away, rather than spend it on clothes which we do not need to keep us warm. To do so is not charitable, or generous. Nor is it the kind of act which philosophers and theologians have called "supererogatory"—an act which it would be good to do, but not wrong not to do. On the contrary, we ought to give the money away, and it is wrong not to do so.

I am not maintaining that there are no acts which are charitable, or that there are no acts which it would be good to do but not wrong not to do. It may be possible to redraw the distinction between duty and charity in some other place. All I am arguing here is that the present way of drawing the distinction, which makes it an act of charity for a man living at the level of affluence which most people in the "developed nations" enjoy to give money to save someone else from starvation, cannot be supported. It is beyond the scope of my argument to consider whether the distinction should be redrawn or abolished altogether. There would be many other possible ways of drawing the distinction—for instance, one might decide that it is good to make other people as happy as possible, but not wrong not to do so.

Despite the limited nature of the revision in our moral conceptual scheme which I am proposing, the revision would, given the extent of both affluence and famine in the world today, have radical implications. These implications may lead to further objections, distinct from those I have already considered. I shall discuss two of these.

One objection to the position I have taken might be simply that it is too drastic a revision of our moral scheme. People do not ordinarily judge in the way I have suggested they should. Most people reserve their moral condemnation for those who violate some moral norm, such as the norm against taking another person's property. They do not condemn those who indulge in luxury instead of giving to famine relief. But given that I did not set out to present a morally neutral description of the way people make moral judgments, the way people do in fact judge has nothing to do with the validity of my conclusion. My conclusion follows from the principle which I advanced earlier, and unless that principle is rejected, or the arguments shown to be unsound, I think the conclusion must stand, however strange it appears. . . .

The second objection to my attack on the present distinction between duty and charity is one which has from time to time been made against utilitarianism. It follows from some forms of utilitarian theory that we all ought, morally, to be working full time to increase the balance of happiness over misery. The position I have taken here would not lead to this conclusion in all circumstances, for if there were no bad occurrences that we could prevent without sacrificing something of comparable moral importance, my argument would have no application. Given the present conditions in many parts of the world, however, it does follow from my argument that we ought, morally, to be working full time to relieve great suffering of the sort that occurs as a result of famine or other disasters. Of course, mitigating circumstances can be adduced—for instance, that if we wear ourselves out through overwork, we shall be less effective than we would otherwise have been. Nevertheless, when all considerations of this sort have been taken into account, the conclusion remains: we ought to be preventing as much suffering as we can without sacrificing something else of comparable moral importance. This conclusion is one which we may be reluctant to face. I cannot see, though, why it should be regarded as a criticism of the position for which I have argued, rather than a criticism of our ordinary standards of behavior. Since most people are self-interested to some degree, very few of us are likely to do everything that we ought to do. It would, however, hardly be honest to take this as evidence that it is not the case that we ought to do it. . . .

The conclusion reached earlier [raises] the question of just how much we all ought to be giving away. One possibility, which has already been mentioned, is that we ought to give until we reach the level of marginal utility—that is, the level at which, by giving more, I would cause as much suffering to myself or my dependents as I would relieve by my gift. This would mean, of course, that one would reduce oneself to very near the material circumstances of a Bengali refugee. It will be recalled that earlier I put forward both a strong and a moderate version of the principle of preventing bad occurrences. The strong version, which required us to prevent bad things from happening unless in doing so we would be sacrificing something of a comparable moral significance, does seem to require reducing ourselves to the level of marginal utility. I should also say that the strong version seems to me to be the correct one. I proposed the more moderate version—that we should prevent bad occurrences unless, to do so, we had to sacrifice something morally significant—only in order to show that even on this surely undeniable principle a great change in our way of life is required. On the more moderate principle, it may not follow that we ought to reduce ourselves to the level of marginal utility, for one might hold that to reduce oneself and one's family to this level is to cause something significantly bad to happen. Whether this is so I shall not discuss, since, as I have said, I can see no good reason for holding the moderate version of the principle rather than the strong version. Even if we accepted the principle only in its moderate form, however, it should be clear that we would have to give away enough to ensure that the consumer society, dependent as it is on people spending on trivia rather than giving to famine relief, would slow down and perhaps disappear entirely. There are several reasons why this would be desirable in itself. The value and necessity of economic growth are now being questioned not only by conservationists, but by economists as well.[2] There is no doubt, too, that the consumer society has had a distorting effect on the goals and purposes of its members. Yet looking at the

---

[2]See, for instance, John Kenneth Galbraith, *The New Industrial State* (Boston, 1967); and E. J. Mishan, *The Costs of Economic Growth* (London, 1967).

matter purely from the point of view of overseas aid, there must be a limit to the extent to which we should deliberately slow down our economy; for it might be the case that if we gave away, say, forty percent of our Gross National Product, we would slow down the economy so much that in absolute terms we would be giving less than if we gave twenty-five percent of the much larger GNP that we would have if we limited our contribution to this smaller percentage.

I mention this only as an indication of the sort of factor that one would have to take into account in working out an ideal. Since Western societies generally consider one percent of the GNP an acceptable level for overseas aid, the matter is entirely academic. Nor does it affect the question of how much an individual should give in a society in which very few are giving substantial amounts.

It is sometimes said, though less often now than it used to be, that philosophers have no special role to play in public affairs, since most public issues depend primarily on an assessment of facts. On questions of fact, it is said, philosophers as such have no special expertise, and so it has been possible to engage in philosophy without committing oneself to any position on major public issues. No doubt there are some issues of social policy and foreign policy about which it can truly be said that a really expert assessment of the facts is required before taking sides or acting, but the issue of famine is surely not one of these. The facts about the existence of suffering are beyond dispute. Nor, I think, is it disputed that we can do something about it, either through orthodox methods of famine relief or through population control or both. This is therefore an issue on which philosophers are competent to take a position. The issue is one which faces everyone who has more money than he needs to support himself and his dependents, or who is in a position to take some sort of political action. These categories must include practically every teacher and student of philosophy in the universities of the Western world. If philosophy is to deal with matters that are relevant to both teachers and students, this is an issue that philosophers should discuss.

Discussion, though, is not enough. What is the point of relating philosophy to public (and personal) affairs if we do not take our conclusions seriously? In this instance, taking our conclusion seriously means acting upon it. The philosopher will not find it any easier than anyone else to alter his attitudes and way of life to the extent that, if I am right, is involved in doing everything that we ought to be doing. At the very least, though, one can make a start. The philosopher who does so will have to sacrifice some of the benefits of the consumer society, but he can find compensation in the satisfaction of a way of life in which theory and practice, if not yet in harmony, are at least coming together.

STUDY QUESTIONS

1. Do you accept Singer's conclusion that you *personally* have a serious moral obligation to do something about world hunger? If not, where do you think his argument goes wrong?
2. Briefly outline Singer's argument. Name two of the strongest objections we can raise against his position. How do you think he would reply to them?
3. If Singer is right, then what we regard as charity is really moral duty. Does this set too high a standard for most people to follow?
4. For utilitarians like Singer the *consequences* of an action determine its moral character. The consequences of not sending food to starving people are the same as sending them poisoned food: in both cases the people die. Are you guilty of the moral equivalent of murder?

World Hunger and Moral Obligation: The Case Against Singer

JOHN ARTHUR

John Arthur is professor of philosophy at the State University of New York at Binghamton. He has published *The Unfinished Constitution*, along with numerous articles and anthologies in areas of ethics and social philosophy.

John Arthur criticizes what he calls "Singer's greater moral evil rule," according to which we ought to sacrifice our own interests if that will result in a greater net welfare to others. (For example, we should all do without luxuries to help those who are starving in Ethiopia.) Singer's premise is the equality of interests: Like amounts of suffering or happiness are of equal moral significance no matter who is experiencing them.

Arthur objects that Singer ignores the part of our common moral code that recognizes rights and deserts as determinants of duty. We have rights to our own lives, to our body parts, to the fruits of our labor—and these qualify our obligations to help others. Arthur denies that others have the *right* to our property whenever our property can reduce their misery without undue sacrifice on our part. "We are . . . entitled to invoke our own rights

WORLD HUNGER AND MORAL OBLIGATION: THE CASE AGAINST SINGER By John Arthur. Excerpted from "Equality, Entitlements and the Distribution of Income." © 1984 by John Arthur. Reprinted by permission.

as justification for our not giving to distant strangers." On the other hand, our moral code does recognize that our *own* children do have rights against us for food and protection.

Rights are one kind of entitlement that qualifies the duty of benevolence. Another is *desert*. We deserve the fruits of our labors. Our common morality does encourage benevolence "especially when it is a friend or someone we are close to geographically, and when the cost is not significant. But it also gives weight to rights and deserts, so we are not usually obligated to give to strangers . . ."

But perhaps Singer can be seen as advocating a reasonable *reform* of our present moral code. Perhaps we, who are in fortunate circumstances, should ignore our current entitlements and *change* our ways. Arthur argues that a call for reform is *un*reasonable and morally suspect. Moral codes are not made for angels, but for human beings with their subjective biases in favor of those close to them. Moreover, ignoring rights and deserts suggests a lack of respect for other persons. So Arthur concludes that our present moral code (that Singer judges to be overly selfish) *is* morally reasonable and in need of no reform in the direction suggested by Singer.

Introduction

My guess is that everyone who reads these words is wealthy by comparison with the poorest millions of people on our planet. Not only do we have plenty of money for food, clothing, housing, and other necessities, but a fair amount is left over for far less important purchases like phonograph records, fancy clothes, trips, intoxicants, movies, and so on. And what's more we don't usually give a thought to whether or not we ought to spend our money on such luxuries rather than to give it to those who need it more; we just assume it's ours to do with as we please.

Peter Singer, "Famine, Affluence, and Morality" argues that our assumption is wrong, that we should not buy luxuries when others are in severe need. But [is he] correct? . . .

He first argues that two general moral principles are widely accepted, and then that those principles imply an obligation to eliminate starvation.

The first principle is simply that "suffering and death from lack of food, shelter and medical care are bad." Some may be inclined to think that the mere existence of such an evil in itself places an obligation on others, but that is, of course, the problem which Singer addresses. I take it that he is not begging the question in this obvious way and will argue from the existence of evil to the obligation of others to eliminate it. But how, exactly, does he establish this? The second principle, he thinks, shows the connection, but it is here that controversy arises.

This principle, which I will call the greater moral evil rule, is as follows:

> If it is in our power to prevent something bad from happening, without thereby sacrificing anything of comparable moral importance, we ought, morally, to do it.[1]

In other words, people are entitled to keep their earnings only if there is no way for them to prevent a greater evil by giving them away. Providing others with food, clothing, and housing would generally be of more importance than buying luxuries, so the greater moral evil rule now requires substantial redistribution of wealth.

Certainly there are few, if any, of us who live by that rule, although that hardly shows we are *justified* in our way of life; we often fail to live up to our own standards. Why does Singer think our shared morality requires that we follow the greater moral evil rule? What arguments does he give for it?

He begins with an analogy. Suppose you came across a child drowning in a shallow pond. Certainly we feel it would be wrong not to help. Even if saving the child meant we must dirty our clothes, we would emphasize that those clothes are not of comparable significance to the child's life. The greater moral evil rule thus seems a natural way of capturing why we think it would be wrong not to help.

---

[1] Singer also offers a "weak" version of this principle which, it seems to me, is *too* weak. It requires giving aid only if the gift is of *no* moral significance to the giver. But since even minor embarrassment or small amounts of happiness are not completely without moral importance, this weak principle implies little or no obligation to aid, even to the drowning child.

But the argument for the greater moral evil rule is not limited to Singer's claim that it explains our feelings about the drowning child or that it appears "uncontroversial." Moral equality also enters the picture. Besides the Jeffersonian idea that we share certain rights equally, most of us are also attracted to another type of equality, namely that like amounts of suffering (or happiness) are of equal significance, no matter who is experiencing them. I cannot reasonably say that, while my pain is no more severe than yours, I am somehow special and it's more important that mine be alleviated. Objectivity requires us to admit the opposite, that no one has a unique status which warrants such special pleading. So equality demands equal consideration of interests as well as respect for certain rights.

But if we fail to give to famine relief and instead purchase a new car when the old one will do, or buy fancy clothes for a friend when his or her old ones are perfectly good, are we not assuming that the relatively minor enjoyment we or our friends may get is as important as another person's life? And that a form of prejudice; we are acting as if people were not equal in the sense that their interests deserve equal consideration. We are giving special consideration to ourselves or to our group, rather like a racist does. Equal consideration of interests thus leads naturally to the greater moral evil rule.

Rights and Desert

Equality, in the sense of giving equal consideration to equally serious needs, is part of our moral code. And so we are led, quite rightly I think, to the conclusion that we should prevent harm to others if in doing so we do not sacrifice anything of comparable moral importance. But there is also another side to the coin, one which Singer ignore[s]. . . . This can be expressed rather awkwardly by the notion of entitlements. These fall into two broad categories, rights and desert. A few examples will show what I mean.

All of us could help others by giving away or allowing others to use our bodies. While your life may be shortened by the loss of a kidney or less enjoyable if lived with only one eye, those costs are probably not comparable to the loss experienced by a person who will die without any kidney or who is totally blind. We can even imagine persons who will actually be harmed in some way by your not granting sexual favors to them. Perhaps the absence of a sexual partner would cause psychological harm or even rape. Now suppose that you can prevent this evil without sacrificing anything of comparable importance. Obviously such relations may not be pleasant, but according to the greater moral evil rule that is not enough; to be justified in refusing, you must show that the unpleasantness you would experience is of equal importance to the harm you are preventing. Otherwise, the rule says you must consent.

If anything is clear, however, it is that our code does not *require* such heroism; you are entitled to keep your second eye and kidney and not bestow sexual favors on anyone who may be harmed without them. The reason for this is often expressed in terms of rights; it's your body, you have a right to it, and that weighs against whatever duty you have to help. To sacrifice a kidney for a stranger is to do more than is required, it's heroic.

Moral rights are normally divided into two categories. Negative rights are rights of noninterference. The right to life, for example, is a right not to be killed. Property rights, the right to privacy, and the right to exercise religious freedom are also negative, requiring only that people leave others alone and not interfere.

Positive rights, however, are rights of recipience. By not putting their children up for adoption, parents give them various positive rights, including rights to be fed, clothed, and housed. If I agree to share in a business venture, my promise creates a right of recipience, so that when I back out of the deal, I've violated your right.

Negative rights also differ from positive in that the former are natural; the ones you have depend on what you are. If lower animals lack rights to life or liberty it is because there is a relevant difference between them and us. But the positive rights you may have are not natural; they arise because others have promised, agreed, or contracted to give you something.

Normally, then, a duty to help a stranger in need is not the result of a right he has. Such a right would be positive, and since no contract or promise was made, no such right exists. An exception to this would be a lifeguard who contracts to watch out for someone's children. The parent whose child drowns would in this case be doubly wronged. First, the lifeguard should not have cruelly or thoughtlessly ignored the child's interests, and second, he ought not to have violated the rights of the parents that he helped. Here, unlike Singer's case, we can say there are rights at stake. Other bystanders also act wrongly by cruelly ignoring the child, but unlike the lifeguard they do not violate anybody's rights. Moral rights are one factor to be weighed, but we also have other obligations; I am not claiming that rights are all we need to consider. That view, like the greater moral evil rule, trades simplicity for accuracy. In fact, our code expects us to help people in need as well as to respect negative and positive rights. But we are also entitled to invoke our own rights as justification for not giving to distant strangers or when the cost to us is substantial, as when we give up an eye or kidney. . . .

Desert is a second form of entitlement. Suppose, for example, an industrious farmer manages through hard work to produce a surplus of food for the winter while a lazy neighbor spends his summer fishing. Must our industrious farmer ignore his hard work and give the surplus away because his neighbor or his family will suffer? What again seems clear is that we have more than one factor to weigh. Not only should we compare the consequences of his keeping it with his giving it away; we also should weigh the fact that one farmer deserves the food, he earned it through his hard work. Perhaps his deserving the product of his labor is outweighed by the greater need of his lazy neighbor, or perhaps it isn't, but being outweighed is in any case not the same as weighing nothing!

Desert can be negative, too. The fact that the Nazi war criminal did what he did means he deserves punishment, that we have a reason to send him to jail. Other considerations, for example the fact that nobody will be deterred by his suffering, or that he is old and harmless, may weigh against punishment and so we may let him go; but again that does not mean he doesn't still deserve to be punished.

Our moral code gives weight to both the greater moral evil principle and entitlements. The former emphasizes equality, claiming that from an objective point of view all comparable suffering, whoever its victim, is equally significant. It encourages us to take an impartial look at all the various effects of our actions; it is thus forward-looking. When we consider matters of entitlement, however, our attention is directed to the past. Whether we have rights to money, property, eyes, or whatever, depends on how we came to possess them. If they were acquired by theft rather than from birth or through gift exchange, then the right is suspect. Desert, like rights, is also backward-looking, emphasizing past effort or past transgressions which now warrant reward or punishment.

Our commonly shared morality thus requires that we ignore neither consequences nor entitlements, neither the future results of our action nor relevant events in the past. It encourages people to help others in need, especially when it's a friend or someone we are close to geographically, and when the cost is not significant. But it also gives weight to rights and desert, so that we are not usually obligated to give to strangers. . . .

But unless we are moral relativists, the mere fact that entitlements are an important part of our moral code does not in itself justify such a role. Singer . . . can perhaps best be seen as a moral reformer advocating the rejection of rules which provide for distribution according to rights and desert. Certainly the fact that in the past our moral code condemned suicide and racial mixing while condoning slavery should not convince us that a more enlightened moral code, one which we would want to support, would take such positions. Rules which define acceptable behavior are continually changing, and we must allow for the replacement of inferior ones.

Why should we not view entitlements as examples of inferior rules we are better off without? What could justify our practice of evaluating actions by looking backward to rights and desert instead of just to their consequences? One answer is that more fundamental values than rights and desert are at stake, namely fairness, justice, and respect. Failure to reward those who earn good grades or promotions is wrong because it's *unfair;* ignoring past guilt shows a lack of regard for *justice;* and failure to respect rights to life, privacy, or religious choice suggests a lack of *respect for other persons.*

Some people may be persuaded by those remarks, feeling that entitlements are now on an acceptably firm foundation. But an advocate of equality may well want to question why fairness, justice, and respect for persons should matter. But since it is no more obvious that preventing suffering matters than that fairness, respect, and justice do, we again seem to have reached an impasse. . . .

The lesson to be learned here is a general one: The moral code it is rational for us to support must be practical; it must actually work. This means, among other things, that it must be able to gain the support of almost everyone.

But the code must be practical in other respects as well. . . . [It] is wrong to ignore the possibilities of altruism, but it is also important that a code not assume people are more unselfish than they are. Rules that would work only for angels are not the ones it is rational to support for humans. Second, an ideal code cannot assume we are more objective than we are; we often tend to rationalize when our own interests are at stake, and a rational person will also keep that in mind when choosing a moral code. Finally, it is not rational to support a code which assumes we have perfect knowledge. We are often mistaken about the consequences of what we do, and a workable code must take that into account as well. . . .

It seems to me, then, that a reasonable code would require people to help when there is no substantial cost to themselves, that is, when what they are sacrificing would not mean *significant* reduction in their own or their families' level of happiness. Since most people's savings accounts and nearly everybody's second kidney are not insignificant, entitlements would in those cases outweigh another's need. But if what is at stake is trivial, as dirtying one's clothes would normally be, then an ideal moral code would not allow rights to override the greater evil that can be prevented. Despite our code's unclear and sometimes schizophrenic posture, it seems to me that these judgments are not that different from our current moral attitudes. We tend to blame people who waste money on trivia when they could help others in need, yet not to expect people to make large sacrifices to distant strangers. An ideal moral code thus might not be a great deal different from our own.

STUDY QUESTIONS

1. What is Singer's greater moral evil rule and why does Arthur object to it?
2. What is the status of the common moral code in Arthur's moral system? How does Arthur deploy the moral code to undermine Singer's general position that utilitarian considerations override parochial loyalties and interests?
3. How does Arthur classify rights? Why is the child's right to parental protection and food a "positive right"? How does Arthur's conception of rights preclude the view that needy but distant strangers have the right to our benevolence?
4. Arthur says "Our commonly shared morality requires that we ignore neither consequences nor entitlements." Is it fair to say that Singer ignores entitlements?

Lifeboat Ethics: The Case Against Helping the Poor

GARRETT HARDIN

Garrett Hardin (b. 1921) is a professor of biology at the University of California at Santa Barbara. He is the author of several books, including *The Limits of Altruism: An Ecologist's View of Survival* (1977) and *Naked Emperors: Essays of a Taboo-Stalker* (1982).

Activists concerned with world hunger claim that the earth is like a "spaceship" whose passengers each have an equal claim to its scarce resources. Hardin rejects the spaceship metaphor, pointing out that a spaceship operates under *one* captain; he prefers to think of the world as consisting of several different lifeboats. Some are quite well stocked and well maintained, and carry a safe number of passengers; others are ill equipped, chaotic, disease ridden, and so overcrowded that passengers constantly fall overboard. Hardin asks, What should the passengers on the wealthy boats do when they see refugees from the poor boats swimming their way? Let them all come aboard and allow the boat to sink? Take a few and eliminate the boat's safety margin? Or allow no one in and guard against boarding parties? Hardin recommends the latter. He not only argues that we should not let the

LIFEBOAT ETHICS: THE CASE AGAINST HELPING THE POOR From *Psychology Today*, September 1974. Reprinted by permission of the author.

world's poor into our own advantaged countries; he also recommends that we be very careful about sending massive aid to countries suffering from extreme poverty and famine. Well-intentioned food programs may lead to a dangerous population increase and a corresponding escalation of misery.

Environmentalists use the metaphor of the earth as a "spaceship" in trying to persuade countries, industries, and people to stop wasting and polluting our natural resources. Since we all share life on this planet, they argue, no single person or institution has the right to destroy, waste, or use more than a fair share of its resources.

But does everyone on earth have an equal right to an equal share of its resources? The spaceship metaphor can be dangerous when used by misguided idealists to justify suicidal policies for sharing our resources through uncontrolled immigration and foreign aid. In their enthusiastic but unrealistic generosity, they confuse the ethics of a spaceship with those of a lifeboat.

A true spaceship would have to be under the control of a captain, since no ship could possibly survive if its course were determined by committee. Spaceship Earth certainly has no captain; the United Nations is merely a toothless tiger, with little power to enforce any policy upon its bickering members.

If we divide the world crudely into rich nations and poor nations, two thirds of them are desperately poor, and only one third comparatively rich, with the United States the wealthiest of all. Metaphorically each rich nation can be seen as a lifeboat full of comparatively rich people. In the ocean outside each lifeboat swim the poor of the world, who would like to get in, or at least to share some of the wealth. What should the lifeboat passengers do?

First, we must recognize the limited capacity of any lifeboat. For example, a nation's land has a limited capacity to support a population and as the current energy crisis has shown us, in some ways we have already exceeded the carrying capacity of our land.

I. Adrift in a Moral Sea

So here we sit, say fifty people in our lifeboat. To be generous, let us assume it has room for ten more, making a total capacity of sixty. Suppose the fifty of us in the lifeboat see 100 others swimming in the water outside, begging for admission to our boat or for handouts. We have several options: We may be tempted to try to live by the Christian ideal of being "our brother's keeper," or by the Marxist ideal of "to each according to his needs." Since the needs of all in the water are the same, and since they can all be seen as "our brothers," we could take them all into our boat, making a total of 150 in a boat designed for sixty. The boat swamps, everyone drowns. Complete justice, complete catastrophe.

Since the boat has an unused excess capacity of ten or more passengers, we could admit just ten more to it. But which ten do we let in? How do we choose? Do we pick the best ten, the neediest ten, "first come, first served"? And what do we say to the ninety we exclude? If we do let an extra ten into our lifeboat, we will have lost our "safety factor," an engineering principle of critical importance. For example, if we don't leave room for excess capacity as a safety factor in our country's agriculture, a new plant disease or a bad change in the weather could have disastrous consequences.

Suppose we decide to preserve our small safety factor and admit no more to the lifeboat. Our survival is then possible, although we shall have to be constantly on guard against boarding parties.

While this last solution clearly offers the only means of our survival, it is morally abhorrent to many people. Some say they feel guilty about their good luck. My reply is simple: "Get out and yield your place to others." This may solve the problem of the guilt-ridden person's conscience, but it does not change the ethics of the lifeboat. The needy person to whom the guilt-ridden person yields his place will not himself feel guilty about his good luck. If he did, he would not climb aboard. The net result of conscience-stricken people giving up their unjustly held seats is the elimination of that sort of conscience from the lifeboat.

This is the basic metaphor within which we must work out our solutions. Let us now enrich the image, step by step, with substantive additions from the real world, a world that must solve real and pressing problems of overpopulation and hunger.

The harsh ethics of the lifeboat become even harsher when we consider the reproductive differences between the rich nations and the poor nations. The people inside the lifeboats are doubling in numbers every eighty-seven years; those swimming around outside are doubling, on the average, every thirty-five years, more than twice as fast as the rich. And since the world's resources are dwindling, the difference in prosperity between the rich and the poor can only increase.

As of 1973, the U.S. had a population of 210 million people, who were increasing by 0.8 percent per year. Outside our lifeboat, let us imagine another 210 million people (say the combined populations of Colombia, Ecuador, Venezuela, Morocco, Pakistan, Thailand, and the Philippines), who are increasing at a rate of 3.3 percent per year. Put differently, the doubling time for this aggregate population is twenty-one years, compared to eighty-seven years for the U.S.

II. Multiplying the Rich and the Poor

Now suppose the U.S. agreed to pool its resources with those seven countries, with everyone receiving an equal share. Initially the ratio of Americans to non-Americans in this model would be one-to-one. But consider what the ratio would be after eighty-seven years, by which time the Americans would have doubled to a population of 420 million. By then, doubling every twenty-one years, the other group would have swollen to 354 billion. Each American would have to share the available resources with more than eight people.

But, one could argue, this discussion assumes that current population trends will continue and they may not. Quite so. Most likely the rate of population increase will decline much faster in the U.S. than it will in the other countries, and there does not seem to be much we can do about it. In sharing with "each according to his needs," we must recognize that needs are determined by population size, which is determined by the rate of reproduction, which at present is regarded as a sovereign right of every nation, poor or not. This being so, the philanthropic load created by the sharing ethic of the spaceship can only increase.

III. The Tragedy of the Commons

The fundamental error of spaceship ethics, and the sharing it requires, is that it leads to what I call "the tragedy of the commons." Under a system of private property, the men who own property recognize their responsibilities to care for it, for if they don't they will eventually suffer. A farmer, for instance, will allow no more cattle in a pasture than its carrying capacity justifies. If he overloads it, erosion sets in, weeds take over, and he loses the use of the pasture.

If a pasture becomes a commons open to all, the right of each to use it may not be matched by a corresponding responsibility to protect it. Asking everyone to use it with discretion will hardly do, for the considerate herdsman who refrains from overloading the commons suffers more than a selfish one who says his needs are greater. If everyone would remain himself, all would be well; but it takes only one less than everyone to ruin a system of voluntary restraint. In a crowded world of less than perfect human beings, mutual ruin is inevitable if there are no controls. This is the tragedy of the commons.

One of the major tasks of education today should be the creation of such an acute awareness of the dangers of the commons that people will recognize its many varieties. For example, the air and water have become polluted because they are treated as commons. Further growth in the population or per capita conversion of natural resources into pollutants will only make the problem worse. The same holds true for the fish of the oceans. Fishing fleets have nearly disappeared in many parts of the world, technological improvements in the art of fishing are hastening the day of complete ruin. Only the replacement of the system of the commons with a responsible system of control will save the land, air, water, and oceanic fisheries.

IV. The World Food Bank

In recent years there has been a push to create a new commons called a world food bank, an international depository of food reserves to which nations would contribute according to their abilities and from which they would draw according to their needs. This humanitarian proposal has received support from many liberal international groups, and from such prominent citizens as Margaret Mead, U.N. Secretary General Kurt Waldheim, and Senators Edward Kennedy and George McGovern.

A world food bank appeals powerfully to our humanitarian impulses. But before we rush ahead with such a plan, let us recognize where the greatest political push comes from, lest we be disillusioned later. Our experience with the "Food for Peace program," or Public Law 480, gives us the answer. This program moved billions of dollars worth of U.S. surplus grain to food-short, population-long countries during the past two decades. But when P.L. 480 first became law, a headline in the business magazine *Forbes* revealed the real power behind it: "Feeding the World's Hungry Millions: How It Will Mean Billions for U.S. Business."

And indeed it did. In the years 1960 to 1970, U.S. taxpayers spent a total of $7.9 billion on the Food for Peace program. Between 1948 and 1970, they also paid an additional $50 billion for other economic-aid programs, some of which went for food and food-producing machinery and technology. Though all U.S. taxpayers were forced to contribute to the cost of P.L. 480, certain special interest groups gained handsomely under the program. Farmers did not have to contribute the grain; the Government, or rather the taxpayers, bought it from them at full market prices. The increased demand raised prices of farm products generally. The manufacturers of farm machinery, fertilizers, and pesticides benefited by the farmers' extra efforts to grow more food. Grain elevators profited from storing the surplus until it could be shipped. Railroads made money hauling it to ports, and shipping lines profited from carrying it overseas. The implementation of P.L. 480 required the creation of a vast Government bureaucracy, which then acquired its own vested interest in continuing the program regardless of its merits.

V. Extracting Dollars

Those who proposed and defended the Food for Peace program in public rarely mentioned its importance to any of these special interests. The public emphasis was always on its humanitarian effects. The combination of silent selfish interests and highly vocal humanitarian apologists made a powerful and successful lobby for extracting money from taxpayers. We can expect the same lobby to push now for the creation of a world food bank.

However great the potential benefit to selfish interests, it should not be a decisive argument against a truly humanitarian program. We must ask if such a program would actually do more good than harm, not only momentarily but also in the long run. Those who propose the food bank usually refer to a current "emergency" or "crisis" in terms of world food supply. But what is an emergency? Although they may be infrequent and sudden, everyone knows that emergencies will occur from time to time. A well-run family, company, organization, or country prepares for the likelihood of accidents and emergencies. It expects them, it budgets for them, it saves for them.

VI. Learning the Hard Way

What happens if some organizations or countries budget for accidents and others do not? If each country is solely responsible for its own well-being, poorly managed ones will suffer. But they can learn from experience. They may mend their ways, and learn to budget for infrequent but certain emergencies. For example, the weather varies from year to year, and periodic crop failures are certain. A wise and competent government saves out of the production of the good years in anticipation of bad years to come. Joseph taught this policy to Pharaoh in Egypt more than 2,000 years ago. Yet the great majority of the governments in the world today do not follow such a policy. They lack either the wisdom or the competence, or both. Should those nations that do manage to put something aside be forced to come to the rescue each time an emergency occurs among the poor nations?

"But it isn't their fault!" some kindhearted liberals argue. "How can we blame the poor people who are caught in an emergency? Why must they suffer for the sins of their government?" The concept of blame is simply not relevant here. The real question is, What are the operational consequences of establishing a world food bank? If it is open to every country every time a need develops, slovenly rulers will not be motivated to take Joseph's advice. Someone will always come to their aid. Some countries will deposit food in the world food bank, and others will withdraw it. There will be almost no overlap. As a result of such solutions to food shortage emergencies, the poor countries will not learn to mend their ways, and will suffer progressively greater emergencies as their populations grow.

VII. Population Control the Crude Way

On the average, poor countries undergo a 2.5 percent increase in population each year; rich countries, about 0.8 percent. Only rich countries have anything in the way of food reserves set aside, and even they do not have as much as they should. Poor countries have none. If poor countries received no food from the outside, the rate of their population growth would be periodically checked by crop failures and famines. But if they can always draw on a world food bank in time of need, their population can continue to grow unchecked, and so will their "need" for aid. In the short run, a world food bank

859

may diminish that need, but in the long run it actually increases the need without limit.

Without some system of worldwide food sharing, the proportion of people in the rich and poor nations might eventually stabilize. The over-populated poor countries would decrease in numbers, while the rich countries that had room for more people would increase. But with a well-meaning system of sharing, such as a world food bank, the growth differential between the rich and the poor countries will not only persist, it will increase. Because of the higher rate of population growth in the poor countries of the world, 88 percent of today's children are born poor, and only 12 percent rich. Year by year the ratio becomes worse, as the fast-reproducing poor outnumber the slow-reproducing rich.

A world food bank is thus a commons in disguise. People will have more motivation to draw from it than to add to any common store. The less provident and less able will multiply at the expense of the abler and more provident, bringing eventual ruin upon all who share in the commons. Besides, any system of "sharing" that amounts to foreign aid from the rich nations to the poor nations will carry the taint of charity, which will contribute little to the world peace so devoutly desired by those who support the idea of a world food bank.

As past U.S. foreign-aid programs have amply and depressingly demonstrated, international charity frequently inspires mistrust and antagonism rather than gratitude on the part of the recipient nation.

VIII. Chinese Fish and Miracle Rice

The modern approach to foreign aid stresses the export of technology and advice, rather than money and food. As an ancient Chinese proverb goes: "Give a man a fish and he will eat for a day; teach him how to fish and he will eat for the rest of his days." Acting on this advice, the Rockefeller and Ford Foundations have financed a number of programs for improving agriculture in the hungry nations. Known as the "Green Revolution," these programs have led to the development of "miracle rice" and "miracle wheat," new strains that offer bigger harvests and greater resistance to crop damage. Norman Borlaug, the Nobel Prize-winning agronomist who, supported by the Rockefeller Foundation, developed "miracle wheat," is one of the most prominent advocates of a world food bank.

Whether or not the Green Revolution can increase food production as much as its champions claim is a debatable but possibly irrelevant point. Those who support this well-intended humanitarian effort should first consider some of the fundamentals of human ecology. Ironically, one man who did was the late Alan Gregg, a vice president of the Rockefeller Foundation. Two decades ago he expressed strong doubts about the wisdom of such attempts to increase food production. He likened the growth and spread of humanity over the surface of the earth to the spread of cancer in the human body, remarking that "cancerous growths demand food; but, as far as I know, they have never been cured by getting it."

IX. Overloading the Environment

Every human born constitutes a draft on all aspects of the environment: food, air, water, forests, beaches, wildlife, scenery, and solitude. Food can, perhaps, be significantly increased to meet a growing demand. But what about clean beaches, unspoiled forests, and solitude? If we satisfy a growing population's need for food, we necessarily decrease its per capita supply of the other resources needed by men.

India, for example, now has a population of 600 million, which increases by 15 million each year. This population already puts a huge load on a relatively impoverished environment. The country's forests are now only a small fraction of what they were three centuries ago, and floods and erosion continually destroy the insufficient farmland that remains. Every one of the 15 million new lives added to India's population puts an additional burden on the environment, and increases the economic and social costs of crowding. However humanitarian our intent, every Indian life saved through medical or nutritional assistance from abroad diminishes the quality of life for those who remain, and for subsequent generations. If rich countries make it possible, through foreign aid, for 600 million Indians to swell to 1.2 billion in a mere twenty-eight years, as their current growth rate threatens, will future generations of Indians thank us for hastening the destruction of their environment? Will our good intentions be sufficient excuse for the consequences of our actions?

My final example of a commons in action is one for which the public has the least desire for rational discussion—immigration.

Anyone who publicly questions the wisdom of current U.S. immigration policy is promptly charged with bigotry, prejudice, ethnocentrism, chauvinism, isolationism, or selfishness. Rather than encounter such accusations, one would rather talk about matters, leaving immigration policy to wallow in the crosscurrents of special interests that take no account of the good of the whole or the interests of posterity.

Perhaps we still feel guilty about things we said in the past. Two generations ago the popular press frequently referred to Dagos, Wops, Polacks, Chinks, and Krauts in articles about how America was being "overrun" by foreigners of supposedly inferior genetic stock. But because the implied inferiority of foreigners was used then as justification for keeping them out, people now assume that restrictive policies could only be based on such misguided notions. There are other grounds.

X. A Nation of Immigrants

Just consider the numbers involved. Our Government acknowledges a new inflow of 400,000 immigrants a year. While we have no hard data on the extent of illegal entries, educated guesses put the figure at about 600,000 a year. Since the natural increase (excess of births over deaths) of the resident population now runs about 1.7 million per year, the yearly gain from immigration amounts to at least 19 percent of the total annual increase, and may be as much as 37 percent if we include the estimate for illegal immigrants. Considering the growing use of birth-control devices, the potential effect of educational campaigns by such organizations as Planned Parenthood Federation of America and Zero Population Growth, and the influence of inflation and the housing shortage, the fertility rate of American women may decline so much that immigration could account for all the yearly increase in population. Should we not at least ask if that is what we want?

For the sake of those who worry about whether the "quality" of the average immigrant compares favorably with the quality of the average resident, let us assume that immigrants and nativeborn citizens are of exactly equal quality, however one defines that term. We will focus here only on quantity; and since our conclusions will depend on nothing else, all charges of bigotry and chauvinism become irrelevant.

862

XI. Immigration vs. Food Supply

World food banks *move food to the people,* hastening the exhaustion of the environment of the poor countries. Unrestricted immigration, on the other hand *moves people to the food,* thus speeding up the destruction of the environment of the rich countries. We can easily understand why poor people should want to make this latter transfer, but why should rich hosts encourage it?

As in the case of foreign-aid programs, immigration receives support from selfish interests and humanitarian impulses. The primary selfish interest in unimpeded immigration is the desire of employers for cheap labor, particularly in industries and trades that offer degrading work. In the past, one wave of foreigners after another was brought into the U.S. to work at wretched jobs for wretched wages. In recent years the Cubans, Puerto Ricans, and Mexicans have had this dubious honor. The interests of the employers of cheap labor mesh well with the guilty silence of the country's liberal intelligentsia. White Anglo-Saxon Protestants are particularly reluctant to call for a closing of the doors to immigration for fear of being called bigots.

But not all countries have such reluctant leadership. Most educated Hawaiians, for example, are keenly aware of the limits of their environment, particularly in terms of population growth. There is only so much room on the islands, and the islanders know it. To Hawaiians, immigrants from the other forty-nine states present as great a threat as those from other nations. At a recent meeting of Hawaiian government officials in Honolulu, I had the ironic delight of hearing a speaker, who like most of his audience was of Japanese ancestry, ask how the country might practically and constitutionally close its doors to further immigration. One member of the audience countered: "How can we shut the doors now? We have many friends and relatives in Japan that we'd like to bring here some day so that they can enjoy Hawaii too." The Japanese-American speaker smiled sympathetically and answered: "Yes, but we have children now, and someday we'll have grandchildren too. We can bring more people here from Japan only by giving away some of the land that we hope to pass on to our grandchildren some day. What right do we have to do that?"

At this point, I can hear U.S. liberals asking: "How can you justify slamming the door once you're inside? You say that immigrants

863

should be kept out. But aren't we all immigrants, or the descendants of immigrants? If we insist on staying, must we not admit all others?" Our craving for intellectual order leads us to seek and prefer symmetrical rules and morals: a single rule for me and everybody else; the same rule yesterday, today, and tomorrow. Justice, we feel, should not change with time and place.

We Americans of non-Indian ancestry can look upon ourselves as the descendants of thieves who are guilty morally, if not legally, of stealing this land from its Indian owners. Should we then give back the land to the now living American descendants of those Indians? However morally or logically sound this proposal may be, I, for one, am unwilling to live by it and I know no one else who is. Besides, the logical consequence would be absurd. Suppose that, intoxicated with a sense of pure justice, we should decide to turn our land over to the Indians. Since all our wealth has also been derived from the land, wouldn't we be morally obliged to give that back to the Indians too?

XII. Pure Justice vs. Reality

Clearly, the concept of pure justice produces an infinite regression to absurdity. Centuries ago, wise men invented statutes of limitations to justify the rejection of such pure justice, in the interest of preventing continual disorder. The law zealously defends property rights, but only relatively recent property rights. Drawing a line after an arbitrary time has elapsed may be unjust, but the alternatives are worse.

We are all the descendants of thieves, and the world's resources are inequitably distributed. But we must begin the journey to tomorrow from the point where we are today. We cannot remake the past. We cannot safely divide the wealth equitably among all peoples so long as people reproduce at different rates. To do so would guarantee that our grandchildren, and everyone else's grandchildren, would have only a ruined world to inhabit.

To be generous with one's own possessions is quite different from being generous with those of posterity. We should call this point to the attention of those who, from a commendable love of justice and equality, would institute a system of the commons, either in the form of a world food bank, or of unrestricted immigration. We must convince them if we wish to save at least some parts of the world from environmental ruin.

Without a true world government to control reproduction and the use of available resources, the sharing ethic of the spaceship is impossible. For the foreseeable future, our survival demands that we govern our actions by the ethics of a lifeboat, harsh though they may be. Posterity will be satisfied with nothing less.

STUDY QUESTIONS

1. Explain the difference between a "lifeboat ethic" and a "spaceship ethic." Defend one or the other.
2. Hardin sees a difference between "reality" and "pure justice." Do you agree?
3. The third-century theologian Tertullian wrote, "The scourges of pestilence, famine, wars, and earthquakes have come to be regarded as a blessing to overcrowded nations, since they serve to prune away the luxuriant growth of the human race." How would Hardin and Singer respond to this remark? With whom do you agree most?

Population and Food: Metaphors and the Reality

WILLIAM W. MURDOCH
and ALLAN OATEN

William Murdoch (b. 1939) is professor of biology at the University of California at Santa Barbara. He has written numerous articles on population, ecology, and famine. He is the author of *The Poverty of Nations: Population, Hunger and Development* (1980).

Allan Oaten is professor of biology at the University of California at Santa Barbara. He has published in the areas of population control and environmentalism.

William Murdoch and Allan Oaten seek to show that Hardin's arguments against famine relief to poor third-world nations are unsound. One mechanism of relief is the proposed world food bank from which needy nations could draw. Hardin had argued that such a resource is a "commons"—people usually deplete a commons without adding to it—that would have the effect of increasing the populations of the poorer nations, eventually bringing disaster to rich and poor alike. Hardin had also argued that aid does not give rise to better birth control; on the contrary, it makes it easy for the poor to continue to

POPULATION AND FOOD: METAPHORS AND THE REALITY By William W. Murdoch and Allan Oaten. Excerpted from *BioScience*, September 9, 1975, pp. 561–567. Copyright 1975 by The American Institute of Biological Sciences. Reprinted by permission of the publisher and the authors.

propagate and thereby to exacerbate the problem that aid is meant to resolve.

According to Murdoch and Oaten, Hardin fails to see that the richer countries in many ways are responsible for the cycle of poverty in the third world. They encourage cash crops instead of food crops; they support repressive rulers for political reasons; they enforce trade policies that exploit the resources of poor countries and do little to help them feed themselves. All this contributes to the endemic state of poverty and to the cycle of famine in the third world. If such policies were revised, the poor nations would be better able to help themselves.

Murdoch and Oaten strongly advocate famine relief. They are unimpressed by Hardin's commons and lifeboat metaphors. And they note, *contra* Hardin, that in some third-world countries birth rates are falling. This occurs when a population is sufficiently well off to enjoy increased literacy, to have some reasonable confidence in the future, and when women enjoy improved status and gain access to birth-control information. None of these events occur, however, in conditions of starvation. Murdoch and Oaten believe that making health education and jobs available to the lowest income groups are prerequisites for a decline in birth rates. They conclude, from the evidence considered, that "The policies dictated by a sense of decency are also the most realistic and rational."

Misleading Metaphors

[Hardin's] "lifeboat" article actually has two messages. The first is that our immigration policy is too generous. This will not concern us here. The second, and more important, is that by helping poor nations we will bring disaster to rich and poor alike:

> Metaphorically, each rich nation amounts to a lifeboat full of comparatively rich people. The poor of the world are in other, much more crowded lifeboats. Continuously, so to speak, the poor fall out of their lifeboats and swim for a while in the water outside, hoping to be admitted to a rich lifeboat, or in some other way to benefit from the "goodies" on board. What should the passengers on a rich lifeboat do?

867

This is the central problem of "the ethics of a lifeboat." (Hardin, 1974, p. 561)[1]

Among these so-called "goodies" are food supplies and technical aid such as that which led to the Green Revolution. Hardin argues that we should withhold such resources from poor nations on the grounds that they help to maintain high rates of population increase, thereby making the problem worse. He foresees the continued supplying and increasing production of food as a process that will be "brought to an end only by the total collapse of the whole system, producing a catastrophe of scarcely imaginable proportions" (p. 564).

Turning to one particular mechanism for distributing these resources, Hardin claims that a world food bank is a commons—people have more motivation to draw from it than to add to it; it will have a ratchet or escalator effect on population because inputs from it will prevent population declines in over-populated countries. Thus "wealth can be steadily moved in one direction only, from the slowly-breeding rich to the rapidly-breeding poor, the process finally coming to a halt only when all countries are equally and miserably poor" (p. 565). Thus our help will not only bring ultimate disaster to poor countries, but it will also be suicidal for us.

As for the "benign demographic transition" to low birth rates, which some aid supporters have predicted, Hardin states flatly that the weight of evidence is against this possibility.

Finally, Hardin claims that the plight of poor nations is partly their own fault: "wise sovereigns seem not to exist in the poor world today. The most anguishing problems are created by poor countries that are governed by rulers insufficiently wise and powerful." Establishing a world food bank will exacerbate this problem: "slovenly rulers" will escape the consequences of their incompetence—"Others will bail them out whenever they are in trouble"; "Far more difficult than the transfer of wealth from one country to another is the transfer of wisdom between sovereign powers or between generations" (p. 563).

What arguments does Hardin present in support of these opinions? Many involve metaphors: lifeboat, commons, and ratchet or escalator. These metaphors are crucial to his thesis, and it is, therefore, important for us to examine them critically.

---

[1]G. Hardin, 1974, "Living on a Lifeboat," *BioScience*, vol. 24, pp. 561–68.

The lifeboat is the major metaphor. It seems attractively simple, but it is in fact simplistic and obscures important issues. As soon as we try to use it to compare various policies, we find that most relevant details of the actual situation are either missing or distorted in the lifeboat metaphor. Let us list some of these details.

Most important, perhaps, Hardin's lifeboats barely interact. The rich lifeboats may drop some handouts over the side and perhaps repel a boarding party now and then, but generally they live their own lives. In the real world, nations interact a great deal, in ways that affect food supply and population size and growth, and the effect of rich nations on poor nations has been strong and not always benevolent.

First, by colonization and actual wars of commerce, and through the international marketplace, rich nations have arranged an exchange of goods that has maintained and even increased the economic imbalance between rich and poor nations. Until recently we have taken or otherwise obtained cheap raw material from poor nations and sold them expensive manufactured goods that they cannot make themselves. In the United States, the structure of tariffs and internal subsidies discriminates selectively against poor nations. In poor countries, the concentration on cash crops rather than on food crops, a legacy of colonial times, is now actively encouraged by western multinational corporations (Barraclough 1975).[2] Indeed, it is claimed that in famine-stricken Sahelian Africa, multinational agribusiness has recently taken land out of food production for cash crops (Transnational Institute 1974).[3] Although we often self-righteously take the "blame" for lowering the death rates of poor nations during the 1940s and 1950s, we are less inclined to accept responsibility for the effects of actions that help maintain poverty and hunger. Yet poverty directly contributes to the high birth rates that Hardin views with such alarm.

Second, U.S. foreign policy, including foreign aid programs, has favored "pro-Western" regimes, many of which govern in the interests of a wealthy elite and some of which are savagely repressive.

---

[2] G. Barraclough, 1975, "The Great World Crisis I, *The New York Review of Books*, vol. 21, pp. 20–29.

[3] Transnational Institute, 1974, *World Hunger: Causes and Remedies* (Washington: Institute for Policy Studies).

Thus, it has often subsidized a gross maldistribution of income and has supported political leaders who have opposed most of the social changes that can lead to reduced birth rates. In this light, Hardin's pronouncements on the alleged wisdom gap between poor leaders and our own, and the difficulty of filling it, appear as a grim joke: our response to leaders with the power and wisdom Hardin yearns for has often been to try to replace them or their policies as soon as possible. Selective giving and withholding of both military and non-military aid has been an important ingredient of our efforts to maintain political leaders we like and to remove those we do not. Brown (1974b),[4] after noting that the withholding of U.S. food aid in 1973 contributed to the downfall of the Allende government in Chile, comments that "although Americans decry the use of petroleum as a political weapon, calling it 'political blackmail,' the United States has been using food aid for political purposes for twenty years—and describing this as 'enlightened diplomacy.'"

Both the quantity and the nature of the supplies on a lifeboat are fixed. In the real world, the quantity has strict limits, but these are far from having been reached (University of California Food Task Force 1974).[5] Nor are we forced to devote fixed proportions of our efforts and energy to automobile travel, pet food, packaging, advertising, corn-fed beef, "defense" and other diversions, many of which cost far more than foreign aid does. The fact is that enough food is now produced to feed the world's population adequately. That people are malnourished is due to distribution and to economics, not to agricultural limits (United Nations Economic and Social Council 1974).[6]

Hardin's lifeboats are divided merely into rich and poor, and it is difficult to talk about birth rates on either. In the real world, however, there are striking differences among the birth rates of the poor countries and even among the birth rates of different parts of single countries. These differences appear to be related to social conditions (also absent from lifeboats) and may guide us to effective aid policies.

---

[4]L. R. Brown, 1974b, *By Bread Alone* (New York: Praeger).

[5]University of California Food Task Force, 1974, *A Hungry World: The Challenge to Agriculture* (University of California, Division of Agricultural Sciences).

[6]United Nations Economic and Social Council, "Assessment: Present Food Situation and Dimensions and Causes of Hunger and Malnutrition in the World" (New York: Economic Conference, May 8, 1974), p. 65.

Hardin's lifeboat metaphor not only conceals facts, but misleads about the effects of his proposals. The rich lifeboat can raise the ladder and sail away. But in real life, the problem will not necessarily go away just because it is ignored. In the real world, there are armies, raw materials in poor nations, and even outraged domestic dissidents prepared to sacrifice their own and others' lives to oppose policies they regard as immoral.

No doubt there are other objections. But even this list shows the lifeboat metaphor to be dangerously inappropriate for serious policy making because it obscures far more than it reveals. Lifeboats and "lifeboat ethics" may be useful topics for those who are shipwrecked; we believe they are worthless—indeed detrimental—in discussions of food-population questions.

The ratchet metaphor is equally flawed. It, too, ignores complex interactions between birth rates and social conditions (including diets), implying as it does that more food will simply mean more babies. Also, it obscures the fact that the decrease in death rates has been caused at least as much by developments such as DDT, improved sanitation, and medical advances, as by increased food supplies, so that cutting out food aid will not necessarily lead to population declines.

The lifeboat article is strangely inadequate in other ways. For example, it shows an astonishing disregard for recent literature. The claim that we can expect no "benign demographic transition" is based on a review written more than a decade ago (Davis 1963).[7] Yet, events and attitudes are changing rapidly in poor countries: for the first time in history, most poor people live in countries with birth control programs; with few exceptions, poor nations are somewhere on the demographic transition to lower birth rates (Demeny 1974);[8] the population-food squeeze is now widely recognized, and governments of poor nations are aware of the relationship. Again, there is a considerable amount of evidence that birth rates can fall rapidly in poor countries given the proper social conditions (as we will discuss later); consequently, crude projections of current population growth rates are quite inadequate for policy making.

---

[7]K. Davis, 1963, "Population," *Scientific American*, vol. 209, pp. 62–71.

[8]P. Demeny, 1974, "The Populations of the Underdeveloped Countries," *Scientific American*, vol. 231, pp. 149–159.

The Tragedy of the Commons

Throughout the lifeboat article, Hardin bolsters his assertions by reference to the "commons" (Hardin 1968).[9] The thesis of the commons, therefore, needs critical evaluation.

Suppose several privately owned flocks, comprising 100 sheep altogether, are grazing on a public commons. They bring in an annual income of $1.00 per sheep. Fred, a herdsman, owns only one sheep. He decides to add another. But 101 is too many: the commons is overgrazed and produces less food. The sheep lose quality and income drops to 90¢ per sheep. Total income is now $90.90 instead of $100.00. Adding the sheep has brought an overall loss. But Fred has gained: *his* income is $1.80 instead of $1.00. The gain from the additional sheep, which is his alone, outweighs the loss from overgrazing, which he shares. Thus he promotes his interest at the expense of the community.

This is the problem of the commons, which seems on the way to becoming an archetype. Hardin, in particular, is not inclined to underrate its importance: "One of the major tasks of education today is to create such an awareness of the dangers of the commons that people will be able to recognize its many varieties, however disguised" (Hardin 1974, p. 562) and "All this is terribly obvious once we are acutely aware of the pervasiveness and danger of the commons. But many people still lack this awareness . . ." (p. 565).

The "commons" affords a handy way of classifying problems: the lifeboat article reveals that sharing, a generous immigration policy, world food banks, air, water, the fish populations of the ocean, and the western range lands are, or produce, a commons. It is also handy to be able to dispose of policies one does not like and "only a particular instance of a class of policies that are in error because they lead to the tragedy of the commons" (p. 561).

But no metaphor, even one as useful as this, should be treated with such awe. Such shorthand can be useful, but it can also mislead by discouraging thought and obscuring important detail. To dismiss a proposal by suggesting that "all you need to know about this proposal is that it institutes a commons and is, therefore, bad" is to assert that the proposed commons is worse than the original

---

[9]G. Hardin, 1968, "The Tragedy of the Commons," *Science*, vol. 162, pp. 1243–48.

problem. This might be so if the problem of the commons were, indeed, a tragedy—that is, if it were insoluble. But it is not.

Hardin favors private ownership as the solution (either through private property or the selling of pollution rights). But, of course, there are solutions other than private ownership; and private ownership itself is no guarantee of carefully husbanded resources.

One alternative to private ownership of the commons is communal ownership of the sheep—or, in general, of the mechanisms and industries that exploit the resource—combined with communal planning for management. (Note, again, how the metaphor favors one solution: perhaps the "tragedy" lay not in the commons but in the sheep. "The Tragedy of the Privately Owned Sheep" lacks zing, unfortunately.) Public ownership of a commons has been tried in Peru to the benefit of the previously privately owned anchoveta fishery (Gulland 1975).[10] The communally owned argiculture of China does not seem to have suffered any greater over-exploitation than that of other Asian nations.

Another alternative is cooperation combined with regulation. For example, Gulland (1975) has shown that Antarctic whale stocks (perhaps the epitome of a commons since they are internationally exploited and no one owns them) are now being properly managed, and stocks are increasing. This has been achieved through cooperation in the International Whaling Commission, which has by agreement set limits to the catch of each nation.

In passing, Hardin's private ownership argument is not generally applicable to nonrenewable resources. Given discount rates, technology substitutes, and no more than an average regard for posterity, privately owned nonrenewable resources, like oil, coal and minerals, are mined at rates that produce maximum profits, rather than at those rates that preserve them for future generations. . . .

Birth Rates: An Alternative View

Is the food-population spiral inevitable? A more optimistic, if less comfortable, hypothesis, presented by Rich (1973)[11] and Brown

---

[10]J. Gulland, 1975, "The Harvest of the Sea," in W. W. Murdoch, ed., *Environment: Resources, Pollution and Society* (Sunderland, MA: Sinauer Associates), pp. 167–189.

[11]W. Rich, 1973, "Smaller Families through Social and Economic Progress" (Washington: Overseas Development Council Monograph #7).

(1974a),[12] is increasingly tenable: contrary to the "ratchet" projection, population growth rates are affected by many complex conditions beside food supply. In particular, a set of socioeconomic conditions can be identified that motivate parents to have fewer children; under these conditions, birth rates can fall quite rapidly, sometimes even before birth control technology is available. Thus, population growth can be controlled more effectively by intelligent human intervention that sets up the appropriate conditions than by doing nothing and trusting to "natural population cycles."

These conditions are: parental confidence about the future, an improved status of women, and literacy. They require low infant mortality rates, widely available rudimentary health care, increased income and employment, and an adequate diet above subsistence levels. Expenditure on schools (especially elementary schools), appropriate health services (especially rural paramedical services), and agricultural reform (especially aid to small farmers) will be needed, and foreign aid can help here. It is essential that these improvements be spread across the population; aid can help here, too, by concentrating on the poor nations' poorest people, encouraging necessary institutional and social reforms, and making it easier for poor nations to use their own resources and initiative to help themselves. It is *not* necessary that per capita GNP be very high, certainly not as high as that of the rich countries during their gradual demographic transition. In other words, low birth rates in poor countries are achievable long before the conditions exist that were present in the rich countries in the late 19th and early 20th centuries.

Twenty or thirty years is not long to discover and assess the factors affecting birth rates, but a body of evidence is now accumulating in favor of this hypothesis. Rich (1973) and Brown (1974a) show that at least 10 developing countries have managed to reduce their birth rates by an average of more than one birth per 1,000 population per year for periods of 5 to 16 years. A reduction of one birth per 1,000 per year would bring birth rates in poor countries to a rough replacement level of about 16/1,000 by the turn of the century, though age distribution effects would prevent a smooth population decline. We have listed these countries in Table 1, together with three other

---

[12]L. R. Brown, 1974a, *In the Human Interest* (New York: W. W. Norton).

TABLE I *Declining Birth Rates and per Capita Income in Selected Developing Countries* These are crude birth rates, uncorrected for age distribution.[13]

Country	Time span	Avg. annual decline in crude birth rate	Crude birth rate 1972	$ per capita per year 1973
			Births/1,000/Year	
Barbados	1960–69	1.5	22	570
Taiwan	1955–71	1.2	24	390
Tunisia	1966–71	1.8	35	250
Mauritius	1961–71	1.5	25	240
Hong Kong	1960–72	1.4	19	970
Singapore	1955–72	1.2	23	920
Costa Rica	1963–72	1.5	32	560
South Korea	1960–70	1.2	29	250
Egypt	1966–70	1.7	37	210
Chile	1963–70	1.2	25	720
China			30	160
Cuba			27	530
Sri Lanka			30	110

nations, including China, that are poor and yet have brought their birth rates down to 30 or less, presumably from rates of over 40 a decade or so ago.

These data show that rapid reduction in birth rates is possible in the developing world. No doubt it can be argued that each of these cases is in some way special. Hong Kong and Singapore are relatively rich; they, Barbados, and Mauritius are also tiny. China is able to exert great social pressure on its citizens; but China is particularly significant. It is enormous; its per capita GNP is almost as low as India's; and it started out in 1949 with a terrible health system. Also, Egypt, Chile, Taiwan, Cuba, South Korea, and Sri Lanka are quite large, and they are poor or very poor (Table 1). In fact, these examples represent an enormous range of religion, political systems, and

---

[13]M. S. Teitelbaum, 1975, "Relevance of Demographic Transition Theory for Developing Countries," *Science*, vol. 188, pp. 420–25.

geography and suggest that such rates of decline in the birth rate can be achieved whenever the appropriate conditions are met. "The common factor in these countries is that the *majority* of the population has shared in the economic and social benefits of significant national progress. . . . [M]aking health, education and jobs more broadly available to lower income groups in poor countries contribute[s] significantly toward the motivation for smaller families that is the prerequisite of a major reduction in birth rates" (Rich 1973).

. . . As a disillusioning quarter-century of aid giving has shown, the obstacles of getting aid to those segments of the population most in need of it are enormous. Aid has typically benefitted a small rich segment of society, partly because of the way aid programs have been designed but also because of human and institutional factors in the poor nations themselves (Owens and Shaw 1972).[14] With some notable exceptions, the distribution of income and services in poor nations is extremely skewed—much more uneven than in rich countries. Indeed, much of the population is essentially outside the economic system. Breaking this pattern will be extremely difficult. It will require not only aid that is designed specifically to benefit the rural poor, but also important institutional changes such as decentralization of decision making and the development of greater autonomy and stronger links to regional and national markets for local groups and industries such as cooperative farms.

Thus, two things are being asked of rich nations and of the United States in particular: to increase nonmilitary foreign aid, including food aid, and to give it in ways, and to governments, that will deliver it to the poorest people and will improve their access to national economic institutions. These are not easy tasks, particularly the second, and there is no guarantee that birth rates will come down quickly in all countries. Still, many poor countries have, in varying degrees, begun the process of reform, and recent evidence suggests that aid and reform together can do much to solve the twin problems of high birth rates and economic underdevelopment. The tasks are far from impossible. Based on the evidence, the policies dictated by a sense of decency are also the most realistic and rational.

---

[14]E. Owens and R. Shaw, 1972, *Development Reconsidered* (Lexington, MA: Heath & Co.).

Majority opinion *in* Roe vs. Wade

JUSTICE HARRY A. BLACKMUN

Justice Harry A. Blackmun (b. 1908) has served on the
United States Supreme Court since 1970.

Before 1973, abortion was illegal in the state of Texas
(except to save the life of the mother). A pregnant single
woman sued under the fictitious name of Jane Roe. Her
case went to the Supreme Court of the United States
where a majority of the justices ruled the Texas law unconstitutional.

Justice Blackmun bases the woman's right to abortion
on "the right to privacy," a right not explicitly mentioned
in the Constitution, but one that has roots in the "pen-
umbra" of interpretations surrounding the Bill of Rights
and the Fourth, Fifth and Ninth Amendments, which do
explicitly respect many personal rights from state interference.

Justice White objects to the majority view: This ruling values the woman's caprice more than it values the
potential life of the fetus. White sees nothing in the
Constitution to warrant this kind of protection. White
acknowledges that the moral issues are complex and
problematic, but he believes that for that very reason the
court's interventions are inappropriate. In his view, the
court should leave the decision to the individual states.

877

. . . [A]t the time of the adoption of our Constitution, and through-out the major portion of the 19th century, abortion was viewed with less disfavor than under most American statutes currently in effect. Phrasing it another way, a woman enjoyed a substantially broader right to terminate a pregnancy than she does in most States today. At least with respect to the early stage of pregnancy, and very possi-bly without such a limitation, the opportunity to make this choice was present in this country well into the 19th century. . . .

Three reasons have been advanced to explain historically the en-actment of criminal abortion laws in the 19th century and to justify their continued existence.

It has been argued occasionally that these laws were the product of a Victorian social concern to discourage illicit sexual conduct. . . .

A second reason is concerned with abortion as a medical proce-dure. When most criminal abortion laws were first enacted, the pro-cedure was a hazardous one for the woman. This was particularly true prior to the development of antisepsis. Antiseptic techniques, of course, were based on discoveries by Lister, Pasteur, and others first announced in 1867, but were not generally accepted and employed until about the turn of the century. Abortion mortality was high. Even after 1900, and perhaps until as late as the development of antibiotics in the 1940's, standard modern techniques such as dilata-tion and curettage were not nearly so safe as they are today. Thus it has been argued that a State's real concern in enacting a criminal abortion law was to protect the pregnant woman, that is, to restrain her from submitting to a procedure that placed her life in serious jeopardy.

Modern medical techniques have altered this situation. Appellants and various *amici* refer to medical data indicating that abortion in early pregnancy, that is, prior to the end of first trimester, although not without its risk, is now relatively safe. Mortality rates for women undergoing early abortions, where the procedure is legal, appear to be as low as or lower than the rates for normal childbirth. Conse-quently, any interest of the State in protecting the woman from an inherently hazardous procedure, except when it would be equally dangerous for her to forgo it, has largely disappeared. Of course, important state interests in the area of health and medical standards do remain. The State has a legitimate interest in seeing to it that abortion, like any other medical procedure, is performed under cir-cumstances that insure maximum safety for the patient. This interest obviously extends at least to the performing physician and his staff, to the facilities involved, to the availability of after-care, and to adequate provision for any complication or emergency that might arise. The prevalence of high mortality rates at illegal "abortion mills" strengthens, rather than weakens, the State's interest in regulating the conditions under which abortions are performed. Moreover, the risk to the woman increases as her pregnancy continues. Thus the State retains a definite interest in protecting the woman's own health and safety when an abortion is performed at a late stage of pregnancy.

The third reason is the State's interest—some phrase it in terms of duty—in protecting prenatal life. Some of the argument for this justification rests on the theory that a new human life is present from the moment of conception. The State's interest and general obligation to protect life then extends, it is argued, to prenatal life. Only when the life of the pregnant mother herself is at stake, balanced against the life she carries within her, should the interest of the embryo or fetus not prevail. Logically, of course, a legitimate state interest in this area need not stand or fall on acceptance of the belief that life begins at conception or at some other point prior to live birth. In assessing the State's interest, recognition may be given to the less rigid claim that as long as at least *potential* life is involved, the State may assert interests beyond the protection of the pregnant woman alone.

Parties challenging state abortion laws have sharply disputed in some courts the contention that a purpose of these laws, when enacted, was to protect prenatal life. Pointing to the absence of legislative history to support the contention, they claim that most state laws were designed solely to protect the woman. Because medical advances have lessened this concern, at least with respect to abortion in early pregnancy, they argue that with respect to such abortions the laws can no longer be justified by any state interest. There is some scholarly support for this view of original purpose. The few state courts called upon to interpret their laws in the late 19th and early 20th centuries did focus on the State's interest in protecting the woman's health rather than in preserving the embryo and fetus. . . .

The Constitution does not explicitly mention any right of privacy. In a line of decisions, however, going back perhaps as far as *Union Pacific R. Co. v. Botsford* (1891), the Court has recognized that a right of personal privacy, or a guarantee of certain areas or zones of privacy, does exist under the Constitution. In varying contexts the

Court or individual Justices have indeed found at least the roots of that right in the First Amendment, . . . in the Fourth and Fifth Amendments . . . in the penumbras of the Bill of Rights . . . in the Ninth Amendment . . . or in the concept of liberty guaranteed by the first section of the Fourteenth Amendment. . . . These decisions make it clear that only personal rights that can be deemed "fundamental" or "implicit in the concept of ordered liberty," . . . are included in this guarantee of personal privacy. They also make it clear that the right has some extension to activities relating to marriage, . . . procreation, . . . contraception, . . . family relationships, . . . and child rearing and education. . . .

This right of privacy, whether it be founded in the Fourteenth Amendment's concept of personal liberty and restrictions upon state action, as we feel it is, or, as the District Court determined, in the Ninth Amendment's reservation of rights to the people, is broad enough to encompass a woman's decision whether or not to terminate her pregnancy. . . .

[S]ome *amici* argue that the woman's right is absolute and that she is entitled to terminate her pregnancy at whatever time, in whatever way, and for whatever reason she alone chooses. With this we do not agree. Appellants' arguments that Texas either has no valid interest at all in regulating the abortion decision, or no interest strong enough to support any limitation upon the woman's sole determination, is unpersuasive. The Court's decisions recognizing a right of privacy also acknowledge that some state regulation in areas protected by that right is appropriate. As noted above, a state may properly assert important interests in safe-guarding health, in maintaining medical standards, and in protecting potential life. At some point in pregnancy, these respective interests become sufficiently compelling to sustain regulation of the factors that govern the abortion decision. . . .

We therefore conclude that the right of personal privacy includes the abortion decision, but that this right is not unqualified and must be considered against important state interests in regulation.

Although the results are divided most (federal and state) courts have agreed that the right of privacy, however based, is broad enough to cover the abortion decision; that the right, nonetheless, is not absolute and is subject to some limitations; and that at some point the state interests as to protection of health, medical standards, and prenatal life, become dominant. We agree. . . .

The appellee and certain *amici* argue that the fetus is a "person" within the language and meaning of the Fourteenth Amendment. In support of this they outline at length and in detail the well-known facts of fetal development. If this suggestion of personhood is established, the appellant's case, of course, collapses, for the fetus' right to life is then guaranteed specifically by the Amendment. The appellant conceded as much on reargument. On the other hand, the appellee conceded on reargument that no case could be cited that holds that a fetus is a person within the meaning of the Fourteenth Amendment. . . .

All this, together with our observation, *supra*, that throughout the major portion of the 19th century prevailing legal abortion practices were far freer than they are today, persuades us that the word "person," as used in the Fourteenth Amendment, does not include the unborn. . . . Indeed, our decision in *United States v. Vuitch* (1971) inferentially is to the same effect, for we there would not have indulged in statutory interpretation favorable to abortion in specified circumstances if the necessary consequence was the termination of life entitled to Fourteenth Amendment protection.

. . . As we have intimated above, it is reasonable and appropriate for a State to decide that at some point in time another interest, that of health of the mother or that of potential human life, becomes significantly involved. The woman's privacy is no longer sole and any right of privacy she possesses must be measured accordingly.

Texas urges that, apart from the Fourteenth Amendment, life begins at conception and is present throughout pregnancy, and that, therefore, the State has a compelling interest in protecting that life from and after conception. We need not resolve the difficult question of when life begins. When those trained in the respective disciplines of medicine, philosophy, and theology are unable to arrive at any consensus, the judiciary, at this point in the development of man's knowledge, is not in a position to speculate as to the answer.

It should be sufficient to note briefly the wide divergence of thinking on this most sensitive and difficult question. There has always been strong support for the view that life does not begin until live birth. This was the belief of the Stoics. It appears to be the predominant, though not the unanimous, attitude of the Jewish faith. It may be taken to represent also the position of a large segment of the Protestant community, insofar as that can be ascertained; organized groups that have taken a formal position on the abortion issue have generally regarded abortion as a matter for the conscience of the individual and her family. As we have noted, the common law found greater significance in quickening. Physicians and their scientific colleagues have regarded that event with less interest and have tended to focus either upon conception or upon live birth or upon the interim point at which the fetus becomes "viable," that is, potentially able to live outside the mother's womb, albeit with artificial aid. Viability is usually placed at about seven months (28 weeks) but may occur earlier.

In areas other than criminal abortion the law has been reluctant to endorse any theory that life, as we recognize it, begins before live birth or to accord legal rights to the unborn except in narrowly defined situations and except when the rights are contingent upon live birth. . . . In short, the unborn have never been recognized in the law as persons in the whole sense.

In view of all this, we do not agree that, by adopting one theory of life, Texas may override the rights of the pregnant woman that are at stake. We repeat, however, that the State does have an important and legitimate interest in preserving and protecting the health of the pregnant woman, whether she be a resident of the State or a nonresident who seeks medical consultation and treatment there, and that it has still *another* important and legitimate interest in protecting the potentiality of human life. These interests are separate and distinct. Each grows in substantiality as the woman approaches term and, at a point during pregnancy, each becomes "compelling."

With respect to the State's important and legitimate interest in the health of the mother, the "compelling" point, in the light of present medical knowledge, is at approximately the end of the first trimester. This is so because of the now established medical fact . . . that until the end of the first trimester mortality in abortion is less than mortality in normal childbirth. It follows that, from and after this point, a State may regulate the abortion procedure to the extent that the regulation reasonably relates to the preservation and protection of maternal health. Examples of permissible state regulation in this area are requirements as to the qualifications of the person who is to perform the abortion; as to licensure of that person; as to the facility in which the procedure is to be performed, that is, whether it must be a hospital or may be a clinic or some other place of less-than-hospital status; as to the licensing of the facility; and the like.

This means, on the other hand, that, for the period of pregnancy prior to this "compelling" point, the attending physician, in consultation with his patient, is free to determine, without regulation by the State, that in his medical judgment the patient's pregnancy should be terminated. If that decision is reached, the judgment may be effectuated by an abortion free of interference by the State.

With respect to the State's important and legitimate interest in potential life, the "compelling" point is at viability. This is so because the fetus then presumably has the capability of meaningful life outside the mother's womb. State regulation protective of fetal life after viability thus has both logical and biological justifications. If the State is interested in protecting fetal life after viability, it may go so far as to proscribe abortion during that period except when it is necessary to preserve the life or health of the mother. . . .

To summarize and repeat:

1. A state criminal abortion statute of the current Texas type, that excepts from criminality only a *life saving* procedure on behalf of the mother, without regard to pregnancy stage and without recognition of the other interests involved, is violative of the Due Process Clause of the Fourteenth Amendment.

(a) For the stage prior to approximately the end of the first trimester, the abortion decision and its effectuation must be left to the medical judgment of the pregnant woman's attending physician.

(b) For the stage subsequent to approximately the end of the first trimester, the State, in promoting its interest in the health of the mother, may, if it chooses, regulate the abortion procedure in ways that are reasonably related to maternal health.

(c) For the stage subsequent to viability the State, in promoting its interest in the potentiality of human life, may, if it chooses, regulate, and even proscribe, abortion except where it is necessary, in appropriate medical judgment, for the preservation of the life or health of the mother.

2. The State may define the term "physician," as it has been employed [here], to mean only a physician currently licensed by the State, and may proscribe any abortion by a person who is not a physician as so defined.

. . . The decision leaves the State free to place increasing restrictions on abortion as the period of pregnancy lengthens, so long as those restrictions are tailored to the recognized state interests. The decision vindicates the right of the physician to administer medical treatment according to his professional judgment up to the points where important state interests provide compelling justifications for intervention. Up to those points the abortion decision in all its aspects is inherently, and primarily, a medical decision, and basic responsibility for it must rest with the physician. . . .

Dissenting Opinion in Roe vs. Wade

JUSTICE BYRON R. WHITE

Justice Byron R. White (b. 1917) has served on the United States Supreme Court since 1962.

At the heart of the controversy are those recurring pregnancies that pose no danger whatsoever to the life or health of the mother but are nevertheless unwanted for any one or more of a variety of reasons—convenience, family planning, economics, dislike of children, the embarrassment of illegitimacy, etc. The common claim before us is that for any one of such reasons, or for no reason at all, and without asserting or claiming any threat to life or health, any woman is entitled to an abortion at her request if she is able to find a medical advisor willing to undertake the procedure.

The Court for the most part sustains this position: During the period prior to the time the fetus becomes viable, the Constitution of the United States values the convenience, whim or caprice of the putative mother more than the life or potential life of the fetus; the Constitution, therefore, guarantees the right to an abortion as against any state law or policy seeking to protect the fetus from an abortion not prompted by more compelling reasons of the mother.

With all due respect, I dissent. I find nothing in the language or history of the Constitution to support the Court's judgment. The Court simply fashions and announces a new constitutional right for pregnant mothers and, with scarcely any reason or authority for its action, invests that right with sufficient substance to override most existing state abortion statutes. The upshot is that the people and the legislatures of the 50 States are constitutionally disentitled to weigh the relative importance of the continued existence and development of the fetus on the one hand against a spectrum of possible impacts on the mother on the other hand. As an exercise of raw judicial power, the Court perhaps has authority to do what it does today; but in my view its judgment is an improvident and extravagant exercise of the power of judicial review which the Constitution extends to this Court.

The Court apparently values the convenience of the pregnant mother more than the continued existence and development of the life or potential life which she carries. Whether or not I might agree with that marshalling of values, I can in no event join the Court's judgment because I find no constitutional warrant for imposing such an order of priorities on the people and legislatures of the States. In a sensitive area such as this, involving as it does issues over which reasonable men may easily and heatedly differ, I cannot accept the Court's exercise of its clear power of choice by interposing a constitutional barrier to state efforts to protect human life and by investing mothers and doctors with the constitutionally protected right to exterminate it. This issue, for the most part, should be left with the people and to the political processes the people have devised to govern their affairs.

STUDY QUESTIONS

1. Read the Bill of Rights carefully, paying special attention to the Fourth, Fifth and Ninth Amendments. Do you find in it an adequate basis for the right to choose to abort? Argue for your answer in the manner of a jurist.

2. Justice Blackmun takes note that religions differ on the status of the fetus. So do ethical writers like Noonan and Warren. How, in the face of these differences of viewpoints, is the best way to proceed to arrive at a valid opinion on abortion?

3. Do you agree with Justice White that since the issues are contro-
    versial and the Constitution is not *explicit*, the federal govern-
    ment should not be ruling to interfere with local decisions?

An Almost Absolute Value in History

JOHN T. NOONAN, JR.

John T. Noonan, Jr. (b. 1926) is a professor of history and
law at the University of California at Berkeley. Among
his many books are *The Morality of Abortion* (1970) and
Persons and Masks of the Law (1976).

According to Noonan the question of abortion turns on
the question of when an individual human life begins.
Noonan's answer is consistent with the answer given by
Christian theologians as well as biologists: Life conceived
by human parents is human from the moment of conception. Noonan's second principle is that human life at any
stage is protected. "A being with a human genetic code is
man." He therefore rejects "viability" as the necessary
condition for being protected. He denies that one can be
more or less human. And he rejects appeals to feelings.
For it may be true that we do not feel much sympathy
with the fetus in its earliest stages, but that is irrelevant.
The only exceptions to the prohibition against abortion
turn on threats to the mother's life.

The most fundamental question involved in the long history of
thought on abortion is: How do you determine the humanity of a

being? To phrase the question that way is to put in comprehensive humanistic terms what the theologians either dealt with as an explicitly theological question under the heading of "ensoulment" or dealt with implicitly in their treatment of abortion. The Christian position as it originated did not depend on a narrow theological or philosophical concept. It had no relation to theories of infant baptism. It appealed to no special theory of instantaneous ensoulment. It took the world's view on ensoulment as that view changed from Aristotle to Zacchia. There was, indeed, theological influence affecting the theory of ensoulment finally adopted, and, of course, ensoulment itself was a theological concept, so that the position was always explained in theological terms. But the theological notion of ensoulment could easily be translated into humanistic language by substituting "human" for "rational soul"; the problem of knowing when a man is a man is common to theology and humanism.

If one steps outside the specific categories used by the theologians, the answer they gave can be analyzed as a refusal to discriminate among human beings on the basis of their varying potentialities. Once conceived, the being was recognized as man because he had man's potential. The criterion for humanity, thus, was simple and all-embracing: if you are conceived by human parents, you are human.

The strength of this position may be tested by a review of some of the other distinctions offered in the contemporary controversy over legalizing abortion. Perhaps the most popular distinction is in terms of viability. Before an age of so many months, the fetus is not viable, that is, it cannot be removed from the mother's womb and live apart from her. To that extent, the life of the fetus is absolutely dependent on the life of the mother. This dependence is made the basis of denying recognition to its humanity.

There are difficulties with this distinction. One is that the perfection of artificial incubation may make the fetus viable at any time: it may be removed and artificially sustained. Experiments with animals already show that such a procedure is possible. This hypothetical extreme case relates to an actual difficulty: there is considerable elasticity to the idea of viability. Mere length of life is not an exact measure. The viability of the fetus depends on the extent of its anatomical and functional development. The weight and length of the fetus are better guides to the state of its development than age, but weight and length vary. Moreover, different racial groups have dif-

887

ferent ages at which their fetuses are viable. Some evidence, for example, suggests that Negro fetuses mature more quickly than white fetuses. If viability is the norm, the standard would vary with race and with many individual circumstances.

The most important objection to this approach is that dependence is not ended by viability. The fetus is still absolutely dependent on someone's care in order to continue existence; indeed a child of one or three or even five years of age is absolutely dependent on another's care for existence; uncared for, the older fetus or the younger child will die as surely as the early fetus detached from the mother. The unsubstantial lessening in dependence at viability does not seem to signify any special acquisition of humanity.

A second distinction has been attempted in terms of experience. A being who has had experience, has lived and suffered, who possesses memories, is more human than one who has not. Humanity depends on formation by experience. The fetus is thus "unformed" in the most basic human sense.

This distinction is not serviceable for the embryo which is already experiencing and reacting. The embryo is responsive to touch after eight weeks and at least at that point is experiencing. At an earlier stage the zygote is certainly alive and responding to its environment. The distinction may also be challenged by the rare case where aphasia has erased adult memory: has it erased humanity? More fundamentally, this distinction leaves even the older fetus or the younger child to be treated as an unformed inhuman thing. Finally, it is not clear why experience as such confers humanity. It could be argued that certain central experiences such as loving or learning are necessary to make a man human. But then human beings who have failed to love or to learn might be excluded from the class called man.

A third distinction is made by appeal to the sentiments of adults. If a fetus dies, the grief of the parents is not the grief they would have for a living child. The fetus is an unnamed "it" till birth, and is not perceived as personality until at least the fourth month of existence when movements in the womb manifest a vigorous presence demanding joyful recognition by the parents.

Yet feeling is notoriously an unsure guide to the humanity of others. Many groups of humans have had difficulty in feeling that persons of another tongue, color, religion, sex, are as human as they. Apart from reactions to alien groups, we mourn the loss of a ten-year-old boy more than the loss of his one-day-old brother or his

90-year-old grandfather. The difference felt and the grief expressed vary with the potentialities extinguished, or the experience wiped out; they do not seem to point to any substantial difference in the humanity of baby, boy, or grandfather.

Distinctions are also made in terms of sensation by the parents. The embryo is felt within the womb only after about the fourth month. The embryo is seen only at birth. What can be neither seen nor felt is different from what is tangible. If the fetus cannot be seen or touched at all, it cannot be perceived as man.

Yet experience shows that sight is even more untrustworthy than feeling in determining humanity. By sight, color became an appropriate index for saying who was a man, and the evil of racial discrimination was given foundation. Nor can touch provide the test; a being confined by sickness, "out of touch" with others, does not thereby seem to lose his humanity. To the extent that touch still has appeal as a criterion, it appears to be a survival of the old English idea of "quickening"—a possible mistranslation of the Latin *animatus* used in the canon law. To that extent touch as a criterion seems to be dependent on the Aristotelian notion of ensoulment, and to fall when this notion is discarded.

Finally, a distinction is sought in social visibility. The fetus is not socially perceived as human. It cannot communicate with others. Thus, both subjectively and objectively, it is not a member of society. As moral rules are rules for the behavior of members of society to each other, they cannot be made for behavior toward what is not yet a member. Excluded from the society of men, the fetus is excluded from the humanity of men.

By force of the argument from the consequences, this distinction is to be rejected. It is more subtle than that founded on an appeal to physical sensation, but it is equally dangerous in its implications. If humanity depends on social recognition, individuals or whole groups may be dehumanized be being denied any status in their society. Such a fate is fictionally portrayed in *1984* and has actually been the lot of many men in many societies. In the Roman empire, for example, condemnation to slavery meant the practical denial of most human rights; in the Chinese Communist world, landlords have been classified as enemies of the people and so treated as nonpersons by the state. Humanity does not depend on social recognition, though often the failure of society to recognize the prisoner, the alien, the heterodox as human has led to the destruction of human beings. Anyone conceived by a man and a woman is human. Recognition of this condition by society follows a real event in the objective order, however imperfect and halting the recognition. Any attempt to limit humanity to exclude some group runs the risk of furnishing authority and precedent for excluding other groups in the name of the consciousness or perception of the controlling group in the society.

A philosopher may reject the appeal to the humanity of the fetus because he views "humanity" as a secular view of the soul and because he doubts the existence of anything real and objective which can be identified as humanity. One answer to such a philosopher is to ask how he reasons about moral questions without supposing that there is a sense in which he and the others of whom he speaks are human. Whatever group is taken as the society which determines who may be killed is thereby taken as human. A second answer is to ask if he does not believe that there is a right and wrong way of deciding moral questions. If there is such a difference, experience may be appealed to: to decide who is human on the basis of the sentiment of a given society has led to consequences which rational men would characterize as monstrous.

The rejection of the attempted distinctions based on viability and visibility, experience and feeling, may be buttressed by the following considerations: Moral judgments often rest on distinctions, but if the distinctions are not to appear arbitrary fiat, they should relate to some real difference in probabilities. There is a kind of continuity in all life, but the earlier stages of the elements of human life possess tiny probabilities of development. Consider for example, the spermatozoa in any normal ejaculate: There are about 200,000,000 in any single ejaculate, of which one has a chance of developing into a zygote. Consider the oocytes which may become ova: there are 100,000 to 1,000,000 oocytes in a female infant, of which a maximum of 390 are ovulated. But once spermatozoon and ovum meet and the conceptus is formed, such studies as have been made show that roughly in only 20 percent of the cases will spontaneous abortion occur. In other words, the chances are about 4 out of 5 that this new being will develop. At this stage in the life of the being there is a sharp shift in probabilities, an immense jump in potentialities. To make a distinction between the rights of spermatozoa and the rights of the fertilized ovum is to respond to an enormous shift in possibil-

890

ities. For about twenty days after conception the egg may split to form twins or combine with another egg to form a chimera, but the probability of either event happening is very small.

It may be asked, What does a change in biological probabilities have to do with establishing humanity? The argument from probabilities is not aimed at establishing humanity but at establishing an objective discontinuity which may be taken into account in moral discourse. As life itself is a matter of probabilities, as most moral reasoning is an estimate of probabilities, so it seems in accord with the structure of reality and the nature of moral thought to found a moral judgment on the change in probabilities at conception. The appeal to probabilities is the most commonsensical of arguments, to a greater or smaller degree all of us base our actions on probabilities, and in morals, as in law, prudence and negligence are often measured by the account one has taken of the probabilities. If the chance is 200,000,000 to 1 that the movement in the bushes into which you shoot is a man's, I doubt if many persons would hold you careless in shooting; but if the chances are 4 out of 5 that the movement is a human being's, few would acquit you of blame. Would the argument be different if only one out of ten children conceived came to term? Of course this argument would be different. This argument is an appeal to probabilities that actually exist, not to any and all states of affairs which may be imagined.

The probabilities as they do exist do not show the humanity of the embryo in the sense of a demonstration in logic any more than the probabilities of the movement in the bush being a man demonstrate beyond all doubt that the being is a man. The appeal is a "buttressing" consideration, showing the plausibility of the standard adopted. The argument focuses on the decisional factor in any moral judgment and assumes that part of the business of a moralist is drawing lines. One evidence of the nonarbitrary character of the line drawn is the difference of probabilities on either side of it. If a spermatozoon is destroyed, one destroys a being which had a chance of far less than 1 in 200 million of developing into a reasonable being, possessed of the genetic code, a heart and other organs, and capable of pain. If a fetus is destroyed, one destroys a being already possessed of the genetic code, organs, and sensitivity to pain, and one which had an 80 percent chance of developing further into a baby outside the womb who, in time, would reason.

The positive argument for conception as the decisive moment of humanization is that at conception the new being receives the genetic code. It is this genetic information which determines his characteristics, which is the biological carrier of the possibility of human wisdom, which makes him a self-evolving being. A being with a human genetic code is man.

This review of current controversy over the humanity of the fetus emphasizes what a fundamental question the theologians resolved in asserting the inviolability of the fetus. To regard the fetus as possessed of equal rights with other humans was not, however, to decide every case where abortion might be employed. It did decide the case where the argument was that the fetus should be aborted for its own good. To say a being was human was to say it had a destiny to decide for itself which could not be taken from it by another man's decision. But human beings with equal rights often come in conflict with each other, and some decision must be made as whose claims are to prevail. Cases of conflict involving the fetus are different only in two respects: the total inability of the fetus to speak for itself and the fact that the right of the fetus regularly at stake is the right to life itself.

The approach taken by the theologians to these conflicts was articulated in terms of "direct" and "indirect." Again, to look at what they were doing from outside their categories, they may be said to have been drawing lines or "balancing values." "Direct" and "indirect" are spatial metaphors; "line-drawing" is another. "To weigh" or "to balance" values is a metaphor of a more complicated mathematical sort hinting at the process which goes on in moral judgments. All the metaphors suggest that, in the moral judgments made, comparisons were necessary, that no value completely controlled. The principle of double effect was no doctrine fallen from heaven, but a method of analysis appropriate where two relative values were being compared. In Catholic moral theology, as it developed, life even of the innocent was not taken as an absolute. Judgments on acts affecting life issued from a process of weighing. In the weighing, the fetus was always given a value greater than zero, always a value separate and independent from its parents. This valuation was crucial and fundamental in all Christian thought on the subject and marked it off from any approach which considered that only the parents' interests needed to be considered.

Even with the fetus weighed as human, one interest could be weighed as equal or superior: that of the mother in her own life. The casuists between 1450 and 1895 were willing to weigh this interest as superior. Since 1895, that interest was given decisive weight only in the two special cases of the cancerous uterus and the ectopic pregnancy. In both of these cases the fetus itself had little chance of survival even if the abortion were not performed. As the balance was once struck in favor of the mother whenever her life was endangered, it could be so struck again. The balance reached between 1895 and 1930 attempted prudentially and pastorally to forestall a multitude of exceptions for interests less than life.

The perception of the humanity of the fetus and the weighing of fetal rights against other human rights constituted the work of the moral analysts. But what spirit animated their abstract judgments? For the Christian community it was the injunction of Scripture to love your neighbor as yourself. The fetus as human was a neighbor; his life had parity with one's own. The commandment gave life to what otherwise would have been only rational calculation.

The commandment could be put in humanistic as well as theological terms: Do not injure your fellow man without reason. In these terms, once the humanity of the fetus is perceived, abortion is never right except in self-defense. When life must be taken to save life, reason alone cannot say that a mother must prefer a child's life to her own. With this exception, now of great rarity, abortion violates the rational humanist tenet of the equality of human lives.

For Christians the commandment to love had received a special imprint in that the exemplar proposed of love was the love of the Lord for his disciples. In the light given by this example, self-sacrifice carried to the point of death seemed in the extreme situations not without meaning. In the less extreme cases, preference for one's own interests to the life of another seemed to express cruelty or selfishness irreconcilable with the demands of love.

STUDY QUESTIONS

1. Many philosophers disagree with Noonan's position that being human is in and of itself a sufficient condition for having an inviolable right to life. They point to brain-dead human beings and ask whether that right applies to them. They argue that the necessary condition for such a right must come some time after conception, perhaps even after birth. Take sides in this dispute.

2. Noonan's argument seems insensitive to considerations that victims of rape should be exceptions to the rule. How would Noonan react to the charge of insensitivity?
3. What role does religion play in Noonan's position? Is a religious standpoint indispensable for holding a strong "right-to-life" point of view?

On the Moral and Legal Status of Abortion

MARY ANNE WARREN

Mary Anne Warren (b. 1946) is an associate professor of philosophy at San Francisco State University. She has written numerous articles in the area of ethics and is the author of *The Nature of Woman; An Encyclopedia and Guide to the Literature* (1980) and *Gendercide: The Implications of Sex Selection* (1985).

Warren distinguishes between being human in the biological sense and being human in the moral sense. She acknowledges that human life begins with conception, but argues that we can only wrong human beings who are also *persons*. To be a person is to have sensitivity to pain, some capacity to reason, some capacity to communicate and some self-awareness. Since the fetus has none of these attributes, it is not a person possessed of a serious right to life. Warren notes that newborn infants also fall short of being persons; nevertheless, a neonate may not be killed, even when the mother does not want the burden

ON THE MORAL AND LEGAL STATUS OF ABORTION, by Mary Anne Warren copyright © 1973. *The Monist.* La Salle, IL 61301. Reprinted with permission.

of caring for it, for others may now want to take over its nurture. Warren does say that unwanted, defective infants may be destroyed, for they are not persons and there is no *prima facie* obligation to keep them alive.

The question which we must answer in order to produce a satisfactory solution to the problem of the moral status of abortion is this: How are we to define the moral community, the set of beings with full and equal moral rights, such that we can decide whether a human fetus is a member of this community or not? What sort of entity, exactly, has the inalienable rights to life, liberty, and the pursuit of happiness? Jefferson attributed these rights to all *men*, and it may or may not be fair to suggest that he intended to attribute them *only* to men. Perhaps he ought to have attributed them to all human beings. If so, then we arrive, first, at Noonan's problem of defining what makes a being human, and, second, at the equally vital question which Noonan does not consider; namely, What reason is there for identifying the moral community with the set of all human beings, in whatever way we have chosen to define that term?

1. On the Definition of "Human"

One reason why this vital second question is so frequently overlooked in the debate over the moral status of abortion is that the term "human" has two distinct, but not often distinguished, senses. This fact results in a slide of meaning, which serves to conceal the fallaciousness of the traditional argument that since (1) it is wrong to kill innocent human beings, and (2) fetuses are innocent human beings, then (3) it is wrong to kill fetuses. For if "human" is used in the same sense in both (1) and (2) then, whichever of the two senses is meant, one of these premises is question-begging. And if it is used in two different senses then of course the conclusion doesn't follow.

Thus, (1) is a self-evident moral truth,[1] and avoids begging the question about abortion, only if "human being" is used to mean

---

[1] Of course, the principle that it is (always) wrong to kill innocent human beings is in need of many other modifications, e.g., that it may be permissible to do so to save a greater number of other innocent human beings, but we may safely ignore these complications here.

something like "a full-fledged member of the moral community." (It may or may not also be meant to refer exclusively to members of the species *Homo sapiens*.) We may call this the *moral* sense of "human." It is not to be confused with what we will call the *genetic* sense, i.e., the sense in which *any* member of the species is a human being, and no member of any other species could be. If (1) is acceptable only if the moral sense is intended, (2) is non-question-begging only if what is intended is the genetic sense.

In "Deciding Who Is Human," Noonan argues for the classifica-tion of fetuses with human beings by pointing to the presence of the full genetic code, and the potential capacity for rational thought.[2] It is clear that what he needs to show, for his version of the traditional argument to be valid, is that fetuses are human in the moral sense, the sense in which it is analytically true that all human beings have full moral rights. But, in the absence of any argument showing that whatever is genetically human is also morally human, and he gives none, nothing more than genetic humanity can be demonstrated by the presence of the human genetic code. And, as we will see, the *potential* capacity for rational thought can at most show that an entity has the potential for *becoming* human in the moral sense.

2. Defining the Moral Community

Can it be established that genetic humanity is sufficient for moral humanity? I think that there are very good reasons for not defining the moral community in this way. I would like to suggest an alter-native way of defining the moral community, which I will argue for only to the extent of explaining why it is, or should be, self-evident. The suggestion is simply that the moral community consists of all and only *people*, rather than all and only human beings;[3] and probably the best way of demonstrating its self-evidence is by considering the concept of personhood, to see what sorts of entity are and are not persons, and what the decision that a being is or is not a person implies about its moral rights.

---

[2]John Noonan, "Deciding Who is Human," *Natural Law Forum*, 13 (1968), 135.

[3]From here on, we will use "human" to mean genetically human, since the moral sense seems closely connected to, and perhaps derived from, the assumption that genetic humanity is sufficient for membership in the moral community.

What characteristics entitle an entity to be considered a person? This is obviously not the place to attempt a complete analysis of the concept of personhood, but we do not need such a fully adequate analysis just to determine whether and why a fetus is or isn't a person. All we need is a rough and approximate list of the most basic criteria of personhood, and some idea of which, or how many, of these an entity must satisfy in order to properly be considered a person.

In searching for such criteria, it is useful to look beyond the set of people with whom we are acquainted, and ask how we would decide whether a totally alien being was a person or not. (For we have no right to assume that genetic humanity is necessary for personhood.) Imagine a space traveler who lands on an unknown planet and encounters a race of beings utterly unlike any he has ever seen or heard of. If he wants to be sure of behaving morally toward these beings, he has to somehow decide whether they are people, and hence have full moral rights, or whether they are the sort of thing which he need not feel guilty about treating as, for example, a source of food.

How should he go about making this decision? If he has some anthropological background, he might look for such things as religion, art, and the manufacturing of tools, weapons, or shelters, since these factors have been used to distinguish our human from our prehuman ancestors, in what seems to be closer to the moral than the genetic sense of "human." And no doubt he would be right to consider the presence of such factors as good evidence that the alien beings were people, and morally human. It would, however, be overly anthropocentric of him to take the absence of these things as adequate evidence that they were not, since we can imagine people who have progressed beyond, or evolved without ever developing, these cultural characteristics.

I suggest that the traits which are most central to the concept of personhood, or humanity in the moral sense, are, very roughly, the following:

1. consciousness (of objects and events external and/or internal to the being), and in particular the capacity to feel pain;
2. reasoning (the *developed* capacity to solve new and relatively complex problems);
3. self-motivated activity (activity which is relatively independent of either genetic or direct external control);

4. the capacity to communicate, by whatever means, messages of an indefinite variety of types, that is, not just with an indefinite number of possible contents, but on indefinitely many possible topics;
5. the presence of self-concepts, and self-awareness, either individual or racial, or both.

Admittedly, there are apt to be a great many problems involved in formulating precise definitions of these criteria, let alone in developing universally valid behavioral criteria for deciding when they apply. But I will assume that both we and our explorer know approximately what (1)-(5) mean, and that he is also able to determine whether or not they apply. How, then, should he use his findings to decide whether or not the alien beings are people? We needn't suppose that an entity must have *all* of these attributes to be properly considered a person; (1) and (2) alone may well be sufficient for personhood, and quite probably (1)-(3) are sufficient. Neither do we need to insist that any one of these criteria is *necessary* for personhood, although once again (1) and (2) look like fairly good candidates for necessary conditions, as does (3), if "activity" is construed so as to include the activity of reasoning.

All we need to claim, to demonstrate that a fetus is not a person, is that any being which satisfies *none* of (1)-(5) is certainly not a person. I consider this claim to be so obvious that I think anyone who denied it, and claimed that a being which satisfied none of (1)-(5) was a person all the same, would thereby demonstrate that he had no notion at all of what a person is—perhaps because he had confused the concept of a person with that of genetic humanity. If the opponents of abortion were to deny the appropriateness of these five criteria, I do not know what further arguments would convince them. We would probably have to admit that our conceptual schemes were indeed irreconcilably different, and that our dispute could not be settled objectively.

I do not expect this to happen, however, since I think that the concept of a person is one which is very nearly universal (to people), and that it is common to both proabortionists and antiabortionists, even though neither group has fully realized the relevance of this concept to the resolution of their dispute. Furthermore, I think that on reflection even the antiabortionists ought to agree not only that (1)-(5) are central to the concept of personhood, but also that it is a part of this concept that all and only people have full moral rights. The concept of a person is in part a moral concept; once we have admitted that *x* is a person we have recognized, even if we have not agreed to respect, *x*'s right to be treated as a member of the moral community. It is true that the claim that *x* is a *human being* is more commonly voiced as part of an appeal to treat *x* decently than is the claim that *x* is a person, but this is either because "human being" is here used in the sense which implies personhood, or because the genetic and moral senses of "human" have been confused.

Now if (1)-(5) are indeed the primary criteria of personhood, then it is clear that genetic humanity is neither necessary nor sufficient for establishing that an entity is a person. Some human beings are not people, and there may well be people who are not human beings. A man or woman whose consciousness has been permanently obliterated but who remains alive is a human being which is no longer a person; defective human beings, with no appreciable mental capacity, are not and presumably never will be people; and a fetus is a human being which is not yet a person, and which therefore cannot coherently be said to have full moral rights. Citizens of the next century should be prepared to recognize highly advanced, self-aware robots or computers, should such be developed, and intelligent inhabitants of other worlds, should such be found, as people in the fullest sense, and to respect their moral rights. But to ascribe full moral rights to an entity which is not a person is as absurd as to ascribe moral obligations and responsibilities to such an entity.

3. Fetal Development and the Right to Life

Two problems arise in the application of these suggestions for the definition of the moral community to the determination of the precise moral status of a human fetus. Given that the paradigm example of a person is a normal adult human being, then (1) How like this paradigm, in particular how far advanced since conception, does a human being need to be before it begins to have a right to life by virtue, not of being fully a person as of yet, but of being *like* a person? and (2) To what extent, if any, does the fact that a fetus has the *potential* for becoming a person endow it with some of the same rights? Each of these questions requires some comment.

In answering the first question, we need not attempt a detailed consideration of the moral rights of organisms which are not developed enough, aware enough, intelligent enough, etc., to be considered people, but which resemble people in some respects. It does seem reasonable to suggest that the more like a person, in the relevant respects, a being is, the stronger is the case for regarding it as having a right to life, and indeed the stronger its right to life is. Thus we ought to take seriously the suggestion that, insofar as "the human individual develops biologically in a continuous fashion . . . the rights of a human person might develop in the same way."[4] But we must keep in mind that the attributes which are relevant in determining whether or not an entity is enough like a person to be regarded as having some of the same moral rights are no different from those which are relevant to determining whether or not it is fully a person—that is, are no different from (1)-(5)—and that being genetically human, or having recognizably human facial and other physical features, or detectable brain activity, or the capacity to survive outside the uterus, are simply not among these relevant attributes.

Thus it is clear that even though a seven- or eight-month fetus has features which make it apt to arouse in us almost the same powerful protective instinct as is commonly aroused by a small infant, nevertheless it is not significantly more personlike than is a very small embryo. It is *somewhat* more personlike; it can apparently feel and respond to pain, and it may even have a rudimentary form of consciousness, insofar as its brain is quite active. Nevertheless, it seems safe to say that it is not fully conscious, in the way that an infant of a few months is, and that it cannot reason, or communicate messages of indefinitely many sorts, does not engage in self-motivated activity, and has no self-awareness. Thus, in the *relevant* respects, a fetus, even a fully developed one, is considerably less personlike than is the average mature mammal, indeed the average fish. And I think that a rational person must conclude that if the right to life of a fetus is to be based upon its resemblance to a person, then it cannot be said to have any more right to life than, let us say, a newborn guppy (which also seems to be capable of feeling pain), and that a right of that magnitude could never override a woman's right to obtain an abortion, at any stage of her pregnancy.

---

[4]Thomas L. Hayes, "A Biological View," *Commonweal*, 85 (March 17, 1967), 677–78; quoted by Daniel Callahan, in *Abortion: Law, Choice and Morality* (London: Macmillan & Co., 1970).

900

There may, of course, be other arguments in favor of placing legal limits upon the stage of pregnancy in which an abortion may be performed. Given the relative safety of the new techniques of artificially inducing labor during the third trimester, the danger to the woman's life or health is no longer such an argument. Neither is the fact that people tend to respond to the thought of abortion in the later stages of pregnancy with emotional repulsion, since mere emotional responses cannot take the place of moral reasoning in determining what ought to be permitted. Nor, finally, is the frequently heard argument that legalizing abortion, especially late in the pregnancy, may erode the level of respect for human life, leading, perhaps, to an increase in unjustified euthanasia and other crimes. For this threat, if it is a threat, can be better met by educating people to the kinds of moral distinctions which we are making here than by limiting access to abortion (which limitation may, in its disregard for the rights of women, be just as damaging to the level of respect for human rights).

Thus, since the fact that even a fully developed fetus is not person-like enough to have any significant right to life on the basis of its personlikeness shows that no legal restrictions upon the stage of pregnancy in which an abortion may be performed can be justified on the grounds that we should protect the rights of the older fetus, and since there is no other apparent justification for such restrictions, we may conclude that they are entirely unjustified. Whether or not it would be *indecent* (whatever that means) for a woman in her seventh month to obtain an abortion just to avoid having to postpone a trip to Europe, it would not, in itself, be *immoral*, and therefore it ought to be permitted.

4. Potential Personhood and the Right to Life

We have seen that a fetus does not resemble a person in any way which can support the claim that it has even some of the same rights. But what about its *potential*, the fact that if nurtured and allowed to develop naturally it will very probably become a person? Doesn't that alone give it at least some right to life? It is hard to deny that the fact that an entity is a potential person is a strong prima facie reason for not destroying it; but we need not conclude from this that a potential person has a right to life, by virtue of that potential. It may be that our feeling that it is better, other things being equal, not to destroy a potential person is better explained by the fact that potential

901

people are still (felt to be) an invaluable resource, not to be lightly squandered. Surely, if every speck of dust were a potential person, we would be much less apt to conclude that every potential person has a right to become actual.

Still, we do not need to insist that a potential person has no right to life whatever. There may well be something immoral, and not just imprudent, about wantonly destroying potential people, when doing so isn't necessary to protect anyone's rights. But even if a potential person does have some prima facie right to life, such a right could not possibly outweigh the right of a woman to obtain an abortion, since the rights of any actual person invariably outweigh those of any potential person, whenever the two conflict. Since this may not be immediately obvious in the case of a human fetus, let us look at another case.

Suppose that our space explorer falls into the hands of an alien culture, whose scientists decide to create a few hundred thousand or more human beings, by breaking his body into its component cells, and using these to create fully developed human beings, with, of course, his genetic code. We may imagine that each of these newly created men will have all of the original man's abilities, skills, knowledge, and so on, and also have an individual self-concept, in short that each of them will be a bona fide (though hardly unique) person. Imagine that the whole project will take only seconds, and that its chances of success are extremely high, and that our explorer knows all of this, and also knows that these people will be treated fairly. I maintain that in such a situation he would have every right to escape if he could, and thus to deprive all of these potential people of their potential lives; for his right to life outweighs all of theirs together, in spite of the fact that they are all genetically human, all innocent, and all have a very high probability of becoming people very soon, if only he refrains from acting.

Indeed, I think he would have a right to escape even if it were not his life which the alien scientists planned to take, but only a year of his freedom, or, indeed, only a day. Nor would he be obligated to stay if he had gotten captured (thus bringing all these people-potentials into existence) because of his own carelessness, or even if he had done so deliberately, knowing the consequences. Regardless of how he got captured, he is not morally obligated to remain in captivity for *any* period of time for the sake of permitting any number of potential people to come into actuality, so great is the margin by which one actual person's right to liberty outweighs whatever right to life even a hundred thousand potential people have. And it seems reasonable to conclude that the rights of a woman will outweigh by a similar margin whatever right to life a fetus may have by virtue of its potential personhood.

Thus, neither a fetus's resemblance to a person, nor its potential for becoming a person provides any basis whatever for the claim that it has any significant right to life. Consequently, a woman's right to protect her health, happiness, freedom, and even her life,[5] by terminating an unwanted pregnancy, will always override whatever right to life it may be appropriate to ascribe to a fetus, even a fully developed one. And thus, in the absence of any overwhelming social need for every possible child, the laws which restrict the right to obtain an abortion, or limit the period of pregnancy during which an abortion may be performed, are a wholly unjustified violation of a woman's most basic moral and constitutional rights.[6]

Postscript on infanticide

Since the publication of this article, many people have written to point out that my argument appears to justify not only abortion, but infanticide as well. For a newborn infant is not significantly more personlike than an advanced fetus, and consequently it would seem that if the destruction of the latter is permissible so too must be that of the former. Inasmuch as most people, regardless of how they feel about the morality of abortion, consider infanticide a form of murder, this might appear to represent a serious flaw in my argument.

Now, if I am right in holding that it is only people who have a full-fledged right to life, and who can be murdered, and if the criteria of personhood are as I have described them, then it obviously follows that killing a new-born infant isn't murder. It does *not* follow, however, that infanticide is permissible, for two reasons. In the first place,

---

[5]That is, insofar as the death rate, for the woman, is higher for childbirth than for early abortion.

[6]My thanks to the following people, who were kind enough to read and criticize an earlier version of this paper: Herbert Gold, Gene Glass, Anne Lauterbach, Judith Thomson, Mary Mothersill, and Timothy Binkley.

it would be wrong, at least in this country and in this period of history, and other things being equal, to kill a new-born infant, because even if its parents do not want it and would not suffer from its destruction, there are other people who would like to have it, and would, in all probability, be deprived of a great deal of pleasure by its destruction. Thus, infanticide is wrong for reasons analogous to those which make it wrong to wantonly destroy natural resources, or great works of art.

Secondly, most people, at least in this country, value infants and would much prefer that they be preserved, even if foster parents are not immediately available. Most of us would rather be taxed to support orphanages than allow unwanted infants to be destroyed. So long as there are people who want an infant preserved, and who are willing and able to provide the means of caring for it, under reasonably humane conditions, it is *ceteris paribus*, wrong to destroy it.

But, it might be replied, if this argument shows that infanticide is wrong, at least at this time and in this country, doesn't it also show that abortion is wrong? After all, many people value fetuses, are disturbed by their destruction, and would much prefer that they be preserved, even at some cost to themselves. Furthermore, as a potential source of pleasure to some foster family, a fetus is just as valuable as an infant. There is, however, a crucial difference between the two cases: so long as the fetus is unborn, its preservation, contrary to the wishes of the pregnant woman, violates her rights to freedom, happiness, and self-determination. Her rights override the rights of those who would like the fetus preserved, just as if someone's life or limb is threatened by a wild animal, his right to protect himself by destroying the animal overrides the rights of those who would prefer that the animal not be harmed.

The minute the infant is born, however, its preservation no longer violates any of its mother's rights, even if she wants it destroyed, because she is free to put it up for adoption. Consequently, while the moment of birth does not mark any sharp discontinuity in the degree to which an infant possesses the right to life, it does mark the end of its mother's right to determine its fate. Indeed, if abortion could be performed without killing the fetus, she would never possess the right to have the fetus destroyed, for the same reasons that she has no right to have an infant destroyed.

On the other hand, it follows from my argument that when an unwanted or defective infant is born into a society which cannot

904

afford and/or is not willing to care for it, then its destruction is permissible. This conclusion will, no doubt, strike many people as heartless and immoral; but remember that the very existence of people who feel this way, and who are willing and able to provide care for unwanted infants, is reason enough to conclude that they should be preserved.

STUDY QUESTIONS

1. You are Stanley Hauerwas (see Hauerwas's reading later in this chapter) and you have just read Mary Anne Warren's article. Write a rejoinder.
2. Discuss the distinction between being human and being a person. Do you agree that being a person is a necessary condition for having a right to life? Obviously Noonan disagrees. What could his arguments be?
3. Suppose you are a doctor in an intensive care unit for neonates. Legal considerations aside, do you apply Warren's position on defective infants in your practice? Why or why not?

A Defense of Abortion*

JUDITH JARVIS THOMSON

Judith Jarvis Thomson (b. 1929) is a professor of philosophy at the Massachusetts Institute of Technology. She has written numerous articles on ethics and is the author of *Acts and Other Events* (1977), *Rights, Restitution and Risk*, (1986) and *The Realm of Rights* (1990).

In her defense of abortion Thomson accepts, for the sake of argument, that the fetus is an innocent human being with a right to live. Her strategy is to show that killing

*I am very much indebted to James Thomson for discussion, criticism, and many helpful suggestions.

an innocent human being is not always wrong. She asks you to imagine yourself waking up one morning and finding that you have been kidnapped, taken to a hospital, and attached to the circulatory system of a famous violinist who will die if you unplug yourself. Apparently, a group of music lovers canvassed local medical records and determined that you alone have the right blood type. Thomson argues that you have the right to unhook yourself even if this will cause the violinist's death. According to Thomson, you might allow the violinist to use your kidneys out of kindness, but you are certainly not *obligated* to do so and may rightfully pull the plug on him. To the objection that in pregnancy the mother in some sense invites the fetus to use her body, Thomson replies that this is more like the negligence of opening a window that permits easy intrusion by an unwanted visitor. You still have the right to cast out the intruder. Thomson concedes that abortion is sometimes a selfish act, but denies that we must refrain from unselfishness; an act may be "self-centered, callous, indecent, but not unjust." No law requires anyone to be even a "Minimally Decent Samaritan." Yet prohibiting abortion forces women to be Good Samaritans.

Thomson's argument does not give blanket permission to abort. Some cases require minimal decency and entail no right to abort. She considers this consequence a merit of her argument. Finally, the right to abort is not the right to kill: If a fetus can be saved once it is taken from its mother's body then she has no right to demand its death.

Most opposition to abortion relies on the premise that the fetus is a human being, a person, from the moment of conception. The premise is argued for, but, as I think, not well. Take, for example, the most common argument. We are asked to notice that the development of a human being from conception through birth into childhood is continuous; then it is said that to draw a line, to choose a point in this development and say "before this point the thing is not a person, after this point it is a person" is to make an arbitrary choice, a choice for which in the nature of things no good reason can be given. It is concluded that the fetus is, or anyway that we had better say it is, a person from the moment of conception. But this conclusion does not follow. Similar things might be said about the development of an acorn into an oak tree, and it does not follow that acorns are oak trees, or that we had better say they are. Arguments of this form are sometimes called "slippery slope arguments"—the phrase is perhaps self-explanatory—and it is dismaying that opponents of abortion rely on them so heavily and uncritically.

I am inclined to agree, however, that the prospects for "drawing a line" in the development of the fetus look dim. I am inclined to think also that we shall probably have to agree that the fetus has already become a human person well before birth. Indeed, it comes as a surprise when one first learns how early in its life it begins to acquire human characteristics. By the tenth week, for example, it already has a face, arms and legs, fingers and toes; it has internal organs, and brain activity is detectable.[1] On the other hand, I think that the premise is false, that the fetus is not a person from the moment of conception. A newly fertilized ovum, a newly implanted clump of cells, is no more a person than an acorn is an oak tree. But I shall not discuss any of this. For it seems to me to be of great interest to ask what happens if, for the sake of argument, we allow the premise. How, precisely, are we supposed to get from there to the conclusion that abortion is morally impermissible? Opponents of abortion commonly spend most of their time establishing that the fetus is a person, and hardly any time explaining the step from there to the impermissibility of abortion. Perhaps they think the step too simple and obvious to require much comment. Or perhaps instead they are simply being economical in argument. Many of those who defend abortion rely on the premise that the fetus is not a person, but only a bit of tissue that will become a person at birth; and why pay out more arguments than you have to? Whatever the explanation, I suggest that the step they take is neither easy nor obvious, that it calls for closer examination than it is commonly given, and that when we do give it this closer examination we shall feel inclined to reject it.

---

[1] Daniel Callahan, *Abortion: Law, Choice and Morality* (New York, 1970), p. 373. This book gives a fascinating survey of the available information on abortion. The Jewish tradition is surveyed in David M. Feldman, *Birth Control in Jewish Law* (New York, 1968), Part 5, the Catholic tradition in John T. Noonan, Jr., "An Almost Absolute Value in History," in *The Morality of Abortion*, ed. John T. Noonan, Jr. (Cambridge, Mass., 1970).

I propose, then, that we grant that the fetus is a person from the moment of conception. How does the argument go from here? Something like this, I take it. Every person has a right to life. So the fetus has a right to life. No doubt the mother has a right to decide what shall happen in and to her body; everyone would grant that. But surely a person's right to life is stronger and more stringent than the mother's right to decide what happens in and to her body, and so outweighs it. So the fetus may not be killed; an abortion may not be performed.

It sounds plausible. But now let me ask you to imagine this. You wake up in the morning and find yourself back to back in bed with an unconscious violinist. A famous unconscious violinist. He has been found to have a fatal kidney ailment, and the Society of Music Lovers has canvassed all the available medical records and found that you alone have the right blood type to help. They have therefore kidnapped you, and last night the violinist's circulatory system was plugged into yours, so that your kidneys can be used to extract poisons from his blood as well as your own. The director of the hospital now tells you, "Look, we're sorry the Society of Music Lovers did this to you—we would never have permitted it if we had known. But still, they did it, and the violinist now is plugged into you. To unplug you would be to kill him. But never mind, it's only for nine months. By then he will have recovered from his ailment, and can safely be unplugged from you." Is it morally incumbent on you to accede to this situation? No doubt it would be very nice of you if you did, a great kindness. But do you *have* to accede to it? What if it were not nine months, but nine years? Or longer still? What if the director of the hospital says, "Tough luck, I agree, but you've now got to stay in bed, with the violinist plugged into you, for the rest of your life. Because remember this. All persons have a right to life, and violinists are persons. Granted you have a right to decide what happens in and to your body, but a person's right to life outweighs your right to decide what happens in and to your body. So you cannot ever be unplugged from him." I imagine you would regard this as outrageous, which suggests that something really is wrong with that plausible-sounding argument I mentioned a moment ago.

In this case, of course, you were kidnapped; you didn't volunteer for this operation that plugged the violinist into your kidneys. Can those who oppose abortion on the ground I mentioned make an exception for a pregnancy due to rape? Certainly. They can say that persons have a right to life only if they didn't come into existence because of rape; or they can say that all persons have a right to life, but that some have less of a right to life than others, in particular, that those who came into existence because of rape have less. But these statements have a rather unpleasant sound. Surely the question of whether you have a right to life at all, or how much of it you have, shouldn't turn on the question of whether or not you are the product of a rape. And in fact the people who oppose abortion on the ground I mentioned do not make this distinction, and hence do not make an exception in case of rape.

Nor do they make an exception for a case in which the mother has to spend the nine months of her pregnancy in bed. They would agree that would be a great pity, and hard on the mother; but all the same, all persons have a right to life, the fetus is a person, and so on. I suspect, in fact, that they would not make an exception for a case in which, miraculously enough, the pregnancy went on for nine years, or even the rest of the mother's life.

Some won't even make an exception for a case in which continuation of the pregnancy is likely to shorten the mother's life; they regard abortion as impermissible even to save the mother's life. Such cases are nowadays very rare, and many opponents of abortion do not accept this extreme view. All the same, it is a good place to begin: a number of points of interest come out in respect to it.

1. Let us call the view that abortion is impermissible even to save the mother's life "the extreme view." I want to suggest first that it does not issue from the argument I mentioned earlier without the addition of some fairly powerful premises. Suppose a woman has become pregnant, and now learns that she has a cardiac condition such that she will die if she carries the baby to term. What may be done for her? The fetus, being a person, has a right to life, but as the mother is a person too, so she has a right to life. Presumably they have an equal right to life. How is it supposed to come out that an abortion may not be performed? If mother and child have an equal right to life, shouldn't we perhaps flip a coin? Or should we add to the mother's right to life her right to decide what happens in and to her body, which everybody seems to be ready to grant—the sum of her rights now outweighing the fetus' right to life?

The most familiar argument here is the following. We are told that performing the abortion would be directly killing[2] the child, whereas doing nothing would not be killing the mother, but only letting her die. Moreover, in killing the child, one would be killing an innocent person, for the child has committed no crime, and is not aiming at his mother's death. And then there are a variety of ways in which this might be continued. (1) But as directly killing an innocent person is always and absolutely impermissible, an abortion may not be performed. Or, (2) as directly killing an innocent person is murder, and murder is always and absolutely impermissible, an abortion may not be performed.[3] Or, (3) as one's duty to refrain from directly killing an innocent person is more stringent than one's duty to keep a person from dying, an abortion may not be performed. Or, (4) if one's only options are directly killing an innocent person or letting a person die, one must prefer letting the person die, and thus an abortion may not be performed.[4]

Some people seem to have thought that these are not further premises which must be added if the conclusion is to be reached, but that they follow from the very fact that an innocent person has a right to life.[5] But this seems to me to be a mistake, and perhaps the simplest way to show this is to bring out that while we must certainly grant that innocent persons have a right to life, the theses in (1) through (4)

---

[2]The term "direct" in the arguments I refer to is a technical one. Roughly, what is meant by "direct killing" is either killing as an end in itself, or killing as a means of some end, for example, the end of saving someone else's life. See footnote 5, for an example of its use.

[3]Cf. *Encyclical Letter of Pope Pius XI on Christian Marriage*, St. Paul Editions (Boston, n.d.), p. 32: "however much we may pity the mother whose health and even life is gravely imperiled in the performance of the duty allotted to her by nature, nevertheless what could ever be a sufficient reason for excusing in any way the direct murder of the innocent? This is precisely what we are dealing with here." Noonan (*The Morality of Abortion*, p. 43) reads this as follows: "What cause can ever avail to excuse in any way the direct killing of the innocent? For it is a question of that."

[4]The thesis in (4) is in an interesting way weaker than those in (1), (2), and (3): they rule out abortion even in cases in which both mother *and* child will die if the abortion is not performed. By contrast, one who held the view expressed in (4) could consistently say that one needn't prefer letting two persons die to killing one.

[5]Cf. the following passage from Pius XII, *Address to the Italian Catholic Society of Midwives*: "The baby in the maternal breast has the right to life immediately from God.—Hence there is no man, no human authority, no science, no medical, eugenic, social, economic or moral 'indication' which can establish or grant a valid juridical

are all false. Take (2), for example. If directly killing an innocent person is murder, and thus is impermissible, then the mother's directly killing the innocent person inside her is murder, and thus is impermissible. But it cannot seriously be thought to be murder if the mother performs an abortion on herself to save her life. It cannot seriously be said that she *must* refrain, that she *must* sit passively by and wait for her death. Let us look again at the case of you and the violinist. There you are, in bed with the violinist, and the director of the hospital says to you, "It's all most distressing, and I deeply sympathize, but you see this is putting an additional strain on your kidneys, and you'll be dead within the month. But you *have* to stay where you are all the same. Because unplugging you would be directly killing an innocent violinist, and that's murder, and that's impermissible." If anything in the world is true, it is that you do not commit murder, you do not do what is impermissible, if you reach around to your back and unplug yourself from that violinist to save your life.

The main focus of attention in writings on abortion has been on what a third party may or may not do in answer to a request from a woman for an abortion. This is in a way understandable. Things being as they are, there isn't much a woman can safely do to abort herself. So the question asked is what a third party may do, and what the mother may do, if it is mentioned at all, is deduced, almost as an afterthought, from what it is concluded that third parties may do. But it seems to me that to treat the matter in this way is to refuse to grant to the mother that very status of person which is so firmly insisted on for the fetus. For we cannot simply read off what a person may do from what a third party may do. Suppose you find yourself trapped in a tiny house with a growing child. I mean a very tiny house, and a rapidly growing child—you are already up against the wall of the house and in a few minutes you'll be crushed to death. The child on the other hand won't be crushed to death; if nothing is done to stop him from growing he'll be hurt, but in the end he'll simply burst open the house and walk out a free man. Now I could

---

ground for a direct deliberate disposition of an innocent human life, that is a disposition which looks to its destruction either as an end or as a means to another end perhaps in itself not illicit.—The baby, still not born, is a man in the same degree and for the same reason as the mother" (quoted in Noonan, *The Morality of Abortion*, p. 45).

well understand it if a bystander were to say, "There's nothing we can do for you. We cannot choose between your life and his, we cannot be the ones to decide who is to live, we cannot intervene." But it cannot be concluded that you too can do nothing, that you cannot attack it to save your life. However innocent the child may be, you do not have to wait passively while it crushes you to death. Perhaps a pregnant woman is vaguely felt to have the status of house, to which we don't allow the right of self-defense. But if the woman houses the child, it should be remembered that she is a person who houses it.

I should perhaps stop to say explicitly that I am not claiming that people have a right to do anything whatever to save their lives. I think, rather, that there are drastic limits to the right of self-defense. If someone threatens you with death unless you torture someone else to death, I think you have not the right, even to save your life, to do so. But the case under consideration here is very different. In our case there are only two people involved, one whose life is threatened, and one who threatens it. Both are innocent: the one who is threatened is not threatened because of any fault, the one who threatens does not threaten because of any fault. For this reason we may feel that we bystanders cannot intervene. But the person threatened can.

In sum, a woman surely can defend her life against the threat to it posed by the unborn child, even if doing so involves its death. And this shows not merely that the theses in (1) through (4) are false; it shows also that the extreme view of abortion is false, and so we need not canvass any other possible ways of arriving at it from the argument I mentioned at the outset.

2. The extreme view could of course be weakened to say that while abortion is permissible to save the mother's life, it may not be performed by a third party, but only by the mother herself. But this cannot be right either. For what we have to keep in mind is that the mother and the unborn child are not like two tenants in a small house which has, by an unfortunate mistake, been rented to both: the mother *owns* the house. The fact that she does add to the offensiveness of deducing that the mother can do nothing from the supposition that third parties can do nothing. But it does more than this: it casts a bright light on the supposition that third parties can do nothing. Certainly it lets us see that a third party who says "I cannot choose between you" is fooling himself if he thinks this is impartiality. If Jones has found and fastened on a certain coat, which he needs

to keep him from freezing, but which Smith also needs to keep him from freezing, then it is not impartiality that says "I cannot choose between you" when Smith owns the coat. Women have said again and again "This body is *my* body!" and they have reason to feel angry, reason to feel that it has been like shouting into the wind. Smith, after all, is hardly likely to bless us if we say to him, "Of course it's your coat, anybody would grant that it is. But no one may choose between you and Jones who is to have it."

We should really ask what it is that says "no one may choose" in the face of the fact that the body that houses the child is the mother's body. It may be simply a failure to appreciate this fact. But it may be something more interesting, namely the sense that one has a right to refuse to lay hands on people, even where it would be just and fair to do so, even where justice seems to require that somebody do so. Thus justice might call for somebody to get Smith's coat back from Jones, and yet you have a right to refuse to be the one to lay hands on Jones, a right to refuse to do physical violence to him. This, I think, must be granted. But then what should be said is not "no one may choose," but only "*I* cannot choose," and indeed not even this, but "*I* will not *act*," leaving it open that somebody else can or should, and in particular that anyone in a position of authority, with the job of securing people's rights, both can and should. So this is no difficulty. I have not been arguing that any given third party must accede to the mother's request that he perform an abortion to save her life, but only that he may.

I suppose that in some views of human life the mother's body is only on loan to her, the loan not being one which gives her any prior claim to it. One who held this view might well think it impartiality to say "I cannot choose." But I shall simply ignore this possibility. My own view is that if a human being has any just, prior claim to anything at all, he has a just, prior claim to his own body. And perhaps this needn't be argued for here anyway, since, as I mentioned, the arguments against abortion we are looking at do grant that the woman has a right to decide what happens in and to her body.

But although they do grant it, I have tried to show that they do not take seriously what is done in granting it. I suggest the same thing will reappear even more clearly when we turn away from cases in which the mother's life is at stake, and attend, as I propose we now do, to the vastly more common cases in which a woman wants an abortion for some less weighty reason than preserving her own life.

3. Where the mother's life is not at stake, the argument I mentioned at the outset seems to have a much stronger pull. "Everyone has a right to life, so the unborn person has a right to life." And isn't the child's right to life weightier than anything other than the mother's own right to life, which she might put forward as ground for an abortion?

This argument treats the right to life as if it were unproblematic. It is not, and this seems to me to be precisely the source of the mistake.

For we should now, at long last, ask what it comes to, to have a right to life. In some views having a right to life includes having a right to be given at least the bare minimum one needs for continued life. But suppose that what in fact *is* the bare minimum a man needs for continued life is something he has no right at all to be given? If I am sick unto death, and the only thing that will save my life is the touch of Henry Fonda's cool hand on my fevered brow, then all the same, I have no right to be given the touch of Henry Fonda's cool hand on my fevered brow. It would be frightfully nice of him to fly in from the West Coast to provide it. It would be less nice, though no doubt well meant, if my friends flew out to the West Coast and carried Henry Fonda back with them. But I have no right at all against anybody that he should do this for me. Or again, to return to the story I told earlier, the fact that for continued life that violinist needs the continued use of your kidneys does not establish that he has a right to be given the continued use of your kidneys. He certainly has no right against you that *you* should give him continued use of your kidneys. For nobody has any right to use your kidneys unless you give him such a right; and nobody has the right against you that you shall give him this right—if you do allow him to go on using your kidneys, this is a kindness on your part, and not something he can claim from you as his due. Nor has he any right against anybody else that *they* should give him continued use of your kidneys. Certainly he had no right against the Society of Music Lovers that they should plug him into you in the first place. And if you now start to unplug yourself, having learned that you will otherwise have to spend nine years in bed with him, there is nobody in the world who must try to prevent you, in order to see to it that he is given something he has a right to be given.

Some people are rather stricter about the right to life. In their view, it does not include the right to be given anything, but amounts to, and only to, the right not to be killed by anybody. But here a related difficulty arises. If everybody must refrain from killing that violinist, then everybody must refrain from doing a great many different sorts of things. Everybody must refrain from slitting his throat, everybody must refrain from shooting him—and everybody must refrain from unplugging you from him. But does he have a right against everybody that they shall refrain from unplugging you from him? To refrain from doing this is to allow him to continue to use your kidneys. It could be argued that he has a right against us that *we* should allow him to continue to use your kidneys. That is, while he had no right against us that we should give him the use of your kidneys, it might be argued that he anyway has a right against us that we shall not now intervene and deprive him of the use of your kidneys. I shall come back to third-party interventions later. But certainly the violinist has no right against you that *you* shall allow him to continue to use your kidneys. As I said, if you do allow him to use them, it is a kindness on your part, and not something you owe him.

The difficulty I point to here is not peculiar to the right to life. It reappears in connection with all the other natural rights; and it is something which an adequate account of rights must deal with. For present purposes it is enough just to draw attention to it. But I would stress that I am not arguing that people do not have a right to life—quite to the contrary, it seems to me that the primary control we must place on the acceptability of an account of rights is that it should turn out in that account to be a truth that all persons have a right to life. I am arguing only that having a right to life does not guarantee having either a right to be given the use of or a right to be allowed continued use of another person's body—even if one needs it for life itself. So the right to life will not serve the opponents of abortion in the very simple and clear way in which they seem to have thought it would.

4. There is another way to bring out the difficulty. In the most ordinary sort of case, to deprive someone of what he has a right to is to treat him unjustly. Suppose a boy and his small brother are jointly given a box of chocolates for Christmas. If the older boy takes the box and refuses to give his brother any of the chocolates, he is unjust to him, for the brother has been given a right to half of them. But suppose that, having learned that otherwise it means nine years in bed with that violinist, you unplug yourself from him. You surely are not being unjust to him, for you gave him no right to use your

kidneys, and no one else can have given him any such right. But we have to notice that, in unplugging yourself, you are killing him; and violinists, like everybody else, have a right to life, and thus in the view we were considering just now, the right not to be killed. So here you do what he supposedly has a right you shall not do, but you do not act unjustly to him in doing it.

The emendation which may be made at this point is this: the right to life consists not in the right not to be killed, but rather in the right not to be killed unjustly. This runs a risk of circularity, but never mind: it would enable us to square the fact that the violinist has a right to life with the fact that you do not act unjustly toward him in unplugging yourself, thereby killing him. For if you do not kill him unjustly, you do not violate his right to life, and so it is no wonder you do him no injustice.

But if this emendation is accepted, the gap in the argument against abortion stares us plainly in the face: it is by no means enough to show that the fetus is a person, and to remind us that all persons have a right to life—we need to be shown also that killing the fetus violates its right to life, i.e., that abortion is unjust killing. And is it?

I suppose we may take it as a datum that in a case of pregnancy due to rape the mother has not given the unborn person a right to the use of her body for food and shelter. Indeed, in what pregnancy could it be supposed that the mother has given the unborn person such a right? It is not as if there were unborn persons drifting about the world, to whom a woman who wants a child says "I invite you in."

But it might be argued that there are other ways one can have acquired a right to the use of another person's body than by having been invited to use it by that person. Suppose a woman voluntarily indulges in intercourse, knowing of the chance it will issue in pregnancy, and then she does become pregnant; is she not in part responsible for the presence, in fact the very existence, of the unborn person inside her? No doubt she did not invite it in. But doesn't her partial responsibility for its being there itself give it a right to the use of her body?[6] If so, then her aborting it would be more like the boy's taking

---

[6]The need for discussion of this argument was brought home to me by members of the Society for Ethical and Legal Philosophy, to whom this paper was originally presented.

away the chocolates, and less like your unplugging yourself from the violinist—doing so would be depriving it of what it does have a right to, and thus would be doing it an injustice.

And then, too, it might be asked whether or not she can kill it even to save her own life: If she voluntarily called it into existence, how can she now kill it, even in self-defense?

The first thing to be said about this is that it is something new. Opponents of abortion have been so concerned to make out the independence of the fetus, in order to establish that it has a right to life, just as its mother does, that they have tended to overlook the possible support they might gain from making out that the fetus is *dependent* on the mother, in order to establish that she has a special kind of responsibility for it, a responsibility that gives it rights against her which are not possessed by any independent person— such as an ailing violinist who is a stranger to her.

On the other hand, this argument would give the unborn person a right to its mother's body only if her pregnancy resulted from a voluntary act, undertaken in full knowledge of the chance a pregnancy might result from it. It would leave out entirely the unborn person whose existence is due to rape. Pending the availability of some further argument, then, we would be left with the conclusion that unborn persons whose existence is due to rape have no right to the use of their mothers' bodies, and thus that aborting them is not depriving them of anything they have a right to and hence is not unjust killing.

And we should also notice that it is not at all plain that this argument really does go even as far as it purports to. For there are cases and cases, and the details make a difference. If the room is stuffy, and I therefore open a window to air it, and a burglar climbs in, it would be absurd to say, "Ah, now he can stay, she's given him a right to the use of her house—for she is partially responsible for his presence there, having voluntarily done what enabled him to get in, in full knowledge that there are such things as burglars, and that burglars burgle." It would be still more absurd to say this if I had had bars installed outside my windows, precisely to prevent burglars from getting in, and a burglar got in only because of a defect in the bars. It remains equally absurd if we imagine it is not a burglar who climbs in, but an innocent person who blunders or falls in. Again, suppose it were like this: people-seeds drift about in the air like pollen, and if you open your windows, one may drift in and take root in your carpets or upholstery. You don't want children, so you fix up your windows with fine mesh screens, the very best you can buy. As can happen, however, and on very, very rare occasions does happen, one of the screens is defective; and a seed drifts in and takes root. Does the person-plant who now develops have a right to the use of your house? Surely not—despite the fact that you voluntarily opened your windows, you knowingly kept carpets and upholstered furniture, and you knew that screens were sometimes defective. Someone may argue that you are responsible for its rooting, that it does have a right to your house, because after all you *could* have lived out your life with bare floors and furniture, or with sealed windows and doors. But this won't do—for by the same token anyone can avoid a pregnancy due to rape by having a hysterectomy, or anyway by never leaving home without a (reliable!) army.

It seems to me that the argument we are looking at can establish at most that there are *some* cases in which the unborn person has a right to the use of its mother's body, and therefore *some* cases in which abortion is unjust killing. There is room for much discussion and argument as to precisely which, if any. But I think we should sidestep this issue and leave it open, for at any rate the argument certainly does not establish that all abortion is unjust killing.

5. There is room for yet another argument here, however. We surely must all grant that there may be cases in which it would be morally indecent to detach a person from your body at the cost of his life. Suppose you learn that what the violinist needs is not nine years of your life, but only one hour: all you need to do to save his life is to spend one hour in that bed with him. Suppose also that letting him use your kidneys for that one hour would not affect your health in the slightest. Admittedly you were kidnapped. Admittedly you did not give anyone permission to plug him into you. Nevertheless it seems to me plain you *ought* to allow him to use your kidneys for that hour—it would be indecent to refuse.

Again, suppose pregnancy lasted only one hour, and constituted no threat to life or health. And suppose that a woman becomes pregnant as a result of rape. Admittedly she did not voluntarily do anything to bring about the existence of a child. Admittedly she did nothing at all which would give the unborn person a right to the use of her body. All the same it might well be said, as in the newly

918

emended violinist story, that she *ought* to allow it to remain for that hour—that it would be indecent in her to refuse.

Now some people are inclined to use the term "right" in such a way that it follows from the fact that you ought to allow a person to use your body for the hour he needs, that he has a right to use your body for the hour he needs, even though he has not been given that right by any person or act. They may say that it follows also that if you refuse, you act unjustly toward him. This use of the term is perhaps so common that it cannot be called wrong; nevertheless it seems to me to be an unfortunate loosening of what we would do better to keep a tight rein on. Suppose that box of chocolates I mentioned earlier had not been given to both boys jointly, but was given only to the older boy. There he sits, stolidly eating his way through the box, his small brother watching enviously. Here we are likely to say "You ought not to be so mean. You ought to give your brother some of those chocolates." My own view is that it just does not follow from the truth of this that the brother has any right to any of the chocolates. If the boy refuses to give his brother any, he is greedy, stingy, callous—but not unjust. I suppose that the people I have in mind will say it does follow that the brother has a right to some of the chocolates, and thus that the boy does act unjustly if he refuses to give his brother any. But the effect of saying this is to obscure what we should keep distinct, namely the difference between the boy's refusal in this case and the boy's refusal in the earlier case, in which the box was given to both boys jointly, and in which the small brother thus had what was from any point of view clear title to half.

A further objection to so using the term "right" that from the fact that A ought to do a thing for B, it follows that B has a right against A that A do it for him, is that it is going to make the question of whether or not a man has a right to a thing turn on how easy it is to provide him with it; and this seems not merely unfortunate, but morally unacceptable. Take the case of Henry Fonda again. I said earlier that I had no right to the touch of his cool hand on my fevered brow, even though I needed it to save my life. I said it would be frightfully nice of him to fly in from the West Coast to provide me with it, but that I had no right against him that he should do so. But suppose he isn't on the West Coast. Suppose he has only to walk across the room, place a hand briefly on my brow—and lo, my life is saved. Then surely he ought to do it, it would be indecent to refuse. Is it to be said "Ah, well, it follows that in this case she has a right to the touch of his hand on her brow, and so it would be an injustice in him to refuse"? So that I have a right to it when it is easy for him to provide it, though no right when it's hard? It's rather a shocking idea that anyone's rights should fade away and disappear as it gets harder and harder to accord them to him.

So my own view is that even though you ought to let the violinist use your kidneys for the one hour he needs, we should not conclude that he has a right to do so—we should say that if you refuse, you are, like the boy who owns all the chocolates and will give none away, self-centered and callous, indecent in fact, but not unjust. And similarly, that even supposing a case in which a woman pregnant due to rape ought to allow the unborn person to use her body for the hour he needs, we should conclude that she is self-centered, callous, indecent, but not unjust, if she refuses. The complaints are no less grave; they are just different. However, there is no need to insist on this point. If anyone does wish to deduce "he has a right" from "you ought," then all the same he must surely grant that there are cases in which it is not morally required of you that you allow that violinist to use your kidneys, and in which he does not have a right to use them, and in which you do not do him an injustice if you refuse. And so also for mother and unborn child. Except in such cases as the unborn person has a right to demand it—and we were leaving open the possibility that there may be such cases—nobody is morally *required* to make large sacrifices, of health, of all other interests and concerns, of all other duties and commitments, for nine years, or even for nine months, in order to keep another person alive.

6. We have in fact to distinguish between two kinds of Samaritan: the Good Samaritan and what we might call the Minimally Decent Samaritan. The story of the Good Samaritan, you will remember, goes like this:

> A certain man went down from Jerusalem to Jericho, and fell among thieves, which stripped him of his raiment, and wounded him, and departed, leaving him half dead.
>
> And by chance there came down a certain priest that way; and when he saw him, he passed by on the other side.
>
> And likewise a Levite, when he was at the place, came and looked on him, and passed by on the other side.

But a certain Samaritan, as he journeyed, came where he was; and when he saw him he had compassion on him.

And went to him, and bound up his wounds, pouring in oil and wine, and set him on his own beast, and brought him to an inn, and took care of him.

And on the morrow, when he departed, he took out two pence, and gave them to the host, and said unto him, "Take care of him; and whatsoever thou spendest more, when I come again, I will repay thee."

(Luke 10:30–35)

The Good Samaritan went out of his way, at some cost to himself, to help one in need of it. We are not told what the options were, that is, whether or not the priest and the Levite could have helped by doing less than the Good Samaritan did, but assuming they could have, then the fact they did nothing at all shows they were not even Minimally Decent Samaritans, not because they were not Samaritans, but because they were not even minimally decent.

These things are a matter of degree, of course, but there is a difference, and it comes out perhaps most clearly in the story of Kitty Genovese, who, as you will remember, was murdered while thirty-eight people watched or listened, and did nothing at all to help her. A Good Samaritan would have rushed out to give direct assistance against the murderer. Or perhaps we had better allow that it would have been a Splendid Samaritan who did this, on the ground that it would have involved a risk of death for himself. But the thirty-eight not only did not do this, they did not even trouble to pick up a phone to call the police. Minimally Decent Samaritanism would call for doing at least that, and their not having done it was monstrous.

After telling the story of the Good Samaritan, Jesus said "Go, and do thou likewise." Perhaps he meant that we are morally required to act as the Good Samaritan did. Perhaps he was urging people to do more than is morally required of them. At all events it seems plain that it was not morally required of any of the thirty-eight that he rush out to give direct assistance at the risk of his own life, and that it is not morally required of anyone that he give long stretches of his life—nine years or nine months—to sustaining the life of a person who has no special right (we were leaving open the possibility of this) to demand it.

Indeed, with one rather striking class of exceptions, no one in any country in the world is *legally* required to do anywhere near as much

921

as this for anyone else. The class of exceptions is obvious. My main concern here is not the state of the law in respect to abortion, but it is worth drawing attention to the fact that in no state in this country is any man compelled by law to be even a Minimally Decent Samaritan to any person; there is no law under which charges could be brought against the thirty-eight who stood by while Kitty Genovese died. By contrast, in most states in this country women are compelled by law to be not merely Minimally Decent Samaritans, but Good Samaritans to unborn persons inside them. This doesn't by itself settle anything one way or the other, because it may well be argued that there should be laws in this country—as there are in many European countries—compelling at least Minimally Decent Samaritanism.[7] But it does show that there is a gross injustice in the existing state of the law. And it shows also that the groups currently working against liberalization of abortion laws, in fact working toward having it declared unconstitutional for a state to permit abortion, had better start working for the adoption of Good Samaritan laws generally, or earn the charge that they are acting in bad faith.

I should think, myself, that Minimally Decent Samaritan laws would be one thing, Good Samaritan laws quite another, and in fact highly improper. But we are not here concerned with the law. What we should ask is not whether anybody should be compelled by law to be a Good Samaritan, but whether we must accede to a situation in which somebody is being compelled—by nature, perhaps—to be a Good Samaritan. We have, in other words, to look now at third-party interventions. I have been arguing that no person is morally required to make large sacrifices to sustain the life of another who has no right to demand them, and this even where the sacrifices do not include life itself; we are not morally required to be Good Samaritans or anyway Very Good Samaritans to one another. But what if a man cannot extricate himself from such a situation? What if he appeals to us to extricate him? It seems to me plain that there are cases in which we can, cases in which a Good Samaritan would extricate him. There you are, you were kidnapped, and nine years in bed with that violinist lie ahead of you. You have your own life to lead. You

---

[7]For a discussion of the difficulties involved, and a survey of the European experience with such laws, see *The Good Samaritan and the Law*, ed. James M. Ratcliffe (New York, 1966).

are sorry, but you simply cannot see giving up so much of your life to the sustaining of his. You cannot extricate yourself, and ask us to do so. I should have thought of that—in light of his having no right to the use of your body—it was obvious that we do not have to accede to your being forced to give up so much. We can do what you ask. There is no injustice to the violinist in our doing so.

7. Following the lead of the opponents of abortion, I have throughout been speaking of the fetus merely as a person, and what I have been asking is whether or not the argument we began with, which proceeds only from the fetus' being a person, really does establish its conclusion. I have argued that it does not.

But of course there are arguments and arguments, and it may be said that I have simply fastened on the wrong one. It may be said that what is important is not merely the fact that the fetus is a person, but that it is a person for whom the woman has a special kind of responsibility issuing from the fact that she is its mother. And it might be argued that all my analogies are therefore irrelevant—for you do not have that special kind of responsibility for that violinist, Henry Fonda does not have that special kind of responsibility for me. And our attention might be drawn to the fact that men and women both *are* compelled by law to provide support for their children.

I have in effect dealt (briefly) with this argument in section 4 above; but a (still briefer) recapitulation now may be in order. Surely we do not have any such "special responsibility" for a person unless we have assumed it, explicitly or implicitly. If a set of parents do not try to prevent pregnancy, do not obtain an abortion, and then at the time of birth of the child do not put it out for adoption, but rather take it home with them, then they have assumed responsibility for it, they have given it rights, and they cannot *now* withdraw support from it at the cost of its life because they now find it difficult to go on providing for it. But if they have taken all reasonable precautions against having a child, they do not simply by virtue of their biological relationship to the child who comes into existence have a special responsibility for it. They may wish to assume responsibility for it, or they may not wish to. And I am suggesting that if assuming responsibility for it would require large sacrifices, then they may refuse. A Good Samaritan would not refuse—or anyway, a Splendid Samaritan, if the sacrifices that had to be made were enormous. But then so would a Good Samaritan assume responsibility for that violinist; so would Henry Fonda, if he is a Good Samaritan, fly in from the West Coast and assume responsibility for me.

8. My argument will be found unsatisfactory on two counts by many of those who want to regard abortion as morally permissible. First, while I do argue that abortion is not permissible, I do not argue that it is always permissible. There may well be cases in which carrying the child to term requires only Minimally Decent Samaritanisms of the mother, and this is a standard we must not fall below. I am inclined to think it a merit of my account precisely that it does *not* give a general yes or a general no. It allows for and supports our sense that, for example, a sick and desperately frightened fourteen-year-old schoolgirl, pregnant due to rape, may *of course* choose abortion, and that any law which rules this out is an insane law. And it also allows for and supports our sense that in other cases resort to abortion is even positively indecent. It would be indecent in the woman to request an abortion, and indecent in a doctor to perform it, if she is in her seventh month, and wants the abortion just to avoid the nuisance of postponing a trip abroad. The very fact that the arguments I have been drawing attention to treat all cases of abortion, or even all cases of abortion in which the mother's life is not at stake, as morally on a par ought to have made them suspect at the outset.

Secondly, while I am arguing for the permissibility of abortion in some cases, I am not arguing for the right to secure the death of the unborn child. It is easy to confuse these two things in that up to a certain point in the life of the fetus it is not able to survive outside the mother's body; hence removing it from her body guarantees its death. But they are importantly different. I have argued that you are not morally required to spend nine months in bed, sustaining the life of that violinist; but to say this is by no means to say that if, when you unplug yourself, there is a miracle and he survives, you then have a right to turn round and slit his throat. You may detach yourself even if this costs him his life; you have no right to be guaranteed his death, by some other means, if unplugging yourself does not kill him. There are some people who will feel dissatisfied by this feature of my argument. A woman may be utterly devastated by the thought of a child, a bit of herself, put out for adoption and never seen or heard of again. She may therefore want not merely that the child be detached from her, but more, that it die. Some opponents of abortion are inclined to regard this as beneath contempt—thereby showing insensitivity to what is surely a powerful source of despair. All the same, I agree that the desire for the child's death is not one which anybody may gratify, should it turn out to be possible to detach the child alive.

At this place, however, it should be remembered that we have only been pretending throughout that the fetus is a human being from the moment of conception. A very early abortion is surely not the killing of a person, and so is not dealt with by anything I have said here.

STUDY QUESTIONS

1. How do you react to Thomson's violinist analogy? Do you think she answers the most serious objections that can be brought against it?
2. What moral responsibility, if any, does a pregnant woman have for the fetus? What is the basis for such a responsibility? Does it make a difference whether the pregnancy is wanted? Imposed?
3. Thomson distinguishes among Good Samaritans, Splendid Samaritans, and Minimally Decent Samaritans. Which are we obligated to be? How does the distinction between being a Good Samaritan and a Minimally Decent Samaritan apply to the woman with an unwanted pregnancy?

Christians and Abortion: The Narrative Context

STANLEY HAUERWAS

Stanley Hauerwas (b. 1940) is a professor of religion at Duke University. He has written numerous articles and several books in the area of theological ethics. His books include: *Truthfulness and Tragedy: Further Investigations in Christian Ethics* (1977) and *A Community of Character: Toward a Constructive Christian Social Ethic* (1981).

Hauerwas does not approach the question of abortion as a conflict of rights (the mother's vs. the fetus's). Instead, he appeals to the Judeo-Christian tradition that respects life "not as an end in itself, but as a gift created by God." "The Christian prohibition of abortion is but the negative side of their positive commitment to welcome new life into their community." Hauerwas holds that respect for human life is but a form of respect for all life and that everyone in the community, even those who are childless, have parental responsibilities. In particular, Christians prefer to live in societies that provide such extended protection to all children.

CHRISTIANS AND ABORTION: THE NARRATIVE CONTEXT. From *A Community of Character: Toward a Constructive Christian Social Ethic* by Stanley Hauerwas. © 1981 by University of Notre Dame Press. Reprinted by permission.

. . . Christians have failed their social order by accepting too easily the terms of argument concerning abortion offered by our society. If we are to serve our society well, and on our own terms, our first task must be to address ourselves by articulating for Christians why abortion can never be regarded as morally indifferent for us. Only by doing this can we witness to our society what kind of people and what kind of society is required if abortion is to be excluded. . . .

To begin with, the first question is not, "Why do Christians think abortion is wrong?" To begin there already presupposes that we know and understand what abortion is. Rather, if we are to understand why Christians assume that by naming abortion they have already said something significant, we have to begin still a step back. We have to ask what it is about the kind of community, and corresponding world, that Christians create that makes them single out abortion in such a way as to exclude it.

For we must remember that "abortion" is not a description of a particular kind of behavior, rather it is a word that teaches us to see a singular kind of behavior from a particular community's moral perspective. The removal of the fetus from the mother's uterus before term can be called an "interruption of pregnancy," the child can be called "fetal matter," and the mother can be called a "patient." But from the Christian perspective, to see the situation in that way changes the self and the community in a decisive way. The Christian insistence on the term "abortion" is a way to remind them that what happens in the removal of the fetus from the mother in order to destroy it strikes at the heart of their community. From this perspective the attempt of Christians to be a community where the term "abortion" remains morally intelligible is a political act.

In this respect the pro-abortionists have always been at a disadvantage. For they have had to carry out the argument in a language created by the moral presuppositions of the Jewish and Christian communities. "Abortion" still carries the connotation that this is not a good thing. Thus to be "pro-abortion" seems to put one in an embarrassing position of recommending a less than good thing. It is not without reason, therefore, that pro-abortion advocates seek to redescribe both the object and act of abortion. We must remind them, however, that by doing so they not only change the description of the act, they also change themselves.

927

Christians insist on the significance of such a change by refusing to live in a world devoid of abortion as a moral description—a world which admittedly may, as a result, involve deep tragedy. There can be no doubt that the insistence that unjust termination of pregnancy be called "abortion" has to do with our respect for life, but this is surely too simple. Jews and Christians are taught to respect life, not as an end in itself, but as a gift created by God. Thus life is respected because all life serves God in its way. Respect for human life is but a form of our respect for all life. . . .

It is the Christian belief, nurtured by the command of Jesus, that we must learn to love one another, that we become more nearly what we were meant to be through the recognition and love of those we did not "choose" to love. Children, the weak, the ill, the dispossessed provide a particularly intense occasion for such love, as they are beings we cannot control. We must love them for what they are rather than what we want or wish them to be, and as a result we discover that we are capable of love. The existence of such love is not unique or limited to Christians. Indeed that is why we have the confidence that our Christian convictions on these matters might ring true even for those who do not share our convictions. The difference between the Christian and the non-Christian is only that what is a possibility for the non-Christian is a duty for the Christian.

But the Christian duty to welcome new life is a joyful duty, as it derives from our very being as God's people. Moreover correlative to the language of duty is the language of gift. Because children are a duty they can also be regarded as a gift, for duty teaches us to accept and welcome a child into the world, not as something that is "ours," but as a gift which comes from another. As a result Christians need not resort to destructive and self-deceiving claims about the qualities they need to have, or the conditions of the world necessary to have children. Perhaps more worrisome than the moral implications of the claim "no unwanted child ought ever to be born," are the ominous assumptions about what is required for one to "want" to have a child.

Christians are thus trained to be the kind of people who are ready to receive and welcome children into the world. For they see children as a sign of the trustworthiness of God's creation and his willingness to abandon the world to the powers of darkness. The Christian prohibition of abortion is but the negative side of the positive commitment to welcome new life into their community: life that they know must challenge and perhaps even change their own interpretation of their tradition, but also life without which the tradition has no means to grow.

It is, of course, true that children will often be conceived and born under less than ideal conditions, but the church lives as a community which assumes that we live in an age which is always dangerous. That we live in such a time is all the more reason we must be the kind of community that can receive children into our midst. Just as we need to be virtuous, not because virtue pays but because we cannot afford to be without virtue where it does not pay, so we must learn how to be people open to new life. We can neither protect them from that suffering nor deny them the joy of participating in the adventure of God's Kingdom.

For Christians, therefore, there can be no question of whether the fetus is or is not a "human being." That way of putting the matter is far too abstract and formal. Rather, because of the kind of community we are, we see in the fetus nothing less than God's continuing creation that is destined in hope to be another citizen of his Kingdom. The question of when human life begins is of little interest to such a people, since their hope is that life will and does continue to begin time after time.

This is the form of life that brings significance to our interaction with the fetus. Our history is the basis for our "natural" sympathies, which have been trained to look forward to the joy and challenges of new life. Wertheimer may well be right that there is no corresponding "natural" welcome for life in our society that would make intelligible the recognition of the fetus as having moral status. Yet I suspect that the expectation of parents, and in particular of women, for the birth of their children remains a powerful form of life that continues to exert a force on everyone. Such an "expectation," however, in the absence of more substantive convictions about parenting, too easily becomes a destructive necessity that distorts the experience of being a parent and a child. Particularly repugnant is the assumption that women are thus primarily defined by the role of "mother," for then we forget that the role of being a parent, even for the childless, is a responsibility for everyone in the Christian community.

Nor should it be thought that the Christian commitment to welcome new life into the world stems from a sentimental fondness for babies. Rather, for Christians the having of children is one of their most significant political acts. From the world's perspective the birth of a child represents but another drain on our material and psychological resources. Children, after all, take up much of our energy that could be spent on making the world a better place and our society more just. But from the Christian perspective the birth of a child represents nothing less than our commitment that God will not have this world "bettered" by destroying life. That is why there is no more profound political act for Christians than taking the time for children. It is but an indication that God, not man, rules this existence, and we have been graciously invited to have a part in God's adventure and his Kingdom through the simple action of having children.

The Immediate Political Task

To some it may seem that I have argued Christians right out of the current controversy, for my argument has made appeal to religious convictions that are inadmissable in the court of our public ethos. But is has certainly not been my intention to make it implausible for Christians to continue to work in the public arena for the protection of all children, nor do I think that this implication follows from the position I have developed. Of course, Christians should prefer to live in societies that provide protection for children. And Christians should certainly wish to encourage those "natural" sentiments that would provide a basis for having and protecting children.

Moreover Christians must be concerned to develop forms of care and support, the absence of which seem to make abortion such a necessity in our society. In particular Christians should, in their own communities, make clear that the role of parent is one we all share. Thus the woman who is pregnant and carrying the child need not be the one to raise it. We must be a people who stand ready to receive and care for any child, not just as if it were one of ours, but because in fact each is one of ours.

But as Christians we must not confuse our political and moral strategies designed to get the best possible care for children in our society with the substance of our convictions. Nor should we hide the latter in the interest of securing the former. For when that is done we abandon our society to its own limits. And then our arguments fall silent in the most regrettable manner, for we forget that our most fundamental political task is to be and to point to that truth which we believe to be the necessary basis for any life-enhancing and just society.

In particular, I think that we will be wise as Christians to state our opposition to abortion in a manner that makes clear our broader concerns for the kind of people we ought to be to welcome children into the world. Therefore, rather than concentrating our energies on whether the fetus is or is not a "person," we would be better advised by example and then argument to make clear why we should hope it is a child. We must show that such a hope involves more than just the question of the status of the fetus, but indeed is the very reason why being a part of God's creation is such an extraordinary and interesting adventure.

STUDY QUESTIONS

1. Could one not use a version of Hauerwas's Christian community argument to defend a woman's right to abortion? It might be argued, for example, that a compassionate Christian community should defer to and respect the decision of a woman to have an abortion. Why, in Hauerwas's view, would this be considered an inadmissable use of the Christian ideal of community?

2. Discuss the contention that every adult in the community has parental responsibilities.

3. *Roe vs. Wade* views the right to choose abortion as one that is protected under individual rights to privacy. Hauerwas emphasizes the responsibility of the community and the mother to care for the unborn human life. How would Hauerwas react to the suggestion that his religious ideal of community conflicts with constitutional principles guaranteeing an individual's right to abort the fetus?

4. The people of Le Chambon (described in Philip Hallie's "From Cruelty to Goodness" in Chapter One) are in many ways a living example of the efficacy of the Christian ethic Hauerwas talks about. Does the example of Le Chambon lend strength to Hauerwas's position that communal responsibility to preserve life is of overriding importance?

5. Hauerwas asks us not to debate the technical legal question of whether or not the fetus is a person, but rather to ask ourselves what kind of community a Christian society should foster. Do

you find Hauerwas's communitarian approach to ethical problems promising? If you do, explain why it is. If you do not, explain why you find it inadequate or unsatisfactory.

SUGGESTED READINGS

Aiken, William and Hugh La Follette, eds. *World Hunger and Moral Obligation*. Englewood Cliffs, NJ: Prentice-Hall, 1977.

Baird, Robert M. and Stuart E. Rosenbaum, eds. *The Ethics of Abortion: Pro-Choice vs. Pro-Life*. Amherst, New York: Prometheus, 1990.

Brown, Peter G. and Douglas MacLean. *Human Rights and U.S. Foreign Policy*. Lexington, MA: Lexington Press, 1979.

Eberstadt, Nick. "Myths of the Food Crisis" in *New York Review of Books*. February 19, 1976, pp. 32–37.

Feinberg, Joel, ed. *The Problem of Abortion*, Belmont, California, Wadsworth, 1984.

Kamm, Frances Myrna. *Creation and Abortion: An Essay in Moral and Legal Philosophy*. New York: Oxford University Press, 1992.

Kleinig, John. *Valuing Life*. Princeton, NJ: Princeton University Press. 1991.

Lucas, George R., and Thomas W. Ogletree, eds. *Lifeboat Ethics: The Moral Dilemma of World Hunger*. New York: Harper and Row, 1976.

Narveson, Jan, ed. *Moral Issues*. Oxford University Press, 1983.

Perkins, Robert, ed. *Abortion Pro and Con*. Cambridge, Mass: Schenkman, 1974.

Shue, Henry. *Basic Rights: Subsistence, Affluence and U. S. Foreign Policy*. Princeton, NJ: Princeton University Press, 1980.

Singer, Peter. *Practical Ethics*. Cambridge, MA: Cambridge University Press, 1979.

Tooley, Michael. *Abortion and Infanticide*. New York: Oxford University Press, 1983.

Wenz, Peter S. *Abortion Rights as Religious Freedom*. Philadelphia: Temple University Press, 1991.

Chapter Ten

THE MEANING OF LIFE

Faced with the knowledge of our own mortality and seeing the misery about us, we ask for meaning. In the popular mind, being "philosophical" is a good thing to be, especially in moments of difficulty. So we look to philosophy, in the old-fashioned sense, to put the human predicament, with all its admitted terrors and inequities, in a perspective that will help us to accept life with composure. The wise, so we hope and sometimes believe, can show us how to mitigate grief and despair by explaining to us the point of our existence thereby giving us the courage to live our lives with a measure of understanding and dignity.

We ask the pundits for "the meaning of life" and two groups of philosophers respond. Those who believe in a divine providence offer us their ideas on divine purpose and the value of faith. Religion, as Leo Tolstoy testifies, can lift us from the slough of despair. But secular or agnostic thinkers like Bertrand Russell and Albert Camus ask us to face a harsher truth: life, they say, has no final meaning. Camus even calls our existence "absurd." To cope with our despair, the skeptics impart a different teaching, one designed for the nonbeliever and adapted to a world that seems to have no purpose and that is indifferent to our finite existence.

There are varieties of religion. In the Judeo–Christian tradition, God, though all-powerful, infinite, and unknowable, is nevertheless viewed as a person to whom one may direct complaints, petitions, and questions. Before any philosophers in that tradition can offer the consolations of faith, they must first somehow come to terms with "the problem of evil": If an all-powerful God is good and merciful, why do so many innocent people live in pain and misery? The biblical figure Job, a man of faith who suffered terrible losses and afflictions, addresses this question to God Himself and is told that no mere mortal creature can possibly fathom the mysteries of creation. "Where were you when I founded the earth?" Chastened, Job realizes that in a world that is beyond man's powers to understand, reason is of no help and unquestioning faith an appropriate response.

For others, it is not suffering, but our finitude that prompts them to ask for the meaning and purpose of our existence. Death seems to render life pointless; why strive if it all must end for everyone? The Chinese poet T'ao Ch'ien does not see this as a theoretical question; rather, it is practical and moral: Since we must die, how should we live our finite lives? T'ao Ch'ien tells us of three answers and recommends the third: "Give yourself to the waves of great change." This note of renunciation is heard in many an Eastern religious classic including the Bhagavad-Gita, a Hindu canon. The God Krishna there exhorts the despairing General Arjuna to practice a detachment to his fate and points out that such detachment will make it easier for him to do the duty that lies ahead.

Moving back to the West, and forward in time, we read *My Confession* of the great Russian novelist, Leo Tolstoy. Tolstoy experienced a prolonged period of melancholy and became obsessed with the idea that human life was pointless. Reason seemed to provide no exit from his despair. Finally, inspired by the lives of peasants who rarely question their hard fates, Tolstoy, like Job, found his salvation in an irrational commitment to living "according to God's law."

For most of us, the problem of the meaning of life comes down to the question of how to live in a world that seems indifferent to our wider purposes. That is a practical problem and the Stoics saw it that way. Our fates, they said, are largely determined and beyond our control. So we face the problem of coping in a dignified manner. According to the Stoics, most of the misery and despair we experience can be avoided if only we change our attitudes. A harsh world owes us no accounts, and the sooner we realize this, the better off we will be. This admonition is reminiscent of T'ao Ch'ien: the Stoics too counsel us to desist from useless attempts at changing the world, turning us instead to the more promising task of changing ourselves to accept life and death more calmly.

In our own century, especially in the West, the breakdown of faith and the turmoil of the Second World War created an atmosphere of disillusionment that exacerbated the problem of the purpose and meaning of life. Modern philosophers are less attracted to the old proposals of renunciation and acceptance, and new attitudes have come to the fore. Camus and Russell believe that those who find consolation in religion are avoiding the brute facts of our arbitrary and finite existence in a world that has *no* creator and *no* ultimate purpose. For Camus, the proper posture to strike in such a predicament is "defiance." We may be doomed and we may be living in a world that offers no answers to our demand for a final purpose; even so, we must not allow ourselves to become ridiculous and acquiescent by giving way to despair. For Russell, the proper posture is pride, in our ability to penetrate nature's secrets, in our ability to make a precarious place in this world and to do in it what we can to dispel ignorance and alleviate suffering.

Thomas Nagel and Joel Feinberg suggest that a world that lacks an over-arching purpose should be confronted with an attitude of irony and a large dose of self-deprecating humor. In any case, as Feinberg reminds us, there is nothing in our predicament to cast serious doubt on the importance of fulfilling ourselves by developing our talents and making a difference to those we love.

Substance, Shadow, and Spirit*

T'AO CH'IEN

T'ao Ch'ien (365–427), a government official and farmer, is one of the great figures in Chinese literature. His philosophical poetry is said to be very direct, personal, and to have universal human appeal. In T'ao Ch'ien's words, "Those who share my tastes will all get what I am driving at."

The question of life's meaning arises acutely when we ponder evil and suffering. It is also prompted by the realization of our finitude. This poem expresses three responses of the poet as he or she faces mortality. "Substance" concentrates on the material consolations: Because we have only a brief time, we should not abjure life's small pleasures. "When wine is offered, don't refuse." "Shadow" argues for the Confucian doctrine that places human goodness above physical pleasure. "Do good, and your love will outlive you." "Spirit," on the other hand, recommends neither the pursuit of pleasure, nor moral activism, but rather surrender and detachment. Spirit's philosophy is Taoist: "Give yourself to the waves of the Great Change."

*This is a Buddhist poem. Substance focuses on the fact of human mortality—life can be made acceptable only by recourse to the wine bottle. Perhaps he believes in Taoist practices which tried alchemy, diet, and breath-control in a search for long life. Shadow is clearly Confucian in desiring a reputation for good deeds that will live after him. Spirit comes out for a stoical acceptance of life and death that has affinities with Taoism. Though the bias is for Spirit's position, all of the attitudes are held by one person—an internal conflict. The Preface states the point of departure for the poem: everyone is attached to life and this attachment is irreconcilable with the inevitability of death.

SUBSTANCE, SHADOW AND SPIRIT From *The Poetry of T'ao Ch'ien* translated by James Robert Hightower (1970). Reprinted by permission of Oxford University Press.

Noble or base, wise or stupid, none but cling tenaciously to life. This is a great delusion. I have put in the strongest terms the complaints of Substance and Shadow and then, to resolve the matter, have made Spirit the spokesman for naturalness. Those who share my tastes will all get what I am driving at.

I

SUBSTANCE TO SHADOW

Earth and heaven endure forever,
Streams and mountains never change.
Plants observe a constant rhythm,
Withered by frost, by dew restored.
But man, most sentient being of all,
In this is not their equal.
He is present here in the world today,
Then leaves abruptly, to return no more.
No one marks there's one man less—
Not even friends and family think of him;
The things that he once used are all that's left
To catch their eye and move them to grief.
I have no way to transcend change,
That it must be, I no longer doubt.
I hope you will take my advice:
When wine is offered, don't refuse.

II

SHADOW TO SUBSTANCE

No use discussing immortality
When just to keep alive is hard enough.
Of course I want to roam in paradise
But it's a long way there and the road is lost.
In all the time since I met up with you
We never differed in our grief and joy.
In shade we may have parted for a time,
But sunshine always brings us close again.
Still this union cannot last forever—
Together we will vanish into darkness.
The body goes; that fame should also end
Is a thought that makes me burn inside.[1]

---

[1] *burn inside*: Confucius has a similar statement in the *Analects*, XV, 19.

Do good, and your love will outlive you;
Surely this is worth your every effort.
While it is true, wine may dissolve care
That is not so good a way as this.

III

SPIRIT'S SOLUTION

The Great Potter cannot intervene—
All creation thrives of itself.
That Man ranks with Earth and Heaven
Is it not because of me?
Though we belong to different orders,
Being alive, I am joined to you,
Bound together for good or ill
I cannot refuse to tell you what I know:
The Three August Ones were great saints[2]
But where are they living today?
Though P'eng-tsu lasted a long time[3]
He still had to go before he was ready.
Die old or die young, the death is the same.[4]
Wise or stupid, there is no difference.
Drunk every day you may forget,
But won't it shorten your life span?
Doing good is always a joyous thing
But no one has to praise you for it.
Too much thinking harms my life;
Just surrender to the cycle of things,
Give yourself to the waves of the Great Change
Neither happy nor yet afraid.
And when it is time to go, then simply go
Without any unnecessary fuss.

---

[2] *Three August Ones*: These cannot be identified with certainty. Various suggestions have been made by Chinese commentators.

[3] *a long time*: Traditionally, he lived eight-hundred years, a record even in Chinese, and he died regretting that he had not lived out his span.

[4] *Die old* . . . . These lines reflect still a passage in the *Lish Tsu* (7.2a): "Among the living there are wise and foolish, noble and mean: this is how they differ. Dead there is corruption and extinction: it is in this that they are the same. . . . Ten-year-olds die and centenarians die, the good and the saintly die and the wicked and the stupid die."

STUDY QUESTIONS

1. Explain the different teachings of "Substance," "Shadow," and "Spirit."
2. How does Spirit resolve the conflict between Substance and Shadow? Do you agree with T'ao Ch'ien that the way of the Spirit is indeed the wisest way?
3. Are there comparable teachings to T'ao Ch'ien's in the Western tradition? Specify and discuss.

The Bhagavad-Gita

The Bhagavad-Gita (The Song of God) is part of a larger epic poem called the *Mahabharata*. It was written in its present classical Sanskrit form in the period between A.D. 300 and 500. *The Bhagavad Gita* occupies a place in Hinduism similar to that of the Gospels in Christianity.

Situations of crisis often bring on reflections about the meaning of life and death. In particular, soldiers getting ready for battle may be led to ask why they are fighting and killing. In this famous epic poem taken from the *Mahabharata*, the narrator Sanjaya tells of Prince Arjuna's anguished doubts as he stood ready to engage the enemy. Arjuna is addressing his charioteer, who is really the God Krishna in disguise. He tells Krishna that he sees no point in killing those who oppose him. "Let them kill me; that will be better." When Krishna says that Arjuna speaks from weakness and self-indulgence, Arjuna begins to doubt whether his scruples are sincere. "Is this real compassion that I feel or only a delusion?" Krishna points out

THE BHAGAVAD–GITA From *The Song of God Bhagavad-Gita* translated by Swami Prabharananda and Christopher Isherwood. Used with permission of the Vendenta Society of Southern California.

that Arjuna's compunctions come from being too attached to pleasures, sentiments, and purposes from which he should be free. Should Arjuna achieve real "nonattachment" he would not shrink from doing his duty (his dharma) which he now finds so disagreeable. This passage gives expression to the Hindu teaching that enjoins a combination of action and renunciation. All Hindus are expected to perform the duties appropriate to their station, at the same time they are to be emotionally detached from the outcome. A soldier is to fight skillfully and valiantly, but he is not to be concerned with the outcome—be it pain and death or glory and wealth.

[T]he prince looked on the array, and in both armies he recognized fathers and grandfathers, teachers, uncles, sons, brothers, grandsons, fathers-in-law, dear friends, and many other familiar faces.

When Kunti's son saw all those ranks of kinsmen he was filled with deep compassion, and he spoke despairingly, as follows:

ARJUNA:
Krishna, Krishna,
Now as I look on
These my kinsmen
Arrayed for battle,
My limbs are weakened,
My mouth is parching,
My body trembles,
My hair stands upright,
My skin seems burning,
The bow Gandiva
Slips from my hand,
My brain is whirling
Round and round,
I can stand no longer:
Krishna, I see such
Omens of evil!
What can we hope from
This killing of kinsmen?

What do I want with
Victory, empire,
Or their enjoyment?
O Govinda,
How can I care for
Power or pleasure,
My own life, even,
When all these others,
Teachers, fathers,
Grandfathers, uncles,
Sons and brothers,
Husbands of sisters,
Grandsons and cousins,
For whose sake only
I could enjoy them
Stand here ready
To risk blood and wealth
In war against us?

Knower of all things,
Though they should slay me
How could I harm them?
I cannot wish it:
Never, never,
Not though it won me
The throne of the three worlds;
How much the less for
Earthly lordship!

Krishna, hearing
The prayers of all men,
Tell me how can
We hope to be happy
Slaying the sons
Of Dhritarashtra?
Evil they may be,
Worst of the wicked,
Yet if we kill them
Our sin is greater.
How could we dare spill
The blood that unites us?

Where is joy in
The killing of kinsmen?

Foul their hearts are
With greed, and blinded:
They see no evil
In breaking of blood-bonds,
See no sin
In treason to comrades.
But we, clear-sighted,
Scanning the ruin
Of families scattered,
Should we not shun
This crime, O Krishna?

We know what fate falls
On families broken:
The rites are forgotten,
Vice rots the remnant
Defiling the women,
And from their corruption
Comes mixing of castes:
The curse of confusion
Degrades the victims
And damns the destroyers.

The rice and the water
No longer are offered;
The ancestors also
Must fall dishonoured
From home in heaven.
Such is the crime
Of the killers of kinsmen:
The ancient, the sacred,
Is broken, forgotten.
Such is the doom
Of the lost, without caste-rites:
Darkness and doubting
And hell for ever.

What is the crime
I am planning, O Krishna?

Murder most hateful,
Murder of brothers!
Am I indeed
So greedy for greatness?

Rather than this
Let the evil children
Of Dhritarashtra
Come with their weapons
Against me in battle:
I shall not struggle,
I shall not strike them.
Now let them kill me,
That will be better.

SANJAYA: (the narrator)

Having spoken thus, Arjuna threw aside his arrows and his bow in the midst of the battlefield. He sat down on the seat of the chariot, and his heart was overcome with sorrow. Then his eyes filled with tears, and his heart grieved and was bewildered with pity. And Sri Krishna spoke to him, saying:

SRI KRISHNA:

Arjuna, is this hour of battle the time for scruples and fancies? Are they worthy of you, who seek enlightenment? Any brave man who merely hopes for fame or heaven would despise them.

What is this weakness? It is beneath you. Is it for nothing men call you the foe-consumer? Shake off this cowardice, Arjuna. Stand up.

ARJUNA:

Bhisma and Drona are noble and ancient, worthy of the deepest reverence. How can I greet them with arrows, in battle? If I kill them, how can I ever enjoy my wealth, or any other pleasure? It will be cursed with bloodguilt. I would much rather spare them, and eat the bread of a beggar.

Which will be worse, to win this war, or to lose it? I scarcely know. Even the sons of Dhritarashtra stand in the enemy ranks. If we kill them, none of us will wish to live.

Is this real compassion that I feel, or only a delusion? My mind gropes about in darkness. I cannot see where my duty lies. Krishna, I beg you, tell me frankly and clearly what I ought to do. I am your disciple. I put myself into your hands. Show me the way.

Not this world's kingdom,
Supreme, unchallenged,
No, nor the throne
Of the gods in heaven,
Could ease this sorrow
That numbs my senses!

SANJAYA:

When Arjuna, the foe-consuming, the never-slothful, had spoken thus to Govinda, ruler of the senses, he added: 'I will not fight,' and was silent. . . .

ARJUNA:

But, Krishna, if you consider knowledge of Brahman superior to any sort of action, why are you telling me to do these terrible deeds?

Your statements seem to contradict each other. They confuse my mind. Tell me one definite way of reaching the highest good. I want to learn the truth about renunciation and non-attachment. What is the difference between these two principles?

SRI KRISHNA:

The sages tell us that renunciation means the complete giving-up of all actions which are motivated by desire. And they say that non-attachment means abandonment of the fruits of action.

Some philosophers declare that all kinds of action should be given up, because action always contains a certain measure of evil. Others say that acts of sacrifice, almsgiving and austerity should not be given up. Now you shall hear the truth of this matter.

Acts of sacrifice, almsgiving and austerity should not be given up: Their performance is necessary. For sacrifice, almsgiving and austerity are a means of purification to those who rightly understand them. But even these acts must be performed without attachment or regard for their fruits. Such is my final and considered judgment.

Renunciation is said to be of three kinds. If a man, in his ignorance, renounces those actions which the scriptures ordain, his renunciation is inspired by tamas. If he abstains from any action merely because it is disagreeable, or because he fears it will cause him bodily pain, his renunciation is inspired by rajas. He will not obtain any spiritual benefit from such renunciation. But when a man performs an action which is sanctioned by the scriptures, and does it for duty's sake only, renouncing all attachment and desire for its fruits, then his renunciation is inspired by sattwa.

When a man is endowed with spiritual discrimination and illumined by knowledge of the Atman, all his doubts are dispelled. He does not shrink from doing what is disagreeable to him, nor does he long to do what is agreeable. No human being can give up action altogether, but he who gives up the fruits of action is said to be non-attached.

To those who have not yet renounced the ego and its desires, action bears three kinds of fruit—pleasant, unpleasant, and a mixture of both. They will be reaped in due season. But those who have renounced ego and desire will reap no fruit at all, either in this world or in the next. . . .

STUDY QUESTIONS

1. Hinduism teaches the doctrine of duty for duty's sake: the baker is to bake bread, the soldier to fight, the farmer to till the soil; but they are to be indifferent to the fruits of their labor—be it pain or pleasure, glory or disgrace. Some critics have said that this Hindu teaching encourages passivity in the face of social injustice. Is this a fair criticism, or does it reflect a basic misunderstanding of Hindu philosophy?
2. Arjuna's scruples about killing seem reasonable. Do you find Krishna's counter arguments as reasonable? Can you mount a better defense of Arjuna's position than he does himself?
3. Compare Arjuna's doubts to Tolstoy's (see next essay). Contrast the ways each has resolved his dilemma. Is resignation an essential part of a balanced approach to life?

My Confession

LEO TOLSTOY

Leo Tolstoy (1828–1910) was a Russian novelist and social critic. His novels were written during the years
1852–1876: Among these are *War and Peace* and *Anna
Karinina*; both are regarded as masterpieces of world literature. He wrote the *Confessions* and other nonfiction
works on religion and morality during the years 1879–
1882. These describe his own spiritual crisis and the salvation he found in Christianity.

Tolstoy describes the feeling of pointlessness that governed him for several years. Reason offered no way out.
Life seemed meaningless. Art was no help. All causes and
enterprises seemed doomed and without purpose. Science seemed to endorse the notion that life was temporary
and that all human endeavor would come to naught.
Tolstoy tells us how he lived for years "in this madness"
but was saved by his love for simple working people
"who carry their own lives and ours upon their shoulders." These people inspired Tolstoy by their irrational
faith that life itself was to be lived "according to God's
law." Death cannot destroy the union with an infinite
God. According to Tolstoy, only an irrational faith can
give meaning to life. "Without faith one cannot live."
Tolstoy came to believe that the lives of the privileged
intelligentsia were empty and futile; by contrast, the hard
lives of the peasants were full and meaningful.

Although I regarded authorship as a waste of time, I continued to write during those fifteen years. I had tasted of the seduction of authorship, of the seduction of enormous monetary remunerations and applauses for my insignificant labour, and so I submitted to it, as being a means for improving my material condition and for stifling in my soul all questions about the meaning of my life and life in general.

In my writings I advocated, what to me was the only truth, that it was necessary to live in such a way as to derive the greatest comfort for oneself and one's family.

Thus I proceeded to live, but five years ago something very strange began to happen with me: I was overcome by minutes at first of perplexity and then of an arrest of life, as though I did not know how to live or what to do, and I lost myself and was dejected. But that passed, and I continued to live as before. Then those minutes of perplexity were repeated oftener and oftener, and always in one and the same form. These arrests of life found their expression in ever the same questions: "Why? Well, and then?"

At first I thought that those were simply aimless, inappropriate questions. It seemed to me that that was all well known and that if I ever wanted to busy myself with their solution, it would not cost me much labour,—that now I had no time to attend to them, but that if I wanted to I should find the proper answers. But the questions began to repeat themselves oftener and oftener, answers were demanded more and more persistently, and, like dots that fall on the same spot, these questions, without any answers, thickened into one black blotch.

There happened what happens with any person who falls ill with a mortal internal disease. At first there appear insignificant symptoms of indisposition, to which the patient pays no attention; then these symptoms are repeated more and more frequently and blend into one temporally indivisible suffering. The suffering keeps growing, and before the patient has had time to look around, he becomes conscious that what he took for an indisposition is the most significant thing in the world to him,—is death.

The same happened with me. I understood that it was not a passing indisposition, but something very important, and that, if the questions were going to repeat themselves, it would be necessary to find an answer for them. And I tried to answer them. The questions seemed to be so foolish, simple, and childish. But the moment I

947

touched them and tried to solve them, I became convinced, in the first place, that they were not childish and foolish, but very important and profound questions in life, and, in the second, that, no matter how much I might try, I should not be able to answer them. Before attending to my Samára estate, to my son's education, or to the writing of a book, I ought to know why I should do that. So long as I did not know why, I could not do anything. I could not live. Amidst my thoughts of farming, which interested me very much during that time, there would suddenly pass through my head a question like this: "All right, you are going to have six thousand desyatínas of land in the Government of Samára, and three hundred horses,—and then?" And I completely lost my senses and did not know what to think farther. Or, when I thought of the education of my children, I said to myself: "Why?" Or, reflecting on the manner in which the masses might obtain their welfare, I suddenly said to myself: "What is that to me?" Or, thinking of the fame which my works would get me, I said to myself: "All right, you will be more famous than Gógol, Púshkin, Shakespeare, Molière, and all the writers in the world,—what of it?" And I was absolutely unable to make any reply. The questions were not waiting, and I had to answer them at once; if I did not answer them, I could not live.

I felt that what I was standing on had given way, that I had no foundation to stand on, that that which I lived by no longer existed, and that I had nothing to live by. . . .

All that happened with me when I was on every side surrounded by what is considered to be complete happiness. I had a good, loving, and beloved wife, good children, and a large estate, which grew and increased without any labour on my part. I was respected by my neighbours and friends, more than ever before, was praised by strangers, and, without any self-deception, could consider my name famous. With all that, I was not deranged or mentally unsound,—on the contrary, I was in full command of my mental and physical powers, such as I had rarely met with in people of my age: physically I could work in a field, mowing, without falling behind a peasant; mentally I could work from eight to ten hours in succession, without experiencing any consequences from the strain. And while in such condition I arrived at the conclusion that I could not live, and, fearing death, I had to use cunning against myself, in order that I might not take my life.

This mental condition expressed itself to me in this form: my life is a stupid, mean trick played on me by somebody. Although I did not recognize that "somebody" as having created me, the form of the conception that some one had played a mean, stupid trick on me by bringing me into the world was the most natural one that presented itself to me.

Involuntarily I imagined that there, somewhere, there was somebody who was now having fun as he looked down upon me and saw me, who had lived for thirty or forty years, learning, developing, growing in body and mind, now that I had become strengthened in mind and had reached that summit of life from which it lay all before me, standing as a complete fool on that summit and seeing clearly that there was nothing in life and never would be. And that was fun to him—

But whether there was or was not that somebody who made fun of me, did not make it easier for me. I could not ascribe any sensible meaning to a single act, or to my whole life. I was only surprised that I had not understood that from the start. All that had long ago been known to everybody. Sooner or later there would come diseases and death (they had come already) to my dear ones and to me, and there would be nothing left but stench and worms. All my affairs, no matter what they might be, would sooner or later be forgotten, and I myself should not exist. So why should I worry about all these things? How could a man fail to see that and live,—that was surprising! A person could live only so long as he was drunk; but the moment he sobered up, he could not help seeing that all that was only a deception, and a stupid deception at that! Really, there was nothing funny and ingenious about it, but only something cruel and stupid.

Long ago has been told the Eastern story about the traveller who in the steppe is overtaken by an infuriated beast. Trying to save himself from the animal, the traveller jumps into a waterless well, but at its bottom he sees a dragon who opens his jaws in order to swallow him. And the unfortunate man does not dare climb out, lest he perish from the infuriated beast, and does not dare jump down to the bottom of the well, lest he be devoured by the dragon, and so clutches the twig of a wild bush growing in a cleft of the well and holds on to it. His hands grow weak and he feels that soon he shall have to surrender to the peril which awaits him at either side; but he still holds on and sees two mice, one white, the other black, in even measure making a circle around the main trunk of the bush to which he is clinging, and nibbling at it on all sides. Now, at any moment, the bush will break and tear off, and he will fall into the dragon's jaws. The traveller sees that and knows that he will inevitably perish; but while he is still clinging, he sees some drops of honey hanging on the leaves of the bush, and so reaches out for them with his tongue and licks the leaves. Just so I hold on to the branch of life, knowing that the dragon of death is waiting inevitably for me, ready to tear me to pieces, and I cannot understand why I have fallen on such suffering. And I try to lick that honey which used to give me pleasure; but now it no longer gives me joy, and the white and the black mouse day and night nibble at the branch to which I am holding on. I clearly see the dragon, and the honey is no longer sweet to me. I see only the inevitable dragon and the mice, and am unable to turn my glance away from them. That is not a fable, but a veritable, indisputable, comprehensible truth.

The former deception of the pleasures of life, which stifled the terror of the dragon, no longer deceives me. No matter how much one should say to me, "You cannot understand the meaning of life, do not think, live!" I am unable to do so, because I have been doing it too long before. Now I cannot help seeing day and night, which run and lead me up to death. I see that alone, because that alone is the truth. Everything else is a lie.

The two drops of honey that have longest turned my eyes away from the cruel truth, the love of family and of authorship, which I have called an art, are no longer sweet to me.

"My family—" I said to myself, "but my family, my wife and children, they are also human beings. They are in precisely the same condition that I am in: they must either live in the lie or see the terrible truth. Why should they live? Why should I love them, why guard, raise, and watch them? Is it for the same despair which is in me, or for dulness of perception? Since I love them, I cannot conceal the truth from them,—every step in cognition leads them up to this truth. And the truth is death."

"Art, poetry?" For a long time, under the influence of the success of human praise, I tried to persuade myself that that was a thing which could be done, even though death should come and destroy everything, my deeds, as well as my memory of them; but soon I came to see that that, too, was a deception. It was clear to me that art was an adornment of life, a decoy of life. But life lost all its attractiveness for me. How, then, could I entrap others? So long as I did not live my own life, and a strange life bore me on its waves; so long as I believed that life had some sense, although I was not able to express it,—the reflections of life of every description in poetry and in the arts afforded me pleasure, and I was delighted to look at life through this little mirror of art; but when I began to look for the meaning of life, when I experienced the necessity of living myself, that little mirror became either useless, superfluous, and ridiculous, or painful to me. I could no longer console myself with what I saw in the mirror, namely, that my situation was stupid and desperate. It was all right for me to rejoice so long as I believed in the depth of my soul that life had some sense. At that time the play of lights—of the comical, the tragical, the touching, the beautiful, the terrible in life— afforded me amusement. But when I knew that life was meaningless and terrible, the play in the little mirror could no longer amuse me. No sweetness of honey could be sweet to me, when I saw the dragon and the mice that were nibbling down my support. . . .

In my search after the question of life I experienced the same feeling which a man who has lost his way in the forest may experience.

He comes to a clearing, climbs a tree, and clearly sees an unlimited space before him; at the same time he sees that there are no houses there, and that there can be none; he goes back to the forest, into the darkness, and he sees darkness, and again there are no houses.

Thus I blundered in this forest of human knowledge, between the clearings of the mathematical and experimental sciences, which disclosed to me clear horizons, but such in the direction of which there could be no house, and between the darkness of the speculative sciences, where I sunk into a deeper darkness, the farther I proceeded, and I convinced myself at last that there was no way out and could not be.

By abandoning myself to the bright side of knowledge I saw that I only turned my eyes away from the question. No matter how enticing and clear the horizons were that were disclosed to me, no matter how enticing it was to bury myself in the infinitude of this knowledge, I comprehended that these sciences were the more clear, the less I needed them, the less they answered my question.

"Well, I know," I said to myself, "all which science wants so persistently to know, but there is no answer to the question about the meaning of my life." But in the speculative sphere I saw that, in spite of the fact that the aim of the knowledge was directed straight to the answer of my question, or because of that fact, there could be no other answer than what I was giving to myself: "What is the meaning of my life?"—"None." Or, "What will come of my life?"—"Nothing." Or, "Why does everything which exists exist, and why do I exist?"—"Because it exists."

Putting the question to the one side of human knowledge, I received an endless quantity of exact answers about what I did not ask: about the chemical composition of the stars, about the movement of the sun toward the constellation of Hercules, about the origin of species and of man, about the forms of infinitely small, imponderable particles of ether; but the answer in this sphere of knowledge to my question what the meaning of my life was, was always: "You are what you call your life; you are a temporal, accidental conglomeration of particles. The interrelation, the change of these particles, produces in you that which you call life. This congeries will last for some time; then the interaction of these particles will cease, and that which you call life and all your questions will come to an end. You are an accidentally cohering globule of something. The globule is fermenting. This fermentation the globule calls its life. The globule falls to pieces, and all fermentation and all questions will come to an end." Thus the clear side of knowledge answers, and it cannot say anything else, if only it strictly follows its principles.

With such an answer it appears that the answer is not a reply to the question. I want to know the meaning of my life, but the fact that it is a particle of the infinite not only gives it no meaning, but even destroys every possible meaning.

Those obscure transactions, which this side of the experimental, exact science has with speculation, when it says that the meaning of life consists in evolution and the coöperation with this evolution, because of their obscurity and inexactness cannot be regarded as answers.

The other side of knowledge, the speculative, so long as it sticks strictly to its fundamental principles in giving a direct answer to the question, everywhere and at all times has answered one and the same: "The world is something infinite and incomprehensible. Human life is an incomprehensible part of this incomprehensible *all*. . . ."

I lived for a long time in this madness, which, not in words, but in deeds, is particularly characteristic of us, the most liberal and learned of men. But, thanks either to my strange, physical love for the real working class, which made me understand it and see that it is not so stupid as we suppose, or to the sincerity of my conviction, which was that I could know nothing and that the best that I could do was to hang myself,—I felt that if I wanted to live and understand the meaning of life, I ought naturally to look for it, not among those who had lost the meaning of life and wanted to kill themselves, but among those billions departed and living men who had been carrying their own lives and ours upon their shoulders. And I looked around at the enormous masses of deceased and living men,—not learned and wealthy, but simple men,—and I saw something quite different. I saw that all these billions of men that lived or had lived, all, with rare exceptions, did not fit into my subdivisions, and that I could not recognize them as not understanding the question, because they themselves put it and answered it with surprising clearness. Nor could I recognize them as Epicureans, because their lives were composed rather of privations and suffering than of enjoyment. Still less could I recognize them as senselessly living out their meaningless lives, because every act of theirs and death itself was explained by them. They regarded it as the greatest evil to kill themselves. It appeared, then, that all humanity was in possession of a knowledge of the meaning of life, which I did not recognize and which I contemned. It turned out that rational knowledge did not give any meaning to life, excluded life, while the meaning which by billions of people, by all humanity, was ascribed to life was based on some despised, false knowledge.

The rational knowledge in the person of the learned and the wise denied the meaning of life, but the enormous masses of men, all humanity, recognized this meaning in an irrational knowledge. This irrational knowledge was faith, the same that I could not help but reject. That was God as one and three, the creation in six days, devils and angels, and all that which I could not accept so long as I had not lost my senses.

My situation was a terrible one. I knew that I should not find anything on the path of rational knowledge but the negation of life, and there, in faith, nothing but the negation of reason, which was still more impossible than the negation of life. From the rational knowledge it followed that life was an evil and men knew it,—it depended on men whether they should cease living, and yet they lived and continued to live, and I myself lived, though I had known long ago that life was meaningless and an evil. From faith it followed that, in order to understand life, I must renounce reason, for which alone a meaning was needed.

There resulted a contradiction, from which there were two ways out: either what I called rational was not so rational as I had thought; or that which to me appeared irrational was not so irrational as I had thought. And I began to verify the train of thoughts of my rational knowledge.

In verifying the train of thoughts of my rational knowledge, I found that it was quite correct. The deduction that life was nothing was inevitable; but I saw a mistake. The mistake was that I had not reasoned in conformity with the question put by me. The question was, "Why should I live?" that is, "What real, indestructible essence will come from my phantasmal, destructible life? What meaning has my finite existence in this infinite world?" And in order to answer this question, I studied life.

The solutions of all possible questions of life apparently could not satisfy me, because my question, no matter how simple it appeared in the beginning, included the necessity of explaining the finite through the infinite, and vice versa.

I asked, "What is the extra-temporal, extra-causal, extra-spatial meaning of life?" But I gave an answer to the question, "What is the temporal, causal, spatial meaning of my life?" The result was that after a long labour of mind I answered, "None."

In my reflections I constantly equated, nor could I do otherwise, the finite with the finite, the infinite with the infinite, and so from that resulted precisely what had to result: force was force, matter was matter, will was will, infinity was infinity, nothing was nothing, — and nothing else could come from it.

There happened something like what at times takes place in mathematics: you think you are solving an equation, when you have only an identity. The reasoning is correct, but you receive as a result the answer: $a = a$, or $x = x$, or $o = o$. The same happened with my reflection in respect to the question about the meaning of my life. The answers given by all science to that question are only identities.

Indeed, the strictly scientific knowledge, that knowledge which, as Descartes did, begins with a full doubt in everything, rejects all knowledge which has been taken on trust, and builds everything anew on the laws of reason and experience, cannot give any other answer to the question of life than what I received,—an indefinite answer. It only seemed to me at first that science gave me a positive answer,—Schopenhauer's answer: "Life has no meaning, it is an evil." But when I analyzed the matter, I saw that the answer was not a positive one, but that it was only my feeling which expressed it as such. The answer, strictly expressed, as it is expressed by the Brahmins, by Solomon, and by Schopenhauer, is only an indefinite answer, or an identity, $o = o$, life is nothing. Thus the philosophical knowledge does not negate anything, but only answers that the question cannot be solved by it, that for philosophy the solution remains insoluble.

When I saw that, I understood that it was not right for me to look for an answer to my question in rational knowledge, and that the answer given by rational knowledge was only an indication that the answer might be got if the question were differently put, but only when into the discussion of the question should be introduced the question of the relation of the finite to the infinite. I also understood that, no matter how irrational and monstrous the answers might be that faith gave, they had this advantage that they introduced into each answer the relation of the finite to the infinite, without which there could be no answer.

No matter how I may put the question, "How must I live?" the answer is, "According to God's law." "What real result will there be from my life?"—"Eternal torment or eternal bliss." "What is the meaning which is not destroyed by death?"—"The union with infinite God, paradise."

Thus, outside the rational knowledge, which had to me appeared as the only one, I was inevitably led to recognize that all living humanity had a certain other irrational knowledge, faith, which made it possible to live.

All the irrationality of faith remained the same for me, but I could not help recognizing that it alone gave to humanity answers to the questions of life, and, in consequence of them, the possibility of living.

The rational knowledge brought me to the recognition that life was meaningless,—my life stopped, and I wanted to destroy myself. When I looked around at people, at all humanity, I saw that people lived and asserted that they knew the meaning of life. I looked back at myself: I lived so long as I knew the meaning of life. As to other people, so even to me, did faith give the meaning of life and the possibility of living.

Looking again at the people of other countries, contemporaries of mine and those passed away, I saw again the same. Where life had been, there faith, ever since humanity had existed, had given the possibility of living, and the chief features of faith were everywhere one and the same.

No matter what answers faith may give, its every answer gives to the finite existence of man the sense of the infinite,—a sense which is not destroyed by suffering, privation, and death. Consequently in faith alone could we find the meaning and possibility of life. What, then, was faith? I understood that faith was not merely an evidence of things not seen, and so forth, not revelation (that is only the description of one of the symptoms of faith), not the relation of man to man (faith has to be defined, and then God, and not first God, and faith through him), not merely an agreement with what a man was told, as faith was generally understood,—that faith was the knowledge of the meaning of human life, in consequence of which man did not destroy himself, but lived. Faith is the power of life. If a man lives he believes in something. If he did not believe that he ought to live for some purpose, he would not live. If he does not see and understand the phantasm of the finite, he believes in that finite; if he understands the phantasm of the finite, he must believe in the infinite. Without faith one cannot live. . . .

In order that all humanity may be able to live, in order that they may continue living, giving a meaning to life, they, those billions, must have another, a real knowledge of faith, for not the fact that I, with Solomon and Schopenhauer, did not kill myself convinced me of the existence of faith, but that these billions had lived and had borne us, me and Solomon, on the waves of life.

Then I began to cultivate the acquaintance of the believers from among the poor, the simple and unlettered folk, of pilgrims, monks, dissenters, peasants. The doctrine of these people from among the masses was also the Christian doctrine that the quasi-believers of our circle professed. With the Christian truths were also mixed in very many superstitions, but there was this difference: the superstitions of our circle were quite unnecessary to them, had no connection with their lives, were only a kind of an Epicurean amusement, while the superstitions of the believers from among the labouring classes were to such an extent blended with their life that it would have been impossible to imagine it without these superstitions,—it was a necessary condition of that life. I began to examine closely the lives and beliefs of these people, and the more I examined them, the more did I become convinced that they had the real faith, that their faith was necessary for them, and that it alone gave them a meaning and possibility of life. In contradistinction to what I saw in our circle, where life without faith was possible, and where hardly one in a thousand professed to be a believer, among them there was hardly one in a thousand who was not a believer. In contradistinction to what I saw in our circle, where all life passed in idleness, amusements, and tedium of life, I saw that the whole life of these people was passed in hard work, and that they were satisfied with life. In contradistinction to the people of our circle, who struggled and murmured against fate because of their privations and their suffering, these people accepted diseases and sorrows without any perplexity or opposition, but with the calm and firm conviction that it was all for good. In contradistinction to the fact that the more intelligent we are, the less do we understand the meaning of life and the more do we see a kind of a bad joke in our suffering and death, these people live, suffer, and approach death, and suffer in peace and more often in joy. In contradistinction to the fact that a calm death, a death without terror or despair, is the greatest exception in our circle, a restless, insubmissive, joyless death is one of the greatest exceptions among the masses. And of such people, who are deprived of everything which for Solomon and for me constitutes the only good of life, and who withal experience the greatest happiness, there is an enormous number. I cast a broader glance about me. I examined the life of past and present vast masses of men, and I saw people who in like manner had understood the meaning of life, who had known how to live and die, not two, not three, not ten, but hundreds, thousands, millions. All of them, infinitely diversified as to habits, intellect, culture, situation, all equally and quite contrary to my ignorance knew the meaning of life and of death, worked calmly, bore privations and suffering, lived and died, seeing in that not vanity, but good.

I began to love those people. The more I penetrated into their life, the life of the men now living, and the life of men departed, of whom I had read and heard, the more did I love them, and the easier it became for me to live. Thus I lived for about two years, and within me took place a transformation, which had long been working within me, and the germ of which had always been in me. What happened with me was that the life of our circle,—of the rich and the learned,—not only disgusted me, but even lost all its meaning. All our acts, reflections, sciences, arts,—all that appeared to me in a new light. I saw that all that was mere pampering of the appetites, and that no meaning could be found in it; but the life of all the working masses, of all humanity, which created life, presented itself to me in its real significance. I saw that that was life itself and that the meaning given to this life was truth, and I accepted it.

STUDY QUESTIONS

1. If believing in God makes our lives richer and happier, is that a good enough reason for believing? Is it any kind of proof of God's presence in the world?

2. Bertrand Russell (see next essay) and Albert Camus are dining together. They have both just read Tolstoy's "My Confession." Write an account of their conversation discussing it.

3. Imagine that Tolstoy has just read Nagel's little essay (selection to follow) on the meaning of life. His reaction to it is very unfavorable. What does he find wrong with it?

4. Both God and the peasants who believe in Him inspire Tolstoy and help him out of the "madness" that overcame him when he thought life was pointless. What inspiration does Tolstoy find in the life of the peasants? How is that related to Tolstoy's faith in God?

A Free Man's Worship

BERTRAND RUSSELL

Bertrand Russell (1872–1970) was a clearheaded and fearless thinker who greatly influenced philosophy in this century. He did groundbreaking work in the logic and the philosophy of language. He wrote many books on morals, politics, religion, education, and history. His style was scintillating and effortless. He worked indefatigably for peace and humanitarian causes throughout his long and productive life. When Russell was awarded the Nobel Prize for literature in 1950, the Nobel Committee described him as "one of our time's most brilliant spokesmen of rationality and humanity, and a fearless champion of free speech and free thought in the West." Readers who want to know more about Russell will enjoy his autobiography. A page from it has been appended to the essay to communicate the flavor of Russell's hatred of injustice and his passion for truth.

Tolstoy had denied that science and reason could provide any grounds for a meaningful existence. Russell's "free man's worship" accepts Tolstoy's challenge to find meaning within the boundaries of a rational, scientific world view. At first, science does seem to present us with a world devoid of meaning. "We arise accidentally." We are constantly subject to the brute power of nature and have but a brief span before extinction. However, blind nature has produced a creature "gifted with sight." Our very

959

consciousness of our predicament is liberating and inspiring. Our desire to know, our capacity to judge, to criticize, to imagine; these all confer meaning on our existence. We find meaning in defying and resisting the brute powers and in cultivating knowledge. Contemplating nature, even contemplating our own inevitable extinction, is liberating. For we are exercising that which is unique in us as visionary and thinking creatures. "Such thought makes us free men." Fate itself is "subdued by the mind."

To Dr. Faustus in his study Mephistophelis told the history of the Creation, saying,

The endless praises of the choirs of angels had begun to grow wearisome; for, after all, did he not deserve their praise? Had he not given them endless joy? Would it not be more amusing to obtain undeserved praise, to be worshiped by beings whom he tortured? He smiled inwardly, and resolved that the great drama should be performed.

For countless ages the hot nebula whirled aimlessly through space. At length it began to take shape, the central mass threw off planets, the planets cooled, boiling seas and burning mountains heaved and tossed, from black masses of cloud hot sheets of rain deluged the barely solid crust. And now the first germ of life grew in the depths of the ocean and developed rapidly in the fructifying warmth into vast forest trees, huge ferns springing from the damp mold, sea monsters breeding, fighting, devouring, and passing away. And from the monsters, as the play unfolded itself, Man was born, with the power of thought, the knowledge of good and evil, and the cruel thirst for worship. And Man saw that all is passing in this mad, monstrous world, that all is struggling to snatch, at any cost, a few brief moments of life before Death's inexorable decree. And Man said, "There is a hidden purpose, could we but fathom it, and the purpose is good; for we must reverence something, and in the visible world there is nothing worthy of reverence." And Man stood aside from the struggle, resolving that God intended harmony to come out of chaos by human efforts. And when he followed the instincts which God had transmitted to him from his ancestry of beasts of prey, he called it Sin, and asked God to forgive him. But he doubted whether he could be justly forgiven, until he invented a divine Plan by which God's wrath was to have been appeased. And seeing the present was bad, he made it yet worse, that thereby the future might be better. And he gave God thanks for the strength that enabled him to forgo even the joys that were possible. And God smiled; and when he saw that Man had become perfect in renunciation and worship, he sent another sun through the sky, which crashed into Man's sun; and all returned again to nebula.

'Yes," he murmured, "it was a good play; I will have it performed again."

Such, in outline, but even more purposeless, more void of meaning, is the world which science presents for our belief. Amid such a world, if anywhere, our ideals henceforward must find a home. That man is the product of causes which had no prevision of the end they were achieving; that his origin, his growth, his hopes and fears, his loves and his beliefs, are but the outcome of accidental collocations of atoms; that no fire, no heroism, no intensity of thought and feeling, can preserve an individual life beyond the grave; that all the labors of the ages, all the devotion, all the inspiration, all the noonday brightness of human genius, are destined to extinction in the vast death of the solar system, and that the whole temple of man's achievement must inevitably be buried beneath the debris of a universe in ruins—all these things, if not quite beyond dispute, are yet so nearly certain that no philosophy which rejects them can hope to stand. Only within the scaffolding of these truths, only on the firm foundation of unyielding despair, can the soul's habitation henceforth be safely built.

How, in such an alien and inhuman world, can so powerless a creature as man preserve his aspirations untarnished? A strange mystery it is that nature, omnipotent but blind, in the revolutions of her secular hurryings through the abysses of space, has brought forth at last a child, subject still to her power, but gifted with sight, with knowledge of good and evil, with the capacity of judging all the works of his unthinking mother. In spite of death, the mark and seal of the parental control, man is yet free, during his brief years, to examine, to criticize, to know, and in imagination to create. To him alone, in the world with which he is acquainted, this freedom be-

961

longs; and in this lies his superiority to the resistless forces that control his outward life.

The savage, like ourselves, feels the oppression of his impotence before the powers of nature; but having in himself nothing that he respects more than power, he is willing to prostrate himself before his gods, without inquiring whether they are worthy of his worship. Pathetic and very terrible is the long history of cruelty and torture, of degradation and human sacrifice, endured in the hope of placating the jealous gods: surely, the trembling believer thinks, when what is most precious has been freely given, their lust for blood must be appeased, and more will not be required. The religion of Moloch—as such creeds may be generically called—is in essence the cringing submission of the slave, who dare not, even in his heart, allow the thought that his master deserves no adulation. Since the independence of ideals is not yet acknowledged, power may be freely worshiped and receive an unlimited respect, despite its wanton infliction of pain.

But gradually, as morality grows bolder, the claim of the ideal world begins to be felt; and worship, if it is not to cease, must be given to gods of another kind than those created by the savage. Some, though they feel the demands of the ideal, will still consciously reject them, still urging that naked power is worthy of worship. Such is the attitude inculcated in God's answer to Job out of the whirlwind: the divine power and knowledge are paraded, but of the divine goodness there is no hint. Such also is the attitude of those who, in our own day, base their morality upon the struggle for survival, maintaining that the survivors are necessarily the fittest. But others, not content with an answer so repugnant to the moral sense, will adopt the position which we have become accustomed to regard as specially religious, maintaining that, in some hidden manner, the world of fact is really harmonious with the world of ideals. Thus man created God, all-powerful and all-good, the mystic unity of what is and what should be.

But the world of fact, after all, is not good; and, in submitting our judgment to it, there is an element of slavishness from which our thoughts must be purged. For in all things it is well to exalt the dignity of man, by freeing him as far as possible from the tyranny of nonhuman power. When we have realized that power is largely bad, that man, with his knowledge of good and evil, is but a helpless atom in a world which has no such knowledge, the choice is again presented to us: Shall we worship force, or shall we worship goodness? Shall our God exist and be evil, or shall he be recognized as the creation of our own conscience?

The answer to this question is very momentous and affects profoundly our whole morality. The worship of force, to which Carlyle and Nietzsche and the creed of militarism have accustomed us, is the result of failure to maintain our own ideals against a hostile universe: it is itself a prostrate submission to evil, a sacrifice of our best to Moloch. If strength indeed is to be respected, let us respect rather the strength of those who refuse that false "recognition of facts" which fails to recognize that facts are often bad. Let us admit that, in the world we know, there are many things that would be better otherwise, and that the ideals to which we do and must adhere are not realized in the realm of matter. Let us preserve our respect for truth, for beauty, for the ideal of perfection which life does not permit us to attain, though none of these things meet with the approval of the unconscious universe. If power is bad, as it seems to be, let us reject it from our hearts. In this lies man's true freedom: in determination to worship only the God created by our own love of the good, to respect only the heaven which inspires the insight of our best moments. In action, in desire, we must submit perpetually to the tyranny of outside forces; but in thought, in aspiration, we are free, free from our fellow men, free from the petty planet on which our bodies impotently crawl, free even, while we live, from the tyranny of death. Let us learn, then, that energy of faith which enables us to live constantly in the vision of the good; and let us descend, in action, into the world of fact, with that vision always before us.

When first the opposition of fact and ideal grows fully visible, a spirit of fiery revolt, of fierce hatred of the gods, seems necessary to the assertion of freedom. To defy with Promethean constancy a hostile universe, to keep its evil always in view, always actively hated, to refuse no pain that the malice of power can invent, appears to be the duty of all who will not bow before the inevitable. But indignation is still a bondage, for it compels our thoughts to be occupied with an evil world; and in the fierceness of desire from which rebellion springs there is a kind of self-assertion which it is necessary for the wise to overcome. Indignation is a submission of our thoughts but not of our desires; the Stoic freedom in which wisdom consists is found in the submission of our desires but not of our thoughts. From the submission of our desires springs the virtue of resignation; from the freedom of our thoughts springs the whole world of art and philosophy, and the vision of beauty by which, at last, we half reconquer the reluctant world. But the vision of beauty is possible only to unfettered contemplation, to thoughts not weighted by the load of eager wishes; and thus freedom comes only to those who no longer ask of life that it shall yield them any of those personal goods that are subject to the mutations of time.

Although the necessity of renunciation is evidence of the existence of evil, yet Christianity, in preaching it, has shown a wisdom exceeding that of the Promethean philosophy of rebellion. It must be admitted that, of the things we desire, some, though they prove impossible, are yet real goods; others, however, as ardently longed for, do not form part of a fully purified ideal. The belief that what must be renounced is bad, though sometimes false, is far less often false than untamed passion supposes; and the creed of religion, by providing a reason for proving that it is never false, has been the means of purifying our hopes by the discovery of many austere truths.

But there is in resignation a further good element: even real goods, when they are unattainable, ought not to be fretfully desired. To every man comes, sooner or later, the great renunciation. For the young, there is nothing unattainable; a good thing desired with the whole force of a passionate will, and yet impossible, is to them not credible. Yet, by death, by illness, by poverty, or by the voice of duty, we must learn, each one of us, that the world was not made for us, and that, however beautiful may be the things we crave, Fate may nevertheless forbid them. It is the part of courage, when misfortune comes, to bear without repining the ruin of our hopes, to turn away our thoughts from vain regrets. This degree of submission to power is not only just and right: it is the very gate of wisdom.

But passive renunciation is not the whole of wisdom; for not by renunciation alone can we build a temple for the worship of our own ideals. Haunting foreshadowings of the temple appear in the realm of imagination, in music, in architecture, in the untroubled kingdom of reason, and in the golden sunset magic of lyrics, where beauty shines and glows, remote from the touch of sorrow, remote from the fear of change, remote from the failures and disenchantments of the world of fact. In the contemplation of these things the vision of heaven will shape itself in our hearts, giving at once a touchstone to judge the world about us and an inspiration by which to fashion to our needs whatever is not incapable of serving as a stone in the sacred temple.

Except for those rare spirits that are born without sin, there is a cavern of darkness to be traversed before that temple can be entered. The gate of the cavern is despair, and its floor is paved with the gravestones of abandoned hopes. There self must die; there the eagerness, the greed of untamed desire, must be slain, for only so can the soul be freed from the empire of Fate. But out of the cavern, the Gate of Renunciation leads again to the daylight of wisdom, by whose radiance a new insight, a new joy, a new tenderness, shine forth to gladden the pilgrim's heart.

When, without the bitterness of impotent rebellion, we have learned both to resign ourselves to the outward rule of Fate and to recognize that the nonhuman world is unworthy of our worship, it becomes possible at last so to transform and refashion the unconscious universe, so to transmute it in the crucible of imagination, that a new image of shining gold replaces the old idol of clay. In all the multiform facts of the world—in the visual shapes of trees and mountains and clouds, in the events of the life of man, even in the very omnipotence of death—the insight of creative idealism can find the reflection of a beauty which its own thoughts first made. In this way mind asserts its subtle mastery over the thoughtless forces of nature. The more evil the material with which it deals, the more thwarting to untrained desire, the greater is its achievement in inducing the reluctant rock to yield up its hidden treasures, the prouder its victory in compelling the opposing forces to swell the pageant of its triumph. Of all the arts, tragedy is the proudest, the most triumphant; for it builds its shining citadel in the very center of the enemy's country, on the very summit of his highest mountain; from its impregnable watchtowers, his camps and arsenals, his columns and forts, are all revealed; within its walls the free life continues, while the legions of death and pain and despair, and all the servile captains of tyrant Fate, afford the burghers of that dauntless city new spectacles of beauty. Happy those sacred ramparts, thrice happy the dwellers on that all-seeing eminence. Honor to those brave warriors who, through countless ages of warfare, have preserved for us the priceless heritage of liberty and have kept undefiled by sacrilegious invaders the home of the unsubdued.

965

But the beauty of tragedy does but make visible a quality which, in more or less obvious shapes, is present always and everywhere in life. In the spectacle of death, in the endurance of intolerable pain, and in the irrevocableness of a vanished past, there is a sacredness, an overpowering awe, a feeling of the vastness, the depth, the inexhaustible mystery of existence, in which, as by some strange marriage of pain, the sufferer is bound to the world by bonds of sorrow. In these moments of insight, we lose all eagerness of temporary desire, all struggling and striving for petty ends, all care for the little trivial things that, to a superficial view, make up the common life of day by day; we see, surrounding the narrow raft illumined by the flickering light of human comradeship, the dark ocean on whose rolling waves we toss for a brief hour; from the great night without, a chill blast breaks in upon our refuge; all the loneliness of humanity amid hostile forces is concentrated upon the individual soul, which must struggle alone, with what of courage it can command, against the whole weight of a universe that cares nothing for its hopes and fears. Victory, in this struggle with the powers of darkness, is the true baptism into the glorious company of heroes, the true initiation into the overmastering beauty of human existence. From that awful encounter of the soul with the outer world, renunciation, wisdom, and charity are born; and with their birth a new life begins. To take into the inmost shrine of the soul the irresistible forces whose puppets we seem to be—death and change, the irrevocableness of the past, and the powerlessness of man before the blind hurry of the universe from vanity to vanity—to feel these things and know them is to conquer them.

This is the reason why the past has such magical power. The beauty of its motionless and silent pictures is like the enchanted purity of late autumn, when the leaves, though one breath would make them fall, still glow against the sky in golden glory. The past does not change or strive; like Duncan, after life's fitful fever it sleeps well; what was eager and grasping, what was petty and transitory, has faded away; the things that were beautiful and eternal shine out of it like stars in the night. Its beauty, to a soul not worthy of it, is unendurable; but to a soul which has conquered Fate it is the key of religion.

The life of man, viewed outwardly, is but a small thing in comparison with the forces of nature. The slave is doomed to worship Time and Fate and Death, because they are greater than anything he finds in himself, and because all his thoughts are of things which they devour. But, great as they are, to think of them greatly, to feel their passionless splendor, is greater still. And such thought makes us free men; we no longer bow before the inevitable in Oriental subjection, but we absorb it and make it a part of ourselves. To abandon the struggle for private happiness, to expel all eagerness of temporary desire, to burn with passion for eternal things—this is emancipation, and this is the free man's worship. And this liberation is effected by contemplation of Fate; for Fate itself is subdued by the mind which leaves nothing to be purged by the purifying fire of time.

United with his fellow men by the strongest of all ties, the tie of a common doom, the free man finds that a new vision is with him always, shedding over every daily task the light of love. The life of man is a long march through the night, surrounded by invisible foes, tortured by weariness and pain, toward a goal that few can hope to reach, and where none may tarry long. One by one, as they march, our comrades vanish from our sight, seized by the silent orders of omnipotent death. Very brief is the time in which we can help them, in which their happiness or misery is decided. Be it ours to shed sunshine on their path, to lighten their sorrows by the balm of sympathy, to give them the pure joy of a never-tiring affection, to strengthen failing courage, to instill faith in hours of despair. Let us not weigh in grudging scales their merits and demerits, but let us think only of their need—of the sorrows, the difficulties, perhaps the blindnesses, that make the misery of their lives; let us remember that they are fellow sufferers in the same darkness, actors in the same tragedy with ourselves. And so, when their day is over, when their good and their evil have become eternal by the immortality of the past, be it ours to feel that, where they suffered, where they failed, no deed of ours was the cause; but wherever a spark of the divine fire kindled in their hearts, we were ready with encouragement, with sympathy, with brave words in which high courage glowed.

Brief and powerless is man's life; on him and all his race the slow, sure doom falls pitiless and dark. Blind to good and evil, reckless of destruction, omnipotent matter rolls on its relentless way; for man, condemned today to lose his dearest, tomorrow himself to pass through the gate of darkness, it remains only to cherish, ere yet the blow fall, the lofty thoughts that ennoble his little day; disdaining the coward terrors of the slave of Fate, to worship at the shrine that his own hands have built; undismayed by the empire of chance, to preserve a mind free from the wanton tyranny that rules his outward life; proudly defiant of the irresistible forces that tolerate, for a moment, his knowledge and his condemnation, to sustain alone, a weary but unyielding Atlas, the world that his own ideals have fashioned despite the trampling march of unconscious power.

. . .

Love, Knowledge, and Pity

Three passions, simple but overwhelmingly strong, have governed my life: the longing for love, the search for knowledge, and unbearable pity for the suffering of mankind. These passions, like great winds, have blown me hither and thither, in a wayward course, over a deep ocean of anguish, reaching to the very verge of despair.

I have sought love, first, because it brings ecstasy—ecstasy so great that I would often have sacrificed all the rest of life for a few hours of this joy. I have sought it, next, because it relieves loneliness—that terrible loneliness in which one shivering consciousness looks over the rim of the world into the cold unfathomable lifeless abyss. I have sought it, finally, because in the union of love I have seen, in a mystic miniature, the prefiguring vision of the heaven that saints and poets have imagined. This is what I sought, and though it might seem too good for human life, this is what—at last—I have found.

With equal passion I have sought knowledge. I have wished to understand the hearts of men. I have wished to know why the stars shine. And I have tried to apprehend the Pythagorean power by which number holds sway above the flux. A little of this, but not much, I have achieved.

Love and knowledge, so far as they were possible, led upward toward the heavens. But always pity brought me back to earth. Echoes of cries of pain reverberate in my heart. Children in famine, victims tortured by oppressors, helpless old people a hated burden to their sons, and the whole world of loneliness, poverty, and pain make a mockery of what human life should be. I long to alleviate the evil, but I cannot, and I too suffer.

This has been my life. I have found it worth living, and would gladly live it again if the chance were offered me.

STUDY QUESTIONS

1. Russell describes the evolution of religions from "the religion of Moloch" to more idealistic and humanitarian forms of worship. Some contemporary cults have rituals reminiscent of ancient, brutal religions. What, in your opinion, is their appeal? Has Russell underestimated the "brute powers" within *us*?

2. Explain Russell's meaning when he says: "Of all the arts, tragedy is the proudest, the most triumphant; for it builds its shining citadel in the very center of the enemy's country . . . "

3. Russell tells us to "burn with passion for eternal things." What are these "eternal things"?

4. If there were a debate between Bertrand Russell and Leo Tolstoy over religion, who do you think would win? Explain.

5. Russell, like Camus, speaks of defiance. But he seems more optimistic and upbeat about life and he does not concede that life is absurd. What in Russell's thinking leads him to reject the fatalistic proposition that life is meaningless? Why does Camus disagree?

The Myth of Sisyphus

ALBERT CAMUS

Albert Camus (1913–1960) was born and educated in Algeria. In 1940 he moved to Paris where he became active in French intellectual life. He was editor of *Le Combat*, an underground publication of the French Resistance. He is the author of several important literary works: most notably *The Stranger*, *The Plague*, and *The Fall*. His philosophical essays include *The Rebel* and *The Myth of*

Sisyphus. In 1957 Camus received the Nobel Prize for literature. He died tragically at age 47 in a car accident.

After the grotesque and brutal behavior of the Nazis in Europe in mid-century, many could no longer believe that "God's in His heaven, all's right with the world." Camus, writing at that time, was addressing a public that had lost faith. Many people felt alien in a world that seemed no longer to offer moral guidance. Camus agreed and sympathized with those who said that life had no meaning. But he rejected despair and asked: Does it follow that life is not worth living? If that did follow, suicide would be reasonable. Camus did not believe he could honestly offer anyone the comfort of a doctrine that attributes meaning to life. But he argued that life's absurdity does not entail suicide. On the contrary, the proper attitude to adopt in the face of absurdity and alienation is defiance. "Revolt gives life its value." To kill oneself is to give in to the absurdity; it is to acquiesce. We must not succumb to meaninglessness. "It is essential to die unreconciled and not of one's own free will."

Absurdity and Suicide

There is but one truly serious philosophical problem, and that is suicide. Judging whether life is or is not worth living amounts to answering the fundamental question of philosophy. . . . A world that can be explained even with bad reasons is a familiar world. But, on the other hand, in a universe suddenly divested of illusions and lights, man feels an alien, a stranger. His exile is without remedy since he is deprived of the memory of a lost home or the hope of a promised land. This divorce between man and his life, the actor and his setting, is properly the feeling of absurdity. All healthy men having thought of their own suicide, it can be seen, without further explanation, that there is a direct connection between this feeling and the longing for death.

The subject of this essay is precisely this relationship between the absurd and suicide, the exact degree to which suicide is a solution to the absurd. The principle can be established that for a man who does not cheat, what he believes to be true must determine his action. Belief in the absurdity of existence must then dictate his conduct. It is legitimate to wonder, clearly and without false pathos, whether a conclusion of this importance requires forsaking as rapidly as possible an incomprehensible condition. . . . Hitherto, and it has not been wasted effort, people have played on words and pretended to believe that refusing to grant a meaning to life necessarily leads to declaring that it is not worth living. In truth, there is no necessary common measure between these two judgments. One merely has to refuse to be misled by the confusions, divorces, and inconsistencies previously pointed out. One must brush everything aside and go straight to the real problem. One kills oneself because life is not worth living, that is certainly a truth—yet an unfruitful one because it is a truism. But does that insult to existence, that flat denial in which it is plunged come from the fact that it has no meaning? Does its absurdity require one to escape it through hope or suicide—this is what must be clarified, hunted down, and elucidated while brushing aside all the rest. Does the Absurd dictate death? This problem must be given priority over others, outside all methods of thought and all exercises of the disinterested mind. . . .

Absurd Freedom

I don't know whether this world has a meaning that transcends it. But I know that I do not know that meaning and that it is impossible for me just now to know it. What can a meaning outside my condition mean to me? I can understand only in human terms. What I touch, what resists me—that is what I understand. And these two certainties—my appetite for the absolute and for unity and the impossibility of reducing this world to a rational and reasonable principle—I also know that I cannot reconcile them. What other truth can I admit without lying, without bringing in a hope I lack and which means nothing within the limits of my condition?

If I were a tree among trees, a cat among animals, this life would have a meaning, or rather this problem would not arise, for I should belong to this world. I should *be* this world to which I am now opposed by my whole consciousness and my whole insistence upon familiarity. This ridiculous reason is what sets me in opposition to all creation. I cannot cross it out with a stroke of the pen. What I believe to be true I must therefore preserve. What seems to me so obvious, even against me, I must support. And what constitutes the basis of that conflict, of that break between the world and my mind, but the awareness of it? If therefore I want to preserve it, I can through a constant awareness, ever revived, ever alert. This is what, for the moment, I must remember. At this moment the absurd, so obvious and yet so hard to win, returns to a man's life and finds its home there. At this moment, too, the mind can leave the arid, dried-up path of lucid effort. That path now emerges in daily life. It encounters the world of the anonymous impersonal pronoun "one," but henceforth man enters in with his revolt and his lucidity. He has forgotten how to hope. This hell of the present is his Kingdom at last. All problems recover their sharp edge. Abstract evidence retreats before the poetry of forms and colors. Spiritual conflicts become embodied and return to the abject and magnificent shelter of man's heart. None of them is settled. But all are transfigured. Is one going to die, escape by the leap, rebuild a mansion of ideas and forms to one's own scale? Is one, on the contrary, going to take up the heart-rending and marvelous wager of the absurd? Let's make a final effort in this regard and draw all our conclusions. The body, affection, creation, action, human nobility will then resume their places in this mad world. At last man will again find there the wine of the absurd and the bread of indifference on which he feeds his greatness.

Let us insist again on the method: it is a matter of persisting. At a certain point on his path the absurd man is tempted. History is not lacking in either religions or prophets, even without gods. He is asked to leap. All he can reply is that he doesn't fully understand, that it is not obvious. Indeed, he does not want to do anything but what he fully understands. He is assured that this is the sin of pride, but he does not understand the notion of sin; that perhaps hell is in store, but he has not enough imagination to visualize that strange future; that he is losing immortal life, but that seems to him an idle consideration. An attempt is made to get him to admit his guilt. He feels innocent. To tell the truth, that is all he feels—his irreparable innocence. This is what allows him everything. Hence, what he demands of himself is to live *solely* with what he knows, to accommodate himself to what is, and to bring in nothing that is not certain. He is told that nothing is. But this at least is a certainty. And it is with this that he is concerned: he wants to find out if it is possible to live *without appeal*.

. . .

Now I can broach the notion of suicide. It has already been felt what solution might be given. At this point the problem is reversed. It was previously a question of finding out whether or not life had to have a meaning to be lived. It now becomes clear, on the contrary, that it will be lived all the better if it has no meaning. Living an experience, a particular fate, is accepting it fully. Now, no one will live this fate, knowing it to be absurd, unless he does everything to keep before him that absurd brought to light by consciousness. Negating one of the terms of the opposition on which he lives amounts to escaping it. To abolish conscious revolt is to elude the problem. The theme of permanent revolution is thus carried into individual experience. Living is keeping the absurd alive. Keeping it alive is, above all, contemplating it. Unlike Eurydice, the absurd dies only when we turn away from it. One of the only coherent philosophical positions is thus revolt. It is a constant confrontation between man and his own obscurity. It is an insistence upon an impossible transparency. It challenges the world anew every second. Just as danger provided man the unique opportunity of seizing awareness, so metaphysical revolt extends awareness to the whole of experience. It is that constant presence of man in his own eyes. It is not aspiration, for it is devoid of hope. That revolt is the certainty of a crushing fate, without the resignation that ought to accompany it.

This is where it is seen to what a degree absurd experience is remote from suicide. It may be thought that suicide follows revolt—but wrongly. For it does not represent the logical outcome of revolt. It is just the contrary by the consent it presupposes. Suicide, like the leap, is acceptance at its extreme. Everything is over and man returns to his essential history. His future, his unique and dreadful future—he sees and rushes toward it. In its way, suicide settles the absurd. It engulfs the absurd in the same death. But I know that in order to keep alive, the absurd cannot be settled. It escapes suicide to the extent that it is simultaneously awareness and rejection of death. It is, at the extreme limit of the condemned man's last thought, that shoelace that despite everything he sees a few yards away, on the very brink of his dizzying fall. The contrary of suicide, in fact, is the man condemned to death.

That revolt gives life its value. Spread out over the whole length of a life, it restores its majesty to that life. To a man devoid of blinders, there is no finer sight than that of the intelligence at grips with a reality that transcends it. The sight of human pride is un-equaled. No disparagement is of any use. That discipline that the mind imposes on itself, that will conjured up out of nothing, that face-to-face struggle have something exceptional about them. To impoverish that reality whose inhumanity constitutes man's majesty is tantamount to impoverishing him himself. I understand then why the doctrines that explain everything to me also debilitate me at the same time. They relieve me of the weight of my own life, and yet I must carry it alone. At this juncture, I cannot conceive that a skeptical metaphysics can be joined to an ethics of renunciation.

Consciousness and revolt, these rejections are the contrary of re-nunciation. Everything that is indomitable and passionate in a human heart quickens them, on the contrary, with its own life. It is essential to die unreconciled and not of one's own free will. Suicide is a repu-diation. The absurd man can only drain everything to the bitter end, and deplete himself. The absurd is his extreme tension, which he maintains constantly by solitary effort, for he knows that in that consciousness and in that day-to-day revolt he gives proof of his only truth, which is defiance.

STUDY QUESTIONS

1. Why does Camus say that the most serious philosophical prob-lem is the problem of suicide? In what sense is life absurd? How does Camus see the relationship between "the absurd" and the question of suicide?

2. Explain what Camus means by saying that "life will be lived all the better if it has no meaning" and "living is keeping the absurd alive." How does he reach these conclusions?

3. Why does Camus think that defiance is the appropriate response to absurdity? Do you agree?

4. Camus believed that those who deny life's absurdity are fooling themselves. Do you agree that life is absurd? If you do not, can you answer Camus's accusation that you are avoiding facing some unpleasant truth about the meaning or meaninglessness of life?

5. Is there any possible world that Camus would *not* find absurd? What sort of world would satisfy his conditions for meaning?

6. Do you think Sisyphus is happy? Before giving your answer, see Feinberg's discussion of the views of Richard Taylor on this question.

The Meaning of Life

THOMAS NAGEL

Thomas Nagel (b. 1937) is a professor of philosophy at New York University. He is the author of numerous books and articles including *Mortal Questions, The View from Nowhere* (1986) and *Equality and Partiality* (1991).

What is the point of living? We'll be dead anyway in two hundred years. One possible answer is that the point of living can be found within our (mortal) lives. We all have large or small chains of projects, such as working to earn money to feed our families, getting ready to go to bed so that we can sleep because we are tired. Each act has a point and the sum of these constitutes the meaning of life. But may we not ask: What is the point of *life as a whole*?

Looking at life in the larger context, "from the outside," we may ask: "Why does my whole existence matter? The *whole* thing does not seem to matter." Nagel acknowledges that the demand for ultimate meaning may be legitimate. Many of us need to feel that our lives are important in the large sense. We want to matter "from the outside" and not merely within our own little scheme of things. But our lives probably do not have any such enduring meanings. On the other hand, we cannot help taking ourselves seriously. Our predicament renders us slightly ridiculous, even absurd.

Perhaps you have had the thought that nothing really matters, because in two hundred years we'll all be dead. This is a peculiar thought, because it's not clear why the fact that we'll be dead in two hundred years should imply that nothing we do now really matters.

The idea seems to be that we are in some kind of rat race, struggling to achieve our goals and make something of our lives, but that this makes sense only if those achievements will be permanent. But they won't be. Even if you produce a great work of literature which continues to be read thousands of years from now, eventually the solar system will cool or the universe will wind down or collapse, and all trace of your efforts will vanish. In any case, we can't hope for even a fraction of this sort of immortality. If there's any point at all to what we do, we have to find it within our own lives.

Why is there any difficulty in that? You can explain the point of most of the things you do. You work to earn money to support yourself and perhaps your family. You eat because you're hungry, sleep because you're tired, go for a walk or call up a friend because you feel like it, read the newspaper to find out what's going on in the world. If you didn't do any of those things you'd be miserable; so what's the big problem?

The problem is that although there are justifications and explanations for most of the things, big and small, that we do *within* life, none of these explanations explain the point of your life as a whole— the whole of which all these activities, successes and failures, strivings and disappointments are parts. If you think about the whole thing, there seems to be no point to it at all. Looking at it from the outside, it wouldn't matter if you had never existed. And after you have gone out of existence, it won't matter that you did exist.

Of course your existence matters to other people—your parents and others who care about you—but taken as a whole, their lives have no point either, so it ultimately doesn't matter that you matter to them. You matter to them and they matter to you, and that may give your life a feeling of significance, but you're just taking in each other's washing, so to speak. Given that any person exists, he has needs and concerns which make particular things and people within his life matter to him. But the *whole thing* doesn't matter.

But does it matter that it doesn't matter? "So what?" you might say. "It's enough that it matters whether I get to the station before my train leaves, or whether I've remembered to feed the cat. I don't need more than that to keep going." This is a perfectly good reply. But it only works if you really can avoid setting your sights higher, and asking what the point of the whole thing is. For once you do that, you open yourself to the possibility that your life is meaningless.

The thought that you'll be dead in two hundred years is just a way of seeing your life embedded in a larger context, so that the point of smaller things inside it seems not to be enough—seems to leave a larger question unanswered. But what if your life as a whole did have a point in relation to something larger? Would that mean that it wasn't meaningless after all?

There are various ways your life could have a larger meaning. You might be part of a political or social movement which changed the world for the better, to the benefit of future generations. Or you might just help provide a good life for your own children and their descendants. Or your life might be thought to have meaning in a religious context, so that your time on Earth was just a preparation for an eternity in direct contact with God.

About the types of meaning that depend on relations to other people, even people in the distant future, I've already indicated what the problem is. If one's life has a point as a part of something larger, it is still possible to ask about that larger thing, what is the point of *it*? Either there's an answer in terms of something still larger or there isn't. If there is, we simply repeat the question. If there isn't, then our search for a point has come to an end with something which has no point. But if that pointlessness is acceptable for the larger thing of which our life is a part, why shouldn't it be acceptable already for our life taken as a whole? Why isn't it all right for your life to be pointless? And if it isn't acceptable there, why should it be acceptable when we get to the larger context? Why don't we have to go on to ask, "But what is the point of all *that*?" (human history, the succession of the generations, or whatever).

The appeal to a religious meaning to life is a bit different. If you believe that the meaning of your life comes from fulfilling the purpose of God, who loves you, and seeing Him in eternity, then it doesn't seem appropriate to ask, "And what is the point of *that*?" It's supposed to be something which is its own point, and can't have a purpose outside itself. But for this very reason it has its own problems.

The idea of God seems to be the idea of something that can explain everything else, without having to be explained itself. But it's very

977

hard to understand how there could be such a thing. If we ask the question, "Why is the world like this?" and are offered a religious answer, how can we be prevented from asking again, "And why is *that* true?" What kind of answer would bring all of our "Why?" questions to a stop, once and for all? And if they can stop there, why couldn't they have stopped earlier?

The same problem seems to arise if God and His purposes are offered as the ultimate explanation of the value and meaning of our lives. The idea that our lives fulfil God's purpose is supposed to give them their point, in a way that doesn't require or admit of any further point. One isn't supposed to ask "What is the point of God?" any more than one is supposed to ask, "What is the explanation of God?"

But my problem here, as with the role of God as ultimate explanation, is that I'm not sure I understand the idea. Can there really be something which gives point to everything else by encompassing it, but which couldn't have, or need, any point itself? Something whose point can't be questioned from outside because there is no outside?

If God is supposed to give our lives a meaning that we can't understand, it's not much of a consolation. God as ultimate justification, like God as ultimate explanation, may be an incomprehensible answer to a question that we can't get rid of. On the other hand, maybe that's the whole point, and I am just failing to understand religious ideas. Perhaps the belief in God is the belief that the universe is intelligible, but not to us.

Leaving that issue aside, let me return to the smaller-scale dimensions of human life. Even if life as a whole is meaningless, perhaps that's nothing to worry about. Perhaps we can recognize it and just go on as before. The trick is to keep your eyes on what's in front of you, and allow justifications to come to an end inside your life, and inside the lives of others to whom you are connected. If you ever ask yourself the question, "But what's the point of being alive at all?"— leading the particular life of a student or bartender or whatever you happen to be—you'll answer "There's no point. It wouldn't matter if I didn't exist at all, or if I didn't care about anything. But I do. That's all there is to it."

Some people find this attitude perfectly satisfying. Others find it depressing, though unavoidable. Part of the problem is that some of us have an incurable tendency to take ourselves seriously. We want to matter to ourselves "from the outside." If our lives as a whole seem pointless, then a part of us is dissatisfied—the part that is always looking over our shoulders at what we are doing. Many human efforts, particularly those in the service of serious ambitions rather than just comfort and survival, get some of their energy from a sense of importance—a sense that what you are doing is not just important to you, but important in some larger sense: important, period. If we have to give this up, it may threaten to take the wind out of our sails. If life is not real, life is not earnest, and the grave is its goal, perhaps it's ridiculous to take ourselves so seriously. On the other hand, if we can't help taking ourselves so seriously, perhaps we just have to put up with being ridiculous. Life may be not only meaningless but absurd.

STUDY QUESTIONS

1. "We want to matter to ourselves 'from the outside.'" What does Nagel mean by this?
2. Explain Nagel's objections to a religious approach to the question of the meaning of life. How might a person of faith answer Nagel?
3. Contrast Nagel and Camus in the way they approach the question of life's meaning. How does each react to the idea that life may be meaningless and absurd?
4. A, despairingly, "Life does not matter."
   B, cynically, "If that is true, why should it matter that it does not matter?"
   What is A's response? Continue the exchange.

Absurd Self-Fulfillment: An Essay on the Moral Perversity of the Gods

JOEL FEINBERG

Joel Feinberg (b. 1926) is a professor of philosophy at the University of Arizona. Among his numerous books are *Social Philosophy* (1973) and *Harm to Others* (1987).

Feinberg aims "to recommend appropriate attitudes to the human condition." By carefully examining the notions of absurdity and fulfillment, he explores the tension between optimistic and pessimistic attitudes to life. On the one hand, life appears absurd to many, offering ground to such negative attitudes as despair and defiance. On the other hand, "insofar as a human life is fulfilled," it is a "good life." Only a temperament pessimistic by nature could find a fulfilled life tragically absurd. Only a temperament optimistic by nature could deny the arbitrariness in the human condition. Feinberg seeks a balanced attitude.

Several modern conceptions of absurdity are compared. The human predicament is absurd, says the philosopher Richard Taylor, because, being finite, all human efforts must come to naught. According to Thomas Nagel, we are absurd because of the importance we attach to our projects, when their importance cannot ultimately be justified. We live in absurdity, according to Albert Camus, because we necessarily crave meaning and order in a world that does not provide it. Feinberg notes that the negative consequences of being absurd or of feeling oneself to be in an absurd predicament can be mitigated by humility. For persons in an absurd situation, humility is essential, otherwise the sense of absurdity will adversely affect their character.

Feinberg goes on to examine modern concepts of human fulfillment. Aristotle had held that human beings fulfil themselves by living a life in which reason plays the most important part. But modern philosophers have emphasized that there is a lot more to being human than the exercise of reason. Furthermore, fulfillment is not necessarily to be conceived in terms of what the whole species of Homo sapiens is like. Individual men and women have their distinctive and variegated ways of individual fulfillment. "We each have within us a number of distinct individual possibilities . . . no one of which is necessary. The most fulfilling ones are those that best *fit* one's latent talents, interests and initial bent . . ."

However, even the fulfilled individual may find life absurd. Feinberg recommends cultivating a strong sense of irony as a way of coping with "the thought that there should be some kind of joke at the heart of human existence."

Richard Taylor adds a twist to the ancient legend of Sisyphus, who was condemned by the gods to perpetual life spent pushing a large rock to the top of a hill from which it falls down the other side, once more to be pushed to the top, and so on forever. "Let us suppose," writes Taylor, "that the gods, while condemning Sisyphus to the fate just described, at the same time, as an afterthought, waxed perversely merciful by implanting in him a strange and irrational impulse, namely a compulsive impulse to roll stones . . . e.g., through implanting some substance that has this effect on his character and drives."[1] Such a modification would be merciful but also 'perverse', Taylor maintains, because "from our point of view there is clearly no reason why anyone should have a persistent and insatiable desire to do something as pointless as that."[2]

Taylor's Sisyphus, meaningless as his activities may seem to us, at least finds his rock-pushing career *fulfilling*. Since a powerful disposition to push rocks has been built into him, he is only doing what he is inclined by his nature to do when he pushes the rock, just as a dog fulfills his nature by chasing a rabbit or a bird by building a nest. One can criticize Taylor, incidentally, for his apparent confusion of self-fulfillment (doing what it is in one's nature to do) with compulsion. In Taylor's example, a substance in Sisyphus' blood forces him to 'want' to push stones, just as repeated injections of heroin into the veins of an unwilling prisoner would impose an addiction for heroin on him and make him 'want' his subsequent 'fixes.' The causal mechanism employed by the gods, however, need not be that crude, and we can imagine that they remake Sisyphus' nature in a more thoroughgoing way so that the disposition to push large objects, stemming from a reconstructed complex of glands and nerves and basic drives, becomes an integral part of Sisyphus' self rather than an alien element restraining him. Let us add a twist to Taylor's twist, then, and have the gods provide Sisyphus with a new nature rather than imposing an addiction on his old one. We can think of a rock-pushing Sisyphus as no more "addicted" to his characteristic activities than we are to walking upright or to speaking a language. Our Sisyphus' activities, furthermore, are self-fulfilling, not simply because they satisfy his desires, nor because they involve his own willful acquiescence, but simply because they express some basic genetic disposition of his nature.

Taylor does not use the word *absurd* in describing Sisyphus' peculiar activities, but a whole tradition, whose most recent prominent member was Albert Camus,[3] finds that term eminently appropriate.

---

[1]Richard Taylor, *Good and Evil*, Macmillan, London, 1970, p. 259.

[2]*Ibid.*

[3]The various essays in which Camus gives his most thorough account of absurdity have been translated into English by Justin O'Brien and published in one volume under the title *The Myth of Sisyphus and Other Essays*, Random House, New York, 1955.

The words Taylor uses are "meaningless," "pointless," and "endless." Perhaps endless repetitive cycles of "pointless" labor to no apparent purpose or result is only one species of absurdity, or perhaps "pointlessness" is only one among many grounds for judging an activity to be absurd. In either case pointlessness and generic absurdity are not identical notions. But few would deny the synthetic judgment that there is an absurdity in pointless labors that come to nothing. Taylor isolates this absurdity by contrasting it both with painfulness and loneliness. It is not because Sisyphus' labors are arduous and body-bruising that they are absurd, for we can imagine that his rock is small and his labors undemanding. They would be no less pointless, and therefore no less absurd for that. Moreover, as Taylor suggests, we could give Sisyphus some partners so that the rock-moving activities are conducted by teams of two or more persons. That would reduce the loneliness of the enterprise but not its silliness. The essential absurdity of pointless activity is captured in a non-Sisyphean example that Taylor provides himself: "Two groups of prisoners, one of them engaged in digging a prodigious hole in the ground that is no sooner finished than it is filled in again by the other group, the latter then digging a new hole that is at once filled in by the first group and so on endlessly."[4]

Many philosophers have said that insofar as human existence is absurd there is a ground for certain negative attitudes—suicidal despair, philosophical pessimism, Camus' "scorn," or defiance. Other philosophers, addressing a somewhat different datum, have said that insofar as a given human life is self-fulfilled it is a good life, and provides a reason for certain positive attitudes toward the human condition—hope, satisfaction, acceptance, or reconciliation. Often the "optimists" say that some lives (at least) are completely fulfilled and most lives fulfilled to some degree or other. There is no necessity that all be fulfilled or that all be unfulfilled; it all depends on luck and skill. "Pessimists," on the other hand, claim that all lives are necessarily absurd (meaningless, pointless), so their view is more sweeping. In any event, "absurdity" and "self-fulfillment" are quite different notions, so the "optimists" and the "pessimists" are not even talking about the same thing. Taylor suggests, quite plausibly, that life might be *both* absurd and (at its best, sometimes) self-fulfilling.

---

[4]Taylor, *op. cit.*, p. 258.

What are we to make of that combination of truths? What are its consequences for optimism and pessimism? What general attitudes are appropriate if it is accepted? These questions call for closer examination of the concepts of "absurdity" and "self-fulfillment" and how they might fit together, and some comments on the question of how we can judge the appropriateness of cosmic attitudes.

I. Absurdity

One element that the various sorts of absurd things have in common is their irrationality, whether that be the apparently knowing assertion of manifestly false propositions or the apparently voluntary making of manifestly unreasonable decisions, or the apparently eager living of a manifestly pointless life.

A second element in all absurdity is implicit in the first, but deserves to be clearly stated on its own. Where there is absurdity there are always two things in clash or disharmony, distinguishable entities that conflict with one another. This element is referred to variously as the "divorce,"[5] disparity, discrepancy, disproportion, or incongruity between discordant objects. In general, things that do not *fit* together—means discrepant with ends, premises incongruous with conclusions, ideals disharmonious with practice, pretensions in conflict with realities—are found wherever there is absurdity. But having located the absurdity, we may attribute it either to the relation of disharmony itself, or exclusively to one, or the other, of the discordant objects.

In D. H. Parker's aesthetic theory,[6] the comic as well as the absurd thrives on discrepancy. One of the two discordant entities in comedy is always a *standard* and the other an object or performance that fails somehow to measure up to the standard. We perceive an object as "pretending but failing to fit" some norm and then take pleasure in the incongruity. In some cases we adopt the point of view of the standard and "laugh down" at the incongruous object, as when we delight in the undignified fall of the pompously powerful. In other cases we take the opposite viewpoint, that of the comically discrepant

---

[5] Albert Camus, *op. cit.*, pp. 22–23.

[6] D. H. Parker, *The Principles of Aesthetics*, 2nd ed., Crofts, New York, 1947, pp. 94–102.

object itself, and we laugh at the standard, as for example when we laugh at cute children masquerading as adults, or in a quite different example, we laugh at a risqué story and thus have some fun with the sexual conventions violated in the tale. Perhaps not all funny things are absurd, and surely not all absurd things are funny, but discordance is an element common to comic and absurd things.

Another form of disparity is described in Thomas Nagel's astute account of absurdity,[7] namely the clash or disharmony between various *perspectives* from which we form attitudes and make judgments. There is an unavoidable discrepancy between the natural subjective way of viewing ourselves—as precious in our own eyes, full of genuinely important projects, whole universes in ourselves, persons who "live only once" and have to make the most of the time allotted them—and various hypothetical judgments made from a more universal perspective—we are mere specks or drops in the ocean, or one of the teeming hive, absolutely inessential to the grand scheme of things, no more lovable in ourselves then are any of the zillions of individual insects whose infinitesimally transitory lives are equally as unimportant in the long run as our own. Our subjective point of view is an expression of the "seriousness" with which all living beings must view their situations, a necessary expression of our biological natures. But the broader perspectives that yield a different and conflicting picture are available to any being with imagination and minimal conceptual development. And judged from those perspectives, the human expenditures of effort and emotion in the pursuit of "important goals" are just so many posturings, and we mortals are absurd figures who strut and fret our hour upon the stage. The absurdity in the human condition, Nagel tells us, consists in a special kind of conspicuous discrepancy, that between unavoidable pretension or aspiration, on the one hand, and reality as perceived from a truer perspective, on the other.

A word should be added here about the conceptual relation between the absurd and the comic. One of the most prominent classes of objects of our laughter is that of the absurdly incongruous.[8] Since

---

[7]Thomas Nagel, "The Absurd," *Journal of Philosophy* 68 (1971), pp. 716–727.

[8]The essence of the comic, according to Arthur Schopenhauer is "the sudden perception of . . . incongruity . . . ," *The World as Will and Idea*, trans. by R. B. Haldane and John Kemp, Trübner, London, 1886, Vol. 1, p. 76.

not all absurdities are funny, however, a philosophical theory must explain what makes some incongruity comic and some not, and also why it is that we should take such pleasure in the incongruous when we do find it funny—why the sudden perception of absurdity in a situation can trigger the biological laugh reflex and produce pleasure in the laughing person. These philosophical problems remain unsolved, but of the standard theories of the comic, that of Max Eastman seems to me to be the most enlightening. We find nothing comic, Eastman reminds us, unless we are in at least a moderately playful mood. Sisyphus will find nothing remotely amusing in the absurdity of his situation if he is (as Camus would have him be) dead serious about it. An outsider, on the other hand, can find amusement in another's plight in proportion to the absurdity he finds in it, if he detaches the absurdity, so to speak, from the serious elements in the situation, and responds to it playfully.

Eastman points out that there are two effective ways of amusing a small child, once you have put him at his ease and restored him to his natural condition of playfulness: you can "make a perfectly terrible face," or you can try a kind of gentle practical joke on him, teasing him in a lighthearted spirit. These two techniques, Eastman points out, correspond to the two most famous definitions of laughter. Corresponding to the frightful face made playfully is Aristotle's definition of the comic as "some defect or ugliness which is not painful or destructive." All perceptual comic objects (what Eastman calls "ludicrousness") fit Aristotle's definition. Corresponding to the practical joke is Kant's account of the cause of laughter as "the sudden transformation of a strained expectation into nothing" (as when a playful adult offers an infant a toy and then suddenly yanks it back with mock laughter). The Kantian definition fits adult humor, where often the funny thing is that "a plausible movement of the mind comes to nothing."[9] Much comedy and perhaps all wit, Eastman tells us, have this Kantian character which in turn is a refinement of a infant's gleeful snatching at the withdrawn toy, in this case a withdrawn meaning. "A trick is played upon our minds—a playful disappointment of their momentary expectation, and a pleasure offered to their underlying trends."[10] Some of the most exquisite comedy is

---

[9] Max Eastman, *The Enjoyment of Laughter*, Simon and Schuster, New York, 1936, p. 38.

[10] *Ibid.*, p. 39.

directed at patently absurd reasonings and ludicrously incongruous situations,[11] but only when we can take them playfully, only, that is, when distracting anxieties, fears, and such emotions as anger, sorrow, compassion, and indignation, have been "paid off" and sent on a holiday. In short, an element of absurdity in an unhappy situation is itself a comic element in that situation no matter how unhappy the whole complex of which it is an element, but that is only to say that *if* we could isolate that element, abstract it from its whole complex and focus narrowly on it in a wholly playful spirit, we would find it amusing. (Why that should be the case even Eastman does not wholly explain.)

II. The Absurdity of Human Life

Taylor, Camus, and Nagel, each in his own way and each making his own special qualifications, looks with favor on the judgment that there is absurdity in the human condition as such. It will be useful here to summarize the reasons given by these authors. We can begin with Taylor, who finds all human activity to be as pointless (in the long run) as that of Sisyphus. He uses the words "meaningless" and "pointless" instead of "absurd," and as we have seen, means by them "endless repetitive activity that comes to nothing." The "endlessness," no doubt, is inessential to the meaninglessness. If Sisyphus pushed his rock continuously for four score and ten years only, before being mercifully killed by the gods, Taylor could and would judge his finite career as a land-mover to be absurd, just as he judges the finite lives of men and mice to be absurd. Meaninglessness for Taylor is mitigated but not canceled by achievement, because achievements do not last. Some achievements, for example *Hamlet*, Beethoven's *Fifth Symphony*, and the Notre Dame cathedral, last longer than others, and might therefore qualify as less absurd than the transient and trivial triumphs in which most perhaps take what pride they can. But from any sufficiently broad point of view, long compared to the

---

[11]Eastman rightly insists on the separation of two distinct species of funny things, those that are funny to look at and those which take one by surprise, the former fitting the Aristotelian and the latter the Kantian model. "There are accordingly, two kinds of humor: taking an unpleasant presentation playfully and taking a frustrated thought or action playfully." Eastman points out that some writers use the term "incongruous" for both comic types, and explains why: "Both practical and perceptual humor can be described loosely as incongruous, the one disrupting a temporal, the other a spatial pattern or congruity" (*op. cit.*, p. 51).

span of human lives or even the lives of nations and planets, but infinitely narrower than the perspective *sub specie aeternitatis*, the difference between the durability of Notre Dame and that of a pioneer's log cabin is utterly insignificant. All of our goals, Taylor says, are of "transitory significance," and "having gained one of them we immediately set forth for the next, as if that one had never been, with this next one being essentially more of the same."[12] Unlike Sisyphus, however, most of us beget children and pass on our values, our modest achievements, and fresh opportunities to them. That fact does not impress Taylor, who replies that "Each man's life thus resembles one of Sisyphus's climbs to the summit of his hill and each day of it one of his steps; the difference is that whereas Sisyphus himself returns to push the stone up again, we leave this to our children."[13] The enterprise is thus collective, but it still comes to nothing in the end.

What could human existence conceivably be like if it were to escape this absurdity? Taylor has us imagine that Sisyphus is permitted to push different stones to the top of his hill and combine them there into a beautiful and enduring temple. This would be different, Taylor says at first, for "activity . . . has a meaning if it has some significant culmination, some more or less lasting end that can be considered to have been the direction and purpose of the activity."[14] But soon he changes his mind. He does not wish to make meaningfulness a matter of "more or less," for then he would have to admit that some human activities and lives are to some degree, at least, meaningful, and comparisons of individual lives in terms of their relative meaningfulness would at least make sense. But that would be to vindicate rather than to destroy common sense on this question, and Taylor quickly withdraws his concession by requiring that the temple must endure—not simply be "more or less lasting"—"adding beauty to the world for the remainder of time."[15] When we look at a meaningless life like that of the legendary Sisyphus or that of a drug-addicted teenage suicide, and compare it with one of the relatively meaningful

---

[12]Taylor, *op. cit.*, p. 262.

[13]*Ibid.*, p. 263.

[14]*Ibid.*, p. 260.

[15]*Ibid.*, p. 263.

human lives suggested by common sense, say that of Jefferson or Shakespeare, the differences at first, are striking. But "if we look at them from a distance" (say from a point in time one hundred million years from now) they "are in outline the same and convey to the mind the same image"—pointless labor coming to nothing.[16] It is the temporal distance that makes the difference. The view from remote distances in time reveals things as they truly are, whereas the detailed close-up picture is distorted and illusory.

Taylor has one final supposition to make. Let us suppose that after a finite period of intense labor Sisyphus finishes a gloriously beautiful temple, and then is allowed by the gods to rest on his laurels and then spend the rest of eternal time in admiring contemplation of his significant achievement. Now at last we seem to have an unchallengeable conception of nonabsurd existence, but Taylor quickly dashes our hopes. Eternal rest, he rightly claims, would be "infinite boredom," and that too would become in due time a kind of pointlessness or absurdity. He does not consider still other possible suppositions: that Sisyphus be allowed to die after a brief rest period but before his proud satisfaction turns to boredom, while his temple is preserved forever by the gods, or that Sisyphus be permitted to live forever, alternating creative activity with replenishing periods of rest, while the gods guarantee the permanence of his achievements. I suspect that Taylor, like Bernard Williams,[17] would find even the latter arrangement no escape from infinite boredom, so that his final view, if he had finished his argument, would be that almost any conceivable form of human life would be absurd, either because it fails to produce lasting achievements or because it leads to infinite boredom.

According to Albert Camus, human beings necessarily crave a certain kind of cosmic order, significant culminations of their efforts,

---

[16]*Ibid.*, p. 264.

[17]Bernard Williams, "The Makropoulos Case: Reflections on the Tedium of Immortality," in *Problems of the Self,* Cambridge University Press, Cambridge, 1973, pp. 82–100. Jonathan Glover replies to Williams: "But I am not convinced that someone with a fairly constant character *need* eventually become intolerably bored, so long as [he] can watch the world continue to unfold and go on asking new questions and thinking, and so long as there are other people to share their feelings and thoughts with. Given the company of the right people, I would be glad of the chance to sample a few million years and see how it went" (*Causing Death and Saving Lives*, Penguin, Harmondsworth, 1977, p. 57).

and a kind of transparent rational intelligibility in the world of experience. But the world has no such order; it works to destroy the point of whatever temporary achievements it permits; and it is in its central core alien, dense, and irrational. Hence the inevitable confrontation and the inevitable absurdity. What should we do about it? Suicide would itself be a pointless gesture. Self-deception is the more common way out. But embracing consoling myths is inconsistent with one's integrity. There is in fact no way of reconciling the cravings inherent in our nature with the uncompromising denials of the alien cosmos. The existentialist hero acknowledges his inherent absurdity without wincing; he cherishes his consciousness of it, keeping it forever alive, as the evidence of his integrity. He has no hope that things could be different, but lives to the hilt and dies well, like a blind person who cannot relinquish his desire to see though he knows the desire is hopeless.[18] In his defiance of what is necessary he achieves his integrity, and in his revolt, his happiness.

Thomas Nagel presents some undeniable examples of absurdity *in* life before raising the subject of the absurdity *of* life. Since the examples are indeed good ones and such that they are easy to respond to playfully, they are irresistibly comic: "Someone gives a complicated speech in support of a motion that has already been passed; a notorious criminal is made president of a major philanthropic foundation; you declare your love over the telephone to a recorded announcement; as you are knighted, your pants fall down." What these and similar examples from ordinary life have in common, Nagel tells us, is "a conspicuous discrepancy between pretension or aspiration and reality."[19] Surely Nagel is right about that, and his examples are right on the mark, but one wonders how useful his instances of absurdity in life are as models for the alleged absurdity of all human lives. Applied to Sisyphus, at any rate, Nagel's "discrepancy between pretension or aspiration and reality" seems less relevant than Taylor's conception of ultimate futility and pointlessness.

Nagel's type of absurdity would add another element to the pointlessness of Sisyphus' labors. Imagine for example that the gods have sentenced Sisyphus only to climb a large mountain and plant a small flag on the top. As soon as he succeeds in doing that, his penalty has

---

[18]Camus, *op. cit., p. 22.*

[19]Nagel, *op cit.*, p. 718.

been paid once and for all. It takes Sisyphus years (or centuries) to climb the mountain but then he finds that he has forgotten the flag. He returns to the base, recovers the flag, and spends another millennium or so climbing a peak only to discover that he is on the wrong mountain. And so on *ad infinitum*. Sisyphus' labors would not be pointless in that case since they would have a sensible aim, but how genuinely absurd he would be! Or suppose that the gods in the original legend had not only assigned Sisyphus his endless self-defeating labor, but had also required him, before each trip to the summit, to write "I am a bad boy" one hundred times on his rock. What an absurd comedown for the proud and once mighty Sisyphus! How discrepant with his pretensions!

Moreover, traditional Sisyphus, before we began tampering with the legend, was *not* absurd on Nagel's definition. He had no illusions or false pretensions, and his resigned "aspiration" was perfectly realistic. If his plight, therefore, is to be taken as a model for the absurdity of the whole human enterprise, we shall have to expand Nagel's account of absurdity to include examples from within human life of the sort that Taylor emphasized, for instance writing novels and then burning them, ordering intricately ornate wedding cakes and then consuming them before they are even wrapped, or in general, giving with one hand and taking away with the other.[20] If in fact we all are like Sisyphus, however, and we pretend to be otherwise, then we are absurd in Nagel's sense too.

The absurdity in the human condition, according to Nagel, derives from the clash of perspectives from which we can view ourselves: that of purposeful actors living out our lives and that of disinterested spectators of the very lives we earnestly live. Only human beings are capable of viewing themselves from a detached and impersonal perspective and of making judgments from that viewpoint of their own

---

[20]Or first taking away and then giving, as in the unfunny example of absurdity from the Civil War: "Lincoln and Brooks lingered at the cot of a wounded soldier who held with a weak white hand a tract given him by a well-dressed lady performing good works that morning. The soldier read the title of the tract and began laughing. Lincoln noticed that the lady of good works was still nearby, and told the soldier that undoubtedly the lady meant well. 'It is hardly fair for you to laugh at her gift.' The soldier gave Lincoln something to remember. 'Mr. President, how can I help laughing a little? She has given me a tract on the "Sin of Dancing," and both my legs are shot off.'" (Carl Sandburg, *Abraham Lincoln: The War Years*, Harcourt, Brace, New York, 1926, Vol. 2, p. 293).

insignificance, and when we do view ourselves in that detached way, then the ordinary way of regarding our lives, which we cannot help but adopt if we are to pursue our lives at all, seems absurd to us. A mouse also regards his own life in the same serious everyday way that humans do, but since "he lacks the capacities for self-consciousness and self-transcendence that would enable him to see that he is only a mouse,"[21] he is not absurd. Human beings can diminish (but probably not eliminate) the absurdity of their own lives by allowing their individual animal natures to drift and respond to impulse, in short by becoming as much like mice as possible, but this would involve "considerable dissociative cost."[22]

Nagel gets confused, or at least confusing, when he talks as if he is making judgments about the absurdity of others' lives when he is only explaining the way in which those lives might come to *seem* absurd, either to those persons themselves or to a sensitive observer. Thus when he talks about possible "escapes" from absurdity and admits that a mindless life spent drifting with impulse is less absurd than more characteristically human lives despite its dissociative cost, he is using "is absurd" to mean "seems absurd," much as psychoanalysts often equate "guilt" and "feelings of guilt." The life of a mouse *is* absurd when we look at it from an imaginatively extended perspective that the mouse itself cannot achieve. When Nagel denies the mouse's absurdity on the ground that it has no transcendental consciousness, he explains why the mouse's life cannot *seem* absurd to it. But the mouse's life can still seem absurd to us, and really be absurd nonetheless. Nagel, in short, at least in much of his discussion, makes the essential discrepancy in an absurd life to be a relation between two components of the being whose life it is—his natural and inevitable seriousness, and his awareness from a higher perspective of his own insignificance. But one could lack that kind of discrepancy, as mice do, and enjoy a more unified consciousness which in turn is discrepant with an *external* reality, the unaccommodating and alien universe. Nagel employs the latter conception of absurdity too when he speaks of the clash between subjective pretension and objective reality, and that is the notion that is used by Taylor and Camus when they make their judgments of real, not merely apparent, absurdity.

---

[21] Nagel, *op. cit.*, p. 718.

[22] *Ibid.*, p. 726.

The distinction between really being and only seeming absurd quickly suggests another, that between absurdity as a property of one's situation, and absurdity as a flaw in one's outlook or self-assessment; put tersely, between *absurd predicaments* and *absurd persons*. It does not follow, of course, from the fact that a person is in an absurd predicament that he is himself an absurd person, for he may have redeeming insights into, and attitudes toward his situation that put him beyond criticism or mockery. The human predicament that we all share is absurd according to Taylor because achievements do not last and there is thus a necessary and objective discrepancy between effort and outcome. It is absurd according to Camus because the universe is resistant to our inherent craving for order and intelligibility and there is thus an ineradicable disharmony between our needs and the world's indifference. The human predicament is absurd according to Nagel because of the irresolvable clash between the importance we attach to our lives and the essential dubitability of all schemes of justification for that importance. All three writers agree that the absurdity of our human predicament is not a matter of "more or less" and not a matter that could be different from what it is. It is otherwise with the absurdity of persons. Some people are obviously more absurd than others in that there is a greater clash between their beliefs and their evidence, their ideals and their practice, their means and their ends, or their pretensions and their real characters and situations.

A person is also absurd—and this is the interesting point—when there is a radical discrepancy between his assessment of his situation and the actual nature of that situation. If one is really in an absurd predicament, if for example all of one's labors are bound to come to nothing in the end whatever one chooses to do about it, and one stubbornly denies that absurdity, adopting inappropriate attitudes and embracing vain hopes, then one becomes more than a little absurd oneself. Thus Sisyphus escapes personal absurdity by correctly appraising the absurdity of his predicament, realistically abandoning hope, and coolly proceeding with his labors in an existentialist spirit of "Let's get on with it,"[23] thus maintaining a kind of dignity and self-respect. But Sisyphus would surely be absurd if, like Don

---

[23]The final line of Jean-Paul Sartre's play, *No Exit (Huis clos)*, translated by Stuart Gilbert, A. A. Knopf, New York, 1946.

Quixote, he talked himself into believing that his labors had an intrinsic worth and importance and were essential to the maintenance of the world order. Indeed, we could imagine a number of possible Sisyphuses varying in their degree of personal absurdity or unabsurdity as their beliefs, assessments, attitudes, and pretensions vary in their degrees of fittingness to their predicament. The situation of all these hypothetical Sisyphuses, however, is the same and as thoroughly absurd as a situation can be, for whatever any Sisyphus chooses to do about it, he must engage in endless repetitive cycles of pointless and unproductive labor.

How can a person be unabsurd if his life as a whole is unavoidably absurd? Some self-attitudes do not further anyone's escape from absurdity, and in the case of the person whose situation itself is absurd and whose projects and enterprises are pointless, they positively accentuate the personal absurdity of their possessor. Vanity, excessive pride or shame, pompous self-importance, even well-grounded self-esteem if taken too seriously, are absurd in a person whose situation guarantees the pointlessness and futility of his activities. Think of Shelley's Ozymandias, for example, who built a monument for posterity directing his descendants to "Look on my works, ye Mighty, and despair!" A tick of cosmic time later only "Two vast and trunkless legs of stone / Stand in the desert. . . . Near them, on the sand, / Half sunk, a shattered visage lies, . . ." How absurd was old Ozymandias, self-declared "king of kings!"[24] Equally absurd would be the towering self-regard of an eminent physicist for having won (and deserved) the Nobel Prize. Think of his proud medal found on some desert of the next millennium by beings whose schoolchildren have a far more advanced understanding of physics than he did. A little bit of genuine humility, perhaps, is a virtue in anyone in any situation, but for a person in an absurd situation it is essential if the absurdity of his predicament is not to rub off on his character.

III. The Concept of Self-Fulfillment

There are various technical concepts of self-fulfillment associated with the writings of such philosophers as Plato, Aristotle, Rousseau, and Hegel, whose histories go back to the earliest beginnings of

---

[24]Percy Bysshe Shelley, *Ozymandias* 2–4, 11, 12.

Western philosophy and are equally venerable in Eastern thought. There also seem to be one or more notions of self-fulfillment, perhaps less clearly conceived and articulable, that are part of ordinary thought, as for example when people say that one kind of life, or one kind of marriage, hobby, or career, is preferred because it is more fulfilling.

In applying the ordinary concept of self-fulfillment, people seem, on different occasions, to use as many as four different models for their understanding. On the first model, fulfillment is simply the answering to *any* anticipatory condition, whether one's own or another's—promises, hopes, expectations, desires, requirements, or whatever. The second is "filling up, being made full." The third is the opposite of the second, namely emptying, unwinding, discharging, untying—draining one's cup of life to the dregs. Each of these familiar models comes with its own metaphors to guide (or obscure) the understanding. It is the fourth model, however, that of "doing what comes naturally," that purports to be more "philosophical," and is the more important one for our present purposes. This model restricts itself to the basic dispositions of one's "nature," and where these differ or conflict, to the "higher" or "better" ones. Moreover, fulfillment on this model is not merely a discharging, but also a maturing and perfecting of our basic dispositions. Finally, fulfillment so interpreted is often said to be a "realizing of one's potential," where the word "potential" refers not only to one's basic natural proclivities to engage in activities of certain kinds, but also to one's natural capacities to acquire skills and talents, to exercise those abilities effectively, and thus to produce achievements. Insofar as one fails to "realize one's potential," one's life is thought, on this as well as the third model, to be "wasted."

This understanding of self-fulfillment is much too general to be useful, and the main challenge to the philosophers, from Aristotle on, who have tried to incorporate it, has been to give it specificity. Almost anything one does can be said to fulfill a prior disposition to act in precisely that way in circumstances of that kind, or to implant or strengthen the habit of acting that way in the future. Thus almost any action can be said to discharge a natural tendency, to be a doing of what it is in one's nature to do. Philosophers who have fashioned a technical concept of self-fulfillment from the vaguer everyday notion have for the most part assigned it a crucial role in the definition of "the good for man." For that reason, most of them have begun the task of specification by ruling out as self-fulfilling, actions that violate objective standards of morality or which are radically defective in other ways. If a man has the bad habit, acquired and reinforced over a lifetime, of stealing purses, then a given act of stealing a purse, even though it fulfills one of the basic dispositions of his (evil) character, cannot be allowed to count as self-fulfilling. The same kind of fiat has excluded evil actions that discharge native propensities, for example the angry tirades or physical assaults of a person who is irascible, hotheaded, or aggressive "by nature." Such arbitrary exclusions do not shock common sense, but there does seem to be at least as much warrant in ordinary conceptions for saying that it may be a bad thing that certain kinds of self be fulfilled, but that the discharging of basic "evil" dispositions remains fulfillment, and properly so called, anyway.

Some philosophers in the grand tradition have also excluded from their conception of self-fulfillment, activities that fulfill dispositions peculiar to individual persons, so as to give special importance to activities that fulfill those dispositions that define our common human nature. The phrase "a person's nature" is of course ambiguous. It may refer to the nature he shares with all and only human beings, his "generic nature" as it were, the nature that makes him classifiable as the kind of being he is, or it may refer to the nature that belongs uniquely to him, his "individual nature," the character that distinguishes him from all other individuals of his kind. My generic nature includes my disposition to walk upright and to speak a language,[25] among other things. It is part of *my* individual nature, on the other hand, to be interested in philosophy, to be punctual at meetings, to be slow at mathematics, and to be irritable when very tired or hungry. Some of the traits that characterize me but not everybody else

---

[25]There have been feral children who have permanently *lost* their ability to learn a language and children born without legs who never acquire the ability to walk. But insofar as these persons are human beings, they are born with the innate *capacity* to acquire the dispositions and skills involved in walking and talking even though circumstances prevent that capacity from being realized. The capacities in question are often conditional ones: all human children have the capacity to learn a language, which is activated between the ages of two and twelve only, and only if they are made part of a language-speaking community during those years. That *conditional capacity* to acquire the dispositions and skills involved in language use *is* common to all human beings.

on the native base. We begin, partly because of our inherited proclivities and talents, to develop tastes, habits, interests, and values. We cultivate the skills that grow naturally out of our aptitudes, and as we get better at them we enjoy them more and exercise them further so that they get better still, while we are inclined to neglect the tasks for which our skills are inadequate, and those abilities wither and decay on the vine.[29] The careers we then select as workers, players, and lovers, should be those that fit our well-informed individual natures, at least insofar as each stage in the emergence of the self grew naturally out of its predecessor in the direction of our native bent.

Emphasis should be given to the further point that fulfillment of one's generic and individual natures are interconnected and interdependent. The passages in *On Liberty* quoted above in which Mill urged fulfillment of the "distinctive endowment" of generic humanity occur, ironically, in a chapter entitled "Individuality as One of the Elements of Well-Being," and nowhere in that chapter can Mill discuss individuality for long without bringing in human nature and vice versa. His view clearly was that it is essential to the generic nature of human beings that each think and decide for himself rather than blindly follow all the rest, so that in cultivating the capacities that human beings share in common, each individual will at the same time be promoting his own distinctive individuality. If I pick a career that fits my individual nature instead of blindly drifting with custom or passively acceding to the choices of another, then I have exercised my generic nature as a thinker and chooser, at the same time that I have promoted the fulfillment of my individual nature as a person with a unique profile of interests and aptitudes.

Useful as it may be for some purposes, the distinction between generic and individual natures is vague and ragged about the edges,

---

[29]John Rawls calls the statement of this psychological tendency "the Aristotelian Principle" and states it as follows: "Other things being equal, human beings enjoy the exercise of their realized capacities (their innate or trained abilities), and this enjoyment increases the more the capacity is realized, or the greater its complexity. The intuitive idea here is that human beings take more pleasure in doing something as they become more proficient at it, and of two activities they do equally well, they prefer the one calling for a larger repertoire of more intricate and subtle discriminations." Rawls cites the preference among good players for chess over checkers and among good mathematicians for algebra over arithmetic. (*A Theory of Justice*, Harvard University Press, Cambridge, Mass., 1971, p. 426).

a point we can appreciate by returning to the plight of Taylor's Sisyphus. Depending on the extent to which the gods had to tamper with him, he has either had a new individual nature grafted on to his basic human nature, or else a new (hence nonhuman) generic nature installed in him. If we say the former, then we must think of his infinite rock-pushing proclivities as merely personal eccentricities, only contingently unshared by other persons who share his human nature. If we say the latter, then the individual nature of Sisyphus and his generic nature coincide, Since he is now one of a kind, the sole member of his new species. A rock-pushing instinct that is so specific would be such a departure from what we normally think of as human nature, so totally unshared by any other humans that perhaps there would be a point in saying that Sisyphus has a new generic nature, humanoid but not human, and that he is now the only member of the biological species *Homo sapiens geopetris*—sapient rock pusher. Still more plausible, perhaps, we might think of the new Sisyphus as a borderline case for our old classifications. Unless we hold to the discredited doctrine of fixed species, we can simply declare that there is no uniquely correct answer to the question of whether Sisyphus' generic nature has been changed, and that considerations of convenience and tidiness are as relevant to its resolution as are any questions of fact.

Moreover, when we consider thoughtfully the whole range of hypothetical Sisyphuses from which we might draw in order to flesh out Taylor's example, we are struck with how very vague the notion of a "nature" is, whether generic or individual. What is in Sisyphus' nature (or the nature of anyone else) is very much like what is in his (cluttered) closet or in his grab bag, including everything from aptitudes and interests to addictive compulsions. Think of all the variations on Taylor's theme: the gods might have implanted in Sisyphus an *appetite* for stone-pushing which makes regular and frequent demands on him, like hunger or the "sex urge" in others, and corresponding in its cycles to the time it takes to push a rock of standard size up Sisyphus' assigned mountain and then return again to the bottom of the hill. "Ye gods!" he might exclaim after each round of labors, "how I hunger for a nice big rock to push," and the accommodating deities always have one ready for him, like the next ball up in a pinball machine. Or the gods might have designed for him a peculiar *talent* for rock-pushing much like others' talents for piano-playing, tennis, or chess. The new Sisyphus starts all over as a perpetual youth, and from the start he is a veritable prodigy at rock-pushing. He comes to enjoy exercising his skills, and makes ever-new challenges for himself. He pushes the rock right-handed, then left-handed, then no-handed, then blindfolded, then does two at a time, then juggles three in the air all the way to the summit, eager to return for another rock so that he can break his record, or equal it next time while dancing a Grecian jig. Or the gods do their job by implanting an *instinct* for rock-pushing so that Sisyphus goes about his chores without giving them so much as a thought (except in rare reflective moments and then only to shrug his shoulders and get on with it). His work is as natural and unremarkable to him as having a language or standing upright is to us, or building a dam to a beaver, or peeling a banana to a chimpanzee. Or (perhaps more plausibly) the gods implant a *drive* or more general proclivity of which stone-pushing is only one of numerous possible fulfillments. If there were only opportunity to do so, Sisyphus would find it equally in his nature to push wooden logs, or plastic bags, or iron bars, or to pull, lift, carry and throw objects or push them while swimming against a current, or to pile, hook, or nail them on to one another as in construction work, and the like. But pushing rocks up a mountain will do as well as any of the other activities as fulfillments of his drive to move and manipulate physical objects and he can be grateful to the gods for that. Or, the gods can use Taylor's own suggested method, and give Sisyphus (say) a shot in the arm after each trip so that he will feel a *"compulsive impulse"* to push the rock up once more in order to get relief in the form of another addicting shot. This technique would keep the gods busier than the others, but they could let some internal gland, timed to secrete the essential substance into Sisyphus' bloodstream at appropriate intervals, do the work for them. There is something especially ingenious in this last scheme, for the "shot" given at the base of the hill creates the impulse to push the rock up the hill and also the addictive need, when its first effect wears off, to be renewed by another shot, and so on, *ad infinitum.*

If the gods' gift to Sisyphus is merely an *appetite* to push rocks he may yet fail to find self-fulfillment on balance in an indefinitely extended lifetime of rock-pushing, just as one of us might fail to be fulfilled in a life that gives us all the food we need, but nothing else. Sisyphus will have the periodic satisfactions of regular appetite-satiation, and that is certainly some benefit to him, but the deepest yearnings of his nature will nevertheless be forever denied. Much the same can be said of his condition if the gods simply addict him chemically to a substance that creates a rock-pushing itch, or if they implant in him an extrahuman instinct to push rocks that fails to dovetail or integrate with the human instincts he must continue to maintain if he is to preserve his identity with his earlier self. The model that makes talk of Sisyphean self-fulfillment most plausible is probably that in which the gods impart to him *talents* for rock-moving that he can forever after exercise and glory in. So endowed, he can find self-fulfillment through his developed virtuosity, in the same way others find fulfillment in lives of skilled cello-playing or cabinet-making.

No conception of self-fulfillment will make much sense unless it allows that fulfillment is a matter of degree. We begin life with a large number of potential careers some of which fit our native bent more closely than others but any of which, if pursued through a lifetime, would lead to substantial fulfillment, so that the pursuit of no *one* of them is indispensable to a fulfilled life. Imagine a warm and loving woman who is superbly equipped by her nature to be a parent, and has thought of herself throughout her girlhood as a potential mother. She marries and then discovers that she is barren. Had she not been infertile she would have achieved fulfillment in a long life-time of nearly full-time motherhood. Is it now impossible for her to be fulfilled in a life without children? Clearly not, for the very traits that make her "superbly equipped" to be a mother will make her more than a little qualified for dozens of other roles, and a fulfilled life could stem from any one of these, from social work to school-teaching,[30] or even from a career based on independent specific

---

[30]Aptitudes and basic dispositions differ in an important way from ordinary desires, plans and ambitions. The latter characteristically tend to be more precise and determinate than the former, and therefore less flexible and easy to "fulfill." Many ambitions are for some relatively specific object and when that object does not come into existence the ambition is denied. General interests, talents, and drives, however, can typically find substitute objects that do equally well. If one has a highly-developed mechanical aptitude, for example, one can employ it equally well as an airplane or an automobile mechanic, as well as a carpenter, as a plumber, or in a hundred other callings. One's ambition to be an automobile mechanic, on the other hand, is squelched once and for all, by the denial of opportunity to enter that particular field. For this reason, fulfillment is, on the whole, less difficult to achieve than successful ambition or "satisfaction."

aptitudes like poetry or basket weaving. She may be disappointed that her chief ambition is squelched and her regrets may last a lifetime, but disappointment and fulfillment can coexist with little friction, as they do to some degree in most human lives. Thus, we each have within us a number of distinct individual possibilities, several (at least) of which would be sufficient for (a degree of) fulfillment, but no one of which is necessary. But the most fulfilling ones are those that best *fit* one's latent talents, interests, and initial bent and with one's evolving self-ideal (as opposed simply to one's conscious desires or formulated ambitions).

Some fulfilled human lives are relatively monochromatic, having a single dominant theme; others are diversely colored, having a harmonious orchestration of themes with equal voices. All of them approach fulfillment insofar as they fill their natural allotment of years with vigorous activity. They need not be "successful," or "triumphant," or even contented on balance in order to be fulfilled, provided they are long lifetimes full of struggles and strivings, achievements and noble failures, contentments and frustrations, friendships and enmities, exertions and relaxations, seriousness and playfulness through all the programmed stages of growth and decay. Most important of all, a fulfilled human life will be a life of planning, designing, making order out of confusion and system out of randomness, a life of building, repairing, rebuilding, creating, pursuing goals, and solving problems. It is in the generic nature of the human animal to address the future, change its course, make the best of his situation. If one's house falls down, if one's cities are in rubble, if disaster comes and goes, the human inclination is to start all over again, rebuilding from scratch. There is no "fulfillment" in resignation and despair.

Sisyphus does seem very human after all, then, when he reshoulders his burden and starts back up his hill. But insofar as his situation is rigidly fixed by the gods, allowing him no discretion to select means, design strategies, and solve problems on his own, his life does not fulfill the governing human propensities. If he can fulfill his nature without these discretionary activities, then he has really assumed the nature of a different species. In all the variations on the Sisyphus myth that we have spun thus far, the gods have assigned a very specific job to Sisyphus that requires no particular judgment or ingenuity on his part to be performed well. They have imposed a duty on him rather than assigning a responsibility.[31] He has a rote job to perform over and over, a mulish task for a mulish fellow, and his is not to reason why or how, but only to get on with it. Suppose, however, that the gods assign to Sisyphus an endless series of rather complex engineering problems and leave it up to him to work out how to solve them. Somehow rocks must be moved to mountain tops and there can be no excuses for failure. "Get it up there somehow," they say; "the methods are up to you. Feel free to experiment and invent. Keep a record of your intermediate successes and failures and be prepared to give us an accounting of the costs. You may hire your own assistants and within certain well-defined limits you have authority to give them commands, so long as you are prepared to answer for the consequences of their work. Now good luck to you." If Sisyphus' subsequent labors are fulfilling, they will be so in a characteristically human way. His individual nature will be fulfilled by a life (endless and pointless thought it may be) that fits his native bent and employs his inherited talents and dispositions to the fullest, as well as fitting his more specific individual tendencies, for example a special fascination (perhaps also a gift of the gods) with rocks.

IV. Why Does Self-Fulfillment Matter?

Why should it "matter" that a person is unfulfilled if, despite his stunted and dwarfed self, the product perhaps of alienating work and other "unfitting" circumstances, he finds a steady diet of satisfaction in delusory occupations, escapist literature, drugs, drink, and television? Why should it "matter," to turn the question around, that a person finds fulfillment when his life looks as absurd from a longer perspective as the life of a shellfish appears to us?

Think first of what a substantially unfulfilled life involves. A person comes into existence with a set of governing dispositions that set him off with others as a being of a certain kind. For twenty years he grows and matures, enlarging and perfecting his inherited propen-

---

[31]The distinction between duty and responsibility is well made by J. Roland Pennock in his essay "The Problem of Responsibility" in C. J. Friedrich (ed.), *Nomos III: Responsibility*, Atherton, New York, 1960, p. 13: "We normally reserve [the word *responsibility*] for cases where the performance of duty requires discernment and choice. We might well say to a child, 'It is your responsibility to take care of your room,' but we would not be likely to say, 'It is your responsibility to do as you are told.'"

sities so that he becomes utterly unique, with a profile of talents and individual traits which, as a group, distinguish him from every other being who has ever existed, and constitute his individual nature. Perhaps he is capable of seeing, from time to time, that this "nature" of his is more than a little absurd. What he does best and most, let us imagine, is play chess and ping-pong and socialize with others who share those interests. He takes those pursuits more seriously than anything else in his life. But he knows that they are, after all, only games, of no cosmic significance whatever, and certainly of no interest to the indifferent Universe, to Posterity, to History, or to any of the other abstract tribunals by which humans in their more magniloquent moods are wont to measure significance. And yet, absurd as it is, it is *his* nature, and the only one he has, so somehow he must make the best of it and seek his own good in pursuit of *its* dominant talents. Whose nature could he try to fulfill, after all, but his own? Where else can his *own* good conceivably be found? It was not up to him to choose his own nature, for that would presuppose that the choosing self already had a nature of its own determining its choice. But given the nature with which he finds himself indissolubly identified for better or worse, he must follow the path discovered in it and identify his good with the goals toward which his nature is already inclined.

Now suppose that he makes a mess of it through impudence, frivolity, or recklessness; or imagine that the world withdraws its opportunities; or that lightning strikes and leaves him critically incapacitated for the realization of his potential. That leaves him still the pleasure of his diminished consciousness, his soma pills and television programs, his comic books and crossword puzzles, but his deepest nature will forever remain unfulfilled. Now we think of that nature, with all of its elaborate neurochemical equipment underlying its distinctive drives and talents and forming its uniquely complex character, as largely *unused, wasted, all for naught*. All wound up, it can never discharge or wind down again. In contrast, the life of fulfillment strikes us as one that comes into being prone and equipped to do its thing, and then uses itself up doing that thing, without waste, blockage, or friction.

When any nature is left unfulfilled it is likely to strike us as a bad thing, an objectively regrettable fact. Perhaps we would withdraw or modify that judgment when we come to appreciate how absurd that nature's preoccupations really were. But from the point of view of the self whose nature it is, nonfulfillment is more than a bad or regrettable thing to be graded down in some negative but modifiable "value judgment." It may or may not be all those things in some final balancing-up, all things considered. But from the point of view of the individual involved, nonfulfillment marks the collapse of his whole universe, the denial once and for all of his *own good*. There is a world of difference in the use of the word "good" as a predicate of evaluation, and its use in the venerable phrase of the philosophers— "one's own good." My good is something peculiarly mine, as determined by my nature alone, and particularly by its most powerful trends and currents. Anything else that is *good for me* (or in my interest) is good because it contributes to my good, the fulfillment of my strongest stable tendencies. One can judge or evaluate that good from some other standpoint, employing some other standard, and the resultant judgment may use the words "good," "bad" or "indifferent." It may not be a good thing that my good be achieved or that it be achieved in a given way, or at a given cost. But it is logically irrelevant to the question of *what my good is* whether my good is itself "good" when judged from an external position. My nonfulfillment may not be a "bad thing on balance" in another's judgment or even in my own. My nonfulfillment may not be "objectively regrettable" or tragic. But my nonfulfillment cannot be *my good* even if it is from all other measuring points, a good thing.

It is perhaps not quite self-evident that my good consists in fulfillment. A hedonist might hold out for the position that my good consists in a balance of pleasant over unpleasant experiences while denying that the basic disposition of my nature is to seek pleasure, thus denying that pleasant experiences as such are fulfilling. I cannot refute such a heroic (and lonely) philosopher. But I would like to urge against the philosopher who is overly impressed with the fact of human absurdity, that *if* my good is fulfillment, it must be fulfillment of *my* nature and not of something else. That my nature is eccentric, absurd, laughable, trivial, cosmically insignificant, is neither here nor there. Such as it is, it is my nature for better or worse. The self whose good is at issue is the self I am and not some other self that I might have been. If I had had any choice in the matter I might have preferred to come into existence with the nature (that is, the potential) of William James, John F. Kennedy, or O. J. Simpson, but I cannot spend all my days lamenting that the only nature whose fulfillment constitutes my good is my own!

The prerequisite to self-fulfillment is a certain amount of clear-eyed, nondeluded *self-love*. A moment ago I spoke of one's own nature "such as it is," "for better or worse." These phrases recall the wedding ceremony and its conception of marital love as loyalty and devotion without condition or reservation. *Totally* unconditional devotion may be too much to ask from any lover, but within wide limits, various kinds of human love of others have a largely unconditional character. Gregory Vlastos describes parental love, for example, in a way that makes it quite familiar: "Constancy of affection in the face of variations of merit is one of the surest tests of whether a parent does love a child."[32] Judgments of merit have nothing to do with love so construed. A child's failures, even moral failures, may disappoint his parents' hopes without weakening their loyalty or affection in the slightest. A parent may admire one child more than another, or like (in the sense of "enjoy") one more than another, as well as judge one higher than the other, but it is a necessary condition of parental love that, short of limiting extremes, it not fluctuate with these responses to merit.

The love which any stable person has toward himself will be similarly constant and independent of perceived merits and demerits. I may (realistically) assign myself very low grades for physique, intellect, talent, even character—indeed I may ascribe deficiencies even to my individual nature itself—while still remaining steadfastly loyal and affectionate to myself. Aristotle was right on target when he said that a wise man ought to have exactly that degree of self-esteem that is dictated by the facts, neither more nor less. But self-esteem is not self-love. I have self-love for myself when I accept my nature as given, without apology or regret, even as I work, within the limits it imposes, for self-improvement. We have been through a lot together, my self and I, sharing everything alike, and as long as I have supported him, he has never let me down. I have scolded him, but never cursed his nature. He is flawed all right, and deeply so, but when the warts show, I smile, fondly and indulgently. His blunders are just what one would expect from anyone with his nature. One cannot come to hate a being with whom one has been so very intimate. Indeed, I would not know how to begin to cope with another

---

[32]Gregory Vlastos, "Justice and Equality," in Richard B. Brandt (ed.), *Social Justice*, Prentice-Hall, Englewood Cliffs, N.J., 1962, p. 44.

self after all my years of dependency, "for better or worse," on this one. In this way self-identity can be conceived as a kind of arranged marriage (I did not select the self that was to be me) that in a stable person ripens into true love, but in an unstable one sours into rancor and self-destruction. And the truest expression of one's self-love is devotion toward one's own good, which is the fulfillment of one's own (who else's?) nature absurd as that may be.

V. The Critique of Cosmic Attitudes

Some lives are manifestly and incontrovertibly absurd. Lives spent moving metaphoric rocks back and forth to no further end and lives spent tangling with metaphoric windmills are cases in point. Other lives are full of achievement and design. In these lives, intermediate goals lend meaning to the pursuits that are instrumental to their achievement, and they in turn are given a point by the more ultimate goals they subserve. No goal is *the* ultimate one, however, for the most general ends are themselves means to a great variety of other ends, all tied together in an intricate and harmonious web of purpose. There may be no purpose to the whole web except its service to its own component parts, but each constituent has a place and a vindicating significance to the person whose life it is. Such a life is, relatively speaking, not absurd. There is no doubt an important practical point in distinguishing human lives in terms of their degree of absurdity, even in highlighting and emphasizing the distinctions. (Marx's doctrine of alienation is an example of the social utility of making such distinctions.) As we have seen, however, philosophers have found reason to claim that there is a kind of cosmic absurdity inherent in the human condition as such. As we stand back and look at ourselves from an extended temporal position, the distinction between absurd and nonabsurd lives begins to fade into insignificance, and finally vanishes altogether.

We also make useful distinctions between relatively fulfilled and unfulfilled selves, or fulfilling and unfulfilling lives. However we interpret "fulfillment"—as the development of one's chief aptitudes into genuine talents in a life that gives them scope, or an unfolding of all basic tendencies and inclinations, or an active realization of the universally human propensities to plan, design, make order—there are wide differences among persons in the degree of fulfillment they achieve. Some lives are wasted; some are partially wasted and partially fulfilled; others are nearly totally fulfilled. Unlike the contrast between absurd and nonabsurd lives, these distinctions seem to be time-resistant. If Hubert Humphrey's life was fulfilling to him, that is a fact like any other, and it never ceases to be true that it was a fact. From any temporal distance from which it can be observed at all it will continue to appear to be a fact (though a diminishingly interesting or important one).

Consider a human life that is near-totally fulfilled, yet from a quite accessible imaginary vantage point is apparently absurd. Insofar as the person in question is fulfilled, he ought to "feel good" about his life, and rejoice that he has achieved his good. Suppose that he realizes then how futile it all was, "coming to nothing in the end." What would be the appropriate attitude in that event to hold toward his life? Unchanged pride and satisfaction? Bitterness and despair? Haughty existential scorn? We can call such responsive attitudes taken toward one's whole life and by implication toward the whole human condition, "cosmic attitudes." One of the traditional tasks of philosophy (and what "philosophy" is entirely about in the minds of innocent persons unacquainted with the academic discipline of that name) is to perform a kind of literary criticism of cosmic attitudes. It used to be the custom for philosophers not only to describe the universe in its more general aspects but to recommend cosmic attitudes toward the world as so described.

I welcome the suggestion of Thomas Nagel that the appropriate responsive attitude toward human lives that are both absurd and fulfilled is *irony*,[33] and I shall conclude by elaborating that suggestion somewhat beyond the bare recommendation that Nagel offers.

None of the familiar senses of irony in language or in objective occurrences seem to make any sense out of the advice that we respond to absurdity with irony. What Nagel had in mind clearly was another sense in which irony is a kind of outlook on events, namely, "an attitude of detached awareness of incongruity."[34] This is a state of

---

[33] Thomas Nagel, *op. cit.*, p. 707: "If *sub specie aeternitatis* there is no reason to believe that anything matters, then that doesn't matter either, and we can approach our absurd lives with irony instead of heroism or despair."

[34] *Webster's New Collegiate Dictionary* (1976), based on *Webster's Third New International Dictionary of the English Language.* Of the five English dictionaries I consulted, only this newest one contained any definition of irony as an attitude. Is that because this sense is relatively new or because dictionary-makers have heretofore overlooked it?

mind halfway between seriousness and playfulness. It may even seem to the person involved that he is both very serious and playful at the same time. The tension between these opposed elements pulling in their opposite ways creates at least temporarily a kind of mental equilibrium not unlike that of the boy in Lincoln's story who was "too scared to laugh and too badly hurt to cry," except that the boy squirms with discomfort whereas irony is on balance an *appreciative* attitude.[35] One appreciates the perceived incongruity much as one does in humor, where the sudden unexpected perception of incongruity produces laughter. Here the appreciation is more deliberate and intellectual. The situation is too unpleasant in some way—sad, threatening, disappointing—to permit the relaxed playfulness of spirit prerequisite to the comic response. There *is* a kind of bittersweet pleasure in it, but not the pleasure of amusement. The situation is surely not seen as funny, though perhaps it would be if only one could achieve a still more detached outlook on it. One contemplates a situation with irony when one looks the facts in the eye and responds in an appreciative way to their incongruous aspects as such. Irony is quite different from despair-cum-tears, scornful defiance-cum-anger, and amusement-cum-laughter. It is pleasant enough to be expressed characteristically in a smile, but a somewhat tired smile, with a touch both of gentleness and mischievousness in it, as befitting the expression of a tempered pleasure.

In one of the most moving scenes of the twenty-seven-part B.B.C. documentary film on the First World War, a group of British reinforcements is shown marching toward the front. We know that they are cannon fodder marching to their own slaughter, and they know it too. They are foot-sore and bone-weary, and splattered with mud, and a steady rain is falling. The song they sing as they march is not a rousing anthem like *La Marseillaise* or *Rule, Britannia!*, not a cocky fight song like *Over There*, not a jolly drinking song like *Waltzing Matilda*, not a sentimental ballad, hymn of lamentation, or a mourn-

---

[35]"The President takes the result of the New York election [a defeat for his party] philosophically, and will doubtless profit by the lesson. When Colonel Forney inquired of him how he felt about New York, he replied: 'Somewhat like the boy in Kentucky who stubbed his toe while running to see his sweetheart. The boy said he was too big to cry, and far too badly hurt to laugh'" (*Frank Leslie's Illustrated Weekly*, November 22, 1862).

ful dirge. Instead they sing to the stirring tune of *Auld Lang Syne* the famous nonsense verse they created for the occasion:

> We're here because we're here
> Because we're here because we're here;
> We're here because we're here
> Because we're here because we're here . . .

The observer of the film feels a sudden pang and finds himself near tears, but quickly he perceives the absurdity in the lyrics and responds appreciatively to it, just as the troops, by selecting those words, are responding to the perceived absurdity in their situation. The sensitive observer sees how fitting the ironic response of the soldiers is (and how dreadfully false any of its standard alternatives would have been) and himself takes a quiet sad pleasure in it. The soldiers were in an inescapably absurd predicament, without hope, and only by their unflinching acceptance of the absurdity of their situation are they saved from absurdity themselves. For us, the unseen audience, there is an inspiration in their example that makes the scene noble.

I do not mean to suggest for a moment that the march of the doomed soldiers is an apt metaphor for the whole of human life. The soldiers' brief lives were tragically wasted. If they had been specially-bred military animals they might have found both a personal and biological fulfillment in their peculiar demises, but they were ordinary humans whose bizarre and untimely deaths climaxed their undeveloped and unfinished lives. In contrast, many individuals do achieve fulfillment in long, active, creative lives. These lives are more than just "worthwhile"; they represent to those who lead them the achievement of the only condition that can plausibly be deemed "their good." So philosophical "Pessimism," the view of Schopenhauer and others that *no* life can *possibly* be worth living given the absurdity of the human condition, must be rejected. Its logical contrary, that cosmic Optimism that holds that all human lives necessarily are, or always can be, good and worthwhile, must also be rejected, in favor of the common-sense view that fulfillment requires luck, and luck is not always good in a world that contains violent passions, accidents, disease, and war.

In this essay, however, I have tried not only to sketch a conception of the good life and the bad but also to recommend an appropriate attitude toward the human condition generally. Imagine a person who both through his own virtues and good luck has led a maximally fulfilling life into his final declining years. He has realized his highest individual potential in a career that perfectly fit his inherited temperamental proclivities. His talents and virtues have unfolded steadily in a life that gave them limitless opportunity for exercise, and he has similarly perfected his generic human powers of discrimination, sympathy, and judgment in a life full of intermeshing purposes and goals. All of this is a source of rich satisfaction to him, until in the philosophical autumn of his days, he chances upon the legend of Sisyphus, the commentary of Camus, and the essays of Taylor and Nagel. In a flash he sees the vanity of all his pursuits, the total permeability of his achievements by time; the lack of any long-term rationale for his purposes, in a word the absurdity of his (otherwise good) life. At first he will feel a keen twinge. But unless he be misled by the sophistries of the philosophical Pessimists who confuse the empty ideal of long-term coherence with the Good for Man, he will soon recover. And then will come a dawning bittersweet appreciation of the cosmic incongruities first called to his attention by the philosophers. The thought that there should be a kind of joke at the heart of human existence begins to please (if not quite tickle) him. Now he can die not with a whine or a snarl, but with an ironic smile.

STUDY QUESTIONS

1. Present and justify your own conception of a fulfilled life.
2. Feinberg councils humility as a way of coping with the human predicament. Camus councils defiance. Discuss and adjudicate.
3. Taylor, Nagel, and Camus describe the human predicament rather differently. In your own view, whose description is more accurate?
4. Do you agree with Feinberg that a sense of irony will mitigate the sense of absurdity? Explain.

The Book of Job

The author of the Book of Job is unknown. It is thought
to have been written sometime between the seventh and
the fifth centuries B.C. Job, whose afflictions cause him
to curse the day he was born, is engaged in a debate on
the mysterious ways of God. The book's arguments and
its style make it one of the masterpieces of religious literature.

The selection is from the later chapters of the Book of
Job. Job, who is a God-fearing man, is being tested by
God. He had been at home in the world, blessed, prosperous and respected; but now he has lost his family, his
health, and all of his possessions. He bitterly protests his
fate, arguing that he does not deserve so much suffering.
Many mock him. He is vulnerable to all malice and evil.
But what were his crimes? "Oh that my accuser would
write out his indictment!"

Job's story illustrates the truism that life is sometimes
terribly unfair. Good people suffer while the wicked
often live very well. Job's plight and plaint are universal.
He begs God for some explanation, some justification.

The Lord addressed Job out of the "whirlwind," neither explaining nor justifying, but pointing out that Job,
a finite being, is in no position to understand the workings of the world. It is not fitting for Job to demand an
explanation that he could not possibly fathom. Thus, despite all appearances to the contrary, Job must have faith

in the ultimate justice of his fate. For he has neither the power to change that fate nor the wisdom to comprehend its meaning in the larger scheme of things. Finally, Job sees that his insistence on moral justification is presumptuous, and he accepts God's will. God then relents. The book ends with Job restored to prosperity and a new family.

29

Job took up his theme anew and said:
Oh, that I were as in the months past!
    as in the days when God watched over me,
While he kept his lamp shining above my head,
    and by his light I walked through darkness;
As I was in my flourishing days,
    when God sheltered my tent;

When the Almighty was yet with me,
    and my children were round about me;
When my footsteps were bathed in milk,
    and the rock flowed with streams of oil;
When I went forth to the gate of the city
    and set up my seat in the square—. . . .

Whoever heard of me blessed me;
    those who saw me commended me.

For I rescued the poor who cried out for help,
    the orphans, and the unassisted;
The blessing of those in extremity came upon me,
    and the heart of the widow I made joyful.
I wore my honesty like a garment;
    justice was my robe and my turban.

I was eyes to the blind,
    and feet to the lame was I;
I was a father to the needy;
    the rights of the stranger I studied,

And I broke the jaws of the wicked man;
　　from his teeth I forced the prey.

Then I said: "In my own nest I shall grow old;
　　I shall multiply years like the phoenix.
My root is spread out to the waters;
　　the dew rests by night on my branches.
My glory is fresh within me,
　　and my bow is renewed in my hand!"

30

But now they hold me in derision
　　who are younger in years than I;
Whose fathers I should have disdained
　　to rank with the dogs of my flock.
Such strength as they had, to me meant nought;
　　they were utterly destitute.
In want and hunger was their lot,
　　they who fled to the parched wastelands:
They plucked saltwort and shrubs;
　　the roots of the broom plant were their food.
They were banished from among men,
　　with an outcry like that against a thief—

To dwell on the slopes of the wadies,
　　in caves of sand and stone;
Among the bushes they raised their raucous cry;
　　under the nettles they huddled together.
Irresponsible, nameless men,
　　they were driven out of the land.

Yet now they sing of me in mockery;
　　I am become a byword among them.
They abhor me, they stand aloof from me,
　　they do not hesitate to spit in my face!
Indeed, they have loosed their bonds; they lord it over me,
　　and have thrown off restraint in my presence.

To subvert my paths they rise up;
    they build their approaches for my ruin.
To destroy me, they attack with none to stay them;
    as through a wide breach they advance.
Amid the uproar they come on in waves;
    over me rolls the terror.
My dignity is borne off on the wind,
    and my welfare vanishes like a cloud.
One with great power lays hold of my clothing;
    by the collar of my tunic he seizes me:
He has cast me into the mire;
    I am leveled with the dust and ashes.

I cry to you, but you do not answer me;
    you stand off and look at me,
Then you turn upon me without mercy
    and with your strong hand you buffet me.
You raise me up and drive me before the wind;
    I am tossed about by the tempest.

Indeed I know you will turn me back in death
    to the destined place of everyone alive.
Yet should not a hand be held out
    to help a wretched man in his calamity?
Or have I not wept for the hardships of others;
    was not my soul grieved for the destitute?
Yet when I looked for good, then evil came;
    when I expected light, then came darkness.

My soul ebbs away from me;
    days of affliction have overtaken me.
My frame takes no rest by night;
    my inward parts seethe and will not be stilled.
I go about in gloom, without the sun;
    I rise up in public to voice my grief.

I have become the brother of jackals,
    companion to the ostrich.
My blackened skin falls away from me;
    the heat scorches my very frame.
My harp is turned to mourning,
    and my reed pipe to sounds of weeping. . . .

31

Had I rejoiced at the destruction of my enemy
    or exulted when evil fell upon him,
Even though I had not suffered my mouth to sin
    by uttering a curse against his life—

Had not the men of my tent exclaimed,
    "Who has not been fed with his meat!"
Because no stranger lodged in the street,
    but I opened my door to wayfarers—

Had I, out of human weakness, hidden my sins
    and buried my guilt in my bosom
Because I feared the noisy multitude
    and the scorn of the tribes terrified me—
    then I should have remained silent, and not come out of doors!

Oh, that I had one to hear my case,
    and that my accuser would write out his indictment!
Surely, I should wear it on my shoulder
    or put it on me like a diadem;
Of all my steps I should give him an account;
    like a prince I should present myself before him.

This is my final plea; let the Almighty answer me!

The words of Job are ended.

The Lord's Speech
38

Then the LORD addressed Job out of the storm and said:

Who is this that obscures divine plans
    with words of ignorance?
Gird up your loins now, like a man;
    I will question you, and you tell me the answers!
Where were you when I founded the earth?
    Tell me, if you have understanding
Who determined its size; do you know?
    Who stretched out the measuring line for it?
Into what were its pedestals sunk,
    and who laid the cornerstone,

While the morning stars sang in chorus
    and all the sons of God shouted for joy?

And who shut within doors the sea,
    when it burst forth from the womb;
When I made the clouds its garment
    and thick darkness its swaddling bands?
When I set limits for it
    and fastened the bar of its door,
And said: Thus far shall you come but no farther,
    and here shall your proud waves be stilled!

Have you ever in your lifetime commanded the morning
    and shown the dawn its place
For taking hold of the ends of the earth,
    till the wicked are shaken from its surface?
The earth is changed as is clay by the seal,
    and dyed as though it were a garment;
But from the wicked the light is withheld,
    and the arm of pride is shattered.

Have you entered into the sources of the sea,
    or walked about in the depths of the abyss?
Have the gates of death been shown to you,
    or have you seen the gates of darkness?
Have you comprehended the breadth of the earth?
    Tell me, if you know all:
Which is the way to the dwelling place of light,
    and where is the abode of darkness,
That you may take them to their boundaries
    and set them on their homeward paths?
You know, because you were born before them,
    and the number of your years is great!

Have you entered the storehouse of the snow,
    and seen the treasury of the hail
Which I have reserved for times of stress,
    for the days of war and of battle?
Which way to the parting of the winds,
    whence the east wind spreads over the earth?

Who has laid out a channel for the downpour
    and for the thunderstorm a path
To bring rain to no man's land,
    the unpeopled wilderness;
To enrich the waste and desolate ground
    till the desert blooms with verdure?

Has the rain a father;
    or who has begotten the drops of dew?
Out of whose womb comes the ice,
    and who gives the hoarfrost its birth in the skies,
When the waters lie covered as though with stone
    that holds captive the surface of the deep?

Have you fitted a curb to the Pleiades,
    or loosened the bonds of Orion?
Can you bring forth the Mazzaroth in their season,
    or guide the Bear with its train?
Do you know the ordinances of the heavens;
    can you put into effect their plan on the earth?

Can you raise your voice among the clouds,
    or veil yourself in the waters of the storm?
Can you send forth the lightnings on their way,
    or will they say to you, "Here we are"?
Who counts the clouds in his wisdom?
    Or who tilts the water jars of heaven
So that the dust of earth is fused into a mass
    and its clods made solid?

Do you hunt the prey for the lioness
    or appease the hunger of her cubs,
While they crouch in their dens,
    or lie in wait in the thicket?
Who puts wisdom in the heart,
    and gives the cock its understanding?
Who provides nourishment for the ravens
    when their young ones cry out to God,
    and they rove abroad without food?

39

Do you know about the birth of the mountain goats,
    watch for the birth pangs of the hinds,
Number the months that they must fulfill,
    and fix the time of their bringing forth?
They crouch down and bear their young;
    they deliver their progeny in the desert.
When their offspring thrive and grow,
    they leave and do not return.

Who has given the wild ass his freedom,
    and who has loosed him from bonds?
I have made the wilderness his home
    and the salt flats his dwelling.
He scoffs at the uproar of the city,
    and hears no shouts of a driver.
He ranges the mountains for pasture,
    and seeks out every patch of green.
Will the wild ox consent to serve you,
    and to pass the nights by your manger?
Will a rope bind him in the furrow,
    and will he harrow the valleys after you?
Will you trust him for his great strength
    and leave to him the fruits of your toil?
Can you rely on him to thresh out your grain
    and gather in the yield of your threshing floor?

The wings of the ostrich beat idly;
    her plumage is lacking in pinions.
When she leaves her eggs on the ground
    and deposits them in the sand,
Unmindful that a foot may crush them,
    that the wild beasts may trample them,
She cruelly disowns her young
    and ruthlessly makes nought of her brood;
For God has withheld wisdom from her
    and has given her no share in understanding.
Yet in her swiftness of foot
    she makes sport of the horse and his rider.

Do you give the horse his strength,
  and endow his neck with splendor?
Do you make the steed to quiver
  while his thunderous snorting spreads terror?
He jubilantly paws the plain
  and rushes in his might against the weapons.
He laughs at fear and cannot be deterred;
  he turns not back from the sword.
Around him rattles the quiver,
  flashes the spear and the javelin.
Frenzied and trembling he devours the ground;
  he holds not back at the sound of the trumpet,
  but at each blast he cries, "Aha!"
Even from afar he scents the battle,
  the roar of the chiefs and the shouting.

Is it by your discernment that the hawk soars,
  that he spreads his wings toward the south?
Does the eagle fly up at your command
  to build his nest aloft?
On the cliff he dwells and spends the night,
  on a spur of the cliff or the fortress.
From thence he watches for his prey;
  his eyes behold it afar off.
His young ones greedily drink blood;
  where the slain are, there is he.

40

The Lord then said to Job:

Will we have arguing with the Almighty by the critic?
  Let him who would correct God give answer!

Then Job answered the Lord and said:

Behold, I am of little account; what can I answer you?
  I put my hand over my mouth.
Though I have spoken once, I will not do so again;
  though twice, I will do so no more.

Then the LORD addressed Job out of the storm and said:

Gird up your loins now, like a man.
    I will question you, and you tell me the answers!
Would you refuse to acknowledge my right?
    Would you condemn me that you may be justified?

Have you an arm like that of God,
    or can you thunder with a voice like his?
Adorn yourself with grandeur and majesty,
    and array yourself with glory and splendor.
Let loose the fury of your wrath;
    tear down the wicked and shatter them.
Bring down the haughty with a glance;
    bury them in the dust together;
    in the hidden world imprison them.
Then will I too acknowledge
    that your own right hand can save you.

See, besides you I made Behemoth,
    that feeds on grass like an ox.
Behold the strength in his loins,
    and his vigor in the sinews of his belly.
He carries his tail like a cedar;
    the sinews of his thighs are like cables.
His bones are like tubes of bronze;
    his frame is like iron rods.
He came at the beginning of God's ways,
    and was made the taskmaster of his fellows;
For the produce of the mountains is brought to him,
    and of all wild animals he makes sport.
Under the lotus trees he lies,
    in coverts of the reedy swamp.
The lotus trees cover him with their shade;
    all about him are the poplars on the bank.
If the river grows violent, he is not disturbed;
    he is tranquil though the torrent surges about his mouth.
Who can capture him by his eyes,
    or pierce his nose with a trap?

Can you lead about Leviathan with a hook,
   or curb his tongue with a bit?
Can you put a rope into his nose,
   or pierce through his cheek with a gaff?
Will he then plead with you, time after time,
   or address you with tender words?
Will he make an agreement with you
   that you may have him as a slave forever?
Can you play with him, as with a bird?
   Can you put him in leash for your maidens?
Will the traders bargain for him?
   Will the merchants divide him up?

Can you fill his hide with barbs,
   or his head with fish spears?
Once you but lay a hand upon him,
   no need to recall any other conflict!

41

Is he not relentless when aroused;
   who then dares stand before him?
Whoever might vainly hope to do so
   need only see him to be overthrown.
Who has assailed him and come off safe—
   Who under all the heavens?

I need hardly mention his limbs,
   his strength, and the fitness of his armor.
Who can strip off his outer garment,
   or penetrate his double corselet?
Who can force open the doors of his mouth,
   close to his terrible teeth?
Rows of scales are on his back,
   tightly sealed together;
They are fitted each so close to the next
   that no space intervenes;
So joined one to another
   that they hold fast and cannot be parted.

When he sneezes, light flashes forth;
   his eyes are like those of the dawn.
Out of his mouth go forth firebrands,
   sparks of fire leap forth.
From his nostrils issues steam,
   as from a seething pot or bowl.
His breath sets coals afire;
   a flame pours from his mouth.
Strength abides in his neck,
   and terror leaps before him.

His heart is hard as stone;
   his flesh, as the lower millstone.
When he rises up, the mighty are afraid;
   the waves of the sea fall back.
Should the sword reach him, it will not avail;
   nor will the spear, nor the dart, nor the javelin.
He regards iron as straw,
   and bronze as rotten wood.
The arrow will not put him to flight;
   slingstones used against him are but straws.
Clubs he esteems as splinters;
   he laughs at the crash of the spear.

His belly is sharp as pottery fragments;
   he spreads like a threshing sledge upon the mire.
He makes the depths boil like a pot;
   the sea he churns like perfume in a kettle.
Behind him he leaves a shining path;
   you would think the deep had the hoary head of age.
Upon the earth there is not his like,
   intrepid he was made.
All, however lofty, fear him;
   he is king over all proud beasts.

42

Then Job answered the LORD and said:

I know that you can do all things,
   and that no purpose of yours can be hindered.

I have dealt with great things that I do not understand;
  things too wonderful for me, which I cannot know.
I had heard of you by word of mouth,
  but now my eye has seen you.
Therefore I disown what I have said,
  and repent in dust and ashes.

STUDY QUESTIONS

1. Job's story illustrates that life is unfair. Does this cast doubts on the foundations of morality? Discuss.
2. Throughout his sufferings Job never doubted God's existence. But many say that the suffering of innocents cannot be squared with the proposition that a benevolent God has created the world. Job himself has no solution to the problem of justifying evil in a world created by God. Why do you think Job's faith in God's existence never wavered?
3. Though Job had no answer to why God permits the suffering of innocents, the Book of Job does have a response to those who raise the question. What is that response? How do you react to it?
4. The story has it that Bertrand Russell went to heaven where he met God who said to him: "You see Russell, you were wrong to deny that I exist!" To which Russell replied: "Not at all; you should have given us more evidence."

   Now imagine Russell meeting Job. Their conversation was longer and more heated (but they parted friends). What was it like?

SUGGESTED READINGS

Klemke, E. D., Ed. *The Meaning of Life*. New York: Oxford University Press, 1981.

Frankl, Victor. *Man's Search for Meaning*. New York: Beacon, 1963.

Fromm, Erich. *Man For Himself*. New York: Holt, Rinehart and Winston, 1947.

Heshel, Abraham. *Man is Not Alone*. New York: Farrar, Strauss, and Giroux, 1951.

James, William. "Is Life Worth Living?" in *The Will To Believe*. New York: Dover, 1960.

Nielsen, Kai. *Ethics Without God*. Buffalo: Prometheus, 1973.

Sanders, Steven and David R. Cheney, eds. *The Meaning of Life*. Englewood Cliffs, NJ: Prentice-Hall, 1980.

Tolstoy, Leo. *The Death of Ivan Ilych*. New York: New American Library, 1960.